Environmental Ethics

BLACKWELL PHILOSOPHY ANTHOLOGIES

Each volume in this outstanding series provides an authoritative and comprehensive collection of the essential primary readings from philosophy's main fields of study. Designed to complement the *Blackwell Companions to Philosophy* series, each volume represents an unparalleled resource in its own right, and will provide the ideal platform for course use.

Environmental Ethics
An Anthology

Edited by
Andrew Light
and
Holmes Rolston III

Blackwell
Publishing

BLACKWELL PUBLISHING
350 Main Street, Malden, MA 02148-5020, USA
9600 Garsington Road, Oxford OX4 2DQ, UK
550 Swanston Street, Carlton, Victoria 3053, Australia

First published 2003 by Blackwell Publishing Ltd

8   2007

Library of Congress Cataloging-in-Publication Data

Environmental ethics : an anthology / edited by Andrew Light and Holmes Rolston.
        p. cm. — (Blackwell philosophy anthologies ; 19)
    Includes bibliographical references and index.
    ISBN 978-0-631-22293-4 (hard : alk. paper) – ISBN 978-0-631-22294-1 (pbk : alk. paper)
        1. Environmental ethics. I. Light, Andrew, 1966– II. Rolston, Holmes, 1932– III.
    Series.

    GE42 .E573   2002
    179'.1—dc21

                                                                        2002066429

A catalogue record for this title is available from the British Library.

Set in 9½ on 11½ pt Ehrhardt
by Kolam Information Services Pvt. Ltd, Pondicherry, India
Printed and bound in Singapore
by C.O.S. Printers Pte Ltd

The publisher's policy is to use permanent paper from mills that operate a sustainable forestry policy, and which has been manufactured from pulp processed using acid-free and elementary chlorine-free practices. Furthermore, the publisher ensures that the text paper and cover board used have met acceptable environmental accreditation standards.

For further information on
Blackwell Publishing, visit our website:
www.blackwellpublishing.com

Contents

Contents

Contents

Acknowledgments

The authors and publishers gratefully acknowledge the following for permission to reproduce copyright material:

Attfield, Robin, "Saving Nature, Feeding People and Ethics," *Environmental Values* 7 (1998) reprinted by permission of The White Horse Press, Cambridge;

Barry, Brian, "Sustainability and Intergenerational Justice," *Theoria* 45 (June 1997), pp. 43–65;

Brennan, Andrew, "Environmental Awareness and Liberal Education," *British Journal of Educational Studies* 39 (1991), reprinted by permission of Blackwell Publishers Ltd/Standing Conference on Studies in Education;

Cahen, Harley, "Against the Moral Considerability of Ecosystems," *Environmental Ethics* 10 (1988), pp. 196–216;

Callicott, J. Baird, "The Case Against Moral Pluralism," *Environmental Ethics* 12 (1990) reprinted by permission of the Center for Environmental Philosophy, University of North Texas, Denton;

Callicott, J. Baird, "A Critique of and an Alternative to the Wilderness Idea," which first appeared in *Wild Earth*, vol. 4, no. 4, 1995 (802–434–4077; www.wild-earth.org) and is used with permission of the author;

Cobb, John B., Jr., "Toward a Just and Sustainable Economic Order," *Journal of Social Issues* 51 (1995);

Elliot, Robert, "Faking Nature," reprinted from *Inquiry* 25 (1982), pp. 81–93, by permission of Taylor & Francis, Oslo, Norway;

Fox, Warwick, "Deep Ecology: A New Philosophy of our Time," *The Ecologist* 14 (1984);

Gaard, Greta and Lori Gruen, "Ecofeminism: Toward Global Justice and Planetary Health," *Society and Nature* 2 (1993);

Hargrove, Eugene, "Weak Anthropocentric Intrinsic Value," *The Monist* 75 (April 1992);

Hartley, Troy W., "Environmental Justice: An Environmental Civil Rights Value Acceptable to All World Views," *Environmental Ethics* 17 (1995), reprinted by permission of Center for Environmental Philosophy, University of North Texas, Denton;

Jamieson, Dale, "Ethics, Public Policy, and Global Warming," *Science, Technology and Human Values* 17 (Spring 1992);

Katz, Eric, "Is There a Place for Animals in the Moral Consideration of Nature?" *Ethics and Animals* 4 (September 1983), reprinted by kind permission of the author;

Katz, Eric, "The Big Lie: Human Restoration of Nature," *Research in Philosophy and Technology* 12 (1992);

Lee, Keekok, "Source and Locus of Intrinsic Value: A Reexamination," *Environmental Ethics* 18 (1996), reprinted by permission of Center for Environmental Philosophy, University of North Texas, Denton;

Leopold, Aldo, "The Land Ethic," from *A Sand County Almanac: And Sketches Here and There* by Aldo Leopold, copyright 1949, 1987, Oxford University Press, Inc. Used by permission of Oxford University Press, Inc.;

Light, Andrew, "Callicott and Naess on Pluralism," reprinted from *Inquiry* 39 (1996), pp. 273–94 by permission of Taylor & Francis, Oslo, Norway;

Light, Andrew, "Ecological Restoration and the Culture of Nature: A Pragmatic Perspective," from *Restoring Nature*, ed. Paul H. Gobster and R. Bruce Hull (Island Press, Washington D.C. 2000), courtesy of Alexander Hoyt Associates, New York);

Minteer, Ben A., and Robert E. Manning, "Pragmatism in Environmental Ethics: Democracy, Pluralism and the Management of Nature," *Environmental Ethics* 21 (1999), reprinted by permission of Center for Environmental Philosophy, University of North Texas, Denton;

Naess, Arne, "The Deep Ecology Movement: Some Philosophical Aspects," *Philosophical Inquiry* 8 (1986). The version reproduced here is a later revision which was first published in *Environmental Philosophy*, Second Edition, ed. Michael Zimmerman, et al. (Prentice-Hall Inc., Englewood Cliffs, NJ, 1998);

Nelson, Michael P., "An Amalgamation of Wilderness Preservation Arguments," from *The Great New Wilderness Debate*, ed. J. Baird Callicott and Michael P. Nelson (University of Georgia Press, Athens, 1998);

Nickel, James W., and Eduardo Viola, "Integrating Environmentalism and Human Rights," *Environmental Ethics* 16 (1994), reprinted by permission of Center for Environmental Philosophy, University of North Texas, Denton;

Norton, Bryan G., "Environmental Ethics and Weak Anthropocentrism," *Environmental Ethics* 6 (1984), reprinted by permission of Center for Environmental Philosophy, University of North Texas, Denton;

Norton, Bryan G., and Bruce Hannon, "Democracy and Sense of Place Values in Environmental Policy," from *Philosophy and Geography III: Philosophies of Place*, ed. Andrew Light and Jonathan M. Smith (Lanham, MD: Rowman & Littlefield Publishers, 1998);

Noss, Reed F., "Wilderness – Now More Than Ever," which first appeared in *Wild Earth*, vol. 4, no. 4, 1995 (802–434–4077; www.wild-earth.org) and is used with permission of the author;

O'Neill, John, "The Varieties of Intrinsic Value," *The Monist* 75 (April, 1992);

Palmer, Clare, "A Bibliographic Essay on Environmental Ethics," *Studies in Christian Ethics* 7 (1994), (T & T Clark Ltd, Edinburgh, 1994);

Regan, Tom, "Animal Rights: What's in a Name?" from *Animal Welfare and the Environment*, ed. Richard D. Ryder (London: Duckworth, 1992);

Regan, Tom, "How to Worry about Endangered Species" from *The Case for Animal Rights*, pp. 359–63, The University of California Press, Berkeley, 1983. Copyright © 1983 The Regents of the University of California;

Rolston, Holmes, III, "Value in Nature and the Nature of Value," from *Philosophy and Natural Environment*, ed. Robin Attfield and Andrew Belsey, © Royal Institute of Philosophy, Supplement, published by Cambridge University Press, 1994;

Rolston, Holmes, III, "Feeding People versus Saving Nature?" from *World Hunger and Morality*, 2nd edn., ed. William Aiken and Hugh LaFollette (Englewood Cliffs: Prentice-Hall Inc., 1996);

Scherer, Donald, "Sustainable Resource Ethics," reprinted from *Encyclopedia of Energy Technology and the Environment*. Copyright © 1995 John Wiley & Sons, Inc., reprinted by permission of John Wiley & Sons, Inc.;

Singer, Peter, "Not for Humans Only: The Place of Nonhumans in Environmental Issues," from *Ethics and Problems of the 21st Century*, ed.

Acknowledgments

K. E. Goodpaster and K. M. Sayre (Notre Dame: University of Notre Dame Press, 1979);

Stone, Christopher D., "Moral Pluralism and the Course of Environmental Ethics," *Environmental Ethics* 10 (1988), reprinted by permission of Center for Environmental Philosophy, University of North Texas, Denton;

Sylvan (Routley), Richard, "Is there a need for a New Environmental Ethic?" from *Philosophy and Science: Morality and Culture: Technology and Man*, Proceedings of the XVth World Congress of Philosophy, Varna, Bulgaria: Sofia, 1973. Reprinted by permission of Nick Griffin on behalf of the author's estate;

Taylor, Paul W., "The Ethics of Respect for Nature," *Environmental Ethics* 3 (1981), reprinted by permission of Center for Environmental Philosophy, University of North Texas, Denton;

Varner, Gary E., "Can Animal Rights Activists be Environmentalists?" from *Environmental Philosophy and Environmental Activism*, ed. Don E. Marietta, Jr. and Lester Embree (Lanham, MD: Rowman & Littlefield Publishers, 1995);

Warren, Karen J., and Jim Cheney, "Ecological Feminism and Ecosystem Ecology," *Hypatia* 6 (Spring 1991), reprinted by permission of Indiana University Press;

Wenz, Peter S., "Minimal, Moderate, and Extreme Moral Pluralism," *Environmental Ethics* 15 (1993), reprinted by permission of Center for Environmental Philosophy, University of North Texas, Denton;

Weston, Anthony, "Beyond Intrinsic Value: Pragmatism in Environmental Ethics," *Environmental Ethics* 7 (1985), reprinted by permission of Center for Environmental Philosophy, University of North Texas, Denton.

The publishers apologize for any errors or omissions in the above list and would be grateful to be notified of any corrections that should be incorporated in the next edition or reprint of this book.

Introduction: Ethics and Environmental Ethics

Andrew Light and Holmes Rolston III

Environmental ethics is a relatively new field of philosophical ethics concerned with describing the values carried by the non-human natural world and prescribing an appropriate ethical response to ensure preservation or restoration of those values. This often urgent concern arises especially in view of threats to nature posed largely by humans. These threats are both to other humans and to non-humans, placing in jeopardy the communities of life on Earth. Environmental ethics as a recognized field within philosophy is now entering its third decade. Interest and development have been spectacular. The International Society for Environmental Ethics (ISEE) has four hundred members in twenty countries and (along with the Center for Environmental Philosophy) maintains an extensive website, with a major bibliography (some 10,000 entries) at http://www.cep.unt.edu/ISEE.html. There are in print over a thousand professional articles, several dozen systematic works, several dozen anthologies, and a number of active academic journals. (Complete lists may be found in the ISEE bibliography under "Anthologies" and "Systematic Works.") Courses are taught in several hundred universities and colleges on several continents (also listed on the website).

Figuring out where to go ahead, it is usually a good idea to look back – rather like looking in the rear view mirror when driving off. So this anthology couples past and present with a view to the future. We need to know where we have come

from to know where we are, and where we ought to be going. While one can trace roots in the field back much further, explicitly and implicitly in the work of philosophers and non-philosophers alike, the first articles in philosophy journals specifically on environmental topics, the first books, the first conferences and the first classes in colleges and universities all began in the early 1970s. This was no coincidence. The environmental movement was then transforming from its earlier phase consisting mainly in practical resource conservation initiatives, such as the creation of the national park system, to a much more active political and social force in its own right.

Heralded by the publication of Rachel Carson's *Silent Spring* in 1963, revealing the toll that agricultural pesticides like DDT were having on animals, plants, ecosystems, and human health, the ecology movement in the late sixties and early seventies emboldened a new generation of thinkers and activists to argue for social and political changes on a par with the peace movement, the civil rights movement, and the women's movement, all insisting on new visions of justice and new legal structures. The overriding concern was that fundamental changes were needed in how we understood the value of nature and how we organize human societies accordingly. Various figures in this movement courted controversy by diagnosing the environmental crisis in the long-prevailing Western, Enlightenment, humanist, scientific, industrial, technological mindsets, and found them all wrong-headed and misdirected. The symptoms were a host of environmental problems that we were then only beginning to understand: deforestation, soil loss, water and air pollution, desertification, loss of species habitat, loss of biodiversity, suburban sprawl, escalating populations, escalating consumption, global warming, and endless other concerns.

Humanists and social scientists in institutions of higher learning heard the call of this movement and responded by starting new areas of research in sociology, politics, history, law, and economics, aimed at contributing something from their discipline to resolving what was beginning to be understood as the environmental crisis. Philosophers, particularly those already involved in struggles against environmental problems, responded as well. Since this time, environmental ethics has been most concerned with the moral grounds for protecting the welfare of non-human animals, the moral foundations for laws protecting endangered species, and the ethical basis for preserving and restoring degraded environments. The principal question underlying such research was how values carried by nature could best be described, often asking whether nature is directly morally considerable in itself, rather than only indirectly morally considerable because it is appreciated or needed by humans. That question remains at issue today, alongside some new concerns.

Nature might be indirectly morally considerable because it is the source of things that humans need, such as natural resources, used to provide the foundations for building and sustaining human communities. As such, we might consider it unfair if one human community has greater access to a share of those resources thought to be held in common – air, water, soil, etc. – over another human community. In contrast, nature might be directly morally considerable if it possesses some kind of value (for example, some kind of value in and of itself not dependent on its value to anything or anyone else) which could further be demonstrated as the sort of value that demanded that we respect or protect it. If nature is the sort of thing that is directly morally considerable (as many ethical theories would claim humans are) then our duties, for example, to preserve whooping cranes and their habitats, would not depend only on describing some value that the cranes have for humans.

The possibility that natural things, such as (nonhuman) animals or plants, might be morally

considerable has launched diverse schools of thought in environmental ethics. This anthology introduces the field by reviewing the debates which have emerged among these different schools of thought. But such dialogue (or disagreements) are in fact healthy in a young field of philosophy. Through such debates we test and retest our assumptions; we evaluate and reevaluate our responsibilities. In fact, the editors of this volume take different perspectives, with one of us (Light) siding more with those who seek to defend the value of nature in indirect terms (a position known as "weak" or "broad anthropocentrism") and the other (Rolston) siding with those who find powerful direct arguments for why nature counts morally (the general position known as "nonanthropocentrism"). We quite agree, however, that environmental ethics prospers only with critical exchange, with deep probing, with argument (notice how positively philosophers use the terms "criticism" and "argument"). We quite agree that "Act now, think later," is unwise advice; action needs to be coupled with serious thinking.

Because this volume includes an opening introductory section that thoroughly describes the history and scope of the field as well as the contents of this volume (chapter 1), we restrict our comments here first, to some general remarks on the nature of ethics (including how it differs from law and how environmental ethics fits in the broader field of ethics), second, to a brief overview of some main themes that have emerged in environmental ethics, and third to a general orientation to the different parts of the volume.

What is Ethics?

Opening a newspaper has become an exercise in a variety of fears. There will be front-page stories about all manner of human suffering, from the mundane to the unusually horrific. Such fears may be exaggerated by the papers themselves. Stories of homicide or armed robbery are reported to titillate us and play on a human desire to view the dark and the grotesque – a hunger identified as far back as the ancient Greek philosopher, Plato. But in many other cases, the fears emerge from a sense that things have gotten out of control; the world is not safe. Famines, political assassinations, military coups, and racial and religious strife are part of our daily diet of news. Often our response is first, "How terrible, this is simply wrong!" And second, "Something must be done about this!"

One resort to comfort such reactions is the realm of law, both as a description of why something is wrong (it is illegal), and second as a prescription for what should be done (those responsible should be punished by the state). We normally think that issues of right and wrong are solely deliberated and assessed in law. Philosophers, however, make a further point: On such occurrences a moral, and not only a legal line has been crossed. The deed is bad, legal or not.

For example, take the case of political terrorism. Imagine a banner headline, "Liberationist Army Strikes Again: Ten Die in Terrorist Attack, Mostly Children." An accompanying picture shows us a policewoman, her face ashen and stunned, her uniform stained with blood, holding a ten year old child gone limp. A bomb was placed in a garbage can just inside a popular fast-food restaurant, frequented by children from a nearby school. The bombing was timed at the end of the school day, when children frequented the restaurant. The Liberationist Army claims responsibility for the attack.

Fear and anger arise within us. We feel indignant; these children did nothing wrong to deserve such an end. The world is a frightening place where such things can happen and the terrorist responsible for the bombing, no matter his or her larger political aims, has done something quite wrong. We mourn the fate of these children, now robbed of their chance to live a full and long life, achieving whatever goals and dreams which they may have only dimly started to formulate. Those responsible for this bombing should be punished to the full extent of the law. No ends justify these means.

Imagine now a new spin on this tale: A similar act of terrorism has occurred in the middle of a recent war zone where no clear legal authority is applicable or enforced. Technically, the newspaper reports, no illegal act of murder was committed because no legal body is responsible for actions taken in that jurisdiction just yet. It's a "no man's land." Children passing through this area were simply in the wrong place at the wrong time. Would our indignation then be muted because the terrorist could not be formally charged with a crime?

Most of us would say no; a wrong was still committed. What we are now claiming then is that a *moral* wrong was committed; an *immoral*

harm has occurred. The bombing was *unethical*. Reading back from this amended case to the first one, we can see that our sense of outrage and our desire for justice was not simply that the bombing at the restaurant was illegal, but also that it was immoral. Ethics underpins law, criticizes it, argues for and with it.

The philosophical discipline of ethics, practiced in the West across the last 2,500 years, has been concerned with making sense of intuitions that actions like this are wrong, legal or not. Ethics becomes a guide to what law ought to be. Philosophers have regularly hoped that the laws that societies pass would embody some considered opinion of what is ethically right and wrong, distributing punishments accordingly. But ethics is not just concerned with such extreme cases of harm. The scope of ethics is in fact much broader than the realm of law. Ethics extends to all our duties and obligations, virtues and vices, as we interact with each other – whether or not we should lie or steal, whether we should be charitable toward those less fortunate than ourselves, whether we should be forgiving, and how to resolve conflicts of interest when we have conflicting obligations to different persons.

Following John Deigh, we can subdivide the field of ethics into six parts:

The general study of goodness
The general study of right action
Applied ethics
Metaethics
Moral psychology
Metaphysics of moral responsibility (the study of free will)[1]

The general study of goodness is directed minimally at two questions: what are the components of a good life, or, what sort of things are good in themselves. Right action concerns the principles of right and wrong that govern our choices and pursuits, understood collectively to constitute a moral code that defines the responsibilities of people who live together. This sort of ethics includes religious traditions, for example the Christian and Jewish traditions, as well as formal philosophical traditions such as deontological or duty-based ethics (illustrated by the eighteenth-century German philosopher, Immanuel Kant), and consequentialist views, or views based on the outcomes served by an ethical decision (illustrated by the utilitarian British philosopher, John Stuart Mill in the nineteenth century).

Applied ethics extends these arguments about principle to particular areas of concern. When applied to medicine, this form of applied ethics is called "medical ethics" (sometimes expanded to include biotechnology and called "bioethics"). When applied to commerce, this becomes "business ethics"; when applied to the press, "journalism ethics"; when applied to engineering, "engineering ethics"; when applied to agriculture, "agricultural ethics," and so on. When applied to issues of environmental policy and regulation, we formulate an "environmental ethics."

One thing is different about the last, however. Many environmental ethicists, alone among various other applied ethicists, envision that the scope of their field moves outside the human sphere. All forms of applied ethics can raise some issues of principle (such as whether "death" has occurred with brain death in medical ethics); but environmental ethics raises deep questions about who counts morally and why – endangered species, old growth forests, wilderness areas – requiring reexamination of the human–nature relationship. In that sense environmental ethics can be as theoretical as it is applied.

Metaethics is the study of the nature and ground of beliefs about ethical beliefs and claims. Ethics moves up a level, so to speak. Metaethics is not a competing field to the various schools of ethics, but rather the study of the methods of justification by which different ethical theories claim to be better adept at describing values and resolving ethical controversies. Metaethics is an important area for applied ethics because we discuss on this terrain the kind of ethics most appropriate to the particular inquiry in which we are engaged. Maybe, for instance, one should be concerned with rights in dealing with individuals, but more utilitarian in dealing with undifferentiated collectives, such as whole nations or future generations. In environmental ethics, many of the debates about the kind of value that nature has (such as whether it has the kind of value which makes it directly or indirectly morally considerable) are debates in metaethics.

Moral psychology is the study of psychological concepts such as desire, emotion, and personality in relation to moral questions. Here we are concerned with whether arguments about what is right in a moral sense do or do not motivate people to change their behavior. Perhaps love (of whales, for instance) moves persons more effectively than argument (about their roles in marine ecosystems) in order to get their support for a ban on commercial whaling; or perhaps love is misplaced without argument. The metaphysics of moral responsibility is the formal study of freedom, or free will, and what it means to act freely in relation to ethical choices. If our actions are predetermined, how can it be true that we can or ought to be held morally responsible for our actions? It might be that "nature" shapes our ethics more than we like to admit; we act selfishly because we are "born that way." Maybe we have to offset our genetic tendencies with moral education, which frees us to do better than we otherwise would do. Then again, maybe what we "naturally" do, what we are (perhaps instinctively) moved to do can be a good thing – as when a mother cares for her children.

One common misconception about ethics concerns the extent of its applicability. For example, in discussions about arguments for informed consent in medical experiments, we have heard people respond: "Why are we talking about requiring some universal rule for informed consent, even in developing countries?" or "The problem with Doctor X is that he only understands ethics in a North American context." This is a substantive metaethical claim about ethics in general and applied ethics in particular. Underpinning the complaint about Doctor X is the claim that ethics cannot be universal (or even aspire to be), and that ethical claims ought to be different from country to country, or region to region.

But to argue that ethics must be different from place to place is to make a metaethical claim, or a claim about the general nature of ethics that must be theoretically defended rather than only stipulated. This sort of relativism is at odds with the way many if not most philosophers think about ethics. Such a position would reduce ethics to an anthropological survey of the different moral attitudes that different people have in the world. To find out what is right for them (whether non-Western physicians should be bound by rules mandating voluntary consent), we go there and find out what most of those people think. Usually the aspirations of ethicists are not merely descriptive in this sense, but prescriptive. Ethicists try to give reasons, for example, why a right to do X should be a right to which everyone is entitled, and correspondingly why interfering with someone's right to X is most often wrong.

Ethicists have of course noticed that different countries have different customs. But most of them do not then say: "When in Rome do as the Romans do," and let it go at that. The historical ideal of ethics is to formulate a set of foundational claims under some description – meaning that when one settles on a fundamental ethical claim, this argument is postulated as true regardless of contexts of time, space, location, or conditions. Ethics has universal intent. So, following our previous example, if we reach an ethical conclusion, "It is morally wrong for terrorists to cause the deaths of politically innocent people," then we are making a claim about all similar acts of terrorism in all places, at all times, past, present, and future.

Of course we might be wrong about some of these universal claims – those about sexuality, gender, and marriage have been much disputed of late, for instance. Ethicists can sometimes argue that some bit of human activity that we once thought was open to universal arguments is really not properly speaking grounded in ethics but instead is a matter of local custom or personal choice. Nonetheless, the question of whether ethics has a universal domain is a lively and on-going debate. There are powerful arguments for always keeping the Golden Rule, or telling the truth, or keeping promises, or being just, though these must be applied in sometimes different and difficult circumstances.

There are many competing theories of morality, or schools of ethics in addition to the few mentioned above (you should consult a good ethics textbook for more background and examples from these various schools). One of the central questions for all of these schools of thought is who counts in ethics. Who deserves moral recognition such that we can meaningfully claim that they have suffered a moral harm? Even if it is settled that ethics properly includes questions of goodness, whose goodness are we interested in? We take it as a matter of course that the children murdered by the terrorists are moral subjects (or more technically, *moral patients*; see below). On most accounts, respect is at least owed to beings capable of having interests that should be respected. There are, however, things that are not morally considerable on most ethical theories, such as inanimate objects, like rocks, or human artifacts such as this book you are reading. It would be a

strange ethical theory that claimed that if you deliberately spilled a cup of coffee on the book you had harmed it in a moral sense. Of course we could give ethical reasons not to damage a book that was the property of another person, but because you owed obligations to the person, not to the book itself.

These debates can get more challenging however when we ask about extending moral consideration to beings not hitherto thought to be moral subjects. Consider slavery. For much of human history, it was considered acceptable practice for one human to own another as a piece of property. Sometimes the considerations owed to slaves were closer to those we now suppose for a book, rather than to free humans. It might be imprudent to harm a slave, but it was not strictly speaking unethical in the sense that a moral wrong was being committed against the slave. But today the considered opinion is that slavery itself is an unethical practice and a grievous moral harm was committed to those historically held in bondage.

Such a conclusion however was only arrived at through much discussion and debate. Other debates have asked about the scope of moral concern and what obligations are owed to whom – whether women should vote, whether children should work in factories, whether there should be a minimum wage and how much, whether a fetus is a person, whether comatose patients are still owed respect as persons. An example en route to environmental ethics is whether animals have rights, or more modestly whether their welfare counts morally.

The issue of whether it is morally wrong to mistreat animals has a longer history than many other debates in environmental ethics. Immanuel Kant and St. Thomas Aquinas offered indirect arguments that it was wrong to harm animals because committing such acts only encouraged people to treat other humans in a similarly callous manner. The nineteenth-century utilitarian Jeremy Bentham went further and offered direct reasons: one ought not to cause needless pain, whether in beast or human.

Deciding (or discovering) that non-human animals can also count morally necessitates changes in the way that we should behave toward them. Depending on how much they suffer, and perhaps also on the kind and extent of the pleasures enjoyed by humans, we might agree that we should not keep animals confined in factory farms, or eat them as meat, or use them as laboratory animals in medical experiments. The claim however that we should so expand the ground of moral considerability is a contentious issue and many ethicists would object to it. As you will see in Eric Katz's contribution (chapter 7), even those who would acknowledge the moral relevance of the environment more broadly may object to extending the same kind of regard to individual animals.

One objection is that, historically, when we have extended the class of those who count morally to include other classes of humans, this goes along with reciprocal responsibilities on their part. Those once slaves are now full citizens with concomitant rights and responsibilities; once women won the right to vote they had a responsibility to vote conscientiously. Would not then recognition of non-human animals as subjects entail that they also owed moral duties as well? But such a conclusion would, absurdly, hold grizzly bears morally responsible for harming humans; or, more bizarre still, fault them for killing elk calves, which they need to eat in the spring. Perhaps then we shouldn't have started down this road at all.

Objections like this however are false starts. Many ethicists accept a distinction between moral *agents* and moral *patients*. The class of moral patients is that class of beings to whom we consider that we owe ethical obligations, when those obligations can be ascertained, and are deserving of what we have been calling moral considerability. Moral agents are defined as that class of moral patients, usually only persons, to whom we owe obligations and who, in turn, are held to be morally responsible for their actions. All moral agents are moral patients but not all moral patients are moral agents. When we accord moral agents moral recognition we can expect them to live up to certain duties related to the respect of those obligations. On the other hand, if a being is only a moral patient and not a moral agent we do not expect it to be morally responsible for its actions. The most often cited examples of moral patients who are not moral agents are human infants and mentally impaired persons. For example, we respect their rights as humans against torture (and codify this in law), even though we do not worry about how they exercise their rights or behave responsibly.

Perhaps animals should be treated morally, and also legally, in a similar way. We can imagine fair methods for assessing the best sense of the interests of animals, even though they may not be able to communicate their interests to us – not in words at least, as also the severely mentally impaired often cannot. Some might argue an important difference between these classes of humans and animals is that infants will someday grow up to be moral agents, if you will, and we have a relevant template of a normal human moral agent with which we can compare the mentally impaired person. But it would appear relevant that many people intuitively understand that the rights we grant to children against undue harm do not depend on the fact that they will grow up to be adults. Rightly or wrongly, many of us chafe at the thought of experimenting with children stricken with incurable diseases in the same way that we would treat animals in medical experiments. Recognizing moral obligations to animals, or more ambitiously, respecting certain narrow classes of rights for animals may not require us to conceive in a new way the connection between rights and obligations in dealing with other humans.

Some arguments made to extend moral considerability to animals will be found in Part II, for example, in the work of Peter Singer and Tom Regan (chapters 4 and 5). In these arguments, counting nonhuman animals morally is at least consistent with counting those human moral patients who are not also moral agents. We have a parallel, or an analogy. But why stop there? Why not count the environment in a moral sense as well? One problem, as we shall see, is that it is not as straightforward to extend moral consideration to entities such as plants, or species, or ecosystems, which either do not have interests at all or do not have interests in the same way as do human and (nonhuman) animals (Cahen, chapter 9). But this unearths a still deeper question, whether having interests is the only criteria which we can use to determine whether a living being deserves our moral respect.

Why an Environmental Ethic?

By now we hope that two conclusions will be fairly uncontroversial: (1) A legitimate goal of ethics is to provide us with a language, with effective arguments, whereby we can claim that some kinds of actions are right or wrong, or at least better or worse, independently of their cultural or legal context. (2) A central question in ethics is how broadly "inclusive" we ought to be in our circle of moral consideration. Looking at the past, there is a good case to be made that ethics has often not been inclusive enough. There has been too much ethical discrimination; a kind of intellectual apartheid. We need to be more discriminating, more sensitive about who counts and why.

Looking at the history of (2), some see a pattern. The history of ethics often appears to be the history of ever-expanding notions of moral respect. We regularly come to criticize our past practices for unduly restricting moral obligation to those we have now more fully brought into the moral circle, such as slaves, African-Americans, women, foreigners, previously denied rights given to others. To claim that the history of ethics is best understood in this way is nonetheless controversial. Still, the goal of many environmental ethicists – now further to expand moral consideration to animals, to plants, to species, even to ecosystems and the Earth – is consistent with this way of reading the history of ethics.

One of the first explicit arguments of this kind in the literature in environmental ethics comes from the "land ethic" of Aldo Leopold (1887–1949), a forester widely recognized as formulating one of the first "holist" environmental ethics. This is an ethic not restricted to individuals (human or not), but inclusive of ecosystems considered as a whole, which he called "the land" (chapter 2). Leopold adopted this expanding, or evolving, theory of ethics, claiming that there has been ethical progress through history. For Leopold, ethics was once thought of as only relevant to individual–individual relations (illustrated by the Ten Commandments), and this hardly included slaves at the start. This inter-personal ethic was expanded eventually to include individual–society relations (such as duties to promote democracy). The next logical step for him is to include individual relations with "the land," the whole community of life, in the scope of ethics.

Leopold's interpretation of progress in the history of ethics is unusual and many philosophers would contest its accuracy. Nonetheless, Leopold's insight is a good one: If ethical considerations govern the relations between individuals and the community around them, why do we restrict our understanding of that community only to the human community? Do not the communities we live in include the myriad other living things with whom we share the Earth, with whom we have entwined destinies? We are all bound up

together. So why should only humans count? Exclusion must at least be carefully justified. Even if we do not think that ecosystems can count morally, it seems clear that human communities cannot grow and thrive without this life support. So we need some way of morally regarding the welfare of those ecosystems either directly or indirectly.

Such intuitions lead us to think globally, cross-culturally, universally, rather like we did earlier with the terrorism case. In our morning newspapers, we read about other calamities, not always involving humans. We learn of threats to rhinos or to amphibians, and recognize that the world is becoming a hazardous home, not only to us, but to the myriad other species that share it with us. The threats to life, to health, to flourishing include many who are not humans. Debate is always going on in our national capitals and legislatures over whether there should be new laws protecting the environment from these harms. But where such laws are considered, often there is an ethical issue as well. If not, are matters of protection of the environment only governed by prudence such that we only recognize an ethical concern in an environmental issue if human health or safety is immediately at risk? The amphibians are like miners' canaries. But perhaps there is more with those rhinos.

Many environmental ethicists argue, rather forcefully, that protection of the environment – of threatened species or habitats, of old-growth forests or even systemic processes such as the oxygen/carbon/carbon dioxide cycle – are valuable in a moral sense for more than the instrumental goods that they provide for humans. These are "vital" on Earth, and what is vital counts morally. These ethicists try to form metaethical theories and accounts of goodness and right action that warrant moral respect for the environment writ large, holistically or systemically. For if the value of nature is restricted only to the instrumental values we attribute to it, then it appears difficult to imagine protecting it in many cases where either no human interest is apparent or where another conflicting human interest seems necessarily to take precedent. We can grow food quite well, maybe even better, if we do not have to worry about endangered warblers' winter habitat in the coffee plantations.

Richard Routley, an Australian logician, formulated a "thought experiment" in one of the first published professional papers in environmental ethics (chapter 3).[2] His experiment was not done in a laboratory but is a conceptual problem to test our intuitions about the scope and limits of morality. (Philosophers often think up test examples like this.) Routley's experiment is aimed at teasing out the common intuition that something is wrong when we think the sole value of nature lies in its use to humans. Imagine that there is only one person left on Earth who both knows that no humans will ever occupy the planet again and who also has the ability (through access to a vast array of nuclear weapons left over from the war that has destroyed everybody else) to destroy all life on this planet. What would be wrong with the last person going out with a big bang, and taking everything else along? Would anything be wrong with this as the last human act?

Most people answer: He shouldn't do it. There is something wrong with such destruction. Routley points to this common response as part of a larger argument that nature has more than instrumental value for humans; also it has intrinsic value, or value such that its existence or flourishing is a morally good thing independently of its relation or use to anything else (in this case, independently of its worth to humans). But we need not resort to such extreme thought experiments to arrive at such conclusions. There are lots of cases, from the snail darter to the Florida panther, of endangered species and subspecies that exist only in particular lakes, streams, swamps, habitats ("local endemics," the biologists call them) which will be wiped out by planned hydroelectric projects, irrigation systems, or highways. Should such species be protected? Do human benefits justify their destruction? One answer popular with many environmental ethicists is that such species have intrinsic value, value on their own, or in themselves, and that this value demands our respect when we determine their fate.

But such conclusions, though widespread, are more intuitive than argued. Environmental ethics still needs convincing argument for the direct moral consideration of nature. That has remained challenging, and is attempted here by Sylvan, Taylor, Rolston, and Lee (chapters 3, 6, 11, and 12).

Bryan Norton and Eugene Hargrove (chapters 13 and 14) argue that, not only do we not have such convincing arguments, we do not need them, because there are adequate concepts of the value of nature for humans that can be extended to cover endangered species and such cases. Environmental ethics does not have to dive into the troubled philosophical waters of knowing whether value is there without us or whether something like intrinsic value can be attributed to entities, such as ecosystems, that many do not believe have "interests" in a morally relevant sense. Considering an expanded and enlightened sense of what benefits humans can do all the moral work we need in justifying an environmental ethic.

This debate over intrinsic value and the moral considerability of nature is part of a larger debate over the status of "anthropocentrism," or human-centered ethical thinking. Tim Hayward argues that most environmental ethicists have understood ethical anthropocentrism as the view that prioritizes those attitudes, values, or practices that give "exclusive or arbitrarily preferential consideration to human interests as opposed to the interests of other beings," or, speaking generally, the environment.[3] Many environmental ethicists have been adamant that if environmental ethics is to be a distinctive field of ethics, it must necessarily reject anthropocentrism understood in this sense. Using Hayward's definition, this amounts to rejecting the claim that ethics should be restricted to obligations, duties, concern among humans and what they have at stake. Such centering of ethics on humans is thought by some to prioritize all human interests over whatever might be assumed are the interests of nonhumans, species, or ecosystems. Justice is for "just us" humans. Charity stays right at home. We humans care about ourselves, only, though we do and ought to care for each other. Nothing else matters, unless something else matters for us. But Hayward goes on to argue that this is too narrow a definition and conception of anthropocentrism, and too strong a set of conclusions to draw from what it might mean to be anthropocentric.

Among the first papers published by professional philosophers in the field (those by Arne Naess, Holmes Rolston, Richard Routley [Sylvan], Val Routley [later Plumwood] and Peter Singer) some version of anthropocentrism was often the target even if not explicitly labeled as such. For Singer the worry was specifically over what he calls "speciesism." Speciesism is the arbitrary assumption that only the interests of members of our human species matter morally. But that, Singer protests, excludes the interests of those nonhumans who can suffer, who ought to be included by the pain/pleasure criterion of utilitarianism (chapter 4). For Richard and Val Routley the worry was over what they called "human chauvinism," or, the claim that "value and morality can ultimately be reduced to matters of interest or concern to the class of humans."[4] Human chauvinism defines who counts morally in ways that necessarily favor capacities found only, or most paradigmatically, in humans, such as rationality or language (see chapter 3).[5]

Fighting anthropocentric views seemed the natural starting point for any environmental ethics. Rightly or wrongly, anthropocentrism was equated with forms of valuation which easily, or even necessarily, lead to nature's destruction. This overlooks, of course, anthropocentric values such as aesthetic values that might count as reasons to preserve nature. A corollary assumption then was that even a limited endorsement of anthropocentric valuation of nature would end up preferring development over preservation – at least when push comes to shove. Centrally preferring human interests seemed an unlikely way to save nature.

It is important to remember that for many environmental ethicists the predominance of anthropocentrism was partly to be explained by the history of Western philosophy. The various schools of ethics, traditionally, classically, had defended, or just assumed, a formal principle that ethical reasoning was limited to, and therefore to be applied only to, human agents and patients. Regardless of continuing disagreements about whether anthropocentrism really is an impediment to making better decisions about the environment, among the various kinds of applied ethics, environmental ethics alone has produced thinkers determined to take on anthropocentrism. This goal was thought further to mark the distinctiveness of the field (a point made by Norton in chapter 13). This task of disciplinary self-correction would constitute a unique contribution that philosophers could make in response to the environmental crisis; it was a task uniquely suited for philosophers.

Meanwhile, there are (and have been all along) environmental ethicists who do not reject anthropocentrism, in part because they have difficulty ascribing intrinsic value to nature or otherwise coming up with reasons why nature might be directly morally considerable. Such philosophers usually argue for some form of "weak" or "broad" anthropocentrism, that is forms of human-centered thinking that admit humanly-based values to nature other than mere resource value. For example, strong reasons may exist to protect the environment out of obligations that we have to

human future generations to protect their welfare and not saddle them with environmental harms. Weak anthropocentrists want to include "amenity" as well as "commodity" values, "ecological" as well as "economic" values. Weak anthropocentrists argue that such values are not only sufficient to generate an adequate environmental ethic but, if appealed to, may more likely motivate people to change their behavior or support stronger environmental policies (an argument in moral psychology). These sorts of values are arguably closer to the prevailing modes of anthropocentric thinking which, after all, most environmental ethicists attribute to humans.

At the start of this section we also mentioned that one goal of ethics is to justify moral claims against cultural traditions to the contrary. In environmental ethics there is a similar goal expressed in much work in the field. Part of the critique of anthropocentrism has been that it only justifies value to nature in instrumental terms, which in turn are embedded within culturally relative environmental policies. Saving nature would depend on nature's being useful to some particular culture at some particular time. Routley provides an example of this worry, concerning a hypothetical culture desirous of saving whales for multiple reasons, mixing economic value with the pleasure people take in whale-watching (chapter 3).

> [I]t would just be a happy accident, it seems, if collective demand ... for a state of the economy with blue whales as a mixed good, were to succeed in outweighing private whaling demands; for if no one in the base class [of citizens] happened to know that blue whales exist or cared a jot that they do then "rational" economic decision-making would do nothing to prevent their extinction.[6]

Paul Taylor brings this claim home further, and more forcefully (and controversially), by suggesting that the problem with anthropocentric value is that it is "entirely relative to culture. If a particular society did not hold ideals that could be symbolized in nature and wildlife (for example, if it happened to value plastic trees more than real ones), then ... there would be no reason for that society to preserve nature or protect wildlife."[7] Fashions come and go. Should the fate of endangered species depend on whether watching whooping cranes is in style?

The problem, these critics say, with weak anthropocentrism is that admitting some humanly based reasons for valuing nature opens the door to other, countervailing anthropocentric reasons for not valuing nature. Some of these critics argue that the values we are trying to save are outside culture, nonanthropocentric, and we need an ethic that escapes these vagaries of different culturally-bound reasons for valuing nature. But that, we have already said, is difficult to get. The anthropocentrists reply that we are better off trying to escape these local fashions of time and place by some broader anthropocentric arguments, such as appealing to our obligations to future generations. We do not know what their fashions will be, and we ought to keep their options for enjoying wild nature open.

Suffice it to say that the terrain of environmental ethics is rich. What we have in environmental ethics, for good or ill, is the attempt to create entirely new foundations and conceptual schemes for a host of questions concerning the moral considerability of the community of life on Earth. Here we have people trying to figure out who they are and where they are, and seeking answers to know what they ought to do to be responsible for, if not to, their planet. Many of these answers are indeed dramatic departures from the history of ethics so far.

Contents of the Volume

Readers should turn to Clare Palmer's bibliographic essay (chapter 1) for a more thorough history of environmental ethics as well as further introduction to the contents of the volume. Our intention is to blend the best classic essays (for example, Aldo Leopold's "Land Ethic," chapter 2; and Richard Sylvan's initial inquiry, chapter 3) with contemporary summaries and works breaking ground with intriguing new paths of scholarship. Parts II, III, and IV take up three of the central debates of environmental ethics: who counts in an environmental ethic? Should we extend ethics to include only other animals or continue with plants, species, or even go as far as ecosystems? Is there a tension between these several forms of extension? Is nature intrinsically valuable, valuable in itself? Are

there one or many ways of valuing nature? There might consequently be several schemes justified in environmental ethics; then again there might be an underlying unifying principle (monism versus pluralism).

In Part V we turn to three alternative approaches to mainstream environmental ethics – continuing the plural possibilities. Deep ecology (chapters 19 and 20) and ecofeminism (chapters 21 and 22) are better established options; environmental pragmatism (chapters 23 and 24) is the newest challenge to the foundations of the field. All three alternatives argue that the classic historical debates started out on the wrong foot, or took wrong turns along the way. We can only hear representatives of these views; but we hope that these essays will stimulate readers to investigate these alternatives further in publications dedicated to these views.[8] One criterion has been to choose representatives that integrate well with (or complement, or challenge, if you prefer) the central questions addressed in Parts I–IV).

For example the paper by Light on moral pluralism (chapter 18) ends by bringing the monist–pluralist controversy into conversation with the material to follow on deep ecology. How does the theoretical discussion of pluralism in environmental ethics connect with the cultural pluralism at the heart of the concerns of deep ecology? The papers by the pragmatists (Weston, and Minteer and Manning) specifically comment on the intrinsic value positions developed in Part III. Minteer and Manning develop further the pragmatism inherent in Norton's weak anthropocentrism (chapter thirteen), thus helping to demonstrate how debates in environmental ethics have evolved over time and stimulated these new alternative voices.

Part VI brings into focus concrete issues and specific cases. This is environmental ethics "on the ground." An Earth ethics needs to get "down to earth." Here we choose three issues: environmental sustainability on the lands we inhabit and use (chapters 25, 26, and 27), ecological restoration on lands we have abused and ought to restore (chapters 28, 29, and 30), and wilderness preservation on lands we do not "use" but ought to keep wild (chapters 31, 32, and 33). We need to think as we act, to think why and how we act. An ethic needs principled practice. So these articles constantly connect up with the theoretical debates and the central questions, as well as with alternative views.

For example, the section on ecological restoration begins with two classic papers by Robert Elliot and Eric Katz criticizing the practice of restoring damaged ecosystems based on the argument that humans (managing nature) can never in principle recreate the intrinsic value of (wild spontaneous) nature as this has been described in some nonanthropocentric value theory. But the section ends with a critique of Elliot's and Katz's worries about "faked nature" from the perspective of environmental pragmatism.

Finally, Part VII opens up the big picture again, moving now from concrete issues back toward a larger worldview: an environmental ethic needs to put humans in their place; the ethic needs to place humans in their cultures significantly on their landscapes. Too often the focus on describing the value of nature in itself leads theorists to neglect questions concerning how humans must and ought to relate themselves to nature. How are humans to value nature in the context of other social problems? The concluding readings step back to take this larger view helping, we hope, to demonstrate the importance of connecting environmental problems with the full social agenda. This move is consistent with current trends in the field which are seeking to broaden discussions of the environment to include other questions of justice and community welfare.

Holmes Rolston claims that we often face conflicts of interest between saving nature and providing food for needy people; and that people, even needy people, ought not always get the priority (chapter 34). At times, we ought not solve our human problems by sacrificing nature. Sometimes, the nonanthropocentric values win, or ought to win, over the anthropocentric ones. Robin Attfield responds (chapter 35), creating an interesting dialogue between two committed proponents of intrinsic value in nature – a dialogue that, we promise, will generate a lively class discussion. There follow articles on environmentalism and human rights (Nickel and Viola, chapter 36), environmental racism and civil rights (Hartley, chapter 37), obligations to human future generations to preserve environmental quality (Barry, chapter 38), environmentalism and democracy (Norton and Hannon, chapter 39) and environmental education (Brennan, chapter 40). Once,

perhaps, you could claim to be literate if you knew your culture and how it fitted into world cultures. But no more. Now, no one is educated unless environmentally literate, knowing how to fit these cultures harmoniously into the landscape.

So there lies ahead a lively and engaging invitation to environmental ethics. And more to the point, an urgent invitation. Here are serious and relevant concerns, central to the global agenda in the new millennium. If these concerns are ever rightly solved, they will need to be solved in the lifetimes of the next generation of decision makers hopefully aided by the next generation of environmental ethicists, today the students in our colleges and universities. The next step is yours.

Notes

1 John Deigh, "Ethics," in *The Cambridge Dictionary of Philosophy*, ed. Robert Audi (Cambridge: Cambridge University Press, 1995), pp. 244–9.

2 Now deceased. Richard Routley later changed his name to Richard Sylvan.

3 Tim Hayward, "Anthropocentrism: A Misunderstood Problem," *Environmental Values* 6 (1997): 51.

4 Richard Routley and Val Routley, "Against the Inevitability of Human Chauvinism," in *Ethics and Problems of the 21st Century*, ed. K. E. Goodpaster and K. M. Sayre (Notre Dame, IN: University of Notre Dame Press, 1979), p. 36.

5 There is some dispute whether speciesism and human chauvinism can or should be equated with each other or with anthropocentrism. See the Hayward article cited above. See also Robyn Eckersley, "Beyond Human Racism," *Environmental Values* 7 (1998): 165–82.

6 Chapter 3, this volume, p. 52.

7 Paul Taylor, "Are Humans Superior to Animals and Plants?" *Environmental Ethics* 6 (1984): 151.

8 See, for example, *Ecofeminism: Women, Animals, Nature*, ed. Greta Gaard (Philadelphia: Temple University Press, 1993) and *Ecological Feminism*, ed. Karen Warren (London: Routledge, 1994). For more on deep ecology see *Deep Ecology for the Twenty-first Century*, ed. George Sessions (Boston: Shambhala, 1995) and *Beneath the Surface: Critical Essays in the Philosophy of Deep Ecology*, ed. Eric Katz, Andrew Light and David Rothenberg (Cambridge, MA: The MIT Press, 2000). For more on environmental pragmatism see *Environmental Pragmatism*, ed. Andrew Light and Eric Katz (London: Routledge, 1996).

PART I

What is Environmental Ethics?

1

An Overview of Environmental Ethics

Clare Palmer

Introduction

Questions concerning the ways in which human beings can and should interact with the nonhuman natural world can hardly be said to be new. Throughout recorded human history prescriptions concerning human behavior towards the nonhuman world have existed. Although with reference to restricted periods of time and restricted geographical locations, attempts have been made to categorize such prescriptions and to consider the attitudes that underlie them, to attempt a comprehensive survey would be an enormous task.[1] This chapter concerns a much smaller, more manageable area, and even within this area, I will not attempt to provide a detailed historical survey.[2] I will be sketching, primarily, approaches to what has become known as "environmental ethics" found in the English-speaking Western world, that is to say, the UK, the USA and Australia, during the last thirty years.[3] (A further area which, while relevant, will not be explicitly covered in this paper is the range of positions on exclusively "animal rights" or "animal liberation" issues.)[4] Any sketch such as this cannot avoid emphasizing some areas at the expense of others, and simplifying that which is complex and contested. It also reflects what might be considered "mainstream" philosophical environmental ethics; and thus is open to the range of criticisms which can be or have been made of such environmental ethics by feminists, environmental policy-makers, activists

and those interested in urban studies, to name but a few. Despite such criticisms, this overview is intended to provide a helpful context in which to read the chapters gathered in this collection.

A Brief Historical Sketch

The publication of Rachel Carson's *Silent Spring* in 1962, warning of the dangers to humans and to wildlife from toxic pesticide residues, is widely regarded as the spark which kindled the environmental movement as it is known today. It was not until some time after this, however, that serious philosophical reflection about ethical issues raised by human action in the nonhuman natural world commenced, in the early 1970s.[5] In 1971 the first conference on environmental philosophy was held at the University of Georgia USA;[6] and in 1973 Richard Sylvan (then Routley) gave the paper, reproduced in this book: "Is There a Need for a New, an Environmental, Ethic?" – a question which he answered positively. In the same year Scandinavian philosopher Arne Naess published, in *Inquiry*, his article "The Shallow and the Deep, Long-Range Ecology Movements," destined to be of peculiar importance in its popular appeal as the founding statement of what later became known as deep ecology.[7] In the field of environmental law, Christopher Stone produced and later published an essay entitled "Should Trees Have Standing?" arguing that "environmental issues should be

Clare Palmer

litigated before federal agencies or federal courts in the name of the inanimate objects about to be despoiled...and where inquiry is the subject of public outrage."[8] Stone's paper, while not in itself contributing substantially to the later philosophical debate, helped to make the application of the language of "rights" and "standing" to nonhuman natural objects and areas more familiar, despite its origin in a legal rather than a philosophical context. The year 1974 also saw the publication of John Passmore's philosophical monograph *Man's Responsibility for Nature.*[9]

By 1975, ethical questions concerning the treatment of nonhumans had begun to become more significant on the philosophical agenda. Peter Singer's *Animal Liberation*, developing a utilitarian approach to the treatment of sentient animals, was published. With the publication of this book, and the subsequent proliferation of philosophical work on this topic, ethical questions concerning the treatment of nonhuman animals were well on the way to achieving philosophical respectability. In the environmental field also, by 1979, there was enough ethical interest in environmental issues for Eugene Hargrove to begin producing the journal *Environmental Ethics*, now indisputably the most significant journal in the field. Shortly after this, in the early 1980s, new and influential collections of essays on environmental philosophy were published, most notably a volume from the Australian National University, *Environmental Philosophy* and another collection, also of Australian origin, sharing the same name.[10] By this time, book length studies of environmental ethics had begun to appear.[11]

From the mid-1980s to the present time, research, publication and teaching in environmental ethics has rapidly expanded. Ethical positions first mooted in articles in *Environmental Ethics* in the early 1980s crystallized into densely argued books; most notable amongst these Holmes Rolston's *Environmental Ethics* and Paul Taylor's *Respect for Nature* (to both of which I shall return).[12] In 1989, the International Society for Environmental Ethics (ISEE) was founded. Several American universities began both undergraduate and graduate courses in environmental ethics, most notably Colorado State University and the University of North Texas in the USA; while Lancaster University in the UK began to offer a taught MA course in Values and the Environment. New journals relevant to environmental ethics were also founded during the 1990s: in the UK *Environmental Values*

in 1992, *Worldviews: Environment, Culture, Religion* in 1997, and *Ethics, Place and Environment* in 1998; in the US *Ethics and the Environment* in 1996 and *Philosophy and Geography* in 1997. By the end of the twentieth century, environmental ethics was a widely studied and hotly debated subject.

Central Questions in Environmental Ethics

A wide spectrum of ethical positions is covered by the umbrella term "environmental ethics." These positions draw on a variety of ethical traditions, from Plato and Aristotle to Mill and Moore. As one might expect, a vigorous debate is being conducted between those advocating such diverse approaches. Certain key questions lie at its heart.

One central area of debate concerns value theory in environmental ethics. What is considered to be valuable, and from where does such value come? A number of differing issues and concerns are raised by this question. It is helpful to begin by noting the commonly drawn distinction in environmental ethics between *instrumental* and *non-instrumental* value. Instrumental value is value assigned to something because of its usefulness, as a means to an end. Water, for instance, is of instrumental value to humans because it helps in achieving another goal – that is, remaining alive. But this does not seem to be the case with all kinds of value – for instance, being alive itself. We do not value our lives for any reason beyond themselves; we do not (usually) regard preserving our life as a means to an end, but rather as an end in itself. Value of this sort is non-instrumental value – often called *intrinsic* value (although as O'Neill's useful chapter "The Varieties of Intrinsic Value" in this book points out, intrinsic value is an expression which can be used in a variety of ways in environmental ethics).

This discussion of intrinsic value, however, inevitably raises a second question about the origin of such value. Is it created by human beings, or is it something already in existence in the world, which human beings recognize rather than bring into being? Again, this is a subject of great debate amongst environmental ethicists, sometimes called the dispute between value *subjectivists* and value *objectivists*. Value subjectivists argue that intrinsic value is something which humans create and attach to their own lives, the lives of other people, and/or to particular states of affairs (such as pleasure or the avoidance of suffering) or perhaps to qualities such as harmony. Value objectivists, on the other hand, think that non-instrumental value is not something which humans create, but something already in the world. From this perspective, valuing nature intrinsically is not *creating* or *projecting* value but rather *recognizing* value already present. Clearly, such an objectivist view creates difficulties. What kind of "thing" or "quality" is value? Is it a quality possessed by objects or individuals, rather like their color?

A third area of significance, for both subjectivists and objectivists alike concerns the *location* of such intrinsic value. What actually *is* of intrinsic value? Here, an even wider array of answers has been advocated. These include attributes of individual living organisms (such as consciousness, sentience, the ability to flourish, or just being alive) and more abstract qualities such as diversity, richness, "naturalness" or balance.

A variety of answers to these questions have been offered by leading environmental ethicists. J. Baird Callicott, some aspects of whose work I will consider later on, argues that all values are *subjective* (human-created, or anthropogenic) but this does not mean they must be human *centered* (anthropocentric). Rather, humans can value the nonhuman world intrinsically, quite apart from its usefulness to humans. Hargrove's chapter "Weak Anthropocentric Intrinsic Value" in this book offers a variant of this view. In contrast, Holmes Rolston (represented in this book by his chapter "Value in Nature and the Value of Nature") argues that value in the natural world is *objective*; it pre-exists human beings, is located in individuals, species, ecosystems and evolutionary processes, and would continue even if humans were to become extinct. For this reason, the natural world objectively contains intrinsic value; and is not only valuable inasmuch as it is useful to humans. Some environmental ethicists have sought to reconcile elements of such arguments. Keekok Lee, for instance, in "Source and Locus of Intrinsic Value: A Reexamination" argues that we need to think of different varieties of intrinsic value: "articulated" intrinsic value, which is created and possessed by humans alone; and "mutely enacted" intrinsic value, which appears in the natural world. The former kind of intrinsic value, she argues, is both subjective and anthropo-

centric; the latter is objective and located in all living beings.

Another area of debate is more directly ethical. How should human beings act in the nonhuman natural world, given the conclusions of value theory? How does one make ethical decisions where perceived values come into conflict? Should one act in order to preserve some kinds of value over others? Obviously, an environmental ethical edifice must, like any other ethical construction, be built on value theory; the two are, ultimately, inseparable. However, whilst it is only just possible that two philosophers with the same value theory might produce different practical ethical responses, it is quite likely that two philosophers with different underlying value theories might draw similar practical ethical conclusions. Indeed, the possible coincidence of practical ethical conclusions despite underlying *theoretical* differences, is something explored and developed within the work of environmental pragmatism, discussed later in this chapter.

One further distinction remains to be made at this point: that between ethical *monism* and ethical *pluralism* (a discussion developed in Part IV of this book). The central question at issue here is whether it is possible, within an ethical constituency so large that it could include the entire planet, to arrive at a single governing ethical principle or set of consistent principles to apply to all ethical problems. Ethical monism – the conviction that such consistency is possible – initially dominated environmental ethics (as indeed, ethics as a whole) and is still championed by some environmental ethicists. More recently, however, some influential figures in environmental ethics have contended that no one ethical principle or set of principles can possibly perform such a comprehensive function. This has led to the advocacy of differing ethical "frameworks" with application to different situations. One might not, for example, expect an ethical framework useful for thinking about a domestic cat to be suitable when dealing with the extinction of species. I will explore this discussion in more detail later.

Having thus introduced some of the questions that lie at the heart of the environmental ethical debate, I will now move on to examine, as concisely as possible, some of the key positions presented by different environmental ethicists. These positions, many of which were first proposed in the early 1980s, have been foundational for more recent discussions in environmental ethics, some of which I will consider later in this chapter. I will summarize each position, some of its major proponents, different possible forms it might take, and some key criticisms of it.

Anthropocentric Approaches to Environmental Ethics

There are a variety of approaches to environmental ethics that can be thought of as being *anthropocentric* or human-centered. Most – but not all – of these approaches (Hargrove's paper in this book is an exception) maintain that the nonhuman natural world is best considered ethically in terms of its instrumental values to human beings. Such instrumental values may be interpreted very broadly. The natural world can be seen as offering humans a range of physical, aesthetic and spiritual instrumental values, to name but a few. And anthropocentric approaches do not necessarily suggest reckless exploitation of the environment; they may instead maintain that natural resources should be very carefully managed for human benefit – including for the benefit of the poor and future human generations (as Barry argues in this volume).[13] Indeed, a broadly anthropocentric approach to environmental values underpins much international environmental policy-making. Most international discussion of central environmental issues – depletion of stratospheric ozone, global warming, marine and atmospheric pollution, treatment of toxic waste, destruction of rainforests – focuses ethically on their effects on human beings. At the level of popular political debate, resource management concerns compose virtually the entire ethical agenda.

Discussion of *sustainable development* also frequently focuses on forms of resource management, with an emphasis on social justice and on the well-being of future generations of humans. Indeed, the most commonly cited definition of sustainable development, taken from the World Commission on Environment and Development (WCED) report *Our Common Future* (1987), is anthropocentric: "sustainable development is development that meets the needs of the present without compromising the ability of future generations to meet their own needs." However, such an understanding of sustainable development is contested in this book. Whilst Cobb in "Toward a Just and Sustainable Economic Order" and Jamieson in "Ethics, Public Policy and Global Warming," worry at various human aspects of sustainable development, Donald Scherer in "Sustainable Resource Ethics" questions the privileging of the human involved in debates about sustainability. He argues that sustainable development needs to take account of "goods other than human well-being and the resources that conduce thereto." Thus Scherer suggests a way in which sustainable development can move beyond the anthropocentric to incorporate a broader understanding of environmental ethics.

Within environmental philosophy, several important thinkers have developed broadly anthropocentric approaches to environmental ethics, though these have taken different forms. John Passmore, for instance, in his early and influential book *Man's Responsibility for Nature* argues – contrary to Routley in the chapter here – that there is no need for a new environmental ethic.[14] At the root of Passmore's objection to a new environmental ethic – an objection shared by R. G. Frey – is the doubt that there are any rigorous grounds on which intrinsic values in the nonhuman natural world can be based.[15] Values are both human-generated and human-focused. Existing Western traditions of environmental management – such as a stewardship tradition – if developed and applied to current ecological problems, can be perfectly adequate.[16]

A rather different, but still anthropocentric, approach to environmental ethics is taken here by Norton in his paper "Environmental Ethics and Weak Anthropocentrism." Norton maintains that environmental ethics need not have recourse to "difficult to justify claims to intrinsic values" in nature. A perfectly sufficient environmental ethic, which can criticize value systems purely exploitative of nature, can be justified on (weakly) anthropocentric grounds alone – which may be the best pragmatic response in a variety of situations where the environment is under threat.[17] From such a perspective, environmental ethics would be principally about "concern for the protection of the resource base through indefinite time."

Such anthropocentric approaches to environmental value have, of course, been attacked from within environmental ethics. Indeed, as reflected by the majority of papers in this collection, one of the central aims of much work in environmental ethics has been to contest an anthropocentric, instrumental valuation of the nonhuman natural world, and to argue that new ways of thinking about and valuing it are needed. The pages of the journal *Environmental Ethics* have reflected such non-anthropocentric views from its early days. Yet outside the academic field of environmental ethics, different kinds of resource management approaches to the nonhuman natural world remain dominant. In recent years, there have been a number of attempts to bring academic environmental ethics and the resource management world of politics and economics together, and to establish shared goals even where the underpinning value approaches may be very different. As I have already suggested, environmental pragmatism is one school of thought in environmental ethics that has adopted this position; I will return to this later in the chapter.

Individualist Consequentialist Approaches

What I have called "individualist consequentialism" covers a spectrum of positions broadly in the utilitarian tradition of Bentham and Mill. As with all utilitarian positions, the aim of ethical behavior is at the best consequences (however "best" might be interpreted). For individualist consequentialism, the unit of ethical concern is always the individual organism rather than, for instance, the ecosystem or the species. However, it is important to make a distinction here: while the individual organism is the unit of ethical concern, it is the state of affairs within the organism, rather than the organism itself, which generates value. In consequentialist ethical systems, it is always states of affairs, rather than things in themselves that are valuable. I hope this distinction will become clearer as I proceed.[18]

Some important advocates of individualist consequentialism in this context are Peter Singer, Donald VanDeVeer, Robin Attfield, and Gary Varner. Singer's position, first articulated in *Animal Liberation*, is perhaps the closest to traditional utilitarianism. This initial view was later developed in his *Practical Ethics* and his article "Killing Humans and Killing Animals," and is represented in this book by his chapter "Not for Humans Only" (first published in 1979).[19] In *Animal Liberation*, Singer's position is that of a straightforward hedonistic utilitarian – that is to say, value is measured in terms of pleasure and pain. The aim of ethical behavior is to maximize

pleasure over pain. Thus to be morally relevant, or "morally considerable," an organism must have the capacity to feel pleasure or pain, or, more fundamentally, to have subjective experience. The capacity to have pleasurable or painful experience means that an organism has "interests": an organism that can feel pain has an interest in avoiding it; an organism which can feel pleasure has an interest in sustaining or increasing it. Thus where an organism cannot feel pleasure or pain it is not morally considerable, and has no interests. (It is, however, the experience – the state of affairs – that is valuable, not the organism that *has* the experience). This, of course, limits Singer's ethical concerns to sentient animals; in "Not for Humans Only" for instance, he states clearly that trees, for example, do not have interests.

Singer himself recognizes that there are possible difficulties with his position (aside from those which environmental ethicists might identify). One difficulty is that of replaceability: that provided killing is painless, and therefore does not generate painful experience, one organism may be killed and replaced by another, since it is total *experience*, and not the organism, which is valuable. (This position, as Varner points out in this book, would allow Singer to accept "therapeutic hunting" – though hunting is usually rejected by animal liberationists). As initially articulated by Singer, replaceability would apply to human beings as well as to nonhuman sentient animals. In order to avoid being seen to uphold this view, in his later articles, Singer "adds-on" to his earlier *hedonistic* utilitarian position what he calls *preference* utilitarianism. He divides the "morally considerable" into two groups: the conscious and the self-conscious. The conscious are organisms which have pleasurable and painful experience, but have no self awareness, no conception of themselves as persisting into the future and hence no preference to go on living. Such organisms are replaceable. However, self-conscious organisms have conceptions of themselves as individuals who endure through time, with desires and preferences about the future, primarily the preference to go on living. These preferences are, for Singer, morally significant, and thus it is worse to kill an animal with a preference to go on living than an animal with no such preference. This allows him to "ring-fence" self-conscious organisms – human beings and a few mammals such as apes and whales – so that they cannot be considered to be replaceable. Singer's position is thus that of a classical utilitarian with preference utilitarianism added on. All non-sentient animals, plants and natural formations are thus morally irrelevant to Singer, except instrumentally in as much as they add pleasurable experience to the lives of sentient animals.

VanDeVeer's position, in his article "Interspecific Justice" is in many respects similar to that of Singer, although he attempts to develop a more discriminating and detailed account.[20] Like Singer, the ability to feel pleasure and pain, and hence to have interests, is the central ethical pillar of his approach. VanDeVeer's particular concern is with decision making where interests conflict (unlike Singer, he does not address the question of replaceability). Instead he develops a two-pronged system of priority principles for the making of ethical decisions. One prong focuses on the psychological complexity of the organism in question: the more complex, the stronger its claim to priority. The second prong concentrates on the importance of the claim for each organism. Is a peripheral or a basic interest at stake in any particular conflict? The more basic the claim, the stronger its priority. The aim of VanDeVeer's principles, as Peter Singer's, is to achieve maximum total utility – the best overall consequences. His account is more meticulous than Singer's, eliding the self-conscious and conscious into one scale of psychological complexity, and also categorizing interests into different degrees of significance. For VanDeVeer, like Singer, non-sentient animals, plants and natural formations, are of no ethical significance, except as instrumentally valuable to those animals which are of direct moral concern.

Robin Attfield acknowledges a considerable debt to Singer and VanDeVeer; a debt which is more obvious in his earlier book *The Ethics of Environmental Concern* than in his later articles and *A Theory of Value and Obligation*.[21] His position contrasts sharply with both Singer and VanDeVeer in that he severs the exclusive link between experience and value, an uncoupling of central importance in environmental ethics. It is not simply the ability to experience, to feel pleasure and pain, which makes an organism morally considerable; it is, rather, its ability to flourish, to exercise the basic capacities of a species. An organism that has the ability to flourish and develop has an interest in doing so. Thus all organisms, regardless of their sentience, are morally considerable; it is only inanimate objects, which cannot flourish,

which are still morally inconsiderable. However, it is important to note, as Attfield is a consequentialist, that *it is the state of affairs of flourishing* which is valuable, rather than the organism itself, and that this leaves him vulnerable to the usual criticisms of individualist consequentialist positions, as will become clear.

This extension of moral considerability makes the need to develop a series of priority principles more pressing, since the greater the number of species admitted to moral consideration, the greater the potential for conflict. In *A Theory of Value and Obligation* Attfield, like VanDeVeer, develops a two-pronged set of priority principles. A sliding scale of psychological complexity, with humans at the top and individual plants at the bottom, forms one prong, while the other is focused around needs, interests, wants, and preferences. Basic and survival needs have priority over wants and preferences; more sophisticated organisms have priority over less sophisticated ones. As with VanDeVeer's priority principles, the aim is to achieve maximum total utility, or the best possible consequences. Attfield works this position out here in the context of sustainability and human hunger in his "Saving Nature, Feeding People and Ethics."

In his 1998 book *In Nature's Interests?* Gary Varner also develops a consequentialist approach to environmental ethics, focusing on the satisfaction of interests, which he argues are possessed by all and only individual living things.[22] Interests, he argues, mean that something "has a welfare or good of its own, that matters from a moral point of view." However, like Attfield and VanDeVeer, Varner creates a value hierarchy; in this instance the hierarchy is based on desires. Some organisms (such as mammals and birds) have desires, and some (such as insects and plants) probably do not. The interests of those organisms who have desires take priority over those organisms who have purely biological interests (such as for water or sunlight) but are not capable of desire. Among those organisms capable of desire, those who have what Varner calls "ground projects" (long-term desires which require satisfaction across a lifetime) take priority over other organisms. With a few possible exceptions, he suggests only humans have this kind of ground project. Thus where human ground projects are at stake, the interests of other organisms are outweighed. However, as Varner insists, this does not mean "anything goes." For instance it is morally important for humans to eat, since this is necessary to continue their ground projects – even though this means the dooming of interests of individuals of other species. However, Varner's hierarchy indicates that it is better to eat (non-desiring) plants than (desiring) animals – so his account of environmental ethics advocates a vegetarian diet (in normal circumstances).

Numerous objections have been leveled at these individualist consequentialist approaches. The identification of value with experience, found in Singer and VanDeVeer, is a particular target of attack from environmental ethicists. John Rodman in his article "The Liberation of Nature" argues that the identification of value with experience is anthropocentric, since it picks a quality paradigmatically possessed by human beings and uses it as a measure by which to judge other species.[23] While Attfield also criticizes the identification of experience with value, a similar criticism can be made of the psychological sliding scale proposed by himself and VanDeVeer. Varner is happy to concede that his account is anthropocentric, inasmuch as some human interests will always trump nonhuman interests.

A second criticism concerns replaceability, a problem which, according to his critics, Singer has not solved by his preference utilitarianism, and which VanDeVeer and Attfield do not acknowledge at all. Both Michael Lockwood in his article "Killing and the Preference for Life" and R. G. Frey in Rights, Killing and Suffering raise serious questions over the ethical adequacy of such positions.[24] If, ultimately, it is maximizing a certain state of affairs – be it pleasure, preferences satisfied or flourishing – which is of value, then the possibility of sacrificing any organism if it might lead to the generation of better states of affairs is always open. From the point of view of ethical deontologists, as I shall move on to consider in the next section, individualist consequentialism thus fails to ascribe enough significance to the organism itself.

A third criticism, leveled both by Rodman and by Tom Regan in The Case for Animal Rights is the degree of subjectivity involved in this kind of moral decision making. How can one decide, for instance, whether meat-eating is of basic or peripheral importance? Or whether a bat is more psychologically sophisticated than a cat? How far are such decisions made on the basis of human prejudice?

In contrast with the criticisms of ethical deontologists that individualist consequentialists fail to give enough ethical significance to individual organisms, other holistic environmental ethicists attack the focus on the individual organism altogether. In his important 1980 paper "Animal Liberation: A Triangular Affair," J. Baird Callicott argued that the individual organism was an inappropriate unit on which to focus when working in the field of environmental ethics.[25] In addition, Callicott argues, individualist consequentialism makes it difficult to accept predation (since all killing is regarded as a loss of value) or to support differential ethical treatment of wild and domestic animals. Others, such as Lawrence Johnson in A Morally Deep World and Holmes Rolston in Environmental Ethics, whilst affirming the value of individual organisms, argue that some value at least should also be assigned to ecological wholes.[26]

Aside from the question whether they are ethically satisfactory in general, it is clear that Singer's and VanDeVeer's positions, which only acknowledge sentient animals as ethically relevant, have difficulty in functioning as environmental ethics. Attfield's and Varner's positions, on the other hand, in acknowledging that all living beings can generate value, offer a broader environmental ethic. However, both are still vulnerable to many of the criticisms made above – as indeed are the next group of environmental ethicists I shall consider, the individualist deontologists.

Individualist Deontological Approaches

I have called these approaches to environmental ethics individualist and deontological both because they reject consequentialism, and because their ethical focus is on individuals rather than on wholes. These environmental ethicists consider that individual organisms have value in themselves, value that is not necessarily linked with experience, nor to do with states of affairs within the organism. It is the organism itself which is valuable, not what it is doing.

Kenneth Goodpaster's 1978 article "On Being Morally Considerable" provides an important basis for many individualist deontological positions.[27] Goodpaster considers the question "what makes something morally considerable?" in some detail, arguing that "X's being a living thing is both necessary and sufficient for moral considerability so understood." Tom Regan considers a similar question in his article "The Nature and Possibility of an Environmental Ethic."[28] Here he suggests that all natural objects have "inherent goodness" whether living or not. However, he finds this position difficult to sustain, and later in *The Case for Animal Rights* he retreats from it, concentrating on "rights" that are possessed by those who are "subjects of a life." Regan's concept of mammalian rights is an individualist deontological position; but one with a scope limited to adult mammals.[29]

More developed deontological approaches to environmental ethics is suggested in the work of Albert Schweitzer (albeit in rather vague fashion); and by Paul Taylor in "The Ethics of Respect for Nature" (in this book) and his influential book *Respect for Nature*. A further version of such a position is proposed by Louis Lombardi in his article "Inherent Worth, Respect and Rights."[30] A consideration of these positions highlights the central divide between deontological individualist environmental ethicists: some suggest that all morally considerable individuals are of equal value, while others argue for a hierarchy of value within the individual deontological framework. Schweitzer and Taylor fall into the former category, while Lombardi is in the latter.

Schweitzer, of course, was writing long before the general period I am considering: *The Philosophy of Civilization* was published in 1923. However, many of his ideas have been developed in more recent environmental philosophy. Central to Schweitzer's thought is the "will-to-live," an impulse to self-realization found in all living things (and even, according to Schweitzer, in crystals and snowflakes: an assertion which immediately generates problems). Recognition of this will-to-live should engender reverence towards all living things by human beings, who experience and wish to actualize their own will-to-live. On this basis, the taking of any life, however necessary, is wrong, and generates a burden of guilt and responsibility. (Though in contrast, on occasion, Schweitzer also talks about "necessary" harms.) Further, Schweitzer asserts that all wills-to-live are of equal value, and that human beings are not in a position to judge the relative values of different species. (Thus to kill an ant is as bad as to kill an antelope.) However, this perspective stands in tension with another that Schweitzer also seems to

hold, where humans are considered to be superior to other species. A parallel tension can be found where Schweitzer hints at the possibility of *restitution*. Restitution in environmental ethics is a kind of ecological compensation: compensating for damage to or death of one individual organism, species or area by good treatment of either the same organism, individual or area at a different time, or of a different organism, species or area. (This raises questions about the possibility of ecological restoration, one of the issues discussed in this volume). Schweitzer, for example, suggests that by helping an insect in difficulties, one is "attempting to cancel out part of man's ever new debt to the animal world."[31] Laying the merits or otherwise of restitution to one side, as a deontologist, Schweitzer cannot consistently advocate restitution, since wrongs cannot be totalled and compensated for (as would be possible for consequentialists).

These tensions are echoed in Paul Taylor's altogether more complex and sophisticated account which urges "respect for nature" rather than "reverence for life." Taylor's background is clearly Aristotelian. He argues that all organisms are teleological centers of life, pursuing their own good in their own way. This telos gives each individual organism *inherent worth*;[32] and this inherent worth is equally possessed by all living organisms, since all have a telos and a good of their own, a good which is as vital to them as a human good is to a human. This forms the basis of his biocentric view, and the scaffolding for his fundamental principle of species impartiality.

Acknowledging the severe difficulties generated by the belief in the inherent worth of every living organism, Taylor devotes much of his book to working out further ethical principles. He argues for four basic principles of duty to the nonhuman natural world: nonmaleficence, noninterference, fidelity, and restitutive justice. In addition to these he suggests five priority principles for resolving situations of conflict: self defense, proportionality, minimum wrong, distributive justice and restitutive justice. While these are too complex to examine in detail here, Taylor considers that careful application of these principles would enable the moral resolution of conflicts between human beings and nonhuman organisms.

Both Schweitzer and Taylor claim to be putting forward a view of "biocentric equality" – where all living beings are of equal moral status. Lombardi, however, develops an individualist deontological approach where values of different organisms are graded. Responding to Taylor, Lombardi maintains that the telos possessed by a living thing is, in fact, a capacity, and that inherent worth is assigned on the basis of this capacity. Lombardi then argues that many living beings have additional capacities that increase inherent worth. A plant, for instance, has vegetative capacities which gives it a little "value-added"; mammals have vegetative capacities, but are also sentient, the added capacity to feel pleasure and pain giving additional value; while human beings, having other additional capacities, such as reflectiveness, have even greater value-added. Thus Lombardi constructs a graded individualist deontological environmental ethic built on difference of capacities between species.

Significant criticisms have been made of the individual deontological positions outlined above. Some of these criticisms relate to the very fact that they are deontological. Since this criticism is not confined to environmental ethics, I will not pursue it here. One aspect which is worth noting, however, is the existence in both Schweitzer and Taylor (where it is particularly significant) of the concept of restitution. As I have already pointed out, such a position cannot be sustained in a deontological system.[33] Indeed, it resembles the much-criticized idea of replaceability, which I considered in the preceding section.

The granting of moral considerability to all living things is also questioned by critics. Both Peter Singer, in his article "The Place of Nonhumans," and W. K. Frankena argue that sentience is necessary for moral considerability.[34] Even more problems are raised by Schweitzer's and Taylor's assertions of the equal value of all living organisms. In actuality, both fail to sustain their positions rigorously. Taylor accepts medical treatment for humans where millions of bacteria may die for one human life; and admits that the infliction of pain makes it worse to kill animals than plants, thus undercutting his egalitarianism. Peter Wenz points out that Taylor also accepts the death and displacement of thousands of organisms to pursue important human projects such as building concert halls.[35] Thus Taylor can be accused of importing a hierarchy by the back door.

The explicit introduction of hierarchy, however, as with Lombardi, opens deontological individual thinking to the same criticism as the individualist consequentialists: that of selecting paradigmatic human qualities and judging the value of other organisms by their possession of them. Lombardi's hierarchy would, for instance, fall victim to Rodman's arguments about anthropocentrism.

Further criticisms of deontological individualism in environmental ethics again echo those made of individualist consequentialists. These criticisms largely stem from holistic ethicists, such as J. Baird Callicott, whom I will consider in the following section. Firstly, again, individualist deontologists are unable to ascribe value to ecosystems or species, except inasmuch as their individual members are valuable. Secondly, again, they are unable to distinguish between domestic and wild animals, and different treatments that may be appropriate to these categories. Diversity is also of no value: a field of wheat and a field of wildflowers are of equal worth, since what is important is the telos or will-to-live of each plant, and not the biological context. Questions about how far humans should "interfere" in wild nature to protect will-to-live are raised. Indeed, Callicott suggests that such individualist environmental ethics are "fundamentally life-denying," failing to accept as good the vital evolutionary processes of predation and death, by suggesting that all dying is an evil.[36]

Holistic Environmental Ethics

In contrast with both the individualist positions considered above, some environmental ethicists focus on ethical consideration of ecological wholes, rather than individuals. By "ecological wholes" I refer to ecosystems and/or species and to the biosphere as a whole, viewed, in this context, as ethical units. Different language can be used to describe these wholes, community and organism being two of the most popular. These holistic approaches to environmental ethics tend to be consequentialist, rather than deontological, aiming at the good of the whole, even where the scale of the whole and what constitutes good for it are in dispute. A variety of scales and putative goods are suggested by different philosophers, enhanced by different uses of scientific ecology and Darwinian evolutionary theory.

Aldo Leopold's *A Sand County Almanac* is often cited as the foundational work in holistic environmental ethics. This book, a collection of autobiographical and philosophical essays, espouses a land ethic (reproduced in this volume) which "enlarges the boundaries of the community to include soils, waters, plants, and animals, or collectively, the land."[37] Leopold's guiding principle is famously expressed "A thing is right when it tends to preserve the integrity, stability and beauty of the biotic community. It is wrong when it tends otherwise."[38] It is important to note that this is a principle of extension, not replacement: human ethics are extended to *include* the land; the land ethic does not replace human ethics.

Owing, in part, to the unsystematic nature of Leopold's writing, there has been some discussion amongst environmental ethicists about how best to interpret Leopold's ideas. The essays collected in *A Companion to a Sand County Almanac*, edited by Callicott, emphasize the importance of the holistic, biotic, non anthropocentric approach Leopold adopts.[39] This stress on the importance of the integrity, stability and beauty of the biotic community contrasts strikingly with both individualist deontologists and individualist consequentialists. First, the community, rather than the individual, is the focus of moral significance. For individualist deontologists, the community has moral significance as a collection of morally valuable individuals; while for individualist consequentialists the community is only valuable inasmuch as it contributes to the improvement of individual experience. Secondly, ecological qualities such as integrity and stability are of primary value.[40] Such qualities cannot be valued in either kind of individualist system where individual living organisms or their experiences are the whole locus of value. Other, more recent interpretations of Leopold's thought have suggested that there are senses in which Leopold's work can be regarded as anthropocentric. For instance, Bryan Norton in "The Constancy of Leopold's Land Ethic," argues that whilst Leopold did consider the biotic community to be an organism, he also considered that humans "must and should" manage it; and that ultimately, as parts of the biotic organism, human and biotic interests would coincide.[41]

Several recent environmental ethicists have put forward views advocating a holistic, rather than an individualistic, environmental ethic. Amongst these is Eric Katz's chapter here: "Is There a Place for Animals in the Moral Consideration of Nature?" Katz argues that the well-being of the ecological community as a whole should be the primary ethical goal or principle of an environmental ethic. Individual natural entities do have value; but this value is a "secondary principle." Another significant holistic view – and one deeply influenced by the work of Leopold – is found in Callicott's paper "Animal Liberation: A Triangular Affair." Here, Callicott placed himself in firm opposition to individualist approaches to environmental ethics.

As already noted, Callicott argued that all value is subjective and anthropogenic (contrasting with the views of, for example, Taylor and Attfield, who consider that values exist in nature independently of conscious valuers).[42] Secondly, Callicott accepted a kind of sociobiology, manifesting itself as a belief in the biological origin of ethics in the community. Ethical behavior in human beings is instinctive, having been evolutionarily selected for, since ethical responses by individuals in a biological community makes the species more likely to survive. Thus, Callicott argued, our ethical impulses are triggered when someone is recognized as being part of the community. If the natural world were to be perceived as part of our "community" humans would consider ethical behavior to be appropriate in this context. And from a Darwinian evolutionary perspective, Callicott argued, such a perception would be a correct one; all living things have the same biological origins and do form an interdependent community. Callicott's third point here, which he claimed emerged in the Platonic tradition, is an emphasis on the ethical priority of the community over the individual. Plato, "shrinks from nothing, as long as it seems to him to be in the interests of the community."[43] This holistic approach contrasts very clearly with the individualist focus of the environmental ethicists considered earlier.

Such a holistic perspective led Callicott to argue that to sustain the health of the biological community of which human beings are a part, some individuals may have to be sacrificed for the whole. The most essential species (such as the pollinating honey bee) are more important than, for instance, higher mammals which play a far less vital role in the biological community. This clearly reflects on human beings, who are not only not vital to the system, but who actually destroy it. Indeed, Callicott suggested that the more misanthropy there is in an ethical system, the more ecological it is, and that the human population should be, in total, about twice that of bears. He also argued that domesticated animals, not being part of the ultimately valuable wild, biotic community, are living arti-facts, lacking natural behavior patterns and unable to be "liberated" as some individualist ethicists would claim.

While Leopold and Callicott focus on commu-nities, the "Gaia hypothesis," and the host of metaphysical and ethical questions raised by it, concerns the entire Earth. The "Gaia hypothesis" originated in the work of scientist James Lovelock in his books *Gaia* and *The Ages of Gaia*.[44] Love-lock contends that the Earth behaves like a single living organism, in that the flora and fauna on Earth act together to regulate the climate and temperature of Earth in order to produce the best conditions for life. Despite scientific criticism, Lovelock argues that this is not a teleological, or purposive process, and dismisses all suggestions that Gaia might be conscious or have a deliberate aim.[45] This point is reinforced in *The Ages of Gaia* by the use of a complex computer model of a fictional world entitled *Daisyworld*. Lovelock him-self has not developed "Gaia" into a thorough-going metaphysical or ethical system, (although periodically, he uses language which suggests this). However, there is no doubt that the Gaia hypothesis can have important ethical implica-tions, although these are dependent on the inter-pretation of Lovelock's hypothesis which is adopted.

Lovelock himself argues that the Earth is not fragile, and that it has survived many potential crises in the past by adapting to changed condi-tions. This may mean that the Earth moves to new equilibria, but that life still continues. He suggests that the Earth may have "vital organs" which, while possibly essential for life on Earth to survive at all, are certainly essential for the Earth to con-tinue at its current equilibrium. These vital organs, he suggests, may be the tropical rainfor-ests, deep sea algae, and prokaryotic bacteria. Their destruction could mean that Gaia moves to a new equilibrium; an equilibrium which may support some kind of life, but which would not support human life. With this background, the ethical implications of Gaia are not focused around protecting Gaia herself, but rather on the preser-vation of human beings from the devastating con-sequences of a new equilibrium. Therefore, actions that might force Gaia to a new equilibrium – such as global warming by an increase in atmos-pheric CO_2 – should be avoided since it may ultimately lead to the destruction of human beings.

This is, as Andrew Dobson points out in *Green Political Thought* provides an anthropocentric reason for the protection of Gaia.[46]

Other groups have, however, developed different ethical conclusions, loosely based on the Gaia hy-pothesis. These highlight the living organismic nature of the Earth, and, in contrast with Lovelock, stress its fragility. This can result in militant ethical stances, such as that put forward by some members of the group Earth First! where the "well-being of the planet" is put before the well-being of individ-ual human beings. A reduction in human popula-tion is thus frequently considered to be an ethical necessity. Such plural ethical interpretations make clear the ambiguous position which Lovelock's hy-pothesis may hold in environmental ethics.

Holistic approaches to environmental ethics have been strongly criticized by individualists, amongst others. Tom Regan, in his chapter "How to Worry about Endangered Species," excerpted from his book *The Case for Animal Rights*, expresses this particularly strongly by describing ethical environ-mental holism as "environmental fascism" since it includes "the clear prospect that the individual may be sacrificed for the greater biotic good, in the name of the 'stability, integrity and beauty of the biotic community.'" The prioritizing of the whole over the individual, in particular when the whole con-cerned is the wild biotic community is widely viewed as ethically unacceptable.

Reconciling Positions

The preceding sections have described a range of different, and sometimes conflicting, positions adopted by those working in environmental ethics – in particular concerning a perceived rift between the individualism of animal liberation positions in contrast with the holism of some environmental ethics. (It should be remembered, however, that there are individualist environmental ethical pos-itions and that animals are still morally relevant to holistic environmental ethics). In response to some of the problems raised, a number of environmental ethicists have attempted to construct approaches to environmental ethics which take into account elements of both individualist and holistic con-cerns. This reconciliation between animal liber-ation and environmental ethics at least can go so far as, in Dale Jamieson's terms, to "have the potential for Hollywood romance"![47] A number of different reconciliatory approaches have been adopted, two of which I will consider below.

Although an important holistic thinker in his earlier work, as we have seen, in later writing, such as "Animal Liberation and Environmental Ethics: Back Together Again" Callicott elaborates a more reconciliatory theory of "nested communities." Here he argues that human beings exist in the center of a series of moral communities which fit, one within the other, as a series of "nests" or concentric circles, with ethical obligations diminishing towards the outside. The major communities Callicott identifies are the human community at the core; the "mixed" community (of human and domestic animals) as the middle "ring"; and the wild or biotic community on the outside. This changes some aspects of Callicott's position in his earlier paper: it allows human concerns to trump those of the wild or biotic community, and it allows for humans to have moral obligations towards animals. (Indeed, his position in this paper has been criticized by Varner as being anthropocentric.[48])

The work of Holmes Rolston represents another key position allowing for both individualist and holistic values. Rolston, whose views are laid out in his systematic work *Environmental Ethics*, is one of the most important figures in the current environmental ethical debate.[49] Like Taylor and Attfield, and unlike Callicott, Rolston argues for objective value in the natural world. The baseline of individual value is the *telos* of each individual organism. Every organism has a good of its own, and is thus a *holder* of value, even if not a *beholder* of it. To this extent, Rolston's views are not dissimilar to those of Taylor. However, Rolston contends that different characteristics – such as sentience or ability for conscious reflection – add value, so that the more sophisticated a living organism, the more valuable it is. Alongside this individualist approach, Rolston also develops an understanding of intrinsic value applicable to ecosystems and species. Species, he argues, provide the normative genetic "set" for the individual, and this genetic set is "as evidently the property of the species as of the individual through whom it passes."[50] A species is a form of life that defends itself and, according to Rolston, thus has value. The ecosystem, and indeed the biosphere as a whole, is a life-creating process. Ethical attention should be not focused on an ecosystem as an individual, but rather as an interconnected matrix within which life evolved and continues to develop. As the womb of life, both producing and nurturing it, the ecosystem is an appropriate unit for moral concern.[51] It would be bizarre, Rolston insists, to value the organisms, the products of the system, without valuing the process which produced them. This wild, systemic value is entirely separate from human culture, exists independently of humans and is increasingly threatened by human development (as well as threatening species and organismic values). Given the extent of this threat, and the significance Rolston considers systemic and species values to have, it is consistent that he should argue in his chapter here "Feeding People versus Saving Nature" that there are occasions when protecting such values takes priority over feeding hungry people. As this book illustrates well, debates over how nature is valued has profound significance for thinking about issues of poverty and sustainability.

Recent Discussions in Environmental Ethics: Monism and Pluralism

This variety of different positions advocated by those working in environmental ethics led to wide-ranging discussion in the 1990s about moral monism and pluralism. Such a diversity of possible objects of moral concern (sentient animals, living organisms, ecosystems, species, the Earth, biodiversity etc.) and so many different approaches to environmental ethics (rights-theories, utilitarianism, virtues theories and so on) were suggested that questions emerged as to whether *any* single ethical approach could be adequate. Moral pluralism, it was suggested by some, might provide a way forward in accommodating so many different approaches and concerns. In the course of this debate, moral monism and pluralism were defined and interpreted in varying ways.[52] Wenz's chapter "Minimal, Moderate, and Extreme Moral Pluralism" is perhaps a good place to start.

Wenz argues that moral pluralism may take different forms, and provides his own three-fold classification, distinguishing extreme, moderate, and minimal moral pluralism. Extreme moral pluralism, in Wenz's classification, is characterized by "alternations between different ethical theories" – theories such as utilitarianism or Kantianism. Moderate moral pluralism is where a single, overarching theory is "pluralistic in the sense that it contains a variety of independent principles, principles that cannot be reduced to or derived from a single master principle." Thirdly, minimal moral pluralism refers to a moral theory which "merely lacks a universal algorithmic decision procedure." Indeed, Wenz goes on to argue that all known moral systems are at least this pluralistic (i.e. there are no monistic systems which provide a perfect algorithmic decision making procedure in all circumstances). (Thus approaches we have already considered in this chapter fall into the category of minimal pluralism, and some arguably into the category of moderate pluralism).

Christopher Stone and Andrew Brennan prefer to use the language of ethical *frameworks* or matrices that can be brought to bear on different situations.[53] Brennan argues that there is no "one set of principles concerning just one form of value that provides ultimate government for our actions."[54] Indeed, he maintains that "an indefinite number of frameworks can be brought to bear. When we restrict our modes of thinking to just one framework, we thereby choose to ignore the perspective supplied by other relevant frameworks."[55] Like Wenz, Brennan notes that moral pluralism may have different forms: first, the acceptance that different considerations may apply in different cases; and secondly (and more controversially) that in any particular situation, there is no single theoretical lens which provides a privileged set of concepts, principles, and structure. Moral pluralism, Brennan argues, allows for exploration of the complexity of ethical issues rather than the imposition of a single reductionist ethical framework onto a complex situation. Andrew Light, in his "The Case for a Practical Pluralism" (in this volume) reads this debate as concerning the relationship between theory-making and practice. Moral pluralists, he suggests, have been interested in environmental ethics as practice; moral theories are seen as "tools developed in the process of addressing specific policy controversies." Moral monists, on the other hand, he considers to be theoretical purists, who start with theories and apply them to complex situations. This analysis allows Light to link moral pluralism with environmental pragmatism, which we shall consider later.

Attractive as some pluralist positions sound, difficulties are generated by them – many of which are discussed by Callicott in his "The Case Against Moral Pluralism." With Stone's work in mind, Callicott asks questions such as: how can one make moral decisions when two frameworks deliver conflicting ethical responses? Would unscrupulous moral agents switch between frameworks in order to make personal gains? Does this all lead to a kind of ethical "musical chairs"? In his 1994 paper "Moral Monism in Environmental Ethics Defended" Callicott argues that the sensitivity to complexity and different contexts highlighted by pluralists such as Stone and Brennan can be achieved within a monistic framework without the need to resort to pluralism.[56]

Pursuing this question would open up an extensive moral debate. It is clear that the moral pluralisms developed (in differing ways) by Wenz, Brennan, and Stone do generate difficulties. However, pluralist approaches to environmental ethics of this sort are context-sensitive, open-ended, and prepared to engage with the profound complexities of making ethical decisions. They acknowledge the impossibility of producing clear-cut answers in many ethical situations – especially when considering the difficult ethical questions engendered by human relations with the nonhuman world.

Recent Discussion in Environmental Ethics: Wilderness and Ecological Restoration

A number of environmentally significant issues – for instance hunting, biodiversity, agriculture – have been debated within environmental ethics. Two of the most significant and hotly debated issues, however, have been the idea of wilderness and the question of the restoration of land after human use. Both these discussions are of considerable importance, illustrating as they do the significance of debates in environmental ethics for thinking about practical policy-making.

Wilderness

In 1964, the US Wilderness Act designated wilderness as "an area where the earth and its community of life are untrammeled by man, where man himself is a visitor who does not remain." This designation reflected the view that wildernesses are untouched, pristine parts of the natural world, formed without human agency and to be protected from permanent human presence. In this pristine condition, wildernesses could be seen as the location of special human values – for recreation, hunting, psychological and spiritual refreshment, scientific study, medicinal possibility, aesthetic wonder – and, for some, a location of intrinsic value. (Nelson's chapter in this book details many of the arguments for wilderness preservation). However, during the 1980s and 1990s, this idea of wilderness was challenged for a variety of reasons (many of the key papers relating to this discussion are collected in Callicott and Michael Nelson's edited volume, *The Great New Wilderness Debate*).[57] One key challenge stemmed from Ramachandra Guha's paper "Radical American Environmentalism and Wilderness Preservation: A Third World Critique."[58] This paper maintained that the idea of wilderness was harmful when exported to developing countries. Many of these countries were densely populated; the creation of wilderness areas from which people were excluded ignored the needs of local people; and inasmuch as such areas become tourist sites for rich visitors, transferred resources from the poor to the rich. Indeed, the whole idea of "setting aside" supposedly pristine areas of land, Guha argues, represents a new, American, imperialist project (both physically and intellectually/spiritually).

Discussion about the idea of wilderness also grew within the US itself, most significantly in a debate between J. Baird Callicott and Holmes Rolston in *The Environmental Professional* in 1991.[59] Callicott contests the idea of wilderness on several grounds. It relies, he suggests, on the idea that humans are separate from nature, and that the wilderness is an "Other" to humans. But this ignores evolutionary theory; humans are "natural." The idea of "preserving" wildernesses also suggests a kind of denial of evolution, and a "freeze-framing" of ecology. In addition, Callicott argues, in the US the wilderness idea is ethnocentric; it depends on the fallacy that when Europeans arrived in the New World it was in "wilderness condition." Yet this either ignores the existence of aboriginal inhabitants, or else it suggests that they are not human beings, so their management of ecosystems can be discounted. Finally, Callicott maintains that the "wilderness idea" is an inappropriate way of dealing with current environmental problems. It can lead to the protection of a few conscience-saving "odds and ends" of remote country whilst outside such locations the environment is devastated. It is better to integrate humans into the natural world and to develop harmonious

living than to work with an idea of wild nature as entirely separate from human culture.

Rolston responds by arguing that wild nature *is* radically different from human culture, and (as we have already seen) that it carries nonhuman intrinsic values that should be respected, and that Callicott's arguments do not recognize. This radical culture/nature difference does not mean "freeze-framing" ecology; it rather means that biological changes in wilderness areas should be driven by evolutionary and ecological processes, not humans. Neither is the view that there is wilderness "untrammeled by man" in the US ethnocentric: Rolston argues that native Americans did not modify the landscape profoundly, did not use high, rough or arid land, and that although they used fire, fire would have occurred anyway.[60] And, overall, the protection of wilderness does not mean that people can do what they like elsewhere; that some places are set aside for wilderness does not mean that in other places greater human/nature harmonious integration should not be an ideal.

This debate continues in different forms amongst environmental ethicists. Reed Noss's chapter for instance maintains, like Rolston, that wildernesses carry intrinsic values, that "huge wild areas are valuable for their own sake." Indeed, to operate healthily with ecosystems containing big predators like wolves, wildernesses may need to be very large; and Noss recommends that about 50 percent of the US should be returned to a wilderness condition to enable the maintenance of biodiversity. What is at stake here are questions about how far humans are viewed as a part of or apart from nature and whether wild nature is thought to be carrying special kinds of intrinsic values. These questions recur with equal force in the debate over restoring nature.

Ecological Restoration

A related central debate in environmental ethics concerns the question whether nature "restored" by humans carries the same value as "wild" nature, understood as nature unmodified by human activity. This issue has been implicit in much work in environmental ethics (as we have seen, restitution was raised in the work of Schweitzer and Taylor, and advocated by Wenz [1988]; and the idea of replaceability in Singer's work raises similar issues). However, environmental ethicists are by no means agreed that restitution or restoration is a principle that should be accepted. Robert Elliott's 1982 paper "Faking Nature" (in this book) importantly raised the profile of this issue. In "Faking Nature" Elliot explores the implications of what he calls "The Restoration Thesis": that the destruction of what has value is compensated for by the later creation (recreation) of something of equal value. (He is particularly concerned where this restoration thesis is used to legitimate environmental harm on the ground that it may later be made good). Elliot argues that part of the reason why humans might value a natural area is its "specific genesis and history." Creating a replica, with a different origin, creates something less valuable, in the same way that faked paintings, however good, are not as valuable as original paintings. As Elliott argues "we value the forest and river in part because they are representative of the world outside our dominion, because this existence is independent of us." This thesis was developed and revised in a book of the same title (1997) which contains a detailed explanation of Elliott's subjectivist understanding of intrinsic value, restates Elliott's commitment to the value of "naturalness of origin," and distinguishes between different *kinds* of restoration, including benign restorations.[61]

Eric Katz, in a series of papers on restoration, including "The Big Lie," develops Elliott's argument. Working with a definition of "natural" as essentially "independent of the actions of humanity," Katz argues that restored nature is not a forgery, but rather an artifact. It is not autonomous and free like wild nature; it is, instead, anthropocentric, and created for human purposes. And such creation, Katz maintains, is an act of human domination of nature. Thus whilst Katz thinks it appropriate that where nature has been harmed (for instance in an oil spill) those responsible should attempt to clean up, this does not amount to a *restoration* of nature, because nature is not the kind of thing humans can restore.

Whilst no one writing in environmental ethics has endorsed the idea that policies of restoration should be used to justify environmental harm, a number of ethicists have disagreed with the premises of Katz's and Elliott's arguments, and with some of their conclusions. This debate has centered around the kind of relationship envisaged for humans to have with the natural world. Both Andrew Light (in this book) and Y. S. Lo explore this question by using analogies from inter-human relationships.[62] Light, for instance, opens up issues about human/nature relationships, suggesting that restoration can be viewed as an attempt to heal relationships between humans and nature, even freeing nature from constraints (such as pollution) that had prevented it from pursuing its autonomy. Engaging in restoration projects may also help humans to understand the natural world better and thus to be more willing to defend it against future harms. Lo questions whether a restored nature is a human artifact, any more than a person who has been healed by human medicine should be regarded as an artifact. She argues that to suggest a nature touched or oppressed by humans is of less value than "free, autonomous" nature is akin to saying that oppressed humans are worth less than free ones (and thus legitimating further domination). Respect for nature may mean assisting dominated nature to become free again – by restoration; and this restoration, though anthropo*genic* need not be anthropo*centric*, but may be aimed at benefiting the nonhuman world.

As the preceding sections have suggested, debates in environmental ethics about intrinsic value, valuing wholes and/or individuals, monism and pluralism and issues such as the concept of wilderness and the value of nature restoration continue. However, these are not the only voices in discussions about such questions.

Responses to Mainstream Environmental Ethics

There are a number of important responses to the more mainstream environmental ethics approaches outlined above. Here I want to consider three broad schools of thought: deep ecology, ecofeminism, and environmental pragmatism. These "schools" are far from homogeneous; they contain considerable inner diversity and debate. I will conclude by looking, briefly, at ways in which ideas about the social construction have begun to enter debates in environmental ethics.

Deep Ecology

The expression "deep ecology" was first used by Arne Naess in his article "The Shallow and the

Deep, Long Range Ecology Movements: A Summary."[63] In this article, Naess suggested that the ecology movement had two strands: the shallow, concerned with pollution and resource depletion; and the deep, which he characterized metaphysically, ethically, and politically. Metaphysically, Naess maintained that deep ecologists reject the idea of humans as separate from their environment, and stress the complex relatedness of all that is. Ethically, deep ecologists espouse biocentric equality in principle (although recognizing that all realistic praxis will require some killing and exploitation) and the equal right of all living organisms to blossom and flourish (an egalitarian, deontological attitude resembling that of Schweitzer and Taylor). Politically, deep ecologists favor diversity and decentralization – and also political action to relate their principles to practice.

Naess's article was the catalyst for a still continuing debate around these issues, which in a variety of ways engages with the environmental ethics questions explored above. Since Naess's article was published, he himself has developed and revised his views, and a number of other significant voices have joined in the discussion. It is only possible to consider a few of these developments here.

The idea of biocentric equality in principle, outlined by Naess in 1973, has been one of the areas of most discussion, obviously linking closely to other debates in environmental ethics. Difficulty in upholding this principle led Naess, and other deep ecologists, to reformulate this idea; some adopted a hierarchical approach.[64] Although the question of biocentric *equality* has been much debated, affirmation of intrinsic value in nature was widely accepted by deep ecologists, including Naess. This affirmation was most powerfully captured in what has become known as the Deep Ecology Platform, a series of eight principles agreed by Naess and a fellow deep ecologist George Sessions in 1984, and published (in slightly varying forms) in a variety of places including Naess's article "The Deep Ecological Movement: Some Philosophical Aspects" in this volume.[65] The first of these principles affirms: "The well-being and flourishing of human and nonhuman life on earth have value in themselves (synonyms: intrinsic value, inherent worth). These values are independent of the usefulness of the nonhuman world for human purposes." The Deep Ecology Platform – maintaining that the flourishing of nonhuman life should be protected

by changes in policy and human lifestyles – lies, as it were, in the middle stage of deep ecological thinking. Underpinning the Deep Ecology Platform, Naess suggests, may lie different metaphysical positions or what Naess calls "ecosophies" (hence Light's argument in "The Case for Practical Pluralism" that Naess may be regarded as in some senses a pluralist) and, resting upon it, a range of political and practical responses and strategies in different situations.

It is the metaphysical underpinning of deep ecology, based on developing and revising Naess's work, which has been of particular significance in deep ecological thinking, even having the effect of making deep ecology seem more like a consciousness movement than an ethical one.[66] This change of consciousness focuses around two key concepts: *holism* and *the extension and realization of the self*. Holism, as used by deep ecologists, is usually based on the claim that everything is fundamentally one. Nothing can be separated from the whole; indeed there are no isolated "things" but an interlocking web of relations in a constant state of flux. Individuals are "knots in a web" or "centers of interaction" – constituted by their relationships. Warwick Fox, in his chapter "Deep Ecology: A New Philosophy of Our Time?" maintains that this holism, the absence of "a firm ontological divide in the field of existence" is "the central intuition of deep ecology." The concept of the extension and realization of the self is closely related to this holism. If everything is fundamentally one, then the distinction between what is self and what is not-self can no longer be simply sustained. Deep ecologists argue that this is true on a physical level since the physical body cannot exist in isolation from its surroundings (a view which deep ecologists reinforce by citing quantum physics and scientific ecology). With this knowledge, human beings can extend their self-identification beyond the confines of their body to include others. Once the factual impossibility of the separation of self from world is recognized, the necessity to extend one's understanding of what constitutes one's self is revealed. If everything is part of one's self, and one is aiming at self-realization (which deep ecologists argue to be the case) then the clear conclusion to be drawn is that the realization of all (living) organisms is necessary for one's own full self-realization.

Politically, deep ecology – both at the metaphysical and the ethical level – has proved an inspiration to a variety of political environmental movements. Many of the members of radical environmental groups such as Earth First! in the US have been influenced by deep ecological thinking.[67] Some deep ecologists, especially in the US, engaged in political activities extending to civil disobedience and sabotage or "monkeywrenching" in order to defend environments threatened by various kinds of harm (such as deforestation or the construction of roads).

At all levels, deep ecology has been severely attacked; most systematically by Richard Sylvan in his "A Critique of Deep Ecology."[68] Ethically, obviously a number of the difficulties associated with affirmation of intrinsic value and egalitarianism in environmental ethics more generally manifest themselves in deep ecology. Metaphysically, the "consciousness-shifting" side of deep ecology has been criticized even more intensely. First, the use of scientific ecology and modern physics has been challenged.[69] Secondly, the philosophical acceptability of the form of holism which Naess appears to be advocating has been subject to philosophical criticism for many years.[70] Being dependent on such holism, the deep ecological concept of the extended self is exposed; and this is not the only difficulty with such an idea. Val Plumwood in *Feminism and the Mastery of Nature* argues that the idea of the extended self in deep ecology suggests that the whole world becomes a kind of extended individual ego incorporating everything that is.[71] It thus fails to acknowledge in any real sense the "otherness" of what is in the world; since everything is viewed as being part of oneself, there is no space for difference. Indeed, ecofeminists such as Plumwood make a variety of criticisms of deep ecology in particular, and of the prevailing debates in environmental ethics in general, as the next section illustrates.

Ecofeminism

Ecofeminism is a term that covers a variety of responses to environmental problems and to theorizing about them. What all these responses have in common is the making of a link between what are often called the "twin oppressions" of women and nature. As Karen Warren and Jim Cheney express it in their chapter "Ecological Feminism and Ecosystem Ecology": "ecofeminists acknowledge up front their basic value commitments: the twin dominations of women and nature exist, are

wrong, and ought to be eliminated." However, the nature of the link between these twin oppressions has been understood in many different ways (as Greta Gaard and Lori Gruen explain in their chapter) and consequently the best way of eliminating these twin oppressions is also contested. Here, I am primarily interested in the ways in which ecofeminists have engaged with debates in environmental ethics, and have attempted to reframe some of the terms of the discussion to counter what Val Plumwood calls "the heavily masculine presence which has inhabited most accounts of environmental philosophy, including those of many deep ecologists."[72]

Many of the approaches to environmental ethics considered above have attempted to develop abstract, theoretical, and universally applicable environmental ethical theories. These approaches – such as the deontological egalitarian theory proposed by Paul Taylor – emphasize the importance of human reason, rather than emotion, in constructing and universalizing ethical theory. Ecofeminist ethicists have tended to reject this abstract, rational, and universalist approach to ethical thinking. Such accounts, ecofeminists argue, assume a single, dominant, detached way of viewing the world at all times and places. In contrast, ecofeminists maintain that there are no such value-neutral, universally applicable, unbiased points of view. Rather, all ethical views, however presented, are products of particular worldviews, contexts, and locations. Many ecofeminists also suggest that environmental ethics, rather than being based on a particular universalizing understanding of reason, can instead be built on relationships of *care* between humans and the nonhumans and particular environments in which they are located.[73] This does not mean that reason should be abandoned altogether; but rather that as Plumwood argues, reason should "find a form which encourages sensitivity to the conditions under which we exist on the earth . . . and enables us to acknowledge our debt to the sustaining others of the earth."[74] Warren also urges that a "felt sensitivity" should become part of environmental ethics, a sensitivity that recognizes the fundamental, essential nature of human relationship with others.[75] The language of relationship resists the kind of incorporation into the extended self for which ecofeminists criticize deep ecology; it allows for the existence of difference. Simultaneously, it makes *relationships*, rather than separate isolated individuals manifesting particular valuable qualities central to ethical decision making. Warren and Cheney argue that ecofeminist ethics grow out of "defining relationships" – relationships that are fundamental in defining who one is.

Ecofeminist approaches to environmental ethics have – as have all the other approaches – been subject to controversy and critique. One difficulty raised concerns the contextual, non-universalist nature of ecofeminist ethics: does this mean that there are no absolutes, that "anything goes"? Ecofeminists have resisted this interpretation by suggesting a series of "boundary conditions" which must be met if an ethic is to be described as "feminist" at all. Warren and Cheney argue that those "boundary conditions" exclude oppressive and patriarchal conceptual frameworks; relationships of an oppressive nature, even where they are defining, cannot be part of ecofeminism. Other questions have been raised about care as the basis for ethics: does it make sense to talk about a relationship of care with the non-living (such as rocks, as Warren does in her article "The Power and Promise of Ecological Feminism")?[76] How does one care for something that has no state that is better or worse for it? And others have defended more traditional approaches, such as an animal rights perspective, against the charges that such systems are abstract, generalizing and insensitive to difference by maintaining that different individuals *can* have the same morally-relevant features.[77]

This brief consideration of deep ecology and ecofeminism, and their engagement with debates in environmental ethics, has provided a glimpse of just how diverse views about environmental ethics might be. The last area of thought I want to consider here, environmental pragmatism, represents in part at least, an attempt to bring some of these diverse ideas together.

Environmental Pragmatism

The term "pragmatism" has two widely acknowledged uses: a general use referring to the adoption of practical strategies to deal with specific situations; and a philosophical use referring to the thought of the classical American philosophers, in particular Dewey and Peirce. The expression "environmental pragmatism" was first advocated by Andrew Light in 1992 at a conference in Budapest, Hungary (although work advocating prag-

matic approaches to environmental ethics, including the chapter by Anthony Weston in this book, had already been published).[78] As with the term pragmatism in general, environmental pragmatism has two strands: a more general, methodological or metaphilosophical approach, represented in the work of Light and Weston; and more specific, philosophical approaches drawing on the work of classic American pragmatic philosophers. These strands are not necessarily in conflict; indeed, some methodological environmental pragmatism has drawn on the ideas of classical philosophical pragmatism. Both strands are represented in Andrew Light and Eric Katz's 1996 edited volume *Environmental Pragmatism*.[79]

The starting point for environmental pragmatism, as argued by Light and Katz, is that debates in environmental ethics – of the kind outlined above – have had little impact on environmental policy-making. Such discussions are philosophers talking to one another, fiddling whilst the environment (in some cases literally!) burns. But as Light and Katz argue "pragmatists cannot tolerate theoretical delays to the contribution that philosophy may make to environmental questions."[80] Environmental pragmatism, then, is concerned to develop strategies by which environmental ethics can contribute to the resolution of practical environmental problems.

Methodologically, this means acceptance of moral pluralism. As with the ecofeminist approaches considered above, environmental pragmatists (such as Weston in "Beyond Intrinsic Value") may argue that environmental ethics is plural and contextual, growing out of the complexity of particular situations and relating to whole webs of needs and desires. This moves environmental ethics debates away from a theoretical search for a single, source of intrinsic value towards working in particular, concrete situations. Environmental pragmatists may also seek ways in which those with different theoretical and practical perspectives can converge in practice with policy-makers and environmental activists (an approach Bryan Norton develops) or argue for a kind of political compatiblism.[81]

Philosophically, the work of classical American pragmatists has also contributed substantially to thinking about environmental pragmatism as Minteer and Manning bear witness in their chapter. In particular, Dewey's work has influenced this, more classical, strand of environmental pragmatism.

Dewey's arguments for anti-foundationalism and "denial of the existence of a priori or self justifying "truths" or "moral absolutes," as well as his arguments for democratic, public conversations about social values, have been central to philosophical environmental pragmatism (and also to methodological environmental pragmatism).

A number of criticisms can be made of environmental pragmatism: inasmuch as, methodologically, it adopts moral pluralism, it is rejected by moral monists on grounds of consistency; in as much as it is contextualist, those who criticize ecofeminist ethics would also critique environmental pragmatists. Some (although not all) of those who argue for forms of intrinsic value in nature consider that environmental pragmatism is not able to give such non-anthropocentric values proper consideration.[82] Others have argued that policy convergence between those with very different ethical perspectives (anthropocentric and non-anthropocentric, or individualist and holist, for instance) is not as common as might be thought, and that different metaethical and ethical positions may issue in conflicting environmental policies.[83] Despite these difficulties, however, the work of environmental pragmatists has been important in bringing together philosophical thinking about the environment with practical environmental issues and problems.

The Social Construction of Nature

A further response to environmental ethics has been suggested by work which might broadly be called social constructivist and may take a variety of weaker and stronger forms.[84] Weaker forms of constructivism argue that "nature" and "the environment" have been interpreted in a variety of different ways at different times; and that "nature" is inescapably viewed through a cultural lens. What is called nature in one culture at one time may be viewed very differently in a different culture influenced by different political, historical, and social factors. Ideas about "nature" or "the environment" are thus inevitably changing and culturally relative. This view does not, however, mean that there is no "real" nature out there, even though our *knowledge* of it may be mediated and partial (in both senses of the word). But stronger versions of social constructivism seem to go further by apparently contesting the idea that there is

a "real" nature at all, working with premises such as: "there is no singular 'nature' as such, only a diversity of contested natures; and ... each such nature is constituted through a variety of sociocultural processes from which such natures cannot be plausibly separated."[85] Here, "nature" or "the environment" is viewed as something socially, culturally, and politically produced in a variety of human discourses and practices. (Even so, not all such claims are intended to be *ontological* – denying that there is any such thing as a "nature" independent of humans – they may rather be *epistemological*, relating to the cultural dependence of all knowledge about nature.)

Such views, especially in stronger forms, raise questions for environmental ethics. If there is no "real" nature independent of human beings, or we can't know about it, what sense can be made of "nature conservation" or "environmental protection"? What could it mean to say that nature (or aspects of it) has (or have) intrinsic value – and what is the political and cultural origin of such claims? If "nature" is a human construction, is it possible to discriminate between more or less "natural" human behavior with respect to it? Strong social constructivism may thus appear to threaten much work in environmental ethics. In response, it has been argued that strong social constructivism is anthropocentrism emerging in new forms – in its most extreme versions now going so far as to maintain that nature has no existence independent of humans.[86] Opponents of strong constructivist claims have argued for forms of realism which insist that humans do have access to meaningful knowledge about nature. Holmes Rolston, for instance, argues that, as organisms, humans do have access to what is "really there" through their senses.[87] Others, accepting weak, or mediated, constructivism, maintain that with this in mind forms of environmental ethics can still be developed.[88] Debates about broadly postmodern thinking in relation to environmental ethics look certain to continue as a location of much future work in environmental ethics.

In Conclusion

The variety of approaches to environmental ethics described in this chapter indicates the diversity and complexity of the current debate. All the approaches to ethics found in current general ethical theory have been applied within environmental ethics. In addition, considering the possible ethical significance of groupings such as ecosystems and of ideas such as diversity, has led to the development of largely new ethical approaches such as that suggested by Callicott or developed out of the Gaia hypothesis. The environmental problems of the present have drawn attention to the insight that ethical questions are raised by human behavior towards not only nonhuman individuals, but towards ecosystems, species and the biosphere itself. Deciding what sort of ethical response is appropriate to such questions is the task of environmental ethics. The importance of such responses is beyond doubt.

Work in environmental ethics over the past three decades has focused, to a considerable degree, on how humans should think about wild environments, and what values they might carry. But it seems likely that in future ethical interest in other kinds of environment will grow. There are a number of obvious reasons for this. Wildernesses are declining, both in size and number. Urbanization is expanding. Most people in the world rarely or never enter wild areas, living and working in urban or rural agricultural areas. Environmental ethicists are now turning to think about such urban and agricultural areas, which raise ethical questions just as much as the wilderness environments which have for so long been the focus of environmental ethics.[89] Thus in the future, debates about environmental ethics are likely to expand to consider ever wider kinds of environments and the ethical issues which these environments raise.

Acknowledgments

I would like to thank Andrew Light and Holmes Rolston for their assistance in rewriting this paper, developed from a much earlier version published in 1994.

Notes

1 Probably the nearest to a comprehensive survey could be found in J. Baird Callicott, *Earth's Insights* (Berkeley: University of California Press, 1996).

2 The closest to a historical survey, though now a little out of date, is Roderick Nash, *The Rights of Nature* (Madison: University of Wisconsin Press, 1989).

3 The expression "environmental ethics" is used here as an umbrella term to cover all kinds of moral debate concerning human attitudes toward, and treatment of, the nonhuman natural world. It is in itself a contentious term, since it could be argued that the very use of the term "environment" separates human beings from the natural world and suggests that the significance of the natural world is as something which surrounds human beings. For this reason, the term "ecological ethics" has been preferred by some ethicists. This has its own difficulties, since it can be interpreted as referring to posited ecological relationships within ecosystems, or with reading ethical approaches out of ecosystems. In this chapter I have elected to use the term "environmental ethics," since it is widely used and less open to misinterpretation than ecological ethics; but its use is not intended to prejudice questions concerning the relationship of humans with the nonhuman natural world.

4 See E. S. Turner, *All Heaven in a Rage* (London: Michael Joseph, 1964); for a collection of readings from various periods, see Tom Regan and Peter Singer (eds.), *Animal Rights and Human Obligations* (New Jersey: Prentice Hall, 1976). The two main approaches to the moral status of animals – utilitarian and "rights" based are put forward most coherently in Peter Singer's *Animal Liberation* (St. Albinos: Paladin, 1975) and Tom Regan's *The Case for Animal Rights* (London: Routledge, 1984).

5 Although there were isolated but significant philosophical considerations of these questions much earlier – most particularly in the work of Albert Schweitzer, and in Aldo Leopold's *A Sand County Almanac* (Oxford: Oxford University Press, 1949, 1987) both of whose work will be considered in this essay.

6 The conference, Philosophy and Environmental Crisis, was held at the University of Georgia, February 18–20, 1971. Proceedings were published in William Blackstone (ed.), *Philosophy and Environmental Crisis* (Athens, GA: University of Georgia Press, 1974).

7 Arne Naess, "The Shallow and the Deep, Long-Range Ecology Movements," *Inquiry* 16 (1973): 95–100.

8 Christopher Stone, "Should Trees Have Standing?" *Southern California Law Review* 45, no. 4 (1972): 462.

9 John Passmore, *Man's Responsibility for Nature* (London: Duckworth, 1974).

10 Don Mannison, Michael McRobbie, and Richard Routley (eds.), *Environmental Philosophy* (Canberra: Research School of Social Sciences, Australian National University, 1980); Robert Elliot and Arran Gare (eds.), *Environmental Philosophy: A Collection of Readings* (University Park, PA.: University of Pennsylvania, 1983).

11 Robin Attfield, *The Ethics of Environmental Concern* (Oxford: Basil Blackwell, 1983).

12 Holmes Rolston III, *Environmental Ethics: Duties to and Values in the Natural World* (Philadelphia: Temple University Press, 1988); Paul Taylor, *Respect for Nature* (Princeton: Princeton University Press, 1986).

13 There is a significant philosophical literature on the moral standing of future generations of humans. See for instance: Derek Parfit, *Reasons and Persons* (Oxford: Clarendon Press, 1984); Robin Attfield, *A Theory of Value and Obligation* (London: Croom Helm, 1987), Avner de-Shalit, *Why Posterity Matters* (London: Routledge, 1995), as well as Andrew Dobson (ed.), *Fairness and Futurity* (Oxford: Oxford University Press, 1999), the original source for the piece by Brian Barry in this volume.

14 Passmore, *Man's Responsibility for Nature*.

15 R. G. Frey, *Rights, Killing and Suffering* (Oxford: Basil Blackwell, 1983).

16 Although it is worth noticing that in later publications, Passmore has been more sympathetic towards a more thoroughgoing environmental ethic. See for instance Passmore's "Attitudes to Nature" in *Nature and Conduct* (Royal Institute of Philosophy, 1975).

17 Norton is an environmental pragmatist, a group of positions discussed later in this chapter, and his approach to value coheres with his pragmatism.

18 I am indebted for the clarity of this distinction to Bernard Williams in J. C. C. Smart and Bernard Williams, *Utilitarianism: For and Against* (Cambridge: Cambridge University Press, 1973), p. 83.

19 Singer, *Animal Liberation*; *Practical Ethics* (Oxford: Oxford University Press, 1979); and "Killing Humans and Killing Animals," *Inquiry* 21 (1978).

20 Donald VanDeVeer, "Interspecific Justice," *Inquiry* 22 (1979): 55–79.

21 For both Attfield volumes see notes 11 and 13.

22 Gary Varner, *In Nature's Interests?* (New York: Oxford University Press, 1998).

23 John Rodman, "The Liberation of Nature," *Inquiry* 20 (1977).

24 Michael Lockwood, "Killing and the Preference for Life," *Inquiry* 22 (1979).

25 J. Baird Callicott, "Animal Liberation: A Triangular Affair," *Environmental Ethics* 2 (1980): 311–38.

26 Lawrence Johnson, *A Morally Deep World* (Cambridge: Cambridge University Press, 1991); Rolston, *Environmental Ethics*.

27 Kenneth Goodpaster, "On Being Morally Considerable," *Journal of Philosophy* 75 (1978): 308–25.

28 Tom Regan, "The Nature and Possibility of an Environmental Ethic," *Environmental Ethics* 3 (1981): 19–34.

29 Though it should be noted, as Varner (in this volume) points out, that Regan is only arguing that

his case applies most clearly to those animals, not that others are necessarily excluded.

30 Taylor, *Respect for Nature*; Louis Lombardi, "Inherent Worth, Respect and Rights," *Environmental Ethics* 5 (1983): 257–70.

31 Albert Schweitzer, *Philosophy of Civilization* (Buffalo, New York: Prometheus Books, 1923, 1987), p. 318.

32 This may sound as if Taylor is straightforwardly equating an "is" with an "ought." In fact, he is most careful not to do this; but it is impossible in a background essay such as this to explain more fully. See Taylor, *Respect for Nature*, p. 71.

33 This same point is made by Peter Wenz in *Environmental Justice* (New York: SUNY Press, 1988).

34 Peter Singer, "The Place of Nonhumans" in K. M. Sayre and K. M. Goodpaster (eds.), *Ethics and Problems of the 21st Century* (Notre Dame: University of Notre Dame Press, 1979), pp. 191–206; W. K. Frankena, "Ethics and the Environment," also in *Ethics and Problems of the 21st Century*, pp. 3–20.

35 Peter Wenz, *Environmental Justice*, p. 286.

36 J. Baird Callicott, "Non-Anthropocentric Value Theory and Environmental Ethics," *American Philosophical Quarterly* 21 (1988): 301.

37 Aldo Leopold, *A Sand County Almanac*, p. 204.

38 Ibid., p. 224.

39 J. Baird Callicott (ed.), *A Companion to a Sand County Almanac* (Wisconsin: University of Wisconsin Press, 1987).

40 Although, as some ecologists have pointed out, neither of these are any longer thought of as necessary qualities of ecological systems.

41 See Bryan Norton, "The Constancy of Leopold's Land Ethic" in Andrew Light and Eric Katz (eds.), *Environmental Pragmatism* (London: Routledge, 1996), pp. 84–102.

42 More recently he has accepted that value may be vertabragenic, generated by all animals with spinal cords; broadly, animals which are conscious (J. Baird Callicott, "Rolston on Intrinsic Values: A Deconstruction," *Environmental Ethics* 14 [1992]: 129–43).

43 Callicott, "Animal Liberation: A Triangular Affair," p. 66.

44 James Lovelock, *Gaia* (Oxford: Oxford University Press, 1979) and *The Ages of Gaia* (Oxford: Oxford University Press, 1982).

45 For the scientific criticism of Gaia, see Richard Dawkins, *The Extended Phenotype* (Oxford: Oxford University Press, 1982), and some of the papers in Stephen H. Schneider and Penelope J. Boston (eds.), *Scientists on Gaia* (MIT Press, 1991).

46 Andrew Dobson, *Green Political Thought* (London: Unwin Hyman, 1990), p. 45.

47 Dale Jamieson, "Animal Liberation is an Environmental Ethic," *Environmental Values* 7, no. 1 (1998).

48 Gary Varner, "No Holism Without Pluralism," *Environmental Ethics* 13 (1991): 175–9.

49 Rolston, *Environmental Ethics*.

50 Ibid., p. 149.

51 Ibid., p. 176.

52 See in particular Christopher Stone, *Earth and Other Ethics* (New York: Harper and Row, 1987) and "Moral Pluralism and the Course of Environmental Ethics" (in this volume); Andrew Brennan, *Thinking About Nature* (London: Routledge, 1988) and "Moral Pluralism and the Environment," *Environmental Values* 1, no. 1 (1992), and other articles in the section on moral pluralism in this volume.

53 See Brennan, *Thinking About Nature*, and also Brennan, "Environmental Awareness and Liberal Education" in this volume.

54 Brennan, "Moral Pluralism and the Environment," p. 6.

55 Brennan, *Thinking About Nature*, p. 3.

56 J. Baird Callicott, "Moral Monism in Environmental Ethics Defended," *Journal of Philosophical Research* 19 (1994).

57 J. Baird Callicott and Michael Nelson (eds.), *The Great New Wilderness Debate* (Athens, GA.: University of Georgia Press, 1998).

58 Ramachandra Guha, "Radical American Environmentalism and Wilderness Preservation: A Third World Critique," *Environmental Ethics* 11 (1989): 71–83.

59 Some of Callicott's arguments are reproduced in "A Critique of and an Alternative to the Wilderness Idea" in this book; the full debate is reproduced in *The Great New Wilderness Debate*, pp. 337–93.

60 This discussion about American Indians forms a small part of a much larger debate about the impacts of American Indians on their environment. See for example, Shepard Krech, *The Ecological Indian* (New York: W. W. Norton and Company, 1999), and Vine Deloria's review article on Krech in *Worldviews: Environment, Culture, Religion* 4, no. 3 (2000).

61 Robert Elliot, *Faking Nature: The Ethics of Environmental Restoration* (London: Routledge, 1997).

62 Y. S. Lo, "Natural and Artifactual: Restored Nature as Subject," *Environmental Ethics* 21 (1999): 247–66. For more on Light's position on restoration see his "Restoration, the Value of Participation, and the Risks of Professionalization" in Paul Gobster and Bruce Hull (eds.), *Restoring Nature: Perspectives from the Social Sciences and Humanities* (Washington, DC: Island Press, 2000), pp. 49–70, and "Restoring Ecological Citizenship" in Ben Minteer and Bob Pepperman-Taylor (eds.), *Democracy and the Claims of Nature* (Lanham, MD: Rowman & Littlefield, 2002).

63 Much of Naess's work, and a wide range of responses to it, has been collected in Nina Witoszek and Andrew Brennan (eds.), *Philosophical Dialogues: Arne Naess and the Development of Ecophilosophy* (Lanham: Rowman and Littlefield, 1999).

64 By 1984, Naess had, for instance, argued that living things could be treated differently without different grades of value being ascribed to them (Arne Naess, "Intuition, Intrinsic Value and Deep Ecology," *The Ecologist* 14, no. 5–6 [1984]). By 1992, he accepted the terminology of value hierarchy in nature (personal communication). Other deep ecologists also accepted this; Warwick Fox suggested a value hierarchy based on complexity of experience.

65 Most prominently in Bill Devall and George Sessions (eds.), *Deep Ecology* (Salt Lake City: Peregrine Smith, 1985), p. 70; and in Witozsek and Brennan, *Philosophical Dialogues*, p. 8.

66 Indeed, in his 1987 Schumacher Lecture, Naess himself comments that "moralizing is not a great force in the world" while Warwick Fox goes so far as to say that deep ecology "renders ethics superfluous." Warwick Fox, *Towards a Transpersonal Ecology* (New York: Shambhala, 1991), p. 225.

67 In particular by Devall and Sessions, *Deep Ecology*.

68 Richard Sylvan, "A Critique of Deep Ecology," *Radical Philosophy* 40/41 (1986).

69 See Brennan, *Thinking About Nature*.

70 See for instance D. C. Phillip, *Holistic Thought in Social Science* (Stanford: Stanford University Press, 1976).

71 Val Plumwood, *Feminism and the Mastery of Nature* (London: Routledge, 1993).

72 Ibid., p. 2.

73 The importance of values associated with particular cherished places is emphasized by Norton and Hannon in this volume.

74 Plumwood, *Feminism and the Mastery of Nature*, p. 196.

75 Karen Warren, "The Power and Promise of Ecological Feminism," *Environmental Ethics* 12 (1990): 125–46.

76 Ibid.

77 See for instance Johnson and Johnson, "The Limits of Partiality," in Karen Warren (ed.), *Ecological Feminism* (London: Routledge, 1994).

78 Light's paper was published later as "Materialists, Ontologists, and Environmental Pragmatists," *Social Theory and Practice*, 21 (1995): 315–33.

79 Light and Katz, *Environmental Pragmatism*.

80 Ibid., p. 4.

81 Bryan Norton, *Towards Unity Amongst Environmentalists* (Oxford: Oxford University Press, 1991) and Norton, "Convergence and Contextualism: Some Clarifications and a Reply to Stephenson," *Environmental Ethics* 19 (1997): 87–100; Andrew Light "Compatiblism in Political Ecology" in Light and Katz, *Environmental Pragmatism*, pp. 161–84, and Light, "Taking Environmental Ethics Public" in David Schmidtz and Elizabeth Willott (eds.), *Envir-*

onmental Ethics: What Really Matters? What Really Works? (Oxford: Oxford University Press, 2001).

82 See for instance Eric Katz "Searching for Intrinsic Value" in Light and Katz, *Environmental Pragmatism*, pp. 307–18. As the next note suggests, however, Katz views on environmental pragmatism in some contexts have changed.

83 This latter point need not be an argument against methodological environmental pragmatism. See Eric Katz, "A Pragmatic Reconsideration of Anthropocentrism," *Environmental Ethics* 21 (1999): 377–90.

84 See Anna Peterson, "Environmental Ethics and the Social Construction of Nature" and Mick Smith, "To Speak of Trees," both in *Environmental Ethics* 12, no. 4 (1999), for more detailed discussion of this debate in the context of environmental ethics.

85 First sentence of Phil Macnaghten and John Urry, *Contested Natures* (London: Sage, 1998). Similar views are put forward in the context of critical theory in Steven Vogel, *Against Nature* (New York: SUNY Press, 1996). The constructivist/realist debate about nature is interestingly discussed in Kate Soper, *What is Nature?* (Oxford: Blackwell, 1995).

86 See Michael Soulé and Gary Lease (eds.), *Reinventing Nature? Responses to Postmodern Deconstruction* (Washington: Island Press, 1995).

87 See Rolston's article "Nature for Real: Is Nature a Social Construct?" in Tim Chappell (ed.), *The Philosophy of the Environment* (Edinburgh: Edinburgh University Press, 1997).

88 See, for instance, Mick Smith, *An Ethics of Place: Radical Ecology, Postmodernity and Social Theory* (New York: SUNY Press, 2001).

89 See for instance Paul Thompson, *Spirit of the Soil* (London: Routledge, 1994); Peter Wenz, "Pragmatism in Practice: The Efficiency of Sustainable Agriculture," *Environmental Ethics* 21 (1999): 391–410; and Andrew Light, "The Urban Blind Spot in Environmental Ethics," *Environmental Politics* 10 (2001): 7–35.

2

The Land Ethic

Aldo Leopold

When god-like Odysseus returned from the wars in Troy, he hanged all on one rope a dozen slave-girls of his household whom he suspected of misbehavior during his absence.

This hanging involved no question of propriety. The girls were property. The disposal of property was then, as now, a matter of expediency, not of right and wrong.

Concepts of right and wrong were not lacking from Odysseus' Greece: witness the fidelity of his wife through the long years before at last his black-prowed galleys clove the wine-dark seas for home. The ethical structure of that day covered wives, but had not yet been extended to human chattels. During the three thousand years which have since elapsed, ethical criteria have been extended to many fields of conduct, with corresponding shrinkages in those judged by expediency only.

The Ethical Sequence

This extension of ethics, so far studied only by philosophers, is actually a process in ecological evolution. Its sequences may be described in ecological as well as in philosophical terms. An ethic, ecologically, is a limitation on freedom of action in the struggle for existence. An ethic, philosophically, is a differentiation of social from anti-social conduct. These are two definitions of one thing. The thing has its origin in the tendency of inter-dependent individuals or groups to evolve modes of co-operation. The ecologist calls these symbioses. Politics and economics are advanced symbioses in which the original free-for-all competition has been replaced, in part, by co-operative mechanisms with an ethical content.

The complexity of co-operative mechanisms has increased with population density, and with the efficiency of tools. It was simpler, for example, to define the anti-social uses of sticks and stones in the days of the mastodons than of bullets and billboards in the age of motors.

The first ethics dealt with the relation between individuals; the Mosaic Decalogue is an example. Later accretions dealt with the relation between the individual and society. The Golden Rule tries to integrate the individual to society; democracy to integrate social organization to the individual.

There is as yet no ethic dealing with man's relation to land and to the animals and plants which grow upon it. Land, like Odysseus' slave-girls, is still property. The land-relation is still strictly economic, entailing privileges but not obligations.

The extension of ethics to this third element in human environment is, if I read the evidence correctly, an evolutionary possibility and an ecological necessity. It is the third step in a sequence. The first two have already been taken. Individual thinkers since the days of Ezekiel and Isaiah have asserted that the despoliation of land is not only inexpedient but wrong. Society, however, has not yet affirmed their belief. I regard the present conservation movement as the embryo of such an affirmation.

An ethic may be regarded as a mode of guidance for meeting ecological situations so new or intricate, or involving such deferred reactions, that the path of social expediency is not discernible to the average individual. Animal instincts are modes of guidance for the individual in meeting such situations. Ethics are possibly a kind of community instinct in-the-making.

The Community Concept

All ethics so far evolved rest upon a single premise: that the individual is a member of a community of interdependant parts. His instincts prompt him to compete for his place in that community, but his ethics prompt him also to cooperate (perhaps in order that there may be a place to compete for).

The land ethic simply enlarges the boundaries of the community to include soils, waters, plants, and animals, or collectively: the land.

This sounds simple: do we not already sing our love for and obligation to the land of the free and the home of the brave? Yes, but just what and whom do we love? Certainly not the soil, which we are sending helter-skelter downriver. Certainly not the waters, which we assume have no function except to turn turbines, float barges, and carry off sewage. Certainly not the plants, of which we exterminate whole communities without batting an eye. Certainly not the animals, of which we have already extirpated many of the largest and most beautiful species. A land ethic of course cannot prevent the alteration, management, and use of these "resources," but it does affirm their right to continued existence, and, at least in spots, their continued existence in a natural state.

In short a land ethic changes the role of *Homo sapiens* from conqueror of the land-community to plain member and citizen of it. It implies respect for his fellow-members, and also respect for the community as such.

In human history, we have learned (I hope) that the conqueror role is eventually self-defeating. Why? Because it is implicit in such a role that the conqueror knows, *ex cathedra*, just what makes the community clock tick, and just what and who is valuable, and what and who is worthless, in community life. It always turns out that he

knows neither, and this is why his conquests eventually defeat themselves.

In the biotic community, a parallel situation exists. Abraham knew exactly what the land was for: it was to drip milk and honey into Abraham's mouth. At the present moment, the assurance with which we regard this assumption is inverse to the degree of our education.

The ordinary citizen today assumes that science knows what makes the community clock tick; the scientist is equally sure that he does not. He knows that the biotic mechanism is so complex that its workings may never be fully understood.

That man is, in fact, only a member of a biotic team is shown by an ecological interpretation of history. Many historical events, hitherto explained solely in terms of human enterprise, were actually biotic interactions between people and land. The characteristics of the land determined the facts quite as potently as the characteristics of the men who lived on it.

Consider, for example, the settlement of the Mississippi valley. In the years following the Revolution, three groups were contending for its control: the native Indian, the French and English traders, and the American settlers. Historians wonder what would have happened if the English at Detroit had thrown a little more weight into the Indian side of those tipsy scales which decided the outcome of the colonial migration into the cane-lands of Kentucky. It is time now to ponder the fact that the cane-lands, when subjected to the particular mixture of forces represented by the cow, plow, fire, and axe of the pioneer, became bluegrass. What if the plant succession inherent in this dark and bloody ground had, under the impact of these forces, given us some worthless sedge, shrub, or weed? Would Boone and Kenton have held out? Would there have been any overflow into Ohio, Indiana, Illinois, and Missouri? Any Louisiana Purchase? Any transcontinental union of new states? Any Civil War?

Kentucky was one sentence in the drama of history. We are commonly told what the human actors in this drama tried to do, but we are seldom told that their success, or the lack of it, hung in large degree on the reaction of particular soils to the impact of the particular forces exerted by their occupancy. In the case of Kentucky, we do not even know where the bluegrass came from – whether it is a native species, or a stowaway from Europe.

Contrast the cane-lands with what hindsight tells us about the Southwest, where the pioneers were equally brave, resourceful, and persevering. The impact of occupancy here brought no bluegrass, or other plant fitted to withstand the bumps and buffetings of hard use. This region, when grazed by livestock, reverted through a series of more and more worthless grasses, shrubs, and weeds to a condition of unstable equilibrium. Each recession of plant types bred erosion; each increment to erosion bred a further recession of plants. The result today is a progressive and mutual deterioration, not only of plants and soils, but of the animal community subsisting thereon. The early settlers did not expect this: on the ciénegas of New Mexico some even cut ditches to hasten it. So subtle has been its progress that few residents of the region are aware of it. It is quite invisible to the tourist who finds this wrecked landscape colorful and charming (as indeed it is, but it bears scant resemblance to what it was in 1848).

This same landscape was "developed" once before, but with quite different results. The Pueblo Indians settled the Southwest in pre-Columbian times, but they happened *not* to be equipped with range livestock. Their civilization expired, but not because their land expired.

In India, regions devoid of any sod-forming grass have been settled, apparently without wrecking the land, by the simple expedient of carrying the grass to the cow, rather than vice versa. (Was this the result of some deep wisdom, or was it just good luck? I do not know.)

In short, the plant succession steered the course of history; the pioneer simply demonstrated, for good or ill, what successions inhered in the land. Is history taught in this spirit? It will be, once the concept of land as a community really penetrates our intellectual life.

The Ecological Conscience

Conservation is a state of harmony between men and land. Despite nearly a century of propaganda, conservation still proceeds at a snail's pace; progress still consists largely of letterhead pieties and convention oratory. On the back forty we still slip two steps backward for each forward stride.

The usual answer to this dilemma is "more conservation education." No one will debate this, but is it certain that only the *volume* of education needs stepping up? Is something lacking in the *content* as well?

It is difficult to give a fair summary of its content in brief form, but, as I understand it, the content is substantially this: obey the law, vote right, join some organizations, and practice what conservation is profitable on your own land; the government will do the rest.

Is not this formula too easy to accomplish anything worth-while? It defines no right or wrong, assigns no obligation, calls for no sacrifice, implies no change in the current philosophy of values. In respect of land-use, it urges only enlightened self-interest. Just how far will such education take us? An example will perhaps yield a partial answer.

By 1930 it had become clear to all except the ecologically blind that southwestern Wisconsin's topsoil was slipping seaward. In 1933 the farmers were told that if they would adopt certain remedial practices for five years, the public would donate CCC labor to install them, plus the necessary machinery and materials. The offer was widely accepted, but the practices were widely forgotten when the five-year contract period was up. The farmers continued only those practices that yielded an immediate and visible economic gain for themselves.

This led to the idea that maybe farmers would learn more quickly if they themselves wrote the rules. Accordingly the Wisconsin Legislature in 1937 passed the Soil Conservation District Law. This said to farmers, in effect: *We, the public, will furnish you free technical service and loan you specialized machinery, if you will write your own rules for land-use. Each county may write its own rules, and these will have the force of law.* Nearly all the counties promptly organized to accept the proffered help, but after a decade of operation, *no county has yet written a single rule*. There has been visible progress in such practices as stripcropping, pasture renovation, and soil liming, but none in fencing woodlots against grazing, and none in excluding plow and cow from steep slopes. The farmers, in short, have selected those remedial practices which were profitable anyhow, and ignored those which were profitable to the community, but not clearly profitable to themselves.

When one asks why no rules have been written, one is told that the community is not yet ready to support them; education must precede rules. But the education actually in progress makes no mention of obligations to land over and above those dictated by self-interest. The net result is that we have more education but less soil, fewer healthy woods, and as many floods as in 1937.

The puzzling aspect of such situations is that the existence of obligations over and above self-interest is taken for granted in such rural community enterprises as the betterment of roads, schools, churches, and baseball teams. Their existence is not taken for granted, nor as yet seriously discussed, in bettering the behavior of the water that falls on the land, or in the preserving of the beauty or diversity of the farm landscape. Land-use ethics are still governed wholly by economic self-interest, just as social ethics were a century ago.

To sum up: we asked the farmer to do what he conveniently could to save his soil, and he has done just that, and only that. The farmer who clears the woods off a 75 per cent slope, turns his cows into the clearing, and dumps its rainfall, rocks, and soil into the community creek, is still (if otherwise decent) a respected member of society. If he puts lime on his fields and plants his crops on contour, he is still entitled to all the privileges and emoluments of his Soil Conservation District. The District is a beautiful piece of social machinery, but it is coughing along on two cylinders because we have been too timid, and too anxious for quick success, to tell the farmer the true magnitude of his obligations. Obligations have no meaning without conscience, and the problem we face is the extension of the social conscience from people to land.

No important change in ethics was ever accomplished without an internal change in our intellectual emphasis, loyalities, affections, and convictions. The proof that conservation has not yet touched these foundations of conduct lies in the fact that philosophy and religion have not yet heard of it. In our attempt to make conservation easy, we have made it trivial.

Substitutes for a Land Ethic

When the logic of history hungers for bread and we hand out a stone, we are at pains to explain how much the stone resembles bread. I now describe some of the stones which serve in lieu of a land ethic.

One basic weakness in a conservation system based wholly on economic motives is that most members of the land community have no economic value. Wildflowers and songbirds are examples. Of the 22,000 higher plants and animals native to Wisconsin, it is doubtful whether more than 5 per cent can be sold, fed, eaten, or otherwise put to economic use. Yet these creatures are members of the biotic community, and if (as I believe) its stability depends on its integrity, they are entitled to continuance.

When one of these non-economic categories is threatened, and if we happen to love it, we invent subterfuges to give it economic importance. At the beginning of the century songbirds were supposed to be disappearing. Ornithologists jumped to the rescue with some distinctly shaky evidence to the effect that insects would eat us up if birds failed to control them. The evidence had to be economic in order to be valid.

It is painful to read these circumlocutions today. We have no land ethic yet, but we have at least drawn nearer the point of admitting that birds should continue as a matter of biotic right, regardless of the presence or absence of economic advantage to us.

A parallel situation exists in respect of predatory mammals, raptorial birds, and fish-eating birds. Time was when biologists somewhat over-worked the evidence that these creatures preserve the health of game by killing weaklings, or that they control rodents for the farmer, or that they prey only on 'worthless' species. Here again, the evidence had to be economic in order to be valid. It is only in recent years that we hear the more honest argument that predators are members of the community, and that no special interest has the right to exterminate them for the sake of a benefit, real or fancied, to itself. Unfortunately this enlightened view is still in the talk stage. In the field the extermination of predators goes merrily on: witness the impending erasure of the timber wolf by fiat of Congress, the Conservation Bureaus, and many state legislatures.

Some species of trees have been 'read out of the party' by economics-minded foresters because they grow too slowly, or have too low a sale value to pay as timber crops: white cedar, tamarack, cypress, beech, and hemlock are examples. In Europe, where forestry is ecologically more advanced, the non-commercial tree species are recognized as members of the native forest community, to be preserved as such, within reason. Moreover some (like beech) have been found to have a valuable function in building up soil fertility. The interdependence of the forest and its constituent tree species, ground flora, and fauna is taken for granted.

Lack of economic value is sometimes a character not only of species or groups, but of entire biotic communities: marshes, bogs, dunes, and 'deserts' are examples. Our formula in such cases is to relegate their conservation to government as refuges, monuments, or parks. The difficulty is that these communities are usually interspersed with more valuable private lands; the government cannot possibly own or control such scattered parcels. The net effect is that we have relegated some of them to ultimate extinction over large areas. If the private owner were ecologically minded, he would be proud to be the custodian of a reasonable proportion of such areas, which add diversity and beauty to his farm and to his community.

In some instances, the assumed lack of profit in these 'waste' areas has proved to be wrong, but only after most of them had been done away with. The present scramble to reflood muskrat marshes is a case in point.

There is a clear tendency in American conservation to relegate to government all necessary jobs that private landowners fail to perform. Government ownership, operation, subsidy, or regulation is now widely prevalent in forestry, range management, soil and watershed management, park and wilderness conservation, fisheries management, and migratory bird management, with more to come. Most of this growth in governmental conservation is proper and logical, some of it is inevitable. That I imply no disapproval of it is implicit in the fact that I have spent most of my life working for it. Nevertheless the question arises: What is the ultimate magnitude of the enterprise? Will the tax base carry its eventual ramifications? At what point will governmental conservation, like the mastodon, become handicapped by its own dimensions? The answer, if there is any, seems to be in a land ethic, or some other force which assigns more obligation to the private landowner.

Industrial landowners and users, especially lumbermen and stockmen, are inclined to wail long and loudly about the extension of government ownership and regulation to land, but (with notable exceptions) they show little disposition to develop the only visible alternative: the voluntary practice of conservation on their own lands.

When the private landowner is asked to perform some unprofitable act for the good of the community, he today assents only with outstretched palm. If the act costs him cash this is fair and proper, but when it costs only forethought, open-mindedness, or time, the issue is at least debatable. The overwhelming growth of land-use subsidies in recent years must be ascribed, in large part, to the government's own agencies for conservation education: the land bureaus, the agricultural colleges, and the extension services. As far as I can detect, no ethical obligation toward land is taught in these institutions.

To sum up: a system of conservation based solely on economic self-interest is hopelessly lopsided. It tends to ignore, and thus eventually to eliminate, many elements in the land community that lack commercial value, but that are (as far as we know) essential to its healthy functioning. It assumes, falsely, I think, that the economic parts of the biotic clock will function without the uneconomic parts. It tends to relegate to government many functions eventually too large, too complex, or too widely dispersed to be performed by government.

An ethical obligation on the part of the private owner is the only visible remedy for these situations.

The Land Pyramid

An ethic to supplement and guide the economic relation to land presupposes the existence of some mental image of land as a biotic mechanism. We can be ethical only in relation to something we can see, feel, understand, love, or otherwise have faith in.

The image commonly employed in conservation education is 'the balance of nature.' For reasons too lengthy to detail here, this figure of speech fails to describe accurately what little we know about the land mechanism. A much truer image is the one employed in ecology: the biotic pyramid. I shall first sketch the pyramid as a symbol of land, and later develop some of its implications in terms of land-use.

Plants absorb energy from the sun. This energy flows through a circuit called the biota, which may be represented by a pyramid consisting of layers. The bottom layer is the soil. A plant layer rests on the soil, an insect layer on the plants, a bird and rodent layer on the insects, and so on up through various animal groups to the apex layer, which consists of the larger carnivores.

The species of a layer are alike not in where they came from, or in what they look like, but rather in what they eat. Each successive layer depends on those below it for food and often for other services, and each in turn furnishes food and services to those above. Proceeding upward, each successive layer decreases in numerical abundance. Thus, for every carnivore there are hundreds of his prey, thousands of their prey, millions of insects, uncountable plants. The pyramidal form of the system reflects this numerical progression from apex to base. Man shares an intermediate layer with the bears, raccoons, and squirrels which eat both meat and vegetables.

The lines of dependency for food and other services are called food chains. Thus soil–oak–deer–Indian is a chain that has now been largely converted to soil–corn–cow–farmer. Each species, including ourselves, is a link in many chains. The deer eats a hundred plants other than oak, and the cow a hundred plants other than corn. Both, then, are links in a hundred chains. The pyramid is a tangle of chains so complex as to seem disorderly, yet the stability of the system proves it to be a highly organized structure. Its functioning depends on the co-operation and competition of its diverse parts.

In the beginning, the pyramid of life was low and squat; the food chains short and simple. Evolution has added layer after layer, link after link. Man is one of thousands of accretions to the height and complexity of the pyramid. Science has given us many doubts, but it has given us at least one certainty: the trend of evolution is to elaborate and diversify the biota.

Land, then, is not merely soil; it is a fountain of energy flowing through a circuit of soils, plants, and animals. Food chains are the living channels which conduct energy upward; death and decay return it to the soil. The circuit is not closed; some energy is dissipated in decay, some is added by absorption from the air, some is stored in soils, peats, and long-lived forests; but it is a sustained circuit, like a slowly augmented revolving fund of life. There is always a net loss by downhill wash, but this is normally small and offset by the decay of rocks. It is deposited in the ocean and, in the course of geological time, raised to form new lands and new pyramids.

The velocity and character of the upward flow of energy depend on the complex structure of the plant and animal community, much as the upward flow of sap in a tree depends on its complex cellular organization. Without this complexity, normal circulation would presumably not occur. Structure means the characteristic numbers, as well as the characteristic kinds and functions, of the component species. This interdependence between the complex structure of the land and its smooth functioning as an energy unit is one of its basic attributes.

When a change occurs in one part of the circuit, many other parts must adjust themselves to it. Change does not necessarily obstruct or divert the flow of energy; evolution is a long series of self-induced changes, the net result of which has been to elaborate the flow mechanism and to lengthen the circuit. Evolutionary changes, however, are usually slow and local. Man's invention of tools has enabled him to make changes of unprecedented violence, rapidity, and scope.

One change is in the composition of floras and faunas. The larger predators are lopped off the apex of the pyramid; food chains, for the first time in history, become shorter rather than longer. Domesticated species from other lands are substituted for wild ones, and wild ones are moved to new habitats. In this world-wide pooling of faunas and floras, some species get out of bounds as pests and diseases, others are extinguished. Such effects are seldom intended or foreseen; they represent unpredicted and often untraceable readjustments in the structure. Agricultural science is largely a race between the emergence of new pests and the emergence of new techniques for their control.

Another change touches the flow of energy through plants and animals and its return to the soil. Fertility is the ability of soil to receive, store, and release energy. Agriculture, by overdrafts on the soil, or by too radical a substitution of domestic for native species in the superstructure, may derange the channels of flow or deplete storage. Soils depleted of their storage, or of the organic matter which anchors it, wash away faster than they form. This is erosion.

Waters, like soil, are part of the energy circuit. Industry, by polluting waters or obstructing them with dams, may exclude the plants and animals necessary to keep energy in circulation.

Transportation brings about another basic change: the plants or animals grown in one region are now consumed and returned to the soil in another. Transportation taps the energy stored in rocks, and in the air, and uses it elsewhere; thus we fertilize the garden with nitrogen gleaned by the guano birds from the fishes of seas on the other side of the Equator. Thus the formerly localized and self-contained circuits are pooled on a world-wide scale.

The process of altering the pyramid for human occupation releases stored energy, and this often gives rise, during the pioneering period, to a deceptive exuberance of plant and animal life, both wild and tame. These releases of biotic capital tend to becloud or postpone the penalties of violence.

This thumbnail sketch of land as an energy circuit conveys three basic ideas:

(1) That land is not merely soil.
(2) That the native plants and animals kept the energy circuit open; others may or may not.
(3) That man-made changes are of a different order than evolutionary changes, and have effects more comprehensive than is intended or foreseen.

These ideas, collectively, raise two basic issues: Can the land adjust itself to the new order? Can the desired alterations be accomplished with less violence?

Biotas seem to differ in their capacity to sustain violent conversion. Western Europe, for example, carries a far different pyramid than Caesar found there. Some large animals are lost; swampy forests have become meadows or plow-land; many new plants and animals are introduced, some of which escape as pests; the remaining natives are greatly changed in distribution and abundance. Yet the soil is still there and, with the help of imported nutrients, still fertile; the waters flow normally; the new structure seems to function and to persist. There is no visible stoppage or derangement of the circuit.

Western Europe, then, has a resistant biota. Its inner processes are tough, elastic, resistant to strain. No matter how violent the alterations, the pyramid, so far, has developed some new *modus vivendi* which preserves its habitability for man, and for most of the other natives.

Japan seems to present another instance of radical conversion without disorganization.

Most other civilized regions, and some as yet barely touched by civilization, display various stages of disorganization, varying from initial symptoms to advanced wastage. In Asia Minor and North Africa diagnosis is confused by climatic changes, which may have been either the cause or

the effect of advanced wastage. In the United States the degree of disorganization varies locally; it is worst in the Southwest, the Ozarks, and parts of the South, and least in New England and the Northwest. Better land-uses may still arrest it in the less advanced regions. In parts of Mexico, South America, South Africa, and Australia a violent and accelerating wastage is in progress, but I cannot assess the prospects.

This almost world-wide display of disorganization in the land seems to be similar to disease in an animal, except that it never culminates in complete disorganization or death. The land recovers, but at some reduced level of complexity, and with a reduced carrying capacity for people, plants, and animals. Many biotas currently regarded as 'lands of opportunity' are in fact already subsisting on exploitative agriculture, i.e. they have already exceeded their sustained carrying capacity. Most of South America is overpopulated in this sense.

In arid regions we attempt to offset the process of wastage by reclamation, but it is only too evident that the prospective longevity of reclamation projects is often short. In our own West, the best of them may not last a century.

The combined evidence of history and ecology seems to support one general deduction: the less violent the manmade changes, the greater the probability of successful readjustment in the pyramid. Violence, in turn, varies with human population density; a dense population requires a more violent conversion. In this respect, North America has a better chance for permanence than Europe, if she can contrive to limit her density.

This deduction runs counter to our current philosophy which assumes that because a small increase in density enriched human life, that an indefinite increase will enrich it indefinitely. Ecology knows of no density relationship that holds for indefinitely wide limits. All gains from density are subject to a law of diminishing returns.

Whatever may be the equation for men and land, it is improbable that we as yet know all its terms. Recent discoveries in mineral and vitamin nutrition reveal unsuspected dependencies in the up-circuit: incredibly minute quantities of certain substances determine the value of soils to plants, of plants to animals. What of the down-circuit? What of the vanishing species, the preservation of which we now regard as an esthetic luxury? They helped build the soil; in what unsuspected ways may they be essential to its maintenance? Professor Weaver proposes that we use prairie flowers to reflocculate the wasting soils of the dust bowl; who knows for what purpose cranes and condors, otters and grizzlies may some day be used?

Land Health and the A–B Cleavage

A land ethic, then, reflects the existence of an ecological conscience, and this in turn reflects a conviction of individual responsibility for the health of the land. Health is the capacity of the land for self-renewal. Conservation is our effort to understand and preserve this capacity.

Conservationists are notorious for their dissensions. Superficially these seem to add up to mere confusion, but a more careful scrutiny reveals a single plane of cleavage common to many specialized fields. In each field one group (A) regards the land as soil, and its function as commodity-production; another group (B) regards the land as a biota, and its function as something broader. How much broader is admittedly in a state of doubt and confusion.

In my own field, forestry, group A is quite content to grow trees like cabbages, with cellulose as the basic forest commodity. It feels no inhibition against violence; its ideology is agronomic. Group B, on the other hand, sees forestry as fundamentally different from agronomy because it employs natural species, and manages a natural environment rather than creating an artificial one. Group B prefers natural reproduction on principle. It worries on biotic as well as economic grounds about the loss of species like chestnut, and the threatened loss of the white pines. It worries about a whole series of secondary forest functions: wildlife, recreation, watersheds, wilderness areas. To my mind, Group B feels the stirrings of an ecological conscience.

In the wildlife field, a parallel cleavage exists. For Group A the basic commodities are sport and meat; the yardsticks of production are ciphers of take in pheasants and trout. Artificial propagation is acceptable as a permanent as well as a temporary recourse – if its unit costs permit. Group B, on the other hand, worries about a whole series of biotic side-issues. What is the cost in predators of producing a game crop? Should we have further recourse to exotics? How can management restore the shrinking species, like prairie grouse, already hopeless as shootable game? How can management restore the threatened rarities, like trumpeter swan and whooping crane? Can management principles be extended to wildflowers? Here again it is clear to me that we have the same A–B cleavage as in forestry.

In the larger field of agriculture I am less competent to speak, but there seem to be somewhat parallel cleavages. Scientific agriculture was actively developing before ecology was born, hence a slower penetration of ecological concepts might be expected. Moreover the farmer, by the very nature of his techniques, must modify the biota more radically than the forester or the wildlife manager. Nevertheless, there are many discontents in agriculture which seem to add up to a new vision of 'biotic farming.'

Perhaps the most important of these is the new evidence that poundage or tonnage is no measure of the food-value of farm crops; the products of fertile soil may be qualitatively as well as quantitatively superior. We can bolster poundage from depleted soils by pouring on imported fertility, but we are not necessarily bolstering food-value. The possible ultimate ramifications of this idea are so immense that I must leave their exposition to abler pens.

The discontent that labels itself 'organic farming,' while bearing some of the earmarks of a cult, is nevertheless biotic in its direction, particularly in its insistence on the importance of soil flora and fauna.

The ecological fundamentals of agriculture are just as poorly known to the public as in other fields of land-use. For example, few educated people realize that the marvelous advances in technique made during recent decades are improvements in the pump, rather than the well. Acre for acre, they have barely sufficed to offset the sinking level of fertility.

In all of these cleavages, we see repeated the same basic paradoxes: man the conqueror *versus* man the biotic citizen; science the sharpener of his sword *versus* science the search-light on his universe; land the slave and servant *versus* land the collective organism. Robinson's injunction to Tristram may well be applied, at this juncture, to *Homo sapiens* as a species in geological time:

Whether you will or not
You are a King, Tristram, for you are one
Of the time-tested few that leave the world,
When they are gone, not the same place it was.
Mark what you leave.

The Outlook

It is inconceivable to me that an ethical relation to land can exist without love, respect, and admiration for land, and a high regard for its value. By value, I of course mean something far broader than mere economic value; I mean value in the philosophical sense.

Perhaps the most serious obstacle impeding the evolution of a land ethic is the fact that our educational and economic system is headed away from, rather than toward, an intense consciousness of land. Your true modern is separated from the land by many middlemen, and by innumerable physical gadgets. He had no vital relation to it; to him it is the space between cities on which crops grow. Turn him loose for a day on the land, and if the spot does not happen to be a golf links or a 'scenic' area, he is bored stiff. If crops could be raised by hydroponics instead of farming, it would suit him very well. Synthetic substitutes for wood, leather, wool, and other natural land products suit him better than the originals. In short, land is something he has 'outgrown.'

Almost equally serious as an obstacle to a land ethic is the attitude of the farmer for whom the land is still an adversary, or a taskmaster that keeps him in slavery. Theoretically, the mechanization of farming ought to cut the farmer's chains, but whether it really does is debatable.

One of the requisites for an ecological comprehension of land is an understanding of ecology, and this is by no means co-extensive with 'education'; in fact, much higher education seems deliberately to avoid ecological concepts. An understanding of ecology does not necessarily originate in courses bearing ecological labels; it is quite as likely to be labeled geography, botany, agronomy, history, or economics. This is as it should be, but whatever the label, ecological training is scarce.

The case for a land ethic would appear hopeless but for the minority which is in obvious revolt against these 'modern' trends.

The 'key-log' which must be moved to release the evolutionary process for an ethic is simply this: quit thinking about decent land-use as solely an economic problem. Examine each question in terms of what is ethically and esthetically right, as well as what is economically expedient. A thing is right when it tends to preserve the integrity, stability, and beauty of the biotic community. It is wrong when it tends otherwise.

It of course goes without saying that economic feasibility limits the tether of what can or cannot be done for land. It always has and it always will. The fallacy the economic determinists have tied around our collective neck, and which we now need to cast off, is the belief that economics determines *all* landuse. This is simply not true. An innumerable host of actions and attitudes, comprising perhaps the bulk of all land relations, is determined by the land-users' tastes and predilections, rather than by his purse. The bulk of all land relations hinges on investments of time, forethought, skill, and faith rather than on investments of cash. As a land-user thinketh, so is he.

I have purposely presented the land ethic as a product of social evolution because nothing so important as an ethic is ever 'written.' Only the most superficial student of history supposes that Moses 'wrote' the Decalogue; it evolved in the minds of a thinking community, and Moses wrote a tentative summary of it for a 'seminar.' I say tentative because evolution never stops.

The evolution of a land ethic is an intellectual as well as emotional process. Conservation is paved with good intentions which prove to be futile, or even dangerous, because they are devoid of critical understanding either of the land, or of economic land-use. I think it is a truism that as the ethical frontier advances from the individual to the community, its intellectual content increases.

The mechanism of operation is the same for any ethic: social approbation for right actions: social disapproval for wrong actions.

By and large, our present problem is one of attitudes and implements. We are remodeling the Alhambra with a steamshovel, and we are proud of our yardage. We shall hardly relinquish the shovel, which after all has many good points, but we are in need of gentler and more objective criteria for its successful use.

Is There a Need for a New, an Environmental, Ethic?

Richard Sylvan (Routley)

1

It is increasingly said that civilization, Western civilization at least, stands in need of a new ethic (and derivatively of a new economics) setting out people's relations to the natural environment, in Leopold's words "an ethic dealing with man's relation to land and to the animals and plants which grow upon it."[1] It is not of course that old and prevailing ethics do not deal with man's relation to nature; they do, and on the prevailing view man is free to deal with nature as he pleases, i.e., his relations with nature, insofar at least as they do not affect others, are not subject to moral censure. Thus assertions such as "Crusoe ought not to be mutilating those trees" are significant and morally determinate but, inasmuch at least as Crusoe's actions do not interfere with others, they are false or do not hold – and trees are not, in a good sense, moral objects.[2] It is to this, to the values and evaluations of the prevailing ethics, that Leopold and others in fact take exception. Leopold regards as subject to moral criticism, as wrong, behavior that on prevailing views is morally permissible. But it is not, as Leopold seems to think, that such behavior is beyond the scope of the prevailing ethics and that an *extension* of traditional morality is required to cover such cases, to fill a moral void. If Leopold is right in his criticism of prevailing conduct what is required is a *change* in the ethics, in attitudes, values and evaluations. For as matters stand, as he himself

explains, men do not feel morally ashamed if they interfere with a wilderness, if they maltreat the land, extract from it whatever it will yield, and then move on; and such conduct is not taken to interfere with and does not rouse the moral indignation of others. "A farmer who clears the woods off a 75% slope, turns his cows into the clearing, and dumps its rainfall, rocks, and soil into the community creek, is still (if otherwise decent) a respected member of society."[3] Under what we shall call *an environmental ethic* such traditionally permissible conduct would be accounted morally wrong, and the farmer subject to proper moral criticism.

Let us grant such evaluations for the purpose of the argument. What is not so clear is that a *new* ethic is required even for such radical judgments. For one thing it is none too clear what is going to count as a new ethic, much as it is often unclear whether a new development in physics counts as a new physics or just as a modification or extension of the old. For, notoriously, ethics are not clearly articulated or at all well worked out, so that the application of identity criteria for ethics may remain obscure.[4] Furthermore we tend to cluster a family of ethical systems which do not differ on core or fundamental principles together as one ethic; e.g. the Christian ethic, which is an umbrella notion covering a cluster of differing and even competing systems. In fact then there are two other possibilities, apart from a new environmental ethic, which might cater for the evaluations, namely that of an extension or modification of the prevailing ethics or that of the development of principles that are already encompassed or latent within the prevailing ethic. The second possibility, that environmental evaluations can be incorporated within (and ecological problems solved within) the framework of prevailing Western ethics, is open because there isn't a single ethical system uniquely assumed in Western civilization: on many issues, and especially on controversial issues such as infanticide, women's rights, and drugs, there are competing sets of principles. Talk of a new ethic and prevailing ethics tends to suggest a sort of monolithic structure, a uniformity, that prevailing ethics, and even a single ethic, need not have.

Indeed Passmore has mapped out three important traditions in Western ethical views concerning man's relation to nature; a dominant tradition, the despotic position, with man as despot (or tyrant), and two lesser traditions, the stewardship position, with man as custodian, and the co-operative position with man as perfecter.[5] Nor are these the only traditions; primitivism is another, and both romanticism and mysticism have influenced Western views.

The dominant Western view is simply inconsistent with an environmental ethic; for according to it nature is the dominion of man and he is free to deal with it as he pleases (since – at least on the mainstream Stoic-Augustine view – it exists only for his sake), whereas on an environmental ethic man is not so free to do as he pleases. But it is not quite so obvious that an environmental ethic cannot be coupled with one of the lesser traditions. Part of the problem is that the lesser traditions are by no means adequately characterized anywhere, especially when the religious backdrop is removed, e.g. *who* is man steward for and responsible to? However both traditions are inconsistent with an environmental ethic because they imply policies of complete interference, whereas on an environmental ethic some worthwhile parts of the earth's surface should be preserved from substantial human interference, whether of the "improving" sort or not. Both traditions would in fact prefer to see the earth's land surfaces reshaped along the lines of the tame and comfortable north-European small farm and village landscape. According to the co-operative position man's proper role is to develop, cultivate and perfect nature – all nature eventually – by bringing out its potentialities, the test of perfection being primarily usefulness for human purposes;

while on the stewardship view man's role, like that of a farm manager, is to make nature productive by his efforts though not by means that will deliberately degrade its resources. Although these positions both depart from the dominant position in a way which enables the incorporation of some evaluations of an environmental ethic, e.g. some of those concerning the irresponsible farmer, they do not go far enough: for in the present situation of expanding populations confined to finite natural areas, they will lead to, and enjoin, the perfecting, farming and utilizing of all natural areas. Indeed these lesser traditions lead to, what a thoroughgoing environmental ethic would reject, a principle of total use, implying that every natural area should be cultivated or otherwise used for human ends, "humanized."[6]

As the important Western traditions exclude an environmental ethic, it would appear that such an ethic, not primitive, mystical or romantic, would be new all right. The matter is not so straightforward; for the dominant ethic has been substantially qualified by the rider that one is not always entitled to do as one pleases where this physically interferes with others. Maybe some such proviso was implicit all along (despite evidence to the contrary), and it was simply assumed that doing what one pleased with natural items would not affect others (the non-interference assumption). Be this as it may, the *modified* dominant position appears, at least for many thinkers, to have supplanted the dominant position; and the modified position can undoubtedly go much further towards an environmental ethic. For example, the farmer's polluting of a community stream may be ruled immoral on the grounds that it physically interferes with others who use or would use the streams. Likewise business enterprises which destroy the natural environment for no satisfactory returns or which cause pollution deleterious to the health of future humans, can be criticized on the sort of welfare basis (e.g. that of Barkley and Seckler) that blends with the modified position; and so on.[7] The position may even serve to restrict the sort of family size one is entitled to have since in a finite situation excessive population levels will interfere with future people. Nonetheless neither the modified dominant position nor its Western variants, obtained by combining it with the lesser traditions, is adequate as an environmental ethic, as I shall try to show. A new ethic *is* wanted.

2

As we noticed (an) *ethic* is ambiguous, as between a specific ethical system, a *specific* ethic, and a more generic notion, a super ethic, under which specific ethics cluster.[8] An ethical system S is, near enough, a propositional system (i.e. a structured set of propositions) or theory which includes (like individuals of a theory) a set of values and (like postulates of a theory) a set of general evaluative judgments concerning conduct, typically of what is obligatory, permissible and wrong, of what are rights, what is valued, and so forth. A general or lawlike proposition of a system is a principle; and certainly if systems S_1 and S_2 contain different principles, then they are different systems. It follows that any environmental ethic differs from the important traditional ethics outlined. Moreover if environmental ethics differ from Western ethical systems on some *core* principle embedded in Western systems, then these systems differ from the Western super ethic (assuming, what seems to be so, that it can be uniquely characterized) – in which case if an environmental ethic *is* needed then a new ethic is wanted. It suffices then to locate a core principle and to provide environmental counter examples to it.

It is commonly assumed that there are what amount to core principles of Western ethical systems, principles that will accordingly belong to the super ethic. The fairness principle inscribed in the Golden Rule provides one example. Directly relevant here, as a good stab at a core principle, is the commonly formulated liberal principle of the modified dominance position. A recent formulation runs as follows:

"The liberal philosophy of the Western world holds that one should be able to do what he wishes, providing (1) that he does not harm others and (2) that he is not likely to harm himself irreparably."[9]

Let us call this principle *basic (human) chauvinism* – because under it humans, or people, come first and everything else a bad last – though sometimes the principle is hailed as a *freedom* principle because it gives permission to perform a wide range of actions (including actions which mess up the environment and natural things) providing they do not harm others. In fact it tends to cunningly shift the onus of proof to others. It is worth remarking that *harming others* in the restriction is narrower than a restriction to the (usual) interests of others; it is not enough that it is in my interests, because I detest you, that you stop breathing; you are free to breathe, for the time being anyway, because it does not harm me. There remains a problem however as to exactly what counts as harm or interference. Moreover the width of the principle is so far obscure because "other" may be filled out in significantly different ways: it makes a difference to the extent, and privilege, of the chauvinism whether "other" expands to "other human" – which is too restrictive – or to "other person" or to "other sentient being"; and it makes a difference to the adequacy of the principle, and inversely to its economic applicability, to which class of others it is intended to apply, whether to future as well as to present others, whether to remote future others or only to non-discountable future others and whether to possible others. The latter would make the principle completely unworkable, and it is generally assumed that it applies at most to present and future others.

It is taken for granted in designing counter examples to basic chauvinist principles, that a semantical analysis of permissibility and obligation statements stretches out over ideal situations (which may be incomplete or even inconsistent), so that what is permissible holds in some ideal situation, what is obligatory in every ideal situation, and what is wrong is excluded in every ideal situation. But the main point to grasp for the counter examples that follow, is that ethical principles if correct are universal and are assessed over the class of ideal situations.

(i) The *last man* example. The last man (or person) surviving the collapse of the world system lays about him, eliminating, as far as he can, every living thing, animal or plant (but painlessly if you like, as at the best abattoirs). What he does is quite permissible according to basic chauvinism, but on environmental grounds what he does is wrong. Moreover one does not have to be committed to esoteric values to regard Mr. Last Man as behaving badly (the reason being perhaps that radical thinking and values have shifted in an environmental direction in advance of corresponding shifts in the formulation of fundamental evaluative principles).

(ii) The *last people* example. The last man example can be broadened to the last people example. We can assume that they know they are the last people, e.g. because they are aware that radiation effects have blocked any chance of reproduction. One considers the last people in order to rule out the possibility that what these people do harms or somehow physically interferes with later people. Otherwise one could as well consider science fiction cases where people arrive at a new planet and destroy its ecosystems, whether with good intentions such as perfecting the planet for their ends and making it more fruitful or, forgetting the lesser traditions, just for the hell of it.

Let us assume that the last people are very numerous. They humanely exterminate every wild animal and they eliminate the fish of the seas, they put all arable land under intensive cultivation, and all remaining forests disappear in favor of quarries or plantations, and so on. They may give various familiar reasons for this, e.g. they believe it is the way to salvation or to perfection, or they are simply satisfying reasonable needs, or even that it is needed to keep the last people employed or occupied so that they do not worry too much about their impending extinction. On an environmental ethic the last people have behaved badly; they have simplified and largely destroyed all the natural ecosystems, and with their demise the world will soon be an ugly and largely wrecked place. But this conduct may conform with the basic chauvinist principle, and as well with the principles enjoined by the lesser traditions. Indeed the main point of elaborating this example is because, as the last man example reveals, basic chauvinism may conflict with stewardship or cooperation principles. The conflict may be removed it seems by conjoining a further proviso to the basic principle, the effect (3) that he does not willfully destroy natural resources. But as the last people do not destroy resources willfully, but perhaps "for the best of reasons," the variant is still environmentally inadequate.

(iii) The *great entrepreneur* example. The last man example can be adjusted so as to not fall foul of clause (3). The last man is an industrialist; he runs a giant complex of automated factories and farms which he proceeds to extend. He produces automobiles among other things, from renewable and recyclable resources of course, only he dumps and recycles these shortly after manufacture and sale to a dummy buyer instead of putting them on the road for a short time as we do. Of course he has the best of reasons for his activity, e.g. he is increasing gross world product, or he is improving output to fulfill some plan, and he will be increas

ing his own and general welfare since he much prefers increased output and productivity. The entrepreneur's behavior is on the Western ethic quite permissible; indeed his conduct is commonly thought to be quite fine and may even meet Pareto optimality requirements given prevailing notions of being "better off."

Just as we can extend the last man example to a class of last people, so we can extend this example to the *industrial society* example: the society looks rather like ours.

(iv) The *vanishing species* example. Consider the blue whale, a mixed good on the economic picture. The blue whale is on the verge of extinction because of his qualities as a private good, as a source of valuable oil and meat. The catching and marketing of blue whales does not harm the whalers; it does not harm or physically interfere with others in any good sense, though it may upset them and they may be prepared to compensate the whalers if they desist; nor need whale hunting be willful destruction. (Slightly different examples which eliminate the hunting aspect of the blue whale example are provided by cases where a species is eliminated or threatened through destruction of its habitat by man's activity or the activities of animals he has introduced, e.g. many plains-dwelling Australian marsupials and the Arabian oryx.) The behavior of the whalers in eliminating this magnificent species of whale is accordingly quite permissible – at least according to basic chauvinism. But on an environmental ethic it is not. However, the free-market mechanism will not cease allocating whales to commercial uses, as a satisfactory environmental economics would; instead the market model will grind inexorably along the private demand curve until the blue whale population is no longer viable – if that point has not already been passed.[10]

In sum, the class of permissible actions that rebound on the environment is more narrowly circumscribed on an environmental ethic than it is in the Western super ethic. But aren't environmentalists going too far in claiming that these people, those of the examples and respected industrialists, fishermen and farmers are behaving, when engaging in environmentally degrading activities of the sort described, in a morally impermissible way? No, what these people do is to a greater or lesser extent evil, and hence in serious cases morally impermissible. For example, insofar as the killing or forced displacement of primitive peoples who stand in the way of an industrial development is morally indefensible and impermissible, so also is the slaughter of the last remaining blue whales for private profit. But how to reformulate basic chauvinism as a satisfactory freedom principle is a more difficult matter. A tentative, but none too adequate beginning might be made by extending (2) to include harm to or interference with others who would be so affected by the action in question were they placed in the environment and (3) to exclude speciecide. It may be preferable, in view of the way the freedom principle sets the onus of proof, simply to scrap it altogether, and instead to specify classes of rights and permissible conduct, as in a bill of rights.

3

A radical change in a theory sometimes forces changes in the meta-theory; e.g. a logic which rejects the Reference Theory in a thoroughgoing way requires a modification of the usual meta-theory which also accepts the Reference Theory and indeed which is tailored to cater only for logics which do conform. A somewhat similar phenomenon seems to occur in the case of a meta-ethic adequate for an environmental ethic. Quite apart from introducing several environmentally important notions, such as *conservation, pollution, growth* and *preservation*, for meta-ethical analysis, an environmental ethic compels reexamination and modified analyses of such characteristic actions as *natural right, ground* of right, and of the relations of obligation and permissibility to rights; it may well require re-assessment of traditional analyses of such notions as *value* and *right*, especially where these are based on chauvinist assumptions; and it forces the rejection of many of the more prominent meta-ethical positions. These points are illustrated by a very brief examination of accounts of *natural right* and then by a sketch of the species bias of some major positions.[11]

Hart accepts, subject to defeating conditions which are here irrelevant, the classical doctrine of natural rights according to which, among other things, "any adult human ... capable of choice is at liberty to do (i.e. is under no obligation to abstain from) any action which is not one coercing or restraining or designed to injure other persons."[12] But this sufficient condition for a human natural right depends on accepting the very human chauvinist principle an environmental ethic rejects, since if a person has a natural right he has a right; so too the *definition* of a natural right adopted by classical theorists and accepted with minor qualifications by Hart presupposes the same defective principle. Accordingly an environmental ethic would have to amend the classical notion of a natural right, a far from straightforward matter now that human rights with respect to animals and the natural environment are, like those with respect to slaves not all that long ago, undergoing major re-evaluation.

An environmental ethic does not commit one to the view that natural objects such as trees have rights (though such a view is occasionally held, e.g. by pantheists. But pantheism is false since artefacts are not alive). For moral prohibitions forbidding certain actions with respect to an object do not award that object a correlative right. That it would be wrong to mutilate a given tree or piece of property does not entail that the tree or piece of property has a correlative right not to be mutilated (without seriously stretching the notion of a right). Environmental views can stick with mainstream theses according to which rights are coupled with corresponding responsibilities and so with bearing obligations, and with corresponding interests and concern; i.e. at least, whatever has a right also has responsibilities and therefore obligations, and whatever has a right has interests. Thus although any person may have a right by no means every living thing can (significantly) have rights, and arguably most sentient objects other than persons cannot have rights. But persons can relate morally, through obligations, prohibitions and so forth, to practically anything at all.

The species bias of certain ethical and economic positions which aim to make principles of conduct or reasonable economic behavior calculable is easily brought out. These positions typically employ a single criterion p, such as preference or happiness, as a *summum bonum;* characteristically each individual of some *base* class, almost always humans, but perhaps including future humans, is supposed to have an ordinal p ranking of the states in question (e.g. of affairs, of the economy); then some principle is supplied to determine a collective p ranking of these states in terms of individual p rankings, and what is best or ought to be done is determined either directly, as in act-utilitarianism under the Greatest Happiness principle, or indirectly, as in rule–utilitarianism, in terms of some optimization principle applied to the collective ranking. The species bias is transparent from the selection of the base class. And even if the base class is extended to embrace persons, or even some animals (at the cost, like that of including remotely future humans, of losing testability), the positions are open to familiar criticism, namely that the whole of the base class may be prejudiced in a way which leads to unjust principles. For example if every member of the base class detests dingoes, on the basis of mistaken data as to dingoes' behavior, then by the Pareto ranking test the collective ranking will rank states where dingoes are exterminated very highly, from which it will generally be concluded that dingoes ought to be exterminated (the evaluation of most Australian farmers anyway). Likewise it would just be a happy accident, it seems, if collective demand (horizontally summed from individual demand) for a state of the economy with blue whales as a mixed good, were to succeed in outweighing private whaling demands: for if no one in the base class happened to know that blue whales exist or cared a jot that they do then "rational" economic decision-making would do nothing to prevent their extinction. Whether the blue whale survives should not have to depend on what humans know or what they see on television. Human interests and preferences are far too parochial to provide a satisfactory basis for deciding on what is environmentally desirable.

These ethical and economic theories are not alone in their species chauvinism; much the same applies to most going meta-ethical theories which, unlike intuitionistic theories, try to offer some rationale for their basic principles. For instance, on social contract positions obligations are a matter of mutual agreements between individuals of the base class; on a social justice picture rights and obligations spring from the application of symmetrical fairness principles to members of the base class, usually a rather special class of persons, while on a Kantian position which has some vague obligations somehow arise from respect for members of the base class persons. In

each case if members of the base class happen to be ill-disposed to items outside the base class then that is too bad for them: that is (rough) justice.

Notes

1 Aldo Leopold, *A Sand Country Almanac with Essays on Conservation from Round River* (New York: Ballantine, 1966), p. 238.

2 A view occasionally tempered by the idea that trees house spirits.

3 Leopold, *Sand County*, p. 245.

4 To the consternation no doubt of Quineans. But the fact is that we can talk perfectly well about inchoate and fragmentary systems the identity of which may be indeterminate.

5 John Passmore, *Man's Responsibility for Nature: Ecological Problems and Western Traditions* (New York: Scribner's, 1974).

6 If "use" is extended, somewhat illicitly, to include use for preservation, this total use principle is rendered innocuous at least as regards its actual effects. Note that the total use principle is tied to the resource view of nature.

7 P. W. Barkley and D. W. Seckler, *Economic Growth and Environmental Decay: The Solution Becomes the Problem* (New York: Harcourt, Brace, Jovanovich, 1972).

8 A *meta-ethic* is, as usual, a theory about ethics, super ethics, their features and fundamental notions.

9 Barkley and Seckler, *Economic Growth and Environmental Decay*, p. 58. A related principle is that (modified) free enterprise can operate within similar limits.

10 The tragedy of the commons type reasons are well explained in Barkley and Seckler, *Economic Growth and Environmental Decay*.

11 Some of these points are developed by those protesting about human maltreatment of animals: see especially the essays collected in S. and R. Godlovitch and J. Harris, eds., *Animals, Men and Morals: An Enquiry into the Maltreatment of Non-humans* (New York: Grove Press, 1971).

12 H. L. A. Hart, "Are There any Natural Rights?" reprinted in A. Quinton, ed., *Political Philosophy* (London: Oxford University Press, 1967).

PART II

Who Counts in Environmental Ethics – Animals? Plants? Ecosystems?

4

Not for Humans Only: The Place of Nonhumans in Environmental Issues

Peter Singer

When we humans change the environment in which we live, we often harm ourselves. If we discharge cadmium into a bay and eat shellfish from that bay, we become ill and may die. When our industries and automobiles pour noxious fumes into the atmosphere, we find a displeasing smell in the air, the long-term results of which may be every bit as deadly as cadmium poisoning. The harm that humans do the environment, however, does not rebound solely, or even chiefly, on humans. It is nonhumans who bear the most direct burden of human interference with nature.

By "nonhumans" I mean to refer to all living things other than human beings, though for reasons to be given later, it is with nonhuman animals, rather than plants, that I am chiefly concerned. It is also important, in the context of environmental issues, to note that living things may be regarded either collectively or as individuals. In debates about the environment the most important way of regarding living things collectively has been to regard them as species. Thus, when environmentalists worry about the future of the blue whale, they usually are thinking of the blue whale as a species, rather than of individual blue whales. But this is not, of course, the only way in which one can think of blue whales, or other animals, and one of the topics I shall discuss is whether we should be concerned about what we are doing to the environment primarily insofar as it threatens entire species of nonhumans, or primarily insofar as it affects individual nonhuman animals.

The general question, then, is how the effects of our actions on the environment of nonhuman beings should figure in our deliberations about what we ought to do. There is an unlimited variety of contexts in which this issue could arise. To take just one: Suppose that it is considered necessary to build a new power station, and there are two sites, A and B, under consideration. In most respects the sites are equally suitable, but building the power station on site A would be more expensive because the greater depth of shifting soil at that site will require deeper foundations; on the other hand to build on site B will destroy a favored breeding ground for thousands of wildfowl. Should the presence of the wildfowl enter into the decision as to where to build? And if so, in what manner should it enter, and how heavily should it weigh?

In a case like this the effects of our actions on nonhuman animals could be taken into account in two quite different ways: directly, giving the lives and welfare of nonhuman animals an intrinsic significance which must count in any moral calculation; or indirectly, so that the effects of our actions on nonhumans are morally significant only if they have consequences for humans.

It is the latter view which has been predominant in the Western tradition. Aristotle was among the founders of this tradition. He regarded nature as a hierarchy, in which the function of the less rational and hence less perfect beings was to serve the more rational and more perfect. So, he wrote:

Plants exist for the sake of animals, and brute beasts for the sake of man – domestic animals for his use and food, wild ones (or at any rate most of them) for food and other accessories of life, such as clothing and various tools.

Since nature makes nothing purposeless or in vain, it is undeniably true that she has made all animals for the sake of man.[1]

If one major strain of Western thought came from Greece, the other dominant influence was that of Christianity. The early Christian writers were no more ready than Aristotle to give moral weight to the lives of nonhuman animals. When St. Paul, in interpreting the old Mosaic law against putting a muzzle on the ox that treads out the corn, asked: "Doth God care for oxen?" it is clear that he was asking a rhetorical question, to which the answer was "No"; the law must have somehow been meant "altogether for our sakes."[2] Augustine agreed, using as evidence for the view that there are no common rights between humans and lesser living things, the incidents in the Gospels when Jesus sent devils into a herd of swine, causing them to hurl themselves into the sea, and with a curse withered a fig tree on which he had found no fruit.[3]

It was Thomas Aquinas, blending Aristotle and the Christian writings, who put most clearly the view that any consideration of the lives or welfare of animals must be because of the indirect consequences of such consideration for humans. Echoing Aristotle, he maintained that plants exist for the sake of animals, and animals for the sake of man. Sins can only be against God, one's human neighbors, or against oneself. Even charity does not extend to "irrational creatures," for, among other things, they are not included in "the fellowship of everlasting happiness." We can love animals only "if we regard them as the good things that we desire for others," that is, "to God's honor and man's use." Yet if this was the correct view, as Aquinas thought, there was one problem that needed explaining: Why does the Old Testament have a few scattered injunctions against cruelty to animals, such as "The just man regardeth the life of his beast, but the bowels of the wicked are cruel?" Aquinas did not overlook such passages, but he did deny that their intention was to spare animals pain. Instead, he wrote, "it is evident that if a man practices a pitiable affection for animals, he is all the more disposed to take pity on his fellow-men." So, for Aquinas, the only sound reason for avoiding cruelty to animals was that it could lead to cruelty to humans.[4]

The influence of Aquinas has been strong in the Roman Catholic church. Not even that oft-quoted exception to the standard Christian view of nature, Francis of Assisi, really broke away from the orthodox theology of his co-religionists. Despite his legendary kindness to animals, Francis could still write: "every creature proclaims: 'God made me for your sake, O man!'"[5] As late as the nineteenth century, Pope Pius IX gave evidence of the continuing hold of the views of Paul, Augustine, and Aquinas by refusing to allow a society for the prevention of cruelty to animals to be established in Rome because to do so would imply that humans have duties toward animals.[6]

It is not, however, only among Roman Catholics that a view like that of Aquinas has found adherents. Calvin, for instance, had no doubt that all of nature was created specifically for its usefulness to man;[7] and in the late eighteenth century, Immanuel Kant, in lecturing on ethics, considered the question of our duties to animals, and told his students: "So far as animals are concerned, we have no direct duties. Animals are not self-conscious and are there merely as a means to an end. That end is man." And Kant then repeated the line that cruelty to animals is to be avoided because it leads to cruelty to humans.[8]

The view that the effects of our actions on other animals has no direct moral significance is not as likely to be openly advocated today as it was in the past; yet it is likely to be accepted implicitly and acted upon. When planners perform cost–benefit studies on new projects, the costs and benefits are costs and benefits for human beings only. This does not mean that the impact of the power station or highway on wildlife is ignored altogether, but it is included only indirectly. That a new reservoir would drown a valley teeming with wildlife is taken into account only under some such heading as the value of the facilities for recreation that the valley affords. In calculating this value, the cost–benefit study will be neutral between forms of recreation like hunting and shooting and those like bird watching and bush walking – in fact hunting and shooting are likely to contribute more to the benefit side of the calculations because larger sums of money are spent on them, and they therefore benefit manufacturers and retailers of firearms as well as the hunters and shooters themselves. The suffering experienced by the animals whose habitat is flooded is not reckoned into the costs of the operation; nor is the recreational value obtained by the hunters and shooters offset by the cost to the animals that their recreation involves.

Despite its venerable origins, the view that the effects of our actions on nonhuman animals have no intrinsic moral significance can be shown to be arbitrary and morally indefensible. If a being suffers, the fact that it is not a member of our own species cannot be a moral reason for failing to take its suffering into account. This becomes obvious if we consider the analogous attempt by white slaveowners to deny consideration to the interests of blacks. These white racists limited their moral concern to their own race, so the suffering of a black did not have the same moral significance as the suffering of a white. We now recognize that in doing so they were making an arbitrary distinction, and that the existence of suffering, rather than the race of the sufferer, is what is really morally significant. The point remains true if "species" is substituted for "race." The logic of racism and the logic of the position we have been discussing, which I have elsewhere referred to as "speciesism," are indistinguishable; and if we reject the former then consistency demands that we reject the latter too.[9]

It should be clearly understood that the rejection of speciesism does not imply that the different species are in fact equal in respect of such characteristics as intelligence, physical strength, ability to communicate, capacity to suffer, ability to damage the environment, or anything else. After all, the moral principle of human equality cannot be taken as implying that all humans are equal in these respects either – if it did, we would have to give up the idea of human equality. That one being is more intelligent than another does not entitle him to enslave, exploit, or disregard the interests of the less intelligent being. The moral basis of equality among humans is not equality in fact, but the principle of equal consideration of interests, and it is this principle that, in consistency, must be extended to any nonhumans who have interests.

There may be some doubt about whether any nonhuman beings have interests. This doubt may arise because of uncertainty about what it is to have an interest, or because of uncertainty about the nature of some nonhuman beings. So far as the concept of "interest" is the cause of doubt, I take the view that only a being with subjective experi-

ences, such as the experience of pleasure or the experience of pain, can have interests in the full sense of the term; and that any being with such experiences does have at least one interest, namely, the interest in experiencing pleasure and avoiding pain. Thus consciousness, or the capacity for subjective experience, is both a necessary and a sufficient condition for having an interest. While there may be a loose sense of the term in which we can say that it is in the interests of a tree to be watered, this attenuated sense of the term is not the sense covered by the principle of equal consideration of interests. All we mean when we say that it is in the interests of a tree to be watered is that the tree needs water if it is to continue to live and grow normally; if we regard this as evidence that the tree has interests, we might almost as well say that it is in the interests of a car to be lubricated regularly because the car needs lubrication if it is to run properly. In neither case can we really mean (unless we impute consciousness to trees or cars) that the tree or car has any preference about the matter.

The remaining doubt about whether nonhuman beings have interests is, then, a doubt about whether nonhuman beings have subjective experiences like the experience of pain. I have argued elsewhere that the commonsense view that birds and mammals feel pain is well founded;[10] but more serious doubts arise as we move down the evolutionary scale. Vertebrate animals have nervous systems broadly similar to our own and behave in ways that resemble our own pain behavior when subjected to stimuli that we would find painful; so the inference that vertebrates are capable of feeling pain is a reasonable one, though not as strong as it is if limited to mammals and birds. When we go beyond vertebrates to insects, crustaceans, mollusks and so on, the existence of subjective states becomes more dubious, and with very simple organisms it is difficult to believe that they could be conscious. As for plants, though there have been sensational claims that plants are not only conscious, but even psychic, there is no hard evidence that supports even the more modest claim.[11]

The boundary of beings who may be taken as having interests is therefore not an abrupt boundary, but a broad range in which the assumption that the being has interests shifts from being so strong as to be virtually certain to being so weak as to be highly improbable. The principle of equal consideration of interests must be applied with this in mind, so that where there is a clash between a virtually certain interest and a highly doubtful one, it is the virtually certain interest that ought to prevail.

In this manner our moral concern ought to extend to all beings who have interests. Unlike race or species, this boundary does not arbitrarily exclude any being; indeed it can truly be said that it excludes nothing at all, not even "the most contemptible clod of earth" from equal consideration of interests – for full consideration of no interests still results in no weight being given to whatever was considered, just as multiplying zero by a million still results in zero.[12]

Giving equal consideration to the interests of two different beings does not mean treating them alike or holding their lives to be of equal value. We may recognize that the interests of one being are greater than those of another, and equal consideration will then lead us to sacrifice the being with lesser interests, if one or the other must be sacrificed. For instance, if for some reason a choice has to be made between saving the life of a normal human being and that of a dog, we might well decide to save the human because he, with his greater awareness of what is going to happen, will suffer more before he dies; we may also take into account the likelihood that it is the family and friends of the human who will suffer more; and finally, it would be the human who had the greater potential for future happiness. This decision would be in accordance with the principle of equal consideration of interests, for the interests of the dog get the same consideration as those of the human, and the loss to the dog is not discounted because the dog is not a member of our species. The outcome is as it is because the balance of interests favors the human. In a different situation – say, if the human were grossly mentally defective and without family or anyone else who would grieve for it – the balance of interests might favor the nonhuman.[13]

The more positive side of the principle of equal consideration is this: where interests are equal, they must be given equal weight. So where human and nonhuman animals share an interest – as in the case of the interest in avoiding physical pain – we must give as much weight to violations of the interest of the nonhumans as we do to similar violations of the human's interest. This does not mean, of course, that it is as bad to hit a horse with a stick as it is to hit a human being, for the same blow would cause less pain to the animal

with the tougher skin. The principle holds between similar amounts of felt pain, and what this is will vary from case to case.

It may be objected that we cannot tell exactly how much pain another animal is suffering, and that therefore the principle is impossible to apply. While I do not deny the difficulty and even, so far as precise measurement is concerned, the impossibility of comparing the subjective experiences of members of different species, I do not think that the problem is different in kind from the problem of comparing the subjective experiences of two members of our own species. Yet this is something we do all the time, for instance when we judge that a wealthy person will suffer less by being taxed at a higher rate than a poor person will gain from the welfare benefits paid for by the tax; or when we decide to take our two children to the beach instead of to a fair, because although the older one would prefer the fair, the younger one has a stronger preference the other way. These comparisons may be very rough, but since there is nothing better, we must use them; it would be irrational to refuse to do so simply because they are rough. Moreover, rough as they are, there are many situations in which we can be reasonably sure which way the balance of interests lies. While a difference of species may make comparisons rougher still, the basic problem is the same, and the comparisons are still often good enough to use, in the absence of anything more precise.

The principle of equal consideration of interests and the indefensibility of limiting this principle to members of our own species means that we cannot deny, as Aquinas and Kant denied, that we have direct duties to members of other species. It may be asked whether this means that members of other species have rights against us. This is an issue on which there has been a certain amount of dispute,[14] but it is, I believe, more a dispute about words than about substantive issues. In one sense of "right," we may say that it follows immediately from the fact that animals come within the scope of the principle of equal consideration of interests that they have at least one right, namely, the right to equal consideration. This is, admittedly, an odd kind of right – it is really a necessary foundation for having rights, rather than a right in itself. But some other rights could be derived from it without difficulty: the right not to have gratuitous pain inflicted would be one such right. There is, however, another sense of "right," according to which rights exist only among those who are part of a community, all members of whom have rights and in turn are capable of respecting the rights of others. On this view, rights are essentially contractual, and hence cannot exist unless both parties are capable of honoring the contract.[15] It would follow that most, if not all, nonhuman animals have no rights. It should be noted, though, that this is a narrower notion of rights than that commonly used in America today, for it follows from this notion of rights that not only nonhuman animals, but also human infants and young children, as well as mentally defective humans, have no rights. Those who put forward this view of rights do not believe that we may do what we like with young or mentally defective humans or nonhuman animals; rather they would say that moral rights are only one kind of constraint on our conduct, and not necessarily the most important. They might, for instance, take account of utilitarian considerations which would apply to all beings capable of pleasure or pain. Thus actions which proponents of the former, broader view of rights may condemn as violations of the rights of animals could also be condemned by those who hold the narrower view, though they would not classify such actions as infringing rights. Seen in this light the question of whether animals have rights becomes less important than it might otherwise appear, for what matters is how we think animals ought to be treated, and not how we employ the concept of a right. Those who deny animals rights will not be likely to refuse to consider their interests, as long as they are reminded that the denial of rights to nonhuman animals does no more than place animals in the same moral category as human infants. Hence I doubt if the claim that animals have rights is worth the effort required in its defense; it is a claim which invites replies which, whatever their philosophical merits, serve as a distraction from the central practical question.

We can now draw at least one conclusion as to how the existence of nonhuman living things should enter into our deliberations about actions affecting the environment: Where our actions are likely to make animals suffer, that suffering must count in our deliberations, and it should count equally with a like amount of suffering by human beings, insofar as rough comparisons can be made.

The difficulty of making the required comparison will mean that the application of this conclu-

sion is controversial in many cases, but there will be some situations in which it is clear enough. Take, for instance, the wholesale poisoning of animals that is euphemistically known as "pest control." The authorities who conduct these campaigns give no consideration to the suffering they inflict on the "pests," and invariably use the method of slaughter they believe to be cheapest and most effective. The result is that hundreds of millions of rabbits have died agonizing deaths from the artificially introduced disease, myxomatosis, or from poisons like "ten-eighty"; coyotes and other wild dogs have died painfully from cyanide poisoning; and all manner of wild animals have endured days of thirst, hunger, and fear with a mangled limb caught in a leg-hold trap.[16] Granting, for the sake of argument, the necessity for pest control – though this has rightly been questioned – the fact remains that no serious attempts have been made to introduce alternative means of control and thereby reduce the incalculable amount of suffering caused by present methods. It would not, presumably, be beyond modern science to produce a substance which, when eaten by rabbits or coyotes, produced sterility instead of a drawn-out death. Such methods might be more expensive, but can anyone doubt that if a similar amount of human suffering were at stake, the expense would be borne?

Another clear instance in which the principle of equal consideration of interests would indicate methods different from those presently used is in the timber industry. There are two basic methods of obtaining timber from forests. One is to cut only selected mature or dead trees, leaving the forest substantially intact. The other, known as clear-cutting, involves chopping down everything that grows in a given area, and then reseeding. Obviously when a large area is clear-cut, wild animals find their whole living area destroyed in a few days, whereas selected felling makes a relatively minor disturbance. But clear-cutting is cheaper, and timber companies therefore use this method and will continue to do so unless forced to do otherwise.[17]

This initial conclusion about how the effects of our actions on nonhuman animals should be taken into account is the only one which follows directly from the argument that I have given against the view that only actions affecting our own species have intrinsic moral significance. There are, however, other suggestions which I shall make more tentatively which are at least consistent with the preceding argument, although much more discussion would be needed to establish them.

The first of these suggestions is that while the suffering of human and nonhuman animals should, as I have said, count equally, the killing of nonhuman animals is in itself not as significant as the killing of normal human beings. Some of the reasons for this have already been discussed – the probable greater grief of the family and friends of the human, and the human's greater potential. To this can be added the fact that other animals will not be made to fear for their own lives, as humans would, by the knowledge that others of their species have been killed. There is also the fact that normal humans are beings with foresight and plans for the future, and to cut these plans off in midstream seems a greater wrong than that which is done in killing a being without the capacity for reflection on the future.

All these reasons will seem to some not to touch the heart of the matter, which is the killing itself and not the circumstances surrounding it; and it is for this reason that I have put forward this view as a suggestion rather than a firm conclusion. For it might be held that the taking of life is intrinsically wrong – and equally wrong whatever the characteristics of the life that was taken. This, perhaps, was the view that Schweitzer held and which has become famous under his memorable if less than crystal-clear phrase, "reverence for life." If this view could be supported, then of course we would have to hold that the killing of nonhuman animals, however painless, is as serious as the killing of humans. Yet I find Schweitzer's position difficult to justify. What is it that is so valuable in the life of, say, a fly, which presumably does not itself have any awareness of the value of its own life, and the death of which will not be a source of regret to any member of its own species or of any other species?

It might be said – and this is a possible interpretation of Schweitzer's remark that there is the same "will-to-live" in all other forms of life as in myself – that while I may see my own life as all-important to me, so is the life of any living thing all-important to it, and hence I cannot justifiably claim greater importance for my own life. If I do, the claim will be true only from my own point of view. But this argument is weak in two respects. First, the idea of a being's life being important *for that being* depends, I think, on the assumption that the being is conscious, and perhaps even on the

stronger assumption that the being is aware that it is alive and that its life is something that it could lose. This would exclude many forms of life from the scope of the argument, particularly if on reflection we decide that it is the stronger assumption that the argument requires. Second, the argument appears to rest on the implicit claim that if two things are each all-important for two independent beings, it is impossible to make a comparison which would show that in some objective or at least intersubjective sense that thing is more important for one than for the other. There is, however, no theoretical difficulty in a comparison of this kind, great as the practical difficulties may be. In theory, all I have to do is imagine myself living simultaneously the lives of both myself and the other being, experiencing whatever the two beings experience. I then ask myself which life I would choose to cease living if I could continue to live only one of the two lives. Since I would be making this decision from a position that is impartial between the two lives, we may conclude that the life I would choose to continue living is objectively or at least intersubjectively of greater value than the life I would choose to give up.[18] If one of the living beings in this thought experiment had *no* conscious experiences, then when imagining myself living the life of this being I would be imagining myself as having no experiences at all. It is hardly necessary to add that it would be no great sacrifice to cease living such a life. This suggests that, just as nonconscious beings have no interests, so nonconscious life lacks intrinsic value.

For Schweitzer, life itself is sacred, not even consciousness being necessary. So the truly ethical man, he says, will not tear a leaf from a tree or break off a flower unnecessarily.[19] Not surprisingly, given the breadth of its coverage, it is impossible for the ethic of reverence for life to be absolute in its prohibitions. We must take plant life, at least, if we are to eat and live. Schweitzer therefore accepts the taking of one form of life to preserve another form of life. Indeed, Schweitzer's whole life as a doctor in Africa makes no sense except on the assumption that the lives of the human beings he was saving are more valuable than the lives of the germs and parasites he was destroying in their bodies, not to mention the plants and probably animals that those humans would kill and eat after Schweitzer had cured them.[20] So I suggest that the idea that all life has equal value, or is equally sacred, lacks a plausible theoretical basis and was not, in practice, adhered to even by the man whose name is most often linked with it.

I shall conclude this discussion of the comparative seriousness of killing human and nonhuman animals by admitting that I have been unable to say anything about *how much* less seriously we should regard the killing of a nonhuman. I do not feel that the death of an animal like a pig or dog is a completely trivial matter, even if it should be painless for the animal concerned and unnoticed by any other members of the species; on the other hand I am quite unable to quantify the issue so as to say that a certain number of porcine or canine deaths adds up to one human death, and in the absence of any such method of comparison, my feeling that the deaths of these animals must count for something lacks both proper justification and practical significance. Perhaps, though, this will not leave practical decision making about the environment in as bad a way as it might seem to. For when an environment decision threatens the lives of animals and birds, it almost always does so in a way that causes suffering to them or to their mates, parents, offspring, or pack-members. Often, the type of death inflicted will itself be a slow and painful one, caused, for instance, by the steady build-up of a noxious chemical. Even when death itself is quick and painless, in many species of birds and mammals it leaves behind survivors whose lives may be disrupted. Birds often mate for life, in some species separating after the young have been reared but meeting again, apparently recognizing each other as individuals, when the breeding season comes round again. There are many species in which a bird who has lost its mate will not mate again. The behavior of mammals who have lost their young also suggests sorrow and distress, and infant mammals left without a mother will usually starve miserably. In other social species the death of one member of a group can cause considerable disturbance, especially if the dead animal is a group leader. Now since, as we have already seen, the suffering of nonhuman animals must count equally with the like suffering of human beings, the upshot of these facts is that quite independently of the intrinsic value we place on the lives of nonhuman animals any morally defensible decision affecting the environment should take care to minimize the loss of animal life, particularly among birds and mammals.

To this point we have been discussing the place of individual nonhuman animals in environmental issues, and we have seen that an impartial consideration of their interests provides sufficient reason to show that present human attitudes and practices involving environmental issues are morally unjustifiable. Although this conclusion is, I think, obvious enough to anyone who thinks about the issue along the lines just discussed, there is one aspect of it that is in sharp contrast to an underlying assumption of much environmental debate, an assumption accepted even by many who consider themselves for animals and against the arrogant "human chauvinism" that sees all of nature as a resource to be harvested or a pit for the disposal of wastes. This assumption is that concern for nonhuman animals is appropriate when a whole species is endangered, but not when the threat is only to individual animals. It is in accordance with this assumption that the National Wildlife Federation has sought and obtained a court injunction preventing the U.S. Department of Transportation from building an interstate highway interchange in an area frequented by the extremely rare Mississippi sandhill crane, while the same organization openly supports what it calls "the hunter-sportsman who, during legal hunting seasons, crops surplus wildlife."[21] Similarly the National Audubon Society has fought to preserve rare birds and other animals but opposed moves to stop the annual slaughter of 40,000 seals on the Pribilof Islands of Alaska on the grounds that this "harvest" could be sustained indefinitely, and the protests were thus "without foundation from a conservation and biological viewpoint."[22] Other "environmentalist" organizations which either actively support or refuse to oppose hunting include the Sierra Club, the Wilderness Society, and the World Wildlife Fund.[23]

Since we have already seen that animals' interests in avoiding suffering are to be given equal weight to our own, and since it is sufficiently obvious that hunting makes animals suffer – for one thing, no hunter kills instantly every time – I shall not discuss the ethics of hunting, though I cannot resist inviting the reader to think about the assumptions behind the use of such images as the "cropping" of "surplus wildlife" or the "harvesting" of seals. The remaining ethical issue that needs to be discussed is whether it is still worse to hunt or otherwise to kill animals of endangered species than it is to kill those of species that are plentiful. In other words, suppose that groups like the National Wildlife Federation were to see the error of their prohunting views, and swing round to opposition to hunting. Would they nevertheless be justified in putting greater efforts into stopping the shooting of the Mississippi sandhill crane than into stopping duck-shooting? If so, why?

Some reasons for an affirmative answer are not hard to find. For instance, if we allow species to become extinct, we shall deprive ourselves and our descendents of the pleasures of observing all of the variety of species that we can observe today. Anyone who has ever regretted not being able to see a great auk must have some sympathy with this view. Then again, we never know what ecological role a given species plays, or may play under some unpredictable change of circumstances. Books on ecology are full of stories about how farmers/the health department/the army/the Forestry Commission decided to get rid of a particular rodent/bird/fish/insect because it was a bit of a nuisance, only to find that that particular animal was the chief restraint on the rate of increase of some much nastier and less easily eradicated pest. Even if a species has already been reduced to the point where its total extinction could not have much "environmental impact" in the sense of triggering off other changes, it is always possible that in the future conditions will change, the species will prove better adapted to the new conditions than its rivals, and will flourish, playing an important part in the new ecological balance in its area to the advantage of humans living there. Yet another reason for seeking to preserve species is that, as is often said, the removal of a species depletes the "gene pool" and thus reduces the possibility of "improving" existing domestic or otherwise useful animals by cross-breeding with related wild animals. We do not know what qualities we may want domestic animals to have in the future. It may be that existing breeds lack resistance to a build-up of toxic chemicals or to a new disease that may break out in some remote place and sweep across our planet; but by interbreeding domestic animals with rare wild varieties, we might be able to confer greater resistance on the former, or greater usefulness to humans on the latter.

These reasons for preserving animals of endangered species have something in common: They are all concerned with benefits or dangers for humans. To regard these as the only reasons for preserving species is to take a position similar to that of Aquinas and Kant, who, as we saw earlier,

thought cruelty to animals wrong only because it might indirectly harm human beings. We dismissed that argument on the grounds that if human suffering is intrinsically bad, then it is arbitrary to maintain that animal suffering is of no intrinsic significance. Can we similarly dismiss the view that species should be preserved only because of the benefits of preservation to humans? It might seem that we should, but it is not easy to justify doing so. While individual animals have interests, and no morally defensible line can be drawn between human interests and the interests of nonhuman animals, species as such are not conscious entities and so do not have interests above and beyond the interests of the individual animals that are members of the species. These individual interests are certainly potent reasons against killing rare animals, but they are no more potent in the case of rare animals than in the case of common animals. The rarity of the blue whale does not cause it to suffer any more (nor any less) when harpooned than the more common sperm whale. On what basis, then, other than the indirect benefits to humans, can we justifiably give preference to the preserving of animals of endangered species rather than animals of species that are not in any danger?

One obvious answer, on the basis of the foregoing, is that we ought to give preference to preserving animals of endangered species if so doing will have indirect benefits for nonhuman animals. This may sometimes be the case, for if the extinction of a species can lead to far-reaching ecological damage, this is likely to be bad for nonhuman animals as well as for humans. Yet this answer to our question, while extending the grounds for preserving species beyond the narrow limits of human benefits, still provides no basis for attributing intrinsic value to preservation. To find such a basis we need an answer to the following modified version of the question asked above: On what basis, other than the indirect benefits to humans or other animals, can we justifiably give preference to the preserving of animals of endangered species rather than animals of species that are not in danger?

To this question I can find no satisfactory answer. The most promising suggestion, perhaps, is that the destruction of a whole species is the destruction of something akin to a great work of art; that the tiger, or any other of the "immensely complex and inimitable items produced in nature" has its own, noninstrumental value, just as a great painting or cathedral has value apart from the pleasure and inspiration it brings to human beings.[24] On this view, to exterminate a species is to commit an act of vandalism, like setting about Michelangelo's *Pietà* with a hammer; while allowing an endangered species to die out without taking steps to save it is like allowing Angkor Wat to fall into ruins and be obliterated by the jungle.

My difficulty with this argument is a difficulty with the allegedly less controversial case on which the analogy is built. If the analogy is to succeed in persuading us that there may be intrinsic value quite independently of any benefits for sentient beings in the existence of a species, we must believe that there is this kind of intrinsic value in the existence of works of art; but how can it be shown that the *Pietà* has value independently of the appreciation of those who have seen or will see it? If, as philosophers are fond of asking, I were the last sentient being on earth, would it matter if, in a moment of boredom, I entertained myself by making a bonfire of all the paintings in the Louvre? My own view is that it would not matter – provided, of course, I really could exclude the possibility that, as I stood around the dying embers, a flying saucer would not land and disgorge a load of tourists from Alpha Centauri who had come all the way solely in order to see the Mona Lisa. But there are those who take the opposite view, and I would agree that *if* works of art have intrinsic value, then it is plausible to suppose that species have too.

I conclude, then, that unless or until better grounds are advanced, the only reasons for being more concerned about the interests of animals from endangered species than about other animals are those which relate the preservation of species to benefits for humans and other animals. The significance of these reasons will vary from case to case, depending on such factors as just how different the endangered species really is from other nonendangered species. For instance, if it takes an expert ornithologist to tell a Mississippi sandhill crane from other, more common cranes (and I have no knowledge of whether this is so), then the argument for preservation based on the pleasures of observing a variety of species cannot carry much weight in this case, for this pleasure would be available only to a few people. Similarly, the value of retaining species that perhaps will one day be usefully crossbred with domestic species will not apply to species that have no connection with any domestic animal; and the importance we

place on this reason for preserving species will also depend on the importance we place on domestic animals. If, as I have argued elsewhere, it is generally both inefficient and inhumane to raise animals for food, we are not going to be greatly moved by the thought of "improving" our livestock.[25] Finally, although the argument that the greater the variety of species, the better the chances of a smooth adjustment to environmental changes, is usually a powerful one, it has little application to endangered species that differ only marginally and in ecologically insignificant ways – like minor differences in the markings of birds – from related, nonendangered species.

This conclusion may seem unfavorable to the efforts of environmental groups to preserve endangered species. I would not wish it to be taken in that way. Often the indirect reasons for preservation will make an overwhelming case for preservation; and in any case we must remember that what we have been discussing is not whether to defend animals against those who would kill them and deprive them of their habitat but whether to give preference to defending animals of endangered species. Defending endangered species is, after all, defending individual animals too. If we are more likely to stop the cruel form of commercial hunting known as whaling by pointing out that blue whales may become extinct than by pointing out that blue whales are sentient creatures with lives of their own to lead, then by all means let us point out that blue whales may become extinct. If, however, the commercial whalers should limit their slaughter to what they call the "maximum sustainable yield" and so cease to be a threat to blue whales as a species, let us not forget that they remain a threat to thousands of individual blue whales. My aim throughout this essay has been to increase the importance we give to individual animals when discussing environmental issues, and not to decrease the importance we presently place on defending animals which are members of endangered species.

Notes

1 *Politics*, 1256b.

2 1 *Corinthians* 9: 9–10.

3 St. Augustine, *The Catholic and Manichean Ways of Life*, tr. D. A. Gallagher and I. J. Gallagher (Boston: Catholic University Press, 1966), p. 102.

4 See the *Summa Theologica*, I, II, Q 72, art. 4; II, I, Q102 art. 6; II, II, Q25 art. 3; II, II, Q64 art. 1; II, II, Q159 art. 2; and the *Summa Contra Gentiles* III, II, 112.

5 *St. Francis of Assisi, His Life and Writings as Recorded by His Contemporaries*, tr. L. Sherely-Price (London, 1959); see also John Passmore, *Man's Responsibility for Nature* (New York: Charles Scribner's Sons, 1974), p. 112.

6 E. S. Turner, *All Heaven in a Rage* (London: Michael Joseph, 1964), p. 163.

7 See the *Institutes of Religion*, tr. F. C. Battles (London, 1961), Bk. 1, chs. 14, 22; vol. 1, p. 182 and elsewhere. I owe this reference to Passmore, *Responsibility for Nature*, p. 13.

8 *Lectures on Ethics*, tr. L. Infield (New York: Harper & Row, 1963) pp. 239–40.

9 For a fuller statement of this argument, see my *Animal Liberation* (New York: A New York Review Book, 1975), esp. ch. 1.

10 Ibid.

11 See, for instance, the comments by Arthur Galston in *Natural History* 83, no. 3 (March 1974): 18, on the "evidence" cited in such books as *The Secret Life of Plants*.

12 The idea that we would logicaly have to consider "the most contemptible clod of earth" as having rights was suggested by Thomas Taylor, the Cambridge Neo-Platonist, in a pamphlet he published anonymously, entitled *A Vindication of the Rights of Brutes* (London, 1792) which appears to be a satirical refutation of the attribution of rights to women by Mary Wollstone-croft in her *Vindication of the Rights of Women* (London, 1792). Logically, Taylor was no doubt correct, but he neglected to specify just what interests such contemptible clods of earth have.

13 Singer, *Animal Liberation*, pp. 20–3.

14 See the selection of articles on this question in part IV of *Animal Rights and Human Obligations*, ed. Tom Regan and Peter Singer (Englewood Cliffs, NJ: Prentice-Hall, 1976).

15 A clear statement of this view is to be found in H. L. A. Hart, "Are There Any Natural Rights?" *The Philosophical Review* 64 (1955).

16 See J. Olsen, *Slaughter the Animals, Poison the Earth* (New York: Simon and Schuster, 1971), especially pp. 153–64.

17 See R. and V. Routley, *The Fight for the Forests* (Canberra: Australian National University Press, 1974), for a thoroughly documented indictment of clear-cutting in Australia; and for a recent report of the controversy about clear-cutting in America, see *Time*, May 17, 1976.

18 This way of putting the question derives from C. I. Lewis, *An Analysis of Knowledge and Valuation* (La Salle, Il.: Open Court, 1946), p. 547, via the work of R. M. Hare, especially *Freedom and Reason* (Oxford: Oxford University Press, 1963) and "Ethical Theory and Utilitarianism," in *Contemporary British Philosophy*, 4th series, ed. H. D. Lewis (London: Allen and Unwin, 1976).

19 *Civilization and Ethics*, tr. John Naish, reprinted in *Animal Rights and Human Obligations*, p. 134. (Nor, says Schweitzer in the same sentence, will the truly ethical man shatter an ice crystal that sparkles in the sun – but he offers no explanation of how this prohibition is derived from the ethic of reverence for life. The example may suggest that for Schweitzer killing is wrong because it is unnecessary destruction, a kind of vandalism.)

20 There is, I suppose, an alternative rationale for Schweitzer's medical activities: that while all life is of equal value, we owe loyalty to our own species and have a duty to save their lives over the lives of members of other species when there is a conflict. But I can find nothing in Schweitzer's writings to suggest that he would take so blatantly a speciesist line, and much to suggest that he would not.

21 For the attempt to obtain a court injunction, see *The Wall Street Journal* January 9, 1976, and for the statement in support of hunting, Lewis Regenstein, *The Politics of Extinction* (New York: Macmillan, 1975), p. 32.

22 Victor Scheffer, *A Voice for Wildlife* (New York: Charles Scribner's Sons, 1974), p. 64, quoting "Protest, Priorities and the Alaska Fur Seal," *Audubon* 72 (1970): 114–15.

23 Regenstein, *Politics of Extinction*, p. 33. There are, of course, some who argue for the preservation of species precisely because otherwise there will be no animals left to hunt; for a brief discussion see Passmore, *Responsibility for Nature*, p. 103.

24 Val Routley, "Critical Notice of *Man's Responsibility for Nature*," *Australasian Journal of Philosophy* 53 no. 2 (1975): 175. Routley uses this argument more as an ad hominem against Passmore (who accepts that works of art can have intrinsic value) than as the basis for her own view. For further discussion of this view, see Passmore, *Responsibility for Nature*, p. 103; and Stanley Benn, "Personal Freedom and Environmental Ethics: The Moral Inequality of Species," paper presented to the World Congress on Philosophy of Law and Social Philosophy, St. Louis, Mo., August 1975, especially p. 21.

25 Singer, *Animal Liberation*, esp. chs. 3 and 4.

5

Animal Rights: What's in a Name?

Tom Regan

Organised efforts to protect other animals are at an historic crossroads. Never before have so many joined in the struggle to bring significant improvements to their lives. Our numbers and shared values are making a difference in the political process, in the marketplace, in the classroom, even – on some occasions, thanks in large part to the indefatigable work of Andrew Linzey – in places of worship. Truly, we are a force to be reckoned with.

This reckoning sometimes takes bitter forms. Especially among those who make a living off the backs of other animals, whether this be in the name of science, commerce in flesh, or entertainment, for example, we are being 'reckoned with' with a vengeance. Steadily increasing amounts of their time, energy and money are being devoted to reckoning with us, not on the merits of the issues involved for the most part, but instead with a view to destroying our movement by discrediting those who comprise it. The old rhetoric of disdainful dismissal, the one that grouped all of us together as 'cranks', 'lunatics', 'freaks', or simple-minded members of an addled army of 'little old ladies in tennis shoes' – this old rhetoric is dead, or dying. In its place is a new rhetoric, an incendiary rhetoric, a rhetoric of vitriolic accusation. Today we are 'fanatics', 'extremists', or – the most frequently used verbal bomb, the one favoured even by the highest ranking public health official in the United States, Health and Human Services Secretary Louis Sullivan – 'terrorists'.

While it is important that we take stock of and combat the fraudulent ways in which we are being described by those who oppose us, we should not be unmindful or insensitive to what we are saying about ourselves, of how *we* are describing who-we-are. For the plain fact is, we are saying many different things. We are against cruelty. We stand for animal welfare, for animal protection, for compassion, for human responsibility to the other animals. Our goal is animal liberation. We are part of a progressive social movement – the Animal Rights Movement. Are we all these things? Can we be?

In the remarks that follow I offer some answers to these questions, make some scattered observations about how these answers relate to concerns about the environment, and indicate where my own sympathies lie.

Why Anti-Cruelty is Not Enough

We do well to remember that societal opposition to cruelty to animals, especially opposition that has the force of law, is a comparatively recent development. In England we can date its beginning with the passage, on 22 June 1822, of the Ill-Treatment of Cattle Act, while in the United States we may point to the passage of anti-cruelty legislation by several of the states, beginning with New York in 1828. Sad to say, there are many countries in which no such laws exist, even to this day.

Laws without strong enforcement are words without deeds, and the tragic truth is that courts in

Tom Regan

both England and the United States have displayed a general unwillingness to mete out harsh punishment to those found guilty of cruelty to animals and an even greater reluctance to render guilty verdicts in the first place. In no small measure this is due to the concept of cruelty with which the judicial system has operated. Historically, to prohibit cruelty to animals has amounted to prohibiting the infliction of *unnecessary* pain, or *unjustified* pain, especially when the pain is *substantial* and the human agent has acted *wantonly* or *maliciously*, and *with intent*. A man who, for the sheer fun of it, intentionally torments and then sets fire to a cat, knowing full well what he is doing, is a paradigm example of what legal and moral opposition to cruelty to animals has meant historically.

Few there are who would speak in favour of cruelty to animals, as thus understood, and I take it that, whatever else our differences might be, at least we all agree that cruelty to other animals is morally vile, and morally vile for the same reasons as cruelty to human children, for example. Indeed I believe we can go further and state that this is a judgment in which the vast majority of British and American citizens agree.

But this consensus conceals important differences, especially those that concern *when* cruelty occurs. To be told that animals are treated cruelly when they are caused *unnecessary* or *unjustified* pain is of little use unless we are told *what counts* as unnecessary or unjustified pain. Not surprisingly, different people count differently.

A case in point is the use of the steel-jawed leghold trap by commercial trappers still common in the United States. For decades people have opposed the use of this trap on grounds of its cruelty, and among those who have done so many have called for the development and utilisation of what are called 'more humane methods' of trapping. For these people use of the steel-jawed leghold trap by commercial trappers is wrong because it causes too much pain, whereas other, 'more humane methods' of trapping would be permissible because the pain they cause, though real enough, is not excessive.

Stated in these simple terms, the anti-cruelty position's most obvious weakness is that it assumes that we already know that trapping wild animals is justified, if only it is done 'as humanely as possible'. However, since this very question – the question whether commercial trapping is morally justified – is open to serious debate, the anti-cruelty position, in its simple form, is question-begging at best, mistaken at worst.

This same observation can be applied to other ways in which we are describing ourselves. People who say they stand for animal protection, for compassion, for human responsibility towards the other animals, speak well and truly, as far as these descriptions go. The problem is, it often is not clear how far this is. If these descriptions assume that the only moral prohibition we must honour is the prohibition against cruelty, then they assume that it is *sometimes* morally permissible to cause animals pain, even substantial pain. Since whether this *is* permissible proves to be a widely disputed proposition, the position that animal protection, or compassion for animals, or our human responsibility to other animals are exhausted by the prohibition against cruelty also are question-begging at best, mistaken at worst.

In addition to these defects, there is another reason why merely being against cruelty to animals is not enough. In the end, all that the prohibition against cruelty forbids is that we unnecessarily or unjustifiably visit evil, in the form of pain, upon another animal. What this prohibition therefore fails to address or account for, is the obligation to *promote the good* of other animals. Perhaps no one sees this point better than St. Francis. Recall his observation: 'Not to hurt our humble brethren is our first duty to them, but to stop there is not enough. We have a higher mission – to be of service to them wherever they require it.'

The Limits of Animal Welfare

If understood in a particular way, this Franciscan insight captures, I believe, the essence of those who stand for the promotion of animal welfare. To be for animal welfare, as distinct from merely being against animal cruelty, is to believe that we have a duty to improve the quality of animal life, by ensuring – so far as this is possible – that other animals are the beneficiaries of what is good for them, not merely that we should avoid being cruel to them.

The difference between these two views can be illustrated by considering the case of endangered species. Animal welfarists, because they are committed to promoting the good of these and other animals, seem to have an intelligible basis on which to rest their call for the preservation of natural habitat. After all, one does not promote the good of elephants and chimpanzees, for example, by destroying their natural homes. Those who limit animal protection to the prohibition against cruelty, by contrast, seem to have a less intelligible basis for preserving natural habitat. If they believe (as they often do) that human needs and interests are more important than the needs and interests of nonhuman animals, then they can – and, in fact, they often do – believe that we are justified in causing significant pain to animals, even if they belong to endangered species. Granting this much, these same people can – and they often do – believe that the destruction of natural habitat is not wrong.

Though the two viewpoints differ in important ways, animal welfarists, I believe, have the same strong public support as those who oppose cruelty to animals. I believe, that is, that most British and American people accept the proposition that we have a positive duty to help other animals when they are in need of it. Moreover, I believe that few people in this room will step forward to denounce the idea of animal welfare, as if it is a matter of indifference whether an animal's life is good or bad. There is, then, *something* in the idea of being for animal welfare we all can accept, just as there is *something* in the ideas of being against cruelty and for human responsibility and animal protection.

Nevertheless, as was true in the case of the anti-cruelty position, the pro-welfare stance is not free from serious problems. I shall comment on only one. Even if all informed people could agree concerning what animal welfare is, and how well various animals are faring – and these are large assumptions – the animal welfarist's position would remain controversial because of how it answers the question 'What may be done in the name of, or in pursuit of, animal welfare?' Historically, those who would describe themselves as 'animal welfarists' have answered this question in the following way.

'The welfare of nonhuman animals is important. But it is not the only thing that is important. Human interests and preferences also are important and, frequently, more important than the interests and preferences of other animals. For example, many people have a serious economic interest in the commercial exploitation of marine life; in addition, many others enjoy eating these animals. These people should be supportive of animal welfare, of course, but with the understanding that being in support of animal welfare is perfectly consistent with utilising animals for human preferences and interests.

'There is no question,' this view continues, 'that when animals in the sea are harvested we shorten their life. But – and this is an important "but" – ending the life of animals is not contrary to supporting animal welfare. If animals in the sea have fared well, all considered, up to the point when they are harvested, and if they are harvested humanely, then we do nothing wrong when we kill them.

'Morever, it is important to realise that a commitment to animal welfare is consistent with striving to improve the *overall* condition of those individuals who have a welfare, both humans and other animals, even if this means decreasing the welfare of some. Such circumstances often arise – in utilising nonhuman animals in biomedical research, for example, or in keeping members of endangered species in zoos. This is regrettable, certainly, and everything should be done to make the lives of these animals as good as practicable. In the end, however, to diminish the welfare of some animals is a price we must be willing to pay for making the world better for others, both human and nonhuman.'

I hope it is clear, from what I have said, that animal welfarists are people who attempt to serve two demanding moral masters. First, there is the demand that *individual animals* have a life that fares well, all considered. This is the demand that leads animal welfarists to call for improved living conditions for animals in laboratories or on the farm, for example. But, secondly, there is the demand that animal (including human) welfare be improved *in general*; and it is this demand that leads animal welfarists to permit the death of some animals, sometimes large numbers of them, and even to permit the agony of some, so that others might benefit.

When viewed in this light it should not be surprising that the loudest, most powerful voices being heard in the name of animal welfare – at least in the United States – are those who have a vested interest in the perpetuation of animal exploitation. By this I mean that those who identify themselves with the cause of animal welfare are increasingly those who speak for the commerical animal agriculture community, the bio-medical community, the hunting and trapping communities, and so on. In the United States, it is fair to say, these people have usurped the idea of animal welfare from the animal welfare societies that historically have helped police them.

And how can traditional advocates of animal welfare prove that these new champions of the welfare of animals must be mistaken? Will it be said that animals raised on close confinement systems, for example, do not fare well, all considered? Well, people who stake their opposition to factory-farming on this kind of consideration should be prepared for a long, heated debate, with one set of 'experts' declaring that thus-and-so is true, while another declares that it is not.

But even if the critics are right, and the quality of life for these animals can be improved, this will not change the system in any fundamental way. True, some more space might be provided; perhaps better ventilation; maybe a change in diet or exercise opportunities. The system of utilisation, that is, might be reformed, with a view to improving the welfare of the animals being utilised. Nevertheless the philosophy of animal welfare by its very nature permits utilising other animals for human purposes, even if this means (as it always does) that most of these animals will experience pain, frustration and other harms, and even if it means, as it almost always does, that these animals will have their life terminated prematurely. This is what I mean by saying that reforms within the system of utilisation will not change the system in any fundamental way.

Animal Rights

Advocates of animal rights believe that more than reform of the system is needed. When a system is unjust to the core, abolition, not reform, is what respect for justice demands. There is, then, a fundamental moral difference between advocates of anti-cruelty, animal welfare and animal rights. Although the first two positions are committed to the view that we are *sometimes* justified in causing nonhuman animals significant pain, in pursuit of institutionalised human interests, animal rightists deny that we are ever justified in doing this. The true objective for which animal advocates should work, according to this view, is not to provide nonhuman animals with larger cages and stalls, but to empty them. If we describe ourselves as advocates of animal rights, therefore, it is quite different from saying that we rest our case with

anti-cruelty or pro-welfare. We are abolitionists, not reformists.

In my view, for reasons I have set forth at length elsewhere, I believe that the philosophy of animal rights is the right philosophy. Am I right to adopt this stance? By my own lights, I think I am. The arguments for the abolitionist position are the best arguments, all considered. Or so I believe, and thus have I argued on numerous occasions in the past. You will be relieved to hear that I shall spare you the details of these arguments on this occasion. My interest here concerns how people who share my views should describe themselves. Not in terms of anti-cruelty. And not in terms of pro-welfare. I hope that is clear. But how, then?

Understanding "Animal Liberation"

People who share my views can, and often do, describe themselves as being in favour of Animal Liberation. I believe this is an appropriate description. But I also believe it can be misunderstood.

One possible basis for Animal Liberation is an egalitarian interpretation of interests. On this view the interests of everyone affected by what we do must be taken into account, and equal interests must be counted equally. If only we would do this, we are to suppose, animals would be liberated.

This understanding of *liberation* is profoundly mistaken. To make this clearer, consider the case of human slavery. There is no question that the interests of slaves were often totally ignored, or that, when they were considered, they often were not counted equitably. This much granted, someone might maintain that the fundamental basis for the call to liberate slaves amounted to the dual demand that, first, their interests not be ignored, and, secondly, their interests be counted equitably.

This is not true. Merely to count the interests of slaves equitably is not equivalent to liberating them. Why? Because slaves can have their interests counted equitably *and still* remain in bondage. Why? Because there is no guarantee that, once their interests are counted equitably, they should be liberated (this will depend on adding up *all* the minuses, and *all* the pluses, for both slaves and those who profit from slavery).

Moreover – and more fundamentally – this way of thinking about Human Liberation has got things backwards. It is not that, in the face of a system of chattel slavery, we first insist on counting everyone's interests equitably and *then* see if slaves should be liberated; it is that we first recognise the moral imperative to liberate them, on grounds *other than* counting equal interests equally. Put another way, *after* human slaves have been liberated, *then* one might attempt to argue that a fair way to decide between competing social policies is to count everyone's interests and count equal interests equally. But it is mistaken to the point of being morally grotesque to argue that, *before* we can decide whether human slaves should be liberated, we first need to count everyone's interests, both slaves' and slave owners' alike, and count equal interests equally. The interests of those who profit from slavery should play no role whatsoever in deciding to abolish the institution from which they profit. The fact that the interests of slaves are not counted equitably by their oppressors proves to be a symptom, not the underlying reason, of the great evil human slaves are made to endure.

This great evil is rooted in systematic injustice. It is the right of slaves *to be free*, their right *not to be treated as another's property*, their right *not to be used as a mere means to another's end* – it is these basic moral *rights* that a system of chattel slavery systematically violates, not the principle that we must count equal interests equally. The very concept of *liberation* makes sense only if it is viewed against the backdrop of unjust oppression, and while the notion of unjust oppression no doubt assumes many guises, it is incomprehensible to me how we might understand it apart from the idea of the violation of basic moral rights.

There is, then, I believe, a much better way in which we can understand Animal Liberation than the way provided by an egalitarian interpretation of interests. It takes its cue from other kinds of liberation, and rests the call for Animal Liberation on the recognition of the rights of nonhuman animals, including in particular their right not to be treated as mere means to human ends. When viewed in this light, Animal Liberation is the goal for which the philosophy of animal rights is the philosophy. The two – Animal Liberation and Animal Rights – go together, like a hand in a glove.

Sources of Resistance

Resistance to the philosophy of animal rights takes many forms, from the incredulous ('You can't be

serious!') to the superficial ('What about carrots?'), and from the arrogant (as in the increasingly heard boast of American researchers, 'I'm a speciesist and proud of it!') to the deep. While most objections are to serious thinking what veneer is to seasoned wood, some – I have in mind objections that some feminists bring against the idea of animal rights in particular and the notion of rights in general – deserve a serious hearing and patient exploration.... A second serious challenge, however, needs our attention here.

This challenge is the one emanating from environmentalists, especially so-called 'deep ecologists'. The fundamental focus of value, according to these thinkers, is the whole, not the part – the ecosystem, not the individuals who comprise it. A healthy ecosystem is one that is diverse, sustainable, and balanced; an unhealthy one is one that lacks one or another of these characteristics. Within a healthy ecosystem, individuals are expendable. Deer can be hunted, for example, whatever the reason, and nothing wrong is done *so long as* they are not overhunted. If that happens, then the ecosystem is thrown out of balance, diversity is diminished, and the community of life loses its sustainability. Sensitive wildlife management programmes, by contrast, developed on the basis of maximum sustainable yields – of seals or whales, deer or quail, or any species of wildlife, for that matter – promote the health of the overall life community.

Here, then, in the deep ecologist's environmental philosophy, the philosophy of animal rights finds a serious (and I dare say powerful) adversary. Notice, moreover, that this philosophy appears to be in harmony, at least in principle, with that of animal welfare and, adding certain plausible assumptions, anti-cruelty. The animal welfarist's position, like the deep ecologist's, is committed to permitting the sacrifice of some individuals for the greater good, and even the deep ecologists, notwithstanding their glorification of sport hunting (I have in mind such legendary figures as Aldo Leopold, Ortega y Gasset and the poet Gary Snyder), might agree that more humane forms of hunting and trapping are preferable to more barbaric ones. In the confrontation with deep ecology, it is the animal rights philosophy, not that of pro-welfare or anti-cruelty, that is the odd position out.

None of this is very surprising, actually. Despite their many differences, deep ecology, animal welfare, and anti-cruelty, have some fundamental similarities, the most important of which is that individuals are morally expendable – expendable for the deep ecologist as long as the good of the biotic community is sustained or promoted, expendable for the animal welfarist as long as the welfare of others is protected or advanced, and expendable for those who accept the anti-cruelty position, as long as worthy ends are not obtained by means that cause excessive suffering.

Not so the philosophy of animal rights. This philosophy regards the individual's right to be treated with respect as inviolate. The rights of the individual are not to be violated in the name of some collective good, whether that good be the good of the ecosystem or the good of sentient life (both human and nonhuman), and independently of whether these rights are violated 'humanely' or otherwise. Thus, as I say, it is hardly surprising that, among those who wish to forge alliances with environmentalists, those who, like myself, work for the goal of animal liberation are likely to find the going rougher than those who are pro-welfare or anti-cruelty.

Even so, there are possible points of agreement – if not in principle, then at least in practice. The most obvious one is commercial animal agriculture in its dominant form. I mean factory-farming, of course. But I also have in mind the massive destruction of delicate, irreplaceable ecosystems (the rain forests of the world are the most obvious example), the massive pollution of the waters of the earth, the massive loss of top soil, the massive contribution to the greenhouse effect, and – lest we forget – the massive assault on human health that can be attributed directly and indirectly to the massive production and consumption of so-called 'food' animals that characterise our times. Unquestionably, this pattern of massive production and consumption is bad for the earth, bad for humans, and bad for the other animals. There is no serious argument against these findings. Only sophistry.

Here, then, we have the most obvious, the most important, opportunity for bridge-building, so obvious and important in fact that, in my view – and here I echo a judgment of Stephen Clark's which in times past I fiercely denied – an individual's or organisation's position on 'meat-eating', so-called, should be regarded as the decisive litmus test of their moral credibility. To the extent that individuals and organisations still support or tolerate meat consumption, to that extent they are part of the moral problem, not part of the moral solution.

By all means, then, I think bridges should be built between the environmental movement and the partisans of anti-cruelty, animal welfare, and animal rights. At the same time, however, I do not think that advocates of animal rights should be willing to sell their soul in order to build a bridge. If part of the deep ecologist's rationale for saving wilderness is so that future generations of humans can savour the orgiastic blood of the hunt (as Ortega y Gasset describes the recreational slaughter of wild animals), animal liberationists can and should unashamedly applaud the efforts to preserve, but not the reasons for doing so.

Aside from these sorts of problems, I believe all of us who presume to speak on behalf of the other animals should worry, not a little but a lot, about the possibility of the Goliath of contemporary environmental concerns co-opting the David of animal protection. Quite apart from questions of environmental impact, there is a distinctive animal-issue agenda we all can share and work on, whether we are pro-welfare, say, or animal rightists. Unless or until we codify this agenda and give it meaning through our cooperative efforts, those of us who care about what is happening to the other animals will remain individual, separate gears that do not mesh.

Here are some concrete examples of what I have in mind. The list that follows is hardly exhaustive. All of you will be able to add to it.

- The philosophy of animal rights calls for an end to the use of animals in cosmetic-testing in particular and product-testing in general.
- The philosophy of animal rights calls for an end to the coercive use of any animal in military research, or in such research topics as the deleterious effects of smoking, maternal deprivation and drug addiction.
- The philosophy of animal rights calls for an end to the traditions of 'sport' hunting and trapping of wildlife.
- The philosophy of animal rights calls for an end to the commerce in the skins of other animals for purposes of human vanity.
- The philosophy of animal rights calls for an end to the capture and training of wild animals, for purposes of entertainment.

Now, unless I am mistaken, those partisans of anti-cruelty or pro-welfare who are gathered here *also* accept these same aspirations. Partisans of these philosophies, in other words, as well as those who prefer to speak in the language of compassion or human responsibility or animal protection, share *some* of the same goals as animal rightists. Granted, the *reasons* each gives in support of these goals differ; and granted, there are *some* goals on the respective agendas of the competing philosophies that are not shared by the others. What is not to be granted is the pessimistic conviction that points of agreement cannot be found.

I conclude, then, not with stirring words of praise for the philosophy of animal rights, or with caustic words of censure for the other philosophies I have mentioned. Rather, I conclude by inviting all of us whose activism is shaped by our concern for what is happening to the other animals to make a renewed, conscientious, patient and determined effort to come together and forge a common agenda, even as we work, both as individuals and organisations, on projects that are uniquely our own. I call upon everyone to begin to work to create such an agenda in the coming months, mindful that each of us may have to make some compromises along the way if we are to end with something in which we all can believe. For the present, what is needed most is more cooperative work, and less competitive philosophising.

A BRIEF EXTRACT FROM *The Case for Animal Rights*

How to Worry About Endangered Species

The rights view is a view about the moral rights of individuals. Species are not individuals, and the rights view does not recognize the moral rights of species to anything, including survival. What it recognizes is the prima facie right of individuals not to be harmed, and thus the prima facie right of individuals not to be killed. That an individual animal is among the last remaining members of a species confers no further right on that animal, and its right not to be harmed must be weighed equitably with the rights of any others who have this right. If, in a prevention situation, we had to choose between saving the last two members of

an endangered species or saving another individual who belonged to a species that was plentiful but whose death would be a greater prima facie harm to that individual than the harm that death would be to the two, then the rights view requires that we save that individual. Moreover, numbers make no difference in such a case. If the choice were between saving the last thousand or million members of the species to which the two belong, that would make no moral difference. The aggregate of their lesser harms does not harm any individual in a way that is prima facie comparable to the harm that would be done to this solitary individual. Nor would aggregating the losses of other interested parties (e.g., human aesthetic or scientific interests) make any difference. The sum of these losses harms no individual in a way that is prima facie comparable to the harm that would be done to the single individual if we chose to override his right.

The rights view is not opposed to efforts to save endangered species. It only insists that we be clear about the reasons for doing so. On the rights view, the reason we ought to save the members of endangered species of animals is not because the species is endangered but because the individual animals have valid claims and thus rights against those who would destroy their natural habitat, for example, or who would make a living off their dead carcasses through poaching and traffic in exotic animals, practices that unjustifiably override the rights of these animals. But though the rights view must look with favor on any attempt to protect the rights of any animal, and so supports efforts to protect the members of endangered species, these very efforts, aimed specifically at protecting the members of species that are endangered, can foster a mentality that is antagonistic to the implications of the rights view. If people are encouraged to believe that the harm done to animals matters morally *only when* these animals belong to endangered species, then these same people will be encouraged to regard the harm done to *other* animals as morally acceptable. In this way people may be encouraged to believe that, for example, the trapping of plentiful animals raises no serious moral question, whereas the trapping of rare animals does. This is not what the rights view implies. The mere size of the relative population of the species to which a given animal belongs makes no moral difference to the grounds for attributing rights to that individual animal or to the basis for determining when that animal's rights may be justifiably overridden or protected.

Though said before, it bears repeating: *the rights view is not indifferent to efforts to save endangered species. It supports these efforts.* It supports them, however, not because these animals are few in number; primarily it supports them because they are equal in value to all who have inherent value, ourselves included, sharing with us the fundamental right to be treated with respect. Since they are not mere receptacles or renewable resources placed here for our use, the harm done to them as individuals cannot be justified merely by aggregating the disparate benefits derived by commercial developers, poachers, and other interested third parties. That is what makes the commercial exploitation of endangered species wrong, not that the species are endangered. On the rights view, the same principles apply to the moral assessment of rare or endangered animals as apply to those that are plentiful, and the same principles apply whether the animals in question are wild or domesticated.

The rights view does not deny, nor is it antagonistic to recognizing, the importance of human aesthetic, scientific, sacramental, and other interests in rare and endangered species or in wild animals generally. What it denies is that (1) the value of these animals is reducible to, or is interchangeable with, the aggregate satisfaction of these human interests, and that (2) the determination of how these animals should be treated, including whether they should be saved in preference to more plentiful animals, is to be fixed by the yardstick of such human interests, either taken individually or aggregatively. Both points cut both ways, concerning, as they do, both how animals may and how they may not be treated. In particular, any and all harm done to rare or endangered animals, done in the name of aggregated human interests, is wrong, according to the rights view, because it violates the individual animal's right to respectful treatment. With regard to wild animals, the general policy recommended by the rights view is: *let them be!* Since this will require increased human intervention in *human* practices that threaten rare or endangered species (e.g., halting the destruction of natural habitat and closer surveillance of poaching, with much stiffer fines and longer prison sentences), the rights view sanctions this intervention, assuming that those humans involved are treated with the respect they are due. Too little is not enough.

Rights and Environmental Ethics: An Aside

The difficulties and implications of developing a rights-based environmental ethic, should be abundantly clear by now and deserve brief comment before moving on. The difficulties include reconciling the *individualistic* nature of moral rights with the more *holistic* view of nature emphasized by many of the leading environmental thinkers. Aldo Leopold is illustrative of this latter tendency. "A thing is right," he states, "when it tends to preserve the integrity, stability, and beauty of the biotic community. It is wrong when it tends otherwise."[5] The implications of this view include the clear prospect that the individual may be sacrificed for the greater biotic good, in the name of "the integrity, stability, and beauty of the biotic community." It is difficult to see how the notion of the rights of the individual could find a home within a view that, emotive connotations to one side, might be fairly dubbed "environmental fascism." To use Leopold's telling phrase, man is "*only* a member of the biotic team,"[6] and as such has the same moral standing as any other "member" of "the team." If, to take an extreme, fanciful but, it is hoped, not unfair example, the situation we faced was either to kill a rare wildflower or a (plentiful) human being, and if the wildflower, as a "team member," would contribute more to "the integrity, stability, and beauty of the biotic community" than the human, then presumably we would not be doing wrong if we killed the human and saved the wildflower. The rights view cannot abide this position, not because the rights view categorically denies that inanimate objects can have rights (more on this momentarily) but because it denies the propriety of deciding what should be done to individuals who have rights by appeal to aggregative considerations, including, therefore, computations about what will or will not maximally "contribute to the integrity, stability, and beauty of the biotic community." Individual rights are not to be outweighed by such considerations (which is not to say that they are never to be outweighed). Environmental fascism and the rights view are like oil and water: they don't mix.

The rights view does not deny the possibility that collections or systems of natural objects might have inherent value – that is, might have a kind of value that is not the same as, is not reducible to, and is incommensurate with any one individual's pleasures, preference-satisfactions, and the like, or with the sum of such goods for any number of individuals. The beauty of an undisturbed, ecologically balanced forest, for example, might be conceived to have value of this kind. The point is certainly arguable. What is far from certain is how moral rights could be meaningfully attributed to the *collection* of trees or the ecosystem. Since neither is an individual, it is unclear how the notion of moral rights can be meaningfully applied. Perhaps this difficulty can be surmounted. It is fair to say, however, that no one writing in this important area of ethics has yet done so.

Because paradigmatic right-holders are individuals, and because the dominant thrust of contemporary environmental efforts (e.g., wilderness preservation) is to focus on the whole rather than on the part (i.e., the individual), there is an understandable reluctance on the part of environmentalists to "take rights seriously," or at least a reluctance to take them as seriously as the rights view contends we should. But this may be a case of environmentalists not seeing the forest for the trees – or, more accurately, of not seeing the trees for the forest. The implications of the successful development of a rights-based environmental ethic, one that made the case that individual inanimate natural objects (e.g., *this* redwood) have inherent value and a basic moral right to treatment respectful of that value,

should be welcomed by environmentalists. If individual trees have inherent value, they have a kind of value that is not the same as, is not reducible to, and is incommensurate with the intrinsic values of the pleasures, preference-satisfactions, and the like, of others, and since the rights of the individual never are to be overridden merely on the grounds of aggregating such values for all those affected by the outcome, a rights-based environmental ethic would bar the door to those who would uproot wilderness in the name of "human progress," whether this progress be aggregated economic, educational, recreational, or other human interests. On the rights view, assuming this could be successfully extended to inanimate natural objects, our general policy regarding wilderness would be precisely what the preservationists want – namely, let it be! Before those who favor such preservation dismiss the rights view in favor of the holistic view more commonly voiced in environmental circles, they might think twice about the implications of the two. There is the danger that the baby will be thrown out with the bath water. A rights-based environmental ethic remains a live option, one that, though far from being established, merits continued exploration. It ought not to be dismissed out of hand by environmentalists as being in principle antagonistic to the goals for which they work. It isn't. Were we to show proper respect for the rights of the individuals who make up the biotic community, would not the *community* be preserved? And is not that what the more holistic, systems-minded environmentalists want?

6

The Ethics of Respect for Nature

Paul W. Taylor

Human-Centered and Life-Centered Systems of Environmental Ethics

When the basic characteristics of the attitude of respect for nature are made clear, it will be seen that a life-centered system of environmental ethics need not be holistic or organicist in its conception of the kinds of entities that are deemed the appropriate objects of moral concern and consideration. Nor does such a system require that the concepts of ecological homeostasis, equilibrium, and integrity provide us with normative principles from which could be derived (with the addition of factual knowledge) our obligations with regard to natural ecosystems. The "balance of nature" is not itself a moral norm, however important may be the role it plays in our general outlook on the natural world that underlies the attitude of respect for nature. I argue that finally it is the good (well-being, welfare) of individual organisms, considered as entities having inherent worth, that determines our moral relations with the Earth's wild communities of life.

In designating the theory to be set forth as life-centered. I intend to contrast it with all anthropocentric views. According to the latter, human actions affecting the natural environment and its nonhuman inhabitants are right (or wrong) by either of two criteria: they have consequences which are favorable (or unfavorable) to human well-being, or they are consistent (or inconsistent) with the system of norms that protect and implement human rights. From this human-centered standpoint it is to humans and only to humans that all duties are ultimately owed. We may have responsibilities *with regard to* the natural ecosystems and biotic communities of our planet, but these responsibilities are in every case based on the contingent fact that our treatment of those ecosystems and communities of life can further the realization of human values and/or human rights. We have no obligation to promote or protect the good of non-human living things, independently of this contingent fact.

A life-centered system of environmental ethics is opposed to human-centered ones precisely on this point. From the perspective of a life-centered theory, we have prima facie moral obligations that are owed to wild plants and animals themselves as members of the Earth's biotic community. We are morally bound (other things being equal) to protect or promote their good for *their* sake. Our duties to respect the integrity of natural ecosystems, to preserve endangered species, and to avoid environmental pollution stem from the fact that these are ways in which we can help make it possible for wild species populations to achieve and maintain a healthy existence in a natural state. Such obligations are due those living things out of recognition of their inherent worth. They are entirely additional to and independent of the obligations we owe to our fellow humans. Although many of the actions that fulfill one set of obligations will also fulfill the other, two different grounds of obligation are involved. Their well-being, as well as human well-being, is something to be realized *as an end in itself.*

If we were to accept a life-centered theory of environmental ethics, a profound reordering of our moral universe would take place. We would begin to look at the whole of the Earth's biosphere in a new light. Our duties with respect to the "world" of nature would be seen as making prima facie claims upon us to be balanced against our duties with respect to the "world" of human civilization. We could no longer simply take the human point of view and consider the effects of our actions exclusively from the perspective of our own good....

We can think of the good of an individual non-human organism as consisting in the full development of its biological powers. Its good is realized to the extent that it is strong and healthy. It possesses whatever capacities it needs for successfully coping with its environment and so preserving its existence throughout the various stages of the normal life cycle of its species. The good of a population or community of such individuals consists in the population or community maintaining itself from generation to generation as a coherent system of genetically and ecologically related organisms whose average good is at an optimum level for the given environment. (Here *average good* means that the degree of realization of the good of *individual organisms* in the population or community is, on average, greater than would be the case under any other ecologically functioning order of interrelations among those species populations in the given ecosystem.)

The idea of a being having a good of its own, as I understand it, does not entail that the being must ... take an interest in what affects its life for better or for worse. We can act in a being's interest or contrary to its interest without its being interested in what we are doing to it in the sense of wanting or not wanting us to do it. It may, indeed, be wholly unaware that favorable and unfavorable events are taking place in its life. I take it that trees, for example, have no knowledge or desires or feelings. Yet is is undoubtedly the case that trees can be harmed or benefited by our actions. We can crush their roots by running a bulldozer too close to them. We can see to it that they get adequate nourishment and moisture by fertilizing and watering the soil

around them. Thus we can help or hinder them in the realization of their good. It is the good of trees themselves that is thereby affected....

When construed in this way, the concept of a being's good is not coextensive with sentience or the capacity for feeling pain. William Frankena has argued for a general theory of environmental ethics in which the ground of a creature's being worthy of moral consideration is its sentience. I have offered some criticisms of this view elsewhere, but the full refutation of such a position, it seems to me, finally depends on the positive reasons for accepting a life-centered theory of the kind I am defending in this essay.... [1]

Since I am concerned only with human treatment of wild organisms, species populations, and communities of life as they occur in our planet's natural ecosystems, it is to those entities alone that the concept "having a good of its own" will here be applied. I am not denying that other living things, whose genetic origin and environmental conditions have been produced, controlled, and manipulated by humans for human ends, do have a good of their own in the same sense as do wild plants and animals. It is not my purpose in this essay, however, to set out or defend the principles that should guide our conduct with regard to their good. It is only insofar as their production and use by humans have good or ill effects upon natural ecosystems and their wild inhabitants that the ethics of respect for nature comes into play....

The Biocentric Outlook on Nature

[The] belief system underlying the attitude of respect for nature I call (for want of a better name) "the biocentric outlook on nature." Since it is not wholly analyzable into empirically confirmable assertions, it should not be thought of as simply a compendium of the biological sciences concerning our planet's ecosystems. It might best be described as a philosophical world view, to distinguish it from a scientific theory or explanatory system. However, one of its major tenets is the great lesson we have learned from the science of ecology: the interdependence of all living things in an organically unified order whose balance and stability are necessary conditions for the realization of the good of its constituent biotic communities.

Paul W. Taylor

Before turning to an account of the main components of the biocentric outlook, it is convenient here to set forth the overall structure of my theory of environmental ethics as it has now emerged. The ethics of respect for nature is made up of three basic elements: a belief system, an ultimate moral attitude, and a set of rules of duty and standards of character. These elements are connected with each other in the following manner. The belief system provides a certain outlook on nature which supports and makes intelligible an autonomous agent's adopting, as an ultimate moral attitude, the attitude of respect for nature. It supports and makes intelligible the attitude in the sense that, when an autonomous agent understands its moral relations to the natural world in terms of this outlook, it recognizes the attitude of respect to be the only *suitable* or *fitting* attitude to take toward all wild forms of life in the Earth's biosphere. Living things are now viewed as *the appropriate objects of the attitude of respect* and are accordingly regarded as entities possessing inherent worth. One then places intrinsic value on the promotion and protection of their good. As a consequence of this, one makes a moral commitment to abide by a set of rules of duty and to fulfill (as far as one can by one's own efforts) certain standards of good character. Given one's adoption of the attitude of respect, one makes that moral commitment because one considers those rules and standards to be validly binding on all moral agents. They are seen as embodying forms of conduct and character structures in which the attitude of respect for nature is manifested.

This three-part complex which internally orders the ethics of respect for nature is symmetrical with a theory of human ethics grounded on respect for persons. Such a theory includes, first, a conception of oneself and others as persons, that is, as centers of autonomous choice. Second, there is the attitude of respect for persons as persons. When this is adopted as an ultimate moral attitude it involves the disposition to treat every person as having inherent worth or "human dignity." Every human being, just in virtue of her or his humanity, is understood to be worthy of moral consideration, and intrinsic value is placed on the autonomy and well-being of each. This is what Kant meant by conceiving of persons as ends in themselves. Third, there is an ethical system of duties which are acknowledged to be owed by everyone to

everyone. These duties are forms of conduct in which public recognition is given to each individual's inherent worth as a person.

This structural framework for a theory of human ethics is meant to leave open the issue of consequentialism (utilitarianism) versus nonconsequentialism (deontology). That issue concerns the particular kind of system of rules defining the duties of moral agents toward persons. Similarly, I am leaving open in this paper the question of what particular kind of system of rules defines our duties with respect to the natural world.

The biocentric outlook on nature has four main components. (1) Humans are thought of as members of the Earth's community of life, holding that membership on the same terms as apply to all the nonhuman members. (2) The Earth's natural ecosystems as a totality are seen as a complex web of interconnected elements, with the sound biological functioning of each being dependent on the sound biological functioning of the others. (This is the component referred to above as the great lesson that the science of ecology has taught us.) (3) Each individual organism is conceived of as a teleological center of life, pursuing its own good in its own way. (4) Whether we are concerned with standards of merit or with the concept of inherent worth, the claim that humans by their very nature are superior to other species is a groundless claim and, in the light of elements (1), (2), and (3) above, must be rejected as nothing more than an irrational bias in our own favor.

The conjunction of these four ideas constitutes the biocentric outlook on nature. In the remainder of this paper I give a brief account of the first three components, followed by a more detailed analysis of the fourth. I then conclude by indicating how this outlook provides a way of justifying the attitude of respect for nature.

Humans as Members of the Earth's Community of Life

We share with other species a common relationship to the Earth. In accepting the biocentric outlook we take the fact of our being an animal species to be a fundamental feature of our existence. We consider it an essential aspect of "the human condition." We do not deny the differences between ourselves and other species, but we keep in the forefront of our consciousness the fact that in relation to our planet's natural ecosystems we are but one species population among many. Thus we acknowledge our origin in the very same evolutionary process that gave rise to all other species and we recognize ourselves to be confronted with similar environmental challenges to those that confront them. The laws of genetics, of natural selection, and of adaptation apply equally to all of us as biological creatures. In this light we consider ourselves as one with them, not set apart from them. We, as well as they, must face certain basic conditions of existence that impose requirements on us for our survival and well-being. Each animal and plant is like us in having a good of its own. Although our human good (what is of true value in human life, including the exercise of individual autonomy in choosing our own particular value systems) is not like the good of a nonhuman animal or plant, it can no more be realized than their good can without the biological necessities for survival and physical health.

When we look at ourselves from the evolutionary point of view, we see that not only are we very recent arrivals on Earth, but that our emergence as a new species on the planet was originally an event of no particular importance to the entire scheme of things. The Earth was teeming with life long before we appeared. Putting the point metaphorically, we are relative newcomers, entering a home that has been the residence of others for hundreds of millions of years, a home that must now be shared by all of us together.

The comparative brevity of human life on Earth may be vividly depicted by imagining the geological time scale in spatial terms. Suppose we start with algae, which have been around for at least 600 million years. (The earliest protozoa actually predated this by several *billion* years.) If the time that algae have been here were represented by the length of a football field (300 feet), then the period during which sharks have been swimming in the world's oceans and spiders have been spinning their webs would occupy three quarters of the length of the field; reptiles would show up at about the center of the field; mammals would cover the last third of the field; hominids (mammals of the family *Hominidae*) the last two feet; and the species *Homo sapiens* the last six inches.

Whether this newcomer is able to survive as long as other species remains to be seen. But there is surely something presumptuous about the way humans look down on the "lower" animals, especially those that have become extinct. We consider the dinosaurs, for example, to be biological failures, though they existed on our planet for 65 million years. One writer has made the point with beautiful simplicity:

> We sometimes speak of the dinosaurs as failures; there will be time enough for that judgment when we have lasted even for one tenth as long. . . . [2]

The possibility of the extinction of the human species, a possibility which starkly confronts us in the contemporary world, makes us aware of another respect in which we should not consider ourselves privileged beings in relation to other species. This is the fact that the well-being of humans is dependent upon the ecological soundness and health of many plant and animal communities, while their soundness and health does not in the least depend upon human well-being. Indeed, from their standpoint the very existence of humans is quite unnecessary. Every last man, woman, and child could disappear from the face of the Earth without any significant detrimental consequence for the good of wild animals and plants. On the contrary, many of them would be greatly benefited. The destruction of their habitats by human "developments" would cease. The poisoning and polluting of their environment would come to an end. The Earth's land, air, and water would no longer be subject to the degradation they are now undergoing as the result of large-scale technology and uncontrolled population growth. Life communities in natural ecosystems would gradually return to their former healthy state. Tropical forests, for example, would again be able to make their full contribution to a life-sustaining atmosphere for the whole planet. The rivers, lakes, and oceans of the world would (perhaps) eventually become clean again. Spilled oil, plastic trash, and even radioactive waste might finally, after many centuries, cease doing their terrible work. Ecosystems would return to their proper balance, suffering only the disruptions of natural events such as volcanic eruptions and glaciation. From these the community of life could recover, as it has so often done in the past. But the ecological disasters now perpetrated on it by humans – disasters from which it might never recover – these it would no longer have to endure.

If, then, the total, final, absolute extermination of our species (by our own hands?) should take place and if we should not carry all the others with us into oblivion, not only would the Earth's community of life continue to exist, but in all probability its well-being would be enhanced. Our presence, in short, is not needed. If we were to take the standpoint of the community and give voice to its true interest, the ending of our six-inch epoch would most likely be greeted with a hearty "Good riddance!"

The Natural World as an Organic System

To accept the biocentric outlook and regard ourselves and our place in the world from its perspective is to see the whole natural order of the Earth's biosphere as a complex but unified web of interconnected organisms, objects, and events. The ecological relationships between any community of living things and their environment form an organic whole of functionally interdependent parts. Each ecosystem is a small universe itself in which the interactions of its various species populations comprise an intricately woven network of cause–effect relations. Such dynamic but at the same time relatively stable structures as food chains, predator–prey relations, and plant succession in a forest are self-regulating, energy-recycling mechanisms that preserve the equilibrium of the whole.

As far as the well-being of wild animals and plants is concerned, this ecological equilibrium must not be destroyed. The same holds true of the well-being of humans. When one views the realm of nature from the perspective of the biocentric outlook, one never forgets that in the long run the integrity of the entire biosphere of our planet is essential to the realization of the good of its constituent communities of life, both human and nonhuman.

Although the importance of this idea cannot be overemphasized, it is by now so familiar and so widely acknowledged that I shall not further elaborate on it here. However, I do wish to point out that this "holistic" view of the Earth's ecological systems does not itself constitute a moral norm. It is a factual aspect of biological reality, to be understood as a set of causal connections in ordinary empirical terms. Its significance for humans is the same as its significance for nonhumans, namely, in setting basic conditions for the realization of the good of living things. Its ethical implications for our treatment of the natural environment lie en-

tirely in the fact that our *knowledge* of these causal connections is an essential *means* to fulfilling the aims we set for ourselves in adopting the attitude of respect for nature. In addition, its theoretical implications for the ethics of respect for nature lie in the fact that it (along with the other elements of the biocentric outlook) makes the adopting of that attitude a rational and intelligible thing to do.

Individual Organisms as Teleological Centers of Life

As our knowledge of living things increases, as we come to a deeper understanding of their life cycles, their interactions with other organisms, and the manifold ways in which they adjust to the environment, we become more fully aware of how each of them is carrying out its biological functions according to the laws of its species-specific nature. But besides this, our increasing knowledge and understanding also develop in us a sharpened awareness of the uniqueness of each individual organism. Scientists who have made careful studies of particular plants and animals, whether in the field or in laboratories, have often acquired a knowledge of their subjects as identifiable individuals. Close observation over extended periods of time has led them to an appreciation of the unique "personalities" of their subjects. Sometimes a scientist may come to take a special interest in a particular animal or plant, all the while remaining strictly objective in the gathering and recording of data. Nonscientists may likewise experience this development of interest when, as amateur naturalists, they make accurate observations over sustained periods of close acquaintance with an individual organism. As one becomes more and more familiar with the organism and its behavior, one becomes fully sensitive to the particular way it is living out its life cycle. One may become fascinated by it and even experience some involvement with its good and bad fortunes (that is, with the occurrence of environmental conditions favorable or unfavorable to the realization of its good). The organism comes to mean something to one as a unique, irreplaceable individual. The final culmination of this process is the achievement of a genuine understanding of its point of view and, with that understanding, an ability to "take" that point of view. *Conceiving of it as a center of life, one is able to look at the world from its perspective.*

This development from objective knowledge to the recognition of individuality, and from the recognition of individuality to full awareness of an organism's standpoint, is a process of heightening our consciousness of what it means to be an individual living thing. We grasp the particularity of the organism as a teleological center of life, striving to preserve itself and to realize its own good in its own unique way.

It is to be noted that we need not be falsely anthropomorphizing when we conceive of individual plants and animals in this manner. Understanding them as teleological centers of life does not necessitate "reading into" them human characteristics. We need not, for example, consider them to have consciousness. Some of them may be aware of the world around them and others may not. Nor need we deny that different kinds and levels of awareness are exemplified when consciousness in some form is present. But conscious or not, all are equally teleological centers of life in the sense that each is a unified system of goal-oriented activities directed toward their preservation and well-being.

When considered from an ethical point of view, a teleological center of life is an entity whose "world" can be viewed from the perspective of *its* life. In looking at the world from that perspective we recognize objects and events occurring in its life as being beneficent, maleficent, or indifferent. The first are occurrences which increase its powers to preserve its existence and realize its good. The second decrease or destroy those powers. The third have neither of these effects on the entity. With regard to our human role as moral agents, we can conceive of a teleological center of life as a being whose standpoint we can take in making judgments about what events in the world are good or evil, desirable or undesirable. In making those judgments it is what promotes or protects the being's own good, not what benefits moral agents themselves, that sets the standard of evaluation. Such judgments can be made about anything that happens to the entity which is favorable or unfavorable in relation to its good. As was pointed out earlier, the entity itself need not have any (conscious) *interest* in what is happening to it for such judgments to be meaningful and true.

It is precisely judgments of this sort that we are disposed to make when we take the attitude of respect for nature. In adopting that attitude those judgments are given weight as reasons for action in our practical deliberation. They become morally relevant facts in the guidance of our conduct.

The Denial of Human Superiority

This fourth component of the biocentric outlook on nature is the single most important idea in establishing the justifiability of the attitude of respect for nature. Its central role is due to the special relationship it bears to the first three components of the outlook. This relationship will be brought out after the concept of human superiority is examined and analyzed.[3]

In what sense are humans alleged to be superior to other animals? We are different from them in having certain capacities that they lack. But why should these capacities be a mark of superiority? From what point of view are they judged to be signs of superiority and what sense of superiority is meant? After all, various nonhuman species have capacities that humans lack. There is the speed of a cheetah, the vision of an eagle, the agility of a monkey. Why should not these be taken as signs of *their* superiority over humans?

One answer that comes immediately to mind is that these capacities are not as *valuable* as the human capacities that are claimed to make us superior. Such uniquely human characteristics as rational thought, aesthetic creativity, autonomy and self-determination, and moral freedom, it might be held, have a higher value than the capacities found in other species. Yet we must ask: valuable to whom, and on what grounds?

The human characteristics mentioned are all valuable to humans. They are essential to the preservation and enrichment of our civilization and culture. Clearly it is from the human standpoint that they are being judged to be desirable and good. It is not difficult here to recognize a begging of the question. Humans are claiming human superiority from a strictly human point of view, that is, from a point of view in which the good of humans is taken as the standard of judgment. All we need to do is to look at the capacities of nonhuman animals (or plants, for that matter) from the standpoint of *their* good to find a contrary judgment of superiority. The speed of the cheetah, for example, is a sign of its superiority to humans when considered from the standpoint of the good of its species. If it were as slow a runner as a human, it would not be able to survive. And so for all the other abilities of nonhumans which further their good but which are lacking in humans. In each case the claim to human superiority would be rejected from a nonhuman standpoint.

When superiority assertions are interpreted in this way, they are based on judgments of *merit*. To judge the merits of a person or an organism one must apply grading or ranking standards to it. (As I show below, this distinguishes judgments of merit from judgments of inherent worth.) Empirical investigation then determines whether it has the "good-making properties" (merits) in virtue of which it fulfills the standards being applied. In the case of humans, merits may be either moral or nonmoral. We can judge one person to be better than (superior to) another from the moral point of view by applying certain standards to their character and conduct. Similarly, we can appeal to nonmoral criteria in judging someone to be an excellent piano player, a fair cook, a poor tennis player, and so on. Different social purposes and roles are implicit in the making of such judgments, providing the frame of reference for the choice of standards by which the nonmoral merits of people are determined. Ultimately such purposes and roles stem from a society's way of life as a whole. Now a society's way of life may be thought of as the cultural form given to the realization of human values. Whether moral or nonmoral standards are being applied, then, all judgments of people's merits finally depend on human values. All are made from an exclusively human standpoint.

The question that naturally arises at this juncture is: why should standards that are based on human values be assumed to be the only valid criteria of merit and hence the only true signs of superiority? This question is especially pressing when humans are being judged superior in merit to nonhumans. It is true that a human being may be a better mathematician than a monkey, but the monkey may be a better tree climber than a human being. If we humans value mathematics more than tree climbing, that is because our conception of civilized life makes the development of mathematical ability more desirable than the ability to climb trees. But is it not

unreasonable to judge nonhumans by the values of human civilization, rather than by values connected with what it is for a member of *that* species to live a good life? If all living things have a good of their own, it at least makes sense to judge the merits of nonhumans by standards derived from *their* good. To use only standards based on human values is already to commit oneself to holding that humans are superior to nonhumans, which is the point in question.

A further logical flaw arises in connection with the widely held conviction that humans are *morally* superior beings because they possess, while others lack, the capacities of a moral agent (free will, accountability, deliberation, judgment, practical reason). This view rests on a conceptual confusion. As far as moral standards are concerned, only beings that have the capacities of a moral agent can properly be judged to be *either* moral (morally good) *or* immoral (morally deficient). Moral standards are simply not applicable to beings that lack such capacities. Animals and plants cannot therefore be said to be morally inferior in merit to humans. Since the only beings that can have moral merits *or be deficient in such merits* are moral agents, it is conceptually incoherent to judge humans as superior to nonhumans on the ground that humans have moral capacities while nonhumans don't.

Up to this point I have been interpreting the claim that humans are superior to other living things as a grading or ranking judgment regarding their comparative merits. There is, however, another way of understanding the idea of human superiority. According to this interpretation, humans are superior to nonhumans not as regards their merits but as regards their inherent worth. Thus the claim of human superiority is to be understood as asserting that all humans, simply in virtue of their humanity, have *a greater inherent worth* than other living things.

The inherent worth of an entity does not depend on its merits.[4] To consider something as possessing inherent worth, we have seen, is to place intrinsic value on the realization of its good. This is done regardless of whatever particular merits it might have or might lack, as judged by a set of grading or ranking standards. In human affairs, we are all familiar with the principle that one's worth as a person does not vary with one's merits or lack of merits. The same can hold true of animals and plants. To regard such entities as possessing inherent worth entails disregarding their merits and deficiencies, whether they are being judged from a human standpoint or from the standpoint of their own species.

The idea of one entity having more merit than another, and so being superior to it in merit, makes perfectly good sense. Merit is a grading or ranking concept, and judgments of comparative merit are based on the different degrees to which things satisfy a given standard. But what can it mean to talk about one thing being superior to another in inherent worth? In order to get at what is being asserted in such a claim it is helpful first to look at the social origin of the concept of degrees of inherent worth.

The idea that humans can possess different degrees of inherent worth originated in societies having rigid class structures. Before the rise of modern democracies with their egalitarian outlook, one's membership in a hereditary class determined one's social status. People in the upper classes were looked up to, while those in the lower classes were looked down upon. In such a society one's social superiors and social inferiors were clearly defined and easily recognized.

Two aspects of these class-structured societies are especially relevant to the idea of degrees of inherent worth. First, those born into the upper classes were deemed more worthy of respect than those born into the lower orders. Second, the superior worth of upper class people had nothing to do with their merits nor did the inferior worth of those in the lower classes rest on their lack of merits. One's superiority or inferiority entirely derived from a social position one was born into. The modern concept of a meritocracy simply did not apply. One could not advance into a higher class by any sort of moral or nonmoral achievement. Similarly, an aristocrat held his title and all the privileges that went with it just because he was the eldest son of a titled nobleman. Unlike the bestowing of knighthood in contemporary Great Britain, one did not earn membership in the nobility by meritorious conduct.

We who live in modern democracies no longer believe in such hereditary social distinctions. Indeed, we would wholeheartedly condemn them on moral grounds as being fundamentally unjust. We have come to think of class systems as a paradigm of social injustice, it being a central principle of the democratic way of life that among humans there are no superiors and no inferiors. Thus we have rejected the whole conceptual framework in which people are judged to have different degrees of inherent worth. That idea is incompatible with our notion of human equality based on the doctrine that all humans, simply in virtue of their humanity, have the same inherent worth. (The belief in universal human rights is one form that this egalitarianism takes.)

The vast majority of people in modern democracies, however, do not maintain an egalitarian outlook when it comes to comparing human beings with other living things. Most people consider our own species to be superior to all other species and this superiority is understood to be a matter of inherent worth, not merit. There may exist thoroughly vicious and depraved humans who lack all merit. Yet because they are human they are thought to belong to a higher class of entities than any plant or animal. That one is born into the species *Homo sapiens* entitles one to have lordship over those who are one's inferiors, namely, those born into other species. The parallel with hereditary social classes is very close. Implicit in this view is a hierarchical conception of nature according to which an organism has a position of superiority or inferiority in the Earth's community of life simply on the basis of its genetic background. The "lower" orders of life are looked down upon and it is considered perfectly proper that they serve the interests of those belonging to the highest order, namely humans. The intrinsic value we place on the well-being of our fellow humans reflects our recognition of their rightful position as our equals. No such intrinsic value is to be placed on the good of other animals, unless we choose to do so out of fondness or affection for them. But their well-being imposes no moral requirement on us. In this respect there is an absolute difference in moral status between ourselves and them.

This is the structure of concepts and beliefs that people are committed to insofar as they regard humans to be superior in inherent worth to all other species. I now wish to argue that this structure of concepts and beliefs is completely groundless. If we accept the first three components of the biocentric outlook and from that perspective look at the major philosophical traditions which have supported that structure, we find it to be at bottom nothing more than the expression of an irrational bias in our own favor. The philosophical traditions themselves rest on very questionable assumptions or else simply beg the question. I briefly consider three of the main traditions to substantiate the point. These are classical Greek humanism, Cartesian dualism, and the Judeo-Christian concept of the Great Chain of Being.

The inherent superiority of humans over other species was implicit in the Greek definition of man as a rational animal. Our animal nature was identified with "brute" desires that need the order and restraint of reason to rule them (just as reason is the special virtue of those who rule in the ideal state). Rationality was then seen to be the key to our superiority over animals. It enables us to live on a higher plane and endows us with a nobility and worth that other creatures lack. This familiar way of comparing humans with other species is deeply ingrained in our Western philosophical outlook. The point to consider here is that this view does not actually provide an argument *for* human superiority but rather makes explicit the framework of thought that is implicitly used by those who think of humans as inherently superior to nonhumans. The Greeks who held that humans, in virtue of their rational capacities, have a kind of worth greater than that of any nonrational being, never looked at rationality as but one capacity of living things among many others. But when we consider rationality from the standpoint of the first three elements of the ecological outlook, we see that its value lies in its importance for *human* life. Other creatures achieve their species-specific good without the need of rationality, although they often make use of capacities that humans lack. So the humanistic outlook of classical Greek thought does not give us a neutral (non-question-begging) ground on which to construct a scale of degrees of inherent worth possessed by different species of living things.

The second tradition, centering on the Cartesian dualism of soul and body, also fails to justify the claim to human superiority. That superiority is supposed to derive from the fact that we have souls while animals do not. Animals are mere automata and lack the divine element that makes us spiritual beings. I won't go into the now familiar criticisms of this two-substance view. I only add the point that, even if humans are composed of an immaterial, unextended soul and a material, extended body, this in itself is not a reason to deem them of greater worth than entities that are only bodies. Why is a soul substance a thing that adds value to its possessor? Unless some theological reasoning is offered here (which many, including

myself, would find unacceptable on epistemological grounds), no logical connection is evident. An immaterial something which thinks is better than a material something which does not think only if thinking itself has value, either intrinsically or instrumentally. Now it is intrinsically valuable to humans alone, who value it as an end in itself, and it is instrumentally valuable to those who benefit from it, namely humans.

For animals that neither enjoy thinking for its own sake nor need it for living the kind of life for which they are best adapted, it has no value. Even if "thinking" is broadened to include all forms of consciousness, there are still many living things that can do without it and yet live what is for their species a good life. The anthropocentricity underlying the claim to human superiority runs throughout Cartesian dualism.

A third major source of the idea of human superiority is the Judeo-Christian concept of the Great Chain of Being. Humans are superior to animals and plants because their Creator has given them a higher place on the chain. It begins with God at the top, and then moves to the angels, who are lower than God but higher than humans, then to humans, positioned between the angels and the beasts (partaking of the nature of both), and then on down to the lower levels occupied by nonhuman animals, plants, and finally inanimate objects. Humans, being "made in God's image," are inherently superior to animals and plants by virtue of their being closer (in their essential nature) to God.

The metaphysical and epistemological difficulties with this conception of a hierarchy of entities are, in my mind, insuperable. Without entering into this matter here, I only point out that if we are unwilling to accept the metaphysics of traditional Judaism and Christianity, we are again left without good reasons for holding to the claim of inherent human superiority.

The foregoing considerations (and others like them) leave us with but one ground for the assertion that a human being, regardless of merit, is a higher kind of entity than any other living thing. This is the mere fact of the genetic makeup of the species *Homo sapiens*. But this is surely irrational and arbitrary. Why should the arrangement of genes of a certain type be a mark of superior value, especially when this fact about an organism is taken by itself, unrelated to any other aspect of its life? We might just as well refer to any other genetic makeup as a ground of superior value.

Clearly we are confronted here with a wholly arbitrary claim that can only be explained as an irrational bias in our own favor.

That the claim is nothing more than a deep-seated prejudice is brought home to us when we look at our relation to other species in the light of the first three elements of the biocentric outlook. Those elements taken conjointly give us a certain overall view of the natural world and of the place of humans in it. When we take this view we come to understand other living things, their environmental conditions, and their ecological relationships in such a way as to awake in us a deep sense of our kinship with them as fellow members of the Earth's community of life. Humans and nonhumans alike are viewed together as integral parts of one unified whole in which all living things are functionally interrelated. Finally, when our awareness focuses on the individual lives of plants and animals, each is seen to share with us the characteristic of being a teleological center of life striving to realize its own good in its own good in its own unique way.

As this entire belief system becomes part of the conceptual framework through which we understand and perceive the world, we come to see ourselves as bearing a certain moral relation to nonhuman forms of life. Our ethical role in nature takes on a new significance. We begin to look at other species as we look at ourselves, seeing them as beings which have a good they are striving to realize just as we have a good we are striving to realize. We accordingly develop the disposition to view the world from the standpoint of their good as well as from the standpoint of our own good. Now if the groundlessness of the claim that humans are inherently superior to other species were brought clearly before our minds, we would not remain intellectually neutral toward that claim but would reject it as being fundamentally at variance with our total world outlook. In the absence of any good reasons for holding it, the assertion of human superiority would then appear simply as the expression of an irrational and self-serving prejudice that favors one particular species over several million others.

Rejecting the notion of human superiority entails its positive counterpart: the doctrine of species impartiality. One who accepts that doctrine regards all living things as possessing inherent worth – the *same* inherent worth, since no one species has been shown to be either "higher" or "lower" than any other. Now we saw earlier that, insofar as one thinks of a living thing as possessing inherent worth, one considers it to be the appropriate object of the attitude of respect and believes that attitude to be the only fitting or suitable one for all moral agents to take toward it.

Here, then, is the key to understanding how the attitude of respect is rooted in the biocentric outlook on nature. The basic connection is made through the denial of human superiority. Once we reject the claim that humans are superior either in merit or in worth to other living things, we are ready to adopt the attitude of respect. The denial of human superiority is itself the result of taking the perspective on nature built into the first three elements of the biocentric outlook.

Now the first three elements of the biocentric outlook, it seems clear, would be found acceptable to any rational and scientifically informed thinker who is fully "open" to the reality of the lives of nonhuman organisms. Without denying our distinctively human characteristics, such a thinker can acknowledge the fundamental respects in which we are members of the Earth's community of life and in which the biological conditions necessary for the realization of our human values are inextricably linked with the whole system of nature. In addition, the conception of individual living things as teleological centers of life simply articulates how a scientifically informed thinker comes to understand them as the result of increasingly careful and detailed observations. Thus, the biocentric outlook recommends itself as an acceptable system of concepts and beliefs to anyone who is clear-minded, unbiased, and factually enlightened, and who has a developed capacity of reality awareness with regard to the lives of individual organisms. This, I submit, is as good a reason for making the moral commitment involved in adopting the attitude of respect for nature as any theory of environmental ethics could possibly have.

Moral Rights and the Matter of Competing Claims

I have not asserted anywhere in the foregoing account that animals or plants have moral rights. This omission was deliberate. I do not think that the reference class of the concept, bearer of moral rights, should be extended to include nonhuman living things. My reasons for taking this position, however, go beyond the scope of this paper. I

Paul W. Taylor

believe I have been able to accomplish many of the same ends which those who ascribe rights to animals or plants wish to accomplish. There is no reason, moreover, why plants and animals, including whole species populations and life communities, cannot be accorded *legal* rights under my theory. To grant them legal protection could be interpreted as giving them legal entitlement to be protected, and this, in fact, would be a means by which a society that subscribed to the ethics of respect for nature could give public recognition to their inherent worth.

There remains the problem of competing claims, even when wild plants and animals are not thought of as bearers of moral rights. If we accept the biocentric outlook and accordingly adopt the attitude of respect for nature as our ultimate moral attitude, how do we resolve conflicts that arise from our respect for persons in the domain of human ethics and our respect for nature in the domain of environmental ethics? This is a question that cannot adequately be dealt with here. My main purpose in this paper has been to try to establish a base point from which we can start working toward a solution to the problem. I have shown why we cannot just begin with an initial presumption in favor of the interests of our own species. It is after all within our power as moral beings to place limits on human population and technology with the deliberate intention of sharing the Earth's bounty with other species. That such sharing is an ideal difficult to realize even in an approximate way does not take away its claim to our deepest moral commitment.

Notes

1 See W. K. Frankena, "Ethics and the Environment," in K. E. Goodpaster and K. M. Sayre, eds., *Ethics and Problems of the 21st Century* (Notre Dame: University of Notre Dame Press, 1979), pp. 3–20. I critically examine Frankena's views in "Frankena on Environmental Ethics," *Monist*, Vol. 64, No. 3 (July 1981), pp. 313–24.

2 Stephen R. L. Clark, *The Moral Status of Animals* (Oxford: Clarendon Press, 1977), pp. 112.

3 My criticisms of the dogma of human superiority gain independent support from a carefully reasoned essay by R. and V. Routley showing the many logical weaknesses in arguments for human-centered theories of environmental ethics. R. and V. Routley, "Against the Inevitability of Human Chauvinism," in K. E. Goodpaster and K. M. Sayre, eds., *Ethics and Problems of the 21st Century* (Notre Dame: University of Notre Dame Press, 1979), pp. 36–59.

4 For this way of distinguishing between merit and inherent worth, I am indebted to Gregory Vlastos, "Justice and Equality," in R. Brandt, ed., *Social Justice* (Englewood Cliffs, NJ: Prentice-Hall, 1962), pp. 31–72.

7

Is There a Place for Animals in the Moral Consideration of Nature?

Eric Katz

I

The compatibility of an "animal liberation" ethic and an environmental ethic depends primarily on how one interprets the meaning and moral structure of a theory of environmental ethics. In part this is because the meaning and moral structure of an animal liberation ethic is fairly straightforward: it focuses on the absence of morally relevant differences between humans and animals, and on the moral significance of animal pain and suffering.[1] But the form of an environmental ethic is not so clear. Does an environmental ethic advocate moral concern for natural individuals, for species, for ecosystems, or perhaps for nature as a whole? An answer to this question is required before one can judge the relationship between animal liberation and environmental ethics, but an answer, unfortunately, is not easily discernible. In what follows I will argue, first, that several versions of an environmental ethic yield problematic environmental and moral conclusions; second, that an environmental ethic must be interpreted as a complex balancing of different kinds of moral concern – i.e., moral concern for individuals, for species, and for natural ecosystems – and third, that this balancing will produce moral results that are troubling to the advocate of an animal liberation ethic.

An analysis of the form of an environmental ethic can proceed most easily if the potential objects for moral concern are divided into three major groups: individuals, species, and ecosyste-mic communities. Thus one interpretation of an environmental ethic will hold that moral obligations, duties, or rules are applicable to all natural individuals – animals, plants, bodies of water, soil, rocks, minerals, etc. Another interpretation of an environmental ethic will consider natural species as the proper object of moral concern. A final interpretation of an environmental ethic will hold that moral concepts are applicable to ecosystems or natural communities as a whole. Restricting the discussion to these possibilities will greatly facilitate the analysis, and the cost in terms of conceptual clarity will not be significant. The form of an environmental ethic that considers obligations to nature as a whole, for example, can easily be assimilated into the ecosystemic interpretation, once one considers the earth's biosphere as one large and complex ecosystemic community.

In analyzing the meaning and form of an environmental ethic, two central points need to be considered. First, is the formal structure of the ethic coherent, reasonable, and in general agreement with normal ethical practice? Of course an environmental ethic is different from traditional ethical theories that consider only human actions, concerns, and institutions the primary objects of moral value – but nonetheless, an environmental ethic cannot be so radically different from traditional ethical theories that it defies credibility. It must be a plausible revision in the meaning and justification of moral concepts. Second, the interpretation of an environmental ethic must be in accord with the general policies of environmentalism, i.e., of environmental protection. Although it might seem strange to cite this as a significant consideration in the analysis of an environmental ethic – isn't it obvious that an environmental ethic is in accord with a policy of environmentalism? – the fact is that certain interpretations of the meaning of an environmental ethic actually undermine environmentalist principles. These interpretations of an environmental ethic will thus be rejected on the practical ground that they fail to achieve the goal of environmental protection.

II

Perhaps the most obvious interpretation of an environmental ethic is the moral consideration of the ecosystem, or the natural community as a whole. Aldo Leopold's oft-quoted definition of the moral rightness of human environmental action is generally used as a thematic signpost for this position: "A thing is right when it tends to preserve the integrity, stability, and beauty of the biotic community. It is wrong when it tends otherwise."[2] J. Baird Callicott and Don Marietta, Jr., have each argued for this model of an environmental ethic. Callicott describes Leopold's vision in this way: "the good of the biotic *community* is the ultimate measure of the moral value, the rightness or wrongness, of actions." Or in other words: "the effect upon ecological systems is the decisive factor in the determination of the ethical quality of actions."[3] Similarly, Marietta writes that "morally acceptable treatment of the environment is that which does not upset the integrity of the ecosystem as it is seen in a diversity of life forms existing in a dynamic and complex but stable interdependency."[4] Thus, in this version of an environmental ethic, the natural ecosystem or community is the primary object of moral concern. The morality of human deliberative action will be judged by various criteria of ecosystemic goodness – the stability, integrity, health, and diversity of the natural biotic community. Actions which affect an ecosystem as a whole – e.g., the damming of a river, the clearing of forest land, the draining of a marsh – will be morally judged by their relation to ecological concepts concerning the entire natural community under consideration. Even actions directed towards individual natural entities will be judged by ecosystemic criteria: shooting a deer or chopping down a single tree will be morally evaluated by the effect the action has on the natural community.

A number of comments can be made about this interpretation of an environmental ethic. First, it is clear that this model of moral concern in an environmental ethic is incompatible, as such, with an ethic of animal liberation. An ethic which evaluates action in terms of communal health and stability cannot be seriously interested in the welfare of individual entities – such as animals – unless these individuals are particularly important to communal functions. As Bryan Norton has recently argued, "the relationship between the individual interests of organisms, individual plants, and nonliving objects, on the one hand, and the healthy functioning and integrity of the ecosystem, on the other hand, is a contingent one."[5] The overall healthy functioning of the natural community may require the death, destruction, or suffering of individual natural entities, animals included. From the perspective of the natural community, the sacrifice of individual entities may be the morally correct course of action. Callicott thus argues that a major thesis of an animal liberation ethic – the moral significance of the suffering of animals – is irrelevant in the moral evaluations of an ecosystemic environmental ethic. "Pain and pleasure seem to have nothing at all to do with good and evil if our appraisal is taken from the vantage point of ecological biology . . . If nature as a whole is good, then pain and death are also good."[6] Or rather, if the well-being of the natural community or ecosystem is the primary good of moral judgment, then pain and death that contributes to this overall good cannot be judged as a moral evil, as an animal liberation ethic would require. Because an animal liberation ethic is concerned with the welfare of individual animals, while a community-based environmental ethic may require the sacrifice of individual animals, the two ethical systems cannot be compatible.

The second point to notice about the interpretation of an environmental ethic that focuses on the natural community is that it may also require the suffering or death of human individuals. The attempt to determine the moral worth of animals in a system of environmental ethics includes the determination of the moral worth of human beings. Callicott, again, notes that in an environmental ethic "the moral worth of individuals (including, n.b., human individuals) is relative, to be assessed in accordance with the particular relation of each to the collective entity," i.e., the natural community.[7] Thus, humans are not to be given their traditionally special moral status based on rationality, moral autonomy, or whatever. Instead, human individuals, just as all other natural entities, will be morally evaluated by their contribution to the welfare, the healthy functioning, of the natural community. This revision of the traditional lofty moral status of human individuals is a source of serious criticism of an environmental ethic. Why, it might be argued, should humans accept a system of moral rules that may require harmful consequences to human individuals or human projects and institutions? One need only consider the existence of species – such as the smallpox virus or disease-bearing mosquitoes – which threaten human individuals. Must the species still be protected at the cost of human life? It does no good to respond to this criticism by arguing that in the long run restricting human activity or sacrificing human individuals for the protection of the natural community will benefit human society. Although this is a popular argument of many environmentalists, it is only a contingent possibility. Indeed, a different point seems more probable: since the primary goal of moral action is the good of the natural community, and since human technology and population growth create many of the threats to environmental health, an environmental ethic may demand the elimination of much of the human race and human civilization. This consideration casts serious doubts on the plausibility of the environmental ethic based on the welfare of the natural community as a whole.

The only possible method of defending an environmental ethic from this criticism is to insist that human life and institutions are part of the natural community whose good is the primary end of all action. Human flourishing is important because it is an essential component of the natural community. An environmental ethic that *excluded* humans from the natural community would clearly threaten the continuation of all human projects and activities – whatever humans did would have an adverse effect on the moral unit, the natural community. An environmental ethic that excluded humans from the natural community, for example, would prohibit humans from filling in a small marsh area in order to expand a pre-existing housing development on its border. But an environmental ethic that considers human well-being as *part* of the natural community (not, of course, the supreme part), as part of the moral end of action, *might* permit the expansion of the housing development after a comparison of the benefits and harms to the human population and the natural environment (the marsh).

At best, however, including humans in the natural community is only a partial deflection of the criticism of an environmental ethic based on its anti-human tendencies. An environmental ethic with an appropriate perspective on the place of humanity in the natural system will save a few human projects and activities, but it will still require major changes in human activity, major human sacrifices for the sake of the overall community. Unfortunately, specifying these changes and sacrifices by means of concrete examples is a difficult – and perhaps impossible – task. The making of environmental decisions is not a job for the armchair philosopher: a proper environmental decision requires a multitude of scientific and sociological data as a factual basis. Nevertheless, even if humans are included in the natural community so that their interests are taken into account in the determination of communal well-being, it should be clear that dumping toxic pollutants into a lake – a lake that is not used in any other way by humans – would be a moral evil, an injury to the natural environment. Whether humans would be permitted to dam a river for electrical power is a more problematic case, since the harm to the natural environment as a whole is less severe; in this kind of case specific facts would be needed to make the moral determination. The crucial point to remember is that this form of an environmental ethic claims that humans are no different than any other species; the measure of their worth and the worth of their activities is decided by the overall well-being of the natural community. If I plan to dig a well on my property in the country I will have to consider the effect of my drawing water not only on my human neighbors and their water supplies, but also on the surrounding countryside and its nonhuman inhabitants. An environmental ethic thus requires a major revision in traditional human moral practice. In an environmental ethic moral decisions transcend inter-human relationships to consider the natural community as a whole. Moral decisions cannot be made by simply considering consequences to human life. But this revision in moral practice is not easily granted; humans must relinquish their special place in the moral universe. Thus an environmental ethic may not be acceptable to humans because it implausibly revises traditional moral practice.

A final comment concerning this interpretation of an environmental ethic undermines its validity even more. The fact is that an environmental ethic that considers the overall well-being of the community as the primary goal of all action cannot explain the moral rightness of all the policies desired by the contemporary environmentalist movement. This version of an environmental ethic is unable to explain the protection of rare and endangered species, species so threatened that they play little or no part in the ecology of their natural communities. In this regard, Lilly-Marlene Russow cites as an example the David deer, a species now preserved only in zoos, a species whose original habitat or natural ecosystem is unknown to humanity.[8] Similarly, the snail darter or the bald eagle are examples of species which have little or no ecological function in their natural habitats. In a sense, then, these species are not members of the natural community, not functioning parts of the ecological system. Their preservation, therefore, cannot be guaranteed by simply securing the moral goal of communal or ecosystemic well-being. An environmental ethic designed to treat communal welfare as the primary good cannot explain the preservation of species so rare that they no longer serve an ecological function. But since the preservation of rare species is an important goal of environmentalists, this interpretation of an environmental ethic must be rejected.

The problem of the role of endangered species in ecological communities leads to a second possible interpretation of an environmental ethic: perhaps an environmental ethic is an ethical system that considers species as the primary object of moral concern. An advocate of this version of an environmental ethic could argue then that rare and endangered species ought to be preserved because natural species are the primary recipients of moral obligation. Destroying a species would be morally wrong, because it is equivalent to the traditional prohibition against killing an individual human being. In addition, a species-based environmental ethic could also explain obligations to ecological communities as a whole, since these communities contain species of living things or they are the habitats necessary for the survival of species. This interpretation of an environmental ethic might therefore be more attuned to the needs of the environmentalist, i.e., to the protection of rare and endangered species and the preservation of natural ecological communities and habitats.

The first point to notice about this "species" interpretation of an environmental ethic is that, like the community model, it is basically incompatible with an animal liberation ethic. Although it restricts moral concern to a much smaller group of entities than the natural community, it still focuses on a *collection* of entities rather than on individuals. Since the primary moral goal is the well-being and survival of species, the pain or death of individual members of the species is of secondary importance. It may be necessary, for example, to manage or "harvest" an animal species that is overpopulating an area and threatening its own food supply. The death (even if painless) of individual animals in order to insure the continuance of the entire species would be a moral evil in a system of animal liberation ethics.

In addition, there are conceptual problems with this interpretation of an environmental ethic. In a practical sense, the moral consideration of species does not provide direct reasons for the protection of the nonliving environmental background, the natural objects that form the material structure of ecosystems. Environmentalists, for example, seek the preservation of beautiful natural rock formations, free-flowing rivers, and undeveloped wetlands. They seek this preservation, not simply because of the life forms which live in and around these natural areas, but because of some direct interest in the nonliving objects themselves. But this concern for nonliving natural objects cannot be explained by a moral consideration of species.

A more serious problem is the justification of an environmental ethic that focuses on species as the primary object of moral consideration. Why should species count so much? Why should species be so important? Joel Feinberg, for one, discounts species entirely as the proper objects of direct moral concern: "A whole collection, as such, cannot have beliefs, expectations, wants, or desires ... Individual elephants can have interests, but the species elephant cannot."[9] For Feinberg, at least, an entity without interests cannot have moral rights or be an object of moral consideration. Now although I am not suggesting agreement with Feinberg's views, he does emphasize the *oddity* of considering a whole species a morally relevant entity. Indeed, this interpretation of an environmental ethic has rather an *ad hoc* aura to it: since environmentalists desire the protection of rare and endangered species, they create an ethic that considers species in themselves as morally valuable. But on what can this moral value be based? Either a species is important because it fulfills an ecological function in the natural community, in which case the community model of an environmental ethic will explain its preservation; or a species is important because the individual members of the species are valuable, in which case an individualistic model of an environmental ethic will explain the act of preservation.[10] In itself, a species-based environmental ethic seems to be an uneasy, groundless compromise between the broad view that the natural community is the environmentally appropriate moral object and the narrow view that natural individuals are themselves the bearers of moral worth.[11]

Thus one arrives at the third interpretation of an environmental ethic: an environmental ethic is a system of ethical rules and obligations pertaining to individual natural entities directly. Natural entities have moral value in themselves, and so they must be protected by environmentally correct policies of action. Human deliberative action will be morally evaluated by its relationship to the individual natural entities in the environment. Draining a marsh or damming a river will be judged by the effects produced on the individual entities in these natural areas. The ecosystem or natural community as a whole will be protected because the individuals who make up the community will be protected in themselves. At first glance, this interpretation has much to recommend it. It has a structure similar to traditional moral theories that consider human individuals the primary objects of moral concern. Since natural individuals are being considered, there is no need to introduce peculiar ontological questions about the interests or desires of collections or communities. Moreover, Leopold suggests an analogy with various historical extensions of moral consideration and rights to groups of human individuals: blacks, women, children, etc.[12] And Christopher Stone has argued that the legal concept of guardianship can be used to provide this moral conception with a substantive content: i.e., the consideration of individual natural entities as the beneficiaries (in themselves) of human action.[13] In sum, the third interpretation of an environmental ethic considers natural entities in themselves, as individuals, the proper objects of moral concern to

whom moral rules and obligations apply. As morally valuable entities they deserve protection and preservation.

Several comments can also be made about this version of an environmental ethic. First, it is clear that this environmental ethic is the most similar to an ethic dealing with the moral status of animals. An animal liberation ethic considers the moral worth of animals in themselves as individuals; this individualistic environmental ethic considers the moral worth of all natural entities. An animal liberation ethic considers as morally relevant certain properties of the animals themselves – e.g., sentience – rather than merely the relationship the animals have to morally "superior" autonomous humans. Animals have intrinsic or inherent value based on some aspect of their existence and not simply an instrumental value for humans. Similarly, an individualistic environmental ethic considers natural entities as inherently valuable because of some objective property they possess in themselves; they are not valuable simply because of their instrumental value to human society and human interests.[14] Thus an environmental ethic conceived on the model of individual rights or moral consideration for natural objects is most similar to an animal liberation ethic; the two ethical theories have identical formal structures.

But there are problems with this version of an environmental ethic. As with the species-based interpretation of an environmental ethic, the problem of justification proves to be insolvable. If one grants that an environmental ethic must find some objective property of natural entities as the source of intrinsic moral value, then one is hard pressed to discover a coherent and plausible candidate. Clearly, the criterion most often chosen by advocates of an animal liberation ethic, sentience or the ability to feel pleasure and pain, is largely irrelevant to an ethic that considers the moral significance of plants and other natural entities that do not feel pain and pleasure. Kenneth Goodpaster has thus argued for the moral considerability of all living entities, and he makes a powerful case in that he does not argue for the moral equivalence of all such living beings.[15] Nevertheless, a reverence for all life criterion cannot justify an environmental ethic. Even assuming that a non-arbitrary or unbiased scale of moral worth could be developed to show when it was morally acceptable to kill other forms of life (Goodpaster, e.g., postpones this extremely difficult task), the ethical consideration of all living entities does not extend the moral boundaries far enough. An environmental ethic that is true to the principles of environmentalism must be able to explain the moral consideration of nonliving natural entities as well as living ones. An environmental ethic that considers the moral worth of all natural entities is considering rocks, bodies of water, and the shifting sands of a beach to be morally considerable. This moral consideration cannot be based on the moral criterion of life, since these natural entities are not alive. On what, then, can the moral consideration be based?

It is at this juncture that one begins to question the entire plan of finding a morally relevant property of all natural objects as the basis of an environmental ethic. As even Goodpaster discovers, in a revision of his earlier views, the extension of moral consideration beyond humans reaches a "breaking point" where talk of morally relevant interests and properties seems highly implausible.[16] The breaking point, of course, is the moral consideration of inanimate natural objects. Can rocks or streams be morally considerable? Unless one postulates an ethical doctrine of the sacredness of all nature, there does not seem to be any method of justifying the moral worth of individual non-living natural entities. But a doctrine of the sacredness of all nature is highly problematic. Does it mean, for example, that disease organisms or disease-carrying insects cannot be exterminated? What about domesticated animals and plants? Do these require an additional moral principle? Basically, the idea that an individual natural nonliving entity has inherent moral worth is too implausible to be seriously considered. Although one may wish to develop a theory that will protect all animals and plants, a moral criterion based on all of natural existence is so broad that it excludes virtually nothing.

The problem with inanimate natural entities forces a return to a community or ecosystemic approach to an environmental ethic. Only if nonliving natural entities are considered as ecologically significant parts of a natural community can they be plausibly judged as morally worthwhile. They do not possess intrinsic or inherent value as such, but as functioning parts of a morally valued natural community. The analysis has thus returned to its starting point, and with disappointing results: all of the interpretations of an environmental ethic considered so far prove to be problematic.

III

Despite the problems encountered in all three of the interpretations of an environmental ethic, it may be feasible to attempt some kind of compromise or combination of the various alternatives. Perhaps a blending of the differing interpretations will yield an environmental ethic that combines the strong points of each version and avoids the implausibilities and areas of contention and criticism. Therefore, I would like to suggest the following version of an environmental ethic, as an outline of a comprehensive and plausible system of ethics to insure the protection of the natural environment.

A meaningful and practical environmental ethic must be composed of two principles or two kinds of moral consideration. The primary form of moral consideration is the moral regard for the ecosystem or the natural community, as discussed above as the first interpretation of an environmental ethic. This must be the *primary* principle of an environmental ethic because environmental protection means more than just the protection of natural individuals and natural species – it means the protection of complete ecological systems. Environmentalists and wilderness preservationists (for example) are interested in protecting *environments*, i.e., ecological systems and natural communities. The preservation of individual natural entities or natural species in isolation from their natural habitats and communities is at best a last ditch effort to prevent extinction; it cannot be the primary goal of a policy of environmentalism. Thus the preeminent goal of action in a theory of environmental ethics is the well-being, health, or stability of the ecological community. Moral rules, obligations, and duties, or the moral evaluation of consequences of action, will be developed and determined by a concept of the *ecological good*, i.e., the good for the ecological community as a whole.

Nonetheless, this primary goal of ecosystemic well-being must be augmented by a secondary goal of the protection of natural individuals. This secondary goal will serve to limit the excessive use of the primary principle in cases where it should not apply. What I have in mind are cases such as the rare endangered species that is no longer a functioning part of the natural ecosystem, or even disease organisms such as the smallpox virus that are on the verge of being totally eradicated. If ecosystemic well-being were the *only* principle of moral action, then it would seem permissible to eliminate the disease organisms or to let the endangered species become extinct. But if an environmental ethic has a secondary moral principle which is activated, so to speak, after questions of ecosystemic well-being are decided, then rare and endangered species can be protected despite their irrelevance to ecosystemic health and stability. Thus in cases where the health or welfare of the natural community is not at issue, human action affecting the environment should be judged by its relationship to natural individuals and species. As long as they do not adversely affect the well-being of the natural ecological community, all individuals and species ought to be preserved and protected. This is the second and subsidiary principle of a practical environmental ethic.

At the risk of repeating myself, let me be a bit more specific about the ordering of these two principles. The primary principle must be the moral consideration of natural communities as a whole, for this is the only method of protecting environmental systems and the inanimate and nonsentient components of these systems. If, on the contrary, the moral consideration of natural individuals was primary, then a coherent and plausible explanation for the protection of inanimate natural objects would have to be given to insure the basic tenets of environmental policy. But it is not at all clear what theory of value could show how inanimate natural entities – stones and streams – are inherently valuable. It seems that only as parts of an ecologically healthy well-functioning community (that is itself valuable) do these inanimate and nonsentient entities become valuable. Moreover, if the consideration of natural individuals was primary, it is not obvious how or why one would protect ecological systems or communities. As long as the individual animals, e.g., were healthy, there would be no need to protect their natural habitats. One could create artificial habitats – parks and preserves – that would maintain the well-being of the individual animals but would not, of course, be consistent with environmentalist principles of preservation. Thus, I have suggested that the moral consideration of ecosystemic communities is the moral principle most compatible with environmental policies; augmenting this principle with a secondary concern for natural individuals – e.g., endangered species of animals – will yield a complete environmental ethic that is plausible and in agreement with environmentalist intuitions.

Although this ordering of two kinds of moral consideration for the environment – i.e., consideration for the natural ecosystemic community and consideration for natural individuals and species – yields a fairly precise practical system of moral action and evaluation, it is not without its hard cases. Perhaps the most intriguing is the case in which the existence of a particular species (or individual) actually threatens the natural community as a whole. Despite environmentalist beliefs about the preservation of species, the use of the two principles in this type of case requires the elimination of the threatening species. Since the primary principle of an environmental ethic, the primary goal of all action relating to the environment, is the health, stability, and well-being of the entire natural community, the community must be protected from the threat. Of course it is likely that in an actual instance the well-being of the ecosystem could be preserved by transfering the species to a different ecosystem where it would not be harmful, or by controlling the size of the species population; nevertheless, if ecosystemic health or stability requires the elimination of the species, the species must be eliminated. If an environmental ethic permitted the destruction of natural environments, natural ecosystems and communities, it would be meaningless or incoherent.

In sum, then, an environmental ethic should be interpreted as a complex balancing of two forms of moral consideration regarding natural entities and systems. Moral consideration should first be directed toward the natural community or ecosystem as a whole, so that the overall good for the ecosystem is the primary goal of action. But this communal good should be supplemented by a consideration of natural individuals and species, so that in cases where ecosystemic well-being is not an issue, the protection of endangered species or natural individuals can be morally justified. This supplementary or secondary moral consideration of individuals will yield a much richer environmental ethic than the mere consideration of ecosystemic good, and it will help avoid the objections to the first community-based environmental ethic discussed above. Augmented by a secondary consideration of natural individuals, this theory will be able to explain the protection of rare endangered species that are no longer functioning members of a natural community. It will also help to soften the revolutionary character of an environmental ethic that considers the ecosystemic good superior to the good of human individuals; because of the secondary principle natural individuals (including humans) will not be excluded from direct moral consideration. Thus, the balancing of these two kinds of moral consideration yields the most plausible and practical environmental ethic, an environmental ethic that is essentially in accord with environmentalist intuitions about the protection of the natural environment, and that is reasonable enough to be accepted by human moral agents.

IV

Finally, then, a comment on the relationship between this environmental ethic and an animal liberation ethic. It should be clear that if the primary ethical goal or principle of an environmental ethic is the well-being of the ecosystemic natural community *as a whole*, then the well-being of individual animals in the community will sometimes be sacrificed for the communal good.[17] The problem is that ecosystems function, develop, and survive by means of the life and death struggle of competing natural forces, competing living beings. Humans cannot act to prevent the suffering and death of all animal life and remain true to an *environmental* ethic. Indeed, there may be times when human action to improve the health of the ecosystemic community will require the death, destruction, or suffering of individual animals or animal species. Humans may have to eliminate disease organisms, insects, or even higher animals – rabbits, deer, or wolves, e.g. – which have overpopulated their natural communities and threaten ecosystemic stability. But an animal liberation ethic holds that the death and suffering of animals is a moral evil, because it violates the moral worth of individual animals. When this death and suffering is a result of human action, even for the sake of ecosystemic well-being, it is a direct violation of the principles of an animal liberation ethic. Thus, as I noted above, an animal liberation ethic and an environmental ethic based on the good of the ecosystemic natural community will tend to be incompatible.

The advocate of an environmental ethic has, I believe, only one method for removing this incompatibility: a revision of the basic structure of an environmental ethic. An environmental ethic can be made compatible with an animal liberation ethic if it is conceived as an ethic primarily concerned with the satisfaction of sentient beings – the higher animals and humans. Natural entities and ecological communities would be preserved, not because of any intrinsic value, but simply because they provide satisfaction or pleasure to sentient beings. But this model of an environmental ethic will not operate as a preserver of environmentalist policies; it makes an environmental ethic compatible with an animal liberation ethic by destroying the essence and the practical application of the environmental ethic. The fact is that the existence of any natural entity or ecological system is only contingently related to the satisfactions of sentient beings. Animals can survive and flourish in habitats that are not their natural homes. Humans, of course, have developed such a multiplicity of artifical enjoyments that there is no real need for the pleasures of the natural world.[18] Now I am not arguing that humans receive no pleasure from the natural environment; my point is that this pleasure is only contingently related to the existence of the natural environment. If the natural environment is only protected, e.g., because it provides humans with aesthetic and recreational satisfactions, then if human interests in aesthetics and recreational activities change (as they seem to be in this increasingly artifical and technological world) there will be no reason to protect the natural environment.[19] The interests of sentient beings cannot provide a secure basis for environmental policies, and thus they cannot be the primary principle of an environmental ethic. The contingent relationship between the existence of the natural environment and the satisfaction or interests of sentient beings prevents the merger of an animal liberation ethic and an environmental ethic. Because an animal liberation ethic only requires the consideration of sentient life, while an environmental ethic requires the preservation of nonsentient entities and systems as well as sentient life, the two systems are basically incompatible.

However, a number of factors serve to modify this bleak picture. First, the environmental ethic here proposed is not based solely on the good of the ecological community as a whole; there is a secondary principle which bases moral evaluation on the good of individual natural entities, including sentient animals. As long as the welfare of the community is not at stake, individual natural entities – including animals – must be protected.

Because I have argued for a balanced set of principles as the structure of an environmental ethic, it is possible to save much of an animal liberation ethic. Individual animals (or species of animals) cannot be harmed, unless there is an overriding and serious need on the part of the entire natural community.

A second factor is the problem of domesticated animals. Advocates of an animal liberation ethic, of course, seek many practical changes in human action affecting domesticated animals. Now Callicott, for one, finds this concern to be almost incoherent from the perspective of an environmental ethic. Since domesticated livestock are a human artifact, their effects on the natural environment should be judged as any other human artifact.[20] Sheep grazing in a meadow, for example, may do as much harm to the natural cycles of the region's plant life as the dumping of toxic chemicals. From Callicott's ecological perspective, the fact that the sheep are animals rather than the instruments of human deliberative action would not justify or excuse the harm done to the natural environment. But I do not think that the advocate of an environmental ethic needs to worry about domesticated animals causing ecological damage. *At worst*, domesticated animals, *because they are not part of the natural community*, are simply an *irrelevancy* from the standpoint of an environmental ethic. Sheep, for example, do not generally graze in natural wilderness areas, but in pasture land that has already been itself domesticated. Their effect on natural ecological cycles is minimal.[21] *At best*, using a two-principle environmental ethic, humans are able to judge the pain and suffering and moral worth of individual domesticated animals as morally significant; as long as questions of environmental health or well-being are not involved, then even domesticated animals can be treated as objects of moral concern.

Finally, it is important to realize that in *practical* terms, a more environmentally appropriate human social policy will greatly benefit animal life. Although from the perspective of ecological theory it may be necessary to sacrifice some animals for the ecological well-being of the natural community, in actual practice more animals are harmed by human actions that *violate* ecological principles. More animals are harmed by humans destroying and degrading ecological communities than by humans attempting to improve them. Adopting principles of an environmental ethic should, in the long run,

benefit the lives of animals, for humans will begin to recognize all natural entities as members of a morally relevant natural community.

Notes

1   I take as prime examples of an animal liberation ethic the work of Peter Singer, *Animal Liberation* (New York: New York Review/Random House, 1975), and Tom Regan, "The Moral Basis of Vegetarianism," *Canadian Journal of Philosophy* 5 (1975): 181–214.

2   Aldo Leopold, "The Land Ethic," in *A Sand County Almanac: With Essays on Conservation from Round River* (1949; rpt. New York: Ballantine, 1970), p. 262.

3   J. Baird Callicott, "Animal Liberation: A Triangular Affair," *Environmental Ethics* 2 (1980): 320.

4   Don E. Marietta, Jr., "The Interrelationship of Ecological Science and Environmental Ethics," *Environmental Ethics* 1 (1979): 197.

5   Bryan G. Norton, "Environmental Ethics and Nonhuman Rights," *Environmental Ethics* 4 (1982): 32.

6   Callicott, "Animal Liberation," pp. 332–3.

7   Ibid., p. 327.

8   Lilly-Marlene Russow, "Why Do Species Matter?" *Environmental Ethics* 3 (1981): 103.

9   Joel Feinberg, "The Rights of Animals and Unborn Generations," in *Philosophy and Environmental Crisis*, ed. William T. Blackstone (Athens, Georgia: University of Georgia Press, 1974), pp. 55–6.

10 Russow, for example, argues that species are important because of the individuals that comprise them.

11 Space limitations prevent a full discussion of the role of species preservation in a system of environmental ethics. Clearly an environmental ethic must recognize that the extinction of species through natural processes – evolutionary defeat by a more successful competitive species – is a morally acceptable event. An environmental ethic does not require humans to prevent naturally occurring extinctions. But of course in reality most of the endangered species that concern environmentalists have been brought to the edge of extinction by human activity, i.e., by human disruption of natural communities. There is thus a duty to attempt to correct our mistakes and to preserve these victims of negligent human actions in the natural environment.

12 Leopold, "The Land Ethic," pp. 237–9.

13 Christopher D. Stone, *Should Trees Have Standing? Towards Legal Rights for Natural Objects* (Los Altos, California: William Kaufmann, 1974), pp. 17–34.

14 For a discussion of intrinsic value see Tom Regan, "The Nature and Possibility of an Environmental Ethic," *Environmental Ethics* 3 (1981): 30–4, and

Evelyn B. Pluhar, "The Justification of an Environmental Ethic," *Environmental Ethics* 5 (1983): 47–61.

15 Kenneth E. Goodpaster, "On Being Morally Considerable," *The Journal of Philosophy* 75 (1978): 308–25.

16 Kenneth E. Goodpaster, "From Egoism to Environmentalism," in *Ethics and Problems of the 21st Century*, ed. K. E. Goodpaster and K. M. Sayre (Notre Dame: University of Notre Dame, 1979), p. 29.

17 Note again that the well-being of individual animals to be sacrificed includes the well-being of human animals. If an environmental ethic limits human projects and activities, then some humans will undoubtedly suffer discomfort, pain, and even death. There may be less energy to be used for recreation or labor-saving devices in the home. Buildings may be colder in the winter and hotter in the summer. Some humans may even die for the sake of environmental well-being: if the mosquito population is not controlled by pesticides, some humans could die from encephalitis, for example.

18 Although some small percentage of the human population may yearn, for example, for the "wilderness experience," it is not clear why this recreational pleasure cannot be satisfied in some other way. As Martin Krieger has argued: "Artificial prairies and wildernesses have been created, and there is no reason to believe that these artificial environments need be unsatisfactory for those who experience them." ("What's Wrong with Plastic Trees?" *Science* 179 (1973): 453.)

19 For a more detailed discussion of the "human interest" arguments for environmentalism, i.e., the arguments based on the instrumental or utilitarian value of the natural environment, see my "Utilitarianism and Preservation," *Environmental Ethics* 1 (1979): 357–64; Mark Sagoff, "On Preserving the Natural Environment," *Yale Law Journal* 84 (1974): 205–67; Sagoff, "Do We Need a Land Use Ethic?" *Environmental Ethics* 3 (1981): 293–308; Laurence H. Tribe, "Ways Not to Think About Plastic Trees," in *When Values Conflict*, ed. Laurence H. Tribe, Corinne S. Schelling, and John Voss (Cambridge, Mass.: Ballinger, 1976): 61–91; and William Godfrey-Smith, "The Value of Wilderness," *Environmental Ethics* 1 (1979): 309–19.

20 Callicott, "Animal Liberation," p. 330.

21 I realize that the issue of domesticated animals and an environmental ethic cannot be adequately discussed in a brief summary paragraph: it requires an entire essay in itself. All that I wish to suggest is that the animal liberationist's concern for the proper treatment of domesticated animals is neither condemned nor condoned in a theory of environmental ethics. The fate of domesticated animals, as such, is not a subject area of environmental ethics. Of course if domesticated animals begin to intrude upon and harm a natural ecological community, then they would be treated like any other human artifact (machines, chemicals, etc.) that harmed the environment. Or if a human began to kill wild natural animals in order to protect his domesticated sheep he would be violating an environmental ethic, just as if he polluted a stream to "protect" his recreational pleasure in speedboating. But the vast majority of cases involving domesticated animals – the morality of factory farming, for example – are in a realm of substantive ethics completely removed from the concerns of an environmental ethic. The question of the compatibility or incompatibility of an environmental ethic and an animal liberation ethic when dealing with the treatment of domesticated animals as such is thus unanswerable and misconceived: these are simply two different subject matters.

8

Can Animal Rights Activists Be Environmentalists?

Gary E. Varner

Introduction

I have never thought of myself as an activist. I occasionally write letters to the editor and to my legislators, but to date, I have only once held a protest sign, and that had nothing to do with the environment or animals.[1] Nevertheless, I began to study and write on questions in environmental ethics and animal rights because I cared about animals and the environment and I believed that philosophical work on these questions would ultimately make a difference in practice. I recall thinking, as early as eighth grade, that humans had commandeered too much of the earth's surface and that we often mistreated animals because we thought that only human beings mattered, morally speaking. I hadn't yet heard the word "anthropocentric," and I was unaware of philosophy as a discipline, but I believed that part of the problem was a question of moral theory.

After coming to Texas A&M in the fall of 1990, I began consciously to distance myself from self-professed activists, especially animal rights activists. For I learned that, to many of the people I was interacting with (animal scientists studying production agriculture and veterinary and medical scientists who use animals in their research, but also older forestry and rangeland people), "activists" were by definition dangerous, unscientific lunatics acting irrationally in the grip of their emotions. I found that, as soon as I was introduced as a philosopher who studies environmental ethics and animal rights,

people jumped to a host of conclusions about me. Many of those conclusions turned out to be true (I vote democratic, I eat tofu, and I ride my bicycle to the office), but as soon as I raised the topic of animal rights, many in the audience would assume that I was against all hunting, all use of animals for food or fiber, and all experimentation, which I am not. I have therefore spent a great deal of time lately emphasizing the ways a critical, more philosophical approach to the animal rights issue yields different conclusions than those endorsed by many self-professed animal rights activists.

Among environmental philosophers there is a parallel tendency to equate "animal rights" and "environmental ethics" with specific views in ethical theory and/or specific accounts of what those views imply. Notoriously, it was J. Baird Callicott who, in his early paper "Animal Liberation: A Triangular Affair," appeared to delight in driving a very deep wedge between environmentalism and animal rights.[2] But the one point on which environmental philosophers reached a general consensus during the field's first decade was that both the theoretical foundations and practical implications of animal rights views were inconsistent with those of environmentalism. Because so many environmental philosophers believed that "the ecological crisis" could be averted only by adopting a non-anthropocentric value theory, there was some hope early on that animal rights philosophies would be of some use in understanding environmental ethics. Tom Regan's early essay "The Nature and Possibility of

Gary E. Varner

an Environmental Ethic"[3] is an example. However, there very quickly emerged a broad-based consensus that animal rights views were no more compatible with sound environmental ethics and sound environmental policy than were anthropocentric views.

To appreciate how hegemonic this view of the animal rights/environmental ethics split has become, consider the following quotations. Under a 1984 title extending Callicott's amorous metaphor (the essay was called "Animal Liberation and Environmental Ethics: Bad Marriage, Quick Divorce") Mark Sagoff wrote:

> Environmentalists cannot be animal liberationists. Animal liberationists cannot be environmentalists. . . . moral obligations to nature cannot be enlightened or explained – one cannot even take the first step – by appealing to the rights of animals . . . [4]

More recently, Eric Katz relied on the now familiar dichotomy in advising businesses engaged in animal research on how to blunt the criticisms of animal rights activists:

> I suggest that the adoption by business of a more conscious environmentalism can serve as a defense against the animal liberation movement. This strategy may seem paradoxical: how can business defend its use of animals by advocating the protection of the environment? But the paradox disappears once we see that animal liberation and environmentalism are incompatible practical moral doctrines.[5]

I myself may have been guilty of perpetuating the perception of dichotomy. In an essay on captive breeding I wrote, very simplistically:

> From the perspective of individual sentient creatures involved in a program, captive breeding [of endangered species] is a moral atrocity.[6]

Although Callicott subsequently regretted the fulminatory rhetoric of his "Triangular Affair" piece,[7] he continues to think of animal rights and environmental ethics as incompatible. For instance, he argues for moral monism on the grounds that a pluralism embracing both animal rights and environmental ethics would be inconsistent, because

animal rights would prohibit controlling the populations of sentient animals by means of hunting, while environmental ethics would permit it.[8]

Even Bryan Norton, whose overarching concern in *Toward Unity Among Environmentalists*, is to find points of agreement at the level of practice amid disagreement at the level of moral principle, writes as if animal rights and environmental ethics can never be reconciled. During a discussion of deep ecologists' profession of biocentric egalitarianism – the view that all organisms are equal (ostensively very similar to animal rights theorists' claim of animal [or at least vertebrate] equality) – Norton states that

> As academics, spokespersons for deep ecology have been able to avoid adopting policies on difficult, real-world cases such as elk destroying their wolf-free ranges, feral goats destroying indigenous vegetation on fragile lands, or park facilities overwhelmed by human visitors.[9]

Norton goes on to explain that equal rights for nonhuman animals is environmentally unsound because

> It can never be "fair" by human standards to kill 10 percent of an elk population because it exceeds the capacity of its range.[10]

That even a consensus-seeking pragmatist like Norton writes as if animal rights views are systematically environmentally unsound suggests just how deeply rooted is the perceived dichotomy between "environmental ethics" and "animal rights."

So the consensus claim among environmental philosophers is that environmental ethics is incompatible, both theoretically and practically, with both anthropocentric and animal rights views. This claim strikes me as multiply confused. First, to identify "environmental ethics" with specifically holistic theories, as the consensus view does, is to deny that thinkers like John Passmore, Bryan Norton, Richard Watson, and Paul Taylor are doing environmental ethics. Yet this strikes me as every bit as arbitrary as denying that environmental ethicists are "doing philosophy." Environmental ethicists should have learned not to define the opposition out of the discipline – for too long, "pure" philosophers succeeded in doing this with "applied" ethicists in general, and with environmental ethicists in particular.

Second, even if we identified "*environmental ethics*" with holistic views, I do not think that either anthropocentric or animal rights views necessarily have environmentally hazardous implications. I think that a sufficiently enlightened anthropocentrism can ground aggressive environmental regulation. In particular, anthropocentrism can be enlightened by an ecologically informed concept of harm of others. On such a concept, no one owns, but everyone has the right to use, ecological processes which (like the hydrologic cycle, or the breeding cycle of migratory waterfowl) necessarily extend beyond the boundaries of private real property. On this view, governments may prohibit uses of land which, when broadly practiced, significantly interfere with such processes, and they may do so without compensating landowners whose activities (e.g. filling wetlands) are prohibited, on the theory that the right to use one's land in a way that harms others was never part of the bundle of rights which the landowner received in the first place. I've argued this at length in a forthcoming paper.[11] Here I want to focus instead on the other claim, that animal rights views are incompatible with environmental ethics.

Self-professed animal rights activists have, I think, contributed to the perception that animal rights views have environmentally unsound implications by truncating and radicalizing their views. Animal rights activists have very little interest in or need for being clear about what their philosophical views are and what those views do and don't imply. In political debates, it is often impossible to describe one's position fully or ineffective to do so even if one has time. "Animals are not ours to eat, wear, or experiment on" is a politically expedient slogan for someone who believes that radical reform is called for, even if that person actually believes that *some* uses are acceptable under *some* conditions. The necessity of producing sound-bite sized quotations for the news media contributes to the truncation of peoples' position statements, but also a general principle of negotiation is to begin with a position which demands more than one is ultimately willing to settle for. So animal rights activists have good reasons for their commonly espoused impatience with philosophical subtlety. The political utility of radicalization and activists' tendency to ignore philosophical subtleties are well documented in Jaspers' and Nelkin's

The Animal Rights Crusade: The Growth of a Moral Protest.[12]

But there *is* a difference between a philosophy and a bumper sticker, and once we move beyond the political posturing and sloganeering, to a careful examination of the philosophical bases of the animal rights movement, we see that convergence is possible at the level of policy between animal rights views and the views of environmentalists. As Norton put it with regard to convergence between anthropocentrism and holism:

> Long-sighted anthropocentrists and ecocentrists tend to adopt more and more similar policies as scientific evidence is gathered, because both value systems – *and several others as well* – point toward the common-denominator objective of protecting ecological contexts.[13]

Our question, practically speaking, is whether or not an animal rights perspective is one of those "several other" value systems which can agree with ecocentrism on broad, long-range policy goals. Given his insistence that "long-sighted anthropocentrists" can agree with ecocentrists about the importance of protecting ecological contexts," it is surprising that Norton never asks whether the goals of "long-sighted animal rights activists" might also converge with those of the ecocentrists.

The Issues

As I understand it, environmental philosophers' antagonism to animal rights views grows out of their perception that the practical implications of such views would be anti-environmental in two basic ways.

1 With regard to wildlife population control the concerns are that:
   a *hunting* would be prohibited, even when it is required to preserve the integrity of an ecosystem, and
   b humans would have an obligation to prevent natural *predation* (including not restoring locally extinct predators).
2 With regard to preserving biodiversity the concerns are that:
   a it would be impermissible to kill destructive *exotics*, and

b it would be impermissible to breed members of *endangered species* in captivity.

In what follows, I am going to begin with, and spend the most time on, hunting. Admittedly, this is the easiest case in which to reconcile the views of animal rights activists and environmentalists, but a careful treatment of this issue sets the stage for a careful treatment of the others.

What I say about hunting will, I think, be met with skepticism by many self-professed animal rights activists. Some will suspect me of being an apologist for the wildlife managers, a philosophical hired gun. And some of what I say (more briefly) about the other three issues will be rejected out of hand by many animal activists. But everything I have to say about these issues is at least *consistent with* a full-blown animal rights philosophy, and that shows, I maintain, that the gulf between animal rights and environmental ethics has been unnecessarily exaggerated.

Therapeutic Hunting of Obligatory Management Species

When teaching the hunting issue, I find it useful to distinguish among three types of hunting in terms of the purposes hunting is taken to serve. By *therapeutic hunting* I mean hunting motivated by and designed to secure the aggregate welfare of the target species and/or the integrity of its ecosystem (I'll discuss later the question of whether the two are separable). By *subsistence* hunting I mean hunting aimed at securing food for human beings. By *sport* hunting I mean hunting aimed at maintaining religious or cultural traditions, reenacting national or evolutionary history, honing certain skills, or just securing a trophy. Many would prefer to recognize a distinction within this third category between hunting for sport and hunting as a ritual. Although there may be some important differences, I class them together because both activities serve human needs (which is what distinguishes both sport and subsistence hunting from therapeutic hunting), but needs which are less fundamental (in the sense of universal) than nutrition (which is what distinguishes subsistence hunting from both ritual and sport hunting).

Obviously these are abstract archetypes. Wildlife managers designing a hunt and hunters going into the field almost always have some composite of these

three goals in mind. Inuits taking a whale are engaged in subsistence hunting, but so is a Hill Country Texan who cherishes venison. And both are engaged in sport hunting as I conceive of it: the Inuits' communal life is structured around hunting – it has great social and religious significance – but so is the Texan's insofar as he views hunting as an expression of his cultural and/or evolutionary history.

Although my typology is an abstraction, sorting out the ends hunting is supposed to serve does help us to say where the prospects for convergence lie. Significantly, the defense hunters and environmentalists most often offer in the face of criticism by animal rights activists – that it is necessary to prevent overpopulation and/or environmental degradation – clearly is a defense of *therapeutic* hunting specifically, not sport or subsistence hunting. The thesis I wish to defend here is that environmentalists and animal rights activists can agree on the moral necessity of therapeutic hunting of *obligatory management species*.

I owe the term "obligatory management species" to Ron Howard of the Texas Agricultural Extension Service, who distinguishes among "obligatory" and "permissive" management species in the following way. An *obligatory management species* is one that has a fairly regular tendency to overshoot the carrying capacity of its range, to the detriment of future generations of it and other species. A *permissive management species* is one that does not normally exhibit this tendency. Examples of obligatory management species would be ungulates (hooved mammals like white-tailed and mule deer, elk, and bison) and elephants. Examples of permissive management species would be mourning doves, cottontail rabbits, gray squirrels, bobwhite, and blue quail.[14] It is not that permissive management species do not become overpopulated. They do every year, in the straightforward sense of producing more young than their habitat can feed through the winter. But they usually do not degrade their habitat in ways that threaten future generations of their own or other species. This is what makes their management environmentally optional, or "merely *permissible*" in Ron Howard's terminology. By contrast, management of ungulates (and some other species) is environmentally necessary, or "*obligatory*" in Howard's terms.[15]

Environmental groups have taken great pains in recent years to distance themselves from animal rights groups, fearing that the widespread perception of animal rights activists as anti-scientific romantics would rub off on them, and much of the distancing has had to do with the hunting issue. In 1990, *Audubon* magazine published an article with the scathing title "Animal Rights: Ignorance About Nature."[16] Also in 1990, the Wisconsin Greens adopted a resolution condemning Madison's Alliance for Animals for disrupting hunts in Blue Mound State Park.[17] And in 1991 a Sierra Club fundraiser said in a phone conversation that the Club was not "doing more to expose the enormous environmental damage caused by factory farming because they wanted to keep their membership as large as possible."[18]

Still, environmentalists do not uniformly support hunting. Audubon and the Sierra Club both oppose hunting in the national parks, and the Texas chapters of both clubs recently opposed a bill which opened the state's parks to recreational hunting. Texas law already allowed hunting in state parks on an *ad hoc* basis, "as sound biological management practices warrant,"[19] e.g. to deal with ungulate population irruptions. But S.B. 179, which was signed into law May 18, 1993, amended the state's Parks and Recreation Code to allow classification of state parks as "game management areas" in addition to as "recreational areas, natural areas, or historical areas."[20] According to its *State Capitol Report*, "The Sierra Club opposes any bill that will shift the burden of proof from no hunting in state parks unless 'biologically necessary', to hunting is allowed unless proven harmful to the area's resources."[21] That's not well written, but the sense is clear enough: the Sierra Club opposes allowing sport hunting on a regular basis in state parks, but it will support sport hunting in the state parks on an *ad hoc* basis, when "biologically necessary."

Sierra's and Audubon's position on hunting in national and state parks shows that the only hunting environmentalists feel *compelled* to support is "biologically necessary" hunting, that is, *therapeutic* hunting, and therapeutic hunting normally is necessary only where obligatory management species are concerned. Officially, both organizations are noncommittal on sport hunting outside of the national and Texas state parks. This mirrors a difference of opinion within the environmental community. Many environmentalists would prefer that sport hunting which is not also therapeutic be stopped, and many would prefer

that natural predators be restored to levels at which human hunting is less often biologically necessary. But many environmentalists are also avid hunters who attach great ritual significance to their hunting.

So the only hunting that environmentalists feel *compelled* to support is therapeutic hunting of obligatory management species. However, the received interpretation of the animal rights/environmental ethics split would have it that animal rights activists must oppose hunting even when it is biologically necessary. When we look behind the sound-bite sized quotations and political slogans of self-professed animal rights *activists*, and examine carefully formulated animal rights *philosophies*, we see that it is *not* necessary for animal rightists to oppose environmentally sound hunting. Animal rightists can support exactly the same policy in regard to hunting which environmental groups like Audubon and the Sierra Club support in regard to the national and state parks. The easiest way to bring this out is by making the now familiar and basic philosophical distinction between an animal liberation or animal welfare view and a true animal rights view, and by beginning with the former's application to the hunting question.

Animal *Liberation* and Therapeutic Hunting

Peter Singer's 1975 book *Animal Liberation*[22] has become the Bible of the "animal rights movement." Singer wrote that book for popular consumption and in it he spoke loosely of animals having "moral rights." But all that he intended by this was that animals (or at least "higher animals," like vertebrates) have some basic moral standing and that there are right and wrong ways of treating them. In later, more philosophically rigorous work (summarized in his *Practical Ethics*, which has just been reissued[23]), he explicitly eschews the term "rights," noting that, as a utilitarian ethical theorist, not only does he deny that animals have moral rights, but in his view, neither do human beings. In *Animal Liberation* Singer was writing in the vernacular in order to make his arguments appeal to the widest variety of audiences – he did not want to tie his critiques of agriculture and animal research to his specific moral philosophy.

Gary E. Varner

When ethical philosophers speak of an individual "having moral rights," they mean something much more specific than that the individual has some basic moral standing and that there are right and wrong ways of treating him or her (or it). Although there is much controversy as to the specifics, there is general agreement on this: to attribute moral rights to an individual is to assert that the individual has some kind of special moral dignity, the cash value of which is that there are certain things which cannot justifiably be done to him or her (or it) for the sake of benefit to others. For this reason, moral rights have been characterized as "trump cards" against utilitarian arguments. Utilitarian arguments are arguments based on aggregate benefits and aggregate harms. Utilitarianism is usually defined as the view that right actions maximize aggregate happiness. In principle, nothing is inherently or intrinsically wrong, according to a utilitarian; any action could be justified under some possible circumstances. One way of characterizing rights views in ethics, by contrast, is that there are some things which, regardless of the consequences, it is simply wrong to do to individuals, and that moral rights single out these things.

Although a technical and stipulative definition of the term, this philosophical usage reflects a familiar concept. One familiar way in which appeals to individuals' rights are used in day-to-day discussions is to assert, in effect, that there is a limit to what individuals can be forced to do, or to the harm that may be inflicted upon them, for the benefit of others. So the philosophical usage of rights talk reflects the common-sense view that there are limits to what we can justifiably do to an individual for the benefit of society.

To defend the moral rights of animals would be to claim that certain ways of treating animals cannot be justified on utilitarian grounds. In the professional philosophical writings cited earlier, Peter Singer explicitly rejects rights views and adopts a utilitarian stance for dealing with our treatment of nonhuman animals. So the author of the Bible of the animal rights movement is not an animal *rights* theorist at all.

When the views of animal rights activists are understood this way, in Singer's theoretical terms, animal rights advocates opposed to hunting actually have a lot in common with wildlife managers and hunters who defend hunting as a means to minimizing suffering in wildlife populations. Both

factions are appealing to the utilitarian tradition in ethics; both believe that it is permissible (at least where nonhuman animals are concerned) to sacrifice (even involuntarily) the life of one individual for the benefit of others, at least where the aggregated benefits to others clearly outweigh the costs to that individual.

Relatedly, the specific conception of happiness which defenders of therapeutic hunting apply to animals is one which Singer himself uses, at least in regard to many or most animals. Since utilitarianism is the view that right actions maximize aggregate *happiness*, it is important for utilitarians to be clear about what happiness consists in. *Hedonistic utilitarians* define happiness in terms of the presence of pleasure and the absence of pain, where both "pleasure" and "pain" are broadly construed to include not only physical pleasures and pains (e.g. those accompanying orgasms and third degree burns), but various kinds of pleasant and unpleasant psychological states (e.g. tension and nervousness, and glee and exhilaration). *Preference utilitarians* define happiness in terms of the satisfaction of preferences (conscious aims, desires, plans, projects), which can, but need not, be accompanied by pleasure.

In *Animal Liberation* Singer employed a strongly hedonistic conception of happiness. He admitted that, "to avoid speciesism," we need *not* hold that

it is as wrong to kill a dog as it is to kill a normal human being ... [Without being guilty of speciesism] we could still hold that, for instance, it is worse to kill a normal adult human, [or any other being] with a capacity for self-awareness, and the ability to plan for the future and have meaningful relations with others, than it is to kill a mouse, which presumably does not share all of these characteristics ...[24]

For this reason he said that "The wrongness of killing a being is more complicated" than the wrongness of inflicting pain. Nevertheless, he there kept the question of killing "in the background," because

in the present state of human tyranny over other species the more simple, straightforward principle of equal consideration of pain or pleasure is a sufficient basis for identifying and protesting against all the major abuses of animals that human beings practice.[25]

In *Practical Ethics*, by contrast, he devotes four chapters (almost 140 pages) to the "more complicated" question. There he stresses that, with regard to "self-conscious individuals, leading their own lives and wanting to go on living,"[26] it is implausible to say that the death of one happy individual is made up for by the birth of an equally happy individual. That is, when dealing with self-conscious beings, preference utilitarianism is more appropriate than hedonistic utilitarianism.

An easy way to clarify Singer's point is with the following example. Suppose I sneak into your bedroom tonight and, without ever disturbing your sleep, kill you (by silently releasing an odorless gas, for instance). Since you led a happy life (hopefully) and died painlessly, on a hedonistic conception of happiness, the only sense we can make of the harm I have done you is in terms of lost future opportunities for pleasure. In the case of human beings, who have complicated desires, intentions, plans, and projects,[27] this seems an inadequate accounting of the harm I've done you. For humans (and any similarly cognitively sophisticated animals) a desire-based conception of harm seems more appropriate. But, Singer argues, self-conscious beings are not replaceable. When a being with future-oriented desires dies, those desires remain unsatisfied even if another being is brought into existence and has similar desires satisfied.

Singer cites research which he says clearly shows that the great apes (chimpanzees, gorillas, and orangutans) have projects,[28] and, without saying what specific research leads him to these conclusions, that fish and chickens do not have projects,[29] but that

> A case can be made, though with varying degrees of confidence, on behalf of whales, dolphins, monkeys, dogs, cats, pigs, seals, bears, cattle, sheep and so on, perhaps even to the point at which it may include all mammals . . .[30]

Elsewhere I have characterized carefully the evidence I think shows that all mammals and birds have desires but fish do not.[31] However, I doubt that either birds or the "lower" mammals (by which I here mean mammals other than primates

and cetaceans) have projects of the kind Singer is interested in, that is, desires that significantly transcend the present. Certainly the desire to go on living (which Singer mentions repeatedly as a sort of *sine qua non* of self-consciousness) constitutes a very sophisticated project. Dogs and cats almost certainly have desires that transcend the present. When a lion flushes a wildebeest in the direction of a hidden pridemate[32] (or, more prosaically, when my cat comes from the back room to where I am sitting and, having gotten my attention by jumping in my lap, leads me to the back door to be let out) it undoubtedly has a desire for something in the future. But it is a very near future about which cats and dogs are concerned. The desire to catch a prey animal here now, or even the desire to get a human being from the other room to come open the door to the outside, is not on a par with aspiring to longer life. Having the desire to go on living involves not only being self-conscious, but having concepts of life and death, and of self.

So I doubt that self-consciousness, as Singer conceives it, extends as far down "the phylogenetic scale" as Singer believes. But for present purposes, I will not try to settle this issue, for two reasons. First, the switch from hedonistic utilitarianism to preference utilitarianism would not in and of itself rule out hunting. As Singer put it, blocking the replaceability argument's application to many mammals

> raised a very large question mark over the justifiability of a great deal of killing of animals carried out by humans, even when this killing takes place painlessly and without causing suffering to other members of the animal community.[33]

But to "raise a very large question mark" is to increase the burden of proof on a justification of killing on preference utilitarian grounds; it is not to rule it out.

Second, in the following section, I will consider the application of a much stronger view – Tom Regan's rights view – to the hunting question, and there I will assume (with Regan) that all mammals have moral rights as he construes them. Since all of the obligatory management species listed above are mammals, this puts a very heavy burden of proof on the defender of therapeutic hunting. My point is that if even Regan's rights view can be used to defend therapeutic hunting of obligatory management species, then certainly a preference utilitarian could defend it as well.

For present purposes, then, let us consider therapeutic hunting from a hedonistic utilitarian perspective. The defense is obvious. Consider the following argument:

(1) We have a moral obligation to minimize pain.
(2) In the case of obligatory management species, more pain would be caused by letting nature take its course than by conducting carefully regulated therapeutic hunts.
(3) Therefore, we are morally obligated to conduct carefully regulated therapeutic hunts of obligatory management species rather than let nature take its course.

Since premise (1) is just a (partial) restatement[34] of the hedonistic utilitarian principle, and the argument is valid, premise (2) is the obvious point of controversy. But premise (2) states an empirical claim. Thus Singer's disagreement with the hunters and wildlife managers is purely empirical. They agree at the level of moral principle; they disagree only about that principle's application in practice.

Specifically, Singer appears to believe that non-lethal means of population control are (or at least could be made) available, and that using them would minimize suffering *vis à vis* therapeutic hunting. Singer has very little to say about hunting specifically. However, in *Practical Ethics* he at one point clearly indicates that a hedonistic utilitarian could endorse hunting under some circumstances.

The replaceability argument is severely limited in its application. It cannot justify factory farming, where animals do not have pleasant lives. Nor does it *normally* justify the killing of wild animals. A duck shot by a hunter ... has probably had a pleasant life, but the shooting of a duck does not lead to its replacement by another. *Unless the duck population is at the maximum that can be sustained by the available food supply*, the killing of a duck ends a pleasant life without starting another, and is for that reason wrong on straightforward utilitarian grounds.[35]

Here Singer admits that the replaceability argument could be used to justify, not just thera-

peutic hunting of obligatory management species, but sport hunting of permissive management species. Ducks are not obligatory management species. Ducks do not, in the normal course of events, overshoot the carrying capacity of their habitat in ways that degrade that habitat for future generations of their own and other species. Their management is therefore environmentally permissible, but not environmentally obligatory. Nevertheless, a hedonistic utilitarian could endorse sport hunting of permissive management species when, as Singer indicates here, their populations are at or above the carrying capacity of their ranges. As noted above, permissive management species regularly overshoot the carrying capacity of their range, producing more young than their habitat can support. Where this is clearly the case, a painlessly killed individual is, in effect, replaced by an individual who survives as a result. So long as the average death ducks suffer at the hands of hunters involves as little or less pain than the average death surplus ducks would have suffered in nature, pain is minimized.

However, in *Animal Liberation* Singer writes:

If it is true that in special circumstances their population grows to such an extent that they damage their own environment and the prospects of their own survival, or that of other animals who share their habitat, then it may be right for humans to take some supervisory action; but obviously if we consider the interests of the animals, this action will not be to allow hunters to kill some animals, inevitably wounding others in the process, but rather to reduce the fertility of the animals.[36]

Here Singer is admitting that therapeutic hunting of obligatory management species is better than letting nature take its course, but he is arguing that there is yet a better option. Singer appears to be substituting into the above argument a different empirical premise:

(2') By using non-lethal means of controlling populations of obligatory management species we would minimize suffering *vis à vis* both letting nature take its course and performing carefully regulated therapeutic hunts.

To reach a different conclusion:

(3′) We are morally obligated to use non-lethal means to control populations of obligatory management species.

When all of the learned dust has settled, the disagreement between the Peter Singers of the world and the self-professed advocates of animal welfare among hunters and wildlife managers boils down to an empirical controversy over the effectiveness of non-lethal wildlife population control measures. Both factions agree at the level of moral principle; they disagree over the facts.

My sense is that, at least in the current state of nonlethal wildlife population control, the defenders of hunting have it right. In a retrospective essay written for the centennial of Aldo Leopold's birth, Dale McCullough (the A. Starker Leopold Professor of Wildlife Management at Berkeley) recounted the controversy over deer management on Angel Island in the San Francisco Bay. Under pressure from the San Francisco Society for the Prevention of Cruelty to Animals, the state of California tried both relocating deer and birth control implants. In a follow-up study, McCullough found that 85% of the relocated deer had died within one year of relocation, and the birth control program was abandoned after the Society was unable to trap and implant enough females to prevent continued population growth (it was estimated that about 60 would need to be implanted). McCullough concluded that "the alternatives to shooting for control of deer populations are expensive, ineffective, and not particularly humane."[37]

For present purposes, however (for assessing convergence of environmentalists' and animal rightists' views on hunting), the point is moot, for two reasons. First, in cases where overpopulation already exists, it is not safe to let all the animals live out their natural lives. If the result of this year's breeding season is a herd already significantly over the carrying capacity of its range, then all the fertility control in the world will not prevent the kind of habitat degradation which Singer admits would justify culling some individuals.

Singer's intention, presumably, is to use fertility control to stabilize populations at sustainable levels. But even with regard to such preemptive population control, for present purposes the choice between therapeutic hunting and non-lethal means is moot. For if, as the defenders of hunting maintain, hunting is in fact the only effective

method of preemptive control, then both environmentalists and the Peter Singers of the world are compelled to support therapeutic hunting. If, on the other hand, effective non-lethal means were currently available, then the Peter Singers of the world would be compelled to support the use of those means rather than therapeutic hunting. Notice, however, that in the latter case an environmentalist would have the same choice open to her. For as we noted earlier, the only hunting environmentalists feel compelled to support is "biologically necessary" hunting. But if nonlethal population control were equally effective, *hunting* would not be biologically necessary, only the disjunctive choice: hunting *or* equivalent nonlethal means. That is, an environmentalist would reach conclusion 3″:

3″) We are morally obligated to use *either* (a) therapeutic hunting *or* (b) biologically equivalent non-lethal means to control populations of obligatory management species.

Just as environmentalists are of two minds with regard to sport hunting which is not also therapeutic, they would be of two minds with regard to the choice between therapeutic hunting and equally effective non-lethal means.

My sense is that the contemporary situation with respect to non-lethal means of deer population management is analogous to the use of hunting as a management tool in Leopold's days. Leopold was skeptical of wildlife managers' ability to control wildlife populations through hunting. He characterized hunting as

a crude, slow, and inaccurate tool, which needs to be supplemented by a precision instrument. The natural aggregation of lions and other predators on an overstocked range, and their natural dispersion from an understocked one, is the only precision instrument known to deer management.[38]

I think that Leopold's skepticism of game management was overblown as a result of his having witnessed the Kaibab irruption in the 1920s and similar population problems in Wisconsin during the 1940s. Decades later, during the 1970s and 1980s, the state of Wisconsin used better censusing techniques and a zone-sensitive permit system[39] to sustain harvests of still wolfless deer in numbers far exceeding the highest yields ever achieved during Leopold's lifetime.[40] Certainly other factors were involved – there was less edge habitat in Wisconsin in the 1940s – but Leopold's dim view of game management probably resulted in large measure from his living during the early days of scientific wildlife management. Non-lethal population control is still slow and crude, and needs to be supplemented with a precision instrument (therapeutic hunting and/or natural predation).

Recognizing that effective non-lethal population control is not currently available, animal rights activists might nevertheless choose to go on opposing therapeutic hunting for political purposes. In doing so, they would be practicing brinkmanship: they would be risking disaster (from the perspective of the individual animals involved) in order to force the development of more precise non-lethal techniques of population control. There is no precise way to determine when such brinkmanship is justified, anymore than there is any precise way to determine when civil disobedience or ecosabotage is justified.[41] In both cases, a rough utilitarian calculation is relied upon: in the case of civil disobedience and sabotage, the adverse effects on public order are weighed against the likely benefit of the law breaking; in the case of brinkmanship, the risk of a disastrous outcome is weighed against the probability of a breakthrough. However, part of the classic defense of civil disobedience and sabotage is that the conscientious lawbreaker has exhausted available legal means to achieve her goal, and in the case of therapeutic hunting, I don't think that activists can plausibly claim to have done this. Just as they have successfully forced private companies (like Mary Kay Cosmetics) and government agencies (like the NIH) to investigate alternatives to animal models in scientific research and product safety testing, activists could force agencies to put more money into investigations of non-lethal population control methods. So my conclusion is that we should not practice brinkmanship in this case. Therapeutic hunting is a precision tool already available, and as advocates of animal welfare, we should push for more research into non-lethal means of population control while supplementing non-lethal means with hunting.

I do, however, think that eventually precision methods of non-lethal wildlife population control will be developed. Recently, extensive experiments with animals have validated the technique of using genetically engineered viruses to spread infertility among wild animals. By inserting part of the protein sheath from the species' sperm into a virus which spreads easily in the population and then distributing food laced with the virus, Australian researchers hope to eradicate the rabbit, an exotic which has devastated their country. Trials of a similar technique to induce *temporary* infertility in other species are now underway.[42] The public in general and animal rights activists in particular are apprehensive of biotechnologies, but I think this method should, with appropriate caution, be embraced by the animal rights movement as a very promising approach to non-lethal control of wildlife populations.

The earlier discussion of environmentalists' ambivalent attitudes towards hunting suggests that if and when effective non-lethal alternatives to therapeutic hunting become available, environmentalists will be split. For some, the availability of non-lethal alternatives will strengthen their opposition to hunting; others will regard the choice between hunting and equally effective non-lethal means as morally moot. For present purposes what is important is this: animal rights activists operating from a hedonistic utilitarian stance will be compelled to support therapeutic hunting of obligatory management species in the absence of precision, non-lethal methods of wildlife population control. Only when such methods are available must such animal rights activists oppose therapeutic hunting, and then they will oppose it only in order to embrace a more humane alternative *with the same environmental effect*.

Animal *Rights* and Therapeutic Hunting

Although Peter Singer's *Animal Liberation* has become the Bible of the animal rights movement, Tom Regan's *The Case for Animal Rights* is the best defense available to date of a true animal rights position. It is impossible to do justice to the argument of a 400 page book in a few paragraphs. In what follows I will simply summarize the conclusions Regan reaches, without trying to reproduce his arguments in detail, and without critically assessing them apart from their application to the hunting controversy. It is my view that without resolving the theoretical question of which individuals (if any) have moral rights, we can still hope to make some progress on the practical question of which hunting policy to adopt. Specifically,

I argue that in the absence of effective non-lethal means of population control, therapeutic hunting of obligatory management species *can* be defended from a true animal rights perspective.

According to Regan, there is basically one moral right – the right not to be harmed on the grounds that doing so benefits others – and at least all normal mammals of a year or more have this basic moral right. In the preface to his most recent anthology, Gene Hargrove characterizes Regan's position as

> more narrowly focused [than Singer's,] on protecting the rights of those nonhuman entities with inherent value – those capable of being the subject of a life – which turn out to be mammals and no other forms of life.[43]

This is misleading. Regan does not deny that any non-mammalian animals have rights. Although he does explicitly restrict the reference of "animal" to "mentally normal mammals of a year or more," Regan does this to avoid the controversy over "line drawing," that is, trying to say precisely where in the phylogenetic scale and where in their ontogeny animals' mental capacities become so impoverished as to make them incapable of being subjects of a life. And Regan clearly says that he chooses mammals in order to make sure that his arguments "refer [to] individuals *well beyond* the point where anyone could reasonably 'draw the line' separating those who have the mental abilities in question from those who lack them."[44] In thus restricting the reference of "animal" he is only acknowledging that the analogical reasoning which would establish that any non-human animal has moral rights is strongest in the case of mentally normal adult mammals and becomes progressively weaker as we consider birds and then reptiles, amphibians, and vertebrate fish.

Regan defends two principles to use in deciding whom to harm where it is impossible not to harm someone who has moral rights: the miniride and worse-off principles. The *worse-off principle* applies where *non-comparable* harms are involved and it requires us to avoid harming the worse-off individual. Regan adopts the kind of desire-based conception of harm discussed earlier in relation to preference utilitarianism. Regan measures harm in terms of the degree to which an individual's capacity to form and satisfy desires has been restricted. The degree of restriction is measured in absolute, rather than relative terms. For if harm were measured relative to the individual's original capacity to form and satisfy desires, rather than in absolute terms, then death would be death wherever it occurs, but Regan reasons that although death is always the greatest harm which any individual can suffer (because it forecloses all opportunity for desire formation and satisfaction), death to a normal human being in the prime of her life is non-comparably worse than death to any non-human animal in the prime of its life, because a normal human being's capacity to form and satisfy desires is so much greater. To illustrate the use of the worse-off principle, Regan imagines that five individuals, four humans and a dog, are in a lifeboat that can support only four of them. Since death to any of the human beings would be non-comparably worse than death to the dog, the worse-off principle applies, and it requires us to avoid harming the human beings, who stand to lose the most.[45]

The *miniride* principle applies to cases where *comparable* harms are involved, and it requires us to harm the few rather than the many. Regan admits that, where it applies, this principle implies the same conclusions as the principle of utility, but he emphasizes that the reasoning is non-utilitarian: the focus is on individuals rather than the aggregate; what the miniride principle instructs us to do is to minimize the overriding of individuals' rights, rather than to maximize aggregate happiness. He says that the rights view (as Regan calls his position) advocates harming the few (at least where *comparable* harms are involved), because it respects all individuals equally. To illustrate the miniride principle's application, Regan imagines that a runaway mine train must be sent down one of two shafts, and that fifty miners would be killed by sending it down the first shaft but only one by sending it down the second. Since the harms that the various individuals in the example would suffer are comparable, the miniride principle applies, and we are obligated to send the runaway train down the second shaft.

Regan argues that the rights view calls for the total abolition of scientific research on animals, of commerical animal agriculture, and of hunting and trapping.[46] He contrasts his views to Singer's in this regard, stressing that, because he is reasoning from a rights-based theory, his conclusions are not contingent upon the facts in the same way as those of a utilitarian like Singer.

At first glance, the prospects for convergence are slim when a true animal rights position like Regan's is opposed to the position of environmentalists. For if having moral rights means that there are certain things that cannot be done to an individual for the sake of the group, and a true animal rights position extends moral rights to animals, then the basic rationale for therapeutic hunting – killing some in order that others may live – appears to be lost. As Regan puts it:

> Put affirmatively, the goal of wildlife managers should be to defend wild animals in the possession of their rights, providing them with the opportunity to live their own life, by their own lights, as best they can, spared that human predation that goes by the name of "sport." ... If, in reply, we are told that [this] will not minimize the total amount of suffering wild animals will suffer over time, our reply should be that this cannot be the overarching goal of wildlife management, once we take the rights of animals seriously.[47]

Regan appears to be opposed even to therapeutic hunting, and his opposition appears to follow from the attribution of moral rights to the animals.

However, Regan never considers the applicability of the miniride principle to hunting. Note that in the passage quoted above, he focuses on the reasoning presented in defense of therapeutic hunting by wildlife managers. They offer an aggregative, utilitarian argument, and as a rights theorist, Regan rejects utilitarian justifications for overriding individual rights. But Regan never considers what the implications would be of applying the miniride principle to the hunting question. Given Regan's conception of harm, death harms all normal individuals of the same species equally. So if it is true that fewer animals will die if therapeutic hunting is used to regulate a wildlife population than if natural attrition is allowed to take its course, then Regan's view implies that therapeutic hunting is not only permissible but a morally mandatory expression of respect for animals' rights.

Similar conclusions could, I think, be reached about certain kinds of medical research using the worse-off principle. Consider AIDS research, for example. Given Regan's conception of harm, the harm that death from AIDS is to a normal human being is non-comparably worse than the harm that death from AIDS is to a mouse or even a chimpanzee. So the worse-off principle would, if applicable, imply that non-human lives may be sacrificed to save human beings from preventable death. Here again, however, Regan does not apply his principle.

With regard to medical research, Regan bases his abolitionist conclusion primarily on the "special consideration" that "*Risks are not morally transferable to those who do not voluntarily choose to take them,*" which, he claims, blocks the application of the worse-off principle.[48] Returning to the hunting question, Regan might similarly cite a "special consideration" which blocks the application of the miniride principle. He might claim that a violation of an individual's moral rights occurs only when a moral agent is responsible for the harm in question, and that while hunters would be responsible for the deaths of the animals they kill in a therapeutic hunt, no one would be responsible for deaths due to natural attrition. Regan and Singer both give the following reason for thinking that natural predators do no wrong when they kill. They point out that only the actions of moral agents can be evaluated as right or wrong, and that presumably only human beings are moral agents (only human beings are capable of recognizing moral principles and altering their behavior accordingly).

But when a responsible agent knowingly allows nature to take its course, is he or she not responsible by omission for the foreseeable deaths which result? Regan's answer would presumably be no, but this does not seem to me to be a plausible position. In a recent article, Dale Jamieson presents a relevant counterexample. Suppose that a boulder is rolling down a hill toward a hiker and that you can save the hiker by calling out to her. Jamieson asks, does it make the slightest difference whether the boulder was dislodged by the wind rather than by a would-be murderer? If we are not responsible for allowing nature to take its course, then although you violate the hiker's rights by failing to warn her in the latter case, in the former case you would do her no wrong. But this seems implausible.[49]

There *would*, I think, be a good reason for not culling overpopulated humans: it is possible for any normal adult human to both understand the gravity of the situation and alter his or her behavior accordingly. A human being can recognize and act on the obligation of individuals to avoid contributing to overpopulation; a deer, an elephant, or a water buffalo cannot. This gives us a reason for being more reticent about involuntarily culling human beings in a situation of overpopulation. However, I would maintain that this is only a reason for *waiting longer* before engaging in involuntary culling, for *letting the situation get significantly worse* before one resorts to such drastic means. Even with regard to humans, it is, I submit, implausible to maintain that the numbers never count. At some point (admittedly unspecifiable in advance), some number of innocent human beings ought to be killed to prevent the foreseeable deaths of some larger number (although again, the minimum required ratio of saved to culled cannot be specified in advance).

Regan claims that the rights view calls for the total abolition of animal research and hunting, and that because he is reasoning from a rights-based theory, his conclusions are not contingent upon the facts in the same way as those of a utilitarian like Singer.[50] But the discussion in this section has suggested that a rights view cannot plausibly be insulated from the facts, and that, therefore, a true animal rights view need not rule out hunting or research *simpliciter*. Where therapeutic hunting is the only means available to prevent a large number of foreseeable deaths, a full-blown animal rights position *can* support therapeutic hunting. And where non-lethal means *are* available, the case against brinkmanship is stronger from Regan's perspective than it is from Singer's. For as I suggested earlier, the defense of brinkmanship would parallel the classic defense of conscientious lawbreaking, and that defense is in terms of a utilitarian balancing of the magnitude and likelihood of the benefits of law breaking (or brinkmanship) against the magnitude and likelihood of the harms of law breaking (or brinkmanship). Although I agree with Jamieson that "Regan's theory has serious problems" and that the remedies "would be less clearly in conflict with consequentialist morality,"[51] I think the case against brinkmanship would remain stronger with Regan. Respect for individuals' rights would seem to require greater aversion to brinkmanship than would treating individuals as receptacles for hedonic utility.

Scrambling Positions on Hunting

A critical look at the philosophical foundations of the animal rights movement shows that an individual genuinely concerned with animal welfare, and even one who attributes moral rights to non-human animals, can support the only kind of hunting environmentalists feel compelled to support, namely therapeutic hunting of obligatory management species.

A critical look at the hunting issue also scrambles the soundbyte-sized positions portrayed in the media. Animal rights activists tend to condemn hunters for being unsportsmanlike, and they tend to condemn management aimed at achieving maximum sustainable yield (MSY) and/or trophy bucks. However, when it comes to designing an actual therapeutic hunt, some animal welfare and animal rights views ought, arguably, to endorse the same management principles that are appropriate to trophy hunting and/or MSY, and the ideal therapeutic hunt would be anything but sportsmanlike. On the latter point, consider that various unsportsmanlike practices would be conducive to killing specific categories of animals as quickly and painlessly as possible. In the ideal therapeutic hunt, deer would be lured to bait stations near blinds from which sharpshooters with high caliber, automatic weapons would be able to kill them selectively and quickly. This is hardly a paradigm of sportsmanlike hunting, but it is, arguably, the ideal which serious animal welfarists should advocate.

The former point, about management principles, cannot be made without a brief discussion of wildlife management principles. For ecologists, the carrying capacity of a deer range is the maximum number of deer the habitat will support on a sustained basis. Wildlife managers, in contrast, have tended to think of carrying capacity in terms of MSY (maximum sustainable yield). To avoid confusion, Dale McCullough advocates calling the former the *K carrying capacity* of the range, the latter its *I carrying capacity*.[52] Deer respond to higher population densities by producing fewer fawns (reabsorption of fetuses becomes more common and twins less common), and denser populations are more susceptible to disease and malnutrition. Consequently, maximum yearly recruitment (addition of new adults) occurs well short of K carrying capacity. Management for MSY therefore requires maintenance of deer populations substantially below K-carrying capacity, where recruitment rates are highest.

The significance is this. Average individual welfare arguably is higher in populations at I carrying capacity than in populations at K carrying capacity, as evidenced both by more fawns surviving and in higher average weights and reduced parasitism and malnutrition among adults. Only a version of utilitarianism which placed preeminent emphasis on the sheer number of animals in the field would find management at K carrying capacity attractive. But McCullough's model suggests that MSY is achieved short of K carrying capacity, where individual welfare is higher. The ironic result that when hunters are harvesting the maximum number of animals, they see fewer afield and expend more effort per kill, has occasioned tension between wildlife managers and hunters.[53] Here is an opportunity for further convergence between pro- and anti-hunting forces. The policy positions of sport hunters educated to accept management at I carrying capacity for the sake of MSY will converge with those of animal welfare advocates educated to see that MSY management maximizes average individual welfare.

Perhaps more surprising is the fact that management practices which produce the best trophy bucks are arguably more consistent with Regan's rights view than is either management for MSY or K carrying capacity. The largest racks occur on older (4 to 6 years), heavier bucks, and heavier animals have to eat more to maintain themselves. So managing a deer herd to produce the best trophy bucks means sustaining fewer total deer and having fewer "hunting opportunities." As one how-to manual for East Texas deer managers puts it:

> On heavily hunted deer ranges, 90 percent of all the bucks are harvested before they reach four years old. Under these conditions deer do not live long enough to become trophy animals ... When managing for maximum quality [read: a preferred trophy], the forked-antlered buck harvest must be at least 30–50 percent less than when managing for maximum harvest.[54]

That is, to produce the best trophy bucks on a range, the population must be maintained below MSY, and this must be accomplished by killing more does and spike bucks[55] and fewer fork-antlered bucks.[56] Although the sex ratio of animals killed changes, by maintaining the population below I carrying capacity and MSY, fewer animals are killed yearly. Here is an opportunity for convergence between the views of trophy hunters and

animal rights activists who think like Tom Regan. The miniride principle implies that it is better to manage herds in ways that minimize killing. The trophy management principles just described do just this, by emphasizing the taking of does and maintenance of the population below MSY. But enlightened trophy hunters will accept this – the manual just cited is designed to get hunters to stop thinking that good trophy management means buck-only hunting.

It would also be possible to endorse the trophy improvement strategy over MSY management from a hedonistic utilitarian perspective. Assuming that on average death is death in hedonistic terms, however it occurs (whether from starvation or human or natural predation), the trophy improvement strategy would minimize pain *vis à vis* the other two management strategies. (Although managing a population at K carrying capacity would involve less hunting than at I carrying capacity, at K carrying capacity total mortality is greatest.)[57]

One further point needs to be emphasized. I defined an obligatory management species as one with "a fairly regular tendency to overshoot the carrying capacity of its range," but this does not mean that obligatory management species *always* need to be hunted. If that were so, then it would not make sense to limit hunting in parks to situations in which hunting becomes "biologically necessary." As McCullough points out:

> Most wildlife biologists and managers can point to situations where deer populations have not been hunted yet do not fluctuate greatly or cause damage to vegetation. Certainly deer reach overpopulation status in some park situations, but the surprising thing is how many parks containing deer populations have no problem.[58]

From an animal welfare or animal rights perspective, the presumption is against hunting. With regard to obligatory management species, it is not unusual for this presumption to be met, although this is not always the case. Ungulates are the classic example of obligatory management species, but even among them there are important variations. In climax-adapted ungulates (like bison, bighorn sheep, mountain goats, muskox, and caribou) the magnifying effects of time lags in vegetation damage are less severe than in subclimax ungulates (like deer, pronghorn antelope, and moose).[59] So the burden of proof necessary to justify therapeutic hunting is more likely to be met with some ungulates (e.g. deer and moose) than others (e.g. mountain goats or bighorn sheep). The parallel point with regard to permissive management species is that although they do not degrade their habitats on anything like a regular basis, they *can* under certain circumstances, and in those circumstances animal rights views can support hunting of them.

Endangered Species, Exotics, and Natural Predators

I said that I would spend most of my time on the hunting issue because a careful treatment of it sets the stage for my treatment of the other issues mentioned earlier: captive breeding of endangered species, removal of exotics, and natural predation. The received view has it that animal rights philosophies have environmentally unsound implications on each of these issues. Environmentalists recognize prima facie duties to remove exotics, to reintroduce locally extinct predators to their former ranges, and to captive breed critically endangered species. My thesis in this section is that a more critical understanding of animal rights philosophies shows how an animal rights activist could recognize each of these prima facie duties on one or the other of two closely related grounds: duties to future generations of animals and/or duties to future generations of human beings.

Let me begin with the latter ground. Singer and Regan both emphasize the formal moral equality of human and (some) non-human animals. Yet, as I had occasion to point out in previous sections, both think hierarchically in the last analysis. For that reason, scientists and agriculturalists who say that, "For an animal rightist, human and animal lives are strictly equal," or "According to animal rights philosophies, 'a rat is a pig is a dog is a boy'," are committing the same intellectual sin they so love to charge animal rights activists with. For they are attacking animal rights philosophies without having troubled to read any of the relevant professional literature (or, if they have read anything it is only *Animal Liberation*, and they have not read it with careful attention to the philosophical arguments). This is every bit as intellectually irresponsible as a follower of Peter Singer refusing to inform himself about the empirical realities of scientific experimentation or animal agriculture. Singer *clearly* states that it is *not* speciesist to hold that killing a normal adult human is as morally serious as killing a mouse,[60] and Regan *clearly* says that death is a greater harm to a normal adult human than it is to any non-human animal. No fair reading of Singer's *Animal Liberation* (let alone his *Practical Ethics*) or Regan's *The Case for Animal Rights* could yield scientists' common, fundamental misunderstanding of their views.

Although fair-minded scientists and agriculturalists will find this inegalitarian aspect of Singer's and Regan's views comforting, no doubt many animal rights activists will reject it. But this is not a point about which animal rights activists need be apologetic. Any workable ethics will recognize *some* hierarchies. Albert Schweitzer is renowned for assiduously refusing to prioritize forms of life and their various interests, maintaining that

> Whenever I in any way sacrifice or injure life, I am not within the sphere of the ethical, but I become guilty, whether it be egoistically guilty for the sake of maintaining my own existence or welfare, or unegoistically guilty for the sake of maintaining a greater number of other existences or their welfare.[61]

Here Schweitzer clearly says that even killing in self preservation incurs guilt. Yet he also admits that "The necessity to destroy and to injure life is imposed upon me" at every step,[62] implying that we cannot help but incur guilt all the time. Elsewhere he appears to contradict himself, saying that "Whenever I injure life of any sort, I must be quite clear whether it is necessary. Beyond the unavoidable, I must never go,"[63] suggesting that "unavoidable" or "necessary" injuries are permissible. It may be that Schweitzer's point was one with which I agree, namely that any adverse impact on the interests of any organism (even a disease microbe) introduces some evil into the world. If this were the meaning of the former passage, then it would be consistent with the latter passage, because (as any utilitarian will admit) the production of some evil can be justified by the preservation or production of good. Speaking in terms of unavoidable guilt is a confusing way of making this point, however. Probably Schweitzer's overarching aim was to urge people, in very dramatic terms, to take more seriously decisions involving injury or death to living things of any species. With that laudable goal I agree. But Schweitzer's own talk about the necessity of injury and death[64] gives the lie to any practically useful ethics entirely free of hierarchies. Any workable ethics must recognize some hierarchy of interests, and from this a hierarchy of life forms follows, if it turns out (as I think it does[65]) that only some forms of life have the favored kinds of interests.

The point of this digression on moral hierarchies is this: if

(1) we have a general duty to preserve the integrity of ecosystems as the necessary context in which future generations of humans can pursue their most important interests,
(2) these interests are of overriding moral importance, and
(3) safeguarding future generations' pursuit of these interests requires us to remove exotics, breed endangered species, and reintroduce predators,

then long-sighted anthropocentrists and animal rights activists can agree that these things should be done (or at least that there is a presumptive, prima facie duty to do these things).

Bryan Norton has offered an anthropocentric defense of the duty to preserve natural variety which leads fairly naturally to the three prima facie duties in question. Norton's argument

> recognizes the crucial role of creative, self-organizing systems in supporting human economic, recreational, aesthetic, and spiritual values. Because self-organizing systems maintain a degree of stable functioning across time, they provide a sufficiently stable context to which human individuals and cultures can adapt their practices.[66]

Norton doubts that adequate indicators of ecosystemic health are currently available, because of the "centrality and intransigence of scaling problems,"[67] but he stresses the general importance of total diversity – a combination of within-habitat diversity and cross-habitat diversity[68] – and the preservation of normal rates of change in environmental systems.[69] He therefore unpacks the duty to preserve natural variety in terms of preserving

(or, where necessary, restoring) the integrity of ecosystems. He says that

> An ecosystem has maintained its integrity . . . if it retains (1) the total diversity of the system – the sum total of the species and associations that have held sway historically – and (2) the systematic organization which maintains that diversity, including, especially, the system's multiple layers of complexity through time.[70]

Preserving "the sum total of the species and associations that have held sway historically" will sometimes require captive breeding of critically endangered species, sometimes it will require us to remove exotics, and sometimes it will require us to reintroduce locally extinct predators.

If future generations of human beings can only fulfill their most important interests against a background of relatively intact ecosystems, then relatively intact ecosystems we must preserve. And if, as environmentalists claim, preserving relatively intact ecosystems necessarily involves (some) breeding of endangered species, (some) removal of exotics, and allowing (some) natural predation, then animal rights activists who acknowledge the primacy of humans' most important interests can agree with both long-sighted anthropocentrists and environmentalists that we have prima facie duties to do these things.

I said that animal rights activists could also recognize prima facie duties to breed critically endangered species, remove exotics, and reintroduce predators as duties to future generations of *animals* and I will end by very briefly outlining how this is so. If human flourishing requires a relatively stable ecological context, then so too, presumably, does the flourishing of the nonhuman animals with which Singer and Regan are concerned. Norton's point about ecological integrity is not (or not just) that intact ecosystems are storehouses of resources useful to future generations of humans. If they were only that, then nontechnological creatures like deer and owls would not need intact ecosystems. But Norton's point is that total diversity is crucial to the dynamic stability of ecosystems through time. Certainly some species (e.g. coyotes and raccoons) are opportunistic and can thrive in newly disturbed ecosystems. Others (e.g. beaver) must disturb ecosystems to survive at all. But only if a patchwork of habitats in various stages of succession is maintained in every region will the needs of such species be met, for cross-habitat diversity provides the species on which these animals' lives depend. Although any one species may require a specific habitat to survive, in the long haul, all species depend on an ecological background of cross-habitat diversity. So without invoking the interests of future generations of humans, an animal rights activist could defend captive breeding, removal of exotics, and reintroduction of predators where these are necessary to preserve the ecological background conditions on which future generations of animals will depend.

Notes

1 It was a demonstration in response to Texas A&M's decision, in early 1991, to remove "sexual orientation" from the list of protected categories in its official anti-discrimination policy. The sign said: "Straight but not narrow." (I wish I could say I made it up, but someone handed it to me!)

2 J. Baird Callicott, "Animal Liberation: A Triangular Affair," *Environmental Ethics* 2 (1980), pp. 311–38; reprinted in Callicott, *In Defense of the Land Ethic* (Albany: SUNY Press, 1989).

3 Tom Regan, "The Nature and Possibility of an Environmental Ethic," *Environmental Ethics* 3 (1981), pp. 19–34.

4 Mark Sagoff, "Animal Liberation and Environmental Ethics: Bad Marriage, Quick Divorce," *Osgood Hall Law Journal* 22 (1984), pp. 297–307, at pp. 304, 306.

5 Eric Katz, "Defending the Use of Animals by Business: Animal Liberation and Environmental Ethics," in W. Michael Hoffman, Robert Frederick, and Edward S. Petry, Jr., eds., *Business, Ethics, and the Environment: The Public Policy Debate* (New York: Quorum Books, 1990), pp. 223–32, at p. 224.

6 Gary E. Varner and Martha C. Monroe, "Ethical Perspectives on Captive Breeding: Is it For the Birds?" *Endangered Species UPDATE*, Vol. 8, No. 1 (November 1990), pp. 27–9, at p. 28.

7 J. Baird Callicott, "Animal Liberation and Environmental Ethics: Back Together Again," in *In Defense of the Land Ethic* (Albany: SUNY Press, 1989), pp. 49–59.

8 Abstract of "Moral Monism in Environmental Ethics Defended," presented to the Central Division Meeting of the American Philosophical Association, April 24, 1993. *Proceedings and Addresses of the American Philosophical Association*, Vol. 66 (1993), No. 6, p. 69.

9 Bryan Norton, *Toward Unity Among Environmentalists* (New York: Oxford University Press, 1991), p. 222.

10 Ibid., p. 223.

11 Gary E. Varner, "Environmental Law and the Eclipse of Land as Private Property," in Frederick Ferré and Peter Hartel, eds., *Ethics and Environmental Policy: Theory Meets Practice* (Athens, GA: University of Georgia Press, 1994) pp. 142–60.

12 James M. Jasper and Dorothy Nelkin, *The Animal Rights Crusade: The Growth of a Moral Protest* (New York: Free Press, 1992).

13 Norton, *Toward Unity Among Environmentalists*, p. 246, emphasis added.

14 Ron Howard, personal communication dated 18 June 1992.

15 It might be preferable to speak in terms of "necessary" and "optional" rather than "obligatory" and "permissible," because Howard's labels are intended to be descriptive, rather than normative. Also, note the qualification, in the penultimate section of this paper, that even among obligatory management species, hunting is not *always* necessary to prevent environmental damage.

16 "Animal Rights: Ignorance About Nature," *Audubon*, November 1990.

17 Julie A. Smith, "Wisconsin Greens Support Hunting – The Alliance Wonders Why?" *The Alliance News*, Vol. 8, No. 1 (February, 1991), pp. 1, 7.

18 Marian Bean, "Environmental Groups and Animal Rights," *The Alliance News*, Vol. 8, No. 1 (February, 1991), p. 6.

19 Title 5 (Hunting and Fishing), §62.062(a).

20 S.B. 179, Section 1; Texas Code, Title 2 (Parks and Recreational Areas), §13.001(b).

21 Lone Star Chapter of the Sierra Club, *State Capitol Report*, Vol. 10, No. 5 (May 1, 1993), p. 2.

22 Peter Singer, *Animal Liberation*, second edition (New York: Avon, 1990).

23 Peter Singer, *Practical Ethics*, second edition (Cambridge: Cambridge University Press, 1993). Hereafter, *Practical Ethics*.

24 *Animal Liberation*, pp. 18–19.

25 Ibid., p. 17.

26 Ibid., p. 125.

27 There are subtle but important differences among these terms. See Michael R. Bratman's treatment in his *Intentions, Plans, and Practical Reason* (Cambridge: Harvard University Press, 1987).

28 *Practical Ethics*, pp. 111–16, 118, and 132.

29 Ibid., pp. 95, 133.

30 Ibid., p. 132.

31 Gary Varner, "Localizing Desire," chapter two of *In Nature's Interests? Interests, Animal Rights, and Environmental Ethics*, (New York: Oxford University Press, 1998), pp. 26–54.

32 See the anecdote reported by Donald Griffin, *Animal Minds* (Chicago: University of Chicago Press, 1992), pp. 64–5.

33 *Practical Ethics*, p. 132.

34 Sans the (possibly incoherent) obligation to maximize simultaneously two variables (minimize pain *and* maximize pleasure).

35 *Practical Ethics*, pp. 133–4, emphasis added.

36 *Animal Liberation*, p. 234. Two points about this argument. First, with regard to obligatory management species, it is not just "in special circumstances" that a population of animals "grows to such an extent that they damage their own environment and the prospects of their own survival, or that of other animals who share their habitat." The regularity with which this happens with obligatory management species is what separates them from permissive management species. Second, the choice is not simply between "allow[ing] hunters to kill some animals, inevitably wounding others in the process" and "reduc[ing] the fertility of the animals" by non-lethal means. Hunting regulations could be radically changed to minimize the wounding of animals. For instance, hunting could (in principle) be confined to bait stations with nearby blinds, from which hunters with high calibre, automatic weapons and telescopic sights would kill habituated animals in a selective way (e.g. only does and sicker animals).

37 Dale McCullough, "North American Deer Ecology: Fifty Years Later," in Thomas Tanner, ed., *Aldo Leopold: The Man and His Legacy* (Ankeny, Iowa: Soil Conservation Society of America, 1987), pp. 115–22, at p. 121.

38 "Report to American Wildlife Institute on the Utah and Oregon Wildlife Units," quoted in Susan Flader, *Thinking Like a Mountain: Aldo Leopold and the Evolution of an Ecological Attitude toward Deer, Wolves, and Forests* (Lincoln: University of Nebraska Press, 1978), p. 176.

39 Described in William Creed et al., "Harvest Management: The Wisconsin Experience," in Lowell K. Halls, ed., *White-Tailed Deer: Ecology and Management* (Harrisburg, Pennsylvania: Stackpole Books, 1984), pp. 211–42.

40 In Leopold's time, it was unusual to harvest over 40,000 animals a year. By the middle 1980s, by contrast, Wisconsin was consistently harvesting over a quarter of a million deer annually. Wisconsin Department of Natural Resources, *Wisconsin Game and Fur Harvest Summary, 1930–1986* (Madison, Wisconsin, 1987), pp. 3–4.

41 Here I am employing Michael Martin's analysis of conscientious law breaking, in "Ecosabotage and Civil Disobedience," *Environmental Ethics* 12 (1990), pp. 291–310, and adapting it to the case of brinkmanship.

42 Malcolm W. Browne, "New Animal Vaccines Spread Like Diseases," *New York Times*, 11 November 1991, pp. B5, B7.

43 Eugene C. Hargrove, "Preface," *The Animal Rights/ Environmental Ethics Debate: The Environmental Perspective*, p. x. See also Callicott's review of Regan's book, *Environmental Ethics 7* (1985), pp. 365–72.

44 Tom Regan, *The Case For Animal Rights* (Berkeley, CA: University of California Press, 1983), p. 78 (emphasis in original).

45 Ibid., pp. 285–6.

46 The phrase "*commercial* animal agriculture" is Regan's. It is not obvious why the qualification "commercial" is included.

47 Regan, *Case for Animal Rights*, p. 357.

48 Regan, *Case for Animal Rights*, pp. 322 and 377, emphasis in original.

49 Dale Jamieson, "Rights, Justice, and Duties to Provide Assistance," *Ethics* 100 (1990), pp. 349–62, at pp. 351ff.

50 Regan, *Case for Animal Rights*, section 6.4.

51 Jamieson, "Rights, Justice, and Duties to Provide Assistance," pp. 349, 362.

52 Dale McCullough, *The George Reserve Deer Herd: Population Ecology of a K-Selected Species* (Ann Arbor: University of Michigan Press, 1979).

53 McCullough, "Lessons from the George Reserve," pp. 219–22.

54 Gary E. Spencer, *Piney Woods Deer Management*, Texas Parks & Wildlife Department bulletin #7000–88 (February 1983), pp. 29, 32.

55 In bad years or on an already overstocked range, spike bucks (bucks 18 months or older with unforked antlers) are the result of poor nutrition rather than genetic "inferiority." But under good conditions such as those obtaining at or below I carrying capacity, bucks who produce spikes as year-lings will never achieve the same degree of antler development as fork-antlered yearlings.

56 McCullough argues that management for MSY simultaneously maximized trophy buck production in the George Reserve. While agreeing that average rack size is correlated with average weight, McCullough denies that heavier bucks must be older: "Record bucks were produced not at high densities, which have the oldest individuals, but rather at the lowest densities . . . having the youngest age structure in both the population and the kill" ("Lessons from the George Reserve," p. 234). But this makes it unclear why he says, earlier in the same article, that "It is ironic that those opposing hunting are most incensed by trophy hunting . . . a practice that assures that the fewest deer will die from gunshots" (p. 230). By his own account, maintaining the population at I carrying capacity involves the *most* animals dying from gunshots.

57 Notice, however, that a single-minded emphasis on eliminating pain would seem to imply that hunting a population of sentient creatures to extinction would be a good thing, since this would prevent an infinite amount of pain. Arthur Schopenhauer, the German pessimist philosopher who placed a premium on the elimination of suffering, advocated extinction of the human race on this ground. Although the hedonistic utilitarian principle as usually formulated involves potentially inconsistent goals (minimizing pain *and* maximizing pleasure), it is therefore preferable to a negative utilitarian principle of minimize pain, simpliciter.

58 McCullough, "Lessons from the George Reserve," pp. 239–40.

59 McCullough, *The George Reserve Deer Herd*, pp. 160 and 172.

60 *Animal Liberation*, p. 17–18, quoted above. See also *Practical Ethics*, ch. three.

61 Albert Schweitzer, *The Philosophy of Civilization* (New York: Macmillan, 1955), p. 325.

62 Ibid., p. 316.

63 Ibid., p. 318.

64 Unanalyzed, the notion of "necessity" is of very little help, however. See Susan Finsen, "On Moderation," in Marc Bekoff and Dale Jamieson, eds., *Interpretation and Explanation in the Study of Animal Behavior*, vol. 2 (Boulder: University of Colorado Press, 1990), pp. 394–419.

65 See generally, my *In Nature's Interests? Interests, Animal Rights, and Environmental Ethics*, (New York: Oxford University Press, 1998).

66 Bryan Norton, "A New Paradigm for Environmental Management," in Robert Costanza and Bryan Norton, eds., *Ecosystem Health: New Goals for Environmental Management* (Washington, DC: Island Press, 1992), pp. 23–41, at p. 24.

67 Ibid., p. 34.

68 Bryan Norton, *Why Preserve Natural Variety?* (Princeton, NJ: Princeton University Press, 1987).

69 Norton, *Toward Unity Among Environmentalists*.

70 "A New Paradigm for Environmental Management," p. 26.

9

Against the Moral Considerability of Ecosystems

Harley Cahen

I

If natural areas had no value at all for human beings, would we still have a duty to preserve them? Some preservationists think that we would. Aldo Leopold, for instance, argues brilliantly for the cultural and psychological value of wilderness; yet he insists that even "enlightened" self-interest is not enough.[1] According to Leopold, an "ecological conscience" recognizes "obligations to land."[2] The ecological conscience sees that preservation is a good thing in itself – something we have a prima facie duty to promote – apart from any contribution it makes to human welfare. For convenience, let us call this conviction the *preservationist intuition*.[3]

I share this intuition. Can we justify it? I see at least four plausible strategies. We might, first, appeal to the intrinsic value of natural ecosystems.[4] A second strategy relies on the interests of the individual creatures that are inevitably harmed when we disturb an ecosystem.[5] A third possibility is a virtue-based approach. Perhaps what offends us – as preservationists – is that anyone who would damage an ecosystem for inadequate reasons falls short of our "ideals of human excellence."[6] Each of these three strategies has something to recommend it. But none captures the element of the preservationist intuition that involves a feeling of obligation *to* "land." This suggests a fourth strategy, the appeal to what Kenneth Goodpaster calls *moral considerability*. This strategy represents an ecosystem as something that has interests of its own, and thus can directly be victimized or benefited by our actions.[7] If ecosystems do have interests of their own, perhaps we owe it to them to consider those interests in our moral deliberations. This fourth strategy is the one that I wish to call into question.

There is a fifth strategy – an appeal to the moral right of a natural ecosystem to be left alone. This strategy is similar to the fourth one but may be distinct. Rights, some would say, automatically "trump" other kinds of moral claim.[8] If so, an appeal to ecosystem rights would be much stronger than an appeal to moral considerability. (Too strong, I suspect: I find it best to regard talk of the rights of nonhumans as an enthusiastic way of asserting moral considerability.[9]) We can leave this question open, though, for if they are trumps, moral rights have at least this much in common with moral considerability: they both presuppose interests.

I contend that ecosystems cannot be morally considerable because they do not have interests – not even in the broad sense in which we commonly say that plants and other nonsentient organisms "have interests." The best we can do on behalf of plant interests, I believe, is the argument from *goal-directedness*. Nonsentient organisms – those not capable of consciously taking an interest in anything – have interests (and thus are candidates for moral considerability) in achieving their biological goals. Should ecosystems, too, turn out to be goal-directed, they would be candidates for moral considerability.[10]

Although the argument from goal-directedness fails, we should not dismiss the argument too hastily. Some ecosystems are strikingly stable and resilient. They definitely have a goal-directed look. Yet there are reasons to doubt whether this apparent goal-directedness is genuine. The key is to distinguish the goals of a system's behavior from other outcomes that are merely behavioral *byproducts*. Armed with this distinction, we can see that the conditions for genuine goal-directedness are tougher than environmental ethicists typically realize. Ecosystems seem unlikely to qualify.

In sections two and three of this paper I define *moral considerability* and distinguish it from other ways that something can matter morally. In section four I establish that goal-directedness plays a key role in arguments for the considerability of plants and other nonsentient organisms. In sections five and six I argue that this appeal to goal-directedness is plausible as long as we keep the goal/byproduct distinction in mind. In sections seven through nine, I argue that ecology and evolutionary biology cast serious doubt on the possibility that ecosystems are genuinely goal-directed.

II

The literature of environmental ethics is full of appeals to the interests of ecosystems. Consider Aldo Leopold's famous remark: "A thing is right when it tends to preserve the integrity, stability, and beauty of the biotic community. It is wrong when it tends otherwise."[11] Is Leopold suggesting that the biotic community has an interest in its own integrity and stability? Some commentators interpret his remark this way. James Heffernan, for instance, defends Leopold by insisting that "even ecosystems . . . are things that have interests and hence, may be benefited or harmed."[12] Holmes Rolston, III likewise would found an "ecological ethic" upon the obligation to promote "ecosystemic interests."[13]

More often the appeal to ecosystem interests is implicit. Consider John Rodman, criticizing animal liberationists such as Peter Singer for drawing the moral considerability boundary to include only sentient beings. Rodman complains: "The moral atomism that focuses on individual animals . . . does not seem well adapted to coping with ecological systems."[14] Why is "atomism" inadequate? Because, Rodman explains, an ecological community as a whole has a good of its own, a "welfare":

> I need only to stand in the midst of clear-cut forest, a strip-mined hillside, a defoliated jungle, or a dammed canyon to feel uneasy with assumptions that could yield the conclusion that no human action can make any difference to the welfare of anything but sentient animals.[15]

Of course, Rodman believes that individual plants and nonsentient animals are morally considerable, too. That is reason enough for him to feel uneasy with Singer's assumptions. It cannot be his only reason, however, for it would leave him as guilty of moral atomism as Singer. Whose *welfare* could Rodman have in mind? The welfare, I take it, of the communities themselves.[16]

III

Moral considerability is a potentially confusing term. Let me clarify and defend my use of it. I take moral considerability to be the moral status x has if, and only if (a) x has interests (a good of its own), (b) it would be prima facie wrong to frustrate x's interests (to harm x), and (c) the wrongness of frustrating x's interests is direct – that is, does not depend on how the interests of any other being are affected. It is the concern with interests that distinguishes moral considerability from the other varieties of moral status upon which the preservationist intuition might possibly be based.

Goodpaster plainly means to restrict moral considerability to beings with *interests*. In his first paper on moral considerability he explains that life is the "key" to moral considerability because living things have interests; this, he points out, is what makes them "capable of being beneficiaries."[17] Goodpaster makes a point of agreeing with Joel Feinberg about what Feinberg calls "mere things." "Mere things," Goodpaster says, are not candidates for moral considerability because they are "incapable of being benefited or harmed – they have no 'well-being' to be sought or acknowledged."[18] That is why he insists that "*x*'s being a living being" is not only sufficient for moral considerability but is also *necessary*.[19]

In Goodpaster's subsequent work, he characterizes the entire biosphere as a "bearer of value."[20] Yet he does not appear to have changed his understanding of the requirements for moral considerability. "The biosystem as a whole" is considerable, he says. Why? Because it is, in effect, an "organism" – "an integrated, self-sustaining unity which puts solar energy to work in the service of growth and maintenance."[21] Goodpaster's focus remains on interests and he expresses his confidence that the "biosystem as a whole" has them.[22]

Some philosophers speak of moral considerability but do not associate it with interests at all. Andrew Brennan, for instance, asserts that natural objects such as ecosystems, mountains, deserts, the air, rocky crests, and rivers may have this moral status though they have no interests and thus can be harmed only "metaphorically." This is no longer moral considerability as I understand it.[23]

Other philosophers equate moral considerability with intrinsic value, holding that both equally presuppose interests. Robin Attfield, for instance, writes, "I follow Goodpaster in holding that things which lack a good of their own cannot be morally considerable . . . or have intrinsic value."[24] J. Baird Callicott attributes to Goodpaster the view that because "life is intrinsically valuable . . . all living beings should be granted moral considerability."[25] As Callicott sums up his own view:

> If the self is intrinsically valuable, then nature is intrinsically valuable. If it is rational for me to act in my own best interest, and I and nature are one, then it is rational for me to act in the best interests of nature.[26]

The association of intrinsic value with interests seems odd to me. Many readers will suppose that "mere things" – things which have no interests, no good of their own – might conceivably be intrinsically valuable. As Eric Katz puts it, "many natural entities worth preserving [i.e., valuable in their own right] are not clearly the possessors of interests."[27]

Is this just a quibble about words? I think not. We have more than one paradigm of moral relevance, and it makes a difference which one we adopt as the model for our ethical thinking about ecosystems. If we aim to justify preservation by appeal to the intrinsic value of natural ecosystems,

our arguments must build on the way ecosystems resemble other things that we preserve for their intrinsic *value*. Moral considerability is another matter. To ground the preservationist intuition upon the *interests* of ecosystems, we have to look for an analogy between ecosystems and beings that clearly have interests. Given that ecosystems are not sentient, the most promising models are plants and other nonsentient organisms.[28]

IV

Some ethicists would object that we cannot even get this argument for ecosystems off the ground – it is absurd, they would say, to think that plants could be morally considerable. Such a dismissal of plants, however, is too quick, for it ignores goal-directedness. Peter Singer, for instance, regards *rocks* as representative of all nonsentient beings. "A stone," he says, "does not have interests because it cannot suffer. Nothing that we can do to it could possibly make any difference to its welfare." He therefore boldly concludes: "If a being is not capable of suffering, or of experiencing enjoyment or happiness, there is nothing to be taken into account."[29]

Although sentience may turn out, after all, to be necessary for moral considerability, this just cannot be as obvious as Singer assumes. There is a world of difference between plants and rocks. Surely there might be something to "take into account" even in the absence of sentience. All we need, as Bryan Norton observes, is something appropriately analogous to sentience. Norton rejects the possibility of ecosystem "rights" because "collectives such as mountain ranges, species, and ecosystems have no significant analogues to human sentience on which to base assignments of interests." Since collectives lack any analogue to sentience, he reasons, "the whole enterprise of assigning interests [to them] becomes virtually arbitrary."[30] Norton reaches this conclusion too quickly, as I argue below, but he makes two crucial points. First, we can plausibly attribute moral considerability to *x* only when we have a nonarbitrary way of identifying *x*'s interests. Second, this project does not require actual sentience. It is plain enough that plants, for instance, have interests in a straightforward sense, though they feel nothing.[31] Paul Taylor puts it this way:

Trees have no knowledge or feelings. Yet it is undoubtedly the case that trees can be harmed or benefited by our actions. We can crush their roots by running a bulldozer too close to them. We can see to it that they get adequate nourishment and moisture.... It is the good of trees themselves that is thereby affected.[32]

In general, Taylor explains, "the good of an individual nonhuman organism [consists in] the full development of its biological powers." Every organism is "a being whose standpoint we can take in making judgments about what events in the world are good or evil."[33]

Let us grant, in spite of Singer and his allies, that there is something about trees that we might intelligibly "take into account" for moral purposes. Can we be more specific? What is it that plants have and rocks do not? The obvious, but unilluminating answer is "life." Just what is it about being alive that makes plants candidates for moral considerability?

Goal-directedness is the key. Taylor, for instance, describes organisms as "teleological centers of life."[34] Goodpaster points to plants' "tendencies [to] maintain and heal themselves" and locates the "core of moral concern" in "respect for self-sustaining organization and integration."[35] Attfield writes of a tree's "latent tendencies, direction of growth and natural fulfillment."[36] Jay Kantor bases his defense of plant interests on their "self-regulating and homeostatic functions."[37] Rodman condemns actions that impose our will upon "natural entities that have their own internal structures, needs, and potentialities," potentialities that are actively "striving to actualize themselves."[38] Finally, James K. Mish'alani points to each living thing's *self-ameliorative competence:* "that is, a power for coordinated movement towards favorable states, a capacity to adjust to its circumstances in a manner to enhance its survival and natural growth."[39]

The goal-directedness of living things gives us a plausible and nonarbitrary standard upon which to "base assignments of interests." If ecosystems, though not sentient, are goal-directed, then we may (without absurdity) attribute interests to them, too. Goodpaster is right: there is no *a priori* reason to think that "the universe of moral considerability [must] map neatly onto our medium-sized framework of organisms."[40] Of course, we must not get carried away with this line of think-

ing. Goal-directedness is certainly not sufficient for moral considerability. One problem is that some machines are goal-directed – e.g., guided missiles, thermostatic heating systems, chess-playing computers, and "The Terminator."[41] The defender of moral considerability for plants must distinguish plants, morally, from goal-directed but inanimate objects.[42] Still, the possession of goals is what makes the notion of a plant's "standpoint" intelligible. Can we locate an ecosystem's standpoint by understanding its goals? Not if it doesn't have any goals.

V

We often know goal-directedness when we see it. The analysis of goal-directedness is, however, a terribly unsettled subject in the philosophy of science.[43] In light of this unsettledness, one must be cautious. Here are three claims. First, the attribution of goal-directedness to organisms can be scientifically and philosophically respectable – even when the organisms in question are nonsentient. Teleology talk need not be vitalistic, anthropomorphic, or rooted in obsolete Aristotelian biology or physics. It does not imply "backward causation." Nor need it run afoul of the "missing goal-object" problem.[44]

Second, some of these respectable accounts of goal-directedness are useful for the environmental ethicist. They enable us to resist crude versions of the common slippery-slope argument against the moral considerability of plants and other nonsentient living things. Once we admit nonsentient beings into the moral considerability club, how can we bar the door to ordinary inanimate objects? Porches, paintings, automobiles, garbage dumps, buildings, and other ordinary objects are allegedly lurking just outside, waiting for us to admit plants.[45] Goal-directedness can keep them out.

Third, we ought to recognize a distinction between goals and behavioral byproducts. A defensible conception of goal-directedness must distinguish true goals from outcomes that a system achieves incidentally. Ecosystem resilience and stability look like goals, but this appearance may deceive us. An ecosystem property such as stability might turn out to be just a byproduct, the incidental result of individual activities aimed exclusively at the individuals' own goals.

I shall discuss two of the main approaches to understanding goal-directedness. The approaches differ in important ways. I favor the second, but either will do for my purposes. The first approach is propounded by Ernest Nagel (among many others). Nagel holds that a system is goal-directed when it can reach (or remain in) some particular state by means of behavior that is sufficiently *persistent* and *plastic*.[46] Persistence refers to the system's ability to "compensate" for interfering factors that would otherwise take the system away from its goal.[47] Plasticity refers to the system's ability to reach the same outcome in a variety of ways.[48]

Nagel assumes that this approach will count all living things as goal-directed. It seems to.[49] There are problems, to be sure. Chief among these is the danger that it will include some behavior that plainly is not goal-directed – the movement of a pendulum, for instance, or the behavior of a buffered chemical solution.[50] Nagel, however, shows that with some plausible tinkering – mainly, by adding a third condition that he calls "orthogonality" – we can deal with these counterexamples.[51]

The second approach, pioneered by Charles Taylor, insists that goal-directed behavior "[really does] occur 'for the sake of' the state of affairs which follows."[52] Subsequent philosophers have developed this basic insight in various ways.

An especially influential exponent of Taylor's approach is Larry Wright. Taylor's considered formulation of his insight requires that the behavior in question be both necessary and sufficient for the goal. Wright finds this unsatisfactory – too generous in some ways and too strict in others.[53] He suggests what he calls an "etiological" account, one that focuses on the causal background of the behavior in question. A system is goal-directed, Wright contends, only if it behaves as it does just because that is the type of behavior that tends to bring about that type of goal. Formally, behavior B occurs for the sake of goal-state G if "(i) B tends to bring about G," and "(ii) B occurs because (i.e. is brought about by the fact that) it tends to bring about G."[54] The key condition is (ii). Some machines, say guided missiles, meet it, for a machine may B because it is designed to B, and it may be designed to B, in turn, because B tends to bring about some G desired by the designer. Organisms meet it, too, because of the way that natural selection operates. The fitness of an organism usually depends on how appropriate its behavior is – that is, the extent to which it does the sort of thing (say, B) that tends to help that kind of organism survive and reproduce. If the disposition to B is heritable,

organisms whose tendency to B helps make them fit will leave descendants that tend to B. Those descendants are disposed to B, then, in part because B is an appropriate type of behavior.[55]

Some people emphatically do not find Wright's approach respectable. He has, for example, recently been accused of "misrepresenting" natural selection as a teleological process in the old-fashioned (and discredited) sense according to which nature selects with certain outcomes in mind.[56] This charge, however, misses the mark, for there is nothing wrong with Wright's understanding of natural selection.[57] In addition, Wright has also dealt effectively with other, better-founded criticisms that need not be discussed here.[58]

Wright's development of Taylor's insight is the best approach for my purposes because alternative versions of Taylor's approach are not as good for sustaining attributions of goal-directedness to plants and lower animals.[59] With regard specifically to the slippery slope and the alleged "needs" of paintings and porches, Nagel's approach seems good enough, for these objects do not act persistently or plastically toward any result that we could seriously be tempted to call a goal. With Wright's criteria, however, we sidestep questions of degree that can plague Nagel. Consider my car, which responds to the upstate New York environment by rusting. The car rusts in spite of my efforts to stop it, and it would rust even if I tried much harder. Eventually it will fall apart. Does this unpleasantly persistent behavior count as goal-directed? A dedicated slippery-sloper might suggest that the car has the goal of rusting, a "need" to rust. Both Nagel and Wright can resist this suggestion, but Nagel would have a tougher time due to the vagueness of his persistence and plasticity conditions. Wright would simply check the behavior's etiology. My car, we may safely say, does not rust because rusting tends to cause cars to fall apart. It rusts because rust is just what happens when steel meets moisture and road salt. The car's behavior fails Wright's condition (ii).

We can imagine an etiology that would make my car's rusting genuinely goal-directed. Assume that car designers know how to make sturdy rust-free cars. Suppose, however, that they greedily conspire to build cars that are susceptible to rust in order to force people to buy new cars more frequently. We would then be unable fully to understand my car's rusting as a purely chemical process, for – on the conspiracy theory of rust – my car would be rusting (in part) because rusting tends to cause cars to fall apart.

Now, what about ecosystems? I concede that the heralded stability and resilience of some ecological systems make them prima facie goal-directed. When such an ecosystem is perturbed in any one of various ways, it bounces back. The members of the ecosystem do just what is necessary (within limits) to restore the system to equilibrium.[60] But are they cooperating in order to restore equilibrium? That is surely imaginable. On the other hand, each creature might instead be "doing its own thing," with the fortunate but incidental result that the ecosystem remains stable. If this is correct, then we are dealing with a behavioral byproduct, not a systemic goal.

The goal/byproduct distinction is well entrenched in the literature on natural selection and biological adaptation. Let me illustrate this distinction with an example from George Williams. Williams asks us to consider the behavior of a panic-stricken crowd rushing from a burning theater. A biologist newly arrived from Mars, he suggests, might be impressed by

> [the group's] rapid 'response' to the stimulus of fire. It went rapidly from a widely dispersed distribution to the formation of dense aggregates that very effectively sealed off the exits.[61]

If the crowd clogs the exits in spite of strenuous crowd-control efforts, would our Martian be entitled to report that he had observed a crowd that was goal-directed toward self-destruction via the sealing off of the exits? Of course not. We know that the clogging of the exits is just incidental. The people are trying to get out. The crowd clogs the exits in spite of the dreadful consequences.

Any theory of goal-directedness ought to be able to avoid the Martian's conclusion. Wright's theory does that easily via condition (ii): G can be a goal of behavior B only if B occurs *because* it tends to bring about G. If G plays no explanatory role it cannot be a genuine goal.[62]

Nagel's account also permits us to distinguish goal from byproduct. The persistence condition does the work here. There is no reason to think that the theater crowd's behavior is truly persistent toward clogging the exits. If there were more exits,

or larger exits, the people would have escaped smoothly. We may be sure that the crowd would not compensate for greater ease of exit by modifying its behavior in order to achieve clogging.

VI

If the idea that organisms have morally considerable "interests" seems plausible, it must, I think, be because organisms are genuinely goal-directed. When Taylor, for instance, characterizes a tree's good as "the full realization of its biological powers," we know what he means. We naturally assume that *powers* does not refer to everything that can happen to a tree – disease, say, or stunting from lack of nutrients. The tree's powers are the capabilities that the tree exercises in the service of its goals of growth, survival, and reproduction. We certify that those are the tree's goals, in turn, by employing criteria such as Wright's or Nagel's.

Should we find moral significance in an organism's goals? Perhaps not. We may coherently admit that plants have goals, yet deny that we have duties to them. Still, there is a tempting analogy between the goal-directed behavior of organisms and the intentional behavior of humans. Recall the rhetorical role that the notion of natural "striving" plays in Paul Taylor's argument for an ethic of respect for nature.[63] Recall Katz's choice of the term *autonomy* to characterize an organism's capacity for independent pursuit of its own interests.[64] Indeed the word *interests* itself conveys the flavor of intention.[65] This flavor lends persuasiveness to arguments such as Taylor's.

Let us, in any event, grant that to have natural goals is to have morally considerable interests. Where does this leave behavioral byproducts? It leaves them where they were – morally irrelevant. We need a nonarbitrary standard for deciding which states of affairs are good ones from the organism's own "standpoint." Sentience gives us such a standard by way of the organism's own preferences (which we are capable of discovering in various ways). By analogy, a nonsentient organism's biological goals – its "preferred" states – can do the same thing. But is there any reason at all for supposing that either mere natural tendencies or behavioral byproducts give rise to interests? I think not. Why, from a given system's "standpoint," should it matter whether some natural tendency, unconnected (except incidentally) to the system's goals, plays itself out?

Consider John Rodman's account of why it is wrong to dam a wild river. Rodman emphasizes that the river "struggles" against the dam "like an instinct struggles against inhibition."[66] One might be tempted to say that this way of talking is unnecessary, that every natural tendency is morally privileged. Such a claim, however, is implausible. What leads Rodman to talk of instinct and struggle is, I take it, the notion that the river actually has goals and would be frustrated, by the dam, in its pursuit of them.

I do not expect this example to be convincing. To see clearly that mere tendencies are in themselves morally irrelevant, we should consider something really drastic – like *death*. Usually, death is something that just happens – by accident, by disease, or simply when the body wears out. Organisms tend to die, but they do not ordinarily aim to die. As Jonathan Bennett puts it: "Every animal is tremendously plastic in respect of becoming dead: throw up what obstacles you may, and death will still be achieved. Yet animals seldom have their deaths as a goal."[67]

Consider a salmon of a species whose members routinely die after spawning. Even here death seems unlikely to be the organism's goal. The salmon dies because the arduous upstream journey has worn it out. If it could spawn without dying, it would do so. Once in a while that actually happens. When it does, do we say (without further evidence) that the salmon has been frustrated in its efforts to die after spawning? No. We would say that the salmon has managed to spawn without having had the misfortune to die.

Behavioral byproducts, like mere tendencies, seem not to generate anything we can comfortably call "interests." The salmon example illustrates this, if we interpret the death of the adult as a byproduct of its spawning. Williams' theater example illustrates it, too. It would be truly bizarre to suggest that the panicky crowd has an interest in being trapped and incinerated.

Although there is much more that needs to be said about whether the argument from goal-directedness can establish the moral considerability of plants, let us go ahead and accept plant moral considerability. But does ecosystem moral considerability follow? No, an obstacle remains: the goal/byproduct distinction. We still need to determine whether stability (or any other property) of an ecosystem is a genuine goal of the whole system rather than merely a byproduct of self-serving individual behavior.

VII

Donald Worster has written in his history of ecological ideas that "More often than not, the ecological text [holistic environmentalists] know and cite is either of their own writing or a pastiche from older, superseded models. Few appreciate that the science they are eagerly pursuing took another fork back yonder up the road."[68] Orthodox ecology, Worster says, has abandoned the "organismic" view of ecosystems and adopted a fundamentally individualistic one.[69] Robert M. May represents this individualistic orthodoxy. Of course, says May, there are "patterns at the level of ecological systems." He insists that these patterns do not represent goals. They are entirely explicable in terms of "the interplay of biological relations that act to confer specific advantages or disadvantages on individual organisms."[70]

What then are we to make of ecosystem stability and resilience? If May is right, the tendency of an ecosystem to bounce back after a disturbance is merely the net result of self-serving responses by individual organisms. We need not view stability as a system "goal." We may not even be entitled to do so. As Robert Ricklefs explains:

> The ability of the community to resist change [is] the sum of the individual properties of component populations.... Relationships between predators and prey, and between competitors, can affect the inherent stability of the community, but trophic structure does not evolve to enhance community stability.[71]

Certain forms of trophic structure typically enhance community stability, Ricklefs agrees, but trophic structure does not take on particular form because that form enhances stability.[72]

Someone might be tempted to conclude that my own argument undermines the moral considerability of organisms. Organisms, after all, consist of cells. The cells have goals of their own. Does my individualism require us to regard the behavior of organisms as merely a byproduct of the selfish behavior of cells? It does not. Cells do have their own goals, but these goals are largely subordinated to the organism's goals, because natural selection selects *bodies*, not cells. If the cells do not cooperate for the body's sake, the body dies and the cells die, too. That, very roughly, is how natural selection coordinates the body's activities.[73] Selection tends to eliminate individuals that are not good at the survival "game" (taking kin selection into account). Eventually this process leaves us with organisms that are good at it, and these organisms are goal-directed toward those states of affairs that have in the past made them winners.

So much for organisms. A familiar process – ordinary, individualistic natural selection – ensures that they are goal-directed. Is there a process that could account for goal-directedness in ecosystems? The only candidate I know of for this job is group selection operating at the community level.[74]

VIII

Does group selection have a part to play in the full explanation of the behavior of species populations or ecosystems? I hold that the answer is no. Now this may seem hard to believe. "Ecosystem behavior," you might counter, "is just too well coordinated for stability to be an accident." To undermine this intuition, let us consider a description of a simple situation in which there is a result that we could construe as "good for the group," but which is strictly speaking a byproduct of self-serving individual action, and then a second situation, a more complicated one, in which an extremely stable group property is, again, a byproduct.[75]

Consider any single-species population. Suppose that some individuals (call them the A-individuals) run into a stretch of bad luck and consequently fail to reproduce. Their failure to reproduce reduces the intensity of competition. This (other things being equal) permits other members of the population (the B-individuals) to reproduce more effectively than they otherwise would have. Should we regard this population as a goal-directed whole, answering a threat to its survival by redirecting its reproductive effort? Of course not. Williams explains the general difficulty in this way:

> Certainly species survival is one result of reproduction. This fact, however, does not constitute evidence that species survival is a function of reproduction. If reproduction is

entirely explainable on the basis of adaptation for individual genetic survival, species survival would have to be considered merely an incidental effect.[76]

There is no reason to think of the B-individuals' increased reproductive success as "compensating" for the failure of the A-individuals. If fact, each of the B-individuals has simply taken advantage of the A-individuals' failure. The net result is survival of the group, to be sure, but a postulated goal of group survival has no explanatory role to play.

Let us now consider a more difficult and controversial example, the clutch size in birds, long a bone of contention between group selectionists and Neo-Darwinians. Clutch size in some species of birds is remarkably constant; certain species of plover, for instance, almost always lay four eggs. If an egg is removed from the plover's nest, the bird lays a replacement, bringing the number back up to four. That is not so strange, in itself; yet it shows that the plover is physiologically able to lay more than four eggs. Why should it lay only four to start with?

Perhaps this is a sign of group selection at work, favoring a population of birds in which individual birds restrain themselves for the good of their group. V. C. Wynne-Edwards, the dean of group selectionism, would say so. Consider what Wynne-Edwards says about "reproductive rate":

> If intraspecific selection was all in favor of the individual, there would be an overwhelming premium on higher and ever higher individual fecundity, provided it resulted in a greater posterity than one's fellows. Manifestly this does not happen in practice; in fact, the reproductive rate in many species . . . is varied according to the current needs of the population.[77]

If this group-selectionist account is correct, then the plover population's behavior is goal-directed, even by Wright's criteria, for the individual birds are laying exactly four fertilized eggs just because of the consequences this activity has – that is, just because their self-restraint meets the "current needs of the population" – and we are entitled to speak of the group's goal of maintaining a certain specified average clutch size.

There is, however, an alternative account, an individualistic Neo-Darwinian explanation. Each individual bird seeks to maximize its own inclusive fitness. If laying more than four eggs were a sound strategy for the individual, then that is the strategy it would pursue. Chances are, however, that if a pair of plovers divide their parental energy and attention among five offspring instead of four, fewer of the offspring will survive than if the parents had been conservative. "Exactly four eggs" is a sound strategy from the standpoint of each individual. Seen in this way, it does not represent individual self-restraint for the good of the group. There is no group goal.[78]

Evolutionary biologists are by and large skeptical about group selection. For one thing, the argument for group selection in nature is essentially negative: as Wynne-Edwards puts it, group selection simply *must* occur, since normal natural selection would not be "at all effective" in generating "the kind of social adaptations . . . in which the interests of the individual are actually submerged or subordinated to those of the community as a whole."[79] This negative argument for group selection is undermined when we discover plausible individualistic explanations – when, as in the clutch size case, we find that the interests of the individual are not "submerged" at all. Williams and others, including Richard Dawkins, have shown that we do not need group selection to explain any of the phenomena upon which Wynne-Edwards builds his case.[80]

Worster is correct about which fork ecology has taken. To be sure, a number of theorists have shown how something they label "group selection" could occur under the right circumstances.[81] These particular theories, however, insofar as they are extensions of kin selection, are fundamentally "individualistic," and are not much like the theories that earlier advocates of group selection had hoped for.[82] We have little or no reason to believe that evolution by group selection, as traditionally conceived, is significant in nature.[83]

IX

When we turn from group selection operating on single-species populations to community selection, the result is much the same. According to Robert May, for instance:

Natural selection acts almost invariably on individuals or on groups of related individuals. Populations, much less communities of interacting populations, cannot be regarded as units subject to Darwinian evolution.[84]

This view has been seconded by Elliott Sober. "Darwinism," Sober asserts, "is a profoundly individualistic doctrine":

[It] rejects the idea that species, communities, and ecosystems have adaptations that exist for their own benefit. These higher-level entities are not conceptualized as goal-directed systems; what properties of organization they possess are viewed as artifacts of processes operating at lower levels of organization.[85]

To be fair, I should report Robert McIntosh's recent lament that "organismic ecology is alive and well." McIntosh worries that parts of the ecosystem-as-organism view survive in "systems" ecology.[86] John L. Harper shares this worry and he warns against "one of the dangers of the systems approach to community productivity" – namely, the temptation to "treat the behavior that [one] discovers as something that can be interpreted *as if* community function is organized." Harper insists that we must resist this temptation: "What we see as the organized behavior of systems is the result of the fate of individuals. Evolution is about individuals and their descendants."[87]

Some systems ecologists contend that ecosystems have some "organismic" features while conceding that "natural selection operates only on a community's constituent populations, not on the community as a whole."[88] These sources, as I read them, hold small comfort for the advocate of ecosystem interests. They support at best an analogy that is too weakly organismic to generate ecosystem goals.[89]

Obviously there is room for rebuttal here. Still, this testimony suggests the scorn with which ecologists and evolutionary biologists typically regard group selection.[90] Could anything else cause individuals to cooperate for the sake of ecosystem goals? I know of no plausible candidates. If the verdict against group selection stands up, I see no way to justify ecosystem moral considerability with the argument from goal-directedness.

X

Earlier I mentioned several distinct strategies for justifying what I call the "preservationist intuition" – intrinsic value, the good of individual plants and animals, and ideals of human excellence. Any of these might be enough. Still, we may find ourselves tempted to believe that whole ecosystems have interests and are therefore morally considerable. This avenue, however, is not promising. Genuine goal-directedness is a step – an essential step – toward moral considerability. It makes sense (as I have argued) to claim that plants and other nonsentient organisms are morally considerable – but only because those beings' own biological goals provide a nonarbitrary standard for our judgments about their welfare. Were ecosystems genuinely goal-directed, we could try for the next step.[91]

Some ecosystems do indeed appear to have goals – stability, for example. There is a complication, however. Mere behavioral byproducts, which are outcomes of no moral significance, can look deceptively like goals. Moreover, on what I take to be our best current ecological and evolutionary understanding, the goal-directed appearance of ecosystems is in fact deceptive. Stability and other ecosystem properties are byproducts, not goals. Ecosystem interests are, I conclude, a shaky foundation for the preservationist intuition.

Notes

1 Aldo Leopold, *A Sand County Almanac: With Essays on Conservation from Round River* (New York: Ballantine, 1966), p. 244. He characterizes economic arguments for preservation as "subterfuges," invented to justify what we know we should do on other grounds (p. 247). He also describes "despoliation of land" as "not only inexpedient but wrong" (p. 239).

2 Ibid., p. 245.

3 Eric Katz expresses the preservationist intuition clearly in "Utilitarianism and Preservation," *Environmental Ethics* 1 (1979): 357–64. The "danger" posed by an ethic based exclusively on human interests, Katz says, is that it "can support a policy of preservation only on a contingent basis" (p. 362).

4 See, e.g., Holmes Rolston, III, "Are Values in Nature Subjective or Objective?" *Environmental Ethics* 4 (1982): 125–51 and Peter Miller, "Value as Richness: Toward a Value Theory for the Expanded Natural-

ism in Environmental Ethics," *Environmental Ethics* 4 (1982): 101–14. Bryan Norton worries, properly, that there are "questionable ontological commitments involved in attributing intrinsic value to nature." "Environmental Ethics and Weak Anthropocentrism," *Environmental Ethics* 6 (1984): 147–8. Some who argue for the "intrinsic value" of nature might be happy with something less worrisome, ontologically – namely, what C. I. Lewis calls "inherent value." See Lewis, *An Analysis of Knowledge and Valuation* (La Salle, Ill.: Open Court, 1946), pp. 382–92. The problem with this strategy is that aesthetic and other kinds of inherent value, though objective, are fundamentally anthropocentric. See Rolston, "Are Values in Nature Subjective or Objective?" p. 151, and Robin Attfield, *The Ethics of Environmental Concern* (New York: Columbia University Press, 1983), pp. 151–2. These waters are very muddy, and J. Baird Callicott has lately stirred them up some more by defining inherent value in a way that is explicitly at odds with Lewis's conception. "Intrinsic Value, Quantum Theory, and Environmental Ethics," *Environmental Ethics* 7 (1985): 262.

5 See Paul W. Taylor, *Respect for Nature: A Theory of Environmental Ethics* (Princeton: Princeton University Press, 1986), pp. 70–1. Taylor makes it clear that when he speaks of the "good of a whole biotic community," he does not imagine that the community – as a whole – has a good of its own. The community's good is, he says, a "statistical concept" compounded out of the interests of the individual creatures that comprise the community.

6 See Thomas E. Hill, Jr., "Ideals of Human Excellence and Preserving Natural Environments," *Environmental Ethics* 5 (1983): 211–24. See also Bryan G. Norton, "Environmental Ethics and Weak Anthropocentrism," *Environmental Ethics* 6 (1984): 131–48. If the "excellence" in question is the ability to recognize intrinsic (or even inherent) value when one encounters it, then this strategy turns out to be a variant of the first one.

7 Goodpaster coined the term *moral considerability* in "On Being Morally Considerable," *Journal of Philosophy* 75 (1978): 308–25. When I speak of an organism's interests I do not mean to imply anything about its state of mind – or even that it has a mind. Throughout this paper I use the terms *interests* and *good of one's own* interchangeably. I recognize that there are good reasons not to equate these terms (see Taylor, *Respect for Nature*, pp. 62–8), but even Taylor concedes that it is "convenient" (pp. 270–1) to speak of whatever furthers a being's good as also promoting its interests. I find it convenient too.

8 See, for example, Ronald Dworkin, *Taking Rights Seriously* (Cambridge, Mass.: Harvard University Press, 1978).

9 According to Joel Feinberg, rights talk is merely a way of referring to *valid claims*. On this view, having rights is equivalent to being morally considerable. See Feinberg, "The Nature and Value of Rights," *Journal of Value Inquiry* 4 (1971): 263–77 and "The Rights of Animals and Unborn Generations," in *Philosophy and Environmental Crisis*, ed. William T. Blackstone (Athens: University of Georgia Press, 1974).

10 I classify all beings that have interests as "candidates" for moral considerability. If my analysis of organismic interests is correct, then having interests is only the first step to moral considerability.

11 Leopold, *Sand County Almanac*, p. 262.

12 James D. Heffernan, "The Land Ethic: A Critical Appraisal," *Environmental Ethics* 4 (1982): 242. On balance I think Heffernan is right: Leopold is asserting moral considerability for ecosystems. In that case, Heffernan's point is well-taken: an ecosystem must be seen as the sort of entity that we can not only damage (i.e., put in a state of diminished value or impaired usefulness), but also *harm* (i.e., make worse off from the standpoint of its own interests).

13 Holmes Rolston, III, "Is There an Ecological Ethic?" *Ethics* 85 (1975): 106. Rolston no longer speaks in these terms, though his talk of "projects" suggests that something like an appeal to goal-directedness is still at work. See "Are Values in Nature Subjective or Objective?" pp. 146–7, where Rolston speaks of achievements that "do not have wills or interests," but do have "headings, trajectories, traits, successions, which give them a tectonic integrity." More recently still, even while conceding that "ecologists... have doubted whether ecosystems exist as anything over their component parts," and agreeing that in ecosystems there are "no policy makers, no social wills, no goals," Rolston is still drawn to speak, tentatively, of "the good of the system" and to claim that "a spontaneous ecosystem is typically healthy." "Valuing Wildlands," *Environmental Ethics* 7 (1985): 26, 30.

14 John Rodman, "The Liberation of Nature?" *Inquiry* 20 (1977): 89.

15 Ibid. See also Rodman's description of a river as a "victim" of a dam (pp. 114–15). A hillside (or even a river) is not likely to be a complete ecosystem, of course. My arguments apply equally, I think, to ecosystems and to ecological communities.

16 Here are two more examples of the sort of language that raises my suspicions. (1) "Deep ecologists" Bill Devall and George Sessions, in "The Development of Natural Resources and the Integrity of Nature," assert that when "humans have distressed an ecosystem," we are obliged to make "reparations" (*Environmental Ethics* 6 [1984]: 305, 312). (2) J. Baird Callicott denies that he wishes to extend "moral considerability" to "inanimate entities such as oceans, lakes, mountains, forests, and wetlands"; yet he refers to the "well-being of the biotic community, the biosphere as a whole," and employs "the good of the community as a whole" as a standard for the assessment of the relative value... of its constitutive parts" ("Animal Liberation: A Triangular Affair," *Environmental Ethics* 2 [1980]: 337, 324–5).

17 Goodpaster, "On Being Morally Considerable," pp. 323, 319.

18 Ibid., p. 318. Feinberg's remarks on "mere things" are in "The Rights of Animals and Unborn Generations," pp. 49–50.

19 Goodpaster, "On Being Morally Considerable," p. 313.

20 Kenneth E. Goodpaster, "From Egoism to Environmentalism," in *Ethics and Problems of the 21st Century*, ed. Goodpaster and Sayre (Notre Dame: Notre Dame University Press, 1979), p. 30.

21 Ibid., pp. 32, 35, n. 25. Here he picks up a suggestion that he had already made in "On Being Morally Considerable," pp. 310, 323.

22 Goodpaster now rejects "generalizations of egoism" that extend moral concern to a class of beneficiaries that includes "forests, lakes, rivers, air and land" ("From Egoism to Environmentalism," p. 28). Moral considerability for ecosystems is in the same "egoistic" spirit, I suppose. Goodpaster prefers to speak of "bearers of value," a term that de-emphasizes the possession of interests. Yet this talk is misleading. It can only obscure Goodpaster's assumptions about what makes the biosphere considerable – including its capacity for "successful self-protection" (p. 32).

23 Andrew Brennan, "The Moral Standing of Natural Objects," *Environmental Ethics* 6 (1984): 53, 49, 51. Brennan uses the term *moral standing*, which he introduces as a synonym for moral considerability (p. 37). I am not attacking the substance of Brennan's view here; I am objecting to his claim to be explicating Goodpaster's concept (p. 35). Brennan has severed moral considerability completely from the notion that Goodpaster finds crucial – that of being a potential beneficiary. I believe that Goodpaster would not recognize the concept after this surgery.

24 Attfield, *The Ethics of Environmental Concern*, p. 149. See also p. 159.

25 Callicott, "Intrinsic Value, Quantum Theory," p. 258.

26 Ibid., p. 275.

27 Eric Katz, "Organism, Community, and the 'Substitution Problem,'" *Environmental Ethics* 7 (1985): 243. Oddly, Katz goes on to associate intrinsic value with "autonomy," which he in turn locates (p. 246) in the fact that "natural individuals... pursue their own *interests* while serving roles in the community."

28 Leaving aside Callicott's argument for nature as one's "extended self."

29 Peter Singer, *Animal Liberation* (New York: Avon Books, 1975), p. 8. Singer repeats this section verbatim in *Practical Ethics* (Cambridge: Cambridge University Press, 1979), p. 50. The leap is surprisingly common. See, e.g., William Frankena, "Ethics and the Environment," in *Ethics and Problems of the 21st Century*, p. 11, and G. J. Warnock, *The Object of Morality* (London: Methuen & Co., 1971), p. 151. Scott Lehmann judges this to be "the standard view among moral philosophers" and rests his case against the "rights" of wilderness areas on the premise that "only subjects of experience can be harmed or benefited" ("Do Wildernesses Have Rights?" *Environmental Ethics* 3 [1981]: 136–8).

30 Norton, "Environmental Ethics and Nonhuman Rights," p. 35.

31 Devastating critiques of claims to have demonstrated plant sentience include Arthur Galston "The Unscientific Method," *Natural History*, March 1974, and Arthur W. Galston and Clifford L. Slayman, "The Not-So-Secret Life of Plants," *American Scientist* 67 (1979): 337–44.

32 Paul Taylor, "The Ethics of Respect for Nature," *Environmental Ethics* 3 (1981): 200. Taylor has reiterated this in *Respect for Nature*.

33 Ibid., p. 199.

34 Ibid., pp. 210–11.

35 Goodpaster, "On Being Morally Considerable," pp. 319, 323.

36 Robin Attfield, "The Good of Trees," *Journal of Value Inquiry* 15 (1981): 37. See also Attfield, *The Ethics of Environmental Concern*, pp. 140–65.

37 Jay Kantor, "The 'Interests' of Natural Objects," *Environmental Ethics* 2 (1980): 169.

38 Rodman, "The Liberation of Nature?" pp. 100, 117.

39 James K. Mish'alani, "The Limits of Moral Community and the Limits of Moral Thought," *Journal of Value Inquiry* 16 (1982): 138.

40 Goodpaster, "On Being Morally Considerable," p. 323.

41 Goodpaster correctly describes the idea that a house's porch has interests as "simply incoherent" ("On Stopping at Everything: A Reply to W. M. Hunt," *Environmental Ethics* 2 [1980]: 282). We cannot dismiss the machines in my list so easily.

42 Mish'alani and Taylor recognize this, but I find their solutions unpersuasive. They seem to imply (implausibly) that if we humans should turn out to be the artifacts of a Creator, we should cease to regard ourselves as morally considerable. Taylor, *Respect for Nature*, p. 124 and Mish'alani, "Limits of Moral Community," p. 139.

43 Even so, it is surprising that environmental ethicists have not looked more often to the philosophy of science literature. Brennan is an exception. See "Moral Standing of Natural Objects," pp. 41–4. (Taylor mentions, in passing, that a philosophical literature about goal-directedness exists, but he does not make much use of it. [*Respect for Nature*, p. 122, n. 8].)

44 The problem of the "missing goal-object" is that behavior may be directed at a goal that happens to be unattainable or even nonexistent. This fact seems fatal for accounts of goal-directedness in terms of feedback. See Israel Scheffler, *The Anatomy of Inquiry* (New York: Alfred A. Knopf, 1963), pp. 112–16. These worries, nevertheless, still trouble many. It is for this reason that William C. Wimsatt insists, defensively, that "teleology, properly so-called, does have a respectable role in the scientific characterization of non-cognitive systems" ("Teleology and the Logical Structure of Function Statements," *Studies in the History and Philosophy of Science* 3 [1972]: 80). Wimsatt maintains that he is innocent of anthropomorphism (p. 65). See also Michael Ruse, *The Philosophy of Biology* (London: Hutchinson, 1973), pp. 174–6.

45 W. Murray Hunt claims that a porch's "needs" (e.g., to be painted) are as evident as a lawn's need to be watered ("Are Mere *Things* Morally Considerable?" *Environmental Ethics* 2 [1980]: 59–66). R. G. Frey asserts that a Rembrandt painting has interests in every sense in which a dog has them, in *Interests and Rights: The Case Against Animals* (Oxford: Clarendon Press, 1980), p. 79. Elliott Sober claims that he cannot see how the needs of plants can be plausibly distinguished from the needs of "automobiles, garbage dumps, and buildings." "Philosophical Problems of Environmentalism," in *The Preservation of Species*, ed. Bryan G. Norton (Princeton, New Jersey: Princeton University Press, 1986), p. 184.

46 Ernest Nagel, *The Structure of Science* (Indianapolis: Hackett, 1961), pp. 398–421 and "Teleology Revisited," in *Teleology Revisited and Other Essays in the Philosophy and History of Science* (New York: Columbia University Press, 1979). See also Richard Braithwaite, *Scientific Explanation* (Cambridge: Cambridge University Press, 1953), pp. 319–41 and Ruse, *Philosophy of Biology*, pp. 174–96.

47 Nagel says that persistence is "the continued maintenance of the system in its goal-directed behavior, by changes occurring in the system that compensate for any disturbances . . . which, were there no compensating changes . . . would prevent the realization of the goal" ("Teleology Revisited," p. 286).

48 In Nagel's words: "the goal . . . can generally be reached by the system following alternate paths or starting from different initial positions" (Ibid). See also Braithwaite, *Scientific Explanation*, pp. 329–34. Braithwaite conducts his analysis entirely in terms of plasticity.

49 Nagel also seems to believe, though, that mechanistic accounts of behavior, when they become available, automatically drive out teleological accounts

("Teleology Revisited," pp. 289–90). He doesn't say whether he thinks we have successful mechanistic accounts of plant behavior yet.

50 For other problems, see Wimsatt, "Teleology," p. 26, David Hull, *Philosophy of Biological Science* (Englewood Cliffs, NJ: Prentice-Hall, 1974), pp. 107–9, and Larry Wright, "The Case Against Teleological Reductionism," *British Journal for the Philosophy of Science* 19 (1968): 211–23.

51 Nagel, *Structure of Science*, pp. 418–21, and "Teleology Revisited," pp. 287–90.

52 Charles Taylor, *The Explanation of Behavior* (London: Routledge and Kegan Paul, 1964), p. 5.

53 Larry Wright, "Explanation and Teleology," *Philosophy of Science* 29 (1972): 204–18. One problem especially relevant to my thesis here is that, as Wright points out, Taylor's formulation admits "all sorts of bizarre accidents into the category of goal-directed activity" (p. 209).

54 Ibid., p. 211. This formulation obviously fails in the case of international but misguided action unless we understand "tends to bring about *G*" as "tends *under normal circumstances* to bring about *G*." If I submit a paper to a defunct journal, that may not tend to bring about the goal of having my paper published, but my behavior is clearly goal-directed. I have submitted the paper in order to have it published.

55 This "because" applies, as Wright acknowledges, in a rather "involuted" way. It applies, nevertheless. See "Explanation and Teleology," pp. 216–17.

56 Kristen Shrader-Frechette, "Organismic Biology and Ecosystems Ecology: Description or Explanation?" in *Current Issues in Teleology*, ed. Nicholas Rescher (Lanham, MD.: University Press of America, 1986), pp. 84–5, n. 28.

57 See Larry Wright, "Functions," *Philosophical Review* 82 (1973): 139–68, esp. 159–64.

58 See, for example, Andrew Woodfield, *Teleology* (Cambridge: Cambridge University Press, 1976), pp. 83–8, and Arthur Minton, "Wright and Taylor: Empiricist Teleology," *Philosophy of Science* 42 (1975): 299. Wright defends himself in "The Ins and Outs of Teleology: A Critical Examination of Woodfield," *Inquiry* 21 (1978): 233–45.

59 Jonathan Bennett, for instance, in *Linguistic Behavior* (Cambridge: Cambridge University Press, 1976), pp. 36–81. Bennett introduces the concept of "registration" and says that a system (*S*) is goal-directed toward *B* when it does *B* because it registers that it is in a situation where *B* will bring about *G*. This analysis does not immediately exclude plants. The question, as Bennett sees it (p. 79), is whether the behavior of plants has a "unitary" mechanistic explanation. Because phototropism in green plants is "controlled by one unitary mechanism," he refuses to count it as a goal-directed behavior.

60 For a sound discussion of ecosystem stability see John Lemons, "Cooperation and Stability as a Basis for Environmental Ethics," *Environmental Ethics* 3 (1981): 219–30.

61 George Williams, *Adaptation and Natural Selection: A Critique of Some Current Evolutionary Thought* (Princeton: Princeton University Press, 1966), pp. 210–11. We can, by the way, imagine a system that is goal-directed toward self-destruction. Wimsatt describes a "suicide machine" in "Teleology," pp. 20–2.

62 Wright is keen on distinguishing goals from byproducts, though not in precisely those terms. "Teleological behavior is not simply appropriate behavior," he insists, "it is appropriate behavior with a certain etiology" ("Explanation and Teleology," p. 215). Byproducts result, after all, from behavior that is appropriate in a trivial sense – appropriate for producing those byproducts. Bennett, too, has a good discussion of "fraudulent" attributions of goal-directedness (*Linguistic Behavior*, pp. 75–7).

63 Taylor, "Respect for Nature," p. 210.

64 See note 27 above. See also Heffernan, "The Land Ethic," p. 242.

65 General treatments of teleology often point this out. In *Linguistic Behavior*, Jonathan Bennett treats human intention as a special case of goal-directedness. Andrew Woodfield reverses the analysis, claiming that attributions of goal-directedness to nonsentient things such as plants and machines are extensions of the "core concept" of having an "intentional" object of desire (*Teleology*, pp. 164–6, 201–2).

66 Rodman, "Liberation of Nature?" p. 115.

67 Bennett, *Linguistic Behavior*, p. 45.

68 Donald Worster, *Nature's Economy: A History of Ecological Ideas* (Cambridge: Cambridge University Press, 1985), pp. 332–3.

69 Here is an "organismic" characterization of ecosystems from an ecology text popular throughout the 1950s: "The community maintains a certain balance, establishes a biotic border, and has a certain unity paralleling the dynamic equilibrium and organization of other living systems. Natural selection operates upon the whole interspecies system, resulting in a slow evolution of adaptive integration and balance. Division of labor, integration and homeostasis characterize the organism.... The interspecies system has also evolved these characteristics of the organism and may thus be called an ecological supraorganism." W. A. Allee et al., *Principles of Animal Ecology* (Philadelphia: W. B. Saunders, 1949), p. 728.

70 Robert M. May, "The Evolution of Ecological Systems," *Scientific American*, September 1987, p. 161. This sort of individualism by no means excludes altruism. Many individual organisms aim to some extent at the survival of their kin.

71 Robert E. Ricklefs, *The Economy of Nature* (Portland, Oreg.: Chiron Press, 1976), p. 355.

72 See also J. Engelberg and L. L. Boyarsky, "The Noncybernetic Nature of Ecosystems," *The American Naturalist* 114 (1979): 317–24. "That a system is stable, that it can resist perturbations, is not a sign that it is cybernetic." Engelberg and Boyarsky's main point is that ecosystems lack the "global information networks" that integrate the parts of goal-directed systems such as organisms.

73 See, for logic similar to mine, Elliott Sober's treatment of "selfish DNA" in *The Nature of Selection: Evolutionary Theory in Philosophical Focus* (Cambridge, Mass.: MIT Press, 1984), pp. 305–14.

74 I agree with William Wimsatt, who suggests that "*all* teleological phenomena are ultimately to be explained in terms of selection processes" ("Teleology," p. 15). David Hull criticizes Wimsatt (unsuccessfully, I think) in *Philosophy of Biological Science*, p. 113.

75 Both of my examples concern single-species populations. I picked them for their simplicity. They make a point that seems to hold, a fortiori, for ecosystems and communities as well.

76 Williams, *Adaptation and Natural Selection*, p. 160. See also pp. 107–8. Jan Narveson also makes this point, observing that as long as some people have children for selfish reasons, then the race is "perpetuated willy-nilly" whether or not anyone has children *in order* to perpetuate the race. Narveson, "On the Survival of Humankind," in *Environmental Philosophy*, ed. Robert Elliot and Arran Gare (St. Lucia: University of Queensland Press, 1983), pp. 51–2.

77 V. C. Wynne-Edwards, *Animal Dispersion in Relation to Social Behavior* (New York: Hafner, 1962), p. 19. See pp. 484–90.

78 David Lack offers evidence that (other things being equal) larger-than-normal clutches typically reduce the number of surviving offspring per nest. David Lack, *The Natural Regulation of Animal Numbers* (Oxford: Clarendon Press, 1954), pp. 21–32, and *Population Studies of Birds* (Oxford: Clarendon Press, 1966), pp. 3–7 and throughout. Reducing the number of eggs does not sufficiently improve each offspring's chances to make that a worthwhile strategy, either. Michael Ruse claims (*The Philosophy of Biology*, pp. 179–81) that the tendency of a bird population toward laying clutches of a particular size *is* goal-directed behavior even though (he assumes) it isn't a result of group selection. He thinks he is using Nagel's conception of goal-directedness. The problem, I suspect, is that he does not subject the population's behavior to a robust version of the persistence test. It is not clear that Ruse can get the right answer even in the theater-crowd case.

79 Wynne-Edwards, *Animal Dispersion*, p. 18.

80 Richard Dawkins, *The Selfish Gene* (Oxford: Oxford University Press, 1976), esp. chaps. 5–7. See, for example, Dawkins' explanation of how sterile castes have evolved in the social insects. Compare Wynne-Edwards' view that it is *inconceivable* that sterile castes could have evolved except where "selection had promoted the interests of the social group, as an evolutionary unit in its own right" (*Animal Dispersion*, p. 19).

81 See, e.g., David Sloan Wilson, *The Natural Selection of Populations and Communities* (Menlo Park, Calif.: Benjamin/Cummings, 1980) and Michael Gilpin, *Group Selection in Predator–Prey Communities* (Princeton: Princeton University Press, 1975).

82 John Cassidy, "Philosophical Aspects of Group Selection," *Philosophy of Science* 45 (1978): 575–94. See also Sober, *The Nature of Selection*, pp. 255–66, 314–68.

83 Some parasites may be an exception. See Peter W. Price, *Evolutionary Biology of Parasites* (Princeton: Princeton University Press, 1980). I am not sure, either, exactly what to say about cases of exceedingly close symbiosis, as in lichens.

84 Robert M. May, "The Evolution of Ecological Systems," *Scientific American*, September 1978, p. 161.

85 Sober, "Philosophical Problems for Environmentalism," p. 185. The upshot? "An environmentalism based on the idea that the ecosystem is directed toward stability and diversity," he says, "must find its foundation elsewhere." Thus Sober has anticipated the central theme of my argument, though in my opinion he is much too quick to draw this conclusion.

86 Robert McIntosh, "The Background and Some Current Problems of Theoretical Ecology," in *Conceptual Issues in Ecology*, ed. Esa Saarinen (Dordrecht, Holland: D. Reidel, 1982), p. 10. The context makes it clear that McIntosh finds this survival lamentable.

87 John L. Harper, "Terrestrial Ecology," in *Changing Scenes in the Natural Sciences, 1776–1976* ed. Clyde E. Goulden (Philadelphia: Academy of Natural Sciences, 1977), pp. 148–9 (emphasis added).

88 See J. L. Richardson, "The Organismic Community: Resilience of an Embattled Ecological Concept," *Bioscience*, July 1980, pp. 465–71. See also R. V. O'Neill et al., *A Hierarchical Concept of Ecosystems* (Princeton: Princeton University Press, 1986), pp. 37–54.

89 See, e.g., Richardson's discussion of "keystone" species.

90 Could my dismissal of group selection be too hasty? A referee points out that group selection is "not a scientific joke like 'Creation Science'." True enough. One respected ecologist who assumes group selection at the community level is Eugene Odum. See *Funda-*

mentals of Ecology, 3rd ed. (Philadelphia: W. B. Saunders, 1971), pp. 251–75. See also M. J. Dunbar, "The Evolution of Stability in Marine Environments: Natural Selection at the Level of the Ecosystem," *American Naturalist* 94 (1960): 129–36. Nevertheless, Wynne-Edwards (whom the referee mentions favorably) has something in common with Creation scientists I have read – he carefully ignores the explanations that his opponents offer. See, for example, Lack's annoyed reply to Wynne-Edwards in *Population Studies*, pp. 299–312.

91 The next step – to ecosystem moral considerability – might not be as tempting as some have thought. It tends to devalue the individual, perhaps too much. See Katz's criticism of Callicott's ethical holism in "Organism, Community, and the 'Substitution Problem'." See also H. J. McCloskey criticism of holistic political philosophies in "The State as an Organism, as a Person, and as an End in Itself," *Philosophical Review* 72 (1963): 306–26.

PART III

Is Nature Intrinsically Valuable?

10

The Varieties of Intrinsic Value

John O'Neill

To hold an environmental ethic is to hold that non-human beings and states of affairs in the natural world have intrinsic value. This seemingly straightforward claim has been the focus of much recent philosophical discussion of environmental issues. Its clarity is, however, illusory. The term 'intrinsic value' has a variety of senses and many arguments on environmental ethics suffer from a conflation of these different senses: specimen hunters for the fallacy of equivocation will find rich pickings in the area. This paper is largely the work of the underlabourer. I distinguish different senses of the concept of intrinsic value, and, relatedly, of the claim that non-human beings in the natural world have intrinsic value; I exhibit the logical relations between these claims and examine the distinct motivations for holding them. The paper is not however merely an exercise in conceptual underlabouring. It also defends one substantive thesis: that while it is the case that natural entities have intrinsic value in the strongest sense of the term, i.e., in the sense of value that exists independently of human valuations, such value does not as such entail any obligations on the part of human beings. The defender of nature's intrinsic value still needs to show that such value contributes to the well-being of human agents.

I

The term 'intrinsic value' is used in at least three different basic senses:

(1) **Intrinsic value$_1$** Intrinsic value is used as a synonym for non-instrumental value. An object has instrumental value insofar as it is a means to some other end. An object has intrinsic value if it is an end in itself. Intrinsic goods are goods that other goods are good for the sake of. It is a well rehearsed point that, under pain of an infinite regress, not everything can have only instrumental value. There must be some objects that have intrinsic value. The defender of an environmental ethic argues that among the entities that have such non-instrumental value are non-human beings and states. It is this claim that Naess makes in defending deep ecology:

> The well-being of non-human life on Earth has value in itself. This value is independent of any instrumental usefulness for limited human purposes.[1]

(2) **Intrinsic value$_2$** Intrinsic value is used to refer to the value an object has solely in virtue of its 'intrinsic properties'. The concept is thus employed by G. E. Moore:

> To say a kind of value is 'intrinsic' means merely that the question whether a thing possesses it, and in what degree it possesses it, depends solely on the intrinsic nature of the thing in question.[2]

This account is in need of some further clarification concerning what is meant by the 'intrinsic nature' of an object or its 'intrinsic properties'. I discuss this further below. However, as a first approximation, I will assume the intrinsic properties of an object to be its non-relational properties, and leave that concept for the moment unanalysed. To hold that non-human beings have intrinsic value given this use is to hold that the value they have depends solely on their non-relational properties.

(3) **Intrinsic value₃** Intrinsic value is used as a synonym for 'objective value' i.e., value that an object possesses independently of the valuations of valuers. As I show below, this sense itself has sub-varieties, depending on the interpretation that is put on the term 'independently'. Here I simply note that if intrinsic value is used in this sense, to claim that non-human beings have intrinsic value is not to make an ethical but a meta-ethical claim. It is to deny the subjectivist view that the source of all value lies in valuers – in their attitudes, preferences and so on.

Which sense of 'intrinsic value' is the proponent of an environmental ethic employing? To hold an environmental ethic is to hold that non-human beings have intrinsic value in the first sense: it is to hold that non-human beings are not simply of value as a means to human ends. However, it might be that to hold a defensible ethical position about the environment, one needs to be committed to the view that they also have intrinsic value in the second or third senses. Whether this is the case is the central concern of this paper.

II

In much of the literature on environmental ethics the different senses of 'intrinsic value' are used interchangeably. In particular senses 1 and 3 are often conflated. Typical is the following passage from Worster's *Nature's Economy*:

One of the most important ethical issues raised anywhere in the past few decades has been whether nature has an order, a pattern, that we humans are bound to understand and respect and preserve. It is the essential question prompting the environmentalist movement in many countries. Generally, those who have answered 'yes' to the question have also believed that such an order has an intrinsic value, which is to say that not all value comes from humans, that value can exist independ-

ently of us: it is not something we bestow. On the other hand, those who have answered 'no' have tended to be in an instrumentalist camp. They look on nature as a storehouse of 'resources' to be organised and used by people, as having no other value than the value some human gives it.[3]

In describing the 'yes' camp Worster characterises the term in sense 3. However, in characterising the 'no's' he presupposes an understanding of the term in both senses 1 and 3. The passage assumes that to deny that natural patterns have value independently of the evaluations of humans is to grant them only instrumental value: a subjectivist meta-ethics entails that non-humans can have only instrumental value. This assumption is widespread.[4] It also underlies the claims of some critics of an environmental ethic who reject it on meta-ethical grounds thus: To claim that items in the non-human world have intrinsic values commits one to an objectivist view of values; an objectivist view of values is indefensible; hence the non-human world contains nothing of intrinsic value.[5]

The assumption that a subjectivist meta-ethics commits one to the view that non-humans have only instrumental value is false. Its apparent plausibility is founded on a confusion of claims about the source of values with claims about their object.[6] The subjectivist claims that the only sources of value are the evaluative attitudes of humans. But this does not entail that the only ultimate objects of value are the states of human beings. Likewise, to be an objectivist about the source of value, i.e., to claim that whether or not something has value does not depend on the attitudes of valuers, is compatible with a thoroughly anthropocentric view of the object of value – that the only things which do in fact have value are humans and their states, such that a world without humans would have no value whatsoever.

To enlarge, consider the emotivist as a standard example of a subjectivist. Evaluative utterances merely evince the speaker's attitudes with the purpose of changing the attitudes of the hearer. They state no facts. Within the emotivist tradition Stevenson provides an admirably clear account of intrinsic value. Intrinsic value is defined as non-instrumental value: ' "intrinsically good" is roughly synonymous with "good for its own sake, as an end, as distinct from good as a means to something else" '.[7] Stevenson then offers the following account of what it is to say something has intrinsic value:

> 'X is intrinsically *good*' asserts that the speaker approves of X intrinsically, and acts emotively to make the hearer or hearers likewise approve of X intrinsically.[8]

There are no reasons why the emotivist should not fill the X place by entities and states of the non-human world. There is nothing in the emotivist's meta-ethical position that precludes her holding basic attitudes that are biocentric. Thus let the H! operator express hurrah attitudes and B! express boo attitudes.[9] Her ultimate values might for example include the following:

> H! (The existence of natural ecosystems)
> B! (The destruction of natural ecosystems by humans).

There is no reason why the emotivist must assume that either egoism or humanism is true, that is that she must assign non-instrumental value only to her own or other humans' states.[10]

It might be objected, however, that there are other difficulties in holding an emotivist meta-ethics and an environmental ethic. In making humans the source of all value, the emotivist is committed to the view that a world without humans contains nothing of value. Hence, while nothing logically precludes the emotivists assigning non-instrumental value to objects in a world which contains humans, it undermines some of the considerations that have led to the belief in the need to assign such value. For example, the standard last man arguments[11] in defence of an environmental ethic fail: the last man whose last act is to destroy a rain forest could on a subjectivist account of value do no wrong, since a world without humans is without value.

This objection fails for just the same reason as did the original assumption that subjectivism entails non-humans have only instrumental value. It confuses the source and object of value. There is nothing in emotivism that forces the emotivist to confine the objects of her attitudes to those that exist at the time at which she expresses them. Her moral utterances might evince attitudes towards events and states of affairs that might happen after her death, for example,

> H! (My great grand-children live in a world without poverty).

Likewise her basic moral attitudes can range over periods in which humans no longer exist, for example,

> H! (Rain forests exist after the extinction of the human species).

Like the rest of us she can deplore the vandalism of the last man. Her moral utterances might evince attitudes not only to other times but also to other possible worlds. Nothing in her meta-ethics stops her asserting with Leibniz that this world is the best of all possible worlds, or, in her despair at the destructiveness of humans, expressing the attitude that it would have been better had humans never existed:

> H! (the possible world in which humans never came into existence).

That humans are the source of value is not incompatible with their assigning value to a world in which they do not exist. To conclude, nothing in the emotivist's meta-ethics dictates the content of her attitudes.

Finally it needs to be stressed that while subjectivism does not rule out non-humans having non-instrumental value, objectivism does not rule it in. To claim that moral utterances have a truth value is not to specify which utterances are true. The objectivist can hold that the moral facts are such that only the states of humans possess value in themselves: everything else has only instrumental value. Ross, for example, held that only states of conscious beings have intrinsic value:

> Contemplate any imaginary universe from which you suppose mind entirely absent, and you will fail to find anything in it you can call good in itself.[12]

Moore allowed that without humans the world might have some, but only very insignificant, value.[13] It does not follow from the claim that values do not have their source in humans that they do not have humans as their sole ultimate object.

The upshot of this discussion is a very traditional one, that meta-ethical commitments are logically independent of ethical ones. However, in the realm of environmental ethics it is one that needs to be re-affirmed. No meta-ethical position is required by an environmental ethic in its basic sense, i.e., an ethic which holds that non-human entities should not be treated merely as a means to the satisfaction of human wants. In particular, one can hold such an ethic and deny objectivism. However, this is not to say that there might not be other reasons for holding an objectivist account of ethics and that some of these reasons might appear particularly pertinent when considering evaluative statements about non-humans. It has not been my purpose in this section of the paper to defend ethical subjectivism and in section IV I defend a version of objectivism about environmental values. First, however, I discuss briefly intrinsic value in its Moorean sense, intrinsic value$_2$ – for this sense of the term is again often confused with intrinsic value$_1$.

III

In its second sense intrinsic value refers to the value an object has solely in virtue of its 'intrinsic properties': it is value that 'depends solely on the intrinsic nature of the thing in question'.[14] I suggested earlier that the intrinsic properties of an object are its non-relational properties. What is meant by 'non-relational properties'? There are two interpretations that might be placed on the phrase:

(i) The non-relational properties of an object are those that persist regardless of the existence or non-existence of other objects (weak interpretation).

(ii) The non-relational properties of an object are those that can be characterised without reference to other objects (strong interpretation).[15]
The distinction between the two senses will not concern me further here, although a similar distinction will take on greater significance in the following section.

If any property is irreducibly relational then rarity is. The rarity of an object depends on the non-existence of other objects, and the property cannot be characterised without reference to other objects. In practical concern about the environment a special status is ascribed to rare entities. The preservation of endangered species of flora and fauna and of unusual habitats and ecological systems is a major practical environmental problem. Rarity appears to confer a special value to an object. This value is related to that of another irreducibly relational property of environmental significance, i.e., diversity. However, it has been argued that such value can have no place in an environmental ethic which places intrinsic value on natural items. The argument runs something as follows:

1 To hold an environmental ethic is to hold that natural objects have intrinsic value.
2 The values objects have in virtue of their relational properties, e.g., their rarity, cannot be intrinsic values.

Hence:

3 The value objects have in virtue of their relational properties have no place in an environmental ethic.[16]

This argument commits a fallacy of equivocation. The term 'intrinsic value' is being used in its Moorean sense, intrinsic value in the second premise, but as synonym for non-instrumental value, intrinsic value, in the first. The senses are distinct. Thus, while it may be true that if an object has only instrumental value it cannot have intrinsic value in the Moorean sense, it is false that an object of non-instrumental value is necessarily also of intrinsic value in the Moorean sense. We might value an object in virtue of its relational properties, for example its rarity, without thereby seeing it as having only instrumental value for human satisfactions.

This point can be stated with greater generality. We need to distinguish:

(1) values objects can have in virtue of their relations to other objects; and
(2) values objects can have in virtue of their relations to human beings.[17]

The second set of values is a proper subset of the first. Moreover, the second set of values is still not co-extensive with

(3) values objects can have in virtue of being instrumental for human satisfaction.

An object might have value in virtue of its relation with human beings without thereby being of only instrumental value for humans. Thus, for example, one might value wilderness in virtue of its not bearing the imprint of human activity, as when John Muir opposed the damming of the Hetch Hetchy valley on the grounds that wild mountain parks should lack 'all...marks of man's work'.[18] To say 'x has value because it is untouched by humans' is to say that it has value in virtue of a relation it has to humans and their activities. Wilderness has such value in virtue of our absence. However, the value is not possessed by wilderness in virtue of its instrumental usefulness for the satisfaction of human desires. The third set of values is a proper subset of both the second and the first. Intrinsic value in the sense of non-instrumental value need not then be intrinsic in the Moorean sense.

What of the relation between Moorean intrinsic value and objective value? Is it the case that if there is value that 'depends solely on the intrinsic nature of the thing in question' then subjectivism about values must be rejected? If an object has value only in virtue of its intrinsic nature, does it follow that it has value independently of human valuations? The answer depends on the interpretation given to the phrases 'depends solely on' and 'only in virtue of'. If these are interpreted to exclude the activity of human evaluation, as I take it Moore intended, then the answer to both questions is immediately 'yes'. However, there is a natural subjectivist reading to the phrases. The subjectivist can talk of the valuing agent *assigning* value to objects solely in virtue of their intrinsic natures. Given a liberal interpretation of the phrases, a subjectivist can hold that some objects have intrinsic value in the Moorean sense.

IV

In section II I argued that the claim that nature has non-instrumental value does not commit one to an objectivist meta-ethics. However, I left open the question as to whether there might be other reasons particularly pertinent in the field of environmental ethics that would lead us to hold an objectivist account of value. I will show in this section that there are.

The ethical objectivist holds that the evaluative properties of objects are real properties of objects, that is, that they are properties that objects possess independently of the valuations of valuers. What is meant by 'independently of the valuations of valuers'? There are two readings of the phrase which parallel the two senses of 'non-relational property' outlined in the last section:

(1) The evaluative properties of objects are properties that exist in the absence of evaluating agents. (Weak interpretation)
(2) The evaluative properties of objects can be characterised without reference to evaluating agents. (Strong interpretation)

The distinction is a particular instance of a more general distinction between two senses in which we can talk of a property being a real property of an object:

(1) A real property is one that exists in the absence of any being experiencing that object. (Weak interpretation)
(2) A real property is one that can be characterised without reference to the experiences of a being who might experience the object. (Strong interpretation)

Is there anything about evaluations of the environment that make the case for objectivism especially compelling? I begin by considering the case for the weak version of objectivism. For the purpose of the rest of the discussion I will assume that only human persons are evaluating agents.

1 Weak objectivity

A popular move in recent work on environmental ethics has been to establish the objectivity of values by invoking an analogy between secondary qualities and evaluative properties in the following manner:

(1) The evaluative properties of objects are analogous to secondary qualities. Both sets of properties are observer dependent.
(2) The Copenhagen interpretation of quantum mechanics has shown the distinction between primary qualities and secondary qualities to be untenable. All the properties of objects are observer dependent.

Hence,

John O'Neill

(3) the evaluative properties of objects are as real as their primary qualities.[19]

The argument fails at every stage. In the first place the conclusion itself is too weak to support objectivism about values: it is no argument for an objectivist theory of values to show that all properties of objects are observer dependent. The second premise should in any case be rejected. Not only is it the case that the Copenhagen interpretation of quantum theory is but one amongst many,[20] it is far from clear that the Copenhagen interpretation is committed to the ontological extravagance that all properties are observer dependent. Rather it can be understood as a straightforward instrumentalist interpretation of quantum theory. As such it involves no ontological commitments about the quantum domain.[21]

More pertinent to the present discussion, there are also good grounds for rejecting the first premise. The analogy between secondary qualities and values has often been used to show that values are not real properties of objects. Thus Hume remarks:

> Vice and virtue . . . may be compared to sounds, heat and cold, which, according to modern philosophy, are not qualities in objects, but perceptions in the mind . . .[22]

For the Humean, both secondary qualities and evaluative properties are not real properties of objects, but, rather, illustrate the mind's 'propensity to spread itself on external objects': as Mackie puts it, moral qualities are the 'projection or objectification of moral attitudes'.[23] The first premise of the argument assumes this Humean view of the analogy between secondary qualities and values. However, there are good grounds for inverting the analogy and that inversion promises to provide a more satisfactory argument for objectivism than that outlined above.

On the weak interpretation of the concept of a real property, secondary qualities are real properties of objects. They persist in the absence of observers. Objects do not lose their colours when we no longer perceive them. In the kingdom of the blind the grass is still green. Secondary qualities are dispositional properties of objects to appear in a certain way to ideal observers in ideal conditions. So, for example, an object is green if and only if it would appear green to a perceptually ideal observer in perceptually ideal conditions.[24] It is consist-

ent with this characterisation of secondary qualities that an object possesses that quality even though it may never actually be perceived by an observer. Thus, while in the strong sense of the term secondary qualities are not real properties of objects – one cannot characterise the properties without referring to the experiences of possible obervers – in the weak sense of the term they are.[25]

This point opens up the possibility of an inversion of the Humean analogy between secondary and evaluative qualities which has been recently exploited by McDowell and others.[26] Like the secondary qualities, evaluative qualities are real properties of objects. An object's evaluative properties are similarly dispositional properties that it has to produce certain attitudes and reactions in ideal observers in ideal conditions. Thus, we might tentatively characterise goodness thus: x is good if and only if x would produce feelings of moral approval in an ideal observer in ideal conditions. Likewise, beauty might be characterised thus: x is beautiful if and only if x would produce feelings of aesthetic delight in ideal observers in ideal conditions. Given this characterisation, an object is beautiful or good even if it never actually appears as such to an observer. The evaluative properties of objects are real in just the same sense that secondary qualities are. Both sets of properties are independent of observers in the sense that they persist in the absence of observers. The first premise of the argument outlined above should therefore be rejected. Furthermore, in rejecting this premise, one arrives at a far more convincing case for the reality of evaluative properties than that provided by excursions into quantum mechanics.

However, the promise of this line of argument for environmental ethics is, I believe, limited. There are a variety of particular arguments that might be raised against it. For example, the Humean might respond by suggesting that the analogy between secondary and evaluative properties is imperfect. The arguments for and against the analogy I will not rehearse here.[27] For even if the analogy is a good one, it is not clear to me that any point of substance about the nature of values divides the Humean and his opponent. The debate is one about preferred modes of speech, specifically about how the term 'real property' is to be read. For the Humean such as Mackie, the term 'real property' is understood in its strong sense. It is a property that can be characterised without reference to the experiences of an observer. Hence neither secondary qualities nor values are real properties of objects. The opponent of the Humean in employing the analogy to establish the reality of evaluative properties merely substitutes a weak interpretation of 'real property' for the strong interpretation. There may be good reasons for doing this, but nothing about the nature of values turns on this move.[28] Moreover, there seems to be nothing about evaluative utterances concerning the natural environment which adds anything to this debate. Nothing about specifically environmental values tells for or against this argument for objectivism.

2   Strong objectivity

A more interesting question is whether there are good reasons for believing that there are objective values in the strong sense: are there evaluative properties that can be characterised without reference to the experiences of human observers? I will now argue that there are and that uses of evaluative utterances about the natural world provide the clearest examples of such values.

Consider the gardener's use of the phrase 'x is good for greenfly'. The term 'good for' can be understood in two distinct ways. It might refer to what is conductive to the destruction of greenfly, as in 'detergent sprays are good for greenfly', or it can be used to describe what causes greenfly to flourish, as in 'mild winters are good for greenfly'. The term 'good for' in the first use describes what is instrumentally good for the gardener: given the ordinary gardener's interest in the flourishing of her rosebushes, detergent sprays satisfy that interest. The second use describes what is instrumentally good for the greenfly, quite independently of the gardener's interests. This instrumental goodness is possible in virtue of the fact that greenflies are the sorts of things that can flourish or be injured. In consequence they have their own goods that are independent of both human interests and any tendency they might have to produce in human observers feelings of approval or disapproval.[29] Such goods I will follow Von Wright in terming the 'goods of X'.[30]

What is the class of entities that can be said to possess such goods? Von Wright in an influential passage offers the following account:

A being, of whose good it is meaningful to talk, is one who can meaningfully be said to be well or ill, to thrive, to flourish, be happy or miserable ... the attributes, which go along with the meaningful use of the phrase 'the good of X', may be called *biological* in a broad sense. By this I do not mean that they were terms, of which biologists make frequent use. 'Happiness' and 'welfare' cannot be said to belong to the professional vocabulary of biologists. What I mean by calling the terms 'biological' is that they are used as attributes of beings, of whom it is meaningful to say they have a *life*. The question 'What kinds or species of being have a good?' is therefore broadly identical with the question 'What kinds or species of being have a life'.[31]

This biological use of the terms 'good for' and 'good of' is at the centre of Aristotelian ethics. The distinction between 'good for' and 'good of' itself corresponds to the Aristotelian distinction between goods externally instrumental to a being's flourishing and those that are constitutive of a being's flourishing.[32] And the central strategy of Aristotle's ethics is to found ethical argument on the basis of this broadly biological use of the term 'good'. I discuss this further below.

The terms 'good' and 'goods' in this biological context characterise items which are real in the strong interpretation of the term. In order to characterise the conditions which are constitutive of the flourishing of a living thing one need make no reference to the experiences of human observers. The goods of an entity are given rather by the characteristic features of the kind or species of being it is. A living thing can be said to flourish if it develops those characteristics which are normal to the species to which it belongs in the normal conditions for that species. If it fails to realise such characteristics then it will be described by terms such as 'defective', 'stunted', 'abnormal' and the like. Correspondingly, the truth of statements about what is good for a living thing, what is conducive to its flourishing, depend on no essential reference to human observers. The use of the evaluative terms in the biological context does then provide good reasons for holding that some evaluative properties are real properties on the strong interpretation of the phrase. Hence, evaluative utterances about living things do have a particular relevance to the debate about the objectivity of values. Specifically biological values tell for objectivism.

However, while the use of value terms in the specifically biological context provides the clearest examples of the existence of objective goods, the class of entities that can be meaningfully said to have such goods is not confined to the biological context. Von Wright's claim that the question 'What kinds or species of being have a good?' is identical with the question 'What kinds or species of being have a life' should be rejected. The problem case for this identity claim is that of collective entities. Von Wright is willing to entertain the possibility that such entities have their own good but only if they can also be said to have their own life in a non-metaphorical sense.

> But what shall we say of social units such as the family, the nation, the state. Have they got a life 'literally' or 'metaphorically' only? I shall not attempt to answer these questions. I doubt whether there is any other way of answering them except by pointing out existing analogies of language. It is a fact that we speak about the life and also the good (welfare) of the family, the nation and the state. This fact about the use of language we must accept and with it the idea that the social units in question *have* a life and a good. What is arguable, however, is whether the life and *a fortiori* also the good (welfare) of a social unit is not somehow 'logically reducible' to the life and therefore the good of the beings – men or animals – who are its members.[33]

This passage conflates two distinct issues: whether collective entities have a life and whether they have their own goods. It does not appear to me that we can talk of collective entities having a life in anything but a metaphorical sense. They clearly lack those properties typical of living things – reproduction, growth, death and such like. However, it does make sense to talk about the conditions in which collective entities flourish and hence of their goods in a non-metaphorical sense. Correspondingly, we can meaningfully talk of what is damaging to them. Furthermore, the goods of collective entities are not reducible to the goods of their members. Thus for example we can refer to the conditions in which bureaucracy flourishes while believing this to be bad for its constituent members. Or to take another example, what is good for members of a workers' cooperative can be quite at odds with what is good for the cooperative itself: the latter is constituted by its relative competitive position in the market place, and members of cooperatives might find themselves forced to forego the satisfaction of their own interests to realise this.[34] The question 'What class of beings has a good?' is identical with the question 'What class of beings can be said to flourish in a non-metaphorical sense?' The class of living things is a proper subset of this class.

This point is central to environmental questions. It makes sense to talk of the goods of collective biological entities – colonies, ecosystems and so on – in a way that is irreducible to that of its members. The realisation of the good of a colony of ants might in certain circumstances involve the death of most of its members. It is not a condition for the flourishing of an individual animal that it be eaten: it often is a condition for the flourishing of the ecosystem of which it is a part. Relatedly, a point central to Darwin's development of the theory of evolution was that living beings have a capacity to reproduce that outstrips the capacity of the environment to support them. Most members of a species die in early life. This is clearly bad for the individuals involved. But it is again essential to the flourishing of the ecosystems of which they are a part. Collective entities have their own goods. In defending this claim one need not show that they have their own life.[35]

Both individual living things and the collective entities of which they are members can be said, then, to have their own goods. These goods are quite independent of human interests and can be characterised without reference to the experiences of human observers. It is a standard at this juncture of the argument to assume that possession of goods entails moral considerability: 'moral standing or considerability belongs to whatever has a good of its own'.[36] This is mistaken. It is possible to talk in an objective sense of what constitutes the goods of entities, without making any claims that these ought to be realised. We can know what is 'good for X' and relatedly what constitutes 'flourishing for X' and yet believe that X is the sort of thing that ought not to exist and hence that the flourishing of X is just the sort of thing we ought to inhibit. The case of the gardener noted earlier is typical in this regard. The gardener knows what it is for greenfly to flourish, recognises they have their own goods, and has a practical knowledge of what is good for them. No moral injunction follows. She can quite consistently believe they ought to be done harm. Likewise one can state the conditions for the flourishing of dictatorship and bureaucracy. The anarchist can claim that 'war is the health of the state'. One can discover what is good both for rain forests and the AIDS virus. One can recognise that something has its own goods, and quite consistently be morally indifferent to these goods or believe one has a moral duty to inhibit their development.[37] That Y is a good of X does not entail that Y should be realised unless we have a prior reason for believing that X is the sort of thing whose good ought to be promoted. While there is not a logical gap between facts and values, in that some value statements are factual, there is a logical gap between facts and oughts. 'Y is a good' does not entail 'Y ought to be realised'.[38]

This gap clearly raises problems for environmental ethics. The existence of objective goods was promising precisely because it appeared to show that items in the non-human world were objects of proper moral concern. The gap outlined threatens to undermine such concern. Can the gap be bridged? There are two ways one might attempt to construct such a bridge. The first is to invoke some general moral claim that linked objective goods and moral duties. One might for example invoke an objectivist version of utilitarianism: we have a moral duty to maximise the total amount of objective good in the world.[39] There are a number of problems of detail with such an approach: What are the units for comparing objective goods? How are different goods to be weighed? However, it also has a more general problem that it shares with hedonistic utilitarianism. Thus, the hedonistic utilitarian must include within his calculus pleasures that ought not to count at all e.g., those of a sadist who gets pleasure from needless suffering. The hedonistic utilitarian fails to allow that pleasures themselves are the direct objects of ethical appraisal. Similarly, there are some entities whose flourishing simply should not enter into any calculations – the flourishing of dictatorships and viruses for example. It is not the case that the goods of viruses should count, even just a very small amount. There is no reason why these goods should count at all as ends in themselves (although there are of course good *instrumental* reasons why some viruses should flourish, in that many are indispensable to the ecosystems of which they are a part). The flourishing of such entities is itself a direct object of ethical appraisal. The quasi-utilitarian approach is unpromising.

A second possible bridge between objective goods and oughts is an Aristotelian one. Human beings like other entities have goods constitutive of their flourishing, and correspondingly other goods instrumental to that flourishing. The flourishing of many other living things ought to be promoted because they are constitutive of our own flourishing. This approach might seem a depressingly familiar one. It looks as if we have taken a long journey into objective value only to arrive back at a narrowly anthropocentric ethic. This however would be mistaken. It is compatible with an Aristotelian ethic that we value items in the natural world for their own sake, not simply as an external means to our own satisfaction. Consider Aristotle's account of the relationship of friendship to human flourishing.[40] It is constitutive of friendship of the best kind that we care for friends for their own sake and not merely for the pleasures or profits they might bring. To do good for a friend purely because one thought they might later return the compliment not for their own sake is to have an ill-formed friendship. Friendship in turn is a constitutive component of a flourishing life. Given the kind of beings we are, to lack friends is to lack part of what makes for a flourishing human existence. Thus the egoist who asks 'why have friends?' or 'why should I do good for my friends' has assumed a narrow range of goods – 'the biggest share of money, honours and bodily pleasures'[41] – and asked how friends can bring such goods. The appropriate response is to point out that he has simply misidentified what the goods of a human life are.

The best case for an environmental ethic should proceed on similar lines. For a large number of, although not all, individual living things and biological collectives, we should recognise and promote their flourishing as an end in itself.[42] Such care for the natural world is constitutive of a flourishing human life. The best human life is one that includes an awareness of and practical concern with the goods of entities in the non-human world. On this view, the last man's act of vandalism reveals the man to be leading an existence below that which is best for a human being, for it exhibits a failure to recognise the goods of non-humans. To outline such an approach is, however, only to provide a promissory note. The claim that care for the natural world for its own sake is a part of the best life for humans requires detailed defence. The most promising general strategy would be to appeal to the claim that a good human life requires a breadth of goods. Part of the problem with egoism is the very narrowness of the goods it involves. The ethical life is one that incorporates a far richer set of goods it involves. The ethical life is one that incorporates a far richer set of goods and relationships than egoism would allow. This form of argument can be made for a connection of care for the natural world with human flourishing: the recognition and promotion of natural goods as ends in themselves involves just such an enrichment.[43]

Notes

Earlier versions of this paper were read to an Open University summer school and to a philosophy seminar at Sussex University. My special thanks to Roger Crisp, Andrew Mason and Ben Gibbs for their comments on these occasions. Thanks are also due to Robin Attfield, John Benson, Stephen Clark, Terry Diffey, Alan Holland and Geoffrey Hunter for conversations on the issues discussed in this paper.

1 A. Naess, 'A Defence of the Deep Ecology Movement', *Environmental Ethics*, 6 (1984), 266. However, Naess's use of the term is unstable and he sometimes uses the phrase 'intrinsic value' to refer to objective value. See n 4, below.

2 G. E. Moore, 'The Conception of Intrinsic Value' in *Philosophical Studies* (London: Routledge and Kegan Paul, 1922), p. 260.

3 D. Worster, *Nature's Economy* (Cambridge: Cambridge University Press, 1985), p. xi.

4 Thus, for example, Naess and Rothenberg in *Ecology, Community and Lifestyle* (Cambridge: Cambridge University Press, 1989) initially define 'intrinsic value' as value which is 'independent of our valuation' (ibid., p. 11) but then in the text characterise it in terms of a contrast with instrumental value (ibid., pp. 74–5). In his own account of deep ecology Naess employs the term in the sense of non-instrumental value (see n 2 and A. Naess, 'The Shallow and the Deep: Long Range Ecology Movement', *Inquiry*, 16, 1973). Others are more careful. Thus, while Attfield is committed to both an objectivist meta-ethics and the view that the states of some non-humans have intrinsic value, in *A Theory of Value and Obligation* (London: Croom Helm, 1987), ch. 2, he *defines* intrinsic value as non-instrumental value and distinguishes this from his 'objectivist understanding of it'. Callicott in 'Intrinsic Value, Quantum Theory, and Environmental Ethics', *Environmental Ethics*, 7 (1989), 257–75, distinguishes non-instrumental

value from objective value, using the term 'inherent value' for the former and 'intrinsic value' for the latter. However, the use of these terms raises its own problems since there is little agreement in the literature as to how they are to be employed. For example, P. Taylor, *Respect for Nature* (Princeton, NJ: Princeton University Press, 1986), pp. 68–77 makes the same distinction but uses 'inherent value' to describe Callicott's 'intrinsic value' and 'intrinsic value' to describe his 'inherent value', while R. Attfield in *The Ethics of Environmental Concern* (Oxford: Blackwell, 1983), ch. 8, uses the term 'inherent value' to refer to something quite different. Another exceptionally clear discussion of the meta-ethical issues surrounding environmental ethics is R. and V. Routley, 'Human Chauvinism and Environmental Ethics' in D. Mannison, M. McRobbie and R. Routley (eds.), *Environmental Philosophy* (Canberra: Australian National University, 1980).

5 This kind of argument is to be found in particular in the work of McCloskey. See H. J. McCloskey, 'Ecological Ethics and its Justification' in Mannison et al., Environmental Philosophy, and *Ecological Ethics and Politics* (Totowa, NJ: Rowman and Littlefield, 1983).

6 Cf. D. Gauthier, *Morals by Agreement* (Oxford: Oxford University Press, 1986), pp. 46–9 and J. B. Callicott, 'Intrinsic Value, Quantum Theory and Environmental Ethics', *Environmental Ethics* 7 (1985), 257–75, who make this point quite emphatically.

7 C. L. Stevenson, *Ethics and Language* (New Haven, CT: Yale University Press, 1944).

8 Ibid., p. 178.

9 I take the operators from S. Blackburn, *Spreading the Word* (Oxford: Clarendon Press, 1984), p. 193ff.

10 Cf. R. and V. Routley, 'Human Chauvinism and Environmental Ethics' in D. Mannison, M. McRobbie and R. Routley (eds.), *Environmental Philosophy* (Canberra: Australian National University, 1980).

11 See ibid., pp. 121–3.

12 W. D. Ross, *The Right and the Good* (Oxford: Clarendon Press, 1930), p. 140. Ross held four things to have intrinsic value – 'virtue, pleasure, the allocation of pleasure to the virtuous, and knowledge' (ibid., p. 140).

13 G. E. Moore, *Principia Ethica* (Cambridge: Cambridge University Press, 1903), pp. 28, 83ff. and 188ff.

14 G. E. Moore, 'The Conception of Intrinsic Value', *Philosophical Studies* (London: Routledge and Kegan Paul, 1922), p. 260.

15 I do not follow Moore's own discussion here. Moore's own use of the term is closer to the weaker than the stronger interpretation. Thus, for example, the method of isolation as a test of intrinsic value proceeds by considering if objects keep their value 'if they existed *by themselves*, in absolute isolation':

G. E. Moore *Principia Ethica* (Cambridge: Cambridge University Press, 1903), p. 187.

16 A similar argument is to be found in A. Gunn, 'Why Should We Care about Rare Species?', *Environmental Ethics*, 2, 1980, pp. 17–37, especially pp. 29–34.

17 J. Thompson partially defines intrinsic value and hence an environmental ethic in terms of a contrast with such values: 'those who find intrinsic value in nature are claiming . . . that things and states which are of value are valuable for what they are in themselves and not because of their relation to us . . .' (J. Thompson, 'A Refutation of Environmental Ethics', p. 148, *Environmental Ethics*, 12 (1990), 147–60). This characterisation is inadequate, in that it rules out of an environmental ethic positions such as that of Muir who values certain parts of nature because of the absence of the marks of humans. I take it that Thompson intends a contrast to the third set of values – values objects can have in virtue of being instrumental for human satisfaction.

18 Cited in R. Dubos, *The Wooing of Earth* (London: The Athlone Press, 1980) p. 135.

19 A relatively sophisticated version of the argument is to be found in Holmes Rolston, III, 'Are Values in Nature Subjective or Objective?', pp. 92–5 in *Philosophy Gone Wild* (Buffalo, NY: Prometheus Books, 1989). Cf. J. B. Callicott, 'Intrinsic Value, Quantum Theory and Environmental Ethics', *Environmental Ethics* 7, (1985), pp. 257–75.

20 M. Jammer, *The Philosophy of Quantum Mechanics* (New York: John Wiley, 1974) remains a good survey of the basic different interpretations of quantum theory.

21 It should also be noted that the view, popular among some Green thinkers (see, for example, F. Capra, *The Tao of Physics* [London: Wildwood House, 1975]), that the Copenhagen interpretation entails a radically new world-view that undermines the old classical Newtonian picture of the world is false. The Copenhagen interpretation is conceptually conservative and denies the possibility that we could replace the concepts of classical physics by any others (see N. Bohr, *Atomic Theory and the Description of Nature* [Cambridge: Cambridge University Press, 1934], p. 94. Cf. W. Heisenberg, *Physics and Philosophy* [London: Allen and Unwin, 1959] p. 46. I discuss this conservativism in J. O'Neill, *Worlds Without Content* [London: Routledge, in press], ch. 6.

22 D. Hume, *A Treatise of Human Nature* (London: Fontana, 1972), Book III, §1, p. 203.

23 J. Mackie, *Ethics* (Harmondsworth, England: Penguin, 1977) p. 42.

24 Cf. J. McDowell, 'Values and Secondary Qualities', p. 111 in T. Honderich (ed.), *Morality and Objectivity* (London: Routledge, 1985).

25 Cf. ibid., p. 113 and J. Dancy, 'Two Conceptions of Moral Realism', *Proceedings of the Aristotelian Society*, Supp. vol. 60, 1986.

26 See J. McDowell, 'Values and secondary qualities' in T. Honderich (ed.), *Morality and Objectivity* (London: Routledge, 1985) and J. McDowell, 'Aesthetic value, objectivity and the fabric of the world' in E. Schaper (ed.), *Pleasure, Preference and Value* (Cambridge: Cambridge University Press, 1983). Cf. D. Wiggins, *Needs, Values, Truth* (Oxford: Blackwell, 1987), Essays III and IV. For critical discussion of this approach see S. Blackburn, 'Errors and the Phenomenology of Value' in T. Honderich (ed.), *Morality and Objectivity*; J. Dancy, 'Two Conceptions of Moral Realism', *Proceedings of the Aristotelian Society*, Supp. vol. 60, 1986; C. Hookway, 'Two Conceptions of Moral Realism', *Proceedings of the Aristotelian Society*, Supp. vol. 60, 1986; C. Wright, 'Moral Values, Projections and Secondary Qualities', *Proceedings of the Aristotelian Society*, Supp. vol. 62, 1988.

27 For such a Humean response see Blackburn, 'Errors and the Phenomenology of Value' in T. Honderich (ed.), *Morality and Objectivity*.

28 Cf. Hookway, 'Two Conceptions of Moral Realism', p. 202.

29 Hence I also reject Feinberg's claim that the goods of plants are reducible to those of humans with an interest in their thriving: 'The Rights of Animals and Unborn Generations' in *Rights, Justice and the Bounds of Liberty* (Princeton, NJ: Princeton University Press, 1980), pp. 169–71. For a similar argument against Feinberg see P. Taylor, *Respect for Nature*, p. 68.

30 G. H. von Wright, *The Varieties of Goodness* (London: Routledge and Kegan Paul, 1963), ch. 3.

31 Ibid., p. 50. Cf. P. Taylor, *Respect for Nature*, pp. 60–71.

32 See J. Cooper, *Reason and Human Good in Aristotle* (Cambridge, MA: Harvard University Press, 1975), p. 19ff.

33 Von Wright, *The Varieties of Goodness*, pp. 50–1.

34 I discuss this example in more detail in J. O'Neill, 'Exploitation and Workers' Councils', *Journal of Applied Philosophy*, 8 (1991), 263–7.

35 Hence, there is no need to invoke scientific hypotheses such as the Gaia hypothesis to defend the existence of such goods, as for example Goodpaster does (K. Goodpaster, 'On Being Morally Considerable', p. 323, *Journal of Philosophy*, 75, 1978, pp. 308–25).

36 R. Attfield, *A Theory of Value and Obligation* (Beckenham: Croom Helm, 1987), p. 21. Cf. Holmes Rolston III, *Environmental Ethics* (Philadelphia: Temple University Press, 1988), K. Goodpaster, 'On Being Morally Considerable' and P. Taylor, *Respect for Nature*.

John O'Neill

37 This point undermines a common objection to objectivism, i.e., that objectivists cannot explain why
value statements necessarily motivate actions. If
values were objective then 'someone might be indifferent to things which he regards as good or actively
hostile to them' (S. Blackburn *Spreading the Word*,
p. 188). The proper reply to this is that not all value
statements do motivate actions, as the example in
the text reveals.

38 Compare Wiggins's point that we need to
discriminate between 'the (spurious) fact-value
distinction and the (real) is-ought distinction'
(D. Wiggins, 'Truth, Invention, and the Meaning
of Life' in *Needs, Values, Truth: Essays in the
Philosophy of Value* [Oxford: Blackwell, 1987]
p. 96). Cf. P. Taylor, *Respect for Nature*, pp.
71–2.

39 See R. Attfield, *A Theory of Value and Obligation*,
for this kind of position. For a different attempt
to bridge the gap between objective goods and

moral oughts see P. Taylor, *Respect for Nature*,
chs. 2–4.

40 Aristotle, *Nicomachean Ethics*, trans. T. Irwin
(Indianapolis, IN: Hackett, 1985), Books viii–ix.

41 Ibid., 1168b.

42 This would clearly involve a rejection of Aristotle's
own view that animals are made for the sake of
humans. (Aristotle, *Politics*, trans. J. Warrington
[London: J. A. Dent and Sons, 1959], 1265b.)

43 This line of argument has the virtue of fitting well
with Aristotle's own account of happiness, given an
inclusive interpretation of his views. Happiness on
this account is inclusive of all goods that are ends in
themselves: a happy life is self-sufficient in that
nothing is lacking. It is a maximally consistent set
of goods. (Aristotle, *Nicomachean Ethics*,
1097b14–20; see J. L. Ackrill, 'Aristotle on *Eudaimo-
nia*' in A. O. Rorty (ed.), *Essays on Aristotle's Ethics*
(Berkeley, CA: University of California Press, 1980)
for a presentation of this interpretation.)

11

Value in Nature and the Nature of Value

Holmes Rolston III

I offer myself as a nature guide, exploring for values. Many before us have got lost and we must look the world over. The unexamined life is not worth living; life in an unexamined world is not worthy living either. We miss too much of value.

Valuable Humans

Let us start from well-mapped ground: humans are able to value. Descartes's *cogito* is as well an indubitable *valeo*. I cannot doubt that I value. Humans are able to value nature instrumentally, to value their own experiential states both intrinsically and instrumentally. Objective natural things and events may contribute to these subjective interest satisfactions, a tree supplies firewood, a sunny day makes a picnic possible.

Taking the first step on our journey into non-human nature, some travellers notice that we must take along this indubitable valuing self; afterwards, along the way, finding these selves always present, they deny any value outside our own minds. Wilhelm Windelband insists: 'Value . . . is never found in the object itself as a property. It consists in a relation to an appreciating mind. . . . Take away will and feeling and there is no such thing as value' (Windelband, 1921, p. 215). Bryan Norton concludes: 'Moralists among environmental ethicists have erred in looking for a value in living things that is *independent* of human valuing. They have

therefore forgotten a most elementary point about valuing anything. Valuing always occurs from the viewpoint of a conscious valuer. . . . Only the humans are valuing agents' (Norton, 1991, p. 251).

Taking an interest in an object gives humans a value-ability. Additionally to valuing nature instrumentally, humans can sometimes value nature intrinsically. When we value a giant sequoia tree, our valuing stops in the tree itself, without further contributory reference. What then is going on? Philosophical travellers, after taking a look at the tree, will want to take a look at their language. 'Intrinsic' means without instrumental reference, but that leaves unsettled whether the value is located in the tree independently, autonomously intrinsic, or placed on the tree upon our arrival. We cannot just take it as elementary that there is no such thing as non-human value. Is this intrinsic value discovered or conferred? There is excitement in the beholder; but what is valued is what is beheld.

If the value-ability of humans is the source of this valued excitement, then value is anthropogenic even though it is not anthropocentric (Callicott, 1984; 1986). Tourists in Yosemite do not value the sequoias as timber but as natural classics, for their age, strength, size, beauty, resilience and majesty. This viewing constitutes the trees' value, which is not present independent of the human valuing. Value thus requires subjectivity to coagulate it in the world. But the value so coagulated, it will be claimed, is placed objectively on the tree. Such value is not self-regarding, or even human-regarding, merely, though it is human-generated. It is not centred on human well-being. That '*n* is valuable' does mean that a human, *H*, takes an interest in *n*, a natural object, but it need not mean '*n* satisfies *H*'s desire', since *H* may take an interest in the trees for what they are in themselves, and not merely to satisfy *H*'s desires. Meanwhile, there is no value until consciousness comes on scene.

Visiting the Grand Canyon, we intrinsically value the rock strata with their colour bands. Visiting Kentucky, we value Mammoth Cave, with its stalactites. Taking any interest whatever constitutes value *ipso facto*. An otherwise valueless object can thus come to have intrinsic value. As travellers we will wonder what was here before, what will remain after. The obvious answer is that there will be whatever properties these trees, canyons, and caves have. Even Descartes found himself unable to doubt the existence of external nature, and no philosopher who doubts that the world exists bothers to take a trip through it.

What account do we give when, excited by a sense of deep time at the Grand Canyon, we realize that humans have rarely been there? At that point, we may wish to give a dispositional twist to value. To say that *n* is valuable means that *n* is able to be valued, if and when human valuers, *H*s, come along, but *n* has these properties whether or not humans arrive. Faced with trilobite fossils, we conclude that the trilobites were potentially intrinsically valuable. By this account there is no actual value ownership autonomous to the valued and valuable trees, canyons, trilobites; there is a value ignition when humans arrive. Intrinsic value in the realized sense emerges relationally with the appearance of the subject-generator.

Despite the language of value conferral, if we try to take the term *intrinsic* seriously, this cannot refer to anything the object gains, to something *within* ('intra') the present tree or the past trilobite, for the human subject does not really place anything on or in the natural object. We have only a 'truncated sense' of *intrinsic* (Callicott, 1986, p. 143). The *attributes* under consideration are objectively there before humans come, but the *attribution* of value is subjective. The object causally affects the subject, who is excited by the incoming data and translates this as value, after which the object, the tree, appears as having value,

rather like it appears to have green colour. But nothing is really added *intrinsically*; everything in the object remains what it was before. Despite the language that humans are the *source* of value which they *locate* in the natural object, no value is really located there at all.

The term *intrinsic*, even when truncated, is misleading. What is meant is better specified by the term *extrinsic*, the *ex* indicating the external, anthropogenic ignition of the value, which is not *in*, *intrinsic*, internal to the nonsentient organism, even though this value, once generated, is apparently conferred on the organism. In the *H-n* encounter, value is conferred by *H* on *n*, and that is really an extrinsic value for *n*, since it comes to *n* from *H*, and likewise it is an extrinsic value for *H*, since it is conferred from *H* to *n*. Neither *H* nor *n*, standing alone, have such value.

We humans carry the lamp that lights up value, although we require the fuel that nature provides. Actual value is an event in our consciousness, though natural items while still in the dark of value have potential intrinsic value. Man is the measure of things, said Protagoras. Humans are the measurers, the valuers of things, even when we measure what they are in themselves.

Valuable Animals

A mother free-tail bat, a mammal like ourselves, can, using sonar, wend her way out of Bracken Cave, in Texas, in total darkness, catch 500–1000 insects each hour on the wing, and return to find and nurse her own young. That gives evidence of bat-valuing; she values the insects and the pup. Now, it seems absurd to say that there are no valuers until humans arrive. Animals do not make humans the measure of things at all. There is no better evidence of non-human values and valuers than spontaneous wildlife, born free and on its own. Animals hunt and howl, find shelter, seek out their habitats and mates, care for their young, flee from threats, grow hungry, thirsty, hot, tired, excited, sleepy. They suffer injury and lick their wounds. Here we are quite convinced that value is non-anthropogenic, to say nothing of anthropocentric.

These wild animals defend their own lives because they have a good of their own. There is somebody there behind the fur or feathers. Our gaze is returned by an animal that itself has a concerned outlook. Here is value right before our eyes, right behind those eyes. Animals are value-able, able to value things in their world. But we may still want to say that value exists only where a subject has an object of interest. David Prall writes: 'The being liked or disliked of the object is its value.... Some sort of a subject is always requisite to there being value at all' (Prall, 1921, p. 227). So at least the higher animals can value too, because they are experiencing subjects and can take an interest in things.

Do animals value anything intrinsically? We may not think that animals have the capacity, earlier claimed for humans, of conferring intrinsic value on anything else. Mostly they seek their own basic needs, food and shelter, and care for their young. But then why not say that an animal values its own life for what it is in itself, intrinsically, without further contributory reference? Else we have an animal world replete with instrumental values and devoid of intrinsic values, everything valuing the resources it needs, nothing valuing itself. That is implausible. Animals maintain a valued self-identity as they cope through the world. Valuing is intrinsic to animal life.

Valuable Organisms

Outdoors it is difficult to get out of sight of plants. It is also difficult for philosophers to 'see' plants philosophically. Few are botanists. Also, it is easy to overlook the insects. Even fewer philosophers are entomologists.

A plant is not a subject, but neither is it an inanimate object, like a stone. Plants, quite alive, are unified entities of the botanical though not of the zoological kind, that is, they are not unitary organisms highly integrated with centred neural control, but they are modular organisms, with a meristem that can repeatedly and indefinitely produce new vegetative modules, additional stem nodes and leaves when there is available space and resources, as well as new reproductive modules, fruits and seeds.

Plants make themselves; they repair injuries; they move water, nutrients, and photosynthate from cell to cell; they store sugars; they make tannin and other toxins and regulate their levels in defence against grazers; they make nectars and emit pheromones to influence the behaviour of pollinating insects and the responses of other plants; they emit allelopathic agents to suppress invaders; they make thorns, trap insects. They can reject genetically incompatible grafts.

A plant, like any other organism, sentient or not, is a spontaneous, self-maintaining system, sustaining and reproducing itself, executing its program, making a way through the world, checking against performance by means of responsive capacities with which to measure success. Something more than physical causes, even when less than sentience, is operating; there is *information* superintending the causes; without it the organism would collapse into a sand heap. The information is used to preserve the plant identity.

All this cargo is carried by the DNA, essentially a *linguistic* molecule. The genetic set is really a *propositional* set – to choose a provocative term – recalling how the Latin *propositum* is an assertion, a set task, a theme, a plan, a proposal, a project, as well as a cognitive statement. These molecules are set to drive the movement from genotypic potential to phenotypic expression. Given a chance, these molecules seek organic self-expression. An organism, unlike an inert rock, claims the environment as source and sink, from which to abstract energy and materials and into which to excrete them. It 'takes advantage' of its environment.

We pass to value when we recognize that the genetic set is a *normative set*; it distinguishes between what *is* and what *ought to be*. The organism is an axiological system, though not a moral system. So the tree grows, reproduces, repairs its wounds, and resists death. The physical state that the organism defends is a valued state. A life is defended for what it is in itself, without necessary further contributory reference. Every organism has a *good-of-its-kind*; it defends its own kind as a *good kind*. In this sense, the genome is a set of conservation molecules.

Does not that mean that the plant is valuable (able to value) itself? If not, we will have to ask, as an open question: Well, the plant has a good of its own, but is there anything of value to it?[1] Possibly, even though plants have a good of their own, they are not able to value because they are not able to feel anything. Nothing matters to a plant. Hence, says Peter Singer, 'there is nothing to be taken into account' (Singer, 1976, p. 154). There is plant good, but not plant value. There is no valuer evaluating anything. Plants can do things that interest us, but the plants are not interested in what they are doing. They do not have any options among which they are choosing. They have only their merely functional goods.

But, though things do not matter *to* plants, things matter *for* them. We ask, of a failing plant: What's the matter *with* that plant? If it is lacking sunshine and soil nutrients, and we arrange for these, we say: The tree is benefiting from the sunshine and the soil nutrients; and *benefit* is – everywhere else we encounter it – a value word. Can we ask, as an open question: The tree is benefiting from the sun and the nutrients, but are those valuable to it? That hardly seems coherent. 'This tree was injured when the elk rubbed its velvet off its antlers, and the tannin secreted there is killing the invading bacteria. But is this valuable to the tree?' Botanists say that the tree is irritable in the biological sense.

Or if trees cannot be irritated, you no doubt think that bees can, even though you may not know what to think about bees as subject valuers. Objectively, it is difficult to dissociate the idea of value from natural selection. Biologists regularly speak of the 'survival value' of plant activities: thorns have survival value. Bees sting and do their waggle dance. These survival traits, though picked out by natural selection, are innate (= intrinsic) in the organism, that is, stored in its genes and expressed in structure and behaviour.

But, it will be protested, careful philosophers will put this kind of 'value' in scare quotes. This is not really value at all, because there is no felt experience choosing from alternatives, no preferences being exercised. This so-called value is not a value, really, not one of interest to philosophers because it is not a value with interest in itself. Meanwhile we humans value many things about which we have no options (photosynthesis and protein), or even no knowledge (perhaps vitamin B_1 or the cytochrome-c molecules). What are we to say of all these functional 'values'? Do they become of real value only upon their discovery, and even then have only instrumental value?

Why is the organism not valuing what it is making resources of? – not consciously, but we do not want to presume that there is only conscious value or valuing. That is what we are debating, not assuming. A valuer is an entity able to defend value. Insentient organisms are the *holders* of value, although not the *beholders* of value. Some value is already present in nonsentient organisms, normative valuative systems, prior to the emergence of further dimensions of value with sentience. Otherwise we have to ask, as an open question: Well, the bee is making use of the nectar, but is the honey valuable to the bee? My mind is not subtle enough to use words with such precision. The bee's defending its own life for what it is in itself is just as much fact of the matter as is its using its stinger or making honey to do so.

No, these are observations of value in nature with just as much certainty as they are biological facts. We are misled to think that all the value of the tree, instrumental or intrinsic, must be subjectively conferred, like the greenness, a secondary quality, or even a tertiary one. A simpler, less anthropically based, more biocentric theory holds that some values, instrumental and intrinsic, are objectively there, discovered not generated by the valuer. Trees may not be coloured without a perceiver, but they exist *per se*; and only if their existence is dynamically defended. That is not an analogue of colour at all. Trees do appear to be green, and perhaps we do not want to call the electromagnetic waves actually there 'greenness'. Trees also photosynthesise with or without humans watching them. Even those who think that all the tree's intrinsic value has to be conferred by humans still think that matters can be better or worse for the tree, and this amounts to saying that the tree on its own has its goods and harms. Norton and Windelband, unable to forget their experiential omnipresence as valuers, have forgotten elementary biology.

Some worry that we here commit the naturalistic fallacy. We find what biologically is in nature and conclude that something valuable is there, something which we may say we ought to protect. But does it not rather seem that the facts here are value facts, when we are describing what benefits the tree? Such value is pretty much fact of the matter. If we refuse to recognize such values being objectively there, have we committed some fallacy? Rather, the danger is the other way round. We commit the subjectivist fallacy if we think all values lie in subjective experience, and, worse still, the anthropocentrist fallacy if we think all values lie in human options and preferences.

Valuable Species

On our travels we may see endangered species. If so, we will value them. But are we seeing, and valuing, species? Or just that trumpeter swan, this grizzly bear, that we were lucky enough to see? That is partly a scientific and partly a philosophical problem. I have seen, and valued, swans and bears in Yellowstone over four decades. But not the same individuals, rather bear replaced by bear replaced by bear, swan–swan–swan.

Certainly humans are able to value species both by instrumental use and by conferring intrinsic value on them. But can a species be value-able all by itself, able to value at the species-level? A species has no self. There is no analogue to the nervous hookups or circulatory flows that characterize the organism. But now we must ask whether singular somatic identity conserved is the only process that is valuable. A species is another level of biological identity reasserted genetically over time. Identity need not attach solely to the centred or modular organism; it can persist as a discrete pattern over time.

The life that the organismic individual has is something passing through the individual as much as something it intrinsically possesses. The genetic set, in which is coded the *telos*, is as evidently the property of the species as of the individual through which it passes. Value is something dynamic to the specific form of life. The species *is* a bigger event than the individual with its interests or sentience. Events can be good for the well-being of the species, considered collectively, although they are harmful if considered as distributed to individuals. When a wolf is tearing up an elk, the individual elk is in distress, but *Cervus canadensis* is in no distress. The species is being improved, shown by the fact that wolves will subsequently find elk harder to catch. If the predators are removed, and the carrying capacity is exceeded, wildlife managers may have to benefit a species by culling its member individuals.

Even the individuals that escape external demise die of old age; and their deaths, always to the disadvantage of individuals, are a necessity for the species. A finite life span makes room for those replacements that enable development, allowing the population to improve in fitness or to adapt to a shifting environment. The surplus of young, with most born to perish prematurely, is disadvantageous to such individuals, but advantageous to the species. Without the 'flawed' reproduction that incorporates mutation and permits variation, without selection of the more fit few, and death of the less fit, which harms most individuals, the species would soon be extinct in a changing environment. The individual is a receptacle of the form, and the receptacles are broken while the form survives, but the form cannot otherwise survive.

Reproduction is typically assumed to be a need of individuals, but since any particular individual can flourish somatically without reproducing at all, indeed may be put through duress and risk or spend much energy reproducing, by another logic we can interpret reproduction as the species staying in place by its replacements. In this sense a female grizzly does not bear cubs to be healthy herself. Rather, her cubs are *Ursus arctos*, threatened by nonbeing, recreating itself by continuous performance. A female animal does not have mammary glands nor a male testicles because the function of these is to preserve its own life; these organs are defending the line of life bigger than the somatic individual. The locus of the value that is defended over generations is as much in the form of life, since the individuals are genetically impelled to sacrifice themselves in the interests of reproducing their kind.

An insistent individualist can claim that species-level phenomena (vitality in a population, danger to a species, reproduction of a life form, tracking a changing environment) are only epiphenomena, byproducts of aggregated individuals in their interrelationships. But our more comprehensive account, interpreting the species itself as a kind of individual, historic lineage over time, is just as plausible. Biologists have often and understandably focused on individual organisms, and some recent trends interpret biological processes from the perspective of genes. But a consideration of species reminds us that many events can be interpreted at this level too. Properly understood, the story at the microscopic genetic level reflects the story at the ecosystemic specific level, with the individual a macroscopic mid-level between. The genome is a kind of map coding the species; the individual is an instance incarnating it.

Much of what we earlier said about individual organisms as nonmoral normative systems can be resaid, *mutatis mutandis*, of species. The single, organismic-directed course is part of a bigger picture in which a species too runs a telic course through the environment, using individuals resourcefully to maintain its course over much longer periods of time. The species line is the *vital* living system, the whole, of which individual organisms are the essential parts. The species defends a particular form of life, pursuing a pathway through the world, resisting death (extinction), by regeneration maintaining a normative identity over time. It is as logical to say that the individual is the species' way of propagating itself as to say that the embryo or egg is the individual's way of propagating itself. The value resides in the dynamic form; the individual inherits this, exemplifies it, and passes it on. If so, what prevents value existing at that level? The appropriate survival unit is the appropriate location of valuing.

Even a species is a kind of valuer. Species as historical lines have a defended biological identity, though they do not have any subjective experience. Species are quite real; that there really is a bear–bear–bear sequence is about as certain as anything we believe about the empirical world. Species are lively and full of life, they are processes, they are wholes, they have a kind of unity and integrity. The species line too is value-able, able to conserve a biological identity. Indeed it is more real, more value-able than the individual, necessary though individuals are for the continuance of this lineage.

We said earlier that natural selection picks out whatever traits an organism has that are valuable to it, relative to its survival. But if we ask what is the essence of this value, it is not the somatic survival of the organismic individual; this value ability is the ability to reproduce. That locates value-ability innate or intrinsic within the organism, but it just as much locates the value-ability as the capacity to re-produce a next generation, and a next generation positioned to produce a next generation after that. Any biocentrism that focuses on individuals has got to argue away the fact that natural selection is rather careless with individuals; the test to which it puts them is whether they can pass on the historical lineage.

Valuable Ecosystems

Exploring, we will see different ecosystems: an oak-hickory forest, a tall grass prairie. At least we see trees and grasses. But do we see ecosystems? Maybe we immerse ourselves in them, for an ecosystem is not so much an object in the focus of vision as an enveloping community, a place in space, a process in time, a set of vital relationships. This can mean that philosophers have difficulty seeing, and valuing, ecosystems. Yet, really, the

ecosystem is the fundamental unit of development and survival.

Humans can value whatever they wish in nature. This can include ecosystems. 'A thing is right,' concluded Aldo Leopold, 'when it tends to preserve the integrity, stability, and beauty of the biotic community. It is wrong when it tends otherwise' (Leopold, 1966, p. 240). Leopold wanted a 'land ethic'. So humans can value ecosystem communities intrinsically – for what they are in themselves – as well as instrumentally. But can ecosystems be valuable all by themselves?

Actually, there is a deeper worry again, partly scientific and partly philosophical. Perhaps ecosystems do not exist – or exist in too loose a way to be valuers. They are nothing but aggregations of their more real members, like a forest is (some say) nothing more than a collection of trees. Even a human will have trouble valuing what does not really exist. We can value collections, as of stamps, but this is just the aggregated value of individual stamps. Still, an ecosystem, if it exists, is rather different. Nothing in the stamp collection is alive; the collection is neither self-generating nor self-maintaining. Neither stamp nor collection is valuable on its own. But perhaps ecosystems are both valuable to humans and, if they exist, value-able as systems in themselves.

We need ecology to discover what biotic community means as an organisational mode. Then we can reflect philosophically to discover the values there. Ecosystems can seem little more than stochastic processes. A sea-shore, a tundra, is a loose collection of externally related parts. Much of the environment is not organic at all (rain, groundwater, rocks, nonbiotic soil particles, air). Some is dead and decaying debris (fallen trees, scat, humus). These things have no organized needs; the collection of them is a jumble. The fortuitous interplay between organisms is simply a matter of the distribution and abundance of organisms, how they get dispersed, birth rates and death rates, population densities, moisture regimes, parasitism and predation, checks and balances. There is really not enough centred process to call community.

An ecosystem has no brain, no genome, no skin, no self-identification, no *telos*, no unified program. It does not defend itself against injury or death. It is not irritable. The parts (foxes, sedges) are more complex than the wholes (forests, grasslands). So it can begin to seem as if an ecosystem is too low a level of organisation to be the direct focus of concern. Ecosystems do not and cannot care; they have no interests about which they or we can care.

But this is to misunderstand ecosystems, to make a category mistake. To fault *communities* as though they ought to be organismic *individuals* is to look at one level for what is appropriate at another. One should look for a matrix of interconnections between centres, for creative stimulus and open-ended potential. Everything will be connected to many other things, sometimes by obligate associations, more often by partial and pliable dependencies; and, among other components, there will be no significant interactions. There will be shunts and criss-crossing pathways, cybernetic subsystems and feedback loops. One looks for selection pressures and adaptive fit, not for irritability or repair of injury, for speciation and life support, not for resisting death. We must think more systemically, and less organismically.

An ecosystem generates a spontaneous order that envelops and produces the richness, beauty, integrity and dynamic stability of the component parts. Though these organized interdependencies are loose in comparison with the tight connections within an organism, all these metabolisms are as vitally linked as are liver and heart. The equilibrating ecosystem is not merely push–pull forces. It is an equilibrating of values.

We do not want in an undiscriminating way to extrapolate criteria of value from organism to biotic community, any more than from person to animal or from animal to plant. Rather, we want to discriminate the criteria appropriate to this level. The selective forces in ecosystems at once transcend and produce the lives of individual plants and animals. Evolutionary ecosystems over geological time have increased the numbers of species on Earth from zero to five million or more. R. H. Whittaker found that on continental scales and for most groups 'increase of species diversity . . . is a self-augmenting evolutionary process without any evident limit'. There is a tendency toward what he called 'species packing' (Whittaker, 1972, p. 214).

Superimposed on this, the quality of individual lives in the upper trophic rungs of ecological pyramids has risen. One-celled organisms evolved into many-celled, highly integrated organisms. Photosynthesis evolved and came to support locomotion – swimming, walking, running, flight. Stimulus-response mechanisms became complex instructive acts. Warm-blooded animals followed cold-blooded ones. Neural complexity, conditioned behaviour, and learning emerged. Sentience appeared – sight, smell, hearing, taste, pleasure, pain. Brains evolved, coupled with hands. Consciousness and self-consciousness arose. Persons appeared with intense concentrated unity. The products are valuable, able to be valued by these humans; but why not say that the process is what is really value-able, able to produce these values?

Ecosystems are selective systems, as surely as organisms are selective systems. The system selects over the long ranges for individuality, for diversity, for adapted fitness, for quantity and quality of life. Organisms defend only their own selves or kinds, but the system spins a bigger story. Organisms defend their continuing survival; ecosystems promote new arrivals. Species increase their kinds, but ecosystems increase kinds, and increase the integration of kinds. The system is a kind of field with characteristics as vital for life as any property contained within particular organisms. The ecosystem is the depth source of individual and species alike.

In the current debate among biologists about the levels at which selection takes place – individual organisms, populations, species, genes – the recent tendency to move selective pressures down to the genetic level forgets that a gene is always emplaced in an organism that is emplaced in an ecosystem. The molecular configurations of DNA are what they are because they record the story of a particular form of life in the macroscopic, historical ecosystem. What is generated arises from molecular mutations, but what survives is selected for adaptive fit in an ecosystem. We cannot make sense of biomolecular life without understanding ecosystemic life, the one level as vital as the other.

Philosophers, sometimes encouraged by biologists, may think ecosystems are just epiphenomenal aggregations. This is a confusion. Any level is real if there is significant downward causation. Thus the atom is real because that pattern shapes the behaviour of electrons; the cell because that pattern shapes the behaviour of amino acids; the organism because that pattern co-ordinates the behaviour of hearts and lungs; the community because the niche shapes the morphology and behaviour of the foxes within it. Being real requires an organisation that shapes the existence and the behaviour of members or parts.

Axiologically, in the more comprehensive levels, the terms 'instrumental' and 'intrinsic' do not work very well. Ecosystems have 'systemic value'. But if we want to know what is value-able, able to create value, why not say that it is the productivity of such ecosystems, bringing into existence these phenomena that, when we arrive, the human consciousness is also able to value? What is incredible is not the existence of ecosystems. What is really incredible is that we humans, arriving late on the evolutionary scene, ourselves products of it, bring all the value into the world, when and as we turn our attention to our sources. That claim has too much subjective bias. It values a late product of the system, psychological life, and subordinates everything else to this. It mistakes a fruit for the whole plant, the last chapter for the whole story.

All value does not end in either human or nonhuman intrinsic value, to which everything else is contributory. Values are intrinsic, instrumental, and systemic, and all three are interwoven, no one with priority over the others in significance, although systemic value is foundational. Each locus of intrinsic value gets folded into instrumental value by the system, and vice versa. There are no intrinsic values, nor instrumental ones either, without the encompassing systemic creativity. It would be foolish to value the golden eggs and disvalue the goose that lays them. It would be a mistake to value the goose only instrumentally. A goose that lays golden eggs is systemically valuable. How much more so is an ecosystem that generates myriads of species, or even, as we next see, an Earth that produces billions of species, ourselves included.

Valuable Earth

I promised to explore the whole world; so let's get the planet in focus. Viewing Earthrise, Edgar Mitchell, was entranced: 'Suddenly from behind the rim of the moon, in long-slow motion moments of immense majesty, there emerges a sparkling blue and white jewel, a light, delicate sky-blue sphere laced with slowly swirling veils of white, rising gradually like a small pearl in a thick sea of black mystery. It takes more than a moment to fully realize this is Earth...home' (Kelley, 1988, at photographs 42–5). Michael Collins was Earthstruck: 'When I travelled to the moon, it wasn't my proximity to that battered rockpile I remember

so vividly, but rather what I saw when I looked back at my fragile home – a glistening, inviting beacon, delicate blue and white, a tiny outpost suspended in the black infinity. Earth is to be treasured and nurtured, something precious that *must* endure' (Gallant, 1980, p. 6).

Pearls are, a philosopher might object, valuable only when humans come around. But this mysterious Earth-pearl, a biologist will reply, is a home long before we humans come. This is the only biosphere, the only planet with an ecology. Earth may not be the only planet where anything is valuable – able to be valued by humans intrinsically or instrumentally – but it is the only place able to produce vitality before humans come. The view from space symbolizes all this.

Earlier the challenge was to evaluate persons, animals, plants, species, ecosystems; but environmental valuing is not over until we have risen to the planetary level. Earth is really the relevant survival unit. But valuing the whole Earth is unfamiliar and needs philosophical analysis. We may seem to be going to extremes. Earth is, after all, just earth. The belief that dirt could have intrinsic value is sometimes taken as a *reductio ad absurdum* in environmental philosophy. Dirt is not the sort of thing that has value by itself. Put like that, we agree. An isolated clod defends no intrinsic value and it is difficult to say that it has much value in itself. But that is not the end of the matter, because a clod of dirt is integrated into an ecosystem; earth is a part, Earth the whole. Dirt is product and process in a systemic nature. We should try to get the global picture, and switch from a lump of dirt to the Earth system in which it has been created.

Earth is, some will insist, a big rockpile like the moon, only one on which the rocks are watered and illuminated in such way that they support life. So maybe it is really the life we value and not the Earth, except as instrumental to life. We do not have duties to rocks, air, ocean, dirt, or Earth; we have duties to people, or living things. We must not confuse duties to the home with duties to the inhabitants. We do not praise so much the dirt as what is in the dirt, not earth so much as what is on Earth. But this is not a systemic view of what is going on. We need some systematic account of the valuable Earth we now behold, before we beheld it, not just some value that is generated in the eye of the beholder. Finding that value will generate a global sense of obligation.

The evolution of rocks into dirt into fauna and flora is one of the great surprises of natural history, one of the rarest events in the astronomical universe. Earth is all dirt, we humans too arise up from the humus, and we find revealed what dirt can do when it is self-organizing under suitable conditions. This is pretty spectacular dirt. Really, the story is little short of a series of 'miracles', wondrous, fortuitous events, unfolding of potential; and when Earth's most complex product, *Homo sapiens*, becomes intelligent enough to reflect over this cosmic wonderland, everyone is left stuttering about the mixtures of accident and necessity out of which we have evolved. For some the black mystery will be numinous and signal transcendence; for some the mystery may be impenetrable. Perhaps we do not have to have all the cosmological answers. Nobody has much doubt that this is a precious place, a pearl in a sea of black mystery.

The elemental chemicals of life – carbon, oxygen, hydrogen, nitrogen – are common enough throughout the universe. They are made in the stars. But life, rare elsewhere, is common on Earth, and the explanation lies in the ordinary elements in an extraordinary setting, the super-special circumstances in which these common chemicals find themselves arranged on Earth, that is, in the self-organizing system. On an everyday scale, earth, dirt, seems to be passive, inert, an unsuitable object of moral concern. But on a global scale?

The scale changes nothing, a critic may protest, the changes are only quantitative. Earth is no doubt precious as life support, but it is not precious in itself. There is nobody there in a planet. There is not even the objective vitality of an organism, or the genetic transmission of a species line. Earth is not even an ecosystem, strictly speaking; it is a loose collection of myriads of ecosystems. So we must be talking loosely, perhaps poetically or romantically, of valuing Earth. Earth is a mere thing, a big thing, a special thing for those who happen to live on it, but still a thing, and not appropriate as an object of intrinsic or systemic valuation. We can, if we insist on being anthropocentrists, say that it is all valueless except as our human resource.

But we will not be valuing Earth objectively until we appreciate this marvellous natural history. This really is a superb planet, the most valuable entity of all, because it is the entity able to produce all the Earthbound values. At this scale of vision, if we ask what is principally to be valued, the value of life arising as a creative process on Earth seems a better description and a more comprehensive category.

Perhaps you think that species are unreal. Perhaps you still insist that ecosystems are unreal, only aggregations, but how about Earth? Will you say that Earth too, being a higher level entity, is unreal? Only an aggregation, and not a systemic whole? There is no such thing as a biosphere? Surely, Earth has some rather clear boundaries, does it not? Will you say that this is a planet where nothing matters? Nothing matters to Earth, perhaps, but everything matters on Earth, for Earth.

Do not humans sometimes value Earth's life-supporting systems because they are valuable, and not always the other way round? Is this value just a matter of late-coming human interests? Or is Earth not historically a remarkable, valuable place, a place able to produce value prior to the human arrival, and even now valuable antecedently to the human uses of it? It seems parochial to say that our part alone in the drama establishes all its worth. The production of value over the millennia of natural history is not something subjective that goes on in the human mind. In that sense, a valuable Earth is not the *reductio ad absurdum* of valuing dirt. It is not even locating the most valuable thing in the world; it is locating the ultimate value of the world itself. The creativity within the natural system we inherit, and the values this generates, are the ground of our being, not just the ground under our feet. Earth could be the ultimate object of duty, short of God, if God exists.

Valuable Nature

William James, toward the beginning of our century, starkly portrayed the utterly valueless world, transfigured as a gift of the human coming:

> Conceive yourself, if possible, suddenly stripped of all the emotion with which your world now inspires you, and try to imagine it *as it exists*, purely by itself, without your favorable or unfavorable, hopeful or apprehensive comment. It will be almost impossible for you to realize such a condition of negativity and deadness. No one portion of the universe would then have importance beyond another; and the whole collection of its things and series of its events would be

without significance, character, expression, or perspective. Whatever of value, interest, or meaning our respective worlds may appear endued with are thus pure gifts of the spectator's mind. (James, 1925, p. 150)

At the end of this century, this is not what the astronauts think at all. They do not see Earth as negativity and deadness, nor do they think that this portion of the universe has no significance beyond any other part, except by gift of our spectating minds. They did not say that the world was valuable only because they took along an indubitable self into space and projected value onto Earth. They rather see that human life arises in a spectacular place, in a nature of whose creative patterns they are part.

According to the old paradigm, so long dominant that to some it now seems elementary, there is no value without an experiencing valuer, just as there are no thoughts without a thinker, no percepts without a perceiver, no deeds without a doer, no targets without an aimer. Valuing is felt preferring by human choosers. Possibly, extending this paradigm, sentient animals may also value. But plants cannot value; they have no options and make no choices. *A fortiori*, Earth and nature cannot be bona fide valuers. One can always hang on to the claim that value, like a tickle or remorse, must be felt to be there. Its *esse* is *percipi*. Nonsensed value is nonsense. It is only beings with 'insides' to them that have value.

But the problem with the 'no value without a valuer' axiom is that it is too individualistic; it looks for some centre of value located in a subjective self. And we nowhere wish to deny that such valuers are sufficient for value. But that is not the whole account of value in a more holistic, systemic, ecological, global account. Perhaps there can be no doing science without a scientist, no religion without a believer, no tickle without somebody tickled. But there can be law without a lawgiver, history without a historian; there is biology without biologists, physics without physicists, creativity without creators, story without storytellers, achievement without achievers – and value without valuers. A sentient valuer is not necessary for value. Another way is for there to be a value-generating system able to generate value. If you like, that is another meaning of value-er; any *x* is a valuer if *x* is value-able, able to produce values.

It is true that humans are the only evaluators who can reflect about what is going on at this global scale, who can deliberate about what they ought to do conserving it. When humans do this, they must set up the scales; and humans are the measurers of things. Animals, organisms, species, ecosystems, Earth, cannot teach us how to do this evaluating. But they can display what it is that is to be valued. The axiological scales we construct do not constitute the value, any more than the scientific scales we erect create what we thereby measure.

Humans are not so much lighting up value in a merely potentially valuable world, as they are psychologically joining ongoing planetary natural history in which there is value wherever there is positive creativity. While such creativity can be present in subjects with their interests and preferences, it can also be present objectively in living organisms with their lives defended, and in species that defend an identity over time, and in systems that are self-organizing and that project storied achievements. The valuing subject in an otherwise valueless world is an insufficient premise for the experienced conclusions of those who value natural history.

Conversion to a biological and geological view seems truer to world experience and more logically compelling. This too is a perspective, but ecologically better informed; we know our place on a home planet. From this more objective viewpoint, there is something subjective, something philosophically naive, and even something hazardous in a time of ecological crisis, about living in a reference frame where one species takes itself as absolute and values everything else in nature relative to its potential to produce value for itself. Such philosophers live in an unexamined world, and, in result, they and those they guide live unworthy lives, because they cannot see their valuable world.

Note

1 Robin Attfield remarks that 'even if trees have needs and a good of their own, they may still have no value of their own' (Attfield, 1981, p. 35).

References

Attfield, Robin 1981. 'The good of trees', *Journal of Value Inquiry* 15, 35–54.

Callicott, J. Baird 1984. 'Non-anthropocentric value theory and environmental ethics', *American Philosophical Quarterly* 21, 299–309.

Callicott, J. Baird 1986. 'On the intrinsic value of nonhuman species', in Bryan G. Norton (ed.), *The Preservation of Species*. Princeton, NJ: Princeton University Press.

Gallant, Roy A. 1980. *Our Universe*. Washington, DC: National Geographic Society.

James, William 1925. *The Varieties of Religious Experience*. New York: Longmans, Green.

Kelley, Kevin W. (ed.) 1988. *The Home Planet*. Reading, MA: Addison-Wesley.

Leopold, Aldo 1966. *A Sand County Almanac*. New York: Oxford University Press.

Norton, Bryan G. 1991. *Toward Unity Among Environmentalists*. New York: Oxford University Press.

Prall, David 1921. *A Study in the Theory of Value*. Berkeley, CA: University of California Press.

Singer, Peter 1976. 'All animals are equal', in Tom Regan and Peter Singer (eds.), *Animal Rights and Human Obligations*. Englewood Cliffs, NJ: Prentice-Hall.

Whittaker, R. H. 1972. 'Evolution and measurement of species diversity', *Taxon* 21, 213–51.

Windelband, Wilhelm 1921. *An Introduction to Philosophy*. London: T. Fisher Unwin.

12

The Source and Locus of Intrinsic Value: A Reexamination

Keekok Lee

I

Callicott distinguishes between the *source* and the *locus* of intrinsic value.[1] By so doing, he makes it possible first to argue that (biotic) nature is the *locus* of intrinsic value even though human consciousness is the *source* of all values and second to argue either that values are no more than the subjective feelings of human individuals or that values exist totally independent of humans. The latter view is vulnerable to Mackie's "argument from queerness."[2] The former is vulnerable to the criticism that it leads to the implausible conclusion that values may be arbitrary and whimsical.

Callicott says that emphasis on the *source* does justice to the insight that a world without human consciousness is a world without values. The emphasis on the *locus* allows one to resist the inference that only humans can be said to possess intrinsic value. He wishes to argue that nonhuman natural beings, too, may be said to be valuable, not "in themselves" but "for themselves." Hume's famous dualism between fact and value has often been used to sustain two theses: (i) that human feelings (and therefore consciousness) create and endow the world with values and (ii) that the world of nature studied by science is devoid of all

value. However, for Callicott, Hume's moral metaphysics is not thus exhausted. Philosophers today often forget that Hume rested the possibility of morality not on any human feeling but specifically on the sentiment of sympathy which humans possess. To this possibility Callicott adds a Darwinian dimension: natural selection leads to an increase in both the extent and the intensity of sympathy in the human species. The study of natural history and ecology completes the argument by informing us that all natural beings are members of the same biotic community. Sympathy for fellow humans can therefore be extended to fellow members of the same biotic community. Human sympathy can thereby be transformed into bioempathy. This Humean/Darwinian bioempathetic moral metaphysics shows how it is possible for values to be conferred by humans without being necessarily homocentric.

Rolston, however, denies the importance of this distinction.[3] If values are anthropogenic (that is, human-generated or conferred),[4] then, even if they are not anthropocentric (because they are not necessarily tied up with human interest or well-being), one is left with a "truncated sense" of intrinsic value, as admitted by Callicott himself. Rolston argues that the theory is unsound because

This chapter limits the discussion about the source and locus of values primarily within a biotic context. For an extended exploration to cover the abiotic, see Lee, *The Natural and the Artefactual: Implications of Science and Technology for Environmental Philosophy* (Lanham: Lexington Books, 1999) where the term "valuable by themselves" is introduced to capture a sense of value which is common to both biotic and abiotic entities.

it commits "a fallacy of the misplaced location of values." For Rolston there are values in natural items which are discovered by the human valuers, not generated by them. The value of a tree is not analogous, for example, to the greenness of its leaves. In "the world out there," there are only electromagnetic waves of 500 nanometers, not greenness. The human perceiver, however, sees the leaves as green. Thus, the greenness may be said to be a projection of the human perception onto the leaves themselves. It is conferred on them by humans. Nevertheless, for Rolston, the tree has *value* whether humans are there or not. Humans are merely the beholders of the value of which the tree is the holder. In other words, nonhuman nature is not merely the *locus* but also the *source* of value, if *source* means "generator" rather than "discoverer." Humans may discover such values but do not generate them.

II

The attempt to resolve the conflict between Callicott and Rolston as well as to do justice to their respective insights involves making the following moves:

(1) We must understand *source*, not as Callicott does, in terms of the Humean thesis of projectivism, but rather in terms of a version of the Cartesian/Kantian[5] thesis of the rational linguistic capacity possessed by humans, a matter which I discuss and defend below in section IV.

(2) We must distinguish between two senses of intrinsic value – (a) being valuable "for itself" and (b) being valuable "in itself." The former is common to human and nonhuman nature (at least its biotic components) and is connected with their capacity to strive to maintain their functioning integrity. The latter is confined only to humans and is connected, as I show below, with their unique type of consciousness, reason, and capacity for language. We must also distinguish two aspects of values (whether instrumental or intrinsic): on the one hand, as recognized articulated values and, on the other, as mutely enacted values. The former are connected with that cluster of characteristics – consciousness, reason, and language – unique to humans and, therefore, with intrinsic value (b). The latter are associated with nonhuman nature and its possession of intrinsic value (a).

(3) The above entails that mutely enacted values may be said to exist independent and irrespective of the presence of human consciousness. In other words, in a world without human consciousness (either before the advent of human evolution, or in the future, when humans have become extinct as a species), there are no recognized-articulated but only mutely enacted values. In a world with human consciousness, there are both. On this view, while humans are the *source* and *locus* of recognized-articulated values regarding themselves and the *source* of recognized-articulated values regarding natural items, natural items are the bearers of mutely enacted values *apropos* themselves. This view supports Rolston's contention that nature is the holder of intrinsic values and humans are their beholders. At the same time, it does justice to the intuition that the evolution of human consciousness does add a complex dimension to the nature of intrinsic value in nature.

This conclusion may be said to be more sympathetic to Rolston than to Callicott because acknowledging that humans may be uniquely intrinsically valuable (b) does not entail the Humean claims. Moreover, if natural nonhuman beings are both the *source* and *locus* of intrinsic value (a), then the Humean claims, as they stand, are false. Nevertheless, even Rolston's position may have to be somewhat qualified, since it fails to distinguish (as does Callicott's, for that matter) between recognized-articulated and mutely enacted values. The former are necessarily anthropogenic just as the latter are necessarily nonanthropogenic.

In the rest of the paper, I set out the detailed steps in the argumentation that sustain the general claims that I have just made.

III

Because the notion of intrinsic value *tout court* in nonhuman nature is notoriously difficult to argue for, I tackle it here, not directly, but obliquely, by starting with something much less uncontentious, namely, instrumental value, which I define as the opposite of intrinsic value. If an object, O, is of use to an entity, A, in satisfying an end or goal, then O has instrumental value for A. If A stands for a human agent and O for a rabbit or a tree, then the nonhuman part of nature (nature for short) clearly has instrumental value for human agents.

However, A may also stand for a nonhuman natural agent, such as a goat, and O may stand for a bush. If so, then it is obvious that one natural entity may have instrumental value or use for another natural entity. As a result, it follows that instrumental values do not uniquely hold between human agents and nature and, therefore, do not disappear with the disappearance of humans. Only those values that involve humans and their relationships with certain parts of nature disappear. Instrumental relationships between entities and items that are part of nonhuman nature continue to exist, irrespective of the human presence. For instance, grass is of instrumental or use value to the cow, the bird to the cat, and so on, whether there are humans in the world or not. Such a world contains instrumental value. It is distinctly counterintuitive to hold otherwise.[6]

The next step of the argument may not be quite so obvious, but it follows from the conclusion above. In a world without humans, if instrumental values exist as argued, then intrinsic values – characterized as intrinsic value (a) – must also exist. As the Routleys have pointed out,[7] an infinite regress is generated unless the end which the means serves to procure is regarded as intrinsically valuable. If the worm is of use to the bird as a means of satisfying its hunger, then the satisfaction of the latter's hunger, or more generally, the maintenance of its functioning integrity must be of intrinsic value (a). Of course, the bird could be of use to the cat in maintaining, in turn, the latter's own functioning integrity. However, if the thesis of external teleology[8] is incorrect, the bird eats the worm not in order to be of use to the cat so that the cat can satisfy its hunger, but to satisfy its own. Its eventual instrumental value to the cat is incidental to its attempt to maintain its own functioning integrity.

Could the same be said of plants? Yes. Plants use water, nutrients from the soil, carbon dioxide and nitrogen from the air, sunlight, etc. to grow and flourish. In turn, they are of instrumental value to the herbivores. Nevertheless, plants use the abiotic parts of nature just mentioned in the way they do, not in order to be of eventual use to the cow or the sheep, but to maintain their own functioning integrity.

If the argument presented so far is correct, then the following theses have been established: (1) The existence of instrumental value in nature is independent of the existence of humans. (2) The existence of intrinsic value (a) in nature is also independent of the existence of humans. (3) It follows from (2) that humans are not the only *source* of values. (4) It follows from (1) and (2) that humans are not the only *loci* or bearers of intrinsic value (a).

IV

The above argument, however, may appear too easy and swift a way of disposing of the view that humans are the sole *source* of values and the unique *locus* of intrinsic value in the world. One could still argue that while the higher animals may possess consciousness and reason which are also shared by humans, it remains true that humans possess a form of consciousness and reason which transcends that of even the higher animals. Minimally, this unique form may be said to manifest itself in the following ways: while humans can recognize (i) instrumental value in nature for humans and (ii) instrumental value in one part of nature (in one type of natural being) for another part of nature (for another type of natural being), an animal can only recognize a limited range of other natural beings as being of instrumental value to it. A cat would recognize a mouse, a bird, a fish, some type of plants as being of use to it, but it would not and could not recognize either that a tiger could be of instrumental use to it (in the sense that the tiger, like the mouse, possesses properties which could be nourishing to the cat) or that a human could be of use to a tiger (in the sense that the tiger could eat the human as food).

This unique capacity is more than the ability to pursue ends, goals, or what is sometimes called in quasi-Aristotelian terms "a good of one's own." Animals are capable of doing the latter – an animal knows when it is hungry, tired, thirsty, where to find food, water, a mate, how to avoid danger, to protect and nurture its young, etc., just as humans do. However, only humans, not animals, can recognize that beings other than themselves have "goods of their own."

If beings that have "goods of their own" can be said to be the bearers of intrinsic value, identified here as (a), then animals clearly can, as we have seen, be such bearers. But humans may be said to be the bearers of intrinsic value, not merely in this sense, but in the different sense of being able to recognize that natural beings, other than themselves, can be the bearers of intrinsic value (a).

In other words, they are the bearers of intrinsic value (b); they do not themselves simply exemplify whatever feature(s) in virtue of which they and other beings may be said to be the bearers of intrinsic value (a), such as having "goods of their own" (or sentience, or whatever), but they can also recognize and articulate that they themselves and other beings possess the feature(s) in question.[9] Humans, uniquely, are the bearers of intrinsic value (b).

Furthermore, because humans are aware that natural beings other than themselves can be the bearers of intrinsic value (a), they can set about *wittingly* either to destroy such bearers, given the technology they possess, or to refrain from destroying them. In contrast, animals, although the bearers of intrinsic value (a), cannot wittingly destroy or refrain from destroying other bearers of such value. When they do destroy such beings, they are simply doing so because these others happen to be of use to them. Given their type of consciousness and reasoning capacity, they are not in a position to appreciate that they have the power to destroy or refrain from destroying others with "goods of their own." Only humans, conceptually, can appreciate this problem.

This difference between humans and animals is sometimes expressed as follows. Humans are valuable not only instrumentally but also intrinsically – they are valuable both "in themselves" and "for themselves." To be valuable "in themselves" is held to be the consequence of possessing not only consciousness but also self-consciousness. Animals are held to possess only the former but not the latter. However, opponents of this form of human chauvinism (derived perhaps from Kantianism) would say that animals do possess self-consciousness and cite evidence in support. To be valuable "for themselves" is held to follow from possessing "a good of one's own." Nevertheless, once again those who challenge human chauvinism can argue quite rightly, as we have seen, that there are other natural beings, such as animals and indeed even plants[10] which appear also to have "goods of their own." Hence, human beings are neither uniquely valuable "in themselves" or "for themselves."

This argument is an adequate reply to one version of the thesis, but not to the first version, in which "valuable in themselves" is derived from that unique character of human consciousness – reason and language – which makes it possible for humans to recognize that not only do they themselves have "goods of their own," but other natural beings may also have "goods of their own." This unique capacity allows them, given their advanced technology, to *ponder* the issue whether it is morally right or permissible for humans to kill individual life forms and/or eliminate species, or to use nature instrumentally to further their own material well-being. This approach is in line with the ethics of Kant, who argues that humans alone, among the species known to us, have the rationality necessary to be capable of morality.[11]

Hence, it is possible to argue that the *locus* and the *source* of intrinsic value (b) is human consciousness and reason. Nevertheless, in a world without human beings there will be instrumental values or natural beings will be intrinsically valuable (a), that is, valuable "for themselves." While we humans can recognize intrinsic value (a) in other natural beings, these beings cannot recognize it in themselves or in others. Recognizing and articulating such recognition can only occur with beings with language, such as we, humans, possess. (This truth is the Kantian/ Cartesian insight.) In other words, in a world without human consciousness, linguistic capacity and reason, there will be no intrinsic value (b), no beings which are valuable "in themselves," but there will still be beings valuable "for themselves" as well as instrumental values. Humans are the *source* and *locus* of intrinsic value (b); they *and* other natural beings are both the *source* and the *locus* of intrinsic value (a).

The claim that humans are the sole *loci* of intrinsic value is, therefore, wrong because it assumes that intrinsic value (b), which indeed is unique to humans, is the only type of intrinsic value that there is. As well as being philosophically invalid, it is flawed as a basis for science. It ignores the long history of the planet, Earth, before the evolution of the human species a mere 100,000 years ago, and also the possibility of the eventual extinction of that species. To ignore the world, ante- and/or posthuman, is to be seriously unhistorical and unscientific, and a philosophy of human chauvinism erected on such a flawed understanding cannot be an adequate philosophy – minimally, it fails the test of comprehensiveness. However, the claim, when suitably revised in the way just proposed above, can do justice to that history of Earth and Earth's evolutionary complexities even in the absence of humans.

V

Moreover, to say that humans can recognize that there are nonhuman bearers of intrinsic value (a) does not imply that such values are the arbitrary projection of human feelings or emotions upon nature, which is presupposed by what Callicott calls scientific naturalism. It is held that the "object-ive, physical world is . . . value-free from a scientific point of view" as "thought, feeling, sensation, and value have ever since been . . . regarded as confined to the subjective realm of consciousness."[12]

Nevertheless, the student of nature, not imbued with the metaphysics of scientific naturalism, can clearly observe and recognize that plants and animals strive to maintain their functioning integ-rity – that is, that they possess intrinsic value (a). To put the same point in different terminology, the student can observe that plants and animals have needs, and that if these are not met, injury is done or harm befalls them. For instance, the eggs of birds whose shells are so thin that they crack before they are hatched, because their mothers have absorbed too much DDT, can be said to have suffered harm. If the level of DDT were to remain sufficiently high, even after the human species, which first introduced the chemical into the birds' environment, were to become extinct, it would remain true that the eggs had been dam-aged. The absence of human consciousness makes no difference to the outcome. The eggs or the bird parents would not *know* that there is "disvalue" created in the world as a result of human interven-tion through the release of DDT. Only humans, with their unique form of consciousness and reason, would know. With the absence of humans, there would also be absence of regret, of a sense of loss. Nonetheless, the absence of humans does not alter the fact that the needs of such natural beings have been subverted, thereby generating "disva-lue" in the world.

The notion of *need* is, moreover, essentially nor-mative or value-laden. However, if natural nonhu-man beings have needs even in the absence of humans, then clearly the metaphysics of scientific naturalism is unacceptable. The world of nature (at least the biotic part) is imbued with value and dis-value – it is not value-free. This line of reasoning also shows the unacceptability of the thesis of pro-jectivism, that value is simply a projection of human feelings or attitudes upon the world. On the revised view above, one is entitled only to conclude that humans alone are capable of *recognizing* that, be-sides themselves, there are other intrinsically valu-able (a) states or beings in the world. When birds coated with oil in an oil spill cannot fly and die as a result, these deaths are relevant evidence (not a feature subjectively/arbitrarily chosen) for saying that these beings have been harmed, thereby gener-ating disvalue in the world.

Of course, harm to natural beings may be brought about in two ways: through the interven-tion of (i) human agents, such as the oil spill and the presence of DDT in the environment, and (ii) other natural beings or physical processes, such as birds eating worms (with the prey suffering harm) or a volcanic eruption killing all animate beings in its vicinity. The terms *value* and *disvalue* have built-in respective "pro" and "con" attitudes, so to speak. If *disvalue* is generated in context (i), it may follow that we humans ought to avoid doing so. Hence, consistency demands that in context (ii), we humans too ought to prevent it from oc-curring – producing the *reductio ad absurdum* that we humans ought to intervene each time a fox eats a rabbit, a bird a worm.

However, this implication does not actually follow, for there is a relevant difference between the two contexts. The processes of life and evolu-tion are such that without the destruction of life there can be no life. In other words, value is predicated upon disvalue. We humans, as part of those processes, also have to destroy life in order to sustain life – those who eschew meat may mis-takenly believe that they fall outside the ambit of this law but this belief, of course, is an illusion. To intervene to prevent the emergence of disvalue in context (ii) would lead ultimately to the death of all living things, and possibly to the annihilation of value itself.

Nevertheless, to prevent the generation of dis-value in context (i) is another matter. Here the issue involves first recognizing that disvalue may be generated by our own attitude of regarding nature in a purely instrumental manner. Of course, humans, like other natural beings, have to use other parts of nature instrumentally in order to preserve their own functioning integrity. How-ever, unlike other natural beings, we have de-veloped technologies, in pursuit of promoting our own well-being, material or otherwise, to such an extent as to deny (in practice, if not in theory) that other beings have intrinsic value (a). Moreover, as we have argued, humans possess a unique form of consciousness, reason, and language in virtue of which they are the bearers of intrinsic value (b), and which enables them to appreciate the problem raised above.

Value and disvalue involve two relevant aspects. In the absence of humans and their unique type of consciousness and reason, values (whether instrumental or intrinsic [a]) are simply mutely enacted in the world. The arrival of human consciousness, reason and language in the world adds a new dimension to the matter – it now makes sense to say that humans can recognize that enactment, that unfolding or that failure to unfold, capture, and articulate those processes in propositional form, debate and discuss such matters linguistically, distinguish between instrumental and intrinsic value, refine the notion of intrinsic value itself to show that it is intelligible to ascribe intrinsic value in a certain sense to nonhuman natural beings, and ask themselves the moral question whether nature is there only to serve human ends.

The existence of this new dimension does not mean that values are no more than the projections of human feelings and attitudes upon nature. To say that human consciousness is the *source* of values does not have to be interpreted according to the metaphysics of scientific naturalism. I argue that it can more plausibly be interpreted so as not to deny the "mute enactment" of value and disvalue in nature as well as acknowledging the recognition and articulation of that enactment linguistically. If values in context (i) are characterized as mutely enacted values and in context (ii) as recognized-articulated values, then to say that human consciousness is the *source* of all values is simply false, and to say it is the *source* of values *simpliciter* is misleading. One can legitimately only say that human consciousness is the *source* of "recognized-articulated values," not of "mutely enacted values."

The distinction between recognized-articulated and mutely enacted values may be further clarified by distinguishing between a sentence and its overt and covert content. Let S stand for the sentence "Ladybirds eat aphids." The *utterance* of S presupposes a conscious being who is linguistically competent in English. But its content, upon philosophical excavation, so to speak, may be said to reveal the following layers of possibilities and significance: (1) At the most obvious surface level, the

utterance asserts a so-called fact, namely, that ladybirds eat aphids. However, (2) the next level reveals that aphids have use or instrumental value for ladybirds. (3) This revelation, in turn, shows that ladybirds strive to maintain their own functioning integrity by eating aphids – that is, ladybirds are the bearers of intrinsic value (a). They are valuable "for themselves." (4) By generating value in devouring aphids, they thereby also generate disvalue as far as the aphids are concerned, which also possess intrinsic value (a). (5) The generation of such values and disvalues is independent of human consciousness and/or human preferences/attitudes. (6) As such, they are mutely enacted values whose *source* and *locus* are nonhuman. (7) Humans with their unique type of consciousness and linguistic capacity can recognize and articulate mutely enacted values which they do by means of further sentences which lie behind the utterance of *S*. (8) Humans then are the *source* and *locus* of recognized-articulated values. (9) As such, they are the bearers not only of intrinsic value (a), but also intrinsic value (b) – they are said to be valuable not merely *for* themselves but also *in* themselves. (10) As humans may value certain plants attacked by aphids (that is, to value them instrumentally), in uttering *S*, they may also intimate that aphids are very bad things, ladybirds are very good things, and ladybirds devouring aphids is a very good thing. (11) This intimation then gives rise to the impression that there is a profound gulf between "ladybirds eating aphids, *per se* as a value-free datum" and "ladybirds devouring aphids as a very good thing" – as a mere projection of human preferences/attitudes on nature. (12) "Ladybirds eating aphids" appears to be value-free simply because it is assumed that the human observer/scientist is indifferent to the well-being of either ladybirds or aphids (which may or may not be correct). However, more to the point, as shown earlier, because aphids have instrumental value for ladybirds and, in general, predators in devouring their prey generate value for themselves but disvalue for their prey, "ladybirds devouring aphids" appears to be a mere projection of human attitudes on nature only if one ignores the distinctions between (i) the indirect instrumental value which ladybirds have for humans in devouring aphids that attack and damage, say, apple trees, (ii) the direct instrumental value which apple trees have for humans, and (iii) the intrinsic value (a) generated by humans for themselves when they devour the apples from the apple trees. Far from there being a gulf between the two contexts, there is, to the contrary, a perfect symmetry between them. It is true that without humans with their unique brand of consciousness, linguistic capacity and rationality, there can be no articulation of mutely enacted values as recognized-articulated values. Nevertheless, such recognition and articulation, to repeat, does not mean that the former are not independent of human presence and existence.

Those eager to uphold the metaphysics of scientific naturalism may still retort that the distinction between "mutely enacted values" and "recognized-articulated values" is simply a distinction made by human consciousness in an arbitrary fashion. However, to say so is to duplicate the ambiguity in the thesis that human consciousness is the *source* of values noted earlier. Undoubtedly, even though the distinction itself can only be made by a being with the peculiar consciousness and rational capacity displayed by humans, the distinction itself is not simply the arbitrary product of human consciousness. To imply that it is is to undermine the very program of scientific naturalism itself, since that program presupposes the idea that it is possible for humans to study the natural world "objectively" without human consciousness itself necessarily producing arbitrary distortions.

VI

I hold that my argument above undermines Mackie's "argument from metaphysical queerness" against the "objectivity" of values. "Recognized-articulated values" are indeed the deliverances, though not the subjective/arbitrary deliverances, of human consciousness.[13] In contrast, however, "mutely enacted values" occur every time natural beings succeed in maintaining their functioning integrity, achieving "goods" that "are their own." In other words, as we have seen, quite unmysteriously, for example, every time a bluetit finds an insect (or seed) to eat when it is hungry, it generates or enacts a value, but at the expense of the insect whose "good" is destroyed, thereby generating or enacting a disvalue. Or, every time a plant grows taller to reach the sunlight, it, too, is generating or enacting a value. These values include both instrumental and intrinsic (a) values. There is nothing

really odd in saying that such values existed in nature before the arrival of human consciousness and will continue to exist even after the disappearance of such consciousness from the world. The *source* and *locus* of recognized-articulated values are indeed humans; the *source* and *locus* of mutely enacted values are, in addition, other natural nonhuman beings.

VII

To sum up these arguments, in which I have tried to resolve the controversy between Callicott and Rolston, one could say that Callicott is correct in distinguishing between the *source* and *locus* of values as well as between entities "valuable *for* themselves" and "valuable *in* themselves." However, he goes wrong in failing to distinguish between recognized-articulated and mutely enacted values and thereby implies that human consciousness is the *source* of all values *tout court*. If the arguments advanced in this paper are correct, then human consciousness is the *source* and *locus* only of recognized-articulated values; humans may, hence, be said to be both valuable *for* and *in* themselves. Callicott is right to say that nonhuman beings are the *loci* only of intrinsic value (a), being valuable *for* themselves but not valuable *in* themselves as humans uniquely are. Nevertheless, he overlooks the fact that nonhumans are not only the *loci* of mutely enacted values but also their *source*. As a result, Rolston is right in his fundamental criticism of Callicott's position, namely, that Callicott has failed to recognize that nature is the holder of values and humans are the beholders. However, Rolston, too, may have overstated his case, as he also fails to distinguish between recognized-articulated and mutely enacted values. Rolston has successfully shown that nature is the holder of mutely enacted values, both instrumental and intrinsic (a) and that humans are their beholders. Because humans have generated recognized-articulated values by beholding, recognizing, and articulating mutely enacted values, Rolston's claim that Callicott is wrong in holding values to be anthropogenic has to be somewhat restated: mutely enacted values are necessarily nonanthropogenic, but recognized-articulated values are anthropogenic.

Callicott is correct in rejecting the Kantian/Cartesian moral metaphysics that confines intrinsic value (a) to rational beings with language, but he is wrong to overlook intrinsic value (b), about which that metaphysics is correct. Moreover, he is unnecessarily overimpressed by the thesis of projectivism which ignores the capacity for language and reason and reason-based morality unique to humans, while emphasizing exclusively their capacity for bioempathy. However, unless that bioempathy at bottom is no more than the mere projection of arbitrary human preferences or sentiments, it must be anchored in the realization that both humans and nonhumans are intrinsically valuable (a), that humans and nonhumans can be of instrumental value mutually to each other, and that the history of Earth's biota has been very much longer than human history and could perhaps even outlast that history. What enables humans to recognize the above is a capacity unique to them, not shared by other life forms. On the other hand, Rolston is better able to recognize this unique form of human consciousness without conceding anything to the thesis of Humean projectivism, while at the same time doing justice to the existence of intrinsic value (a) in nature. Perhaps one could conclude that Rolston is more right than wrong and that Callicott more wrong than right. Callicott, by refraining from challenging the non-rational foundation of much of modern Western moral philosophy, ends up being unable (in spite of his explicit attempts) to do justice to the geological, evolutionary, and ecological prehuman history of the planet Earth and also to its possible posthuman existence.

Notes

1 J. Baird Callicott, "On the Intrinsic Value of Nonhuman Species," in *The Preservation of Species*, ed. Bryan G. Norton (Princeton: Princeton University Press, 1986), p. 142.

2 John L. Mackie, *Ethics: Inventing Right and Wrong* (Middlesex: Penguin Books, 1977), pp. 38–42.

3 Holmes Rolston, III, *Environmental Ethics: Duties to and Values in Nature* (Philadelphia: Temple University Press, 1988), pp. 112–17.

4 In so doing, Rolston challenges the modern philosophical foundation for values.

5 The Cartesian element comes from the claim that humans are uniquely rational because they possess language. The Kantian element comes from the thesis that humans are uniquely rational moral beings, amongst natural beings. (Of course, Kant also holds that there are rational beings which are neither human nor natural. Moreover, he holds that there *could* exist other rational moral species, although at the moment we know of none.)

6 Eugene Hargrove makes the same point. See "Weak Anthropocentrism," *The Monist* 75 (1992): 186–7.

7 Richard and Val Routley, "Against the Inevitability of Human Chauvinism," in *Ethics and Problems of the 21st Century*, ed. K. E. Goodpaster and K. M. Sayre (Notre Dame and London: University of Notre Dame Press, 1979), pp. 36–59.

8 This sense of teleology refers back to the medieval notion of "the great chain of beings," and earlier to that famous passage in Aristotle's *The Politics* in which he says that plants exist for the sake of animals which, in turn, exist for the sake of humans. But this sense is to be distinguished from another thesis of Aristotle, namely, that organisms possess their own respective *tele* (or "goods of their own"), which may be called intrinsic or immanent teleology.

9 One kind of critical response to this point must be faced here. Such a response concedes that humans can and may recognize intrinsic value (a) in organisms, but insists that the mere recognition of it is insufficient to determine moral judgements in contexts where the interests of two beings, each intrinsically valuable, clash. This line of argument implies that as the AIDS virus may be recognized to be intrinsically valuable (a), it ought to live and multiply, and that the human victim ought not to kill it. It further implies that if the claim entails such a conclusion, then the argument is suspect as the conclusion is counterintuitive and absurd. Through *reductio ad absurdum*, the premises of the argument may be dismissed as equally absurd. However, does this charge succeed? The claim that it does is based on confusing two very different issues: (i) whether an entity is intrinsically valuable (a) and (ii) in a specific conflict between two beings – the one which is intrinsically valuable (a) and (b), the other which is only intrinsically valuable (a) – which ought to yield? To settle the first issue does not *ipso facto* settle the second. When the two entities involved are humans, the critics do not appear to get the issues confused. But when one of the two entities is human and the other nonhuman, they become confused. Consider the following example. A teacher who intervenes to stop child A from bullying B and to discipline A is fully aware that both children are intrinsically valuable. All the same he or she judges that A's behavior is wrong, guided by considerations other than their possessing intrinsic value (a) and (b). Another possible source of confusion is a misconstrual of Kant's maxim about regarding fellow humans as ends in themselves, not as means to one's own ends. Kant and Kantians do not say: *always* regard them as ends in themselves, *never* as means to one's ends. Instead they say: *do not*

merely regard them as means to one's ends, but also as ends in themselves. Kantians realize that the former is quite unworkable as, inevitably, situations exist where it is impossible to avoid treating another intrinsically valuable being as a means to one's ends. Analogously, recognizing that organisms have intrinsic value (a) in no way entails or even suggests that we may never treat them in certain contexts as means to our ends. Quite simply, if we did not, we would not survive at all. But having said that, it does not mean that it is right to treat them always merely as means to our ends, never as ends in themselves. To recognize that they are intrinsically valuable (a) is to admit that contexts exist where it would *not* be right to treat them as mere means to our ends. To claim none exists amounts to denying that they are intrinsically valuable (a), thereby implying they have only instrumental value for humans.

10 See Paul W. Taylor, *Respect for Nature: A Theory of Environmental Ethics* (Princeton: Princeton University Press, 1986) and Robin Attfield, "The Good of Trees," *Journal of Value Inquiry* 15 (1981): 35–54.

11 When Rolston refers to the superiority of the human over others species, it is this feature that he has in mind. He talks about "this latecoming species in which mind has flowered and morals have emerged" and "this sole moral species" (*Environmental Ethics*, p. 157). If so, Callicott is somewhat unfair to Rolston when he accuses him of "conveniently forget-[ting] that [for] Kant... the *value of reason* depends ultimately upon the value *ascribed* to itself by a rational being" ("Rolston on Intrinsic Value," *Environmental Ethics* 14[1992]: 135). In the light of the clarification offered here, Rolston could accept that nod to Kant without jeopardizing the claim that such rational/moral agents can recognize and appreciate that organisms have built-in goods of their own which are worthy of respect.

12 Callicott, "On the Intrinsic Value of Nonhuman Species," p. 141.

13 In a trivial sense of *subjective*, such deliverances are indeed subjective as they are the products of a particular type of consciousness, and consciousness itself, necessarily, is subjective. But they are not subjective when that term is used as a synonym or implicate of "arbitrary."

13

Environmental Ethics and Weak Anthropocentrism

Bryan G. Norton

I Introduction

In two essays already published in the journal *Environmental Ethics*, I have argued that an environmental ethic cannot be derived, first, from rights or interests of nonhumans and, second, from rights or interests of future generations of humans.[1] Those negative conclusions pave the way for a more positive discussion of the nature and shape of environmental ethics and, in the present paper, I undertake that task. In particular, I address the question of whether there must be a distinctively environmental ethic.

Discussions of this question in the literature have equated a negative answer with the belief that the standard categories of rights, interests, and duties of individual human beings are adequate to furnish ethical guidance in environmental decision making. A positive answer is equated with the suggestion that nature has, in some sense, intrinsic value. In other words, the question of whether environmental ethics is distinctive is taken as equivalent to the question of whether an environmental ethic must reject anthropocentrism, the view that only humans are loci of fundamental value.[2] Environmental ethics is seen as distinctive vis-à-vis standard ethics if and only if environmental ethics can be founded upon principles which assert or presuppose that nonhuman natural entities have value independent of human value.

I argue that this equivalence is mistaken by showing that the anthropocentrism/nonanthropocentr-

ism debate is far less important than is usually assumed. Once an ambiguity is noted in its central terms, it becomes clear that nonanthropocentrism is not the only adequate basis for a truly environmental ethic.[3] I then argue that another dichotomy, that of individualism versus nonindividualism, should be seen as crucial to the distinctiveness of environmental ethics and that a successful environmental ethic cannot be individualistic in the way that standard contemporary ethical systems are. Finally, I examine the consequences of these conclusions for the nature and shape of an environmental ethic.

Before beginning these arguments, I need to clarify how I propose to test an adequate environmental ethic. I begin by assuming that all environmentally sensitive individuals believe that there is a set of human behaviors which do or would damage the environment. Further, I assume that there is considerable agreement among such individuals about what behaviors are included in that set. Most would decry, for example, careless storage of toxic wastes, grossly overpopulating the world with humans, wanton destruction of other species, air and water pollution, and so forth. There are other behaviors which would be more controversial, but I take the initial task of constructing an adequate environmental ethic to be the statement of some set of principles from which rules can be derived proscribing the behaviors included in the set which virtually all environmentally sensitive individuals agree are environmentally destructive. The further task of refining an environmental ethic then involves moving back and forth between the basic principles and the more or less controversial behaviors, adjusting principles and/or rejecting intuitions until the best possible fit between principles and sets of proscribed behaviors is obtained for the whole environmental community. In the present paper I address the prior question of basic principles. I am here only seeking to clarify which principles do (and which do not) support the large set of relatively uncontroversial cases of behaviors damaging to the environment. An ethic will be adequate, on this approach, if its principles are sufficient to entail rules proscribing the behaviors involved in the noncontroversial set. My arguments, then, are not directed at determining which principles are *true*, but which are *adequate* to uphold certain shared intuitions. Questions concerning the truth of such principles must be left for another occasion.

II Anthropocentrism and Nonanthropocentrism

I suggest that the distinction between anthropocentrism and nonanthropocentrism has been given more importance in discussions of the foundations of environmental ethics than it warrants because a crucial ambiguity in the term *anthropocentrism* has gone unnoticed.[4] Writers on both sides of the controversy apply this term to positions which treat humans as the only loci of intrinsic value.[5] Anthropocentrists are therefore taken to believe that every instance of value originates in a contribution to human values and that all elements of nature can, at most, have value instrumental to the satisfaction of human interests.[6] Note that anthropocentrism is defined by reference to the position taken on *loci* of value. Some nonanthropocentrists say that human beings are the *source* of all values, but that they can designate nonhuman objects as loci of fundamental value.[7]

It has also become common to explain and test views on this point by reference to "last man examples" which are formulated as follows.[8] Assume that a human being, *S*, is the last living member of *Homo sapiens* and that *S* faces imminent death. Would *S* do wrong to wantonly destroy some object *X*? A positive answer to this question with regard to any nonhuman *X* is taken to entail nonanthropocentrism. If the variable *X* refers to some natural object, a species, an ecosystem, a geological formation, etc., then it is thought that positions on such questions determine whether a person is an anthropocentrist or not, because the action in question cannot conceivably harm any human individual. If it is wrong to destroy *X*, the wrongness must derive from harm to *X* or to some other natural object. But one can harm something only if it is a good in its own right in the sense of being a locus of fundamental value.

Or so the story goes. I am unconvinced because not nearly enough has been said about what counts as a human interest. In order to explore this difficult area, I introduce two useful definitions. A *felt preference* is any desire or need of a human individual that can at least temporarily be sated by some specifiable experience of that individual. A *considered preference* is any desire or need that a human individual would express after careful deliberation, including a judgment that the desire or need is consistent with a rationally adopted world view – a world view which includes fully supported scientific theories and a metaphysical framework interpreting those theories, as well as a set of rationally supported aesthetic and moral ideals.

When interests are assumed to be constructed merely from felt preferences, they are thereby insulated from any criticism or objection. Economic approaches to decision making often adopt this approach because it eschews "value judgments" – decision makers need only ask people what they want, perhaps correct these preferences for intensity, compute the preferences satisfied by the various possible courses of action, and let the resulting ordinal ranking imply a decision.

A considered preference, on the other hand, is an idealization in the sense that it can only be adopted after a person has rationally accepted an entire world view and, further, has succeeded in altering his felt preferences so that they are consonant with that world view. Since this is a process no one has ever completed, references to considered preferences are hypothetical – they refer to preferences the individual would have if certain contrary-to-fact conditions were fulfilled. Nonetheless, references to considered preferences remain useful because it is possible to distinguish felt preferences from considered preferences when there are convincing arguments that felt preferences are not consistent with some element of a world view that appears worthy of rational support.

It is now possible to define two forms of anthropocentrism. A value theory is *strongly anthropocentric* if all value countenanced by it is explained by reference to satisfactions of felt preferences of human individuals. A value theory is *weakly anthropocentric* if all value countenanced by it is explained by reference to satisfaction of some felt preference of a human individual or by reference to its bearing upon the ideals which exist as elements in a world view essential to determinations of considered preferences.

Strong anthropocentrism, as here defined, takes unquestioned felt preferences of human individuals as determining value. Consequently, if humans have a strongly consumptive value system, then their "interests" (which are taken merely to be their felt preferences) dictate that nature will be used in an exploitative manner. Since there is no check upon the felt preferences of individuals in the value system of strong anthropocentrism, there exists no means to criticize the behavior of individuals who use nature merely as a storehouse of raw materials to be extracted and used for products serving human preferences.

Weak anthropocentrism, on the other hand, recognizes that felt preferences can be either rational or not (in the sense that they can be judged not consonant with a rational world view). Hence, weak anthropocentrism provides a basis for criticism of value systems which are purely exploitative of nature. In this way, weak anthropocentrism makes available two ethical resources of crucial importance to environmentalists. First, to the extent that environmental ethicists can make a case for a world view that emphasizes the close relationship between the human species and other living species, they can also make a case for ideals of human behavior extolling harmony with nature. These ideals are then available as a basis for criticizing preferences that merely exploit nature.

Second, weak anthropocentrism as here defined also places value on human experiences that provide the basis for value formation. Because weak anthropocentrism places value not only on felt preferences, but also on the process of value formation embodied in the criticism and replacement of felt preferences with more rational ones, it makes possible appeals to the value of experiences of natural objects and undisturbed places in human value formation. To the extent that environmentalists can show that values are formed and informed by contact with nature, nature takes on value as a

teacher of human values. Nature need no longer be seen as a mere satisfier of fixed and often consumptive values – it also becomes an important source of inspiration in value formation.[9]

In the final section of this paper I develop these two sources of value in nature more fully. Even there my goal is not to defend these two bases for environmental protection as embodying true claims about the value of nature – that, as I said at the outset is a larger and later task. My point is only that, within the limits set by weak anthropocentrism as here defined, there exists a framework for developing powerful reasons for protecting nature. Further, these reasons do not resemble the extractive and exploitative reasons normally associated with strong anthropocentrism.

And they do not differ from strongly anthropocentric reasons in merely theoretical ways. Weakly anthropocentric reasoning can affect behavior as can be seen by applying it to last man situations. Suppose that human beings choose, for rational or religious reasons, to live according to an ideal of maximum harmony with nature. Suppose also that this ideal is taken seriously and that anyone who impairs that harmony (by destroying another species, by polluting air and water, etc.) would be judged harshly. But such an ideal need not attribute intrinsic value to natural objects, nor need the prohibitions implied by it be justified with nonanthropocentric reasoning attributing intrinsic value to nonhuman natural objects. Rather, they can be justified as being implied by the ideal of harmony with nature. This ideal, in turn, can be justified either on religious grounds referring to human spiritual development or as being a fitting part of a rationally defensible world view.

Indeed, there exist examples of well developed world views that exhibit these characteristics. The Hindus and Jains, in proscribing the killing of insects, etc., show concern for their own spiritual development rather than for the actual lives of those insects. Likewise, Henry David Thoreau is careful not to attribute independent, intrinsic value to nature. Rather he believes that nature expresses a deeper spiritual reality and that humans can learn spiritual values from it.[10] Nor should it be inferred that only spiritually oriented positions can uphold weakly anthropocentric reasons. In a post-Darwinian world, one could give rational and scientific support for a world view that includes ideals of living in harmony with nature, but which involve no attributions of intrinsic value to nature.

Views such as those just described are weakly anthropocentric because they refer only to human values, but they are not strongly so because human behavior is limited by concerns other than those derivable from prohibitions against interfering with the satisfaction of human felt preferences. And practically speaking, the difference in behavior between strong anthropocentrists and weak anthropocentrists of the sort just described and exemplified is very great. In particular, the reaction of these weak anthropocentrists to last man situations is undoubtedly more similar to that of nonanthropocentrists than to that of strong anthropocentrists. Ideals such as that of living in harmony with nature imply rules proscribing the wanton destruction of other species or ecosystems even if the human species faces imminent extinction.

But it might be objected that positions such as those here sketched only appear to avoid attributions of intrinsic value to nature and natural objects. For example, Tom Regan has argued that a position similar to them makes covert appeal to the intrinsic value of nonhuman objects and hence fails to embody a purely anthropocentric argument for the preservation of nature. He writes:

> If we are told that treating the environment in certain ways offends against an ideal of human conduct, we are not being given a position that is an alternative to, or inconsistent with, the view that nonconscious objects have a value of their own. The fatal objection which the offense against an ideal argument encounters, is that, rather than offering an alternative to the view that some nonconscious objects have inherent value, it presupposes that they do.[11]

Prior to this conclusion, Regan states three propositions which are intended to support it:

> The fitting way to act in regard to X clearly involves a commitment to regarding X as having value.... An ideal which enjoins us not to act toward X in a certain way but which denies that X has any value is either unintelligible or pointless. Ideals, in short, involve the recognition of the value of *that toward which* one acts.[12]

Regan's three propositions, however, are either false or they fail to support his conclusion. If the value they refer to is inclusive of intrinsic and instrumental value, the propositions are true but do not support the conclusion that all ideals of human conduct imply intrinsic value of the object protected by the ideal. Ideals regarding the treatment of my neighbor's horse (viewed as a piece of private property) imply only that the horse has instrumental, not intrinsic, value. If, on the other hand, Regan intends the references to value in the three propositions to refer to *intrinsic* value exclusively, then all three propositions are clearly false. I can accept that there is a fitting way to act in regard to my neighbor's horse, without thereby accepting any commitment to accord intrinsic value to it. Nor am I thereby committed to anything either unintelligible or pointless. I need not recognize the intrinsic value of the horse; I can, alternatively, recognize the intrinsic value of my neighbor and her preference that the horse not be harmed.

The example of the horse provides a counterexample to Regan's argument, thereby showing that the argument is unsound. It does so, admittedly, by appealing to the instrumental value of the horse for human preference satisfaction. It does not, therefore, directly address the question of whether there are ideals of environmental protection supportable on weakly anthropocentric grounds, but which imply no intrinsic value for the protected objects. The examples mentioned earlier, however, fulfill this function. If the Hindu, the Jainist, or the follower of Thoreau appeals to ideals designed to improve humans spiritually, then they can justify those ideals without attributing intrinsic value to the objects protected. Nor are the spiritual aspects of these examples essential. If ideals of human behavior are justified as fitting parts of a world view which can be rationally supported from a human perspective, then these ideals, too, escape Regan's argument – they might support protection of nature as a fitting thing for humans to strive toward, without attributing intrinsic value to nature.

Nor need weak anthropocentrism collapse into strong anthropocentrism. It would do so if the dichotomy between preferences and ideals were indefensible. If all values can, ultimately, be interpreted as satisfactions of preferences, then ideals are simply human preferences. The controversy here is reminiscent of that discussed by early utilitarians. John Stuart Mill, for example, argued that because higher pleasures ultimately can be seen to provide greater satisfactions, there is thus only a single scale of values – preference satisfaction.[13] It is true that weak anthopocentrists must deny that preference satisfaction is the only measure of human value. They must take human ideals seriously enough so that they can be set against preference satisfactions as a limit upon them. It is therefore no surprise that weak anthropocentrists reject the reductionistic position popular among utilitarians. Indeed, it is precisely the rejection of that reductionism that allows them to steer their way between strong anthropocentrism and nonanthropocentrism. The rejection of this reduction is, of course, a commitment that weak anthropocentrists share with nonanthropocentrists. Both believe there are values distinct from human preference satisfaction, rejecting the reduction of ideals to preferences. They differ not on this point, but on whether the justification of those ideals must appeal to the intrinsic value of nonhuman objects.

Weak anthropocentrism is, therefore, an attractive position for environmentalists. It requires no radical, difficult-to-justify claims about the intrinsic value of nonhuman objects and, at the same time, it provides a framework for stating obligations that goes beyond concern for satisfying human preferences. It, rather, allows the development of arguments to the effect that current, largely consumptive attitudes toward nature are indefensible, because they do not fit into a world view that is rationally defensible in terms not implying intrinsic value for nonhumans. It can also emphasize the value of nature in forming, rather than in satisfying human preferences, as preferences can be modified in the process of striving toward a consistent and rationally defensible world view.

III Individualism and Nonindividualism

The distinctions and arguments presented above convince me that, while the development of a nonanthropocentric axiology committed to intrinsic value for nonhuman natural entities remains an interesting philosophical enterprise, the dichotomy on which it is based has less importance for the nature of environmental ethics than is usually thought. In particular, I see no reason to think that, if environmental ethics is distinctive, its distinctiveness derives from the necessity of appeals to the intrinsic value of nonhuman natural objects. Once two forms of anthropocentrism are distinguished, it appears that from one, weak anthropocentrism, an adequate environmental ethic can be derived. If that is true, authors who equate the question of the distinctiveness of an adequate environmental ethic with the claim that nature or natural objects have intrinsic value are mistaken.

There is, nevertheless, reason to believe that an adequate environmental ethic is distinctive. In this section, I argue that no successful environmental ethic can be derived from an individualistic basis, whether the individuals in question are human or nonhuman. Since most contemporary ethical systems are essentially individualistic, an adequate environmental ethic is distinctive, not by being necessarily nonanthropocentric as many environmental ethicists have argued or assumed, but, rather, by being nonindividualistic.

Standard contemporary ethical theories, at least in the United States and Western Europe are essentially individualistic. By this I mean that the behavioral prohibitions embodied in them derive from the principle that actions ought not to harm other individuals unjustifiably. Utilitarians derive ethical rules from the general principle that all actions should promote the greatest possible happiness for the greatest possible number of individuals. This means that actions (or rules) are judged to be legitimate or not according to whether more good (and less harm) for individuals will result from the action than from any alternative. On this view, the satisfaction of each individual interest is afforded an initial prima facie value. Some such interests are not to be satisfied because the information available indicates that if they are, some greater interest or sets of interests of some individuals cannot be satisfied concurrently with them. The utilitarian principle, supplemented by empirical predictions about the consequences of actions for individuals, filters happiness-maximizing actions from others that do not maximize happiness. For present purposes, the important point is that the satisfaction of individual interests are the basic unit of value for utilitarians, and in this sense, utilitarianism (either of the act or rule variety) is essentially individualistic.[14]

Contemporary deontologists derive ethical prohibitions from individual rights and obligations to protect those rights.[15] Individuals make claims, and when these claims conflict with claims made by other individuals, they are judged to be legitimate or illegitimate according to a set of ethical rules designed to make such decisions. Although these rules, in essence, are the embodiment of a system of justice and fairness, the rules adjudicate between claims of individuals, and consequently modern deontology is essentially individualistic.[16] Therefore, both utilitarianism and modern deontology are essentially individualistic in the sense that the basic units of ethical concern are interests or claims of individuals.

It is characteristic of the rules of environmental ethics that they must prohibit current behaviors that have effects upon the long-range future as well as the present. For example, storage of radioactive wastes with a half-life of thousands of years in containers that will deteriorate in a few centuries must be prohibited by an adequate environmental ethic, even if such actions, on the whole, provide the most benefits and no harms to currently living individuals. Likewise, human demographic growth, if subsequent generations continue that policy, will create severe overpopulation, a behavior negatively affecting the future of the environment, and hence human reproductive behavior must be governed by an adequate environmental ethic. An adequate environmental ethic must therefore prohibit current activities generally agreed to have negative effects on the environment of the future.

I have argued at length elsewhere that a paradox, due to Derek Parfit, effectively precludes systems of ethics which are individualistic in the sense defined above from governing current decisions by reference to their effects on future individuals.[17] To summarize that argument briefly, it exploits the insight that no system of ethics built exclusively upon adjudications of interests of present and future individuals can govern current decisions and their effects on future individuals because current environmental decisions determine what individuals will exist in the future. Parfit's argument notes that current decisions regarding consumption determine how many individuals and which individuals will be born in the future. On a policy of fast demographic growth and high consumption, different individuals will exist a century from now than would exist if the current generation adopts a policy of low growth and moderate consumption. Assume, as most environmentalists do, that a policy of high growth and immoderate consumption will leave the future

with a lower quality of life than more moderate growth policies would. The individuals who are, in fact, born as a result of the immoderate growth policies cannot complain that they would have been better off had the policies been different – for they would not even have existed had moderate policies been adopted. That is, Parfit's paradox shows that current policy cannot be governed by reference to harms to the interests of future individuals, because those policies determine who those individuals will be and what interests they will have. Attempts to govern behaviors affecting the distant future cannot, therefore, be governed by appeal to individual interests of future persons, since the very existence of such individuals hangs in the balance until all relevant decisions are made.

Since the ethical intuitions shared by all environmentally sensitive individuals include prohibitions against behaviors which may have negative effects only in the long-term future (and not in the present), the rules of environmental ethics cannot be derived from the usual, individualistic systems of ethics currently in vogue. Note, also, that my argument concerning individualism makes no assumption that only human individuals make claims or have interests and rights. Future nonhuman individuals are, likewise, affected by human policies regarding consumption and reproduction. Consequently, expansion of the loss of individual rights holders, or preference havers to include nonhumans in no way affects the argument. No ethical system which is essentially individualistic, regardless of how broadly the reference category of individuals is construed, can offer ethical guidance concerning current environmental policy in all cases.

IV   A Proposal for an Adequate Anthropocentric Environmental Ethic

The arguments of the last section are surprisingly simple and general, but if they are sound, they explain the fairly general intuition that environmental ethics must be distinctive in some sense, although not in the sense usually assumed. So far my conclusions have all been negative – I have argued that an adequate environmental ethic *need not* be nonanthropocentric and that an adequate environmental ethic *must not* be limited to considerations of individual interests. From these conclusions a new direction for environmental ethics emerges which is weakly anthropocentric – it finds all value in human loci – and which is also non-individualistic in the sense that value is not restricted to satisfactions of felt preferences of human individuals. In other words, the arguments of the first two sections of the paper (1) positively define a space by establishing the possibility of a weakly, but not strongly, anthropocentric environmental ethic and (2) negatively constrain that ethic by eliminating the possibility that it be purely individualistic.

My purpose now is not to demonstrate that the ethical principles I have set out are definitely correct or that they are the only adequate principles available. My goal, rather, is to present a valid alternative for environmental ethics that is adequate in a manner that no purely individualistic, strongly anthropocentric ethic can be, while avoiding difficult-to-defend references to the intrinsic value of nonhuman natural objects.

I begin my explication with an analogy. Suppose an extremely wealthy individual, through a will, sets up a very large trust fund "to be managed for the economic well-being of my descendants." Over the years, descendants will be born and die, and the class of beneficiaries will change through time. Suppose, also, that the family drifts apart emotionally and becomes highly contentious. I suggest that two sorts of controversies, each with its own distinctive logic, could arise concerning the fund. First, there may be issues about the *fair distribution* of proceeds of the trust. Some descendants might claim that other descendants are not entitled to full shares, because they are, or are descended from, an illegitimate offspring of a member of the family. Or it might be disputed whether adopted children of descendants are included in the terms of the will.

Second, there may well be disputes about the *management* of the trust. Here, there may be questions concerning what sorts of investments are "good investments." Should all investments be safe ones, thereby insuring a continued, although smaller income? Might the principle of the trust be invaded in years where the income from investments is unusually low? Might one generation simply spend the principle, dividing it fairly among themselves, showing no concern for future descendants?

To apply this analogy in obvious ways, ethical questions about the environment can be divided into ones concerning distributional fairness within generations and others concerning longer-term, cross-generational issues. If the arguments in the third section are correct, then the latter are not reducible to the former; nor do they have the same logic. It can be assumed that many environmental concerns, as well as nonenvironmental ones, can be resolved as issues of distributional fairness. If a property owner pollutes a stream running through his property, this action raises a question of fairness between him and his downstream neighbors.[18] These moral issues are, presumably, as amenable to resolution using the categories and rules of standard, individualistic ethics as are nonenvironmental ones.

But there are also many questions in environmental ethics that are analogous to questions of management of a trust across time. Soil, water, forests, coal, oil, etc. are analogous to the principle of the trust. If they are used up, destroyed, or degraded, they no longer provide benefits. The income from the trust provides an analogy for renewable resources. As long as the productive resource (analogous to the principle of the trust) is intact, one can expect a steady flow of benefits.

One feature that makes environmental ethics distinctive is concern for protection of the resource base through indefinite time. Parfit's paradox shows that these concerns cannot be accounted for by reference to concerns for individuals and to the obligation not to harm other individuals unjustifiably. The obligations are analogous to those accepted by an individual who is appointed executor of the trust fund. Although decisions made by the executor affect individuals and their well-being, the obligation is to the integrity of the trust, not to those individuals. While one might be tempted to say that the obligation of the executor is to future individuals who will be born, but who are at this time unknown, this conceptualization also involves a failure to perceive the profundity of Parfit's paradox. Suppose all of the members of a given generation of the family in question sign an agreement not to have offspring and thereby convince the executor to disburse the principle of the trust equally among current beneficiaries. Perhaps this is consistent with the terms of the trust, but it shows that the current choices of the executor cannot be guided by abstract conceptions of "future individuals." When current decisions about management are interlocked with not-yet-decided questions affecting the future existence of individuals, it is impossible to refer to those individuals as the basis of guidance in making current management decisions.

Suppose a generation of the entire human species freely decided to sterilize itself, thereby freeing itself to consume without fear of harming future individuals. Would they do wrong? Yes.[19] The perpetuation of the human species is a good thing because a universe containing human consciousness is preferable to one without it.[20] This value claim implies that current generations must show concern for future generations. They must take steps to avoid the extinction of the species and they must provide a reasonably stable resource base so that future generations will not suffer great deprivation. These are the bases of rules of management analogous to the rules for administering a trust fund. They do not have individuals or individual interests as their reference point, but they do govern behavior that will affect future individuals.

It is now possible to outline a weakly anthropocentric, nonindividualistic environmental ethic. Such an ethic has two levels. The distributional level has as its principle that one ought not to harm other human individuals unjustifiably. This principle rests upon the assumption that felt preferences, desires that occur within individual human consciousness, have equal prima facie value. Rules for the fair treatment of individuals are derived from the principle of no harm and prescribe fair treatment of individuals, whether regarding benefits derived from the environment or from other sources. Since there is nothing distinctive about the environmental prescriptions and proscriptions that occur on this level – they do not differ in nature from other issues of individual fairness – I do not discuss them further.

Decisions on the second level of environmental ethics, which I call the level of "allocation," cannot, however, be based upon individual considerations. The central value placed on human consciousness is not a result of aggregating the value of individual consciousnesses, because the value of ongoing consciousness cannot be derived from the value of individual consciousnesses – they cannot be identified or counted prior to the making of decisions on resource allocation.[21] Therefore, obligations on this level are owed to no individual and can be called "generalized obligations." They are obligations of the current generation to maintain a stable flow of resources into the indefinite future and, consequently, they

are stated vis-à-vis resources necessary for ongoing human life, not vis-à-vis individual requirements. Resources represent the means for supporting life looked at from a nonindividual perspective. The individual perspective determines needs and wants and then seeks means to fulfill them. Concern for the continued flow of resources insures that sources of goods and services such as ecosystems, soil, forests, etc. remain "healthy" and are not deteriorating. In this way, options are held open and reasonable needs of individuals for whatever goods and services can be fulfilled with reasonable labor, technology, and ingenuity. The emphasis of this concern, however, is not individualistic since it is not focused on the fulfillment of specifiable needs, but rather on the integrity and health of ongoing ecosystems as holistic entities.

While the long-term nature of the concern implies that the stability of the resource base must be protected, this stability is not the same thing as ecological stability. It is an open (and controversial) question as to what the stability of ecosystems means. Further, there are controversies concerning the extent to which there are scientifically supportable generalizations about what is necessary to protect ecological stability. For example, it is highly controversial whether diversity, in general, promotes and/or is necessary for ecological stability.[22] These controversies are too complex to enter into here, but they are relevant. To the extent that scientists know what is necessary to protect the resource base, there is an obligation to act upon it. Even if there are few sweeping generalizations such as those concerning diversity and stability, there are a wide variety of less general rules that are well supported and are being systematically ignored in environmental policy. Ecologists and resource managers know that clear-cutting tropical forests on steep slopes causes disastrous erosion, that intensely tilling monocultures causes loss of topsoil, and that overexploitation of fisheries can cause new and far less productive species compositions. Further, there is an obligation, where knowledge is lacking, to seek that knowledge in order to avoid unintentional destruction.

An ethic of resource allocation should apply to nonrenewable resources as well as to renewable ones and should also imply a population policy. The general injunction to maintain the stability of the resource base across generations follows from the value of human consciousness. It implies that, with respect to renewable, or interest-bearing resources, present generations should not harvest more than the maximum sustainable yield of the resource. But what does stability imply with respect to nonrenewable resources? Although at first glance it would seem to suggest that a stable supply can only be sustained if no utilization takes place, this reasoning is based on a confusion – it is not the case that there is an obligation to have a certain, fixed amount of goods in supply, but rather there is an obligation to maintain a stable level of goods *available for use*. The ethical principle, in other words, is directed at maintaining the possibility of human consciousness which requires resource use. What is required, then, is a constant supply of resources available for utilization by succeeding generations. Once the problem is framed in this manner, human technology and the phenomenon of substitutability of products become relevant. Present humans may use up nonrenewable resources, provided they take steps to provide suitable substitutes. If, for example, the present generation uses up a major portion of the accumulated fossil fuels available, they will have done nothing wrong if they leave the next generation with a technology capable of deriving energy from renewable sources such as the sun, wind, or ocean currents.[23] There are significant trade-offs available back and forth between renewable and nonrenewable resources.

Note also that this system implies a population principle – the level of population in any given generation should be determined by the requirements for the stability of the resource flow. Such a determination would be based on an assessment of (a) how many people are consistent with the maximal sustainable yield of renewable resources and (b) how many people are consistent with a level of use for nonrenewable resources which does not outstrip the ability of the existing technology to produce suitable substitutes. A population principle follows, in turn, from this stability principle. One need not identify future individuals or worry about utilities of possible individuals on this approach. The obligation is to maintain maximum sustainable yield consistent with the stability of the resource flow. The population principle sets a population policy for a generation as a whole based on the carrying capacity of the environment. Questions about who, in a given generation, should have children and how many each individual can have, may be treated as questions of interpersonal equity among the existing individuals of any given generation.

The ethical obligations constituting an ethic of allocation are quite simple as they derive from a single value – that of ongoing human consciousness. In general form, however, they do not state specifically what to do; they only require actions necessary to retain a stable resource base through indefinite time. Scientific knowledge can, in principle, nevertheless, indicate specific actions necessary in order to fulfill that obligation. Scientific evidence is sufficient to imply that many currently widespread practices violate those obligations either directly or cumulatively and are, in terms of this system, immoral. There are also areas where scientific knowledge is insufficient to decide whether and how certain practices are destructive. Here, the obligation is to be cautious and to proceed to obtain the information necessary.

While science plays a crucial role in this system, the system is not naturalistic. It does not derive moral obligations from purely scientific statements. Central to all obligations of present individuals to the future is an obligation to perpetuate the value of human consciousness. Science elucidates and makes concrete the specific obligations flowing from that central obligation but does not support it.

V   Relating the Two Levels

The ethic proposed has two levels – one has the prima facie equality of felt preferences of individual humans as its central value principle; the other has the value of ongoing human life and consciousness as its central value principle. Rules and behaviors justified on these two levels can, of course, conflict. If felt preferences are overly consumptive, then the future of human life may be threatened. Conversely, one can imagine situations where concern for the future of the human species might lead to draconian measures threatening the life or livelihood of current individuals by limiting the satisfaction of felt preferences. Weak anthropocentrism, nevertheless, because it recognizes the important difference between felt and considered preferences, can adjudicate these disputes.

The most common conflict, the one many environmentalists fear we now face, exists when overly consumptive felt preferences cause serious overexploitation of nature and thereby threaten the resource base necessary for continued human life. This conflict can be resolved by taking human ideals into consideration. If, for example, one's total world view contains as an ideal the continuation of human life and consciousness, then the felt preferences in question are irrational – they are inconsistent with an important ethical ideal. Similarly, if a rational world view recognizing that the human species evolved from other life forms includes an ideal calling for harmony with nature, this ideal, likewise, can function to criticize and alter felt preferences. By building ecological principles and ideals regarding the proper human treatment of nature into a rationally supported world view, weak anthropocentrists can develop vast resources for criticizing felt preferences of human individuals which threaten environmental stability and harmony.

It can be argued that experiences of nature are essential in constructing a rational world view. Likewise, scientific understanding of nature seems essential for the construction of such a world view. Nor would it be very surprising if it turned out that analogies, symbols, and metaphors drawn from nature provided an essential source of guidance in choosing ethical and aesthetic ideals as well.[24] Other species and unspoiled places would thereby have great value to humans not only for the way in which they satisfy human felt preferences, but also for the way they serve to enlighten those preferences. Once one recognizes the distinction between felt preferences and considered preferences, nature assumes a crucial role in informing values by contributing to the formation of a rational world view, the criterion by which felt preferences are criticized.

VI Environmental Ethics and Intrinsic Value

The conflicts that exist between the levels of distributive fairness and allocation require thoughtful discussion and debate, but that discussion and debate can take place without appeal to the intrinsic value of nonhuman natural objects. The value of ongoing human consciousness and the rules it implies for resource allocation can serve as a basis for criticism of consumptive and exploitative felt preferences. Further, ideas such as that of human harmony with nature and the human species' evolutionary affinity to other species, can serve to

strengthen and add flesh to the world view available for the critique of current environmentally destructive behaviors.

When I refer to an environmental ethic, then, I refer, first of all, to the rules of distributive fairness guiding behaviors affecting other human beings' use of the environment. Second, I refer to the rules of allocation affecting the long-term health of the biosphere as a functioning, organic unit. An environmental ethic, nevertheless, is more than these rules: it also encompasses the ideals, values, and principles that constitute a rational world view regarding the human species' relationship to nature. In these sources are bases for evaluating the rules of right action and for criticizing currently felt preferences. Aesthetic experience of nature is an essential part of the process of forming and applying these ideals and, hence, is also a central part of the environmental ethic here described.

Some nonanthropocentrists, such as J. Baird Callicott, have developed in more detail such ideas as the human affinity to other species and have concluded that it is rational for humans to "attribute" intrinsic value to other species on the basis of affective feelings toward them,[25] but if, as I have argued, a sense of harmony with nature can, once it becomes an entrenched part of our world view, serve to correct felt preferences, then it can also serve to bring felt preferences more in line with the requirements of resource allocation without any talk about intrinsic value. Of course, since human beings, as highly evolved animals, share many needs for clean air, clean water, ecosystem services, etc., in the long term with other species it would not be surprising that *speaking as if* nature has intrinsic value could provide useful guidance in adjusting human felt preferences. And since these preferences are now far too exploitative and too consumptive for the good of our own species, showing concern for other species that share our long-term needs for survival might be one useful tool in a very large kit.

The point of this essay, however, has been to show that one need not make the questionable ontological commitments involved in attributing intrinsic value to nature, since weak anthropocentrism provides a framework adequate to criticize current destructive practices to incorporate concepts of human affinity to nature, and to account for the distinctive nature of environmental ethics. All of these are essential elements in an ethic that recognizes the distinction between felt and considered preferences and includes important aesthetic and ethical ideals. These ideals, which can be derived from spiritual sources or from a rationally constructed world view, can be based on and find their locus in human values. And yet they are sufficient to provide the basis of criticism of currently overconsumptive felt preferences. As such they adjudicate between ethical concerns for distributional fairness in the present and concerns of allocation which have reference to the long-term future. Essential to this adjudication is the development of principles of conduct that respect the ongoing integrity of functioning ecosystems seen as wholes. In this way they transcend concern for individualistically expressed felt preferences and focus attention on the stable functioning of ongoing systems. If all of this is true, Occam's razor surely provides a basis for favoring weak anthropocentrism over nonanthropocentrism.

Notes

1 Bryan G. Norton, "Environmental Ethics and Nonhuman Rights," *Environmental Ethics* 4 (1982): 17–36, and "Environmental Ethics and the Rights of Future Generations," *Environmental Ethics* 4 (1982): 319–37.

2 See, for example, Richard Routley, "Is There a Need for a New, an Environmental Ethics?" *Proceedings of the XV World Congress of Philosophy*, vol. 1 (1973), pp. 205–10; Holmes Rolston, III, "Is There an Ecological Ethic?" *Ethics* 85 (1975): 93–109; Tom Regan, "The Nature and Possibility of an Environmental Ethic," *Environmental Ethics* 3 (1981): 19–34; and Evelyn B. Pluhar, "The Justification of an Environmental Ethic," *Environmental Ethics* 4 (1982): 319–37.

3 See Regan, "The Nature and Possibility of an Environmental Ethic," who distinguishes "an ethic of the environment" from "an ethic for the use of the environment" (p. 20), where the former, but not the latter, recognizes the intrinsic (inherent) value of nonhuman elements of nature. If the arguments of this paper are persuasive, Regan's distinction will lose interest.

4 My thoughts on this subject have been deeply affected by discussions of the work of Donald Regan and J. Baird Callicott. See, Donald Regan, "Duties of Preservation," and J. Baird Callicott, "On the Intrinsic Value of Nonhuman Species," in *The Preservation of Species*, edited by Bryan G. Norton (Princeton: Princeton University Press, 1986).

5 I borrow this phrase from Donald Scherer, "Anthropocentrism, Atomism, and Environmental Ethics," *Environmental Ethics* 4 (1982): 115–23.

6 I take anthropocentrism to be interchangeable with homocentrism. See R. and V. Routley, "Against the Inevitability of Human Chauvinism," in *Ethics and Problems of the 21st Century*, edited by K. E. Goodpaster and K. M. Sayre (Notre Dame, Ind.: University of Notre Dame Press, 1979), pp. 56–7. Routley and Routley show that "human chauvinism" (anthropocentrism, homocentrism) are equivalent to the thesis of man's "dominion," which they describe as "the view that the earth and all its nonhuman contents exist or are available for man's benefit and to serve his interests."

7 See J. Baird Callicott, "On the Intrinsic Value of Nonhuman Species," in Norton, *The Preservation of Species* (in preparation), and Pluhar, "The Justification of an Environmental Ethic."

8 See, for example, Richard Routley, "Is There a Need for a New, an Environmental, Ethic?" p. 207; Routley and Routley, "Human Chauvinism and Environmental Ethics," in *Environmental Philosophy*, edited by D. S. Mannison, M. A. McRobbie and R. Routley (Canberra: Australian National University, Department of Philosophy, 1980), p. 121; and Donald Regan, "Duties of Preservation," in Norton, *The Preservation of Species*.

9 For fuller discussions of this point, see Mark Sagoff, "On Preserving the Natural Environment," *Yale Law Journal* 84 (1974): 205–67; and Holmes Rolston, III, "Can and Ought We to Follow Nature?" *Environmental Ethics* 1 (1979): 7–21.

10 See Henry David Thoreau, *Walden* (New York: Harper and Row, 1958). Note page 64, for example, where Thoreau writes: "One value of even the smallest well is, that when you look into it you see that earth is not continent but insular. This is as important as that it keeps butter cool."

11 Regan, "The Nature and Possibility of an Environmental Ethic," pp. 25–6. It involves no distortion, I think, to equate Regan's use of *inherent* with mine of *intrinsic*.

12 Ibid., p. 25.

13 John Stuart Mill, *Utilitarianism*, chap. 2.

14 I do not intend to imply here that utilitarians are limited to treating human interests as felt preferences. Utilitarians adopt varied interpretations of interests in relation to happiness. My point is only that human individual interests, however determined, are the basis of their moral calculus.

15 I qualify the position here discussed as "contemporary" deontology because there is a strain of thought in Kant which emphasizes that the imperatives are abstract principles. Modern neo-Kantians such as Rawls, however, emphasize the more individualistic

strains in Kant, placing him more in the contractarian tradition. Contractarian deontologists – those that fit clearly into the liberal tradition – are my concern here. (I am indebted to Douglas Berggren for clarifying this point.)

16 For a clear explanation of how rights function to adjudicate individual claims, see Joel Feinberg, "The Nature and Value of Rights," *Journal of Value Inquiry* 4 (1970): 243–57. While not all writers agree that rights originate in claims, the disputes are immaterial here. For example, McCloskey's linkage of rights to "entitlements" is not inconsistent with my point. H. J. McCloskey, "Rights," *Philosophical Quarterly* 15 (1965): 115–27.

17 See, "Energy and the Further Future," in *Energy and the Future*, edited by Douglas MacLean and Peter G. Brown (Totowa, NJ: Rowman and Littlefield, 1983). I apply Parfit's "paradox" to environmental ethics in "Environmental Ethics and the Rights of Future Generations," *Environmental Ethics* 4 (1982): 321. See that essay for a more detailed discussion.

18 This is not to suggest, of course, that such action could not also have more long-term effects raising issues of the second sort as well.

19 This answer implies a disanalogy with the trust fund situation, provided one accepts the judgment that no wrong would be committed if a generation of the family chose not to reproduce. I think there is a disanalogy here, as different reproductive obligations would arise if the future of the human species were at stake. Suppose one answers this question negatively regarding the future of human kind and then considers the possibility that the last human individual might wantonly destroy other species, natural places, etc. I would still reject such wanton acts as inconsistent with good human behavior, relying upon weakly anthropocentric arguments as described above.

20 I willingly accept the implication of this value claim that, in a situation of severely contracting human population, some or all individuals would have an obligation to reproduce, but I will not defend this central claim here. Although I believe it can be defended, I am more interested in integrating it into a coherent ethical system than in defending it.

21 On a closely related point, see Brian Barry, "Circumstances of Justice and Future Generations," in Sikora and Barry, eds., *Obligations to Future Generations* (Philadelphia: Temple University Press, 1978).

22 See Norton, *The Spice of Life*.

23 I am, for the sake of the example, ignoring other long-term effects of the use of fossil fuels. Problems due to the greenhouse effect would, of course, also have to be solved.

24 See references in note 9 above.

25 Callicott, "On the Intrinsic Value of Nonhuman Species." Also see Pluhar, "The Justification of an Environmental Ethic" for a somewhat different approach to attribution of intrinsic value.

14

Weak Anthropocentric Intrinsic Value

Eugene Hargrove

Introduction

Professional environmental ethics arose directly out of the interest in the environment created by Earth Day in 1970. At that time many environmentalists, primarily because they had read Aldo Leopold's essay, "The Land Ethic," were convinced that the foundations of environmental problems were philosophical.[1] Moreover, these environmentalists were dissatisfied with the instrumental arguments based on human use and benefit – which they felt compelled to invoke in defense of nature – because they thought these arguments were part of the problem. Wanting to counter instrumental arguments in some way with non- or even anti-instrumental arguments, and unable to think of anything else to say, they began wistfully suggesting that perhaps nature had or ought to have rights.[2] When professional environmental ethics came into its own in the early 1980s, rights for nature were one of the first subjects to be debated in detail.[3] Unfortunately, however, no one could come up with a theory to support such rights attributions. Nevertheless, because rights had been invoked by environmentalists to challenge the preeminent role of instrumental value arguments, and because the field of environmental ethics developed in support of environmental concerns and arguments, environmental ethicists turned to an examination of noninstrumental or intrinsic value arguments for the preservation of nature.

As these investigations progressed, it soon became clear that most environmental ethicists, and indeed most environmentalists, did not believe that traditional intrinsic value – for example, the kind of intrinsic value which is attributed to art – was an adequate counter to instrumental value.[4] To find a kind of intrinsic value that could trump instrumental value – in the way that rights can – they started looking for nonanthropocentric intrinsic value. This search, unfortunately, has been a confusing one because of definitional problems with the word *nonanthropocentric*. A nonanthropocentric value was simply assumed to be the opposite of an instrumental value, making *anthropocentric* for all practical purposes a synonym for the word *instrumental*.[5] In environmental policy, there is perhaps some basis for such a definition, since nearly all arguments, economic and otherwise, are formulated routinely in terms of instrumental value to human beings. Nevertheless, *anthropocentric* is not and has never been a synonym for *instrumental*. It simply means "human-centered," and refers to a humanoriented perspective – seeing from the standpoint of a human being.[6] This confusion results from an assault on intrinsic value undertaken by pragmatists at the beginning of this century, who tried to eliminate intrinsic value talk and substitute instrumental value talk across the board. Although no one today can remember, let alone clearly formulate, the pragmatic reasons for abandoning intrinsic value, the idea that intrinsic value is an unnecessary concept has managed to trickle-down to the level of ordinary people, who now *believe* that only instrumental value arguments work – but nevertheless *wish* that it were not so.[7] Moreover, the situation has been further aggravated by another even more widely believed corollary of logical positivism which has also successfully trickled-down – viz., the belief that all value judgments are meaningless, arbitrary, subjective, irrational expressions of emotion.[8]

There are actually two kinds of nonanthropocentric intrinsic value theory, an objectivist version of which Paul Taylor and Holmes Rolston, III are the most prominent proponents, and a subjectivist version proposed by J. Baird Callicott. In this essay, I discuss both objective and subjective nonanthropocentric intrinsic value in contrast to a counter-position, weak anthropocentric intrinsic value. I argue (1) that objectivist nonanthropocentric intrinsic value theory requires and is complemented by weak anthropocentric intrinsic value theory, (2) that the most plausible version of subjectivist nonanthropocentric intrinsic value theory is actually a form of weak anthropocentric intrinsic value theory, (3) that a weak anthropocentric intrinsic value theory is superior to a weak anthropocentric value theory based on pragmatic instrumentalism, and (4) that most nonanthropocentric value theories are in various ways really anthropocentric.

Objectivist Nonanthropocentric Intrinsic Value Theory

Any examination of objective nonanthropocentric value should begin with an examination of its practical role in environmental ethics and indeed ethics in general. In the three periods of Western civilization, there have been two very different approaches to ethical decision making. The first is a virtue approach, according to which people are trained to develop good moral character on the assumption that moral persons will act morally. The second is a rule approach which aims at establishing a set of universal rules that are to be followed without deviation.[9] The former is the characteristic approach of the ancient and medieval periods, the latter of the modern period. As I have argued elsewhere, the effect, if not the intention, of the rule approach is to limit the range of ethical decision making, turning moral decision into either/or situations, in which following a rule, without regard to consequences, is what

being ethical is all about.[10] This approach has gained support in the modern period because of "fear that the open form in which decisions naturally and normally take place will allow unscrupulous or weak moral agents to waver and modify principles to their own immoral advantage."[11] Efforts to establish unmodifiable universal rules for ethical decision-making usually come at the end of a period of emotivism – *Sturm und Drang* followed by Kantianism in the last century, and positivistic emotivism followed by prescriptivism in this century.[12]

The motivation behind the quest for an objective nonanthropocentric value theory seems to be of this kind, for objective intrinsic value is supposed to be independent of and override individual human judgment and the relative and evolving cultural ideals, which though currently supportive of nature preservation, might change leaving nature without moral defense. This concern is explicit in the writings of Paul Taylor, for example, who, citing Mark Sagoff's anthropocentric symbolic value theory, argues that he wants to develop a nonanthropocentric value theory because anthropocentric value is "entirely relative to culture: if a particular society did not hold ideals that could be symbolized in nature and wildlife (for example, if it happened to value plastic trees more than real ones), then ... there would be no reason for that society to preserve nature or protect wildlife."[13] On analogy with the distinction between the basic rules of a game and rules of good play, I have distinguished between two kinds of rules, constitutive rules and nonconstitutive rules.[14] The first are rules which must be followed without deviation. Not doing so automatically produces an immoral act. The second are guides which may or may not be followed depending on specific circumstances in specific situations. Objective nonanthropocentric intrinsic value is supposed to play a limiting role similar to that of constitutive rules. Recognition of the existence of these values in nature, independent of human judgment and culturally evolved values, putatively automatically triggers specific moral behavior.

Since the field of environmental ethics first began, environmental ethicists have always been very much aware that educated attitudes toward nature in the Middle Ages – according to which nature is not beautiful – would not have been supportive of twentieth-century-style environmental concern, and that it is possible that current supportive values might change again.[15] This concern is also shared by most environmentalists. When I speak on behalf of weak anthropocentric value, I am frequently asked by environmentalists, "But what if people change their minds and stop thinking that nature is beautiful?" The possibility that our culturally evolved environmental values might change is, of course, a serious concern, given that these values, though derived from aesthetic tastes in art – primarily, from landscape painting, but also from nature poetry, landscape gardening, and natural history science – have now been out of fashion in art circles for more than a century. Nevertheless, although constitutive values might produce a trumping effect similar to rights for nature, if and when people ever come to be convinced that such values exist, I doubt that attempts to persuade ordinary people that such values exist independently in nature is a wise long-term environmentalist strategy. The best way, in my view, to deal with this concern is actively to defend these values as part of our cultural heritage, not to try to develop a metaphysical/epistemological theory of objective nonanthropocentric intrinsic values that constitutively trumps individual judgment and culturally evolved values. Defending these values as culturally derived values will focus attention on the merits of these values and presumably help strengthen them. In contrast, an objective nonanthropocentric value theory will draw attention away from their merits as cultural values (the point of the objectivist effort) and refocus it on metaphysical and epistemological issues that ordinary people are unlikely to understand or be persuaded by. While this approach might succeed for a time in freezing current values (by embedding them in our constitutive moral framework), it certainly cannot strengthen them (since they are supposed to be independent of human judgment and culture, humans should not be able to alter them one way or the other). In the event that aesthetic tastes toward nature do start to change (for example, "catching up" with those of modern art), a spirited defense of these values as cultural values might prevail. Whether an argument that these values are independent of and trump human judgment, and therefore cannot be changed, would succeed, however, seems less likely, given that ordinary people can easily refute the argument without providing any counterargument of their own simply by changing their values.

To be sure, there is a lot of room for legitimate nonanthropocentric value theory in environmental ethics, for most values, whether instrumental or intrinsic, *are* independent of human judgment. At the most general level, four kinds of values are possible: (1) nonanthropocentric instrumental value, (2) anthropocentric instrumental value, (3) nonanthropocentric intrinsic value, and (4) anthropocentric intrinsic value. In environmental matters nonanthropocentric instrumental values – concerning the instrumental relationships of benefit and harm between nonhuman plants and animals – are quite common and completely uncontroversial. Such values, which can easily be converted into facts, are indeed discovered in the world and are independent of human judgment. One thing in nature either instrumentally benefits other things or it does not, regardless of what humans think about it and whether or not humans even know that these instrumental relationships exist. Bambu is either instrumentally valuable to pandas or it is not. What we believe, know, and how we value it makes no difference. Anthropocentric instrumental value judgments, if they are simply the same relationships applied to humans, are likewise common and uncontroversial. Fluoride is either instrumentally valuable to humans or not, whether we humans know it, believe it, or value it. Even if *anthropocentric* is taken to require human judgment, producing judgments or beliefs that one thing is instrumentally valuable or harmful to another thing (human or otherwise) without adequate or complete factual evidence, such anthropocentric instrumental value judgments are also uncontroversial when they can be converted into the form of scientific hypotheses, making them potential or possible facts, and irrelevant (rather than controversial) when they are merely whimsical or irrational expressions of belief. Smoking tobacco is widely judged to be instrumentally harmful to human health, even though it is sometimes scientifically disputed by tobacco companies; in contrast, even though chicken-noodle soup is generally judged to be instrumentally beneficial to humans with colds, this judgment is not supported by medical evidence. Similarly, the basic nonanthropocentric maneuver, notably exemplified by Paul Taylor and Holmes Rolston, III – defining living organisms as centers of purpose in accordance with Aristotle's ends/means distinction – is also noncontroversial, if all that is claimed is that these entities have sakes or

Eugene Hargrove

goods of their own (independent of human interests) and that they are using nature instrumentally for the benefit of their own sakes, which are then defined as (intrinsically valuable) ends (to them).[16] Because such intrinsic value assignments are also a matter of discovery rather than judgment, they too can be treated as disguised facts – we can discover facts through scientific research that such and such kinds of organisms do or do not instrumentally use other parts of nature for their own ends. It is actually only anthropocentric intrinsic value assignments – judgments made by humans that such and such living and nonliving entities are noninstrumentally (intrinsically) valuable – that fully and truly depend upon human judgment, rather than mere discovery, and are not ever reducible to facts or scientific hypotheses.

There seem to be two basic reasons why objectivist nonanthropocentric value theorists object to doing away with or at least radically deemphasizing anthropocentric intrinsic value judgments. First, as noted above, they want values that operate much like constitutive rules in order to trump anthropocentric instrumental values. Second, they hold that there can only be (or should only be) one kind of intrinsic value.[17] It is this second reason which I find most problematic. Given that there are many kinds of instrumental value, nearly all of which have something to do with environmental ethics, it seems strange to me that anyone would want to claim that there can only be one kind of intrinsic value, or, if it is acknowledged that there may be more than one kind, that only one kind is relevant to environmental ethic.[18] It is almost as if there is a competition between various conceptions of intrinsic value such that recognition of one kind of intrinsic value, anthropocentric intrinsic value, somehow damages the other, nonanthropocentric intrinsic value. In opposition to this strange view, I want to argue here that anthropocentric intrinsic value judgments, rather than being in competition with nonanthropocentric intrinsic values, are absolutely essential if humans are to muster any environmental concern about nonhuman living centers of purpose (as well as many other natural entities) objectively existing out in the world.

Paul Taylor, a proponent of nonanthropocentric intrinsic value, which he calls inherent worth, has made a noteworthy attempt to distinguish and separate nonanthropocentric and anthropocentric intrinsic value. After briefly mentioning instrumental value, commercial value, and merit or excellence,

Taylor offers three kinds of intrinsic value: the immediately good, the intrinsically valued, and inherent worth. After defining (1) *instrumental value*, (2) *commercial value*, and (3) *merit or excellence*, none of which are important for the purposes of this paper, he defines (4) *the immediately good* as "any experience or activity of a conscious being which it finds to be enjoyable, satisfying, pleasant, or worthwhile in itself," noting that it "is sometimes called *intrinsic value*." He then provides two long definitions for (5) *the intrinsically valued* and (6) *inherent worth*, complete with examples, which I quote here in full:

(5) *the intrinsically valued*. An entity is intrinsically valued in this sense only in relation to its being valued in a certain way by some human valuer. The entity may be a person, animal, or plant, a physical object, a place, or even a social practice. Any such entity is intrinsically valued insofar as some person cherishes it, holds it dear or precious, loves, admires, or appreciates it for what it is in itself, or so places intrinsic value on its existence. This value is independent of whatever instrumental or commercial value it might have. When something is intrinsically valued by someone, it is deemed by that person to be worthy of being preserved and protected because it is the particular thing that it is. Thus, the people of a society may place intrinsic value on a ceremonial occasion (the coronation of a king), on historically significant objects (the original Declaration of Independence) and places (the battlefield at Gettysburg), on ruins of ancient cultures (Stonehenge), on natural wonders (the Grand Canyon), and of course on works of art. Intrinsic value may also be placed on living things, which then are intrinsically valuable to (have intrinsic value for) the human valuers. A pet dog or cat, an endangered population of rare plants, or a whole wilderness area can be considered worth preserving for just what they are. Finally, anyone we love and care about has this kind of value for us. From a moral point of view, correlative with intrinsically valuing something is the recognition of a negative duty not to destroy, harm, damage, vandalize, or misuse the thing and a positive duty to protect it from being destroyed, harmed, damaged, vandalized, or misused by others.

178

(6) *Inherent worth*. This is the value something has simply in virtue of the fact that it has a good of its own. To say that an entity has inherent worth is to say that its good (welfare, well-being) is deserving of the concern and consideration of all moral agents and that the realization of its good is something to be promoted or protected as an end in itself and for the sake of the being whose good it is. Since it is only with reference to living things, (humans, animals, or plants) that it makes sense to speak of promoting or protecting their well-being and of doing this for their sake, the class of entities having inherent worth is extensionally equivalent to the class of living beings.[19]

The immediately good, as Taylor defines it, is the product of an instrumental relationship between a "good" object and a human being exposed to it. As Taylor presents it here (rightly, I think), it does not involve human judgment, merely spontaneous emotional reaction to sensory events triggered by an external source. Taylor's discussion of the intrinsically valued is a good presentation of what I mean by anthropocentric intrinsic value – intrinsic value assigned or attributed by a human being or a group of human beings from an independent ahistorical human perspective or from a culturally dependent historical human perspective. Taylor's inherent worth is a fairly standard version of nonanthropocentric intrinsic value attributed to entities which have a sake, instrumentally use other parts of nature for their own intrinsic ends, or, as Taylor puts it, have goods of their own.

From my perspective, the key issue concerning Taylor's account of intrinsic value is whether the intrinsically valued and inherent worth can be radically separated. If they can't, then a creature having inherent worth or a good of its own is simply one of the various kinds of things that humans may, if they wish, collectively or individually, value intrinsically. Immediately following the definitions and discussions of the various kinds of values listed, Taylor writes:

When a living thing is regarded as possessing inherent worth, it is seen to be the appropriate object of the moral attitude of respect. This kind of respect, "recognition respect," should not be confused with the attitudes of love,

admiration, and appreciation directed toward entities that are intrinsically valued in sense (5) above.[20]

Two questions occur to me about these two sentences and the discussion that follows them. First, has Taylor shown that respecting something is different from intrinsically valuing it? At a minimum, Taylor has correctly pointed out that respect is different from love, admiration, and appreciation. One can respect one's enemies, for example, without loving them. He has, however, as far as I can determine, merely asserted, but not shown, that respect is something so different that it should not be placed together with love, admiration, and appreciation as a form of intrinsic valuing. Second, when "it is seen" (passive voice) that such and such an entity is "the appropriate object of respect," why does this not simply mean that some human decides to value this entity intrinsically – that is, by means of an act of judgment, attributes (active voice) intrinsic value to the thing in accordance with some personal or culturally derived standard? The use of the passive voice together with the introduction of the term *recognition respect* seems to suggest that there is no human value judgment involved – that the human simply "sees" or discovers that the entity has a good of its own, automatically triggering a feeling of respect analogous to the instrumental relationship characteristic of the immediately good.[21] Such an account of respect as automatic recognition bypassing human judgment seems to me to be implausible.

Consider the alien monsters of the films *Alien* and *Aliens*, which require the deaths of many other living creatures, indifferently including humans, in order to reproduce and survive as a species. The newly hatched alien monster emerges from its (his or her) egg and immediately enters a host organism, which it keeps alive and feeds on while continuing its development. When it no longer needs the host, it explodes out of the chest of the organism, killing the host with some fanfare. Up until this moment, the human host is conscious and aware of his or her situation. Because these creatures have goods of their own, according to Taylor, they have inherent worth. But does it follow from the fact that such a creature has a good of its own that we humans are *required*, in accordance with Taylor's definition of *inherent worth*, "to say that its good (welfare, well-being) is deserving of the concern and consideration of all moral agents and that the realization of its good is something to be promoted or protected as an end in itself for the sake of the being whose good it is?" I think not. Rather, the (nonanthropocentric) inherent worth or good of its own of the alien monster produces a concern and consideration if and only if a human decides (or humans collectively decide) to intrinsically value the creature, thereby producing, in accordance with Taylor's definition of *the intrinsically valued*, "the recognition of a negative duty not to destroy, harm, damage, vandalize, or misuse the thing and a positive duty to protect it from being destroyed, harmed, damaged, vandalized, or misused by others." The circumstances under which the necessary anthropocentric intrinsic value attribution might be generated are fairly limited. First, the human and all other humans (and all other inappropriate potential hosts) would have to be safe from the organism (a point with which, I believe, Taylor would agree). Second, the creature would have to be in its natural ecosystem, rather than in some other ecosystem, where it would be regarded as an improper (and very destructive) pest. In the two films, two characters (an android and a human) do value alien monsters and try to preserve them, but they do so because of their instrumental value as military weapons (such creatures once released could presumably destroy all human life fairly easily, given the speed with which they are able to reproduce). It is true that humans might quickly develop a (healthy) respect for such creatures, but this respect would not be based on the recognition that these creatures have goods of their own, but rather would be out of fear, having recognized that the creatures are very dangerous.

Note that I am not claiming that a creature's good of its own is irrelevant to the moral concern of humans, merely that the fact that a particular creature has a good of its own is not enough automatically to produce moral behavior on behalf of the creature. After discovering that something has a good of its own, the human or humans must decide to intrinsically value it, and in doing so, the specter of cultural (and historical) relativity reappears, which was avoided by omitting mention of the need for intrinsic value attribution.

Note also that even though objectivist nonanthropocentrists are committed to doing away with anthropocentric intrinsic value, as an anthropocentrist, I have no similar desire to bring the quest for nonanthropocentric intrinsic value to an end. [I hold that "weak anthropocentrism" (the view, as I define it, that *anthropocentric* does not simply mean instrumental) can serve environmental ethics well until such time, if ever, that a convincing nonanthropocentric theory appears that will sweep strong and weak anthropocentrism aside.[22]] Moreover, I hold that whether the quest succeeds or fails, it will further enhance anthropocentric intrinsic value theory by providing new grounds for intrinsically valuing nonhuman life anthropocentrically. I confess, however, that I am not very optimistic that a nonanthropocentric theory will be successfully formulated, because the search for nonanthropocentric intrinsic value seems to me to be comparable to a Kantian search for actual objects in the noumenal world. To succeed, the nonanthropocentrists apparently need to go beyond valuing based on the human perspective – which seems impossible.

Note, finally, that even if a persuasive nonanthropocentric theory of intrinsic value can be constructed, environmentalists and environmental policy and decision makers will probably still need to make some anthropocentric intrinsic value judgments. Currently, nonanthropocentric theory, based as it is on the goods of individual organisms, leaves nonliving natural objects out of the moral account. As Taylor notes in his definition and discussion of inherent worth, cited above, the "class of entities having inherent worth is extensionally equivalent to the class of living beings." Thus, nonliving objects can only be defended on the grounds that they are instrumentally valuable to living centers of purpose that use them for their own intrinsically valuable ends.

Such an approach is, however, woefully inadequate with regard to the kinds of objects that I was principally interested in protecting when I undertook work in the field of environmental ethics – caves. Strictly speaking, caves are not objects at all. Paraphrasing Wittgenstein on pain, they are not a something but not a nothing either – that is, they are hollow spaces in layers of sediments. As a cave conservationist, I quickly learned that it is difficult to produce winning arguments to protect caves in terms of the creatures who live in them. Bats, worms, insects, and blind fish, though less distasteful than alien monsters, generate little preservationist concern or sympathy. Many people, for example, foolishly think that it would be a good idea for all bats to be killed on sight. The strongest arguments for protecting caves, in contrast, depend upon the willingness of humans to act so as to preserve natural beauty, which in turn depends upon intrinsic valuing on the model of the aesthetic appreciation of art objects. As long as nonanthropocentric theorists concentrate on the class of living objects, nonliving beauty will continue to be left out, and will require anthropocentric intrinsic value attributions in order to receive any protection at all. Although protection of living organisms may require the partial abandonment of an anthropocentric perspective (to the degree that that may be possible), protection of nonliving objects requires a return to an anthropocentric perspective, unless these objects are to be valued instrumentally only. That approach, however, would run counter to our basic environmental intuitions and unnecessarily abandon very strong arguments for nature preservation, given that the historical/cultural foundations of environmental ethics (going back three hundred years) are primarily aesthetic.[23]

Because I consider my conception of intrinsic value to be (1) a necessary element in the valuing of nonanthropocentric intrinsic value and (2) complementary to nonanthropocentric valuing, since only anthropocentric intrinsic value can be applied to nonliving objects, I have no quarrel with the objectivist nonanthropocentrists and their quest as long as they do not insist that (1) only living entities with goods of their own matter morally and that (2) they matter in a way that is independent of human (anthropocentric) intrinsic valuing.

Accepting anthropocentric and nonanthropocentric value as complementary and interrelated, moreover, can even improve some objectivist nonanthropocentric theories. For example, Rolston's narrow focus on an organism's good ultimately denies a central role to natural beauty in his theory because natural beauty is too subjective to fit in comfortably with Rolston's desire to develop an objective approach. When Rolston finally reaches natural beauty in his book, he is only prepared to go through the motions of a discussion, and ultimately has little to say about it, because he can't effectively tie it into his objective theory: "With beauty we cross a threshold into a realm of higher value; the experience of beauty is something humans bring into the world."[24] According to Rolston, the value focus in natural systems is on the organism with its good of its own.[25] In this context, he divides the world up into beholders of value (humans) and

holders of value (organisms with goods of their own), the value that the beholders behold. To find a way to include value beyond holders and beholders, Rolston adds value producers (the ecosystem) which provide (instrumental) support for organisms, the value holders. According to Rolston, the value produced by ecosystems, *systemic value*, flashes back and forth between instrumental and intrinsic value, on the model of particles and waves of light.[26] In addition, however, to maintain the dualism between holders and beholders, Rolston goes on to maintain that an ecosystem as a value producer is really a value holder "in the sense that it projects, conserves, elaborates value holders (organisms)."[27] When he finally turns to beauty directly, he addresses two fairly trivial questions, whether nothing in nature is beautiful and whether everything in nature is beautiful, and argues that the answer is somewhere in between, if we accept that the sublime is also beautiful.[28] The insignificant role of natural beauty in his theory, brought about by the quest for nonanthropocentric intrinsic value, is truly unfortunate, because, as is evident in virtually every sentence Rolston writes, no philosopher has a better feel for and appreciation of natural beauty than he does. To provide a place in his theory for his own aesthetic values, all that Rolston needs to do is simply to go beyond nonanthropocentric intrinsic value, defined in terms of the good of its own of an organism, and reintroduce anthropocentric intrinsic valuing into his theory. (This is advice that I also recommend to all other nonanthropocentrists who have pointlessly lost touch with natural beauty by trying to be too objective.)

Subjectivist Nonanthropocentric Intrinsic Value

Although there is only one prominent subjective nonanthropocentric value theorist, J. Baird Callicott, there are two theories. First, Callicott has argued that intrinsic value is conferred on the natural world by humans valuing it for itself. Second, he has flirted with the Self-realization approach of deep ecology, in which nature comes to have intrinsic value because a Self-realizing human becomes one with it. I deal with the Self-realization theory only in passing and focus my discussion on the first theory.

Callicott summarizes his Self-realization approach as follows:

> Now *if* we assume, (a)...that nature is one and continuous with self, and (b) that self-interested behavior has a prima facie claim to be at the same time rational behavior, then the central axiological problem of environmental ethics, the problem of intrinsic value in nature may be directly and simply solved. If quantum theory and ecology both imply in structurally similar ways in both the physical and organic domains of nature the continuity of self and nature, and *if* the self is intrinsically valuable, then nature is intrinsically valuable. If it is rational for me to act in my own interest, and I and nature are one, then it is rational for me to act in the best interest of nature.[29]

This approach is said to produce nonanthropocentric value, rather than anthropocentric value, because the human self is only a small part of nature as a whole, which is the Self with a capital *S*. Nevertheless, an alternative interpretation is available, according to which Self-realization is anthropocentric and nothing more than Cartesianism commandeered for environmental purposes. Note that nature acquires (or borrows) its intrinsic value from the human self, which is established on supposedly noncontroversial traditional grounds (the uncritical belief that humans have intrinsic value).[30] Seen in this way, the intrinsic value of nature is a product of the humanizing of nature, and the model is nineteenth-century idealism and solipsism, arising out of the Cartesian puzzle about whether humans can know that the world exists.[31] Because such humanizing is frequently considered one of the causes of our environmental problems, this approach is suspect.

Turning to the other theory, Callicott has also claimed that values depend entirely on human judgment – that there are no values in the world until they are imposed by humans: "Value is, as it were, projected onto natural objects or events by the subjective feelings of observers. If all consciousness were annihilated at a stroke, there would be no good and evil, no beauty and ugliness, no right and wrong; only impassive phenomena would remain."[32] Nevertheless, Callicott insists that he can develop a nonanthropocentric intrinsic value theory within this domain of humanly generated values, which he calls his "truncated" theory of intrinsic value:

> I concede that, from the point of view of scientific naturalism, the *source* of all value is human consciousness, but it by no means follows that the *locus* of all vaue is consciousness itself or a mode of consciousness like reason, pleasure, or knowledge. In other words, something may be valuable only because someone values it, but it may also be valued for itself, not for the sake of any subjective experience (pleasure, knowledge, aesthetic satisfaction, and so forth) it may afford the valuers. Value may be subjective and affective, but it is intentional, not self-referential. For example, a newborn infant is of value to its parents for its own sake as well as for the joy or any other experience it may afford them. In and of itself an infant child is as value-neutral as a stone or a hydrogen atom, considered in strict accordance with the subject-object/fact-value dichotomy of modern science. Yet we still may wish to say that a newborn infant is "intrinsically valuable" (even though its value depends, in the last analysis, on human consciousness) in order to distinguish the *noninstrumental* value it has for its parents, relatives, and the human community generally from its actual or potential instrumental value – the pleasure it gives its parents, the pride it affords its relatives, the contribution it makes to society, and so forth. In doing so, however, "intrinsic value" retains only half its traditional meaning. An intrinsically valuable thing on this reading is valuable *for* its own sake, *for* itself, but it is not valuable in itself, that is, completely independently of any consciousness, since no value can, in principle, from the point of view of classical normal science, be altogether independent of a valuing consciousness.[33]

According to Callicott, this view is nonanthropocentric, rather than anthropocentric, because human valuers (anthropogenically) value things other than themselves, and it is intrinsic, because human valuers value these other things for their own sakes. Nevertheless, it is truncated because although human valuers value things *for* themselves, nonhuman things are not valuable *in* themselves – because there is no objective nonanthropocentric intrinsic value *in* nature.

Although there are a number of problems with this position, fairly minor adjustments could transform it into a weak anthropocentric position. First, it is a bit of an overstatement to claim that *all* value depends on the subjective feelings of *human* observers and that value does not exist in nature unless it is projected on it by human valuing. As I indicated at the beginning of this paper, there are many kinds of nonanthropocentric instrumental values that exist in nature independent of human judgment. In addition, I see no reason why Callicott should dismiss entirely the claim that nonhuman creatures have independent intrinsic value in the sense that they have goods of their own – that is, that they are ends instrumentally using their environment for their own sake. Problems arise with this kind of value only when it is declared to be the only kind of intrinsic value or the only kind that matters. Just as objectivist nonanthropocentrists need to acknowledge that human intrinsic valuing takes place and matters, subjectivist nonanthropocentrists need to acknowledge that nonanthropocentric intrinsic value, the good of its own of an organism, even though it exists independently of human valuing, is something that humans can (whenever they so choose) value for its own sake. Finally, I question whether humans are the only beings who value nature. Given that Callicott accepts a Darwinian evolutionary approach, it seems strange that he *sometimes* suggests that while humans can value (like or dislike, for example) some parts of nature, nonhumans cannot.

Second, I find it questionable whether Callicott's subjectivist position should be called nonanthropocentric. If it is true that "the *source* of all values is human consciousness" and that value "is, as it were, projected onto natural objects or events by the subjective feelings of observers," then all value (both instrumental and intrinsic) is centered *in* humans and radiates outward from humans *onto* things in nature. Given that I believe that other creatures also sometimes value (both instrumentally and intrinsically), Callicott's position is, in my terminology, a slightly stronger (weak) anthropocentrism than my own. For him to insist that his position is nonanthropocentric creates unnecessary and pointless confusion.

Third, I consider Callicott's position to be overly subjective. As I have argued elsewhere, human values are not entirely dependent upon the arbitrary value preferences of individuals.[34] In an Aristotelian sense, there are cultural values that are the product of social evolution. These values are not entirely subjective. At any given moment in the history of a particular society they can be objectively identified and described. Moreover, in most cases they are the foundation for the values of individual people. It is no accident that nearly all people in a particular society share the same values. They pick them up as children without formal teaching. They are the context and starting point out of which individual differences develop. Simply to call these social values subjective misrepresents their very substantial objective character.

Pragmatic Instrumentalism

The most serious attack on anthropocentric intrinsic value theory, and indeed intrinsic value in general, comes from the pragmatic instrumentalists, who like the turn-of-the-century pragmatists mentioned at the beginning of this paper want to convert such values into instrumental terms.[35] Rather curiously my chief quarrel is with my fellow weak anthropocentrist, Bryan Norton.[36] His arguments for denying that humans can (or should?) make anthropocentric intrinsic value judgments seem to be (1) that ordinary people find the word *intrinsic* confusing because it sounds mystical and (2) that presenting anthropocentric intrinsic value judgments in instrumental terms simplifies value theory, making ethics easier for ordinary people to understand.

Concerning the second claim, while I do not deny that it is certainly possible to simplify value theory in this way, most environmentalists, as noted above, have been unwilling to accept this simplification because they find instrumental presentations of noninstrumental values inappropriate and demeaning (to the natural entity), as evidenced, for example, by the fact that they still want a rights theory for nature.[37] When an aesthetic intrinsic value judgment is converted into instrumental terms, the person having the aesthetic experience is depicted as using natural scenery as a trigger for feelings of pleasure. When these feelings of pleasure are then compared with the other instrumental values that can be obtained, for example, by clear-cutting or strip-mining, the value of the aesthetic experience then appears trivial, ridiculous, and indeed indefensible.[38] In short, anthropocentric instrumental scientific and aesthetic values fail to mimic the desired trumping effect of rights theory over basic instrumental values because they are treated either as questionable or inferior instrumental values.

With regard to the first claim, people are confused about intrinsic value only because they have become disoriented by the trickle-down effect of the pragmatic instrumentalist attack on intrinsic value at the beginning of this century. Before pragmatism created the confusion about the relationship of intrinsic and instrumental value, the distinction was clear and serviceable to ordinary people. The confusion caused by the blurring of this distinction is, therefore, not adequate grounds for continuing the confusion by insisting on the pragmatic instrumentalist conversion of intrinsic value into instrumental value in opposition to the clear calls by environmentalists, policy makers, and the general public for a return to intrinsic value theory. Norton has provided no evidence that we have reached a point of no return. Quite to the contrary, the dissatisfaction with instrumental arguments among environmentalists, policy makers, and the general public suggests that a return to straightforward intrinsic value talk is probably the easiest solution.

The way Norton converts intrinsic value into instrumental value is itself very confusing and, I believe, limited. According to Norton, natural objects should be valued because they have *transformative value* – value which transforms humans or changes their lives. As far as I am able to tell, this transformative value is similar to, and perhaps a general label for, what Rolston means by "character building value," "therapeutic value," and "religious value."[39] If it is, then it is too limited as a replacement for anthropocentric intrinsic value, for I do not see that the intrinsic valuing of some natural object necessarily involves an instrumental transformation of the human triggered by the object valued. Many intrinsic value attributions in art, for example, depend upon the application of historical aesthetic standards that at various times go out of fashion and, as a result, no longer move viewers emotionally (transform their lives). Although it is universally agreed that the Mona Lisa is worthy of being intrinsically valued, many, indeed, most people have no idea why it is considered to be such a valuable painting, and, lacking detailed training in the history of art, are not transformed by it when they see it. Should we say that it continues to be valuable because it

once transformed people's lives and perhaps has the potential to do so again? If the value of the Mona Lisa were calculated in such terms, I think the concern of the nonanthropocentrists about the cultural relativity of anthropocentric value judgments would be justified. In real life, however, the value of a painting does not depend on the occurrence of particular emotional experiences in the general public. Rather it depends on the judgment of experts who interpret social ideals – the equivalent of the perception of Aristotle's "good man." Precise aesthetic judgments, comparable to those provided by art critics, can also be obtained by consulting professional nature interpreters, naturalists, and most environmentalists.

In practice, there is nothing confusing (or mystical or metaphysical) about anthropocentric intrinsic value judgments. Consider the value of an ornamental knife, made of precious metals and covered with jewels. Because the knife can function as a knife, it has the normal instrumental value that any other knife would have, not simply potentially, but also actually. Nevertheless, because the knife is beautiful, the judgment of the owner and others who take time to consider the matter will likely be that it is too beautiful (or good) to use (assuming that using the knife will mar its beauty). This judgment, to value the knife for its beauty, rather than its use, involves no confusing detours into metaphysics or mysticism. All that is required is an act of judgment. An individual or group of individuals or a society decides. In real life, it does not even require a defense. We do not customarily begin an instrumental argument with a general defense of instrumental arguments – for example, that instrumental value exists. We simply present the instrumental argument within the implicit framework in which such arguments are generally acceptable. The same is true of anthropocentric intrinsic value arguments. We do not need to begin such an argument with a proof that intrinsic value exists, for the existence of this kind of intrinsic value is not an issue. This kind of intrinsic value is the product of human valuing, human decision making, and everyone already knows what valuing, deciding, and judging means. The issue in such an argument is not the mental process (or the metaphysical status of the value produced), but whether the value judgment is an appropriate one – that is, in accordance with recognized social standards and ideals. The person who decides that the knife should not be used will not justify his judgment by claiming that the knife is intrinsically valuable, but rather by pointing out that the knife is beautiful. Talk about intrinsic value will occur only if someone chooses to claim that beauty is itself a use (an instrumental value), invoking the pragmatic instrumentalist maneuver. At this point, the answer could be a nonanthropocentric excursion into metaphysics; however, a simple reminder that humans are fully capable of valuing things noninstrumentally and have been doing so for thousands of years is really all that is needed.

The reintroduction of anthropocentric intrinsic value judgments is not only a simple matter, but also a very useful one. As I indicated above, the reduction of intrinsic value to instrumental terms demeans and trivializes it, giving a counterintuitive advantage to (instrumental) resource exploitation by turning nature preservation into a peculiar, and largely indefensible, special case of resource exploitation and consumption. Maintaining the distinction between intrinsic and instrumental value, in contrast, allows us to set certain things aside and exempt them from use. Because the instrumentalist approach to valuing natural objects is the primary approach in economics, the valuable contribution that can be made by an intrinsic value approach has been neglected. In the nineteenth century, nevertheless, newly formed national parks were valued in two ways – in terms of their use as sources of raw materials and in terms of their intrinsic value as aesthetically and scientifically interesting collections of natural object. Proponents of these parks argued that these geographical areas, though instrumentally worthless (Yellowstone was said to have no minerals worth extracting and to be unsuited for agriculture), were priceless (off the monetary scale) aesthetically and scientifically. In these arguments, intrinsic and instrumental values were juxtaposed against each other as competing perspectives, both of which could to some degree be expressed in economic terms. Interestingly, however, arguments in terms of intrinsic value were always estimated in extreme terms – the natural objects were declared to be priceless, or off the economic scale, too valuable for any reasonable price to be set upon them. What we have here is an attempt to produce the trumping effect of the rights for nature arguments of the twentieth century, without corresponding theoretical problems. All that is being said is that these areas are valuable in a noninstru-

mental way, such that they should be removed from the market system, specifically, instrumental resource exploitation. The judgmental process is identical to the one that excludes the ornamental knife from use. In effect, the assignment of aesthetic and scientific intrinsic value to these natural areas is an attempt to give them the status of economic externalities, providing a useful tie with standard economic valuational theory. The public incurs the social costs involved in not exploiting these natural areas in much the same way that it incurs the social costs involved in exploiting other parts of nature – for example, covering the cost of pollution not included directly in the cost of the manufacturing of specific products.[40]

In part, to be sure, the high economic valuations (that they are priceless) are sometimes produced, as a matter of strategy (when the valuations are inflated), to override any possible instrumental argument. Nevertheless, they generally reflect people's basic evaluational intuitions, and can usually be justified (provided they are in accordance with social standards and ideals) on the grounds that their economic value (from an aesthetic/scientific intrinsic value perspective), though high, is indeterminate and speculative, given that the routine economic transactions that determine worth in the market system do not occur (or at least seldom occur) with regard to natural objects.[41] Recent sales of houses in a particular area, for example, largely determine the value of houses in future sales. Because natural areas (and species) are not bought and sold like houses on an everyday basis, their value cannot be determined in this way. To come close to this kind of valuing, we have to ask ordinary people to engage in contrary-to-fact thought experiments in which they imagine what dollar values might be assigned if natural areas and species were bought and sold like houses and if there actually were large numbers of humans who traded in them on a regular (and quotable) basis. This problem is analogous to the problem of determining the value of paintings and other art objects, most of which are also not bought and sold in the marketplace (having been removed from the market system by being placed in publicly supported museums). The value of the Mona Lisa, though very high (essentially priceless), is indeterminate and speculative because there is nothing comparable to housing sales to bracket the price range, which is another way of saying that the Mona Lisa, and similar paintings, are

Eugene Hargrove

external to the market system that determines the value of less highly valued paintings and reproductions. Note that this valuing is not mystical or confusing. It clearly reflects our desire as individuals, as a society, and as a historically evolved culture to value some things noninstrumentally and to set them aside and protect them from exploitation. It is justified by the fact that the valuational methods of the market system are designed to provide values for things that are in the market and subject to market forces, not for things that have been removed from the market and are, therefore, external to it.

Anthropocentrism Revisited

I have used the term *weak anthropocentrism*, rather than simply *anthropocentrism*, in the title of this paper to help call attention to the fact that not all anthropocentric valuing is instrumental. Without the addition of the word *weak*, no doubt many nonanthropocentrists would probably conclude that the title contained a typographical error or was a contradiction in terms: "instrumental intrinsic value." While I do not think that labels are important, it is useful to call the view I represent weak anthropocentrism at least until it becomes generally recognized that anthropocentrism does not imply instrumentalism. I do not think that it is possible for humans to avoid being anthropocentric, given that whatever we humans value will always be from a human (or anthropocentric) point of view. Even when we try to imagine what it might be like to have the point of view of (or be) a bat, a tree, or a mountain, in my view, we are still looking at the world anthropocentrically – the way a human imagines that a nonhuman might look at the world.

This kind of anthropocentrism, as I noted above, is built into Callicott's anthropogenic position that "the *source* of all value is human consciousness" and Rolston's aesthetic position that "the experience of beauty is something that humans bring into the world."[42] Although Rolston tries to deemphasize such human values, covering beauty almost as an afterthought after elaborately developing his nonanthropocentric value theory, these values do play a major role in his environmental ethics. For example, as Rolston acknowledges at the end of his chapter on the objective intrinsic value of organisms, the good of human

(anthropocentric) aesthetic appreciation can easily override the good of its own of a wildflower:

> the goods preserved by the human destruction of plants must outweigh the goods of the organisms destroyed; thus, to be justified in picking flowers for a bouquet one would have to judge correctly that the aesthetic appreciation of the bouquet outweighed the goods of the flowers destroyed. One might pluck flowers for a bouquet but refuse to uproot the whole plant, or pick common flowers (daisies) and refuse to pick rare ones (trailing arbutus) or those that reproduce slowly (wild orchids).[43]

In this example, the deciding factors are purely anthropocentric: the human is the judge and the issue is the amount of aesthetic pleasure the human believes he or she will receive by destroying the nonanthropocentric good of the plant.

Rolston's nonanthropocentrism is also infected with anthropocentrism in an even more fundamental sense, for he argues, against the biocentrism of Taylor, that humans are superior to the rest of nature and deserve special consideration, a *strong* anthropocentric claim.[44] The practical effect of this position is an anthropocentric point of view in which humans receive special or superior attention because of their special or superior status. Rolston's arguments that nonhuman organisms have nonanthropocentric goods of their own have no *practical* impact on this anthropocentrism, which retains its traditionally anthropocentric character, as a kind of stewardship, rather than as a form of dominion.[45] (It is probably because humans are superior to wildflowers that picking the latter for the aesthetic enjoyment of the former can be justified.)

The term *nonanthropocentric intrinsic value* is really more problematic than the term *anthropocentric intrinsic value*, for the former comes very close to being redundant. The word *intrinsic*, which here is supposed to mean "for its own sake," clearly distinguishes the value of the valuable thing from the value of the valuer, indicating that the value is tied to the sake of the thing said to be intrinsically valued, not to the sake of the valuer. At best, the word *nonanthropocentric*, which is supposed to refer to value that is not human centered and independent of human judgment, merely asserts that the value of the thing valued does not derive its value from the value of a human valuer, a point already made more generally (with regard to any valuer) by the term *intrinsic*. If we come to accept, as I have argued above, that most values are independent of human judgment, and that when we do value, we value necessarily from a human perspective but not necessarily in terms of human instrumental interests, then the term *intrinsic value* (referring both to intrinsic value conferred through human judgment and intrinsic value defined as the goods of their own of living organisms), will make the terms *non-anthropocentric* and *anthropocentric* unnecessary.

Notes

1 Aldo Leopold, "The Land Ethic," in *A Sand County Almanac, and Sketches Here and There* (New York: Oxford University Press, 1949), pp. 209–10.

2 There are two references to rights of nature in Aldo Leopold's "The Land Ethic," *Sand County Almanac*, pp. 204, 211. Environmentalists were also influenced by Christopher Stone, *Should Trees Have Standing? Toward Legal Rights for Natural Objects* (Los Altos, CA: William Kaufman, 1972), which, though not focused on moral rights for nature, left open the possibility. This book was inspired by and associated with a Supreme Court case involving a wilderness area called Mineral King in California, in which Justice William O. Douglas, in a minority opinion, suggested rights for natural areas, citing Stone's views (reprinted in the appendix of Stone's book, pp. 73–87). Because animal liberation and environmental ethics were ambiguously interrelated in the early seventies, calls for rights for domestic animals were also frequently considered to be calls for rights for nature. Rights for animals were being championed at that time by Peter Singer, *Animal Liberation: A New Ethic for Our Treatment of Animals* (New York: New York Review/Random House, 1975), although Singer later declared that his rights view was inessential to his position in "The Fable of the Fox and the Unliberated Animals," *Ethics*, 88 (1978), 122. I first heard an environmentalist suggest that a river, the Meramec River, south of St. Louis, had rights in 1972. Rights talk was so common among environmentlists by the mid-seventies that John Passmore considered it to be the basic preservationist position. See John Passmore, *Man's Responsibility for Nature: Ecological Problems and Western Traditions* (London: Duckworth, 1974), pp. 115–17. See also Norman Myers, *The Sinking Ark* (Oxford: Pergamon Press, 1979), p. 46; David Ehrenfeld, *The Arrogance of Humanism* (New York: Oxford University Press, 1978), pp. 207–9; Paul and Anne Ehrlich, *Extinction* (New York: Random House, 1981), p. 48. For detailed discussion of people holding this view at the movement level, see Roderick Frazier Nash, *The Rights of Nature: A History of Environmental Ethics* (Madison, WI: University of Wisconsin Press, 1989).

3 Discussion of rights for nature was a basic theme of many issues of *Environmental Ethics* in the first five years. See especially Charles Hartshorne, "The Rights of the Subhuman World," *Environmental Ethics*, 1 (1979), 49–60; Richard A. Watson, "Self-Consciousness and the Rights of Nonhuman Animals and the Rights of Nonhuman Animals and Nature," *Environmental Ethics*, 1 (1979), 99–129; Roland C. Clement, "Watson's Reciprocity of Rights and Duties," *Environmental Ethics*, 1 (1979), 353–5; Anthony Povilitis, "On Assigning Rights to Animals and Nature," *Environmental Ethics*, 2 (1980), 67–71; Tom Regan, "Animal Rights, Human Wrong," *Environmental Ethics*, 2 (1980), 99–100; Meredith Williams, "Rights, Interests, and Moral Equality," *Environmental Ethics*, 2 (1980), 149–61; Jay E. Kantor, "The 'Interests' of Natural Objects," *Environmental Ethics*, 2 (1980), 163–71; James E. Scarff, "Ethical Issues in Whale and Small Cetacean Management," *Environmental Ethics*, 2 (1980), 241–79; J. Baird Callicott, "Animal Liberation: A Triangular Affair," *Environmental Ethics*, 2 (1980) 311–38; Scott Lehmann, "Do Wildernesses Have Rights?", *Environmental Ethics*, 3 (1981), 167–71; Edward Johnson, "Animal Liberation versus the Land Ethic," *Environmental Ethics*, 3 (1981), 265–73; Bryan G. Norton, "Environmental Ethics and Nonhuman Rights," *Environmental Ethics*, 4 (1982), 17–36; George S. Cave, "Animals, Heidegger, and the Right to Life," *Environmental Ethics*, 4 (1982), 249–54; Steve F. Sapontzis, "The Moral Significance of Interests," *Environmental Ethics*, 4 (1982), 345–58; Alastair S. Gunn, "Traditional Ethics and the Moral Status of Animals," *Environmental Ethics*, 5 (1983), 133–54; Louis G. Lombardi, "Inherent Worth, Respect, and Rights," *Environmental Ethics*, 5 (1983), 257–70; Peter Miller, "Do Animals Have Interests Worthy of Our Moral Interest?" *Environmental Ethics*, 5 (1983), 319–33. According to Roderick Nash (*The Rights of Nature*), rights for nature is still the dominate view in environmental ethics.

4 For example, according to Samuel Alexander, beauty, whether artistic or natural, is contemplated for its own sake – that is, is regarded as being intrinsically valuable. Samuel Alexander, *Beauty and Other Forms of Value* (London: Macmillan and Co., 1933), pp. 13–14. The idea that art objects are intrinsically valuable is so well established that it was seldom overtly expressed. It appears primarily in analogies extending intrinsic value from art to nature and in contrasts of intrinsic value with instrumental and utilitarian value. See, for example, Thomas Cole, "Essay on American Scenery," in John W. McCoubrey, ed., *American Art: 1700–1960* (Englewood

Cliffs, NJ: Prentice-Hall, 1965), pp. 99–100. According to Emerson, "art aims at beauty as an end," that is, as an intrinsic rather than an instrumental value, and beauty, both in nature and in art, gives us delight *in and for itself*. See Ralph Waldo Emerson, "Thoughts on Art," in McCoubrey, *American Art*, p. 76, and "Nature," in *The Writings of Ralph Waldo Emerson*, ed. Brooks Atkinson (New York: Modern Library, 1940), p. 9. At the beginning of this century, G. E. Moore argued that things that are beautiful in art and nature are good for their own sakes and "the proper appreciation of a beautiful object is a good thing in itself" and he compared landscape paintings with natural landscapes. G. E. Moore, *Principia Ethica* (Cambridge: At the University Press, 1903), pp. 188–9. In accordance with this tradition, Aldo Leopold draws similar comparisons in "The Conservation Esthetic," in *Sand County Almanac*, p. 168, and "Means and Ends in Wild Life Management," *Environmental Ethics*, 12 (1990), 330.

5 Although this definition is implicit in virtually all the writings of the deep ecologists, it has been explicitly stated by J. Baird Callicott (who is not a deep ecologist): "An anthropocentric value theory (or axiology), by common consensus, confers intrinsic value on human beings and regards all other things, including other forms of life, as being only instrumentally valuable, i.e., valuable only to the extent that they are means or instruments which may serve human beings. A non-anthropocentric value theory (or axiology), on the other hand, would confer intrinsic value on some non-human beings." J. Baird Callicott, "Non-Anthropocentric Value Theory and Environmental Ethics," *American Philosophical Quarterly*, 21 (1984), 299.

6 See Henryk Skolimowski, "The Dogma of Anti-Anthropocentrism and Ecophilosophy," *Environmental Ethics*, 6 (1984), 283–8.

7 See, for example, Monroe Beardsley, "Intrinsic Value," in Monroe Beardsley, *The Aesthetic Point of View: Selected Essays*, ed. Michael J. Wren and Donald M. Callen (Ithaca, NY, and London: Cornell University Press, 1982). After applauding Dewey's attack on intrinsic value and adding arguments of his own, Beardsley admits in his concluding remarks that he himself finds Dewey's attack confusing: "I am always frustrated in reading Dewey, trying to separate the enormously good points from the confusing ones. Much of Dewey's famous attack on intrinsic value is really concerned with something else, namely ends-in-themselves (as opposed to ends-in-view). What he really exposes over and over again is the danger of fixing goals without reasonable regard to their means and consequences, and he is convinced that the belief in intrinsic value fosters this fixation, with its attendant train of ills: fanaticism, utopianism, opportunism, and the rest. Of course, it does not

logically follow that if there are intrinsically valuable things, then there are necessarily ends-in-themselves" (p. 63). Other frustrations and confusions are not difficult to find. For example, in speaking of the consummatory phase of experience (happily, consummation, not consumption), Dewey warns against "the joys of egotistic success" replacing "the fulfillment of an experience for its own sake." He then claims to solve this problem by expanding the definition of "instrumental" (his quotation marks) to cover such matters – scolding, in passing, "persons who draw back at the mention of 'instrumental' in connection with art" (that is, who hold that aesthetic experiences involve intrinsic value, not just expanded instrumental value). He fails, however, fully to explain how the quotation marks take care of the problem of intrinsic value. John Dewey, *Art as Experience* (New York: G. P. Putnam's Sons, 1934), p. 139. Amazingly, Beardsley discusses Dewey's attack on intrinsic value without ever bothering to cite any book or essay by Dewey on the subject, leaving uninformed and skeptical readers like myself no opportunity to judge for themselves whether or not the attack was truly successful. The difficulties involved in finding and unscrambling Dewey's attack suggest that it was more an ideological pronouncement than a real argument.

8 See A. J. Ayer, "Critique of Ethics and Theology," in *Language, Truth and Logic* (New York: Dover Publications, 1950), pp. 102–20.

9 See Alasdair MacIntyre, *After Virtue*, 2nd edn. (Notre Dame, IN: University of Notre Dame Press, 1984).

10 Eugene C. Hargrove, "The Role of Rules in Ethical Decision Making," *Inquiry*, 28 (1985), 3–42.

11 Ibid., p. 26.

12 Ibid., p. 27.

13 See, for example, Paul W. Taylor, "Are Humans Superior to Animals and Plants?", *Environmental Ethics*, 6 (1984), 151, n5.

14 Hargrove, "Role of Rules," pp. 10–11. I go on to argue that the treatment of nonconstitutive rules in a constitutive manner in chess and ethics limits a player's or moral agent's perception (in an Aristotelian sense), causing the player to miss winning opportunities and the moral agent to overlook important aspects of and solutions to moral problems (pp. 18–23).

15 As John Passmore once noted, in criticism of environmental ethics theory in general, "It is a considerable presumption, indeed, that our descendants will continue to admire wildernesses aesthetically, just as it is a considerable assumption that they will continue to enjoy solitude.... We ought...to preserve wildernesses because they may turn out to be useful and because they may afford recreational pleasures, scientific opportunities and aesthetic delight, to our

successors. The first of these considerations . . . is a powerful one, the others less powerful in that they rest upon the presumption that our descendants will still delight in what now delights only some of us and did not delight our predecessors." Passmore, *Man's Responsibility*, pp. 109–10.

16 Paul W. Taylor, *Respect for Nature: A Theory of Environmental Ethics* (Princeton, NJ: Princeton University Press, 1986); Holmes Rolston, III. *Environmental Ethics: Duties to and Values in Nature* (Philadelphia: Temple University Press, 1988).

17 The issue is apparently what Callicott calls "moral monism." See J. Baird Callicott, "The Case against Moral Pluralism," *Environmental Ethics*, 12 (1990), 99–124. Callicott classifies Christopher Stone and myself, among others, as moral pluralists and cites himself and Holmes Rolston, III as moral monists.

18 William Frankena lists utility values, extrinsic values, contributory values, and perhaps inherent values, and other formulations are possible. William Frankena, *Ethics*, 2nd edn. (Englewood Cliffs, NJ: Prentice-Hall, 1973).

19 Paul W. Taylor, "Are Humans Superior to Animals and Plants?" pp. 150–1.

20 Ibid., p. 151–2.

21 See Hargrove, *Foundations of Environmental Ethics*, pp. 124–9; 165–6; 208–9.

22 See Bryan G. Norton, "Environmental Ethics and Weak Anthropocentrism," *Environmental Ethics* 6 (1984), 133–8. Although my remarks here are in the spirit of Norton's paper, we differ concerning the meaning of weak anthropocentrism (personal communication). At the time he wrote this paper, Norton believed that all intrinsic value was nonanthropocentric, a view which he apparently no longer holds (see the introduction to his essay in *The Monist*, 75 (1992), 208–26).

23 I develop this point at great length in my book, *Foundations of Environmental Ethics* (Englewood Cliffs, NJ: Prentice-Hall, 1989).

24 Holmes Rolston, III, *Environmental Ethics* (Philadelphia: Temple University Press, 1988), pp. 97–104, 169, 186–7, 232–45.

25 Ibid., p. 169.

26 Ibid., 218.

27 Ibid., p. 187. Apparently the claim is that anything that is instrumentally valuable to a holder of intrinsic value, an organism, in some way shares in the intrinsic value of that organism.

28 Ibid., pp. 233–45.

29 J. Baird Callicott, *In Defense of the Land Ethic* (Albany, NJ: SUNY Press, 1989), p. 173.

30 I use the word *uncritical* to describe the claim that humans have intrinsic value because Callicott introduces the claim on the basis of the following sentence: "The intrinsic value of oneself has *for some*

reason been taken for granted. . . ." Ibid., p. 172 (emphasis added).

31 I am aware that deep ecologists try to overcome this problem by taking a Spinozistic approach. See George Sessions, "Spinoza and Jeffers on Man in Nature," *Inquiry* 20 (1977), 481–528. I do not, however, see any evidence that Callicott is a Spinozan.

32 Callicott, *In Defense*, p. 147.

33 Ibid., pp. 133–4.

34 See Hargrove, "The Role of Rules," p. 21 and n22, p. 40.

35 See, for example, Anthony Weston, "Beyond Intrinsic Value: Pragmatism in Environmental Ethics," *Environmental Ethics*, 7 (1985), 321–39, who relies on Beardsley, "Intrinsic Value," cited above, and Bryan G. Norton, "Environmental Ethics and Weak Anthropocentrism," *Environmental Ethics*, 6 (1984), 131–48. Norton himself (personal communication) backed into pragmatism as a result of the ontological complications of nonanthropocentric intrinsic value, but did not fully embrace pragmatism until he wrote "Conservation and Preservation: A Conceptual Rehabilitation," *Environmental Ethics*, 8 (1986), 195–220. There are, of course, also anti-environmental pragmatic instrumentalists. Passmore, *Man's Responsibility for Nature*, for example, argues that nature preservation can only be supported instrumentally (pp. 101–26), claiming eventually that "whatever exists in nature is of some use to [humans]." He notes that though this claim is not "an empirical hypothesis, for there is no way to falsify it," it is, nevertheless, a useful "guiding principle," which should not be "set aside" (p. 180).

36 Norton, "Environmental Ethics and Weak Anthropocentrism." Although Norton leaves open the door for anthropocentric intrinsic value in his paper in this volume, he continues to be preoccupied with his attack on nonanthropocentric intrinsic value.

37 See Nash, *Rights of Nature*. See also F. Fraser Darling, "Man's Responsibility for the Environment," in F. J. Ebling, ed., *Biology and Ethics*, Symposia of the Institute of Biology, no. 18 (London, 1969), p. 119. He writes, "I am not greatly moved when I hear supporters of the national park and nature reserve movement argue that living things have educational value, that the beauties of nature give pleasure to humanity, that they are of scientific value . . . and that we cannot afford to lose them" for "the essential attitude is not far in advance of the timber merchant."

38 For a more detailed discussion, see Eugene C. Hargrove, *Foundations of Environmental Ethics* (Englewood Cliffs, NJ: Prentice-Hall, 1989), pp. 124–9.

39 Rolston, *Environmental Ethics*, pp. 16–17, 25–6.

Eugene Hargrove

40 For a longer discussion of this matter, see Hargrove, *Foundations of Environmental Ethics*, pp. 210–14.

41 While there are undoubtedly millions of people who have sold a piece of land with trees on it, a much smaller number of people have bought or sold a forest. Although forests are apparently bought and sold all the time, I have never had regular contact at any time in my life with anyone who has either bought or sold a forest. I would guess that the number of people who have consciously bought or sold a species is less than one hundred, if that many.

42 Callicott, *In Defense of the Land Ethic*, p. 133; Rolston, *Environmental Ethics*, p. 233.

43 Rolston, *Environmental Ethics*, p. 120.

44 Ibid., pp. 62–78.

45 Anthropocentrism of this kind has even appeared in the more recent writings of Callicott, who also gives special attention to humans over domestic animals and to domestic animals over wild ones. See Callicott, "Animal Liberation and Environmental Ethics: Back Together Again," in *In Defense of the Land Ethic*. "Domestic animals are members of the mixed community and ought to enjoy, therefore, all the rights and privileges, whatever they turn out to be, attendant upon that membership. Wild animals are, by definition, not members of the mixed community and therefore should not lie on the same spectrum of graded moral standing as family members, neighbors, fellow citizens, fellow human beings, pets, and other domestic animals" (p. 56). "We are still subject to all the other more particular and individually oriented duties to the members of our various more circumscribed and intimate communities. And *since they are closer to home*, they come first" (p. 58; emphasis added).

PART IV

Is There One Environmental Ethic? Monism versus Pluralism

quantum leap more perplexing than the task of putting together (or discovering) an ethics for our conduct respecting persons.

The Metaethical Assumptions

The larger – in all events, prior – questions require further consideration of the implicit metaethical assumptions. What are environmental ethicists trying to achieve, and what are the standards for success? In other words, what, more exactly, is an ethics supposed to look like and do? To illustrate, for years environmental ethicists have been stimulated by Aldo Leopold's conviction that we should develop a "land ethic." But how much thought has been given to what such a project implies? Are the proponents of a land ethic committed to coming up with a capacious replacement for all existing ethics, one capable of mediating all moral questions touching man, beast and mountain, but by reference to a grander, more all-encompassing set of principles? Or can the land ethic be an ethic that governs man's relations with land alone, leaving intact other principles to govern actions touching humankind (and yet others for actions touching, say, lower animals, and so on)?

If we are implying that there are different ethics, then there are a host of questions to face. What is an ethical system, and what are its minimum requirements? Need its "proofs" be as irresistible as a geometry's? Is it required to provide for each moral dilemma that it recognizes as a dilemma one right, tightly defined answer? Or is it enough to identify several courses of action equally acceptable, perhaps identifying for elimination those that are wrong or unwelcome? How – by reference to what elements – can one ethic differ from another? What possibilities of conflicting judgments are introduced by multiple frameworks, and how are they to be resolved?

These are among the questions that, sooner or later, environmental ethicists will have to confront. Upon their answer hinges nothing less than the legitimacy of environmental ethics as a distinct enterprise.

Moral Monism

The environmental ethics movement has always known that if it is to succeed, it has to challenge the prevailing orthodoxy. But the orthodoxy it has targeted is only the more obvious one, the orthodoxy of morals: that man is the measure (and not merely the measurer) of all value. Certainly calling that gross presumption to question is a valid part of the program. But the orthodoxy we have to question first is that of metaethics – of how moral philosophy ought to be conducted, of the ground rules.

Note that I am not claiming that we lack controversy at the level of *morals*. There is no shortage of lively contention in the philosophy literature. But underneath it all there is a striking, if ordinarily only implicit agreement on the metaethical sense of mission. It is widely presumed, by implication when it is not made explicit, that the ethicist's task is to put forward and defend a single overarching principle (or coherent body of principles), such as utilitarianism's "greatest good for the greatest number" or Kant's categorical imperative, and to demonstrate how it (the one correct viewpoint) guides us through all moral dilemmas to the one right solution.

This attitude, which I call moral monism, implies that in defending, say, the preservation of a forest or the protection of a laboratory animal, we are expected to bring our argument under the same principles that dictate our obligations to kin or the just deserts of terrorists. It suggests that moral considerateness is a matter of either-or; that is, the single viewpoint is presumably built upon a single salient moral property, such as, typically, sentience, intelligence, being the subject of a conscious life, etc. Various entities (depending on whether they are blessed with the one salient property) are *either* morally relevant (each in the same way, according to the same rules) *or* utterly inconsiderate, out in the moral cold.[3]

Environmentalists, more than most philosophers, have at least an intuitive reason for supposing that this attitude is mistaken, for it is they whom the attitude is the first to bridle. Environmentalists wonder about the possible value in a river (or in preserving a river), but cannot rationalize those feelings in the familiar anthropocentric terms of pains and life-projects that they would apply to their own situations. By contrast, mainstream ethicists, concentrating on interpersonal relations, constrict their attention to a relatively narrow and uncontroversial band of morally salient qualities. Persons can speak for themselves, exercise moral choice, and – because they share a community assert and waive many sorts of claims that are useful in governing their reciprocal relationships. Orthodox ethics has understandably tended to identify all ethics with this one set of morally salient properties: the paradigmatic moral problems have historically been interpersonal problems; the paradigmatic rules, person-regarding.

Thus, while vying camps have arisen within the orthodox tradition, none is ordinarily forced to account for the significance of properties that lie outside the common pool of human attributes. It is only when one starts to wonder about exotic clients, such as future generations, the dead, embryos, animals, the spatially remote, tribes, trees, robots, mountains, and art works, that the assumptions which unify ordinary morals are called into question. Need the rules that apply be in some sense, and at some level of generality, "the same" in all cases? The term *environmental ethics* suggests the possibility of a distinct moral regime for managing our way through environment-affecting conduct. But in what respects that regime is distinct from other regimes and how conflicts among the regimes are to be mediated are crucial matters that have not been generally and directly addressed.

In default of well-worked out answers, the prevailing strategy of those who represent nonhumans is one of extension: to force one of the familiar person-oriented frameworks outward and apply one of the familiar arguments to some nonhuman entity. But such arguments too often appear just that – forced. Utilitarianism's efforts to draw future generations under its mantle (a relatively easy extension, one would suppose) ties it in some awkward, if not paradoxical knots. Do we include, for example, those who might be born – obliging us to bring as many as possible of them into existence in order to aggregate more pleasures? Nor is it clear that utilitarianism, unqualified by a complex and ill-fitting rights appendage, can satisfy the concerns that drive the animal liberation movement.

The shortcomings of (let us call it) moral extensionism[4] are not peculiar to utilitarianism. Extensions of utilitarianism's principal contenders all require, in various ways and with various justifications, putting oneself in the place of another to test whether we can really wish the conduct under evaluation if we assume the other's position, role, and/or natural endowment. While such hypothetical trading of places and comparable techniques of thought experiment are always problematical, they are most satisfactory when we are trading places with (or universalizing about) persons who share our culture, and whose interests, values, and tastes we can therefore presume with some confidence. But even that slender assurance is destined to erode the further we venture beyond the domain of the most familiar natural persons. With what conviction can we trade places with members of spatially and temporally remote cultures, or with our own descendants in some future century? And, of course, if we wish to explore our obligations in regard to the dead, trees, rocks, fetuses, artificial intelligence, species, or corporate bodies, trading places is essentially a blind alley. It is one thing to put oneself in the shoes of a stranger, perhaps even in the hooves of a horse – but quite another to put oneself in the banks of a river.

Certainly, the fact that orthodox moral philosophies, each with its own ordinary-person orientation, have difficulty accommodating various nonhumans is not, in itself, proof that the conventional moral schools are wrong, or have to be amended beyond recognition. One alternative, the position of an ardent adherent to one of the predominant schools, is that any unconventional moral client that it cannot account for, except perhaps in a certain limited way, cannot (save in that limited way) have any independent moral significance or standing.

But there is another response to the dilemma, one that is more challenging to the assumptions that dominate conventional moral thought. In accordance with this approach we need to ask several new questions. How imperialistic need a moral framework be? Need we accept as inevitable that there be one set of axioms or principles or paradigm cases for all morals – operable across all moral activities and all diverse entities? Are we constrained to come forward with a single coherent set of principles that will govern throughout, so that any ethic we champion has to absorb its contenders with a more general, abstract and plenary intellectual framework? My own view is that monism's ambitions, to unify all ethics within a single framework capable of yielding the one right answer to all our quandaries, are simply quixotic.

First, the monists's mission sits uneasily with the fact that morality involves not one, but several distinguishable *activities* – choosing among courses of conduct, praising and blaming actors, evaluating institutions, and so on. Is it self-evident that someone who is, say, utilitarian in his or her act evaluation is committed to utilitarianism in the grading of character?

Second, we have to account for the *variety of things* whose considerateness commands some intuitive appeal: normal persons in a common moral community, persons remote in time and space, embryos and fetuses, nations and nightingales, beautiful things and sacred things. Some of these things we wish to account for because of their high degree of intelligence (higher animals); with others, sentience seems the key (lower life); the moral standing of membership groups, such as nation-states, cultures, and species has to stand on some additional footing, since the group itself (the species, as distinct from the individual whale) manifests no intelligence and experiences no pain. Other entities are genetically human, either capable of experiencing pain (advanced fetuses) or nonsentient (early embryos), but lack, at the time of our dealings with them, full human capacities. Trying to force all these diverse entities into a single mold – the one big, sparsely principled comprehensive theory – forces us to disregard some of our moral intuitions, and to dilate our overworked person-wrought precepts into unhelpfully bland generalities. The commitment is not only chimerical; it imposes strictures on thought that stifle the emergence of more valid approaches to moral reasoning.

Moral Pluralism

The alternative conception toward which I have been inviting discussion, what I call *moral pluralism*,[5] takes exception to monism point by point. It refuses to presume that all ethical activities (evaluating acts, actors, social institutions, rules, states of affairs, etc.) are in all contexts (in normal interpersonal relations, across large spaces and many generations, between species) determined by the same features (intelligence, sentience, capacity for emotions, life) or even that they are subject, in each case, to the same overarching principles (utilitarianism, Kantianism, nonmaleficence, etc.). Pluralism invites us to conceive the intellectual activities of which morals consist as being partitioned into several distinct frameworks, each governed by its own appropriate principles.

Certainly, one would expect pain-regarding principles to emerge as pivotal in establishing obligations toward all those things that experience

pain. Not pain alone, but preferences of some sort, e.g., the projection of a life plan, have to be accounted for in our relations with a second level of creature. Still richer threads (such as a sense of justice, and rights of a sort that can be consensually created, extinguished, traded, and waived) form the fabric of the moral tapestry that connects humans who share a common moral community. Other principles, perhaps invoking respect for life, for a natural unfolding, seem fit as a basis for forming our relations with plants.[6] Indeed, should we pursue this path, we would multiply subdivisions even within the interpersonal realm. The Kantians, emphasizing the place of nonwelfarist duties, make rightful ado about our not saving our child from drowning because it is "best on the whole." But this does not mean that classic utilitarianism is wrong. Maybe it is of only limited force in parsing out obligations among associates and kin. Utilitarianism strikes me as having considerable validity for legislation (an activity) affecting large numbers of largely unrelated persons (an entity set) who are therefore relatively unacquainted with each other's cardinal preferences.

That monism should have become so firmly established in morals is understandable (it echoes one God, one grand unified theory), but is hardly inevitable. Geometers have long relinquished the belief that Euclid's is the only geometry.

This discovery led to the pluralization of mathematics (itself already a strangely plural noun); where we once had geometry, we now have geometries and, ultimately, algebras rather than algebra, and number systems rather than a number system.[7]

A comparable partitioning has taken place in the empirical and social sciences. The body politic is commonly viewed as being comprised of groups: groups of humans, each of which is made up of more groups, groups of cells, molecules, atoms, and subatomic particles, and/or waves. What happens at one level of description is undoubtedly a product, in some complex way, of what is occurring at another. Many, perhaps most scientists feel that "in principle" there is a single unifying body of law – the laws of nature – that at some level of simple generality hold throughout. If so, one may harbor the hope not only of abolishing all lingering pockets of ignorance and chaos, but of connecting phenomena on every plane with phenomena on another, of someday unifying, say, the laws that govern the movement of subatomic particles with those that govern social conduct. But we are far from it. What we actually work with, for all intents and purposes, and to almost everyone's satisfaction, are separate bodies of law and knowledge.

The issue I am raising is this. If, as I maintain, ethics comprises several activities and if it has to deal with subject matters as diverse as persons, dolphins, cultural groups, and trees, why has ethics not pursued the same path as the sciences – or, rather, paths? That is, why not explore the possibility that ethics can also be partitioned?

Perhaps the analogy is simply too weak. However free science may be to partition, one might argue, ethics appears to be under peculiarly strong constraints to remain monistic. The argument might go like this. Alternative descriptions of how the world is (or might be) can peacefully coexist over a broad latitude without logical conflict, – e.g., in most contexts, one can indulge either in a particle or a wave version of light without chafing. And even where apparently irreconcilable conflict does erupt at one level (say, at the subatomic) the participants at other levels (those doing cellular biology) can ordinarily remain agnostic. By contrast, ethics (one is tempted to say) is not merely descriptive. It has as its ultimate aim choosing the right *action*. Unlike describing, in which subtly overlapping nuances of adjective and predicate are tolerable, acting seems to lend itself to, if not to demand, binary yes/no, right/wrong alternatives.

If this is the argument why morals require monism, it appears to me unpersuasive. There is, to begin with, the question of agenda: one wants from moral reasoning not merely the verdict, whether or not to do act *a*, but also what the choice set is: *a*, *b*, *c*, ... ? Moral thought is a service when it is populating and clarifying the range of morally creditable alternatives. Hence, attention to plural approaches would find justification if, by stimulating us to define and come at problems from different angles, it were to advance our grasp of alternatives.[8]

Perhaps most importantly, let us remind ourselves that actions are in the physical world; the evaluation of them is intellectual. Many persons (are these the "moralists"?) would probably be pleased if our moral reasoning had the power to map a unique, precise moral evaluation for each alternative action. It would give us much the same

pleasure (tinged with a not entirely ingenuous surprise) that mathematicians derive from confirmation that the world "out there," while theoretically at liberty to go its own haphazard way, is conforming in general to the elegant inventions of our intellects.[9] Why, when we set out to apply our best moral theories to the unruly world of human conduct should we confidently expect more – a more meticulous isomorphism, more freedom from inconsistency, more power of resolution?

Specifically, it may be a (not terribly interesting) truth that an act can be defined in such a way that we are left with no alternative but to do it or not – a feature of the world that makes monism superficially attractive. But even if so, it is a fact about the world that our best moral reasoning may just not be able to rise to or to map. The rightness and wrongness of some acts may lie beyond our power to deduce or otherwise discover. Key moral properties may not lend themselves to produce a transitive ordering across the choice set.

The Variables

If we are to explore bringing our relations with different sorts of things under different moral governances, then we face the question: by reference to what intellectual elements might governances vary domain to domain?

(a) *Grain of description.* Morals is concerned with comparing actions, characters, and states of affairs. To compare alternatives, as a logical first step, we have to settle upon the appropriate vocabulary of description. For example, in evaluating our impact on humans, we consistently adopt a grain of description that individuates organisms: each person counts equally. In evaluating other actions, there is often intuitive support for some other unit, e.g., the hive or the herd or the habitat. I am not claiming that these intuitions are self-validating, only that they, and their implications, merit sustained and systematic attention. Each vying grain of description is integral to a separate editorial viewpoint. Suppose that a bison naturally (of its own action) faces drowning in a river in a national park. Should we rescue it, or let "nature take its course"? One viewpoint emphasizes the individual animal; another (favored, apparently, by the park service)[10] consigns the individual animal to the background and emphasizes the larger unit, the park ecosystem. Another viewpoint emphasizes species. Each focus brings along its allied constellation of concepts. In invoking the finer grain, focusing upon the individual animal, we scan for such properties as the animal's capacity to feel pain, its intelligence, its understanding of the situation, and its suffering. None of these terms apply to the park. Instead, the ecosystem version brings out stability, resilience, uniqueness, and energy flow.

(b) *Mood.* What I mean by mood may best be illustrated by a contrast between morals and law. Law, like morals, often speaks in negative injunctions, i.e., "Thou shalt not kill . . ." and "Thou shalt not park in the red zone. . . ." But the law always proceeds to specify, in each case, a sanction which expresses the relative severity of the offense, viz., " . . . or face the death penalty," " . . . or face a $12 fine." The result is a legal discussion endowed with fine-tuned nuances. By contrast, much of moral philosophy, inspirited with monism, is conducted at a level of abstraction at which every act is assumed to be either–or, either good or bad; there is either a duty to do *x* or a duty not to do *x*; a right to *y* or no right to *y*. Monist moral discourse, then, lacks the refinements of expression that enrich legal discourse. As long as monism reigns, significant distinctions between cases, distinctions marked by nuances of feeling and belief that moral reflection might investigate and amplify, lack a semantic foothold.

By contrast, pluralism welcomes diversified material out of which moral judgments can be fashioned, particularly as we cross from one domain to another. Moral regard for lakes may seem silly – or even unintelligible – if we are required to flesh it out by reference to the same rules, and express our judgments in the same mood, as those that apply to a person. But there are prospective middle grounds. Our lake-affecting actions might have to be judged in terms of distinct deontic operators understood to convey a relatively lenient mood, perhaps something like "that which is morally welcome" or that which will bring credit or discredit to our character.

(c) *Logical (formal) texture.* Every system of intellectual rules is girded on a number of properties that endow it with a distinct logical texture. These range from whether it is subject to closure (whether it is capable of yielding one unique solution for each question that can be opened within it) to its attitude on contradictions and inconsisten-

cies. As to closure, the monist implicitly assumes that morals must be modelled on ordinary arithmetic. There is one and only one solution to $4 + 7$; so too there should be, for each dilemma of morals, one right answer. And monism rejects, too, any system of ethical postulates from which we could derive conflicting and contradictory prescriptions. After all, what would we think of a system of geometry from whose postulates we could derive both that two triangles were, and that they were not, congruent?

Pluralism is not so dogmatic – or perhaps one should just say not so "optimistic" – about the prospects of assimilating morals to (slightly idealized conceptions of) arithmetic or geometry. We simply may not be able to devise a single system of morals, operative throughout, that is subject to closure, and in which the laws of noncontradiction[11] and excluded middle[12] are in vigilant command.[13]

Reconciling the Differences

There are many problems with this pluralistic approach. Many of the stumbling blocks – those that I could identify by myself, or with a little help from my friends – are dealt with in *Earth and Other Ethics*.[14] It can be defended from the obvious charge that it must stumble into moral relativism of the rankest sort.[15] But it faces comparable problems that are not so easy to dismiss. It would appear that a pluralist, analyzing some choice situation in one framework (say, one that accounts for species in an appropriate way) may conclude that act *a* is right. The same person, analyzing the situation in another framework (one built, say, from a person-regarding viewpoint) concludes *b*. Are not such conflicts paralyzing? And do they not therefore render pluralism methodologically unacceptable?

To begin with, the fact that morals might admit of several allowable viewpoints does not mean that each and every dilemma will require several competing analyses. Assuming that remotely probable and minimal consequences can be ignored, some choices may be carried through solely within one framework. For example, whatever morality has to say about whether to uproot an individual plant could be provided, presumably, by the appropriate one-plant framework. No excursion into the agent's obligations to the plant's species, or to mankind, or to kin or whatever would be called for.

We can anticipate myriad other circumstances in which thorough analysis requires defining and processing the situation in each of several frameworks. But in some subset of those situations each of the various analyses will endorse the same action. We all know that vegetarianism, for example, can be supported both within a framework that posits the moral considerateness of animals and one that values humans alone, viz., that by eating animals the planet uses protein inefficiently, therefore reducing aggregate human welfare, even robbing badly undernourished persons of a minimally human existence. (What we do not know – and ought to examine – is why approaching such a question from several angles, a technique well-accepted in other areas,[16] should be indicted as an ignoble and impure way to go about doing philosophy).

There is a third set of cases in which more than one framework will appear appropriate, and the different frameworks, rather than mutually endorsing the same result, reinforce different, even inconsistent actions. The potential for conflicts is there – but no more so than in any moral system that deems the proper choice to be a function of several independent criteria: welfare maximization, duties to kin, respect for life, the values of community and friendship. How do we "combine," where rights analysis says one thing, utility analysis, another?

One possibility is to formulate a lexical ordering rule. For example, our obligations to neighbor-persons, as determined on a framework built on neo-Kantian principles, might claim priority up to the point where our neighbor persons have reached a certain level of comfort and protection. But when that level has been reached, considerations of, say, species preservation as determined per another framework, or of future generations per another, would be brought into play.

One might claim, with partial justification, that in those circumstances in which we accepted mediation by reference to a master rule, we are reintroducing a sort of monism "after all." But even in these cases, it is an "after all" significant enough to keep pluralism from collapsing into monism. Under monism, a problem is defined appropriately for evaluation by the relevant standard, in such a way that all the "irrelevant" descriptions are left behind from the outset. The problem, so defined, is worked through to solution without further distraction. Under pluralism, a single situation,

variously described, may produce several analyses and various conclusions. If a master rule is to be introduced, it is to be introduced only after the separate reasoning processes have gone their separate ways to yield a conflicting set of conclusions, a, b, c, d. The master rule is brought to bear on that set, none of whose members would necessarily have been constructed had the procedure been subjected to the monist stricture that a single standard, such as utilitarianism, had to be applied consistently and exclusively from the start.

Finally, and most troublesomely, there are quandaries for which each of our multiple analyses not only endorse inconsistent actions, but for which no lexical rule is available, and for which further intuitive reflection[17] reveals no further, best-of-all, alternative. We can imagine as a "worst case scenario" an outcome not merely of the form a is mandatory per one framework and b is mandatory per the other (and we cannot do both), but rather of the form a is mandatory and -a is mandatory (a is impermissible). One must, and must not, pull the trigger. What then?

This much is clear: those two edicts, taken together, tell us (logically) nothing. We would say of the total system of beliefs that it had *disappointed us in the particular case*. We would have to agree, too, that if such out-and-out conflicts were in each and every case endemic to pluralist methodology, the whole system we constructed, would have to be abandoned. But suppose that such outcomes, while possible, should prove exceptional. Then we could regard their occasional occurrences as a particularly poignant indication of the total system's indeterminacy.

This prospect illustrates one of the principal monist–pluralist dividing lines referred to earlier: How fatal is it to a system of moral rules if it fails to furnish a single unambiguous answer to each choice we recognize as morally significant? If we cannot devise a whale-regarding moral framework that gives us one confident right answer to every action affecting whales, do we have to withdraw whales from consideration (except as resources in a human-oriented framework) entirely? If our whale-regarding and our person-regarding edicts conflict, does one or the other or both of the systems responsible have to be dismantled?

As I have already indicated, such a standard, if to be applied with an even hand (and fin) throughout, would cramp the range of morals significantly. Better to come right out and consider the alternative: that we may have to abandon the ambition to find perfect consistency and the "one right answer" to every moral quandary, either because a single answer does not exist, or because our best analytical methods are not up to finding it.[18]

In some circumstances, if we can identify and eliminate the options that are morally unacceptable, we may have gone as far as moral thought can take us. It may be that the choices that remain are equally good or equally evil or equally perplexing.[19]

This does not mean that as a moral community we are relieved from striving for a higher, if ultimately imperfect consensus on progressively better answers.[20] Nor does it mean that, as regards the indeterminate set, one can be arbitrary – as though, from that point on, flipping a coin is as good as we can do. It is by the choices we affirm in this zone of ultimate uncertainty that we have our highest opportunity to exercise our freedoms and define our characters. Particularly as the range of moral considerateness is extended outward from those who are (in various ways) "near" us, people who take morals seriously, who are committed to giving good reasons, will come to irreconcilably conflicting judgments on many issues. But the main question now is this: what model of decision process provides the best prospect for constructing the best answers reason can furnish?

Notes

1 See J. Baird Callicott, "Non-Anthropocentric Value Theory and Environmental Ethics," *American Philosophical Quarterly* 21 (1984): 299–300.

2 See Lynn Arthur Steen, "Mathematics Today," in *Mathematics Today*, ed. Steen (New York: Springer-Verlag, 1970), pp. 7–8. Note that in the model of mathematics Steen presents the flow of ideas and valuable information runs in two directions: the inventory of the most highly abstract ideas in the core are available for equipping application in the outer regions; in turn, the core is fueled with the new ideas that concrete application sends back from the field.

3 Consider the argument that a proponent of using animals in medical research throws up to the animal rights advocate: "If all forms of animal life ... must be treated equally, and if therefore ... the pains of a rodent count equally with the pains of a human, we are forced to conclude (1) that neither humans nor rodents possess rights, or (2) that rodents possess all the rights that humans possess." Carl Cohen, "The Case for the Use of Animals in Biomedical Research," *New England Journal of Medicine* 315 (1986): 865, 867.

An alternative "pluralist" position would examine the possibility that a laboratory bred animal has rights, but not the same as humans. The rodent might have no "right" to life, but have a "right" to be free from suffering. This distinction could be operationalized by saying that the proponent of an experiment that took a laboratory animal's life painlessly would only have to show a clear likelihood of an advance of human welfare; animal suffering, however, would (alternatively) never be allowed, or allowed only when it could be shown that there was a very high probability that the experiment would result in the saving of human lives or the reduction of human suffering – never because it would alleviate mere inconveniences in human life, such as baggy eyelids.

4 The term was suggested to me by Holmes Rolston.

5 Moral pluralism ought not to be confused with moral relativism, the view, roughly, that all morals are context-dependent. A pluralist can be agnostic with respect to the moral realist position that there are absolutely true answers to moral quandaries, as invariable across time, space, and communities as the value of pi. There may be "really right" and not just relatively right answers, but the way to find them is by reference not to one single principle, constellation of concepts, etc., but by reference to several distinct frameworks, each appropriate to its own domain of entities and/or moral activities (evaluating character, ranking options for conduct, etc.).

6 See Paul W. Taylor, *Respect for Nature* (Princeton: Princeton University Press, 1986); J. L. Arbor presents a coherent and persuasive plea for plants – coldly logical, however heartfelt – in "Animal Chauvinism, Plant-Regarding Ethics, and the Torture of Trees," *Australasian Journal of Philosophy* 64 (1986): 335.

7 Steen, "Mathematics Today," pp. 4–5. To pursue the mathematical model for a further moment, Godel and others have laid to rest the hope of ever producing a complete and consistent formal system powerful enough to prove or to refute every statement it can formulate. Although what happens in math is hardly a conclusive model of what should go on in morals, it does make one wonder how much of moral philosophy implicitly proceeds on the assumption that a morality not only has axioms (or even solider starting points), but that they are axioms more powerful than math's! And if that is not the assumption, what takes its place?

8 Note that this rationale for pluralism could be endorsed on heuristic grounds by a monist, even by a moral realist who presumed (as I do not) that all the candidates for truth *disclosed* by this many-angled attack on the problem will in the end be submitted to a single adjudicatory principle to decide which of them is *uniquely and truly right*. Compare the position Paul Feyerabend adopts with respect to the natural sciences, viz., that the history of sciences reveals an incompleteness and even inconsistency of each

framework which should be regarded as routine and inevitable, and that a pluralism of theories and metaphysical viewpoints should be nourished as a means of advancing on the truth. Feyerabend, *Against Method* (London: Verso, 1978): 35–53.

9   See E. P. Wigner, "The Unreasonable Effectiveness of Mathematics in the Natural Sciences," in Wigner, *Symmetries and Reflections* (Cambridge: MIT Press, 1970).

10 See Jim Robbins, "Do not Feed the Bears?" *Natural History*, January 1984, p. 12.

11 The law of contradiction holds that it cannot be the case that both a proposition p and its negation $-p$ are true.

12 The law of excluded middle maintains that either a proposition p or its negation $-p$ must be true; there is no middle possibility.

13 See Freidrich Waismann, "Language Strata", in *Logic and Language*, ed. Anthony Flew (New York: Anchor Books, 1965), p. 237. The notion I present of multiple conceptual planes with systematically varying formal requirements owes much to Waismann's musings about "language strata."

14 Christopher D. Stone, *Earth and Other Ethics* (New York: Harper & Row, 1987).

15 See note 5 above.

16 I do not mean only lawyers, who do this sort of thing unabashedly all of the time. As for the natural sciences, see Feyerabend, *Against Method*. In mathematics, Gorg Polya, *How to Solve It* (Princeton: Princeton University Press, 1957) is a classic exposition of how mathematicians may stalk a single problem with widely assorted techniques (indirect proofs, reductio ad absurdums, analogy), ultimately to be convinced of the truth of a solution by the dual standards of formal proof and intuition.

17 I mean by intuitive reflection a process of analysis that leads to a right-feeling judgment, but one for which, even after the conclusion, we cannot offer any proof, perhaps not even specify the premises.

18 As Hilary Putnam puts it, "The question whether there is one objectively best morality or a number of objectively best moralities which, hopefully, agree on a good many principles or in a good many cases, is simply the question whether, given the desiderata...[of] the enterprise...will it turn out that these desiderata select a best morality or a group of moralities which have a significant measure of agreement on a number of significant questions." Hilary Putnam, *Meaning and the Moral Sciences* (Boston: Routledge & Kegan Paul; 1978), p. 84.

19 See Leibniz's stumper: "It is certain that God sets greater store by a man than a lion; nevertheless it can hardly be said with certainty that God prefers a single man in all respects to the whole of lion-kind." *Theodicy*, trans. E. M. Hoggard (New Haven: Yale University Press, 1952), sec. 118.

20 One might even expect this endeavor to take the form of integrating, or at least striving to integrate, originally independent "plural" frameworks into something grander and more unified – much as the theoretical physicist will continue to scout about for a grand unified field theory. But in the meantime, the practical and even playful work of significance will take place on humbler levels.

16

The Case against Moral Pluralism

J. Baird Callicott

Why Moral Pluralism Should Arise Especially in Connection with Environmental Ethics

It is not at all accidental – or, now that it is here, surprising – that moral pluralism would pop up in close association with *environmental* ethics. Fifteen years ago a few academic philosophers, I among them, went looking for a moral theory that would ethically enfranchise nonhuman natural entities and nature as a whole. We wanted to articulate, as Tom Regan so forcefully put it in the third volume of the journal *Environmental Ethics*, not an ethic for the *use* of the environment, a "management ethic," but an ethic *of* the environment.[1] Or, put another way, we wanted to develop what I then called a "direct," not an "indirect," "environmental ethic," or what Holmes Rolston, III, still earlier called a "primary," not a "secondary," "ecological ethic" – an ethic, in any case, which situates the environment as the object, not merely the arena, of human moral concern.[2]

We wanted to bring the natural environment within the purview of ethics, to be sure, but we also wanted to keep human well-being and the human social fabric in sharp moral focus.[3] Between lay a spectrum of concerns – the welfare of future people, of domestic animals, and so on – neglected in traditional Western moral theories that many other philosophers also felt compelled, either by novel circumstances (modern technology) or by the dialectic of rapidly evolving moral

sensibility (civil rights, followed by women's liberation, followed by universal human rights), to try to bring within the reach of ethical theory. By working with *one* ethical theory, chosen to accommodate our special concern for the environment, how could we also account for our traditional interpersonal responsibilities and social duties, accommodate all these intermediate new moral concerns to boot, and then order and mutually reconcile the whole spectrum of traditional and novel ethical domains?

Christopher Stone, one of the fathers of environmental ethics and an early architect of the extensionist enterprise, now claims, in *Earth and Other Ethics: The Case for Moral Pluralism*, that we cannot. The Earth and other ethical requirements simply stretch any given moral theory to the breaking point. One thus seems confronted with two choices: moral cynicism or moral pluralism. We can either give in to moral overload and theoretical burn out, or pick up the pieces, one by one, and work theoretically with each separately. I am not attracted to either alternative and propose a third in the last section of this discussion.

In a *précis* of his book, published in these pages, Stone laments that environmental ethics has "reached a plateau. The signs include a tendency to reiterate the well-worn 'need' for an environmental ethic 'whose time has come' and then work over the increasingly familiar themes about the restricted reach of mainstream theories, *et cetera*."[4] Stone claims to draw this conclusion from a survey of the first ten volumes of *Environmental Ethics* (which he modestly declines to "presume to summarize") and allied monographs that appeared during the same decade – 1979–89.[5] But both his book and the spinoff article give the lie to that claim. The "need" for an environmental ethic was in fact the burden of the 1970s generation of philosophical environmental literature.[6] Over the 1980s, thanks in large measure to the forum for exploration and critical discussion provided here by Eugene C. Hargrove, environmental philosophers have actually developed an impressive array of fairly well worked out theories of environmental ethics.[7] State-of-the-art environmental ethics also exhibits lateral theoretical diversity; in other words, as each theoretician attempts his or her own vertical integration of multiple moral spheres. It is partly our success in creating a wide variety of compelling, but distinct and mutually inconsistent, environmental ethical systems – however great their tendency may be to weaken when asked to cover all our moral concerns – that has resulted in an embarrassment of riches, ripe for pluralist plucking.

As the 1990s arrive and *Environmental Ethics* the journal settles into its second decade, there exist a fairly wide selection of nonanthropocentric ethical theories, each of which, proclaim its proponents, is superior to all the others. Though many distinct voices have been heard in the environmental ethics choir during the past decade, most are improvising on one or another familiar melody.

A neo-Kantian family of environmental ethics (united by conation as a criterion for moral considerability) seems to be attracting more converts as time goes on. Paul Taylor's biocentrism is the purest neoclassical exemplar of this type. But more baroque variations on the conation theme have been set out by Robin Attfield and Holmes Rolston.[8] Although Rolston frequently quotes Aldo Leopold and shares certain temperamental affinities with the great American conservationist, the immediate intellectual ancestor of contemporary conativism is Albert Schweitzer's reverence-for-life ethic.[9]

A second family of environmental ethics (united by "a more tender and widely diffused" altruism, to quote Darwin, with intellectual roots in Hume) has sprung, in fact, from the Aldo Leopold land ethic. I have been the most vocal champion of this theoretical approach, but fellow travelers include Edward O. Wilson, William Godfrey-Smith, and Richard and Val Routley (now Sylvan and Plumwood, respectively).[10]

A third family – centered upon Self-realization (with a capital *S*), based upon the unity between self and world suggested by ecology – has been advocated by the more philosophical exponents of deep ecology.[11]

Now that we had a good feel for the lay of the theoretical land, I assumed – before Stone came along with his powerful and seductive case for moral pluralism – that we could begin to work toward the creation of an intellectual federation and try to put an end to the Balkanization of nonanthropocentric moral philosophy. Recently, I took a step in that direction. Back in 1981, in "Animal Liberation: A Triangular Affair," I contemptuously dismissed the moral enfranchisement of *individual* animals *qua* individuals, because the ecocentric ethic adumbrated by Leopold – that had at first inspired me, and that I was attempting rigorously to ground – enthroned the integrity, stability, and beauty of the biotic *community* as the ultimate measure of the rightness and wrongness of human actions. Although I now wince at its stridency when I reread "Triangular Affair," and wish that I were not so closely identified with this particular piece of work, that essay did serve to delineate sharply the theoretical differences between animal welfare ethics and one approach – ecocentrism, as it has come to be called – to a primary or direct environmental ethic. Personally, however, I am not unmoved by the pain and suffering of individual sentient animals and believe that we ought to extend them moral considerability, if not rights. Thus, I have recently tried to effect a reconciliation between animal welfare ethics and environmental ethics with a little palinode entitled "Animal Liberation and Environmental Ethics: Back Together Again," which I held out as an olive branch to our colleagues interested primarily in the study of ethics and individual animals.[12] Nevertheless, in that paper I didn't simply say, "Where animals are concerned, I'll go with Singer or Regan, if they meet me half way and agree to go with me (or Rolston) on species and ecosystems." Rather, I tried to find a coherent theory that would provide at once for the moral considerability of individual animals – differently "textured," incidentally, for domestic animals on the one hand and for wild animals on the other – *and* for species and ecosystems.[13]

In "Triangular Affair" I even argued that the worth of individual *human* beings must, *if* one acceded to a demand for ruthless consistency, be measured against Leopold's holistic *summum bonum*, and suggested that its degree of misanthropy might be the litmus test of whether a stance or policy is in agreement with the land ethic. I never actually endorsed such a position, since it is obnoxious and untenable, and I now no longer think that antihuman prescriptions can be deduced from the Leopold land ethic, as I have subsequently explained.[14] I certainly feel that we have duties and obligations to fellow humans (and to humanity as a whole) that supersede the land ethic, although I have by no means abandoned the land ethic. Before Stone, I just *assumed* that a complete environmental ethic would begin with a carefully chosen theory of interpersonal and social human ethics, and unite animal welfare and environmental ethics under the same theoretical umbrella. Although I still think that this is the appropriate way to proceed, Stone has offered an easy and appealing alternative that demands a thoughtful reply.

Moral pluralism, crudely characterized – I hope not crudely caricatured – invites us to adopt one theory to steer a course in our relations with friends and neighbors, another to define our obligations to fellow citizens, a third to clarify our duties to more distantly related people, a fourth to express the concern we feel for future generations, a fifth to govern our relationship with nonhuman animals, a sixth to bring plants within the purview of morals, a seventh to tell us how to treat the elemental environment, an eighth to cover species, ecosystems, and other environmental collectives, and perhaps a ninth to explain our obligations to the planet, Gaia, as a whole and organically unified living thing. Stone himself provides an illustration of a pluralist posture in the following image:

> The Moral Pluralist holds that a public representative, a senator, for example, might rightly embrace utilitarianism when it comes to legislating a rule for social conduct (say, in deciding what sort of toxic waste program to establish). Yet, this same representative need not be principally utilitarian, nor even a consequentialist of any style, in arranging his personal affairs among kin or friends, or deciding whether it is right to poke out the eyes of pigeons. And surely being committed to utilitarianism as a basis for choosing legislation does not entail judging a

person's character solely by reference to whether, on balance, he advances the greatest good for the greatest number of persons.[15]

Those Who Advocate Pluralism in Environmental Ethics and Those Who Don't

Because environmental ethics invites pluralist parsing, and because Christopher Stone has now put together such a frank, strong, and eminently reasonable case for moral pluralism, one wonders if a pluralistic turn can be detected in the earlier unconventional environmental ethics literature.

In "Back Together Again" I gave critical attention to Mary Anne Warren's plea for moral pluralism published in the early 1980s. Although Warren argues that animals, like human beings, have rights, she also argues that animals do not enjoy the same rights as human beings and, *pace* Regan, that the rights of animals do not equal human rights. Animal rights and human rights are grounded in different metaphysics of morals. Human beings have "strong" rights because we are autonomous (à la Kant). Animals have "weaker rights" because they are sentient (à la Bentham). Because plant liberation (à la Paul Taylor) had not been vociferously championed or well-formulated when Warren was writing, she has nothing specifically to say about the moral entitlements of individual living things. Nevertheless, a holistic environmental ethic, Warren suggests, rests upon still other foundations – the instrumental value of "natural resources" to us and to future generations (à la Gifford Pinchot) and the "intrinsic value" we may intuitively find in species, "mountains, oceans, and the like" (à la Aldo Leopold).[16] Warren doesn't come right out and say that she is advocating moral pluralism, but that's what her eclectic program amounts to. In "Back Together Again" I (mistakenly) thought that it was enough simply to point out that Warren's approach was eclectic and pluralistic, in order to set it aside and get on with the serious business of searching for the Holy Grail of environmental ethics – the coherent, inclusive super-theory.

Although he does not actually so label his posture, moral pluralism is, nevertheless, also detectable in Eugene C. Hargrove's metaethical discussion of the role of rules in ethical decision making. In light of recently emerged "moral perceptions" respecting animals and the environment, writes Hargrove, "moral philosophers will have to abandon for the most part the search for a rational set of universal principles which moral agents can mechanically follow."[17] Hargrove, incidentally, anticipates Stone's comparison of moral theorizing to map making. Hargrove, in another conceit (that Stone seems not to have thought of but might find useful), suggests that we understand moral rules to be similar to nonconstitutive chess rules – not the rules of the game that inflexibly govern the movement of the pieces, but the ad hoc rules for effective play in various situations. According to Hargrove, in ethics as in chess,

> the body of rules has no ultimate unifying principle, the principles themselves are not logically related to one another (the omission of one or the addition of another in no way affects the group as whole), they are not organized in any meaningful hierarchy, ... and there are innumerable cases which can be brought forward with regard to each of them in which following the proper rule leads to disaster in a board [or, analogously, in a real–life] situation.[18]

Almost simultaneously with Stone's extensive case for moral pluralism, Andrew Brennan and Peter Wenz have expressly advocated "ethical polymorphism" and a "pluralistic theory" of environmental ethics, respectively.[19] Brennan remarks that

> an ethic by which to live is not to be found by adopting one fundamental, substantive principle relative to which all our deliberations are to be resolved. Instead we are prey to numerous different kinds of consideration originating from different directions, many of them with a good claim to be ethical ones.[20]

Brennan goes on to rummage through a few of these different kinds of consideration, showering most of his attention on the competing claims of environmental individualism and environmental holism to which our ethical intuitions are prey. Wenz, for his part, after glossing the same (by now familiar) biocentric (Taylorian) and ecocentric (Callicottian) theories, as something of an afterthought at the end of an elaborate review of conventional theories of justice and an evaluation

of the direction they each give for equitably dividing the environmental pie, feels less inclined to settle on one best approach than to float them all at once:[21]

> We found ... that none of the above theories of justice was flexible enough to accommodate all of our considered views about how particular matters of environmental justice should be decided.... But because each theory and many of the principles contained in each theory seem reasonable when applied to certain kinds of cases, they should not be abandoned entirely. They should be modified and blended to form an all embracing pluralistic theory. A theory is pluralistic when it contains a variety of principles that cannot be reduced to or derived from a single master principle.[22]

G. E. Varner's review of *Earth and Other Ethics*, underscores, *correctly* I think, "the fundamental metaethical challenge" to environmental ethics posed by Stone.[23] In casting about for harbingers of pluralism, however, Varner, quite understandably, completely overlooks Warren's essay – one small, dated item in a literature that is growing exponentially – and Hargrove's which is about ethics in general, not environmental and animal welfare ethics specifically. Wenz's and Brennan's very recent books, on the other hand, could not have come to his attention before his review of Stone was all but set in stone.

Yet, Varner goes on to find, *incorrectly* I think, intimations of pluralism in Paul Taylor's work and my own. He writes,

> There are hints – but still only hints – of pluralism emerging in recent work by Paul Taylor and Baird Callicott. In *Respect for Nature*, Taylor stresses that environmental ethics rests on very different foundations than human ethics, and that it accordingly embodies very different principles. In his recent "Search for an Environmental Ethic," Callicott similarly abandons the vitriolic rhetoric of his "Triangular Affair" article and stresses that Leopold characterizes the land ethic as an accretion that supplements, rather than replaces, previous ethics.[24]

How accurately my work may be characterized as pluralistic may be gathered from this essay. As to

Paul Taylor's, his theory strikes me as about as clear a case of what Stone calls moral monism as any theory of environmental ethics could possibly be. While Taylor grants moral rights to human teleological centers of life and withholds them from nonhuman teleological centers of life, he insists that, their rights notwithstanding, the former are in no way morally superior to the latter and that *all* teleological centers of life are of *equal* inherent worth.[25]

Basically, Taylor slips conation into the slot reason fills in Kant's moral philosophy.[26] To be sure, Taylor, a neo-Kantian, cannot bring himself to completely renounce the classical Kantian emphasis on special respect for persons and sometimes speaks of "both systems of ethics" – respect for persons and respect for nature – as if he were juggling two independent principles. But Taylor's moral theory is monistic, as Wenz clearly recognizes. When he considers conflicts of interest, Taylor does not treat respect for persons and respect for nature as two mutually incommensurable systems of ethics. For Taylor, "the good of other species and the good of humans make claims that must equally be taken into consideration."[27] It's just that human beings, as self-conscious and morally autonomous beings, have certain goods that other teleological centers of life lack. Thus, while it may be contrary to a tree's good to cut it down, it is not contrary to a tree's good, as it is to a human being's, to be lied to or to be fenced in. Respect for persons (and associated human rights) takes into account the peculiar, but not better making, endowment of human beings in comparison with other forms of life.

Taylor does not, in other words, resort to other theories than his basic biocentrism in order to guarantee that we human beings (at least we genteel, culturally rich, but materially modest human beings) can go on living the lives to which we have grown accustomed. He tries to make things come out right – so that we can eat vegetables, build wooden houses, and generally get on with our human projects (at least our more refined, low-impact human projects) – by means of an elaborate set of hedges enabling us consumptively to use our fellow entelechies within the limits of his extremely broad egalitarian theory.[28] To show that Taylor's attempt to deal, under the auspices of a single theory, with all our considered moral sensibilities – from respect for human rights to the moral enfranchisement of individual plants – collapses

under the load, Wenz employs, very effectively in my opinion, a technique of philosophical refutation delightfully satirized by Stone: he "volleys hypothetical quandaries onto" Taylor that his "principles cannot handle."[29]

Varner might somewhat more profitably have looked into Holmes Rolston's theory of environmental ethics for "hints" of pluralism. In his 1988 book *Environmental Ethics* (a consolidated and definitive statement of his revolutionary moral theory) Rolston devotes a chapter each to the intrinsic value of, and corresponding duties owed to, "higher animals," "organisms," "species," and "ecosystems." Along the way he finds intrinsic value in evolutionary *processes* – going all the way back to the Big Bang.

Because Rolston does not strive for unambiguous clarity and clean, crisp definitions, as Taylor does, it may seem that in each of these chapters he develops independent arguments – not all of which, even within each chapter, are univocal – for the value of each of these natural things. Nevertheless, I think that most of his arguments for intrinsic value in nature cluster around a central, pivotal notion – conation, once again. Organisms have, each of them, a *telos*, Rolston reminds us – unconscious drives and aims, or (at least) latent tendencies, directions of growth and natural fulfillments. His defense of their intrinsic value seems to settle upon the fact that organisms, even unconscious organisms, compete for nutrients and a place in the sun, and defend their own lives – in an astonishing variety of ingenious ways. They have, thus, a good of their own. Sentient organisms are aware of their strivings, and feel urges and impulses, some more keenly than others; and we human organisms are *self*-aware, conscious of ourselves as beings with wishes, desires, hopes, and goals. Unlike Taylor, Rolston assigns a value bonus to consciousness and a double bonus to self-consciousness which he adds on to the value base constituted by conation.

From this value epicenter, conation, Rolston hoes the row the other way. Each organism, Rolston says, in a characteristic argument by verbal trope, represents – i.e., "re-presents" – its species.[30] Each struggles, not only to survive and flourish, but also to reproduce. Each is a token of its type. Its type is indeed its *telos*, just as Aristotle would have it. Each strives to be "good-of-its-kind" and to "defend its own kind of good."[31]

Hence, each kind – each species – is intrinsically valuable, even though species are holistic entities which are not conative *per se*. Ecosystems, similarly, are the matrices which give birth to the myriad intrinsically valuable kinds. Rolston says that ecosystems and evolutionary processes are "projective."[32] They do not themselves possess *teloi* (Rolston observes with strict consistency the ateleological conventions of evolutionary biology), but they have "projected," or thrown up, a good many ordered systems and organized entities. The quasi-conative character of ecosystems and evolutionary processes earns them a value dividend in Rolston's theory of environmental ethics.

Given that even Rolston is not really a pluralist after all, one begins to wonder why our best, most systematic, and thoroughgoing environmental philosophers cling to moral monism. Although one can find scattered outbreaks of pluralism in the literature, so far pluralism has not become epidemic. Stone, a lawyer, does make moral pluralism seem so reasonable, and its opposite a silly and parochial preoccupation; yet, Taylor and Rolston have mounted veritably epic efforts to save the philosophical integrities of their respective systems. Taylor will save his biocentrism at the cost of patent sophistries (which Wenz revels in exposing) and Rolston can save his only by resorting to ambiguity and courting equivocation. Why? Why don't we all just become merry moral pluralists? I take this to be the metaethical challenge that Varner says that Stone has thrown down.

Moral Pluralism's Achilles Heel: The Hard Choice Between Contradictory Indications

Wenz, pluralist convert though he may have become, clearly articulates one reason to beware of its siren lure:

> Without a single master principle in the background, what is to be done . . . when one of the independent principles in the pluralistic theory requires a course of action different from and incompatible with the course of action required by one of the other independent principles . . . ? In this kind of situation, the theory yields

either no recommended course of action or contradictory recommendations.[33]

Consistency is not just a shrine before which philosophers worship. There is a reason for wanting consistency, insured by organization around or derivation from a "master principle," among one's practical precepts. Attempting to *act* upon inconsistent or mutually contradictory ethical principles results in frustration of action altogether or in actions that are either incoherent or mutually canceling.

Stone, of course, has thought of this problem. It is worth noting, he points out, that a multiplicity of independent principles might just as well all converge on a single course of action. The practical necessity of such a plurally mandated course of action would be reinforced, rather than frustrated or negated. *Earth and Other Ethics* is wonderfully creative, not only in its advocacy of the idea of pluralistic ethics, but in working out methods for solving ethical conundrums drawing upon the resources of a variety of moral systems. Stone asks us to think of various maps of a single territory. One map might show human population distribution, another land-use patterns, a third the vegetation types, a fourth contours, and so on. If we regard a situation in which we must do something as the "territory" and various theories as the "maps" (or "planes," as Stone later calls them), we may overlay the "planes"/"maps" and see if they indicate a clear path of action. Why, he asks, should we expect several overlays to yield interference patterns more usually than sympathetic vibrations?

Still, what do we do when we put all our systems down, each "plane" layered over the "territory" (the actual or hypothetical moral quandary in which we find ourselves), and the indications are inconsistent or contradictory? The actual case of a bison trapped in a frozen Yellowstone river, a case that Stone fully develops in his book, serves as a good example. Animal welfare ethics indicate that we ought to try to save individual animals from unnecessary pain, suffering, and eventual death, while ecocentric environmental ethics indicate that we ought to let bison (and all the other nonhuman members of the biotic community) alone to struggle for their lives and live and pass their tested genes on to the next generation or die and become food for the carrion eaters. Stone tells us what happened to this particular bison on this particular occasion, and how the moral theories that various people held affected their actions and inactions, but he never tells us what these people ought to have done or not done for the animal.

One problem with moral pluralism, noticed by Hargrove – but that neither Wenz nor Stone directly address – is that it invites a kind of moral promiscuity. Hargrove notes a potential "fear that the open form in which decisions naturally and normally take place will allow unscrupulous or weak moral agents to waver and [choose] principles to their own immoral advantage."[34] With a variety of theories at our disposal, each indicating different, inconsistent, or contradictory courses of action, we may be tempted to espouse the one that seems most convenient or self-serving in the circumstances.

If Stone can, in a charming and friendly way, tweak us philosophers about our foibles, then turn about is fair play. Lawyers are notoriously adversarial. They are trained to use scholarship and logic, not to seek the truth, or implement justice, but to represent a client or win a case – regardless of where the truth and the right lie. The overall structure of *Earth and Other Ethics* does not give one much comfort about the worry that moral pluralism might provide a sophisticated scoundrel with a bag of tricks to rationalize his or her convenience or self-interest – rather than a box of tools to work his or her way through the moral complexities of life in the twentieth and twenty-first centuries.

In the early 1970s, Stone began with a *desideratum* – how *legally* to enfranchise "non-persons," as he calls everything from ships and corporations to wild rivers and endangered species. Extending them (limited) legal rights, operationally defined, was his answer in "Should Trees Have Standing?".[35] Since then the courts have considerably liberalized standing, but "standing ... does nothing but get you through the courthouse door."[36] The law can provide all sorts of legal fictions and devices for the legal considerateness of non-persons. That's no problem. But once environmentalists or animal liberationists get a hearing for their "wards," Stone asks, then how do they go about "justifying" legal accommodation and how can they prevail against competing interests?[37] This question leads Stone from the realm of law to the realm of ethics. In other words, like a lawyer, he begins with a spectrum of practical ends in view – leaving some resources and wilderness

for the use and enjoyment of future generations, protecting animals from pointless or needless experimentation, saving species, etc. – and looks for a spectrum of persuasive theories, as means, to secure those ends. Then finally, the apparent hopelessness of ordering that very caboodle of practical ends and kit of theoretical means within a single comprehensive moral philosophy leads him on to plead for pluralism and to challenge the very impetus to univocal theory construction.

To the worry that moral pluralism invites moral promiscuity, had Stone expressly confronted it, he might have replied, more or less as Hargrove does, that all moral philosophy presupposes persons of good will. Pluralism may supply a scoundrel with another sort of rationalization for ducking his or her responsibilities, but moral philosophy generally – monistic no less than pluralistic – is underdeterminate and, in the hands of a skilled, but unscrupulous, advocate can be made to justify all manner of action or inaction. (Didn't lesser Nazi war criminals at their Nüremberg trials hide behind Kant's noble notions of apodictic duty?) One might argue, by parity of reasoning, that the ethical lives of sincere persons of good will are proportionately enriched and empowered by moral pluralism, thus offsetting the invitation to the abuse that pluralism inadvertently affords persons less noble of character.

Granted that moral pluralists may be sincere persons of good will, how *do* they decide between the inconsistent or contradictory indications of their several theories? Stone, of course, has thought about this too. He suggests we bring to bear a "lexical" procedure for reaching a decision.

Lexical, in this context, is a euphemism for hierarchical ordering – prioritizing, if you will. Baldly put, what Stone suggests is this: we take our many moral "maps," "planes," and "frameworks" (our polyglot ethical systems or theories), lay them out over the "territory" (the problem, quandary, or conundrum) and, if they jibe, fine. If they don't, then we prioritize them.

But how? For pluralists there's no "master principle," no super-theory, by definition. His back against the wall, Stone frankly endorses appeal to what Regan calls "considered intuition," and to cultivated moral tastes, sensibilities, feelings, and "moral faculties."[38] (Wenz similarly, asks us to use unspecified "good judgment," while Hargrove, for his part, is simply willing to live with more of a mess than Stone.[39])

But what does that really tell us? When push comes to shove, how do we choose between theory A with its recommended course of action a, B with b, and C with c? According to Stone, "when we turn to the selection of planes – what things [people, animals, plants, species], as bundled in what governance [utility-maximizing, person-respecting], count? – we are removed to another jurisdiction. . . ."[40] The final resolution of the intractable dilemmas that will inevitably confront the moral pluralist, Stone tells us, lies in "selecting a version of the world."[41] Stone points in his final pages, in other words, to metaphysics. To "buy into" a "plane" – a set of ethically enfranchised entities (a "moral ontology") as Stone revealingly calls such a set, and a "governance" (how exactly those entities are endowed with rights or equal consideration of interests, respect, or whatever) – is to buy into a world view. When we are forced to choose between "planes," we make a metaphysical commitment as well as a moral choice.

But then the real work, the ethical *Grundlegung* should commence anew. We might think of our hard moral choices (in my opinion misleadingly mystified by Stone with his talk about intuition, literature, art, and humor) as actually revelatory of the deeper – but because deeper less fully conscious – structures of our thinking.[42] The task then is to call these organizing concepts up on the screen – to articulate in a more self-conscious and deliberate way the world view, the metaphysics, which has rationally (we hope), but subconsciously, arbitrated among the divers moral "maps." However, once we have carried through on that project, then the many "maps," and the whole apparatus of moral pluralism become otiose. Some of the "maps" will be seen to assume untenable versions of the world or versions of human nature and we may readily consign them to the historical rubbish heap – along with "maps" to ferret out and punish blasphemy and hunt and burn witches, which involve concepts like God's literal word and efficacious satanic rites (and verses), and other notions belonging to a version of the world which centuries of experience and critical thinking have, let's face it, invalidated.

Stone seems to think, however, that such metaphysical questions lie beyond philosophical competence: "It is just that these 'big' questions lie outside the province of academic and legal philosophy, which are more at home working *within* or talking *about* planes."[43] Here, finally, is the crux of what I think is wrong with moral pluralism. It severs ethical theory from moral philosophy, from the metaphysical foundations in which ethical theory is, whether we are conscious of it or not, grounded.

The Case for a Unified Moral Philosophy

Can ethics be so severed from moral philosophy, the metaphysical groundwork of ethical theories? The medieval world view seems to most latter-day moderns to be a quaint anachronism and its associated moral "maps" to be curious – when they are not sinister – relics of a bygone mentality. But the modern world view is itself rapidly becoming history. How, therefore, can we reject, out of hand, condemnations and death sentences for "blasphemy," witch hunts, and book burnings, and continue uncritically to ascribe, in a pluralistic spirit, to equally – though more recently – obsolete eighteenth-century moral theories like hedonic utilitarianism or "pure reason" Kantianism?

Why, more pointedly, we may ask, has Stone borrowed his "maps" and "planes" from the moral philosophies of Bentham, Mill, Kant, and other modern philosophers, and from those of Schweitzer, Singer, Leopold, Taylor and other contemporary philosophers, but neglected to borrow with equal alacrity from medieval philosophers like St. Thomas, and St. Augustine, and ancient philosophers like Plato and Aristotle? Or why do we not find "maps" and "planes" featured in *Earth and Other Ethics* taken from the Old Testament – say the Mosaic Decalogue – or from the Koran? The answer is, I suggest, that Stone and most of us who are thoughtful enough to worry about the human treatment of whales, rain forests, and the ozone layer do not buy into divine revelation of moral commandments or the independent existence of the Good (with a capital *G*) – concepts that are among the various metaphysical background assumptions of Aquinas, Augustine, Plato, Aristotle, the late Ayatolla Ruholla Khomeini, and the Reverend Jerry Falwell.

Nevertheless, each of the modern ethical systems which Stone so deftly employs in his pluralistic ethical tool kit also comes wrapped in its metaphysical vestments. Consider the threadbare metaphysical cloth from which classical utilitarianism is cut. Utilitarianism assumes a radical individualism or rank social atomism completely at odds with the relational sense of self that is consistent with a more fully informed evolutionary and ecological understanding of terrestrial and human nature. Bentham could not have more clearly revealed his reductive assumptions when he wrote, "the community is a fictitious body composed of the individual persons who are considered as constituting as it were its members. The interest of the community then is what? – the sum of the interests of the several members who compose it."[44]

Bentham, the founder of utilitarianism, also invests intrinsic value and disvalue exclusively in psychological experiences – pleasure and pain, in all their protean forms. Such a psychologized understanding of good and evil is historically linked with, if it does not literally follow from, the radical Cartesian split, ubiquitous in modern philosophy, between subject and object, and the resulting alienation of the self from the "external world" – which includes our own bodies. "Sense data" and sensations are, from the prevailing modern point of view, the nearest – and hence the dearest – realities.

To employ Stone's several utilitarian "planes," therefore, involves buying into a vision of human (and animal) nature in which isolated egos (*subjects*-of-a-life) are imprisoned within alien mechanical objects (their bodies), and look fearfully out on a foreign "external world." The only "things" to which good and evil can attach, given such a world view, are, naturally, positive and negative private *subjective* psychological states.

To adopt Kant's moral theory is to buy into a vintage European Enlightenment philosophy of human nature in which Reason (with a capital R) constitutes the essence of "man," somewhat in the way that the "image of God" constitutes the essence of "man" in the biblical conception of human nature. It is revealing, I think, to note that Kant himself never considers the "marginal cases," which animal welfare ethicists routinely volley onto contemporary Kantians. He never seems to notice, in other words, that, by his principles, subrational human beings such as infants, imbeciles, and the senile are also "mere things" (as he characterizes sentient animals lacking reason) and might be treated accordingly. That's not because Kant didn't think his theory through, but because he understood reason to be less an organic function or capacity than a kind of philosophically

sanitized, Enlightenment equivalent of the *imago dei* inhabiting all human beings, quite irrespective of their functional rationality.

Now let's return once more to Stone's senator, a model moral pluralist, and consider a variation on Stone's description of her agile ethical experience. After "embracing utilitarianism" on a floor vote in the morning "(deciding what sort of toxic waste program to establish)," her staff reminds her that in the afternoon a vote will be taken on a forest service plan to "road" the Gila wilderness. Our senator has read *A Sand County Almanac* and added the land ethic to her moral repertoire. So, having given utilitarianism a turn in the morning, embracing the land ethic in the afternoon, she votes against the forest service. This means that over lunch she has blithely stepped out of the atomized, mechanical, and dualistic view of nature and human nature inspiring utilitarianism and into the organic, internally related, holistic view of nature and human nature animating the land ethic – a world view in which human beings are not privatized pleasure-loving egos, but integrated plain members and citizens of social and biotic communities. Then upon leaving the Capitol, she remembers that she has promised to help her son write a school essay that evening. So, tired though she may be with handling the public business all day long, during dinner she slips into a Kantian mode, and considers that a promise is a promise, and that (as Stone represents it at least) one should not use utilitarian cost–benefit analyses appropriate to funding toxic waste programs in deciding what to do in family affairs. Thus, buying into a Prussian view of iron-clad categorical, apodictic imperatives, grounded in metaphysical Reason, she works past her bedtime editing her son's essay, "How I Spent My Summer Vacation."

Moral pluralism, in short, implies metaphysical musical chairs. I think, however, that we human beings deeply need and mightily strive for consistency, coherency, and closure in our personal and shared outlook on the world and on ourselves in relation to the world and to one another. Stone is skeptical that Truth, with a capital T, may be had in matters metaphysical.[45] I am no more sanguine than he, but I do think that we can expect to generate comprehensive conceptual systems that fully embrace our ever-growing body of empirical knowledge, scientific theory, and self-discovery. Although in many ways *Earth and Other Ethics* is

J. Baird Callicott

a much better book than *Should Trees Have Standing?* in the years between *Trees* and *Earth* Stone seems to have abandoned a project that I think it is more important now than ever to try to advance. In the earlier book he wrote,

> The time may be on hand when these sentiments, and the early stirrings of the law, can be coalesced into a radical new theory or myth – felt as well as intellectualized – of man's relationships to the rest of nature. I do not mean "myth" in the demeaning sense of the term, but in the sense in which, at different times in history, our social "facts" and relationships have been comprehended and integrated by reference to the "myths" that we are co-signers of a social contract, that the Pope is God's agent, and that all men are created equal.... What is needed is a [new] myth that can fit our growing body of knowledge of geophysics, biology, and the cosmos. In this vein, I do not think it too remote that we may come to regard the Earth, as some have suggested, as one organism, of which mankind is a functional part – the mind, perhaps: different from the rest of nature, but different from the rest of nature as a man's brain is from his lungs.[46]

The Disturbing Connection Between Moral Pluralism and Deconstructive Postmodernism

Absent such a comprehensive model to focus and order our competing moral concerns, we are left with kaleidoscopic and random, albeit enriched, moral lives – individually. Collectively, socially, we are left with irreconcilable fractional disputes. Stone's happy-go-lucky moral pluralism, culturally generalized and interpreted, is allied with – if not equivalent to – deconstructive postmodernism. Absent a comprehensive and culturally shared new myth, we are left with plural points of view, perspectives, multiple outlooks – each of which has an equal claim on "truth."

The "postmodern turn" in environmental philosophy has recently been taken by Jim Cheney.[47] Joining other ecofeminists running out to bark at deep ecology, Cheney snaps at deep ecology's "totalizing" vision – a vision not unlike Stone's regrettably abandoned one – which attempts to "colonize" other outlooks. By *totalizing* vision

Cheney seems to mean one that is comprehensive. By *colonizing* outlook he seems to mean one that claims to be the best available. Cheney employs these neologisms repeatedly and they have the distinct ring of an argot or cant. This is the closest Cheney comes to defining them:

> One form that understanding can take is that of the construction of a totalizing theory designed to assimilate the other into a unifying conceptual framework.... One of the functions of a totalizing theory is to rationalize the "colonizing" of the other, the control of the other by means of control over naming.[48]

A metaphysical system which tries to embrace our ever-expanding human experience, to comprehend it, *and* to make sense of it is part of the problem, Cheney thinks, not the solution. In any case, comprehensive system building, Cheney also seems to think, is a decidedly modern preoccupation. With the "demise of modernism" there has occurred a "shattering into a world of difference, the postmodern world."[49]

Postmodernism is a term associated with two very different things. One we might call "constructive" postmodernism, following Frederick Ferré.[50] Modern natural philosophy, essentially classical mechanics, has been overturned by the new physics. Everything else modern – capitalism (and anticapitalist Marxism) in economics, utilitarianism in ethics, the social contract theory in political philosophy, etc. – that has orbited modern natural philosophy has been left without a center or a foundation. We live in a time not unlike that of Plato or Descartes. The old order has passed, but the new one has not yet arrived. For Plato the old order was the Homeric–Hesiodic world; for Descartes, it was the Aristotelian–Thomistic cosmos; for us it is the Cartesian–Newtonian universe. In our time, contemporary academic and legal philosophers "working within and talking about planes," as Stone puts it, are like the poets and rhapsodes scorned by Plato, and the Schoolmen contemned by Descartes – an army of craftspersons working frantically to keep a crumbling old edifice (to employ Descartes' architectural metaphor) in some semblance of repair.

In the Ferréian sense of the term, *postmodernism* is a place marker. While we revolutionary philosophers turn to the task of razing the old structures and rebuilding a new metaphysics from the ground up – by distilling the abstract ideas out of quantum theory and ecology, as Descartes distilled the abstract ideas out of Copernican astronomy and Galilean mechanics – and while we remodel, accordingly, such satellite areas of philosophy as ethics and political theory, we call this interlude "postmodernism," since all we know for sure is that modernism is dead (though not gone). Because we can't be quite sure yet what modernity's successor will turn out to be be, we remain cautious and wait for "organicism" or "systems theory" or some such label to take hold.

The other sense of postmodernism, following Jacques Derrida and Richard Rorty, is exclusively deconstructive – and essentially nihilistic.[51] For the constructive postmodernists the fractured present is an existentially distressing moment, but a moment of great creative intellectual opportunity – exhilarating, exciting, and stimulating. Deconstructive postmodernists, on the other hand, are content to deconstruct the old texts and declare that there will be no new master narratives, no new *Organons*, *Meditations*, or *Principia* to set the course for generations to come. We don't just need a *new* metaphysics, they seem to think, we need to get off the metaphysical treadmill altogether; we don't just need to reorganize our world *view* – to respond to and accommodate fundamental changes in natural philosophy – we need to see (oops, realize, rather) that a "view," a "vision" of any sort is a modernist hang-up.

Cheney's references to deep ecology's metaphysical pretensions and vision-constructing aspirations drip with contempt. "Why would it occur to one," Cheney writes, "that alienation is to be overcome by, of all things, metaphysics, by the empathetic internalization of a highly abstract, humanly constructed *vision* of wholeness, connectedness, and health."[52] It seems that like Ronald Reagan, who consigned "liberal" to the dictionary of dirty words, Cheney wants us to smirk at the deep ecologists' innocent description of their "vision."

Who knows whether future postmodern philosophy will be constructive or deconstructive. If deconstructivism is the wave of the future, however, then we should not call it "postmodernism," but "post-Western civilizationism," since metaphysics and comprehensive intellectual system building, with natural philosophy at the core, go way back in the Western tradition, considerably further back than the modern period.

Although the impetus to deconstructive postmodernism is largely political, its argumentative fulcrum is epistemological. We have given up on Truth (with a capital *T*). To mirror nature with the mind has been a common ambition of philosophers from Thales to Russell in the Western tradition. Past Western philosophers hoped to arrive at and guarantee the truth by inductive/empirical methods, or by deductive/rational methods, or by a judicious combination of the two. Through centuries of error, they kept the faith that we would eventually arrive at a conceptual model that would correspond, point for point, to Reality (with a capital *R*). That dream has become more elusive now than ever. Newton seemed at last to have grasped Reality by the tail and to have put a lock on Truth. But then along came Planck, Einstein, and finally Heisenberg. Uncertainty is now a cornerstone of foundational physics.

Grant skepticism the freest rein. Must we, therefore, accede to nihilism and relativism, as the deconstructive postmodernists seem to think? Not necessarily, I would argue. Though we may not hope to marry Truth to Reality, we may hope to find an intellectual construct that comprehends and systematizes more of our experience and does so more coherently than any other. That's exactly what Stone meant in *Trees*, I think, when he urged us not to make a final assault on Reality and Truth, but to seek a new "*myth*" – one "that can fit our growing body of knowledge."

But such an honest and reasonable compromise between old fashioned truth seeking and nihilism is politically suspect. According to Cheney, it represents a last ditch effort to "colonize" "other" points of view – though he wouldn't want to own the visual metaphor – for there is no one true view. Hence, everyone is entitled to his or her own myth, one that grows out of his or her own personal experience, however limited and uninformed it may be. We require a "politics of difference" in which truth (with a small *t*) is reached by "social negotiation," not "colonization."

To my knowledge none of the philosophical deep ecologists who are the targets of Cheney's attack has proposed conversion to Ecosophy T or Ecosophy S at sword point, as the colonizing Spanish spread Christianity; nor have they suggested that harmony with nature grows out of the barrel of a gun. It seems, rather, that they are guilty of assuming that people can agree about what is what – if they are willing to come up to speed on our growing body of knowledge and rationally think through how that knowledge may be integrated into a single coherent world view. They have put their best foot (or feet) forward with Ecosophy T and Ecosophy S and I think that they are willing to argue these ecosophies on their merits. Why must we resort to *negotiation* between intractable parties when hope of agreement remains? Why not listen to one another... and be open to *persuasion?*

Because, it seems clear from Cheney's paper, the ground rules for persuasion themselves are totalizing/colonizing. Our growing body of knowledge comes from science and "science has constructed itself in such a way that it has insulated itself from social negotiation."[53] Never mind that science is an international activity, the hallmark of which is the falsifiable hypothesis and the repeatable experiment. Cheney even considers it to be politically suspect to suggest making *reason* an arbiter of what is worth believing and what isn't – since reason may be a colonizing device of patriarchy.

Thus, in the new dark age of deconstructive *différence*, without even the minimum methodological agreements required for resolving differences of opinion by informed, reasoned argument, negotiation is our only recourse. Or is it? Mention of the Spanish Conquistadores' technique for securing consensus reminds us that a far more likely option for a *Realpolitik* of difference in a shattered and fragmented world is naked power – backed either by bullets or bucks. Why negotiate with someone with whom agreement is hopeless when you can have your own way – when the "other" can be bombed, terrorized, bought, pacified, or sweet-talked?

A Single Moral Philosophy Uniting Multiple Moral Communities

The moral pluralists' inability clearly to articulate a criterion for choosing among several inconsistent courses of action, indicated by several incommensurable moral theories, is not itself a terribly serious problem. (Monistic theories – Kant's notoriously, with its conflicting *categorical* duties – sometimes run aground on the same sorts of intractable practical contradictions.) Rather, in my opinion, it is a symptom of a deeper, more distressing malaise – the disengagement of ethics

from metaphysics and moral philosophy. Hargrove, for example, simply regards the recent emergence of environmental and animal welfare ethics to have proceeded from new "moral perceptions" – rather than from newly acquired cognitive lenses which have reorganized what our senses have perceived all along – as if suddenly we acquired keener senses for empirical moral properties.[54] The environment and animals have been around all along. That we now regard them as appropriate beneficiaries of ethics depends not on our recent perception of something in them that we didn't perceive before, but on our recent understanding of what and who they are in relation to what and who we are.

On the other hand, I completely agree with Stone, who is too kind to put it so flatly, that a monistic system like Paul Taylor's simply fails to integrate our many and genuinely diverse moral concerns. So how can we have our cake and eat it too? We must operate effectively within a multiplicity of moral spheres – family obligations, the duties associated with our professional lives, our public lives, our interspecies, and ecosystemic and biospheric relationships – each with its very different set of demands that often compete, one with another. At the same time we feel (or at least I feel) that we must maintain a coherent sense of self and world, a unified moral world view. Such unity enables us rationally to select among or balance out the contradictory or inconsistent demands made upon us when the multiple social circles in which we operate overlap and come into conflict. More importantly, a unified world view gives our lives purpose, direction, coherency, and sanity.

Stone's term *lexical*, which he uses when talking about setting priorities among the multiple moral spheres through which we move, not only connotes an alphabetical hierarchy, but also, ever so subtly, a hierarchy that has a principle in a home-base or root notion – for what "lexical (in contradistinction to *grammatical*) meaning" means is the base or root meaning of a word (in contradistinction to the multiple but clustered meanings of its grammatical forms and variations). In my view, the base or root moral concept – which may serve as a univocal "lexical" root, with a multiplicity of "grammatical" permutations – is what Aldo Leopold called "the community concept."[55] The version of the world or "myth" in which the community concept is embedded is provided by Charles Darwin's general evolutionary epic.

In *The Descent of Man* Darwin constructed a communitarian moral philosophy consistent with and embedded in the larger evolutionary world view outlined in *The Origin of Species*. It goes something like this: the proto-moral sentiments of affection and sympathy (upon which David Hume and Adam Smith erected their moral philosophies) were naturally selected in mammals as a device to ensure reproductive success. The mammal mother in whom these sentiments were strong more successfully reared her offspring to maturity. For those species in which larger and more complex social organization led to even greater reproductive success, the filial affections and sympathies spilled over to other family members – fathers, siblings, grandparents and grandchildren, uncles and aunts, nephews and nieces, cousins, and so on. Human beings evolved from highly social primates in a complex social matrix, and inherited highly refined and tender social sentiments and sympathies. With the acquisition of the power of speech and some capacity for abstraction, our ancestors began to codify the kinds of behavior concordant and discordant with their inherited communal-emotional bonds. They dubbed the former good and the latter evil. Ethics, thus, came into being.

As human gens began to merge to form tribes, and social organization and relationships grew more varied and complex, the circle of morally enfranchised persons expanded apace and ethical prescriptions and precepts grew more varied and complex in response to and as a reflection of the newer, more varied and complex social structures. Capping off his description of this process, Darwin writes,

As man advances in civilization, and small tribes are united into larger communities, the simplest reason would tell each individual that he ought to extend his social instincts and sympathies to all the members of the same nation, though personally unknown to him. This point being once reached there is only an artificial barrier to prevent his sympathies extending to the men of all nations and races. If, indeed, such men are separated from him by great differences of appearance and habits, experience unfortunately shews us how long it is, before we look at them as our fellow-creatures.[56]

Ontogeny recapitulates phylogeny in our social lives and moral institutions as well as in our phenotypic growth and development. The primitive family, clan, and tribal communities, which Darwin imagines to have gradually evolved, did not simply disappear upon their merger into larger and looser social wholes. They remained intact and became, rather, encircled by these larger communal spheres. Not only do we still retain the more ancient bonds, we feel them to be stronger than those of more recently evolved associations. Correspondingly, we feel the mores of the more venerable and intimate communities to be more binding.

Darwin himself anticipated the recent layering of the human–animal community orbit, and quite appropriately so, since it was he who first suggested that we conceptually reorganize contemporary animals as members of a wider community or kinship group i.e., as beings descended along parallel evolutionary lines from common ancestors. "Sympathy beyond the confines of man," he writes,

that is humanity to the lower animals, seems to be one of the latest moral acquisitions . . . . This virtue, one of the noblest with which man is endowed, seems to arise incidentally from our sympathies becoming more tender and widely diffused until they are extended to all sentient beings.[57]

Half a century later, Charles Elton added the most recent addition to the nested social circles to which we now regard ourselves to belong. Elton suggested that we conceive of ecological relationships as uniting plants, animals, soil, airs, waters, and so on into "biotic communities."[58] Leopold simply plugged Elton's community concept in ecology into Darwin's analysis of the origin and evolution of ethics, and articulated a land or environmental ethic.[59]

We have before us then the bare bones of a *univocal* ethical theory embedded in a coherent world view that provides, nevertheless, for a *multiplicity* of hierarchically ordered and variously "textured" moral relationships (and thus duties, responsibilities, and so on) each corresponding to and supporting our multiple, varied, and hierarchically ordered social relationships. If we accept it, we can then discard the competing and inconsistent metaphysics of morals – Kant's, Bentham's, and the lot – that make up the theoretical menagerie of moral pluralism and, in the last analysis, that only serve to obfuscate the actual basis of our multiple moral sensibilities, the interplay between them, and the lexical principle of their delicate arrangement.[60]

Borrowing an image that seems to have been original with Richard Sylvan and Val Plumwood, I suggest that we graphically represent the expansion of our moral sensibilities from narrower to wider circles, not as Peter Singer would have us represent it, like the expansion of the circumference of a ballon, but like the annular growth rings of a tree.[61] In such a figure the inner rings remain visible and present and the outer are added on, each more remote from the center, from the moral heartwood.[62]

The Hume–Darwin–Leopold line of social, humane, and environmental ethics – univocal in its world view and moral philosophy, but multiple in its moral domains – has not been widely endorsed or even critically debated as an alternative to moral pluralism. Because this community-centered complex is rooted in a theory of moral sentiments, it was confused with emotivism, after the ascendency of logical positivism, then associated with "rank relativism" (as Stone calls it), and finally went completely out of fashion in philosophy. Ethics grounded in a theory of moral sentiments emerged as a part of the romantic revolt against the apotheosis of reason in the Enlightenment and has recently survived primarily in the biological literature, having been established there by no less great a figure than Darwin. It has reemerged in contemporary sociobiology – which by itself makes such a theory a philosophical pariah.

I emphatically do not think that such a moral philosophy as I have here outlined – although it involves a multiplicity of overlapping and competing community entanglements – is pluralistic. It is not – because it involves one metaphysics of morals: one concept of the nature of morality (as rooted in moral sentiments), one concept of human nature (that we are social animals voyaging with fellow creatures in the odyssey of evolution), one moral psychology (that we respond in subtly shaded ways to the fellow members of our multiple, diverse, tiered communities and to those communities *per se*). Certainly, it does not suggest that we follow Kant here, Bentham and Mill there,

Singer and/or Regan yonder, and Leopold at the frontier. It posits a single coherent strand of moral thought: David Hume and Adam Smith set out its elements in the eighteenth century, Charles Darwin grounded them in an evolutionary account of human nature in the nineteenth, and Leopold (making moral hay of Elton's ecological paradigm) provided its outermost "accretion" in the twentieth.

Notes

1 Tom Regan, "The Nature and Possibility of an Environmental Ethic," *Environmental Ethics* 3 (1982): 19–34.

2 J. Baird Callicott, "Elements of an Environmental Ethic: Moral Considerability and the Biotic Community," *Environmental Ethics* 1 (1979): 71–81; and Holmes Rolston, III, "Is There an Ecological Ethic?," *Ethics* 85 (1975): 93–109.

3 Dave Foreman, editor of *Earth First!*, and associated environmental activists have been accused of going over the the top and recommending that we substitute an environmental ethic for a human social ethic. See George Bradford, "How Deep is Deep Ecology? A Challenge to Radical Environmentalism" *The Fifth Estate* 22 (Fall 1987): 3–33.

4 Christopher D. Stone, "Moral Pluralism and the Course of Environmental Ethics," *Environmental Ethics* 10 (1988): 139.

5 Ibid., p. 140.

6 In addition to Rolston's "Is There an Ecological Ethic?" notable seventies-generation papers "calling for" the development of primary or direct environmental ethics are Richard Routley (now Sylvan), "Is There a Need for a New, an Environmental Ethic?" in Bulgarian Organizing Committee, ed., *Proceedings of the Fifteenth World Congress of Philosophy* (Sophia: Sophia Press, 1973), pp. 205–10; and Kenneth E. Goodpaster, "From Egoism to Environmentalism," in K. E. Goodpaster and K. M. Sayre, eds., *Ethics and Problems of the 21st Century* (Notre Dame: University of Notre Dame Press, 1979), pp. 21–35.

7 For a representative sample see Robin Attfield, *The Ethics of Environmental Concern* (New York: Columbia University Press, 1983); Paul W. Taylor, *Respect for Nature: A Theory of Environmental Ethics* (Princeton: Princeton University Press, 1986); Holmes Rolston, III, *Philosophy Gone Wild: Essays in Environmental Ethics* (Buffalo: Prometheus Books, 1986), and *Environmental Ethics: Duties to and Values in the Natural World* (Philadelphia: Temple University Press, 1988); Eugene C. Hargrove, *Foundations of*

Environmental Ethics (Englewood Cliffs, N.J.: Prentice Hall 1989); and J. Baird Callicott, *In Defense of the Land Ethic: Essays in Environmental Philosophy* (Albany: State University of New York Press, 1989). Many of these full-dress theories of environmental ethics were first broached in the pages of this journal.

8 See Taylor, *Respect for Nature*; Robin Attfield is clearest about his position, I think, in "The Good of Trees," *Journal of Value Inquiry* 15 (1981): 35–54. Rolston's earlier work was theoretically promiscuous, in my opinion, but has, in *Environmental Ethics*, settled into a stable relationship with conativism. Contemporary conativism in environmental ethics is traceable to a loose remark made by Joel Feinberg in "The Rights of Animals and Unborn Generations," in William Blackstone, ed., *Philosophy and Environmental Crisis* (Athens: University of Georgia Press, 1974): "A mere thing . . . has no good of its own. The explanation of that fact, I suspect, consists in the fact that mere things have no conative life: no conscious wishes, desires, and hopes; or urges and impulses; or unconscious drives, aims, and goals; or latent tendencies, direction of growth, and natural fulfillments" (p. 49). The implication, clearly, is that a minimally conative life, absent conscious wishes, desires, hopes, urges, and impulses, but possessing latent tendencies, directions of growth, and natural fulfillments has a good of its own. Tom Regan toyed with the theoretical possibilities for environmental ethics, inadvertently provided by Feinberg, in "Feinberg on What Sorts of Beings Can Have Rights," *Southern Journal of Philosophy* 14 (1976): 485–98, but eventually gave up on conations as a sufficient condition for something having a good of its own in favor of conscious wishes, desires, hopes, urges, and impulses, summed up in his concept of "subject-of-a-life." Kenneth Goodpaster, next picked up on the idea in "On Being Morally Considerable," *Journal of Philosophy* 75 (1978): 306–25; however, after publishing one more paper in environmental philosophy, "From Egoism to Environmentalism" (in which conation plays no crucial role), Goodpaster defected from environmental ethics to business ethics and has not been heard from since. Paul Taylor brought Feinberg's offhanded remark to its full fruition – inventing, parallel to Regan's notion of a subject-of-a-life, the notion of a teleological-center-of-a-life – in "The Ethics of Respect for Nature," *Environmental Ethics* 3 (1981): 197–218 and then, more fully still, in his book, *Respect for Nature*.

9 See Albert Schweitzer, *Philosophy and Civilization*, trans. John Naish (London: A. & C. Black, 1923). The intellectual affinities between Schweitzer and an earlier generation of environmental conativists is developed in J. Baird Callicott, "Non-anthropocentric

Value Theory and Environmental Ethics," *American Philosophical Quarterly* 21 (1984): 299–309.

10 See J. Baird Callicott, *In Defense of the Land Ethic*; Edward O. Wilson, *Biophilia* (Cambridge: Harvard University Press, 1984); William Godfrey-Smith "The Rights of Non-humans and Intrinsic Values," and Richard and Val Routley, "Human Chauvinism and Environmental Ethics," both in D. Mannison, M. McRobbie, and R. Routley, eds., *Environmental Philosophy*, Monograph Series no. 2 (Canberra: Department of Philosophy, Australian National University, 1980), pp. 30–47 and 96–189, respectively.

11 See Arne Naess, "Self-Realization: An Ecological Approach to Being in the World," in John Seed, Joanna Macy, Pat Fleming, and Arne Naess, ·ed., *Thinking Like a Mountain: Towards a Council of All Beings* (Philadelphia: New Society Publishers, 1988); Warwick Fox, *Approaching Deep Ecology: A Response to Richard Sylvan's Critique of Deep Ecology*, Occasional Paper no. 20 (Hobart: University of Tasmania, 1986) and Freya Matthews, "Conservation and Self-Realization: A Deep Ecology Perspective," *Environmental Ethics* (1988): 347–55.

12 J. Baird Callicott, "Animal Liberation and Environmental Ethics: Back Together Again," *Between the Species* 4 (1988): 163–9.

13 *Texture* is one of the many quasi-technical terms in Stone's wonderfully rich and creative book. I hope that I have used it correctly here.

14 See J. Baird Callicott, "The Search for an Environmental Ethic," in Tom Regan, ed., *Matters of Life and Death*, 2nd edn. (New York: Random House, 1986); and "The Conceptual Foundations of the Land Ethic," in J. Baird Callicott, ed., *Companion to A Sand County Almanac: Interpretive and Critical Essays* (Madison: University of Wisconsin Press, 1987), pp. 186–217.

15 Stone, *Earth and Other Ethics*, p. 118.

16 Mary Anne Warren, "The Rights of the Nonhuman World," in Robert Elliot and Aaran Gare, ed., *Environmental Philosophy: A Collection of Readings* (University Park: The Pennsylvania State University Press, 1983), pp. 130–1.

17 Eugene C. Hargrove, "The Role of Rules in Ethical Decision Making," *Inquiry* 28 (1985): 30.

18 Ibid., p. 22.

19 Andrew Brennan, *Thinking About Nature: An Investigation of Nature, Value, and Ecology* (Athens: The University of Georgia Press, 1988); Peter S. Wenz, *Environmental Justice* (Albany: State University of New York Press, 1988).

20 Brennan, *Thinking About Nature*, p. 186.

21 In the introduction to *Environmental Justice*, Wenz tells how as a boy he and his friend Billy used to divide a pizza. One cut it in half and the other chose first. Wenz often returns to this childhood image of

J. Baird Callicott

distributive justice throughout his discussion. For Wenz, the environment is a big pizza. The ethical question is how to divide it equitably among human consumers. Rolston notices this feature of Wenz's discussion in his review of *Environmental Justice* in *Between the Species* 5 (1989): 147–53.

22 Wenz, *Environmental Justice*, p. 310. Wenz is aware that the phrase "pluralistic theory" may seem an oxymoron to many philosophers.

23 G. E. Varner's review of Christopher D. Stone, *Earth and Other Ethics*, in *Environmental Ethics* 10 (1983): 264.

24 Ibid.

25 Taylor, *Respect for Nature*, p. 260.

26 See Bryan Norton's review of Paul Taylor, *Respect for Nature*, in *Environmental Ethics* 9 (1987): 261–7.

27 Taylor, *Respect for Nature*, p. 259.

28 Ibid., chap. 6.

29 Wenz, *Environmental Justice*, chap. 13. The quotations are from Stone, *Earth and Other Ethics*, p. 117.

30 Rolston, *Environmental Ethics*, p. 143.

31 Ibid., p. 101.

32 Ibid., chap. 6.

33 Wenz, *Environmental Justice*, p. 313.

34 Hargrove, "The Role of Rules," p. 26.

35 Christopher D. Stone, "Should Trees Have Standing? – Towards Legal Rights for Natural Objects," *Southern California Law Review* 45 (1972): 450–501.

36 Stone, *Earth and Other Ethics*, p. 10.

37 Ibid., p. 42.

38 Regan endorses "considered" or "reflective" intuition in *The Case for Animal Rights*. Taylor, the consummate neo-classical monist spurns them in *Respect for Nature*, on the grounds that we should always follow the dictates of principle, whether they conform to our intuitions or not.

39 Wenz, *Environmental Justice*, p. 314; Eugene C. Hargrove, personal communication.

40 Stone, *Earth and Other Ethics*, p. 256.

41 Ibid.

42 Stone writes that "we are removed to another jurisdiction in which our minds operate less by appeals to consistency than provocations of irony and humor. Here the dynamic involves the demonstration of buried contradictions in our lives, rather than of inconsistency among our ideas. Emotion has a more legitimate rein (or reign); suppressed feeling and insight are released and mobilized....[we] are less under the sway of the stuff we academics do than of literature, folk songs, war, art, landscape, and poetry.... Poetry and literature, obviously, are high forms of intellect; but rather than to derive 'truths,' they make them manifest" (*Earth and Other Ethics*, p. 256).

43 Ibid.

44 Jeremy Bentham, *An Introduction to the Principles of Morals and Legislation* (Oxford: The Clarendon Press, 1823), chap. 1, sec. 4.

45 Stone writes, "No simple formula about truth is available when we ascend to the level of selecting a version of the world for scientific purposes, that is in deciding whether and in what form to posit matter, space, energy, time, and their relationships" (*Earth and Other Ethics*, p. 256).

46 Christopher D. Stone, *Should Trees Have Standing?: Toward Legal Rights for Natural Objects* (Los Altos, Calif.: William Kaufmann, 1974), pp. 51–2. Notice the rhetorical allusion in the first sentence to Bentham's famous remark, quoted *ad nauseum* in the animal welfare literature: "The day may come when the rest of the animal creation may acquire those rights...." Stone was writing in the early 1970s before the phrase "animal liberation" had been coined by Peter Singer and before women's liberation had made a reference to a "man's brain" and "his lungs" appear gender-biased.

47 Jim Cheney, "Postmodern Environmental Ethics: Ethics as Bioregional Narrative," *Environmental Ethics* 11 (1989): 117–34; and "The Neo-Stoicism of Radical Environmentalism," *Environmental Ethics* 11 (1989): 293–325.

48 Cheney, "Neo-Stoicism," p. 310. The neologism, *totalizing*, seems to be a hybrid intended to evoke the political ogre of totalitarianism in the vocabulary of a Valley Girl, as in, "I was *totally* totalized."

49 Ibid. p. 302.

50 See Frederick Ferré, "Toward a Postmodern Science and Technology," in David Ray Griffin, ed., *Spirituality and Society: Postmodern Visions* (Albany: State University of New York Press, 1988). David Ray Griffin has established a Center for a Postmodern World in Santa Barbara, California to further postmodernism of this "constructive" sort and edits a series for SUNY Press called "Constructive Postmodern Thought."

51 See Jacques Derrida, *Positions*, trans. Alan Bass (Chicago: University of Chicago Press, 1981); and Richard Rorty, *Philosophy and the Mirror of Nature* (Princeton: Princeton University Press, 1979).

52 Cheney, "Neo-Stoicism," p. 301; emphasis in original.

53 Ibid., p. 308.

54 Hargrove, "The Role of Rules."

55 Aldo Leopold, *A Sand County Almanac* (New York: Oxford University Press, 1949).

56 Charles Darwin, *The Descent of Man and Selection in Relation to Sex* (New York: J. A. Hill and Company, 1904), p. 124.

57 Darwin, *Descent*, p. 124.

58 Charles Elton, *Animal Ecology* (New York: Macmillan, 1927).

59 See Aldo Leopold, *Sand County Almanac*; and Callicott, "The Conceptual Foundations of the Land Ethic."

60 I have more fully expounded this theory in *In Defense of the Land Ethic*.

61 See Peter Singer, *The Expanding Circle: Ethics and Sociology* (New York: Farrar, Straus, and Giroux, 1982).

62 See Richard and Val Routley, "Human Chauvinism and Environmental Ethics."

17

Minimal, Moderate, and Extreme Moral Pluralism

Peter S. Wenz

I Introduction

It is no surprise that moral pluralism is discussed in environmental ethics, for such ethics concerns human beings, animals of various sorts, species, ecosystems, wilderness areas, and evolutionary and ecological processes. Some philosophers have maintained that no single ethic can encompass this variety, and have, therefore, advocated moral pluralism. Although moral pluralism is usually referred to as if it is a single position, there are actually three different kinds of views that have been discussed by environmental ethicists as being pluralistic without the differences among them being recognized. To dispel this confusion, I distinguish between minimal, moderate, and extreme forms of moral pluralism and defend moderate moral pluralism against its chief critic, J. Baird Callicott.[1]

In section II, I examine minimal moral pluralism, using as its exemplar a general characterization of moral pluralism given by Christopher Stone in *Earth and Other Ethics: The Case for Moral Pluralism*.[2] I reject this characterization as unhelpful because, contrary to its author's probable intentions, it makes all moral theories pluralistic. In section III, I draw from Stone's work a definition of what I call extreme moral pluralism, and reject it on grounds given by Callicott.[3] In section IV, I argue that the source of Stone's error is a faulty analogy between compartmentalization in the sciences, social sciences, and arts, on one hand, and one's moral life, on the other. In section V, I discuss moderate

pluralism, which I have endorsed in *Environmental Justice*.[4] Such pluralism, I argue, is reasonable and free of the defects that justify rejecting extreme pluralism. Finally, in section VI, I show that Callicott, who believes himself to be rejecting all moral pluralism, actually incorporates moderate pluralism in his version of the land ethic. In doing so, I distinguish my position concerning Callicott's pluralism from Gary E. Varner's as yet unsubstantiated contention that the *foundations* of Callicott's theory are pluralistic.[5]

II Minimal Moral Pluralism

Stone defines pluralistic theories by contrasting them with monistic theories. At one point he writes that a monistic theory, unlike pluralistic theories, contains "a single coherent set of principles capable of governing all moral quandaries" and yielding "for each quandary one right answer."[6] Pluralistic theories, by contrast, do not provide a single right answer to every moral question. Callicott seems initially to interpret Stone as holding that, as a practical matter, monistic theories provide ordinary moral agents with unique and specific prescriptions in every situation involving moral choice, while pluralistic theories do not. In other words, monistic theories, unlike pluralistic theories, provide algorithms that people can as a practical matter use to determine their duty in any situation. Although I am not particularly comfortable with this use of terms, I follow this usage here because I am joining a discussion in which the terms are already so defined. To avoid confusion, however, I call this form of pluralism "minimal moral pluralism" because the requirements for being pluralistic are minimal. For a theory to be pluralistic in this sense, it is sufficient that the theory merely lack a universal algorithmic decision procedure.

In the present section, I discuss Callicott's two objections to minimal pluralism, and then show that these objections are misplaced. I argue that all known moral theories are pluralistic in this minimal sense. As a result, if such pluralism is objectionable, it is the state of human moral knowledge in general that is to blame, not Stone's or any other particular moral theory. In short, when pluralism is defined in this way, as minimal pluralism, there are no monistic theories with which it can be contrasted at all, much less invidiously.

Callicott objects, first, that in many situations a pluralistic theory does not provide practical guidance to ordinary people. This objection arises directly out of Stone's characterization of what I have called minimal pluralism. The lack of specific guidance troubles Callicott. He cites an example given by Stone in which considerations related to animal welfare suggest that an animal stuck in the ice in the Yellowstone River be rescued, while considerations related to ecocentric environmental ethics suggest that the animal be allowed to suffer and perish to preserve the normal routine of natural processes. Stone's pluralistic theory, like my own, places value on both the avoidance of animal suffering and on the preservation of natural balances in wilderness areas. In the situation described, these values suggest different, conflicting courses of action. Since Stone supplies no master rule to determine how to resolve such conflicts, Callicott objects that Stone "never tells us what . . . people ought to have done or not done for the animal."[7] The objection is that pluralistic theories fail to supply a single correct answer to such moral queries. The implication is that monistic theories do not suffer from this defect, that, presumably, they do not, as a practical matter, leave ordinary people in doubt about what they ought to do.

Callicott's second objection is a corollary of the first. Because pluralistic theories do not tell people unambiguously what to do, such theories "might provide a sophisticated scoundrel with a bag of tricks to rationalize his or her convenience or self interest. . . ."[8] Presumably, again, monistic theor-

ies are free of this defect. However, they can be in this favored position only if, unlike pluralistic theories, they supply such unambiguous answers to all moral quandaries as to leave scoundrels no room to rationalize immoral behavior.

Note that the problem Callicott identifies persists in a theory that provides unity at a *theoretical* level, but not at the *practical* level. If the failure to provide unambiguous prescriptions risks self-serving rationalizations, as Callicott maintains, a theory can overcome this defect only by supplying to ordinary people unambiguous, practical prescriptions in all situations where moral choices must be made.

A moment's reflection suggests, however, that no theory is monistic in this sense. Consider two prominent theories that are often presented as monistic, utilitarianism and Kantianism. Although utilitarianism is often, though not invariably, presented as a monistic theory, R. M. Hare, a major proponent of what he considers a monistic form of utilitarianism, does not consider his theory monistic in the sense required by Callicott. First, even if utilitarian calculations could, at least sometimes, be performed (a matter of some debate that need not detain us here), there is the possibility that two or more courses of action could be calculated to produce the same, maximum utility in a given situation. In such cases, Hare's utilitarianism fails to prescribe a unique course of action and so becomes minimally pluralistic.

More importantly, Hare has little faith in people's direct recourse to utilitarianism's single, master principle. Such recourse is too complex for most people most of the time, for, according to Hare, only an archangel can reliably calculate utility. When the rest of us try, "we may easily, being human, 'cook' our moral thinking to suit our own interest."[9] Thus, even Hare, who thinks that in principle utilitarianism supplies one right answer to all moral quandaries, does not think this one right answer is available in practice to most human beings most of the time. As a result, his act utilitarianism is not monistic according to the stipulations of Stone and Callicott, who require of monistic theories that they supply to ordinary people definite, practical advice in all circumstances. On the definition given above, Hare's utilitarianism is at least minimally pluralistic.

Rule utilitarianism is no improvement on the utilitarianism just considered. Moral dilemmas are created when two rules apply to the same situation and indicate different, incompatible courses of action. Direct utilitarian calculations are, however, necessary to decide which action is obligatory. But, as we have just seen, people are, at least sometimes, incapable of accurately performing such calculations. Thus, until reasons are given to suppose that this incapacity never afflicts rule utilitarians confronted with conflicting rules, Stone and Callicott have to deny that rule utilitarianism is monistic, for their definition of monism requires that monistic theories always supply unambiguous advice to ordinary people.

Kantianism is another theory, often considered to be monistic, that fails always to supply unambiguous moral guidance. Thus, it too cannot be considered monistic by Stone and Callicott. A classic case concerns lying. Kant condemned all lies as violating the categorical imperative.[10] Others, however, considering Kant's own example of a lie told to save the life of an innocent third party, think a lie would be justified, and perhaps obligatory in such a case.[11] There is, of course, disagreement here about limits and exceptions to the general condemnation of lying. Disagreement can exist also concerning the propriety of a lie to conceal how one voted in an election by secret ballot. Which is more important, the rule against lying, or the principle supporting the privacy of electoral behavior? Moreover, what if the lie in question is told to a spouse? Reasonable people may disagree about the relative importance of rules protecting electoral versus marital integrity. Lying may be controversial also when the lie serves to cover up betrayal of an agreement to vote in a certain way. Reasonable people can differ about the relative importance of rules protecting electoral integrity and those against lying and against covering up betrayal. With cases like these in mind, it seems safe to say that, absent a clear demonstration to the contrary, the merits of competing rules, generalizations, and maxims cannot be weighed so accurately as to permit algorithmic solutions to all moral controversies. Indeed, I am unaware of any rule deontologist who even claims to have a universally applicable algorithm for settling moral disagreements. Thus, Kantianism, in particular, and rule deontological approaches to ethics, in general, do not appear better than utilitarianism at providing practical, definite moral directives to ordinary people in all situations.

Aristotelian approaches to ethics have, of course, always denied that "moral understanding lends itself to scientific systematization. . . ." According to Aristotle and his followers, "ethics deals with a multitude of particular concrete situations, which are themselves so variable that they resist all attempts to generalize about them in universal terms."[12]

In sum, it seems that all moral theories are pluralistic in the minimal sense that they fail always to inform ordinary people through the application of a practically available algorithmic procedure of a uniquely correct action. While it is important that we recognize this point, doing so gives us no reason to prefer any moral theory over its rival, and certainly not monistic over pluralistic theories, as there are no monistic theories to prefer to those that are minimally pluralistic. Curiously, after predicating two arguments on the assumption of a contrast that has no application, Callicott himself seems to recognize the contrast's inapplicability.[13]

III The Rejection of Extreme Moral Pluralism

Stone also employs a more robust notion of pluralism that does not render all theories pluralistic. I call this kind "extreme pluralism." I now discuss this type of pluralism and second Callicott's reasons for rejecting it.

Extreme pluralism is characterized by alternations among several ethical theories. Although each such theory is accepted in its entirety, the range of application of each is limited. The extreme pluralist adopts different ethical theories for different contexts, and/or for different general subjects, of application. Stone writes that

> . . . a senator, for example, might rightly embrace utilitarianism when it comes to legislating a general rule for social conduct (say, in deciding what sort of toxic waste program to establish). Yet this same representative need not be principally utilitarian, nor even a consequentialist of any style, in arranging his personal affairs among kin or friends, or deciding whether it is right to poke out the eyes of pigeons.[14]

Stone suggests here that a senator might be a thorough utilitarian when choosing among legislative proposals, but a Kantian in his or her relationships with family and friends, and a Leopoldian land ethicist when wilderness areas are at issue.

Callicott rejects the idea that a sane individual could reasonably alternate among three such different ethical theories. "Utilitarianism assumes a radical individualism," according to which "the community is a fictitious body," whereas the land ethic takes the community to be the fundamental unit within which individuals are organically and internally related. "To adopt Kant's moral theory is to buy into a . . . philosophy of human nature in which Reason (with a capital R) constitutes the essence of 'man,'" and all nonhumans are mere things.[16] The Kantian rejects the utilitarian concern for pleasures, pains, and preference satisfactions among human beings and other animals, and the land ethic's concern for biotic communities, wilderness areas and endangered species. Callicott finds unreasonable an individual's alternations among such different views about the nature of human life and its place in the cosmos.

> Moral pluralism, in short, implies metaphysical musical chairs. I think, however, that we human beings deeply need and mightily strive for consistency, coherence, and closure in our personal and shared outlook on the world and on ourselves in relation to the world and to one another.[17]

I do not know if Stone meant to endorse "metaphysical musical chairs," but his statements do lend themselves to Callicott's interpretation. Whatever Stone's particular views, however, Callicott argues powerfully against any version of moral pluralism that requires alternations among radically different metaphysical perspectives. I join Callicott in his rejection of it.

IV   The Source of Stone's Error

While Callicott accurately identifies the weakness of extreme pluralism, he does not explain the source of Stone's error. I do so here. Stone's view results from combining a keen observation with a mistaken analogy. The keen observation is that philosophers often seek more unity than is reasonable. The mistaken analogy is between scientific and social scientific discourse, on the one hand, and moral judgments, on the other. Stone assumes that compartmentalization in morality is justified by analogy with compartmentalization in science and social science.

Philosophers tend to claim that what appears to be many is really just one thing. Some pre-Socratic Milesian philosophers declared the world to be composed of a single substance. More recently, philosophers resigned to a plurality of physical elements and subatomic particles have sought unity in reductionism. Early in this century, it was still claimed that, in principle, all natural science can be explained in terms of physics, and all social sciences in terms of natural science. Sociobiology is a current example of reductionist thinking. In the hands of Richard Dawkins, the driving force behind evolution is simply the tendency of genes to replicate.[18]

In ethics, as we have already seen, some philosophers have found the single criterion for moral behavior in the greatest happiness principle, others in the categorical imperative. In political philosophy, some philosophers have found a single basis for political obligation in the principle of maximum individual liberty, others in the social contract, and still others in the sovereign's access to overwhelming coercive force.

Reductionists in science have generally retreated, as they should, in response to the existence and behavior of emergent properties. Properties exist at the level of material organization studied in chemistry and biology that do not exist at the level studied in physics. For example, although there are no colors among subatomic particles, there are among chemicals. Subatomic particles do not grow or reproduce as biological organisms do. Most importantly, changes in these emergent aspects of reality cannot be explained as functions of changes in the properties studied by physicists. Moreover, aspects of social groups, such as mutual loyalty and social hierarchies, cannot be explained by purely physical variables.

Stone is apparently so impressed by the failure of reductionist projects in the sciences and social sciences that he largely predicates his case for moral pluralism upon it. In a chapter entitled "Foundations for Moral Pluralism," he writes, "Pluralism conceives the realm of morals to be partitioned into several planes. The planes are intellectual frameworks. . . ."[19] He compares these to the distinct planes of geometry and arithmetic,[20] of mathematics and poetry,[21] and of chemistry and art criticism.[22] He is explicit in a later article that his moral pluralism is inspired by the inability of investigators to "unify . . . the laws that govern the movement of subatomic particles with those that govern social conduct."[23] In his book, he reasons that "just as the rules of solid geometry are not the rules of arithmetic, so the rules that govern our relations with animals are not the same rules that govern the relations among corporate bodies."[24] Similarly, different rules govern our friend dilemmas and our stranger dilemmas,[25] as well as the personal and professional responsibilities of senators.[26]

Stone's analogy is fatally flawed. He compares differences among the sciences, social sciences, and arts, on the one hand, to differences among domains of ethical application, on the other. The crucial disanalogy rests on the fact that moral judgments about conduct are ideally made only after all relevant matters have been considered. Doing so restricts the propriety of compartmentalization, since one is expected to take ethical considerations into account wherever, and in whatever combinations, they appear.

Assume for a moment, as Stone does, that in addition to utilitarian and Kantian obligations concerning human beings, people have obligations to avoid unnecessary cruelty to animals and to promote the preservation of wilderness areas and species diversity. In accordance with these assumptions, which are common enough among environmental philosophers, a legislator cannot be simply a utilitarian, as Stone maintains, when acting in his or her professional capacity. If legislation under consideration concerns, for example, granting permission to the U.S. Forest Service to allow clear-cutting in national forests, considerations related to wilderness preservation and species diversity are relevant. From the moral point of view, they must be considered, notwithstanding the forum in which they arose. The senator cannot employ utilitarianism in his or her professional capacity to the exclusion of other ethical considerations without risking immoral behavior. Similarly, while, as an environmentalist, I am interested in promoting the preservation of wilderness areas, as a parent I risk immoral behavior unless I consider my work on behalf of the environment in light of my parental obligations.

More generally, moral behavior requires a disposition to be responsive simultaneously to all of one's roles and commitments. This moral requirement follows from the fact that moral judgments are properly made *all things considered*. Whenever and wherever a factor of moral relevance arises, it must be considered, even though it may not appear prima facie to be the dominant factor.

Unlike moral judgments, however, judgments within certain disciplines can be isolated from judgments within other disciplines. Stone correctly notes, for example, that "the rules of solid geometry are not the rules of arithmetic...."[27] To the extent that the rules are different, one can legitimately ignore completely the rules of one while reasoning in the other domain. Stone writes also, "What makes a statement of chemistry true is not what makes true the verdict of an art critic."[28] Again, he is correct. Judgments in these areas can be compartmentalized and isolated. As we have seen, however, different areas of the moral life cannot similarly be isolated from one another.

Stone seems to have been misled by his failure to perceive that disciplinary compartmentalization in the sciences, social sciences, and arts does not imply similar compartmentalization in morality. The difference is between acceptable specialization and unacceptable incoherence. In sum, Callicott's criticisms of what I call extreme moral pluralism are justified. Such pluralism is built on a faulty analogy and invites inconsistency and incoherence where consistency and reason are needed most – in our moral lives.

V Moderate Moral Pluralism

Moderate moral pluralism, the view endorsed in this paper, avoids the defects of extreme pluralism. First, moderate pluralism does not involve alternations among different ethical theories, for it is itself a single ethical theory. It is pluralistic only in the sense that it "contains a variety of *independent* principles, principles that cannot all be reduced to or derived from a single master principle."[29] Whereas extreme pluralism involves a plurality of theories, moderate pluralism includes only a plurality of principles (in a *single* theory).

Second, moderate pluralism does not compartmentalize the moral life. Because the moderate pluralist confronts all situations with the same ethical theory, he or she can entertain in any situation the full range of relevant principles. For example, a senator can, and should, give some weight to the principle that promises should be kept (all other things being equal) whenever and wherever he or she has the opportunity to keep or break a promise. Subject matter, forum, and role do not affect this general principle. All other things being equal, promises should be kept concerning presents for children, pledges to the Environmental Defense Fund, and agreements to vote for minimum wage legislation. They should be kept on the floor of the Senate, in the living room and on camping trips. They should be kept by parents, teachers, and senators. The same is true of other principles, i.e., that unnecessary pain is to be avoided, that persuasion is preferable to coercion, and that wilderness areas should be preserved. Each is to be considered whenever it is applicable. Since the individual meets all situations with the same set of moral principles, his or her ethical life is coherent.

The weight accorded a principle sometimes varies with context. When I am asked to join a toast to salute the beauty of a bride, for example, the principle of honesty is outweighed by the principle of consideration for people's feelings. However, when evaluating a student's work, honesty takes precedence. Some hurt feelings are acceptable if they unavoidably accompany honest communication. Similarly, a defense lawyer may place a higher priority on promoting general human welfare when soliciting for United Way than when defending a client. Having agreed to defend the client, he or she must do so even when believing that a conviction would better serve general human welfare.

Adjustment of priorities to specific context does not require renouncing in some contexts principles that are considered of singular importance in others. Nor does it involve "metaphysical musical chairs." The individual remains prepared in all contexts to apply the full range of relevant moral principles. Thus, the lawyer defending an unsavory client may withdraw from the case if defending that client conflicts too strongly with his or her principle that human welfare should be fostered.

Coherent thinking is not jeopardized by responsiveness to more than one consideration at a time. Rather, such responsiveness is a common aspect of human life. For example, while making dinner I can choose ingredients, in part, for their nutritional value and, in part, because they are perishable and getting spoiled. I can choose to cook the potatoes (one of those ingredients) in the microwave to save electricity, at some sacrifice to my pleasure (crisp potato crusts). I can at the same time listen for my wife's call on the telephone (telling me when she will arrive home), and monitor the play of neighbor children on our old swing set. My thinking is not made incoherent because

I am sensitive simultaneously to several considerations, to considerations of several different types, and to considerations that suggest incompatible courses of action (saving electricity versus enjoying crisp potato crusts). Such thinking is simply normal.

Harold I. Brown argues, convincingly, I believe, in *Rationality* that most thinking that we consider rational is of this nature.[30] Eugene C. Hargrove argues, equally convincingly, that we should "abandon for the most part the search for a rational set of universal principles which moral agents can mechanically follow," because most rational thinking does not involve the mechanical application of rules.[31] Moderately pluralistic moral theories are not made incoherent by their simultaneous application of several moral principles to a given moral quandary. The failure to provide algorithmic decision procedures in these situations merely means that moderately pluralistic theories are also minimally pluralistic. This fact is not surprising, since, as I argued in section two above, all moral theories are at least minimally pluralistic. Such pluralism can be equated with incoherence only by imposing an unusually demanding standard for coherence. Since this standard is new, and would label "incoherent" much of what we presently consider rational, it is up to those who want to impose it to argue for its adoption.

VI The Land Ethic as Moderately Pluralistic

The theory of environmental ethics that Callicott explains in "The Conceptual Foundations of the Land Ethic"[32] and "The Search for an Environmental Ethic"[33] is pluralistic in the same way and to the same degree as the concentric circle theory that I offer in *Environmental Justice*. Callicott maintains that the land ethic adds environmental duties to our other obligations. It does not displace or override those other obligations.[34] We retain all familiar obligations toward family, friends, country, and humanity in general. What is more, "Family obligations in general come before nationalistic duties and humanitarian obligations in general come before environmental duties," because, "as a general rule, the duties correlative to the inner social circles to which we belong eclipse those correlative to the rings farther from the heartwood."[35]

Peter S. Wenz

Since environmental obligations are farthest from the heartwood, one may think that their demands are always overridden by whatever demands may exist in a more interior social–ethical circle. However, this approach is not Callicott's position at all, for it would constitute abandoning the land ethic altogether in favor of the culture's predominant anthropocentrism. Callicott maintains, instead:

> The land ethic may ... as with any new accretion, demand choices which affect, in turn, the demands of the more interior social-ethical circles. Taxes and the military draft may conflict with family-level obligations. While the land ethic certainly does not cancel human morality, neither does it leave it unaffected.[36]

This remark accords with Callicott's statement elsewhere that

> [J]ust as it is not unreasonable for one to suppose that he or she has *some* obligation and should make *some* sacrifice for the "wretched of the earth," so it is not unreasonable to suppose that the human community should assume *some* obligation and make *some* sacrifice for the beleaguered and abused biotic community.[37]

I agree with this position completely. My obligations toward my daughters are among the strongest that I have. It would certainly be wrong to sacrifice a daughter's life to save a bear. Nevertheless, it makes perfect sense to curtail her snowmobiling to protect a wilderness area. The strength of an obligation varies not only with one's relationship to its object, but also with the nature of the object's claim. The claim to protection of one's life is much stronger than the claim to enjoy a preferred pattern of recreation. It is for this reason that there often are, for example, restrictions on the display of fireworks. Although some people prefer firework displays in their backyards, such displays endanger the lives of others, and human lives are (usually) more important than preferred enjoyments. The importance of the protection of wilderness areas, which is of moral concern in the land ethic, may generally be placed in between the protection of individual human lives, which is more important, and the accommodation of people's preferred patterns of recreation, which is less important. Thus, reverting to the example

of my daughter, preserving her life can override environmental considerations which, in turn, override her increased satisfaction in winter recreation.

I assume that the foregoing fairly reflects Callicott's general approach to these matters. If so, he is clearly a moderate pluralist. He has many moral principles, and they are not all derived from a single, master principle. Some moral principles concern which relationships are more important than which others, i.e., parenthood more than friendship, friendship more than citizenship, etc. Other principles concern the relative values attached to different kinds of outcomes, e.g., death is generally worse than dissatisfaction, at least where human beings are concerned. Still other principles are used to identify when the normal priorities do not apply, i.e., when citizen obligations override familial duties and the value of life so as to justify going to war. Callicott neither presents, nor claims to possess, any master rule or principle from which one can deduce uniquely correct moral conduct in situations of moral conflict. Indeed, he writes, "How obligations ... may be weighed and compared is admittedly uncertain ...."[38] Nor does he claim that the many principles he employs can be derived from any *action-guiding*, universal master rule or master principle. Thus, *at the level of action-guiding norms*, Callicott's version of the land ethic is both minimally and moderately pluralistic. It "contains a variety of *independent* principles ... that cannot all be reduced to or derived from a single master principle."[39]

To avoid confusion, this demonstration of the pluralism in Callicott's version of the land ethic should be distinguished from the argument offered by Gary Varner. Varner defines "a pluralistic theory" as "one which acknowledges distinct, theoretically incommensurable bases for direct moral consideration."[40] He argues that Callicott's theory must be pluralistic because Callicott considers both people and biotic communities to be directly morally considerable. However, if biotic communities are directly morally considerable, "it must be for very different reasons than is usually given for saying that individual human beings are directly morally considerable ...."[41] Thus, Varner concludes, if pluralism exists wherever there are "theoretically incommensurable bases for direct moral consideration," Callicott's theory must be pluralistic.

I have three comments about Varner's contribution. First, Varner's principal argument is at best inconclusive as it stands. Callicott considers both people and biotic communities to be directly morally considerable. His theory is pluralistic in terms of Varner's understanding of pluralism only if the bases Callicott uses for these and other such judgments are incommensurable. Varner, however, does not tell us what basis *Callicott* gives for maintaining that people are directly morally considerable. Varner merely refers to reasons that are *usually* given for maintaining that people are directly morally considerable. Whatever these usual reasons are, they may or may not be Callicott's. Thus, Varner cannot claim to have shown that Callicott's basis for maintaining that people are directly morally considerable is incommensurable with Callicott's basis for according direct moral consideration to biotic communities. As a result, in terms of Varner's definition of moral pluralism, Callicott may or may not be a pluralist.

Second, Varner's argument addresses the *foundations* of Callicott's version of the land ethic. In this respect, it differs from the subject matter of the present paper, which concerns pluralism at the level of normative principles.

Finally, Varner may be suggesting that normative pluralism inevitably involves pluralism at the foundational, or metaphysical, level. Such a position would involve the claim that moderate pluralism presupposes extreme pluralism, and so shares the defects of extreme pluralism. This claim is a generalization of Varner's claim that Callicott's moderate pluralism lacks a unitary foundation. Nevertheless, there is no *a priori* reason to accept this view. W. D. Ross's position in *The Right and the Good* is moderately, but not extremely (i.e., metaphysically), pluralistic.[42] Several independent moral principles coexist within a single metaphysical vision. A controversial, and in my view ultimately unacceptable, foundationalist epistemology ties it all together. One cannot rule out *a priori* a more acceptable epistemology attaching the land ethic's moderate moral pluralism to a unitary metaphysical vision. This possibility, however, is a matter for future consideration.

fines his pluralism in this minimal way, Callicott's arguments against Stone's position founder because the contrast with monistic theories that Callicott relies upon is vacuous.

A question worth exploring is whether those minimally pluralistic theories that claim to be monistic at a deeper (theoretical) level, such as some forms of utilitarianism and Kantianism, are monistic in any meaningful sense at all. It may be that any single, master principle featured in such a theory is more symbolic than operative, like a corporate chairman of the board who is merely a figurehead. This situation would exist if and when there were no reasonably reliable method of using the master principle either (a) to generate the mid-level principles that the theory employs, or (b) to justify reliance upon, or preference for, one such mid-level principle over others in cases of practical conflicts among them. In such cases, the putatively monistic theories in question would, in effect, be at least moderately, as well as minimally, pluralistic. Since the master principle would not meaningfully authorize mid-level principles, nor meaningfully adjudicate among them, the mid-level principles would be independent of one another as in a moderately pluralistic theory. I leave to another occasion arguments that putatively monistic (minimally pluralistic) theories are actually moderately pluralistic.

I conclude also that extremely pluralistic theories, including Stone's, are properly criticized by Callicott as lacking the unity and integrity necessary for a coherent moral life.

I conclude, finally, that there is a significant conceptual distinction between moderate and extreme pluralism that allows the former to avoid charges of incoherence that are properly leveled at the latter. There is no *a priori* reason why moderate pluralism cannot coexist with unity at the metaphysical, foundational level. Thus, in the absence of additional argument, there is no reason why the moderate pluralism of Callicott's land ethic should be considered incoherent, as if it were an extremely pluralistic theory like Stone's.

VII.   Conclusion

I conclude, first of all, that all known moral theories are at least minimally pluralistic, as none provides algorithms for the solution of each and every moral quandary that may arise. When Stone de-

Notes

1   Outside of the contexts of environmental philosophy, the term *moral pluralism* and similar terms have been associated with several topics and views. In Michael Walzer, *Spheres of Justice: A Defense of Pluralism and*

Equality (New York: Basic Books, 1983), it stands for the view that different principles of distributive justice are appropriate in different contexts. To the extent that this view resembles the extreme pluralism of Christopher Stone, discussed and criticized below, it is susceptible of the same critique. However, because Walzer's view is more subtle than Stone's, criticisms of the latter cannot be transferred automatically to the former. The term *pluralist lexical consequentialist* is used in Samuel Scheffler, *The Rejection of Consequentialism* (Oxford: Clarendon Press, 1982), pp. 27–8, to refer to the idea that there is a plurality of basic goods that are not commensurable. This position somewhat resembles the moderate pluralism that I endorse. A similar view is found also in Thomas Nagel, "The Fragmentation of Value," in *Mortal Questions* (New York: Cambridge University Press, 1979), pp. 128–41. Finally, cultural relativism in ethics, individual relativism, and subjectivism have all been referred to from time to time as pluralist views, because they allow for more than one moral view to be considered correct. I trust that neither my moderate nor Stone's extreme pluralism will be confused with any of these.

2 Christopher D. Stone, *Earth and Other Ethics: The Case for Moral Pluralism* (New York: Harper and Row, 1987).

3 J. Baird Callicott, "The Case against Moral Pluralism," *Environmental Ethics* 12 (1990): 99–112.

4 Peter S. Wenz, *Environmental Justice* (Albany: State University of New York Press, 1988).

5 Gary E. Varner, "No Holism without Pluralism," *Environmental Ethics* 13 (1991): 175–9.

6 Stone, *Earth*, p. 116. He repeats this point in "Moral Pluralism and the Course of Environmental Ethics," *Environmental Ethics* 10 (1988): 145.

7 Callicott, "The Case against Moral Pluralism," p. 110.

8 Ibid., p. 111.

9 R. M. Hare, *Moral Thinking: Its Levels, Method and Point* (New York: Oxford University Press, 1981), p. 38.

10 Immanuel Kant, "On a Supposed Right to Lie from Altruistic Motives," in *Critique of Practical Reason and Other Writings in Moral Philosophy*, ed. and trans. Lewis White Beck (Chicago: University of Chicago Press, 1949), pp. 346–50.

11 See Sissela Bok, *Lying* (New York: Vintage Books, 1979), pp. 41–4.

12 Albert R. Jonsen and Stephen Toulmin, *The Abuse of Casuistry* (Berkeley, Calif.: University of California Press, 1988), p. 19.

13 Callicott, "The Case against Moral Pluralism," p. 120.

14 Stone, *Earth*, p. 118.

15 Callicott, "The Case against Moral Pluralism," p. 114, where he quotes Jeremy Bentham, *An Introduction to the Principles of Morals and Legislation* (Oxford: The Clarendon Press, 1823), chap. 1, sec. 4.

16 Callicott, "The Case against Moral Pluralism," pp. 114–15.

17 Ibid., p. 115.

18 Richard Dawkins, *The Selfish Gene* (New York: Oxford University Press, 1978).

19 Stone, *Earth*, p. 133.

20 Ibid., p. 134.

21 Ibid., p. 150.

22 Ibid., p. 151.

23 Stone, "Moral Pluralism," p. 147.

24 Stone, *Earth*, p. 134.

25 Ibid., p. 142.

26 Ibid., p. 118.

27 Ibid., p. 134.

28 Ibid., p. 151.

29 Wenz, *Environmental Justice*, p. 313 (emphasis in the original).

30 Harold I. Brown, *Rationality* (New York: Routledge, 1988).

31 Eugene C. Hargrove, "The Role of Rules in Ethical Decision Making," *Inquiry* 28 (1987): 3–42.

32 J. Baird Callicott, "The Conceptual Foundations of the Land Ethic," in J. Baird Callicott, *A Companion to a Sand County Almanac* (Madison: University of Wisconsin Press, 1987), pp. 186–217.

33 J. Baird Callicott, "The Search for an Environmental Ethic," in Tom Regan, ed., *Matters of Life and Death*, 2nd edn. (New York: Random House, 1986), pp. 381–424.

34 Callicott, "Conceptual Foundations," p. 208.

35 Ibid.

36 Ibid.

37 Callicott, "The Search for an Environmental Ethic," p. 412.

38 Ibid.

39 Wenz, *Environmental Justice*, p. 313.

40 Varner, "No Holism without Pluralism," p. 177.

41 Ibid., p. 179.

42 W. D. Ross, *The Right and the Good* (New York: Oxford University Press, 1930).

18

The Case for a Practical Pluralism

Andrew Light

As environmental ethics approaches its third decade it finds itself at a curious crossroad. On the one hand, it has produced an array of moral theories attempting to extend ethics beyond its traditional human domain to include arguments for the moral consideration of nonhumans as well as ecosystems.[1] On the other hand, many leading figures in the field often appear inclined to restrict this plurality of positions by arguing that only a narrow set of theoretical approaches could possibly generate an adequate environmental ethic. Some of these theorists argue that a coherent environmental ethics must embrace a restricted set of properties: nonanthropocentrism, holism, moral monism, and, perhaps, a commitment to some form of intrinsic value.

Certainly, it is not unusual, nor should it be discouraged, to have philosophers insisting that one approach to a topic is better than its competitors. But the situation in environmental ethics is not always one of healthy philosophical disagreement, entailing sober but vigorous assessment of competing moral positions. Instead, conversations in environmental ethics tend to be dominated by what Gary Varner has aptly described as inadequately defended "dogmas."[2] For example, Varner claims that the predominant rejection of even moderate forms of anthropocentrism in the field is not based so much on a set of sound philosophical arguments, but instead amounts to an undefended prejudice that an ethic devoted to protection of the environment could not feasibly be based on considerations of human welfare. So, for example, arguments that morally responsible environmental policies can be ground in more traditional philosophical appeals to the ethical obligations we may have to human future generations (e.g., to leave them with a healthy and sustainable environment) have been dismissed out of hand. The reason has not been because of a careful consideration and rejection of the best defenses of such a theory, but more simply because this approach is human centered, even if it is an example of what Bryan Norton calls "weak (or broad) anthropocentrism." Claims that such anthropocentric justifications for better environmental polices overlap and compliment nonanthropocentric approaches (which entail more controversial arguments for why nature is valuable in and of itself) fall on deaf ears to those philosophers only interested in deciphering nonanthropocentric reasons why nature is morally valuable in and of itself.

Examples of attempts to narrow the field abound. Here I will focus on the debate between those positions formally defined as "moral monism" and "moral pluralism" as an instance of this trend. Monists in environmental ethics generally argue that a single moral philosophy or value theory is necessary and sufficient to ground our extended duties and obligations towards the environment. Pluralists, again, generally speaking, argue that this cannot be the case either (1) theoretically, because the sources of value in nature are too diverse to account for in any single value theory, or (2), practically, because an environmental ethics sufficient to motivate enough people to extend moral consideration to the nonhuman natural world would have to appeal to a broader range of intuitions about the value of nature than is found in the work of any single approach to environmental ethics. Because people find nature valuable for so many different reasons, "practical" pluralists argue that no single ethical theory could be made attractive to a sufficient number of people to generate the support for meaningful environmental change. In the example offered above, pluralists would not reject arguments for environmental policies ground in claims about obligations to human future generations merely because such arguments were anthropocentric. Even if a pluralist was committed to the priority of grounding environmental values in some form of nonanthropocentrism they ought still acknowledge the practical importance of developing alternatives to nonanthropocentrism so long as these alternatives could be used to justify the same policy ends. On the other hand, a monist would necessarily be committed to rejecting the philosophical basis of any scheme of environmental value that differed from the one they were committed to defending, and would most likely be compelled to reject alternative schemes of value even if these schemes justified the same policy end for different reasons.

The debate between monists and pluralists in environmental ethics has proved quite lively and at times has become a bit caustic. For example, in an early article attempting to cut short the move toward pluralism, J. Baird Callicott argued that until Christopher Stone's book on pluralism in environmental ethics came along in 1988 (*Earth and Other Ethics*), he was prepared for the discipline to "begin to work toward the creation of an intellectual federation and try to put an end to the Balkanization of nonanthropocentric moral philosophy."[3] In this article Callicott assumed that it was settled that a workable environmental ethic would have to reject pluralism in favor of a non-anthropocentric moral monism. Indeed, on Callicott's account, a commitment to monism is one of the strongest stances that must be maintained in environmental ethics. After arguing that the dean of North American environmental ethics, Holmes Rolston III, is a monist, he remarks: "Given that even Rolston is not really a pluralist after all, one begins to wonder why *our best, most systematic, and thoroughgoing* environmental philosophers cling to moral monism."[4]

Responses to such claims have been numerous and vigorous. Many well-respected theorists in the field, such as Stone, Andrew Brennan, Gary Varner, Peter Wenz, Anthony Weston, Eugene Hargrove, and others count themselves on the pluralist side of this debate.[5] Here, I will take up the monism–pluralism debate through a critical commentary on one of Callicott's more recent contributions to this exchange in a 1994 article in the *Journal of Philosophical Research*. From there however I will take a different turn from this discussion as it has played out so far. Specifically, I will take up the question of where Arne Naess's environmental philosophy fits into the monism–pluralism debate. In the discussions of monism and pluralism in environmental ethics so far there is little or no mention of Naess's "deep ecology," even though in developing this view he may have worked out some of the most interesting defenses of pluralism in environmental thought. Unfortunately, Naess's work has generally been relegated to the historical background to debates like this rather than being read as an active voice in the field. But Naess has consistently argued that the premises of the eight-point deep ecology platform are derivable from a plurality of competing traditions.[6] Even though I do not count myself as a deep ecologist, or a devotee of Naess's work, it is worth having a look at what we might call his "operationalized pluralism" as it has not only been theoretically advanced but as it has been put into practice in the deep ecology movement.

The conclusion I will work toward is that even if one rejects Naess's overall approach to environmental philosophy, he does defend a form of pluralism that avoids the foibles of that position which Callicott fears: the descent from pluralism to moral relativism and deconstructive postmodernism. But before getting to that conclusion I will first examine Callicott's arguments against pluralism. I will argue that the best frame within which to evaluate the monism–pluralism debate is the extent to which monism or pluralism helps to bridge the gap between environmental theory and practice. In the end we will see a perhaps surprising convergence between my more practical and pragmatist take on the monism–pluralism debate and Naess's approach to the same set of issues.

1 Callicott's Theoretical Monism

Calls for the reassessment of the current direction and possible dogmas of environmental ethics ought to carry some weight given the object of our study: the troubling state of the environment and the complicity of humans in the creation of these hazardous conditions – hazardous to humans, non-humans, future generations of both, and the biosphere itself. Environmental philosophy, broadly speaking, and environmental ethics itself, is the attempt to bring the traditions, history, and skills of philosophy to bear on the questions of how to maintain the long-term sustainability of a diversity of life on this planet. In that context, clarifying the direction of our discipline in relation to our contribution to the resolution of environmental problems is an important theoretical enterprise. I say this as a philosopher very hesitant to reduce environmental ethics to a set of metaethical debates – arguments, largely between ethicists, about how to do ethics. The debate between monists and pluralists is one of these metaethical debates, as are many of the claims made in debates like this one that try to restrict what counts as an environmental ethics to a discrete set of properties (nonanthropocentrism, etc.). Nonetheless, some metaethics is required to get beyond these debates. My reason for trying to settle such arguments is to encourage more contributions in the field which are more practical and immediate in relation to the environmental problems we are aimed at helping to resolve.

The call for caution in thinking it is appropriate to settle now on one particular metaethical approach for environmental philosophy, as Callicott is inclined, is helped by an argument by Anthony Weston that given the early, or "originary" stages of environmental ethics, we should defer to more pluralistic approaches for understanding the value of nature. In an influential article titled "Before Environmental Ethics," Weston, partly in response to the anti-pluralist claims cited earlier by Callicott, put the point this way:

At the originary stage we should ... expect a variety of fairly incompatible outlines coupled with a wide range of proto-practices, even social experiments of various sorts, all contributing to a kind of cultural working-through of a new set of possibilities. In environmental ethics, we arrive at exactly the opposite view from that of J. Baird Callicott, for example, who insists that we attempt to formulate, right now, a complete, unified, even "closed" (his term) theory of environmental ethics. Callicott even argues that contemporary environ-

mental ethics should not tolerate more than one basic type of value, insisting on a "univocal" environmental ethic. In fact, however ... originary stages are the worst possible times at which to demand that we all speak with one voice. Once a set of values is culturally consolidated, it may well be possible, perhaps even necessary, to reduce them to some kind of consistency. But environmental values are unlikely to be in such a position for a very long time. The necessary period of ferment, cultural experimentation, and thus *multi*-vocality is only *beginning*.[7]

For Weston, the burden of proof in environmental ethics, because it is a new field of ethics, is on those who would wish to restrict the field to a single and preferred path for the pursuit of moral theories regarding our treatment of nature. The argumentative burden for monism should therefore be quite high.

Callicott has replied to such sentiments that those same demands which make continual re-evaluation of the discipline important also make stabilization on a narrow path of work equally important. Given the environmental crisis we face, how could we afford the sorts of delays seemingly implicit in such talk of "cultural experiments"? We should instead develop a strong theory of the moral consideration of nature and press it forward in different cases.

Additionally, an endorsement of moral pluralism could lead to an embrace of the relativism sometimes associated with deconstructive postmodernism.[8] And relativism is something that we may agree ought to be avoided when our goal is to form a moral response to the deepening environmental crisis. Why? Because relativism entails abandoning the view that there are some moral stances better than others which could guide our ethical claims about how we should treat nature. If we admit relativism then, one could argue, we would give up on attempts to form a moral response to the cultural justifications put forward to defend the abuse or destruction of other animals, species or ecosystems. Relativism may entail that ethics is relative to different cultural traditions. But given the trans-cultural nature of environmental problems, how could we possibly give up on the search for a moral viewpoint from which we could critique different cultures' treatment of the environment and still hope to be contributing an ethical response to the environmental crisis? A relativist environmental ethics might not be adequate to protect the environment with any kind of normative force.

But pluralism does not necessarily entail relativism. So, assuming for the moment that we can answer the relativist charge against pluralism (a point I will return to later), what else would motivate us to follow Callicott down the path of moral monism? In "Moral Monism in Environmental Ethics Defended," Callicott answers the criticisms of various pluralists (Wenz, Varner, Brennan, Weston, and Hargrove) and advances the cause of monism by describing his approach to environmental ethics as a form of "communitarianism," where "all our duties – to people, to animals, to nature – are expressible in a common vocabulary of community," and so "may be weighed and compared in commensurable terms."[9] Before criticizing this view, I will unpack Callicott's justification for this position and outline how he thinks it is a good alternative to pluralism.

Callicott begins this article with a summary of his now familiar objections to the pluralism of Christopher Stone. The argument is that Stone's form of pluralism, termed by Callicott "intrapersonal pluralism," is ultimately "facile" and incoherent. Callicott describes Stone's position as one that supposes that an agent can adopt different moral principles for determining either reasons for ascribing moral value or ethical grounds for action depending on the situation at hand (becoming, for example, a utilitarian for one purpose and a Kantian for another). Why would anyone hold such a view? Because an ethics extended to include our relationships with nature would of necessity include a broad variety of relationships – human–human, human–nonhuman animals, and human–ecosystem. It is therefore not inconceivable that balancing the demands of these differing relationships would require movement from one ethical view to another given the very different kinds of relationships subsumed in an environmental ethic. Perhaps our moral relationships with other animals are best captured by reference to a consequentialist ethic that uses a non-linguistic criteria for moral obligation such as the presumed interests of an entity not to experience pain. Perhaps our moral relationships with ecosystems are best captured by some other criteria (such as its existence value) since ecosystems are not the sorts of entities which can have interests concerning pain. And perhaps we need further to appeal to some other kind of

moral theory altogether when our duties to ecosystems and to other animals come into conflict. Stone's pluralism would at least allow us the flexibility to move from one moral theory to another depending on the kind of moral controversy at hand (e.g., what sort of relationship is under discussion in a particular situation). Unfortunately, this pluralism is even more extreme in that it does not hold agents to one kind of moral theory for each type of relationship. We can imagine a more moderate form of pluralism which would at least demand consistency depending on the kind of relationship at hand (i.e., always use a utility calculus when assessing the welfare of animals and always use a land ethic when assessing the welfare of ecosystems, etc.).

For Callicott, however, such distinctions are irrelevant. Our many moral concerns as environmentalists, though difficult to negotiate under the terms of one moral theory, cannot be resolved simply by accepting the apparent necessity of moving from one moral theory to another depending on the sort of problem that needs to be resolved. According to Callicott:

> When an agent adopts an ethical theory, an ethical "intellectual framework" as Stone defines his neologism, he or she adopts a moral psychology, a notion of the supreme good, a criterion of moral considerability, among other foundational ideas. Facilely becoming a utilitarian for this purpose, a deontologist for that, an Aristotelian for another, and so on, implies either that the pluralist simultaneously hold all the contradictory foundational ideas supporting each theory, or first affirm one set, then reject it in favor of another, and then reject that set for yet another, only to return to the first later, back and forth, round and round. A mature moral agent, I submit, wants a coherent outlook – the one that seems true. He or she cannot comfortably live in a state of self-contradiction or as the philosophical equivalent of an individual with a multiple personality disorder.[10]

Monism avoids such problems by providing a secure philosophical foundation to right action in relation to humans, other animals and nature, ground in one measure of moral value and one system of valuing. Callicott's particular monistic environmental ethic is ground in his reading of Aldo Leopold's land ethic. While I will not recount the particulars of that view here, I will summarize his description of it as a form of monism.

Callicott's communitarian monism works like this: since we are all members of different communities – families, regions, nations, and so on – it follows that each membership generates particular duties and obligations. Therefore, says Callicott, "we can hold a single moral philosophy and a univocal ethical theory, but one that provides for a multiplicity of community memberships, each with its peculiar ethic."[11] So, when faced with the infamous choice between preserving the habitat of spotted owls and the livelihood of Pacific Northwest logging communities, we have to realize that we are connected to both of these communities, with each membership resulting in different obligations. Still, realizing that our membership in the "larger biotic community generates duties to preserve the old-growth forest ecosystem and the endangered species . . . that depend on it," the moral choice is between "temporarily preserving a human life-system that is doomed in any event and reserving in perpetuity an ecosystem and the species that depend upon it."[12] On Callicott's account, our duties to the ecosystem outweigh our duties to the loggers even though we are members of communities that encompass both as sources of moral value. Balancing our obligations to the various communities in which we belong is therefore key to Callicott's solution to the problem of how we balance moral concerns to different subjects, in an ethic extended to be inclusive of nature, without resorting to pluralism.

The issue that immediately springs to mind is whether Callicott's communitarianism really answers the original questions raised by pluralists in environmental ethics. If Callicott's communitarianism is enough to get us an answer to the problem of valuing all types of things in an environment under one ethical system, then why has the monism–pluralism debate continued? The answer may be that the original concern of pluralists was not so much about the ability to adequately cover the variety of moral relationships encompassed in an environmental ethic, but more over the extent to which the body of moral theories developing in the field were adequately responding to the practical dilemmas of forming a moral consensus around environmental issues.

As I said at the start, two sorts of distinguishable concerns are cited in the literature on pluralism in environmental philosophy, both a theoretical and a practical issue. The first is about the complexity of the subject of our theoretical enterprise which we have just discussed. The second issue however concerns finding a practical solution to disagreements over reasons for valuing nature between and among theorists and practitioners, and further how a broader moral consensus on environmental issues can be forged among those who do not normally count themselves as "environmentalists." For even if it were true that one approach to understanding the value of natural objects (such as Callicott's version of Leopold's land ethic) best captured the reasons for our moral obligations entailed in the variety of moral relationships subsumed in an environmental ethic, could we ever rest comfortably in assuming that simply articulating that one approach exhausted our philosophical duties in response to the environmental crisis? Because different people embrace a variety of moral frameworks, isn't there some utility in describing how these different frameworks variously entail the recognition of moral obligations to protect the environment? As it appears unlikely that any single approach to environmental ethics could adequately ignite the morally reflective passions of a critical mass of people needed to effect environmental change, there would seem to be an argument for the necessity of casting one's moral net in broader terms.

Andrew Brennan, defending another form of pluralism puts the point this way:

> By adopting the pluralist stance, we not only start to do justice to the complexity of real situations, but we also can start to look for ways by which environmental ethics can be linked up with other modes of valuing and ways of responding to our surroundings. Utilitarianism and its rivals need not be abandoned, but can be considered as partial accounts of the moral life. There is scope, for example, for developing notions such as attention, humility and selflessness in our dealings with nature as part of the story of what makes a worthwhile human life. These notions should not be thought of as the truth about morality – any more than utilitarianism is. Rather they provide greater depth in characterizing our situation. Abandoning reductive monism about

values and valuing makes even more sense once the force of moral pluralism in this latest form is recognized.[13]

For Brennan, the impetus for pluralism in environmental ethics is more to build stronger connections to a larger array of human moral practices and ethical beliefs thus widening the appeal of the ethical dimensions of environmental concerns. A pluralist environmental ethic could then encourage a variety of moral reasons for ethically defending any particular environmental end.

It is not clear from Callicott's account that his communitarianism captures this result as conceived by Brennan and other pluralists. Recognizing that we are parts of different moral communities will not necessarily get us joint pursuit of similar environmental ends by rival schemes of value, or translation of one environmental end into multiple moral frameworks. We can easily imagine, and even expect, for example, that the ethical dilemmas raised by the case of the owls versus loggers will remain for those agents closer to the logging communities (through parental ties, etc.). Brennan's goal would be to find a way of describing the importance of the old growth forests in ways compatible with the moral assumptions undergirding those familial ties. Pluralism opens up the possibility of finding such an appeal by making it the work of environmental philosophy to create links between already existing moral priorities in specific human communities and the ends of environmental concern. This does not mean that pluralists must endorse jumping from one ethical system to another depending on the situation, but rather that we should consistently look for multiple ways of describing the value of any bit of nature that we want to preserve or restore so as to appeal to a range of interests, both anthropocentric and nonanthropocentric alike.

It is this more practical notion of pluralism as a kind of compatibilism among competing moral frameworks that I think is the most interesting issue in the literature on pluralism in environmental philosophy. And, to his credit, Callicott does acknowledge that at least in one sense he is something like a pluralist, albeit what he calls an "interpersonal pluralist." By this he means that he upholds "everyone else's right to explore or to adopt a moral philosophy and ethical theory that seems persuasive to them."[14] Along with this "commitment to the flourishing of philosophy"

is a belief in the necessary unified end to a process of reasoned persuasion: "Intelligent people of good will should eventually reach agreement if they take the time to thrash out their initial differences."[15]

But surely this form of pluralism is not the same as that championed by Brennan. Mere toleration of the expression of different views does not get us the kind of cooperation among moral frameworks (be they traditional ethical views or new environmental approaches) that Brennan seems to have in mind. Callicott's pluralist need only acknowledge that different people adopt different moral philosophies and then is free to set aside those other approaches for whatever reasons – perhaps because they do not really count as an environmental ethic because they are not nonanthropocentric, monistic, or holist.

The kind of pluralism I embrace, to be explained in more detail below, argues that as long as our different moral frameworks are oriented toward the same environmental priorities, we can ignore for the time being many of the issues of the truth about which reason for valuing nature is actually right. So, for example, my pluralist would not worry too much whether an agent adopts weak anthropocentric or nonanthropocentric reasons for endorsing a particular policy, such as saving old growth forests to protect the habitat of the endangered spotted owl so long as saving the spotted owl was defensible within her preferred moral framework. A nonanthropocentrist might argue that we have direct duties to protect the interest of the owl because ensuring its survival is a desired moral end in itself; a weak anthropocentrist might argue that our duties are much more indirect – that we should preserve the habitat to make sure that future human generations will either benefit from the existence of the owl (for example for aesthetic reasons) or not be harmed by its disappearance (citing a principle of precaution in cases like this where we do not fully understand the consequences which would follow from the loss of this species). A third position might combine weak anthropocentric and nonanthropocentric reasons by arguing that our national character as stewards of the environment entails a responsibility for protecting the remains of old growth forests and the species contained therein. The point to focus on practically is that the differing theoretical bases of these views need not be resolved further for the pluralist so long as they offer reasons for achieving the same policy end: protecting the old growth forests and the habitat of the owls. If the different views conflict on some other end or on the ultimate enactment of this end then we have a moral issue which must be investigated further.

As the ends of environmental ethics should be to better the environment, we must be concerned at least as much with creating agreement on those policies we all support as with finding the philosophical truth of how to value nature. Practically oriented pluralists do not advocate, as Callicott puts it, "deconstructive postmodern *différance*," but instead acknowledge that the environmental situation we face requires us be more flexible about our philosophical differences, even if we are at heart moral realists. The pluralist and the monist (even one with interpersonal pluralist inclinations like Callicott) disagree on these priorities. For the monist our goal should be theoretical agreement all the way down, from policy ends to ethical foundations. For my version of practical, or "pragmatic pluralism," the fact that the environmental problems we face are so pressing provides a warrant for setting aside agreement on ethical foundations when possible. Outside of extreme cases (say, an environmentalist who wants to save old growth forests as part of a larger defense of a fascist state) we not only can afford disagreement on ethical foundations but our situation with respect to environmental priorities requires it. We literally do not have the time to await agreement all the way down (though admittedly, it would be the odd monist who insisted on criticizing every positive policy outcome just because it wasn't achieved for the reasons they thought were right). My version of this argument maintains that when possible we should work within the traditional moral psychologies and ethical theories that most people already have and direct them, where we can, at the same environmental ends. Such a theoretical response is more practical for the pluralist than spending time proving the superiority of one set of ethical foundations over another. (Beyond this, an additional theoretical point, which need not be defended here, is that it may actually be true that no single ethical view can exhaust the reasons why old growth forests and the like should be preserved given the myriad values represented in an entity like a forest.)

Perhaps Callicott is not really concerned with this question of the relationship between theory and practice. Since his original target was Stone's

argument that one can adopt different assessments of obligation generating value for different situations, maybe the issue of how pluralism can help build a moral consensus on the same ends is not a concern for him? There does not appear to be anything explicit in Callicott's account that would prohibit him from consenting to something like Bryan Norton's "convergence hypothesis." The convergence hypothesis identifies and encourages the apparent agreement on most ends of environmental policy among, for example, environmentalists embracing anthropocentrism or non-anthropocentrism, even if they do not agree on the philosophical foundations for those common ends.[16] In this sense, there seems to be no objection in Callicott's argument to the motivation behind the pluralism embraced by Brennan, only to the way in which pluralism is theoretically endorsed interpersonally by theorists like Stone. Let us then say that Callicott appears to reject Stone's theory, which I now will call "theoretical pluralism" – a pluralism justified by an argument concerning the diverse values that must be covered in an environmental ethic – while he may assent to the "practical pluralism" implied in Brennan's, mine, and Norton's views. (Brennan is most likely a theoretical pluralist as well but I will leave that point aside for now.) Practical pluralism then is a kind of view which defends the need for divergent ethical theories to work together in a single moral enterprise (such as defending the same policy end) despite their theoretical differences. Unlike the theoretical pluralist, the practical pluralist does not necessarily advocate the need for a single agent to shift from one moral theory to another depending on the moral relationship at hand, but rather encourages the articulation of a diversity of moral arguments for the same end. The practical pluralist would encourage theorists to work together to coordinate a variety of arguments in service at the same ends.

In fact, even though Callicott does not take up the issue of Brennan's practical pluralism in the defense of his own views against the pluralists, he does acknowledge the accusation of Anthony Weston that he (Callicott) is trying "prematurely ...[to] shut off further discussion and development of the field."[17] Callicott objects that Weston has confused his rejection of intrapersonal pluralism with his position on interpersonal pluralism. Callicott states that he does not want to close off discussion in environmental ethics but rather "keep the interpersonal debate going." One might suppose that this is enough of an answer to the question of how Callicott's views compare with practical pluralists such as Norton or Brennan, or myself. There is no monism–pluralism debate here so long as we exclude extreme theoretical pluralists such as Stone. If Callicott tolerates the existence of competing forms of valuation, then surely he must tolerate the idea of divergent theories working together in a common enterprise, be they anthropocentric, nonanthropocentric or some other variation. If practical pluralism really is the interesting issue raised by the pluralists, then given what we can determine is Callicott's tacit agreement to it, perhaps his communitarianism (combined with his "interpersonalism") is sufficient as a substitute for pluralism after all.

But here we must be cautious. There is no reason to believe that Callicott would make the turn from toleration of the expression of different theories (which is the heart of his interpersonal stance) to embrace cooperation among theories of the sort advocated by Brennan. Since Callicott uses an allusion to communitarianism to clarify his argument, I will do the same.

Suppose that two human communities exist which both embrace some right to free expression. Suppose next that they differ in respect to the reasons they both positively value and wish to protect something else outside of, but lying in-between, their two communities, for example, a common wetland. One of these communities values the wetland for nonanthropocentric and intrinsic reasons while the other values it for its instrumental value for their human community only. Let us also assume that both communities agree on the full range of entities and systems that need to be preserved in the wetland, even though they do so for different reasons. Now finally, suppose that an opportunity arises such that both groups could cooperate to protect the long-term welfare of the wetland, perhaps because redrawn boundaries of the region demonstrate that the wetland crosses into both communities' territories thus raising the issue that it should be jointly managed.

It does not follow merely from of the fact that both communities embrace a right of free expression of ideas, and further actively encourage and tolerate such expressions in their communities (which is relevantly similar to Callicott's interpersonal pluralism), that they will then proceed to cooperate with each other to protect the wetland.

It is possible that the community valuing the wetland for intrinsic reasons would find too crude and repugnant the instrumental valuation of the other community. Or perhaps those valuing the wetland for intrinsic reasons would not participate with the instrumentalists for fear that the instrumentalists would eventually renege on their commitment to the welfare of the shared ecosystem, since, after all, they are instrumentalists. On the other side, the instrumentalists might find cooperating with people who have such obviously false views distasteful. An openness to the formation of other moral theories or accounts of natural value does not necessarily entail even a strategic acceptance of these competing accounts in a unified project to promote a shared end. Toleration endorsed in a community does not necessarily extend in theory or in practice outside of a community. Setting aside obvious counterexamples of not wanting to endorse the ends of fascists, it is clear that toleration could stop at the level of theory formation absent an additional argument for why communities with different moral viewpoints should cooperate on shared ends. So, even if Callicott himself did endorse practical pluralism, his version of interpersonal pluralism does not in itself require it.

So, what alternatives exist? In previous work I argued for what I now call "methodological environmental pragmatism" (my earlier term was the inelegant "metaphilosophical pragmatism"), intended in part to provide a more coherent framework for the sort of practical pluralism embraced by Brennan.[18] The exact details of this position need not concern us here. Suffice to say that it is a way of clarifying how it might be possible for almost any environmental ethicist to embrace something like the practical pluralism described above, toward the goal of promoting greater coherence between the activity of formulating moral theories and the production of useful ethical tools to promote better environmental practices. On such a view, the "extreme pluralism," criticized throughout this essay by Callicott (the idea that one would adopt Aristotle's theory on one occasion, Kant's on another, etc.) would be rejected. A practical pluralist, bound by my pragmatist views must at least be consistent in the application of what she thought was the best (all things considered) moral theory to a particular type of object of valuation, and not change theories with the evaluation of each situation. Practical pluralists need not be ethical situationalists, and presumably would not apply theories in a self-defeating manner (as Callicott, at the end of his paper, hints an extreme pluralist would).

Most important, and hence distinct from Callicott's view, my methodological pragmatist would not simply tolerate some form of interpersonal pluralism (like advocating a right to free speech) but would actively advocate the expression of multiple arguments for describing the value of some thing in nature in order to generate as broad a basis of support as possible for the polices designed to protect or restore that entity. As long as we are not contradictory about our ends, and as long as we are not advocating obviously morally suspicious schemes of value, environmental ethicists should be making as many arguments as possible to appeal to as wide an audience as possible: both anthropocentric and nonanthropocentric claims, both moral claims about our environmental obligations to human future generations and claims about the non-instrumental value of nature. The goal of practical pluralism, and the particular version I endorse in my pragmatist version of it, is to transform the work of environmental ethicists to one where their first priority is to aid in forging a moral consensus on environmental issues. The path to this consensus is not the traditional philosophical task of staking a claim on some moral theory and defending it against all comers, but instead generating creative ways of persuading a variety of people, with very different ethical views, to look kindly and favorably on the same environmental ends. Unlike Callicott, I do not believe that consensus is always reached by "intelligent people of good will." (I also do not believe that we can actually count on people to patiently listen to alternative accounts of how they should value things in the world.) Given these assumptions, we need to find more ways of convincing people within these existing moral frameworks, why they should endorse the same positive environmental ends.

Callicott characterizes Weston's project in "Before Environmental Ethics" as an attempt to radically refocus the goal of environmental philosophy. But this is not what I am up to here. I still think, along with Callicott, that what we should be doing is "systematic environmental philosophy." But systematic environmental philosophy cannot be systematic philosophy in a vacuum. Not to sound too vulgar (especially since I have a great admiration for philosophers who work in modal logic), but our object of concern is not the question

of the spatio-temporal existence of other possible worlds but the future of the one world we are confident we do inhabit. Surely our method of interacting as philosophers must push the envelope of Callicott's interpersonal pluralism, beyond what we would expect it to be for any well-trained philosopher working on any topic. Any philosopher who thought it appropriate to censure the work of his colleagues only because it is different from his own, or failed to give it a fair hearing, would simply be a bad philosopher. We need not theorize about varieties of pluralism to get to that conclusion. The most interesting question concerning pluralism in environmental ethics is a practical, not a theoretical question, different from the one Callicott has taken up. Again, Andrew Brennan provides a valuable insight:

> If we accept moral pluralism as a philosophical position, the project of environmental ethics can be seen in a new light. The challenge of nonanthropocentric ethics to the western, human-centered tradition need not be described as an attempt to supplant one set of principles ... with some new overarching set that embrace not only human concerns but also the interests, whatever they are, of other natural things.... [E]nvironmental ethics is less a competitor for a certain moral position, but an investigation of a more sophisticated turn that moral philosophy has taken. Embarking upon it is a partial recognition of the complexity of our moral situation. Note, once more, that the complexity in question is intrinsic to the business of being moral. Moral pluralism is a philosophical, not a moral, thesis.[19]

Though a bit cryptic in the distinction employed at the end, the gist of Brennan's argument is friendly to my views. The impetus for moral pluralism is not to defeat one or another monistic ethics, but instead to help mature environmental ethics so that it more adequately responds to the task of broadening the ethical horizons of all approaches to moral problems so that they are inclusive of environmental concerns.

If we follow Brennan's line of reasoning, an argument that I think is both crucial to and lost in discussions of pluralism in this literature, then most practically inclined pluralists can grant Callicott's arguments against Stone for now.[20] But we

Andrew Light

should not stop there. We must also insist that Callicott, and many others who consider these questions, rethink what is at stake in the monism–pluralism debate in environmental ethics. As I said at the beginning, environmental ethics is unfortunately marked by certain dogmas, not the least of which is how we have constructed some of the defining debates in the discipline. We need to ask whether the way we approach the practice of doing philosophy best coheres with what is arguably the most effective contribution we can make as philosophers to the struggle to help resolve environmental problems.

2 Naess's Metatheoretical Pluralism

In hopes of helping to clarify it, I would add one caveat to Brennan's claim that moral pluralism is a philosophical rather than a moral thesis. More accurately stated, pluralism is a practical philosophical thesis, meaning that it is not simply a claim about how to do philosophy but rather how to do philosophy in response to a certain set of problems. Bryan Norton has argued for a distinction between practical and applied philosophy which explains this comment. On Norton's account, we should use the term "applied philosophy" for the practice of top-down philosophical reflection about a problem in the world. "Practical philosophy," in contrast, "is problem-oriented; it treats theories as tools of the understanding, tools that are developed in the process of addressing specific policy controversies." Practical philosophers therefore do not assume that "theoretical issues can be resolved in isolation to real problems." While the practical philosopher can work toward developing a "unified vision of environmental goals and objectives," in the meantime, theoretical differences can be set aside provided all disputants can "agree on important management principles...despite disagreement on ultimate values."[21]

Given this distinction, Norton argues that the difference between monism and pluralism is much more profound than may at first be assumed. Echoing Brennan, Norton suggests that these are two entirely different ways of doing philosophy in the context of its relationship to practice. Approvingly citing Weston's remarks on this subject, Norton characterizes monists as those who do not want to muck up the activity of theory formation with the "details of everyday environmental man-

agement practice." Somewhat hyperbolically, Norton puts it this way:

As applied philosophers, they [monists] hope to resolve environmental problems by throwing fully formed theories and principles over the edge of the ivory tower, to be used as intellectual armaments by the currently outgunned environmental activists, to aid them against the economic philistines in the political street wars that determine the fate of natural environments. This heroic version of applied philosophy's role in the policy process will only be realized if environmental ethicists, laboring in the tower, can agree on which theory to throw down to the street fighters.[22]

We may wish to discount such a description as being a bit unfair to monists. Nonetheless, the point remains that the activity of environmental philosophy as described by some pluralists is very different from an even more charitable description of the monist's project. Norton goes on in the rest of his article to criticize Callicott's monism further, toward the claim that nonanthropocentrism itself, surely thought of as the bulwark of environmental ethics, should be challenged along with its monistic ground. If we are going to be pluralists (either theoretical or practical) we have to at least be willing to consider the validity of other forms of valuing nature, not just those which have traditionally passed for the range of positions in nonanthropocentric value theory.

But I do not want to take this argument any further in this direction. I do not wish to shore up Norton's criticisms of Callicott here (even though I think they are very serious), consider Callicott's response to it, or turn what I take to be the approach to pluralism that I share with Norton, Brennan, and perhaps Weston, into a criticism of any other ethical monist.[23] Instead I want to turn this discussion toward a more positive appraisal of another kind of pluralism in environmental philosophy as found in the work of another theorist. If we are going to reshape the debate between monism and pluralism along more practical lines then we also need to reassess what theories have normally been placed on which side of the dividing line between the two sides of this disagreement as it has more traditionally been conceived. In particular, I will argue here that this turn to a new terrain for the monism–pluralism debate demands that we bring into this conversation the work of Arne Naess.

It is difficult these days to find hard-nosed environmental ethicists willing to spend much time on Naess's work. Many think that it is only of use to the "true-believers" of deep ecology. Though he can at times be agonizingly vague, I think that there is still a wealth of material in Naess's later work that deserves our attention. His comments on the monism–pluralism debate are a good case in point. But if we were to give this work a serious look, it is also probably true that many environmental ethicists would consider Naess's formal philosophical system (his "Ecosophy T") to be a paradigm case of moral monism, since it seems to emanate from a single source. Naess argues that humans are ontologically connected with the world around them. (In other words, Naess argues that what it means to be a human is to be an indistinguishable part of nature. See chapters 19 and 20 for more details on this set of arguments.) Naess's philosophical views about how we should treat nature then follow from his understanding that humans are a part of nature. Once we recognize this fact then, for Naess, our ethics concerning nature is in some respects only an expanded sense of self-regard and self-respect. Other theorists like Warwick Fox have argued that the point of deep ecology is that there is no meaningful ontological distinction to be made between humans and non-humans, or nature itself. This fundamental principle of deep ecology could be seen as the monistic foundation from which our duties to each other and the environment can be derived.[24]

But Naess's formal system ought to be interpreted as theoretically pluralist, and his comments on how to do environmental philosophy point out that he is also a practical pluralist as well. Since I think that the practical argument is the more interesting ground for the monism–pluralism debate, I will spend most of my time on that part of Naess's view. Perhaps Norton would be surprised that I should consider Naess in this way, especially since Norton has famously argued that deep ecologists are anti-pluralists, and that the entire deep ecology–shallow ecology distinction did more to interrupt convergence on environmental policies among theorists and activists than almost any other distinction in the literature.[25] But Naess, perhaps more than any other deep ecologist, has worked to foster a form of practical plur-

alism both inside and outside deep ecology circles. And since Naess never really got involved in the old monism–pluralism debate as its ground was defined by Callicott and others, we can safely say that for Naess the issue of pluralism in environmental philosophy has always been the question of how to do philosophy, rather than an argument over the specific content of our ethical theories or principles.[26]

It is well known that along with George Sessions, Naess formulated eight principles of deep ecology in 1984 with the goal of providing guidance for how those who accepted his basic philosophical views ought to act in the world. For example, principle three states that, "Humans have no right to reduce [the] richness and diversity [of the world] except to satisfy vital needs." Naess has pointed out time and time again that behind the eight principles of deep ecology are at least three possible overlapping sources of deep ecological thought. One can come to embrace the eight principles from any one of these foundations, so no one foundation constitutes the sole basis for endorsing the eight principles.[27] The foundations are: Christian – some will argue there is strong ground for the intrinsic connection between humans and nature even in the stewardship view from Genesis; Buddhist – primarily according to Naess as found in the work of Dogen;[28] and philosophical – specifically from Whitehead's process philosophy and from Naess's readings of Spinoza on the connection between mind and matter. We need not go into the details of how the diverse foundations inform the principles of deep ecology. As far as theoretical pluralism goes, this should be enough to get us at least the "moderate moral pluralism" described by Peter Wenz, where a single ethical theory is pluralistic in so far as it "contains a variety of independent principles, principles that cannot all be reduced to or derived from a single master principle."[29] One need not assent to even the coherence of any one of the foundations in order to derive the principles out of another of the foundations.[30]

We can test this approach as a form of pluralism by comparing it with the previously established example of moral monism. Recall that for Callicott, our differing moral obligations stem from the different moral communities in which we take part. Still, the foundation for the different principles that we can assume would emerge from our different obligations to different communities is

Andrew Light

common: it is Callicott's version of the general theory of value found in Leopold's land ethic.[31] So, all principles, no matter which communities we belong to, ought to be derived from the same foundational conception of value. Naess, on the other hand, does not find the rationale for his multiple principles in one source or even a specific collection of sources. It is crucial for him that one can come to the principles of deep ecology from a variety of foundations. Importantly, they need not even be the same three foundations that Naess identifies. He assumes that there are other foundations that could lead others to embrace the eight principles. Different people will assent to the principles of deep ecology for different reasons, hopefully building a broader movement around the policies endorsed by deep ecologists.[32] One goal of the philosopher then following Naess's lead is to describe how other world views could be interpreted such that they are compatible with the eight principles. The principles amount to a version of the policy ends which I previously argued would be the focus of my pragmatic practical pluralist.

We can however go further in understanding this connection between Naess's views and the preferred form of pluralism identified above. Naess helps this cause considerably in a little known article titled, "The Encouraging Richness and Diversity of Ultimate Premises in Environmental Philosophy."[33] In this piece Naess acknowledges early on that the style of his approach to the issue of pluralism belongs to "a somewhat different tradition of metaethical discussion and methodology than the chief participants of the ethical monism/pluralism debate."[34] His first claim is that one of the central tasks of environmental philosophers should be "to study different positions but not to try to reduce the ultimate differences" between those positions.[35] Such a view is consistent with the practical pluralism I am advocating, and may even go beyond it. What Naess has in mind is a principle of respect for different cultural approaches to environmental problems. In fact, in this article he embraces an explicitly cultural form of pluralism. I will return to the question of cultural pluralism later, and compare it with Callicott's similar argument taking up this same challenge. But for now I want to suggest that the argument Naess works out in this paper is not restricted to issues of cultural pluralism and is consistent with the positions previously outlined by Brennan and Norton.

Naess gives two reasons for embracing a practical form of pluralism. First, he argues that a uniformity in views on valuing nature would indicate a stagnation rather than a strength in environmental ethics. Going beyond Callicott's embrace of interpersonal pluralism, Naess sees not only a potential for fruitful philosophical argument in a diversity of views, but also the basis for a claim to the strength of environmental thought ground in that diversity. Like Weston's remarks about how we ought to find any discipline at its beginning, investigating a variety of ethical approaches, Naess suggests that the cultural richness and diversity that we may think are part of a good environmental philosophy cannot be sustained "under conditions of increasing similarity of ultimate views."[36] There is also an inherent translation problem: why would we ever think that a unified moral view would be coherent to every cultural tradition? According to Naess, even if it could be shown that we could attain something as ambitious as a unified theory of the relationship between humans and nature, "it does not follow that adequate, verbal accounts of this oneness should or must converge or be practically translatable into each other."[37]

Such a claim may appear in tension with my earlier arguments for practical pluralism. Naess's argument seems to value diversity writ large rather than as a means to an end, namely generating a larger moral consensus on environmental policies. But Naess does not endorse pluralism wholesale. In a passage very similar to Norton's defense of the convergence hypothesis, Naess argues that we do not have to accept all ethical views concerning the environment: "The only reason to attack a religious or philosophical ultimate premise seems to be the assumption that a particular environmentally unacceptable position follows with necessity from it."[38]

Finally, on this point, any discussion of deep ecology must keep in mind that it is as much, if not more, a social movement than an academic philosophy. Few environmentalists walk the streets calling themselves "nonanthropocentric monists" or "weak anthropocentrists" (no surprises there). But a surprisingly large number do call themselves deep ecologists. Naess is one of the few environmental philosophers in the world who can claim to have directly and determinably affected a movement of practitioners, and possibly even some policy-makers. For example, through the early part of its history, many leaders of the American environmental group Earth First! claimed to be deep ecologists and were ardent followers of Naess's work. Naess's desire to forge some sort of ground for agreement among them is a practical, not an applied or even theoretical problem. Seen as such, we can read Naess's comments as more properly addressing the variety of positions, or even factions, of the deep ecology movement. In a passage similar to the ones cited at the beginning of this discussion, Naess remarks that: "Most deep ecologists have fundamental differences from each other, and speak in a variety of terminologies. Questioning one's motives leads inevitably to philosophical positions and from there back to practice."[39] While some may consider this concern with one group of activists and philosophers a limitation in Naess's practical pluralism, I think instead that it is a sign of why we environmental ethicists should heed his advice more keenly than that of others.

A second reason for practical pluralism in the "Encouraging Richness" article is found in Naess's distinction between the background assumptions of our moral views and the way we voice those views in ethical conflicts. The two need not be the same. As suggested earlier, Naess is skeptical about the prospects of formulating a logically complete and foundational environmental ethic which could be definitively shown to best capture the value of nature and our moral obligations to it.[40] Even if we disagree with Naess on this point however, his argument about the gap between theory and practice is still quite interesting.

For Naess, a good environmental philosopher needs to be something of a practical anthropologist, with a sound understanding of various moral customs in order to help forge a greater propensity for cooperation among environmentalists. Naess outlines two goals for environmental philosophy in this context: on the one hand we should aim toward perfecting our theories and making them more philosophically rigorous – monist, theoretical pluralist, or whatever – and on the other hand, we ought to try to work with the moral assumptions of those with whom we must cooperate to achieve environmental reforms, even if we disagree with some of their principles. For Naess, the need for a philosophical response to the environmental crisis drives these twin goals rather than some generic aspiration of the practice of philosophy. Again, Naess uses an intramural example from

deep ecology circles to make his point: "The supporters of the deep ecology movement cooperate in the fight to implement decisions on the level of concrete situations with everybody who sincerely supports a decision."[41]

Now, it is generally regarded by most who have followed the course of Naess's work that the limits to such a drive for pluralistic cooperation would be drawn at collaboration with "shallow" or reform oriented ecologists and environmentalists. Naess's original designation of a specifically "deep ecology," in his first article in environmental philosophy, distinguished it from a "shallow" ecological approach which stops short of analyzing the fundamental causes of environmental problems. Damning them in the comparison, Naess argued that shallow ecologists do not go as far as some deep ecologists, for example, in questioning the systemic roots of the environmental crisis in our economic systems. Like the example of the two communities and the wetland offered earlier, at first glance there appears to be no reason why Naess's argument for cooperation between different schools of deep ecologists would imply broader forms of tolerance and cooperation between deep and shallow ecologists.

But in the very next sentence after the one quoted at the end of the previous paragraph, Naess sets these worries to rest. Naess asks the rhetorical question: "What could the supporters [of the deep ecology movement] achieve *without* cooperation with people whose general argumentation pattern for instance in terms of premise/conclusion relations, is shallow or merely concerned with reforms?"[42] Presumably, very little. One of the most striking things about this passage is that it brings Naess much closer to Norton's convergence hypothesis (again, which argues that environmentalists of all varieties (anthropocentrist and nonanthropocentrist, shallow and deep) can and do converge on the same ends of environmental policy albeit for different reasons). Perhaps Naess still thinks there is a sharper divide between deep and shallow ecologists than Norton is ready to admit. But for Naess those differences apparently dissolve given the necessity of a practical pluralism designed to encourage convergence on the ends of environmental reform. While other deep ecologists might disagree with how far Naess is willing to take his pluralism, we may be encouraged that at least one deep ecologist, and a very important one at that, does not see any persuasive reason why deep ecologists cannot find good news in Norton's convergence hypothesis.

Naess ends this paper with perhaps one of the most succinct and elegant statements of the need for practical pluralism, which again, points to the need to revisit Naess's work in the context of a recast monism–pluralism debate: "The richness and diversity of philosophical and religious ultimate premises suitable for action in the ecological crisis may be in itself considered part of the richness and diversity of life forms on Earth."[43] Practical pluralism is thus the activity of environmental philosophers who wish to emulate the patterns of the objects of their concern.

3   Conclusions

Before closing, there are two issues to take up that could be important in the reintroduction of Naess's work into a reformed monism–pluralism debate, fulfilling two promissory notes given before. First there is the question of the role of cultural pluralism in this debate, which at times is the issue on which Naess hangs his comments on pluralism. Second, there is the remaining issue of whether Callicott's worries concerning the relationship between pluralism and relativism still hold for the form of pluralism I endorse and am attributing to Brennan, Norton, and now Naess.

At least since the late 1980s, cultural pluralism has been on the agenda of environmental ethics. Still smarting a bit from the critiques of theorists like Ramachandra Guha and Vandana Shiva, that much of environmental philosophy is almost exclusively First World in its orientation and expectations, environmental ethicists of almost all schools of thought have begun thinking seriously about the issue of whether their approaches to understanding the value of nature are either compatible with, or respectful of the way other cultures understand the place of nature in their understanding of themselves.[44] Is an environmental ethic which champions the value of nature as part of our overall set of obligations to protect the interests of human future generations appropriate from a more traditional society which may see its obligations to nature in a much more immediate and direct framework? Is the predominant focus in environmental ethics on the preservation of wilderness as a plot of land set apart from human influence appropriate for a culture which does not

accept such divides between realms of human culture and realms of untrammeled nature? For his part, Callicott has demonstrated a clear commitment to cultural pluralism in his book, *Earth's Insights*.[45] In many ways this book is more thorough than anything Naess or almost anyone else has written to aid in understanding how a variety of global cultural traditions can be understood to be compatible with a Western environmental ethic.

In this book Callicott provides a very helpful survey of the implicit environmental philosophies at work in a variety of intellectual and religious traditions from around the world. The details of this account are not important here, only the unique structure of Callicott's argument.[46] Callicott not only surveys these various traditions but also uses them to bolster the case for his particular brand of environmental ethics. It is this last part of his argument that shows the differences between a pluralist and monist approach to the problem of cultural pluralism.

The penultimate chapter of *Earth's Insights* rehearses Callicott's defense of an expanded communitarian version of a Leopoldian land ethic. Such an ethic is the "one" in what Callicott calls the "one-many problem," or the need to have a single cross-cultural environmental ethic consistent with the science of ecology while at the same time acknowledging the importance of a multiplicity of "traditional cultural environmental ethics, resonant with such an international, scientifically grounded environmental ethic and helping to articulate it."[47] The "one" and the "many" represent, respectively, our quality of being one species facing a global environmental crisis and the historical reality that we are many people from many cultures and different places. These two aspects of the human experience are not at odds for Callicott; each needs to be integrated into a unified world ecological view.

Callicott's move toward cultural pluralism is not practically pluralist. All of the competing cultural environmental traditions in Callicott's work are evaluated through the lens of his nonanthropocentric version of Leopold's land ethic. Leopold's view becomes for Callicott the "Rosetta stone of environmental philosophy," needed to "translate one indigenous environmental ethic into another, if we are to avoid balkanizing environmental philosophy."[48] Accordingly, the veracity of one or another cultural environmental view is accepted or rejected by how closely it approximates Callicott's interpretation of Leopold's ethic.

But it is tempting to see Callicott's interpretation of Leopold's work as a potential yardstick for evaluating all indigenous environmental traditions, as encouraging more balkanization than discouraging it. What we are left with is not a compatibility and tolerance of different cultural environmental traditions but a convenient guide for dividing between those environmental traditions which are acceptable and those which are not. If we may call into question the singular vision of this kind of ethic, then we may also call into question some of Callicott's appraisals of these other systems. Callicott claims for example that, "Africa looms as a big blank spot on the world map of indigenous environmental ethics."[49] Why would Callicott make such a claim? Because African environmental thought tends to be anthropocentric in contrast to Callicott's nonanthropocentric, Leopoldian ethic. Surely such an abstract reason for rejection of an entire cultural tradition is question begging at best. What Callicott is doing here certainly is an example of just what Naess warns us against. Callicott has judged (and sometimes denigrated) different traditional environmental views by holding them up to the measure of a Leopoldian ethic. But why isn't Naess doing the same thing? After all, Naess also argues that different religious, cultural and philosophical approaches – Christianity, Buddhism, and some schools of philosophy – all provide a basis within which we can derive support for the eight principles of the deep ecology platform. The difference however is that Naess, unlike Callicott, does not evaluate different forms of thought on the basis of their amenability to the foundations or even specific principles of deep ecology. Naess only points out that these different traditions can be interpreted such that they support a set of common principles. Naess does not reject Christianity, for example, because it could be used to support a reform environmentalism, or even an anti-environmental stance. Naess's appropriation of these competing traditions, unlike Callicott's, is at the level of interpretation not evaluation. Naess also suggests that while we can "infer traits of an environmental ethic" from different world literatures, we cannot "pretend to be able to compare in a methodologically neutral and adequate way meanings and validity of the ultimate premises of total views."[50] While he limits this somewhat puzzling comment to the problem of

translating simple expressions of environmental protection into complex theoretical positions, I think the point holds in general to his approach to divergent cultural–environmental traditions. Therefore, excluding the rejection of views from which we can derive necessary and unassailable anti-environmental conclusions, or morally offensive conclusions (fascism, etc.), the goal of cultural pluralism in environmental ethics is not necessarily evaluation of different world views, but a finding of means for convergence of environmental policies, activities, and theories through these different views.

It is probably the case that some question still remains of whether Callicott's or Naess's approach to cultural pluralism is preferable in environmental ethics. After all, there is something to be said for having some means for evaluating competing world views on the environment.[51] Because environmental problems are not restricted by cultural borders, we often find ourselves in situations of cross-cultural disagreement over a common problem. Consider for example the differences between the support for a ban on whaling in most Western countries, and the popular insistence in Norway and Japan that whaling is an important cultural institution that must be continued. Part of resolving the issue of which approach to cultural pluralism is best will necessarily involve some answer to the original question posed by Callicott, and cited at the beginning of this paper: does pluralism lead to a deconstructive, or more simply, destructive relativism? If it does then pluralists who are opposed to whaling may have no answer to those who find the practice integral to their cultural integrity.

A theoretical or practical pluralism is not necessarily relativist, nor incommensurable with a workable, robust, and critical environmental philosophy. Callicott is right in suggesting that there could be a tendency to move from theoretical pluralism to relativism. Still, without an argument for their necessary connection (which has yet to be made in this debate), it seems that each version of pluralism has to be individually evaluated. Callicott's strongest case so far is therefore against Stone. But following from the earlier analysis in Part I, "What is Environmental Ethics?" Callicott's worries with regard to relativism need to be rephrased against a practical pluralism. Practical pluralism, especially given the comments on its importance found in Brennan, Norton and

Andrew Light

Naess, may provide the guidelines for formulating an environmental ethic adequate to the task of informing better environmental polices and practices within diverging cultural traditions. It is no doubt true that we can ill afford relativism in environmental philosophy right now. Otherwise, we would be impotent in the face of the abundant cultural claims denying that we have any ethical obligations to non-humans or ecosystems on any grounds. A practical pluralism however, could help to mitigate this problem by providing a non-relative array of answers to the general skepticism toward the moral dimensions of environmental problems in the language of a variety of traditional and non-traditional ethical perspectives. Practical pluralists do not give up in the face of a potentially anti-environmental position justified through an appeal to local customs or cultural traditions. They simply look first for a response from within those customs and traditions. If none is forthcoming then we move outside to take recourse to another set of arguments. If some framework is provided to prevent pluralism from lapsing into an indecisive form of relativism, and if pluralism can be argued to be important for the development of a more practical environmental ethics, then the next question becomes how we go about doing environmental philosophy so that we get the right sort of pluralism.

I have argued elsewhere that environmental pragmatism provides us with just the sort of framework we need to temper pluralism toward these goals.[52] But the question of whether this strategy, or an embrace of Naess's form of deep ecology, or something else, is best for this kind of theory development is an empirical question. If theorists and practitioners followed our views to their logical conclusions, and were able both to cooperate on ends and avoid relativism (or even the unproductive debates about relativism that seems to paralyze much of contemporary philosophy), then we could actually see which form of pluralism best serves the broader goals of a more practical environmental philosophy. Of all the views examined here, only Naess's pluralism seems likely to be testable in this manner anytime soon since his views have the broadest following in the world of activists and practitioners. In this respect, a careful analysis of the reception of Naess's pluralism in the deep ecology movement is one of the best next steps in advancing a reformed monism–pluralism debate.

244

Acknowledgments

I am grateful to Avner de-Shalit, Alastair Hannay, Eric Katz, Zev Trachtenberg, Allen Carlson, Wayne Ouderkirk and Anne Naess for helpful comments on earlier versions of this article. This chapter has been substantially revised from its original (titled "Callicott and Naess on Pluralism"), appearing in *Inquiry*, Vol. 39, No. 2, June 1996, pp. 273–94. It should supplant revised versions of that essay reprinted in *Beneath the Surface: Critical Essays in the Philosophy of Deep Ecology*, eds. E. Katz, A. Light, and D. Rothenberg (Cambridge, MA: MIT Press, 2000), and in *Land, Value, Community: Callicott and Environmental Philosophy*, eds. W. Ouderkirk and J. Hill (Albany, NY: SUNY Press, 2002).

Notes

1 J. Baird Callicott marks three types of non-human centered (nonanthropocentric) theories: neo-Kantian (e.g., Paul Taylor, Robin Attfield, Holmes Rolston), "Leopoldian" (Callicott, William Godfrey-Smith, Richard Sylvan and Val Plumwood) and Self-Realized (deep ecologists). See Callicott's "The Case Against Moral Pluralism," *Environmental Ethics* 12:2 (1990): 101–2. In this paper Callicott gives an interesting genealogy of the development of these areas. A strong case can be made that a complete list of all types of environmental philosophies, contra Callicott, would also have to include non-anthropocentric theories like those of animal liberationists Peter Singer and Tom Regan, as well as anthropocentric holists such as Bryan Norton, and Gary Varner's biocentric individualism, just to name a few other representative approaches in the field.

2 See Gary Varner, *In Nature's Interests?* (Oxford: Oxford University Press, 1998).

3 Callicott, "The Case Against Moral Pluralism," p. 102.

4 Ibid., p. 109. My emphasis.

5 Some of the most frequently cited papers on the pluralist side are: Christopher D. Stone, "Moral Pluralism and the Course of Environmental Ethics," *Environmental Ethics* 10:2 (1988): 139–54; Gary E. Varner, "No Holism Without Pluralism," *Environmental Ethics* 13:2 (1991): 175–9; Andrew Brennan, "Moral Pluralism and the Environment," *Environmental Values* 1:1 (1992): 15–33; Peter Wenz "Minimal, Moderate, and Extreme Moral Pluralism," *Environmental Ethics* 15:1 (1993): 61–74; and two unpublished papers, Anthony Weston, "What Are We Arguing About?," and Eugene Hargrove, "Callicott and Moral Pluralism," both presented at the Central Division meeting of the American Philosophical Association, April 24, 1993.

6   For reasons that may become apparent later, I count Naess's "environmental philosophy" as both his attempt to characterize the deep ecology movement, and his argument for a definite "total view," his Ecosophy T.

7   Anthony Weston, "Before Environmental Ethics," *Environmental Ethics* 14:4 (1992): 333. The reference to Callicott in the quote is to "The Case against Moral Pluralism," pp. 99–124.

8   Callicott, "The Case against Moral Pluralism," pp. 116–20.

9   J. Baird Callicott, "Moral Monism in Environmental Ethics Defended," *Journal of Philosophical Research* 19 (1994): 53. There are problems with Callicott's description of his view as "communitarian," problems that unnecessarily confuse this argument with the more familiar communitarianism of Michael Walzer, Michael Sandel, Charles Taylor, Avner de-Shalit, and others. Callicott's work does not share much with these other views, especially in light of the fact that most communitarians include a substantial role for political and moral pluralism in their work. For a specific example of a more robust environmental communitarianism, see Avner de-Shalit, *Why Posterity Matters: Environmental Policies and Future Generations* (London: Routledge Press, 1995). For de-Shalit, pluralism comes into play in communitarianism in the way that communities open themselves to the values of other communities, regarding these other valuation schemes "as potential truths rather than as something inimical" (p. 62). Ultimately, of course, this problem of nomenclature is not philosophically very serious for Callicott, only a bit inelegant of him. For an update of de-Shalit's views see his *The Environment Between Theory and Practice* (Oxford: Oxford University Press, 2000).

10 Ibid., p. 52.

11 Ibid., p. 53.

12 Ibid.

13 Brennan, "Moral Pluralism and the Environment," p. 30. Brennan's thesis is that "there is no single theoretical lens which provides a privileged set of concepts, principles and structure in terms of which a situation is to be viewed" (p. 29).

14 Callicott, "Moral Monism in Environmental Ethics Defended," p. 54.

15 Ibid.

16 See Bryan Norton, *Toward Unity Among Environmentalists* (Oxford: Oxford University Press, 1991), esp. ch. 10.

17 Callicott, "Moral Monism in Environmental Ethics Defended," p. 56. Callicott is referring to Weston's remark on Callicott cited in the first section of this paper.

18 For what I hope is a clear summary of this position see Andrew Light, "Taking Environmental Ethics Public," in *Environmental Ethics: What Really Matters? What Really Works?*, eds. D. Schmidtz and E. Willott (Oxford: Oxford University Press, 2002). For the background of the view see my contributions to *Environmental Pragmatism*, eds. A. Light and E. Katz (London: Routledge, 1996).

19 Brennan, "Moral Pluralism and the Environment," p. 30.

20 I am not yet ready to completely concede Callicott's arguments against Stone, Varner, Hargrove, and Brennan on theoretical moral pluralism, or what Callicott winds up calling "pluralism at the level of theory." Strategically, however, I am ready to let the issue rest. It seems that Callicott has made an interesting argument here that needs to be responded to by those original proponents of theoretical pluralism. I still have some worries about what exactly Callicott is embracing. Even though he claims to be a pluralist with respect to principles, it is unclear that this really individuates his theory at all. What environmental ethicist would argue that one single principle is sufficient to generate all duties toward the environment? Who holds such a view? If no one, then we still have a monism–pluralism debate at the level of theory which is at least philosophically interesting.

21 Bryan Norton, "Why I am not a Nonanthropocentrist," *Environmental Ethics* 17:4 (1995): 344. Also see Norton's expanded version of this paper, "Reduction or Integration: Two Approaches to Environmental Values," in Andrew Light and Eric Katz (eds.), *Environmental Pragmatism*, pp. 105–38.

22 Ibid., p. 345.

23 I would hesitate to too closely connect moral monism exclusively with the applied philosophy program which Norton is criticizing. If practical philosophy is an improved way of doing philosophy, then why couldn't a monist, at least in principle, do philosophy in that way? Surely again we are talking about the difference between a way of doing philosophy and a methodological approach. Even as firmly ground a monist as Callicott could presumably embrace a practical form of pluralism based on an argument for the theoretical responsibilities of environmental ethicists interacting in broader arenas than philosophy departments and journals. Such a position could be derivable through a more applied philosophy. In support of this position I note that for Norton, monism and applied philosophy only "tend" to go together. For Callicott's reply to Norton's criticisms of him see "On Norton and the Failure of Monistic Inherentism," *Environmental Ethics* 18:2 (1996): 219–21.

24 See Warwick Fox, "Approaching Deep Ecology: A Response to Richard Sylvan's Critique of Deep Ecology." Hobart: University of Tasmania Environmental Studies Occasional Paper 20, 1986.

25 See Norton's *Toward Unity Among Environmentalists*, and the discussion by Harold Glasser of the convergence argument in his "Naess's Deep Ecology Approach and Environmental Policy," *Inquiry* 39:2 (1996): pp. 157–87.

26 Because I do not count myself as a deep ecologist I do not have anything at stake in proving some form of inherent pluralism in deep ecology.

27 See chapter 20, this volume. For a listing of the eight principles see Bill Devall and George Sessions, *Deep Ecology: Living as if Nature Mattered* (Salt Lake City, UT: Peregrine Smith Books, 1985), p. 70.

28 The validity of this claim has been called into question most notably by Deane Curtin in "A State of Mind Like Water: Ecosophy T and the Buddhist Traditions," *Inquiry* 39:2 (1996): 239–84.

29 Peter Wenz, "Minimal, Moderate, and Extreme Moral Pluralism," p. 69, cited by Wenz from his *Environmental Justice* (Albany, NY: State University of New York Press, 1988), p. 313.

30 One worry would be whether the principles of deep ecology are independent of each other. But even though this issue is not taken up by Naess it is clear from the context in which they are introduced that he does not have their necessary interdependence in mind. He acknowledges the validity, for example, of the derivation of a different set of deep ecological principles from the shallow–deep distinction, and that the views of the platform of deep ecology are "not basic in an absolute sense, but basic among the views that supporters [of deep ecology] have in common" (Naess, *Ecology, Community and Lifestyle*, trans. D. Rothenberg [Cambridge: Cambridge University Press], 1989, pp. 28–9). Another objection is that the real foundation of the deep ecology principles is the set of intuitions behind the shallow–deep distinction. Accordingly, Naess may have only identified those religious and intellectual traditions which implicitly agree with the rationale behind the distinction. If someone can prove this claim then I will concede that in this sense at least Naess's formal system is monistic. But even if Naess is a theoretical monist he could still embrace a practical pluralism.

31 Callicott argues persuasively that his form of monism is at the level of theory but not of principle. Still, I believe the contrast with Naess still holds. For some of Callicott's more important papers explicating this view, see J. Baird Callicott, *In Defense of the Land Ethic. Essays in Environmental Philosophy* (Albany, NY: State University of New York Press, 1989), and *Beyond the Land Ethic* (Albany, NY: State University of New York Press, 1999).

32 The question remains as to whether Naess is correct that people with different philosophical or theological foundations will embrace the principles of deep ecology. A case can be made that they already have, but we can only verify this empirically. I will return to the importance of empirical verification of arguments for pluralism at the end of this chapter.

33 Arne Naess, "The Encouraging Richness and Diversity of Ultimate Premises in Environmental Philosophy," *The Trumpeter* 9:2 (1992): 53–90. My thanks to Harold Glasser for calling my attention to this article.

34 Ibid., p. 54.

35 Ibid., p. 53.

36 Ibid., p. 55.

37 Ibid.

38 Ibid. I completely agree with this limitation by Naess on the compatibilism of practical pluralism employed for environmental ends. The point of this pluralism is to strengthen "pro-environmental" claims. If this pluralism began covering "anti-environmental" views then it would violate its environmental predicate. I will leave for another time a discussion of the ramifications of this caveat.

39 David Rothenberg, *Is It Painful To Think? Conversations with Arne Naess* (Minneapolis: University of Minnesota Press, 1993), p. 136.

40 Naess could find support in advancing this position from Wim J. van der Steen, who has embraced a kind of default theoretical pluralism. Says van der Steen: "Although I opt for pluralism, I do so in a qualified way. The issue is whether we can elaborate a single, overarching theory for environmental ethics. In a sense we can if we use the term *theory* for highly abstract, general guidelines that are far removed from practical applications. However if we use the term *theory* for the mundane entities that we come across in most disciplines, pluralism is our only option. Modesty is my ultimate defense of pluralism. We should recognize our limitations, and we should be aware of fundamental limitations of science and philosophy. Plain methodology alone suffices to show that the search for grand theories that satisfy all the goals we may cherish is misguided." "The Demise of Monism and Pluralism in Environmental Ethics," *Environmental Ethics* 17:2 (1995): 218. Naess too bases some of his arguments for pluralism on an analogy with science. Callicott argues explicitly in "Moral Monism in Environmental Ethics Defended," that this analogy does not work. For Callicott, theoretical pluralism in science may be a necessity, even a virtue, but in moral reasoning it may only be a sign of sloppy reasoning. Though I like van der Steen's argument, I share Callicott's worry that the analogy doesn't really do much philosophical work. Still, for an example of a more rigorous pluralism see Nicholas Rescher's *Pluralism: Against the Demand for Consensus* (Oxford: Oxford University Press, 1993).

41 Naess, "Encouraging Richness and Diversity," p. 58.

42 Ibid. My emphasis.

43 Ibid., p. 60.

44 See Ramachandra Guha, "Radical American Environmentalism and Wilderness Preservation: A Third World Critique," *Environmental Ethics* 11 (1989): 71–83; and Maria Mies and Vandana Shiva, *Ecofeminism* (London: Zed Books, 1993).

45 J. Baird Callicott, *Earth's Insights: A Multicultural Survey of Ecological Ethics from the Mediterranean Basin to the Australian Outback* (Berkeley: University of California Press, 1994).

46 I am in no position to evaluate Callicott's descriptive project, though from what little I do know about world environmental traditions, his account seems good. Anyone interested in comparative environmental philosophy or theology surely will benefit from Callicott's work.

47 *Earth's Insights*, p. 186.

48 Ibid., p. 186.

49 Ibid., p. 158.

50 Naess, "Encouraging Richness and Diversity," p. 60.

51 I should mention one over-simple answer to the question of how to evaluate world environmental views: simply look and see which ones cause more harm to the environment. But here I agree with Callicott who explicitly refuses to make such an argument, suggesting that such a criteria is not clear, and probably unfair as a means of evaluation. See, e.g., Callicott's discussion of the relationship between Japan's intellectual heritage and its current environmental situation (*Earth's Insights*, p. 106).

52 See Light, "Taking Environmental Ethics Public."

PART V

Reframing Environmental Ethics: What Alternatives Exist

Deep Ecology

19

Deep Ecology:
A New Philosophy of our Time?

Warwick Fox

The Australian philosopher William Godfrey-Smith has remarked that "deep ecology ... has an unfortunate tendency to discuss everything at once. Thus a social critique of deep ecology may be backed by such disparate authorities as Ginsberg, Castenada, Thoreau, Spinoza, Buddhist visionaries, and Taoist physics. With a cast of prima donnas like this on stage it is very hard to follow the script."[1] In this paper, I shall try not to "discuss everything at once" by confining my attention mainly to what I take to be the central intuition of deep ecology, and to some considerations related to that intuition. Even so, I shall still be making reference to "Buddhist visionaries and Taoist physics" for at least one compelling reason: not to refer to the parallels between deep ecology, the mystical traditions,[2] and the so-called "new physics" (i.e. post 1920s physics) might well indicate that one had *missed* the central intuition of deep ecology since, fundamentally, each of these fields of understanding subscribes to a similar structure of reality, a similar cosmology. Deep ecology's "disparate authorities" turn out to be not as disparate as they at first appear. Moreover, comparison with these other fields can, I believe, be fruitful in clarifying some of deep ecology's vaguer or more contradictory aspects.

The distinction between 'shallow' and 'deep' ecology was made in 1972 (and published the following year) by the distinguished Norwegian philosopher Arne Naess, and has subsequently been developed by a number of thinkers (most notably, Bill Devall and George Sessions) to the point where we may now reasonably refer to an intellectual 'deep ecology movement.'[3] The shallow/deep ecology distinction has generated so much discussion that it has become difficult to distil to any simple essence but, for the sake of brevity, it could be characterized by the following three points.

First, shallow ecology views humans as separate from their environment. Figure/ground boundaries are sharply drawn such that humans are perceived as the significant figures against a ground that only assumes significance in so far as it enhances humans' images of themselves *qua* important figures. Shallow ecology thus views humans as the source of all value and ascribes only instrumental (or use) value to the nonhuman world.[4] It is, in short, anthropocentric, representing that attitude to conservation that says: "We ought to preserve the environment (i.e., what lies outside the boundary) not for its own sake but because of its value to us (i.e., what lies inside the boundary)." Deep ecology, on the other hand, rejects "the (human)-in-environment image in favour of the relational, total-field image."[5] Organisms are then viewed rather "as knots in the biospherical net or field of intrinsic relations."[6] Figure/ground boundaries are replaced by a holistic or gestalt view where, in Devall's words, "the person is not above or outside of nature ... (but) ... is part of creation on-going."[7] This 'total-field' conception dissolves not only the notion of humans as separate from their environment but the very notion of the world as composed of discrete, compact, separate 'things'. When we do talk about the world as if it were a collection of discrete, isolable 'things' we are, in Naess's view, *"talking at a superficial or preliminary level of communication."*[8] Deep ecology thus strives to be non-anthropocentric by viewing humans as just one constituency among others in the biotic community, just one particular strand in the web of life, just one kind of knot in the biospherical net. The intrinsic value of the nonhuman members of the biotic community is recognized and the right of these members to pursue their own evolutionary destinies is taken as "an intuitively clear and obvious value axiom."[9] In contrast, the idea that humans are the source or ground of all value ('the measure of all things') is viewed as the arrogant conceit of those who dwell in the moral equivalent of a Ptolemaic universe. Deep ecologists are concerned to move heaven and earth in this universe in order to effect a 'paradigm shift'[10] of comparable significance to that associated with Copernicus.

Second (and directly related to the above), in its acceptance of what Sessions refers to as 'discrete entity metaphysics'[11] shallow ecology accepts by default or positively endorses the dominant metaphysics of mechanistic materialism. Viewing knowledge, too, as amenable to discrete compartmentalization, the shallow approach considers ethics in isolation from metaphysics with the consequence that the dominant metaphysics is usually implicitly assumed. Deep ecology, however, is concerned to criticize mechanistic materialism and to replace it with a better 'code for reading nature.'[12] This code can be generally described as one of 'unity in process.'[13] By this is indicated both the idea that all 'things' are fundamentally (i.e., internally) related and the idea that these interrelationships are in constant flux (i.e., they are characterized by process/dynamism/instability/novelty/creativity, etc). This conception of the world lends itself far more readily to organismic rather than mechanical metaphors, and thus to panpsychic or pantheistic rather than inert, dead-matter conceptions of the nonhuman world. Among Western philosophers, Spinoza, Whitehead and Heidegger are most often invoked for the purposes of articulating this vision of the world or, particularly in the case of Heidegger, for the purposes of articulating the 'letting be' mode of being most appropriate to such a deep ecological

understanding of the world.[14] Deep ecology also has an enormous respect for many non-Western views since 'unity in process' and panpsychic conceptions of the world have received sophisticated elaboration in Eastern spiritual traditions and in the mythological systems of other non-Western peoples. This respect also extends to the entire sensibility or mode of being-in-the-world of some of these traditions since this often accords with the non-power-seeking sensibility of deep ecology.[15] In stressing the interconnection between ethics and metaphysics, deep ecology recognizes that an ecologically effective ethics can only arise within the context of a more persuasive and more enchanting cosmology than that of mechanistic materialism.[16]

Third, in terms of its social, political and economic project, shallow ecology tends to accept by default or positively endorse the ideology of economic growth which characterizes industrial and developing societies of all political complexions. It is thus often referred to as the 'Resource Management' or 'Resource Conservation and Development' approach. As such, it is content to operate in a reformist fashion within the 'dominant social paradigm'[17] and, often, to accept the economic reduction (i.e., the reduction of all values to economic terms) for the purposes of decision making. Deep ecology on the other hand, is concerned to address existing social, political and economic arrangements and to replace the ideology of economic growth with the ideology of ecological sustainability. It is insisted that economics (etymologically: 'management of the household') must be seen as subsidiary to ecology ('study of the household'), and the economic reduction of values is thus firmly resisted.[18] Key ideas in deep ecology's social, political and economic project include those of a just and sustainable society, carrying capacity, frugality (or 'voluntary simplicity'), dwelling in place, cultural and biological diversity, local autonomy and decentralization, soft energy paths, appropriate technology, reinhabitation, and bioregionalism. These last two perhaps require some elaboration. Reinhabitation refers to the process of relearning how to live in place, how to establish a 'sense of place', how to dwell in and care for a place. Some people are attempting to cultivate consciously this sense, under the most difficult of circumstances, by moving into areas that have been degraded by industrial 'development' and participating in the re-establishment of a rich and diverse ecosystem. Bioregions refer to areas possessing common characteristics of soils, watersheds, plants and animals (e.g., the Amazon jungle). It is argued that bioregions should replace nation-states as the fundamental geographical unit in terms of which humans think and live. The human carrying capacity for each bioregion should be determined in terms of the number of humans that can be supported living at a level of resource use that is adequate for their needs but minimally intrusive on their environment. Here, of course, lie a multitude of difficult questions for the political agenda of deep ecology. However, these questions have, in various forms, been addressed by numerous societies in the past (including a minority tradition in Western society) and are now being taken up by increasing numbers of thinkers in highly industrialized societies.

It should be clear from this summary that many writers whose work falls within the ambit of deep ecology do not necessarily describe themselves as 'deep ecologists'. A good example is Theodore Roszak who, in his 1972 book *Where the Wasteland Ends*, pointed to the same kind of distinction as Naess:

> Ecology stands at a critical cross-roads. Is it, too, to become another anthropocentric technique of efficient manipulation, a matter of enlightened self-interest and expert, long-range resource budgeting? Or will it meet the nature mystics on their own terms and so recognize that we are to embrace nature as if indeed it were a beloved person in whom, as in ourselves, something sacred dwells? . . . The question remains open: which will ecology be, the last of the old sciences or the first of the new?[19]

However, despite this and other attempts by philosophers, historians and sociologists to distinguish between various streams of environmentalism, Naess's twelve year old shallow/deep ecology terminology seems to have stuck as the most economical and striking way of referring to the major division within contemporary environmental thought. The conceptualization of this division clearly constitutes a powerful organizing idea in terms of providing a focal point from which to view the relationships between a number of otherwise very diffuse strands of ecologically oriented thought.

The Intuition of Deep Ecology

It should be clear from my brief outline of the shallow/deep ecology distinction that many of the views held by deep ecologists go well beyond the data of ecology conceived as an empiric-analytic science. As Arne Naess said when introducing the shallow/deep ecology distinction: " . . . the norms and tendencies of the Deep Ecology movement are not derived from ecology by logic or induction. Ecological knowledge and the life-style of the ecological field-worker have *suggested, inspired, and fortified* the perspectives of the Deep Ecology movement."[20] Deep ecologists have, therefore, taken the point made by Donald Worster in his study of the history of ecological ideas from the eighteenth century to the early 1970s:

> In the case of the ecological ethic . . . one might say that its proponents picked out their values first and only afterward came to science for its stamp of approval. It might have been the better part of honesty if they had come out and announced that, for some reason or by some personal standard of value, they were constrained to promote a deeper sense of integration between (humans) and nature, a more-than-economic relatedness – and to let all the appended scientific arguments go. 'Ought' might then be its own justification, its own defence, its own persuasion, regardless of what 'is.'
>
> That more straightforward stance has now and again been adopted by a few intuitionists, mystics, and transcendentalists. Most people, however, have not been so willing to trust their inner voices, perhaps due to lack of self-confidence or out of fear that such wholly individual exercise of choice will lead to the general disintegration of the moral community.[21]

Deep ecologists *are* 'willing to trust their inner voices' in the hope that the dominant social paradigm (within which the moral community is situated) *will* disintegrate – although in a creative rather than a destructive manner. Again, Arne Naess is quite explicit on these points in a recent interview in *The Ten Directions*, a magazine published by the Zen Centre of Los Angeles:

> *Ten Directions*: This brings us back to the question of information versus intuition. Your feeling

is that we can't expect to have an ideal amount of information but must somehow act on what we know?

Naess: Yes. It's easier for deep ecologists than for others because we have certain fundamental values, a fundamental view of what's meaningful in life, what's worth maintaining, which makes it completely clear that we are opposed to further development for the sake of increased domination and an increased standard of living. The material standard of living should be drastically reduced and the quality of life, in the sense of basic satisfaction in the depths of one's heart or soul, should be maintained or increased. This view is intuitive, as are all important views, in the sense that it can't be proven. As Aristotle said, it shows a lack of education to try to prove everything because you have to have a starting point. You can't prove the methodology of science, you can't prove logic, because logic presupposes fundamental premisses.[22]

However, the *central* intuition of deep ecology, the one from which Naess's views on practice flow, is the first point I made in my summary of the shallow/deep ecology distinction. This is the idea that there is no firm ontological divide in the field of existence. In other words, the world simply is not divided up into independently existing subjects and objects, nor is there any bifurcation in reality between the human and non-human realms. Rather all entities are constituted by their relationships. To the extent that we perceive boundaries, we fall short of a deep ecological consciousness. In Devall's words: "Deep ecology begins with unity rather than dualism which has been the dominant theme of Western philosophy."[23]

The Intuition of Deep Ecology and Cross-Disciplinary Parallels

The central intuition of deep ecology finds a profound resonance in both the mystical traditions and the 'new physics'. For example, the 'perennial philosophy' tells us, and the meditative process is claimed to reveal, that 'Thou art That.'[24] In other words, it is claimed that by subtracting your own self-centred and self-serving thoughts from the world you come to realize that "the other is none other than yourself: that the fundamental delusion of humanity is to suppose I am here and you are out there."[25] This understanding permeates

the mystical traditions and is exemplified in the Taoist advice to "identify yourself with non-distinction."[26] Likewise, the Zen teacher Chü-chih would answer any question he was asked by holding up one finger, while the contemporary Zen roshi Robert Aitken says that "we save all beings by including them."[27] The mystical traditions are simply full of differing illustrations of this same point.[28] Ken Wilber, editor of the journal *Revision* and perhaps the most significant recent integrator of Eastern and Western worldviews, expresses the mystical understanding in these terms: "We fall from Heaven in this moment and this moment and this, every time we embrace boundaries and live as a separate self sense."[29] Just so, adds the deep ecologist, do we fall short of a *deep* ecological consciousness.

It is now becoming commonplace to point to the fundamentally similar cosmologies embodied in the mystical traditions on the one hand and the 'new physics' on the other.[30] What is *structurally* similar about these cosmologies is that they reveal a 'seamless web' view of the universe. As David Bohm, the distinguished Professor of Theoretical Physics at Birbeck College, University of London, has said in an interview with the philosopher Renée Weber:

Bohm: . . . the present state of theoretical physics implies that empty space has all this energy and matter is a slight increase of the energy, and therefore matter is like a small ripple on this tremendous ocean of energy, having some relative stability, and being manifest. (Thus, my suggestion of an 'implicate order') implies a reality immensely beyond what we call matter. Matter itself is merely a ripple in this background . . . in this ocean of energy . . .

Weber: This view is of course very beautiful, breath taking in fact, but would a physicist who pressed you on this . . . find some kind of basis *in physics* for allowing such a vision to be postulated?

Bohm: Well, I should think it's what physics directly implies.[31]

Both the mystical traditions and the 'new physics' serve to generate, *inter alia*, what we might now call 'ecological awareness', that is, awareness of the fundamental interrelatedness of all things or, more accurately, all events.[32] The theoretical physicist Fritjof Capra has been quite explicit about this: "I think what physics can do is help to generate ecological awareness. You see, in my

Warwick Fox

view now the Western version of mystical awareness, our version of Buddhism or Taoism, will be ecological awareness."[33] Where the physicist, the mystic, and the deep ecologist (as philosopher) differ is in their *means* of arriving at an 'ecological awareness'. In terms of Wilber's typology of modes of inquiry, we could say that the physicist (like the 'scientific' ecologist) emphasizes 'empiric-analytic inquiry' (i.e. analysis of measurements), the mystic emphasizes 'transcendental inquiry' (i.e. contemplation), and the deep ecologist (as philosopher) emphasizes 'mental-phenomenological inquiry' (i.e. analysis of meaning: here we include such things as reflection on personal experience, the analysis of valuational arguments, and the meaning of knowledge furnished by the other two modes of inquiry).[34] However, all three modes of inquiry lead to a similar conception of the underlying structure of reality. Like the mystic and the 'new physicist', the deep ecologist is drawn to a cosmology of (in David Bohm's words) "unbroken wholeness which denies the classical idea of the analyzability of the world into separately and independently existing parts."[35]

A New Cosmology

While I refer to this view as the central *intuition* of deep ecology, I do not in any way mean that it is irrational or ungrounded. The deep ecologist who is pressed to say whether there is a basis *in ecology* for "allowing such a vision to be postulated" can reply, in the manner of David Bohm, that this cosmology is what ecology directly implies. Moreover, the deep ecologist can argue that if there is substance to the "hypothesis of emerging cross-disciplinary parallels" advocated by the neurophysiologist Roger Walsh, then the parallels between the structures of reality advanced by deep ecology, the mystical traditions and the 'new physics' are enormously significant rather than trivial coincidences or accidents of language. Briefly, Walsh's hypothesis is that we can enhance our perceptual sensitivity by the augmentation of normal sensory perception (as in science), by intellectual conceptual analysis (as in philosophy), or by direct perceptual training (as in meditation), and that:

no matter how it is obtained, (perceptual) enhancement of sufficient degree may reveal a

different order or reality from that to which we are accustomed. Furthermore, the properties so revealed will be essentially more fundamental and veridical than the usual, and will display a greater degree of commonality across disciplines. Thus as empirical disciplines evolve and become more sensitive, they might be expected to uncover phenomena and properties which point toward underlying commonalities and parallels between disciplines and across levels.[37]

On the basis of emerging cross-disciplinary parallels such as those I discuss above, Walsh proceeds to argue that the classical Greek and, later, Cartesian concept of the universe as "essentially atomistic, divisible, isolable, static, nonrelativistic, and comprehensible by reductionism, is in the process of replacement, not just for physics where evidence for such a shift was first obtained, but for all sciences."[37] Deep ecology throws its full weight behind this shift, and is in accord with Walsh that the fundamental ontology now being revealed can be described as "largely dynamic, fluid, impermanent, holistic, interconnected, interdependent, foundationless, self-consistent, empty, paradoxical, probabilistic, infinitely over-determined, and inextricably linked to the consciousness of the observer."[38]

But beyond what the data of ecology – or of science generally – seem to imply, and beyond the significance or otherwise of emerging cross-disciplinary parallels, the central vision of deep ecologists *is* a matter of intuition in Worster's and Naess's sense. That is, it is a matter of trusting one's inner voice in the adoption of a value stance or a view that can not itself be proven or disconfirmed. There is nothing alarming or even unusual in the use of intuition understood in this sense. Philosophers of science generally accept that scientific theories, let alone metaphysical systems (or 'ontic theories' as Quine calls them), are *constrained* by facts but are *underdetermined* by them. In other words, the same data can always be theorized or interpreted in a number of ways that are nevertheless *consistent* with the data. How then are we to decide between competing theories and world-views? An evaluative stance must ultimately be adopted and, for the deep ecologists, this means the promotion of, in Worster's words, "a deeper sense of integration between (humans) and nature."[39]

Ecological Justice and 'Procrustean Ethics'

In their zeal to effect this integration, deep ecologists have firmly coupled their central intuition of no boundaries in the biospherical field to the notion of 'biospherical egalitarianism – in principle.'[40] As a result, these notions tend to go everywhere together, almost as if they implied each other (although I shall argue they do not). These two ideas constituted the first two points in Naess's original seven-point outline of deep ecology, while Devall commented in his 1980 overview of the 'deep ecology movement' that "in deep ecology, the wholeness and integrity of person/ planet together with the principle of what Arne Naess calls 'biological equalitarianism' are the most important ideas."[41]

'Biospherical egalitarianism' effectively refers to the equal intrinsic worth of all members of the biosphere: "the equal right to live and blossom is (taken as) an intuitively clear and obvious value axiom."[42] The 'in principle' clause is added to this value axiom because it is recognized that "any realistic praxis necessitates some killing, exploitation and suppression."[43]

The idea that, in principle, no organism possesses greater intrinsic value than any other means that two major classes of value-theory have been condemned by deep ecologists as anthropocentric. First are those theories of value whose practical application implies that the nonhuman world possesses *only* instrumental (or use) value. Traditional, mainstream Christian ethics, secular Western ethics such as utilitarianism and Kantian ethics, and modern economic theory are typically included in this class. In the second class are those recent attempts to develop a practical ecological ethics which recognizes the intrinsic value of the nonhuman world but which ascribes *differential* intrinsic value to organisms depending on their complexity and, hence, capacity for richness of experience.

Now those theories of value which fall into the first class are clearly anthropocentric in the most obvious sense – they embody that essential 'arrogance of humanism'[44] which views the nonhuman world purely as a means to human ends. But to the extent that we can describe those theories of value in the second class as anthropocentric, we are using that term in a very different sense. The second class of value-theory (often inspired by Whitehead's thought) can be considered as philosophy catching up with the biological news. Humans are not posited as the source of all value, nor is it denied that organisms possessing nervous systems of comparable complexity to that of humans (such as whales and dolphins) also possess comparable intrinsic value. Moreover, and most importantly, it is *not* assumed or implied that organisms possessing greater intrinsic value have any right to exploit those possessing lesser intrinsic value. Quite the contrary. For example, in Birch and Cobb's recent elaboration of this second kind of value theory, their central ethic is that we have an obligation to act so as to *maximize richness of experience in general* – which includes the richness of experience on the nonhuman world.[45]

Yet deep ecologists dismiss this second class of value-theory, along with the first, as anthropocentric. For example, with respect to the second class, Sessions refers to the 'pecking order in this moral barnyard' and argues that:

> The point is not whether humans do in fact have the greatest degree of sentience on this planet ... (but that, for deep ecologists) ... the degree of sentience is *irrelevant* in terms of how humans relate to the rest of Nature. And so, contemporary Whiteheadian ecological ethics does not meet the deep ecology insistence on 'ecological egalitarianism in principle.'[46]

I think deep ecologists tend to conflate principle and practice when they make judgements such as this. As Birch and Cobb's ethic makes clear, the second class of value theorists need have no argument with the axiom that all organisms have an 'equal right to live and blossom' *when genuine conflicts of value are absent.* And this, I think, does satisfy the deep ecologist's insistence on ecological egalitarianism *in principle.* But as Naess points out, value conflicts can never be completely avoided in practice; the process of living entails some forms of "killing, exploitation, and suppression." To this extent, then, the degree of sentience becomes extremely relevant in terms of how humans relate to the rest of nature *if* they are to resolve *genuine* conflicts of value in anything other than a capricious or expedient manner.

The deep ecologist who is 'thoroughgoing' in confusing ecological egalitarianism in principle with ecological egalitarianism in practice is forced into the position that they might as well eat meat as vegetables since all organisms possess equal intrinsic value. In stark contrast to this position is the comment by Alan Watts that he was a vegetarian "because cows scream louder than carrots",[47] and this is, in essence, the argument of the second class of value theorists – and the view, I am sure, that deep ecologists tend to adopt *in practice*. Deep ecology thus does itself a disservice by employing a definition of anthropocentrism which is so overly exclusive that it condemns more or less *any* theory of value that attempts to guide 'realistic praxis'. This observation explains why deep ecological theorizing has shied away from considering situations of genuine value conflict and why it has not come forth with ethical guidelines for those situations where some form of killing, exploitation or suppression *is* necessitated. Unless deep ecologists take up this challenge and employ a workable definition of anthropocentrism, they may well become known as the advocates of 'Procrustean Ethics' as they attempt to fit all organisms to the same dimensions of intrinsic value. Again, diversity is the key.

Cross-disciplinary analogies may add emphasis to the above. When the 'new physicist' considers matter as a ripple on a tremendous ocean of energy, this conception of 'unity in process' does not then imply that, at any given moment, all ripples are of equal magnitude. In terms of cosmic time, these ripples are continuously rising and falling, but at any given moment real differences exist. Likewise, the mystic's conception of 'unity in process' does not deny that, at any given moment, some forms are more significant expressions of pure consciousness than others – notwithstanding the knowledge that, from the aspect of eternity, all forms are fleeting. In fact, the notion of a hierarchy of states of mind/being, with greater value being ascribed to the higher states, is central to all mystical traditions. Similarly, the deep ecologist's conception of 'unity in process' need not imply that, at any given moment, all 'knots' (i.e. organisms) in the 'biospherical net' are constituted of equally complex relations. To the extent that value inheres in complexity of relations, and to the extent that complexity of relations is evidenced in the degree of an organism's central organization (and therefore capacity for richness of experience), then organisms are entitled to moral consideration commensurate with their degree of central organization (or capacity for richness of experience) for the duration of their existence – as transient as that may be in terms of evolutionary time.

In pursuing their central intuition of 'unity' (i.e. of no boundaries in the biospherical field), deep ecologists have possibly lost sight of the significance of the 'in process' aspect of their 'unity in process' metaphysics. Attention to this latter aspect suggests that any process continuously produces impermanent, uneven distributions (i.e., different values) of various attributes (and in the process of the world these attributes may be money, information, complexity of relations, and so on). If this were not so then we would have no process but a perfectly uniform, homogenous and, therefore, lifeless field. The only universe where value is spread evenly across the field is a dead universe.[48] Recognizing this, we should be clear that the central intuition of deep ecology does not entail the view that intrinsic value is spread evenly across the membership of the biotic community. Moreover, in situations of genuine value conflict, justice is better served by *not* subscribing to the view of ecological egalitarianism. Cows do scream louder than carrots. As Charles Birch and John Cobb have remarked: "Justice does not require equality. It does require that we share one another's fate."[49] There is, however, a shallow and a deep sense of sharing one another's fate. The shallow sense is simply that of being subject to the same forces. It does not involve caring. The deep sense, intended by Birch and Cobb, involves love and compassion. It involves the *enlargement of one's sphere of identification*. The lesson of ecology is that we do share one another's fate in the shallow sense since we all share the fate of the earth. The message of deep ecology is that we ought to care as deeply and as compassionately as possible about that fate – not because it *affects* us but because it *is* us.

Notes

This text is a revised version of a paper delivered to the "Environment, Ethics and Ecology Conference", Australian National University, 26–28 August, 1983. A considerable number of people have read this paper in its original version and offered detailed criticisms, comments, and/or encouragement. In particular, I am grateful to Robin Attfield, Baird Callicott, John Cobb, Bill Devall, Brian Easlea, Jeremy Evans, Patsy Hallen, Judy Lockhart, Arne Naess, John Seed, George Sessions, Swami Shankarananda, Michael Zimmerman and, especially, Charles Birch.

1 Godfrey-Smith, W. Environmental philosophy. *Habitat*, June, 1980, 24–25, p. 24.

2 Where I refer to the "mystical traditions". Aldous Huxley uses the phrase "perennial philosophy", while the neurophysiologist Roger Walsh refers to the "consciousness disciplines". (See: Huxley, A. *The Perennial Philosophy*, New York: Harper Colophon Books, 1970 (originally 1944); Walsh, R. Emerging cross-disciplinary parallels: suggestions from the neurosciences. *The Journal of Transpersonal Psychology*, 1979, 11: 175–84; and Walsh, R. *Towards an Ecology of Brain*, New York: Spectrum Publications, 1981). Huxley, Walsh and I are referring to a similar, if not identical, corpus of knowledge, the authors of which are commonly referred to as "mystics".

3 Articles marked by an asterisk in this note appear in Devall, B. and Sessions, G. *Deep Ecology*, Layton, Utah: Peregrine Smith Books, 1984.

Devall, B.	Reform environmentalism. *Humboldt Journal of Social Relations*, 1979, 6:129–58*.
Devall, B.	The deep ecology movement. *Natural Resources Journal*, 1980, 20:299–322*.
Devall, B.	Muir redux: from conservation to ecology, 1890–1990. *Humboldt Journal of Social Relations*, 1982(a) 9:172–97*.
Devall, B.	Ecological consciousness and ecological resisting: guidelines for comprehension and research. *Humboldt Journal of Social Relations*, 1982(b), 9 (2).
Devall, B.	Ecological realism. In: Tobias, M. (ed.) *Deep Ecology*, San Diego: Avant Books, 1984(a).
Devall, B.	New age and deep ecology: contrasting paradigms. Manuscript.
Devall, B. and Sessions, G.	The development of natural resources and the integrity of nature: Contrasting views of management. *Environmental Ethics*, 1984(a), 6 (4):293–322.
Devall, B. and Sessions, G.	*Deep Ecology*, Layton. Utah: Peregrine Smith Books, 1984(b).
Naess, A.	The shallow and the deep, long-range ecology movement. A summary. *Inquiry*, 1973, 16:95–100.
Naess, A.	Notes on the methodology of normative systems. *Methodology and Science*, 1977(a), 10:64–79.
Naess, A.	Spinoza and ecology, *Philosophia*, 1977(b), 7:45–54.
Naess, A.	Validity of norms – but which norms? Self-realisation? Reply to Harald Afstad. In: Gullvag, I. and Wetlesen, J. (eds.) *In Sceptical Wonder: Inquiries into the philosophy of Arne Naess on the occasion of his 70th birthday*, Oslo: Universitetsforlaget, 1982, pp. 257–69.
Naess, A.	A defence of the deep ecology movement. *Environmental Ethics*, 1984, 6 (3):265–70.
Naess, A. and Bodian, S.	Simple in means, rich in ends: a conversation with Arne Naess. *The Ten Directions*, 1982, 3(2): 7, 10–12.
Sessions, G. E	Ecophilosophy 1, April 1976, 14p. Ecophilosophy 2, May 1979, 48p. Ecophilosophy 3, April 1981, 20p. Ecophilosophy 4, May 1982, 34p. Ecophilosophy 5, May 1983, 24p. c/o George Sessions, Philosophy Dept., Sierra College, Rocklin, Calif. 95677.
Sessions, G.	Anthropocentrism and the environmental crisis. *Humboldt Journal of Social Relations*, 1974(a), 2:1–12.
Sessions, G.	Panpsychism versus modern materialism: some implications for an ecological ethics. Revised and extended version of a paper delivered at the conference on "The Rights of Non-Human Nature", Pitzer College, Claremont, California, April 18–20, 1974(b), 39p.
Sessions, G.	Spinoza and Jeffers on man in nature. *Inquiry*, 1977, 20:481–528*.
Sessions, G.	Spinoza, perennial philosophy and deep ecology. Paper presented to first national "Reminding" conference ("Philosophy, Where Are You?"). Dominican College, San Raphael, California, June 29–July 4, 1979, 34p*.
Sessions, G.	Shallow and deep ecology: a review of the philosophical literature. In: Schultz, R. and Hughes, J. (eds.) *Ecological Consciousness: Essays for the Earthday X colloquium. University of Denver, April 21–24, 1980*. Washington D.C.: University Press of America, 1981, p. 391–462*.
Sessions, G.	Ecophilosophy, utopias, and education. *Journal of Environmental Education*, 1983, 15:27–42*.
Sessions, G.	Ecological consciousness and paradigm change. In: Tobias, M. (ed.) *Deep Ecology*, San Diego: Avant Books, 1984.

4 For an illuminating characterisation of various classes of instrumental value, see: Godfrey-Smith, W. "The value of wilderness," *Environmental Ethics*, 1979, 1:309–19.

5 Naess, "The shallow and the deep", p. 95.

6 Ibid.

7 Devall, "The deep ecology movement", p. 303.

8 Naess, "The shallow and the deep", p. 95.

9 Ibid., p. 96.

10 Kuhn, T. *The Structure of Scientific Revolutions*, University of Chicago Press, 1970.

11 Sessions, 1983, "Ecophilosophy", p. 29.

12 Skolimowski, H. *Eco-philosophy: Designing new tactics for living*, London, Marion Boyars, 1981, p. vii.

13 Roszak, T. *Where the Wasteland Ends: Politics and transcendence in post-industrial society*. London: Faber, 1973, p. 400.

14 For more on internal relations, process metaphysics, organismic metaphors, and Whitehead, see my review of Birch and Cobb entitled "Liberating Life" in *The Ecologist*, 1984, No. 4 (Birch and Cobb's book is cited at note 32 below.)

15 Roszak (ibid.) describes the sensibility of ecology in its "subversive", or deeper, aspect as: "wholistic, receptive, trustful, largely non-tampering, deeply grounded in aesthetic intuition".

16 The German sociologist Max Weber believed that with the "rationalisation" of the world by scientific techniques (i.e., the rendering of all aspects of the world as *potentially* controllable and calculable) we have lost our sense of the sacred and the world has become "disenchanted". See Baum, G. Does the world remain disenchanted? *Social Research*, 1970, 37:153–203: Chapter 1 in Freund, J. *The Sociology of Max Weber*, London: Penguin, 1968; and Weber's essay "Science as a Vocation" in Gerth. H. and Mills, C. *From Max Weber: Essays in Sociology*, London: Routledge and Kegan Paul, 1948.

17 "Reformist environmentalism" and the "dominant social paradigm" are characterized by Devall. On the "dominant social paradigm" see also Devall, 1980, "The deep ecology movement".

18 On the commensurability and incommensurability of economic and other values, see Godfrey-Smith, "The value of wilderness".

19 Roszak, *Where the Wasteland Ends*, pp. 403–4.

20 Naess, "The shallow and the deep", p. 98.

21 Worster, D. *Nature's Economy: The roots of ecology*. San Francisco: Sierra Club Books, 1977, pp. 336–7.

22 Naess, "Validity of norms", pp. 11–12.

23 Devall, "The deep ecology movement", p. 309. The ecologist Paul Shepard speaks eloquently to this point: "Ecological thinking . . . requires a kind of vision across boundaries. The epidermis of the skin is ecologically like a pond surface or a forest soil, not a shell so much as a delicate interpenetration" (Sessions, "Spinoza, perennial philosophy" p. 8).

24 This phrase derives from the Sanskrit formulation "tat tvam asi" and is rendered "That art Thou" by Huxley (*The Perennial Philosophy*) and "Thou art That" in Juan Mascaro's translation of *The Upanishads* (Harmondsworth: Penguin 1965).

25 Aitken, R. *Taking the Path of Zen*, San Francisco: North Point Press, 1982, p. 33 and p. 77 respectively. See also: Aitken, R. Gandhi, Dogen, and deep ecology. *Nothing Special*, July 1980.

26 Smart, N. and Hecht, R. (eds.) *Sacred Texts of the World: A universal anthology*, London: Macmillan, 1982, p. 298.

27 Aitken, *Taking the Path of Zen*, p. 26 and p. 73 respectively.

28 For a brief but illuminating demonstration of this claim see chapter 9 ("The one in world scriptures") in: Cooper, J. *Yin and Yang: the Taoist harmony of opposites*, Wellingborough: The Aquarian Press, 1982.

29 Wilber, K. Odyssey: "A personal inquiry into humanistic and transpersonal psychology." *Journal of Humanistic Psychology*, 1982, 22:57–90, p. 71.

30 Some books either on, or which embody, this theme include David Bohm's *Wholeness and the Implicate Order* (London: Routledge and Kegan Paul, 1980): Fritjof Capra's *The Tao of Physics* (Glasgow: Fontana, 1976); Michael Talbot's *Mysticism and the New Physics* (New York: Bantam Books, 1981); and Gary Zukav's *The Dancing Wu Li Masters: An overview of the new physics* (Bungay, Suffolk: Fontana, 1981). Despite this recent spate of books; it would be a mistake to assume that reference to the parallels between the cosmologies of physics and the mystical traditions is a "New Age" phenomenon. Oppenheimer explicitly pointed to such parallels in 1954 (*Science and the Common Understanding*, London: Oxford University Press) as did Bohr in 1958 (*Atomic Physics and Human Knowledge*, New York: John Wiley). That being said, for an erudite critique of the *dangers* involved in drawing such parallels see Wilber's essay entitled "Physics, mysticism and the new holographic paradigm" in: Wilber K. (ed) *The Holographic Paradigm and Other Paradoxes: Exploring the leading edge of science*, Boulder: Shambhala, 1982. (Reprinted in: Wilber, K. *Eye to Eye: The quest for the new paradigm*, New York: Anchor Books, 1983). Against Wilber's criticisms, however, one should balance Walsh's observations on the *significance* of these "emerging cross-disciplinary parallels" (see Walsh, "Emerging cross-disciplinary parallels" and *Towards an Ecology*).

31 Bohm, D. and Weber, R. "The enfolding unfolding universe: A conversation with David Bohm con-

ducted by Renée Weber." In: Wilber (ed.), *The Holographic Paradigm*, pp. 56–7.

32 For an introduction to a "process" conception of life (via Whitehead) whereby "things", so-called, are viewed as *enduring societies of events*, see Charles Birch and John Cobb's *The Liberation of Life: From the cell to the community* (Cambridge: Cambridge University Press, 1981).

33 Capra, F. and Weber, R. " 'The Tao of Physics' revisited: A conversation with Fritjof Capra conducted by Renée Weber." In: Wilber (ed.), 1982, *The Holographic Paradigm*, p. 229.

34 Wilber, *Eye to Eye*. See Chapter 2: "The problem of proof."

35 In: Capra, *The Tao of Physics*, pp. 141–2.

36 Walsh, "Emerging cross-disciplinary parallels", p. 175.

37 Ibid., p. 176.

38 Ibid., p. 180.

39 Worster, *Nature's Economy*, p. 337. Mary Hesse argues that "we can observe by hindsight that in the early stages of a science, value judgements (such as the centrality of (humans) in the universe) provide some of the reasons for choice among competing underdetermined theories" (*Revolutions and Reconstructions in the Philosophy of Science*, Brighton, Sussex: Harvester, 1980, p. 190). For deep ecologists the situation is just the opposite: value judgements such as the *lack* of centrality of humans in the universe provide some of the reasons for choice among competing underdetermined theories (and here I include metaphysical views or "ontic theories").

40 Naess, "The shallow and the deep", p. 95.

41 Devall, "The deep ecology movement", p. 310.

42 Naess, "The shallow and the deep", p. 96.

43 Ibid., p. 95.

44 Ehrenfeld, D. *The Arrogance of Humanism*, Oxford: Oxford University Press, 1981.

45 Birch and Cobb, *The Liberation of Life*.

46 Sessions, "Spinoza, perennial philosophy", p. 18. The phrase "a pecking order in this moral barnyard" comes from John Rodman who used it in his insightful critique of Peter Singer's "Animal Liberation" and Christopher Stone's "Should Trees Have Standing?" See Rodman, J. The liberation of nature? *Inquiry*, 1977, 20:83–145, p. 93.

47 Aitken, *Taking the Path of Zen*, p. 81.

48 In a slightly different context, Wilber (1983, *Eye to Eye*, p. 295) argues that statements like "all is one" or "all is Brahman" typically give rise to a false picture of the universe that reduces all diversity and multiplicity to "uniform, homogenous, and unchanging mush" or to "uniform, all-pervading, featureless but divine goo."

49 Birch and Cobb, *The Liberation of Life*, p. 165.

20

The Deep Ecological Movement: Some Philosophical Aspects

Arne Naess

1 Deep Ecology on the Defensive

Increasing pressures for continued growth and development have placed the vast majority of environmental professionals on the defensive. By way of illustration:

The field-ecologist Ivar Mysterud, who both professionally and vigorously advocated deep ecological principles in the late 1960s, encountered considerable resistance. Colleagues at his university said he should keep to his science and not meddle in philosophical and political matters. He should resist the temptation to become a prominent "popularizer" through mass media exposure. Nevertheless, he persisted and influenced thousands of people (including myself).

Mysterud became a well-known professional "expert" at assessing the damage done when bears killed or maimed sheep and other domestic animals in Norway. According to the law, their owners are paid damages. And licensed hunters receive permission to shoot bears if their misdeeds become considerable.[1] Continued growth and development required that the sheep industry consolidate, and sheepowners became fewer, richer, and tended to live in cities. As a result of wage increases, they could not afford to hire shepherds to watch the flocks, so the sheep were left on their own even more than before. Continued growth also required moving sheep to what was traditionally considered "bear territory." In spite of this invasion, bear populations grew and troubles multiplied.

How did Mysterud react to these new problems? Did he set limits to the amount of human/sheep encroachment on bear territory? Did he attempt a direct application of his deep ecological perspective to these issues? Quite the contrary. He adopted what appeared to be a shallow wildlife management perspective, and defended the sheepowners: more money to compensate for losses, quicker compensation, and the immediate hiring of hunters who killed mostly "juvenile delinquent" bears accused of killing many sheep.

Protectors of big carnivores noted with concern the change of Mysterud's public "image"; had he really abandoned his former value priorities? Privately he insisted that he hadn't. But in public he tended to remain silent.

The reason for M.'s unexpected actions was not difficult to find: the force of economic growth was so strong that the laws protecting bears would be changed in a highly unfavorable direction if the sheepowners were not soon pacified by accepting some of their not unreasonable demands. After all, it did cost a lot of money to hire and equip people to locate a flock of sheep which had been harassed by a bear and, further, to prove the bear's guilt. And the bureaucratic procedures involved were time-consuming. M. had not changed his basic value priorities at all. Rather, he had adopted a purely defensive compromise. He stopped promoting his deep ecology philosophy publicly in order to retain credibility and standing among opponents of his principles and to retain his friendships with sheepowners.

And what is true of Mysterud is also true of thousands of other professional ecologists and environmentalists. These people often hold responsible positions in society where they might strengthen responsible environmental policy, but, given the exponential forces of growth, their publications, if any, are limited to narrowly professional and specialized concerns. Their writings are surely competent, but lack a deeper and more comprehensive perspective (although I admit that there are some brilliant exceptions to this).

If professional ecologists persist in voicing their value priorities, their jobs are often in danger, or they tend to lose influence and status among those who are in charge of overall policies.[2] Privately, they admit the necessity for deep and far-ranging changes, but they no longer speak out in public. As a result, people deeply concerned about ecology and the environment feel abandoned and even betrayed by the "experts" who work within the "establishment."

In ecological debates, many participants know a lot about particular conservation policies in particular places, and many others have strong views concerning fundamental philosophical questions of environmental ethics, but only a few have both qualities. When these people are silent, the loss is formidable.

For example, the complicated question concerning how industrial societies can increase energy production with the least undesirable consequences is largely a waste of time if this increase is pointless in relation to ultimate human ends. Thousands of experts hired by the government and other big institutions devote their time to this complicated problem, yet it is difficult for the public to find out or realize that many of these same experts consider the problem to be pointless and irrelevant. What these experts consider relevant are the problems of how to stabilize and eventually decrease consumption without losing genuine quality of life for humans. But they continue to work on the irrelevant problems assigned to them while, at the same time, failing to speak out, because the ultimate power is not in their hands.

2   A Call to Speak Out

What I am arguing for is this: even those who completely subsume ecological policies under the narrow ends of human health and well-being cannot attain their modest aims, at least not fully, without being joined by the supporters of deep ecology. They need what these people have to contribute, and this will work in their favor more often than it will work against them. Those in charge of environmental policies, even if they are resource-oriented (and growth tolerating?) decision makers, will increasingly welcome, if only for tactical and not fundamental reasons, what deep ecology supporters have to say. Even though the more radical ethic may seem nonsensical or untenable to them, they know that its advocates are, in practice, doing conservation work that sooner or later must be done. They concur with the practice even though they operate from diverging theories. The time is ripe for professional ecologists to break their silence and express their deepest concerns more freely. A bolder advocacy of deep ecological concerns by those working within the shallow, resource-oriented environmental sphere is the best strategy for regaining some of the strength of this movement among the general public, thereby contributing, however modestly, to a turning of the tide.

What do I mean by saying that even the more modest aims of shallow environmentalism have a need for deep ecology? We can see this by considering the World Conservation Strategy – prepared by the International Union for the Conservation of Nature and Natural Resources (IUCN) in cooperation with the United Nations Environmental Programme (UNEP) and the World Wildlife Fund (WWF). The argument in this important document is thoroughly anthropocentric in the sense that all its recommendations are justified exclusively in terms of their effects upon human health and basic well-being.[3]

A more ecocentric environmental ethic is also recommended apparently for tactical reasons: "A new ethic, embracing plants and animals as well as people, is required for human societies to live in harmony with the natural world on which they depend for survival and well-being." But such an ethic would surely be more effective if it were acted upon by people who believe in its validity, rather than merely its usefulness. This, I think, will come to be understood more and more by those in charge of educational policies. Quite simply, it is indecent for a teacher to proclaim an ethic for tactical reasons only.

Furthermore, this point applies to all aspects of a world conservation strategy. Conservation strategies are more eagerly implemented by people who love what they are conserving, and who are convinced that what they love is intrinsically lovable. Such lovers will not want to hide their attitudes and values, rather they will increasingly give voice to them in public. They possess a genuine ethics of conservation, not merely a tactically useful instrument for human survival.

In short, environmental education campaigns can fortunately combine human-centered arguments with a practical environmental ethic based on either a deeper and more fundamental philosophic or religious perspective, and on a set of norms resting on intrinsic values. But the inherent strength of this overall position will be lost if those who work professionally on environmental problems do not freely give testimony to fundamental norms.

The above is hortatory in the positive etymological sense of that word. I seek "to urge, incite, instigate, encourage, cheer" (Latin: *hortari*). This may seem unacademic but I consider it justifiable because of an intimate relationship between hortatory sentences and basic philosophical views which I formulate in section 8. To trace what follows from fundamental norms and hypotheses is eminently philosophical.

3 What is Deep Ecology?

The phrase "deep ecology movement" has been used up to this point without trying to define it. One should not expect too much from definitions of movements; think, for example, of terms like "conservatism," "liberalism," or the "feminist movement." And there is no reason why supporters of movements should adhere exactly to the same definition, or to any definition, for that matter. It is the same with characterizations, criteria, or a set of proposed necessary conditions for application of the term or phrase. In what follows, a platform or key terms and phrases, agreed upon by George Sessions and myself, are tentatively proposed as basic to deep ecology.[4] More accurately, the sentences have a double function. They are meant to express important points which the great majority of supporters accept, implicitly or explicitly, at a high level of generality. Furthermore, they express a proposal to the effect that those who solidly reject one or more of these points should not be viewed as supporters of

deep ecology. This might result because they are supporters of a shallow (or reform) environmental movement or rather they may simply dislike one or more of the eight points for semantical or other reasons. But they may well accept a different set of points which, to me, has roughly the same meaning, in which case I shall call them supporters of the deep ecology movement, but add that they *think* they disagree (maybe Henryk Skolimowski is an example of the latter). The eight points are:

1 The well-being and flourishing of human and non-human life on Earth have value in themselves (synonyms: intrinsic value, inherent worth). These values are independent of the usefulness of the non-human world for human purposes.

2 Richness and diversity of life forms contribute to the realization of these values and are also values in themselves.

3 Humans have no right to reduce this richness and diversity except to satisfy vital needs.

4 The flourishing of human life and cultures is compatible with a substantially smaller human population. The flourishing of non-human life *requires* a smaller human population.

5 Present human interference with the non-human world is excessive, and the situation is rapidly worsening.

6 Policies must therefore be changed. These policies affect basic economic, technological, and ideological structures. The resulting state of affairs will be deeply different from the present.

7 The ideological change will be mainly that of appreciating life quality (dwelling in situations of inherent value) rather than adhering to an increasingly higher standard of living. There will be a profound awareness of the difference between bigness and greatness.

8 Those who subscribe to the foregoing points have an obligation directly or indirectly to try to implement the necessary changes.

Comments on the eight points of the platform

RE (1): This formulation refers to the biosphere, or more professionally, to the ecosphere as a whole (this is also referred to as "ecocentrism"). This includes individuals, species, populations, habitat, as well as human and non-human cultures. Given our current knowledge of all-pervasive intimate relationships, this implies a fundamental concern and respect.

The term "life" is used here in a more comprehensive non-technical way also to refer to what biologists classify as "non-living": rivers (watersheds), landscapes, ecosystems. For supporters of deep ecology, slogans such as "let the river live" illustrate this broader usage so common in many cultures.

Inherent value, as used in (1), is common in deep ecology literature (e.g., "The presence of inherent value in a natural object is independent of any awareness, interest, or appreciation of it by any conscious being").[5]

RE (2): The so-called simple, lower, or primitive species of plants and animals contribute essentially to the richness and diversity of life. They have value in themselves and are not merely steps toward the so-called higher or rational life forms. The second principle presupposes that life itself, as a process over evolutionary time, implies an increase of diversity and richness.

Complexity, as referred to here, is different from complication. For example, urban life may be more complicated than life in a natural setting without being more complex in the sense of multifaceted quality.

RE (3): The term "vital need" is deliberately left vague to allow for considerable latitude in judgment. Differences in climate and related factors, together with differences in the structures of societies as they now exist, need to be taken into consideration.

RE (4): People in the materially richest countries cannot be expected to reduce their excessive interference with the non-human world overnight. The stabilization and reduction of the human population will take time. Hundreds of years! Interim strategies need to be developed. But in no way does this excuse the present complacency. The extreme seriousness of our current situation must first be realized. And the longer we wait to make the necessary changes, the more drastic will be the measures needed. Until deep changes are made, substantial decreases in richness and diversity are liable to occur: the rate of extinction of species will be ten to one hundred or more times greater than in any other short period of earth history.

RE (5): This formulation is mild. For a realistic assessment, see the annual reports of the Worldwatch Institute in Washington, D.C.

The slogan of "non-interference" does not imply that humans should not modify some ecosystems, as do other species. Humans have modified the earth over their entire history and will probably continue to do so. At issue is the *nature and extent* of such interference. The per capita destruction of wild (ancient) forests and other wild ecosystems has been excessive in rich countries; it is essential that the poor do not imitate the rich in this regard.

The fight to preserve and extend areas of wilderness and near-wilderness ("free Nature") should continue. The rationale for such preservation should focus mainly on the ecological functions of these areas (one such function: large wilderness areas are required in the biosphere for the continued evolutionary speciation of plants and animals). Most of the present designated wilderness areas and game reserves are not large enough to allow for such speciation.

RE (6): Economic growth as it is conceived of and implemented today by the industrial states is incompatible with points (1) through (5). There is only a faint resemblance between ideal sustainable forms of economic growth and the present policies of industrial societies.

Present ideology tends to value things because they are scarce and because they have a commodity value. There is prestige in vast consumption and waste (to mention only several relevant factors).

Whereas "self-determination," "local community," and "think globally, act locally," will remain key terms in the ecology of human societies, nevertheless the implementation of deep changes requires increasingly global action: Action across borders.

Governments in Third World countries are mostly uninterested in deep ecological issues. When institutions in the industrial societies try to promote ecological measures through Third World governments, practically nothing is accomplished (e.g., with problems of desertification). Given this situation, support for global action through non-governmental international organizations becomes increasingly important. Many of these organizations are able to act globally "from grassroots to grassroots" thus avoiding negative governmental interference.

Cultural diversity today requires advanced technology, that is, techniques that advance the basic goals of each culture. So-called soft, intermediate, and alternative technologies are steps in this direction.

RE (7): Some economists criticize the term "quality of life" because it is supposedly vague. But, on closer inspection, what they consider to be vague is actually the nonquantifiable nature of the term. One cannot quantify adequately what is important for the quality of life as discussed here, and there is no need to do so.

RE (8): There is ample room for different opinions about priorities: What should be done first; what next? What is the most urgent? What is clearly necessary to be done, as opposed to what is highly desirable but not absolutely pressing? The frontier of the environmental crisis is long and varied, and there is a place for everyone.

The above formulations of the eight points may be useful to many supporters of the deep ecology movement. But some will certainly feel that they are imperfect, even misleading. If they need to formulate in a few words what is basic to deep ecology, then they will propose an alternative set of sentences. I shall of course be glad to refer to them as alternatives. There ought to be a measure of diversity in what is considered basic and common.

Why should we call the movement "the deep ecological movement"?[6] There are at least six other designations which cover most of the same issues: "Ecological Resistance," used by John Rodman in important discussions; "The New Natural Philosophy" coined by Joseph Meeker; "Eco-philosophy," used by Sigmund Kvaloy and others to emphasize (1) a highly critical assessment of the industrial growth societies from a general ecological point of view, and (2) the ecology of the human species; "Green Philosophy and Politics" (while the term "green" is often used in Europe, in the United States "green" has a misleading association with the rather "blue" Green agricultural revolution); "Sustainable Earth Ethics," as used by G. Tyler Miller; and "Ecosophy" (ecowisdom), which is my own favorite term. Others could be mentioned as well.

And so, why use the adjective "deep"? This question will be easier to answer after the contrast is made between shallow and deep ecological concerns. "Deep ecology" is not a philosophy in any proper academic sense, nor is it institutionalized as a religion or an ideology. Rather, what happens is that various persons come together in campaigns and direct actions. They form a circle of friends supporting the same kind of lifestyle which others

may think to be "simple," but which they themselves see as rich and many-sided. They agree on a vast array of political issues, although they may otherwise support different political parties. As in all social movements, slogans and rhetoric are indispensable for in-group coherence. They react together against the same threats in a predominantly nonviolent way. Perhaps the most influential participants are artists and writers who do not articulate their insights in terms of professional philosophy, expressing themselves rather in art or poetry. For these reasons, I use the term "movement" rather than "philosophy." But it is essential that fundamental attitudes and beliefs are involved as part of the motivation for action.

4 Deep versus Shallow Ecology

A number of key terms and slogans from the environmental debate will clarify the contrast between the shallow and the deep ecology movements.[7]

A Pollution

Shallow Approach: Technology seeks to purify the air and water and to spread pollution more evenly. Laws limit permissible pollution. Polluting industries are preferably exported to developing countries.

Deep Approach: Pollution is evaluated from a biospheric point of view, not focusing exclusively on its effects on human health, but rather on life as a whole, including the life conditions of every species and system. The shallow reaction to acid rain, for example, is to tend to avoid action by demanding more research, and the attempt to find species of trees which will tolerate high acidity, etc. The deep approach concentrates on what is going on in the total ecosystem and calls for a high priority fight against the economic conditions and the technology responsible for producing the acid rain. The long-range concerns are one hundred years, at least.

The priority is to fight the deep causes of pollution, not merely the superficial, short-range effects. The Third and Fourth World countries cannot afford to pay the total costs of the war against pollution in their regions; consequently they require the assistance of the First and Second

World countries. Exporting pollution is not only a crime against humanity, it is a crime against life in general.

B Resources

Shallow Approach: The emphasis is upon resources for humans, especially for the present generation in affluent societies. In this view, the resources of the earth belong to those who have the technology to exploit them. There is confidence that resources will not be depleted because, as they get rarer, a high market price will conserve them, and substitutes will be found through technological progress. Further, plants, animals, and natural objects are valuable only as resources for humans. If no human use is known, or seems likely ever to be found, it does not matter if they are destroyed.

Deep Approach: The concern here is with resources and habitats for all life-forms for their own sake. No natural object is conceived of solely as a resource. This leads, then, to a critical evaluation of human modes of production and consumption. The question arises: to what extent does an increase in production and consumption foster ultimate human values? To what extent does it satisfy vital needs, locally or globally? How can economic, legal, and educational institutions be changed to counteract destructive increases? How can resource use serve the quality of life rather than the economic standard of living as generally promoted by consumerism? From a deep perspective, there is an emphasis upon an ecosystem approach rather than the consideration merely of isolated life-forms or local situations. There is a long-range maximal perspective of time and place.

C Population

Shallow Approach: The threat of (human) "overpopulation" is seen mainly as a problem for developing countries. One condones or even applauds population increases in one's own country for short-sighted economic, military, or other reasons; an increase in the number of humans is considered as valuable in itself or as economically profitable. The issue of an "optimum population" for humans is discussed without reference to the question of an "optimum population" for other life-forms. The destruction of wild habitats caused by increasing human population is accepted as an inevitable evil, and drastic decreases of wildlife forms tend to be accepted insofar as species are not driven to extinction. Further, the social relations of animals are ignored. A long-term substantial reduction of the global human population is not seen to be a desirable goal. In addition, the right is claimed to defend one's borders against "illegal aliens," regardless of what the population pressures are elsewhere.

Deep Approach: It is recognized that excessive pressures on planetary life stem from the human population explosion. The pressure stemming from the industrial societies is a major factor, and population reduction must have the highest priority in those societies.

D Cultural diversity and appropriate technology

Shallow Approach: Industrialization of the Western industrial type is held to be the goal of developing countries. The universal adoption of Western technology is held to be compatible with cultural diversity, together with the conservation of the positive elements (from a Western perspective) of present non-industrial societies. There is a low estimate of deep cultural differences in non-industrial societies which deviate significantly from contemporary Western standards.

Deep Approach: Protection of non-industrial cultures from invasion by industrial societies. The goals of the former should not be seen as promoting lifestyles similar to those in the rich countries. Deep cultural diversity is an analogue on the human level to the biological richness and diversity of life-forms. A high priority should be given to cultural anthropology in general education programs in industrial societies.

There should be limits on the impact of Western technology upon present existing non-industrial countries and the Fourth World should be defended against foreign domination. Political and economic policies should favor subcultures within industrial societies. Local, soft technologies should allow for a basic cultural assessment of any technical innovations, together with freely expressed criticism of so-called advanced technology when this has the potential to be culturally destructive.

E Land and sea ethics

Shallow Approach: Landscapes, ecosystems, rivers, and other whole entities of nature are conceptually cut into fragments, thus disregarding larger units and comprehensive gestalts. These fragments are regarded as the properties and resources of individuals, organizations or states. Conservation is argued in terms of "multiple use" and "cost/benefit analysis." The social costs and long-term global ecological costs of resource extraction and use are usually not considered. Wildlife management is conceived of as conserving nature for "future generations of humans." Soil erosion or the deterioration of ground water quality, for example, is noted as a human loss, but a strong belief in future technological progress makes deep changes seem unnecessary.

Deep Approach: The earth does not belong to humans. For example, the Norwegian landscapes, rivers, flora and fauna, and the neighboring sea are not the property of Norwegians. Similarly, the oil under the North Sea or anywhere else does not belong to any state or to humanity. And the "free nature" surrounding a local community does not belong to the local community.

Humans only inhabit the lands, using resources to satisfy vital needs. And if their non-vital needs come in conflict with the vital needs of nonhumans, then humans should defer to the latter. The ecological destruction now going on will not be cured by a technological fix. Current arrogant notions in industrial (and other) societies must be resisted.

F Education and the scientific enterprise

Shallow Approach: The degradation of the environment and resource depletion requires the training of more and more "experts" who can provide advice concerning how to continue combining economic growth with maintaining a healthy environment. We are likely to need an increasingly more dominating and manipulative technology to "manage the planet" when global economic growth makes further environmental degradation inevitable. The scientific enterprise must continue giving priority to the "hard sciences" (physics and chemistry). High educational standards with intense competition in the relevant "tough" areas of learning will be required.

Deep Approach: If sane ecological policies are adopted, then education should concentrate on an increased sensitivity to non-consumptive goods, and on such consumables where there is enough for all. Education should therefore counteract the excessive emphasis upon things with a price tag. There should be a shift in concentration from the "hard" to the "soft" sciences which stress the importance of the local and global cultures. The educational objective of the World Conservation Strategy ("building support for conservation") should be given a high priority, but within the deeper framework of respect for the biosphere.

In the future, there will be no shallow environmental movement if deep policies are increasingly adopted by governments, and thus no need for a special deep ecological social movement.

5 But Why a "Deep" Ecology?

The decisive difference between a shallow and a deep ecology, in practice, concerns the willingness to question, and an appreciation of the importance of questioning, every economic and political policy in public. This questioning is both "deep" and public. It asks "why" insistently and consistently, taking nothing for granted!

Deep ecology can readily admit to the practical effectiveness of homocentric arguments:

> It is essential for conservation to be seen as central to human interests and aspirations. At the same time, people – from heads of state to the members of rural communities – will most readily be brought to demand conservation if they themselves recognize the contribution of conservation to the achievement of their needs as perceived by them, and the solution of their problems, as perceived by them.[8]

There are several dangers in arguing solely from the point of view of narrow human interests. Some policies based upon successful homocentric arguments turn out to violate or unduly compromise the objectives of deeper argumentation. Further, homocentric arguments tend to weaken the motivation to fight for necessary social change, together with the willingness to serve a great cause. In addition, the complicated arguments in human-centered conservation documents such as the World Conservation Strategy go beyond the time and ability of many people to assimilate and understand. They also tend to provoke interminable technical disagreements among experts. Special interest groups with narrow short-term exploitive objectives, which run counter to saner ecological policies, often exploit these disagreements and thereby stall the debate and steps toward effective action.

When arguing from deep ecological premises, most of the complicated proposed technological fixes need not be discussed at all. The relative merits of alternative technological proposals are pointless if our vital needs have already been met. A focus on vital issues activates mental energy and strengthens motivation. On the other hand, the shallow environmental approach, by focusing almost exclusively on the technical aspects of environmental problems, tends to make the public more passive and disinterested in the more crucial non-technical, lifestyle-related, environmental issues.

Writers within the deep ecology movement try to articulate the fundamental presuppositions underlying the dominant economic approach in terms of value priorities, philosophy, and religion. In the shallow movement, questioning and argumentation comes to a halt long before this. The deep ecology movement is therefore "the ecology movement which questions deeper." A realization of the deep changes which are required, as outlined in the deep ecology eight point platform (discussed in #3 above) makes us realize the necessity of "questioning everything."

The terms "egalitarianism," "homocentrism," "anthropocentrism," and "human chauvinism" are often used to characterize points of view on the shallow–deep spectrum. But these terms usually function as slogans which are often open to misinterpretation. They can properly imply that man is in some respects only a "plain citizen" (Aldo Leopold) of the planet on a par with all other species, but they are sometimes interpreted as denying that humans have any "extraordinary" traits, or that, in situations involving vital interests, humans have no overriding obligations towards their own kind. But this would be a mistake: they have!

In any social movement, rhetoric has an essential function in keeping members fighting together under the same banner. Rhetorical formulations also serve to provoke interest among outsiders.

Of the many excellent slogans, one might mention "nature knows best," "small is beautiful," and "all things hang together." But sometimes one may safely say that nature does not always know best, that small is sometimes dreadful, and that fortunately things hang together sometimes only loosely, or not at all.

Only a minority of deep ecology supporters are academic philosophers, such as myself. And while deep ecology cannot be a finished philosophical system, this does not mean that its philosophers should not try to be as clear as possible. So a discussion of deep ecology as a derivational system may be of value to clarify the many important premise/conclusion relations.

6 Deep Ecology Illustrated as a Derivational System

Underlying the eight tenets or principles presented in section 3, there are even more basic positions and norms which reside in philosophical systems and in various world religions. Schematically we may represent the total views logically implied in the deep ecology movement by streams of derivations from the most fundamental norms and descriptive assumptions (level 1) to the particular decisions in actual life situations (level 4).

The pyramidal model has some features in common with hypotheticodeductive systems. The main difference, however, is that some sentences at the top (= deepest) level are normative, and preferably are expressed by imperatives. This makes it possible to arrive at imperatives at the lowest derivational level: the crucial level in terms of decisions. Thus, there are "oughts" in our premises as well as in our conclusions. We never move from an "is" to an "ought," or vice versa. From a logical standpoint, this is decisive!

The above premise/conclusion structure (or diagram) of a total view must not be taken too seriously (fig. 20.1). It is not meant in any restrictive way to characterize creative thinking within the deep ecology movement. Creative thinking moves freely in any direction. But many of us with a professional background in science and analytical philosophy find such a diagram helpful.

As we dig deeper into the premises of our thinking, we eventually stop. Those premises we stop at are our ultimates. When we philosophize, we all stop at different places. But we all use premises

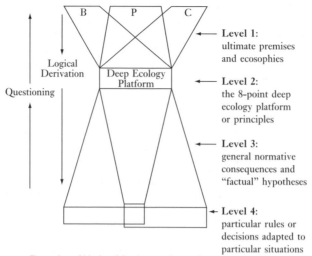

Examples of kinds of fundamental premises:
B = Buddhist
C = Christian
P = Philosophical (e.g., Spinozist or Whiteheadian)

Figure 20.1

which, for us, are ultimate. They belong to level 1 in the diagram. Some will use a sentence like "Every life form has intrinsic value" as an ultimate premise, and therefore place it at level 1. Others try, as I do, to conceive of it as a conclusion based on a set of premises. For these people, this sentence does not belong to level 1. There will be different ecosophies corresponding to such differences.

Obviously, point 6 of the 8 point deep ecology tenets (see section 3) cannot belong to level 1 of the diagram. The statement "there must be new policies affecting basic economic structures" needs to be justified. If no logical justification is forthcoming, why not just assert instead that ecologically destructive "business as usual" economic policies should continue? In the diagram I have had ecosophies as ultimate premises in mind at level 1. None of the 8 points of the deep ecology principles belong at the ultimate level; they are derived as conclusions from premises at level 1.

Different supporters of the deep ecology movement may have different ultimates (level 1), but will nevertheless agree about level 2 (the 8 points). Level 4 will comprise concrete decisions in concrete situations which appear as conclusions from deliberations involving premises at levels 1 to 3. An important point: supporters of the deep ecology movement act from deep premises. They are

motivated, in part, from a philosophical or religious position.

7 Multiple Roots of the Deep Ecology Platform

The deep ecology movement seriously questions the presuppositions of shallow argumentation. Even what counts as a rational decision is challenged, because what is "rational" is always defined in relation to specific aims and goals. If a decision is rational in relation to the lower level aims and goals of our pyramid, but not in relation to the highest level, then this decision should not be judged to be rational. This is an important point! If an environmentally oriented policy decision is not linked to intrinsic values or ultimates, then its rationality has yet to be determined. The deep ecology movement connects rationality with a set of philosophical or religious foundations. But one cannot expect the ultimate premises to constitute rational conclusions. There are no "deeper" premises available.

Deep ecological questioning thus reveals the fundamental normative orientations of differing positions. Shallow argumentation stops before reaching fundamentals, or it jumps from the ultimate to the particular; that is, from level 1 to level 4.

But it is not only normative claims that are at issue. Most (perhaps all) norms presuppose ideas about how the world functions. Typically the vast majority of assertions needed in normative systems are descriptive (or factual). This holds at all the levels.

As mentioned before, it does not follow that supporters of deep ecology must have identical beliefs about ultimate issues. They do have common attitudes about intrinsic values in nature, but these can, in turn (at a still deeper level), be derived from different, mutually incompatible sets of ultimate beliefs.

Thus, while a specific decision may be judged as rational from within the derivational system (if there is such) of shallow ecology, it might be judged as irrational from within the derivational system of deep ecology. Again, it should be emphasized that what is rational from within the deep ecology derivational pyramid does not require unanimity in ontology and fundamental ethics. Deep ecology as a conviction, with its subsequently derived practical recommendations, can follow from a number of more comprehensive world views, from differing ecosophies.

Those engaged in the deep ecology movement have so far revealed their philosophical or religious homes to be mainly in Christianity, Buddhism, Taoism, Baha'i, or in various philosophies. The top level of the derivational pyramid can, in such cases, be made up of normative and descriptive principles which belong to these religions and philosophies.

Since the late 1970s, numerous Christians in Europe and America, including some theologians, have actively taken part in the deep ecology movement. Their interpretations of the Bible, and their theological positions in general, have been reformed from what was, until recently, a crude dominating anthropocentric emphasis.

There is an intimate relationship between some forms of Buddhism and the deep ecology movement. The history of Buddhist thought and practice, especially the principles of non-violence, non-injury, and reverence for life, sometimes makes it easier for Buddhists to understand and appreciate deep ecology than it is for Christians, despite a (sometimes overlooked) blessedness which Jesus recommended in peace-making. I mention Taoism chiefly because there is some basis for calling John Muir a Taoist, for instance, and Baha'i because of Lawrence Arturo.

Ecosophies are not religions in the classical sense. They are better characterized as *general* philosophies, in the sense of total views, inspired in part by the science of ecology. At level 1, a traditional religion may enter the derivational pyramid through a set of normative and descriptive assumptions which would be characteristic of contemporary interpretations (hermeneutical efforts) of that religion.

Supporters of the deep ecology movement act in contemporary conflicts on the basis of their fundamental beliefs and attitudes. This gives them a particular strength and a joyful expectation or hope for a greener future. But, naturally, few of them are actively engaged in a systematic verbal articulation of where they stand.

8 Ecosophy T as an Example of a Deep Ecological Derivational System

I call the ecosophy I feel at home with "Ecosophy T." My main purpose in announcing that I feel at home with Ecosophy T is didactic and dialectic. I hope to get others to announce their philosophy. If they say they have none, I maintain that they have, but perhaps don't know their own views, or are too modest or inhibited to proclaim what they believe. Following Socrates, I want to provoke questioning until others know where they stand on basic matters of life and death. This is done using ecological issues, and also by using Ecosophy T as a foil. But Socrates pretended in debate that he knew nothing. My posture seems to be the opposite. I may seem to know everything and to derive it magically from a small set of hypotheses about the world. But both interpretations are misleading! Socrates did not consistently claim to know nothing, nor do I in my Ecosophy T pretend to have comprehensive knowledge. Socrates claimed to know, for instance, about the fallibility of human claims to have knowledge.

Ecosophy T has only one ultimate norm: "Self-realization!" I do not use this expression in any narrow, individualistic sense. I want to give it an expanded meaning based on the distinction between a large comprehensive Self and narrow egoistic self as conceived of in certain Eastern traditions of *atman*.[9] This large comprehensive Self (with a capital "S") embraces all the life forms on the planet (and elsewhere?) together with their individual selves (jivas). If I were to

Arne Naess

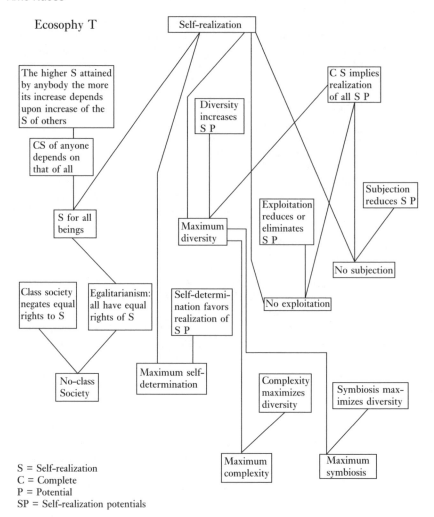

Figure 20.2

S = Self-realization
C = Complete
P = Potential
SP = Self-realization potentials

express this ultimate norm in a few words, I would say: "Maximize (long-range, universal) Self-realization!" Another more colloquial way to express this ultimate norm would be to say "Live and let live!" (referring to all of the life forms and natural processes on the planet). If I had to give up the term fearing its inevitable misunderstanding, I would use the term "universal symbiosis." "Maximize Self-realization!" could, of course, be misinterpreted in the direction of colossal ego trips. But "Maximize symbiosis!" could be misinterpreted in the opposite direction of eliminating individuality in favor of collectivity.

Viewed systematically, not individually, maximum Self-realization implies maximizing the manifestations of all life. So next I derive the second term, "Maximize (long-range, universal) diversity!" A corollary is that the higher the levels of Self-realization attained by any person, the more any further increase depends upon the Self-realization of others. Increased self-identity involves increased identification with others. "Altruism" is a natural consequence of this identification.

This leads to a hypothesis concerning an inescapable increase of identification with other beings when one's own self-realization increases. As a result, we increasingly see ourselves in other beings, and others see themselves in us. In this way, the self is extended and deepened as a natural process of the realization of its potentialities in others.

By universalizing the above, we can derive the norm, "Self-realization for every being!" From the norm, "Maximize diversity!" and a hypothesis that maximum diversity implies a maximum of symbiosis, we can derive the norm "Maximize symbiosis!" Further, we work for life conditions such that there is a minimum of coercion in the lives of others. And so on![10] The eight points of the deep ecology platform are derived in a fairly simple way.

A philosophy as a world view inevitably has implications for practical situations. Like other ecosophies, Ecosophy T therefore moves on, without apologies, to the concrete questions of lifestyles. These will obviously show great variation because of differences in hypotheses about the world in which each of us lives, and in the "factual" statements about the concrete situations in which we make decisions.

I shall limit myself to a discussion of a couple of areas in which my "style" of thinking and behaving seem somewhat strange to friends and others who know a little about my philosophy.

First, I have a somewhat extreme appreciation of diversity; a positive appreciation of the existence of styles and behavior which I personally detest or find nonsensical (but which are not clearly incompatible with symbiosis); an enthusiasm for the "mere" diversity of species, or varieties within a genus of plants or animals; I support, as the head of a philosophy department, doctrinal theses completely at odds with my own inclinations, with the requirement only that the authors are able to understand fairly adequately some basic features of the kind of philosophy I myself feel at home with; an appreciation of combinations of *seemingly* incompatible interests and behaviors, which makes for an increase of subcultures within industrial states and which might to some extent help future cultural diversity. So much for "diversity!"

Second, I have a somewhat extreme appreciation of what Kant calls "beautiful actions" (good actions based on inclination), in contrast with actions which are performed out of a sense of duty or obligation. The choice of the formulation "Self-realization!" is in part motivated by the belief that maturity in humans can be measured along a scale from selfishness to an increased realization of Self, that is, by broadening and deepening the self, rather than being measured by degrees of dutiful altruism. I see joyful sharing

and caring as a natural process of growth in humans.

Third, I believe that multifaceted high-level Self-realization is more easily reached through a lifestyle which is "simple in means but rich in ends" rather than through the material standard of living of the average citizens of industrial states.

The simple formulations of the deep ecology platform and Ecosophy T are not meant primarily to be used among philosophers, but also in dialogues with the "experts." When I wrote to the "experts" and environmental professionals personally, asking whether they accept the eight points of the platform, many answered positively in relation to most or all of the points. And this includes top people in the ministries of oil and energy! Nearly all were willing to let their written answers be widely published. It is an open question, however, as to what extent they will try to influence their colleagues who use only shallow argumentation. But the main conclusion to be drawn is moderately encouraging: there are views of the human/nature relationship, widely accepted among established experts responsible for environmental decisions, which require a pervasive, substantial change of present policies in favor of our "living" planet, and these views are held not only on the basis of shortsighted human interests.

Notes

1 For more about interspecific community relationships, see Arne Naess, "Self-realization in Mixed Communities of Humans, Bears, Sheep, and Wolves," *Inquiry* 22 (1979): 321–41; Naess and Ivar Mysterud, "Philosophy of Wolf Policies I: General Principles and Preliminary Exploration of Selected Norms," *Conservation Biology* 1, 1 (1987): 22–34.

2 These problems are discussed further in Naess's keynote address to the second international Conference Conservation on Biology held at the University of Michigan in May 1985; published as "Intrinsic Value: Will the Defenders of Nature Please Rise?" *Conservation Biology* (1986): 504–15.

3 IUCN, *World Conservation Strategy: Living Resource Conservation for Sustainable Development* (Gland, Switzerland, 1980), section 13 ("Building Support for Conservation").

4 The deep ecology principles (or platform) were agreed upon during a camping trip in Death Valley, California (April 1984) and first published in George Sessions (ed.), *Ecophilosophy VI* newsletter (May

1984). They have subsequently appeared in a number of publications.

5 Tom Regan, "The Nature and Possibility of an Environmental Ethics," *Environmental Ethics* 3 (1981): 19–34, citation on p. 30.

6 I proposed the name "Deep, Long-Range Ecology Movement" in a lecture at the Third World Future Research conference in Bucharest in September 1972. A summary of that lecture ("The Shallow and the Deep, Long-Range Ecology Movement") was published in *Inquiry* 16 (1973): 95–100. Within the deep ecology movement it is fairly common to use the term "deep ecologist," whereas "shallow ecologist," I am glad to say is rather uncommon. Both terms may be considered arrogant and slightly misleading. I prefer to use the awkward, but more egalitarian expression "supporter of the deep (or shallow) ecology movement," avoiding personification. Also, it is common to call deep ecology consistently anti-anthropocentric. This has led to misconceptions: see my "A Defense of the Deep Ecology Movement," *Environmental Ethics* 5 (1983).

7 The "shallow/deep" dichotomy is rough. Richard Sylvan has proposed a much more subtle classification; see his "A Critique of Deep Ecology," *Discussion Papers in Environmental Philosophy*, RSSS, Australian National University, No. 12 (1985).

8 *World Conservation Strategy*, section 13 (concluding paragraph).

9 The term *atman* is not taken in its absolutistic senses (not as a permanent indestructible "soul"). This makes it consistent with those Buddhist denials (the *avatman doctrine*) that the *atman* is to be taken in absolutist senses. Within the Christian tradition some theologians distinguish "ego" and "true self"

in ways similar to these distinctions in Eastern religions. See the ecophilosophical interpretation of the gospel of Luke in Stephen Verney's *Onto the New Age* (Glasgow: Collins, 1976), pp. 33–41.

10 Many authors take some steps toward derivational structures, offering mild systematizations. The chapter "Environmental Ethics and Hope" (in G. Tyler Miller, *Living in the Environment*, 3rd ed. [Belmont: Wadsworth, 1983]) is a valuable start, but the derivational relations are unclear. The logic and semantics of simple models of normative systems are briefly discussed in my "Notes on the Methodology of Normative Systems," *Methodology and Science* 10 (1977): 64–79. For a defense of the thesis that as soon as people assert anything at all, they assume a total view, implicitly involving an ontology, methodology, epistemology, and ethics, see my "Reflections about Total Views," *Philosophy and Phenomenological Research* 25 (1964–65): 16–29. The best and wittiest warning against taking systematizations too seriously is to be found in Søren Kierkegaard, *Concluding Unscientific Postscript*.

For criticism and defense of my fundamental norm ("Self-realization"), together with my answer, see *In Sceptical Wonder: Essays in Honor of Arne Naess* (Oslo: University Press, 1982). My main exposition of Ecosophy T was originally offered in the Norwegian work, *Okologi, samfunn og livsstil* (Oslo: University Press, 5th ed., 1976). Even there, the exposition is sketchy. (Editor's note: Naess's Norwegian book has been revised and reissued as Arne Naess (translated and edited by David Rothenberg), *Ecology, Community and Lifestyle* [Cambridge: Cambridge University Press, 1989].)

Ecofeminism

21

Ecofeminism: Toward Global Justice and Planetary Health

Greta Gaard and Lori Gruen

Like many other modern progressive movements, ecofeminism has its roots in the social change movements of the 1960s and 1970s.[1] Texts such as Rachel Carson's *Silent Spring* (1962), Rosemary Radford Ruether's *New Woman/ New Earth* (1975), Mary Daly's *Gyn/ Ecology* (1978), Susan Griffin's *Woman and Nature: The Roaring Inside Her* (1978), Elizabeth Dodson Gray's *Green Paradise Lost* (1979), and Carolyn Merchant's *The Death of Nature* (1980) provided the foundation for what would become a full-blown feminist approach to ecology and environmentalism in the 1980s. The first conference to address the parallel oppression of women and nature, "Women and the Environment," was held at the University of California, Berkeley, in 1974, and was later followed by a number of other conferences.[2] To date, four anthologies, a number of articles, and whole volumes of journals have been devoted to the topic of ecofeminism.[3] Initially, writers sought to accomplish two goals: to establish the connection between feminism and ecology, and to demonstrate the inadequacies of environmental theory for accommodating the insights of feminism. In these essays, writers legitimized the project of ecofeminism by showing why such a theory is useful and how it is unique in relation to other environmental theories.

This confluence of writers, scholars, and activists has answered four questions in developing a theory of ecofeminism: what are the problems that ecofeminism has addressed; how did these problems arise; why should these problems concern feminists; and why might ecofeminism offer the best framework for analyzing them? In this essay, we will explore ways that ecofeminists have answered each of these questions.

What Are the Problems?

Even in the United States, which is among the most affluent of nations, most people will acknowledge that the world is not what it should be. While many people are aware of the gross injustice in the distribution of wealth globally, for example, few realize its magnitude – 85 percent of the world's income goes to 23 percent of the world's people.[4] In effect, the industrialized countries (the 'North') are draining the Third World[5] (the 'South') of resources. "A person in the North consumes 52 times as much meat, 115 times more paper, and 35 times more energy than a Latin American," according to Margarita Arias of Costa Rica.[6] With only 5 percent of the world's people, the United States uses one-third of the world's non-renewable resources and one-fourth of the planet's commodities; the average US citizen uses 300 times the energy that a Third World citizen does.[7] As a result of this overconsumption, there is a corresponding overproduction of waste. Based on 1991 statistics, it appears that the average US resident produces more than one-half a ton of solid waste each year. At that rate, by the year 2009, 80 percent of all remaining landfills will be full.[8]

Pollution is affecting our water globally – approximately 1.2 billion people lack safe drinking water.[9] In developing countries, diarrhea and associated diseases kill four million children under the age of five each year.[10] Though it doesn't compare with water degradation in the South, water quality in the United States is also declining. According to 1991 estimates, one in six people drink water with excessive amounts of lead, a known cause of impaired IQ in children. Additionally, US water may contain PCBs, DDT, mercury, asbestos, and other toxic chemicals and pesticides which are dumped directly into waterways or that leak into the groundwater supplies from agricultural spraying and improperly disposed of industrial waste.[11]

In addition to losing fresh water supplies globally, we are also losing our forests. The United States has lost all but 10 percent of its ancient forests. Canada has lost 60 percent of its old-growth forests to logging, and less than 20 percent of what remains lies in protected areas. At current logging rates, all unprotected old-growth forests in Washington and Oregon will be gone by the year 2023.[12] Globally, forests are vanishing at a rate of some 17 million hectares per year.[13]

Certainly a forest does not consist merely of trees. Forests are dynamic ecosystems, home to insects and animals alike, producers of fresh air and water when left unharmed by human pollution. For example, a single Douglas fir keeps an estimated 400 tons of carbon out of the atmosphere over the course of its lifetime, which can be as long as 400 to 1,000 years. During that time, it provides food or shelter to at least 45 vertebrate species.[14] When we lose forests, we lose the animals they shelter as well; current estimates are that a minimum of 140 plant and animal species become extinct each day.[15] Forests are intricately connected with human survival, as they supply a majority of the world's people with food and fuel.

World hunger and food security continue to be global problems. According to the Institute for Food and Development Policy, 40 thousand children starve to death on this planet every day.[16] Ruth Engo Tjega, a founding member of Advocates for African Food Security, reminds us that every minute 15 children in the world die of hunger.[17] Many of those concerned with the environment consider the problem of starvation to be a problem of overpopulation. They tell us that world population is growing by 92 million people annually, of which 88 million are being added in the developing world.[18]

These are facts that people live with daily. Because an acute awareness of such facts would probably make it difficult to go about our day-to-day business, many people choose to deny the severity or the probability of such facts.[19] Collectively, we act like ostriches, believing what we can't see or don't look at doesn't exist. Yet denying these critical facts virtually ensures their inevitability.

Standing at the crossroads of environmentalism and feminism, ecofeminist theory is uniquely positioned to undertake a holistic analysis of these problems in both their human and natural contexts. Ecofeminism's central claim is that these problems stem from the mutually reinforcing oppression of humans and of the natural world. It is no longer possible to discuss environmental change without addressing social change; moreover, it is not possible to address women's oppression without addressing environmental degradation. That these two worlds, the human and the natural, are inextricably interconnected, may seem so obvious that it's hard to imagine that they are usually addressed separately.

How Did These Problems Arise?

Ecofeminists have offered or drawn upon a number of approaches for understanding the present functioning of global oppression.[20] Here, we will survey the most predominant explanations for the separation of the human from the natural world.

Some ecofeminists, such as Carolyn Merchant, see the separation of culture from nature as a product of the scientific revolution.[21] Where nature was previously seen as alive, with the scientific revolution, and most notably the works of Francis Bacon and René Descartes, nature was increasingly viewed as a machine which could be analyzed, experimented with, and understood through reason. This theory located animals in nature and authorized unlimited animal experimentation without anesthesia. Animals, thought to be particularly well-fashioned machines, could be tortured at will because the animals' cries of pain were not real but rather like the striking of a well-timed clock. According to this mind-set, nature was dead, inert, and mechanistic. Thus, the domination or oppression of nature was not considered to be unethical, but rather a judicious use of resources.

Other ecofeminists cite patriarchal religion as the origin of this separation. They date the origin of the oppression of nature back to 4500 b.c., well before the scientific revolution, when the shift from goddess-worshipping cultures to male deities began.[22] In the goddess religions, both the earth and women's fertility were seen as sacred. There was no gender hierarchy, and divinity was seen as immanent. With the advent of patriarchal religions, people worshipped a sky god, and nature was seen as his creation. The role of the male in reproduction was elevated above the role of the female; women were compared to fields which would gestate and bear the male seed. Certainly this shift from goddess-centered cultures to male deities didn't happen overnight, and many men and women resisted, but by the time of the Jews and the Greeks, the change had been largely effected. In the Judeo-Christian tradition, a great chain of being was established with god at the top, appointing Adam to be in charge of his entire creation. Woman was created from Adam's rib and placed below him, and below the divinely appointed heterosexuals were the animals and the rest of nature, all to serve man. The patriarchal domination of both nature and women was divinely commanded.

Others have suggested that patriarchal domination is the result of human evolutionary development.[23] According to one very popular anthropological story, an evolutionary shift occurred as the result of the emergence of hunting behavior in male hominids. The hunter's destructive, competitive, and violent activity directed toward his prey is what originally distinguished man from nature. According to this theory of human social evolution, woman's body, which is smaller, weaker, and reproductive, prevents her from full participation in the hunt and thus relegates her to the realm of non-culture. Her reproductive capacity and life-bearing activities stood in sharp contrast to the death-oriented activities that underlie culture. Thus, women, animals, and nature are considered inferior to the cultural activities of men and can be thought of as separate from them.

Still other ecofeminists use metaphorical or ideological explanations of the separation of culture from nature and look at the way that patriarchal culture describes the world in terms of self and other dualisms. These value dualisms give rise to value hierarchies, where all things associated with self are valued, and all things described as other are of lesser value.[24] These dualisms of self/other are manifested as culture/nature, man/woman, white/non-white, human/non-human animal, civilized/wild, heterosexual/homosexual, reason/emotion, wealthy/poor, etc.[25] Domination is built in to such dualisms because the other is negated in the process of defining a powerful self. Because the privileged self in such dualisms is always male, and the devalued other is always female, all valued components of such dualisms are also associated with the male, and all devalued components with the female.

Ecofeminists who use this approach see the self/other separation as an effective means for explaining the twin dominations of women and nature, since both are always configured as 'other'.

Those ecofeminists particularly concerned with the place of animals within ecofeminism emphasize the woman–animal connection as both are seen as Other. They observe that the feminization, naturalization, or animalization of an Other is often requisite to its ensuing subordination.[26] They point to the metaphors of language which reveal its ideological underpinnings: phrases such as 'the rape of nature', 'mother nature', and 'virgin forests' all feminize nature and, thus, in a culture where women are seen as subordinate, authorize the subordination of nature. In turn, colloquialisms for women, such as 'pussy', 'bitch', 'old hen', 'sow', and the like, serve to animalize women and thereby reinforce women's inferior status by appealing to women's animal (and thus non-human) nature.

Ecofeminists who look to psychology or the internalization of gender roles base their insights on the feminist psychoanalytic work of Carol Gilligan and Nancy Chodorow.[27] Chodorow's work on object-relations theory as it pertains to the patriarchal family suggests that masculine identification stresses differentiation from others, a denial of connection, and an increasing propensity toward abstraction. In contrast, feminine identities are relational, connected, and embodied. Gilligan's studies on moral development show that a rights-based ethic is more characteristic of men and a responsibilities–based ethic is more characteristic of women. Ethical decision making is based on a person's sense of self in relationship to others and to society. These theorists suggest that men's self-identity is established through separation from the mother, whereas women's sense of self is founded on a sense of continuity and self-in-relationship. In making ethical decisions, men often look at the people involved or affected by such a decision as separate individuals having competing interests; men are more likely to base ethical decisions on an appeal to abstract rules. In contrast, women tend to consider the net effect of ethical decisions on all people involved and make choices which may be considered ethical only within the specific context of that decision. Gilligan emphasizes that while both ethical outlooks are available to men and women, it is the 'focus' phenomenon, that is, which voice we listen to, that is gendered. Drawing on these insights, ecofeminists observe that the separation of culture from nature parallels the separation of self from other, a separation fundamental to the social construction of masculinity.

Those ecofeminists who explain the separation from an economic perspective look to the Marxist insights about feudalism and the rise of capitalism, as well as colonialist practices. In Europe, the enclosure of the commons and the creation of private property caused a hierarchy between land-owning lords and landless peasants. According to Engels, the development of private property also led to "the world historical defeat of the female sex."[28] Spreading throughout Europe and eventually to Asia and Africa, this system enslaved indigenous people and captured the land for the use and profit of a few.[29] Thus began what Vandana Shiva appropriately terms "systematic underdevelopment." The Europeans described the living conditions of the Asian and African people as total poverty, and told themselves they would take on the 'white man's burden' by bringing Western civilization and industrialization to these countries. In fact, what the Europeans described as poverty was subsistence living, and the 'improvements' brought about through colonialism and development created real material poverty.

The indigenous people were a cheap labor supply. Based on the division of labor by gender roles, the men were employed for cash by the colonizers while the women fulfilled all the household duties, providing food for the whole family. The colonizers, under the guise of benevolence,

loaned the indigenous people money to establish industries modeled after those in Europe. The industry loaned from the Europeans then took the natural resources – the trees, the animals, and the crops – and employed the indigenous people, at very low wages, to participate in their own exploitation. The colonizers replaced the native food crops with cash crops for export, arguing that such exchange would bring about a cash flow for the people. In fact, such development over a period of time created severe material hardships for the indigenous people. Without the native tree cover, the land did not absorb the rains as well, and massive erosion began, depleting the fields of precious topsoil. The intensive logging practices of the colonizers meant that women had to walk farther each day to gather wood for fuel, since this was considered a woman's task. Finally, the monoculture crops depleted the soil. Where there used to be just food enough, now there was famine, environmental degradation, and an enormous debt to the colonial lenders. This is the system of 'development' ecofeminists see as causing the oppression of women, indigenous people, and the natural world today.

It's easy to see that these are not competing explanations of the present global situation. Rather, each perspective maps out a particular explanation of oppression. Taken together, these analyses describe a global shift in orientation, from reverence and respect for women and nature, and a view of all life as interconnected, to a world-view which is based on separation, and which conceptualizes women, nature, animals, and non-dominant people as inferior and subordinate objects to be dominated.

Why Should Global Environmental Problems Concern Feminists?

The current system of global inequity, interpersonal and international violence, and environmental degradation may seem beyond the scope of feminist analysis at first glance. However, if we can establish that a proposed activity or practice contributes to the subordination of women, then by necessity it becomes a feminist concern. Certainly toxic waste, air pollution, contaminated groundwater, increased militarization, and the like are not exclusively women's issues; they are human issues which affect everybody. But, ecofeminists claim that environmental issues are femi-

Greta Gaard and Lori Gruen

nist issues because it is women and children who are the first to suffer the consequences of injustice and environmental destruction.

To some, it may seem particularly absurd to have to convince 'first world' feminists that nature is a feminist concern. For those who live outside the wealth of the world's industrialized economy, environmental degradation has immediate, tangible results – hunger, thirst, and fuel scarcity, to mention only a few – and under these conditions environmental activism is a form of self-defense.[30] That the privileged minority of the industrialized world does not feel the full and immediate consequences of this pollution does not mitigate its effect on the majority of the world's less privileged. And it is only a matter of time, if the present course runs unchecked, that even the most privileged will be forced to pull their heads out of the sand.

To demonstrate the connections between environmentalism and feminism, ecofeminists point to a number of ways in which environmental degradation causes a decrease in the quality of life for women, children, and people of color. Specifically, ecofeminists have noted the connections between women's oppression and the oppression of nature by examining global economics, Third World debt, underdevelopment, food production and distribution, reproductive rights, militarism, and environmental racism. We will address each of these in turn.

On the international market, the United Nations System of National Accounts (UNSNA) has no method of accounting for nature's own production or destruction until the products of nature enter the cash economy, nor does it account for the majority of the work done by women. For example, Marilyn Waring has observed that the water rural women carry from the wells to their homes has no cash value, but the water carried through pipes has value.[31] Moreover, a clean lake which offers women fresh water supplies has no value in these accounting systems; once it is polluted, however, and companies must pay to clean it up, then the clean-up activity itself is performed by men and recorded as generating income. Similarly, living forests which supply women with food, fuel, and fodder have no recorded value in the UNSNA until they are logged and their products can be manufactured into commodities for sale – then all related industry and manufacture, usually seen as men's work, is recorded as income generating. Yet carrying water, collecting fire-

wood, weeding and hoeing, bearing children, preparing food, all usually seen as women's work because these tasks take place in the 'private' sector or home, are not factored into a nation's Gross National Product (GNP). In this way, both nature and women do not 'count' in the international market economy.

Yet it is women and nature who are called upon to pay the Third World debt. As we have already observed, the colonial heritage of the European invasion in Asia and Africa replaced subsistence farming with cash crops for export. The gender division of labor requires men to be in charge of the cash crops while the women manage the food crops; however, since hoeing and weeding are also seen as women's work, women are called upon to maintain the men's fields as well as their own. Presently, African women perform 60 percent of the agricultural work and 60 to 80 percent of the food production work.[32] Thus, to create cash crops which will generate income to pay the national debt, women work harder than men and receive no compensation. Only men are allowed to manage cash or to obtain credit in most developing countries; the assumption is that the money will 'trickle down', but it seldom does.

Moreover, the cash crops are draining these developing countries of their natural resources. In India, for example, the mixed tropical forests were replaced with the non-native cash crops of eucalyptus tree and sugarcane, both of which require enormous amounts of water for such a semi-arid region. The resulting deforestation and water loss has meant longer and longer walks each day for rural women to gather fuel wood and to haul water.[33] According to one estimate, women in New Delhi walk an average of 10 kilometers every three out of four days for an average of seven hours at a time, just to obtain firewood.[34] Again, women bear a disproportionate burden within systems of underdevelopment.

Wealthy nations of the North need to acknowledge their role in creating this system of underdevelopment and the debt repayments from which they benefit. The affluence of the North is founded on the natural resources and labor of the South; the recent popularity of the 'debt-for-nature' swaps, whereby Third World nations can exchange a portion of their natural resources to pay a percentage of their national debt, is yet another injustice in this repressive system. One debtor nation, the Philippines, is among 70 countries which annually remit over $50 billion in interest alone to First World creditors.[35] At this rate, the Third World will be perpetually indentured servants of the industrialized nations, an outcome well suited to the goals of capitalism. Because classism and economic imperialism (or neo-colonialism) are feminist concerns, and because this system of international accounting extracts the most severe payments from women and nature, the oppression inherent in the international market can best be understood from an ecofeminist perspective.

Globally, women produce approximately 80 percent of the world's food supplies, and for this reason women are most severely affected by food and fuel shortages and the pollution of water sources. Though women produce the food, most of the agricultural development training has been directed towards men; in addition, the men and boys are served first and provided with the most nutritious foods.[36] The phenomenon of world hunger is surely a product of underdevelopment and the international market, which demands that Third World countries export more food and resources in order to pay off their national debts.[37] In fact, on the average, governments in developing nations devote less than 10 percent of their budgets to agriculture which will feed their own people.[38] In addition to inequities in trade and food production, a major factor in world hunger is the widespread growth of meat production and consumption.

International development agencies have encouraged livestock production in developing countries and have funded a number of livestock projects.[39] Where domesticated animals used to play an integral role in household economies, providing a buffer against the changes in the market and the weather, and creating precious fertilizer and fuel for rural families, the mass production of livestock for export has become a major factor in desertification, water pollution and scarcity, ozone destruction, and hunger. Instead of producing crops for food, large areas of the world's cropland are devoted to feeding livestock: roughly 38 percent of the world's grain globally and 70 percent in the United States alone.[40] It is estimated that if the land devoted to livestock production in the United States were converted to producing grain for human consumption, it would free up more than 130 million tons of food, enough for 400 million people.[41] Of course, the availability of this food will not ensure that 400 million people will be fed; feeding the world also requires a just political policy for distribution. Nonetheless, eating high on the food chain must be seen as catering to the tastes of the affluent industrialized nations at the cost of between 40 and 60 million people – mostly children – who die each year of hunger or malnutrition.

Livestock production is a major cause of desertification, as more and more forests are cleared to provide rangeland for cattle. In Central America, more than 25 percent of the forests have been cleared to provide rangeland since 1960, and in Mexico alone, 37 million acres of forests have been converted since 1987.[42] It takes 55 square feet of cleared tropical forest to produce enough beef to make a quarter pound hamburger.[43] The combination of persistent overgrazing along with the dense soil compaction caused by the cattle's heavy hooves makes the ground impermeable to rainwater, which then runs off the surface and carries away topsoil. And cattle production requires an enormous amount of water: more than 3,000 litres of water are used to produce a kilogram of beef.[44] In a context where women may walk up to seven hours a day to provide water for their families, livestock production and its toll on the environment become ecofeminist concerns.

Intensive cattle production is also a major source of pollution. In belches, flatulence, and solid waste, cattle emit methane, the second most destructive greenhouse gas. Currently, livestock produce between 15 and 20 percent of methane emissions globally.[45] The nitrogen from their manure escapes into the air as gaseous ammonia, which causes acid rain. Animal agriculture produces 2 billion tons of waste each year.[46] Not all of this pollution is 'natural' either. Intensively reared animals are pumped full of antibiotics and growth hormones, chemicals that remain in their flesh and are transferred to humans when we consume the contaminated meat.

The use of these chemicals is thought to increase production, which in turn increases profit. However, such biotechnological intervention is not without its costs. Both humans and animals suffer from the introduction of scientific manipulation into production and reproduction. Dairy cows, for example, who are already over-milked are now forced to produce even more through the introduction of the Bovine Growth Hormones (BGH).[47] The hormonal manipulation of dairy cows affects not just the animals who are turned into "fast-food factories,"[48] but also small farmers who can no longer compete with the mega-industries. As these farmers have pointed out, such technological intervention benefits multinational pharmaceutical companies at their expense.[49] The US market is already saturated with dairy products, which has caused a dramatic drop in dairy prices. With the advent of BGH and the production of even more dairy products, the price reduction will force approximately 50 percent of US dairy farmers into bankruptcy.[50]

The increase in biological manipulation in agriculture and the widespread growth of biotechnological industry are of concern to ecofeminists. These endeavors involve the objectification and domination of both women's bodies and animals' bodies as well as the further economic exploitation of working class and Third World peoples. While technological intervention is often seen as a panacea – a means to progress and development, a way of increasing production and thus quality of life – it is becoming increasingly obvious that these technologies are creating more serious problems than those they were meant to solve. As Vandana Shiva has suggested, the so-called advances of the 'Green Revolution' turned the seed into a commodity, which was owned and controlled by a few wealthy Western corporations who stripped the farmers and their products of integrity and power: "The social and political planning that went into the Green Revolution aimed at engineering not just seeds but social relations as well."[51] Biotechnological intervention in agriculture served to perpetuate the dependence relation between poorer nations and their inhabitants and the wealthy 'innovators' of the super-seed.

A parallel dependence can be observed between women and those who control knowledge about women's bodies. The dangers of scientific intervention into the bodies and lives of women is particularly acute in the area of new reproductive technologies. Gena Corea has documented just how women may suffer from reproductive experimentation: hormonal treatment to create superovulation can damage ovaries, and long-term effects of such treatment have not been studied; surgical manipulation may damage ovaries and the uterus; and the danger of anesthetic and risk of infection are often downplayed.[52] In addition, the ideology of motherhood, which forces women to believe that they are failures if they cannot conceive and produce children, is so strong that those women

who can afford it 'consent' to the medical manipulation of their bodies. Science, which has been developed and practiced primarily by white, middle-class Western men, has systematically exploited women, animals, and the environment. Such practices are justified based on the prevailing conception of women and nature as different and inferior and their manipulation as legitimate in the name of 'progress'.

Feminists recognize the negative implications of the scientific control of women's bodies and reproduction. Nowhere are these implications more apparent than in the debate about global population. It's important to distinguish population control from reproductive choice, both in terminology and in terms of the underlying assumptions of each. As Betsy Hartmann observes, population control policy assumes that overpopulation is the primary cause of all the problems in the Third World, from hunger to deforestation and economic and political malaise.[53] Based on this assumption, population control ideology argues that people must be persuaded or forced to have fewer children and that this can be effected by delivering birth control to Third World women in a top-down fashion. While population is certainly a cause for concern – UN estimations project world population to be at 10.5 billion by the year 2110 – to place environmental degradation and economic distress on the population of the Third World is just another form of racism, sexism, and victim-blaming.

The issue of world population cannot be ignored, but from an ecofeminist perspective, 'population' does not describe the problem in a way that it can be solved. It is the North's overconsumption, coupled with the globally unjust distribution of wealth, resources, and power, which is causing world hunger and environmental degradation. Population control obscures the very real issues of women's lives and holds women responsible for overpopulating the world. From an ecofeminist perspective, the problem of population may more adequately be addressed by looking at the intersection of several factors: reproductive control, socioeconomics, and particularly the social status of women.

Reproductive control includes access to free, safe methods of contraception, including elective abortion; it means freedom from compulsory sterilization as well as compulsory motherhood, and the freedom to control the number and spacing of one's children. Yet the contraceptive methods currently available often endanger women's lives. For example, poor women who come to health officials are routinely given a choice between such unsafe methods as an IUD (intra-uterine device), the implant of a hormone-releasing device such as Norplant, injectable contraception such as Depo-Provera, or sterilization. While the first three methods are known causes of irregular bleeding, infection, illness and possibly death, in many countries the option of sterilization may also ensure a woman's starvation or death. A sterilized woman may be seen as an unfit wife, unable to bear the desired sons, and since her survival will depend on her role as a part of a family's production unit, she may be forced into begging or prostitution to support herself or her children.

But birth control programs alone have been shown to account for only 15 to 20 percent of overall fertility decline; the remaining percentage is attributed to socioeconomic factors such as economic security, increased literacy rates, better education, better health care, and better job opportunities for women. In rural agricultural communities, a family's well-being may depend on having more workers to grow the food, haul the water, and gather firewood. The vast majority of families in the Third World don't have pension plans or social security, and thus children are their only form of security for their old age. Moreover, not all those children born to Third World families will survive to adulthood. The average infant mortality rate in the Third World generally is 90 deaths per 1,000 live births – 150 deaths per 1,000 births in 16 African countries – as compared to 20 in the industrialized nations. In addition, women's reproductive systems and children's vulnerable immune systems and their rapid rates of growth make them particularly susceptible to environmentally-induced illness. But as the economy changes, even the poorest don't need to have as many children. When women have access to education and employment, they tend to want fewer children. As Hartmann's research shows, "no country has ever achieved low birth rates as long as it has had a high infant mortality rate."[54] Until women are valued in ways other than reproduction, and men's virility proven in ways other than producing many male offspring, there will be little hope of reducing birth rates.

With this kind of gross imbalance in population and the distribution of food and resources, it makes sense that the wealthy few in power would feel the need to protect their grossly unjust share of the earth's resources from the majority. Thus we have witnessed in this century alone the tremendous growth of militarism, predicated upon an enormous sense of fear and its resulting need to control. Feminist peace activists have analyzed the root cause of militarism as lying in the social construction of masculinity: based on a sense of self as separate, the masculine self is so isolated that the only way to break these rigid ego boundaries is through a conflict which could result in death.[55] Given the problems of masculine embodiment, heroism has been seen as the answer, for masculinity must be continually proved. Heroism, according to Nancy Hartsock, requires several steps: first, the exclusion of women; second, a zero–sum competition, in which one man's gain is another man's loss; third, a heroic action, which can only take place in separation from daily life and daily needs; and fourth, a sense of abstraction of the self and the moment from the larger whole.[56] Heroic actions cannot occur unless the situation is so dangerous that it threatens a man's continued existence. Ecofeminists have suggested it is the heroic mentality itself which has brought the world to a state of ecological devastation, but unfortunately, it is not until the crisis is of sufficiently epidemic proportions that heroes will respond.[57]

In fact, zero sum competition is taking place right now, where the military's gain is a loss that is suffered disproportionately by women and children. In 1987, the US military budget was $293 billion, accounting for 27.8 percent of all federal spending.[58] In 1990, global military spending was at $980 billion, or $185 per individual on the planet; in contrast, global spending on family planning totaled $4.5 billion.[59] Our international priorities are clearly set on killing people rather than on creating or preserving quality of life. To the millions of poor households suffering from malnutrition, hunger, poor to nonexistent health care, polluted water, and all the related problems of poverty, the continued increase in military spending is a kind of warfare in itself.

The military is a primary cause of global homelessness, a problem which women and children suffer the most. Globally, there are now more than 15 million refugees of war, with women and children comprising from 75 to 95 percent of these homeless.[60] One example, from the Palestinian–Israeli war, are the 600,000 refugees living on the

Gaza strip, at a density of 5,440 people per square mile.[61] More than 50 percent of their population are children under the age of 14. In India, 150,000 refugees from the desertified rural areas created by colonial economic policies of underdevelopment now live on the sidewalks of Bombay.[62] Around the world, poor city dwellers suffer a disproportionate share of urban hazards, ranging from toxic waste dumps and polluted water sources to high-speed traffic, simply because they lack the economic and political resources to prevent these conditions.

Moreover, the armed forces are the number one polluters globally: the production and testing of their weapons; their toxic, chemical, and nuclear wastes; and their acts of violence have caused needless damage to women, to children, to the earth and the animals, human and nonhuman, that live on it.[63] For example, 80 percent of Kuwait's camel population was destroyed during the Gulf War. That is 8,000 camels in addition to the estimated 15–30,000 birds who died in oil slicks. In the civil wars in various African countries, rhinos, elephants, hippos, and most recently the mountain gorillas have been slaughtered at an alarming rate. The effects of war on wilderness and wildlife are nowhere more devastating than in Vietnam. The conflict in Vietnam was by far the most ecologically damaging, with 5.43 million acres of tropical rainforests literally reduced to ashes. Eleven animal species that only live in the Southeast Asian war zone are seriously endangered. If the few remaining wild forest ox and pileated gibbon die, these species will be gone forever.[64]

Ecofeminists are especially concerned with environmental racism, defined as "the dumping, siting or placement of environmentally hazardous substances or facilities in the communities of color in North America and around the world, primarily because of the race and powerlessness of people in those communities."[65] In the United States, for example, race is a major factor in the location of hazardous waste: three out of every five Blacks and Hispanics live in areas with uncontrolled toxic waste sites; 75 percent of the residents in the rural Southwest, the majority of whom are Hispanic, drink pesticide-contaminated water; over 700,000 inner-city children suffer from lead poisoning, which results in learning disorders; and over two million tons of uranium tailings have been dumped on Indian reservations, resulting in reproductive organ cancer in Navajo teenagers at 17 times the national average.[66]

The needs and the cultures of indigenous people are rarely considered in the siting of development projects. In Papua New Guinea, the Panguna copper mine on Bougainville displaced local residents with a token compensation for their homes and land, creating a mine which was enormously profitable for the government: before 1989, when the displaced residents finally succeeded in closing it down, the mine was yielding 17 percent of the country's operating revenue and 40 percent of its export income.[67] Presently, in the Amazon, the indigenous Yanomami are being displaced by mining operations in the northern Brazilian states of Roraima and Amazonas. These mines are polluting local rivers with sediment and mercury, and are causing the deaths of at least 15 percent of the Yanomami.[68] In Hawaii, geothermal drilling is underway on the slopes of the active Mauna Loa volcano at Kilauea. Such drilling is an act of environmental racism in that it violates the religious and cultural beliefs of the native Hawaiians, for whom the Mauna Loa volcano is a manifestation of the Goddess Pele. This geothermal drilling releases a toxic corrosive gas, hydrogen sulfide, which is sickening at low levels and at high levels can kill. Drilling on an active volcano means that a single eruption could destroy wells and pipelines, releasing a toxic cloud over thousands of homes. The energy generated from such drilling will be used for increased industrialization on Oahu and Maui. One projected development, a metals smelting plant, will convert metal-bearing ocean crust into manganese, cobalt, and nickel, producing a huge toxic waste problem, with the poisons to be dumped into ocean trenches – the current source of the richest fishing grounds for indigenous people.[69]

From this plethora of examples, it's easy to see why planetary health and global ecological destruction are feminist issues. A commitment to women's health – reproductive health (freedom from compulsory motherhood, freedom to choose motherhood and to regulate it), labor health (safe conditions and fair compensation), and general health (in terms of unpolluted and sufficient sources of food, fuel, water, and shelter) – requires a commitment to planetary health. Yet around the world, more economic and natural resources are channeled into the destruction of life and away from the support of life. More than 1.5 million children under the age of five die in the Third World each year from measles; more than three quarters of a million children die annually from neonatal tetanus.[70] Inexpensive and effective health care could save 14 million lives of those under five years of age for a cost of $2.5 billion per year – which amounts to the cost of the entire world's military spending for one day.[71] Industrialization, militarism, and overconsumption are requiring the majority of the earth's resources and polluting the air, water, and soil of the planet, while women, children, people of color, and the earth itself pay for this with their health and their lives. Ecofeminism is a feminist movement for global health, but health cannot happen in the context of injustice. Ecofeminists believe the costs of ignoring women's needs are many: uncontrolled population growth, high infant and child mortality, a diminished economy, ineffective agriculture, a deteriorating environment, a divided society, and a poorer life for all.[72] If we truly want to make a change, the oppressions of women and the earth can no longer be addressed in isolation.

Developing an Ecofeminist Framework

Much like US socialist feminists who, in the 1970s, began analyzing the oppression of women in terms not just of patriarchy or capitalism, but both, ecofeminists are developing a 'multisystems' approach to understanding the interconnected forces that operate to oppress women and the natural world. Drawing heavily on the initial insights of socialist feminist theories[73] as well as the experiences of activists in the peace, anti-nuclear, anti-racist, anti-colonialist, environmental, and animal liberation movements, ecofeminist theory provides a historical, contextualized, inclusive approach for solving the problems discussed above. Ecofeminists believe that the current global crises are the result of the mutually reinforcing ideologies of racism, sexism, classism, imperialism, naturism, and speciesism. These ideologies, while conceptually isolatable, are best understood, according to ecofeminists, as force fields that intersect one another (to greater or lesser extents, depending on the actual context) to create complex systems of oppression.

To illustrate how an ecofeminist analysis differs from, yet draws on, other theories, we will examine one particular issue – intensive animal agriculture, a system of keeping animals indoors, in large sheds, where every aspect of their existence can be regulated to produce maximum output at minimum cost – through the theoretical lens of a number of distinct approaches. These analyses are necessarily brief and are meant simply to indicate how different theorists, using different arguments and points of reference, come to sometimes different, although not incompatible, conclusions about the same issue.

Feminists might respond to the practice of intensive animal agriculture in a variety of ways. From a liberal feminist perspective, for example, the use of animals for food, however the animals are raised, may be unproblematic. For liberal feminists, moral considerability is grounded on the ability to reason, an ability that presumably animals lack. The traditional liberal split between culture and nature is preserved with this view.[74] Their primary concerns are that women be recognized as fully rational creatures and thus allowed the full privilege of participation in human culture. Animals, like the natural world, are outside of the realm of culture; they can be used to further human ends. In addition, the liberal feminist would focus on the autonomy of individual humans to choose what they eat. According to liberal theory, individuals can do whatever they find pleasurable or fulfilling, as long as no humans are harmed by such action. Since animals are excluded from consideration, the concern a liberal feminist would have with intensive animal agriculture would be one that focuses on the inequitable distribution of animal protein and the effect such a distribution would have on women's lives, rather than on the effects factory farming has on animal lives.[75]

Socialist feminists also traditionally have focused exclusively on humans. Yet their analysis of intensive animal agriculture would have a different emphasis than that of the liberal feminists. The socialist feminist criticism of animal rearing practices and the consumption of factory farmed animal protein would focus on the patriarchal capitalist nature of animal production. They might point out, for example, that in the United States, eight corporations, responsible for the deaths of 5.3 million birds annually, control over 50 percent of the chicken market.[76] They might also point out that 95 percent of all poultry workers are black women who are required to scrape the insides out of 5000 chickens per hour and as a result suffer various disorders caused by repetitive motion and stress.[77] Those who profit from industrialized animal production do so by exploiting traditionally underprivileged groups, namely working-class white women and people of color. The socialist feminist analysis might also include an examination of the commodification of animal bodies and the marketing of these bodies to women who are represented culturally as those responsible for the reproduction of raw flesh into dinner for husbands and children. In addition, these feminists would undoubtedly examine the social status that is associated with those who, in this country for example, can afford to consume filet mignon as opposed to ground beef and brisket and the implications such consumption patterns have for broader socioeconomic relationships between classes.

Environmental theorists view human consumption of animals as an integral part of the ecological food chain: "the natural world as actually constituted is one in which one being lives at the expense of others."[78] Environmental theorists concentrate on holistic, biocentric analyses and thus reject vegetarianism as a choice that removes human beings from the workings of nature.[79] That is not to say, however, that all environmental theorists would approve of intensive animal agriculture. Quite the contrary. However, their analysis of such practices focuses on "the transmogrification of organic to mechanical processes."[80] What is objectionable about industrialized animal agriculture is the process whereby organic creatures are domesticated, manipulated through breeding and biotechnological intervention, and ultimately reduced to food-producing units. In addition, the very process of industrialized food production, which requires massive amounts of energy, water, and grazing land and produces large quantities of waste, is environmentally destructive in itself.

A Third World analysis of industrial animal production would focus on this institution as one of the many that contribute to overconsumption in the North.[81] As we indicated earlier, this type of analysis would examine the ways in which intensive animal production wastes vast amounts of protein that could otherwise be used to feed the millions of people around the globe who go to sleep hungry. Only about 17 percent of the grain and food energy that is fed to dairy cows is recovered in milk, while only about 6 percent is recovered from beef.[82] In addition, a Third World analysis might link the rise of industrialized animal agriculture to other problematic economic developments that occurred after the second World War when multinational agribusiness corporations began exploiting the Third World by instituting certain agricultural policies

such as cash cropping, monoculture, and consolidation. These policies led to a state of affairs in which small independent food producers lost their autonomy and could no longer afford to produce. This situation parallels that which is presently going on in first world intensive agriculture, where small 'mom and pop' farms are going out of business because they simply cannot compete. In addition, agribusiness conglomerates go into Third World countries, cut down their forests, displace their people, and disrupt their economic system, in order to usurp land for intensive animal production.

The animal liberation perspective is one that would suggest that factory farming is immoral in itself. Animal proponents argue that nonhuman animals are beings whose lives can go better or worse, who can feel pain and experience pleasure, and who have interests in living free from confinement. Conditions on factory farms ignore the animals' most basic needs and interests, and because of this humans should refrain from consuming factory farmed food products and become vegetarians.[83] While philosophically there are differences in the arguments that are advanced on behalf of animals,[84] there is a rough consensus that because animals are enough like humans in morally relevant ways, their interests should not be excluded from ethical deliberations. To fail to morally consider the fate that animals suffer on factory farms would be 'speciesist', a position that maintains that nonhuman animals are inherently less worthy of consideration simply because they are not human.[85]

These analyses of animal agriculture are not mutually exclusive. A socialist feminist, for example, may also be inspired by an environmental perspective and/or a Third World analysis. Animal liberationists are informed by the environmental perspective insofar as factory farming affects not just domestic animals but wild animals whose habitats are destroyed by it. The point we are trying to highlight is that each of these different approaches focuses on one or two elements of oppression as primary in its analysis. An ecofeminist framework will view *all* of the various forms of oppression as central to an understanding of particular institutions. So, for example, an ecofeminist analysis of factory farming is one which would examine the way in which the logic of domination[86] supports this institution not only as it affects animals' lives, but also as it affects workers, women, and nature.

By examining the connections between these various oppressions, ecofeminists provide a distinct critique of institutionalized animal agriculture. It is interesting to note that as far back as 1964 the beginings of just such an analysis appeared in Ruth Harrison's *Animal Machines*, which offered the first major exposé of factory farming. Her book was heralded by ecofeminist forerunner Rachel Carson, who wrote in the foreword, "wherever [*Animal Machines*] is read it will certainly provoke feelings of dismay, revulsion, and outrage."[87] More recently, ecofeminists have argued for a contextual moral vegetarianism, one that is capable of accounting for the injustices associated with factory farming while at the same time allowing for the moral justifiability of traditional food practices of indigenous people.[88]

Focusing on context and diversity is one of the strengths of ecofeminist theorizing. However, during the past decade or so, the polyphony of perspectives known as ecofeminism has created interesting theoretical tensions. For example, not all ecofeminists agree about the importance of taking the suffering of animals seriously.[89] Another area of some controversy involves the place of spirituality in ecofeminist theory. Some consider spirituality to be historically significant and personally empowering,[90] while others have maintained that spirituality is not a necessary condition of ecofeminist theory.[91] The use of feminized and sexualized metaphors for nature, such as 'mother nature' and 'the rape of the wild', has also been a topic of constructive debate.[92] Clearly, ecofeminist theory is theory in process. What is thought to be important at this particular historical and cultural moment may not be important to ecofeminists in another place at another time. Although the vision of a just and sustainable future for all is shared by ecofeminists, what this future looks like and how it is to be arrived at varies according to the diverse voices and experiences of those people engaged in developing ecofeminist theories.

Indeed, ecofeminist theory is theory built on community-based knowing and valuing, and the strength of this knowledge is dependent on the inclusivity, flexibility, and reflexivity of the community in which it is generated. Ecofeminist theory grows out of dialogue and focuses on reaching consensus. One method for accomplishing this is to focus on commonality while at the same time respecting difference, building coalitions with any number of individuals or groups struggling against oppression – such as deep ecologists, social ecologists, bioregionalists, Native American traditionalists, anti-imperialists, ecosocialists, greens, and others. In solidarity, these efforts to encourage dialogue across difference must emphasize a principled unity-in-diversity. Nothing less than the future of the earth and all of its inhabitants may well depend on how effectively we all can work together to achieve global justice and planetary health.

Notes

1 Francoise d'Eaubonne's *Le feminisme ou la mort* (1974) is often credited for the first usage of the word 'eco-feminism', but as Ariel Salleh has pointed out in *Hypatia*, Vol. 6, No. 1 (Spring 1991), pp. 206–14, esp. p. 206, the text was not translated into English until 15 years later, so it would have had little effect on those articles and texts published before 1989. The spontaneous appearance of the word or the concept of 'eco-feminism' across several continents would indicate it arose out of a real, internationally observable phenomenon rather than the influence of a single writer.

2 See the list of conferences at the end of this article.

3 See the reading list at the end of the article as well as the sources listed in the notes.

4 Lester R. Brown et al., *State of the World: 1992* (New York: W. W. Norton & Co., 1992), p. 4.

5 Our use of 'Third World', following Gita Sen and Caren Grown, is meant to convey respect for those women who self-identify as 'Third World Women' based on their "struggles against the multiple oppression of nation, gender, class, and ethnicity," *Development, Crises, and Alternative Visions: Third World Women's Perspectives* (New York: New Feminist Library, 1987), p. 9.

6 Official Report from the World Women's Congress for a Healthy Planet, 8–12 Nov. 1991, Miami, Florida (New York: Women's Environment & Development Organization, 1992), p. 6.

7 Ibid., p. 21.

8 World Resources Institute, *The 1992 "Information Please" Environmental Almanac* (Boston: Houghton Mifflin Company, 1992), pp. 107–11.

9 Brown, *State of the World: 1992*, p. 4.

10 Lloyd Timberlake and Laura Thomas, *When the Bough Breaks... Our Children, Our Environment* (London: Earthscan Publications, 1990), p. 128.

11 "Is Your Water Safe?" *U.S. News and World Report* (29 July 1991), pp. 48–55; Lewis Regenstein, *How to Survive in America the Poisoned* (Washington, DC: Acropolis Books, 1986), pp. 168–88.

12 *1992 Environmental Almanac*, pp. 143–5.

13 Brown, *State of the World: 1992*, p. 3.

14 *1992 Environmental Almanac*, p. 146. See also G. Jon Roush, "The Disintegrating Web: The Causes and Consequences of Extinction," *The Nature Conservancy Magazine* (Nov./Dec. 1989), pp. 4–15.

15 Brown, *State of the World: 1992*, p. 3.

16 John Robbins, *Diet for a New America* (Walpole, NH: Stillpoint Publishing, 1987), p. 352.

17 As reported at the "World Women's Congress for a Healthy Planet."

18 Brown, *State of the World: 1992*, p. 3.

19 In Brown, *State of the World: 1992*, the Worldwatch Institute writers use the metaphor of addiction to describe this denial, arguing that what is needed is a massive intervention. We find the paradigm of addiction to be inadequate for developing ecofeminist theory for a variety of reasons. Aside from the fact that the metaphor of addiction medicalizes and thereby potentially depoliticizes the problem of overconsumption and related injustices, there is the more practical problem of choosing a treatment center large enough to accommodate patriarchy.

20 For a philosophical taxonomy of these approaches, see Karen Warren, "Feminism and the Environment: An Overview of the Issues," *APA Newsletter on Feminism and Philosophy*, Vol. 90, No. 3 (Fall 1991), pp. 108–16.

21 See Carolyn Merchant, *The Death of Nature: Women, Ecology, and the Scientific Revolution* (New York: Harper & Row, 1980).

22 See Marija Gimbutas, *The Gods and Goddesses of Old Europe – 6500–3500 B. C.* (Berkeley and Los Angeles: University of California Press, 1982); Monica Sjoo and Barbara Mor, *The Great Cosmic Mother: Rediscovering the Religion of the Earth* (San Francisco: Harper & Row, 1987); Merlin Stone, *When God Was a Woman* (New York: Harcourt Brace Jovanovich, 1976); Riane Eisler, *The Chalice and the Blade: Our History, Our Future* (New York: Harper Collins, 1987).

23 For extensive anthropological discussions, see Elizabeth Fisher, *Woman's Creation* (New York: McGraw Hill, 1979); Donna Haraway, *Primate Visions* (New York: Routledge, 1989); and Andrée Collard with Joyce Contrucci, *Rape of the Wild: Man's Violence Against Animals and the Earth* (London: The Women's Press, 1988).

24 See Karen Warren, "Feminism and Ecology: Making Connections," *Environmental Ethics*, Vol. 9 (Spring 1987), pp. 3–20, and "The Power and the Promise of Ecological Feminism," *Environmental Ethics*, Vol. 12, No. 2 (Summer 1990), pp. 125–46.

25 See Elizabeth Dodson Gray, *Green Paradise Lost* (Wellesley, MA: Roundtable Press, 1981); and Susan Griffin, *Woman and Nature: The Roaring Inside Her* (San Francisco: Harper & Row, 1978).

26 See Carol Adams, *The Sexual Politics of Meat: A Feminist–Vegetarian Critical Theory* (New York: Continuum, 1990); Andrée Collard with Joyce Contrucci, *Rape of the Wild*; Lori Gruen, "Dismantling Oppression: An Analysis of the Connection Between Women and Animals," in *Ecofeminism: Women, Animals, Nature*, Greta Gaard, ed. (Philadelphia: Temple University Press, 1993), and "Exclusion and Difference: Reflections on 'On Women, Animals and Nature'," *APA Newsletter on Feminism and Philosophy* (Spring 1992); Marti Kheel, "Ecofeminism and Deep Ecology: Reflections on Identity and Difference," pp. 128–37, in *Reweaving the World: The Emergence of Ecofeminism*, Irene Diamond and Gloria Feman Orenstein, eds. (San Francisco: Sierra Club Books)

27 See Nancy Chodorow, *The Reproduction of Mothering* (Berkeley: University of California Press, 1978); Carol Gilligan, *In a Different Voice: Psychological Theory and Women's Development* (Cambridge, Mass.: Harvard University Press, 1982); Carol Gilligan, Janie Victoria Ward, Jill McLean, and Betty Bardige, eds., *Mapping the Moral Domain: A Contribution of Women's Thinking to Psychological Theory and Education* (Cambridge, Mass.: Harvard University Press, 1988). Gilligan's work has been critiqued in a number of feminist analyses for its racial and class biases. See, for example, Joan C. Tronto, "Beyond Gender Difference to a Theory of Care," *Signs*, Vol. 12, No. 4 (Summer 1987), pp. 644–63.

28 According to Fredrick Engels, *The Origin of the Family, Private Property and the State* (New York: International Publishers, reprinted 1990), p. 120, with the advent of private property, men were, for the first time, able to accumulate wealth, which they wished to pass on to their offspring. These conditions led to what Engels called the overthrow of mother right, which was the beginning of the decline in the social status of women.

29 For a Marxist account of this spread in Africa, see Walter Rodney, *How Europe Underdeveloped Africa* (Washington, D.C.: Howard University Press, 1981). For an ecofeminist analysis of British colonialism in India, see Vandana Shiva, *Staying Alive: Women, Ecology and Development* (London: Zed Books, 1988) For an account of US colonialism in Hawaii, see Haunani-Kay Trask, *From a Native Daughter: Colonialism and Sovereignty in Hawaii* (Monroe, ME: Common Courage Press, 1993).

30 For an overview of environmental activism as survival strategy, see Alan B. Durning, "Environmentalism South," *The Amicus Journal* (Summer 1990), pp. 12–18. For a sampling on the impacts of environmental degradation on women in particular, see Maggie Black, "Mothers of the Earth," *Earthwatch*, Vol. 32 (1988), pp. 5–7; Gita Sen and Caren Grown, *Development, Crises, and Alternative Visions: Third*

World Women's Perspectives (New York: Monthly Review Press, 1987); The Manushi Collective, "Drought: God-sent or Man-made Disaster?" *Heresies*, Vol. 13 (1981), pp. 56–8; Vandana Shiva, "Where Has All the Water Gone? – Women and the Water Crisis," *Ecoforum*, Vol. 10, No. 3 (Apr. 1985), p. 16; and Sally Sontheimer, ed., *Women and the Environment: Crisis and Development in the Third World* (New York: Monthly Review Press, 1991).

31 See Marilyn Waring, *If Women Counted: A New Feminist Economics* (San Francisco: HarperCollins, 1988); and Susan Meeker-Lowry, *Economics As If the Earth Really Mattered* (Philadelphia: New Society, 1988).

32 Anne V. Akeroyd, "Gender, Food Production and Property Rights: Constraints on Women Farmers in Southern Africa," pp. 139–47, in *Women, Development and Survival in the Third World* (London: Longman Group, 1991).

33 See Vandana Shiva, *Staying Alive: Women, Ecology and Development*, and "Where Has All the Water Gone?"

34 Waring, *If Women Counted*, p. 263.

35 Leonor Briones, Philippines, speaking at the World Women's Congress in Miami, Florida, 8–12 Nov. 1991.

36 Brown, *State of the World: 1992*, p. 87.

37 In addition to *World Hunger* (1986), a number of studies have proven that world hunger is a product of underdevelopment and colonialism. For example, see Tom Barry, *Roots of Rebellion: Land and Hunger in Central America* (Boston: South End Press, 1987); Susan George, *How the Other Half Dies: The Real Reasons for Hunger* (Penguin, 1976), and *Ill Fares the Land: Essays on Food, Hunger, and Power* (Washington, D.C.: Institute for Policy Studies, 1984); Betsy Hartmann and James Boyce, *Needless Hunger: Voices from a Bangladesh Village* (San Francisco: Institute for Food and Development Policy, 1979); Frances Moore Lappe, Joseph Collins, and David Kinley, *Aid as Obstacle: Twenty Questions About Our Foreign Aid and the Hungry* (San Francisco: Institute for Food and Development Policy, 1980).

38 These facts are corroborated in Akeroyd, "Gender, Food Production and Property Rights," pp. 153–4; Ruth Engo Tjega, Cameroon *Official Report from the World Women's Congress*, pp. 9–10.

39 Brown, *State of the World: 1992*, pp. 66–82.

40 Ibid., p. 69.

41 See Jeremy Rifkin, "Beyond Beef," *The Utne Reader*, Vol. 50 (March/Apr. 1992), pp. 96–109. Rifkin now has a book, *Beyond Beef: The Rise and Fall of the Cattle Culture* (New York: Penguin/Pume, 1992). According to John Robbins, "The livestock population of the U.S. today consumes enough grain and soybeans to feed over five times

the entire human population of the country...." (Robbins, *Diet for a New America*, pp. 350–1).

42 Rifkin, "Beyond Beef," pp. 98–9.

43 *Environmental Almanac 1992*, p. 39.

44 Brown, *State of the World: 1992*, p. 71.

45 Ibid., p. 74.

46 Jim Mason and Peter Singer, *Animal Factories* (New York: Crown, 1980), p. 84.

47 See Gruen, in *Ecofeminism: Women, Animals, Nature*, Gaard, ed.

48 Pat Hynes, *The Recurring Silent Spring* (New York: Pergamon Press, 1989), p. 185.

49 As reported in Peter Singer, *Animal Liberation* (New York: Avon, 1990), p. 138.

50 Hynes, *The Recurring Silent Spring*, p. 185.

51 Vandana Shiva, *The Violence of the Green Revolution* (London: Zed Books Ltd., 1991), p. 16.

52 Gena Corea, *The Mother Machine* (New York: Harper and Row, 1985).

53 See Betsy Hartmann, *Reproductive Rights and Wrongs: The Global Politics of Population Control and Reproductive Choice* (New York: Harper & Row, 1987).

54 See Betsy Hartmann, *Reproductive Rights and Wrongs*, p. 9.

55 See Nancy C. M. Hartsock, "Masculinity, Heroism, and the Making of War," pp. 133–52, in *Rocking the Ship of State: Toward a Feminist Peace Politics*, Adrienne Harris and Ynestra King, eds. (Boulder: Westview Press, 1989).

56 Ibid., p. 141.

57 See Chaia Heller, "For the Love of Nature: Ecology and the Cult of the Romantic"; and Marti Kheel, "From Heroic to Holistic Ethics: The Ecofeminist Challenge," in *Ecofeminism: Women, Animals, Nature*, Greta Gaard, ed.

58 Lourdes Beneria and Rebecca Blank, "Women and the Economics of Military Spending," pp. 191–203, in *Rocking the Ship of State*, Adrienne Harris and Ynestra King, eds.

59 Brown, *State of the World: 1992*, p. 5.

60 Official Report from the World Women's Congress, p. 10.

61 Najwa M. Sa'd, "In a Stateless Environment," *Women and Environments*, Vol. 10, No. 3 (Spring 1988), pp. 11–12.

62 Prema Gopalan, "Bombay Pavement Dwellers Struggle for Permanent Shelter," *Women and Environments*, Vol. 10, No. 3 (Spring 1988), pp. 13–15.

63 See Rosalie Bertell, "Charting a New Environmental Course," *Women and Environments*, Vol. 13, No. 2 (Winter/Spring 1991), pp. 6–9.

64 National Wildlife Federation information.

65 Official Statement of the World Women's Congress, p. 32.

66 See Cynthia Hamilton, "Women, Home, and Community: The Struggle in an Urban Environment,"

Woman of Power, Vol. 20 (Spring 1991), pp. 42–5; Official Statement of the World Women's Congress, p. 35; Margo Nikitas, "The 'Silent Bomb': Racism, War and Toxic Wastes," *The WREE View of Women: Newsmagazine of Women for Racial and Economic Equality (WREE)*, Vol. 16, Nos. 1/2 (Spring/Summer 1991), p. 15; "The Military's Toxic Legacy," *Newsweek* (6 Aug. 1990), p. 21.

67 Brown, *State of the World: 1992*, p. 115.

68 Ibid., p. 115.

69 The Pele Defense Fund, "The Violation of the Goddess Pele: Geothermal Development on Mauna Loa Volcano," *Woman of Power*, Vol. 20 (Spring 1991), pp. 40–1. See also, Trask, *From a Native Daughter*.

70 Timberlake and Thomas, *When the Bough Breaks*, p. 161.

71 Ibid., p. 168.

72 Janet Henshall Momsen, *Women and Development in the Third World* (New York: Routledge, 1991).

73 It is certainly true that many insights of the early radical feminists were important in the development of ecofeminism; however, contrary to what Val Plumwood suggests in "Beyond the Dualistic Assumptions of Women, Men and Nature," in *The Ecologist*, Vol. 22, No. 1 (Jan./Feb. 1992), most contemporary ecofeminist theorists reject the essentialist basis that cultural feminism maintains. Socialist Feminist theory, which recognizes the reinforcing oppressions of gender, race, and class and argues that liberation cannot occur when the exploitation of any group by another is occurring, is much closer in principle to recent work in ecofeminist theory. For examples of socialist feminist writing, see Karen V. Hansen and Ilene J. Philipson, eds. *Women, Class, and the Feminist Imagination* (Philadelphia: Temple University Press, 1990); and Ann Ferguson, *Blood at the Root* (London: Pandora Press, 1989); and *Sexual Democracy: Women, Oppression, and Revolution* (Boulder: Westview Press, 1991).

74 See Alison Jaggar, *Feminist Politics and Human Nature* (Totowa, NJ: Rowman & Allanheld, 1983), Ch. 3.

75 For example, Kathryn George might be read as adopting a liberal feminist approach to factory farming and vegetarianism more generally. In her article "So Human an Animal...., or the Moral Relevance of Being an Omnivore," *The Journal of Agricultural Ethics*, Vol. 3, No. 2 (1990), she suggests that people who are not as nutritionally privileged as most white, middle-class men should be morally permitted to eat factory farmed animals though not "to eat as much meat or animal products as they wish." She argues that moral vegetarianism precludes women from full participation in moral activities and is thus problematic.

76 *Broiler Industry* (Dec. 1987), p. 22, as cited in Singer, *Animal Liberation*, p. 98.

77 Carol Adams, "Ecofeminism and the Eating of Animals," *Hypatia*, Vol. 6, No. 1 (1991), p. 130.

78 J. Baird Callicott, *In Defense of the Land Ethic* (Albany: State University of New York Press, 1989), p. 33.

79 As Ned Hettinger writes in "Bambi Lovers Versus Tree Huggers: A Critique of Rolston's Environmental Ethics," *Environmental Ethics*, Vol. 16, No. 1 (1994): 3–20: "Rolston thinks there are positive values in the lives of (some) hunters and (all?) meat eaters that are lacking in the lives of vegetarians and nonhunters. 'Meat eaters', he says, 'know their ecology and natural history in a way that vegetarians do not ... I'm not sure a vegetarian even understands the way the world is built'." Rolston argues that vegetarians, in their refusal to eat meat, even factory farmed meat, are repudiating nature and their natural origins.

80 J. Baird Callicott, *In Defense of the Land Ethic*, p. 35.

81 Of course, we recognize that, as with the environmental theorists previously discussed, there is no single Third World viewpoint.

82 Mason and Singer, "Animal Factories," p. 74.

83 See, for example, Peter Singer, ed., *In Defense of Animals* (Oxford: Basil Blackwell, 1985), and Tom Regan, *The Case for Animal Rights* (Berkeley: University of California Press, 1983).

84 See Lori Gruen, "Animals" in Peter Singer, ed., *A Companion to Ethics* (Oxford: Basil Blackwell, 1991), pp. 343–53.

85 There is some debate about what exactly constitutes speciesism, a term originally coined by Richard Ryder and picked up by Singer. For an interesting feminist take on the issue, see the Comment and Reply between Nel Noddings and Josephine Donovan in *Signs*, Vol. 16, No. 2 (Winter 1991), pp. 418–25.

86 A concept discussed by Warren, "The Power and the Promise."

87 Ruth Harrison, *Animal Machines* (Vincent Stuart Ltd: London, 1964), p. viii.

88 See, especially, Deane Curtin, "Toward an Ecological Ethic of Care," *Hypatia*, Vol. 6, No. 1 (Spring 1991), pp. 60–74.

89 Those who do take animal suffering seriously include Carol Adams, *The Sexual Politics of Meat: A Feminist–Vegetarian Critical Theory* (New York: Continuum, 1990), "The Feminist Traffic in Animals," in *Ecofeminism: Women, Animals, Nature*, Gaard, ed., and "Ecofeminism and the Eating of Animals," *Hypatia*, Vol. 6, No. 1 (Spring 1991), pp. 125–45; Andrée Collard with Joyce Contrucci, *Rape of the Wild;* Deborah Slicer, "Your Daughter or Your Dog? A Feminist Assessment of the Animal Research Issue," *Hypatia*, Vol. 6, No. 1 (Spring 1991), pp. 108–24; Norma Benney, "All of One Flesh: The Rights of Animals," in *Reclaim the Earth: Women Speak Out for Life on Earth*, Leonie

Caldecott and Stephanie Leland, eds. (London: The Women's Press, 1983); Lori Gruen in *Ecofeminism: Women, Animals, Nature*, Gaard, ed. While some ecofeminists have failed to address the role of animals in their theories, none have specifically argued against considering animal suffering.

90　See, for example, Starhawk, "Power, Authority and Mystery: Ecofeminism and Earth-based Spirituality," pp. 73–86; Riane Eisler, "The Gaia Tradition and the Partnership Future: An Ecofeminist Manifesto," pp. 23–34; Mara Lynn Keller, "The Eleusinian Mysteries: Ancient Nature Religion of Demeter and Persephone," pp. 41–51; Carol P. Christ, "Rethinking Theology and Nature," pp. 58–68, all found in *Reweaving the World*, Diamond and Orenstein, eds. See also Charlene Spretnak, "Toward an Ecofeminist Spirituality," pp. 127–32; Rosemary Radford Ruether, "Toward an Ecological–Feminist Theory of Nature," pp. 145–50; Margot Adler, "The Juice and the Mystery," pp. 151–4; Dolores LaChapelle, "Sacred Land, Sacred Sex," pp. 155–67; Starhawk, "Feminist Earth-based Spirituality and Ecofeminism," pp. 174–85, all found in *Healing the Wounds*, Judith Plant, ed.

91　See Greta Gaard, "Ecofeminism and Native American Cultures: Pushing the Limits of Cultural Imperialism?" in *Ecofeminism: Women, Animals, Nature*, Gaard, ed., and Karen Warren, "Ecofeminist Spiritualities: An Ecofeminist Philosophical Perspective," in *Ecofeminism and the Sacred*, Carol Adams, ed. (New York: Continuum, 1993), pp. 119–32.

92　See Catherine Roach, "Loving Your Mother: On the Woman–Nature Relation," *Hypatia*, Vol. 6, No. 1 (Spring 1991), pp. 46–59; Lori Gruen, "Exclusion and Difference: Reflections on 'On Women, Nature, and Animals'," *APA Newsletter on Feminism and Philosophy*, Spring 1992; Yaakov Jerome Garb, "Perspective of Escape? Ecofeminist Musings on Contemporary Earth Imagery," pp. 264–78, in *Reweaving the World*, Diamond and Orenstein, eds.; Patrick D. Murphy, "Sex-Typing the Planet: Gaia Imagery and the Problem of Subverting Patriarchy," *Environmental Ethics*, Vol. 10, No. 2 (Summer 1988), pp. 155–68; Ellen Cronan Rose, "The Good Mother: From Gaia to Gilead," *Frontiers*, Vol. 11, No. 1 (1991), pp. 77–97; Chaia Heller, "For the Love of Nature: Ecology and the Cult of the Romantic," in *Ecofeminism: Women, Animals, Nature*, Gaard, ed.: Greta Gaard, "Ecofeminism and Native American Cultures," in *Ecofeminism: Women, Animals, Nature*, Gaard, ed.

Further Reading

Overview

For an overview of ecofeminist beginnings, see:

Spretnak, Charlene. "Ecofeminism: Our Roots and Flowering." *Woman of Power*, Vol. 9 (Spring 1988), pp. 6–10, reprinted in *Reweaving the World: The Emergence of Ecofeminism*, Irene Diamond and Gloria Feman Orenstein, eds. San Francisco: Sierra Club Books, 1990.

Anthologies

In order of appearance, they are:

Caldecott, Leonie and Stephanie Leland, eds. *Reclaim the Earth: Women Speak Out for Life on Earth*. London: The Women's Press, 1983.

Plant, Judith, ed. *Healing the Wounds: The Promise of Ecofeminism*. Philadelphia: New Society, 1989.

Diamond, Irene and Gloria Feman Orenstein, eds. *Reweaving the World: The Emergence of Ecofeminism*. San Francisco: Sierra Club Books, 1990.

Gaard, Greta, ed. *Ecofeminism: Women, Animals, Nature*. Philadelphia: Temple University Press, 1993.

Articles

Brown, Margaret. "Ecofeminism: An Idea Whose Time Has Come." *Utne Reader* (Apr. 1988).

Griffin, Susan. "Split Culture." *ReVISION*, Vol. 9, No. 2 (Winter/Spring 1987), pp. 17–23.

Griscom, Joan L. "On Healing the Nature/History Split in Feminist Thought." *Heresies*, Vol. 13 (1981), pp. 4–9.

King, Ynestra. "Healing the Wounds: Feminism, Ecology, and the Nature/Culture Dualism." *Gender/Body/Knowledge: Feminist Reconstructions of Being and Knowing*, Alison Jaggar and Susan Bordo, eds. New Jersey: Rutgers University Press, 1989.

Peterson, Abby and Carolyn Merchant. "'Peace with the Earth': Women and the Environmental Movement in Sweden." *Women's Studies International Forum*, Vol. 9, Nos. 5/6 (1986), pp. 465–79.

Plant, Judith. "Searching for Common Ground: Ecofeminism and Bioregionalism." *The New Catalyst* (Winter 1987/88).

Plumwood, Val. "Ecofeminism: An Overview and Discussion of Positions and Arguments." *Australasian Journal of Philosophy*, Supplement to Vol. 64 (June 1986), pp. 120–37.

Sale, Kirkpatrick. "Ecofeminism – A New Perspective." *The Nation* (Sept. 1987), pp. 302–5.

Greta Gaard and Lori Gruen

Salleh, Ariel. "Living with Nature: Reciprocity or Control?" *Ethics of Environment and Development*, R. and J. Engel, eds. Tucson: University of Arizona Press, 1990.

Warren, Karen. "Toward an Ecofeminist Ethic." *Studies in the Humanities*, Vol. 15 (1988), pp. 140–56.

Wyman, Miriam. "Explorations of Ecofeminism." *Women and Environments* (Spring 1987), pp. 6–7.

Young, Iris. " 'Feminism and Ecology' and 'Women and Life on Earth: Ecofeminism in the 80s'." *Environmental Ethics*, Vol. 5, No. 2 (1983), pp. 173–80.

Articles that take the connection between feminism and ecology as their central project include:

Bushwick, Nancy. "Women and the Environment: Seeing the Linkages in Economic Development." *Ecoforum*, Vol. 10, No. 2 (Apr. 1985), p. 3.

Davies, Katherine. "What Is Ecofeminism?" *Women and Environments* (Spring 1988), pp. 4–6.

—— "Why Talk About Women and the Environment? A Panel Discussion." *Women and Environments* (Winter/Spring 1991), pp. 10–12.

Henderson, Hazel. "The Warp and the Weft: The Coming Synthesis of Eco-Philosophy and Eco-Feminism." *Development: Seeds of Change*, Vol. 4 (1984), pp. 64–8.

King, Ynestra. "May the Circle Be Unbroken: The Eco-Feminist Imperative." *Tidings* (May 1981), pp. 1–5.

—— "The Ecology of Feminism and the Feminism of Ecology." *Harbinger: The Journal of Social Ecology*, Vol. 1 (1983).

—— "Feminism and the Revolt of Nature." *Heresies*, Vol. 13 (1981), pp. 12–16.

—— "Ecofeminism: The Necessity of History and Mystery." *Woman of Power* (1988).

—— "What is Ecofeminism?" *The Nation*, Vol. 12 (Dec. 1987), pp. 702, 730–1.

Warren, Karen. "Feminism and Ecology: Making Connections." *Environmental Ethics*, Vol. 9 (1987), pp. 3–21.

Articles on the debate between advocates of deep ecology and ecofeminism include the following:

Biehl, Janet. "Ecofeminism and Deep Ecology: Unresolvable Conflict?" *Our Generation*, Vol. 19 (1988), pp. 19–31.

Cheney, Jim. "Eco-Feminism and Deep Ecology." *Environmental Ethics*, Vol. 9 (1987), pp. 115–45.

Doubiago, Sharon. "Deeper Than Deep Ecology: Men Must Become Feminists." *The New Catalyst* (Winter 1987/88).

Kheel, Marti. "Ecofeminism and Deep Ecology: Reflections on Identity and Difference." *Reweaving the World*, Diamond and Orenstein, eds., pp. 128–37.

Salleh, Ariel. "Deeper Than Deep Ecology: The Eco-Feminist Connection." *Environmental Ethics*, Vol. 3 (1984), pp. 339–45.

—— "The Ecofeminist/Deep Ecology Debate: A Response to Patriarchal Reason." *Environmental Ethics*, Vol. 14, No. 3 (Fall 1992).

Sells, Jennifer. "An Eco-feminist Critique of Deep Ecology: A Question of Social Ethics." *Feminist Ethics* (Winter 1989/90), pp. 12–27.

Sessions, Robert. "Deep Ecology Versus Ecofeminism: Healthy Differences or Incompatible Philosophies?" *Hypatia*, Vol. 6, No. 1 (Spring 1991), pp. 90–107.

Zimmerman, Michael. "Feminism, Deep Ecology, and Environmental Ethics." *Environmental Ethics*, Vol. 9 (1987), pp. 21–44.

A more complete listing of the articles on ecofeminism can be found throughout the notes in this essay; as of Fall 1991, the most comprehensive listing of texts on ecofeminism was offered in the "Special Issue: Feminism and the Environment," *APA Newsletter on Feminism and Philosophy*, Vol. 90, No. 3 (Fall 1991).

Journals
In order of appearance, they are:

"Feminism and Ecology." *Heresies*, Vol. 13 (1981).

"Woman/Earth Speaking: Feminism and Ecology." *New Catalyst*, Vol. 10 (Winter 1987/88).

Woman of Power (Spring 1988).

"Feminism, Ecology, and the Future of the Humanities." *Studies in the Humanities*, Vol. 15, No. 2 (Dec. 1988).

"A Sense of Wilderness." *Creation*, Vol. 5, No. 2 (May/June 1989).

"Women and the Environment." *World Women News*, Vol. 1, No. 4 (1989).

"Paradise Found: How the Environmental Crisis Can Improve Our Lives." *Utne Reader*, Vol. 36 (Nov./Dec. 1989).

Woman of Power (Spring 1991).

"Special Issue: Feminism and the Environment." *APA Newsletter on Feminism and Philosophy*, Vol. 90, No. 3 (Fall 1991).

"Feminism, Nature, Development." *The Ecologist*, Vol. 22, No. 1 (Jan./Feb. 1992).

List of conferences
"Women and Life on Earth: Ecofeminism in the 1980s," held at Amherst, Massachusetts in 1980.

"Women and the Environment: The First West Coast Ecofeminist Conference," held at Sonoma State University in 1981.

"Women and Life on Earth," held in London in 1981.

"United Nations World Women Conference," held in Nairobi in 1985.

"Ecofeminist Perspectives: Culture, Nature, and Theory," held at the University of Southern California in 1987.

"Healing the Earth: Women's Strategies for the Environment," held at the University of British Columbia in Vancouver in 1991.

"World Women's Congress for a Healthy Planet," held in Miami, Florida in 1991.

"Midwest Environmental Ethics Conference on Ecological Feminism," held in Iowa in 1992.

While the international conferences in 1985 and 1991 did not explicitly use the term "ecofeminism" in their titles, their content and goals exemplify the principles of ecofeminism, and many of those who attended the 1991 conferences identified themselves as ecofeminists.

22

Ecological Feminism and Ecosystem Ecology

Karen J. Warren and Jim Cheney

Ecological feminism is a feminism which attempts to unite the demands of the women's movement with those of the ecological movement in order to bring about a world and worldview that are not based on socioeconomic and conceptual structures of domination. Many ecological feminists have claimed that what is needed is a feminism that is ecological and an ecology that is feminist (see King 1983, 1989). They have shown ways in which ecology, understood in its broadest sense as environmentalism, is a feminist issue.[1] What has yet to be shown is that ecology, understood in its narrower sense as "the science of ecology" (or, scientific ecology) also is or might be a feminist issue. Establishing *that* claim involves showing that ecological feminism makes good scientific ecological sense.[2]

In this paper we discuss ten noteworthy similarities between themes in ecological feminism and ecosystem ecology – similarities that show the two are engaged in complementary, mutually supportive projects. Our goal is modest and suggestive. We are *not* arguing for the stronger claims that ecosystem (or, more generally, scientific) ecology must be feminist, that feminists must be ecologists, or that these similarities establish that ecosystem ecology is feminist. To establish these claims, much more would be needed than is provided in this paper.[3] Rather, we are identifying theoretical points of intersection between ecofeminism and ecosystem ecology in the interest of furthering discussion on the nature and

direction of future bridge-building between the two.[4]

Ecological Feminism and Ecofeminist Ethics

We take ecological feminism to refer "to a sensibility, an intimation, that feminist concerns run parallel to, are bound up with, or, perhaps, are one with concern for a natural world which has been subjected to much the same abuse and ambivalent behavior as have women" (Cheney 1987, 115). Although there are a variety of ecofeminist positions (Warren 1987), the common thread that runs through ecofeminist scholarship is that the domination of women and the domination of nature are "intimately connected and mutually reinforcing" (King 1989, 18). All ecofeminists endorse the view that an adequate understanding of the nature of the connections between the twin dominations of women and nature requires a feminist theory and practice informed by an ecological perspective and an environmentalism informed by a feminist perspective (Warren 1987, 4–5).

Much of ecofeminist scholarship concerns the ethical nature of human relationships to the nonhuman natural world. Like feminist ethics generally, "ecofeminist ethics" includes a variety of positions. What makes ecofeminist ethics feminist is a twofold commitment to critique male bias in ethics and to develop analyses which are not male-biased (see Jaggar 1990, 23). However, ecofeminist ethics extends feminist ethical critiques of sexism and other social "isms of domination" to include critiques of "naturism," i.e., the unjustified domination of nonhuman animals and nature by humans. As such, ecofeminist ethics critiques not only androcentric but also anthrocentric and naturist bias in ethics. Ecofeminist ethics is grounded in the assumption that the dominations of women and of nature are morally wrong and ought to be eliminated. Like feminist ethics (see Jaggar 1990, 24–5), the practical import of ecofeminist ethics is as a guide to action on issues in the pre-feminist, patriarchal present. This guidance is aimed at assisting persons in resisting sexist, naturist, and interconnected racist, classist, heterosexist practices, and in envisioning and creating morally desirable alternatives. The women-initiated nonviolent Chipko movement begun in 1974 in Reni, India is one such alternative action (see Shiva 1988 and Warren 1988).

One way to image ecofeminist ethics is as a quilt-in-the-making (see Warren 1988, 1990). Like the AIDS Names Project Quilt, ecofeminist ethics is a quilt-in-process, constructed from "patches" contributed by persons located in different socioeconomic, cultural, historical circumstances. Since these patches will reflect the histories of the various quilters, no two patches will be just the same. Nonetheless, the quilts-in-process will each have borders that not only delimit the spatiotemporal dimensions of the quilt, but also put some necessary conditions, "boundary conditions," on what can become part of the quilt. What these boundary conditions do *not* do is delimit the interior of the quilt, what the design or actual pattern of the quilt will be. That design will emerge out of the life experiences, ethical concerns, and specific socioeconomic historical contexts of the quilters (see Warren 1990).

What are some of the boundary conditions of ecofeminist ethics? Just what does, and what does not, belong on the quilt? Since ecofeminism is a critique of interrelated social systems of domination, no "isms of domination" (for example, sexism, racism, classism, heterosexism, naturism) belong on the quilt (Warren 1990). This means that any conceptual framework (or, set of basic beliefs, values, attitudes, and assumptions which grow out of and reflect one's view of oneself and one's world) which sanctions, justifies, or perpetuates these "isms of domination" – oppressive and

patriarchal conceptual frameworks – does not belong on the quilt. What *does* belong on the quilt are those descriptions and prescriptions of social reality that do not maintain, perpetuate, or attempt to justify social "isms of domination" and the power-over relationships used to keep them intact. These will include patches that make visible and challenge local and global forms of environmental abuse, the disproportional effects of environmental pollution on women, children, the poor, dislocated indigenous persons, and peoples in so-called less developed countries; patches that provide present-day alternatives to environmental exploitation; patches that document and celebrate the morally respectful dimensions of women's experiences with the nonhuman world; and patches that include the experiences of indigenous people, when those experiences are neither sexist nor naturist. Taken together, the patches on the quilt provide the ethical theorist with concrete, pictoral ways of understanding the nature of a morality which treats both women's moral experiences and human interactions with the nonhuman natural world respectfully.

Ecosystem Ecology

Many controversies in modern ecosystem ecology about the nature of ecosystems can be understood as arguments between two approaches to the study of ecosystems: the "population-community" approach and the "process-functional" approach.[5] The population-community approach focuses on the growth of populations, the structure and composition of communities of organisms, and the interactions among individual organisms. It is grounded in Darwinian theory of natural selection. It "tends to view ecosystems as networks of interacting populations whereby the biota *are* the ecosystem and abiotic components such as soil or sediments are external influences" (O'Neill et al. 1986, 8). The population-community approach typically is identified with the work of such ecologists as Clements, Lotka, Gause, and Whittaker.

In contrast, the process-functional approach is based on a quantitative, mathematical, thermodynamic, biophysical model which emphasizes energy flows and nutrient cycling. It assumes that the fundamental units of ecosystems include both organisms and physical components, biotic and abiotic components. The process-functional approach was developed during this century by such ecologists as Tansley, Lindeman, and Odum.

Although discussions of ecosystems ecology often present "the ecological perspective" as if there were only one perspective, debates arising from differences between the population-community and process-functional approaches to ecosystems ecology reveal that there currently is *no single model* of ecosystems.[6] Furthermore, there is a third alternative way to conceive ecosystems. That alternative is "hierarchy theory" or what, for important feminist reasons, we prefer to refer to as "observation set theory."[7] We understand hierarchy theory to be the most viable attempt to date by scientific ecologists to provide an inclusive theoretical framework for the variety of ecosystem analyses. Ecologists such as O'Neill, DeAngelis, Waide and Allen are among its main advocates (O'Neill et al. 1986).

Central to hierarchy (observation set) theory is the notion of an *observation set*. O'Neill et al. describe an observation set as "a particular way of viewing the natural world. It includes the phenomena of interest, the specific measurements taken, and the techniques used to analyze the data" (1986, 7). Although specific problems always call for particular observation sets, theory making calls for consideration of multiple observation sets:

> Each of these points of view emphasizes different phenomena and quite different measurements. But since neither encompasses all possible observations, neither can be considered to be more fundamental. When studying a specific problem, the scientists must always focus on a single observation set. However, when developing theory, many observation sets must be considered. (O'Neill et al. 1986, 7)

According to hierarchy theory, both an adequate conception of the complexity of ecosystems and meaningful ecosystem comparisons require that one consider multiple observation sets.

Spatiotemporal scale is an important characteristic of an observation set both because it changes as the ecological problem changes and because "ecological principles often do not translate well across these scales" (O'Neill et al. 1986, 20). The meanings of such basic ecological concepts as "stability," "equilibrium," "temporary," "enduring," "local," and "global," are relative to some particular scale. Depending on the spatiotemporal scale

used in any given observation set, "ecosystems have been seen as static or dynamic, as steady-state or as fluctuating, as integrated systems or as collections of individuals" (O'Neill et al. 1986, 20). For example, a forest stand can be looked at from an organismic standpoint (e.g., as enduring, stable individual trees or populations of trees) *or* from an energy flow and nutrient cycling standpoint (e.g., as fluxes and flows of carbon and oxygen recycled through photosynthesis). Because the forest stand may accurately be viewed in either way, it is incorrect, in fact impossible, "to designate *the* components of *the* ecosystem" – the designation depends on the spatiotemporal scale and changes as that scale changes (O'Neill et al. 1986, 83).

The basic contribution of hierarchy (observation set) theory is to call attention to the importance of observation sets and spatiotemporal scales to ecosystem ecology. The complexity of natural systems is overlooked or discounted when one focuses on a single observation set. An exclusivist "either-or" approach to describing or studying ecosystems (e.g., an exclusivist population-community or functional process approach) is thereby viewed as based on a false dichotomy which results in an inadequate, because incomplete, *theory* of ecosystems (O'Neill et al. 1986, 209).[8]

Similarities Between Ecofeminism and Ecosystems Ecology

We are now in a position to show some of the similarities between ecofeminism (particularly ecofeminist ethics) and ecosystem ecology seen through the lens of hierarchy (observation set) theory. These similarities suggest various ways in which ecofeminism and ecosystem ecology inform and support one another.[9]

First, central to hierarchy theory is the view that space–time dependent observation sets provide different vantage points or frameworks from which one makes ecological observations and engages in ecological theory building. It is through the notion of multiple observation sets that the idea of one single model of ecosystems is rejected. In this respect, hierarchy theory rules out any notion of an observation set free or *decontextualized* science: how one views ecosystems will depend on the observation sets one employs.

One is immediately struck by the similarity between the hierarchy theorist's emphasis on observation sets, "windows through which one views the world," and the ecofeminist's emphasis on "ways of thinking," "world-views," and "conceptual frameworks," especially oppressive and patriarchal ones (see Warren 1987, 1990). The notion of a patriarchal and oppressive conceptual framework is as central to ecofeminism and ecofeminist ethics as the notion of an observation set is to hierarchy theory in ecosystem ecology: one could not generate the observations and conclusions of each without them. An attention to observation sets is also an acknowledgment of the importance of the contexts in and through which one observes, measures, and theorizes. One's observation set, like one's conceptual framework, will quite literally shape and affect what one sees; both provide a *context* for theorizing.

There are at least three interrelated reasons why attention to context is of importance to ecofeminist ethics. First, *what* a thing (person, community, population, species, animal, river) is, is in part a function of *where* it is, a function of the relationships in which it stands to other things and to its history, including (where applicable) its evolutionary history. It is this attention to *place* that fuels bioregionalist ecofeminism (see Plant, 1990) and the importance many ecofeminists give to narratives, myth, and ritual in the construction of ecofeminist ethics (see Cheney 1987, 1989a; Diamond and Orenstein 1990; Warren 1990). Second, an understanding of context is important in assessing the putatively universal claims of reason and ethical deliberation. Feminist worries about ahistorical and allegedly gender-neutral conceptions of reason and rationality in the Western philosophical tradition provide one way of understanding the importance of context – historical location and gender identity in theory building in the prefeminist present.[10] Ecofeminist theory building seeks to rid prevailing conceptions of reason, rationality, and morality of whatever male and naturist bias they have.

More than this, however, and this is our third point, an attention to context permits one to stress the idiographic dimension of our ethical journeys through this world and of ethics itself. Holmes Rolston has been a strong advocate for recognizing this aspect of ethical thought in environmental ethics, and this advocacy derives from his understanding that a thing is what it is in part because of where it is. As Rolston puts it:

An ethics should be rational, but rationality inhabits a historical system. The place that is to be counted morally has a history; the ethics that befits such a place will take on historical form; the ethics will itself have a history. The place to be mapped ... will have twin foci. One focus will be nomothetic, recurrent; the other will be idiographic, uniquely particular. ...

The rationality of the ethic, as well as the area to be mapped, will be historical. That is, logic will be mixed with story. The move from *is* to *ought* ... is transformed into movement along a story line (Rolston 1988, 341–2). An attention to context does not split off the idiographic as what ethics permits, provided that the universal demands of morality are met. Instead, the ethically idiographic is the very center of each individual's ethical life; it is the place from which we not only test the claims of the "universal" and the "rational," but from which we construct the "universal" claims of "rationality." In this way, the "universal" and the "rational" are always in some manner or other inflected with historicity. The "universal" and "rational" are themselves moments in a story, reflecting some observation set.

The ecological dimension of ethical reflection stems in large part from the fact that ecology is context (or observation set) dependent. We agree with Brennan that:

what ecology shows is not simply that the context makes a difference to the kind of action we engage in. It shows, rather, that what kinds of things we are, what sort of thing an individual person is, and what sort of options for fulfillment and self-realisation are open, are themselves very much context-dependent. (Brennan 1988, 162)

One way ecofeminist ethics centralizes this context-dependent feature of ethical discourse is by conceiving of ethics as growing out of what Cheney (1987, 144) calls defining relationships, that is, relationships understood as in some sense defining who one is. These relationships include those of moral agents with the nonhuman natural world, including animals.

Second, hierarchy theory provides a methodological means of investigating ecological problems. According to hierarchy theory, the "ontology" that emerges from any particular investigation is relative to the observation set that produces it. This does not make the ontology "subjective" in any pernicious sense; but it does mean that to accept a solution to a particular problem is not thereby to make any ontological commitments in any absolute (i.e., non-observation set dependent) sense. Thus, the methodology of hierarchy theory makes it imperative that the epistemological requirements of particular problems, given in terms of observer-affected observation sets, dictate to ontology (rather than the converse); ecology does not determine that an ecological problem must be pressed into the shape of a preferred ontology. According to hierarchy theory, it would be quixotic to think in terms of striving for an articulation of *the* structure (even *the* hierarchical structure) of an ecosystem.

As a methodological stance, hierarchy theory rejects the view that there is only one way to describe ecological phenomena. Which description is appropriate will depend upon the observation set and on what it is one is attempting to describe, explain, or predict. In this respect, hierarchy theory privileges methodological and epistemological considerations over ontology, the attempt to specify what is "really" in the world. The ontology embedded in both explanation and phenomena being explained is always a function of the appropriate observation set. Any grand attempt to provide one metaphysics of morals seems doomed because misguided: it puts the metaphysical/ontological cart before the epistemological/methodological horse.

Like hierarchy theory, ecofeminism makes no attempt to provide *the* point of view, one single model, an "objective" (i.e., value-neutral, unbiased) point of view – none, that is, beyond the very "boundary conditions" of ecofeminism itself. Ecofeminists criticize up–down, value-hierarchical, value dualistic thinking which they say characterizes Western philosophical thinking about women and nature as being both patriarchal and insular – as if what is observed, prescribed, and theorized are independent of *any* conceptual framework (Gray 1981; Griffin 1978; King 1983, 1989; Ruether 1975; Warren 1987, 1988, 1990). Ecofeminists acknowledge up front their basic feminist value commitments: the twin dominations of women and nature exist, are wrong, and ought to be eliminated. Ecofeminists see these twin dominations as social problems rooted in very concrete, historical, socioeconomic conditions, as well as in oppressive, patriarchal conceptual frameworks that maintain and sanction these conditions.

As a methodological and epistemological stance, all ecofeminists centralize, in one way or another, the "voices" and experiences of women (and others) with regard to an understanding of the nonhuman natural world. Like hierarchy theory, this is not to say that an ecofeminist "ontology" does not include material objects – real trees, rivers, and animals. It does! But it acknowledges that these objects are in important senses both materially given and socially constructed: what counts as a tree, river, or animal, how natural "objects" are conceived, described, and treated, must be understood in the context of broader social and institutional practices. Centralizing women's voices is important methodologically and epistemologically to the overall critique and revisioning of the concept of nature and the moral dimensions of human–nature relationships.

Third, hierarchy theory is antireductionist. Population-community based observation sets cannot be reduced to process-functional based observation sets (or vice versa). Consequently, a functional-process understanding of organisms does not render an "object ontology" of discrete organisms (trees, rivers, animals) obsolete, or render organisms mere conduits or configurations of energy, as environmental ethicist J. Baird Callicott has claimed (1986). There *is no* ontologically prior or privileged or fundamental description of nature. Hierarchy theory rules out a view of individual entities (e.g., animals) as ontologically parasitic on something more fundamental (e.g., energy flows or nutrient cycles), a point we return to shortly. If hierarchy theory is correct, then in contemporary scientific ecology, there is no place for a notion of degrees of reality. *Both* individuals and energy flows are real.

Because it is antireductionist, hierarchy theory centralizes diversity; it takes difference or diversity to be a fundamental feature of phenomena, not reducible to talk of the "sameness" of organisms or the "oneness" of energy flows. That would be the case only if one approach had epistemological, metaphysical, or ontological priority over the other. In fact, one of the most interesting features of hierarchy theory is that it privileges the notion of diversity or difference when studying interactions between different subsystems ("holons") of ecosystems, *and* the notion of commonalities among members of the same subsystem. Hierarchy theory is therefore a framework which provides for both an ecology of differences and an ecology of commonalities, depending on the context and observation set.[11]

Ecofeminist ethics is also antireductionist. It is a structurally pluralistic framework that centralizes both diversity or difference (e.g., among women, among people of color, between humans and non-humans) *and* commonalities (e.g., among women, among people of color, between humans and non-humans). A nonreductionist ecofeminist stance acknowledges differences between humans and members or elements of nonhuman nature, while nonetheless affirming that humans are animals and members of an ecological community. An ecology of differences and commonalities fits well with an ecofeminist politics and ethics of differences and commonalities.

Fourth, hierarchy theory is an inclusivist theory that offers a framework for mediating between historically opposed approaches to ecosystem ecology, making a central place for the insights of each without inheriting the defects of either when viewed exclusively as the right or correct way to study ecosystems. Hierarchy theory suggests that the future of at least ecosystem ecology may well lie in successfully integrating these two approaches into a model that centralizes the importance of observation sets and locates any particular ecosystem analysis in or relative to a particular observation set.

Similarly, ecofeminist ethics is an inclusivist ethic (see Warren 1990) that offers a framework for mediating between two historically opposed approaches in environmental ethics: deontological rights-, virtues-, or holistic-based ethics and consequentialist-based ethics. Warren has argued that ecofeminism "involves a shift *from* a conception of ethics as primarily a matter of rights, rules, or principles [whether deontological or consequentialist] determined and applied in specific cases to entities viewed as competitors in the contest of moral standing," *to* one which "makes a central place for values . . . that presuppose that our relationships to others are central to our understanding of who we are" (Warren 1990, 143). An ecofeminist ethic may involve a commitment to rights in certain contexts and for certain purposes (for example, in the protection of individual animals against unnecessary pain or suffering); it may use consequentialist considerations in other contexts and for other purposes (for example,

when considering behavior toward ecosystems). Like hierarchy theory, ecofeminist ethics is one possible framework for developing such an inclusivist alternative.[12]

As a fifth and related point, hierarchy theory provides a framework for viewing historically opposed approaches as complementary. Dualisms fade into the complexity of multiple vantage points and find complementarity where once there was only oppositionality (e.g., stability or instability, diversity or sameness, energy flow or discrete organism). This rejection of oppositional polarities is accomplished *not* by reducing population-community to process-functional accounts, or vice versa, or by reducing both to a still more basic or primitive ontological framework; it is accomplished by providing a unifying framework for studying and relating to one another various analyses, each with their own epistemology and context-dependent ontology. As a "unified theory," it is a unity which does not erase difference.

The earliest ecofeminist literature was grounded in a rejection of oppositional value dualisms (see Gray 1981; Griffin 1978). Ecofeminist ethics needs to follow suit[13] by emphasizing difference in a way that does not reduce difference to the terms of some (reductionist) privileged discourse.

Sixth, because it centralizes diversity, hierarchy theory complexifies rather than simplifies the variety of ways natural phenomena can be described. It does this by emphasizing the sorts of interrelationships that exist among organisms and the relevance of scalar and other dimensions to the observations made. It rejects exclusivist models of ecosystems (i.e., population-community or process-functional models) that simplify rather than complexify the nature of ecosystems, typically by an imposed naive reductionism that focuses on sameness, similarity, or shared traits. Interrelationships among biotic and abiotic nature that are based on a single, unitary model of ecosystems are viewed as misrepresentations of the variety of relationships in nature.

Similarly, as a context-dependent, inclusivist framework that centralizes difference, ecofeminism complexifies the variety of ways in which ethics is conceived and practiced, in which humans may be in relationship with others (including the nonhuman natural environment), and in which human–nature, women–nature connections may be described. As we have argued elsewhere (Warren 1988, 1990; Cheney 1987, 1989a) ecofeminist ethics complexifies the moral arena by making a central place for values often lost or overlooked in mainstream ethics (e.g., values of care, love, friendship, diversity, appropriate reciprocity) in the context of human–nonhuman relationships. This includes taking seriously the sort of "indigenous technical knowledge" that women and others who work closely with the land have (see Warren 1988).

Seventh, and perhaps most importantly for ethics, hierarchy theory permits meaningful ecological talk of "individual" and "other" without the caveat that these are nonprimitive notions, ultimately reducible to notions of energy flow and pattern. At the same time, it also permits meaningful talk of "whole-system" behavior in both population-community and process-functional terms, neither of which is reducible to the other. Hierarchy theory thus permits meaningful discussion of discrete (and, in varying degrees and modes, autonomous) individual objects as well as of whole systems. Hierarchy theory shows that "object theory" is not obsolete; it is an acceptable and alternative way to describe organisms – appropriate for some observation sets and not others.

This alternative way of describing ecosystems is accomplished in hierarchy theory in part by an eighth characteristic, one shared by ecofeminism and ecofeminist ethics: it encourages a network or relational view of organisms, whether conceived as "knots in a biospherical web of relationships" or as separate (although not isolated or solitary), discrete individuals, members of species, populations, or communities. In both cases, ecosystems are networks, either networks of interacting individuals, populations, and communities or of interacting energy and nutrient flows and cycles.

This dual acknowledgment of the autonomous existence of individuals (characteristic seven) and the relational existence of individuals in webs of relationships (characteristic eight) fits nicely with those feminist ethics which insist that it is of primary importance to acknowledge and foster individual autonomy (after all, oppressed persons are still trying to have their autonomy recognized) *and* to recognize that people exist in webs of relationships that are to some extent constitutive of who they are. Much work in feminist ethics (often strongly influenced by the work of Gilligan 1982) has emphasized the centrality of relationships in women's ethical thinking. Others (e.g., Friedman

1989 and Young 1986) have critiqued communitarian ideals and stressed the importance for women of autonomy and a politics of difference in a world in which the penchant for defining oneself relationally can easily be turned into sacrifice of the self. Many feminists have been concerned to develop conceptions of self and society that avoid the problems of what Alison Jaggar calls abstract individualism, that is, the position that it is possible to identify a human essence or human nature that exists independently of any particular historical context (Jaggar 1990, 29).

This concern carries over into ecofeminist ethical reflection on nature. An ecofeminist ethic that emphasizes the nature of individuals or "others" as beings-in-relationships permits meaningful ecological discussion of *both* "self" and "other," of "individuals" (populations, communities) and "webs of relationships." For ecofeminists the contexts and relationships that help construct "the self" include ecological contexts and relationships with non-human nature. For an ecofeminist one cannot give an adequate account of what it is to be human in terms that do not acknowledge humans as members of ecological communities.

That hierarchy theory provides for meaningful discussion of "self" and "other" suggests one reason ecofeminists are and ought to be suspicious of some of the claims about scientific ecology made by other, allegedly "minority position" environmental ethics. For example, in "The Metaphysical Implications of Ecology," Callicott argues that scientific ecology "undermines the concept of a separable ego and thus renders obsolete any ethics which involves the concepts of 'self' and 'other' as primitive terms" (1986, 301). Callicott's overarching conclusion is that scientific ecology ontologically subordinates matter and living natural objects (e.g., humans, deer, trees) to energy flows, making an "object ontology" inappropriate as an ecological description of the natural environment.

Views such as Callicott's are not borne out by state-of-the-art hierarchy theory in ecosystem ecology. Hierarchy theory shows that even if at some level of inquiry it is plausible to hold that the universe and everything in it are constituted of energy, that everything is a perturbation in an all-encompassing energy field, this does *not* imply that entities revealed through other observation sets (e.g., as individual organisms, populations, or communities) are not "primitive," that they are reducible to the ontology of some other observation set. Hierarchy theory not only permits but demands meaningful ecological discussion of "self" and "other" on the one hand *and* of "whole-system behavior" on the other. Certain ecological observation sets relevant to ethics yield an ontology of autonomous individual organisms interacting with one another. Other observation sets paint a holistic picture of ecosystem function. But there is no a priori or ecological reason (other than a misguided reductionism) to give (ethical or metaphysical) pride of place to the latter.[14]

What *is* crucial is our particular mode of access to the objects of our moral concern. We need to formulate our "ethical ontology" and ethical theory in light of an understanding of our epistemological relationship to the objects of moral concern. In terms of actual practice, we certainly can say things, significant and important things, about individuals without drawing in the rest of the universe. We can gain at least certain kinds of knowledge of individuals without an analysis of the relations that constitute or produce the individual as the individual it is; that is, we can come to know the individual without knowing anything much about the shaping factors.

Ninth, hierarchy theory makes a place for whatever "hard" scientific data scientific ecology produces regarding the natural environment, although it always contextualizes that data relative to a given observation set with specific scalar dimension. It is *always* scientifically relevant to ask about particular observation sets within which and from which the "hard" data are gathered. According to hierarchy theory, all scientific data and questions of ecology come with and have a context; proper scientific theorizing involves making visible the observation sets (contexts) within which one conducts the observations and analyses. Hierarchy theory thereby leaves open the door for saying that whatever ecologists learn about organisms or ecosystems from computer modeling techniques, mathematical or statistical models, or data projections conducted within the closed system of a laboratory may not tell us all there is to know, or even the most relevant information and material we need to know, about terrestrial organisms and ecosystems – i.e., nature outside the laboratory. But we may need to know it, nonetheless, to solve pressing environmental problems.[15]

Ecofeminism welcomes appropriate ecological science and technology. Environmental problems demand scientific and technological responses as part of the solution. These "data" represent a piece of the ecological pie. What ecofeminists insist on is that the perspectives of women and indigenous peoples with regard to the natural environment also be recognized as relevant "data." As a *feminism*, ecofeminism insists that relevant "data" about the historical and interconnected twin exploitations of women (and other oppressed peoples) and nature be included in solutions to environmental problems; as an *ecological* feminism, ecofeminism insists upon the inclusion of appropriate insights and "data" of scientific ecology. What ecological feminism opposes is the practice of one without the other.

Lastly, hierarchy theory invites a reconceiving of ecosystems research and methodology, objectivity, and knowledge. In its rejection of the view that there is one ahistorical, context-free, neutral observation stance, in its incorporation of multiple observation sets and its refusal to privilege the ontology of one over the ontology of any other, in its acceptance of multiple understandings of ecosystems and the complexity of the relationships that exist within them, hierarchy theory exemplifies, to some extent, what Donna Haraway (1988) has called embodied objectivity. What is obviously absent in hierarchy theory is an ethical and political dimension, however, which is present in Haraway's notion.

Objectivity, as Haraway puts it, is "about particular and specific embodiment and definitely not about the false vision promising transcendence of all limits and responsibility" (Haraway 1988, 582–3). Because all knowledge is "situated knowledge" (Haraway 1988, 581), no knowledge is innocent; all knowledge involves risks and implies responsibility. As Haraway argues:

> admitted or not, politics and ethics ground struggles over knowledge projects in the exact, natural, social, and human sciences. Otherwise, rationality is simply impossible, an optical illusion projected from nowhere comprehensively. (1988, 587)

The ethical and political dimensions of knowledge and objectivity suggest an important contribution that ecofeminism can offer hierarchy theory. The "partial knowledges" that emerge from various observation sets do not constitute an innocent plurality of bodies of knowledge. Both the positions taken (with their resultant situated knowledges) and the connections made are "power-sensitive" (Haraway 1988, 589). Situated knowledges are partial knowledges,

> not partiality for its own sake but, rather, for the sake of the connections and unexpected openings situated knowledges make possible. Situated knowledges are about communities, not about isolated individuals. The only way to find a larger vision is to be somewhere in particular. (Haraway 1988, 590)

Since ecofeminism sees theory building, objectivity, and knowledge as historically situated, illuminated, and created, theory is not something static – it is both "situated" (in Haraway's sense) and "in process," emerging from people's different experiences and observations and changing over time. It *is* like quilting.

Are there, then, any ethical implications of ecosystem ecology? It depends. The ethical implications of ecosystem ecology, like the hierarchy theory that might be used to support them, only have axiological status within and from the vantage points of certain observation sets. As ecologist Mark Davis claims of any ecological model, "any set of ethical implications derived or inspired from the model must always be regarded as only one of many possible such sets" (Davis 1988, 4).

The contextualist conception of objectivity at work in hierarchy theory is consistent with the notion of objectivity being developed in some feminist postmodernist theorizing. The problem faced by postmodern science, as Haraway puts it, is "how to have *simultaneously* an account of radical historical contingency for all knowledge claims and knowing subjects ... *and* a no-nonsense commitment to faithful accounts of a 'real' world" (Haraway 1988, 579). But just as Haraway would insist upon an ethical and political basis for objectivity in the sciences, so she would add the idea of the "object" of knowledge as an active agent in the construction of knowledge. She rightly points out that feminists have been suspicious of scientific accounts of objectivity that portray the "object" of knowledge as passive and inert. Haraway's view in response to this passive understanding of the object of scientific inquiry is as follows:

> Situated knowledges require that the object of knowledge be pictured as an actor and agent, not as a screen or a ground or a resource, never

finally as slave to the master that closes off the dialectic in his unique agency and his authorship of "objective" knowledge. The point is paradigmatically clear in critical approaches to the social and human sciences.... But the same point must apply to the other knowledge projects called sciences. (Haraway 1988, 592–3)

If we understand the objects of scientific inquiry as actors and agents *and* insist upon an ethical and political basis for objectivity, accounts of the world based "on a logic of 'discovery'" give way to "a power-charged social relation of 'conversation.' The world neither speaks itself nor disappears in favor of a master decoder" (Haraway 1988, 593). In this regard, Haraway herself calls attention to the promise of ecofeminism:

> Ecofeminists have perhaps been most insistent on some version of the world as active subject. ... Acknowledging the agency of the world in knowledge makes room for some unsettling possibilities, including a sense of the world's independent sense of humor.... There are ... richly evocative figures to promote feminist visualizations of the world as witty agent. We need not lapse into appeals to a primal mother resisting her translation into resource. The Coyote or Trickster ... suggests the situation we are in when we give up mastery but keep searching for fidelity, knowing all the while that we will be hoodwinked.... We are not in charge of the world. We just live here and try to strike up noninnocent conversations. (Haraway 1988, 593–4)

We agree with Haraway's concluding words: "Perhaps our hopes for accountability, for politics, for ecofeminism, turn on revisioning the world as coding trickster with whom we must learn to converse" (Haraway 1988, 596). The significance of the finding that ecofeminism and ecosystem ecology are involved in complementary, mutually reinforcing projects would then lie in what they can contribute together to our conversation with the world as "coding trickster."

Notes

We gratefully acknowledge the helpful comments received on an earlier draft of this paper from Roxanne Gudeman, Donna Haraway, Sandra Harding, Alison M.

Jaggar, Ruthanne Kurth-Schai, Toby McAdams, Michal McCall, Lindsay Powers, Truman Schwartz, Geoff Sutton, Nancy Tuana, Leslie Vaughn, Anthony Weston, and Cathy Zabinski.

1   See ecofeminist critiques of environmental practices cross-culturally in Caldecott and Leland (1983), Diamond and Orenstein (1990), Merchant (1980), Peterson and Merchant (1986), Plant (1989), Shiva (1988), and Warren (1988).

2   Showing that scientific ecology is a feminist issue is not as easy as one might expect. As scientific ecologists are quick to point out, there is a difference between the ecology movement (or, popular environmentalism) and the science of ecology. Even if the women's movement and the ecology movement are inextricably connected, and even if understanding the connections between the domination of women and the domination of nature is crucial to an adequate feminism, environmentalism, or ethic, still, none of this shows any respects in which the *science* of ecology must be feminist. In this paper, we attempt to put into place some considerations which bear on *that* issue.

3   In helpful comments on an earlier draft of this paper, Sandra Harding pointed out that even if there are striking similarities between ecological feminism and ecosystem ecology, there might be very good reasons for feminists to reject some claims of ecosystem ecology, and vice versa. One such reason would be the inattention to issues of power in ecosystem theory construction and practice. Since an analysis of power is central to feminist critiques of socially constructed "isms of domination," one would need very good reasons for accepting *as feminist* any theory or practice in scientific ecology which did not include an analysis of power and power-over relationships.

4   Our discussion of ecological feminism is limited to emerging themes in ecofeminism and ecofeminist ethics which are not tied to any one feminism. This is because there is not *one* ecological feminism anymore than there is *one* feminism; the varieties of ecofeminisms will reflect differing feminist commitments of liberal, marxist, radical, socialist feminisms as well as feminisms of women of color (nationally and internationally). Similarly, our discussion of scientific ecology is limited to ecosystem ecology, since it is ecosystem analysis that is the focus of much of the current literature in environmental ethics on the ethical or metaphysical implications, if any, of ecology (see Brennan 1988; Callicott 1986; Cheney 1991b; Golley 1987; Rolston 1988, 1989).

5   We express our gratitude to Mark Davis, Department of Biology and Director of Environmental Studies at Macalester College, for the information he provided

about the population-community and functional-process approaches to ecosystem ecology and hierarchy theory. Much of that information is presented in his unpublished article "Should Moral Philosophers Be Listening to Ecologists?" (1988).

6   There are also feminist reasons to worry about construing these two approaches as the only approaches to studying ecosystems, reasons having to do both with a general concern about theoretical descriptions of material reality in terms of mutually exclusive polarities. (See, e.g., Gray, 1981.)

7   Insofar as so much feminist, including ecofeminist, theory has focused on a critique of value hierarchical thinking and its function in creating, maintaining, and perpetuating social systems of domination, the name "hierarchy theory" is most unfortunate from a feminist point of view. In her comments on an earlier draft of this paper, Alison Jaggar suggested that the name is "toxic" and could well predispose feminists to be antagonistic towards hierarchy theory from the outset. Since, as will be shown, the notion of an "observation set" is central to hierarchy theory and yet does not connote problematic value hierarchies, we have chosen to refer to hierarchy theory frequently throughout this paper as "hierarchy (observation set) theory." (We do not discuss here that aspect of hierarchy theory which gives it its name, though we do in our forthcoming book *Ecological Feminism*, Westview Press.) If it were not for the established usage of the expression "hierarchy theory" within the scientific ecological community, we would refer to the theory simply as "observation set theory."

8   O'Neill et al. stress that they have exaggerated the differences between the population-community and process-functional approaches and that "few ecologists would hold to either extreme of the spectrum" (1986, 10). The distinction between the two approaches is better viewed on a continuum, with the population-community and process-functional approaches at each end and ecologists "drawn in one direction or the other by the specific problems that interest them" (1986, 10).

9   That the discussion format moves from hierarchy (observation set) theory to ecofeminism is not intended to privilege either perspective. Furthermore, more space is provided below to ecosystem ecology when discussing similarities than to ecofeminism for two main reasons: first, there is a virtual absence in the literature of ecofeminism of any attempt to spell out the details of just how ecological feminism might draw support for its position from, or impart its own insights to, ecological science. To begin to remedy this omission, we deliberately have chosen to focus on ecosystem ecology (rather than on ecological feminism) and *then* show important similarities between the two – similarities that are more

Karen J. Warren and Jim Cheney

detailed and specific about "ecology" than are general appeals to the importance of ecosystems, interconnectedness among life forms, or ecological well-being to the survival of the planet. Second, we have presented elsewhere our views on ecological feminism and ecofeminist ethics (Cheney 1987, 1989a; 1991a; Warren 1987, 1988, 1990) and did not want to duplicate those efforts here.

10 For essays and a literature overview on this issue, see the American Philosophical Association *Newsletter on Feminism and Philosophy* Special Issue on "Reason, Rationality and Gender," edited by Nancy Tuana and Karen J. Warren, vol 88, no. 2 (March 1989).

11 This argument is developed in more detail in Warren's *Ecofeminist Philosophy*.

12 Warren has argued that ecofeminist ethics needs to evaluate ethical claims partly in terms of a condition of inclusiveness: *Those claims are morally and epistemologically favored (preferred, better, less partial, less biased) which are more inclusive of the perspectives and felt, lived experiences of the most amount of people, particularly including the perspectives and experiences of oppressed persons* (Warren 1988, 1990).

13 We say "needs to" because some ecofeminists have been criticized for substituting a value-hierarchical "women *are* closer to nature than men" ontology and ethics for an unacceptable patriarchal value-hierarchical schema which puts nature and what is female gender-identified together as inferior and opposed to that which is male gender-identified. The criticism is that the very oppositional dualism which prompts the question "Are women closer to nature than men?" is itself the problem. Switching the answer by elevating women and nature (in opposition to men) only perpetuates the problem. (See Griscom, 1981; King, 1981; Ortner, 1974; Warren, 1987.)

14 The implication is clear: just as "it is quite feasible and even reasonable to maintain an individualistic (i.e., Gleasonian) concept of the community and a holistic concept of ecosystem function" (O'Neill et al. 1986, 189) so too it is quite feasible and reasonable to understand the moral community as consisting, in part, of autonomous agents with properties in their own right while at the same time treating that community as in some respects holistic.

15 A popular environmentalist slogan, sometimes endorsed by ecofeminists, is that everything is connected: a tug on any part of the system has an effect on every other part of the system. This image of ecosystems is one that O'Neill et al. take great pains to dispel (1986, 86). Critical to the stability of an ecosystem is the relative insulation or *dis*connection of sub-systems ("holons") from one another (with strong interaction within holons and weak interaction between holons). Overconnectedness in a system, where tugs on any part of the system produce effects on all parts of the system, are *un*stable (94). This perspective renders problematic the oft-repeated remark that ecology demonstrates that everything is connected with everything else – the interconnection is only within holons, not between holons.

An adequate ecofeminist ecology, then, must acknowledge that the world, so to speak, "strives" to organize itself into discrete and relatively autonomous holons as a condition of its own stability. This is at least as important a feature of our world as is its connectedness. And, indeed, individuals still come into their own with the same sterling ontological credentials as the energy flow patterns which emerge from process-functional analyses. Everything may be tied to everything else in *some* sense, but hierarchy (observation set) theory suggests that it is not in any metaphysically reductionist, holistic sense.

References

Brennan, Andrew. 1988. *Thinking About Nature: An investigation of nature, value and ecology*. Athens, GA: University of Georgia Press.

Caldecott, Léonie and Stephanie Leland, eds. 1983. *Reclaim the Earth: Women speak out for life on earth*. London: The Women's Press.

Callicott, J. Baird. 1986. The metaphysical implications of ecology. *Environmental Ethics* 8: 301–16.

Cheney, Jim. 1987. Eco-feminism and deep ecology. *Environmental Ethics* 9: 115–45.

——. 1989a. Postmodern environmental ethics: Ethics as bioregional narrative. *Environmental Ethics* 11: 117–34.

——. 1989b. The Neo-stoicism of radical environmentalism. *Environmental Ethics* 11: 293–325.

——. 1991a. Review of Arne Naess, *Ecology, Community and Life-style*. *Environmental Ethics*, 13: 263–73.

——. 1991b. Callicott's "Metaphysics of morals." *Environmental Ethics*, 13: 311–25.

Davis, Mark. 1988. Should moral philosophers be listening to ecologists? Unpublished manuscript.

Diamond, Irene and Gloria Femen Orenstein, eds. 1990. *Reweaving the World: The emergence of ecofeminism*. San Fransisco: Sierra Club Books.

Friedman, Marilyn. 1989. Feminism and modern friendship: Dislocating the community. *Ethics* 99: 275–90.

Gilligan, Carol. 1982. *In a Different Voice: Psychological theory and women's development*. Cambridge: Harvard University Press.

Golley, Frank B. 1987. Deep ecology from the perspective of environmental science. *Environmental Ethics* 9(1): 45–55.

Gray, Elizabeth Dodson. 1981. *Green Paradise Lost*. Wellesley, MA: Roundtable Press.

Griffin, Susan. 1978. *Women and Nature: The roaring inside her*. San Francisco: Harper and Row.

Griscom, Joan L. 1981. On healing the nature/history split in feminist thought. In *Heresies #13: Feminism and Ecology* 4(1): 4–9.

Haraway, Donna. 1988. Situated knowledges: The science question in feminism and the privilege of partial perspective. *Feminist Studies* 14: 575–99.

Jaggar, Alison M. 1990. Feminist ethics: Problems, projects, problems. In *Feminist Ethics*. Claudia Card, ed. Lawrence, KS: University Press of Kansas.

King, Ynestra. 1981. Feminism and the revolt of nature. *Heresies #13: Feminism and Ecology* 4(1): 12–16.

——. 1983. Toward an ecological feminism and a feminist ecology. In *Machina ex dea: Feminist perspectives on technology*. Joan Rothschild, ed. New York: Pergamon Press.

——. 1989. The ecology of feminism and the feminism of ecology. In *Healing the Wounds: The power of ecological feminism*. Judith Plant, ed. Philadelphia and Santa Cruz: New Society Publishers.

Leopold, Aldo. 1970. *A Sand County Almanac*. New York: Ballantine Books.

Merchant, Carolyn. 1980. *The Death of Nature: Women, ecology, and the scientific revolution*. San Francisco: Harper and Row.

Murphy, Patrick, ed. 1988. Feminism, ecology and the future of the humanities. Special issue of *Studies in the Humanities*. 15(2).

O'Neill, R. V., D. L. DeAngelis, J. B. Waide, and T. F. H. Allen. 1986. *A Hierarchical Concept of Ecosystems*. Princeton: Princeton University Press.

Ortner, Sherry B. 1974. Is female to male as nature is to culture? In *Women, Culture, and Society*. Michelle Rosaldo and Louise Lamphere, eds. Stanford, CA: Stanford University Press.

Peterson, Abby and Carolyn Merchant. 1986. Peace with the earth: Women and the environmental movement in Sweden. *Women's Studies International Forum*. 9(5–6): 465–79.

Plant, Judith. 1990. Searching for common ground: Ecofeminism and bioregionalism. In *Reweaving the World: The emergence of ecofeminism*. Irene Diamond and Gloria Feman Orenstein, eds. San Francisco: Sierra Club Books.

Plant, Judith, ed. 1989. *Healing the wounds: The Power of Ecological Feminism*. Philadelphia and Santa Cruz: New Society Publishers.

Rolston, Holmes, III. 1988. *Environmental Ethics: Duties to and values in the natural world*. Philadelphia: Temple University Press.

——. 1989. Review of Andrew Brennan, "Thinking about nature: An investigation of nature, value and ecology." *Environmental Ethics* 11: 259–67.

Ruether, Rosemary Radford. 1975. *New Woman/New Earth: Sexist ideologies and human liberation*. New York: Seabury Press.

Salleh, Ariel Kay. 1984. Deeper than deep ecology: The eco-feminist connection. *Environmental Ethics* 6: 339–45.

Shiva, Vandana. 1988. *Staying Alive: Women, ecology, and development*. London: Zed Books.

Warren, Karen J. 1987. Feminism and ecology: Making connections. *Environmental Ethics* 9: 3–21.

——. 1988. Toward an ecofeminist ethic. *Studies in the Humanities* 15 (2): 140–56.

——. 1990. The power and promise of ecological feminism. *Environmental Ethics* 12: 125–46.

——. 2000. Ecofeminist Philosophy. Lanham, MD: Rowman and Littlefield Publishers.

Young, Iris. 1986. The ideal of community and the politics of difference. *Social Theory and Practice* 12: 1–26.

Zimmerman, Michael. 1987. Feminism, deep ecology, and environmental ethics. *Environmental Ethics* 9: 21–44.

Environmental Pragmatism

23

Beyond Intrinsic Value: Pragmatism in Environmental Ethics

Anthony Weston

I Introduction

"Pragmatism" sounds like just what environmental ethics is against: shortsighted, human-centered instrumentalism. In popular usage that connotation is certainly common. *Philosophical* pragmatism, however, offers a theory of values which is by no means committed to that crude anthropocentrism, or indeed to any anthropocentrism at all. True, pragmatism rejects the mean–ends distinction, and consequently rejects the notion of fixed, final ends objectively grounding the entire field of human striving. True, pragmatism takes valuing to be a certain kind of desiring, and possibly only human beings desire in this way. But neither of these starting points rules out a genuine environmental ethic. I argue that the truth is closer to the reverse: only these starting points may make a workable environmental ethic possible.

One charge of anthropocentrism should not detain us.[1] Pragmatism is a form of subjectivism – it makes valuing an activity of subjects, possibly only of human subjects – but subjectivism is not necessarily anthropocentric. Even if only human beings value in this sense, it does not follow that only human beings *have* value; it does not follow that human beings must be the sole or final objects of valuation. Subjectivism does not imply, so to say, subject-*centrism*; our actual values can be much more complex and world-directed.

Pragmatism insists most centrally on the *interrelatedness* of our values. The notion of fixed ends is replaced by a picture of values dynamically interdepending with other values and with beliefs, choices, and exemplars: pragmatism offers, metaphorically at least, a kind of "ecology" of values. Values so conceived are resilient under stress, because, when put to question, a value can draw upon those other values, beliefs, etc. which hold it in place in the larger system. At the same time, though, every value is open to critical challenge and change, because each value is also *at stake* precisely with those related values, beliefs, etc. which on other occasions reinforce it. We are thus left with a plurality of concrete values, in which many different kinds of value, and many different sources of value, can be recognized as serious and deep without requiring further reduction to some single all end in itself. And there is every reason to think that respect for other life forms and concern for natural environments are among those values. The problem is not to devise still more imaginative or exotic justifications for environmental values. We do not need to *ground* these values, pragmatists would say, but rather to situate them in their supporting contexts and to adjudicate their conflicts with others – a subtle enough difference at first glance, perhaps, but in fact a radical shift in philosophical perspective.

II Intrinsic Value and Contemporary Environmental Ethics

We seem to be compelled to distinguish means and ends almost as soon as we begin thinking about environmental values. Nature has certain obvious appeals: recreational and aesthetic satisfactions, "ecosystem stabilization" values (seemingly useless species may play a role in controlling pests, or fixing nitrogen), research and teaching uses, the attraction of natural objects and lifeforms simply as exemplars of survival, and so on.[2] In making these appeals, however, we value nature not "for its own sake," but for a further end: because it is necessary, useful, or satisfying to *us*. Even aesthetic appreciation does not necessarily require valuing nature for itself, since we might be tempted to say that only aesthetic *experience* is valued intrinsically. Beauty is in the mind of the beholder: aesthetic objects are only means to it.

The familiar next step is to ask whether nature could also be valuable in its own right. Could nature have *intrinsic* value, could it have worth as an end in itself, and not just because it serves human ends?[3] This question, of course, frames much of the debate in contemporary environmental ethics. If human beings, or some particular and unique human characteristics (e.g., a certain kind of conscious experience), are the only ends in themselves, then we have, for better or worse, "anthropocentrism." If some broader, but not universal class of beings has intrinsic value, and if, as usual, this class is taken to be the class of sentient or (even more broadly) living beings, then we have what might be called "sentientism" or (more broadly) "biocentrism." If *all* ("natural"?) beings, living or not, have intrinsic value and must not be treated merely as means, then we have what might be called "universalism." There is a continuum of possible ethical relations to nature, then, ranging from views which limit the bearers of intrinsic value strictly to human beings through views which progressively extend the franchise until finally it is (nearly?) universal.[4]

This much seems perfectly innocent. No views are actually endorsed, after all: only a range of possibilities is set out. In fact, however, I think that this "frame" is far from innocent. This seemingly uncommitted range of possibilities is in fact narrowly restricted by the underlying notion of intrinsic value itself.

Consider, after all, how that range of possibilities is determined in the first place: each option is defined precisely by the set of beings to which it attributes intrinsic value. Richard and Val Routley, for instance, argue that anthropocentrism represents a kind of moral "chauvinism," as egregious as the egoist's blindness to values beyond his or her self or the racist's failure to look beyond his or her race;[5] they insist upon the existence of *other* intrinsic values besides conscious human experience, values which deserve similar respect. Tom Regan *defines* an environmental ethic as a view which attributes "inherent goodness" to at least some non-human natural objects, where "inherent goodness" is an "objective property" of objects which compels us to respect its bearers.[6]

That notion of intrinsic or "inherent" value, however, is itself extremely specific and demanding. A great deal of philosophical baggage comes with it. Regan already weighs in with some of it, as Evelyn Pluhar points out, by construing inherent value as a "supervenient," "nonnatural" property, notions whose Moorean ancestry and problematic metaphysical commitments are plain to see.[7] But there is more to come. Let me try to set out the traditional requirements for intrinsic values more systematically.

(1) To qualify as intrinsic a value must be *self-sufficient*. G. E. Moore – the patron saint of intrinsic values – wrote that "to say that a kind of value is 'intrinsic' means . . . that the question whether a thing possesses it . . . depends solely on the intrinsic nature of the thing in question."[8] In his famous thought experiment in *Principia Ethica*, Moore says that to decide what things have intrinsic value "it is necessary to consider what things are such that, if they existed *by themselves*, in absolute isolation, we should yet judge their existence to be good."[9] While everything else is dependent and, by itself, valueless, intrinsic values hold the sufficient grounds of their worth within themselves.

Moore appears to find it conceivable that anything at all could be valued intrinsically. In practice, however, self-sufficiency may not be such a neutral requirement. Even Moore came in the end to the conclusion that nothing but an experience can be intrinsically good; his argument turns on the claim that only experiences can be "worth having even if [they] exist quite alone."[10] Here Moore invokes a fundamentally Cartesian outlook. Consciousness is aloof from, not implicated in, the failures and ambiguities of actual objects and states of affairs in the world. Descartes argued that while my beliefs may or may not correspond to something in the world, I am sure at least that I have them. Perhaps Moore is arguing that while my acts too, in the world, may be incomplete, damaging, or uncertain, at least my conscious enjoyment of them, taken by itself, is solid and unquestionable. Just as Descartes' way of setting up the problem of knowledge made consciousness the natural and necessary standard-bearer against skepticism, so the demand that intrinsic values be self-sufficient may make consciousness the natural and necessary standard-bearer of the intrinsic. Only a commitment to a philosophical "paradigm" of this sort, I think, can explain the strikingly *unargued* insistence, even by such careful writers as W. K. Frankena, that "[no]thing can have intrinsic value except the activities, experiences, and lives of conscious, sentient beings."[11] Frankena just *"cannot see"* that "we ought morally to consider unconscious animals, plants, rocks, etc."[12]

(2) Philosophical tradition also demands, at least by implication, that intrinsic values be *abstract*. Intrinsic values are, after all, special: not everything can be intrinsically valuable. But the distinction between special ends and ordinary means, perhaps innocent enough at first, sets in motion increasingly radical demands. Everyday values are integrated as means under fewer and somewhat more general ends. On the next tier these still proximate ends become means themselves, to be unified in turn under still fewer and more general ends. Already this is a kind of "slippery slope" – upward, as it were. The supercession of each proximate end seems to deprive it of any independent value at all: now they are only means to the ends on a still higher tier. But these ends too may be superseded. Nothing will stop this regress, we say, except the most general, not-to-be-superseded ends in themselves: traditionally, values like "happiness" or respect for persons. Having reached this point, moreover, there is a familiar and strong impulse towards erecting a *single* end on the first and highest level. Traditional value theory tends towards a kind of monism. We are

not inclined to leave two or five values at the top of this pyramid when we might abstract down to one: on the most general level we want unity. Respect for persons might be reinterpreted as another source of happiness; happiness might be reinterpreted, as in Aristotle or Rawls, as valuable insofar as it represents the self-actualization of autonomous persons; but in any case, as Kenneth Goodpaster puts it, "one has the impression that it just *goes without saying*...that there must be some unified account of our considered moral judgments and principles," some sort of "common denominator."[13]

This monism too, moreover, may not be so neutral in practice. Conscious experience is supposed to be a single, unified sort of thing, abstract and self-sufficient enough, given Cartesian presuppositions, to be a bearer of intrinsic value. Adding a second sort of thing as another bearer of intrinsic value would destroy this tight unity. Thus, the implicit demand to reduce intrinsic values to a single common denominator may incline us once again towards the anthropocentric-sentientist end of the range of possible environmental ethics. Goodpaster reminds us, for instance, that many philosophers have been tempted to underwrite environmental values by extension from familiar "interest" or "dignity" ethics, respectively Humean or Kantian. Both are monistic models, tied at least historically to human beings as exemplars, and therefore run the risk of "constraining our moral sensitivity to the size of our self-wrought paradigms," just as they gain plausibility from the very same appeal.[14]

On the speculative side, some metaphysical consciousness monisms have become attractive. Some environmental ethicists want to attribute conscious experience even to the seemingly inanimate world: Po-Keung Ip, for example, uses a panpsychic Taoism to vindicate the intrinsic value of nature; Jay McDaniel uses a Whiteheadian reading of quantum mechanics.[15] Christopher Stone suggests that we regard the whole planet as a conscious entity.[16] Nature itself is thus animated, and all of us can enter the Kingdom of Ends together. At this extreme, then, a monism of intrinsic values is perhaps compatible with a powerful environmental ethic after all. The cost, however, is a radical revision of our metaphysics – in itself not unattractive, perhaps, but in the process we must also reaffirm, rather than escape, the absolute ethical centrality of sentience.

(3) Intrinsic values demand *special justification*. Given their supposed self-sufficiency, they cannot be justified by reference to other values. Given their abstractness, they are too special, too philosophically fragile, to exist unproblematically in the world. But merely to assert them is insufficient: that would make them arbitrary, or condemn us to speechlessness about them, and so would cast our whole system of values adrift. Justification, we say instead, must take a special form: a "grounding" of intrinsic values is called for. Value as such must be derived, ontologically, from something else. Thus, intrinsic values have been construed as God's commands, as a priori truths about a special moral world revealed by intuition, as deliverances of Pure Reason, as aspirations fundamental to "human nature," and so forth. It is not surprising, then, that when Regan tries to ground his "inherent values," he feels driven to an ontology of "nonnatural properties" – despite the irony of appealing to "nonnatural" properties precisely in order to vindicate the value of *nature*! Some such ontology seems necessary. David Ehrenfeld holds that only the religious tradition will do: only a transcendental perspective can transfigure nature into "the present expression of a continuing historical process of immense antiquity and majesty."[17]

Many philosophers, however, no longer accept any of the traditional ontologies of values. Once again the result is to make some form of anthropocentrism or sentientism seem the only live option. Human concerns can always be counted upon to motivate, and the intrinsic value of conscious experience is often accepted without a fight. Thus, the temptation is to eschew the traditional ontology and to try to "build out" from these readily available anthropocentric starting points. Bryan Norton, for instance, proposes what he calls "weak anthropocentrism," a view which countenances not only occurrent human desires but also "ideals," like living in harmony with nature, which represent patterns of *considered* desire. Norton explicitly "avoids attributing intrinsic value to nature" because of the "questionable ontological commitment" that attribution would involve.[18] "Strong" anthropocentrists are often similarly motivated. Some utilitarians argue that cost–benefit analysis can accommodate environmental values more effectively than they have so far.[19] Here dubious ontological claims are avoided because only human interests are considered: utilitarianism is the epitome of an ontologically unadventurous theory of values. Mark Sagoff holds that we may value in nature expressions of things we value intrinsically in our own lives: freedom, nobility, etc.,[20] and, in a similar way, Thomas Hill, Jr. argues that the best moral attitudes towards persons – humility, self-acceptance, gratitude – are mirrored and promoted by more respectful environmental values.[21] Both Sagoff and Hill, however, are still "building out" from human-centered value systems, from expressions or personal qualities which we value in our own and other *human* lives.[22]

Regan has argued effectively that no strong anthropocentrism can vindicate environmental values to the extent that our convictions demand.[23] Sagoff, Hill and others may well disagree, but all the same they often convey a sense that they consider even their own approaches somewhat "second best." Hill writes at one point that "even if there is no convincing way to show that [environmentally] destructive acts are wrong... we may find that the willingness to indulge in them reflects an absence of human traits that we admire and regard as morally important."[24] *Even if...* we *may* find: the suggestion seems to be that modified anthropocentrism is the best we can do, though definitely not the best we might wish. Regan, meanwhile, according to Pluhar, draws the opposite conclusion from the same premise: Regan, she says, "seems to find it preferable to make the commitment to dubious property instances and thus salvage the possibility of the kind of ethical justification he wants. The possibility is remote, but he may reason that it is better than nothing."[25] So "better than nothing" is the bottom line on both sides. We are in a sorry state indeed.

Only occasionally are there hints of anything truly different. Some of these are attempts to formulate a new language for values in nature. Holmes Rolston's essay "Values Gone Wild," for instance, is striking in this regard for its plays on "source" and "resource," "neighbor," etc.[26] Later I will suggest that Rolston's promising start too is partially undercut by his attempts to meet the demands of intrinsic value: what *is* promising, I hold, is precisely the part that has worked free of those shackles. So far I am only trying to show how confining those shackles are. In short, not only has environmental ethics taken over from philosophical ethics an extremely specific and demanding notion of intrinsic value, rooted in various ways in Cartesian metaphysics and in time-honored philosophical temptations to abstraction and special justification; those very roots in turn put extraordinary constraints on any attempt to demonstrate intrinsic values in nature. At the deepest level, non-anthropocentric environmental ethics may simply be impossible within the inherited framework of intrinsic values. In itself, of course, this is not necessarily an objection to the tradition: may be environmental ethics finally *is* impossible. But it is time to ask whether that tradition has any compelling defense.

III Against Intrinsic Value

Moore argues that some notion of "valuable for its own sake" or "valuable in itself" is required simply to *understand* the notion of "valuable for the sake of something else," the everyday notion of instrumental value which we usually take for granted. If we speak of means, then logically we must also be able to conceive of ends, since an end seems to be implicated in the very concept of a means. Thus Moore reads the phrase "good as a means" as equivalent to "a means to good," where the "good" in the second case seems to be intrinsic.[27]

This rationale fails, however, for a simple reason. We can also understand the notion of instrumental value by reference to further, but non-intrinsic values. Values may refer beyond themselves without ever necessitating a value which must be self-explanatory. The value of a day's hike in the woods need not be explained either by the intrinsic value of my appreciation of the woods or by the intrinsic value of the woods themselves; instead, both the appreciation and the woods may be valuable for further reasons, the same may be true of *those* reasons, and so forth. Appreciation may be valued, as Hill points out, partly because it can lead to greater sensitivity to others; but greater sensitivity to others may in turn make us better watchers of animals and storms, and so on. The woods may be valued not only as an expression of freedom and nobility, but also as a refuge for wildlife, and both of these values may in turn be explained by still other, not necessarily human-centered values.

Someone may respond that explanations such as these must still have stopping points somewhere. If X is valuable because it leads to or enhances Y, we might seem to be required to say that X's value is "passed on" from Y. Y's value in turn may be passed on from Z. But – the argument goes – there must be some origin to the value which is thus "passed on." Like a bucket of water in a fire chain, it must have started in some reservoir which is not merely another bucket. Monroe Beardsley likens this argument to the first cause argument for the existence of God: "... the existence of any instrumental value [is supposed to] prove the existence of some intrinsic value just as the occurrence of any event is said to prove the existence of a First Cause."[28]

Beardsley's analogy, however, suggests an initial objection. The "first value" argument may beg the very question it is trying to answer. Just as the first cause argument must assume that the chain of causes it invokes cannot be infinite, so the "first value" argument assumes that the long process of tracing means back to ends must have a final stopping point. But actually this is just what it was supposed to *show*.

Most importantly, however, there are many ways of not having a stopping point. We need not think of an endless series of means each necessitating the next like a long line of falling dominoes. It is more appropriate to think in quite different terms. Consider a more holistic picture conception according to which values are connected in a weblike way, so that any value can be justified by referring to those "adjacent" to it. On this model there is no ultimate reference or stopping point simply because the series of justifications is ultimately, in a sense, circular: to justify or to explain a value is to reveal its organic place among our others. These justifications need not wind their way only in a single direction or even towards a single type of value. If sometimes I value the mountain air because in it I feel (and *am*) healthy, other times I value health because it enables me to reach the mountains. If sometimes I value the melancholy glory of the autumn because it mirrors the closure of my own year, other times I value the rhythms of my yearly schedule because they mirror the glories of the seasons. The web image also emphasizes the *multiple* "adjacencies" of most values. To explain why I climb mountains may take hours; Henry Beston took a whole book to chart the riches of a year spent living alone on Cape Cod. By extension we may think of multiple circularities and feedback loops, multiple arcs returning to completion, so that the summation of those arcs is a rough map of one's whole system of values. To explain why I climb mountains may take hours, but it is not an endless task: although the story has no final stopping point or ultimate appeal, it is *complete* when I have articulated the manifold connections between mountain climbing and the other values, beliefs, etc. which make up my self.

Conceiving values in this holistic way undercuts the very center of the traditional notion of intrinsic value. Self-sufficiency, in the first place, is just what we should *not* want in our values. Beardsley argues that the notion of "intrinsic value" is almost a *contradiction* precisely because it insists on cutting values off from their relations with others in order to consider them "just in themselves." Following Richard Brandt's suggestion that the statement "X is desirable" means something like "desiring X is justified," Beardsley argues:

> What "desirable" adds to "desired" is this claim to justifiability. But the only way this claim can be made good is by considering X in the wider context of other things, in relation to a segment of life or of many lives. Thus the term "intrinsic desirability" pulls in two directions: the noun tells us to look farther afield, the adjective tells us to pay no attention to anything but X itself.[29]

What would it actually be like, after all, to value a conscious experience for itself, "in absolute isolation"? Clearly it could qualify only in so far as it approximates the Cartesian self-sufficiency of dreams or visions: it could not matter whether the experience is connected to anything else in the world. But it is not obvious that this self-sufficiency makes an experience good at all, let alone good intrinsically – and the reasons are precisely the considerations that the self-sufficiency criterion requires us to rule out. What can exist and attract in isolation from everything else may be, for just that reason, *bad*: like the dream world of the drug user, it seduces us away from the complexity of our lives, substitutes solipsism for sociality, divides certain parts of our lives from the rest. We should prefer a conception of values which ties them to their contexts and insists not on their separability but on their relatedness and interdependence.

Beardsley himself has a somewhat different line of response to the "first value" argument. It is not so much a challenge to the alleged self-sufficiency of intrinsic values as a challenge to their abstractness. He begins by recalling Hume's response to the first cause argument. In ordinary life, Hume points out, we are not only familiar with specific causal relations, but are entirely capable of dealing with them concretely. The ultimate nature of causality, by contrast, is neither knowable nor important: it is "merely speculative," as Hume put it, both in the sense that it is endlessly debatable and in the sense that it is irrelevant to practical purposes. Beardsley makes just this argument with respect to intrinsic values. "We have a good deal of sound knowledge about instrumental values," he writes, "but we are in considerable doubt about intrinsic values."[30] In ordinary life we are not only familiar with specific values, but are eminently capable of dealing with them concretely. We know that it is better to be healthy than to be sick, better to live amidst beauty than monotony or ugliness, better to walk in a virgin forest than along the median strip of Interstate 84, and so on. But we do not know whether these things are good because they maximize our net hedonic quality, or good because they cultivate a good will, or what. So far from being the absolutely central project of any philosophy of values, the search for an ultimate end seems "merely speculative." It is better to think of values more concretely, in all their richness and plurality.

Besides, why *should* there be something which all values have in common? It is more plausible to deny that there *is* any final end from which all the others flow and which plays end to all the others' means. We have instead an irreducibly pluralistic system of desires. Some are straightforwardly biological, others culturally rooted, others more personal, and many are mixtures of all three. If anything we are doomed to hopelessly *conflicting* desires. Neither our biological predispositions nor our cultural heritage are even self-consistent, let alone fully compatible with the other.

These last points, however, may lead us to a third and final argument for intrinsic values. It may be urged that, in fact, intrinsic values *can* be concrete, plural, and possibly even inconsistent. This is Holmes Rolston's view, and a version of it has been held even by some pragmatists, such as C. I. Lewis. There are times, Rolston or Lewis would say, when we apprehend value concretely and directly, without having to look farther afield or into the future in order to recognize it. Lewis echoes Moore by comparing this recognition to the way we see redness or hear shrillness.[31] Rolston speaks of the intrinsic value of "point experiences," like the warmth of the spring sun, calling it "as fleeting and plural as any other kind of value."[32] Rolston's intrinsic values need not be abstract, then, and they need no justification at all, let alone "special" justification. A day's hike in the woods is worthwhile even if it does not contribute to peace of mind or animal-watching ability or job performance: the experience, as well as the woods itself considered even apart from my experience, is simply good "for what it is in itself."[33]

Undeniably, Lewis and Rolston are pointing to a real kind of experience; the question is what this kind of experience shows. It is, at least, an experience of what we might call *immediate* value. John Dewey argued, however, that "to pass from immediacy of enjoyment to something called 'intrinsic value' is a leap for which there is no ground."[34] When we do endorse something in an immediate and non-inferential way, according to Dewey, we do not usually make a judgment of value at all, and so *a fortiori* do not make a judgment of intrinsic value. Instead, that endorsement is a "statement to the effect that no judgment is required, because there is no conflict of values, no occasion for deliberation and choice."[35] Even obviously instrumental activities – doing the dishes, driving the highways – are sometimes appreciated in this immediate and non-referential way. Even something that destroys, a virus or a tornado, can sometimes be arrestingly beautiful. *Arresting* is the right word, too: our response to them precisely *disconnects* the frame of reference in which value questions even arise.

When values do become problematic, when choice is required, then they need articulation and defense. But to call them "intrinsic," in Rolston's sense, now offers no help. Since we have to disconnect objects and actions from their contexts in order to value them just "for what they are in themselves," what they are in relation to everything else is pushed out of focus. If I lose myself in the beauty of the tornado, I may not reach shelter in time. Rolston insists that immediate values must be put in context, like any others, and that they are sometimes ambiguous or even downright bad when contextualized. The upshot, however, is that the attribution of intrinsic value, in his sense, carries no special force in the real world. A thousand other "point experiences" of values press in upon us from every side, just as ordinary values have always pressed in upon us, and what we *do* will and should be determined, just as it has always been determined, by the balances and synergies

and trade-offs between them. By all means let us remember that this is a world lavish with its moments of beauty and preciousness – but let us honor those moments without cutting them off from the practical living of our lives.

Earlier I called into question the traditional demands for self-sufficiency and abstractness in intrinsic values. Here, finally, the task of justification too is reconceived. It is not the task of "grounding" values: what Rolston's defense of the notion of intrinsic values may finally illustrate, in fact, is the way in which the project of "grounding" natural values (or, perhaps, any values) finally cuts itself off from the real-life task of assessment and choice. For assessment and choice we must learn, again, to *relate* values. Any adequate theory of valuation must recognize that valuation involves desires with a complex internal structure, desires interlinked, and mutually dependent with a large number of other desires, beliefs, exemplars and choices.[36] Love, for example, interlinks with a wide range of desires and beliefs, from the tenderness of "being with" to sexual desires, from one's complex understanding of the other person to the culture's images and exemplars of love, and so on. Justification draws on these interdependencies. We justify a value by articulating the supporting role it plays with respect to other values, which in turn play a supporting role with respect to it, and by referring to the beliefs which make it natural, which it in turn makes natural by reaffirming those choices and models which link it to the living of our lives. Precisely this is Beardsley's "wider context of things."

Interdependent values are not closed to criticism: it may actually be this sort of interdependence, indeed, which makes the most effective criticism *possible*. Criticism becomes an attempt to alter certain desires by altering something in the constellation of other desires, beliefs. choices, etc. to which they are linked.[37] Some of the beliefs in question may be false, desires artificial or shallow, and so forth. Norton is right to point out that "felt preferences" exploitative of nature can often be criticized on the basis of "considered preferences." Too often we are simply thoughtless, or not thoughtful enough. But the power of this sort of criticism goes far beyond the dialectic of "ideals": only Norton's wish to set up shop on the edge of the concept of intrinsic value, I think, leads him to conceive considered preferences on the model of ideals, thus making them seem far more marginal than they are.[38] As Pluhar writes:

It is amazing how much prejudice and ignorance fuel ethical disputes, not to mention bad reasoning.... How much lack of impartiality and empathy underlie common attitudes towards animals...? How much greed (a prime source of partiality), ignorance, and muddled thinking fuel common attitudes about ecosystems and natural objects?

As she points out, visiting a meat factory makes many vegetarians! Although Pluhar, oddly, regards this pragmatic sort of criticism as an alternative way of defending Regan's "inherent values," she offers no argument that the values which might emerge from this procedure are in any sense "inherent" or intrinsic.[40] I suspect that no such arguments can be found. It is time to abandon the old preoccupation with intrinsic values entirely: let practical criticism be practical.

Not even radical criticism is excluded. The culture to which we owe so many of our explicit desires and their interlinkings also includes an attic full of latent ideals, inconsistent perhaps with its main tendencies, but still there waiting to be drawn out. God may have given us dominion over land and sea, but He also gave us St Francis; against the swashbuckling exploitation of the Industrial Revolution we have the romantic poets, landscape painting, Rousseau, Emerson, Thoreau; against factory farms we have the still compelling image of the solitary farmer close to the soil. The wide-ranging recent debates about Christian and Judaic attitudes towards nature underscore this fundamental dissonance.[41] It is a mistake to try to find *the* Christian (or *the* American, etc.) attitude towards nature: there are many. Our traditions, I want to suggest (I have tried to argue this general point elsewhere[42]), contain their dialectical opposites within themselves. Even our biologically rooted desires are far from monolithic and static. Sometimes criticism simply needs the time and the patience to draw these latent elements out.

IV Pragmatism in Environmental Ethics

The real power of the pragmatic approach lies in what it does *not* say, in what it has removed the need to say. Thus my concern here is emphatically not to devise new arguments for environmental values, but instead to show that the familiar ones are laboring under needless constraints. Still, this may be a modest, if unexotic, bit of progress, and I expect that it will be controversial all the same. I think that if values are conceived along the lines just sketched, then the case we can already make for environmental values – and in quite simple terms – is far stronger than most environmental ethicists themselves seem to believe.

We know that the experience of nature can awaken respect and concern for it. We know indeed that these feelings can become deep and synergistic desires in some lives, and we have before us exemplars of such lives in Muir, Thoreau, Leopold and others. Most of us are not so single-minded, but we too know how essential a return to nature can be, how Thoreau felt returning to Walden Pond from town, and why Yeats yearned for the bee-loud glade. While there are varied motives behind the recent boom in backpacking, cross-country skiing, canoeing, camping, and the like, at least part of the cause is surely a growing appreciation of nature, not just as another frame for our exercise and relaxation, but for its own unique voices, from the silence of the winter woods to the roar of waterfalls in spring.

These feelings are essential starting points for a pragmatic defense of environmental values. They are *not* "second best," "weak" anthropocentric substitutes for the intrinsic values philosophers want but cannot find. They do not need a philosophical "grounding." The questions that arise for us are of quite a different sort. Again, we need to know how to articulate, to ourselves and to others, the *relation* of these values to other parts of our system of desires, to other things that are important, and to the solution of concrete problems. For ourselves we want to understand and strengthen these values; in others we want to nourish and extend them. Nor, finally, need we start by trying to assimilate environmental values to our other values. Even our respect and concern for each other may be of quite a different type, and have entirely different sources, from our respect and concern for the environment.

The articulation of these values is not the province of philosophy alone. Poetry and biography are just as vital. Think of Wordsworth:

> And I have felt
> A presence that disturbs me with the joy

Of elevated thoughts; a sense sublime
Of something far more deeply interfused,
Whose dwelling is the light of setting suns,
And the round ocean and the living air . . .
   Therefore let the moon
Shine on thee in thy solitary walk;

And let the misty mountain winds be free
To blow against thee. . . . [43]

We must not read this as an incomplete statement of pantheism, in need of philosophical clarification. Maybe Wordsworth was a closet metaphysician, but the possible linkage to Spinoza is not what makes us ache to feel those winds. Wordsworth offers a way to begin to describe a kind of experience which for our purposes may not need a stricter formulation. It is not a "grounding": it is a kind of *portrait*. Likewise, what is finally important in *Walden* is not Thoreau's misanthropic philosophizing, but the way in which he shows us, in his own person, how a human being can meet the evening, between the squirrels and the shadows, or how to look at a lake:

A lake is the landscape's most . . . expressive feature. It is earth's eye, looking into which the beholder measures the depth of his own nature. The fluviate trees next to the shore are the slender eyelashes which fringe it, and the wooded hills and cliffs around are its overhanging brows. [44]

Nietzsche suggests more than once that philosophers are too clumsy to handle real values. He may exaggerate, but all the same we do know that philosophy has too long failed to take seriously what it cannot itself fully articulate. By rejecting the demand to "ground" these values, then, pragmatism also begins to undercut the demand that we articulate them in philosophy's peculiar, epistemically oriented way.

Still, on the whole, many philosophical arguments fare well in terms of the new set of questions I am advancing. Indeed many of them fare *better* when measured against this new set of questions than against the set of questions that they are actually trying to answer. Let us first return to Rolston's "Values Gone Wild." Rolston begins with a critique of the idea of nature as a "resource." The idea that "everything is a resource," he argues, like the idea that "everybody is selfish," becomes simply trivial at the extremes,

"eating up everything, as if humans had no other operating mode *vis-à-vis* wilderness." In fact, we must enter wilderness "on its own terms" – not, or not primarily, as a means to "high quality experience." In this way, he argues, "one is not so much looking to *resources* as to *sources*, seeking relationships in an elemental stream of being with transcending integrities." [45] At this point, however, Rolston goes on to suggest that nature is intrinsically valuable because it is a source, in this sense, of whatever (else) we intrinsically value. This seems to me to add nothing: it only *weakens* the evocative force of the notion of "sourcehood." Although "elemental . . . transcending integrities" make a certain ecosystemic sense, trying to make their *value* transcendental either introduces an extremely problematic ontology, as I argued in part II, or represents only one way of talking, as I argued in part III, with no special force in actual moral thinking. "Sourcehood" is a perfectly understandable and powerful model of value in its own right: why force it into the mold of intrinsic values?

Consider one other example. Rolston writes of "sympathetically turning to value what does not stand directly in our lineage or underpinning" – our "kin" and "neighbors" in the animal world. [46] This too is genuinely perceptive: we do have a latent sense of community with animals which close acquaintance may bring out. But here too Rolston tries to wring intrinsic values out of facts which are better left alone. He argues, for instance, that the similarity between our reactions and those of animals suggests that we should take their reactions to express imperatives – values – as well, presumably including intrinsic values. Why these imperatives also bear on *us*, however, is not clear, and the claim that they do bear on us involves analogic arguments problematic in both philosophy of mind and moral theory. Once again Rolston's concrete notions, here of "kinship" and of being "neighbors," capture the values at stake much more freshly and directly than the philosophically problematic analogies necessary to make them over into intrinsic values. Moreover, as Rolston also points out, even within the animate world the notion of kinship eventually stretches beyond the breaking point: certainly we have little kinship with spiders. If another kind of value must be invoked for such "aliens," then it is not clear why this should not be so even for "neighbors." There is no need to fit all values into a single model.

Anthony Weston

Even more standard philosophical arguments – or at least their basic intentions – fit naturally into this framework. Recall Sagoff's argument that we may value in nature expressions of things that we value intrinsically in our lives: freedom, nobility, etc. Critics have pointed out that this cannot demonstrate the intrinsic value of nature itself.[47] Pragmatists, however, want to know simply how this value relates to others and can form an organic part of our lives. This is exactly what Sagoff helps to show us, locating it partly in the orbit of the desire for freedom. Or again, the persistent inclination to attribute "rights" directly to nature might now be reapproached and understood. In part, certainly, that attribution is a straightforward political attempt to state environmental values with enough force that others will take them seriously. But it is also an attempt to articulate a specific and familiar attitude towards nature. Alone in the woods we find ourselves feeling a sense of gratefulness, of "awe," finally almost of intrusion, a feeling which probably has its closest parallel in those responses to other *people* which make us want to attribute *them* rights. But how closely these feelings are actually parallel remains an open question. Here we first need a careful phenomenology. This may be true even of human rights: real respect for others comes only through the concrete experience and finally "awe" of the other. It is the conditions and nature of this feeling which we really need to understand. Reversing the usual deduction entirely, we might even take rights talk itself as a first and rather crude attempt at just such a phenomenology – but surely we can do better.

Let me conclude by returning to the level of practical problems in environmental ethics. Why, for instance, should we value wilderness? What sort of justification can we give for keeping exploitable land and resources in their natural state? Not surprisingly, it is necessary to begin with a reorientation. Notice that this question is already posed in abstraction from any specific situation. This may itself give rise to absurdities. If we answer that wilderness indeed has intrinsic value, then presumably we are required to go to any lengths to support as much of it as possible, and wherever possible, at least consistent with other intrinsic values. But too many other things of equal or greater importance in the *situation* will not be captured by a hierarchical scheme of intrinsic values. Of course, there are other ways out,

perhaps invoking intrinsic principles of such generality that they can be used to justify anything. The response I am urging, however, is the abandonment of these very ways of posing the question. The important questions for pragmatism are the ones posed by specific situations, and while the answers across different situations will probably bear a strong family resemblance, they will not always be the same.

Why should we protect the new Alaskan national parks, for example? Now the answers are much easier: because the new parks are both exceptionally wild and exceptionally fragile; because the non-preservationist pressures in at least this case are exceptionally unworthy, tied largely to the exploitation of energy resources to which there are any number of more intelligent alternatives; perhaps also because their protection is still possible. These arguments do indeed seem to dodge the original question. They do not say why wilderness as such should be protected. On the other hand, one certainly does not have to be an anthropocentrist to doubt whether it *should* be protected "as such." This is why the *exceptional* nature of the Alaskan wilderness makes that particular case so powerful. These "practical" arguments are precisely the kinds offered by the Sierra Club, the Nature Conservancy, and most of the other environmentally oriented organizations. Are these arguments offered merely for lack of better (philosophical?) ones? Or might those organizations actually have a more reasonable position after all?

"What about those people, though, who simply could not care less about wilderness? What about the many cases in which such values simply cannot be assumed? Tame rivers are much nicer than wild ones if one owns a motorboat; exploitation in Alaska might lower our fuel bills and make America more self-sufficient in some vital resources; and so on." Let me respond in several ways. First, even these cases may not be real cases of "could not care less." Nearly everyone recognizes *some* value in nature; think of how often natural scenes turn up on wall calendars and church bulletins. Even motorboaters like to see woods. Wilderness values may just seem to them less significant than other values at stake in the particular situation. Common ground remains. If we begin by treating others as absolutists, we run the risk of turning them into just what we fear. But this is only a caricature, and we can instead approach them from a standpoint of complex mutuality. Then,

316

though, if some shared values can indeed be agreed upon, the real issue shifts to the question of alternatives, and this is a recognizably factual issue on both sides, and also negotiable. Motorboats don't have to go everywhere.

The pragmatic approach defended here forswears the search for knockdown arguments that will convince absolutely everyone that natural values are important. We cannot defeat the occasional extremist who sees no value at all in nature. But if this is a defect, it is certainly not unique to pragmatism. No other approach has knockdown arguments to offer either; otherwise, environmental ethics would not be a *problem*. The real difference is that pragmatists are not looking for knockdown arguments; we propose to concern ourselves with defending environmental values in other ways. It is striking, actually, that the search for a proof of the intrinsic value of nature is almost always *post hoc*. Even if someone were finally to discover a knockdown proof, it would not be the reason that most of us who are in search of such a proof do in fact value nature, since our present accounts of natural values differ so markedly. *We* learned the values of nature through experience and effort, through mistakes and mishaps, through poetry and stargazing, and, if we were lucky, a few inspired friends. What guarantees that there is a shortcut? It is wiser to accept the fact that many of our contemporaries, even our most thoughtful contemporaries, hold deeply different, probably irreconcilable, visions of the ideal world.[48] Pragmatism, indeed, celebrates a wide-open and diverse culture; it is the prerequisite of all the central Deweyan virtues: intelligence, freedom, autonomy, growth. What we have yet to accept is its inconclusiveness and open-endedness, its demand that we struggle for our own values without being closed to the values and the hopes of others. The search for intrinsic values substitutes a kind of shadowboxing for what must always be a good fight.

Acknowledgments

"Beyond Intrinsic Value: Pragmatism in Environmental Ethics" first appeared in *Environmental Ethics* Vol. 7, No. 4 (Winter 1985). I am indebted to Holmes Rolston, III, and to an anonymous reviewer for *Environmental Ethics* for extensive comments on earlier versions of this essay. It has also benefited greatly from a colloquium discussion at the Vassar College Department of Philosophy and from several careful readings by Jennifer Church.

Notes

1 The confusion of subjectivism with "subject-centrism" is dissected, though not in these terms, by Richard and Val Routley in "Against the Inevitability of Human Chauvinism," in K. E. Goodpaster and K. M. Sayre, eds, *Ethics and the Problems of the 21st Century* (Notre Dame: University of Notre Dame Press, 1979), pp. 42–7.

2 For an extensive list, see David Ehrenfeld, *The Arrogance of Humanism* (Oxford: Oxford University Press, 1978), Chap. 5; or Holmes Rolston, III, "Valuing Wildlands," *Environmental Ethics* 7 (1985): 24–30.

3 I am equating intrinsic values with ends in themselves, instrumental values with means to ends. For present purposes I think that subtle distinctions between these concepts can be ignored.

4 See W. K. Frankena, "Ethics and the Environment," in Goodpaster and Sayre, *Ethics*, pp. 5–6 and pp. 18–19; and J. Baird Callicott, "Non-anthropocentric Value Theory and Environmental Ethics," *American Philosophical Quarterly* 21 (1984), pp. 299–309.

5 Routley and Routley, "Against the Inevitability," pp. 36–62.

6 Tom Regan, "The Nature and Possibility of an Environmental Ethic," *Environmental Ethics* 3 (1981): 30–4. Frankena, C. I. Lewis, and others use *inherent value* to refer to objects or actions the contemplation of which leads to intrinsically valuable experience. Regan, however, clearly means by *inherent* what Frankena and Lewis mean by *intrinsic*. "If an object is inherently good," he tells us, "its value must inhere in the object itself" (p. 30). Its value does not depend upon experience at all.

7 Evelyn Pluhar, "The Justification of an Environmental Ethic," *Environmental Ethics* 5 (1983): 55–8.

8 G. E. Moore, *Philosophical Studies* (London: Paul, Trench, Trubner, 1922), p. 260.

9 G. E. Moore, *Principia Ethica* (Cambridge: Cambridge University Press, 1903), p. 187.

10 G. E. Moore, "Is Goodness a Quality?" in *Philosophical Papers* (London: Allen and Unwin, 1959), p. 95.

11 Frankena, "Ethics and the Environment," p. 17. Pluhar makes some sharp comments on this claim in "The Justification of an Environmental Ethic," p. 54.

12 Ibid., p. 15. My emphasis.

13 K. E. Goodpaster, "From Egoism to Environmentalism," in Goodpaster and Sayre, *Ethics*, p. 25 and

p. 34, his emphasis. Strictly speaking the claim here is only about ethics in the Humean tradition, but he soon allows that the Kantian tradition has still stronger monistic tendencies.

14 Ibid., p. 32.

15 Po-Keung Ip, "Taoism and the Foundations of Environmental Ethics," *Environmental Ethics* 5 (1983): 335–44, and Jay McDaniel, "Physical Matter as Creative and Sentient," *Environmental Ethics* 5 (1983): 291–318.

16 Christopher Stone, *Should Trees Have Standing?* (Los Altos: William Kaufmann, 1974), pp. 52–3.

17 Ehrenfeld, *Arrogance of Humanism*, p. 208.

18 Bryan Norton, "Environmental Ethics and Weak Anthropocentrism," *Environmental Ethics* 6 (1984): 131, 136, 138.

19 J. V. Krutilla and A. C. Fisher, *The Economics of Natural Environments* (Baltimore: Johns Hopkins, 1975).

20 Mark Sagoff, "On Preserving the Natural Environment," *Yale Law Journal* 84 (1974): 205–67; reprinted in Richard Wasserstrom, *Today's Moral Problems* (New York: Macmillan, 1979).

21 Thomas E. Hill, Jr., "Ideals of Human Excellence and Preserving Natural Environments," *Environmental Ethics* 5 (1983): 211–24.

22 See Hill, "Ideals," p. 233, or p. 220: "It may be that, given the sort of beings we are, we would never learn humility *before persons* without developing the general capacity to cherish...many [other] things for their own sakes" (my emphasis). Sagoff speaks of our obligation to nature as finally an obligation "to our national values, to our history, and, therefore, to ourselves" (Wasserstrom, *Today's Moral Problems*, p. 620).

23 Regan, "Nature and Possibility," pp. 24–30.

24 Hill, "Ideals," p. 215.

25 Pluhar, "Justification," p. 58.

26 Holmes Rolston, III, "Values Gone Wild," *Inquiry* 26 (1983): 181–207.

27 Moore, *Principia Ethica*, p. 24.

28 Monroe Beardsley, "Intrinsic Value," *Philosophy and Phenomenological Research* 26 (1965): 6. The critique offered here is indebted to Beardsley's fine article.

29 Ibid., p. 13.

30 Ibid., p. 7.

31 C. I. Lewis, *An Analysis of Knowledge and Valuation* (LaSalle, Ill.: Open Court, 1946), pp. 374–5.

32 Rolston was generous enough to comment extensively on an earlier draft of this paper, and I am quoting from his comments. Obviously he should not be held to these exact words, though I think his position here is a natural completion of what he has said in print. See Rolston, "Values Gone Wild" and Holmes Rolston, III, "Are Values in Nature Objective or Subjective?" *Environmental Ethics* 4 (1982): 125–52; reprinted in Robert Elliot and Arran Gare, eds, *Environmental Philosophy* (University Park: Pennsylvania State Press, 1983), pp. 135–65.

33 Rolston, "Are Values in Nature Objective or Subjective?" in Elliot and Gare, *Environmental Philosophy*, p. 158.

34 John Dewey, *Theory of Valuation* (Chicago: International Encyclopedia of Unified Science, 1939), 2:41.

35 Beardsley, "Intrinsic Value," p. 16.

36 See Anthony Weston, "Toward the Reconstruction of Subjectivism: Love as a Paradigm of Values," *Journal of Value Inquiry* 18 (1984): 181–94.

37 Ibid. and R. B. Brandt, *Theory of the Good and the Right* (Oxford: Clarendon Press, 1979), part I.

38 Norton ends up arguing that having ideals need not presuppose the intrinsic value of the things or states of affairs idealized: see Norton, "Weak Anthropocentrism," p. 137.

39 Pluhar, "Justification," p. 60.

40 Ibid., p. 58. This curious inference also mars J. Baird Callicott's otherwise fine survey: see Callicott, "Non-anthropocentric Value Theory," p. 305.

41 See Robin Attfield, "Western Traditions and Environmental Ethics," in Elliot and Gare, *Environmental Philosophy*, pp. 201–30.

42 See Anthony Weston, "Subjectivism and the Question of Social Criticism," *Metaphilosophy* 16 (1985): 57–65.

43 William Wordsworth, "Lines Composed a Few Miles above Tintern Abbey," lines 93–8 and 134–7.

44 H. D. Thoreau, *Walden* (New York: Signet, 1960), p. 128.

45 Rolston, "Values Gone Wild," pp. 181–3.

46 Ibid., pp. 188, 191.

47 For instance, Louis Lombardi, "Inherent Worth, Respect, and Rights." *Environmental Ethics* 5 (1983): 260.

48 A particularly striking example is Steven S. Schwarzschild, "The Unnatural Jew", *Environmental Ethics* 6 (1984): 347–62.

24

Pragmatism in Environmental Ethics: Democracy, Pluralism, and the Management of Nature

Ben A. Minteer and Robert E. Manning

I Introduction

In a recent paper appearing in *Environmental Ethics*, Bryan Norton argues for a more "useful" environmental philosophical mission – one that avoids sterile abstraction and a "hypothetical case-study approach" to moral dilemmas.[1] A growing number of environmental ethicists have become dissatisfied with the limits of monistic philosophy as the paradigmatic operating mode in the field. Accordingly, many writers have begun to outline a pragmatic agenda for environmental ethics by proffering approaches that attempt to shift the field's mode of inquiry to a more practical conversation about the multiple values at play in specific matters of environmental policy. Norton's work, along with that of Anthony Weston and Andrew Light, among others, represents the leading edge of a swelling wave of contributions to this pragmatic turn in environmental ethics.[2]

One of the clearest messages emerging from this work is the notion that in order for the field of environmental ethics to gain a greater purchase on environmental problem solving, a number of changes must occur – from the rhetorical to the metaphysical – changes which entail a more critical appraisal of the role of environmental ethics in policy deliberation and decision making. As the new environmental pragmatists note, however, such reconstructions pose fundamental challenges to the traditional preoccupations of the field. For

example, much of the work in environmental ethics to date has been committed to the often vocal discussion of antipodal conceptual issues – intrinsic versus instrumental value, anthropocentrism versus biocentrism, monism versus pluralism, and so on. The consequence of this discussion, many observers note, has been the field's conspicuous silence regarding concrete solutions to real world environmental dilemmas. Also, many writers have suggested that the practical aims of environmental philosophy are not well served by ethicists' penchant for employing esoteric forms of discourse that make it difficult for a large audience to connect with the more immediate content of their arguments. Perhaps most importantly, several of these contributors have observed that the field's search for a new metaphysical framework – a "seismic shift" in thinking about the status of human–nature relationships – has operated at the expense of understanding more clearly the integrated connections between human culture and the natural world. In other words, there is a feeling that environmental ethicists' urgent calls for new environmental world views and radically revised ontological schemes, rather than leading to improved environmental solutions and conditions, only leads ethicists' attention away from the resources already present within our shared moral and political traditions.[3]

We believe that the field of environmental ethics has much to contribute to the clarification and evaluation of the options available to us as a democratic community to improve our ability to achieve more informed, effective, and equitable resolutions in environmental decision making and policy formation. Because we hold that environmental problems possess an undeniable, if complex and not always understood political character, we argue that a more democratic and pluralistic approach to the countenance of ethical orientations regarding the natural world must be accepted in environmental discourse and policy deliberation. A "culture of democracy" in the Deweyan sense – a democratic temperament exhibited in both the method and substance of ethical inquiry into the public's moral claims about the natural world – is required if environmental ethics is to respect the values of democratic life in its practice. We believe that a pragmatic approach to the role of environmental ethics in policy making holds great promise for directing the environmentalist project in such a manner, and that it is also uniquely capable of bringing the insights of environmental ethics into various natural resource management settings. This is especially true with respect to debates over American public lands, which we will take up at the end of our discussion here.

In support of our arguments, we offer the results of an empirical study of environmental ethics to reinforce the claim that public environmental ethics are broadly diverse in their metaphysical character and normative implications. Our results suggest that any form of rigid monistic prescriptivism, thus, runs the risk of a priori excluding alternative ethical sentiments, jeopardizing in principle a democratic toleration of public ethical pluralism by failing to fully engage these multiple values in environmental decision making. We maintain that the diversity of moral positions regarding nonhuman nature requires theoretical and procedural frameworks for incorporating a range of ethical concerns in policy making, methods which we believe are most effectively provided by a pluralistic and pragmatic approach to environmental values and their implementation in policy and management.

II The Promise of Environmental Pragmatism

Taking its namesake, as well as its ethos from the American philosophical school represented chiefly in the late nineteenth and early twentieth-century

writings of Charles Sanders Peirce, William James, and John Dewey, environmental pragmatism draws upon a rich philosophical and political tradition in American thought. The work of Peirce, James, and Dewey is marked most notably by its anti-foundational character; the denial of the existence of a priori or self-justifying "truths" and moral absolutes. The pragmatists' support (especially James and Dewey) for a robustly experimental and contextual view of individuals' moral universes testifies to these writers' overarching faith in the ability of human experience to produce from within itself the means for justifying and evaluating moral beliefs and values. This reliance on the critical potential of cultural experience allowed pragmatists to dismiss the relevance of various claims surrounding a host of philosophical dualisms, from Cartesian mind–body/subject–object antinomies to divisions relating to theory and practice and instrumental and intrinsic values. The experiential thrust of pragmatism is buttressed by its pervasive empirical temper; a sensibility which for Dewey meant that the general method of experimental science, in the form of organized, cooperative "intelligence," offered the best hope for ethical understanding, the sharpest blade for philosophical criticism, and the only effective and democratic means for reconstructing the moral and political community.[4]

In light of this brief characterization, it becomes clear how creatively and powerfully new environmental pragmatists such as Norton have incorporated key elements of the pragmatists' work in their own environmental projects. Norton's approach, which advocates a "practical" environmental ethics – one that begins with environmental policy dilemmas themselves and then appeals, in experimental fashion, to the tools of ethical theory in achieving a resolution – strives to place environmental philosophy on more relevant and useful footing than the "applied" ethical programs of monistic theorists. Applied environmental ethicists, Norton believes, depend upon an abstract foundational theory building that dilutes the usefulness of their work for environmental problem solving.[5] In contrast, Norton's pragmatism promises a way out of the arid theoretical preoccupations of applied ethical theory by emphasizing the complex and contextual nature of environmental policy, a condition dependent upon the unpredictable variability of human experience with the natural world. It also incorporates the ethical pluralists' understanding of the existence of a host of ethical possibilities for human–nature relationships by appealing to those moral programs that best help resolve policy contests.[6] In this manner, programs like Norton's in environmental ethics demonstrate a sensitivity to changing environmental values across time, space, and culture; dimensions which are not well served by monistic environmental ethics.

Politically speaking, there are important implications and opportunities resulting from the acceptance of a practical and experimental cast for environmental values. A pluralistic accounting of environmental ethics dovetails with democratic culture, which thrives on such diversity in moral thinking and experience. Democracy as a "way of life" entails the genuine conversation about new meanings and values, a discussion which challenges participants to both clearly articulate their own positions as well as to understand those of others. Indeed, this kind of public political "talk" is at the center of a strong participatory mode of democracy, and the legitimacy it bestows upon public values, including those relating to the environment, is of central importance.[7] It therefore becomes critical, for environmental ethicists as well as natural resource managers and environmental policy makers, to understand just exactly what the public has to say about the shape and extent of environmental values in their daily lives.

III Environmental Ethics: An Empirical Study

For both political and philosophical reasons, we strongly believe that public beliefs and values are crucial data for assessing our conceptual assumptions about the meaning and form of environmental ethical sentiments. One of the virtues that we hope environmental pragmatists have inherited from their forebears is an openness to experimental investigations into the nature of ethical thinking and policy formulation. For decades, social scientists have been employing survey methods to understand the structure and substance of public opinion on a variety of social, economic, and political issues. While environmental opinion data has enjoyed a great deal of attention in this respect, empirical research in what readers of *Environmental Ethics* would consider "environmental ethics" is largely absent from the scholarly literature.

Previous studies of public environmentalism have generally been concerned with either measures of general environmental values, or more narrowly construed attitudes about specific elements of environmental policy. The classic example of the former is the "new environmental paradigm" research carried out by Dunlap and Van Liere in the late 1970s, which measured public beliefs about notions such as the limits to growth, fragility of nature, and the need for a steady state economy.[8] More issue-specific empirical treatments of environmental attitudes have appeared in work investigating a variety of subjects, including views of wildlife and endangered species, land management policies, and global environmental problems.[9]

A recent and innovative contribution to the social scientific research on public environmentalism has been made by a group of cognitive anthropologists investigating the structure of environmental beliefs and values as "cultural models" of human–environment relationships. Using both qualitative and quantitative research methods with representative samples of the general public as well as targeted groups like "radical environmentalists" and resource industry employees, the researchers found that there is a surprisingly strong consensus among individuals regarding their environmental beliefs and values. Further, they determined that such values were integrated with a number of core American values like personal responsibility, obligations to future generations, and religious traditions.[10]

We are particularly intrigued by this conclusion, as it suggests that much of the divisiveness and acrimony surrounding disputes over environmental policy may be overstated. Moreover, such debates may be constructed around assumed philosophical loggerheads which do not actually exist in practice. But while we believe there is significant public consensus to be found when we look at the larger shape of "cultural systems" or "world views" relating to environmental values, we also feel that public moral commitments to nature demonstrate a strong diversity – a variability that we are interested in exploring. We do so with an eye toward understanding how this ethical pluralism can profitably contribute to integrative and context-sensitive environmental policy. In this vein, we are encouraged by the growing number of scholarly contributions measuring various typologies of environmental values from a number of disciplinary and methodological perspectives, including sociology and anthropology, but also history, economics, and political science.[11] The shape of human–nature relationships emerging from this scholarship is undeniably pluralistic and multidimensional in character.

Building upon our own interests in a pragmatic and pluralistic approach to understanding environmental values, our support for interdisciplinary investigations of the beliefs and commitments attached to public environmentalism, and our conviction that environmental ethics must demonstrate a democratic respect for public values and attitudes toward the natural world, we constructed an empirically based study to test public support

for a broad spectrum of ethical positions regarding the environment. We devised a typology of potential environmental ethics, informed by a number of sources in the philosophical and historical literature.[12] Table 24.1 presents the resulting typology of environmental ethics gleaned from this material. These ethics are clustered into five conceptual categories. We do not imply that these clusters of ethical positions exist as thematic "wholes" in the minds of individuals. Instead, they are merely heuristic tools for understanding the philosophical relationships among potential environmental ethics. A representative statement for each ethical position is also included in table 24.1. These state-

Table 24.1 Environmental ethics: A pluralistic typology

Environmental Ethics	Representative Statement
Anti-Environment	
1. Physical Threat	1. Nature can be dangerous to human survival.
2. Spiritual Evil	2. Nature can be spiritually evil.
Benign Indifference	
3. Storehouse of Raw Materials	3. Nature is a storehouse of raw materials that should be used by humans as needed.
4. Religious Dualism	4. Humans were created as more important than the rest of nature.
5. Intellectual Dualism	5. Because humans can think, they are more important than the rest of nature.
Utilitarian Conservation	
6. Old Humanitarianism	6. Cruelty toward animals makes people less human.
7. Efficiency	7. The supply of goods and services provided by nature is limited.
8. Quality of Life	8. Nature adds to the quality of our lives (for example, outdoor recreation, natural beauty).
9. Ecological Survival	9. Human survival depends on nature and natural processes.
Stewardship	
10. Religious/Spiritual Duty	10. It is our religious responsibility to take care of nature.
11. Future Generations	11. Nature will be important to future generations.
12. God's Creation	12. Nature is God's creation.
13. Life-Based/Mysticism	13. All living things are sacred.
Radical Environmentalism	
14. Humanitarianism	14. Animals should be free from needless pain and suffering.
15. Organicism/Animism	15. All living things are interconnected.
16. Pantheism	16. All living things have a spirit.
17. Natural Rights	17. All living things have a moral right to exist.

ments, joined by others of similar phrasing, were employed as scale items in the survey.

Study Design

A mail-back questionnaire was constructed which included the scales designed to measure the multiple environmental ethics described above. The study questionnaire was administered to a representative sample of Vermont households chosen from telephone directories covering the state. The questionnaire was administered following procedures recommended by Dillman.[13] Of a total of 1228 deliverable questionnaires, 612 were completed and returned, yielding a response rate of 50 percent.[14]

A total of forty-two environmental ethics statements were employed as scale items for the seventeen environmental ethics in the questionnaire. Two dimensions of support for each statement were measured. The first measured the extent to which the respondents agreed with each ethical statement. An eleven-point response scale was employed, anchored at "strongly agree" and "strongly disagree." The second dimension measured the importance that respondents placed upon each statement in influencing their attitudes toward environmental policy. A six-point response scale was used, anchored at "not-at-all important" and "extremely important."

Results

Results of the measurements of agreement and importance for each of the seventeen environmental ethics are presented in figures 24.1 and 24.2, respectively. A number of observations are in order. First, and most importantly for our arguments here, it is clear that the study sample subscribed to a number of environmental ethical positions, as is evident from the high level of agreement and importance placed upon multiple environmental ethics. All four environmental ethics in the utilitarian conservation category received high mean agreement and importance ratings, particularly "ecological survival" and "quality of life" ethics. Stewardship ethics also received a substantial amount of support from respondents, especially the "future generations" ethic, which drew the highest score on both measurement scales.

A number of radical environmental ethics, which revolve around a set of arguments for the intrinsic value of nonhuman nature, were embraced by respondents, especially "organicism/animism," "humanitarianism (new)," and "natural rights." Environmental ethics in the Benign Indifference category, which represent views of the human–nature relationship that set nature apart from human moral and intellectual life, received an equivocal response from the study sample. Lastly, anti-environmental ethics, the most robustly anthropocentric of all categories, received the lowest agreement and importance scores of all the ethics in the typology, suggesting that their currency among respondents is weak.

IV Ethical Pluralism and the Democratic Public

The study results indicate that there is a broad range of moral sentiments about human–nature relationships "out there," so to speak, a number of which demonstrate a high degree of acceptability in public thinking. While our study sample of the Vermont public possesses obvious geographic and demographic limitations, we believe that the data provide us with powerful support for a pluralistic reading of environmental values. Of course, many contributors to environmental philosophy (especially those with a monistic disposition) may point out that a survey of environmental ethics embraced by the public, while polling individuals on what they *do* think about the place of humans in the natural world, does not get at the burning issue of what they *should* think. In other words, an "unacceptable" moral relativism is encouraged by this kind of pluralistic and empirical framework.

Because we do not have space in the present paper to engage such concerns in sufficient detail, we can only offer the briefest of defenses here. Philosophically speaking, the search for analytically constructed moral "truths" – whether about human nature or environmental obligations – from a detached, external perspective is not the only way to go about the work of ethical inquiry. Michael Walzer writes that instead of striving for independent ground for moral theory building and social criticism, it is far better to conceive of such activities as coming from within communities,

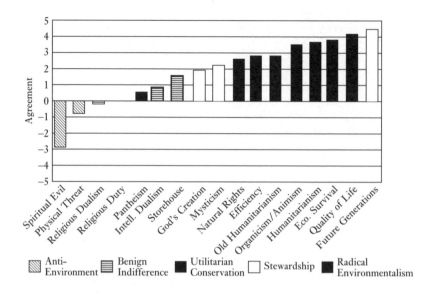

Figure 24.1 Environmental ethics: agreement

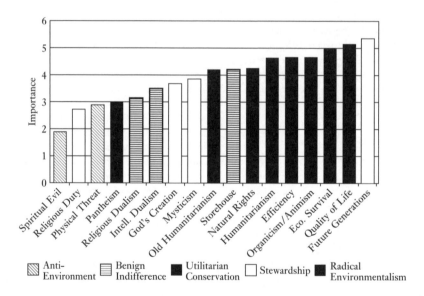

Figure 24.2 Environmental ethics: importance

within cultural traditions, and within public life in general. "It is better to tell stories," Walzer concludes, "even though there is no definitive and best story." Moral inquiry is thus an "inside job," a process of "thick description" directed by the attributes and tensions of existing values and commitments already present within democratic communities.[15]

There is a potentially more distressing consequence lying in the claims of many monistic environmental ethicists, however. The notion that the charge of environmental philosophy is to prescribe the "correct" environmental decision in every case based upon a single set of coherent moral principles possesses an undemocratic strain that we find troubling. Many, if not most monistic approaches to environmental ethics leave little room for public discussion, debate, and criticism of their arguments for respecting the intrinsic value of nonhuman nature (be it located in sentience, consciousness, or ecological creativity). The emphasis on ethical foundationalism in this work (either epistemic or metaphysical) generally renders such arguments impervious to public deliberation and critical evaluation, grounded as they are in unshakable philosophical bedrock. As a result, it seems that monistic environmental philosophy is designed to avoid such public deliberation (which necessarily requires mediation and concession) altogether.[16]

This monistic approach is especially unfortunate because we feel that public debate and criticism are activities that we believe are central to the justification of moral sentiments as well as the construction of environmental policy. In other words, running against the grain of much monistic environmental philosophy, we hold that no single outcome is necessarily guaranteed ahead of time. Public deliberation is experimental, open, and creative; as such, it does not conform to the circumscribed procedures of analytic philosophy. As Christopher Lasch concluded, "[public] argument is risky and unpredictable, therefore educational."[17] Indeed, it is this very activity – the conversation about moral claims regarding nature within democratic communities – that ultimately legitimizes environmental ethics and allows us to creatively address our myriad concerns surrounding the natural world.[18]

No one, of course, grasped this notion more fully or deeply than Dewey, who saw public deliberation in a free and open setting as the only vehicle by which a truly democratic life could be fashioned.

> For what is the faith in democracy in the role of consultation, of conference, of persuasion, of discussion, in formation of public opinion, which in the long run is self-corrective, except faith in the capacity of the intelligence of the common man to respond with common sense to the free play of facts and ideas which are secured by effective guarantees of free inquiry, free assembly, and free communication?[19]

Dewey realized, however, as we must, that despite the apparent universal acceptance of this sentiment in American political culture, real democratic life is never easy, and never guaranteed. Therefore, to have authentic democratic communication and discussion about environmental values in both professional environmental philosophy and general public discourse, we need to be respectful of the moral languages spoken by others, even when they sound different from our own. Dewey's lesson applied to environmental ethics would have us always remember that those who care about the health of the environment have the potential to contribute to this discussion, whether they speak with a biocentric "accent," an anthropocentric one, or with something else altogether.

V   Pragmatism in Public Land Management

To provide a brief illustration of how a pragmatic and pluralist account of environmental ethics can operate along with a respect for democratic values, we can look to the case of public land management in the United States. Here we find both empirical and normative implications for a pragmatic spirit in environmental ethics. Public land management represents one of the more visible and challenging environmental policy matters facing the nation. Occupying nearly one third of the area of the United States, public lands present an especially intriguing set of management issues for local communities, federal land management agencies, and the general public. These issues become evident when one considers the different values associated with various land types managed by the federal agencies. A broad ethical mosaic can be seen clearly with respect to three categories of public lands of interest here: national forests, national parks, and wilderness.

National forests have been managed historically for utilitarian purposes – the provision of material benefits such as timber, minerals, and forage to American society. Under the canons of science, professionalism, and efficiency, national forest lands in the twentieth century have been viewed predominantly as storehouses of raw materials to be managed on a "sustained-yield" basis. The national parks were born out of an aesthetic appreciation of natural wonders and the romanticist association of spiritual values with nature and its elevation as a source of American cultural pride.[20] Although the national parks share an anthropocentric foundation with the national forests – both are creatures of the conservationism of the progressive era – the efforts of such early park advocates as John Muir ensured that, from the beginning, the parks were guided by a strong preservationist philosophy. Finally, legally designated wilderness reveals an even more resolute preservationist underpinning. The passage of the Wilderness Act in 1964 provided that these lands would become the most "primitive" and "natural" on the public domain.

What this mix of public land types suggests, we believe, is that as a democratic society we have attempted to "map out" our environmental values onto the public land system, and by doing so have fashioned a diverse, "patchy" landscape, one that admits to the array of human–nature experiences and sentiments found in our contemporary culture. We do not claim that the mapping out has always been entirely successful or completely fair. Indeed, as any student of public land history knows, this process has often been carried out under less than fully democratic conditions. Most notoriously, these cases have at times involved the infiltration of imbalances of power and influence in public discourse and decision making. In addition, our maps have traditionally not reflected the ecological facts of life. As the science of ecology grows, so too does our recognition of the inadequacy of many of our public land management units for serving ecological functions such as securing viable biological populations and energy flows within ecosystems. This recognition brings to bear a whole new set of challenging questions for public land management, and, by extension, for public discussion about the course of human–nature relationships in places such as national forests, parks, and wilderness.

Toward and perhaps in light of these considerations, we believe that the model of environmental pragmatism holds great potential for encouraging more critical and democratic deliberation over environmental ethics at various social and political levels. This practical and pluralistic approach to the role of environmental philosophy in addressing environmental policy offers a useful framework for locating environmental ethics in deliberative exchanges through the open discussion of a range of alternative environmental sentiments. We believe

that this activity is necessary if public land management is to continue to evolve in response to shifting citizen values.

The discussion of a diverse set of environmental ethics in management debates can lead to effective, equitable forms of compromise that allow a broad spectrum of values and ethics to be served through responsive land management decisions. Such discussions are possible, and indeed, desirable at a number of organizational levels – from localized debates like whether bison should be shot as they wander outside of Yellowstone National Park, to large scale considerations of ecosystem management policies that may include a complex association of issues regarding numerous public, state, and private land holdings. For example, within national forests, competing demands for timber, forage, recreation, aesthetics, and so on may be met by molding forest management to accentuate or deemphasize particular values and uses based upon each forest's unique set of biophysical properties and ascribed sociohistorical attributes. A corollary to this biophysical and social diversity is that some forest lands could be allocated to advocates of more utilitarian commodity production, while others would be set aside for proponents of positions falling within aesthetic or moral preservationism.[21] While this scenario is obviously an oversimplification, it suggests the attractiveness of a pragmatic spirit in public land use decision making.

As mentioned above, this mode of thinking can also be extended to the larger public land system, where the historical record attests to the effectiveness of democratic deliberation in guiding land management decisions. Witness the debate over the establishment of Olympic National Park in Washington state in the 1930s, where, after much contentious discussion, land under the administration of the U.S. Forest Service was placed in the National Park Service's domain as various segments of the citizenry articulated their desire to preserve this land for non–commodity values.[22] A similar course of events has just taken place in Utah, where lands administered by the Bureau of Land Management have been transferred to the National Park Service as national monument status. The recent decision to forego mine development in the Yellowstone region in favor of another less "culturally treasured" location demonstrates the potential flexibility and responsiveness in land management policy decisions that allow for the engagement of multiple ethical perspectives in public discourse.

Finally, if our investigations are correct, environmental pragmatism also reflects the shape of public thinking about human–nature relationships. Our study data show that the public does subscribe to a pluralistic notion of environmental ethics – orientations that involve a broad array of environmental values and moral sentiments. According to Norton, we can expect such diverse ethical positions to "converge" when a sufficiently long-sighted and pluralistic perspective toward human–nature relationships is captured in environmental policy.[23] While not designed explicitly to test for such a hypothesis, we believe our data on public environmentalism do lend credence to Norton's position regarding environmental values and policy, and would suggest that on this count a pragmatic approach to philosophy and practice is especially useful in generating democratically authentic and inclusive environmental policy and management.[24]

VI Conclusion

We believe our conceptual and empirical study of environmental ethics demonstrates that pluralism in environmental value theory possesses conceptual and practical validity, and that this demonstration suggests the shortcomings of a vision of public environmental philosophy that appeals to any form of rigid monism in depicting the moral component of human–nature relationships. Such monistic thinking is not irrelevant for it informs and persuades public debate in relations to its substance and merit. It should not be assumed, however, to be universally prescriptive on either the public intellect or landscape. Therefore, we have argued that for environmental philosophy to be useful to the formulation of policy and the resolution of environmental debates and dilemmas, a full array of environmental ethics must be incorporated in a critical, open discussion about specific management issues and ethical alternatives. Our commitment in this paper has thus been to an inclusive model of ethical relationships rather than to a partisan engagement of either side of the dualisms in environmental ethics scholarship. This approach hinges on our belief that environmental pragmatism is capable, and, per-

haps, uniquely situated to accommodate a range of environmental values as well as classically framed anthropocentric and more biocentric ethical positions when contributing to public deliberation over policy. If our position is valid, monistic ethical programs guided by the recognition of intrinsic natural value will turn out to be only one type among many possible moral positions that encourage environmental protection.

Moreover, we strongly feel that for environmental policy debates to be fair and just, diverse moral claims must be accorded equal respect in democratic discourse. Of course, respect does not mean agreement, and the selection of "appropriate" philosophical arguments is ultimately left to the procedures of free and open debate over policy alternatives. There is growing evidence that democratic deliberation is capable, and, in fact, conducive to promoting strong environmental protection.[25] The task thus remains to expand and stimulate opportunities for democratic debate over environmental policy at various organizational and institutional levels. While we recognize that many moral monists in environmental ethics will take issue with the robust pluralistic tenor of our conclusions, we feel that a focus on practical environmental policy issues with appeals to multiple ethics for problem solving is a more beneficial and effective activity than an exclusive emphasis on monistic ethical prescriptivism. More attention needs to be paid to the illumination of the meanings of the natural world for human culture and society – in all its richness and diversity – and the moral demands upon environmental policy these meanings may place.

Environmental ethics can do much to enhance and substantively contribute to public deliberation about the character of our moral commitments to nature, including whatever obligations, duties, and other relationships with the natural world we may find ourselves assuming as a democratic community. In this sense, we believe that environmental pragmatists are especially well positioned to speak not only out of a respect for the natural community, but from a respect for the democratic values of the human community in their environmental projects. Ultimately, we feel that it is only this kind of political and moral conversation that will legitimately set the course of human–nature relationships, be it in national forests, parks, wilderness, or elsewhere.

Notes

1 Bryan Norton, "Why I am Not a Nonanthropocentrist: Callicott and the Failure of Monistic Inherentism," *Environmental Ethics* 17 (1995): 341–58.

2 See, for example, Anthony Weston, *Toward Better Problems: New Perspectives on Abortion, Animal Rights, the Environment, and Justice* (Philadelphia: Temple University Press, 1992); Frederick Ferré and Peter Hartel, eds., *Ethics and Environmental Policy: Theory Meets Practice* (Athens: University of Georgia Press, 1994); Don Marietta and Lester Embree, eds. *Environmental Philosophy and Environmental Activism* (Lanham, Md.: Rowman and Littlefield, 1995); and especially Andrew Light and Eric Katz, eds., *Environmental Pragmatism* (London: Routledge, 1996) for recent work in environmental philosophy in the pragmatic mode.

3 See the essays appearing in Light and Katz, *Environmental Pragmatism*, for a thorough summary of the pragmatic critique of monistic environmental ethics.

4 Dewey's philosophical and political projects are elaborated most powerfully in *Reconstruction in Philosophy* (New York: Henry Holt and Co., 1920) and *The Public and its Problems* (New York: Henry Holt and Co., 1927).

5 Norton, "Why I am Not a Nonanthropocentrist."

6 A pluralistic account of moral and social life seems to more accurately reflect our empirical and normative experiences than a monistic philosophical stance. As Nicholas Rescher writes, the experiential diversity of individuals differently situated in various social, historical, and cultural contexts means that people are destined to reach variant conclusions about "the nature of things." See his *Pluralism: Against the Demand for Consensus* (Oxford: Clarendon Press, 1993). The most developed and systematic treatment of pluralism in environmental ethics is still Christopher Stone's *Earth and Other Ethics* (New York: Harper and Row, 1987). See J. Baird Callicott's "The Case against Moral Pluralism," *Environmental Ethics* 12 (1990): 9–24, for a response to Stone's program from within monistic environmental philosophy.

7 An argument forcefully made by Benjamin Barber in his *Strong Democracy* (Berkeley: University of California Press, 1984). Barber believes that there can be no robust and lasting democratic legitimacy without ongoing citizen consent in the form of public deliberation. Only this kind of citizen activity, involving the creative reconstruction of privately held values as public norms through communication and identification, will, Barber claims, support a strong democratic politics. Following this line of argument, we suggest that environmental ethics do not enjoy special status as unimpeachable philosophical concepts; they are public values which must be debated, disassembled, and reconstructed through citizen deliberation.

8 Riley Dunlap and Kent Van Liere, "The New Environmental Paradigm," *Journal of Environmental Education* 9 (1978): 10–19. A selection of similar empirical treatments of general environmental values would include Stephen Cotgrove, *Catastrophe of Cornucopia: The Environment, Politics, and the Future* (Chichester: Wiley, 1982); Lester Milbrath, *Environmentalists: Vanguard for a New Society* (Albany: State University of New York Press, 1984), Robert C. Mitchell, "Public Opinion and Environmental Politics in the 1970s and 1980s," in *Environmental Policy in the 1980s: Reagan's New Agenda*, ed. N. J. Vig and M. E. Kraft (Washington, D.C.: Congressional Quarterly Press, 1984), pp. 51–74; Riley Dunlap, "Trends in Public Opinion Toward Environmental Issues: 1965–1990," in *American Environmentalism: The U. S. Environmental Movement, 1970–1990*, ed. R. Dunlap and A. Mertig (Washington, DC: Taylor and Francis, 1992), pp. 89–116; Marvin Olsen, Doral Lodwick, and Riley Dunlap, eds., *Viewing the World Ecologically* (Boulder: Westview Press, 1992); and Stephen Kellert's *The Value of Life* (Washington, D.C.: Island Press, 1996).

9 Wildlife attitude research has blossomed into an expansive literature; see Kellert, *The Value of Life*, for a useful discussion and summary of this work and also the relevant papers appearing in the new journal *Human Dimensions of Wildlife*. Examples of research focused on public attitudes toward land management and global environmental problems include work such as Bruce Shindler, Peter List, and Brent Steel, "Managing Federal Forests: Public Attitudes in Oregon and Nationwide," *Journal of Forestry* 91 (1993): 36–42; Frederick Buttel and Peter Taylor, "Environmental Sociology and Global Environmental Change: A Critical Assessment." *Society and Natural Resources* 5 (1993): 211–30; and Riley Dunlap, George Gallup, Jr., and Alec Gallup, "Of Global Concern: Results of the Health of the Planet Survey," *Environment* 35 (1993): 7–15, 33–9.

10 Willett Kempton, James Boster, and Jennifer Hartley, *Environmental Values in American Culture* (Cambridge, MA: MIT Press, 1995).

11 For an interesting discussion of this multidisciplinary attention to environmental values, see David Bengston, "Changing Forest Values and Ecosystem Management," *Society and Natural Resources* 7 (1994): 515–33.

12 Sources consulted include Robin Attfield, *The Ethics of Environmental Concern* (Athens: University of Georgia Press, 1991); John Black, *The Dominion of Man: The Search for Ecological Responsibility* (Edinburgh: Edinburgh University Press, 1970);

J. Baird Callicott, *In Defense of the Land Ethic* (Albany: State University of New York Press, 1989); Warwick Fox, *Toward a Transpersonal Ecology* (Albany: State University of New York Press, 1995); Eugene Hargrove, *Foundations of Environmental Ethics* (Engelwood Cliffs: Prentice Hall, 1989); Samuel Hays, *Conservation and the Gospel of Efficiency* (Cambridge, MA: Harvard University Press, 1959); Hans Huth, *Nature and the American* (Lincoln: University of Nebraska Press, 1990); Roderick Nash, *The Rights of Nature: A History of Environmental Ethics* (Madison: University of Wisconsin Press, 1989); Max Oelschlaeger, *The Idea of Wilderness* (New Haven: Yale University Press, 1991); Holmes Rolston, III, *Environmental Ethics: Duties to and Values in the Natural World* (Philadelphia: Temple University Press, 1988); and Donald Worster, *Nature's Economy: A History of Ecological Ideas* (Cambridge: Cambridge University Press, 1994).

13 Don Dillman, *Mail and Telephone Surveys: The Total Design Method* (New York: John Wiley, 1978).

14 A telephone survey of a random sample of nonrespondents was conducted to test for nonresponse bias. On only two scale items was there a statistical difference between respondents and nonrespondents with respect to mean agreement scores.

15 Michael Walzer, *Interpretation and Social Criticism* (New York: Basic Books, 1988).

16 As Bob Pepperman Taylor observes, rather than proceeding to develop arguments about specific environmental issues and guiding us in our assessment of different moral claims, monistic environmental ethics (especially biocentric theory) demands that we transform our "environmental ideology" before we even start talking about environmental policy. Such approaches seem to squelch democratic debate before it even begins. Bob Pepperman Taylor, "Democracy and Environmental Ethics," in *Democracy and the Environment*, ed. William Lafferty and James Meadowcroft (Cheltenham, UK: Edward Elgar, 1996), pp. 86–107.

17 Lasch, following Dewey, proposes that such public discussion and respectful argument allows us to subject our preferences and values to the test of debate – a test which tells us what we know and what we still need to learn; an epistemological and political point also made by Barber (note 7 above). Christopher Lasch, *The Revolt of the Elites and the Betrayal of Democracy* (New York: W. W. Norton, 1995), pp. 170–1.

18 Kai Lee has written a persuasive account of the potential benefits an experimental "civic science" of public deliberation and social learning can yield when citizens engage in democratic argument about ecological knowledge and policy approaches. Kai Lee, *Compass and Gyroscope* (Washington, D.C.

Island Press, 1993). We might also note that the indeterminacy of much of our ecological knowledge suggests that environmental philosophers might do well to adopt what Robert Kirkman calls an "epistemological modesty" when constructing moral claims about the environment around biological and ecological concepts. See his insightful "The Problem of Knowledge in Environmental Thought: A Counterchallenge," in Roger Gottlieb, ed., *The Ecological Community* (New York: Routledge, 1997), pp. 193–206.

19 John Dewey, "Creative Democracy – The Task Before Us," in Jo Ann Boydston, ed., *The Later Works of John Dewey, 1925–1953*, vol. 14 (Carbondale: Southern Illinois University Press, 1988), p. 227.

20 Alfred Runte, *National Parks: The American Experience* (Lincoln: University of Nebraska Press, 1987).

21 For a discussion of these types of scenarios, see R. W. Behan, "Multiresource Forest Management: A Paradigmatic Challenge to Professional Forestry," *Journal of Forestry* 88 (1990): 12–18; and Alan McQuillan, "Is National Forest Planning Incompatible with a Land Ethic?" *Journal of Forestry* 88 (1990): 31–7.

22 Ben Twight, *Organizational Values and Political Power: The Forest Service Versus the Olympic National Park* (College Park: Pennsylvania State University Press, 1983).

23 Norton's "convergence hypothesis" offers a succinct, yet powerful claim "provided anthropocentrists consider the full breadth of human values as they unfold into the indefinite future, and provided nonanthropocentrists endorse a consistent and coherent version of the view that nature has intrinsic value, all sides may be able to endorse a common policy direction." Such a conception of the integrative potential of long-sighted environmental policy leads Norton to conclude that there is not as much at stake between anthropocentric and biocentric positions as many practitioners would lead one to conclude; a position we find appealing and persuasive. Bryan Norton, "Convergence and Contextualism: Some Clarifications and a Reply to Steverson," *Environmental Ethics* 19 (1997): 87–100.

24 The empirical data reported here are part of a larger study of the Vermont public's environmental ethical orientations and policy attitudes toward national forest management. In this research we have conceptually and empirically investigated the relationship between the public's philosophical commitments to nature and their preferences for specific policy approaches on Vermont's Green Mountain National Forest. Our initial results tend to support Norton's theory that ethical positions do, in fact, "converge" in the sense that individuals, even if they express an affinity for radically different ethical

positions as conventionally understood in the ethics literature, nevertheless demonstrate a strong consensus for sustainable "ecosystem" oriented forest management in their policy attitudes. Ben A. Minteer and Robert E. Manning, "Convergence and Environmental Values: An Empirical and Conceptual Defense," *Ethics, Place and Environment* 3 (no. 1, 2000): 47–60.

25 Adolf Gunderson, *The Environmental Promise of Democratic Deliberation* (Madison: University of Wisconsin Press, 1995). Through the employment of interview methodology, Gunderson provides compelling support for how extended debate between citizens can encourage more rational and protective environmental policy attitudes in deliberative democratic systems.

PART VI

Focusing on Central Issues: Sustaining, Restoring, Preserving Nature

Is Sustainability Possible?

25

The Ethics of Sustainable Resources

Donald Scherer

An article on the ethics of sustainable energy requires elaboration of what sustainability means and clarification of what an ethic is. On these bases an evaluation of energy choices can build.

Heraclitus, the pre-Socratic philosopher, cryptically pronounced that one cannot step into the same river twice. The Heraclitian view has been that, after the step is taken, neither the river nor the one who steps, is ever again the same. Philosophers thereafter have taken his paradoxical pronouncement as a challenge to the concept and criteria of identity or sameness. From Plato's forms to Wittgenstein's aphorism that "same" does not mean the same, philosophers have sought to understand sameness. Heraclitus' remark is pertinent to understanding sustainability. To call an energy *choice* sustainable is to assert that persons like us can make that same energy choice continually and indefinitely. To claim that a *lifestyle* is sustainable is to claim that the impacts of that lifestyle cause no degeneration of the environment incompatible with continuation of that lifestyle. To designate water a sustainable *resource* is to presume its reusability. To affirm that biomass is a renewable and hence sustainable energy *resource* is to assert that, within the limits of regeneration, biomass can continue to be available for human use. In all these formulations sustainability implies at least that what we do will not constrain others like us from carrying on as we have. That human beings ought not act in any such way as to constrain future human beings from acting in

that same way is sometimes affirmed as the basic obligation to future generations underlying an ethic of sustainability. Our lives should not diminish theirs. The same choices, the same lifestyle, the same resources ought to be available to them as to us.

Sustainability of Choice

The idea that choices should be sustainable opens this discussion. The most obvious way in which an energy choice might not be sustainable would be if the processes of making energy available consumed materials faster than such materials accumulate. In different parts of the world, for example, people continue to burn wood and other forms of biomass more quickly than the biomass grows, rendering their choice and use of biomass non-sustainable.

Within this mode of thinking, sustainability is conceptually tied to renewability. Through the water cycle, water is transported to higher places so that turbines placed in the mist of falling water can continue to turn, generating electricity. Calling hydroelectric power a sustainable energy choice assumes a minimum rate of flow within a river, the rate sustained in even the driest season. The choice of electric energy generated from falling water will not constrain our successors from making that choice later on, up to the amount generated by that minimum flow.

Scale

An immediate corollary of our example is that even sustainable energy is limited. The sustainability of an energy choice depends on the rate of the renewability of the energy supply. The theoretical limit of recoverable energy from hydroelectric power is set by the operation of the water cycle. Only below that limit is the choice of hydroelectric power sustainable. Similarly, the sustainability of a choice to burn biomass is relative to the size of a population and the efficiency of its energy conversion. Increased use of a forest, resulting from increased human population, increased per person use or decreased efficiency of use, can make a sustainable choice insustainable. Equivalently, decreased use of a forest, resulting from decreased human population, decreased per person use or increased efficiency, can make an insustainable choice sustainable.

Multipurpose projects

A second implication of our example derives from the multipurpose nature of many human actions, for instance, the construction of large dams. Large dams are typically constructed not only to provide energy but to assure minimal water supply, provide flood protection and create lake recreation. Contention surrounding the issue of whether a choice is sustainable often arises from divergent foci on the purposes the choice serves. Siltation, for instance, may compromise the long-term use of the lake for recreation without compromising minimal water supply. Accordingly, a choice may be literally sustainable and insustainable at once, for different purposes. Whether a present-day choice is sustainable, therefore, often rests on different evaluations about which purposes need to continue to be pursued.

Unintended consequences

The siltation and salination associated with large dams both illustrate another conceptual complexity of sustainability: the consequences of our choices are often unintended, and some unintended consequences are not benign. Certainly the United States never intended that its construction of dams would increase the salinity of water flowing from the United States into Mexico. Yet by the early 1970s increased salinity threatened Mexican agriculture, whatever the blessings of hydroenergy and an assured minimum water supply. The decision of the United States government to construct water desalinization facilities to clean water entering Mexico reflects the need to evaluate sustainability in terms of actual effects, not merely in terms of the intentions that frame a choice.

A further point emerges from combining considerations of scale, multipurpose projects and unintended consequences. *Thresholds and synergisms*, particularly in light of our *ignorance*, often render the aggregate of our choices insustainable. For example, trace salts, alone and by themselves, seldom affect crop fertility. The fact that the toxicity of a substance is defined as a concentration capable of producing a statistically significant harmful or lethal effect, reflects human awareness that equal increments of an accumulating substance are not equally consequential.

Synergisms are particularly troublesome because of their complexity and therefore because of our more likely ignorance of their workings. It is a standard fact of elementary chemistry that there is no proportion between the effects of relatively benign elements and of the compounds derived from them. When particularly active elements, like chlorine, are components of benign compounds released into an environmental commons, recombination there may produce dangerous compounds. Predicting synergistic effects is extremely difficult, given the lack of laboratory conditions, the novelty resulting from rapidly changing technologies and the variety of harms to which organisms and ecosystems are susceptible. If this complexity were not itself sufficient to engender significant ignorance of synergisms and their ecological effects, public ignorance is regularly increased because the commons contains the emissions and run-off products of many manufacturers, the value of whose manufacturing processes vouchsafes to them, within Anglo-American law, a right to keep secret chemical formulae intrinsic to their manufacture of products. Thus, if synergisms regularly compete with sustainability, the political value of liberty exacerbates public ignorance of their effects and minimizes public prospects for fortifying sustainability.

Negative fecundity

For a particularly untoward set of consequences Jeremy Bentham (1748–1832) invented the term 'negative fecundity.' An act has negative fecundity when doing the act in order to achieve some effect today increases the difficulty of bringing about the same effect tomorrow (or some later time) through the same action. It is manifest that the increased expense of new generations of pesticides, required to contend effectively against pests selectively evolved for their resistance to older pesticides, has made protection against those pests more difficult. Likewise, the political difficulty of finding adequately safe long-term storage for spent nuclear fuels has increased the difficulty of siting additional fission plants.

From all the above criticisms we may conclude that sustainability is not a simple function of choice. When an individual makes a choice, the sustainability of that choice is a function of the environment in which the choice is made. How often is the choice being made? What other choices, as well as conditions of the physical environment, mitigate that choice? Does making the choice today increase or decrease the costs of repeating it tomorrow? Accordingly, the environment of a sustainable choice includes both the nonhuman environment in which conditions of regeneration occur and the human environment in which further resource-use choices are made.

In summary, then, speaking about sustainable choices is not well advised for, against this understanding, one might urge that a plurality of purposes can make a given choice both sustainable and insustainable, that choices have unintended consequences, and that insustainability, as derived from threshold and synergistic effects, is not directly the product of a given choice.

Sustainability of Lifestyles

It is often thought that the fundamental problem with defining sustainability in terms of choice is that reality is more systemic, less linear, than coheres well with the concept of the consequences of a choice. Defining sustainability in terms of lifestyles, gives sustainability an explicitly systemic character. If the accumulative effects of choices affect sustainability, then the concept of a lifestyle can incorporate the facts that societies are composed of many choice-making individuals, that individuals repeat their choices, and that many effects of choices arise from or are magnified by the organization of the society within which they arise.

A significant advantage of defining sustainability with reference to lifestyle is its focus on social organization. The distancing of residences from workplaces increases energy expended on transportation. A throw-away society creates problems of waste management that impinge its sustainability. The size of residences affects the costs of controlling their temperature. Stereotypes of exercise clothing and dress for work reinforce the inappropriateness of bicycling to work. Ultimately, sustainability, whether of a lifestyle, a resource or a society, is in significant part the sustainability of a pattern of practices. Practices, for example, that reinforce short time lines and impulse buying, thereby reinforce the inefficiency that threatens sustainability. Despite the advantages of holism, defining sustainability as the sustainability of a lifestyle has several disadvantages.

Holism and choice

Whatever the disadvantages of a definition of sustainability in terms of choice, the existence of options enhances self-realization. Inversely, marketing bundles human choices in packages. On speculation a builder constructs a new home. When a customer buys the home, the customer may feel that the choice made is of the features of the home, not its location. Or the customer may feel that the choice is one of living space, not of insulation and heating system. Yet the builder speculated that the money paid for the package of features enhanced the ability of the new home to be sold. In other words, people's options are typically concrete, encompassing many factors outside the focus of choice. The ability of a product in a market to be sold reflects the holistic appeal of the product. Thus although customer appeal and sustainability both require holistic definitions, nothing guarantees their coherence with one another.

Fascism

The very holism that makes a definition of sustainability in terms of lifestyle attractive carries with it the distinct disadvantage that holism can be antiliberal. If a lifestyle is a style of a society, then maintenance of the lifestyle is compatible with the repulsive treatment of some (dispensable) individuals. Air-pollution-induced emphysema, landfill-leached disease and water-pollution-induced birth defects are all compatible with a society's maintaining a lifestyle. Thus the objection here to defining sustainability in terms of lifestyle is that a lifestyle may produce as its by-product significant hazards for disadvantaged populations. The holism of the definition then encourages a society to look past so basic a right as an individual's right to health, not in the strong sense that others are obliged to provide health care for the needy, but in the very weak sense that others do not have the right to impair or destroy one's health, particularly without one's consent.

Size of cohort

A lifestyle is not rigidly defined by the number of its participants. Yet the number of participants may be crucial to the sustainability of the lifestyle. The importance of thresholds is that it is often the aggregate concentration of substances that makes them effective. Inversely, some pollutant, benign at a given concentration, may be lethal at another. The greatest mid-range challenge to the sustainability of a western affluent lifestyle will come from the Asian rim, particularly from China, and its attempt to import consumption-driven markets. The adoption of the automobile in Taiwan and Korea and the Chinese (not to mention Eastern European) use of dirty coal flag the problem of cohort-size for sustainability. When 5% of the human population consumes approximately 30% of the human energy supply and emits over 20% of the world's anthropogenic pollutants, the adoption of the lifestyle by increasingly larger cohorts strains thresholds.

Energy sources

This strain is particularly awkward because of the character of prevalent energy sources. Affluent lifestyles are built largely on nonrenewable energy sources while many marginal lifestyles rely centrally on insustainable use rates of biomass. A nonrenewable energy source is by definition not a sustainable source. To call a lifestyle built on nonrenewable energy a sustainable lifestyle is to postulate that an adequate functional substitute will be found when the nonrenewable resource is exhausted. That is, the lifestyle is sustainable only if the substitute that replaces the nonrenewable energy source continues to allow the energy expenditures the lifestyle requires. To say that calling affluent lifestyles sustainable involves a postulate is a euphemistic way of saying that calling them sustainable involves a perhaps self-indulgent act of faith or, worse, a self-deceptive delusion.

Substitution

Focusing on lifestyle sustainability draws the focus away from the materials and processes that support that lifestyle. These processes may undermine their own continuation, as when rates of use vastly exceed rates of renewability or when pollution emissions destroy resources or undermine health. In such cases lifestyle maintenance is likely to require substitution of materials, the modification of processes and the redistribution of human well-being. A limitation of a definition of sustainability in terms of lifestyle is that it obscures what such adjustments might be and how they take place.

Privileged persons

Defining sustainability in terms of lifestyle invites the question, "Whose lifestyle?" Advocates will exercise their political ideologies to the extent that a particular lifestyle advantages some race or class or other social grouping. Egalitarian criticisms of traditional treatments of women make points both about women's self-respect and about the costs to human society of the suppression of women. Not only are energies spent reinforcing the suppression but the advantages of the full expression of women's capabilities is lost to the society. Similarly, criticisms arise concerning the developing world. The export of repetitious manufacturing jobs from developed countries, while integrating the workers of developing countries into the world economy, also curtails the roles and opportunities of those workers.

Anthropocentrism

Beyond these issues of intraspecies comparison lies the privileging of the human. Whosever lifestyle the definition addresses is the lifestyle of some cohort of human beings. A definition of sustainability in terms of lifestyle captures some of the holism of human life, but it ignores ecosystemic holism. The sustainability of human energy use, however, rests not simply on lifestyle factors but on renewability rates and the effects of pollutants on nonhuman systems upon which humans ultimately rely. Edward Wilson's hypothesis that the sixth great extinction in the history of life is human-driven casts doubt on the wisdom of defining sustainability in terms of lifestyle.

Sustainability, then, is not well-defined in terms of lifestyle. For such a definition at least controversially, if not illicitly, relies on implicit assumptions about whom the lifestyle privileges. Such a bias makes the use of such a definition of sustainability an often powerful rhetorical ploy. Yet it also undermines its ability to justify the treatment it prescribes for the lives falling outside its privilege. Social and natural feedback systems imply that the long-term consequence of the use of such a definition is both the felt need to suppress the negative feedback the privileging generates and the long-term necessity of adjusting to the rhythms of a more encompassing system than the lifestyle acknowledges.

Sustainability of Resources

When sustainability is understood as the sustainability of neither choices nor lifestyles, discussion may be recast as discussion about the sustainability of a resource. Within the framework a resource is in the broadest sense any material for which a use is established. The material is then a resource for that use. Similarly, a material for which no use is established is at most and at least a potential re-

source. That is, while the absence of an established use must rather undermine the claim that the material is a resource, the undeniable possibility of devising and establishing a use leaves open the possibility of the material becoming a resource. By the same temporal relativity, much of today's wastes are materials for which uses have ceased being established.

It is typical of human beings that they often take the term "resource" to mean "resource for human beings." Since nothing in the preceding account implies that resources are resources for human beings, the assumption that "resource" is an anthropocentric concept is at once plausible and challengeable. In any event, certain understandings underlie discussion of the sustainability of resources:

Relativity to use

Sustainability, when glossed as resource sustainability, retains significant relativity. That is, when a material is called a resource, we mean that the material is effective when put to a particular use. The Ollagala Reservoir, beneath much of the Great Plains, is replenished quickly enough to provide drinking water for far more human beings than currently live above it. Yet Great Plains agriculture is arguably unsustainable because of its threatened depletion of the reservoir. Thus, the simple term "resource" can hide from us that a material can be both renewable and nonrenewable, sustainable and unsustainable, as the material is put to different uses.

Even if one confines the view of materials to the energy they can provide, a multiplicity of uses can obscure discussion about sustainability. Energy is used for transportation and for temperature control, for manufacturing and in agriculture. Whether a resource is renewable is a function of the rate of total consumption of the material, not of a particular use to which it is put.

Sustainability of resources vs sustainability of choices

An advantage of defining sustainability as the sustainability of resource uses, rather than the repeatability of choices, arises in the case where a choice may seem sustainable, but the resource may seem unsustainable. Consider fissionable fuels. The choice of fissionable materials as fuels would probably by itself be sustainable for a very long time. While the problem of the continued use of radioactive fuels is in part a practical and political problem of whether safe long-term use can be provided, beyond that problem is the potential problem that fissionable materials potentially refinable into fuels, have other uses, say in armaments. In this way it is possible that a (theoretically sustainable) resource becomes unavailable because a competing and nonsustainable use of the material undermines the market within which the theoretically sustainable resource exists.

Inelasticity of supply

When it is said that the theoretical limit of hydroelectric power is set by the water cycle, it is often assumed that "the rain falleth where it will," beyond the control of human beings to increase. Likewise, when it is said that the theoretical limit to the use of lumber is the rate at which trees grow, it has similarly been assumed that climatic conditions beyond human control determine tree growth. Contrarily, of course, we have the ability to predict, principally from the age of a tree, its species and the light available to its crown, by how many board feet it will grow in a given time span. Since the mean age of trees in a plot, the species of those trees and the mean light available to each of their crowns are all subject to human calculation and manipulation over time, theoretical limits to the use of lumber have been exceeded in many terrains.

Efficiency of use

The board feet of timber available from a forest is also relative to the efficiency with which a tree is converted to lumber. The use of computers to calculate the most productive cut of the wood and the development of saw blades that create less saw dust per board foot have both increased production beyond increases in timber supply. The considerable gains in motor efficiency and building insulation that followed the energy crises of the 1970s, notwithstanding, inefficiency of energy use remains a considerable obstacle to sustainability.

Sustainability and Substitutability

Energy from different sources is renewable at different rates. When the rate of consumption vastly exceeds (in orders of magnitude) the rate of renewal, as it does for the common fossil fuels, the energy resource is called nonrenewable. The assumption in this assertion is that efficiencies neither of new technologies nor of social organization will suffice to reduce the resource's rate of consumption to the rate of its renewal.

A significant complexity of the discussion of sustainability has arisen from the reality of substituting one material for another. In the 1840s, for example, whale oil was being used more quickly than whales reproduce. The rate of the resource's use was not sustainable, given the relative constancy of supply. In this circumstance the result was neither the extermination of whales nor the curtailment of oil use. Instead, crude oil was discovered at Titusville, Pa., whaling for whale oil declined, and petroleum use increased. This has been the kind of case in virtue of which economists rest contentions of sustainability not on reuse but on substitution.

Discussion at this point often turns to discounting. Financial or technical resources invested, at a given point in time, in extending the known supply of a form of energy, represent opportunities diverted from other uses of those resources. It is standardly argued that knowing the availability of a form of energy is valuable only because of the time required to devise technologies for accessing that energy and converting it to usable form. In this way, knowing of more than a twenty year supply of petroleum is regularly thought to be worthless. Accordingly, it is inferred that the fact that the known supply of petroleum (at present rates of use) will not last a generation reflects the discounted value of such knowledge, not the absolute shortness of the supply of the energy resource.

The twin arguments of substitutability and discounting are often combined. The argument from discounting is thought to show that supply probably substantially exceeds known supply, and the argument from substitutability is used to conclude that the case in which supply is actually limited to known supply will only occasion the development of new technologies that convert what are now useless materials into tomorrow's resources. In this vein it has even been argued that the present generation's landfills, far from marking the decadence of consumerism, amount instead to the storage of inventoried materials whose recovery will be inexpensive when their future uses become established.

Sustainability and justice

One of the ethical shortcomings of that argument comes into focus when we shift our attention from cities to rural areas and from countries that use nonrenewable energy resources intensively to countries that rely much more centrally on human labor. When we shift our attention from the center to the peripheries of economic power, we encounter disease, poverty and people who lack opportunities to live in the style either of their parents or of their powerful contemporaries. The likelihood of the siting of hazardous waste in a given area is known to be a function of the race and poverty of its human inhabitants. The effect of a given resource shortage on a particular local human population is a function of the strength of the network of other resources available to that population.

In light of the differential effects of resource shortages on human populations, some rethinking of the concept of sustainability is appropriate. "We should not imperil the availability for future generations of what we have available to us now." When is "now" and who is "us"? Is there a future population that is less deserving of what more affluent societies now have available to them?

Here the ethics of sustainable energy become an ethics of the just use of power. In its starkest form, the danger is that the concept of sustainable energy itself is loaded. The very concept comes under scrutiny from the suspicion that concern about sustainability is no more than a concern of an elite to retain its privileged status.

Justice is an issue of the use of power. Accordingly if sustainability is to escape the label of an ideological concept that imposes the legitimacy of the interests of an established class, then at some level just patterns of resource use or changes in the pattern of resource use must be patterns or changes acceptable to the least powerful. That is, acceptable uses of power among competent adult human beings are largely confined to uses that have the consent of those upon whom power is wielded. Accordingly, there is nothing just about the (forced) imposition of patterns of resource use.

Although this line of argument seems plausible as far as it goes, it leaves significant questions unresolved. Suppose a society establishes a set of conventions or a code of law governing the rightful possession and use of things, in a word, property. Suppose that members of that society are amenable to what they have established, to a set of rules of acquisition and transfer, say. Imagine that those rules include rules governing inheritance. Imagine also that the rules include models of what materials are useful (resources, as we say), models the society outgrows over a period of generations. What facts and principles then ground the justification of the agreement? Who all is bound by this original agreement? Under what conditions, by whom, and to what ends, can it legitimately be modified?

The conservative value of social order is that much human coordination presupposes a large degree, but not a particular definition, of social order. Driving on the right is not better than driving on the left, but having everyone driving on the same side maintains life, health, and property values. Changes in the ongoing definition of an established order always occasions some disruption of coordination mutually beneficial for the parties directly involved. When right turn on red first became the default norm in the United States, pedestrian deaths at intersections rose. At least somewhat contrary to this good, regularly lies the point that certain changes in the ongoing definition of that order would clearly benefit society in general or at least one of the parties directly involved without clear harm, at least in the long run, to anyone. United States pedestrian deaths have since declined and average mileage is increased because time spent idling at intersections is reduced. The point–counterpoint of these assertions defines much of the battle ground for conventional aspects of what justice amounts to.

Justice and the meaning of opportunity

The frequent context of these questions has been the still-influential view of John Locke (1632–1702) on property. "In the beginning," Locke said, "all the world was America." By this statement, Locke contrasted England with the new world. In 1661 England had passed the Enclosure Laws that remain to this day the legal foundation of property law in the Anglo-American, liberal tradition. In 1689 when Locke wrote, England was a land parceled into plots to which owners had titles. If one wished to acquire land in England, one's only option was to buy it from its owner. Such was the implication of earlier claims and enacted laws of transfer.

America, as Locke saw it, was a land to which, until recently, no property claims had been made. For in Locke's eye, one can claim previously unworked land as one's own when and only when the value of the land has become, substantially, the product of the labor one has invested in it. Since Locke believed that all American Indians were nomads, he saw them lacking an agriculturalist's investment in, and hence the agriculturalist's claim to, the land. In Locke's eyes, then, America, being inhabited only by nomads (here Locke believed a false premise), was an unclaimed land.

Locke's conclusion was that people come to own previously unowned land by the investment of their labor in the land. Locke reasoned as follows: 90 to 99% of the value of cultivated land has derived from its having been cultivated. Thus, almost nothing of what one claimed after such work would have been available except for one's labor. Indeed inasmuch as the basis of the claim was the creation of value resulting from cultivation, others have been benefited if, because they have also used their labor to create value, they can exchange the value they have created for the value others create and they lack. Therefore, provided that one leaves as much and as good for others (so that they are not deprived of the opportunity to labor and to enjoy the fruits of their labor), the claim of the land as property benefited the claimant (by securing value the claimant has created) without harming anyone else.

This formulation of the view emphasizes Locke's reliance on America as a frontier open for future claimants. The virtual closing of that frontier in the late nineteenth century therefore reopened the question of justice and the meaning of opportunity. The Square Deal, the New Deal, the Fair Deal, and the New Frontier are the prominent slogans of attempts in the United States to address that question.

Of these, Theodore Roosevelt's Square Deal, Truman's Fair Deal, and the Kennedy–Johnson years are central for understanding the meaning 'sustainability' has acquired in the United States. For Roosevelt, the closing of the frontier and the ongoing importance of equal opportunity imply the need for policies that sustain opportunities for future generations. Where Jefferson at the outset of the nineteenth century had inferred from Locke that he ought to buy the Louisiana Territory to secure agricultural opportunities for future generations, Roosevelt inferred at the outset of the twentieth century that efficiency in resource use, through conservation and technological innovation, were required for the United States to succeed in the impending competition among nations. A significant continuing relevance of Roosevelt's view is that the frontiers of energy efficiency and renewable energy remain substantially open.

The relevant plank of Truman's Fair Deal was the GI Bill that created an entitlement to a college education for World War II veterans. The use of this entitlement marked the beginning of mass higher education. Where before the war, the percentage of college educated Americans resembled the percentage of college educated (largely upper class) Britons, enrollments in United States colleges after the war began a 500% increase that has made the United States unique in enrolling over half its population in post-secondary education in the second half of the twentieth century. This development created knowledge acquisition as a new frontier, breathing new life into the meaning of equality of opportunity. In the 1980s countries as diverse as Taiwan and Argentina began following the United States in the pursuit of that frontier.

The Kennedy–Johnson years contribute dialectically to the contemporary meaning of sustainability. Outer space has been a new frontier because going to the moon can provide new resources and new platforms on which to develop technology, in a word, new opportunities. The meaning of opportunities, however, has vastly changed. Science education has been seen as vital to prepare people for work on the new frontier so that the frontier will itself become a frontier for the development of further scientific and technical knowledge.

The progressivism of the Roosevelt administration, in other words, has rested on the importance of maintaining equality as an American ideal. New frontiers, whether in education, technology, space, the sea bottom, battery technology or solar energy, are similarly focused on sustaining opportunity by increasing the production of value. Questions of the justice of previous generations' conventions of property are often effectively postponed by the demonstration that their further employment retains promise for the less fortunate.

Donald Scherer

Sustainability and the well-being of ecosystems

As straightforwardly as these ideas develop Roosevelt's vision, the meaning of 'sustainability' also developed during the Kennedy–Johnson years out of an emerging ecological understanding of both conservation and wilderness preservation. Although late-nineteenth century preservationism had rested on maintaining vestiges of wilderness experience, natural curiosities and the "people's temples" with their remarkable aesthetic–religious appeal, early attempts at applying the preservation ethic in Yellowstone National Park began to convince field biologists that their work required systemic understandings, just as Aldo Leopold reached this conclusion from his early attempts to apply the conservation ethic to forestry and ranching in New Mexico and Arizona. Although Stewart Udall began his tenure as Secretary of the Interior with many older conservationistic and preservationistic attitudes, the Secretary became the champion of more ecological approaches. Since that time "sustainability" has tended to reflect an understanding of the systemic connections that sustain the components of ecosystems we call our resources.

This ecosystemic emphasis, however, does not fit easily with a Lockean conception of property. Most fundamentally, ecology has been called a subversive science because so influential an ecologist as Aldo Leopold seems committed to the view that it makes as much sense to speak of the good of the ecological community inhabiting a mountainside as it does to speak of the good of a human being. An overpopulation of deer, brought about by the human extermination of the deer's predators, harms the mountain, Leopold has argued, as surely as an injury to one's body harms a human being.

Leopold concluded that we are no more justified in harming a mountainside than Odysseus was in hanging several slave girls on his return from Troy. While neither extant morality nor law gives more status to ecosystems than to slaves, Leopold saw the harm done to mountainsides and slave girls as undermining whatever conventions ignore and justify that harm.

Leopold's observation that extant morality and law did not condemn Odysseus' hanging of his slaves highlights a conflict concerning the property

of persons: some hold that value exists precisely because people actually value something. If 1850s Lake Michigan lumbermen saw trees with ten inch trunk diameters as worthless hindrances to the harvesting of the larger-diametered trees Chicago lumberyard dealers were alone willing to buy at that time, then, with no voices raised in dissent, the trees were without value. If 1870s lumber men saw trees of that same size as the largest and most desirable of available trees, then the trees had acquired value. In accord with this mode of thinking, some economists argue that in circumstances of abundance, the destruction of potential resources is justified as often as it is efficient.

The alternative viewpoint is that all organisms (and perhaps ecosystems as well) have goods of their own. A suitable premise here is that organisms are disentropic entities: they absorb energy from their environment; they have capacities, unlike a stone, for maintaining a supply of usable energy, and they have mechanisms within them, unlike an automobile, through which, within limits, they maintain their own functionality. When an entity has both energy-absorbing and self-maintaining capacities it makes sense to speak of the good of the entity. The trees Chicago-based lumbermen saw as worthless in 1850 certainly had a good of their own. The soil that blew off Iowa farms in the 1960s, although not an organism with a good of its own, is a component of a prairie ecosystem that absorbs energy and, in some views, has capacities of self-maintenance. If any entity has a good of its own, then certainly impairing the capacities that underlie that good amount to harming the entity.

Humans continually learn to recognize harms previously invisible to them. The ability to recognize such harms, however, challenges sets of conventions for the acquisition and transfer of property. For "sustainability" within a philosophy oriented to human resources has often meant the sustainability of what the human beings treat as materials to be manipulated by the human beings for their own purposes and therefore independent of any so-called good of non-human entities. In this light, the challenge of Leopold's land ethic, as it is called, is that it is no more right wantonly to ignore the good of an ecosystem than it is to ignore the good of a slave.

The good of a person and the good of an ecosystem compared

Maiming, by definition, is injuring in such a way as to cause the loss of some functional capacity. Since a forest, like any ecosystem, has functional capacities, maiming it is a real possibility. A forest has parts that cannot live independently of the forest as a whole anymore than one's leg continues to live after its amputation. The positive good realized in the maintaining of functional capacities implies that something undesirable and, all things being equal, wrong happens when a forest is maimed.

If, however, one is to look for duties of human beings towards ecosystems, those duties must be relative to the entities ecosystems are and thus to what the good of an ecosystem amounts to. The good of an ecosystem is, of course, far different from the good of an enslaved human being. Even if laws made it illegal to teach slaves to read (perhaps on the ground that they would be incapable of learning), human slaves, whose brains evolved as products of cohort-monitoring, are capable of directing their lives autonomously. A slave's degrading treatment by the master may demean the slave. The resultant loss of self-respect may impair the slave's capacities. Those underlying capacities, nevertheless, justify a respect for the slave, laws and cultural mores notwithstanding. Nothing like the centralized self-directing capacities of a human being, however, are present in an ecosystem.

The good of an ecosystem is in its functional capacities. Rather than the thwarting of a will, the thwarting of an ecosystem is the disassembly of its structure, the destruction of its resilience or the degradation of its diversity. It is these function-enabling capacities that justify human respect for them and their well-being. Accordingly, the well-guided tree-hugger hugs the tree not in the misguided conviction that a tree has the capacities and deserves the respect of a "similarly" mistreated human slave. Instead, the clear thinking tree-hugger urges protection of self-sustaining systems.

Both the magnificence of the integrated living system a forest is and the future resource value for human beings of forest components require respect for the integrity of that system. Edward Wilson has recently noted that human beings are dangerously ignorant of how they (frequently) pre-cipitate the collapse of apparently stable but volatile ecosystems. At the same time, not all human use of forests maims them. The regenerative resilience of a forest, whatever its limits, is real. The reality of such resilience implies that the human use of resources is not categorically wrong. One does well to remember that, even in a world where no human beings live, resource relationships are implicit in the concepts of a water cycle or a nitrogen cycle or a food chain. It is not intrinsically wrong for an entity to be a resource. The hope that an encyclopedia of energy is a useful resource is not on its face an immoral hope. The teacher one most greatly respects may be one's mentor and one's most valuable resource. The fact that resources are often treated without respect does not imply that what is one's resource one uses without respect. Respect for an ecosystem is respect for the capacities that give it a good of its own, its structure, its resilience, its diversity.

The ecosystemic concept of sustainability reaches into the discussion of development. Once sustainability is defined ecosystemically, it is clear that many environments are degraded. They are functionally impaired. The question then arises whether the impairment can be corrected. Both the state of technology and the scale of costs immediately enter the discussion. It is, in general, clear that new development conjoined with restoration of the abandoned, previously developed area is more expensive, less feasible and regularly less successful than redevelopment of a previously developed area that leaves undeveloped areas thriving, or, more anthropocentrically, undeveloped. Thus, the sustainability of both ecosystems and of human life regularly favors redevelopment over new.

Sustainability, then, if understood ecosystemically, includes the recognition of goods other than human well-being and the resources that conduce thereto. Once these other goods are recognized, conditions of their stable maintenance exist. The recognition of these goods expands the meaning of 'sustainability' to include the conditions that assure that stable maintenance. Respect for those goods, along perhaps with prudence as well, requires aiming to maintain the conditions that those goods require. Accordingly, human actions thought right or at least permissible, on the grounds that they promote or at least do not harm human well-being, are arguably wrong if and when they contravene broadened, ecosystemic conditions of sustainability.

Ecosystemic goods as public goods

The good of an ecosystem regularly involves public goods for human beings. Clean air and water are the most obvious and universal examples, but there are others. Recently much has been made of the fact that extinction involves loss of genetic information and of the ecosystemic setting in which the emergence of human life was possible. Similarly, the regular flow of energy relative to the rhythms of life promotes the stability and helps to maintain the diversity of complex ecosystems.

A standard social problem about public goods is that individuals will free ride, taking the benefit of the good without contributing to maintaining it, depleting without helping to restore it. Each individual may be tempted to think that an individual defection or contribution is insignificant. Each individual may be concerned that defections by others will leave the contributing individual a hapless sucker. When the good of the individual agent and the good of some larger entity diverge, the agent may act in rationally self-interested fashion. The interest of the larger entity will then move toward managing the options agents encounter.

Managing common resources

The management of common resources has sometimes been in government hands (international peace keeping forces, harbors, dams, roadways) and sometimes in the hands of government-regulated monopolies (public utilities, turnpike authorities). This management has grown out of the efficiencies surrounding capital investment for construction and out of the conviction that the community (world, national or local) would benefit, collectively and individually, from a co-ordinated investment.

What does not follow from these premises is that the resulting management will also be beneficial. To the contrary, a historically prominent result has been that from some egalitarian premise, the further conclusion has been drawn that all individuals are entitled to equal access to the investment and its potential fruits. Accordingly we see user fees in United States National Parks that cover only 7% of the cost of the parks; we see electric utility companies charging customers equally whether the utility's least or most efficient generator produces the customer's energy; we see public tax money subsidizing western cattlemen's access to public land and reservoir water; and we see neither urban companies nor their employees seeking to end rush-hour tie-ups by staggering work days and hours.

Sustainability requires efficiency. The management of common resources is often inefficient. Yet societies often secure individual and collective welfare through institutions that allow nonexclusive access to particular resources. By eliminating the cost of the roadway as part of decisions about travel, the provision of free public roads encourages personal transportation in private vehicles. By leaving unallocated the access to open-water fishing grounds, the provision of public harbors encourages overfishing of targeted areas. Typical features of unsustainably managed resources are that access to them is not borne specially by those who use them and that the benefits of overuse rebound primarily to the user with the costs of overuse distributed primarily to others, especially to future generations, and non-human organisms that suffer largely through habitat degradation, including pollution.

Economists and philosophers have noted, however, that both governmental and private action can effectively structure social environments so that individuals choose to promote, rather than diminish, the public good. The size and community structure of small town neighborhoods has made voluntary curb-side recycling much more successful than was widely predicted as recently as the late 1980s. If energy producers pay full costs on the pollution resulting from the use of some fossil fuel, the producers are induced to avoid the costs through energy production that avoids the pollution. Moreover, such structuring is not aimed merely at preventing losses. While clean air reduces respiratory disease, public goods can be used to generate further public goods. Clean water facilitates an attractive park. Genetic knowledge facilitates health.

The advantage of competition among suppliers is that consumers expand their choice beyond purchasing or not purchasing to a choice of purchases. An upshot of deregulation of the telephone industry, for instance, is that competing companies offer alternative products for alternative prices. Similarly, one might distinguish between the advantages, for the public, of a common provision for universal education and the disadvantages of the noncompetitive expenditure of tax revenue allocated to education.

Public goods and governmental involvement

Public goods create accountability problems because their disrupters are not regularly the victims of the disruption they cause. The run-off from an open strip mine, for example, creates standard upstream/downstream problems. It does not follow, however, that government regulation, permits and fines, are typically required to police disrupters and protect victims. A quarter century of experience has taught the Environmental Protection Agency and environmental cabinet ministries in other countries that heavy regulation is not only prohibitively expensive but also often unnecessary.

The role of government as facilitator of public goods, therefore, takes on different meanings in different cases. (1) The years that utilities found capital tied up in unapproved fission plants taught the value of up-front agreements. Foresight about acceptable forms of action avoids both industrial consternation about invested capital and public concern about implementations that require excessive monitoring because of their embodiment of temptations for industry to choose between its own interests and a broader public or environmental interest. (2) Sometimes a one-time financial incentive provides the capital base for an ongoing, long-term payoff. Thus, energy tax credits have been legislated to induce investment in insulation or efficient machinery. (3) Sometimes a good name is so significant an asset that support for the public good benefits the benefactor. For such reasons, ARCO, with its technological investments, has found taking a public spirited perspective beneficial. Indeed, certain other companies in the energy industry, lacking similar technologies, have found aping ARCO through token but visible environmental benevolence to be the best strategy available to them with an increasingly environmentally literate public. Clearly, efficiency in social systems argues that people should not fear government involvement per se, especially involvements that surely stabilize the availability and increase of public goods or the decrease or elimination of public bads. Entirely compatible with government involvement for the

sake of public goods is the citizen concern of prudence to seek minimal, nonintrusive, one-time or short-term governmental involvements.

In summary, communities and their residents do benefit from the public availability of various goods. Yet common access to those goods often results in inefficient resource use. Therefore, one key to true sustainability lies in alternative management of public goods to avoid the inefficiencies of common access while maintaining the benefits of public availability. While different resources will require different management decisions, the goal of sustainability is to increase the efficiency of public availability. Although a common objection to competitive management is its effects on access for the most disadvantaged, a frequent result of competitive management is increases in efficiency more than offsetting increases in cost. Of course, since this correlation is less rigid than a law of nature, the endeavor to increase efficiency by constraining the terms of public availability must include a caution that constraining the terms of availability without improving efficiency amounts simply to a loss (at least in part) of public goods, typically by poorer individuals.

Proper resource pricing

The thesis that a market system produces efficiency involves the assumption that in a market prices reflect costs. Public goods, like clean air and clean water, are threatened and markets become less efficient and less supportive of sustainability when costs are externalized from the market. How, then, are unpriced costs reflected?

The costs of pollution are regularly borne by the polluted. That is, when an Ohio coal-burning electric utility feeds air-conditioning systems by emitting sulfur compounds that contaminate an area two to five hundred miles downwind, it is the lungs of people in New York and Ontario that sustain injury. Similarly, the cost of the emissions from an Alabama plant is a smoggy view of the Shenandoah Valley for summer visitors to the national park.

A "right" to emit pollutants into waterways or the atmosphere would amount to a right to impose costs upon others without their consent. Many of the norms of Anglo-American society, indeed of any human society, function to monitor, constrain and chastise impositions of harm, especially when

Donald Scherer

they are nonconsensual. Without an argument that the harmed eventually benefit from the harm imposed upon them, their innocence would make it extremely difficult to justify any nonconsensual imposition of harm. While the presumption of a frontier society may be that the normal dilution of pollutants will nullify any toxic effect, the present-day intensity and multiplicity of nearby pollutants, especially new, artifactual pollutants, renders that presumption inappropriate.

A small but significant loophole in the preceding argument arises from thresholds. A right to emit pollutants into commons could be a right merely to emit pollutants below the threshold of their harmfulness. If a level of a pollutant can be vouchsafed as harmless to entities whose good would be affected by a greater emission, then the liberty to emit below-threshold amounts of sulfur dioxide and other effluents is a liberty so to act in ways that cause no harm. The Environmental Defense Fund was instrumental in the incorporation of such thinking into the "Emissions Trading" section (Title IV) of the Clean Air Act of 1990.

Justice, opportunity, and public goods

The important relationship between social structure and public goods is typically obscured in frontier situations. Pollution is a central public bad as energy supply is a central public good for an interdependent society. But since pollution is a threshold phenomenon, it is often not critical on a spatial frontier. "Six miles of free-flowing water purifies itself," is an oft-cited rule of thumb. Yet while frontier experiences were forming the national psyche of maximal liberty combined with a minimal conception of harm in late nineteenth century United States, the sophisticated observation of settled life in eastern United States was moving towards different norms.

Ellen Swallow Richards (1842–1911) was at the forefront of much of this movement. Early Massachusetts efforts to establish standards of clean water, early efforts to develop a science of air standards, and early efforts to establish sound practices of public health, glowed from the luster of her pioneering efforts. She matched her keen awareness of physical endangerment of public environmental goods not only with her own tireless and energetic devotion but also with her early mobilization of educated women and of home

economists as sources of knowledge and expertise that needed to be structured so as to facilitate public goods. Perhaps through her efforts, more than any one else, there was established a heritage of concern for environmental public goods, a heritage devoted to articulating the elaborate interplay between danger to people, especially less fortunate people, harm to people and harm to non-human life. Great women from Rachel Carson (1907–64) to Kristin Shrader-Frechette, with her work on siting hazardous wastes, and Theo Colburn, with her work on genetically linked degeneracies arising out of organochlorides in the food chain, have advanced the line Ellen Swallow Richards first developed.

Pollution: Prevention versus clean-up

Once pollution is distributed into a fluid medium, isolating and removing pollutants is extremely costly and not very effective. Analyses comparing the costs of preventing the emission of pollutants with the costs of cleaning up after such emissions, regularly conclude the preferability of prevention. The right of the society to avoid, for itself and for its members, the public bad of pollution suggests a rationale for resource pricing that internalizes the costs of appropriate disposal of unwanted by-products of production.

For example, an electric utility that has been mandated to pay the cost of disposing of unwanted by-products of its production of electricity. The cost of this disposal now increases the price of the electricity. A monopoly may succeed in passing those costs along to customers, for the monopoly will argue to its regulators that, with the increase of its legitimate costs, it is entitled to an increase in price to sustain its profit margin. If that utility is in a competitive market, however, it must weigh the advantage of alternative means of internalizing its costs. The utility must at least consider the possibilities of cleaning gaseous by-products before emitting them versus compensating victims of long-term emissions.

An enterprising utility will explore further possibilities. Efficiencies will result if cheaper resources can be used to generate electricity. Efficiencies will result if the by-product is eliminated from the generation process. Profits will rise if, instead of the polluting by-product, a salable product is produced. Imagine, then, a process of converting high sulfur coal in conjunction with such landfilled wastes as automobile tires. Let high temperatures, in the absence of oxygen, reduce complex hydrocarbons in coal to hydrogen and carbon monoxide. Let the by-products of the conversion, rather than any polluting gas, be a solid useful for paving highways and making construction blocks. Imagine that utility companies can burn the produced gases with no need to use post-combustion pollution controls. With an entrepreneurial enterprise like Calderon Energy Company seriously working with utility companies to bring such a process to market, we see fleshed out a promising prospect: even with huge externalized costs in much of the electricity generated from high sulfur coal, a process could be profitable if it reduced what would otherwise become a waste product, to usable forms of energy, created salable by-products rather than unsalable pollutants and converted otherwise landfilled wastes into components of such salable products. A society that mandated the morally appropriate internalization of the costs of producing electricity from high sulfur coal would thereby speed the technological, and enhance the economic success of such processes.

Even when prices reflect full costs, resources may be improperly priced because different units of the resource are not priced relative to their different costs. For example, the most expensive energy an electric utility generates is that which it generates in middle afternoon on a hot summer weekday. Then, when demand is highest, the company will use its less efficient generators and the average cost per-watt hour will climb. Suppose, however, that pricing does not reflect this cost. For instance, a large user, whose use is increased by air-conditioning demand, may actually pay less if billed at a decreasing block rate. In many other areas flat rates are standard. In any such case, improper pricing is failing to signal to the customer the reasonability of avoiding peak time use. Producers and investors also receive faulty signals from improper price structures.

The most dramatic proof of the efficacy of pricing structures resulted from the "energy crises" of 1973 and 1979. The steeply increased price of energy signaled consumers to improve the efficiency of their energy use. It, "accordingly," signaled producers and investors to develop and market improved efficiency. From insulation to motor efficiency, from temperature controls to construction techniques, long-term efficiencies have resulted.

Sustainability and Reusability

Using a reusable resource is equivalent to making use of it, with the presumption that such use is at least compatible with the reuse of the resource. The presumption in such cases is that using the resource is not equivalent to using it up; that is, transforming it so that it cannot again function as the resource it once was. Water and atmospheric gases are said to be sustainable resources because they are deemed indefinitely reusable.

The value of the reuse of a product, as opposed to recycling of a material, is often noted in this context. The reuse of a cloth shopping bag implies almost no degeneration of the product over time. The recycling of a paper or plastic shopping bag costs tens to hundreds of dollars per ton. Such costs overshadow such cleaning or transportation costs as reuse often involves. Consider water used in cleaning. When water scarcity grows, as in a long-lasting California drought, a processor using water to clean reusable bottles may abandon the practice of disposing of gray water. Rational self-interest demands the reuse of gray water if the scarce supply of water makes cleaning and disinfecting the gray water cheaper than procuring a new supply. Theoretically, the loop of the water, through cleaning bottles, to being cleaned, to cleaning more bottles, is unending.

Similarly, if more complexly, the nitrogen cycle is a cycle of nitrogen from being free in the atmosphere to being fixed in processes of plant growth, perhaps to be tracked into soils, perhaps to be tracked through animals, but eventually to return in free form to the atmosphere, undegraded in its ability to participate in the cycle. Accordingly, one of the worries about green house gases is that oxides of nitrogen will accumulate in the atmosphere. Does such an accumulation interfere with the functioning of the nitrogen cycle? If so, insustainability is threatened in the form of degradation of theoretically reusable resources. Even if not, the concept of global warming rests in part on the assumption that deflecting nitrogen out of the cycle threatens sustainability by violating temperature parameters. Accordingly, we see that the harm in the disruption of reusability may result not only from threatened scarcity of the consumed or diverted resource but also from the transformation of the reusable resource into a pollutant that itself threatens sustainability.

Sustainability and limits of reusability

Important as reuse is to the promotion of sustainability, unending cycles of reuse are of course a theoretical ideal only approachable in practice. The degree to which recycling reduces the average fiber length of recycled paper quantifies the degradation of the paper and thus the limit of its reuse through recycling. In such cases reuse extends the life of a material without indefinitely, much less unendingly, sustaining the material as a resource.

The use of motor oil as a lubricant further illuminates the practical limits of reusability. Just as a scarcity of water may prompt its cleaning and reuse, so the supply of motor oil, in conjunction with the polluting effects of non-reused motor oil, have led to its cleaning and reuse. And, as some nitrogen may be diverted from its cycle into accumulating nitrogen oxides, so some motor oil may be burned or lose viscosity within an engine.

With lubricants, however, a further serious concern is dissipation. Dissipation here is essentially a distributional concept. The distribution of a lubricant throughout a space reduces the amount of lubricant at any one place. The more accessible that space is, the greater the potential for contamination. Both the distribution and the potential contamination increase the cost of recollecting the lubricant for cleaning or for reuse.

Evaluating whether resource loss is superfluous.

These examples of reusability all suggest that actual conditions of use significantly compromise theoretical reusability. The question whether these compromises are significant for the sustainability of resources is often discussed with reference to the example of agricultural practice and soil erosion. Certainly much of Iowa once had more top soil than sustainable agricultural practice requires. The initial abundance of the resource, however, meant that markets did not protect against the early, casual discarding of 'superfluous' materials. Under these conditions loss of some top soil was

thought "harmless" on the presumption that the erosive practices would be curtailed and replaced by practices that used top soil up only as fast as new soil accumulates. The advent of low- and no-till plowing has significantly lessened soil erosion since the early 1980s. Familiar, then, is the pattern of resource use by which an abundant and theoretically reusable resource is at first degradingly used and is only later the subject of conservation efforts. Many economists have assumed that, under such conditions, the early unsustainable practice is morally benign.

As degradation of a given resource becomes more threatening to property owners or others who benefit directly from the sustainability of the resource, many have hoped, argued, or trusted that those persons with direct interests will move to ensure reusability. Although the recent history of forestry is often cited as a case in point, real problems remain in replanting some of the steeper harvested slopes or Northwest forest land. Therefore, whether an early "unsustainable" practice is actually morally benign rests upon a falsifiable assumption: that a hypothesized future sustainability will be achievable. Some risk is always involved in such a judgment, a risk likely borne largely by those who are not well off, or freely and easily borne by those who are affluent.

The argument that the loss of Iowa topsoil is superfluous because less topsoil is adequate for agricultural needs also rests on the assumption that the value of Iowa topsoil is confined to its agricultural value for human beings. The "superfluous" loss of materials may be harmful in each of three ways in which this assumption can be challenged. It can be challenged by noting that increased frequency of floods on the Mississippi River between 1950 and 1980 resulted in part from increased siltation of the river itself arising from traditional post-war agriculture. Even when a material is superfluous as a resource, it may be dangerous as a pollutant. The assumption can also be challenged by noting that topsoil may take on nonagricultural value for human beings. Topsoil loss, for example, may curtail shade tree growth. Finally, the assumption can be challenged as anthropocentric. The topsoil is beneficial for the ecosystem it supports. Hundreds of species are benefited by the topsoil and harmed by its loss. A maimed ecosystem is weakened in its diversity and stability.

Resource reusability and ecosystem sustainability

Even though many resources that are theoretically indefinitely reusable are in fact to some extent degraded through use, the question of the sustainability of those resources remains open. For with respect to many reusable resources, ecosystem sustainability is key to resource sustainability. Slowly, atmospheric pollutants precipitate out, wetlands purify waters, soil accumulates, and trees grow. Therefore, many resources can be refreshed or renewed. Accordingly, the sustainability of many reusable resources rests ultimately on a complex social fact: the relationship between demand, (partially degrading) reuse, and renewal (contravened or facilitated by humans). Lower demand, minimized degradation, and swifter renewal are the friends of sustainability.

The sustainability of a useful material, accordingly, cannot be a function simply of the physical properties of the material and its 'inherent' capacities for reuse or renewal. Contrarily, the concept of sustainability builds on the concept of availability. Rather than a question of theoretical physics, the question of energy sustainability is the question of the human capacity to use some portion of the potential energy in some material. This statement may be either a question of material technology or of social organization. If, for example, food is cooked over a wood stove, the question need not be the technical one of the stove's efficiency in converting the potential energy within the wood into heat. Instead, the question may be to what extent and in what ways the social organization of food preparation detracts from theoretical efficiency.

Distributing proven technologies

Social organization can be as important as technology in creating efficiencies. Most obviously, many proven technologies are unavailable to almost all of the approximately 85% of underdeveloped countries' populations that are rural. Similarly, efficient technologies are often unavailable to the lower class in advanced societies. Typically, a strong contrast exists between low absolute costs of the technologies and high marginal costs for selected populations. The social value of many of these technologies is two-fold: avoided social costs provide a short-term justifying pay-back for original expenditures,

and improved resource efficiency and decreased pollution enhance prospects of sustainability.

Empowering individuals

The power to reproduce is often the greatest power available to a couple. To the extent that overpopulation is a root cause of poverty and resource degradation, the power to reproduce must be supplemented to avoid poverty and its correlates of disease and violence, and to improve prospects of resource sustainability. Demographic and economic studies concur that literacy and control over some land are changes that by themselves regularly and more effectively than other changes, increase the power and decrease the reproduction of the world's poor. While the trend in rural areas continues toward increased farm size, production per acre is most efficient on small farms. In urban areas worldwide the percentage of illegal aliens undercuts the social practices that would otherwise support individual empowerment.

Reforming management

The role of the manager is often buffered from economic shocks. If the manager is the decision-maker, the self-interested decision is usually to continue the manager's work. When circumstances change, different management teams, created for different purposes, find their jurisdictions impinging on each other's resulting in conflicts. Again self-interest may stir parties away from coordination because they insist on their own legitimacy. The social environments in which management will itself be reformed are therefore environments in which managers are not insulated from the effects of their decisions. While older models emphasized the accountability of a common authority (in the business or in the government) to whom conflicting managers would report, newer models emphasize both how stockholders can make managers accountable and how the disintegration of the core corporation has given markets more leverage to make managers accountable.

Coping with congestion

The plurality of ways in which disruption of the nitrogen cycle might disrupt sustainability occasions a usual schema of environmental degenerations. In addition to resource depletion and pollution accumulation, sustainability can be threatened by congestion, it is often said. The point is that congestion implies a local exhaustion of resources (road space, living accommodations) or a local accumulation of pollution (climatological inversion, smoke stack emission) that could be remedied by changing the local concentration of resources or pollution. Often the build up of (human) population in a locale and therefore the localization of resource demand and pollution output account for congestion. Congestion, in other words, is a distributional, not a purely aggregative, concept.

This said, one might infer that the category of congestion is theoretically redundant. Still there seem four reasons for retaining the category: first, we must remember that degradation is sometimes a function of the concentration of causes at a site rather than of the absolute amount of the cause. Similarly, the duration of an effect is often a function of the intensity of the cause. Third, "the intensity of the cause" is regularly tied either to the intensity of human resource use or to the sheer prevalence of human beings on the planet. Fourth, remedies for environmental degradation being tied to the above three points, it is salient to focus on actual local conditions of congestion as a means of alleviating degradation and restoring sustainability.

Improved monitoring

Underlying many of the above problems lie issues of information flow. When information is missing, obscure or difficult and expensive to obtain, persons often proceed in ignorance. Possible efficiencies may go unrealized; realized efficiencies may not be signaled; signaled efficiencies may be obscured by further noise in the social system; market inefficiencies may go undetected; nonmarket coordinations may be obscured: common values may be hidden and common aspirations may be unassumed. What, then, do we know about human beings as monitors?

Every species has evolved in response to vulnerabilities imposed on it and opportunities presented to it by the environment in which its ancestors have lived. The human species is biologically unique because of the ratio of its brain to body size. The human brain is an amazing organ. Requiring an extraordinary amount of continuous energy, the vulnerability the organ brings to the organism argues that only some extraordinary environmental complexity would have stimulated its development. Yet if we begin with the imprecise but consensus view that the hominid line developed on the African savannah, then we have as yet no explanation of why, among the large hunting mammals living on the savannah, brain size increased remarkably only in the hominid line; why when the hominid line proper had a distinctly large brain at its outset at least two million years ago, brains continued to enlarge over the next 1.8 million years.

Accordingly, biologists hold that the complex environment to which hominid's brains have responded is the society of their cohorts. In other words the fundamental problem driving this evolution has been social: how to gain knowledge about and assurances concerning others of one's kind. The reading of facial expressions and vocalizations and the memory of the dispositions of a cohort have been central to the hominid environment for millions of years. Humankind thus evolved in an environment already intricately social.

Human abilities to monitor each other, then, have developed within the traditional social environments of human life. Interpersonal cooperation, nonsymmetrical reliances of individuals on others, possibilities of alliances and possibilities of betrayals have been the stuff of human evolution. The abilities to comprehend gestures and read intentions off their smallest signs, the abilities to assure and to detect phony assurances are the stock in trade of a hominid's mastery of its (social!) environment. Detailed observations of a small number of constant cohorts were the hard work that drove the evolution of the hominid line.

Clearly, however, the social environments of most human beings have altered dramatically in historical times, especially since the industrial revolution. Cohorts of repeated interaction and cohorts of association are much larger than ever in human history. Intricate systems have sprung up for the organization of anonymous, mass society. While in some ways modern life has allowed individuality to flower, in other respects it has required that much human behavior become role-bound and institution-bound so that interactions can proceed easily in the absence of personal histories.

These changes in human society notwithstanding, it is well to focus the environments for which human cognitive and motivational responses are honed. Without affirming the perfection of those responses and without deprecating the capacities of human beings to adapt to social novelty, it is reasonable to believe that maximizing the opportunities of people to respond directly to the voices, faces, gestures, affirmations, assertions and assurances of others improves the quality of the information on the basis of which the humans respond.

Consider the particular success of small communities with curbside recycling. In general transportation expenses make curbside recycling prohibitively expensive in rural areas. Leaving them aside, however, studies find the percentage of participation and the percentage of waste reduction greatest in smaller towns. The apparent explanation of this difference is the nonovert pressure small town people sense to do their part for their town. Part of the confirmation of this explanation is that transients, whom one would expect to identify less with the town, recycle less. Part of the confirmation is that apartment dwellers, whose (non-)recycling is less observable, recycle less. Fluctuating membership of groups and the anonymity of members each detract from community participation.

Similarly, scale is central in delivery systems. Communication theorists have long known the geometrically increasing costs of communication lines in urban areas. Transportation theorists appreciate the complexity and importance of efficiency in delivery routes. These theories have become parts of the basis for movements within large cities toward neighborhood revitalization. The link is that vital neighborhoods contain a multitude of interlinked ties. People, in other words, repeatedly engage a reduced number of cohorts. Given that modern society is defined by a multiplicity of roles, vocational, economic, familial, educational, recreational, religious, etc., a plausible hypothesis is that neighborhoods so organized as to encompass all or most of these roles will so interactively and repeatedly engage persons as to reinforce their concern for each other and for the well-being of their community.

The Grounding of Ethics in Natural History

An ethic of sustainability is an ethic. Humans have not been especially perspicuous in understanding their ethics. Since ethics has something to do with

advocacy grounded in the distinction of right from wrong, ethical discussion often focuses on advocacy rather than on understanding the place of ethics in human life. The following is a melded discussion, first of what an ethic is, and then of what norms are appropriate for an ethic of sustainability.

The kind of creature that has an ethic is social and linguistic, for an ethic is a linguistic means of coordination of cohort behavior. A look at the history of the hominid line places what an ethic is and whatever justifiability an ethic may have in focus. The goal of social coordination is to enhance the well-being of individuals without, through coordination, imposing new harms or excessive limits. Eventually norms of social coordination emerge to that end. An ethic is the articulation, justification and criticism of those norms. A slice of history will suggest how society with an ethic emerges.

Four million years ago the climate was getting colder and less rain was falling in the tropical forest, which was consequently shrinking. Some of the primates who were thus losing their habitat for reasons they did not comprehend, our remote ancestors among them, began to move out onto the surrounding savannah. There they encountered many established large mammal species, both herbivorous and carnivorous. Stereoscopic vision they probably had. In the perspective of evolutionary time, they moved quickly, as populations in strange habitats often do, toward a fully upright gait and a loss of brachiation. These animals, already social, also underwent a swift evolution in brain size. Surprisingly, in the line leading to *Homo sapiens*, brain size continued to increase until approximately 100,000 years ago, reaching a point where it requires approximately 20% of an adult's total energy intake and up to 50% of the intake of a human infant.

Evolutionary biologists agree that, however stressful the savannah environment might have been for its mammalian inhabitants, those common stresses cannot explain why one line developed such an extraordinary brain. Instead they find the root of increasing brain size in the extraordinary stress faced by that line arising from the complexity of its intense social living. Exactly how that complexity formed is unknown, but some of its outlines are clear: The lengthening of childhood implied the strengthening of ties among adult support networks. Peer interaction among juveniles promoted the exercising and development of social skills. Squabbles among juveniles provoked partisan adult intervention. The advantages of social harmony promoted adult learning about interventions that avoid not only violence but also hard feelings within support networks. The cessation of estrus, ongoing moderate adult female sexual receptivity, extended relationships between sexual partners, food sharing, and a significant contribution of an adult male's labor to the well-being of his sexual partner(s) and her or their offspring are somehow comingled in the formation of the family as a social unit.

In other words, given that the hominid line lacked the adaptations that secured success for other savannah species, the hominid line relied heavily on strength emerging from numbers and social cohesion. A division of hominid labor, however, unlike a division of bee or ant labor, is not rigidly genetically determined. If instead it is a division to be worked out, then it is a division requiring the likes of trust and assurance. At the same time, the need for trust and assurance amounts to the social possibility of betrayal. For all communities, spread over many generations, circumstances will continually vary between those in which an individual benefits from the existence of mutual aid networks and those in which an individual benefits from striking his (more often than her) own path or ignoring an opportunity for aiding one's cohorts.

The problem then for hominid society becomes centrally social: how to scrutinize the social scene so as to discern the trustworthiness of cohorts. Associated are the individual's problems both of providing the assurance that will make others willing to cooperate and of gaining the freedom to go one's own way or tend one's own concerns without endangering either one's self, one's offspring or the future reliability of one's social network.

In this context the ability to read the motivation of others and the abilities both to show one's genuineness well enough to enlist the aid of others and to conceal one's disposition well enough to avoid becoming others' transparent dupe undergo intense stress. Many coordinations may occur, but breakdowns of coordination will be dangerous and may become violent. It is of course relevant to note how often the advent of modern warfare is interpreted in the light of energy supplies.

Intracohort violence can threaten the security of a social species by reducing numbers, by weakening cohorts to attack from outside the community, and by poisoning the social atmosphere against future cooperation. Intracohort violence, therefore, is dangerous to the survival of a species whose strength emerges from its social ties. At this juncture, the social value of the emotional predisposition toward shame at being implicated in the death of a dear (to one) or valuable (to one) cohort may be that the predisposition may move an animal to shrink in horror from bringing about such a result. Such a predisposition will have the effect of reducing violence and replacing much possible violence with posturing.

The point of speaking of an emotional predisposition is two-fold. First, all social primates have emotional dispositions. Such dispositions are mechanisms much older than language, and consequently, ethics, for regulating social intercourse. Their regulative capacity builds on not only the fundamental social character of those primates' lives but, in a layered fashion, on the fact that behavioral and monitoring problems have become evolutionary problems for earlier generations that had emotional capacities. Thus, emotions respond to the emotions of others and even to the emotions of the self. (One may be frustrated or ashamed that one is angry, for instance.)

Second, a primate emotional disposition is not always overwhelming. Clearly, human behavior does not follow rigidly and inevitably from such dispositions. Circumstances may be so dangerous that expression of the disposition may be preempted. Circumstances may be so suspicious that expression of the disposition is checked. In ongoingly oppressive environments the repression of those predispositions may be learned.

In summary, if in social insects social coordination results from a genetically pre-established harmony, in primates the harmony requires significant reading of peer behavior, the stimulus of social emotions and trial-and-error learning about social interaction. Norms of behavior, intact not only with sanctions against violation but also with socially astute tolerances for indiscretions, are already displayed in baboon and chimpanzee societies. Whatever the limitations of such norms, they tend to contribute to social stability and a degree of harmony.

All of the preceding observations and language are among the human tools for the social coordination central to the general animalian capacity for behavior. Animals have evolved from the advantage an organism may obtain from movement. That is, what is good for an animal regularly requires some behavior by the animal for its realization. The animal does a right, or fitting, or appropriate, thing if the behavior in which it engages is at least behavior that tends to be effective in bringing about or maintaining or restoring some facet of well-being. For social species, a right behavior often does not by itself bring about, maintain, or restore any facet of well-being. If the right behavior affects well-being at all, it does so because it is part of a network of behaviors that affect well-being interdependently.

Whenever language had become a part of human life, all of the preceding was already in the fabric of human society. Actual human practices show us that eventually our social emotions have been supplemented both by articulations of them and by reasonings about the underlying goods and bads of human life and about strategies for promoting the goods and avoiding the bads. Language has become integral to what ethics is. As much as humans may be repulsed by the wrong or tempted to it, they can also articulate what is wrong with it, if it indeed is wrong, and what is attractive about it, if indeed it is attractive. They can reason whether the articulated wrong and the articulated attractiveness are finally incompatible with each other. They can reason about whether their belief that the two are compatible is insight or desire-induced delusion. When they define the bads and who is likely to suffer them, they can devise strategies and new norms for avoiding the bads or for making the suffering fairer. (As such, this article has attempted to define and discuss sustainability as a norm of energy use.)

Language is useful directly for improving the social coordination through which a hominid society pursues the good. Language provides its users with means of abstract foci of attention (on the shape or the movement of an object, for instance). Language allows its users to speak of what is not present (the animal that will come to the watering hole) and to use such talk to plan (a sequence of coordinated actions). Language allows its speakers to interpret themselves to others ("What I really want is . . ." "I believe that . . ."), thereby obviating problems of interpretation for trusted or desired allies, while increasing the complexity of problems of interpretation for those who are distrusted and those who are not convinced they are viewed kindly.

Human ethics, then, are not framed simply by emotional dispositions. Part of human intelligence is the ability to observe a recurrence of circumstances and to note that more and less happy effects result from different initiatives. Some behavioral dispositions, human beings may come to believe, are so generally conducive to social facility or harmony that those dispositions are generally or universally to be endorsed, commended, encouraged, and reinforced.

Honesty, courage, and wisdom are often commended as universal human virtues precisely on the argument that the (social) character of human life, regardless of the eccentricities of social organization, is bound to benefit from these dispositions. That is, the veracity of information, resoluteness in the face of danger and discernment of subtle distinctions through which beneficial and enriching pursuits become feasible, is bound to be valuable in human life because of the complex phenomenon that human society is. Because social life is bound to benefit from information-sharing and coordinated planning, for example, honesty and promise-keeping are bound to be excellences; that is, behavioral dispositions such that a society whose members have and act upon, will benefit as a society but whose members lack or do not act upon those dispositions will not.

The evaluation of sustainability

The virtue of sustainability is similar; that is, organisms require energy to maintain themselves. Organisms use some of the energy available to them to enhance the assurance of a reliable energy supply. A social animal places its reliance in its creation of a social network. Inconstancy in the supply of energy will mean either that individuals directly suffer a curtailment of energy available to them or that the energy devoted to the social network for assuring energy supplies, is itself curtailed. In the first of these cases, the quality of individuals' lives is diminished. In the second, the well-being of a society's future is jeopardized. In this way a social network establishes itself because having the network improves a population's ability to survive (and reproduce). Within primates, such social networks involve patterns of behavior that evolve, are learned by individuals, and are monitored and reinforced by concerned community members. Obviously, then, if an ethic is the articulation, justification, and criticism of a set of social norms, and if the norms themselves are justified by the social well-being they maintain, then sustainability must be a virtue because, regardless of the eccentricities of social organization, the character of human life is bound to benefit if people act not only honestly, courageously and wisely, but also sustainably.

A corollary concerns the place of actions that are not sustainable. If reliance upon those actions for energy supplies, either for individuals or for maintaining the society's assurance structure, is wrong because it is not sustainable, then the more fitting use of non-renewable resources is for boot-strapping. If, having created enhancements of human well-being, the resources needed for the enhancements are no longer needed for its maintenance, then the nonrenewability of the resource is morally unproblematic. To be sure, it is sometimes difficult to foresee whether a present use of a nonrenewable resource will later become superfluous. It is not difficult, however, to observe that many present human uses of resources is the non-boot-strapping use of nonrenewables. It is also possible and prudent, when planning the use of a nonrenewable, both to monitor the confinement of its use and to take systematic and diligent steps to outgrow its use.

If some dispositions are universally beneficial, others are less so. In particular, many matters of convention gain the benefit they have, partly or totally, from the establishment of the convention. Property rights in Anglo-American society imply that trespassing is wrong. Property rights in Scandinavian society do not prohibit temporary, non-degrading uses, say of pasture lands. While it is obvious that well-known, widely respected conventions promote the meeting, rather than the frustrating, of expectations, it is not obvious that one of these conventions is better in the sense that a society having it enriches the society or improves its sustainability.

At the same time, it is clear that a convention, established at a given time, is designed to handle a foreseen range of cases. For instance, the so-called taking clause of the Fifth Amendment to the Constitution of the United States prohibits the government's taking of a person's property without compensation. Seizure, eviction, preemptive use of the land for public purposes, all of these were foreseen cases. Case law on the prohibition of coal excavation because of its impact on surface useful-ness, on zoning against the downwind effects of smelting and other polluting activities, and on government limitations on the filling of wetlands, have all raised unforeseen issues about when the use of property is rightly restricted to prevent public nuisance or harm versus when an owner has been deprived of economic benefit for the sake of promoting a public good.

Whether, then, a social norm is appropriate, can be evaluated in four distinct ways: to what extent is the norm one of those that reinforces and promotes the dispositions that are valuable in any human society? To what extent does a norm promote the improvement of well-being without, through the use of nonrenewables or the creation of pollutants, substantially endangering well-being elsewhere? To what extent have emerging natural, technical, demographic, or social circumstances skewed the reliance on established norms so that they are not so beneficial or at least neutral as they had been or had been interpreted to have been? And, finally, to what extent is the norm one of those that establishes and facilitates human coordination and, thus, social harmony through means that disrupt goods in either the natural or the social world?

In the light of these criteria, we may evaluate the development of norms for international cooperation regarding environmental concerns. An older practice of norm development for the sake of international cooperation about energy sustainability had been a lowest common denominator standard. From the premise that the international order includes few means of imposing cooperation, it was inferred both that cooperation cannot be constrained and that the only universally achievable standard would be the lowest standard acceptable to any of the nations seeking an agreement.

That practice has been substantially superseded since the early 1980s. The lowest common denominator standard, it has been realized, discouraged nations from seeking mutually beneficial higher standards, misestimated the effect of higher standards on nations obviously falling below those standards, and ignored the often-positive dynamic of higher standards towards the creations of technologies and conventions that facilitate compliance from previously noncomplying countries.

The emerging standard is one of a patch-work of boot-strapping agreements. The dynamics of such agreements not only boast the floor of coordination. Rather, they also encourage new coordinations and additional partnerships. Instead of a norm focused on the avoidance of problems, emerging international norms are focused on the pursuit of goods.

The Ethics of Sustainability

Trends in energy conservation, pollution control, population growth, urban planning, and economic development have brought the concept of sustainability to international attention. Yet substantial fuzziness remains in the concept. That fuzziness arises partly from the multiplicity of goods at which actions aim, the multiple uses of resources and the multiple effects of these uses. Different foci then allow the construction of plausible arguments that resources are both sustainable and insustainable and that fuzziness arises significantly from disagreement about what is to be sustained. Set aside the idea that choice is to be sustained and sustainability can either be a matter of lifestyles or of resources. With each of those discussions, one must question how holistically sustainability is to be understood. The key to a non-fascistic but holistic understanding of the sustainability of resources is to conceive resources themselves non-anthropocentrically: all forms of life use resources. From that perspective the functional value intrinsic to an ecosystem provides the only clarity humans presently have about what value sustainability has and why. The most clearly sustainable resources are renewable. The danger that no adequate substitute will be found for some nonrenewable resource grounds the argument that nonsustainable resources, if used, should be used for bootstrapping, not for lifestyle maintenance.

Indeed, the hardest and riskiest way to fulfill the obligation of sustainability to our descendants is to predicate sustainability as the product of an unending substitution of resources. As many substitutions as human history records, the record clearly shows much suffering and non-sustainability for individuals in the midst of substitution. Even the attribution of that suffering to normal market adjustments will not gainsay the moral significance the suffering retains, both because lives are centrally disrupted and because the vulnerability of the disrupted lives underlines the nonconsensual character of their disruption.

The Ethics of Sustainable Energy

The application of these norms to the achievement of energy sustainability, however, requires effort in several areas, for "energy sustainability" continues to have different meanings. It is entirely possible that "energy sustainability" will come to mean the continual availability of adequate energy for human beings of means. If one focuses on the sustainability of human society in the aggregate, then local societies and poorer classes may be dispensable to that sustainability (a matter of fact, true to some degree depending on violence resulting from discontent, etc) and judged and accounted as such (a matter of practice, policy and ethics). It is entirely possible that "energy sustainability" will come to mean the continued availability of adequate energy for human beings if acceptable materials and technologies continue to replace exhausted energy resources. If one focuses on the possible gains of a high-risk energy policy, then a larger group of human beings, perhaps persons of all classes, might suffer substantially from misfortunate calculation. The very suffering that sustainability is primarily directed at averting is made more probable by reliance on scarce, non-renewable energy sources, or on ones the use of which creates significant pollution. It is entirely possible that "energy sustainability" will come to mean making the planet not metaphorically but literally "spaceship earth," a planet composed almost exclusively of human beings, materials used as resources for them, and the technologies required for that use. In that case our immense ignorance of ecosystems will assure that before the planet becomes so composed, the human beings will cease to be one of the components.

When Plato advanced the thesis he called the unity of the virtues, the view that each virtue is identical with the several others, he defended it by arguing both that in the ideal case the virtues coincide and that in the total absence of the one, the others are also impossible. Whatever the considerable difficulties of Plato's argumentation, the wisdom of this view is that of cautiously maintaining the coherence that allows several goods to be achieved, or at least approached, simultaneously. Since it is impossible to maximize simultaneously for more than one desideratum, the achievement of several goals requires caution not to make any of them one's sole, or even predominant, guiding light and, indeed, deliberately to pursue each only in ways that facilitate, rather than hinder, the achievement of others.

The outlines of the achievement of energy sustainability are therefore three-fold. First, sufficient poverty exists to drive human population growth, thereby increasing the energy supply required to sustain human life. Honesty requires humans to affirm that the problem is hard enough and that making the problem harder will increase the likelihood that wide-spread social and ecological harm will precede energy sustainability. From this caution must derive the fundamental courage to attack poverty worldwide as a prerequisite of achieving energy sustainability. Otherwise, in wisdom, we discern that the price of sustainability for some will be ongoing social tension, violence, bloodshed, and warfare.

Second, the scale of the operation of maintaining energy supplies for human beings implies a moral demand not only for increasing the efficiency with which the demand is met but, quite significantly, with constraining the pollution of present-day demand meeting. The harms of pollution and their projectable ballooning as developing nations command larger supplies of dirty energy, combine with the unevenness of access to such energy to demand the courage of the immediate pursuit of both the short-term goals of purity and efficiency of using non-renewable energy supplies, and, the longer-term goal of conversion to solar (including wind) and other, hydral forms of renewable energy. Premises about the probable half-century lag time in developing new energy technologies and stabilizing world human population aid discernment of the wisdom of immediate deployment of these strategies. And honesty requires a clear, undiluted statement of the risks, lest people be self-deceptively lulled into ignoring them.

Third, the fuzziness of our understanding of ecosystems and of the myriad species that compose them, argues, in conjunction with the importance of understanding sustainability, for improving human biological knowledge. In our current state of considerable ignorance, the fuzziness of our understanding of ecosystems argues, in light of the value of sustainability, for prudence. Prudence implies relieving the poverty that provides the impetus to human population growth, encouraging healthy, energy-efficient lifestyles chosen informedly in the light of prices that thoroughly reflect

costs, and converting energy production to renewable, non-polluting forms. Interestingly, the pursuit of a lifestyle that is not oriented around consumption helps to bring human beings occasions evoking the wisdom involved in discerning and appreciating the good that the integrity of an ecosystem is. Honesty, however, requires the acknowledgment that, like an ecological ethic, a wide-spread ecological consciousness remains no more than what Aldo Leopold called an evolutionary possibility.

Bibliography

Caring for the Earth: A Strategy for Sustainable Living, Earthscan, London, 1991.

A Compendium of Energy Conservation Success Stories, U.S. Department of Energy, Office of Conservation, Washington, D.C., 1988.

Comprehensive National Energy Policy Act of 1992, House of Representatives, One Hundred Second Congress, second session, April 9, 1992, Washington, U.S. Government Printing Office, Supt. of Documents, Congressional Sales Office, 1992.

Controlling Summer Heat Islands: Workshop on Saving Energy and Reducing Atmospheric Pollution by Controlling Summer Heat Islands, Washington, D.C.: U.S. Dept. of Energy, Building Systems Division, Office of Building and Community Systems, 1989.

Energy Efficiency and Renewable Energy Research, Development, and Demonstration, United States Senate, One Hundred First Congress, first session, on S. 488, S. 964 June 15, 1989, Washington, U.S. Government Printing Office, Supt. of Documents, Congressional Sales Office, 1989.

Energy Tax Incentives, United States Senate, One Hundred Second Congress, first session, on S. 26, S. 83, S. 129, S. 141, S. 201, S. 326, S. 466, S. 661, S. 679, S. 731, S. 741, S. 743, S. 992, S. 1157, and S. 1178, June 13 and 14, 1991, Washington, U.S. Government Printing Office, Supt. of Documents, Congressional Sales Office, 1991.

Energy 2000: A Global Strategy for Sustainable Development: A Report for the World Commission on Environment and Development, London, Zed Books, Atlantic Highlands, N.J., 1987.

Global Environment: A National Energy Strategy, House of Representatives, One Hundred First Congress, second session, on H.R. 5521 a bill to establish the global environmental consequences of current trends in atmospheric concentrations of greenhouse gases, September 13, 1990, Washington, U.S. Government Printing Office, Supt. of Documents, Congressional Sales Office, 1991.

Industrial Competitiveness through Energy Efficiency and Waste Minimization, United States Senate, One Hundred Third Congress, first session, April 29, 1993, Washington, U.S. Government Printing Office, Supt. of Documents, Congressional Sales Office, 1993.

Old Growth Forests: Hearing before the Subcommittee on National Parks and Public Lands of the Committee on Interior and Insular Affairs, House of Representatives, One Hundred Second Congress, first session, on H.R. 842, Ancient Forest Protection Act of 1991, H.R. 1590, Ancient Forest Act of 1991, hearing held in Washington, DC, April 25, 1991, Washington, U.S. Government Printing Office, Supt. of Documents, Congressional Sales Office, 1992.

Renewable Energy and Energy Efficiency Technology Competitiveness Act of 1989, U.S. House of Representatives, One Hundred First Congress, first session, May 23, 1989, Washington, U.S. Government Printing Office, Supt. of Documents, Congressional Sales Office, 1989.

Renewable Energy Technologies, House of Representatives, One Hundred First Congress, first session, on H.R. 1216, April 26, 1989, Washington, U.S. Government Printing Office, Supt. of Documents, Congressional Sales Office, 1989.

Regulation of Registered Electric Utility Holding Companies, United States Senate, One Hundred Second Congress, second session, on S. 2607, hearing held on May 14, 1992, Washington, U.S. Government Printing Office, Supt. of Documents, Congressional Sales Office, 1992.

Report to Congress: Coal Refineries – A Definition and Example Concepts, Washington, D. C., United States Department of Energy, July, 1991, pp. 38–44.

Retiring Old Cars: Programs to Save Gasoline and Reduce Emissions, Washington, D.C., U.S. Government Printing Office, Supt. of Documents, Congressional Sales Office, 1992.

State Initiatives to Promote a Diversified Energy Resource Base, U.S. House of Representatives, One Hundred Second Congress, first session, December 12, 1991, Washington, U.S. Government Printing Office, Supt. of Documents, Congressional Sales Office, 1992.

W. Aiken, "Human Rights in an Ecological Era," *Environmental Values*, The White Horse Press, Cambridge, UK, Autumn, 1992.

H. S. Burness, "Risk: Accounting for the Future," *Natural Resources Journal* (Oct. 1981).

B. R. Barkovich, *Regulatory Interventionism in the Utility Industry: Fairness, Efficiency, and the Pursuit of Energy Conservation*, Quorum Books, New York, 1989.

R. Costanza, ed., *Ecological Economics: The Science and Management of Sustainability*, Columbia University Press, New York, 1991.

H. Daly and J. Cobb, *For Our Common Good*, Beacon Press, Boston, Mass., 1989.

P. L. Fiedler and S. K. Jain, eds., *Conservation Biology: The Theory and Practice of Nature Conservation, Pre-servation, and Management*, Chapman and Hall, New York, 1992.

W. Fox, *Toward a Transpersonal Ecology: Developing New Foundations for Environmentalism*, Shambhala Publications Inc., Boston, Mass., 1990.

B. Furze, "Ecologically Sustainable Rural Development and the Difficulty of Social Change," *Environmental Values*. The White Horse Press, Cambridge, UK, Summer, 1992.

A. M. Friend, "Economics, Ecology and Sustainable Development: Are They Compatible?" *Environmental Values*. The White Horse Press, Cambridge, UK, Summer, 1992.

J. Garbarino, *Toward a Sustainable Society: An Economic, Social and Environmental Agenda for Our Children's Future*, Noble Press, Chicago, Ill., 1993.

J. P. Gates, *Sustainable or Alternative Agriculture: January 1990–September 1992*, National Agricultural Library, Beltsville, Md., 1993.

D. Hafemeister, H. Kelly, and B. Levi, eds., *Energy Sources: Conservation and Renewables*, American Institute of Physics, New York, 1985.

Heraclitus, *Heraclitus: Fragments*, translation with a commentary by T.M. Robinson, Toronto, Ont., and London, University of Toronto Press, 1987.

J. M. Hollander, ed., *The Energy–Environment Connection*, Island Press, Washington, D.C., 1992.

R. B. Howarth, "Intergenerational Justice and the Chain of Obligation," *Environmental Values*, The White Horse Press, Cambridge, Summer, 1992.

R. Howes, and A. Fainberg, eds., *The Energy Sourcebook: A Guide to Technology, Resources, and Policy*, American Institute of Physics, New York, 1991.

F. A. Khavari, *Environomics: the Economics of Environmentally Safe Prosperity*, Praeger, Westport, Conn., 1993.

J. T. MacLean, *Sustainable or Alternative Agriculture, January 1982–December 1989*, National Agricultural Library, Beltsville, Md., 1990.

M. V. Melosi, *Coping with Abundance: Energy and Environment in Industrial America*. Temple University Press, Philadelphia, Pa., 1985.

J. S. Mill "The Stationary State," in *Principles of Political Economy*, 5th edn: Appleton and Company, New York, 1897.

B. G. Norton, "Sustainability, Human Welfare and Ecosystem Health," *Environmental Values*, The White Horse Press, Cambridge, UK, Summer, 1992.

B. G. Norton, *Why Preserve Natural Variety?*. Princeton University Press, Princeton, N.J., 1987.

D. Parfit, "Energy Policy and the Further Future," Center for Philosophy and Public Policy, University of Maryland College, Park, Md., Feb. 23, 1981.

E. Partridge, "On the Rights of Future Generations," in Scherer, D., ed., *Upstream / Downstream Issues in Environmental Ethics*, Temple University Press, Philadelphia, Pa., 1991.

Donald Scherer

E. Partridge, *Responsibilities to Future Generations*, Prometheus Books, Buffalo, N.Y., 1981, c1980.

D. Pearce, and co-workers, *Blueprint 2: Greening the World Economy*, London, Earthscan Publications in association with the London Environmental Economics Centre, London, 1991.

D. W. Pearce, and J. J. Warford, *World without End: Economics, Environment, and Sustainable Development*. Published for the World Bank [by] Oxford University Press, New York, 1993.

J. Pezzey, "Sustainability: An Interdisciplinary Guide," *Environmental Values*, The White Horse Press, Cambridge, UK, Winter, 1992.

S. L. Pimm, *The Balance of Nature?: Ecological Issues in the Conservation of Species and Communities*, University of Chicago Press, Chicago Ill., 1991.

D. Rothenberg, "Individual or Community? Two Approaches to Ecophilosophy in Practice," *Environmental Values*, The White Horse Press, Cambridge, UK, Summer, 1992.

J. W. Russell, *Economic Disincentives for Energy Conservation*. Ballinger Publishing Co., Cambridge, Mass., 1979.

M. Sagoff, *The Economy of the Earth*, Cambridge University Press, New York, 1988.

M. Sagoff, "Property Rights and Environmental Law," *Philosophy and Public Policy* (Spring 1988).

D. Saxe, "The Fiduciary Duty of Corporate Directors to Protect the Environment for Future Generations," *Environmental Values*, The White Horse Press, Cambridge, UK, Autumn, 1992.

D. Scherer, "A Disentropic Ethic," *The Monist* (Winter, 1988).

D. Scherer, "Towards an Upstream/Downstream Morality for our Upstream/Downstream World," in R. Blatz, ed., *Water Resources, Water Ethics*, University of Idaho Press, 1990.

K. R. Schneider, *Alternative Farming Systems, Economic Aspects: January 1991–January 1993*, National Agricultural Library, Beltsville, Md., 1993.

K. Shrader-Frechette, "Ethical Dilemmas and Radioactive Waste: A Survey of the Issues," *Environmental Ethics* (Winter, 1991).

K. Shrader-Frechette, *Risk Analysis and Scientific Method*, D. Reidel, Boston, Mass., 1985.

K. Shrader-Frechette, *Risk and Rationality: Philosophical Foundations for Populist Reforms*, University of California Press, Berkeley, Calif., 1991.

K. Shrader-Frechette, "Models, Scientific Method and Environmental Ethics," in Scherer, D., ed., *Upstream / Downstream Issues in Environmental Ethics*, Temple University Press, Philadelphia, Pa., 1991.

M. E. Soule, and K. A. Kohm, eds., *Research Priorities for Conservation Biology*, Island Press, Washington, D.C., 1989.

I. F. Spellberg, *Evaluation and Assessment for Conservation: Ecological Guidelines for Determining Priorities for Nature Conservation*, Chapman & Hall, London, 1992.

C. D. Stone, *Earth and Other Ethics: The Case for Moral Pluralism*, Harper & Row, New York, 1987.

E. O. Wilson, *The Diversity of Life*, Belknap Press of Harvard University Press, Cambridge, Mass., 1992.

L. Wittgenstein, *Philosophical Investigations*, trans. G. E. M. Anscombe, New York, Macmillan, 1953.

26

Toward a Just and Sustainable Economic Order

John B. Cobb, Jr.

Many morally concerned people today believe we should make moderate changes in the present economic order so as to render it just and sustainable. Others, however, and I am one of them, believe the basic principles that govern the global economy today inherently lead to increasing injustice and unsustainability. Policies based on these principles concentrate wealth in fewer hands, leaving the poor more destitute. They transfer wealth from poorer to richer countries. And they speed the destruction of natural resources, especially in the poorer countries. Reforms within the system can moderate these tendencies, but they cannot basically change them. If we are concerned for either justice or sustainability, we must envision, and work for, a different economic system.

At present there is little discussion of alternatives. Many assume that the only options are the present global market economy, on the one hand, and the bureaucratically managed economy, on the other. The latter has shown itself, particularly in eastern Europe and China, to be inseparable from political injustice and oppression. It has also shown itself to be inefficient in its use of resources, whereas sustainability requires efficiency. To suppose that these are the only options limits us to a choice between two unjust and unsustainable systems. We need to envision ways of organizing the global economy that differ from both.

This article offers some principles and outlines of an alternative economic system that has the possibility of being both sustainable and just.

After expounding the vision that now shapes our national and international policies and institutions, their achievements and limitations are addressed. The principle of "sustainable development" is analyzed, its shortcomings noted, and an alternative proposed.

The Vision That Now Guides Us

The most important change in the global order after World War II was the shift from a primarily political world system to a primarily economic one. This shift is not manifest in the United Nations. It *was* clearly expressed at the 1944 meeting at Bretton Woods, where the International Monetary Fund (IMF), and the World Bank were established, and shortly thereafter with the General Agreement on Tariffs and Trade (GATT; Kock, 1969; Van Dormael, 1978). Whereas the United Nations was designed to deal with international affairs, assuming the continuing sovereignty of states, the institutions generated at Bretton Woods were designed to deal with the global economy. The most powerful nations are now cooperating for the sake of the growth of the global economy. Competition is among firms across national boundaries. Through trade agreements, the governments of even the most powerful nations have systematically given up their ability to control these economic actors by raising tariffs or other actions deemed to be in restraint of trade. They have also greatly restricted the ability of the weaker nations to do so (Raghavan, 1990).

This massive shift of power from nations to transnational corporations was long obscured by the cold war. The shift occurred within the First World, but public attention was riveted on the confrontation between the First and Second Worlds. At the deepest level this, too, was economic, and it was the vastly greater growth of the First World system that led to the collapse of the Second. But the political and military conflict was more visible. Now that this conflict has drastically diminished, and the Second World is seeking entry into the First World system, the primacy of the global economic order is apparent.

In the past the United Nations provided a forum for debate about economic issues in which the concerns of the poorer nations were voiced. But this debate had little influence on actual global economic policies, and today it has been largely silenced. Serious discussion of economic matters takes place only in those institutions created after World War II to give new shape to the planet. Political agreements needed to attain the goals of the global economic institutions are made through negotiations among the major economic powers, most visibly through the annual economic summit of leaders from the big seven economic powers.

The policies of these powers, and of the global institutions they largely control, are shaped for their economic benefit. However, one should not view this cynically. The goal of Bretton Woods was to increase the rate of economic growth *globally*. It has been assumed throughout that global economic growth benefits all. The enemy is not the self-interest of individual nations but is seen as policies that slow this global growth.

Economic theory from the time of Adam Smith (1776/1991) has viewed the one engine of growth as being rational, competitive behavior in the market. In this view all sell their labor and goods as dearly as possible and acquire the labor and goods of others as cheaply as possible. This brings about efficient allocation of resources, improved organization, and technological development. These, in turn, cause increased production and lower prices; in short, economic growth. The chief obstacle to such growth is viewed as imposition of restrictions by governments. Although all governments necessarily impose some restrictions, according to standard economic theory these should be kept to a minimum.

Equally important is the size of the market. The larger the market, the more specialization can be achieved within it. Increased specialization leads to "economies of scale," that is, to increased efficiency, lower prices, and more consumption. Most nations have national markets within which investments and goods flow freely and a high degree of specialization is possible. Since World War II the goal has been a global free market that allows for much greater specialization internationally.

The major obstacle to this global market is restriction placed on economic action across national boundaries. Tariffs are imposed, exports are controlled, and ownership of business by outsiders is limited. These policies cause the people of a country to produce for themselves what could be produced more cheaply by others. Total production is less than it could be.

The global economic institutions work to reduce all such barriers to trade with their accompanying inefficiencies. Ratification by all national participants of the recently completed GATT negotiations (called the Uruguay Round) will go a long way toward realizing these goals. It will establish the World Trade Organization (WTO) as the arbiter of international disputes. Meanwhile, short of global economic integration, the free market can be expanded regionally. The two most important expansions thus far have been the European Community and the North American Free Trade Agreement (NAFTA).

Success and Limitations

The single-minded pursuit of global economic growth has achieved many of its goals. From the end of World War II until around 1980 the global economy grew at a remarkable rate (Green, 1984). Some countries moved from poverty to affluence, inspiring others to see this as a possibility for themselves as well. At the same time, the already affluent nations greatly increased their wealth. The market magic worked. The growth of some was not at the expense of others but rather facilitated the growth of others.

Nonenvironmental issues

When one goal is pursued in this way, it is inevitable that there will be unintended side effects.

John B. C

Successful cases of rapid growth, such as South Korea, Taiwan, and Singapore, all had highly authoritarian governments during the important take-off stage. These were needed to maintain discipline in a laboring class that was being severely exploited (Bello and Rosenfeld, 1990). However, when growth reached a certain level, some of the prosperity was shared with the workers, and at that point the governments could become less authoritarian. Although few citizens of democracies are attracted to these methods, the promise that in time the exploited would also profit from the policies required for growth has come true to a considerable degree. Thus the general conviction that rapid economic growth makes possible the solution of other problems, including those it creates, has been reinforced.

A second problem has been that the breakdown of established communities, inherent in growth-oriented policies, has led to the moral decay of some societies. For example, in many tropical countries the displacement of peasant farms with modern agribusiness monoculture has reduced the need for farm labor and sent millions of people to the slums surrounding cities. There traditional social values are hard to maintain. This breakdown can be illustrated in the United States as well, where levels of family instability, crime, drugs, and social alienation have increased along with the urbanization associated with growth of the gross national product (GNP). This raises questions about the wisdom of our primary commitment to growth-oriented policies. The reply is often that more growth is needed in order to reintegrate alienated people into the economic system and to have the resources to deal with all social needs.

A third problem is that, alongside the success stories, there are other countries in which economic growth has not kept up with the increase of population (Brown, 1987). This is especially common in sub-Saharan Africa. In many of these countries growth-oriented policies have concentrated wealth in fewer hands, so that masses of the people are much poorer than they were before these policies were put into effect.

The response is usually that this results from imperfect implementation of market policies. Too many governments have tried to manage economic developments bureaucratically, have taxed business too much, have inhibited free trade, have yielded to political pressures (David, 1985). On this assump-

tion the task is to overcome t business activity and allow the rapidly enough to absorb the ur prove the standard of living of a ing agreements imposed by the countries move in this direction

Environmental issues

A fourth problem has been environmental. When firms compete with each other in the free market, their decisions are not guided by environmental considerations. They can produce more cheaply when they dispose of their wastes in the least expensive way – for example, in the nearest river. The loss of fish is costly to fishermen, and the loss of recreational areas diminishes the quality of life for others, but as long as competitors are also disposing of wastes in this cheap way, no manufacturer can afford to do otherwise. The cost is borne by society as a whole. Recognizing this, all advanced industrial nations have rules governing the disposal of industrial waste.

Most advocates of the free market affirm the need of such rules. They recognize that market activity has unintended side effects that transfer costs to third parties. These are called "externalities" (Daly and Cobb, 1994). In an ideal market all externalities would be internalized, so that the purchaser pays the full cost of the goods. As long as all producers within the market abide by the same rules, there is "a level playing field."

Unfortunately, the desirability of internalizing social costs through governmental regulations has not been assimilated into the thinking of most of the economists who influence policies. The problem is particularly acute as free markets are expanded beyond national boundaries. When this happens, differing regulations in the countries involved destroy the level playing field and give the advantage to industries in the country with the lowest standards.

The progressive reduction of barriers to trade between the United States and Mexico during the 1980s serves as an example of the problem. As tariffs were reduced, many U.S. companies found it more economical to relocate production across the border. One reason they could produce more cheaply there was that they did not have to spend money on expensive waste disposal. They could dump their wastes into the Rio Grande. They ship their products back into the United States to undersell the goods of competitors who were subject to U.S. rules. Now it is recognized that the river should be cleaned up. The best proposals now being considered at the governmental level are for an expenditure of nine billion dollars for this purpose. The Sierra Club estimates that the cost for a real cleanup would be twenty-one billion dollars (Sierra Club, 1993, p. 16). In any case, these costs are to be borne primarily by the taxpayers and concerned citizens of Mexico and the United States, rather than by the polluters.

In the negotiation of NAFTA under the Bush administration, little attention was given to these environmental matters. The goal was to secure existing U.S. investments in Mexico, improve the climate for additional investment, and thus increase the total growth rate of North America. The Clinton administration was more concerned with environmental issues, but the basic problem of the lack of a level playing field was still dealt with only tangentially in a side agreement to NAFTA.

The problem is not only with regard to those plants that actually move across the border. The problem is also with legislation within the United States. If a state desires, for environmental reasons, to enact new restrictive legislation, it is told that more of its businesses will move away. In view of the number of polluting industries that have already moved across the Mexican border, it is clear that this is not always an idle threat! If the industry wishes to remain in the United States, it may still find it advantageous to move – from California to Utah, for example. The extension of the free market beyond political boundaries inherently makes it more difficult to slow environmental decay within those boundaries.

The exhaustion of resources is a somewhat different problem. With regard to pollution, the problem is that those committed to economic growth fail to pay attention to an accepted economic principle, namely, that external costs should be internalized. With regard to resources, the problem is that economic thinking has not developed the needed principle – instead, it is based on the idea that natural resources are, for practical purposes, inexhaustible.

The assumption of inexhaustible resources has gained repeated reinforcement from experience. For example, when an ore is said to be exhausted, this means only that mining the remaining inferior grades of ore is not profitable at current prices

with current technology. As prices rise and new technology is developed, more ore can be extracted. Also, plastics can be devised as substitutes for scarce minerals. Thus economists typically hold that we should give technological ingenuity a free hand and allow the market to provide the needed incentives.

Unfortunately, this theory has led to blindness to the actual effects of the free market in many parts of the world. Since industry is the sector of the economy capable of continuing growth, growth-oriented policies emphasize the export of whatever is available in order to bring in the capital needed for industrialization. In many countries the available resource most desired by the global market is lumber. Accordingly, the earth as a whole is being rapidly deforested.

To understand what is happening, Allen Durning asks us to imagine a time lapse film of the earth.

> Since 1950 vast tracts of forest vanish from Japan, the Philippines, and the mainland of Southeast Asia, from most of Central America and the horn of Africa, from western North America and eastern South America, from the Indian subcontinent and sub-Saharan Africa. Fires rage in the Amazon basin where they never did before. Central Europe's forests die, poisoned by the air and the rain. Southeast Asia looks like a dog with the mange. Malaysian Borneo is scalped.... The clearing spreads to Siberia and the Canadian north. (Durning, 1994, p. 22)

It is almost meaningless to speak of substituting other resources for forest cover. The loss of forest cover leads to extensive erosion, which limits the possibility of reforestation. It also destroys large tracts of agricultural land. It leads to the extinction of species. It takes away the livelihood of those who have depended on this resource. It changes the weather both locally and globally. There is no way in which its costs could be adequately internalized, although, if economists had undertaken such calculations, this might have helped to slow down the process of deforestation. Technology, in the form of developing new types of trees that grow more rapidly and survive on poorer soil, can play a positive role once the devastation has occurred, but it is a small compensation for what has been permanently lost.

The global economic system is not the only cause of the reduction of forest cover, but it has been and continues to be the major factor. The growth-oriented switch from peasant farms to agribusiness displaces many lowland farmers onto forested hillsides, which they must then clear if they are to survive. Many countries export lumber on an unsustainable basis in order to get the capital for industrialization. Those governments that do wish to preserve this basic resource for use by their own people are inhibited from doing so by the need to increase their exports as part of the structural adjustment imposed by the IMF (Bello, 1994).

Advocates of growth-oriented policies sometimes argue that, however regrettable some of these environmental losses are, economic growth will offer rewards that more than compensate. Growth also enables societies to afford the luxury of setting aside selected areas for scenic and recreational enjoyment. These supporters of the growth solution point out that it is affluent nations that best protect their environment. If we pursue growth-oriented policies unflinchingly, they claim, eventually all countries will be able to give high priority to reducing the pollution of their environment and to protecting natural resources. Thus the response to issues of unsustainability is like the response to problems of social breakdown and injustice. For standard economic thinking, economic growth is the only solution.

Sustainable Growth

Most advocates of growth-oriented solutions now recognize that some actions taken for the sake of growth are not sustainable. For example, the extensive use of chemicals that deplete the ozone layer is recognized as unsustainable. An agreement was reached in 1987, The Montreal Protocol, to curtail the production of these chemicals (Meadows, Meadows, and Randers, 1992). Although some economists might argue that the elimination of some popular species of fish would not much matter, since others could be substituted or technology could invent substitutes for our table, most agree that it is better to aim at sustainable limits of fishing particular stocks, at least on a global basis. Accordingly, there is general consensus that some forms of economic growth are better than others –

that is, economic growth that is not destructive of the natural environment (or of social order) is preferable to that which is.

This recognition is given its most influential expression in what is often called "the Brundtland Report" by the United Nations World Commission on Environment and Development headed by a former prime minister of Norway, Gro Brundtland. The official title of the report is *Our Common Future* (Brundtland, 1987).

This report describes well the multiple interrelated environmental and human problems afflicting the planet. It recognizes that economic development thus far has not led to a decrease in human misery. It shows utmost sensitivity for the suffering of the global poor. It argues that overriding priority should be given to their needs, and also that development should meet the needs of the present without compromising the ability of future generations to meet theirs.

The report points out that current practices are wasteful. It leans heavily on the sorts of insights that Hunter and Amory Lovins have so effectively highlighted – namely, that if we used our resources more efficiently, we could continue present high levels of consumption with much less pressure on the environment (Lovins, 1977).

Our Common Future proposes that the global poor need greatly increased per capita consumption in order to have a decent life. Since their numbers will also continue to increase, the report calls for a five- to tenfold increase of goods and services for them. This might appear to be threatening to those who are committed to continuing and strengthening the present global economic system, since it prepares us to think of restricting growth in the already affluent nations and concentrating it in the poorer ones, while making sure that wealth in these countries is fairly distributed.

In fact, no such proposal is made. Instead, the report assumes that the present global system will continue. In this system the poor can be benefited only as the rich grow richer, that is, only by, and in proportion to, an increase in the total economy. Hence, a five- to tenfold increase of consumption by the poor requires a similar increase in consumption by the rich. The only answer to how such growth can occur without intensifying ecological destruction is that resources can be used more efficiently and that particularly destructive channels of growth can be avoided.

Those who are primarily concerned for justice and sustainability agree that many of the poor need greatly increased consumption. The increase in total global production required to make this possible could be covered by more efficient use of resources. Care in avoiding especially dangerous types of growth might enable humanity to find its way through the current crisis, increasing the consumption by the poor and maintaining the affluence of the rich, while relating sustainably to the environment. But the proposal that the rich must grow richer by the same percentage as the poor is disastrous.

When a family with $1500 a year increases its income to $4500, this is an increase of only $3000. The family needs it and the earth can afford it. When a family with $150,000 a year increases its income to $450,000, this is an increase of $300,000. The family does not need it, and the earth cannot afford the additional consumption.

It may be claimed, nevertheless, that this is the only realistic possibility for helping the poor. The forces that now rule the world will not accept any form of development for the poor that does not increase their own wealth and power. Any program designed to help the poor while leaving the affluent where they are would require a massive shift of power that is now unthinkable.

But is this true "realism?" Is a five- to tenfold increase in global industrial output possible? Even if half of this increase came from greater efficiency in the use of resources, the answer is "No." Present levels of resource use and pollution are unsustainable (Postel, 1994). Tripling or quadrupling these levels is not a realistic option.

Furthermore, the policies directed to the end of increasing production have always proved costly to the poor. In some instances, as noted above, successful countries have been able to compensate their poor at later stages of development with improved living standards. But on a global basis such success is impossible. To continue policies that harm the poor now for the sake of a later improvement that cannot occur is profoundly unjust.

The disastrous consequences of the global system are already visible in many parts of the world, and especially in parts of Africa. In "The Coming Anarchy," Robert D. Kaplan (1994) describes the vast migration to the cities throughout the "developing" world and the rise of slums as major centers of population. He details the situation in West Africa, and especially Sierra Leone, as a warning of where tendencies in many other places are leading.

The exploitation of the people and resources of this part of Africa goes back to the slave trade and the colonial period. However, it was accelerated with the neocolonial system that developed after World War II with political independence. Forests covered 60% of Sierra Leone at independence in 1961. Now this area has been reduced to 6%, and the export of logs continues. Deforestation has resulted in widespread erosion of former farmland, and deforested land has become swampy, ideal breeding grounds for malarial mosquitoes. The population has continued to grow, while the basis of livelihood in the rural area declined. The result has been massive urban migration, chiefly to new slums where water supply and sewers are not distinguished.

The Sierra Leone government maintains some order in the cities during the day, none by night. Other armies roam the countryside. AIDS and tuberculosis spread rapidly. Malaria is extremely widespread, and is no longer responsive to earlier forms of treatment. Fear of malaria keeps outsiders away. In any case, with the disappearance of the forests and the end of the cold war, foreign powers have little interest in what happens.

Countering the Idealization of Growth

The Brundtland Report assumes that increased consumption is a good thing, needed especially by the poor. It accepts the trickledown approach to their economic well-being as the only one available. Given these assumptions, its proposals may be as good as can be found. But since they lead to an impasse, and since policies based on this report will continue to sacrifice the poor and add to the pressure on the environment, we need to think about an alternative global economic system. This, of course, will be seen as "unrealistic," since "realism" requires that we accept the present system and only propose policies that are compatible with it. But it is better to be unrealistic than to support a global direction that has already brought catastrophe to many and will eventually lead to catastrophe for all.

Little progress can be made toward a different way of envisaging the global system as long as "growth" is viewed as a, indeed *the*, self-evident good. Demystification of growth requires recognition that increased per capita GNP, which is the standard meaning of "growth," is not identical with improvement in the economic well-being of real human beings. To promote this demystification, I have worked with others (especially Clifford W. Cobb) to develop an Index of Sustainable Economic Welfare (ISEW) for the United States (Cobb and Cobb, 1994).

Computation of the ISEW begins with personal consumption, but then adjusts this in relation to income distribution. (Our assumption is that the well-being of the society as a whole is affected by the condition of the poorest.) The index then adds for household services, chiefly the contribution of housewives. It subtracts for "defensive costs," that is, costs that result from economic growth and the social changes, such as urbanization, that accompany it. (For example, the cost of commuting to work should not be viewed as an addition to welfare just because it adds to the GNP.) This applies also to the cost of pollution. Since it is an index of *sustainable* welfare, it subtracts for the reduction of natural capital, and adds or subtracts for change in the net international position.

The index can be used to compare growth as measured by per capita GNP with economic welfare as measured by per capita ISEW. From 1951 to 1990, (in 1972 dollars) per capita GNP for the U.S. more than doubled from $3741 to $7756; per capita ISEW rose less than 15% from $2793 to $3253. This suggests that economic well-being can be improved better in other ways than by simply seeking GNP growth. This suggestion is reinforced by figures for the second half of this period. From 1971 to 1990, per capita GNP rose from $5405 to $7756, or 43%; per capita ISEW *fell* from $3425 to $3253, or 5%.

Only *economic* welfare is considered in these calculations. Other indicators of social health in the United States, such as family stability, the quality of public education, crime, alcohol and drug abuse, and citizen participation in political life, show that significant social decline has accompanied growth of production.

The disconnection between economic growth and social well-being can be illustrated by international comparisons as well. One example is infant mortality rates. In 1990, Sri Lanka, with a per capita GNP of only one twenty-eighth that of the United States, and in the midst of ethnic strife amounting to civil war, had an infant mortality

rate of 19 per 1000, only slightly more than the 17.6 figure for black citizens of the United States (Jackson, 1993). Clearly the reduction of infant mortality is not dependent on, or guaranteed by, the increase of GNP.

Over a broader front, the state of Kerala in India shows that many social needs can be met without significant economic growth. The per capita income in Kerala is about the same as that for India as a whole. But, with regard to infant mortality and life expectancy, it ranks well in comparison with highly industrialized nations. At the same time it has greatly reduced its rate of population growth without resorting to authoritarian measures. It has achieved this by educating its people, and especially its women, about health and population issues, providing inexpensive care to all, and meeting other basic needs (Alexander, 1994; Franke and Chasin, 1989).

The danger of using GNP growth as an indicator of well-being can be illustrated in another way. When peasants lose their land to multinational agribusiness, some of them are employed. Their wages show up in GNP. Their basic inability to feed and house themselves is not counted as a loss. Hence, even though they are less well fed and housed as employees than they were as independent peasants, the GNP goes up. If these large estates were broken up again into peasant holdings, the new owners would be better off. But this could not be ascertained from GNP figures.

This means that even the idealistic proposal to which the Brundtland Report *might* lead, that is, increase of per capita consumption by the poor without increasing that of the rich, is a poor guide to what is needed. Our concern should be that the poor have access to the means of production whereby they can feed, clothe, and house themselves and have an enjoyable life free from external oppression. How this would show up in GNP figures should be a secondary consideration or not one at all. The question is whether we can envision a world in which the basic needs of all, and some less basic ones as well, are met without continuing unsustainable pressures on the environment.

An Alternative Global Economic System

The centerpiece of the present global economic system is the principle that the greater the specialization in production, the more efficiently workers can produce. The larger the market, the more specialization is possible. Hence the ideal is a global free market in which everyone everywhere concentrates on producing what is best produced in that location and imports everything else from other regions. The ideal is complete global interdependence.

The intended and actual consequence of present economic policy is that no community or nation feeds, or houses, or clothes itself. All of this is to depend on trade. This trade is "free" in the sense that the firms engaged in it are free from interference or restriction by governments. But the people of each region are not free *not* to trade. They cannot live without importing the necessities for their livelihood, however unfavorable the terms of trade may be.

An alternate ideal is one in which relatively small regions are relatively self-sufficient economically. People of such regions can then make basic decisions about themselves and about the rules by which they are governed. They are free to trade or not according to the terms of trade that are attractive to them. Not to trade means to deny themselves many desirable goods, but it does not threaten their healthy survival.

Within such regions the market should be as free as possible. The community should set the terms on which all firms compete, including standards dealing with minimum wages, workplace safety, and the environment. These requirements on the producers will internalize the social costs that result from inadequate wages, poor health, and pollution.

If these requirements are not to be unfair to producers, then goods produced elsewhere, where low wages, poor working conditions, and extensive pollution are tolerated, cannot be allowed to undersell local products. Tariffs at least equal to the extra costs of production within the region must be assessed. The region would establish its trading policies with its social goals in view – not for the sake of minimizing prices and maximizing global specialization and production. One of its goals would be to encourage other regions to organize their economies in similar ways, and tariffs could be used to this end.

The terms "relatively small" and "relatively self-sufficient" are intentionally vague. There may be places where this can realistically refer to a single village. In other instances it may be pointless to seek anything resembling self-sufficiency at

a level smaller than a nation. In either case it requires that several competing producers can be supported in the region.

In most cases, there would be several levels of organization with different types of production involved. For example, in the United States a region the size of a county might become relatively self-sufficient with regard to most of the necessities of life. But the production of cars would make sense only in a region including several states, and aircraft production might be at the national level.

Each productive activity should take place in as small a region as is practical, with the recognition that for some purposes this region will be quite large. The smaller regions are communities, and the larger regions are communities of communities and communities of communities of communities. In all cases, the political unit will include the economic one and set conditions for competition within it. No subordination of political institutions to economic ones will be allowed.

The communities of communities would be governed by representatives of the communities governed. They should also have responsibility to ensure that the local communities function as such, that is, that they not exclude any of their residents from the rights and privileges of citizenship. They also would not allow any community to export pollution to its neighbors.

Although there is little need for production to take place at the global level, there are many problems that can only be dealt with there. The United Nations already functions as a community of nations. That is, its decisions are made by representatives of nations, which themselves should be transformed into communities of communities. The United Nations should be strengthened in order to deal with those issues that can only be confronted globally, such as the protection of local resources whose value is global, as well as countering and mitigating international conflict. On the other hand, the Bretton Woods institutions should be dismantled, since they embody the principle of the independence of economic institutions from political ones. Their necessary functions should be taken over by agencies fully responsible to the General Assembly of the United Nations. This would restore the subordination of economic institutions to political ones in which the will of the people *can* be expressed.

The primacy of the political over the economic, combined with weakening global economic institutions, would make possible economic decentralization. It would be possible for nations and even regions within nations to develop relatively self-sufficient economies. They would then trade with one another only as this did not weaken their capacity to meet their own basic needs. They would cooperate in establishing larger markets for goods that cannot be efficiently produced for smaller ones.

Since much of the unsustainability of the present economy stems from the appropriation of the resources of the poorer countries by the richer ones, the ending of the present global economic system would counter this. For example, most of the rapid deforestation of the planet is for the sake of export, either of lumber or of beef that can be raised on formerly forested land. If the focus of attention is on the local economy, the value of the standing forest counts for more. In this and other ways, in regions which were not heavily oriented to export, the people would often be concerned that their region continue to provide a habitable home to their children, and they would be more likely to adopt sustainable relations to the environment.

Nevertheless, policies that commend themselves locally may have negative consequences globally. An example is production of ozone-destroying chemicals. They may be produced in a part of the world where destruction of the ozone layer does not seem a pressing problem. The most threatened regions may have little direct political clout with those that cause the danger. Global political institutions must have the power to protect the global environment from such local infringements. Global warming may prove another problem that will require strict rules from the global level to be enforced in every region.

Fantasy or Possible Future?

I have proposed a global order that *could* be relatively just and sustainable. Economic decentralization would reduce pressure on the environment and give people more participation in the decisions that are important for their lives. It would not guarantee that those decisions would be wise, however. This is not a utopia. It *does* offer a chance for a decent survival, one that continuation of present policies precludes.

It can still be objected that this is too different from the structures and practices to which we are accustomed, that it appeals to motives that have been subordinated to profit and consumerism, that it implies a transfer of power that no one is in a position to effect, that it requires changes that would be painful. One's response to these objections will depend on the degree of one's distress about what is now taking place and the impending catastrophes. Those who are relatively content with what has been happening and are able to avoid thinking of catastrophes to come will conclude that it is better to continue muddling along, mitigating suffering where possible, and adapting to the rest. Those who are truly concerned about the suffering now occurring because of dominant policies, and those who are unable to accept continued movement toward the precipice as "realistic," will acknowledge the extreme difficulty of changing direction, but will take the first step.

That step is the acknowledgment that the redirection of efforts is urgent. Only in that context can there be serious discussion of further steps that can and should be taken. Hoping that some of my readers share with me the sense of urgency, I will describe further steps that are now possible in order to begin the shift of direction.

The next step is to raise the consciousness of those who are already deeply concerned about injustice and unsustainability. Too many of them have accepted the idea that justice and sustainability can be attained by, or in tandem with, the pursuit of growth-oriented policies, assuming that economic growth is inherently beneficial. Exposing the fallacy of this assumption may make it possible to mobilize the natural constituencies for economic policies that would make for justice and sustainability.

The environmental movement is one such constituency. A substantial part of this movement has begun to understand the close connection between environmental decay and policies aimed at economic growth. Several major environmental organizations, such as the Sierra Club and Greenpeace, opposed NAFTA, along with the Humane Society. On the other hand, many environmental organizations, including the Natural Resources Defense Council, the Environmental Defense Fund, and the National Audubon Society, supported it. They were pleased that with its side agreements it

John B. Cobb, Jr.

introduced environmental considerations into a trade agreement for the first time, and they see that it offers promise in dealing with specific environmental problems such as the polluted Rio Grande. They see the basic relation between economic growth and environmental protection as positive.

Rosemary Ostergen (personal communication, March 2, 1994), Director of Membership of the Environmental Defense Fund, wrote to those supporters of the Fund who had questioned its advocacy of NAFTA. She stated, "We believe that collective action and economic growth will prove to be a more effective vehicle to prevent further environmental degradation from occurring in North America." Not mentioned were the facts that it is precisely the sort of undirected economic growth promoted by the agreement that polluted the Rio Grande, that the expansion of such growth will add to pollution elsewhere, that NAFTA's promotion of agribusiness will displace millions of peasants and degrade the soil, and that it will speed up the exploitation of other resources in Mexico. In other words, like many environmentalists, the Environmental Defense Fund does not see the inherent conflict between sustaining the environment and policies directed toward increasing the GNP.

Labor is a second natural constituency for changing the direction of the global economy. In relation to the test case of NAFTA, organized labor understood its interests better than many of the environmentalists. Since the globalization of the economy has already depressed wages in the United States, and it was easy to see that NAFTA was one more step in this direction, the leaders of organized labor were united in opposition. Unfortunately, the globalization of the economy has already greatly weakened organized labor. Also, labor leaders did not articulate an alternative vision for the economic future; so they appeared to be opposing "progress" for the sake of "special interests."

The growing underclass is a third group that, if it were able to function as a constituency, would certainly have reason to support change. This underclass is created by the global economy and will continue to grow as long as the present growth-oriented, globalizing policies are in effect. Unfortunately, the underclass is poorly organized and is forced to exist on a day-by-day basis, rather than to dream dreams of a new economic order.

Communitarians constitute a fourth natural constituency of support for change. Unfortunately, many of them are also neoliberals in economic thinking, not recognizing that it is the application of standard economic principles that systematically undermines community (e.g., Etzioni, 1983). Other communitarians ignore economic issues, concentrating on social and political ones, not realizing that all the progress they make there can often be wiped out by a single decision made by a distant corporation.

Humanitarians are a fifth such constituency. The present policies are brutal in their effects on billions of people. The suffering will grow worse and will not be compensated in most countries by an eventual improvement. Nevertheless, most humanitarians are persuaded that economic growth is an essential part of the solution to human problems. Most continue to suppose that an increase in per capita GNP indicates that the lot of human beings is improving. Most do not see that the catastrophes that are coming upon humanity are the result of just these growth-oriented policies (e.g., Sherman, 1992; Weaver, 1994).

Even if all these natural constituencies for change were mobilized, could they give a different direction to the global system? Each year the transnational corporations and the elites all over the world, who profit from the present global system, grow more powerful. By supporting trade that cannot be controlled or regulated at the national level, governments are surrendering to these corporations control not only over international economic transactions but also over the laws that operate within their own countries (Nader, 1994). This surrender is now embodied in binding international agreements such as NAFTA and GATT. Billions of people have been persuaded that political institutions are inefficient and corrupt and that only business leaders can get "the job" done. Could all this be reversed?

Not easily, certainly. Probably not until more catastrophes strike and people grow more desperate. But desperation by itself is more likely to lead to acceptance of totalitarian governments than to decentralization of economic and political power, unless a vision of a livable alternative already has strong support. Otherwise, most will continue to believe the solution to the problems caused by global economic integration is more rigorous application of the policies directed to that end.

Meanwhile, in addition to raising consciousness about the incompatibility of aiming primarily at economic growth with the attainment of justice and sustainability, we can form alliances to oppose further steps in the direction now called "progress." We can also support subdominant trends that appear in many areas. Even within business there is growing recognition that highly centralized control is not efficient. Decentralization of decision making does occur. There are political movements in the same direction.

There is increasing recognition that top-down development projects do not work. For example, the World Bank, after much criticism, finally withdrew from the Narmada Project in India, the largest water project ever undertaken. Development for the sake of the people should begin instead where they are and help them attain their own goals along the lines articulated in "Another Development" (Ekins, 1992, chap. 5).

There are significant movements in agriculture away from land-exploiting agribusiness toward small scale stewardship of land by families. And there are many communities that are, as far as the present economy allows, taking more responsibility for their own lives (Fisher, 1993). Some institutions are beginning to support local farmers and business rather than tie into the national and global economies (Valen, 1992). Some colleges and universities are introducing programs of study that clarify the present functioning of the global economy and its consequences and promote thinking about alternatives. Many individuals are reordering their lives around service rather than around gaining wealth, and the New Roadmap Foundation works to encourage this decision (Dominguez and Robin, 1992). Thus, while the dominant trends at the top lead to injustice and unsustainability, there is a new ferment among the peoples of the world calling for and embodying new directions.

References

Alexander, W. M. (1994, April). *Exceptional Kerala: Efficient and sustainable human behavior.* Paper distributed at the Seventh International Conference for Human Ecology, Michigan State University, East Lansing, MI.

Bello, W., with Cunningham, S., and Rau, B. (1994). *Dark Victory: The United States, structural adjustment and global poverty.* London: Pluto Press.

Bello, W., and Rosenfeld, S. (1990). *Dragons in Distress: Asia's miracle economies in crisis.* San Francisco: Food First.

Brown, L. R. (1987). Analyzing the demographic trap. In L. R. Brown (ed.), *State of the World* (pp. 20–37). New York: W. W. Norton.

Brundtland, G. (ed.). (1987). *Our Common Future.* New York: World Commission on Environment and Trade.

Cobb, C. W., and Cobb, J. B., Jr. (1994). *The Green National Product: A proposed index of sustainable economic welfare.* Lanham, MD: University Press of America.

Cobb, J. B., Jr. (1994). *Sustaining the Common Good: A Christian perspective on the global economy.* Cleveland, OH: Pilgrim Press.

Daly, H. F., and Cobb, J. B., Jr. (1994). *For the Common Good: Redirecting the economy toward community, the environment, and a sustainable future.* Boston: Beacon Press.

David, W. L. (1985). *The IMF Policy Paradigm: The macroeconomics of stabilization, structural adjustment, and economic development.* New York: Praeger Publishers.

Dominguez, J., and Robin, V. (1992). *Your Money or Your Life.* New York: Viking/Penguin.

Durning, A. T. (1994). Redesigning the forest economy. In L. R. Brown (ed.), *State of the World* (pp. 22–40). New York: W. W. Norton.

Ekins, P. (1992). *A New World Order: Grassroots movements for global change.* London: Routledge.

Etzioni, A. (1983). *An Immodest Agenda.* New York: McGraw-Hill.

Fisher, J. (1993). *The Road From Rio: Sustainable development and the nongovernmental movement in the Third World.* Westport, CT: Praeger.

Franke, R., and Chasin, B. (1989). *Kerala: Radical reform as development in an Indian state.* San Francisco: Food First Institute.

Green, R. H. (ed.). (1984). *The International Financial System: An ecumenical critique.* Geneva: World Council of Churches.

Jackson, R. L. (1993, December 16). Panel calls for U.S. to curb infant deaths. *Los Angeles Times*, p. A37.

Kaplan, R. D. (1994, February). The coming anarchy. *The Atlantic Monthly*, pp. 44–76.

Kock, K. (1969). *International Trade Policy and the Gatt.* Stockholm: Almquist & Wiksell.

Lovins, A. B. (1977). *Soft Energy Paths: Toward a durable peace.* San Francisco: Friends of the Earth.

Meadows, D. H., Meadows, D. L. and Randers, J. (1992). *Beyond the Limits: Confronting global collapse: Envisioning a sustainable future.* Post Mills, VT: Chelsea Green.

Nader, R. (1994, May/June). GATT threatens U.S. environment, consumer protection laws. *Public Citizen*, pp. 18–21.

Postel, S. (1994). Carrying capacity: Earth's bottom line. In L. R. Brown (ed.), *State of the World* (pp. 3–21). New York: W. W. Norton.

Raghavan, C. (1990). *Recolonization: GATT, the Uruguay round, & the Third World.* Penang: Third World Network.

Sherman, A. (1992, December 9). Rethinking development: A market-friendly strategy for the poor. *Christian Century*, pp. 1130–4.

Sierra Club. (1993, October 6). *Analysis of the North American Free Trade Agreement and the North American Agreement on Environmental Cooperation.* Washington, DC: Author.

Smith, A. (1991). *An Inquiry into the Nature and Causes of the Wealth of Nations.* New York: Alfred Knopf. (Original work published 1776.)

Valen, G. L. (1992). Hendrix College local food project. In D. J. Eagan and D. W. Orr (eds.), *The Campus and Environmental Responsibility* (pp. 77–87). San Francisco: Jossey-Bass.

Van Dormael, A. (1978). *Bretton Woods: Birth of a monetary system.* New York: Holmes & Meier.

Weaver, J. H. (1994, March 16). Can we achieve broad-based sustainable development? *Christian Century*, pp. 282–4.

27

Ethics, Public Policy, and Global Warming

Dale Jamieson

There has been speculation about the possibility of anthropogenic global warming since at least the late nineteenth century (Arrhenius 1896, 1908). At times the prospect of such a warming has been welcomed, for it has been thought that it would increase agricultural productivity and delay the onset of the next ice age (Callendar 1938). Other times, and more recently, the prospect of global warming has been the stuff of "doomsday narratives," as various writers have focused on the possibility of widespread drought, flood, famine, and the economic and political dislocations that might result from a "greenhouse warming"-induced climate change (Flavin 1989).

Although high-level meetings have been convened to discuss the greenhouse effect since at least 1963 (see Conservation Foundation 1963), the emergence of a rough, international consensus about the likelihood and extent of anthropogenic global warming began with a National Academy Report in 1983 (National Academy of Sciences/ National Research Council 1983); meetings in Villach, Austria, and Bellagio, Italy, in 1985 (World Climate Program 1985); and in Toronto, Canada, in 1988 (Conference Statement 1988). The most recent influential statement of the consensus holds that although there are uncertainties, a doubling of atmospheric carbon dioxide from its preindustrial baseline is likely to lead to a 2.5 degree centigrade increase in the earth's mean surface temperature by the middle of the next century (Intergovernmental Panel on Climate Change [IPCC] 1990). (Interestingly, this estimate is within the range predicted by Arrhenius [1896]). This increase is expected to have a profound impact on climate and therefore on plants, animals, and human activities of all kinds. Moreover, there is no reason to suppose that without policy interventions, atmospheric carbon dioxide will stabilize at twice preindustrial levels. According to the IPCC (1990), we would need immediate 60% reductions in net emissions in order to stabilize at a carbon dioxide doubling by the end of this century. Since these reductions are very unlikely to occur, we may well see increases of 4 degrees centigrade by the end of the twenty-first century.

The emerging consensus about climate change was brought home to the American public on 23 June 1988, a sweltering day in Washington, D.C., in the middle of a severe national drought, when James Hansen testified to the U.S. Senate Committee on Energy and Natural Resources that it was 99% probable that global warming had begun. Hansen's testimony was front page news in the *New York Times* and was extensively covered by other media as well. By the end of the summer of 1988, the greenhouse effect had become an important public issue. According to a June 1989 Gallup poll, 35% of the American public worried "a great deal" about the greenhouse effect, while 28% worried about it "a fair amount" (Gallup Organization 1989).

Beginning in 1989 there was a media "backlash" against the "hawkish" views of Hansen and others (for the typology of "hawks," "doves," and "owls," see Glantz 1988). In 1989 the *Washington Post* (8 February), the *Wall Street Journal* (10 April), and the *New York Times* (13 December) all published major articles expressing skepticism about the predictions of global warming or minimizing its potential impacts. These themes were picked up by other media, including such mass circulation periodicals as *Reader's Digest* (February 1990). In its December 1989 issue *Forbes* published a hard-hitting cover story titled "The Global Warming Panic" and later took out a full-page ad in the *New York Times* (7 February 1990) congratulating itself for its courage in confronting the "doom-and-gloomers."

The Bush administration seems to have been influenced by this backlash. The April 1990 White House conference on global warming concluded with a ringing call for more research, disappointing several European countries that were hoping for concerted action. In July at the Houston Economic Summit, the Bush administration reiterated its position, warning against precipitous action. In a series of meetings, convened as part of the IPCC process, the American government has stood virtually alone in opposing specific targets and timetables for stabilizing carbon dioxide emissions. The Bush administration has continually emphasized the scientific uncertainties involved in forecasts of global warming and also expressed concern about the economic impacts of carbon dioxide stabilization policies.

It is a fact that there are a number of different hypotheses about the future development of the global climate and its impact on human and other biological activities; and several of these are dramatically at variance with the consensus. For example, Budyko (1988) and Idso (1989) think that global warming is good for us, and Ephron (1988) argues that the injection of greenhouse gases will trigger a new ice age. Others, influenced by the "Gaia Hypothesis" (see Lovelock 1988), believe that there are self-regulating planetary mechanisms that may preserve climate stability even in the face of anthropogenic forcings of greenhouse gases.

Although there are some outlying views, most of the differences of opinion within the scientific community are differences of emphasis rather than differences of kind. Rather than highlighting the degree of certainty that attaches to predictions of global warming, as does Schneider (1989), for example, some emphasize the degree of uncertainty that attaches to such predictions (for example, Abelson 1990).

However, in my view, the most important force driving the backlash is not concerns about the weakness of the science but the realization that slowing global warming or responding to its effects may involve large economic costs and redistributions, as well as radical revisions in lifestyle. Various interest groups argue that they are already doing enough in response to global warming, while some economists have begun to express doubt about whether it is worth trying to prevent substantial warming (*New York Times*, 11 November 1989; White House Council of Economic Advisors 1990). What seems to be emerging as the dominant view among economists is that chlorofluorocarbons (CFCs) should be eliminated, but emissions of carbon dioxide or other trace gases should be reduced only slightly if at all (see Nordhaus 1990; Darmstadter 1991).

There are many uncertainties concerning anthropogenic climate change, yet we cannot wait until all the facts are in before we respond. All the facts may never be in. New knowledge may resolve old uncertainties, but it may bring with it new uncertainties. And it is an important dimension of this problem that our insults to the biosphere outrun our ability to understand them. We may suffer the worst effects of the greenhouse before we can prove to everyone's satisfaction that they will occur (Jamieson 1991).

The most important point I wish to make, however, is that the problem we face is not a purely scientific problem that can be solved by the accumulation of scientific information. Science has alerted us to a problem, but the problem also concerns our values. It is about how we ought to live, and how humans should relate to each other and to the rest of nature. These are problems of ethics and politics as well as problems of science.

In the first section I examine what I call the "management" approach to assessing the impacts of, and our responses to, climate change. I argue that this approach cannot succeed, for it does not have the resources to answer the most fundamental questions that we face. In the second section I explain why the problem of anthropogenic global change is to a great extent an ethical problem, and why our conventional value system is not adequate for addressing it. Finally I draw some conclusions.

Why Management Approaches Must Fail

From the perspective of conventional policy studies, the possibility of anthropogenic climate change and its attendant consequences are problems to be "managed." Management techniques mainly are drawn from neoclassical economic theory and are directed toward manipulating behavior by controlling economic incentives through taxes, regulations, and subsidies.

In recent years economic vocabularies and ways of reasoning have dominated the discussion of social issues. Participants in the public dialogue have internalized the neoclassical economic perspective to such an extent that its assumptions and biases have become almost invisible. It is only a mild exaggeration to say that in recent years debates over policies have largely become debates over economics.

The Environmental Protection Agency's draft report *Policy Options for Stabilizing Global Climate* (U.S. Environmental Protection Agency 1989) is a good example. Despite its title, only one of nine chapters is specifically devoted to policy options, and in that chapter only "internalizing the cost of climate change risks" and "regulations and standards" are considered. For many people questions of regulation are not distinct from questions about internalizing costs. According to one influential view, the role of regulations and standards is precisely to internalize costs, thus (to echo a parody of our forefathers) "creating a more perfect market." For people with this view, political questions about regulation are really disguised economic questions (for discussion, see Sagoff 1988).

It would be both wrong and foolish to deny the importance of economic information. Such information is important when making policy decisions, for some policies or programs that would otherwise appear to be attractive may be economically prohibitive. Or in some cases there may be alternative policies that would achieve the same ends and also conserve resources.

However, these days it is common for people to make more grandiose claims on behalf of economics. As philosophers and clergymen have become increasingly modest and reluctant to tell people what to do, economists have become bolder. Some economists or their champions believe not only that economics provides important information for making policy decisions but that it provides the most important information. Some even appear to believe that economics provides the only relevant information. According to this view, when faced with a policy decision, what we need to do is assess the benefits and costs of various alternatives. The alternative that maximizes the benefits less the costs is the one we should prefer. This alternative is "efficient" and choosing it is "rational."

Unfortunately, too often we lose sight of the fact that economic efficiency is only one value, and it may not be the most important one. Consider, for example, the idea of imposing a carbon tax as one policy response to the prospect of global warming (Moomaw [1988] 1989). What we think of this proposal may depend to some extent on how it affects other concerns that are important to us. Equity is sometimes mentioned as one other such concern, but most of us have very little idea about what equity means or exactly what role it should play in policy considerations.

One reason for the hegemony of economic analysis and prescriptions is that many people have come to think that neoclassical economics provides the only social theory that accurately represents human motivation. According to the neoclassical paradigm, welfare can be defined in terms of preference-satisfaction, and preferences are defined in terms of choice behavior. From this, many (illicitly) infer that the perception of self-interest is the only motivator for human beings. This view suggests the following "management technique": If you want people to do something give them a carrot; if you want them to desist, give them a stick. (For the view that self-interest is the "soul of modern economic man," see Myers 1983).

Many times the claim that people do what they believe is in their interests is understood in such a way as to be circular, therefore unfalsifiable and trivial. We know that something is perceived as being in a person's interests because the person pursues it; and if the person pursues it, then we know that the person must perceive it as being in his or her interests. On the other hand if we take it as an empirical claim that people always do what they believe is in their interests, it appears to be false. If we look around the world we see people risking or even sacrificing their own interests in attempts to overthrow oppressive governments or to realize ideals to which they are committed. Each year more people die in wars fighting for some perceived collective good than die in criminal attempts to further their own individual interests. It is implausible to suppose that the behavior (much less the motivations) of a revolutionary, a radical environmentalist, or a friend or lover can be revealed by a benefit–cost analysis (even one that appeals to the "selfish gene").

It seems plain that people are motivated by a broad range of concerns, including concern for family and friends, and religious, moral, and political ideals. And it seems just as plain that people sometimes sacrifice their own interests for what they regard to be a greater, sometimes impersonal, good. (Increasingly these facts are being appreciated in the social science literature; see, for example, Mansbridge [1990], Opp [1989], and Scitovsky [1976]).

People often act in ways that are contrary to what we might predict on narrowly economic grounds, and moreover, they sometimes believe that it would be wrong or inappropriate even to take economic considerations into account. Many people would say that choosing spouses, lovers, friends, or religious or political commitments on economic grounds is simply wrong. People who behave in this way are often seen as manipulative, not to be trusted, without character or virtue. One way of understanding some environmentalists is to see them as wanting us to think about nature in the way that many of us think of friends and lovers – to see nature not as a resource to be exploited but as a partner with whom to share our lives.

What I have been suggesting in this section is that it is not always rational to make decisions solely on narrowly economic grounds. Although economic efficiency may be a value, there are other values as well, and in many areas of life, values other than economic efficiency should take precedence. I have also suggested that people's motivational patterns are complex and that exploiting people's perceptions of self-interest may not be the only way to move them. This amounts to a general critique of viewing all social issues as management problems to be solved by the application of received economic techniques.

There is a further reason why economic considerations should take a back seat in our thinking about global climate change: There is no way to assess accurately all the possible impacts and to assign economic values to alternative courses of action. A greenhouse warming, if it occurs, will have impacts that are so broad, diverse, and uncertain that conventional economic analysis is practically useless. (Our inability to perform reliably the economic calculations also counts against the "insurance" view favored by many "hawks": but that is another story.)

Consider first the uncertainty of the potential impacts. Some uncertainties about the global effects of loading the atmosphere with carbon dioxide and other greenhouse gases have already been noted. But even if the consensus is correct that global mean surface temperatures will increase 1.5–4 degrees centigrade sometime in the next century because of a doubling of atmospheric carbon dioxide, there is still great uncertainty about the impact of this warming on regional climate. One thing is certain: The impacts will not be homogeneous. Some areas will become warmer, some will probably become colder, and overall variability is likely to increase. Precipitation patterns will also change, and there is much less confidence in the projections about precipitation than in those about temperature. These uncertainties about the regional effects make estimates of the economic consequences of climate change radically uncertain.

There is also another source of uncertainty regarding these estimates. In general, predicting human behavior is difficult, as recent events in Central and Eastern Europe have demonstrated. These difficulties are especially acute in the case that we are considering because climate change, if it occurs, will affect a wide range of social, economic, and political activities. Changes in these sectors will affect emissions of "greenhouse gases," which will in turn affect climate, and around we go again (Jamieson 1990). Climate change is itself uncertain, and its human effects are even more radically so. It is for reasons such as these that in general, the area of environment and energy has been full of surprises.

A second reason why the benefits and costs of the impacts of global climate change cannot reliably be assessed concerns the breadth of the impacts. Global climate change will affect all regions of the globe. About many of these regions – those in which most of the world's population live – we know very little. Some of these regions do not even have monetarized economies. It is ludicrous to suppose that we could assess the economic impacts of global climate change when we have such little understanding of the global economy in the first place. (Nordhaus [1990], for example, implausibly extrapolates the sectorial analysis of the American economy to the world economy for the purposes of his study.)

Finally, consider the diversity of the potential impacts. Global climate change will affect agriculture; fishing, forestry, and tourism. It will affect "unmanaged" ecosystems and patterns of urbanization. International trade and relations will be affected. Some nations and sectors may benefit at the expense of others. There will be complex interactions between these effects. For this reason we cannot reliably aggregate the effects by evaluating each impact and combining them by simple addition. But since the interactions are so complex, we have no idea what the proper mathematical function would be for aggregating them (if the idea of aggregation even makes sense in this context.) It is difficult enough to assess the economic benefits and costs of small-scale, local activities. It is almost unimaginable to suppose that we could aggregate the diverse impacts of global climate change in such a way as to dictate policy responses.

In response to skeptical arguments like the one that I have given, it is sometimes admitted that our present ability to provide reliable economic analyses is limited, but then it is asserted that any analysis is better than none. I think that this is incorrect and that one way to see this is by considering an example.

Imagine a century ago a government doing an economic analysis in order to decide whether to build its national transportation system around the private automobile. No one could have imagined the secondary effects: the attendant roads, the loss of life, the effects on wildlife, on communities; the impact on air quality, noise, travel time, and quality of life. Given our inability to reliably predict and evaluate the effects of even small-scale technology (e.g., the artificial heart, see Jamieson 1988), the idea that we could predict the impact of global climate change reliably enough to permit meaningful economic analysis seems fatuous indeed.

When our ignorance is so extreme, it is a leap of faith to say that some analysis is better than none. A bad analysis can be so wrong that it can lead us to do bad things, outrageous things – things that are much worse than what we would have done had we not tried to assess the costs and benefits at all (this may be the wisdom in the old adage that "a little knowledge can be a dangerous thing").

What I have been arguing is that the idea of managing global climate change is a dangerous

conceit. The tools of economic evaluation are not up to the task. However, the most fundamental reason why management approaches are doomed to failure is that the questions they can answer are not the ones that are most important and profound. The problems posed by anthropogenic global climate change are ethical as well as economic and scientific. I will explain this claim in the next section.

Ethics and Global Change

Since the end of World War II, humans have attained a kind of power that is unprecedented in history. While in the past entire peoples could be destroyed, now all people are vulnerable. While once particular human societies had the power to upset the natural processes that made their lives and cultures possible, now people have the power to alter the fundamental global conditions that permitted human life to evolve and that continue to sustain it. While our species dances with the devil, the rest of nature is held hostage. Even if we step back from the precipice, it will be too late for many or even perhaps most of the plant and animal life with which we share the planet (Borza and Jamieson 1990). Even if global climate can be stabilized, the future may be one without wild nature (McKibben 1989). Humans will live in a humanized world with a few domestic plants and animals that can survive or thrive on their relationships with humans.

The questions that such possibilities pose are fundamental questions of morality. They concern how we ought to live, what kinds of societies we want, and how we should relate to nature and other forms of life. Seen from this perspective, it is not surprising that economics cannot tell us everything we want to know about how we should respond to global warming and global change. Economics may be able to tell us how to reach our goals efficiently, but it cannot tell us what our goals should be or even whether we should be concerned to reach them efficiently.

It is a striking fact about modern intellectual life that we often seek to evade the value dimensions of fundamental social questions. Social scientists tend to eschew explicit talk about values, and this is part of the reason why we have so little understanding of how value change occurs in individuals and societies. Policy professionals are also often reluctant to talk about values. Many think that rational reflection on values and value change is impossible, unnecessary, impractical, or dangerous. Others see it as a professional, political, or bureaucratic threat (Amy 1984). Generally, in the political process, value language tends to function as code words for policies and attitudes that cannot be discussed directly.

A system of values, in the sense in which I will use this notion, specifies permissions, norms, duties, and obligations; it assigns blame, praise, and responsibility; and it provides an account of what is valuable and what is not. A system of values provides a standard for assessing our behavior and that of others. Perhaps indirectly it also provides a measure of the acceptability of government action and regulation.

Values are more objective than mere preferences (Andrews and Waits 1978). A value has force for a range of people who are similarly situated. A preference may have force only for the individual whose preference it is. Whether or not someone should have a particular value depends on reasons and arguments. We can rationally discuss values, while preferences may be rooted simply in desire, without supporting reasons.

A system of values may govern someone's behavior without these values being fully explicit. They may figure in people's motivations and in their attempts to justify or criticize their own actions or those of others. Yet it may require a theorist or a therapist to make these values explicit.

In this respect a system of values may be like an iceberg – most of what is important may be submerged and invisible even to the person whose values they are. Because values are often opaque to the person who holds them, there can be inconsistencies and incoherencies in a system of values. Indeed much debate and dialogue about values involves attempts to resolve inconsistencies and incoherencies in one direction or another.

A system of values is generally a cultural construction rather than an individual one (Weiskel 1990). It makes sense to speak of contemporary American values, or those of eighteenth-century England or tenth-century India. Our individual differences tend to occur around the edges of our value system. The vast areas of agreement often seem invisible because they are presupposed or assumed without argument.

I believe that our dominant value system is inadequate and inappropriate for guiding our thinking

about global environmental problems, such as those entailed by climate changes caused by human activity. This value system, as it impinges on the environment, can be thought of as a relatively recent construction, coincident with the rise of capitalism and modern science, and expressed in the writings of such philosophers as Francis Bacon ([1620] 1870), John Locke ([1690] 1952), and Bernard Mandeville ([1714] 1970; see also Hirschman 1977). It evolved in low-population-density and low-technology societies, with seemingly unlimited access to land and other resources. This value system is reflected in attitudes toward population, consumption, technology, and social justice, as well as toward the environment.

The feature of this value system that I will discuss is its conception of responsibility. Our current value system presupposes that harms and their causes are individual, that they can readily be identified, and that they are local in space and time. It is these aspects of our conception of responsibility on which I want to focus.

Consider an example of the sort of case with which our value system deals best. Jones breaks into Smith's house and steals Smith's television set. Jones's intent is clear: she wants Smith's TV set. Smith suffers a clear harm; he is made worse off by having lost the television set. Jones is responsible for Smith's loss, for she was the cause of the harm and no one else was involved.

What we have in this case is a clear, self-contained story about Smith's loss. We know how to identify the harms and how to assign responsibility. We respond to this breach of our norms by punishing Jones in order to prevent her from doing it again and to deter others from such acts, or we require compensation from Jones so that Smith may be restored to his former position.

It is my contention that this paradigm collapses when we try to apply it to global environmental problems, such as those associated with human-induced global climate change. It is for this reason that we are often left feeling confused about how to think about these problems.

There are three important dimensions along which global environmental problems such as those involved with climate change vary from the paradigm: Apparently innocent acts can have devastating consequences, causes and harms may be diffuse, and causes and harms may be remote in space and time. (Other important dimensions may concern nonlinear causation, threshold effects, and the relative unimportance of political boundaries, but I cannot discuss these here [see Lee 1989].)

Consider an example. Some projections suggest that one effect of greenhouse warming may be to shift the Southern Hemisphere cyclone belt to the south. If this occurs the frequency of cyclones in Sydney, Australia, will increase enormously, resulting in great death and destruction. The causes of this death and destruction will be diffuse. There is no one whom we can identify as the cause of destruction in the way in which we can identify Jones as the cause of Smith's loss. Instead of a single cause, millions of people will have made tiny, almost imperceptible causal contributions – by driving cars, cutting trees, using electricity, and so on. They will have made these contributions in the course of their daily lives performing apparently "innocent" acts, without intending to bring about this harm. Moreover, most of these people will be geographically remote from Sydney, Australia. (Many of them will have no idea where Sydney, Australia, is.) Further, some people who are harmed will be remote in time from those who have harmed them. Sydney may suffer in the twenty-first century in part because of people's behavior in the nineteenth and twentieth centuries. Many small people doing small things over a long period of time together will cause unimaginable harms.

Despite the fact that serious, clearly identifiable harms will have occurred because of human agency, conventional morality would have trouble finding anyone to blame. For no one intended the bad outcome or brought it about or even was able to foresee it.

Today we face the possibility that the global environment may be destroyed, yet no one will be responsible. This is a new problem. It takes a great many people and a high level of consumption and production to change the earth's climate. It could not have been done in low-density, low-technology societies. Nor could it have been done in societies like ours until recently. London could be polluted by its inhabitants in the eighteenth century, but its reach was limited. Today no part of the planet is safe. Unless we develop new values and conceptions of responsibility, we will have enormous difficulty in motivating people to respond to this problem.

Some may think that discussion about new values is idealistic. Human nature cannot be changed, it is sometimes said. But as anyone who takes anthropology or history seriously knows, our current values are at least in part historically constructed, rooted in the conditions of life in which they developed. What we need are new values that reflect the interconnectedness of life on a dense, high-technology planet.

Others may think that a search for new values is excessively individualistic and that what is needed are collective and institutional solutions. This overlooks the fact that our values permeate our institutions and practices. Reforming our values is part of constructing new moral, political, and legal concepts.

One of the most important benefits of viewing global environmental problems as moral problems is that this brings them into the domain of dialogue, discussion, and participation. Rather than being management problems that governments or experts can solve for us, when seen as ethical problems, they become problems for all of us to address, both as political actors and as everyday moral agents.

In this essay I cannot hope to say what new values are needed or to provide a recipe for how to bring them about. Values are collectively created rather than individually dictated, and the dominance of economic models has meant that the study of values and value change has been neglected (but see Wolfe 1989; Reich 1988). However, I do have one positive suggestion: We should focus more on character and less on calculating probable outcomes. Focusing on outcomes has made us cynical calculators and has institutionalized hypocrisy. We can each reason: Since my contribution is small, outcomes are likely to be determined by the behavior of others. Reasoning in this way we can each justify driving cars while advocating bicycles or using fireplaces while favoring regulations against them. In such a climate we do not condemn or even find it surprising that Congress exempts itself from civil rights laws. Even David Brower, the "archdruid" of the environmental movement, owns two cars, four color televisions, two video cameras, three video recorders, and a dozen tape recorders, and he justifies this by saying that "it will help him in his work to save the Earth" (*San Diego Union*, 1 April 1990).

Calculating probable outcomes leads to unraveling the patterns of collective behavior that are needed in order to respond successfully to many of the global environmental problems that we face. When we "economize" our behavior in the way that is required for calculating, we systematically

Dale Jamieson

neglect the subtle and indirect effects of our actions, and for this reason we see individual action as inefficacious. For social change to occur it is important that there be people of integrity and character who act on the basis of principles and ideals.

The content of our principles and ideals is, of course, important. Principles and ideals can be eccentric or even demented. In my opinion, in order to address such problems as global climate change, we need to nurture and give new content to some old virtues such as humility, courage, and moderation and perhaps develop such new virtues as those of simplicity and conservatism. But whatever the best candidates are for twenty-first century virtues, what is important to recognize is the importance and centrality of the virtues in bringing about value change.

Conclusion

Science has alerted us to the impact of humankind on the planet, each other, and all life. This dramatically confronts us with questions about who we are, our relations to nature, and what we are willing to sacrifice for various possible futures. We should confront this as a fundamental challenge to our values and not treat it as if it were simply another technical problem to be managed.

Some who seek quick fixes may find this concern with values frustrating. A moral argument will not change the world overnight. Collective moral change is fundamentally cooperative rather than coercive. No one will fall over, mortally wounded, in the face of an argument. Yet if there is to be meaningful change that makes a difference over the long term, it must be both collective and thoroughgoing. Developing a deeper understanding of who we are, as well as how our best conceptions of ourselves can guide change, is the fundamental issue that we face.

References

Abelson, Philip. 1990. Uncertainties about global warming. *Science* 247 (30 March): 1529.

Amy, Douglas R. 1984. Why policy analysis and ethics are incompatible. *Journal of Policy Analysis and Management* 3: 573–91.

Andrews, Richard, and Mary Jo Waits. 1978. *Environmental Values in Public Decisions: A research agenda*. Ann Arbor: University of Michigan, School of Natural Resources.

Arrhenius, S. 1896. On the influence of carbonic acid in the air upon the temperature of the ground. *Philosophical Magazine* 41: 237.

——. 1908. *Worlds in the Making*. New York: Harper & Brothers.

Bacon, F. [1620] 1870. *Works*, edited by James Spedding, Robert Leslie Ellis, and Douglas Devon Heath. London: Longmans Green.

Borza, K., and D. Jamieson. 1990. *Global Change and Biodiversity Loss: Some impediments to response*. Boulder: University of Colorado, Center for Space and Geoscience Policy.

Budyko, M. I. 1988. Anthropogenic climate change. Paper presented at the World Congress on Climate and Development, Hamburg, Federal Republic of Germany.

Callendar, G. S. 1938. The artificial production of carbon dioxide and its influence on temperature. *Quarterly Journal of the Royal Meteorological Society* 64: 223–40.

Conference Statement. 1988. The changing atmosphere: Implications for global security. Toronto, Canada, 27–30 June.

Conservation Foundation. 1963. *Implications of Rising Carbon Dioxide Content of the Atmosphere*. New York.

Darmstadter, Joel. 1991. The Economic Cost of CO_2 Mitigation: A review of estimates for selected world regions. Discussion paper ENR 91–06. Washington, DC: Resources for the Future.

Ephron, L. 1988. *The End: The imminent ice age and how we can stop it*. Berkeley, CA: Celestial Arts.

Flavin, C. 1989. *Slowing Global Warming: A worldwide strategy*. Worldwatch Paper 91. Washington, DC: Worldwatch Institute.

Gallup Organization. 1989. *The Gallup Report #285: Concern about the environment*. Washington, DC.

Glantz, M. 1988. Politics and the air around us: International policy action on atmospheric pollution by trace gases. In *Societal Responses to Regional Climate Change: Forecasting by analogy*, edited by M. Glantz, 41–72. Boulder, CO: Westview.

Hirschman, Albert. 1977. *The Passions and the Interests*. Princeton, NJ: Princeton University Press.

Idso, Sherwood B. 1989. *Carbon Dioxide and Global Change: The earth in transition*. Tempe, AZ: IBR Press.

Intergovernmental Panel on Climate Change. 1990. *Policymakers' Summary: Working group III*. Geneva: World Meteorological Association and United Nations Environment Programme.

Jamieson, Dale. 1988. The artificial heart: Reevaluating the investment. In *Organ Substitution Technology*, edited by D. Mathieu, 277–96. Boulder, CO: Westview.

———. 1990. Managing the future: Public policy, scientific uncertainty, and global warming. In *Upstream/ Downstream: New essays in environmental ethics*, edited by D. Scherer, 67–89. Philadelphia: Temple University Press.

———. 1991. The epistemology of climate change: Some morals for managers. *Society and Natural Resources* 4: 319–29.

Lee, Keekok. 1989. *Social Philosophy and Ecological Scarcity*. New York: Routledge.

Locke, John. [1690] 1952. *The Second Treatise of Government*. Indianapolis, IN: Bobbs-Merrill.

Lovelock, J. E. 1988. *The Ages of Gaia: A biography of our living earth*. New York: Norton.

Mandeville, B. [1714] 1970. *The Fable of the Bees*, trans. P. Harth. Hammersmith, England: Penguin.

Mansbridge, Jane, ed. 1990. *Beyond Self-Interest*. Chicago: University of Chicago Press.

McKibben, W. 1989. *The End of Nature*. New York: Knopf.

Moomaw, William R. [1988] 1989. Near-term Congressional options for responding to global climate change. Reprinted in *The Challenge of Global Warming*, edited by Dean Edwin Abrahamson, 305–26. Washington, DC: Island.

Myers, Milton. L. 1983. *The Soul of Modern Economic Man*. Chicago: University of Chicago Press.

National Academy of Sciences/National Research Council. 1983. *Changing Climate*. Washington, DC: National Academy Press.

Nordhaus, W. 1990. To slow or not to slow: The economics of the greenhouse effect. Paper presented at the American Association for the Advancement of Science, New Orleans, LA.

Opp, Karl-Dieter. 1989. *The Rationality of Political Protest*. Boulder, CO: Westview.

Reich, Robert, ed. 1988. *The Power of Public Ideas*. Cambridge: Harvard University Press.

Sagoff, Mark. 1988. *The Economy of the Earth*. New York: Cambridge University Press.

Schneider, Stephen H. 1989. *Global Warming: Are we entering the greenhouse century?* San Francisco: Sierra Club Books.

Scitovsky, Tibor. 1976. *The Joyless Economy: An inquiry into human satisfaction and consumer dissatisfaction*. New York: Oxford University Press.

U.S. Environmental Protection Agency. 1989. *Policy Options for Stabilizing Global Climate, Draft Report to Congress*, edited by D. Lashof and D. A. Tirpak. Washington, DC: GPO.

Weiskel, Timothy. 1990. Cultural values and their environmental implications: An essay on knowledge, belief and global survival. Paper presented at the American Association for the Advancement of Science, New Orleans, LA.

White House Council of Economic Advisors. 1990. *The Economic Report of the President*. Washington, DC: Executive Office of the President, Publication Services.

Wolfe, Alan. 1989. *Whose Keeper? Social science and moral obligation*. Berkeley: University of California Press.

World Climate Program. 1985. *Report of the International Conference on the Assessment of the Role of Carbon Dioxide and of Other Greenhouse Gases in Climate Variations and Associated Impacts: Report on an international conference held at Villach, Austria, 9–15 October 1985*. Geneva: World Meteorological Organization.

Can and Ought We Restore Nature?

28

Faking Nature

Robert Elliot

I

Consider the following case. There is a proposal to mine beach sands for rutile. Large areas of dune are to be cleared of vegetation and the dunes themselves destroyed. It is agreed, by all parties concerned, that the dune area has value quite apart from a utilitarian one. It is agreed, in other words, that it would be a bad thing considered in itself for the dune area to be dramatically altered. Acknowledging this the mining company expresses its willingness, indeed its desire, to restore the dune area to its original condition after the minerals have been extracted.[1] The company goes on to argue that any loss of value is merely temporary and that full value will in fact be restored. In other words they are claiming that the destruction of what has value is compensated for by the later creation (recreation) of something of equal value. I shall call this "the restoration thesis."

In the actual world many such proposals are made, not because of shared conservationist principles, but as a way of undermining the arguments of conservationists. Such proposals are in fact effective in defeating environmentalist protest. They are also notoriously ineffective in putting right, or indeed even seeming to put right, the particular wrong that has been done to the environment. The sandmining case is just one of a number of similar cases involving such things as open-cut mining, clear-felling of forests, river di-version, and highway construction. Across a range of such cases some concession is made by way of acknowledging the value of pieces of landscape, rivers, forests and so forth, and a suggestion is made that this value can be restored once the environmentally disruptive process has been completed.

Imagine, contrary to fact, that restoration projects are largely successful, that the environment is brought back to its original condition, and that even a close inspection will fail to reveal that the area has been mined, clear-felled, or whatever. If this is so then there is temptation to think that one particular environmentalist objection is defeated. The issue is by no means merely academic. I have already claimed that restoration promises do in fact carry weight against environmental arguments. Thus Mr. Doug Anthony, the Australian deputy prime minister, saw fit to suggest that sand-mining on Fraser Island could be resumed once "the community becomes more informed and more enlightened as to what reclamation work is being carried out by mining companies. . . . "[2] Or consider how the protests of environmentalists might be deflected in the light of the following report of environmental engineering in the United States.

about 2 km of creek 25 feet wide has been moved to accommodate a highway and in doing so engineers with the aid of landscape architects and biologists have rebuilt the creek to the same standard as before. Boulders, bends, irregularities and natural vegetation have all been designed into the new section. In addition, special log structures have been built to improve the habitat as part of a fish development program.[3]

Not surprisingly the claim that revegetation, rehabilitation, and the like restore value has been strongly contested. J. G. Mosley reports that:

> The Fraser Island Environmental Inquiry Commissioners did in fact face up to the question of the relevance of successful rehabilitation to the decision on whether to ban exports (of beach sand minerals) and were quite unequivocal in saying that if the aim was to protect a natural area such success was irrelevant.... The Inquiry said: "... even if, contrary to the overwhelming weight of evidence before the Commission, successful rehabilitation of the flora after mining is found to be ecologically possible on all mined sites on the Island ... the overall impression of a wild, uncultivated island refuge will be destroyed forever by mining."[4]

I want to show both that there is a rational, coherent ethical system which supports decisive objections to the restoration thesis, and that that system is not lacking in normative appeal. The system I have in mind will make valuation depend, in part, on the presence of properties which cannot survive the disruption–restoration process. There is, however, one point that needs clarifying before discussion proceeds. Establishing that restoration projects, even if empirically successful, do not fully restore value does not by any means constitute a knock-down argument against some environmentally disruptive policy. The value that would be lost if such a policy were implemented may be just one value among many which conflict in this situation. Countervailing considerations may be decisive and the policy thereby shown to be the right one. If my argument turns out to be correct it will provide an extra, though by no means decisive, reason for adopting certain environmentalist policies. It will show that the resistance which environmentalists display in the face of restoration promises is not merely silly, or emotional, or irrational. This is important because so much of the debate assumes that settling the dispute about what is ecologically possible automatically settles the value question. The thrust of much of the discussion is that if restoration is shown to be possible, and economically feasible, then recalcitrant environmentalists are behaving irrationally, being merely obstinate, or being selfish.

There are indeed familiar ethical systems which will serve to explain what is wrong with the restoration thesis in a certain range of cases. Thus preference utilitarianism will support objections to some restoration proposal if that proposal fails to maximally satisfy preferences. Likewise classical utilitarianism will lend support to a conservationist stance provided that the restoration proposal fails to maximize happiness and pleasure. However, in both cases the support offered is contingent upon the way in which the preferences and utilities line up. And it is simply not clear that they line up in such a way that the conservationist position is even usually vindicated. While appeal to utilitarian considerations might be strategically useful in certain cases they do not reflect the underlying motivation of the conservationists. The conservationists seem committed to an account of what has value which allows that restoration proposals fail to compensate for environmental destruction despite the fact that such proposals would maximize utility. What, then, is this distinct source of value which motivates and underpins the stance taken by, among others, the Commissioners of the Fraser Island Environmental Inquiry?

II

It is instructive to list some reasons that might be given in support of the claim that something of value would be lost if a certain bit of the environment were destroyed. It may be that the area supports a diversity of plant and animal life, it may be that it is the habitat of some endangered species, it may be that it contains striking rock formations or particularly fine specimens of mountain ash. If it is only considerations such as these that contribute to the area's value then perhaps opposition to the environmentally disruptive project would be irrational provided certain firm guarantees were available; for instance that the mining company or timber company would carry out the restoration and that it would be successful. Presumably there are steps that could be taken to ensure the continuance of species diversity and the continued existence of the endangered species. Some of the other requirements might prove harder to meet, but in some sense or other it is possible to recreate the rock formations and to plant mountain ash that will turn out to be particularly fine specimens. If value consists of the presence of objects of these various kinds, independently of what explains their presence, then the restoration thesis would seem to hold. The environmentalist needs to appeal to some feature which cannot be replicated as a source of some part of a natural area's value.

Putting the point thus indicates the direction the environmentalist could take. He might suggest that an area is valuable, partly, because it is a natural area, one that has not been modified by human hand, one that is undeveloped, unspoiled, or even unsullied. This suggestion is in accordance with much environmentalist rhetoric, and something like it at least must be at the basis of resistance to restoration proposals. One way of teasing out the suggestion and giving it a normative basis is to take over a notion from aesthetics. Thus we might claim that what the environmental engineers are proposing is that we accept a fake or a forgery instead of the real thing. If the claim can be made good then perhaps an adequate response to restoration proposals is to point out that they merely fake nature: that they offer us something less than was taken away.[5] Certainly there is a weight of opinion to the effect that, in art at least, fakes lack a value possessed by the real thing.[6]

One way in which this argument might be nipped in the bud is by claiming that it is bound to exploit an ultimately unworkable distinction between what is natural and what is not. Admittedly the distinction between the natural and the nonnatural requires detailed working out. This is something I do not propose doing. However, I do think the distinction can be made good in a way sufficient to the present need. For present purposes I shall take it that "natural" means something like "unmodified by human activity." Obviously some areas will be more natural than others according to the degree to which they have been shaped by human hands. Indeed most rural landscapes will, on this view, count as nonnatural to a very high degree. Nor do I intend the natural/non-natural distinction to exactly parallel some dependent moral evaluation; that is, I do not want to be taken as claiming that what is natural is good and what is nonnatural is not. The distinction between natural and nonnatural connects with valuation in a much more subtle way than that. This is something to which I shall presently return. My claim, then, is that restoration policies do not always fully restore value because part of the reason that we value bits of the environment is because they are natural to a high degree. It is time to consider some counterarguments.

An environmental engineer might urge that the exact similarity which holds between the original and the perfectly restored environment leaves no room for a value discrimination between them. He may urge that if they are *exactly* alike, down to the minutest detail (and let us imagine for the sake of argument that this is a technological possibility), then they must be *equally* valuable. The suggestion is that value-discriminations depend on there being intrinsic differences between the states of affairs evaluated. This begs the question against the environmentalist, since it simply discounts the possibility that events temporally and spatially outside the immediate landscape in question can serve as the basis of some valuation of it. It discounts the possibility that the manner of the landscape's genesis, for example, has a legitimate role in determining its value. Here are some examples which suggest that an object's origins do affect its value and our valuations of it.

Imagine that I have a piece of sculpture in my garden which is too fragile to be moved at all. For some reason it would suit the local council to lay sewage pipes just where the sculpture happens to be. The council engineer informs me of this and explains that my sculpture will have to go. However, I need not despair because he promises to replace it with an exactly similar artifact, one which, he assures me, not even the very best experts could tell was not the original. The example may be unlikely, but it does have some point. While I may concede that the replica would be better than nothing at all (and I may not even concede that), it is utterly improbable that I would accept it as full compensation for the original. Nor is my reluctance entirely explained by the monetary value of the original work. My reluctance springs from the fact that I value the original as an aesthetic object, as an object with a specific genesis and history.

Alternatively, imagine I have been promised a Vermeer for my birthday. The day arrives and I am given a painting which looks just like a Vermeer. I am understandably pleased. However, my pleasure does not last for long. I am told that the painting I am holding is not a Vermeer but instead an exact replica of one previously destroyed. Any attempt to allay my disappointment by insisting that there just is no difference between the replica and the original misses the mark completely. There is a difference and it is one which affects my perception, and consequent valuation, of the painting. The difference, of course, lies in the painting's genesis.

I shall offer one last example which perhaps bears even more closely on the environmental issue. I am given a rather beautiful, delicately constructed object. It is something I treasure and admire, something in which I find considerable aesthetic value. Everything is fine until I discover certain facts about its origin. I discover that it is carved out of the bone of someone killed especially for that purpose. This discovery affects me deeply and I cease to value the object in the way that I once did. I regard it as in some sense sullied, spoiled by the facts of its origin. The object itself has not changed but my perceptions of it have. I now know that it is not quite the kind of thing I thought it was, and that my prior valuation of it was mistaken. The discovery is like the discovery that a painting one believed to be an original is in fact a forgery. The discovery about the object's origin changes the valuation made of it, since it reveals that the object is not of the kind that I value.

What these examples suggest is that there is at least a prima facie case for partially explaining the value of objects in terms of their origins, in terms of the kinds of processes that brought them into being. It is easy to find evidence in the writings of people who have valued nature that things extrinsic to the present, immediate environment determine valuations of it. John Muir's remarks about Hetch Hetchy Valley are a case in point.[7] Muir regarded the valley as a place where he could have direct contact with primeval nature; he valued it not just because it was a place of great beauty, but because it was also a part of the world that had not been shaped by human hand. Muir's valuation was conditional upon certain facts about the valley's genesis; his valuation was of a literally natural object, of an object with a special kind of continuity with the past. The news that it was a carefully contrived elaborate *ecological* artifact would have transformed that valuation immediately and radically.

The appeal that many find in areas of wilderness, in natural forests and wild rivers, depends very much on the naturalness of such places. There may be similarities between the experience one has when confronted with the multifaceted complexity, the magnitude, the awesomeness of a very large city, and the experience one has walking through a rain forest. There may be similarities between the feeling one has listening to the roar of water over the spillway of a dam and the feeling one has listening to a similar roar as a wild river tumbles down rapids. Despite the similarities there are also differences. We value the forest and river in part because they are representative of the world outside our dominion, because their existence is independent of us. We may value the city and the dam because of what they represent of human achievement. Pointing out the differences is not necessarily to denigrate either. However, there will be cases where we rightly judge that it is better to have the natural object than it is to have the artifact.

It is appropriate to return to a point mentioned earlier concerning the relationship between the natural and the valuable. It will not do to argue that what is natural is necessarily of value. The environmentalist can comfortably concede this point. He is not claiming that all natural phenomena have value in virtue of being natural. Sickness and disease are natural in a straightforward sense and are certainly not good. Natural phenomena such as fires, hurricanes, and volcanic eruptions can totally alter landscapes, and alter them for the worse. All of this can be conceded. What the environmentalist wants to claim is that within certain constraints, the naturalness of a landscape is a reason for preserving it, a determinant of its value. Artificially transforming an utterly barren, ecologically bankrupt landscape into something richer and more subtle may be a good thing. That is a view quite compatible with the belief that replacing a rich natural environment with a rich artificial one is a bad thing. What the environmentalist insists on is that naturalness is one factor in determining the value of pieces of the environment. But that, as I have tried to suggest, is no news. The castle by the Scottish loch is a very different kind of object, value-wise, from the exact replica in the appropriately shaped environment of some Disneyland of the future. The barrenness of some Cycladic island would stand in a different, better perspective if it were not brought about by human intervention.

As I have glossed it, the environmentalist's complaint concerning restoration proposals is that nature is not replaceable without depreciation in one aspect of its value which has to do with its genesis, its history. Given this, an opponent might be tempted to argue that there is no longer any such thing as "natural" wilderness, since the preservation of those bits of it which remain is achievable only by deliberate policy. The idea is that by placing boundaries around national parks; by actively discouraging grazing, trail-biking, and the like; by prohibiting sandmining, we are turning the wilderness into an artifact, that in some negative or indirect way we are creating an environment. There is some truth in this suggestion. In fact we need to take notice of it if we do value wilderness, since positive policies are required to preserve it. But as an argument against my overall claim, it fails. What is significant about wilderness is its causal continuity with the past. This is something that is not destroyed by demarcating an area and declaring it a national park. There is a distinction between the "naturalness" of the wilderness itself and the means used to maintain and protect it. What remains within the park boundaries is, as it were, the real thing. The environmentalist may regret that such positive policy is required to preserve the wilderness against human, or even natural, assault.[8] However, the regret does not follow from the belief that what remains is of depreciated value. There is a significant difference between preventing damage and repairing damage once it is done. That is the difference that leaves room for an argument in favor of a preservation policy over and above a restoration policy.

There is another important issue which needs highlighting. It might be thought that naturalness only matters insofar as it is perceived. In other words, it might be thought that if the environmental engineer could perform the restoration quickly and secretly, then there would be no room for complaint. Of course, in one sense there would not be, since the knowledge which would motivate complaint would be missing. What this shows is that there can be loss of value without the loss being perceived. It allows room for valuations to be mistaken because of ignorance concerning relevant facts. Thus my Vermeer can be removed and secretly replaced with the perfect replica. I have lost something of value without knowing that I have. This is possible because it is not simply the states of mind engendered by looking at the painting, by gloatingly contemplating my possession of it, by giving myself over to aesthetic pleasure, and so on, which explain why it has value. It has value because of the kind of thing that it is, and one thing that it is is a painting executed by a man with certain intentions, at a certain stage of his artistic development, living in a certain aesthetic milieu. Similarly, it is not just those things which make me feel the joy that wilderness makes me feel that I value. That would be a reason for desiring such things, but that is a distinct consideration. I value the forest because it is of a specific kind, because there is a certain kind of causal history which explains its existence. Of course I can be deceived into thinking that a piece of landscape has that kind of history, has developed in the appropriate way. The success of the deception does not elevate the restored landscape to the level of the original, no more than the success of the deception in the previous example confers on the fake the value of a real Vermeer. What has value in both cases are objects which are of the kind that I value, not merely objects which I think are of that kind. This point, it should be noted, is appropriate independently of views concerning the subjectivity or objectivity of value.

An example might bring the point home. Imagine that John is someone who values wilderness. John may find himself in one of the following situations:

(1) He falls into the clutches of a utilitarian-minded supertechnologist. John's captor has erected a rather incredible device which he calls an experience machine. Once the electrodes are attached and the right buttons pressed one can be brought to experience anything whatsoever. John is plugged into the machine, and, since his captor knows full well John's love of wilderness, given an extended experience as of hiking through a spectacular wilderness. This is environmental engineering at its most extreme. Quite assuredly John is being shortchanged. John wants there to be wilderness and he wants to experience it. He wants the world to be a

certain way and he wants to have experiences of a certain kind; veridical.

(2) John is abducted, blindfolded, and taken to a simulated, plastic wilderness area. When the blindfold is removed John is thrilled by what he sees around him: the tall gums, the wattles, the lichen on the rocks. At least that is what he thinks is there. We know better: We know that John is deceived, that he is once again being shortchanged. He has been presented with an environment which he thinks is of value but isn't. If he knew that the leaves through which the artificially generated breeze now stirred were synthetic he would be profoundly disappointed, perhaps even disgusted at what at best is a cruel joke.

(3) John is taken to a place which was once devastated by strip-mining. The forest which had stood there for some thousands of years had been felled and the earth torn up, and the animals either killed or driven from their habitat. Times have changed, however, and the area has been restored. Trees of the species which grew there before the devastation grow there again, and the animal species have returned. John knows nothing of this and thinks he is in pristine forest. Once again, he has been shortchanged, presented with less than what he values most.

In the same way that the plastic trees may be thought a (minimal) improvement on the experience machine, so too the real trees are an improvement on the plastic ones. In fact, in the third situation there is incomparably more of value than in the second, but there could be more. The forest, though real, is not genuinely what John wants it to be. If it were not the product of contrivance he would value it more. It is a product of contrivance. Even in the situation where the devastated area regenerates rather than is restored, it is possible to understand and sympathize with John's claim that the environment does not have the fullest possible value. Admittedly in this case there is not so much room for that claim, since the environment has regenerated of its own accord. Still, the regenerated environment does not have the right kind of continuity with the forest that stood there initially; that continuity has been interfered with by the earlier devastation. (In actual fact the regenerated forest is likely to be perceivably quite different to the kind of thing originally there.)

III

I have argued that the causal genesis of forests, rivers, lakes, and so on is important in establishing their value. I have also tried to give an indication of why this is. In the course of my argument I drew various analogies, implicit rather than explicit, between faking art and faking nature. This should not be taken to suggest, however, that the concepts of aesthetic evaluation and judgment are to be carried straight over to evaluations of, and judgments about, the natural environment. Indeed there is good reason to believe that this cannot be done. For one thing, an apparently integral part of aesthetic evaluation depends on viewing the aesthetic object as an intentional object, as an artifact, as something that is shaped by the purposes and designs of its author. Evaluating works of art involves explaining them, and judging them, in terms of their author's intentions; it involves placing them within the author's corpus of work; it involves locating them in some tradition and in some special milieu. Nature is not a work of art, though works of art (in some suitably broad sense) may look very much like natural objects.

None of this is to deny that certain concepts which are frequently deployed in aesthetic evaluation cannot usefully and legitimately be deployed in evaluations of the environment. We admire the intricacy and delicacy of coloring in paintings as we might admire the intricate and delicate shadings in a eucalyptus forest. We admire the solid grandeur of a building as we might admire the solidity and grandeur of a massive rock outcrop. And of course the ubiquitous notion of the beautiful has a purchase in environmental evaluations as it does in aesthetic evaluations. Even granted all this, there are various arguments which might be developed to drive a wedge between the two kinds of evaluation which would weaken the analogies between faking art and faking nature. One such argument turns on the claim that aesthetic evaluation has, as a central component, a judgmental factor concerning the author's intentions and the like, in the way that was sketched above.[9] The idea is that nature, like works of art, may elicit any of a range of emotional responses in viewers. We may be awed by a mountain, soothed by the sound of water over rocks, excited by the power of a waterfall, and so on. However, the judgmental element in aesthetic evaluation serves to differentiate it from environmental evaluation and serves to explain, or so the argument would go, exactly what it is about fakes and forgeries in art which discounts their value with respect to the original. The claim is that if there is no judgmental element in environmental evaluation, then there is no rational basis for preferring real to faked nature when the latter is a good replica. The argument can, I think, be met.

Meeting the argument does not require arguing that responses to nature count as aesthetic responses. I agree that they are not. Nevertheless there are analogies which go beyond emotional content, and which may persuade us to take more seriously the claim that faked nature is inferior. It is important to make the point that only in fanciful situations dreamt up by philosophers are there no detectable differences between fakes and originals, both in the case of artifacts and in the case of natural objects. By taking a realistic example where there are discernible, and possibly discernible, differences between the fake and the real thing, it is possible to bring out the judgmental element in responses to, and evaluations of, the environment. Right now I may not be able to tell a real Vermeer from a Van Meegeren, though I might learn to do so. By the same token I might not be able to tell apart a naturally evolved stand of mountain ash from one which has been planted, but might later acquire the ability to make the requisite judgment. Perhaps an anecdote is appropriate here. There is a particular stand of mountain ash that I had long admired. The trees were straight and tall, of uniform stature, neither densely packed nor too openspaced. I then discovered what would have been obvious to a more expert eye, namely that the stand of mountain ash had been planted to replace original forest which had been burnt out. This explained the uniformity in size, the density and so on: It also changed my attitude to that piece of landscape. The evaluation that I make now of that landscape is to a certain extent informed, the response is not merely emotive but cognitive as well. The evaluation is informed and directed by my beliefs about the forest, the type of forest it is, its condition as a member of that kind, its causal genesis, and so on. What is more, the judgmental element affects the emotive one. Knowing that the forest is not a naturally evolved forest causes me to feel differently about it: It causes me to perceive the forest differently and to assign it less value than naturally evolved forests.

Val Routley has eloquently reminded us that people who value wilderness do not do so merely because they like to soak up pretty scenery.[10] They see much more and value much more than this. What they do see, and what they value, is very much a function of the degree to which they understand the ecological mechanisms which maintain the landscape and which determine that it appears the way it does. Similarly, knowledge of art history, of painting techniques and the like, will inform aesthetic evaluations and alter aesthetic perceptions. Knowledge of this kind is capable of transforming a hitherto uninteresting landscape into one that is compelling. Holmes Rolston has discussed at length the way in which an understanding and appreciation of ecology generates new values.[11] He does not claim that ecology reveals values previously unnoticed, but rather that the understanding of the complexity, diversity, and integration of the natural world which ecology affords us opens up a new area of valuation. As the facts are uncovered, the values are generated. What the remarks of Routley and Rolston highlight is the judgmental factor which is present in environmental appraisal. Understanding and evaluation do go hand in hand; and the responses individuals have to forests, wild rivers, and the like are not merely raw, emotional responses.

IV

Not all forests are alike, not all rain forests are alike. There are countless possible discriminations that the informed observer may make. Comparative judgments between areas of the natural environment are possible with regard to ecological richness, stage of development, stability, peculiar local circumstance, and the like. Judgments of this kind will very often underlie hierarchical orderings of environments in terms of their intrinsic worth. Appeal to judgments of this kind will frequently strengthen the case for preserving some bit of the environment. Thus one strong argument against the Tasmanian Hydroelectricity Commission's proposal to dam the Lower Gordon River turns on the fact that it threatens the inundation of an exceedingly fine stand of Huon pine. If the stand of Huon pines could not justifiably be ranked so high on the appropriate ecological scale then the argument against the dam would be to that extent weakened.

One reason that a faked forest is not just as good as a naturally evolved forest is that there is always the possibility that the trained eye will tell the difference.[12] It takes some time to discriminate areas of Alpine plain which are naturally clear of snow gums from those that have been cleared. It takes some time to discriminate regrowth forest which has been logged from forest which has not been touched. These are discriminations which it is possible to make and which are made. Moreover, they are discriminations which affect valuations. The reasons why the "faked" forest counts for less, more often than not, than the real thing are similar to the reasons why faked works of art count for less than the real thing.

Origin is important as an integral part of the evaluation process. It is important because our beliefs about it determine the valuations we make. It is also important in that the discovery that something has an origin quite different to the origin we initially believe that it has can literally alter the way we perceive that thing.[13] The point concerning the possibility of detecting fakes is important in that it stresses just how much detail must be written into the claim that environmental engineers can replicate nature. Even if environmental engineering could achieve such exactitude, there is, I suggest, no compelling reason for accepting the restoration thesis. It is worth stressing, though, that as a matter of strategy, environmentalists must argue the empirical inadequacy of restoration proposals. This is the strongest argument against restoration ploys, because it appeals to diverse value frameworks, and because such proposals are promises to deliver a specific good. Showing that the good won't be delivered is thus a useful move to make.

Notes

1 In this case *full* restoration will be literally impossible because the minerals are not going to be replaced.

2 J. G. Mosley, "The Revegetation 'Debate': A Trap For Conservationists," *Australian Conservation Foundation Newsletter* 12, no. 8 (1980): 1.

3 Peter Dunk, "How New Engineering Can Work with the Environment," *Habitat Australia* 7, no. 5 (1979): 12.

4 See Mosley, "The Revegetation 'Debate,' " p. 1.

5 Offering something less is not, of course, always the same as offering nothing. If diversity of animal and plant life, stability of complex ecosystems, tall trees, and so on are things that we value in themselves, then certainly we are offered something. I am not denying this, and I doubt that many would qualify their valuations of the above-mentioned items in a way that leaves the restored environment devoid of value. Environmentalists would count as of worth programs designed to render polluted rivers reinhabitable by fish species. The point is rather that they may, as I hope to show, rationally deem it less valuable than what was originally there.

6 See, e.g., Colin Radford, "Fakes," *Mind* 87, no. 345 (1978): 66–76; and Nelson Goodman, *Languages of Art* (New York: Bobbs–Merrill, 1968) pp. 99–122, though Radford and Goodman have different accounts of why genesis matters.

7 See chap. 10 of Roderick Nash, *Wilderness and the American Mind* (New Haven: Yale University Press, 1973).

8 For example, protecting the Great Barrier Reef from damage by the crown-of-thorns starfish.

9 See, e.g., Don Mannison, "A Prolegomenon to a Human Chauvinist Aesthetic," in *Environmental Philosophy*, ed. D. S. Mannison, M. A. McRobbie, and R. Routley, (Canberra: Research and School of Social Sciences, Australian National University. 1980), pp. 212–16.

10 Val Routley, "Critical Notice of Passmore's *Man's Responsibility for Nature*." *Australasian Journal of Philosophy* 53, no. 2 (1975): 171–85.

11 Holmes Rolston III, "Is There an Ecological Ethic?" *Ethics* 85, no. 2 (1975): 93–109.

12 For a discussion of this point with respect to art forgeries, see Goodman, *Languages of Art*, esp. pp. 103–12.

13 For an excellent discussion of this same point with respect to artifacts, see Radford, "Fakes," esp. pp. 73–6.

References

Dunk, Peter. "How Engineering Can Work with the Environment." *Habitat Australia* 7, no. 5 (1979).

Goodman, Nelson. *Languages of Art*. New York: Bobbs-Merrill, 1968.

Mannison, Don. "A Prolegomenon to a Human Chauvinist Aesthetic." In *Environmental Philosophy*, edited by D. S. Mannison, M. A. McRobbie, and R. Routley. Canberra: Research School of Social Sciences, Australian National University, 1980.

Mosley, J. G. "The Revegetation 'Debate': A Trap for Conservationists." *Australian Conservation Foundation Newsletter* 12, no. 8 (1980).

Nash, Roderick. *Wilderness and the American Mind.* New Haven: Yale University Press, 1973.

Radford, Colin. "Fakes." *Mind* 87, no. 345 (1978).

Rolston, Holmes III. "Is There an Ecological Ethic?" *Ethics* 85, no. 2 (1975): 93–109.

Routley, Val. "Critical Notice of Passmore's *Man's Responsibility for Nature*." *Australasian Journal of Philosophy* 53, no. 2 (1975).

29

The Big Lie: Human Restoration of Nature

Eric Katz

The trail of the human serpent is thus over everything.

William James, *Pragmatism*

I

I begin with an empirical point, based on my own random observations: the idea that humanity can restore or repair the natural environment has begun to play an important part in decisions regarding environmental policy. We are urged to plant trees to reverse the "greenhouse effect." Real estate developers are obligated to restore previously damaged acreage in exchange for building permits.[1] The U.S. National Park Service spends $33 million to "rehabilitate" 39,000 acres of the Redwood Creek watershed.[2] And the U.S. Forest Service is criticized for its "plantation" mentality: it is harvesting trees from old-growth forests rather than "redesigning" forests according to the sustainable principles of nature. "Restoration forestry is the only true forestry," claims an environmentally conscious former employee of the Bureau of Land Management.[3]

These policies present the message that humanity should repair the damage that human intervention has caused the natural environment. The message is an optimistic one, for it implies that we recognize the harm we have caused in the natural environment and that we possess the means and will to correct these harms. These

policies also make us feel good; the prospect of restoration relieves the guilt we feel about the destruction of nature. The wounds we have inflicted on the natural world are not permanent; nature can be made "whole" again. Our natural resource base and foundation for survival can be saved by the appropriate policies of restoration, regeneration, and redesign.

It is also apparent that these ideas are not restricted to policymakers, environmentalists, or the general public – they have begun to pervade the normative principles of philosophers concerned with developing an adequate environmental ethic. Paul Taylor uses a concept of "restitutive justice" both as one of the basic rules of duty in his biocentric ethic and as a "priority principle" to resolve competing claims.[4] The basic idea of this rule is that human violators of nature will in some way repair or compensate injured natural entities and systems. Peter Wenz also endorses a principle of restitution as being essential to an adequate theory of environmental ethics; he then attacks Taylor's theory for not presenting a coherent principle.[5] The idea that humanity is morally responsible for reconstructing natural areas and entities – species, communities, ecosystems – thus becomes a central concern of an applied environmental ethic.

In this essay I question the environmentalists' concern for the restoration of nature and argue against the optimistic view that humanity has the obligation and ability to repair or reconstruct damaged natural systems. This conception of environmental policy and environmental ethics is based on a misperception of natural reality and a misguided understanding of the human place in the natural environment. On a simple level, it is the same kind of "technological fix" that has engendered the environmental crisis. Human science and technology will fix, repair, and improve natural processes. On a deeper level, it is an expression of an anthropocentric world view, in which human interests shape and redesign a comfortable natural reality. A "restored" nature is an artifact created to meet human satisfactions and interests. Thus, on the most fundamental level, it is an unrecognized manifestation of the insidious dream of the human domination of nature. Once and for all, humanity will demonstrate its mastery of nature by "restoring" and repairing the degraded ecosystems of the biosphere. Cloaked in an environmental consciousness, human power will reign supreme.

II

It has been many years since Robert Elliot published his sharp and accurate criticism of "the restoration thesis."[6] In an article entitled "Faking Nature," Elliot examined the moral objections to the practical environmental policy of restoring damaged natural systems, locations, and landscapes. For the sake of argument, Elliot assumed that the restoration of a damaged area could be recreated perfectly, so that the area would appear in its original condition after the restoration was completed. He then argued that the perfect copy of the natural area would be of less value than the original, for the newly restored natural area would be analogous to an art forgery. Two points seem crucial to Elliot's argument. First, the value of objects can be explained "in terms of their origins, in terms of the kinds of processes that brought them into being."[7] We value an art work in part because of the fact that a particular artist, a human individual, created the work at a precise moment in historical time. Similarly, we value a natural area because of its "special kind of continuity with the past." But to understand the art work or the natural area in its historical context we require a special kind of insight or knowledge. Thus, the second crucial point of Elliot's argument is the co-existence of "understanding and evaluation." The art expert brings to the analysis and evaluation of a

work of art a full range of information about the artist, the period, the intentions of the work, and so on. In a similar way, the evaluation of a natural area is informed by a detailed knowledge of ecological processes, a knowledge that can be learned as easily as the history of art.[8] To value the restored landscape as much as the original is thus a kind of ignorance; we are being fooled by the superficial similarities to the natural area, just as the ignorant art "appreciator" is fooled by the appearance of the art forgery.

Although Elliot's argument has had a profound effect on my own thinking about environmental issues, I believed that the problem he uses as a starting point is purely theoretical, almost fanciful.[9] After all, who would possibly believe that a land developer or a strip mining company would actually restore a natural area to its original state? Elliot himself claims that "the restoration thesis" is generally used "as a way of undermining the arguments of conservationists."[10] Thus it is with concern that I discover that serious environmentalist thinkers, as noted above, have argued for a position similar to Elliot's "restoration thesis." The restoration of a damaged nature is seen not only as a practical option for environmental policy but also as a moral obligation for right-thinking environmentalists. If we are to continue human projects which (unfortunately) impinge on the natural environment (it is claimed), then we must repair the damage. In a few short years a "sea-change" has occurred: what Elliot attacked as both a physical impossibility and a moral mistake is now advocated as proper environmental policy. Am I alone in thinking that something has gone wrong here?

Perhaps not enough people have read Elliot's arguments; neither Taylor nor Wenz, the principal advocates of restitutive environmental justice, list this article in their notes or bibliographies. Perhaps we need to re-examine the idea of re-creating a natural landscape; in what sense is this action analogous to an art forgery? Perhaps we need to push beyond Elliot's analysis, to use his arguments as a starting point for a deeper investigation into the fundamental errors of restoration policy.

III

My initial reaction to the possibility of restoration policy is almost entirely visceral: I am outraged by the idea that a technologically created "nature"

Eric Katz

will be passed off as reality. The human presumption that we are capable of this technological fix demonstrates (once again) the arrogance with which humanity surveys the natural world. Whatever the problem may be, there will be a technological, mechanical, or scientific solution. Human engineering will modify the secrets of natural processes and effect a satisfactory result. Chemical fertilizers will increase food production; pesticides will control disease-carrying insects; hydroelectric dams will harness the power of our rivers. The familiar list goes on and on.

The relationship between this technological mind-set and the environmental crisis has been amply demonstrated, and need not concern us here.[11] My interest is narrower. I want to focus on the creation of artifacts, for that is what technology does. The re-created natural environment that is the end result of a restoration project is nothing more than an artifact created for human use. The problem for an applied environmental ethic is the determination of the moral value of this artifact.

Recently, Michael Losonsky has pointed out how little we know about the nature, structure, and meaning of artifacts. "[C]ompared to the scientific study of nature, the scientific study of artifacts is in its infancy."[12] What is clear, of course, is that an artifact is not equivalent to a natural object; but the precise difference, or set of differences, is not readily apparent. Indeed, when we consider objects such as beaver dams, we are unsure if we are dealing with natural objects or artifacts. Fortunately, however, these kinds of animal-created artifacts can be safely ignored in the present investigation. Nature restoration projects are obviously human. A human built dam is clearly artifactual.

The concepts of function and purpose are central to an understanding of artifacts. Losonsky rejects the Aristotelian view that artifacts (as distinguished from natural objects) have no inner nature or hidden essence that can be discovered. Artifacts have a "nature" that is partially comprised of three features: "internal structure, purpose, and manner of use." This nature, in turn, explains why artifacts "have predictable lifespans during which they undergo regular and predictable changes."[13] The structure, function, and use of the artifacts determine to some extent the changes which they undergo. Clocks would not develop in a manner which prevented the measurement of time.

Natural objects lack the kind of purpose and function found in artifacts. As Andrew Brennan has argued, natural entities have no "intrinsic functions," as he calls them, for they were not the result of design. They were not created for a particular purpose; they have no set manner of use. Although we often speak as if natural individuals (for example, predators) have roles to play in ecosystemic well-being (the maintenance of optimum population levels), this kind of talk is either metaphorical or fallacious. No one created or designed the mountain lion as a regulator of the deer population.[14]

This is the key point. Natural individuals were not designed for a purpose. They lack intrinsic functions, making them different from human-created artifacts. Artifacts, I claim, are essentially anthropocentric. They are created for human use, human purpose – they serve a function for human life. Their existence is centered on human life. It would be impossible to imagine an artifact not designed to meet a human purpose. Without a foreseen use the object would not be created. This is completely different from the way natural entities and species evolve to fill ecological niches in the biosphere.

The doctrine of anthropocentrism is thus an essential element in understanding the meaning of artifacts. This conceptual relationship is not generally problematic, for most artifacts are human creations designed for use in human social and cultural contexts. But once we begin to re-design natural systems and processes, once we begin to create restored natural environments, we impose our anthropocentric purposes on areas that exist outside human society. We will construct so-called natural objects on the model of human desires, interests, and satisfactions. Depending on the adequacy of our technology, these restored and redesigned natural areas will appear more or less natural, but they will never be natural – they will be anthropocentrically designed human artifacts.

A disturbing example of this conceptual problem applied to environmental policy can be found in Chris Maser's *The Redesigned Forest*. Maser is a former research scientist for the United States Department of Interior Bureau of Land Management. His book attests to his deeply felt commitment to the policy of "sustainable" forestry, as opposed to the short-term expediency of present-day forestry practices. Maser argues for a forestry policy that "restores" the forest as it harvests it; we must be true foresters and not "plantation" managers.

Nonetheless, Maser's plans for "redesigning" forests reveal several problems about the concepts and values implicit in restoration policy. First, Maser consistently compares the human design of forests with Nature's design. The entire first chapter is a series of short sections comparing the two "designs." In the "Introduction," he writes, "[W]e are redesigning our forests from Nature's blueprint to humanity's blueprint."[15] But Nature, of course, does not have a blueprint, nor a design. As a zoologist, Maser knows this, but his metaphorical talk is dangerous. It implies that we can discover the plan, the methods, the processes of nature, and mold them to our purposes.

Maser himself often writes as if he accepts that implication. The second problem with his argument is the comparison of nature to a mechanism that we do not fully understand. The crucial error we make in simplifying forest ecology – turning forests into plantations – is that we are assuming our design for the forest mechanism is better than nature's. "Forests are not automobiles in which we can tailor artificially substituted parts for original parts."[16] How true. But Maser's argument against this substitution is empirical: "A forest cannot be 'rebuilt' and remain the same forest, but we could probably rebuild a forest similar to the original if we knew how. No one has ever done it. . . . [W]e do not have a parts catalog, or a maintenance manual. . . ."[17] The implication is that if we did have a catalog and manual, if nature were known as well as artifactual machines, then the restoration of forests would be morally and practically acceptable. This conclusion serves as Maser's chief argument for the preservation of old-growth and other unmanaged forests: "We have to maintain some original, unmanaged old-growth forest, mature forest, and young-growth forest as parts catalog, maintenance manual, and service department from which to learn to practice restoration forestry."[18] Is the forest-as-parts-catalog a better guiding metaphor than the forest-as-plantation?

This mechanistic conception of nature underlies, or explains, the third problem with Maser's argument. His goal for restoration forestry, his purpose in criticizing the short-term plantation mentality, is irredeemably anthropocentric. The problem with present-day forestry practices is that they are "exclusive of all other human values except production of fast-grown wood fiber."[19] It

is the elimination of other human values and interests that concerns Maser. "We need to learn to see the forest as the factory that produces raw materials. . . ." to meet our "common goal[:] . . . a sustainable forest for a sustainable industry for a sustainable environment for a sustainable human population."[20] Restoration forestry is necessary because it is the best method for achieving the human goods which we extract from nature. Our goal is to build a better "factory-forest," using the complex knowledge of forest ecology.

What is disturbing about Maser's position is that it comes from an environmentalist. Unlike Elliot's theoretical opponents of conservation, who wished to subvert the environmentalist position with the "restoration thesis," Maser advocates the human design of forests as a method of environmental protection and conservation for human use. His conclusion shows us the danger of using anthropocentric and mechanistic models of thought in the formulation of environmental policy. These models leave us with forests that are "factories" for the production of human commodities, spare-parts catalogs for the maintenance of the machine.

But Maser's view can be considered an extreme version of restoration thinking. Is Steve Packard's work with The Nature Conservancy a better expression of the underlying principles and values of restoration policy?[21] Is Packard's work more aligned with natural processes? Is it less technological, artifactual, and anthropocentric? Unfortunately not: even this more benign and less interventionist project of ecological restoration is based on problematic assumptions about the management of nature.

Packard describes the research and actions undertaken to rediscover and restore the tallgrass savanna or oak opening community of the Midwest. As he relates, the rediscovery of the savanna was an accidental by-product of a different project, the restoration of prairie landscapes which included a bur oak edge. Involving seven small sites with degraded "prairies," the project entailed the enlargement of the areas by clearing brush and planting prairie species in its place. "Our objective was clear," he writes. "It was to restore these tracts to their original natural condition."

But how was this goal achieved? Packard asserts that he wanted to use "natural forces" such as fire to clear the brush; but this methodology is soon abandoned: "the question was, did we have enough determination and patience to give natural processes two or three hundred years to work themselves out? Or could we find something quicker?" Thus, he writes, "we decided to leap-frog the persistent brushy border and to recut our fire lines. . . ." Although Packard is using the natural force of fire, he is employing it in an artificially accelerated manner to achieve the desired results more quickly. A similar process is used when the "seeding process" begins: naturally occurring seeds are used, but the process involves the preparation of a "savanna mix," and human decisions regarding the placement and release of the seeds.

Although I have nothing but admiration for Packard's work, and I sincerely applaud his success, the significant philosophical lesson from his restoration project is that even such a "benign" and minimal intervention compromises the natural integrity of the system being restored. Despite his goal of restoring an original natural condition, Packard is actually creating an artifactual substitute for the real savanna, one based on human technologies and designed for human purposes: a pure and grand vision of the old Midwest. The most telling passage in his chronicle of the savanna restoration is his report of the "farsighted" 1913 law which established the Forest Preserve District, a law whose statement of purpose "emboldened" Packard to accelerate the burning process. He quotes the law, with emphasis added: "to *restore*, restock, protect and preserve the natural forests and said lands . . . as nearly as may be, in their natural state and condition, for the purpose of the education, pleasure, and recreation of the public." Note that the purpose of the preservation and restoration is the production of human goods; as with all artifacts, the goal is a human benefit. Packard calls this a "noble statement." Clearly the aim of restoration is the creation of environments that are pleasing to the human population. If the restoration is done well, as in the case of Packard's savannas, the area may appear natural; but it will not be natural, since it is the result of a technological acceleration of natural forces.

I began this section with a report of my visceral reaction to the technological re-creation of natural environments. This reaction has now been explained and analyzed. Nature restoration projects are the creations of human technologies, and as such, are artifacts. But artifacts are essentially the constructs of an anthropocentric world view. They

are designed by humans for humans to satisfy human interests and needs. Artifactual restored nature is thus fundamentally different from natural objects and systems which exist without human design. It is not surprising, then, that we view restored nature with a value different from the original.

IV

To this point, my analysis has supported the argument and conclusions of Elliot's criticism of "the restoration thesis." But further reflection on the nature of artifacts, and the comparison of forests to well run machines, makes me doubt the central analogy which serves as the foundation of his case. Can we compare an undisturbed natural environment to a work of art? Should we?

As noted in Section II, Elliot uses the art/nature analogy to make two fundamental points about the process of evaluation: (1) the importance of a continuous causal history; and (2) the use of knowledge about this causal history to make appropriate judgments. A work of art or a natural entity which lacks a continuous causal history, as understood by the expert in the field, would be judged inferior. If the object is "passed off" as an original, with its causal history intact, then we would judge it to be a forgery or an instance of "faked" nature.

I do not deny that this is a powerful analogy. It demonstrates the crucial importance of causal history in the analysis of value. But the analogy should not be pushed too far, for the comparison suggests that we possess an understanding of art forgery that is now simply being applied to natural objects. I doubt that our understanding of art forgery is adequate for this task. L. B. Cebik argues that an analysis of forgery involves basic ontological questions about the meaning of art. Cebik claims that it is a mistake to focus exclusively on questions of value when analyzing art forgeries, for the practice of forgery raises fundamental issues about the status of art itself.[22]

According to Cebik, an analysis of forgeries demonstrates that our understanding of art is dominated by a limiting paradigm – "production by individuals." We focus almost exclusively on the individual identity of the artist as the determining factor in assessing authenticity. "Nowhere . . . is there room for paradigmatic art being fluid, unfinished, evolving, and continuous in its creation." Cebik has in mind a dynamic, communally based art, an ever-changing neighborhood mural or music passed on for generations.[23] Another example would be classical ballet, a performance of which is a unique dynamic movement, different from every other performance of the same ballet.

These suggestions about a different paradigm of art show clearly, I think, what is wrong with the art/nature analogy as a useful analytical tool. Natural entities and systems are much more akin to the fluid evolving art of Cebik's alternative model than they are to the static, finished, individual artworks of the dominant paradigm. It is thus an error to use criteria of forgery and authenticity that derive from an individualistic, static conception of art for an evaluation of natural entities and systems. Natural entities and systems are nothing like static, finished objects of art. They are fluid, evolving systems which completely transcend the category of artist or creator. The perceived disvalue in restored natural objects does not derive from a misunderstanding over the identity of the creator of the objects. It derives instead from the misplaced category of "creator" – for natural objects do not have creators or designers as human artworks do. Once we realize that the natural entity we are viewing has been "restored" by a human artisan it ceases to be a natural object. It is not a forgery; it is an artifact.

We thus return to artifacts, and their essential anthropocentric nature. We cannot (and should not) think of natural objects as artifacts, for this imposes a human purpose or design on their very essence. As artifacts, they are evaluated by their success in meeting human interests and needs, not by their own intrinsic being. Using the art/nature analogy of forgery reinforces the impression that natural objects are similar to artifacts – artworks – and that they can be evaluated using the same anthropocentric criteria. Natural entities have to be evaluated on their own terms, not as artworks, machines, factories, or any other human-created artifact.

V

But what are the terms appropriate for the evaluation of natural objects? What criteria should be used? To answer this question we need to do more than differentiate natural objects from artifacts; we need to examine the essence or nature of natural

objects. What does it mean to say that an entity is natural (and hence, not an artifact)? Is there a distinguishing mark or characteristic that determines the descriptive judgment? What makes an object natural, and why is the standard not met through the restoration process?

The simple answer to this question – a response I basically support – is that the natural is defined as being independent of the actions of humanity. Thus, Taylor advocates a principle of noninterference as a primary moral duty in his ethic of respect for nature. "[W]e put aside our personal likes and our human interests.... Our respect for nature means that we acknowledge the sufficiency of the natural world to sustain its own proper order throughout the whole domain of life."[24] The processes of the natural world that are free of human interference are the most natural.

There are two obvious problems with this first simple answer. First, there is the empirical point that the human effect on the environment is, by now, fairly pervasive. No part of the natural world lies untouched by our pollution and technology. In a sense, then, nothing natural truly exists (anymore). Second, there is the logical point that humans themselves are naturally evolved beings, and so all human actions would be "natural," regardless of the amount of technology used or the interference on nonhuman nature. The creation of artifacts is a natural human activity, and thus the distinction between artifact and natural object begins to blur.

These problems in the relationship of humanity to nature are not new. Mill raised similar objections to the idea of "nature" as a moral norm over a hundred years ago, and I need not review his arguments.[25] The answer to these problems is twofold. First, we admit that the concepts of "natural" and "artifactual" are not absolutes; they exist along a spectrum, where various gradations of both concepts can be discerned. The human effect on the natural world is pervasive, but there are differences in human actions that make a descriptive difference. A toxic waste dump is different from a compost heap of organic material. To claim that both are equally non-natural would obscure important distinctions.

A second response is presented by Brennan.[26] Although a broad definition of "natural" denotes independence from human management or interference, a more useful notion (because it has implications for value theory and ethics) can be derived from the consideration of evolutionary adaptations. Our natural diet is the one we are adapted for, that is "in keeping with our nature." All human activity is not unnatural, only that activity which goes beyond our biological and evolutionary capacities. As an example, Brennan cites the procedure of "natural childbirth," that is, childbirth free of technological medical interventions. "Childbirth is an especially striking example of the wildness within us... where we can appreciate the natural at first hand...." It is natural, free, and wild not because it is a nonhuman activity – after all, it is human childbirth – but because it is independent of a certain type of human activity, actions designed to control or to manipulate natural processes.

The "natural" then is a term we use to designate objects and processes that exist as far as possible from human manipulation and control. Natural entities are autonomous in ways that human-created artifacts are not; as Taylor writes, "to be free to pursue the realization of one's good according to the laws of one's nature."[27] When we thus judge natural objects, and evaluate them more highly than artifacts, we are focusing on the extent of their independence from human domination. In this sense, then, human actions can also be judged to be natural – these are the human actions that exist as evolutionary adaptations, free of the control and alteration of technological processes.

If these reflections on the meaning of "natural" are plausible, then it should be clear why the restoration process fails to meet the criteria of naturalness. The attempt to redesign, recreate, and restore natural areas and objects is a radical intervention in natural processes. Although there is an obvious spectrum of possible restoration and redesign projects which differ in their value – Maser's redesigned sustainable forest is better than a tree plantation – all of these projects involve the manipulation and domination of natural areas. All of these projects involve the creation of artifactual natural realities, the imposition of anthropocentric interests on the processes and objects of nature. Nature is not permitted to be free, to pursue its own independent course of development.

The fundamental error is thus domination, the denial of freedom and autonomy. Anthropocentrism, the major concern of most environmental philosophers, is only one species of the more basic attack on the preeminent value of self-realization.

From within the perspective of anthropocentrism, humanity believes it is justified in dominating and molding the nonhuman world to its own human purposes. But a policy of domination transcends the anthropocentric subversion of natural processes. A policy of domination subverts both nature and human existence; it denies both the cultural and natural realization of individual good, human and nonhuman. Liberation from all forms of domination is thus the chief goal of any ethical or political system.

It is difficult to awaken from the dream of domination. We are all impressed by the power and breadth of human technological achievements. Why is it not possible to extend this power further, until we control, manipulate, and dominate the entire natural universe? This is the illusion that the restoration of nature presents to us. But it is only an illusion. Once we dominate nature, once we restore and redesign nature for our own purposes, then we have destroyed nature – we have created an artifactual reality, in a sense, a false reality, which merely provides us the pleasant illusory appearance of the natural environment.

VI

As a concluding note, let me leave the realm of philosophical speculation and return to the world of practical environmental policy. Nothing I have said in this essay should be taken as an endorsement of actions that develop, exploit, or injure areas of the natural environment and leave them in a damaged state. I believe, for example, that Exxon should attempt to clean up and restore the Alaskan waterways and land that was harmed by its corporate negligence. The point of my argument here is that we must not misunderstand what we humans are doing when we attempt to restore or repair natural areas. We are not restoring nature; we are not making it whole and healthy again. Nature restoration is a compromise; it should not be a basic policy goal. It is a policy that makes the best of a bad situation; it cleans up our mess. We are putting a piece of furniture over the stain in the carpet, for it provides a better appearance. As a matter of policy, however, it would be much more significant to prevent the causes of the stains.

Notes

1 In Islip Town, New York, real-estate developers have cited the New York State Department of Environmental Conservation policy of "no-net loss" in proposing the restoration of parts of their property to a natural state, in exchange for permission to develop. A report in *Newsday* discusses a controversial case: "In hopes of gaining town-board approval, Blankman has promised to return a three-quarter-mile dirt road on his property to its natural habitat...." Katti Gray, "Wetlands in the Eye of a Storm," Islip Special, *Newsday*, April 22, 1990; pp. 1, 5.

2 *Garbage: The Practical Journal for the Environment*, May/June 1990, rear cover.

3 Chris Maser, *The Redesigned Forest* (San Pedro, Calif.: R. & E. Miles, 1988), p. 173. It is also interesting to note that there now exists a dissident group within the U.S. Forest Service, called the Association of Forest Service Employees for Environmental Ethics (AFSEEE). They advocate a return to sustainable forestry.

4 Paul Taylor, *Respect for Nature: A Theory of Environmental Ethics* (Princeton: Princeton University Press, 1986), pp. 186–92, 304–6, and ch. 4 and 6 generally.

5 Peter S. Wenz, *Environmental Justice* (Albany: SUNY Press, 1988), pp. 287–91.

6 Robert Elliot, "Faking Nature," *Inquiry* 25 (1982): 81–93; reprinted in Donald VanDeVeer and Christine Pierce, eds., *People, Penguins, and Plastic Trees: Basic Issues in Environmental Ethics* (Belmont, Calif.: Wadsworth, 1986), pp. 142–50.

7 Ibid., p. 86 (VanDeVeer and Pierce, p. 145).

8 Ibid., p. 91 (VanDeVeer and Pierce, p. 149).

9 Eric Katz, "Organism, Community, and the 'Substitution Problem,'" *Environmental Ethics* 7 (1985): 253–5.

10 Elliot, p. 81 (VanDeVeer and Pierce, p. 142).

11 See, for example, Barry Commoner, *The Closing Circle* (New York: Knopf, 1971) and Arnold Pacey, *The Culture of Technology* (Cambridge, MA: MIT Press, 1983).

12 Michael Losonsky, "The Nature of Artifacts," *Philosophy* 65 (1990): 88.

13 Ibid., p. 84.

14 Andrew Brennan, "The Moral Standing of Natural Objects," *Environmental Ethics* 6 (1984): 41–4.

15 Maser, *The Redesigned Forest*, p. xvii.

16 Ibid., pp. 176–7.

17 Ibid., pp. 88–9.

18 Ibid., p. 174.

19 Ibid., p. 94.

20 Ibid., pp. 148–9.

21 Steve Packard, "Just a Few Oddball Species: Restoration and the Rediscovery of the Tallgrass Savanna," *Restoration and Management Notes* 6:1 (Summer 1988): 13–22.

22 L. B. Cebik, "Forging Issues from Forged Art," *Southern Journal of Philosophy* 27 (1989): 331–46.

23 Ibid., p. 342.

24 Taylor, *Respect for Nature*, p. 177. The rule of non-interference is discussed on pp. 173–9.

25 J. S. Mill, "Nature," in *Three Essays on Religion* (London: 1874).

26 Andrew Brennan, *Thinking About Nature: An Investigation of Nature, Value, and Ecology* (Athens: University of Georgia Press, 1988), pp. 88–91.

27 Taylor, *Respect for Nature*, p. 174.

30

Ecological Restoration and the Culture of Nature: a Pragmatic Perspective

Andrew Light

Most environmental philosophers have failed to understand the theoretical and practical importance of ecological restoration. I believe this failure is primarily due to the mistaken impression that ecological restoration is only an attempt to restore nature itself, rather than an effort to restore an important part of the human relationship with nonhuman nature. In investigating this claim, I will first discuss the possibility of transforming environmental philosophy into a more pragmatic discipline, one better suited to contributing to the formation of sound environmental policies, including ecological restoration. Specifically, I will advocate an alternative philosophical approach to the ideas about the value of ecological restoration raised by Eric Katz and other philosophers who claim that restored nature can never reproduce the actual value of nature. I will make this contrast more explicit and further argue that Katz's views in particular are not sufficiently sensitive to the values at work in the variety of projects falling within the category of ecological restoration. We need a more practically oriented philosophical contribution to discussions of ecological restoration policies than environmental philosophers have provided so far. A richer description of the ethical implications of restoration will identify a large part of its value in the revitalization of the human culture of nature. Before reaching this conclusion, however, I will briefly consider an alternative framework for environmental philosophy as a whole.

Environmental Philosophy: What and for Whom?

Two underlying questions that I believe still confound most environmental philosophers are "What is our discipline actually for?" and, consequently, "Who is our audience?" So far, most work in environmental ethics has been concerned with describing the nonanthropocentric value of nature – that is, the value of nature independent of human concerns and reasons for valuing nature – and determining the duties, obligations, or rights that follow from that description. But one can easily wonder whether such work is directed only toward other environmental philosophers as a contribution to the literature on value theory or whether it has a broader aim. Certainly, given the history of the field – formally beginning in the early 1970s with the work of thinkers as diverse as Arne Naess, Val Plumwood, Holmes Rolston, Peter Singer, and Richard Sylvan, all concerned with how philosophers could make some sort of contribution to the resolution of environmental problems – one would think that the aspirations of environmental philosophy would be greater than simply continuing an intramural discussion about the value of nature.

But if environmental philosophy is more than a discussion among philosophers about natural value, to what broader purposes and audiences should it reach? I pose at least four responses. Environmental philosophy might serve as (1) a guide for environmental activists searching for ethical justifications for their activities in defense of other animals and ecosystems, (2) an applied ethic for resource managers, (3) a general tool for policy makers, helping them to shape more responsible environmental policies, and (4) a beacon for the public at large, attempting to expand their notions of moral obligation beyond the traditional confines of anthropocentric (human-centered) moral concerns.

Environmental philosophy should, of course, aim to serve all of these purposes and groups, although I think that most importantly we should focus our energies on guiding policy makers and the public. My rationale is this: If the original reason that philosophers established this field was to make a philosophical contribution to the resolution of environmental problems (consistent with other professionals' response to environmental concerns in the early 1970s), then the continuation – indeed, the urgency – of those problems demands that philosophers do all they can to actually help change present policies and attitudes involving environmental problems. If we talk only to each other about value theory, we have failed as environmental professionals. But if we can help convince policy makers to formulate better policies and make the case to the public at large to support these policies for ethical reasons, then we can join other environmental professionals in making more productive contributions to the resolution of environmental problems.

As it now stands, however, the current focus in environmental philosophy on describing the non-anthropocentric value of nature often ends up separating environmental philosophy from other forms of environmental inquiry. One prime example of this disconnection from practical considerations is that many environmental philosophers do not think of restoration ecology in a positive light. My friend and colleague Eric Katz comes near the top of the list of these philosophers; his chapter [in the volume in which the original of this essay appeared] is the latest in a series of articles in which he argues that ecological restoration does not result in a restoration of nature and, in fact, may even create a disvalue in nature. Robert Elliot is another influential thinker in this camp, although his views have moderated significantly in recent years. Katz, Elliot, and others maintain that if the goal of environmental philosophy is to describe the non-human-centered value of nature and to distinguish nature from human ap-

preciation of it, then presumably nature cannot be the sort of thing that is associated with human creation or manipulation. Thus, if restorations are human creations, argue philosophical critics such as Katz, they can never count as the sort of thing that contains natural value.

In this view, restorations are not natural – they are artifacts. To claim that environmental philosophers should be concerned with ecological restoration is therefore to commit a kind of category mistake: it is to ask that they talk about something that is not part of nature. But to label ecological restorations a philosophical category mistake is the best-case scenario in this view; at worst, restorations represent the tyranny of humans over nature and should not be practiced at all. Katz has put it most emphatically in arguing that "the practice of ecological restoration *can only* represent a misguided faith in the hegemony and infallibility of the human power to control the natural world" (Katz 1996, 222, my emphasis).

I have long disagreed with claims like this one. My early response to such positions was to simply set them aside in my search for broader ethical and political questions useful for a more public discussion of policies concerning ecological restoration (e.g., Light and Higgs 1996). But I now think it is dangerous to ignore the arguments of Katz and Elliot, for at least two reasons. First, their arguments represent the most sustained attempt yet to make a philosophical contribution to the overall literature on restoration and thus ought to be answered by philosophers also interested in restoration. Second, the larger restoration community is increasingly coming to believe that the sorts of questions being addressed by Katz and Elliot are the only kind of contribution that philosophy as a discipline can make to discussions of restoration. And since Katz has explicitly rejected the idea that ecological restoration is an acceptable environmental practice, the restoration community's assumption that environmental ethicists tend to be hostile to the idea of ecological restoration is a fair one. Given this disjunction, there would be no ground left for a philosophical contribution to public policy questions concerning ecological restoration, since none of these issues would count as moral or ethical questions.[1]

I believe that philosophers can make constructive contributions to ecological restoration and to environmental issues in general by helping to articulate the normative foundations for environmental policies in ways that are translatable to the public. But making such contributions requires doing environmental philosophy in some different ways. Specifically, it requires a more public philosophy, one focused on making the kinds of arguments that resonate with the moral intuitions most people carry around with them every day. Such intuitions usually resonate more with human-centered notions of value than with abstract non-anthropocentric conceptions of natural value.

"Environmental pragmatism" is my term for the view that makes it plausible for me to make this claim about the importance of appealing to human motivations in valuing nature. By this I do not mean an application of the traditional writings of the American pragmatists – Dewey, James, and Pierce, for example – to environmental problems. Instead, I simply mean the recognition that a responsible and complete environmental philosophy includes a public component with a clear policy emphasis (see, for example, Light 1996a, 1996b, 1996c). It is certainly appropriate for philosophers to continue their search for a true and foundational nonanthropocentric description of the value of nature. But environmental philosophers would be remiss if they did not also try to make other, perhaps more appealing ethical arguments that may have an audience in an anthropocentric public. Environmental pragmatism in my sense is agnostic concerning the existence of nonanthropocentric natural value. It is simply a methodology permitting environmental philosophers to endorse a pluralism allowing for one kind of philosophical task inside the philosophy community – searching for the "real" value of nature – and another task outside of that community – articulating a value for nature that resonates with the public and therefore has more impact on discussions of projects such as ecological restorations that may be performed by the public.

This approach modifies the philosophical contribution to questions about restoration ecology in a positive way. As mentioned, many philosophers have criticized ecological restoration because it is a human intervention into natural processes. In contrast, I have argued that such projects as the prairie restorations at the University of Wisconsin–Madison Arboretum would be fully supported by a pragmatic environmental philosophy (Light 1996b). Restoration makes sense because on the whole it results in many advantages over mere preservation of ecosystems that have been substan-

tially damaged by humans. More significantly, this pragmatic approach exposes other salient ethical issues involving the practice of ecological restoration beyond the discussion of natural value, such as whether there are moral grounds that justify encouraging public participation in restoration (see Light and Higgs 1996). It is therefore the duty of the pragmatic environmental philosopher to become involved in debates with practitioners about what the value of restoration is in human terms, rather than to keep the discussion restricted to a private debate among philosophers on whether restored nature is really nature. In the rest of this chapter, I will offer a specific critique of Katz's claims about the value of restoration, a critique, however, that does not rely on a pragmatist foundation for environmental philosophy. I will then go on to and discuss some pragmatic issues that contribute to a fuller philosophical analysis of the practice and ethics of ecological restoration.

Ecological Restoration: A Preliminary Distinction

Following the project described above, in previous work I have outlined some preliminary distinctions that paint a broader picture of the philosophical terrain up for grabs in restoration than that presented by Katz and Elliot. Specifically, in response to Elliot's early critique of restoration (1982), I have tried to distinguish between two categories of ecological restoration that have differing moral implications.

Elliot begins his seminal article on restoration, "Faking Nature," by identifying a particularly pernicious kind of restoration – restoration that is used to rationalize the destruction of nature. On this claim, any harm done to nature by humans is ultimately repairable through restoration, so the harm should be discounted. Elliot calls this view the "restoration thesis" and states that it implies that "the destruction of what has value [in nature] is compensated for by the later creation (re-creation) of something of equal value" (Elliot 1982, 82). Elliot rejects the restoration thesis through an analogy based on the relationship between original and replicated works of art and nature. Just as we would not value a replication of a work of art as much as we would the original, we would not value a replicated piece of nature as much as we would the original, such as some bit of wilderness. Elliot's argument that the two sorts of value choices are similar is persuasive.

In responding to Elliot's (1982) criticisms of the value of restoration, I have suggested a distinction implicit in his analysis of restoration to help us think through the value of ecological restoration (Light 2002). The distinction is based on an acknowledgment Elliot makes in his 1982 article (and expands upon in his 1997 book): "Artificially transforming an utterly barren, ecologically bankrupt landscape into something richer and more subtle may be a good thing. That is a view quite compatible with the belief that replacing a rich natural environment with a rich artificial one is a bad thing" (Elliot 1982, 87).

Following Elliot's lead that some kinds of restoration may be beneficial, I distinguished between two sorts of restorations: (1) malicious restorations, such as the kind described in the restoration thesis, and (2) benevolent restorations, or those undertaken to remedy a past harm done to nature although not offered as a justification for harming nature. Benevolent restorations, unlike malicious restorations, cannot serve as justifications for the conditions that would warrant their engagement.

If this distinction holds, then we can claim that Elliot's original target was not all of restoration, but only a particular kind of restoration, namely malicious restorations. While there is mixed evidence to support the claim that Elliot was originally going after only malicious restorations in his first work on the topic, the distinction is nonetheless intuitively plausible. The sorts of restorations undertaken at the Wisconsin Arboretum, for example, are certainly not offered as excuses or rationales for the destruction of nature. In contrast, the restorations involved in mountaintop mining projects in rural West Virginia can definitely be seen as examples of malicious restorations. Mountaintop mining – where tops of mountains are destroyed and dumped into adjacent valleys – is in part rationalized through a requirement that the damaged streambeds in the adjacent valleys be restored. The presumed ability to restore these streambeds is used as a justification for allowing mountaintop mining, making this practice a clear instantiation of Elliot's restoration thesis. The upshot of this malicious–benevolent distinction is that one may be able to grant much of Elliot's claim that restored nature is not original nature while still not denying that there is some

kind of positive value to the act of ecological restoration in many cases. Even if benevolent restorations are not restorations of original nature, and hence more akin to art forgeries than to original works of art, they can still have some kind of positive content.

The idea that many restorations can have positive content may be developed more by pushing the art analogy a bit further. If ecological restoration is a material practice like making a piece of art (fake or not), why isn't it like art restoration rather than art forgery? After all, we know that some parallels can be drawn between restoration projects and mitigation projects. A mitigation often involves the wholesale creation of a new ecosystem designed to look like a bit of nature that may have absolutely no historical continuity with the natural history of the land on which it is placed. For example, in order to meet an environmental standard that demands no net loss of wetlands, some environmental managers will sanction the creation of a wetland to replace a destroyed one on a piece of land where there had been no wetland. Conversely, a restoration must be tied to some claim about the historical continuity of the land on which the restoration is taking place. In some cases, this might simply entail linking original pieces of nature together to restore the integrity of the original ecosystem without creating a new landscape altogether (as in the case of the Wildlands Project to link the great western parks in the United States and Canada with protected corridors). In that sense, a restoration could be more like repairing a damaged work of art than like creating a fake one.[2]

The possibility of having benevolent restorations does much to clear the way for a positive philosophical contribution to questions of restoration. Katz, however, unlike Elliot, denies the positive value of any kind of restoration. For him, a restoration can only be malicious because all restorations represent evidence of human domination and arrogance toward nature. But surprisingly, even though Katz draws on Elliot's work in formulating his own position, he seems to ignore the fact that Elliot's original description of the restoration thesis was primarily directed against particular kinds of restorations. In his earliest and most famous article on restoration, "The Big Lie: Human Restoration of Nature," Katz acknowledged that while Elliot claimed that the restoration thesis mostly was advocated as a way of undermining conservation

efforts by big business, he (Katz) was surprised to
see environmental thinkers (such as forest biologist
Chris Maser) advocating "a position similar to
Elliot's 'restoration thesis.'" This position, as
Katz interprets it, is that "restoration of damaged
nature is seen not only as a practical option for
environmental policy but also as a moral obligation
for right-thinking environmentalists" (reprinted in
1997, 96). But Maser's position is not the restoration thesis as Elliot defines it. Katz never shows
that Maser, or any other restoration advocate whom
he analyzes, actually argues for restoration as a
rationale for destruction of nature. He never demonstrates that those in the restoration community
endorse restorations for malicious reasons. If in fact
they do not, then what is wrong with restoration, in
Katz's view?

Katz Against Restoration

Just as Elliot's original target of the restoration
thesis has faded from philosophical memory,
Katz's original target has also been somewhat lost
in the years since he began writing on this topic in
1992. At first, Katz seemed most concerned with
the arguments of fellow environmental ethicists
like Paul Taylor and Peter Wenz, who advocated
variously "restitutive justice" and a "principle of
restitution" as part of our fulfillment of possible
human obligations to nature. If we harmed nature,
according to Taylor and Wenz, we should have to
compensate it. Restoration would be part of a
reasonable package of restitution. According to
Katz, in these views humans have an "*obligation*
and *ability* to repair or reconstruct damaged ecosystems" (1997, 95, my emphasis). But I think it is
crucial here to note the argument Katz is actually
taking on and the objection he proceeds to make.

As Katz describes it, there are actually two separable questions to put to Taylor, Wenz, and other
advocates of restoration: (1) Do we have an obligation to try to restore damaged nature? and (2) Do
we have the ability to restore damaged nature? Katz
argues quite forcefully that we do not have the
ability to restore nature because what we actually
create in ecological restorations are humanly produced artifacts – not nature, nonanthropocentri-
cally conceived. Based on this claim, he assumes
that the first question – whether we have an obligation to try to restore nature – is moot. Katz's logic is

simple: we do not have an obligation to do what we
cannot in actuality do.

But even if we were to grant Katz his position
that it is impossible to restore nature, we may still
have moral obligations to try to restore nature.
How can this be true? There are a number of
reasons, but before fully explicating this view, we
need to first better understand Katz's arguments.

In examining Katz's papers on this topic,[3] I
have identified five separable but often overlapping arguments he has made against both the idea
that we can restore nature and the practice of
trying to restore it. I call these arguments KR1–
5. They are listed below in the order they arise in
his work, each accompanied by an example of
supporting evidence from Katz's various papers
on restoration.

KR1. The Duplicitous Argument
       "I am outraged by the idea that a techno-
       logically created 'nature' will be passed
       off as reality" (1997, 97).[4]

KR2. The Arrogance (or Hubris) Argument
       "The human presumption that we are
       capable of this technological fix demon-
       strates (once again) the arrogance with
       which humanity surveys the natural
       world" (1997, 97).

KR3. The Artifact Argument
       "The re-created natural environment
       that is the end result of a restoration
       project is nothing more than an artifact
       created for human use" (1997, 97).[5]

KR4. The Domination Argument
       "The attempt to redesign, recreate and
       restore natural areas and objects is a
       radical intervention in natural processes.
       Although there is an obvious spectrum
       of possible restoration[s]...all of these
       projects involve the manipulation and
       domination of natural areas. All of these
       projects involve the creation of artifac-
       tual realities, the imposition of anthro-
       pocentric interests on the processes and
       objects of value. Nature is not permitted
       to be free, to pursue its own independent
       course of development" (1997, 105).[6]

KR5. The Replacement Argument
       "If a restored environment is an ade-
       quate replacement for the previously
       existing natural environment [which for
       Katz it can never be], then humans can

use, degrade, destroy, and replace natural entities and habitats with no moral consequence whatsoever. The value in the original natural entity does not require preservation." (1997, 113)[7]

I disagree with all of these arguments and have articulated what I hope are thorough responses of them elsewhere. Here I will focus on KR4, the domination argument, which is perhaps the one that arises most often throughout all of Katz's restoration papers. It is arguably the case that one can answer all of Katz's arguments by conceding one important premise of all of his claims as long as KR4 can be independently answered. KR4 also is interesting to me because his original articulation of it involved a very slim admission that there is some sort of difference between various kinds of restoration projects. Even though these differences are not ultimately important for Katz, he still nonetheless acknowledged them, and they give me a space in which I can critique his position.

In addition, I believe that KR1–3 and KR5 can be ignored in rejecting Katz's position as long as we are prepared to concede for now one important premise of all of his arguments. This is Katz's ontological assumption (a claim concerning the nature or essence of a thing) that humans and nature can be meaningfully separated so as to definitively argue that restored nature is an artifact, a part of human culture, rather than a part of nature. As Katz has admitted in a soon to be published forum on his work, he is a nature–culture dualist. This means that for Katz, nature and culture are separate things entirely.[8] If one rejects this overall ontological view, then one may reject most of Katz's objections to restoration. But metaphysical debates are often intractable, and rarely does either side give quarter.[9] Thus, even though I disagree with it, I will accept Katz's underlying assumption that restored nature does not reproduce nature.

But even if I grant this point that restored nature is not really nature, KR4 is still false because it is arguably the case that restoration does not dominate nature in any coherent sense but instead often helps nature to be free of just the sort of domination that Katz is concerned about. The reasoning here is straightforward enough. If I can show that restorations are valuable for nature, even if I concede that they do not re-create nature, then the various motivations for restoration will

distinguish whether a restoration is duplicitous (KR1) or arrogant (KR2). A benevolent restoration, for example, would not risk KR1 or KR2 because in principle it is not trying to fool anyone, nor is it necessarily arrogant. Further, and more simply, conceding Katz's ontological claim about the distinction between nature and culture eliminates the significance of KR3 – since we no longer care whether what is created is an artifact – as well as KR5, since we have given up hope that a restoration could ever actually serve as a replacement for "real" nature.

Now, back to the domination argument. KR4 is a claim that could hold even for a view that conceded Katz's nature–culture distinction. The reason, following Katz, would be that even a failed attempt to duplicate natural value – or create something akin to nature while conceding that in principle real nature can never be restored by humans – could still count as an instance of domination as Katz has defined it. An attempt at restoration, according to Katz's reasoning, would still prohibit nature from ever being able to pursue its own development. The reason is that for Katz, restoration is always a substitute for whatever would have occurred at a particular site without human interference. The idea is that even if humans can produce a valuable landscape of some sort on a denuded acreage, this act of production is still an instance of domination over the alternative of a natural evolution of this same acreage, even if a significant natural change would take ten times as long as the human-induced change and would be arguably less valuable for the species making use of it. Still, one can muster several arguments against KR4 (I will provide four) and still play largely within Katz's biggest and most contentious assumption about the ontological status of restored nature. After going through these arguments, we will see that these claims can lead to a new philosophical context for the evaluation of restoration, which I believe in the end also undermines the other KR arguments.

1 We can imagine cases in which nature cannot pursue its own interests (however one wishes to understand this sense of nature having interests) because of something we have done to it. For example, many restorations are limited to bioactivation of soil that has become contaminated by hazardous industrial waste. If restoration necessar-

ily prohibits nature from being free, as KR4 maintains, then how do we reconcile this claim with the relative freedom that bioactivation makes possible? Restoration need not determine exactly what grows in a certain place, but may in fact simply be the act of allowing nature to again pursue its own interests rather than shackling it to perpetual human-induced trauma. In many cases of restoration, this point can be underscored when we see how anthropogenically damaged land (or soil) can be uniquely put at risk of invasion by anthropogenically introduced exotic plants. South African ice plant, an exotic in southern California that destroys the soil it is introduced into, is highly opportunistic and can easily spread onto degraded land, thus ensuring that native plants will not be able to reestablish themselves. I highlight here this contentious native–exotic distinction because I suspect that given Katz's strong nature–culture distinction, he would necessarily have to prefer a landscape of native plants over a landscape of exotics where the existence of the exotics is a result of an act of human (cultural) interference in nature. Allowing nature to pursue its own interests, given prior anthropogenic interference, thus involves at least as strong a claim to protect it from further anthropogenic risk through restoration practices as does the case Katz makes for leaving it alone.

2 Even if we do agree with Katz that restorations produce only artifacts, can't it still be the case that the harm we cause nature still requires us to engage in what Katz would have to term "attempted restorations"? It simply does not follow from the premise that something is more natural when it is relatively free of human interference that we must therefore always avoid interfering with nature (this is actually a point that Katz finally recognizes in a later paper, "Imperialism and Environmentalism"). It is a classic premise of holism in environmental ethics (the theory that obligations to the nonhuman natural world are to whole ecosystems and not to individual entities, a view that Katz endorses) that some interference is warranted when we are the cause of an imbalance in nature. For example, hunting of white-tailed deer is thought to be permissible under holism since humans have caused that species' population explosion. If such interventions are permissible to help "rectify the balance of nature," then why are there not comparable cases with the use of restoration as an aid to the original, real nature? We can

even imagine that such cases would be less controversial than holistic defenses of hunting.

There are cases where restoration, even if it results in the production of an artifact, does not lead to the domination described by Katz. Imagine a case in which the restoration project is one that will restore a corridor between two wilderness preserves. If there is positive natural value in the two preserves that is threatened because wildlife is not allowed to move freely between them, then restoration projects that would restore a corridor (by removing roads, for example) would actually not only be morally permissible but also possibly ethically required depending on one's views of the value of the nature in the preserves. This is not restoration as a second best to preservation or a distraction from preservation; it is restoration as an integral and critical part of the maintenance of natural value. So even if we agree with Katz that humans cannot really restore nature, it does not follow that they ought not to engage in restoration projects that actually repair the damage caused by past domination rather than further that domination.

Given objections like the two discussed so far, it is important to try to get a better handle on exactly what sort of damage is caused by domination in the sense described by Katz. It turns out that the worst damage to nature for Katz is domination that prevents the "self-realization" of nature:

> The fundamental error is thus domination, the denial of freedom and autonomy. Anthropocentrism, the major concern of most environmental philosophers, is only one species of the more basic attack on the preeminent value of self-realization. From within the perspective of anthropocentrism, humanity believes it is justified in dominating and molding the nonhuman world to its own human purposes. (1997, 105)

Thus, the problem with restoration is that it restricts natural self-realization in order to force nature onto a path that we find more appealing.

3 With this clarification, we can then further object to Katz that his sense of restoration confuses restoration with mitigation. The force of the charge of domination is that we mold nature to fit our own human purposes. But most restorationists would counter that it is nonanthropocentric nature that

sets the goals for restoration, not humans. While there is indeed some subjectivity in determining what should be restored at a particular site (which period do we restore to?) and uncertainty about how we should do it (limitations in scientific and technical expertise), we cannot restore a landscape any way we wish and still have a good restoration in scientific terms. If Katz's objection is that when we restore a denuded bit of land, we are at least making something that fits our need to have more attractive natural surroundings – an argument he often makes – we can reply that because of the constraints on restoration (as opposed to mitigation), the fact that we find a restored landscape appealing is only contingently true. It is often the case that what we must restore to is not the preferred landscape of most people. The controversy over the "Chicago Wilderness" project [a decade long attempt to restore tens of thousands of acres of forest preserves around Chicago to their arguably original state as oak savanna and tallgrass prairie] is a good example of this: many local residents see restoration activities as destroying the aesthetically pleasing forests that now exist in order to restore the prairie and oak savanna ecosystems that were present prior to European settlement. But philosophically, because a restored landscape can never necessarily be tied only to our own desires (since our desires are not historically and scientifically determined in the same way that the parameters of a restoration are), then those desires cannot actually be the direct cause of any restriction on the self-realization of nature.

4 Finally, we must wonder about this value of self-realization. Setting aside the inherent philosophical problems with understanding what self-realization means in the case of nature, one has to wonder how we could know what natural self-realization would be in any particular case, and why we would totally reject a human role in helping to make it happen if we could discern it. In an analogous case involving two humans, we do not say that a human right to (or value of) self-realization is abrogated when a criminal who harms someone is forced to pay restitution. Even if the restitution is forced against the will of the victim, and even if the compensation in principle can never make up for the harm done, we would not say that somehow the victim's self-realization has been restricted by the act of restitution by the criminal. Again, there seems to be no clear argument here for why the moral obligation to try to restore has been diminished by Katz's arguments that we do not have the ability to really restore nature or pass off an artifact as nature.

Restoring Environmental Philosophy

If I am justified in setting aside the rest of Katz's arguments (KR1–3 and KR5) by accepting his claim that humans cannot restore real nature, what sort of conclusions can we draw about the role of philosophy in sorting out the normative issues involved in restoration? As it turns out, Katz gives us an insight that is helpful in figuring out the next step.

After explaining the harm we do to nature in the domination we visit upon it through acts of restoration, Katz briefly assesses the harm that we do to ourselves through such actions:

> But a policy of domination transcends the anthropocentric subversion of natural processes. A policy of domination subverts both nature and human existence; it denies both the cultural and natural realization of individual good, human and nonhuman. Liberation from all forms of domination is thus the chief goal of any ethical or political system. (1997, 105)

Although not very clearly explained by Katz, this intuition represents a crucial point for proceeding further. In addition to connecting environmental philosophy to larger projects of social liberation, Katz here opens the door to a consideration of the consequences of restoration on humans and human communities. As such, Katz allows an implicit assertion that there is a value involved in restoration that must be evaluated in addition to the value of the objects that are produced by restoration.

But the problem with drawing this conclusion is that this passage is also perhaps the most cryptic in all of Katz's work on restoration. What does Katz mean by this claim? How exactly does restoration deny the realization of an individual human, or cultural, good? This claim can be made understandable only by assuming that some kind of cultural value connected to nature is risked through the act of dominating or otherwise causing harm to nature. But what is this value?

I think the value Katz is alluding to here, although he never explores it seriously, is related to the part of human culture that is connected to external, nonhuman nature. This is not simply a suggestion that we humans are part of nature; it also points out that we have a relationship with nature that exists on moral as well as physical terrain in such a way that our actions toward nature can reciprocally harm us. If this is the view implicit in this claim, then it is still consistent with much of the rest of Katz's larger views about the value of nature. We have a relationship with nature even if we are separable from it. I will accept this basic tenet of Katz's argument: we do exist in some kind of moral relationship with nature. And without fully explicating the content of that relationship, it seems that Katz is right in assuming that somehow our actions toward nature morally implicate us in a particular way. In the same sense, when we morally mistreat another human, we not only harm them but harm ourselves (by diminishing our character, by implicating ourselves in evil – however you want to put it). Katz is suggesting that our relationship with nature has a determinant effect on our moral character – or, perhaps more accurately, this suggestion is necessary for Katz's comment to make sense, even though he never expresses it himself.

If this assumption is correct, and if there is any truth in the arguments I have put forward so far that there can be some kind of positive value to our interaction with nature, then doing right by nature will have the same reciprocal effect of morally implicating us in a positive value as occurs when we do right by other persons. Perhaps Katz would agree. He would disagree, however, with the suggestion I would want to add: that there is some part of many kinds of restorations (if not most kinds) that contains positive value. Aside from the other suggestions I have already made concerning the possible positive content of restoration, one can also consider that the relationship with nature that is implied in Katz's view has a moral content in itself that is not reducible to the value of fulfilling this relationship's concomitant obligations. The relationship between humans and nature imbues restoration with a positive value even if it cannot replicate natural value in its products. But understanding this point will require some explanation.

Consider that if I have a reciprocal relationship with another human (in which I do right by them

and they do right by me), then, to generalize Katz's view, there is a moral content to both of our actions that implicates each of us as persons. Each of us is a better person morally because of the way we interact with each other in the relationship. But the relationship itself, or rather just the fact of the existence of the relationship, has a moral content of its own (or what we could call a normative content, meaning that the relationship can be assessed as being in a better or worse state) that is independent of the fulfillment of any obligations.

If this point of the possible separation between the value of a relationship and the value of the fulfillment of obligations does not follow intuitively, imagine a case in which two people act according to duty toward each other without building a relationship of substantive normative content between them. For example, I have a brother with whom I am not terribly close. While I always act according to duty to him – I never knowingly do harm to him, and I even extend special family obligations to him – I do not have a substantive relationship with him that in itself has a normative content. Thus, if I do not speak to him for a year, nothing is lost because there is no relationship to maintain or that requires maintenance for normative reasons. But if my brother needed a kidney transplant, I would give him my kidney unhesitatingly out of a sense of obligation – something I would not feel obliged to do for someone outside my family – even though I still do not feel intimately comfortable around him in the same way I do with my closest friends. (It isn't necessarily a disvalue, only a sense of indifference, a lack of closeness.) Our relationship as persons has no positive value for me – as distinct from my relationships with friends, which include a sense of intimate affection and care for each other. Thus I can have interaction with another person, even interaction that involves substantial components of obligation and duty (and, in Katz's terms, I will never put myself in a position to dominate the other person) but still not have a relationship with that person that involves any kind of positive value or that has normative standards of maintenance.

I don't think I have any obligation to have a relationship with normative content with my brother, even though my mother would like it if I did. But if I did have that kind of a relationship with him, it would have a value above and beyond the moral interaction I have with him now (the obligations I have to him, which can be iterated) that aids in a determination of our moral characters.[10] If we had a relationship with normative content, there would be a positive or negative value that could be assessed if I lost touch with him or ceased to care about his welfare. (I could very well claim that it would be better for me to have such a relationship with him, but this would require an additional argument.)

Consider further: If I wanted to rectify or create anew a substantive normative relationship with my brother, like the relationship I have with several close friends, how would I do it? One thing I could do would be to engage in activities with him – the same sorts of activities (let's call them material interactions) that I do with my friends now. I might work with him to put up a fence or help him plant his garden. I might begin to talk over my personal and professional problems with him. I might go on a long journey with him that demanded some kind of mutual reliance, such as white-water rafting or visiting a foreign city where neither of us spoke the native language. In short, although there are, of course, no guarantees, I could begin to have some kind of material relationship with him as a prelude to having some kind of substantive normative relationship with him. Many factors might limit the success of such a project: for one thing, the distance between the two of us – he lives in our hometown of Atlanta and I live in New York. So if I were really serious about this project of building a relationship between us that had value independent of the value of the fulfillment of our mutual obligations to each other, I'd have to come up with ways around these interfering factors. Importantly, though, I couldn't form a substantive normative relationship with him merely by respecting his right of self-realization and autonomy as a person; I would have to somehow become actively involved with him.

When we compare the case of the estranged brother to that of nature, many parallels arise. We know that we can fulfill obligations to nature in terms of respecting its autonomy and self-realization as a subject (in Katz's terms) without ever forming a substantive normative relationship with it. Assuming also that a kind of relationship with nature is possible according to Katz's scheme (for this is in part what we harm when we dominate nature), it is fair to say that a relationship consisting of positive normative value with nature is compatible with Katz's overall view of the

human–nature relationship. Because he says so little about what our positive relationship to nature could be, he is in no position to restrict it a priori. We also know that, as in the case of the estranged brother, we need some kind of material bridge in order to create a relationship with nature.

How do we build that bridge? Suggesting ways to overcome the gap between humans and nature (without necessarily disvaluing it) seems in part to be the role of environmental philosophy in questions of ecological restoration. Certainly, as in the case of my brother, distance is a problem. Numerous environmental professionals have emphasized the importance of being in nature in order to care for nature. Also, acts of preservation are important for there to be nature to have a relationship with. But what about restoration? Can restoration help engender such a positive normative relationship with nature?

It seems clear to me that it can. When we engage in acts of benevolent restoration, we are bound *by* nature in the sense that we are obligated to respect what it once was attempting to realize before we interfered with it. In Katz's terms, we are attempting to respect it as an autonomous subject. But we are also bound *to* nature in the act of restoring. In addition to the substantial personal and social benefits that accrue to people who engage in benevolent forms of restoration, we can also say that restoration restores the human connection to nature by restoring the part of culture that has historically contained a connection to nature. This kind of relationship goes well beyond mere reciprocity; it involves the creation of a value in relationship with nature beyond obligation. While it would take further argument to prove, I believe that this kind of relationship is a necessary condition for encouraging people to protect natural systems and landscapes around them rather than trade them for short-term monetary gains from development. If I am in a normative relationship with the land around me (whether it is "real" nature or not), I am less likely to allow it to be harmed further.

Specifying the parameters of restoration that help to achieve this moral relationship with nature will be the task of a more pragmatic environmental philosophy. As mentioned at the outset of this chapter, environmental pragmatism allows for and encourages the development of human-centered notions of the value of nature. Pragmatists are not restricted to identifying obligations to nature in the existence of nonanthropocentric conceptions of value but may embrace an expression of environmental values in human terms. More adequately developing the idea of restoration in terms of the human–nature relationship is thus appropriately under the pragmatist's purview. More importantly, however, the value articulated here exists between anthropocentrism and nonanthropocentrism, fully relying on the capacities of both sides of the human–nature relationship.[11]

We can even look to Katz for help in completing this pragmatic task. We don't want restorations that try to pass themselves off as the real thing when they are actually "fakes" (KR1) or are pursued through arrogance (KR2); nor are we interested in those that are offered as justifications for replacing or destroying nature (KR5). We would not want our comparable human relationships to exhibit those properties either. But even given the legacy of inhuman treatment of each other, we know that it is possible to restore human relationships in ways that do not resemble KR1, KR2, or KR5. There is, however, one possible concern to attend to in KR3, the artifact argument. Although earlier I said that the importance of KR3 is diminished by granting Katz's nature–culture distinction, there is a way that it can still cause us problems in grounding attempts at restoration in the positive value of strengthening the human–nature relationship.

If we allow Katz's claim that what has been restored is not really nature, then he may argue that we are not restoring a cultural relationship with nature but, in a sense, only extending the artifactual material culture of humans. At best, all we can have with restoration is a relationship with artifacts, not nature. Maybe he will allow that we improve our relationships with each other through cooperative acts of restoration, but this is not the same as a restoration of a relationship with nature itself.

But it should be clear by now that Katz would be mistaken to make such an objection for several reasons, stemming in part from my earlier remarks:

1 Even if we admit that restored nature is an artifact and not real nature, restored nature can also serve as a way for real nature to free itself from the shackles we have previously placed upon it. Restoration can allow nature to engage in its own autonomous restitution. Of the different sorts of restoration projects that I have mentioned earlier, many amount to aids to nature rather than creations of new nature.

2 Even if restoration is the production of an artifact, these artifacts do bear a striking resemblance to the real thing. This is not to say that restorations can be good enough to fool us (KR1). Rather, it is simply to point out that an opportunity to interact with the flora and fauna of the sort most common in benevolent restorations will increase the bonds of care that people will have with nonrestored nature. If a denuded and abandoned lot in the middle of an inner-city ghetto is restored by local residents who have never been outside of their city, it will help them better appreciate the fragility and complexity of the natural processes of nature itself should they encounter them. The fact that restorationists are engaged in a technological process does not necessarily mean that their practices do not serve the broader purpose of restoring a relationship with nature. Similarly, while beginning some form of mediated communication with my brother (such as e-mail or regular phone calls) does not restore a fully healthy communicative relationship with him in the way that face-to-face conversation might, it still helps me get used to the idea of some form of immediate and substantive communication.

3 Finally, if Katz persists in his concern that the act of restoration reifies domination by reaffirming our power over nature through the creation of artifacts, we can say that exactly the opposite is likely the case (at least in the case of benevolent restorations) when the goal is restoring the culture of nature, if not nature itself. Restorationists get firsthand (rather than anecdotal and textbook) exposure to the actual consequences of human domination of nature. A better understanding of the problems of bioactivating soil, for example, gives us a better idea of the complexity of the harm we have caused to natural processes. In a much healthier way than Katz seems willing to admit, knowing about that harm can empower us to learn more precisely why we should object to the kinds of activities that can cause the harm in the first place. As a parallel human case, imagine a carrier of a disease that is deadly and contagious (but not, for some reason, fatal to her) who ignores warnings about taking precautions to avoid spreading the disease to other people. If that person passes on her deadly disease to others, would it not in the end benefit her to volunteer in a hospital ward full of people dying from this particular disease? If the

disease were incurable, she could never restore health to its victims even if she sought to (either out of reciprocity or a desire to form helpful normative relationships with others), but the experience might teach her the importance of taking precautions against giving the disease to others. Restoration similarly teaches us the actual consequences of our actions rather than allowing us to ignore them by restricting our interaction with nature to those parts we have not yet damaged.[12]

Conclusion

In a follow-up essay to "The Big Lie" called "The Call of the Wild," which used the image of the "wildness" in the white-tailed deer population at his summer home on Fire Island to help distinguish nature from culture, Katz embraced a kind of reciprocal relationship with nature. The wild white-tailed deer, which he admitted in the essay were now quite tame, were described as "members of my moral and natural community. The deer and I are partners in the continuous struggle for the preservation of autonomy, freedom, and integrity. This shared partnership creates obligations on the part of humanity for the preservation and protection of the natural world" (1997, 117). Surely we would respond that this relationship also creates obligations of benevolent restoration as well. If the deer were threatened with harm without a needed restoration of a breeding ground, for example, would Katz not be obliged to do it? And, in doing this restoration, would he not help to generate positive value in his relationship with those deer?

It seems clear that benevolent restorations of this sort are valuable because they help us restore our relationship with nature, by restoring what could be termed our "culture of nature." This is true even if Katz is correct that restored nature has the ontological property of an artifact. Restoration is an obligation exercised in the interests of forming a positive community with nature and thus is well within the boundaries of a positive, pragmatic environmental philosophy. Just as artifacts can serve valuable relationship goals by creating material bridges to other subjects, artifactual landscapes can help restore the culture of nature. Further defining the normative ground of benevolent restorations should be the contribution that

philosophy can make to the public consideration and practice of ecological restoration. It is a contribution directed at a larger audience, beyond the professional philosophy community, and aimed toward the practical end of helping to resolve environmental problems.

Notes

This chapter is based on a presentation originally given at a plenary session (with Eric Katz and William Jordan) of the International Symposium on Society and Resource Management, University of Missouri, Columbia, in May 1998. Subsequent versions were presented as the keynote address of the Eastern Pennsylvania Philosophy Association annual meeting, Bloomsburg University, November 1998; and at Georgia State University, the State University of New York at Binghamton, and Lancaster University in the United Kingdom. I have benefited much from the discussions at all of these occasions and especially from the helpful comments provided by Cari Dzuris, Cheryl Foster, Warwick Fox, Paul Gobster, Leslie Heywood, Bruce Hull, Bryan Norton, George Rainbolt, and Christopher Wellman.

1   If we accept Katz's position, a philosophical inquiry into restoration would actually be an investigation of some kinds of questions other than those legitimately posed by environmental philosophers. Since Katz argues that restored nature is only an artifact, philosophers of technology would presumably still be doing philosophy when they were involved in an investigation of ecological restoration. The suggestion that Katz is trying to define certain practices as outside the field of environmental ethics is no red herring. In a public forum discussing his work at the Central Division meeting of the American Philosophical Association in Chicago in 1998, Katz stated publicly that agriculture was not the proper purview of environmental ethics. Philosophers working on questions of ethics and agriculture could be doing agricultural ethics but not environmental ethics. Katz's original comments are forthcoming as "Understanding Moral Limits in the Duality of Artifacts and Nature," in *Ethics and the Environment*, 2002. The comments on agriculture, however, only occurred in the discussion at the session.

2   From the early aesthetic theory of Mark Sagoff (before he ever turned to environmental questions), one can also extract the following distinction to deepen the discussion of different kinds of benevolent restorations: (1) integral restorations, or restorations that "put new pieces in the place of original fragments that have been lost," and (2) purist

Andrew Light

restorations, or restorations that "limit [themselves] to cleaning works of art and to reattaching original pieces that may have fallen" (Sagoff 1978, 457). As it turns out, one can argue that integral restorations are aesthetically (and possibly ethically) worrisome, since they seem to create hybrid works of art (created by both the artist and the restorationist). But this does not really undermine the analogy with ecological restorations, since many of these restorations are more akin to purist restorations – for example, cleaning land by bioactivating soil – than to integral ones. Perhaps more common would be a subclass of purist restoration that we might call rehabilitative restoration – for example, cleaning out exotic plants that had been introduced into a site and allowing the native plants to reestablish themselves. Such activity is akin to the work of a purist art restorationist who corrects the work of a restorationist who had come before her. If a restorationist, for example, were to remove an eighteenth-century integral addition to a sixteenth-century painting, we would assume that this rehabilitative act was consistent with a purist restoration. I provide a much more thorough discussion of the import of this distinction for ecological restoration in Light (2002).

3 Katz has four main papers on restoration: "The Big Lie: Human Restoration of Nature" (1992), "The Call of the Wild: The Struggle Against Domination and the Technological Fix of Nature" (1992), "Artifacts and Functions: A Note on the Value of Nature" (1993), and "Imperialism and Environmentalism" (1993). All of these papers are collected in Katz (1997), and it is these later versions that I have drawn on for this chapter.

4 Originally in "The Big Lie" (as are KR2–KR4). KR1 is restated later in "The Call of the Wild": "what makes value in the artifactually restored natural environment questionable is its ostensible claim to be the original" (Katz 1997, 114).

5 KR3 is most thoroughly elaborated later in "Artifacts and Functions."

6 The domination argument is repeated in "The Call of the Wild" (Katz 1997, 115) with the addition of an imported quote from Eugene Hargrove: domination "reduces [nature's] ability to be creative." The argument is also repeated in "Artifacts and Functions" and further explicated in "Imperialism and Environmentalism." As far as I can determine, though, Katz does not really expand the argument for domination in this last paper, except to deem imperialism wrong because it makes nature into an artifact (KR3).

7 Originally in "The Call of the Wild" and repeated in "Imperialism and Environmentalism" (Katz 1997, 139).

8 The forum here is the same as the one referenced in note 1.

9 The absence of any perceptible progress in Katz's views following his debate with Donald Scherer is a case in point. Scherer spends too much time, I think, trying to advance a critique of Katz's ontology and metaphysics. The resulting debate appears intractable. See Scherer (1995) and Katz (1996).

10 On a broader scale, just as there can be a town full of decent, law-abiding citizens, those citizens may not constitute a moral community in any significant sense.

11 It is also the case that restoration will be only one of a large collection of practices available for adaptive management. Indeed, there could even be cases where something akin to mitigation (albeit a benevolent kind) rather than restoration would be justified if a claim to sustaining some form of natural value warranted it. In a project to clean up an abandoned mine site, for example, restoring the site to a landscape that was there before might not be the best choice; instead, a sustainable landscape that would help preserve an endangered species now in the area might be more appropriate. But overall, environmentalists must consider human interaction with nature to be an acceptable practice in order to begin the ethical assessment of any case of environmental management. I am indebted to Anne Chapman for pressing me to clarify this point.

12 Katz can legitimately respond that there seems to be no unique reason why people couldn't have experiences that generate a closer relationship with nature as a result of activities other than restoration. Why couldn't we just use this sort of argument to encourage more acts of preservation, or to simply promote taking more walks though nature? Such an objection would, however, miss a crucial point. Even if it can be proved that we can have these kinds of positive experiences with nature through ways other than acts of restoration (and I see no reason why we couldn't), this does not diminish the case being built here: that restoration does not necessarily result in the domination of nature. The goal of my argument is not to show that restoration provides a unique value compared with other environmental practices, but only to reject the claim that there is no kind of positive value that restoration can contribute to nature in some sense. So an objection by Katz of this sort would miss the target of our substantive disagreement. Additionally, one could argue that (1) restoration does, in fact, produce some unique values in our relationship with nature and that (2) even if not unique in itself, restoration helps to improve other sorts of unique values in nature. A case for (2) could be made, for example, in Allen Carlson's work on the importance of scientific understanding for appreciating the aesthetic value of nature (Carlson 1995). Arguably, our experiences as restorationists give us some of the kinds of understandings of natural processes required for

410

aesthetic appreciation, in Carlson's view. Importantly, this understanding is a transitive property: it gives us an ability to aesthetically appreciate not only the nature we are trying to restore but also the nature we are not trying to restore. Restoration thus can provide a unique avenue to the aesthetic appreciation of all nature, restored or not. The main point, however, should not be lost: restoration is an important component in a mosaic of efforts to revive the culture of nature. Given that there is no reason to believe that it has other disastrous effects, restoration seems warranted within a prescribed context even if it is not a cure-all.

References

Carlson, A. 1995. "Nature, Aesthetic Appreciation, and Knowledge." *The Journal of Aesthetics and Art Criticism* 53: 393–400.

Elliot, R. 1982. "Faking Nature." *Inquiry* 25: 81–3.

Elliot, R. 1997. *Faking Nature*. London: Routledge.

Katz, E. 1996. "The Problem of Ecological Restoration." *Environmental Ethics* 18: 222–4.

Katz, E. 1997. *Nature as Subject: Human Obligation and Natural Community*. Lanham, MD: Rowman & Littlefield Publishers.

Light, A. 1996a. "Environmental Pragmatism as Philosophy or Metaphilosophy." In *Environmental Pragmatism*, edited by A. Light and E. Katz, 325–38. London: Routledge.

Light, A. 1996b. "Compatibilism in Political Ecology." In *Environmental Pragmatism*, edited by A. Light and E. Katz, 161–84. London: Routledge.

Light, A. 1996c. "Callicott and Naess on Pluralism." *Inquiry* 39: 273–94. [Expanded and reprinted as chapter 18 in this volume.]

Light, A. 2002. "Faking Nature Revisited." In *The Beauty Around Us*, edited by D. Michelfelder and B. Wilcox, forthcoming. Albany, NY: SUNY Press.

Light, A., and E. Higgs. 1996. "The Politics of Ecological Restoration." *Environmental Ethics* 18: 227–47.

Sagoff, M. 1978. "On Restoring and Reproducing Art." *The Journal of Philosophy* 75: 453–70.

Scherer, D. 1995. "Evolution, Human Living, and the Practice of Ecological Restoration." *Environmental Ethics* 17: 359–79.

Should We Preserve Wilderness?

31

An Amalgamation of Wilderness Preservation Arguments

Michael P. Nelson

Numerous and diverse arguments have been put forth by people of sundry backgrounds and times on behalf of the preservation of what they took to be wilderness. From backpackers to bureaucrats, Romantics to rednecks, socialists to suburbanites, historians to hunters, philosophers to philanthropists, people have sung the praises of areas which they assumed to exist in their "pristine state." It is safe to think that there will continue to be wilderness defenders regardless of the challenge presented to the very concept of wilderness. In the present essay I attempt to summarize in one place the many traditional and contemporary arguments proffered on behalf of "wilderness."

To review such arguments for the sake of historical interest and to observe how the received view of wilderness is tellingly manifested in such arguments is worthwhile. But there is another reason for wanting such a review. The rationales we employ on behalf of anything, including wilderness preservation, reflect our attitudes and values. Our attitudes toward and valuation of those places we have thought of as wilderness are revealed in the many traditional defenses of those places. Moreover, our attitudes and values profoundly affect the manner in which we treat something, including the places we call "wilderness." As environmental historian Roderick Nash observes, "So it is that attitudes and values can shape a nation's environment just as do bulldozers and chain saws."[1] Consequently, we might better understand our current environmental policies if we look at the historical rationales for protecting and defending certain wild places. And if we indeed do need to rethink our classical concept of wilderness – and therefore our current policies with regard to those places taken to be wilderness – a review of where we came from can surely aid us in such an undertaking.[2]

Wilderness preservation arguments have been previously catalogued by Roderick Nash, Holmes Rolston III, William Godfrey-Smith (now William Grey), Warwick Fox, George Sessions, and Michael McCloskey. Here I try to integrate and reconcile these disparate compilations. In the process, I rename and recategorize many of the arguments found in these sources. To them, I add hitherto unexplored wilderness preservation rationales. Hence, what follows is more an amalgamation than a taxonomy or typology; although there is a general attempt to move from narrowly instrumental, egocentric, and anthropocentric values to broader social, biocentric, and even intrinsic values attributed to putative wilderness.

Admittedly, an inherent tension exists in such a project. Most of the wilderness preservation arguments contained herein take the existence of wilderness for granted. However, the usefulness of the concept of wilderness is correctly subject to intense debate: a great new wilderness debate.

Further, all of the following arguments for wilderness preservation are significantly biased in two major ways. First, they assume a terrestrial and not an oceanic or even extraterrestrial sense of wilderness. One might argue that they really ought also to apply to marine wildernesses and to the other, so far untrammeled, planets. Accordingly, I will interject a non-terrestrial perspective into the following arguments when it seems appropriate to do so. Second, the received wilderness idea, and hence many of these arguments for wilderness preservation, has an Australian–American bias. Many Europeans, for example, have no wilderness to worry about preserving. As histories of land settlement and tenure differ so do senses and views of the landscape. Arguably, it takes designated wilderness areas, or at least some recent memory of or belief in a once pristine landscape, to have a received view of wilderness. Actually, then, we are only referring to certain cultures – Protestant Christian, colonial, and postcolonial cultures in particular – when we refer to "a received view of wilderness."

1   The Natural Resources Argument

In many of those areas we refer to as wilderness, there exist significant quantities of untapped yet precious physical resources. Certain designated wilderness areas are great repositories of a wide variety of natural resources and we humans can render our future more secure by preserving these resource reserves. Clearly this is the most narrowly anthropocentric, instrumental, and simpleminded preservation argument that one could advance. It is, therefore, also the most popular and effective argument for the preservation of purported wilderness.

Some writers even suggest that their value as physical resources for *present* or *immediate* exploitation is a rationale for wilderness *preservation!* "Market Value," is what Rolston calls this liquidatable wilderness value.[3] B. L. Driver, Nash, and Glenn Haas refer to wilderness resources as individual and societal "Commodity-Related Benefits," and cite water, timber, minerals, and forage as examples of what they mean by wilderness-area-produced resources.[4] However, a bit of reflection suggests that this entire argument is actually paradoxical, if not thoroughly self-contradictory. In theory, *designated wilderness areas are places where the extraction of resources is strictly prohibited;* ideally wilderness and resource extraction don't mix.[5] It would seem that if we use an area as a goods resource then we are no longer entitled to call it wilderness. Can we have our wilderness and

eat it too? Can we extract resources from an area and still call it wilderness? Maybe we could harvest an area's resources on a very small, sustainable, and non-trammeling scale and the area might still fit the description of wilderness. This argument, however, advanced by Rolston, is conceptually problematic as even small-scale natural resource exploitation arguably runs contrary to the received view of wilderness as untouched by human hands. Moreover, resource use is a matter of degree and "small scale" is a relative term. Such ambiguities leave the present resource extraction argument for wilderness preservation paradoxical and troubling. Less problematic is the argument that we could look at wilderness areas as resource reserves to be exploited only by future generations. Obviously, this is not paradoxical. If we are saving vast resource-rich areas, not exploiting them, we are preserving them. And if future generations did use those presently preserved wilderness areas for resource extraction then they would, at that point, no longer be wilderness areas. Resource reserves, then, are only wilderness areas insofar as their use is potential and not actual. Further, one might argue for preserving as wilderness some areas that may harbor *potential* resources whose existence and instrumental worth has not yet been discovered.[6]

Proponents of the resource reserve argument for wilderness preservation seem to assume that the world without wilderness areas is a world without the many natural resources found (and unfound) in them. That is, they seem to assume that natural resource conservation depends upon wilderness preservation. Wilderness is the untapped pool of natural resources. And this may be true of some resources. Old growth timber and grizzly bear hides come immediately to mind.

Some types of natural resources are so commonly cited as depending upon wilderness preservation that they merit separate discussion – to wit, hunting and medicine.

2   The Hunting Argument

One of the earliest and most popular wilderness preservation arguments asserted that areas of what was taken to be wilderness were worthy of protection because some of them provided terrific venues for hunting or supplied the natural resource of wild game.

Aldo Leopold, one of the earliest and most passionate advocates of wilderness preservation, was keen on what he thought of as wilderness hunting. He traveled to places like the Sierra Madre Occidental in northern Mexico to hunt wild game. He wrote essays with titles like "A Plea for Wilderness Hunting Grounds." And he urged the U.S. Forest Service to set aside certain bits of pristine land dedicated to nothing but wilderness hunting. "The establishment of wilderness areas," he wrote, "would provide an opportunity to produce and hunt certain kinds of game, such as elk, sheep, and bears, which do not always 'mix well' with settlement.... Wilderness areas are primarily a proposal to conserve at least a sample of a certain kind of recreational environment, of which game and hunting is an essential part."[7] Hence, in order to hunt these more charismatic and "wilderness" dependent megafauna, their home ranges (purported wilderness) must be maintained.

This special case of wilderness preservation as a sort of big, fierce, almost tribal proving grounds has been especially championed or ridiculed because of its identification with virility, masculinity, and machismo. Leopold once wrote, "Public wilderness areas are essentially a means for allowing the more virile and primitive forms of outdoor recreation to survive."[8] But nowhere was the association of wilderness preservation, hunting, and masculinity more vehemently expressed than in the thoughts and writings of rough-riding U.S. President Theodore Roosevelt. In the twenty-three volumes of his collected written works, Roosevelt often refers to what was in his mind wilderness as a hunting grounds and laments its loss as such. Referring to modern Americans as overcivilized, slothful, and flabby, Roosevelt calls upon Americans to regain and develop those "fundamental frontier values," to lead a "life of strenuous endeavor," and to revel in the "savage virtues."[9] For Roosevelt, what he referred to as wilderness hunting was the means to accomplish this; for only in such wilderness hunting can a person (man) "show the qualities of hardihood, self-reliance, and resolution."[10] Roosevelt declared:

> Every believer in manliness and therefore in manly sport, and every lover of nature, every man who appreciates the majesty and beauty of wilderness and of wild life, should strike hands with the farsighted men who wish to preserve

our material resources, in an effort to keep our forests and our game beasts, game-birds, and game-fish – indeed, all the living creatures.[11]

Three comments on this argument. First, we can easily expand on this argument and include fishing as well. In certain terrestrial designated wilderness areas the surface waters harbor the biggest trout that put up the fiercest fight. And deep-sea fishing is reported to be some of the most exciting fishing there is. Second, this argument pertains, however, only to certain putative wilderness areas and not to others. Places inhabited by animals that humans desire to hunt or have a historical predator/prey relationship with are worth preserving as wilderness, but those that are largely devoid of big game are not. Third, a century later the big-game-hunting argument for wilderness preservation is an embarrassment to many wilderness advocates. This is not an argument that contemporary wilderness advocates often employ. It would be like mounting an argument for the establishment of zoos as places where people could go to taunt animals. In fact, many would ban hunting from wilderness areas as the epitome of an intrusive, exploitative, and destructive use of wild places and their denizens.

3 The Pharmacopoeia Argument

Another special case of ostensible wilderness resource extraction is medicine.[12] The actual and potential pharmaceutical use of what some of us think of as wilderness is perhaps the single most prevalent and persuasive contemporary wilderness preservation argument. The areas of the earth many commonly referred to as wilderness – such as the Amazon Rainforest and the forests of the Pacific Northwest – contain and support the most species on earth.[13] Since around 80 percent of the world's medicines are derived from life forms,[14] these "wilderness" areas therefore contain the greatest source of medicinal natural resources. As these places are "developed," many of the species that live in them become extinct. Thus, we lose forever any medicinal use they may have had. Donella Meadows calls this the "Madagascar periwinkle argument," referring to the celebrated rosy periwinkle (*Catharanthus roseus*) plant of Madagascar from which were

Michael P. Nelson

derived the drugs vincristine and vinblastine, used in the treatment of leukemia.[15]

This argument seems unpersuasive if constructed in terms of the proven medicinal uses of wild species, since many medically useful species can be cultivated in plantations and laboratories or their active ingredients can be isolated and synthesized. The argument is most forceful in reference to potential, and yet unknown, medicinal uses of wild species. As noted, rainforests, old-growth forests, and the world's oceans house the greatest numbers of species. Most such species have not been described by systematists, let alone assayed for their medicinal potential. Therefore, these same areas arguably also house the greatest source of potential medicines. If these areas are destructively developed, we will lose a significant portion of the species that live in them, and thus we will lose any medicinal use of those species as well. Hence, it is argued, these purported wilderness areas should be saved because they shelter both potential as well as actual medicinal resources.

This argument deserves comment as well. First, many designated wilderness areas in North America and Australia are not species-rich rainforests and old-growth forests. Hence the Madagascar periwinkle argument does little to support their preservation. Second, in conjunction with this argument, it is often noted that the people most knowledgeable about the medicinal uses of rainforest species are the local indigenous inhabitants. But an area inhabited and used by human beings is not, by definition, wilderness.

4 The Service Argument

In addition to the natural resource goods provided by certain putative wilderness areas, innumerable and invaluable services are said to be provided by many of these areas as well. Wetlands benefit humans indirectly by serving to protect important river headways. Unbroken forests remove carbon dioxide from the atmosphere and replenish its oxygen, as do the world's oceans. Since we humans depend upon clean air and water, such services are vital to our continued existence.

Thinking critically about this argument for a moment, we realize that wilderness is indeed a sufficient condition for the performance of these services, but it does not seem to be a necessary one. That is, these services are not unique to uninhab-

ited or uncultivated places; they are performed by non-wilderness ecosystems as well. Iowa corn plants purify air and remove atmospheric carbon dioxide just as Douglas firs do. Moreover, recovering forests composed of fast-growing young trees do an even better job of this than do old-growth forests.

Nevertheless, certain ecological services can only be performed in large tracts of relatively untouched land. For example, some designated wilderness areas provide nurseries for species such as salmon. Conservation biologists tell us that certain species, like the grizzly bear, require large tracts of unbroken land to exist. And the earth's oceans help to moderate temperatures. Again, to be sure, certain non-wilderness areas do perform some of these same services. But they do not perform these services as efficiently and thriftily as alleged wilderness areas do. Some wilderness areas are irreplaceable sources of clean air and pure water.

Potentiality comes into play in this argument as well. Since we are not entirely sure exactly what all is in those areas we think of as wilderness, we cannot be entirely confident of all the unique and crucial services provided by them. Hence, for their potential services we ought to preserve them as well.

5 The Life-Support Argument

Holmes Rolston explains that there exists "a parallel between the good of the system and that of the individual." Further, we depend upon the healthy functioning of various ecosystems. Ecosystems often have the greatest value for us when they are the most independent of us; or, as Rolston concludes, "So far as [we] are entwined with ecosystems, our choices ... need to be within the capacities of biological systems, paying some attention to ecosystem value."[16]

George Sessions points out that this prudential argument was made famous in the 1960s and 1970s "ecological revolution" by thinkers such as Rachel Carson, Barry Commoner, and Anne and Paul Ehrlich. The Ehrlichs, for example, liken species eradication to the popping of an airplane's rivets. Rivet-popping will eventually lead to the demise of spaceship Earth.[17]

So, as a mechanism for supporting and ensuring human existence (and the existence of many other species for that matter), so-called wilderness areas not only should but must be preserved, it is argued.

Is this argument persuasive? As an argument for wilderness, over and above an argument for species preservation, its proponents must prove that the only way to preserve species is to preserve wilderness. They must explain how species diversity coexisted with people in species-rich areas of the world for hundreds, even thousands of years. Indeed, if this argument is to work, two links must be made. The preservation of wilderness must be linked with the preservation of species, and the preservation of species must be linked with human survival. This latter link is also questionable. Are species rivets? Is Earth a spaceship? One might take "survival" in a literal sense. We might survive, but only in diminished numbers as impoverished creatures in an ecologically impoverished environment. In sum, such an argument opens up a virtual Pandora's box of difficult questions with tough answers.

6 The Physical Therapy Argument

It is argued that designated wilderness area-related activities are wonderful and essential ways to enhance and even remedy our physical health. Primitivists, for example, claim that the more closely we are associated with nature the more physically healthy we will be. Hence, if putative wilderness is the purest representative form of nature, we would be healthier if we took our physical exercise in such places, some argue. Socialist, wilderness advocate, and cofounder of the Wilderness Society, Robert Marshall once asserted that there exist great physical benefits to "wilderness activities."[18]

This may appear to be quite a weak argument for wilderness preservation, since people in many parts of the world are physically fit despite having no access to designated wilderness areas. Traditionally the world's greatest middle-distance runners have been British. And there are no wilderness areas in Britain. Exercising in what Marshall took to be wilderness is at best only a sufficient, not a necessary, condition for physical well-being. However, wilderness advocates might still argue that these proffered wilderness areas are the *best* source and measure of physical health. Hence to lose them is to lose the *greatest* source and measure of physical therapy.

This wilderness preservation argument is what Godfrey-Smith refers to as the Gymnasium argument. However, it seems that his classification

actually has two separate arguments: one is that designated wilderness areas provide us with a source and measure of physical health and the other is that these places serve as a great place to engage in certain sports (which may also aid our physical health), or what I refer to here as the Arena argument.

7 The Arena Argument

Even more elementary than supplying a source and measure of physical fitness, wilderness preservation is sometimes urged on the grounds that many designated wilderness areas provide us with superb and incomparable locales for athletic and recreational pursuits.

In various designated wilderness areas we can engage in a variety of activities: we can go cross-country skiing, hunting, scuba diving, snowmobiling, rock climbing, swimming, kayaking, backpacking, canoeing, horseback riding, hiking, camping, and mountaineering. Those engaged in these pursuits argue that designated wilderness areas allow us an unprecedented place to test our skills, hone our muscles, and experience all of the joys associated with these activities. Aldo Leopold saw this as one of the primary goals of public wilderness areas:

> Wilderness areas are, first of all, a means of perpetuating, in sport form, the ... primitive skills in pioneering travel and subsistence ... a series of sanctuaries for the primitive arts of wilderness travel, especially canoeing and packing [he was referring here to mule and horse packing]. ... Recreation is valuable in proportion to the intensity of its experiences, and to the degree to which it differs from and contrasts with workaday life.[19]

We need places to roam, to use our leg muscles, places to use our hands in the grasping of natural things, so the argument goes. In the civilized world we keep fit and tone our bodies by running on the indoor treadmill, lifting weights, swimming laps, and going to aerobics classes at the local health spa. Wilderness areas provide us with places where we can develop our muscles and realize our strength by hiking, climbing, paddling, and so forth. ... Obviously, it can contribute to physical well-being and even rehabilitate the disabled.

Michael P. Nelson

But we might ask why we need designated wilderness areas to do these things; I can paddle my canoe in a dam-created reservoir, hike in an industrial monoculture pine forest, and climb on a modern climbing-wall. The wilderness advocate may respond by claiming that these "artificial" places are pale substitutes for the "real" thing; that designated wilderness areas provide the *best* locales for these sorts of activities. They are unmatched and unmatchable outdoor gymnasia, places to play. They have all – and more – of the sporting accoutrements that our more "civilized" physical fitness facilities have.

Some wilderness advocates even argue that just as we require certain cultural spaces for certain cultural activities (e.g., football fields to play football on, theaters to see movies in, etc.), so some wilderness athletic activities simply require wilderness areas to do them in. Just as deep-powder skiers require deep powder, mountain climbers mountains, and deep-sea divers deep seas, wilderness backpackers require wilderness to do their thing. It seems that an essential ingredient in these activities is solitude and a pristine natural arena. Without a "wilderness" condition, enthusiasts of wilderness activities cannot pursue those activities.

There are really two different arguments here: first, wilderness is the best locale for certain activities; and, second, wilderness as the only locale for other activities. While one might grant that designated wilderness areas provide the *best* locale for certain activities – say deep-powder skiing and deep-sea diving – they do not provide the *sole* locale. Deep powder may lie a mere saunter from a ski resort. Deep seas exist under shipping lanes. These activities do not depend solely on the existence of designated or even *de facto* wilderness. On the other hand, it seems tautological and circular to claim that wilderness backpackers need wilderness. Still, it is an argument for wilderness preservation: one can hardly deny that wilderness recreationalists need wilderness in order to pursue their sports.

8 The Mental Therapy Argument

Perhaps even more prevalent than the above physical benefits of proffered wilderness is the argument for wilderness preservation on behalf of its actual and potential psychological health benefits.

Wilderness advocates have often claimed that what are taken to be wilderness experiences can be psychologically therapeutic and can even significantly help treat psychologically disturbed persons.

Reflecting on the ever-increasing human desire to visit America's national parks, John Muir cites psychological dysfunction as a major cause, and refers to city people as "tired, nerve-shaken, over-civilized," "half-insane," "choked with care like clocks full of dust," and bursting with "rust and disease," "sins and cobweb cares."[20] According to Muir, visiting designated wilderness – which, as he realized, both necessitates and threatens its preservation – is the cure to these problems. In Muir's prescription for mental health, "wilderness is a necessity," and wild places are "fountains of life."[21] Others, such as Sigurd Olson, Robert Marshall, and even Sigmund Freud have argued that civilization represses, frustrates, and often breeds unhappiness and discontent in humans that can best be alleviated by periodic escape to what they took to be wilderness. More contemporary studies show that drug abusers, juvenile delinquents, and over-stressed executives can and do often benefit from an occasional dose of wilderness experience.[22]

Wilderness helps us to put our "civilized" lives in perspective; it simplifies living; reacquaints us with pain, fear, and solitude; provides us with a necessary sense of challenge; and helps us discover what is really important and essential to our existence. Or so some say. Wilderness experience is also said to be a great form of stress relief and serves as a superb pressure release for those living in metropolitan areas. Primitivists claim that just as there are great physical benefits to close association with nature in wilderness, such association also has the mentally therapeutic benefits of making us happier and more psychologically stable and balanced. On this same note, Rolston claims that "wildlands absorb a kind of urban negative disvalue...and provide a 'niche' that meets deep seated psychosomatic needs."[23]

If one believes that the collective mental well-being of a society is but an aggregate of the mental well-being of its individual members, then the individual mental health of those who visit designated wilderness areas arguably contributes to the quality of a society's life and vitality. Some wilderness advocates even go so far as to assert that experience with wild places functions as a gauge or measure for our individual and collective sanity. Wallace Stegner, for example, asserts that his vision of wilderness is a "means of reassuring ourselves of our sanity as creatures."[24]

None of the proponents of the mental health argument for wilderness preservation explain exactly how the existence of designated wilderness areas contributes to sanity. But even if we did grant that the existence of designated wilderness areas is a sufficient condition for instilling mental health, is it a necessary condition? There are seemingly many psychologically fit people who have never visited a designated wilderness area and there are undoubtedly "wilderness junkies" who are not mentally healthy or stable. Surely other methods of ensuring and gauging our mental health and sanity exist.

Nevertheless, some wilderness proponents claim that purported wilderness is necessary for human mental health. In his book *Nature and Madness*, ecologist Paul Shepard argues that we humans *need* wilderness. He claims that in the natural and healthy growth process there needs to be close association, experience, and bonding with the wild things that inhabit wild places.[25] Warwick Fox echoes Shepard's sentiments when he claims that this sort of wilderness preservation argument "emphasizes the importance of the non-human world to humans for the development of healthy (sane) minds."[26]

However, even if these areas of alleged wilderness are only sufficient conditions for mental well-being, one might still wish to argue that they are the best means of assuring mental health. Moreover, one might argue that these "wild" places succor our souls in a much more socially and individually cost-effective manner than do therapists, twelve-step programs, support groups, churches, prisons, and mental institutions.

9 The Art Gallery Argument

Many people search out putative wilderness areas for aesthetic experience. Both beauty and sublimity may be found in these places, they say. Therefore, we should preserve them because they are sites of the beautiful and the sublime. "Wild" places, it is argued, are like gigantic art galleries.[27]

In fact, some have argued that aesthetic experience, of the sort so-called wilderness offers, can border on the religious or mystical. Roderick Nash, for example, maintains that the experience of wild things involves "awe in the face of large,

unmodified natural forces and places – such as storms, waterfalls, mountains and deserts."[28] And William Wordsworth wrote that experiencing the beauty of what his vision of wilderness was produces "a motion and a spirit, that impels... and rolls through all things."[29] Further, some argue that designated wilderness areas are places where the very meaning of aesthetic quality can be ascertained and that, therefore, all beauty is dependent upon such sites. Muir, for example, claims that "None of Nature's landscapes are ugly so long as they are wild."[30]

The destruction of a designated wilderness area – and hence wilderness-dependent species such as wolves and grizzlies – it is claimed, would be as bad as, even worse than, the destruction of a painting by da Vinci or a sculpture by Michelangelo. In principle, works of art can be recreated, but wilderness-dependent species – like any species – cannot. As Aldo Leopold puts it in his essay "Goose Music," "In dire necessity somebody might write another Iliad, or paint another 'Angelus,' but fashion a goose?"[31] Now, geese are admittedly not a wilderness–dependent species and Leopold is not speaking directly of wilderness in this essay, but Leopold's point clearly applies to wolves and grizzlies as well as to geese. What cannot almost unequivocally be recreated (*Jurassic Park*-considerations to the side) is an extinct species. And since species like wolves and grizzlies are dependent upon wilderness for their continued existence, the loss of wilderness is tantamount to the *permanent* loss of those species.

The intensity and type of beauty found in unique land forms, waterfalls, mountains, oceans, outer space, deserts, plants, and animals – all shaped by natural forces – cannot be replicated in urban or even pastoral settings, some wilderness advocates maintain. According to them, these places are both necessary and sufficient conditions for a true sense of beauty. Hence, if the loss of this beauty is to be avoided the preservation of wilderness areas is mandated.

10 The Inspiration Argument

Many claim that putative wilderness areas are important to maintain because they provide inspiration for the artistically and intellectually inclined. In the process, these designated wilderness areas add to and help shape culture. Numerous artists –

Michael P. Nelson

such as painters Thomas Cole, Thomas Moran, and Albert Bierstadt; photographers Ansel Adams and Galen Rowell; writers James Fenimore Cooper, Colin Fletcher, and "Cactus" Ed Abbey (not to mention Emerson and Thoreau); musicians John Denver and "Walkin'" Jim Stoltz; and poets Walt Whitman, William Wordsworth, and Robinson Jeffers, to name but a few – find their inspiration in what they take to be wilderness. For them, "wilderness" provides an excellent and unique motif for art.

Some even assert that wilderness serves to inspire those in the intellectual arts as well. Philosophers, for example – especially environmental philosophers – often regard what they take to be wilderness experience to be a contemplative catalyst or cognitive genesis for the really big questions of philosophy: What is the meaning of the universe (a question evoked especially by extraterrestrial wilderness, it seems); where we all came from; what we are all doing here; where we are going; what the character of our existence is, and what our moral place in the world is. Now of course there are other catalysts for artistic and philosophic inspiration: cattle, cities, and factories to name but a few. The point is not that wilderness areas are the only muses for art, but rather that they are excellent and unique ones, and that to lose any such inspirational kindling would be tragic.

11   The Cathedral Argument

For some, ostensible wilderness is a site for spiritual, mystical, or religious encounters: places to experience mystery, moral regeneration, spiritual revival, meaning, oneness, unity, wonder, awe, inspiration, or a sense of harmony with the rest of creation – all essentially religious experiences. Wilderness areas are also said to be places where one can come to an understanding of and engage in the celebration of the creation – an essentially religious activity. Hence, for people who think like this, designated wilderness areas can and do serve as a sort of (or in lieu of) a church, mosque, tabernacle, synagogue, or cathedral. We should, then, no more destroy wilderness areas than we should raze Mecca or turn the Sistine Chapel into a giant grain silo. For some, wild places represent and reflect the various spiritual and religious values that they hold dear.

To go one step further, some even claim that since designated wilderness areas are the closest thing we have on earth to the original work of God, to destroy them would be tantamount to the destruction of God's handiwork, forever altering God's original intent.

John Muir believed that the closer one was to nature, the closer one was to God. To Muir, "wilderness" was the highest manifestation of nature and so was a "window opening into heaven, a mirror reflecting the Creator," and all parts of it were seen as "sparks of the Divine Soul."[32] Yosemite's Hetch Hetchy Valley was, for Muir, a place epitomizing wilderness, a shrine to a higher existence, the destruction of which was tantamount to sacrilege. For this reason, Muir vehemently defended Hetch Hetchy and said of its would-be desecrators:

These temple destroyers, devotees of ravaging commercialism, seem to have a perfect contempt for Nature, and, instead of lifting their eyes to the God of the mountains, lift them to the Almighty Dollar.

Dam Hetch Hetchy! As well dam for water-tanks the people's cathedrals and churches, for no holier temple has ever been consecrated by the heart of man.[33]

Transcendentalists, such as Ralph Waldo Emerson, Thoreau, and William Cullen Bryant, went so far as to claim that one could only genuinely understand moral and aesthetic truths in what they took to be a wilderness setting. For these thinkers, civilization only fragments and taints one's genuine moral and aesthetic understanding.

Actually, this appears to be a quite powerful political argument for legally preserving designated wilderness areas. In the United States, for example, if the sorts of experiences and activities just listed are presumed to be essentially religious experiences and activities, then designated wilderness areas can be said to serve a religious function. Hence, designated American wilderness areas could be defended on the constitutional grounds of freedom to worship as one chooses. Regardless of concerns about the size or type of the area required or the fact that only a minority of people actually "go to church in the woods," designated wilderness areas might still merit protection, both ethically and legally, as places of worship.

12   The Laboratory Argument

Some (mostly wildlife, marine, and conservation biologists) argue that the preservation of designated areas of wilderness is important because it provides scientists with an unprecedented location and the raw materials for certain kinds of scientific inquiry. In order to conduct their scientific queries, these wilderness advocates require many types and varieties of geographical locales which remain in their pristine state. This scientific study is said to be important not only for the sake of knowledge itself but also more instrumentally because a society can use this knowledge to form a better understanding of itself, the world around it, and hence its proper role in that world. Wilderness is viewed by these people as one end of the spectrum of locales for such study.

Admittedly, there is a potential paradox involved with this argument – as there is with all wilderness preservation arguments that entail the use of areas of putative wilderness by humans. If we use wilderness areas as laboratories (or gymnasiums, cathedrals, resource pools, etc. . . .) in too dense or intrusive a fashion, they would then cease to be wilderness areas. The use, then, of wilderness areas by humans possibly is or could be a threat to such areas themselves. This tension ought always to be kept in mind when considering these sorts of arguments.

13   The Standard of Land Health Argument

Aldo Leopold's arguments on behalf of wilderness preservation shifted and expanded as his thought progressed. The more mature Leopold believed that what he took to be wilderness was important for scientific as well as for recreational reasons. Leopold proclaimed that "all wild areas . . . have value . . . for land science. . . . Recreation is not their only, or even their principal, utility." For Leopold, the main scientific use of "wilderness" was as a base-datum or measure of land health and as a model of a normal ecologically balanced landscape. According to Leopold, wilderness areas serve as a measure "of what the land was, what it is, and what it ought to be," providing us with both an actual ecological control sample of healthy land and a normative measure of what we ought to strive toward.

Throughout his life, Leopold became increasingly interested in land use and the science of land health. In order to have such a science, Leopold declared that we need "first of all, a base datum of normality, a picture of how healthy land maintains itself as an organism." According to Leopold, the "most perfect norm is wilderness" for "in many cases we literally do not know how good a performance to expect of healthy land unless we have a wild area for comparison with sick ones." Hence, we can easily see how "wilderness," in Leopold's words, "assumes unexpected importance as a laboratory for the study of land-health."[34]

Rolston develops Leopold's original idea: "We want to know what the unmolested system was in order to fit ourselves more intelligently in with its operations when we do alter it."[35] Further, as a measure of healthy land, areas of "wilderness" are said to be of value, according to Warwick Fox, as a sort of "early warning system" whose job it is "to warn us of more general kinds of deterioration in the quality or quantity of the free 'goods and services' that are provided *by* our 'life support system'"; wilderness can function as the proverbial canary in the coal mine.[36]

"But," one might ask, "why do we need *so much* wilderness; *so many* wilderness areas?" "Couldn't we have a base datum and measure of ecological health with but one wilderness area?" The answer is no. In order to serve as a measure of land health, it is argued, designated wilderness areas must be large and varied; for there are many distinct types of biotic communities. Leopold tells us – in a passage remarkably in line with contemporary conservation biology – that "each biotic province needs its own wilderness for comparative studies of used and unused land. . . . In short all available wild areas, large or small, are likely to have value as norms for land science."[37]

Interestingly, this argument avoids the potential paradox of overuse found in all use-oriented arguments because such control areas are *not* places to conduct invasive or manipulative research. Science only takes the pulse of these areas – so to speak.

Although this appears to be a strong argument for preserving designated wilderness areas it also appears, at least in part, to buy into the ontologically impossible notion that there are places totally untouched and unaffected by human actions. In order for "wilderness" to serve as a standard of land health, we must recognize that "wilderness" needs to be conceived of as a relative and tenuous concept.

14 The Storage Silo Argument

Taking the Laboratory argument one step further, it is often asserted by conservation biologists, among others, that many supposed terrestrial and aquatic wilderness areas are worth saving because they contain vast amounts of biodiversity; especially genetic information or species diversity, or what Harvard biologist E. O. Wilson refers to as the "diversity of life." Beyond the argument that humans have no moral right to muck with the evolutionary and ecological workings of *all* ecosystems of a given type, maintaining these genetic reservoirs intact is instrumentally important because they function as a great safety device; holding a large portion of the world's accumulated evolutionary and ecological wisdom as they do. These proponents of wilderness claim that the whole of this information can only be properly maintained in its original context. Hence, some wilderness areas can serve as places where various forms of biodiversity can be stored for a time when they might be needed for genetic engineering, agricultural rejuvenation, or some other crucial purpose. Biotically rich and untrammeled wilderness areas are better than trammeled areas at providing for the continuation of the crucial processes of evolution and ecology since biotically rich and untrammeled areas have larger gene pools and are places where evolution can work unfettered to bring forth new species. Hence, biotically rich and untrammeled wilderness areas store the information that can help us to better manage and rebuild our natural environment. Certain wilderness areas, some believe, are therefore the key to life on earth. As David Brower puts it, "Wilderness holds the answers to the questions we do not yet know how to ask."[38]

Obviously, it would be foolish to knowingly extirpate natural processes. According to Aldo Leopold, "To keep every cog and wheel is the first precaution of intelligent tinkering."[39] Hence, to destroy biotically rich wilderness areas is tantamount to the destruction of vast amounts of hitherto untapped and unused, but crucial, information; or, as Holmes Rolston analogizes, "destroying wildlands is like burning unread books."[40]

15 The Classroom Argument

Those of us who regularly or only occasionally visit designated wilderness areas are very aware that these locales often function as a sort of classroom where a plethora of valuable lessons can be learned.

Obviously, these experiences can increase our taxonomical environmental education: we can learn to identify Norway maples, magnolia warblers, spotted joe-pye, or timber wolf scat, for example. Granted, we can learn taxonomy elsewhere, but only in would-be wilderness can we encounter and learn of the habits and behaviors of some of these "others"; for only in large tracts of unbroken land do certain animals exist. According to many, "wilderness" experiences are also the *best* way to teach us such tangible skills as navigation and survival, and help us attain a feeling for a particular geographic region and features. However, it is also thought that additional important lessons can be learned through exposure to what many refer to as wilderness.

Nearly all advocates of wilderness preservation note the way that "wilderness experience" can help us put things in perspective or put our priorities in order, how it can teach us proper values and a sense of valuation, how it can instill within us a sense of humility and help build our individual and collective characters. Many also claim that periodic trips to designated wilderness areas force us to recognize our proper place as stewards, not masters, of the land; endow us with long-sighted and ecological vision; train us to make better public-policy decisions; furnish us with a sense of individual responsibility; promote our self-confidence and self-image; teach us how to cooperate successfully with others and how to assess and take wise and appropriate risks; and instill within us a reverence for all life and a proper sense of beauty. Groups such as Outward Bound and the Girl and Boy Scouts, for example, depend upon and utilize designated wilderness areas as classrooms to teach such lessons. In addition, if considered as places where natural processes continue unfettered, designated wilderness areas might also be said to provide a necessary and unique place to glean insights into the precious scientific studies of evolution and ecology.

And finally, for some environmental ethicists at least, the most important pedagogical aspect of "wilderness experience" lies in the fact that the lessons learned through and only through such exposure play a necessary role in the development and support of a proper and sound environmental ethic. Hence, they argue, one could not develop an ethical relation toward the nonhuman natural environment without the presence of wilderness areas. Given arguments against the very existence of wilderness, then, this would seem to imply that if there is no such thing as wilderness then there would be no such thing as an appropriate environmental ethic.

On a critical note: one must ask two questions. First, does this classroom argument for the preservation of designated wilderness areas hold true for all of these areas? That is, are all, or only some, designated wilderness areas sources of these important lessons? And second, while it may be true that the presence of designated wilderness areas is a sufficient condition for providing these valuable lessons, is it a necessary one? Can we not learn these lessons elsewhere? Or, is the argument that these are nonduplicable locales for environmental, life, and ethical wisdom? This argument appears to be weakened either if it does not hold true for all designated wilderness areas or if there are other ways or places to learn these lessons.

16 The Ontogeny Argument

Individually and collectively we human beings, like all living things, have evolved within a specific context. We are what we are, have become what we have become, because of the environment in which we have flourished. Some argue that the context of this historical development includes "wilderness" to a great extent – originally cosmic, then aquatic, and most recently terrestrial.

Homo sapiens and their communities, like all species and their respective communities, are deeply entrenched in nature and nature's processes. In other words, we fit our context. One might go on from this simple premise to argue that since what is thought of as wilderness is the paradigmatic form of nature and its processes, that this wilderness – first oceanic and then terrestrial – is and continues to be the source of our evolution. Hence, putative wilderness in its many forms not only ought to but must be preserved for continued human evolution.

We could, then, view wilderness preservation as a symbolic gesture of love and respect for our evolutionary ontogeny and perhaps as a defense of our evolutionary future. Edward Abbey adds such an argument to his list of wilderness preservation rationales. "The love of wilderness...," he wrote, "is...an expression of loyalty to the earth, the earth which bore us and sustains us, the only home we shall ever know, the only paradise we ever need – if only we had the eyes to see." Abbey goes on to claim that the destruction of these areas of "wilderness" would be a sin, then, against our origins, or the "true original sin."[41]

Additionally, there is a nonsymbolic sense of this argument. Walt Whitman believed that those who remain closer and more in touch with their evolutionary context become better people. As he wrote in *Leaves of Grass*, "Now I see the secret of the making of the best persons./It is to grow in the open air, and to eat and sleep with the earth."[42] Nash points out that a variety of primitivists – from Jean-Jacques Rousseau to Edgar Rice Burroughs – concur with Whitman and likewise declare that "the wild world produces a superior human being."[43]

Our ontogenetic setting, for Whitman and Nash at least, deserves special consideration since our evolutionary past, present, and future is intimately tied to what we now call wilderness. Therefore, according to this argument, these places should be preserved in order to ensure our context, our physio/psycho-genesis and natural individual development. And excursions to these areas, then, appear to function as visitations to our ancestral residence or what Abbey once referred to as the "journey home."

There is a definite irony to this argument. If "wilderness" is a place where humans are but visitors who do not remain or an area beyond that which is cultivated or inhabited continuously by humans, how in the world could it be our literal ancestral home? In fact, "wilderness," designated or not, is often portrayed as an area undefiled by human habitation, a place where people do not live. So how could it be our home? And if we have evicted ourselves from our ancestral paradise home irrevocably, how can wilderness be the locus or future of our human evolution?

17 The Cultural Diversity Argument

In one of his most familiar works, "Walking," Thoreau writes,

Our ancestors were savages. The story of Romulus and Remus being suckled by a wolf is not a meaningless fable. The founders of every state which has risen to eminence have drawn their nourishment and vigor from similar wild sources. . . . In such soil grew Homer and Confucius and the rest, and out of such a wilderness comes the Reformer eating locusts and wild honey.[44]

So it is argued that, just as human beings generically derive from a context, specific cultures are derived from and are dependent upon a certain ontogenetic context as well. And the wide variety of cultural variation or diversity stems from the fact that there has been a wide variety of natural ecosystems. As Leopold put it, "The rich diversity of the world's cultures reflects a corresponding diversity in the wilds that gave them birth."[45] The vigor for culture, some deduce, comes from wilderness. Or, as Nash writes, "The wild world is cultural raw material."[46]

A wide variety of designated wilderness areas ought to be preserved, it is thought, because they function as the foundation for the world's myriad cultures. As much as we value individual cultures and the diversity of cultures, we must to the same extent value their respective areas of purported wilderness. "We want some wilderness preserved," Rolston claims, "because it comes to express the values of the culture superimposed on it, entering our sense of belongingness and identity."[47]

There seems to be a paradox implicit in this argument. If the diverse cultures remain in the wilderness that gave them birth, then the places they are in are not, by definition, wilderness. If various areas of the world are *designated* wilderness areas and the cultures they spawned are expelled from them (if these cultures still exist), as the Ik were from the Kidepo in Uganda and the !Kung were from the Etosha National Park in Namibia, then the cultures are exterminated in order to preserve the wilderness that spawned them.[48]

Furthermore, to argue that areas of wilderness ought to be preserved as museum pieces in honor of a part of the environment that helped shape each unique culture commits the fallacy of appeal to tradition. Slavery helped to form much of the American Deep South; the oppressive Hindu caste system largely shaped modern India; various acts of violence, wars, and systems of patriarchy have helped to mold various world cultures. Should

remnant enclaves of these institutions likewise be preserved because they are the roots of various cultures? Should we designate one or two counties in Mississippi as Old South cultural reserves in which the plantation system, including slavery, is preserved? And so on.

18   The National Character Argument

A specific example of the above two arguments is national character, and even more specific is colonial American national character.

In the United States, many see designated wilderness areas as monuments; symbolically enshrining national values. Our Euro-American cultural identity, for example, is often said to be deeply entwined with the existence of designated wilderness areas. For many Euro-Americans, the United States is the place where the eagle flies, the buffalo roam, and the deer and the antelope play. Wallace Stegner calls the wilderness idea "something that has helped form our character and that has certainly shaped our history as a people." Designated wilderness areas ought to be preserved then, because they are a "part of the geography of hope."[49] Many seminal American historical thinkers – such as Gertrude Stein and Frederick Jackson Turner – felt that designated wilderness areas in the United States serve as what Roderick Nash refers to as the "crucible of American character."[50]

Hence it is argued that designated wilderness areas ought to be preserved because they and their resident species helped form and continue to enshrine our most fundamental and powerful Euro-American values. Nash notes that American president Theodore Roosevelt was particularly fond of the argument which asserts that since "wilderness shaped our national values and institutions, it follows that one of the most important roles of nature reserves is keeping those values and institutions alive."[51] Environmental philosopher Mark Sagoff even goes so far as to submit that wilderness preservation has constitutional clout:

If restraints on the exploitation of our environment are to be adequate, then, they must be found in the Constitution itself. . . . To say that an environmental policy can be based on the Constitution does not require, of course, a constitutional passage or article which directly concerns the environment; rather the argument would rest on the concept of nationhood, the structure created by the Constitution as a single instrument functioning in all of its parts. It is reasonable to think that cultural traditions and values constitute a condition – at least a causal one – of our political and legal freedom; and therefore insofar as the Constitution safeguards our nation as a political entity, it must safeguard our cultural integrity as well. Citizenship, then, can be seen to involve not only legal and political but also cultural rights and responsibilities . . . The right to . . . demand that the mountains be left as a symbol of the sublime, a quality which is extremely important in our cultural history, . . . the right to cherish traditional national symbols, the right to preserve in the environment the qualities we associate with our character as a people, belongs to us as Americans. The concept of nationhood implies this right; and for this reason, it is constitutionally based.[52]

Moreover, for all the reasons that we preserve in perpetuity the dwelling places of Americans of European descent (e.g., Puritans or Mormons) as national landmarks denoting their cultural heritage, we ought also to preserve many areas of putative wilderness as well. These designated wilderness areas, we might argue, would function as a similar sort of cultural monument, since they are seen by some to be the historical home of aboriginal American peoples like the Sioux, Hopi, Iroquois, or Inuit.[53] As such, of course, they were not wilderness areas, since these people were people (not wildlife) and did live there (not just visit).

Now there is admittedly yet another inherent paradox involved with the above three ontogeny-type arguments, and especially with the National Character argument. If wilderness preservation is a good thing because it is a representation of Euro-American ontogeny then wilderness destruction seems to be a good thing as well. That part of our Euro-American ontogeny, most recently evolved is the tendency to work to destroy, or at least to severely alter and interrupt, what colonizing Euro-Americans took to be wilderness. Like belief in the existence of a vast North American wilderness, the transformation of that wilderness could be said to be an important aspect of our national character. So, we might argue that Euro-Americans and Euro-American wilderness colonization and destruction is part of Euro-American national character. Hence, destroying designated

wilderness areas would be more consistent with the Euro-American national character than preserving it. Wilderness preservation might be seen as both good and bad at the same time then. It is good because the North American "wilderness" is the raw material of Euro-American culture and is valuable as such. It is bad because the destruction of those same places is part of that same national ontogeny and we would be interfering with that ontogeny if we were to artificially restrain or frustrate it. The root problem, it seems, is to make the argument that X is good merely because X is part of our heritage. Slavery, violence, and sexism are parts of our heritage, but that is no reason to keep them around as treasured national institutions. Logicians call this the Genetic Fallacy.

19   The Self-Realization Argument

One of the fundamental tenets of Deep Ecology is the notion of self-realization. Relying heavily upon the works of Muir, Thoreau, Leopold, and the Romantic and American Transcendental traditions, Deep Ecologists assert that – in order truly and appropriately to perceive and understand the world, our place in it, and our duties to it – we must first dismiss the assumed but inaccurate bifurcation between self and nature. We must grasp the depth of the relational reality of all things, including the non-human world. In addition to the general character and self-image building mentioned above, wilderness preservation becomes crucial for Deep Ecologists because designated wilderness areas are, for them, necessary components in this process of self-realization – a sort of asylum of reorientation where this relational self ideal can take form. We must, therefore, maintain areas of "wilderness" in order to achieve a complete and appropriate view of self. Designated wilderness areas are crucial, according to this argument, for individual development and continued existence. No designated wilderness areas means no self-realization; no Deep Ecology; no proper view of self and world; no appropriate treatment of self and world; no continued self-existence.[54]

On a more critical note, this argument appears to fall prey to the recurring problem of confusing necessary and sufficient conditions. Merely because designated wilderness areas provide an arguably sufficient condition for self-realization, it remains to be proven that they are a necessary condition for such self-realization.

20 The Disease Sequestration Argument

This is a very new and perhaps very worthy wilderness preservation argument.

As noted, more than half of the earth's extant species live in the tropics; and most of these species are not known to science. Since most all species host viruses, we can assume that there are at least as many viruses as there are living species, if not some multiple of that number.

One thing we do know is that viruses adapt to their hosts. A successful virus either does not, or "learns" not to, kill its host so as to have a residence for its continued existence. However, as human population continues to surge and human invasion into places such as tropical habitats becomes more prevalent, humans cross never-before-traversed ecological and spatial boundaries. Hence, humans increasingly encounter new species; in Star Trek phraseology, we "boldly go where no one has gone before." As humans intrude, put pressure upon, or destroy supposed wilderness, viruses will adapt and jump hosts, taking humans as their new hosts. The effects of this "host jumping" are unknown and potentially dreadful, especially when dealing with lethal viruses for which there is no vaccine nor cure. Known viruses, such as Guanarito and Marburg, and currently "emerging" viruses like Q fever and Monkeypox, are part of a long list of viruses which have already jumped to human hosts with deleterious results.[55] In his insightful – and truly frightening – essay in *The New Yorker*, Richard Preston explains:

> When an ecosystem suffers degradation, many species die out and a few survivor-species have population explosions. Viruses in a damaged ecosystem can come under extreme selective pressure. Viruses are adaptable: they react to change and can mutate fast, and they can jump among species of hosts. As people enter the forest and clear it, viruses come out, carried in their survivor-hosts – rodents, insects, soft ticks – and the viruses meet Homo sapiens.[56]

In fact, human immunodeficiency virus (HIV) is another, more familiar, contemporary example. The reigning theory asserts that HIV is a mutant zoonotic virus that originally resided in the rain forests of Central Africa which jumped to humans when they had some sort of intimate contact (i.e., sexual contact, hunters touching the bloody tissue of the victim, etc.) with the sooty mangabey, an African monkey. We do not know the source for certain; HIV may have come from chimpanzees or even from other previously isolated humans, or it may just be a viral mutation of some sort. Nevertheless, as Preston points out,

> The emergence of AIDS appears to be a natural consequence of the ruin of the tropical biosphere. Unknown viruses are coming out of the equatorial wildernesses of the earth and discovering the human race. It seems to be happening as a result of the destruction of tropical habitats. You might call AIDS the revenge of the rain forest. AIDS is arguably the worst environmental disaster of the twentieth century, so far.[57]

And HIV is not even as dangerous as some. Yes, it is lethal, but it is relatively noninfectious considering how it might be transmitted. Just imagine HIV as an airborne pathogen, which is not impossible. Ebola Zaire, a lethal airborne filovirus that emerged in fifty-five African villages in 1976 and subjected nine out of ten of its victims to hideous deaths within days of infection, is an example of an encountered virus even more lethal than HIV. And viruses are only part of this gloom-and-doom story. As Preston tells us, "mutant bacteria, such as the strains that cause multidrug-resistant tuberculosis, and protozoans, such as mutant strains of malaria, have become major and growing threats to the [world's] population" as well.[58]

Since these disease-causing agents are for the most part sequestered in many of the earth's remaining wild areas, our intrusion into these areas is a definite issue – one that deserves our utmost attention. So, not only do many of the wild areas of the earth serve as a disaster hedge by acting as a buffer, but much ostensible wilderness left intact is thought to protect us from potential viral and bacterial decimation. For this reason, any sane person would agree, some regions of the Earth – those harboring tropical viruses – deserve special consideration and preservation.

However, this argument appears to be less an argument for preserving designated wilderness areas and more an argument for not intruding into those areas where these viruses thrive; less an argument for preserving the Bob Marshall Wilderness Area and more an argument for staying out of some very specific (i.e., tropical) places. Moreover, with this argument also there are elements of paradox and irony. These lairs of deadly viruses are not exactly those places that we wish to *visit* for recreation, inspiration, religious awe, and so forth.

21 The Salvation of Freedom Argument

In his novel celebrating the arenaceous wilds of southern Utah's Arches National Monument, *Desert Solitaire*, Edward Abbey defends the preservation of what he imagines to be wilderness for what he calls "political reasons." He claims that we need designated and de facto wilderness areas, whether or not we ever set foot in them, to serve as potential sanctuaries from oppressive governmental structures. As Abbey writes,

> We may need it [wilderness] someday not only as a refuge from excessive industrialism but also as a refuge from authoritarian government, from political oppression. Grand Canyon, Big Bend, Yellowstone and the High Sierras may be required to function as bases for guerrilla warfare against tyranny.

Abbey reminds us of some of the supposed findings of modern political science – that our cities might easily be transformed into concentration camps and that one of the key strategies in the imposition of any dictatorial regime in any country is to "Raze the wilderness. Dam the rivers, flood the canyons, drain the swamps, log the forests, strip-mine the hills, bulldoze the mountains, irrigate the deserts and improve the national parks into national parking lots."

In order to attempt to alleviate the obvious charge that this is only a paranoid survivalist-type fantasy, Abbey cites as historical fact that the worst of the world's tyrannies have occurred in those countries with the most industry and the least of what Abbey thinks of as wilderness. Centralized oppressive domination flourished in Germany, Hungary, and the Dominican Republic, according

to Abbey, because "an urbanized environment gives the advantage to the power with the technological equipment." On the other hand, more rural insurrections, such as those in Cuba, Algeria, the American colonies, and Vietnam, have favored the revolutionaries since there remained in those countries "mountains, desert, and jungle hinterlands;" or areas of would-be wilderness.[59] Further support for Abbey's wilderness preservation argument might be drawn from the Old Testament story of the Exodus and the New Testament story of John the Baptist. The political dangers of a "wilderness-free" world are fictionally portrayed in Aldous Huxley's *Brave New World* and George Orwell's *1984*.

It should be noted, however, that Abbey's evidence is quite shaky since the counter-examples of the Soviet Union, with its vast expanses of "wilderness," and Cuba, since Castro, throw a monkey wrench into his political theory. Moreover, philosopher Michael Zimmerman has recently chronicled how the Nazi Germans advocated nature preservation more ardently than any other Europeans.[60]

To sum up, according to this argument, areas of "wilderness" in general provide us with a place to escape to and combat a totalitarian police state; as well as providing us with the very standard or meaning of freedom. Hence, in the minds of those such as Ed Abbey, in order to preserve freedom we must preserve alleged wilderness areas.

Now, obviously, not all designated wilderness areas would provide us with base camps for guerrilla warfare against tyrannical governments and one has to allow for the possibility at least that there might be some non-wilderness areas which would. This argument seems, then, to be more an argument for areas from which to oppose tyranny rather than necessarily an argument for the preservation of designated wilderness areas.

Moreover, the fact that something would provide us with the means to oppose tyrannical government is *not* sufficient justification for its preservation. Private atomic-bomb factories in each of our basements would put us in a good position to oppose tyrannical governments too, but clearly (or hopefully) Abbey would not advocate *that*.

22 The Mythopoetic Argument

Some contemporary thinkers, such as Deep Ecologists and postmodernists, argue that wilderness preservation is critical for mythopoetic reasons. Those places they view as wilderness serve as the optimum location for the viewing of the history of myth and are absolutely crucial for the building of the myth of the future. In his mythopoetic book *The Idea of Wilderness*, Max Oelschlaeger writes, in reference to a postmodern conception of nature, "the idea of wilderness in postmodern context is...a search for meaning – for a new creation story or mythology – that is leading humankind out of a homocentric prison into the cosmic wilderness."[61] Putative wilderness areas function as an essential source of meaning, vital for the future of humanity.

The current "Men's Movement" is an excellent example of a mythopoetic use of putative wilderness. In their search for a new way of understanding or realizing their manhood, those involved in the movement have a strong tendency to gather in "wild places" because they seek to recover the roots of their maleness as hunters and companions of animals originally thought to be found in "wilderness." Adding to this, Robert Bly (the central figure in the "mythopoetic" branch of the movement) promotes the ideal of the "wildman," which has central significance as one of the movement's goals. Men should strive, according to Bly, to be whole, healthy, and energized by realizing the "wildman" deep inside their psyches. He is not here referring to any irrational lunatic sense of wild but rather arguing that men need to get in touch with their more primitive or natural roots. Male mythologizing, accordingly, requires areas of would-be wilderness, and for those in the Men's Movement and others, without this "wilderness" a sense of the history of, standard for, or place for the future of myth-building is lost.

This argument appears to rest on some unproved premises: that "wilderness" is the sole or best source of future mythologizing, that our future is impoverished without this source of myth, and that areas other than designated wilderness areas cannot serve as adequate or even more appropriate mythological sources.

23 The Necessity Argument

As we have seen above, certain wilderness advocates believe in the truism that, historically speaking, no civilized world would have evolved without the prior existence of wilderness. As Leopold

claims, "wilderness is the raw material out of which man has hammered the artifact called civilization."[62] But one could, on a more conceptual level, argue that "wilderness" is *necessary* in a more philosophical sense. One might claim that an idea or concept of wilderness is logically and metaphysically necessary (a sense of necessity not historically dependent) for the existence and complete understanding of the concepts of culture and civilization.

Although some may contend that this is more of an explanation of than a justification for wilderness, and that it does not require the preservation of anything but, at the most, a very small bit of wilderness (and at the least only the concept of wilderness and hence no areas of wilderness at all), others might argue that to truly understand concepts such as culture, civilization, freedom, primitive, development, and perhaps others, we need physical wildness (such as that found in designated wilderness areas) to serve as a model or foil of contrast. Holmes Rolston explains:

> Humans can think about ultimates: they can espouse worldviews: indeed, they are not fully human until they do. No one can form a comprehensive worldview without a concept of nature, and no one can form a view of nature without evaluating it in the wild.... In that sense, one of the highest cultural values, an examined worldview, is impossible to achieve without wild nature to be evaluated as a foil to and indeed source of culture.[63]

There can be no finish without a start; no good without evil; no yin without yang; and (according to folksinger Arlo Guthrie) "no light without a dark to stick it in." Similarly then, wilderness might be said to be logically (wherever "civilization" has meaning, "wilderness" does also) and metaphysically (where one thing exists, its opposite must also) necessary for a complete and proper understanding of civilization. According to this argument, there can be no proper understanding of civilization when there is no concept of wilderness, and there can be no complete and proper understanding of the concept of wilderness without genuine designated wilderness areas. Thus the move to rid the world of designated wilderness areas is tantamount to an attempt to deny and dismantle a necessary component for a complete understanding of the world.[64]

24 The Defense of Democracy Argument

Enemies of wilderness preservation and environmentalism in general are fond of charging wilderness advocates and environmentalists with committing the sin of elitism. They claim that wilderness preservation ought *not* be pursued since only a minority of people ever visit designated wilderness areas. Environmentalists, they allege, are selfish people who want to set aside vast stretches of land that only the physically fit and economically able can experience. Wilderness preservation, then, only benefits the elite few and therefore does not serve the general welfare – the greatest good for the greatest number.

However, even though this populist argument is often quite effective, it is also quite easy to "set it on its ear" and turn the charge of elitism into a pro-wilderness preservation argument. Without denying the charge of elitism made by the opponents of wilderness preservation, it could be claimed that precisely because wilderness preservation shows respect for the needs of a minority, wilderness preservation is, therefore, indicative of good democracy. The existence of things like opera houses, softball diamonds, art galleries, public swimming pools and designated wilderness areas – all places used by only a minority – is a display of respect for minority rights or, as Nash says, "the fact that these things can exist is a tribute to nations that cherish and defend minority interests as part of their political ideology."[65] Concerning such an argument, Leopold wrote:

> There are those who decry wilderness sports as "undemocratic" because the recreational carrying capacity of a wilderness is small, as compared with a golf links or a tourist camp. The basic error in such argument is that it applies the philosophy of mass-production to what is intended to counteract mass-production.... Mechanized recreation already has seized nine-tenths of the woods and mountains; a decent respect of minorities should dedicate the other tenth to wilderness.[66]

Robert Marshall was also quite fond of pointing to this as a benefit of designated wilderness areas. "As long as we prize individuality and competence," Marshall says, "it is imperative to provide the opportunity for complete self-sufficiency."[67]

In fact, the original charge of elitism may even be more severely wrong-headed. We might argue that designating areas as wilderness does not limit but rather opens up access to more people than would privatization or land development, especially if we consider future generations of humans, since these wilderness areas are public access lands.

Now, there seems to be an irony or paradox involved with this argument as well. If privatization keeps people out and public ownership allows them in, then designating an area as publicly owned wilderness will guarantee that it will be overrun by hordes of backpackers, camera hunters, and the like.

25 The Social Bonding Argument

Expanding on all of those arguments espousing individual benefits, one could argue that many designated wilderness areas serve as valuable mechanisms in the critical process of social bonding. Those who collectively recreate in designated wilderness areas often attest to the benefits that come from social interaction in such a setting. Driver, Nash, and Haas illustrate these benefits when they claim that one of the most pervasive reasons that people choose to spend time in designated wilderness areas

> relates to family cohesiveness and solidarity. Others include strengthening social bonds with small groups of significant others, sharing skills with others, and gaining social recognition or status from demonstration of skills to others and later sharing tales or photographs of enviable experiences.[68]

Because, and to the extent that, we are social animals and our continued survival depends on effective social interaction, we ought to value social bonding. Exposure to "wilderness" is thought to intensify experience and provide a vector for high-level and successful interpersonal cohesion. Therefore, as an important social mechanism, designated wilderness areas are assumed to be valuable and worthy of preservation.

As an expansion of individual-use values of designated wilderness areas, this argument is subject to the same criticisms leveled at many of the other arguments catalogued here. Surely designated wilderness areas are sufficient and effective in facilitating social bonding, but just as surely they are not necessary. Social bonding can and does take place in highly artificial settings like classrooms, concert halls, offices, saloons, and salons. Moreover, we can just as easily imagine the cohesiveness of a group being completely destroyed by the pressures of wilderness travel. And furthermore, the use of designated wilderness areas by groups of people greatly jeopardizes the "wilderness" integrity of a place.

26 The Animal Welfare Argument

By exploring a non-anthropocentric justification for wilderness preservation we might claim that, like us, wild animals too depend upon their respective home environments for their existence. And since they should be considered as members of the community of beings deserving moral consideration, we owe it to those animals not to destroy their homes. Along similar lines, it was popular in the 1970s to argue that the "wild" things on earth had the right to go about their business unmolested and unharmed by Homo sapiens. We humans, therefore, had no right to interfere with their freedom and dignity. And, since designated wilderness areas were seen as the places where this freedom was most fully realized, these areas should be preserved as "reservoirs of ecological freedom."

As intuitively attractive as this sounds, it must be recognized that most of the animals that animal welfare ethicists are concerned with do not depend on designated wilderness areas for their habitat needs: chickens and cows live on farms, squirrels and pigeons live in cities, deer live in rural areas around farms, cats and dogs live in human homes. Indeed, most animals, both wild and domestic, do not require "wilderness" at all. However, some few animals do require large tracts of unbroken land as habitat: wolves and bears are good examples. For the proper respect of and caring for these animals, then, it might be argued that those areas which are their homes, which would include only certain designated wilderness areas, ought to be preserved.

Bringing this argument back to the human realm by reinserting the anthropocentric side of the coin

for a moment, one might argue, as does Paul Shepard, that wild animals are a human necessity. Shepard claims that "the human mind needs [animals to exist in their wild habitats] in order to develop and work. Human intelligence is bound to the presence of [these wild] animals."[69] This would apparently include "wilderness" dwelling animals. Therefore, wild animals (including wilderness dwellers) and their habitats (including wilderness areas) deserve moral consideration, albeit indirect, in this sense as well.

The more mature Leopold also believed that designated wilderness areas were valuable for the sake of wildlife such as wolves, mountain sheep, and grizzly bears. Moreover, given the validity of these arguments, such areas would have to be large and unbroken so as to be able to accommodate these "far-ranging species." Arguing for permanent grizzly ranges, for example, Leopold once wrote that,

> saving the grizzly requires a series of large areas from which roads and livestock are excluded. ...Relegating grizzlies to Alaska is about like relegating happiness to heaven; one may never get there.... Only those able to see the pageant of evolution can be expected to value its theater, the wilderness, or its outstanding achievement, the grizzly.[70]

In fact, this argument has now become the principal conservation biology argument for wilderness preservation – big reserves for biodiversity.[71]

27 The Gaia Hypothesis Argument

Expanding on the above argument, we might apply non-anthropocentric moral consideration to yet another sort of living organism: namely, the earth or Gaia. Scientists such as James Lovelock posit and defend what they call the Gaia Hypothesis, which postulates that the earth itself, as a self-correcting system, is alive or is tantamount to a living organism. Like any living thing, certain of its parts are imperative to its proper functioning and viability. With regard to the earth, or Gaia, certain wild ecosystems are arguably vital to its prospering. Wild ecosystems might be likened to the internal organs of a multicelled organism – or what we traditionally think of as an organism. With Gaia, designated wilderness areas could be said to perform certain services invaluable to the smooth functioning of the earth organism, just as a human liver provides a service invaluable to the human organism. Without a liver a human cannot live; without wilderness earth perhaps cannot either. So, if planetary homeostasis is to continue, and Gaia is to live, areas of "wilderness" must be preserved.

If we owe moral consideration to living beings, and if the earth itself is alive, as the Gaia Hypothesis maintains, then the earth deserves moral consideration. Disrupting Gaia's vital organs, such as putative wilderness, becomes, then, immoral. So, in order to show proper moral respect to the earth organism, these areas ought to be maintained.

Leopold was inspired by the Russian philosopher and mystic P. D. Ouspensky. In his essay "Some Fundamentals of Conservation in the Southwest," Leopold toys with a Gaia-type defense of earth and wilderness preservation. "Philosophy," he writes, " . . . suggests one reason why we can not destroy the earth with moral impunity; namely, that the 'dead' earth is an organism possessing a certain kind and degree of life, which we intuitively respect as such."[72]

The objections to the above two arguments are too complex to cover here. In sum, these arguments rest on the premise(s) that animals and Gaia deserve moral consideration, which corresponds to actions of preservation on behalf of humans. Clearly, one would have to justify this argument prior to making the larger argument stick. Moreover, with regard to the Gaia argument, one would have to prove that designated wilderness areas really are crucial to the life of Gaia.

28 The Future Generations Argument

Another common defense of wilderness preservation revolves around the supposed moral obligations that existing human beings have with regard to future generations of human beings. One might maintain that, among other debts owed, current humans ought to pass the world on to future generations as we inherited it, with as many designated wilderness areas intact as possible. As the old American Indian saying goes, "We do not inherit the earth from our ancestors; we only borrow it from our children."

Destroying putative wilderness areas, when taking into account these future generations, would then become a matter of injustice and unfairness. When we destroy these areas we can also be said to be depriving future generations of valuable resources and services: we are taking away their heritage and identity; we are not providing them with a place for enjoyment, education, aesthetic experience, and self-discovery; we are subjecting them to the consequences of our irreversible land-use decisions; all those things we commonly think of "wilderness" as providing for us. If we accept that future generations merit at least some degree of moral consideration, many of the "wilderness benefits" mentioned above would also apply to future generations of humans. In short, "wilderness" destruction is wrong, according to this argument, because future generations of humans would mourn its loss.

The truth is that we really do not know for certain what future generations will want or need. And, as hard as it is for some to believe, perhaps they will not want or need designated wilderness areas. However, one might argue that this lack of knowledge is reason enough to save designated wilderness areas, not ravage them. We don't *know* what future generations will want or need. Therefore, we should keep their options open. Wilderness preserved is an option for future generations. They can keep and use their wilderness areas or develop them. But if we develop them now, they won't have the option. Further, our protection of "wilderness" arguably sets a good example for future generations, and displays a good ethic of stewardship, which would encourage them, in turn, to keep land use options open to future future generations. Interestingly, all future generations might arguably be forced to preserve designated wilderness areas because they would be locked into the same "logic of wilderness preservation for future generations" argument that compelled us to save wilderness for them. This logical compulsion might then propel wilderness preservation indefinitely.

Nevertheless, this argument appears to be contingent upon the validity of the other arguments that attempt to show that a world with designated wilderness areas is better than a world without them. Hence, we might note that this is not an entirely independent argument.

29 The Unknown and Indirect Benefits Argument

For some, one of the greatest reasons why we ought to err on the side of caution, and preserve and designate more wilderness areas, is that theoretically speaking most of the benefits emanating from these areas are thought to be indirect (what Driver, Nash, and Haas refer to as "spinoff" value and what economists commonly refer to in part as "option value") or unknown. The potential for goods and services may be unlimited, and the possible harms unknown. Many of the indirect social benefits can only be guessed at. We simply do not have all the information in as of yet. E. O. Wilson maintains that "the wildlands are like a magic well: the more that is drawn from them in knowledge and benefits, the more there will be to draw."[73] But if we destroy designated wilderness areas, we would then apparently destroy tremendous amounts of information and potential benefits along with them. Hence, it would seem to be prudent to save designated wilderness areas because of these unknown and indirect benefits, and as many and as large of these areas as possible at that. The downside to this argument is that it makes the preservation of wilderness contingent only on its potential utility.

For certain wilderness proponents the promise of wilderness preservation lies ahead, in the future. Aldo Leopold echoes this sentiment by pronouncing that we "should be aware of the fact that the richest values of wilderness lies not in the days of Daniel Boone, nor even in the present, but rather, in the future."[74] Hence, because we have a responsibility to follow a wise course of action, and since this would include conserving potential benefits to all of humanity, we apparently then have a responsibility to keep designated wilderness areas in existence.

30   The Intrinsic Value Argument

Many, many wilderness boosters claim that simply knowing that there exist designated wilderness areas, regardless of whether or not they ever get to experience such areas, is reason enough for them to want to preserve them. For these people, "wilderness" is valuable just because it exists, just because it is. Designated wilderness areas, in this sense, have value in and of themselves; regardless of, or in addition to, their value as a means to some other end – like clean water, recreation, or medicine. "Wilderness," then, is said to possess intrinsic value.

E. O. Wilson asserts that designated wilderness areas have uses not to be ignored: but he quickly points out that the argument for the preservation of these areas does not end there. As he writes, "I do not mean to suggest that every ecosystem now be viewed as a factory of useful products." Utility is not the only measure of "wilderness" value, he declares, "Wilderness has virtue unto itself and needs no extraneous justification."[75] Reiterating Wilson's conviction, and issuing a call to action, Edward Abbey once wrote, "The idea of wilderness needs no defense. It only needs more defenders."[76] Clearly what Wilson, Abbey, and many other wilderness-minded folks are claiming is that, ultimately, "wilderness" defense needs no articulation. Designated wilderness areas just *are* valuable. Such locales, then, join the list of other things, like friends, relatives, children, family heirlooms, and so forth, whose worth is not contingent upon anything other than their mere existence, whose value is intrinsic.

For many environmentalists, to categorize and quantify the benefits of what they take to be wilderness is a fundamentally flawed approach to wilderness preservation. It is, in effect, to play the game of your opponent by trying to bolster your side by including on your team bigger, better, and more players (or, in this case, more human benefit arguments), while the question of whether or not the correct game is being played in the first place goes unanswered and unasked. Many people would challenge the dominant cult of perpetual growth by instead making the more radical claim that areas of "wilderness" are not for humans in the first place, that wild species and ecosystems themselves have a right to exist apart from their uses to humans. "Diffuse but deeply felt," Rolston declares, "such values are difficult to bring into decisions; nevertheless, it does not follow that they ought to be ignored."[77]

If we accept this reasoning, we might get the feeling that designated wilderness areas are important and valuable just because they are there; regardless of whether or not we ever decide to visit, experience, scientifically monitor, or even contemplate them. But this seems to be the real challenge of wilderness preservation. According to William Godfrey-Smith, "the philosophical task is to try to provide adequate justification, or at least clear the way for a scheme of values according to which concern and sympathy for our environment is immediate and natural, and the desirability of protecting and preserving wilderness self-evident."[78]

The initial assumption in this argument is that if purported wilderness areas do indeed possess intrinsic value, their defense and preservation become self-evident; they just *are* of value and, therefore, worthy of preservation. However, there is obviously a lot more to the debate surrounding intrinsic value and the intrinsic value of "wilderness" than I have presented here. In fact, as Godfrey-Smith says, providing for or grounding the intrinsic value of things like "wilderness" is where the real work needs to be done. This might be seen as perhaps one of the central roles of environmental philosophy in this debate; and we might urge philosophers to begin dealing with and answering questions about how we ground the claim that putative wilderness has intrinsic value, how to sort out both instrumental and intrinsic competing value claims, and how, when, and why the intrinsic value of something like wilderness – if such a thing actually exists – trumps these other value claims.

If we can justify the intrinsic value of designated wilderness areas, and if we can locate their level of moral consideration, then wilderness preservation immediately becomes a moral issue. Designated wilderness areas would gain considerable ethical clout. And this changes the argument about wilderness preservation quite a bit; the burden of proof would apparently be shifted. Those who would destroy designated wilderness areas would then have the burden of proof; they would have to demonstrate that something of great social value would be lost if a wilderness area stood in its way; they would have the difficult task of showing that something possessing intrinsic value should be sacrificed for the sake of something of merely instrumental value. "Wilderness is innocent 'til proven guilty," David Brower once quipped, "and they're going to have a tough time proving it guilty."[79]

Notes

I owe debts of gratitude to Don Fadner, Alan Holland, Kate Rawles, John Vollrath, Dôna Warren, Mark Woods, and especially Baird Callicott for assistance with this essay.

1 Roderick Nash, "The Value of Wilderness," *Environmental Review* 3 (1977): 14–25, p. 25.

2 Nash's wilderness preservation arguments originally appear in *Wilderness and the American Mind*, all editions (New Haven: Yale University Press, 1982), and are later summarized and indexed in "The Value of Wilderness"; see also Nash, "Why Wilderness?," in Vance Morton, ed., *For the Conservation of the Earth* (Golden, Col.: Fulcrum, 1988), pp. 194–201; and Nash with B. L. Driver and Glenn Haas, "Wilderness Benefits: A State-of-Knowledge Review," in Robert Lucus, ed., *Proceedings – National Wilderness Research Conference*, Intermountain Research Station General Technical Report, INT-220 (Ogden, Utah: U.S. Forest Service, 1987), pp. 294–319. Holmes Rolston III presents his wilderness preservation rationales in "Valuing Wildlands," *Environmental Ethics* 7 (1985): 23–48; and in "Values in Nature" and "Values Gone Wild," both in Rolston, *Philosophy Gone Wild: Essays in Environmental Philosophy* (Buffalo, NY: Prometheus, 1986), pp. 74–90 and 118–42, respectively. William Godfrey-Smith's arguments appear in "The Value of Wilderness," *Environmental Ethics* 1 (1979): 309–19. Warwick Fox expands on Godfrey-Smith's work in *Toward a Transpersonal Ecology: Developing New Foundations for Environmentalism* (Boston: Shambhala, 1990), pp. 154–61. George Sessions adds to this lineage in "Ecosystem, Wilderness, and Global Ecosystem Protection," in Max Oelschlaeger, ed., *The Wilderness Condition: Essays on Environment and Civilization* (Washington, D.C.: Island Press, 1992), pp. 90–130. And Michael McCloskey's taxonomy of wilderness values and benefits is in "Evolving Perspectives on Wilderness Values: Putting Wilderness Values in Order," in Patrick C. Reed, ed., *Preparing to Manage Wilderness in the 21st Century: Proceedings of the Conference*, "Southeastern Forest Experiment Station General Technical Report," SE-66 (Athens, Ga.: U.S. Forest Service, 1990), pp. 13–18.

3 Rolston, "Valuing Wildlands," p. 27.

4 Driver, Nash, and Haas, "Wilderness Benefits," p. 304.

5 I say "in theory" and "ideally" because, as Mark Woods indicates, this is not true in practice. See Woods, "Federal Wilderness Preservation in the United States: The Preservation of Wilderness?" in J. Baird Callicott and Michael P. Nelson, eds., *The Great New Wilderness Debate* (Athens, GA: University of Georgia Press, 1998), pp. 154–98. Grazing and other extractive uses *are* permitted in some designated wilderness. It would appear that the resource view is that there are a suite of commodities that are "wilderness commodities" – timber, fodder, game. The difference between these and other commodities is that they are there for the taking and do not have to be planted and tended.

6 To avoid confusion, two senses of "potential" need to be distinguished. First is the notion of postponing the

use of those resources whose uses we are aware of (e.g., turning trees into timber). Second is the sense of the yet unknown uses of something (e.g., undiscovered medicinal uses of known and unknown plants).

7   Aldo Leopold, "A Plea for Wilderness Hunting Grounds," in David E. Brown and Neil B. Carmony, *Aldo Leopold's Wilderness: Selected Early Writings by the Author of A Sand County Almanac* (Harrisburg, Penn.: Stackpole Books, 1990), p. 160; originally published in *Outdoor Life*, November 1925.

8   Leopold, "Wilderness as a Form of Land Use," in Susan Flader and J. Baird Callicott, eds., *The River of the Mother of God and Other Essays by Aldo Leopold* (Madison, Wis.: University of Wisconsin Press, 1991), p. 138; this essay was originally published in *The Journal of Land and Public Utility Economics*, October 1925.

9   Theodore Roosevelt, "The Pioneer Spirit and American Problems," in *The Works of Theodore Roosevelt* (New York: Charles Scribner's Sons, 1923), 18:23.

10   Roosevelt, "The American Wilderness: Wilderness Hunters and Wilderness Game," in *Works*, 2:19.

11   Roosevelt, "Wilderness Reserves: The Yellowstone Park," in *Works*, 3:267–8.

12   Some medical researchers might discontinue using this argument because of their increased confidence in the ability of computers to generate synthetic models of medicines and the ability to be able to artificially produce such medicines in laboratories. If their optimism were justified, we would no longer need to "mess about in the jungle" for medicine and, as an argument for wilderness preservation, this argument would become contingent only upon the state of our ability to artificially produce medicine.

13   In fact, in her recent book *Coyotes and Town Dogs: Earth First! and the Environmental Movement* (New York: Viking Penguin, 1993), a review of American environmentalism of the past few decades as seen through the eyes, lives, and voices of members of Earth First!, Susan Zakin tells us that ecologist Jerry Franklin discovered upon study "that the Pacific Northwest forest is the most densely green place on earth. One acre of old-growth Douglas fir forest contains more than twice the living matter of an acre of tropical rainforest. Some stands of trees harbor as many as 1,500 species of plants and animals" (p. 240). This finding is substantiated in a recent book on biodiversity by conservation biologists Reed Noss and Allen Cooperrider, *Saving Nature's Legacy: Protecting and Restoring Biodiversity* (Washington, D.C.: Island Press, 1994), p. 101.

14   N. R. Farnsworth, "Screening Plants for New Medicines," in E. O. Wilson, ed., *Biodiversity* (Washington, D.C.: National Academy Press, 1988), pp. 83–97.

15   Donella Meadows, "Biodiversity: The Key to Saving Life on Earth," *Land Stewardship Letter* (Summer 1990).

16   Rolston, "Valuing Wildlands," pp. 26 and 27, respectively. Note that it is quite common for wilderness advocates to equate "wilderness" with "nature" or "environment" and to use these terms interchangeably. Rolston is a good example of someone who quite liberally uses these terms in such a manner. However, these are not the same things and it seems improper to conflate them. But note also that the life-support argument turns not on the equivocation of these terms but rather on the relationship that exists between nature and wilderness.

17   Sessions, "Ecocentrism, Wilderness, and Global Ecosystem Protection," p. 99. Paul and Anne Ehrlich, *Extinction: The Causes and Consequences of the Disappearance of Species* (New York: Random House, 1981), pp. xi–xiv, 77–100; and Paul Ehrlich, "The Loss of Biodiversity: Causes and Consequences," in E. O. Wilson, *Biodiversity*, pp. 21–7, both cited in Sessions.

18   Robert Marshall, "The Problem of the Wilderness," *The Scientific Monthly* 30 (February 1930); 142.

19   Leopold, *A Sand County Almanac: With Essays on Conservation from Round River* (New York: Ballantine, 1966; originally published in 1949), pp. 269–72, his emphasis. See also Leopold, "Wilderness as a Form of Land Use."

20   John Muir, *Our National Parks* (Boston: Houghton Mifflin, 1901; San Francisco: Sierra Club Books, 1991), ch. 1.

21   Ibid., p. 1.

22   See the studies cited in Driver, Nash, and Haas, "Wilderness Benefits," p. 301.

23   Rolston, "Valuing Wildlands," p. 30.

24   Wallace Stegner, "The Wilderness Idea," in David Brower, ed., *Wilderness: America's Living Heritage* (San Francisco: Sierra Club Books, 1961), p. 102.

25   Paul Shepard, *Nature and Madness* (San Francisco: Sierra Club Books, 1982).

26   Fox, *Toward a Transpersonal Ecology*, p. 160.

27   See, for example, Robert Marshall's "The Problem of the Wilderness" in *The Great New Wilderness Debate*, pp. 85–96.

28   Nash, "Why Wilderness?," p. 198.

29   William Wordsworth, "Lines Composed a Few Miles Above Tintern Abbey" (1798).

30   Muir, *Our National Parks*, p. 4. This point has also been made by Allen Carlson in "Nature and Positive Aesthetics," *Environmental Ethics* 6 (1984): 5–34.

31   Aldo Leopold, "Goose Music," in Luna B. Leopold, ed., *Round River: From the Journals of Aldo*

Leopold (Minocqua, Wis.: NorthWord Press, 1991), p. 245.

32 Muir, quoted in Nash, "The Value of Wilderness," p. 23.

33 Muir, *The Yosemite* (San Francisco: Sierra Club Books, 1988), pp. 196–7.

34 These three quotations, respectively, are from Leopold, *A Sand County Almanac*, p. 276; Leopold, "The Arboretum and the University," *Parks and Recreation* 78 (1934): 60 (interestingly, this quotation is used by Nash in *Wilderness and the American Mind* and "The Value of Wilderness," as well as by others, to refer to wilderness; however, what Leopold is actually referring to is the Arboretum at the University of Wisconsin, which is nothing remotely like a wilderness area. It seems safe to assume, as Nash and I do, however, that Leopold would say the same of putative wilderness); and *A Sand County Almanac*, pp. 274–5.

35 Rolston, "Valuing Wildlands," p. 27.

36 Fox, *Toward a Transpersonal Ecology*, p. 158 (his emphasis).

37 Leopold, *A Sand County Almanac*, pp. 274 and 276, respectively (my emphasis).

38 David Brower, quoted in Nash, "Why Wilderness?," p. 198.

39 Leopold, *A Sand County Almanac*, p. 190.

40 Rolston, "Valuing Wildlands," p. 28.

41 Edward Abbey, *Desert Solitaire: A Season in the Wilderness* (New York: Avon Books, 1968), p. 190.

42 Walt Whitman, *Leaves of Grass* (Ithaca, NY: Cornell University Press, 1961; originally published in 1860), p. 319.

43 Nash, "Why Wilderness?," p. 199.

44 Henry David Thoreau, "Walking," in *Excursions* (Boston: Ticknor and Fields, 1863), pp. 185 and 191, respectively.

45 Leopold, *A Sand County Almanac*, p. 264.

46 Nash, "Why Wilderness?," p. 199.

47 Rolston, "Valuing Wildlands," p. 29.

48 A good example of this type of wilderness preservation rationale is found in Aldo Leopold's essay "Conserving the Covered Wagon," in Flader and Callicott, eds., *The River of the Mother of God*, pp. 128–32.

49 Stegner, "The Wilderness Idea," pp. 97 and 102, respectively.

50 Nash quoted in McCloskey, "Evolving Perspectives on Wilderness Values," p. 15.

51 Nash, "The Value of Wilderness," p. 22.

52 Mark Sagoff, "On Preserving the Natural Environment," *The Yale Law Review* 84 (1974): 266–7.

53 To take this line of thought even further, if that which is unspoiled is of value, and if completely pristine wilderness no longer really does exist, then our current wilderness areas (no matter how tainted by human interference), stand as a memorial to and a symbol of hope for the lost unsullied wildness of the earth and should be preserved as such.

54 Michael Zimmerman makes this point in *Contesting Earth's Future: Radical Ecology and Postmodernism* (Berkeley: University of California Press, 1994), p. 120.

55 The eradication of a virus's familiar host species exacerbates this problem by forcing the virus to jump hosts in order to survive.

56 Richard Preston, "A Reporter at Large: Crisis in the Hot Zone," *The New Yorker*, October 26, 1994: 62.

57 Ibid., p. 62.

58 Ibid., p. 80. See also Preston's book-length treatment of this issue, *The Hot Zone* (New York: Random House, 1994). This is also the topic of the 1995 Hollywood movie *Outbreak*.

59 Edward Abbey, *Desert Solitaire*, pp. 148–51.

60 Michael Zimmerman, "The Threat of Ecofascism," *Social Theory and Practice* 21 (1995): 207–38.

61 Max Oelschlaeger, *The Idea of Wilderness* (New York and London: Yale Univ. Press, 1991), p. 231.

62 Leopold, *A Sand County Almanac*, p. 264.

63 Rolston, *Conserving Natural Value* (New York: Columbia University Press, 1994), p. 15.

64 Note that both Nash and Oelschlaeger see wilderness as a contrasting value. For the ideas and insights in this section I owe much credit to the thought and work of Arthur Herman in *The Problem of Evil and Indian Thought*, 2nd edn. (New Delhi: Motilal Bansaridas, 1993), in which he discusses the logical and metaphysical necessity of evil as a possible solution to the philosophical and theological problem of evil.

65 Nash, "The Value of Wilderness," p. 24.

66 Leopold, *A Sand County Almanac*, pp. 271–2.

67 Marshall, "The Problem of the Wilderness," p. 143.

68 Driver, Nash, and Haas, "Wilderness Benefits," p. 302.

69 Paul Shepard, *Thinking Animals: Animals and the Development of Human Intelligence* (New York: Viking Press, 1978), pp. 246–52. See also Shepard's new book, *The Others: How Animals Made Us Human* (Washington, D.C.: Island Press, 1996) on this topic.

70 Leopold, *A Sand County Almanac*, pp. 276–8.

71 For an explanation of modern conservation biology and the plight of the grizzly bear, see R. Edward Grumbine, *Ghost Bears: Exploring the Biodiversity Crisis* (Washington, D.C.: Island Press, 1992). See also Noss and Cooperrider, *Saving Nature's Legacy*.

Michael P. Nelson

72 Leopold, "Some Fundamentals of Conservation in the Southwest," *Environmental Ethics* 1 (1979): 140; originally written in the early 1920s.

73 E. O. Wilson, *The Diversity of Life* (Cambridge: Harvard University Press, 1992), p. 282.

74 Leopold, "Wilderness Values," *1941 Yearbook of the Parks and Recreational Services* (Washington, D.C.: National Park Service, 1941), p. 28.

75 Wilson, *The Diversity of Life*, p. 303.

76 Edward Abbey, *The Journey Home* (New York: Dutton, 1977), p. 223.

77 Rolston, "Valuing Wildlands," p. 30.

78 Godfrey-Smith, "The Value of Wilderness," p. 319.

79 David Brower, quoted in *Wild by Law*, a film by Lawrence Hott and Dianne Garey, Florentine Films, 1990.

32

A Critique of and an Alternative to the Wilderness Idea

J. Baird Callicott

Last March, I gave a talk at a symposium in Bozeman, Montana, celebrating the thirtieth anniversary of the 1964 Wilderness Act. I was preceded at the podium by a well-spoken, Amherst College-educated cattleman, Chase Hibbard, who described himself as the token redneck at this gathering of the wilderness faithful. He proclaimed his love of things wild and free and his dedication to steward the lands, private and public, grazed by his stock. He urged us all to find consensus and strike a balance between wilderness preservation and economic necessity.

When it was my turn to speak, I began by saying that if Mr. Hibbard was the token redneck, I was fixing to be the skunk at this garden party – a little simile I borrowed (without attribution) from a piece by Dave Foreman in *Wild Earth*. Thus at once I endeared myself to the audience – people can't hate a self-proclaimed skunk – and put them on notice that I might have something unsettling to say. There are two debates about the value of wilderness, I went on to note. One we just heard about, that between wilderness preservation and "jobs." (And, I pointed out, *profits*, doubtless the most important consideration to Mr. Hibbard, who doesn't work for wages, but one he never mentioned in his speech.) The other debate – *within* the community of conservationists, not between conservationists and cowboys – is about the value of the wilderness ideal to the conservation of biological diversity.

As a dedicated conservationist and environmentalist, I think we must reexamine the *received* wilderness idea, that is, the idea that wilderness is "an area where the earth and its community of life are untrammeled by man, where man is a visitor who does not remain." I want to emphasize that my intent in doing so is not to discredit the *areas* designated "Wilderness," and thus make them more vulnerable to development pressures. On the contrary, we need to multiply and expand such areas. Here I criticize rather the *concept* of wilderness, that is, how we conceive of the areas that we call wilderness. I do so hoping to strengthen conservation efforts by helping to ground conservation policy in a sound environmental philosophy.

After the existence of an "environmental crisis" was widely acknowledged in the late 1960s, the benchmark of environmental quality was the wilderness ideal of pristine, untouched nature. Accordingly, the new breed of environmentalists believed that the best way to preserve nature, if not the only way, was to exclude all human economic activities from representative ecosystems and designate them as wilderness preserves. In them, some old-growth forests could remain standing, wild animals could have a little habitat, and so on. In effect, we attempted to achieve environmental preservation by zoning the planet into areas where environmentally destructive human economic activities – like grazing, mining, logging, agriculture, mechanized recreation, manufacturing, and real estate development – would be permitted and areas where such activities would be excluded. Several recent and not so recent realizations are subverting this simple philosophy of nature conservation through wilderness preservation.

First, at the practical level, the original rationale for wilderness preservation was not articulated in terms of biological conservation by turn-of-the-century environmentalists like John Muir. Instead, they emphasized the way wilderness satisfies human aesthetic, psychological, and spiritual needs. Wilderness, in short, was originally regarded as a psycho-spiritual *resource*. Often the most haunting, beautiful, silent, and solitary places are too remote, rugged, barren, or arid to be farmed or logged or even mined. Hence, an early criterion for identifying suitable areas for National Parks, such as Yellowstone and Yosemite, long before the Wilderness Act of 1964 and public acknowledgment of the environmental crisis, was their *uselessness* for practically any other purpose. Consequently, as Dave Foreman puts it with his characteristic bluntness, much designated wilderness is "rock and ice," great for "scenery and solitude" but not so great for biological conservation.

Second, at the political level, the wilderness preservation philosophy of nature conservation is defensive and ultimately represents a losing strategy. The development-permitted zones greatly exceed the development-excluded zones in number and size. More acreage of the contiguous United States is under pavement than is under protection as Wilderness. Less than five percent of the Lower Forty-eight is in a designated or de facto wilderness condition. As the human population and economy grow, the pressure on these ragtag wild areas becomes ever greater. In temperate North America, wilderness reserves, national parks, and conservancy districts have become small islands in a rising tide of cities, suburbs, farms, ranches, interstates, and clearcuts. And they are all seriously compromised by human recreation and by exotic species colonization. Big wilderness has receded to the subarctic and arctic latitudes. Even these remote hinterlands are threatened by logging, hydropower schemes, oil exploration and other industrial intrusions, not to mention the threats posed by global warming and by exposure to sharply increased levels of ultraviolet radiation. The wilderness idea, hopefully and enthusiastically popularized by John Muir's best-sellers at the close of the nineteenth century, has played itself out, here at the close of the twentieth, in the pessimism and despair of Bill McKibben's recent best-seller, *The End of Nature*. McKibben's thesis needs no elaboration by me because his title says it all.

Third, at the international level, the uniquely American wilderness idea is not a universalizable approach to conservation. But the environmental crisis, and particularly the erosion of biodiversity, is global in scope. Thus we need a conservation philosophy that *is* universalizable. In Western Europe, conservation via wilderness preservation is meaningless. In India, Africa, and South America, American-style national parks have been created by forcibly evicting resident peoples, sometimes with tragic consequences. The Ik, for example, were hunter-gatherers living sustainably, from time immemorial, in the remote Kidepo Valley of northeast Uganda. In 1962, they were removed in order to create the Kidepo National Park, an area where the community of life would henceforth be untrammeled by man, where man would be a visitor who does not remain. Forced to settle in crowded villages outside the park and to farm, their culture disintegrated and the Ik degenerated into the travesty of humanity made infamous by Colin Turnbull.

Fourth, at the historical level, we are beginning to realize that wilderness is an ethnocentric concept. Europeans came to what they called the "New World" and since it did not look like the humanized landscape that they had left behind in the "Old World," they thought it was a pristine wilderness, where, as David Brower put it, the hand of man had never set foot. But the Western Hemisphere was full of Indians when Columbus stumbled upon it. In 1492, the only continental-size wilderness on the planet was Antarctica. The aboriginal inhabitants of North and South America, further, were not passive denizens of the forests, prairies, and deserts; they actively managed their lands – principally with fire. Some paleo-ecologists believe that in the absence of Indian burning, the vast, biologically diverse open prairies of North and South American would not have existed; that the American heartland would have instead been grown over with brush. Some believe that the North American forests would not have been as rich and diverse in the absence of the Indian's pyro-technology.

By the seventeenth century, when English colonists began to settle the eastern seaboard of North America, the native peoples had suffered the greatest demographic debacle of human history. Their populations were reduced by perhaps 90% due to the ravages of Old World diseases, which had swept through the hemisphere transmitted first from European to Indian and then from Indian to Indian. So, the Pilgrims *did* find themselves in a relatively desolate and howling wilderness, as they lamented, but it was, ironically, an *artificial* wilderness – though that combination of words seems oxymoronic. Europeans inadvertently created the New World wilderness condition by means of an unintended but utterly devastating biological warfare on the aboriginal inhabitants.

Fifth, at the theoretical ecology level, ecosystems were once thought to remain stable unless disturbed; and if disturbed, to return eventually to their stable states, called climax communities. To be constantly changing and unstable is now believed to be their usual, rather than exceptional, condition. Thus, whether we humans interfere with them or not, ecosystems will undergo metamorphosis. But wilderness *preservation* has often meant freeze-framing the status quo ante, maintaining things as they were when the "white man" first came on the scene. Hence the wilderness ideal, *so interpreted*, represents a conservation goal that would be possible to attain, paradoxically, only through intensive management efforts to keep things the way they were in defiance of nature's inherent dynamism.

Sixth, at the philosophical level, the wilderness idea perpetuates the pre-Darwinian myth that "man" exists apart from nature. Our oldest and most influential cultural traditions have taught us that we human beings are exclusively created in the image of God, or that we are somehow uniquely endowed with divine rationality. Thus we, and all the products of our essentially supernatural minds, were thought to exist apart from and over-against nature. For a wilderness purist, encountering any human artifact (not his or her own) in a wilderness setting spoils his or her experience of pristine nature. But Darwin broadcast the unwelcome news that we self-exalting human beings are mere accidents of natural selection, no less than any other large mammal. We are one of five living species of great ape. We are, to put it bluntly, just big monkeys – very precocious ones, to be sure, but monkeys nonetheless. And everything we do – from bowling and bungee-jumping to writing *Iliads* and engineering space shuttles (and committing acts of ecotage, most definitely) – is monkey business. For many people, Darwin's news was bad news because it seemed to demean us and to undermine our noblest pretensions and aspirations. But I think it's good news. If we are a part of nature, then we have a rightful place and role in nature no less than any other creature – no less than elephants, or whales, or redwoods. And what we may do in and to nature – the transformations that we impose upon the environment – are in principle no better or no worse than what elephants, or whales, or redwoods, may do in and to nature.

I say "in principle" because I certainly do not wish to leave anyone with the impression that I think because we are just as natural as all other organisms, everything we do in and to nature – every change we impose upon the environment – is okay. My name is not Alston Chase. (This brought a howl of laughter and applause from the Bozeman crowd, since Chase is a resident villain in the local environmental philosophy melodrama.) Most anthropogenic change is certainly not okay. Indeed, most of what we do in and to nature is very destructive.

But other species, too, may have either beneficial or harmful effects on the rest of nature. If there were five billion elephants on the planet instead of five billion people (or remembering that an adult elephant is more than a hundred times as heavy as an adult human, if there were as much elephant biomass as presently there is human biomass), then planet Earth would still be in the throes of an ecological crisis. Elephants, in other words, can also be very destructive citizens of their biotic communities. On the other hand, the biomass of bees and other insect pollinators of plants is probably greater than the human biomass (I don't know, I'm not a biologist) and certainly the bee population far exceeds the human population; but the ecological effect of all these bees is undoubtedly beneficial. So, if the ecological impact of the activities of bees and elephants can be either good or bad, then why can't the ecological impact of human activities be good as well as bad? Measured by the wilderness standard, all human impact is bad, not because human beings are inherently bad, but because human beings are not a part of nature – or so the wilderness idea assumes.

Personally, I hope that those of us affluent North Americans who wish to do so can go on enjoying the luxury of respectfully, worshipfully visiting Wilderness Areas. In my opinion, the greatest value of the Wilderness Act of 1964 is ethical. It formally acknowledges a human commitment to humility, forbearance, and restraint. But as the centerpiece of a nature *conservation* philosophy, we need to find an alternative to the wilderness idea. Fortunately, we need not look far. We find the appropriate alternative in the concept of biosphere reserves, a concept hatched in Europe, focused on the tropics, and given the imprimatur of the United Nations. Thus, it has genuine international currency. Further, biosphere reserves are selected not on the basis of scenic qualities and not because they are otherwise useless, but on the basis of ecological qualities. Such reserves, intended to preserve biological diversity and ecosystem health, should be designed not only to harbor the charismatic megafauna – bears, wolves, bison, and the like – but the entire spectrum of indigenous species, invertebrates as well as vertebrates, plants as well as animals.

A policy of invasive human management – by means of, say, prescribed burning or carefully planned culling – is cognitively dissonant with the wilderness idea, but not with the biosphere (or biodiversity) reserve idea. Indeed, one of the signal differences between the old wilderness idea and the new concept of biosphere reserves is a provision for compatible human residence and economic activity in and around reserves. Had the Kidepo National Park been conceived as the Kidepo Biosphere Reserve (though of course to think that it actually might have been is anachronistic) then the Ik and their culture could have been part of what was preserved. Looking toward the future, the Buffalo Commons, envisioned by Frank and Deborah Popper, was, upon first hearing, so violently opposed because it was originally uncritically cast in the wilderness mode. It is becoming politically more palatable, even attractive, as residents of the target regions see an opportunity to stay, not leave, and switch from farming and livestock ranching to various ways of sustainably exploiting American Bison, Elk, deer, and Pronghorn antelope. As I envision a Buffalo Commons, private herds of cattle and sheep would be removed all over the arid the semi-arid West. Absent domestic stock, the native vegetation could reclothe the range. And with the fences down, the native ungulates could roam free and wild. Erstwhile ranchers and farmers could retain a home forty and form management co-ops to allot themselves culling rights, proportional perhaps to how much land each put into the commons. If the Blackfeet, Arapaho, Cheyenne, and Lakota could cull the unowned Elk and Buffalo herds without compromising biological diversity, why can't the contemporary residents of the same region?

The biosphere reserve idea may be the centerpiece of a coherent and universalizable conservation philosophy, but not the whole of such a philosophy. The wilderness idea is half of an either/or dichotomy: *either* devote an area to human inhabitation and destructive economic development, *or* preserve it in its pristine condition as wilderness. The classic wilderness advocates, such as Roderick Nash, in other words, envisioned no alternative to industrial civilization offset by wilderness preservation. As long as it stayed on its side of the fence, industrial civilization went unchallenged.

The core-buffer-corridor concept of The Wildlands Project casts it in the new biosphere reserve paradigm. But the authors of "The Wildlands Project Mission Statement" still, in my opinion, concede too much to industrial civilization as we know it, when they write, "Intensive human activity associated with civilization – agriculture, industrial production, urban centers – could continue outside the buffers." Complementing the biodiversity reserve idea in a sound nature conservation philosophy are the ideas of appropriate technology and sustainable livelihood – *if* by "sustainable livelihood" is meant human economic activity that does not compromise ecological health and integrity. Solar alternatives to hydroelectric and fossil fuel energy should be aggressively explored. Alternatives to industrial agriculture should be encouraged by means of policy changes. Urban sprawl should be controlled by better planning and stricter zoning. Timber reserves should be harvested ecologically as well as sustainably, as now ostensibly mandated by the new Forest Service policy on National Forests. And so on. Thus some biological conservation might be integrated with economic activities in areas not designated as biodiversity reserves (cum buffers and corridors), just as some economic activities might be integrated with biological conservation in those that are.

I was impressed with how the Greater Yellowstone Ecosystem seemed to be a looming presence in the collective consciousness of Bozeman. Almost all the symposium speakers mentioned it. Some dwelled on it. A few spoke of nothing else. It being my spring break and all, I had set aside a few days afterward to go trekking. The Park pulled me like a magnet. I rented a car and drove up the Paradise Valley to the north gate. Then I poked around the valley of the Yellowstone River and those of the Lamar and Gardiner, two of its tributaries, on foot.

Tired of a long, bitter Wisconsin winter and with my crosscountry skis back home in my shack, I never got anywhere near the backcountry. Climbing up on McMinn Bench near Mt. Everts, I could see the Park Headquarters village in the vicinity of Mammoth Hot Springs, the town of Gardiner off to the north, US 89 running south to Norris Geyser Basin, and US 212, which is kept open all winter as far east as Cooke City, Montana. But the difference between inside and outside the Park boundaries was like the difference between night and day. Inside, the headquarters village, the roads, the camp grounds, all had hard edges. And there were no fences. Outside, the gate town had a long filament of gas stations, motels, fly shops, and whatnot strung out along the highway. New-looking houses were scattered here and there on the nearby bluffs. Though I was usually walking through a mixture of mud and Elk manure, the Park seemed clean. Beyond, the landscape seemed marred and cluttered.

Both outside and inside the Park I saw Elk, Mule, and White-tailed Deer, and Pronghorn. Inside the Park I saw plenty of Bison. At close range the evidence of Elk overpopulation was ubiquitous: aspen were absent, an Elk-eye-level browse line was on the Douglas-firs and Whitebark Pines, game trails traversed the slopes every 50 feet or so of elevation, the river banks were denuded and eroding, and everywhere I stepped, I stepped in Elk scat.

The Greater Yellowstone Ecosystem (comprising Yellowstone and Grand Teton National Parks, the Bridger-Teton, Targhee, Gallatin, Custer, Caribou, and Beaverhead National Forests, three National Wildlife Refuges, and BLM, state, and private lands) is the biggest relatively intact ecosystem in the Lower Forty-eight. The Park is a listed UNESCO Biosphere Reserve and World Heritage Site. What the Yellowstone Biosphere Reserve lacks is a thoughtful buffer zone policy and well-articulated corridors connecting it with the Bitterroot, Bob Marshall, Glacier, and Cascade core habitats. I have no personal experience with potential corridors, but the Paradise Valley is an ideal candidate for a buffer zone on the north boundary of Yellowstone National Park. Under the new mandate for ecosystem management, the Forest Service should manage its "multiple use" forests as buffer zones to the adjoining parks and to its designated Wilderness Areas in the Greater Yellowstone Ecosystem. Up to now, the Forest Service has extensively roaded and permitted clearcut logging, especially in the Targhee and Gallatin National Forests, "treatments" not consistent with biosphere reserve buffer zone management. Stock grazing is permitted on nearly half the public lands in the Ecosystem, including (incredibly) designated Wilderness Areas in the National Forests and parts of Grand Teton National Park. But what hope can we entertain that the absolutely essential winter ungulate habitat represented by a multitude of private properties in the Paradise Valley will be managed as a buffer zone?

Let's look at what's going on in the Valley now. With my first quart of cold beer in three days on the seat between my legs, my left hand on the wheel, and the right taking notes as I drove from Gardiner to Livingston, this is what I saw:

Immediately beyond the Park boundaries a good deal of open land in the side hills between the Yellowstone River valley and the mountains has been bought for winter range by the Rocky Mountain Elk Foundation. But virtually within sight of the Park gate and only a stone's throw from the river, some enterprising entrepreneur has dug a gravel pit. As I drove by, a bulldozer was pushing loose rock around in a cloud of dust.

The next notable manmark on the landscape is the former alpine estate, Royal Teton Ranch, of the late Malcolm Forbes, who must not have known that his view opened on the Gallatins, not the Tetons. As his last rite to Mammon, Forbes got top dollar for his prime Montana property from a California survivalist cult, the Church Universal and Triumphant. Right on the river bank the hard core cultists live in a tacky shanty town (and the rest in places like Livingston and Bozeman). Back in the side hills of the Gallatin Range they have erected bomb shelters, the fuel storage tanks of which were found leaking diesel oil. As I drove by at eventide, cult cattle were watering in the Yellowstone and trampling its banks. It so happens that the old Forbes place has geothermal

441

J. Baird Callicott

"resources"; and I saw steam rising near the little settlement. The "Church" plans to develop these resources, putting the Park's geysers at the risk of extinguishment.

Then, on the side of the road away from the river, I passed an "elk farm," a rundown house and some ramshackle outbuildings beside a small, grassless paddock enclosed by a high fence. I was told that game wardens had finally caught the wily proprietor luring hungry wild Elk into his compound by night. Later he would sell them as pen-raised animals.

A little relief from this world of wounds came when I drove into Yankee Jim Canyon, most of which is part of the Gallatin National Forest, where the mountains on either side of the Valley narrow and the river flows fast through a shallow gorge.

Down north of the Yankee Jim respite, the valley widens, framed on the east by the Absoroka and on the west by the Gallatin ranges. Once more the property is mostly private. Ranches. Cattle. I wasn't around long enough to know whether or not the ranchers in the Paradise Valley were conscientious land stewards, like Mr. Hibbard. But what I could see through the windshield at sixty miles per hour was the meaning of "trammeled"—to be caught or held in, or as if in, a net; enmeshed; to be prevented or impeded; confined, according to Webster's Collegiate. The valley was trammeled, enmeshed, and impeded by a network of fences.

Interspersed with the ranches, closer to a wide spot on the road called Emigrant and on into Livingston, are riparian smallholds with mansions sitting on them, belonging to gentry from elsewhere who found their little piece of paradise on the Yellowstone River. Two miles east of Emigrant on a big bend of the river is Chico, a hot springs resort. I didn't go there, since I had just had an *au naturel* soak in the Park.

To accommodate itinerant pilgrims to the valley, someone was rearranging the river bluff with a bulldozer and building an RV "camp-ground," farther down the road. The hookups were all installed. When I passed by, the driveways were just going in.

As I got closer to Livingston, the gentrification of the riparian zone became more intense. The mountains pinch in again and stop at the north end of Paradise Valley, near a place called Allen Spur. I rolled on into town – gradually. The highway is lined with modest houses along the

river, lumber yards, gas station/seven–eleven stores, motels, fast food joints, trashy empty lots – the usual mishmash of totally planless strip development, Anyplace, USA.

And what could the valley become? A Buffalo Commons. Or, more precisely, an Ungulate Commons.

Most cults – the Branch Davidians were an especially spectacular example – eventually self-destruct. Hopefully the Church Universal and Triumphant will be no exception to the rule. Then the federal government can do what it tried before to do, purchase the old Forbes place and devote it to wildlife.

The government thought it couldn't afford Forbes's asking price, and so probably would shrink from the thought of buying the whole Paradise Valley, much of which may not be for sale. So what can be done? Convince the ranchers to tear down their fences, the most ubiquitously trammeling presence on the land; get rid of their cattle; and invite in the Elk, Bison, antelope, and deer. Coyotes will keep the ground squirrels in check; Black-footed Ferrets will hold down the prairie dog population; Gray Wolves and Mountain Lions will take out old, sick, and less fit large herbivores, leaving the cream of the freeranging crop for the erstwhile cattle ranchers to skim. The gentry should love to look out their picture windows and see free wild animals, rather than their neighbors' fenced cattle. And the tourists might pay even more money to park their Winne-bagoes in the midst of "free nature" – as Arne Naess dubs this fair mix of people and wildlife – instead of in just another roadside attraction.

But how to avoid the tragedy of the commons? Through cooperation. The Paradise Valley is well defined and self-contained. A ranchers' co-op could hire its own wildlife ecologists and, in consultation with the Fish and Wildlife, Forest, and Park Services, set their own sustainable harvest quotas.

After my talk at the wilderness symposium, Chase Hibbard was asked what he thought of my remarks about switching from cattle ranching to market hunting native ungulates. He was opposed to it. Categorically. I asked him, Why?, if market analyses suggest that such a scheme would be more economically attractive than cattle ranching. You know, business is business. Are cattle a religion in Montana, or what? He answered, Yes, they are. (This symposium was full of surprises.) And he went on to lay down the usual line of bullshit (pun intended) about how cattle are a part of what makes the West the West (in the Hollywood-mediated American mind), and how his family has been running cattle here a long time. A long time!, I wanted to say, but didn't – a blip on the trajectory of the true history and future of the West which belongs to the Bison and to those whose livelihood once did and may soon again center on this shaggy symbol of North America's high, semi-arid country and on the other native grazers and browsers.

Thinking over this exchange of opinions, I came to the conclusion that cattle were not the real cult-object of the Western ranchers' religion. Private property is. In addition to the Church Universal and Triumphant, the Paradise Valley is not home to neo-Baal cultists. No, John Locke is the theologian of cattlepersons. As I envision a Paradise Valley Ungulate Commons – a key part of the Greater Yellowstone Biosphere Reserve Buffer Zone – private "real" property would remain in private hands. Privately owned "animal units" are what would go, along with fences, one purpose of which is to mark real estate boundaries and segregate one rancher's privately owned herd from another's.

Would this be so unAmerican? Not if we think more expansively, in historical terms. That's more or less the way the Indians – bona fide Americans if anyone is – did it. Each group had a territory, the property rights to which they claimed and enforced. But the animals were their own bosses. And if, to get a hearing, we must confine ourselves

to the short-term scale of Euro-American history, pelagic fisherpersons, traditionally, own their boats and tackle, but the fish go where they will, owned by no one. So the precedent and paradigm for an economically exploited native Ungulate Commons should perhaps be marine fisheries rather than terrestrial ranches. With this difference: A network of North American Ungulate Commons would be far less liable to overexploitation, because the stocks are composed of large, visible specimens that are fairly easy to count and they fall under national jurisdictions (those of the United States, Canada, and Mexico, now, for better or worse, coordinated by NAFTA).

The biosphere reserve conservation concept includes another, less often discussed zone, the transition zone. Here too, the key is appropriate technologies and sustainable economies. Starting at Livingston and going east, montane Montana gives way to high plains Montana. The Great Plains region is already moving in the direction of a Buffalo Commons. The fences are still up, but several big ranches – most famously, the one belonging to Ted and Jane – are switching from cattle to Buffalo. While Buffalo are certainly less tractable and more difficult to contain, they need less care than cattle, and so are becoming an increasingly attractive alternative for imaginative and well-landed high plains entrepreneurs. And many Indian groups are expressing a keen interest in restoring Buffalo herds to reservation land, with the added incentive of the Bison's place in their histories, cultures, and religions.

33

Wilderness – Now More Than Ever: A Response to Callicott

Reed F. Noss

Callicott's essay is peculiar. It is nicely written, erudite, and definitely provokes thought. But it also provokes, at least in me, a good deal of frustration. Many of us in the conservation movement have worked hard for years to promote ecological and evolutionary understanding as the logical foundation for land conservation (land in the sense Leopold used it, including air, soil, water, and biota), but coupled with the aesthetic and ethical appreciation of wild things and wild places for their own sakes. Following Leopold, we have tried to unite brain and heart, rationality and intuition, in the struggle to defend wild nature. Yet here comes Callicott, a leading environmental ethicist, a Leopold scholar, a professed lover of wildness, mounting an attack on the *concept* of wilderness. His article in *Wild Earth* is only the latest in a series of essays in which Callicott assails the idea of wilderness as anachronistic, ecologically uninformed, ethnocentric, historically naive, and politically counterproductive. I believe Callicott is dead wrong and I will try to tell you why.

First, I must state emphatically that I agree with much of Callicott's essay. His progressive interpretations of biosphere reserves, buffer zones, transition zones, sustainable livelihood, and ecological management are all in line with what I and many others affiliated with The Wildlands Project have supported and proposed. But Callicott portrays all these integrative concepts as *alternatives* to wilderness protection, as things conservationists should spend their time on instead of defending

wildlands. To support his contention that the wilderness idea no longer has merit, Callicott erects a straw man of wilderness (based essentially on the Wilderness Act of 1964) that is 30 years out of date. No one I know today thinks of wilderness in the way Callicott depicts it. Everyone with any brain knows that wilderness boundaries are permeable, that ecosystems are dynamic entities, that humans are fundamentally part of nature (though arguably a malignant part), and that ecological management is essential in most modern wilderness areas and other reserves if we want to maintain biodiversity and ecological integrity. To "let nature run its course" in small, isolated reserves burgeoning with alien species and uncontrolled herbivores is to watch passively while an accident victim bleeds to death.

Callicott claims that "several recent and not so recent realizations are subverting this simple philosophy of nature conservation through wilderness preservation." He goes on to provide a number of arguments in support of his thesis that the wilderness ideal is no longer useful. I will agree that "hands-off" wilderness areas in human–dominated landscapes often have minimal ecological value. But they do have some worth, for instance in serving as reference sites (though imperfect) for restoration and management experiments and as micro–refugia for species sensitive to human disturbances. It is an overstatement to claim that wilderness preservation has failed. Indeed, one could more easily conclude from recent evidence over most of the continent that it is *multiple-use management* that has failed. Multiple-use areas, which constitute the vast majority of public lands, have been degraded far more than virtually any of our Wilderness Areas (Callicott himself provides several examples from the Greater Yellowstone Ecosystem). Roads run everywhere, the last old-growth forests are being converted to two-by-fours, cows munch and shit their way across public rangelands, and "ecosystem management" propaganda is being used to justify continuation of the status quo under a new guise. This evidence only strengthens the argument that we need more – not less – area off limits to intensive human exploitation. The more degraded the overall landscape becomes, the greater the value of real wilderness, even though it becomes ever harder to protect.

Callicott is absolutely correct that biological conservation was not a major consideration in the designation of existing Wilderness Areas. The biased allocation of land to Wilderness – where areas of little economic value, except for recreation and tourism, are protected instead of more productive and biodiverse areas – is well known. That warped, unecological approach to wilderness protection has been thoroughly exposed in the technical and popular literature of conservation. Modern conservation programs, from mainstream government projects such as the National Biological Survey's Gap Analysis to avante garde efforts such as The Wildlands Project, are trying to correct this imbalance and better represent the full spectrum of biodiversity in protected areas. Callicott's criticism of the wilderness movement on these grounds is disingenuous; we have learned and we have matured. We will no longer tolerate sacrifices of productive wildlands in exchange for a few scraps of rock and ice. Callicott's claim that wilderness preservation is purely "defensive" only reflects the assaults wild areas face everywhere. Of course we are defensive. If we did not defend the last remaining wild areas, they would soon be gone. We lose most battles as it is; if we gave up, nothing would remain for long. Anyway, the wilderness movement today is not purely defensive. Indeed, The Wildlands Project seeks to move away from defensive, last-ditch efforts, away from saying what *should not* be done toward saying what *should* be done to restore whole ecosystems in all regions.

Callicott devotes quite a bit of space in his article to the problem of excluding humans from wilderness when humans are really part of nature. I know of no philosophical problem more recalcitrant than the whole question of "what is natural?" Hell if I know. But Callicott doesn't make much headway toward resolving this issue either. I agree it was a mistake to extend the standard American model of national parks to developing countries and exclude indigenous hunter-gatherer cultures from these areas. The idea that wilderness can include all primates except for the genus *Homo* is ridiculous. It is not ridiculous, however, to exclude people living profligate, subsidized, unsustainable, industrial lifestyles (including Callicott and me) from permanent habitation in Wilderness Areas. Even to exclude "native" people from some reserves is not ridiculous when these people have acquired guns, snowmobiles, ATVs, bulldozers, and modern medicine. It is not exclusion from these reserves that separates us from nature; it is our culture and our lifestyles, which had already separated us long before we began designating Wilderness Areas. Yes, the Darwinian revolution united us with nature intellectually; but we have been trying our damnedest to separate ourselves from nature emotionally and physically since Neolithic times (at least).

The problem of our estrangement from nature may lie in the increasing dominance of cultural over biological evolution in the last few millennia of our history. This cultural-biological schism also requires that we take measures to protect wild areas and other species from human exploitation, if they are to survive. The adaptations of most species are determined by biological evolution acting through natural selection. Except for bacteria species and some invertebrate species that have very short "generation" times, biological evolution is much slower than cultural evolution, taking hundreds or thousands of years to express itself. Through cultural evolution humans can respond much faster than most other species to environmental change. Because most environmental change today is human generated, we have created a situation where our short-term survival is much more assured than that of less adaptable species. Some of these species are extremely sensitive to human activities. It seems to me that an environmental ethic, as Leopold, Callicott, and others have expressed it, gives us an obligation to protect species that depend on wilderness because

Reed F. Noss

they are sensitive to human persecution and harassment. I hasten to add that few species "depend" on wilderness because they prefer wilderness over human-occupied lands; rather, they require wilderness because humans exterminate them elsewhere. Roadlessness defines wilderness. Where there are roads or other means of human access, large carnivores and other species vulnerable to human persecution often cannot survive.

Callicott correctly criticizes the idea of wilderness as a totally "unmanaged" landscape. I differ from some modern wilderness advocates in emphasizing that most Wilderness Areas today must be actively managed if they are to maintain the "natural" conditions for which they were set aside (see my book with Allen Cooperrider, *Saving Nature's Legacy: Protecting and Restoring Biodiversity*, Island Press, 1994). Certainly native Americans managed the ecosystems in which they lived, principally through the use of fire. I think the evidence is plain that at some level of management *Homo sapiens* can be a true "keystone species" in the most positive sense, in that we can enrich the diversity of habitats and species in the landscape. We can play a role similar to that of the Beaver, prairie dog, Bison, woodpecker, or Gopher Tortoise, by providing habitats upon which many other species depend. Above some threshold of manipulation, though, biodiversity enhancement becomes biodiversity destruction. Diversification becomes homogenization. Man as part of nature becomes man at war with nature. We become too damn clever for our own good. I do not believe that human management or technology is inherently bad; but once we have crossed the threshold, we become a tumor instead of a vital part of the ecosystem. Again, this transformation provides all the more reason to set wild areas aside and protect them from human invasion. Those wild areas may very well require management, but the most positive management will usually be protection from over-use by people, restoration of structures and processes damaged by past human activities, and disturbance management (for instance, prescribed burning) to substitute for natural processes that have been disrupted.

Callicott's straw man of wilderness reaches its zenith in his statement that "wilderness *preservation* [his emphasis] suggests freeze-framing the status quo ante, maintaining the way things were when the 'white man' first came on the scene..." While logically consistent, such an interpretation

of the wilderness ideal is idiotic. No ecologist interprets wilderness in the static, pristine, climax sense that Callicott caricatures it. Nonetheless, to throw out knowledge of the historical, pre-European condition of North American landscapes would be equally stupid. Those presettlement ecosystems developed through thousands and even millions of years of evolution of their component species without significant human intervention [excepting the possible role of human hunters in eliminating many of North America's large mammals 10–15,000 years ago]. Sure, the environment in which these communities developed was dynamic, but the rate and magnitude of change was nothing like that experienced today. As ecologists Steward Pickett, Tom Parker, and Peggy Fiedler (1991, in *Conservation Biology*, edited by P. L. Fiedler and S. K. Jain; Chapman and Hall) pointed out with regard to the "new paradigm in ecology," the knowledge that nature is a shifting mosaic in essentially continuous flux should not be misconstrued to suggest that human-generated changes are nothing to worry about. Instead, "human-generated changes must be constrained because nature has *functional*, *historical*, and *evolutionary* limits. Nature has a range of ways to be, but there is a limit to those ways, and therefore, human changes must be within those limits."

Yes, many North American ecosystems were managed by Indian burning for perhaps as long as 10,000 years; but in most cases, the Indians did not create new ecosystems. They simply maintained and expanded grasslands and savannas that developed naturally during climatic periods with high fire frequency. Furthermore, the importance of Indian burning is often exaggerated. As many ecologists have pointed out, the natural thunderstorm frequency in some regions, such as the Southeastern Coastal Plain, is more than enough to explain the dominance of pyrogenic vegetation there. In any case, the native Americans in most cases (megafaunal extinctions of the late Pleistocene aside) clearly operated more within the functional, historical, and evolutionary limits of their ecosystems than the Europeans, who transformed most of the North American continent in less than 200 years. The modern wilderness idea, as embodied in The Wildlands Project, does not say humans are apart from nature. It simply says, in line with Leopold's land ethic, that *we need to impose restraints on our actions*. We need to keep

446

ourselves within the limits set by the evolutionary histories of the landscapes we inhabit. Until we can bring our numbers down and walk humbly everywhere, let us at least do so within our remaining wild areas.

Callicott discusses the biosphere reserve model as if it were an alternative to wilderness. I agree that the biosphere reserve model is useful – we base our Wildlands Project reserve network proposals on an extension of that model. Biosphere reserves are not, however, an alternative to wilderness. In fact, wilderness is the central part of the biosphere reserve model: the core area. Without a wilderness core, a biosphere reserve could not fulfill its function of maintaining the full suite of native species and natural processes. A wilderness core area may still require ecological management, especially if it is too small to take care of itself (i.e., less than several million acres). A healthy long-term goal is to recreate core areas (ideally at least one in every ecoregion) big enough to be essentially self-managing, areas that do not require our constant vigilance and nurturing. Those true wilderness areas will have much to teach us about how we might dwell harmoniously with nature in the buffer zones.

Callicott's alleged dichotomy of "*either* devote an area to human inhabitation and destructive economic development, *or* preserve it in its pristine condition as wilderness" is false. The reserve network model applied by The Wildlands Project recognizes a gradient of wild to developed land, but encourages a continual movement toward the wild end of the gradient over time as the scale and intensity of human activities decline. And human activities *must* decline if this earth is to have any future. Callicott's idea of "sustainable livelihood" is entirely consistent with this model. But how are we to figure out how to manage resources sustainably (while sustaining *all* native species and ecological processes) without wild areas as benchmarks and blueprints? How are we to show restraint in our management of resources in the landscape matrix when we don't have enough respect to set aside big, wild areas for their own sake?

We need no alternative to wilderness. Rather, we need to incorporate the wilderness ideal into a broader vision of recovered but dynamic landscapes dominated by wildland but complemented by true civilization. As Ed Abbey stated, a society worthy of the name of civilization is one that recognizes the values of keeping much of its land as wilderness. We need the wilderness ideal in these days of frivolous "ecosystem management" more than ever before. We need it to provide a "base-datum of normality," as Leopold put it, to give us reference sites for comparison with more intensively managed lands. We need it to counter the arrogant belief that we can manage and control everything. We need it to inspire us, to put our lives at risk, to humble us. And, more important, the bears need it too.

PART VII

What on Earth Do We Want?
Human Social Issues and
Environmental Values

34

Feeding People versus Saving Nature?

Holmes Rolston III

When we must choose between feeding the hungry and conserving nature, people ought to come first. A bumper sticker reads: Hungry loggers eat spotted owls. That pinpoints an ethical issue, pure and simple, and often one where the humanist protagonist, taking high moral ground, intends to put the environmentalist on the defensive. You wouldn't let the Ethiopians starve to save some butterfly, would you?

"Human beings are at the centre of concerns for sustainable development." So the *Rio Declaration* begins. Once this was to be an *Earth Charter*, but the developing nations were more interested in getting the needs of their poor met. The developed nations are wealthy enough to be concerned about saving nature. The developing nations want the anthropocentrism, loud and clear. These humans, they add, "are entitled to a healthy and productive life in harmony with nature," but there too they seem as concerned with their entitlements as with any care for nature.[1] Can we fault them for it?

We have to be circumspect. To isolate so simple a trade-off as hungry people versus nature is perhaps artificial. If too far abstracted from the complex circumstances of decision, we may not be facing any serious operational issue. When we have simplified the question, it may have become, minus its many qualifications, a different question. The gestalt configures the question, and the same question reconfigured can be different. So we must analyze the general matrix, and then confront the more particular people-versus-nature issue.

Humans win? Nature loses? After analysis, sometimes it turns out that humans are not really winning, if they are sacrificing the nature that is their life support system. Humans win by conserving nature – and these winners include the poor and the hungry. "In order to achieve sustainable development, environmental protection shall constitute an integral part of the development process and cannot be considered in isolation from it."[2] After all, food has to be produced by growing it in some reasonably healthy natural system, and the clean water that the poor need is also good for fauna and flora. Extractive reserves give people an incentive to conserve. Tourism can often benefit both the local poor and the wildlife, as well as tourists. One ought to seek win–win solutions wherever one can. Pragmatically, these are often the only kind likely to succeed.

Yet there are times when nature is sacrificed for human development; most development is of this kind. By no means all is warranted, but that which gets people fed seems basic and urgent. Then nature should lose and people win. Or are there times when at least some humans should lose and some nature should win? We are here interested in these latter occasions. Can we ever say that we should save nature rather than feed people?

Feed People First? Do We? Ought We?

"Feed people first!" That has a ring of righteousness. The *Rio Declaration* insists, "All States and all people shall cooperate in the essential task of eradicating poverty as an indispensable requirement."[3] In the biblical parable of the great judgment, the righteous had ministered to the needy, and Jesus welcomes them to their reward. "I was hungry and you gave me food, I was thirsty and you gave me drink." Those who refused to help are damned (Matthew 28:31–46). The vision of heaven is that "they shall hunger no more, neither thirst any more" (Revelation 7.16), and Jesus teaches his disciples to pray that this will of God be done on earth, as it is in heaven. "Give us this day our daily bread" (Matthew 5.11). These are such basic values, if there is to be any ethics at all, surely food comes first.

Or does it? If giving others their daily bread were always the first concern, the Christians would never have built an organ or a sanctuary with a stained glass window, but rather always given all to the poor. There is also the biblical story of the woman who washed Jesus' feet with expensive ointment. When the disciples complained that it should have been sold and given to the poor, Jesus replied, "you always have the poor with you. She has done a beautiful thing" (Matthew 26.10–11). While the poor are a continuing concern, with whom Jesus demonstrated ample solidarity, there are other commendable values in human life, "beautiful things," in Jesus' phrase. The poor are always there, and if we did nothing else of value until there were no more poor, we would do nothing else of value at all.

Eradicating poverty is an indispensable requirement! Yes, but set these ideals beside the plain fact that we all daily prefer other values. Every time we buy a Christmas gift for a wife or husband, or go to a symphony concert, or give a college education to a child, or drive a late model car home, or turn on the air conditioner, we spend money that might have helped to eradicate poverty. We mostly choose to do things we value more than feeding the hungry.

An ethicist may reply, yes, that is the fact of the matter. But no normative ought follows from the description of this behavior. We ought not to behave so. But such widespread behavior, engaged in almost universally by persons who regard themselves as being ethical, including readers of this article, is strong evidence that we in fact not only have these norms but think we ought to have them. To be sure, we also think that charity is

appropriate, and we censure those who are wholly insensitive to the plight of others. But we place decisions here on a scale of degree, and we do not feel guilty about all these other values we pursue, while yet some people somewhere on earth are starving.

If one were to advocate always feeding the hungry first, doing nothing else until no one in the world is hungry, this would paralyze civilization. People would not have invented writing, or smelted iron, or written music, or invented airplanes. Plato would not have written his dialogues, or Aquinas the *Summa Theologica*; Edison would not have discovered the electric light bulb or Einstein the theory of relativity. We both do and ought to devote ourselves to various worthy causes, while yet persons in our own communities and elsewhere go hungry.

A few of these activities redound subsequently to help the poor, but the possible feedback to alleviating poverty cannot be the sole justification of advancing these multiple cultural values. Let us remember this when we ask whether saving natural values might sometimes take precedence. Our moral systems in fact do not teach us to feed the poor first. The Ten Commandments do not say that; the Golden Rule does not; Kant did not say that; nor does the utilitarian greatest good for the greatest number imply that. Eradicating poverty may be indispensable but not always prior to all other cultural values. It may not always be prior to conserving natural values either.

Choosing for People to Die

But food is absolutely vital. "Thou shalt not kill" is one of the commandments. Next to the evil of taking life is taking the sustenance for life. Is not saving nature, thereby preventing hunting, harvesting, or development by those who need the produce of that land to put food in their mouths, almost like killing? Surely one ought not to choose for someone else to die, an innocent who is only trying to eat; everyone has a right to life. To fence out the hungry is choosing that people will die. That can't be right.

Or can it? In broader social policy we make many decisions that cause people to die. When in 1988 we increased the national speed limit on rural Interstate highways from 55 to 65 miles per hour, we chose for 400 persons to die each year. We decide against hiring more police, though if we did some murders would be avoided. The city council spends that money on a new art museum, or to give the schoolteachers a raise. Congress decides not to pass a national health care program that would subsidize medical insurance for some now uninsured, who cannot otherwise afford it; and some such persons will, in result, fail to get, timely medical care and die of preventable diseases.

We may decide to leave existing air pollution standards in place because it is expensive for industry to install new scrubbers, even though there is statistical evidence that a certain number of persons will contract diseases and die prematurely. All money budgeted for the National Endowment for the Humanities, and almost all that budgeted for the National Science Foundation, could be spent to prevent the deaths of babies that die from malnutrition. We do not know exactly who will die, but we know that some will; we often have reasonable estimates how many. The situation would be similar, should we choose to save nature rather than to feed people.

U.S. soldiers go abroad to stabilize an African nation, from which starving refugees are fleeing, and we feel good about it. All those unfortunate people cannot come here, but at least we can go there and help. All this masks, however, how we really choose to fight others rather than to feed them. The developed countries spend as much on military power in a year as the poorest two billion people on Earth earn in total income. The developed countries in 1990 provided 56 billion dollars in economic aid to the poorer countries but they also sold 36 billion dollars worth of arms to them. At a cost of less than half their military expenditures, the developing countries could provide a package of basic health care services and clinical care that would save 10 million lives a year. World military spending in 1992 exceeded 600 billion dollars. U.S. military spending accounted for nearly half this amount, yet in the United States one person in seven lives below the poverty line and over 37 million people lack any form of health care coverage.[5] These are choices that cause people to die, both abroad and at home.

But such spending, a moralist critic will object, is wrong. This only reports what people do decide, not what they ought to decide. Yes, but few are going to argue that we ought to spend nothing on military defense until all the poor are fed, clothed, and housed. We believe that many of the values achieved in the United States, which place us among the wealthier nations, are worth protecting, even while others starve. Europeans and others will give similar arguments. Say if you like that this only puts our self-interest over theirs, but in fact we all do act to protect what we value, even if this decision results in death for those beyond our borders. That seems to mean that a majority of citizens think such decisions are right.

Wealthy and poverty-stricken nations alike put up borders across which the poor are forbidden to pass. Rich nations will not let them in; their own governments will not let them out. We may have misgivings about this on both sides, but if we believe in immigration laws at all, we, on the richer side of the border, think that protecting our lifestyle counts more than their betterment, even if they just want to be better fed. If we let anyone who pleased enter the United States, and gave them free passage, hundreds of millions would come. Already 30 percent of our population growth is by immigration, legal and illegal. Sooner or later we must fence them out, or face the loss of prosperity that we value. We may not think this is always right, but when one faces the escalating numbers that would swamp the United States, it is hard not to conclude that it is sometimes right. Admitting refugees is humane, but it lets such persons flee their own national problems and does not contribute to any long-term solutions in the nations from which they emigrate. Meanwhile, people die as a result of such decisions.

Some of these choices address the question whether we ought to save nature if this causes people to die. Inside our U.S. boundaries, we have a welfare system, refusing to let anyone starve. Fortunately, we are wealthy enough to afford this as well as nature conservation. But if it came to this, we would think it wrong-headed to put animals (or art, or well-paid teachers) over starving people. Does that not show that, as domestic policy, we take care of our own? We feed people first – or at least second, after military defense. Yet we let foreigners die, when we are not willing to open our five hundred wilderness areas, nearly 100 million acres, to Cubans and Ethiopians.

Hunger and Social Justice

The welfare concept introduces another possibility, that the wealthy should be taxed to feed the poor. We should do that first, rather than cut into much else that we treasure, possibly losing our wildlife, or wilderness areas, or giving up art, or underpaying the teachers. In fact, there is a way greatly to relieve this tragedy, could there be a just distribution of the goods of culture, now often so inequitably distributed. Few persons would need to go without enough if we could use the produce of the already domesticated landscape justly and charitably. It is better to try to fix this problem where it arises, within society, than to try to enlarge the sphere of society by the sacrifice of remnant natural values, by, say, opening up the wilderness areas to settlement. Indeed, the latter only postpones the problem.

Peoples in the South (a code word for the lesser developed countries, or the poor) complain about the overconsumption of peoples in the North (the industrial rich), often legitimately so. But Brazil has within its own boundaries the most skewed income distribution in the world. The U.S. ratio between personal income for the top 20 percent of people to the bottom 20 percent is 9 to 1; the ratio in Brazil is 26 to 1. Just one percent of Brazilians control 45 percent of the agricultural land. The biggest 20 landowners own more land between them than the 3.3 million smallest farmers. With the Amazon still largely undeveloped, there is already more arable land per person in Brazil than in the United States. Much land is held for speculation; 330 million hectares of farm land, an area larger than India, is lying idle. The top 10 percent of Brazilians spend 51 percent of the national income.[6] This anthropocentric inequity ought to be put "at the center of concern" when we decide about saving nature versus feeding people.

Save the Amazon! No! The howler monkeys and toucans may delight tourists, but we ought not save them if people need to eat. Such either–or choices mask how marginalized peoples are forced onto marginal lands; and those lands become easily stressed, both because the lands are by nature marginal for agriculture, range, and life support, and also because by human nature marginalized peoples find it difficult to plan for the long-range. They are caught up in meeting their immediate needs; their stress forces them to stress a fragile landscape.

Prime agricultural or residential lands can also be stressed to produce more, because there is a growing population to feed, or to grow an export crop, because there is an international debt to pay. Prime agricultural lands in southern Brazil, formerly used for growing food and worked by tenants who lived on these lands and ate their produce, as well as sent food into the cities, have been converted to growing coffee as an export crop, using mechanized farming, to help pay Brazil's massive debt, contracted by a military government since overthrown. Peoples forced off these lands were resettled in the Amazon basin, aided by development schemes fostered by the military government, resettled on lands really not suitable for agriculture. The integrity of the Amazon, to say nothing of the integrity of these peoples, is being sacrificed to cover for misguided loans. Meanwhile the wealthy in Brazil pay little or no income tax that might be used for such loan repayment.

The world is full enough of societies that have squandered their resources, inequitably distributed wealth, degraded their landscapes, and who will be tempted to jeopardize what natural values remain as an alternative to solving hard social problems. The decision about social welfare, poor people over nature, usually lies in the context of another decision, often a tacit one, to protect vested interests, wealthy people over poor people, wealthy people who have exploited nature already, ready to exploit anything they can. At this point in our logic, en route to any conclusion such as let-people-starve, we regularly reach an if-then, go-to decision point, where before we face the people-over-nature choice we have to reaffirm or let stand the wealthy-over-poor choice.

South Africa is seeking an ethic of ecojustice enabling five million privileged whites and twenty nine million exploited blacks (as well as several million underprivileged "Coloureds") to live in harmony on their marvelously rich but often fragile landscape.[7] Whites earn nearly ten times the per capita income of blacks. White farmers, 50,000 of them, own 70 percent of farmland; 700,000 black farmers own 13 percent of the land (17% other). Black ownership of land was long severely restricted by law. Forced relocations of blacks and black birth rates have combined to give the homelands, small areas carved out within the South African nation, an extremely high-average population density. When ownership patterns in the homelands are combined with those in the rest of the nation, land ownership is as skewed as anywhere on Earth. Compounding the problem is that the black population is growing, and is already more than ten times what it was before the Europeans came.

The land health is poor. South African farmers lose twenty tons of topsoil to produce one ton of crops. Water resources are running out; the limited wetlands in an essentially arid nation are exploited for development; water is polluted by unregulated industry. Natal, one of the nation's greenest and most glorious areas, is especially troubled with polluted winds. Everywhere, herbicides float downwind with adverse human, vegetative, and wildlife effects on nontarget organisms.

With an abundance of coal, South Africa generates 60 percent of the electricity on the African continent, sold at some of the cheapest rates in the world, although less than a third of South Africans have electricity. The Eskom coal-burning power plants in the Transvaal are the worst offenders in air pollution, leaving the high veld as polluted as was Eastern Germany, also threatening an area producing 50 percent of South Africa's timber industry and 50 percent of the nation's high potential agricultural soils. As a result of all this, many blacks go poorly nourished; some, in weakened condition, catch diseases and die.

What is the solution? South Africa also has some of the finest wildlife conservation reserves in Africa. Some are public; some are private. They are visited mostly by white tourists, often from abroad. One hears the cry that conserving elitist reserves, in which the wealthy enjoy watching lions and wildebeest, cannot be justified where poor blacks are starving. What South Africa needs is development, not conservation. In an industry-financed study, Brian Huntley, Roy Siegfried, and Clem Sunter conclude: "What is needed is a much larger cake, not a sudden change in the way it is cut."[8] One way to get a bigger cake would be to take over the lands presently held as wildlife reserves.

But more cake, just as unequally cut, is not the right solution in a nation that already stresses the carrying capacity of its landscape. Laissez-faire capitalists propose growth so that every one can become more prosperous, oblivious to the obvious fact that even the present South African relationship to the landscape is neither sustainable nor healthy. They seem humane; they do not want anyone to starve. The rhetoric, and even the intent, is laudable. At the same time, they want growth because this will avoid redistribution of wealth. The result, under the rubric of feeding

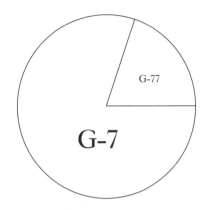

Figure 34.1 Proportionate production and consumption among nations

people versus saving nature, is in fact favoring the wealthy over the poor.

What is happening is that an unjust lack of sharing between whites and blacks is destroying the green. It would be foolish for all, even for white South Africans acting in their own self-interest, further to jeopardize environmental health, rather than to look first and resolutely to solving their social problems. It would not really be right, if South Africans were to open their magnificent wildlife reserves, seemingly in the interests of the poor, while the cake remains as inequitably divided as ever. Fortunately, many South Africans have realized the deeper imperative, and the recent historic election there, and efforts toward a new constitution, promise deep social changes. This, in turn, will make possible a more intelligent conservation of natural values.[9]

In the more fortunate nations, we may distribute wealth more equitably, perhaps through taxes or minimum wage laws, or by labor unions, or educational opportunities, and we do have in place the welfare systems referred to earlier, refusing to let anyone starve. But lest we seem too righteous, we also recall that we have such policies only domestically. The international picture puts this in a different light. There are two major blocs, the G-7 nations (the Group of 7, the big nations of North America, Europe, and Japan, "the North"), and the G-77 nations, once 77 but now including

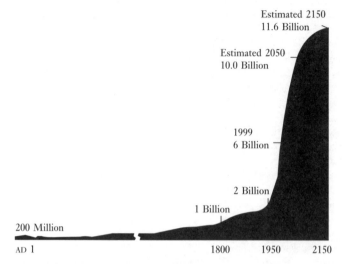

Estimated 2150
11.6 Billion

Estimated 2050
10.0 Billion

1999
6 Billion

2 Billion

1 Billion

200 Million

AD 1   1800   1950   2150

Figure 34.2 Adapted from data in U.S. Bureau of the Census, *Statistical Abstract of the United States: 2000* (120th edition). Washington, DC, 2000, p. 821.

some 128 lesser developed nations, often south of the industrial north. The G-7 nations hold about one fifth of the world's five billion persons, and they produce and consume about four fifths of all goods and services. The G-77 nations, with four fifths of the world's people, produce and consume one fifth. (See figure 34.1.) For every person added to the population of the North, twenty are added in the South. For every dollar of economic growth per person in the South, 20 dollars accrue in the North.[10]

The distribution problem is complex. Earth's natural resources are unevenly distributed by nature. Diverse societies have often taken different directions of development; they have different governments, ideologies, and religions; they have made different social choices, valued material prosperity differently. Typically, where there is agricultural and industrial development, people think of this as an impressive achievement. Pies have to be produced before they can be divided, and who has produced this pie? Who deserves the pie? People ought to get what they earn. Fairness nowhere commands rewarding all parties equally; justice is giving each his or her due. We treat equals equally; we treat unequals equitably, and that typically means unequal treatment proportionately to merit. There is nothing evidently unfair in the pie diagram, not at least until we have inquired about earnings. Some distribution

patterns reflect achievement. Not all of the asymmetrical distribution is a result of social injustice.

Meanwhile, it is difficult to look at a distribution chart and not think that something is unfair. Is some of the richness on one side related to the poverty on the other? Regularly, the poor come off poorly when they bargain with the rich; and wealth that originates as impressive achievement can further accumulate through exploitation. Certainly many of the hungry people have worked just as hard as many of the rich.

Some will say that what the poorer nations need to do is to imitate the productive people. Unproductive people need to learn how to make more pies. Then they can feed themselves. Those in the G-7 nations who emphasize the earnings model tend to recommend to the G-77 nations that they produce more, often offering to help them produce by investments which can also be productive for the G-7 nations. Those in the G-77 nations do indeed wish to produce, but they also see the exploitation and realize that the problem is sharing as well as producing. Meanwhile the growth graphs caution us that producing can be as much part of the problem as part of the solution. One way to think of the circular pie chart is that this is planet Earth, and we do not have any way of producing a bigger planet. We could, though, feed more people by sacrificing more nature.

such decisions take place
‹-4/5ths, 4/5ths-gets-1/5
ʿust the Brazilians and the
ƒ us in the United States,
well that have to face an
ı point, reaffirming and
‹ealthy-over-poor division of
at we enjoy. This is what
e the bumper sticker ethical
ımply that others may simply

ıan Populations

ı population growth. (See figure
ʿy have the numbers of persons
pectations have grown, so that we
ʿse one exploding curve on top
uperficial reading of such a graph
really start winning big in the
ıry. There are lots of them, and
⁓, ..., ...d many get, lots of things. If one is a
moral humanist, this can seem a good thing.
Wouldn't it be marvelous if all could get what
they want, and none hunger and thirst any
more?

But when we come to our senses, we realize that
this kind of winning, if it keeps on escalating, is
really losing. Humans will lose, and nature will be
destroyed as well. Cultures have become consumptive, with ever-escalating insatiable desires,
overlaid on ever-escalating population growth.
Culture does not know how to say "Enough!"
and that is not satisfactory. Starkly put, the growth
of culture has become cancerous. That is hardly a
metaphor, for a cancer is essentially an explosion
of unregulated growth. Feeding people always
seems humane, but, when we face up to what is
really going on, by just feeding people, without
attention to the larger social results, we could be
feeding a kind of cancer.

One can say that where there is a hungry mouth,
one should do what it takes to get food into it. But
when there are two mouths there the next day, and
four the day after that, and sixteen the day after
that, one needs a more complex answer. The
population of Egypt was less than 3 million for
over five millennia, fluctuating between 1.5 to 2.5
million, even when Napoleon went there in the
early 1800s. Today the population of Egypt is
about 55 million. Egypt has to import more than

half its food. The effects on nature, both on land
health and on wildlife, have been adversely proportional.

If, in this picture, we look at individual persons,
caught up in this uncontrolled growth, and if
we try to save nature, some persons will go
hungry. Surely, that is a bad thing. Would anyone
want to say that such persons ought not to sacrifice
nature, if needs be, to alleviate such harm as
best they can? From their perspective, they are
only doing what humans have always done,
making a resourceful use of nature to meet their
own needs. Isn't that a good thing anymore? Such
persons are doomed, unless they can capture natural values.

But here we face a time-bound truth, in which
too much of a good thing becomes a bad thing.
We have to figure in where such persons are located on the population curve, and realize that a
good thing when human numbers are manageable
is no longer a good thing when such a person is
really another cell of cancerous growth. That
sounds cruel, and it is tragic, but it does not
cease to be true for these reasons. For a couple to
have two children may be a blessing; but the tenth
child is a tragedy. When the child comes, one has
to be as humane as possible, but one will only be
making the best of a tragic situation, and if the
tenth child is reared, and has ten children in turn,
that will only multiply the tragedy. The quality of
human lives deteriorates; the poor get poorer.
Natural resources are further stressed; ecosystem
health and integrity degenerate; and this compounds the losses again – a lose–lose situation. In
a social system misfitted to its landscape, one's
wins can only be temporary in a losing human
ecology.

Even if there were an equitable distribution of
wealth, the human population cannot go on escalating without people becoming all equally poor. Of
the 90 million new people who will come on board
planet Earth this year, 85 million will appear in the
Third World, the countries least able to support
such population growth. At the same time, each
North American will consume 200 times as much
energy, and many other resources. The 5 million
new people in the industrial countries will put as
much strain on the environment as the 85 million
new poor. There are three problems: overpopulation, over-consumption, and underdistribution.
Sacrificing nature for development does not solve
any of these problems, none at all. It only brings

further loss. The poor, after a meal for a day or two, perhaps a decade or two, are soon hungry all over again, only now poorer still because their natural wealth is also gone.

To say that we ought always to feed the poor first commits a good–better–best fallacy. If a little is good, more must be better, most is best. If feeding some humans is good, feeding more is better. And more. And more! Feeding all of them is best? That sounds right. We can hardly bring ourselves to say that anyone ought to starve. But we reach a point of diminishing returns, when the goods put at threat lead us to wonder.

Endangered Natural Values

Natural values are endangered at every scale: global, regional, and local, at levels of ecosystems, species, organisms, populations, fauna and flora, terrestrial and marine, charismatic megafauna down to mollusks and beetles. This is true in both developed and developing nations, though we have under discussion here places where poverty threatens biodiversity.

Humans now control 40 percent of the planet's land-based primary net productivity, that is, the basic plant growth that captures the energy on which everything else depends.[11] If the human population doubles again, the capture will rise to 60 to 80 percent, and little habitat will remain for natural forms of life that cannot be accommodated after we have put people first. Humans do not use the lands they have domesticated effectively. A World Bank study found that 35 percent of the Earth's land has now become degraded.[12] Daniel Hillel, in a soils study, concludes, "Present yields are extremely low in many of the developing countries, and as they can be boosted substantially and rapidly, there should be no need to reclaim new land and to encroach further upon natural habitats."[13]

Africa is a case in point, and Madagascar epitomizes Africa's future. Its fauna and flora evolved independently from the mainland continent; there are 30 primates, all lemurs; the reptiles and amphibians are 90 percent endemic, including two thirds of all the chameleons of the world, and 10,000 plant species, of which 80 percent are endemic, including a thousand kinds of orchids. Humans came there about 1,500 years ago and lived with the fauna and flora more or less intact

until this century. Now an escalating population of impoverished Malagasy people rely heavily on slash-and-burn agriculture, and the forest cover is one third of the original (27.6 million acres to 9.4 million acres), most of the loss occurring since 1950.[14] Madagascar is the most eroded nation on Earth, and little or none of the fauna and flora is safely conserved. Population is expanding at 3.2 percent a year; remaining forest is shrinking at 3 percent, almost all to provide for the expanding population. Are we to say that none ought to be conserved until after no person is hungry?

Tigers are sliding toward extinction. Populations have declined 95 percent in this century; the two main factors are loss of habitat and a ferocious black market in bones and other body parts used in traditional medicine and folklore in China, Taiwan, and Korea, uses that are given no medical credence. Ranthambhore National Park in Rajasthan, India, is a tiger sanctuary; there were 40 tigers during the late 1980s, reduced in a few years by human pressures – illicit cattle grazing and poaching – to 20 to 25 tigers today. There are 200,000 Indians within three miles of the core of the park – more than double the population when the park was launched, 21 years ago. Most depend on wood from the 150 square miles of park to cook their food. They graze in and around the park some 150,000 head of scrawny cattle, buffalo, goats, and camels. The cattle impoverish habitat and carry diseases to the ungulates that are the tiger's prey base. In May 1993, a young tigress gave birth to four cubs; that month 316 babies were born in the villages surrounding the park.[15]

The tigers may be doomed, but ought they to be? Consider, for instance, that there are minimal reforestation efforts, or that cattle dung can be used for fuel with much greater efficiency than is being done, or that, in an experimental herd of jersey and holstein cattle there, the yield of milk increased ten times that of the gaunt, free-ranging local cattle, and that a small group of dairy producers has increased milk production 1,000 percent in just 3 years. In some moods we may insist that people are more important than tigers. But in other moods these majestic animals seem the casualties of human inabilities to manage themselves and their resources intelligently, a tragic story that leaves us wondering whether the tigers should always lose and the people win.

When Nature Comes First

Ought we to save nature if this results in people going hungry? In people dying? Regrettably, sometimes, the answer is yes. In 20 years Africa's black rhinoceros population declined from 65,000 to 2,500, a loss of 97 percent; the species faces imminent extinction. Again, as with the tigers, there has been loss of habitat caused by human population growth, an important and indirect cause; but the primary direct cause is poaching, this time for horns. People cannot eat horns: but they can buy food with the money from selling them. Zimbabwe has a hard-line shoot-to-kill policy for poachers, and over 150 poachers have been killed.[16]

So Zimbabweans do not always put people first; they are willing to kill some, and to let others to go hungry rather than sacrifice the rhino. If we always put people first, there will be no rhinos at all. Always too, we must guard against inhumanity, and take care, so far as we can, that poachers have other alternatives for overcoming their poverty. Still, if it comes to this, the Zimbabwean policy is right. Given the fact that rhinos have been so precipitously reduced, given that the Zimbabwean population is escalating (the average married woman there desires to have six children),[17] one ought to put the black rhino as a species first, even if this costs human lives.

But the poachers are doing something illegal. What about ordinary people, who are not breaking any laws? The sensitive moralist may object that, even when the multiple causal factors are known, and lamented, when it comes to dealing with individual persons caught up in these social forces, we should factor out overpopulation, overconsumption, and maldistribution, none of which are the fault of the particular persons who may wish to develop their lands. "I did not ask to be born; I am poor, not overconsuming; I am not the cause but rather the victim of the inequitable distribution of wealth." Surely there still remains for such an innocent person a right to use whatever natural resources one has available, as best one can, under the exigencies of one's particular life, set though this is in these unfortunate circumstances. "I only want enough to eat, is that not my right?"

Human rights must include, if anything at all, the right to subsistence. So even if particular persons are located at the wrong point on the global growth graph, even if they are willy-nilly part of a cancerous and consumptive society, even if there is some better social solution than the wrong one that is in fact happening, have they not a right that will override the conservation of natural value? Will it not just be a further wrong to them to deprive them of their right to what little they have? Can basic human rights ever be overridden by a society that wants to do better by conserving natural value?

This requires some weighing of the endangered natural values. Consider the tropical forests. There is more richness there than in other regions of the planet – half of all known species. In South America, for example, there are one fifth of the planet's species of terrestrial mammals (800 species); there are one third of the planet's flowering plants.[18] The peak of global plant diversity is in the three Andean countries of Columbia, Ecuador, and Peru, where over 40,000 species occur on just 2 percent of the world's land surface.[19] But population growth in South America has been as high as anywhere in the world,[20] and people are flowing into the forests, often crowded off other lands.

What about these hungry people? Consider first people who are not now there but might move there. This is not good agricultural soil, and such would-be settlers are likely to find only a short-term bargain, a long-term loss. Consider the people who already live there. If they are indigenous peoples, and wish to continue to live as they have already for hundreds and even thousands of years, there will be no threat to the forest. If they are cabaclos (of mixed European and native races), they can also continue the lifestyles known for hundreds of years, without serious destruction of the forests. Such peoples may continue the opportunities that they have long had. Nothing is taken away from them. They have been reasonably well fed, though often poor.

Can these peoples modernize? Can they multiply? Ought there to be a policy of feeding first all the children they bear, sacrificing nature as we must to accomplish this goal? Modern medicine and technology have enabled them to multiply, curing childhood diseases and providing better nutrition, even if these peoples often remain at thresholds of poverty. Do not such people have the right to develop? A first answer is that they do, but with the qualification that all rights are not absolute, some are weaker, some stronger, and the exercise of any right has to be balanced against values destroyed in the exercise of that right.

The qualification brings a second answer. If one concludes that the natural values at stake are quite high, and that the opportunities for development are low, because the envisioned development is inadvisable, then a possible answer is: No, there will be no development of these reserved areas, even if people there remain in the relative poverty of many centuries, or even if, with escalating populations, they become more poor. We are not always obligated to cover human mistakes with the sacrifice of natural values.

Again, one ought to be as humane as possible. Perhaps there can be development elsewhere, to which persons in the escalating population can be facilitated to move, if they wish. Indeed, this often happens, as such persons flee to the cities, though they often only encounter further poverty there, owing to the inequitable distribution of resources which we have lamented. If they remain in these areas of high biological diversity, they must stay under the traditional lifestyles of their present and past circumstances.

Does this violate human rights? Anywhere that there is legal zoning, persons are told what they may and may not do, in order to protect various social and natural values. Land ownership is limited ("imperfect," as lawyers term it) when the rights of use conflict with the rights of other persons. One's rights are constrained by the harm one does to others, and we legislate to enforce this (under what lawyers call "police power"). Environmental policy may and ought to regulate the harms that people do on the lands on which they live ("policing"), and it is perfectly appropriate to set aside conservation reserves to protect the cultural, ecological, scientific, economic, historical, aesthetic, religious, and other values people have at stake here, as well as for values that the fauna and flora have intrinsically in themselves. Indeed, unless there is such reserving of natural areas, counterbalancing the high pressures for development, there will be almost no conservation at all. Every person on Earth is told that he or she cannot develop some areas.

Persons are not told that they must starve, but they are told that they cannot save themselves from starving by sacrificing the nature set aside in reserves – not at least beyond the traditional kinds of uses that did leave the biodiversity on the landscape. If one is already residing in a location where development is constrained, this may seem unfair, and the invitation to move elsewhere a forced relocation. Relocation may be difficult proportionately to how vigorously the prevailing inequitable distribution of wealth is enforced elsewhere.

Human rights to development, even by those who are poor, though they are to be taken quite seriously, are not everywhere absolute, but have to be weighed against the other values at stake. An individual sees at a local scale; the farmer wants only to plant crops on the now forested land. But environmental ethics sees that the actions of individuals cumulate and produce larger scale changes that go on over the heads of these individuals. This ethic will regularly be constraining individuals in the interest of some larger ecological and social goods. That will regularly seem cruel, unfair to the individual caught in such constraints. This is the tragedy of the commons; individuals cannot see far enough ahead, under the pressures of the moment, to operate at intelligent ecological scales. Social policy must be set synoptically. This invokes both ecology and ethics, and blends them, if we are to respect life at all relevant scales.

These poor may not have so much a right to develop in any way they please, as a right to a more equitable distribution of the goods of the Earth that we, the wealthy, think we absolutely own.

Our traditional focus on individuals, and their rights, can blind us to how the mistakes (as well as the wisdom) of the parents can curse (and bless) the children, as the Ten Commandments put it, how "the iniquity of the fathers is visited upon the children to the third and fourth generation" (cf. Exodus 20.5). All this has a deeply tragic dimension, made worse by the coupling of human foibles with ecological realities. We have little reason to think that misguided compassion that puts food into every hungry mouth, be the consequences whatever they may, will relieve the tragedy. We also have no reason to think that the problem will be solved without wise compassion, balancing a love for persons and a love for nature.

Ought we to feed people first, and save nature last? We never face so simple a question. The practical question is more complex.

If persons widely demonstrate that they value many other worthwhile things over feeding the hungry (Christmas gifts, college educations, symphony concerts), and if developed countries, to protect what they value, post national boundaries across which the poor may not pass (immigration laws),

and if there is unequal and unjust distribution of wealth, and if just redistribution to alleviate poverty is refused,

and if charitable redistribution of justified unequal distribution of wealth is refused,

and if one fifth of the world continues to consume four fifths of the production of goods and four fifths consumes one fifth,

and if escalating birthrates continue so that there are no real gains in alleviating poverty, only larger numbers of poor in the next generation,

and if low productivity on domesticated lands continues, and if the natural lands to be sacrificed are likely to be low in productivity,

and if significant natural values are at stake, including extinctions of species –

then one ought not always to feed people first, but rather one ought sometimes to save nature.

Many of the "ands" in this conjunction can be replaced with "ors" and the statement will remain true, though we cannot say outside of particular contexts how many. The logic is not so much that of implication as of the weighing up of values and disvalues, natural and human, and of human rights and wrongs, past, present, and future.

Some will protest that this risks becoming misanthropic and morally callous. The Ten Commandments order us not to kill, and saving nature can never justify what amounts to killing people. Yes, but there is another kind of killing here, one not envisioned at Sinai, where humans are superkilling species. Extinction kills forms (*species*) – not just individuals; it kills collectively, not just distributively. Killing a natural kind is the death of birth, not just of an individual life. The historical lineage is stopped forever. Preceding the Ten Commandments is the Noah myth, when nature was primordially put at peril as great as the actual threat today. There, God seems more concerned about species than about the humans who had then gone so far astray. In the covenant re-established with humans on the promised Earth, the beasts are specifically included. "Keep them alive with you . . . according to their kinds" (Genesis 6.19–20). There is something ungodly about an ethic by which the late-coming *Homo sapiens* arrogantly regards the welfare of one's own species as absolute, with the welfare of all the other five million species sacrificed to that. The commandment not to kill is as old as Cain and Abel, but the most archaic commandment of all is the divine, "Let the earth bring forth" (Genesis 1). Stopping that genesis is the most destructive event possible, and we humans have no right to do that. Saving nature is not always morally naive; it can deepen our understanding of the human place in the scheme of things entire, and of our duties on this majestic home planet.

Notes

1 *Rio Declaration on Environment and Development*, Principle 1, UNCED document A/CONF.151/26, vol. I, ps. 15–25.

2 *Rio Declaration*, Principle 4.

3 *Rio Declaration*, Principle 5.

4 Insurance Institute for Highway Safety (Arlington, Virginia), *Status Report*, vol. 29 (no. 10, September 10, 1994): 3.

5 Ruth Leger Sivard, *World Military and Social Expenditures*, 15th edn., Washington, DC: World Priorities, Inc., 1993.

6 Jonathan Power, 1992. "Despite Its Gifts, Brazil Is a Basket Case," *The Miami Herald*, June 22, p. 10A.

7 The empirical data below are in: Brian Huntley, Roy Siegfried, and Clem Sunter, *South African Environments into the 21st Century*, Cape Town: Human and Rousseau, Ltd, and Tafelberg Publishers Ltd., 1989; Rob Preston-Whyte and Graham House, eds., *Rotating the Cube: Environmental Strategies for the 1990s*, Durban: Department of Geographical and Environmental Sciences and Indicator Project South Africa, University of Natal, 1990; and Alan B. Durning, *Apartheid's Environmental Toll*, Washington, DC: Worldwatch Institute, 1990.

8 Huntley, Siegfried, and Sunter, *South African Environments*, p. 85.

9 Mamphela Ramphele, ed., *Restoring the Land: Environment and Change in Post-Apartheid South Africa*, London: Panos Publications, 1991.

10 The pie chart summarizes data in the *World Development Report 1991*, New York: Oxford University Press, 1991.

11 Peter M. Vitousek, Paul R. Ehrlich, Anne H. Ehrlich, and Pamela A. Matson, "Human Appropriation of the Products of Biosynthesis," *BioScience* 36(1986): 368–73.

12 Robert Goodland, "The Case That the World Has Reached Limits," pp. 3–22 in Robert Goodland, Herman E. Daly, and Salah El Serafy, eds., *Popula-*

tion, Technology, and Lifestyle, Washington, DC: Island Press, 1992.

13 Daniel Hillel, *Out of the Earth*, New York: Free Press, Macmillan, 1991, p. 279.

14 E. O. Wilson, *The Diversity of Life*, Cambridge, MA: Harvard University Press, 1992, p. 267; Alison Jolly, *A World Like Our Own: Man and Nature in Madagascar*, New Haven: Yale University Press, 1980.

15 Geoffrey C. Ward, "The People and the Tiger," *Audubon* 96 (no. 4, July–August 1994):62–9.

16 Joel Berger and Carol Cunningham, "Active Intervention and Conservation: Africa's Pachyderm Problem," *Science* 263(1994):1241–2.

17 John Bongaarts, "Population Policy Options in the Developing World," *Science* 263(1994):771–6.

18 Michael A. Mares, "Conservation in South America: Problems, Consequences, and Solutions," *Science* 233(1986):734–9.

19 Wilson, *The Diversity of Life*, p. 197.

20 Ansley J. Coale, "Recent Trends in Fertility in the Less Developed Countries," *Science* 221(1983):828–32.

35

Saving Nature, Feeding People, and Ethics

Robin Attfield

1 Introduction

'Given the fact that rhinos have been so precipit-ously reduced, given that the Zimbabwean popu-lation is escalating (the average married woman there desires to have six children), one ought to put the black rhino as a species first, even if this costs human lives'.[1] Thus Holmes Rolston about the black rhinos of Zimbabwe. Rolston goes on to argue that feeding the hungry is not always our first obligation,[2] and that it may sometimes be right to allow not just poachers to be shot (as is authorised by the law of Zimbabwe) but even ordinary inoffensive malnourished people to starve, granted that they have other options which could fend off starvation, rather than allow within nature reserves the kind of development which might alleviate the poverty of people already living there.[3] This paper discusses ethical and related issues arising from problems about conser-vation, population growth and feeding people, as raised in Rolston's paper, together with some al-ternative responses to these issues.

Those of Rolston's readers who reject capital punishment or favour due process are likely to be unenthusiastic about any shoot-to-kill policy; but resorting to violence against poachers (including violence designed to incapacitate) might still be approved. Approving it, however, need not in-volve endorsement of Rolston's grounds; and the same applies to his grounds for prohibiting devel-opment in nature reserves. The issue is not a straightforward conflict of interests of the human population of Zimbabwe versus Zimbabwean rhinos. For the grounds for conservation include the interests of future Zimbabweans (some of whom may be saved from starvation thereby) and also, to some degree, the interests of future rhinos. These interests show that the sharp decline in the rhino population has moral relevance; but it is much less clear that the growth of the human population of Zimbabwe constitutes a reason for letting some of its citizens die, any more than the growth of Western affluence does, and much less still that the supposed desires of Zimbabwean mothers supply such a reason. Some rather differ-ent responses to population growth will be pre-sented later in this essay.

2 Priorities, Preservation and Development

What, then, is to be said about priorities between saving nature and feeding people? Compared with many American environmentalists, Rolston is rela-tively moderate in these matters. Thus he does not write of population growth as a kind of pollution, or advocate the removal of indigenous peoples from their forests. However, he is prepared to argue from the actual moral assumptions of people in the actual world that meeting people's needs does not always take priority. For example, he is prepared to argue from people's willingness to deploy surplus resources on Christmas gifts, college education or symphony concerts rather than on relieving poverty, and from other suchlike existing priorities, for the conclusion that morality does not always require us to feed people first.

To such reasoning, we need not object that it moves from sociological facts to value judgements. For Rolston is aware that he is reliant on the acceptability of the moral assumptions of existing agents and communities, and that without such a premise his premises about Christmas presents and the rest have little relevance. Hence he could not object to this premise being made explicit: the moral assumptions of existing agents and communities (particularly Western ones) are acceptable, at least to some degree, he supposes. Yet this same premise still warrants criticism; the assumptions underlying Christmas expenditure could easily be morally indefensible. Indeed the annual spending spree of nominally Christian societies is frequently a target for moral criticism, whether from utilitarians, Kantians or religious believers. More generally, the moral assumptions of behaviour in the contemporary world cannot be allowed to form the basis of critical normative ethics; for on this basis it would make no sense to urge that the *status quo* warrants criticism and ought to change. Yet this is something which environmental ethicists usually both want and need to urge.

To be fair to Rolston, he is not in general a supporter of the *status quo*, he recognises the general moral importance of satisfying human needs,[4] and he allows that in many cases there will be no conflict between feeding people and upholding the interests of nature.[5] Indeed his argument is partly that feeding people first cannot always be given the highest priority, or prioritising anything else would always be wrong – which (I agree) is implausible. He also holds that most development (agricultural development included) is of a kind where nature is sacrificed. While it is undeniable that some so-called 'development' is of this kind, the limited scope of such conflicts is worthy of a few moments' reflection.

Conflicts between nature and development would be frequent if development happens whenever a change is generated by human beings which

someone regards as an improvement (and this seems to be the sense in which Rolston is using the term). For if the concept of nature applies not only to wilderness but also to whatever exists without significant modification from human purposive activity or contrivance, then most building projects will constitute development in this sense, and will also subvert a larger or smaller segment of nature. Conflicts will, however, be less frequent where the concept of development is given its more usual sense, and relates to social and/or economic change which genuinely satisfies human needs,[6] and not just change believed by someone to be for the better; for the relevant criteria will plausibly now include those of social justice, and will exclude much which would otherwise count as 'development'.

Now a further defensible criterion of development as genuine improvement is sustainability; for development which is unsustainable will seldom if ever comprise an improvement. Thus we already know, once we know that it is unsustainable, that either it will undermine itself, or that it will be undermined by other predictable processes; and this already casts considerable doubt on whether an improvement is present at all. Even if, with regard to human interests, there will be temporary gains (even for a thousand years), an unsustainable change scarcely counts as development if there is an alternative change which would be both beneficial and sustainable.

Sustainable changes, however, will typically allow affected tracts of nature to remain self-renewing and sustainable. For where affected tracts of nature are subverted or cease to be sustainable, the processes of production, whether of food or shelter or of other services, will more often than not be unsustainable themselves, because natural systems have ceased to be self-renewing and sustainable, and cannot sustain them indefinitely. (Rolston has suggested that processes which last for several centuries are thereby sustainable, but might also sacrifice much biodiversity;[7] in my view, if ecosystems are disrupted or undermined for the sake of processes which cannot be sustained indefinitely, these processes are not sustainable.) Accordingly, development will seldom be worthy of the name where it is not sustainable, and sustainable not only in the form of stable systems of production but also with respect to the stability of the natural world. And if so, then it will not be the case that most development is of a kind where nature is sacrificed. Where nature is sacrificed, what is going on will usually fall short of being development, at least in the more usual sense of that term.

3 Grounds for Preservation

This is, however, a somewhat *a priori* defence of development; and in any case the impression should not be given that I would seek to argue against Rolston's conclusions about saving nature at all points. Specifically, the arguments for preserving wild species should be recognised, and require the preservation of some wild habitats (as Rolston argues with regard to black rhinos in Zimbabwe). These arguments derive from the interests both of future humans and also from those of the future wildlife whose existence we can either facilitate or prevent, plus obviously the interests of current wildlife and those current humans who derive benefit from the existence of wildlife.

Further, as Rolston concludes, this means that there are some areas which could be colonised by hungry humans, if only temporarily rather than sustainably, who might thereby temporarily satisfy their needs for food, fuel and shelter, but which should be denied to them in order to save the wild creatures (such as black rhinos) which depend on these same areas. The hungry humans would not be required to starve, being free, for example, to move to areas of development elsewhere. Nor would the indigenous people who already inhabit such reserves be required to leave, as long as their lifestyles are compatible with nature preservation. The only kind of prohibited actions would be ones which meet human interests through the kind of so-called 'development' which destroys the reserve, because of the value of the thriving of wild nature, because of the importance of this for future humans, and because of the importance of the intactness of habitats necessary if the thriving of wild nature is to be facilitated.

Now one of Rolston's background assumptions should be challenged. Rolston cites Peter M. Vitousek and others as having shown that 40 percent of the planet's land-based net primary product (i.e. basic plant growth) has been captured by human begins, and claims that if the human population and its economic demand doubles, this capture could rise as high as 80 percent, leaving little for 'natural forms of life that cannot be accommodated after we have put people first'.[8] But Mark

Sagoff has pointed out that this argument wrongly assumes that increases in the size of the economy require a proportional increase in the percentage of net primary product calculated by this method as having been 'captured'.

Vitousek and his colleagues only reached their 40 percent by including all the material used in human-dominated ecosystems by communities of organisms different from those in corresponding natural systems, or in other words all the plants indirectly affected through human-caused changes in land use, including all the plants of areas of countryside which are not strictly wilderness. Otherwise their figure for human use would have been around 5 percent. Sagoff proceeds to argue that virtually the whole of North America had already been thus 'captured' (in the Vitousek sense) by 1492, and certainly by one hundred years ago, and that since there has been large-scale economic growth since then, the proportionality assumption must be rejected, as it implies that in the absence of increased capture of net primary product no economic growth in North America since then could possibly have occurred.

Obviously there was an increase in the actual exploitation of net primary product between 1492 and a century ago, but this does not detract from Sagoff's reply to Vitousek. Wary as we should often be of economic growth, such growth turns out to be partially independent of capture of net primary product,[9] a proposition assumed by Rolston himself when he remarks that agricultural production in many developing countries could be boosted without further encroachment on natural habitats.[10]

But as this last point exhibits, the unacceptability of Rolston's use of Vitousek's claims about net primary product does not entirely undermine his argument against the development of such habitats. For natural ecosystems and the valuable wild creatures which populate them continue to be under threat, not least through land hunger in areas of human population growth. Even if growth need not be at the expense of natural vegetation, it often is, and this is true of population growth as well as of economic growth.

A key aspect of Rolston's argument, however, is that the areas in question could not support human colonisers sustainably. Neither the moral philosopher nor, I suggest, the consistent environmentalist can rest content with the conclusion that some such areas should be forbidden to people altogether (and, to his credit, Rolston does not favour this[11]). Besides (although here Rolston might disagree), if the needs of starving people could be satisfied sustainably from a given area, there is a strong case in favour of letting them colonise it and thereby meet their needs, unless these needs both could be met elsewhere, and probably would be met if this were attempted. If the needs of future people count, so do the needs of current people.

The qualification about starving people may seem to suggest that my view is that priority should always go to human interests over nonhuman interests. In fact, this is a stance which I should reject. Often, for example, the human interests at stake will not be basic needs, while the nonhuman interests will comprise basic needs for the nonhuman creatures concerned. Besides, although I differ from Rolston in holding that some colonising of wild habitats is allowable, I still favour most current reserves remaining such, and more being created, in full recognition of the fact that this involves one or another kind of zoning, and the designating of these areas as prohibited to uses which would harm either other people or wild nature. The difference between us concerns the permissibility of sustainable development in some areas which are predominantly natural at present (such as the siting of solar energy plant in deserts close to areas needing an enhanced energy supply). In cases where such development could be and would be so planned and organised as to involve a sustainable relation between the human participants and nature, it should in my view be permitted for the sake of human needs.

Even so, it would have to be limited for the sake of species preservation. In previous centuries, poor people have been able to colonise wild areas, and this should not be wholly prohibited to the poor people of the present. Yet the ethical case for preservation means that this process must have its limits. Preserving the last members of a wild species can make a much greater difference to the total of value in the world than preserving the same number of members of a currently plentiful species would. For it preserves not only current lives but also the possibility of countless future members of the species coming into being in the future. This justifies preserving the territorial niches necessary for such preservation. While the case for such preservation could conflict with sustainable colonisation, in practice such conflicts

would be rare, granted the argument already put forward concerning the way in which sustainable development allows of the sustaining of wild species and systems.

4 Population and Sustainability

Certainly, population policies are important, so that we do not get into dilemmas such as choosing between exterminating wild species and/or allowing their extinction, and failing to make provision for an increased human population. Population policies (if voluntary, and integrated with policies of development) have the potential for eventually limiting the incidence of conflicts between preservation and human needs.

For many reasons including this one, population policies should aim at attaining a sustainable level of population. Even if the level at which the global human population eventually stabilises is substantially greater than the current population of the planet, a sustainable population could mean an end to encroachments on the remaining areas of countryside and of wilderness. Or rather, it could mean this as long as the level is not so high that next to no wilderness by then remains, and also as long as the introduction of sustainable processes of production and of food-supply by then prevents the need to extract resources from yet more and more wild places.

Even before the human population stabilises, there will be a tendency for conflicts between human colonisation of wild places and the preservation of such places to become fewer, as long as the trend is in the direction of stabilisation; for the demand for additional territory will steadily reduce. Naturally the reasons for aiming at population stability are unlikely to be confined to the desire to avoid such conflicts; the interests of the human beings of that day are likely to be central. Nonetheless the eventual attainment of zero population growth on a sustainable basis remains likely to contribute strongly towards the preservation of wildlife and wilderness.

5 Are People a Cancer?

Rolston, however, is not alone in representing much of the current human population of the world as resembling a cancer (glossed on his previous page as 'an explosion of unregulated growth'[12]), and many of its individuals as 'another cell of cancerous growth'. 'For a couple to have two children', he concedes, 'may be a blessing'. But the tenth child, he claims, is 'a tragedy'. 'When the child comes, one has to be as humane as possible, but one will only be making the best of a tragic situation, and if the tenth child is reared, and has ten children in turn, that will only multiply the tragedy.' Such tragic growth, he maintains, leads to a deteriorating quality of life and to deteriorating natural resources, declining ecosystem health and disappearing integrity. And in these circumstances, it is a fallacy to claim, he suggests, that we ought always to feed the poor first.[13]

While I agree that there are some measures which should not be taken to feed the poor because they are unsustainable methods and would destroy wild habitats, much of what Rolston here says is unacceptable. Admittedly my agreement that some means towards the feeding of the poor would be misguided commits me to the view that feeding the poor should not always be everyone's highest priority. But Rolston's argument would, if valid, prove too much, and would suggest that with regard to certain humans, or to all humans above certain vague numerical ceilings for certain territories, there is no obligation to feed these people at all.

First, it should be pointed out that if the conception and birth of anyone is a blessing and has positive value, then this should be true of the conception and birth of everyone, except perhaps those whose quality of life is going to be nil or negative. The intrinsic value of the life of a given person cannot simply disappear through the fact that this is the tenth child of their parents. At most, there might, alongside the positive intrinsic value attaching to such lives, be a negative instrumental value in the simultaneous existence of all ten children plus the other human inhabitants of the planet. Whether there actually would be such negative instrumental value might depend on factors such as the possible overcrowding which might sometimes result from the addition of extra people, the possible strain for those involved in supporting extra people through childhood, or the possible indirect effects of extra people on ecosystems.

Yet these very factors could easily be exaggerated. Overcrowding of dwelling-places is avoidable if enough are built to prevent houses being excessively crowded, and overcrowding of streets and squares if people refrain from gathering in excessive crowds. Attaining this would often involve few extra resources. As for strain for existing people, the addition of children to poor families in the Third World involves less strain than Westerners might expect, as such children soon become economically active, and thus usually supply pairs of hands which can assist in the work of providing for the family or the community. As for strain on ecosystems, sometimes no extra fuel will be involved (as the newcomers may share the same hearth as their elders), and whether their needs for food and for sanitation cause ecosystems to degenerate is much more a function of social arrangements than of these extra people's mere existence.

A little more should be said about the property of tenthness (or of ordinality in general) not undermining the intrinsic value of lives of positive quality. Rolston seems to be saying that additional children after some threshold number have no such value. But imagine that after the birth of such an additional child, one or more siblings die, and the total number falls below the threshold number. His view seems to imply that the life of this child now acquires the intrinsic value it would have had if her/his birth had occurred before the threshold was reached. But such miraculous changes to intrinsic value are incredible, particularly since no qualitative change may have befallen the child in question; for the child may be too young to be affected by the deaths of the siblings. Besides, if this child's life has intrinsic value after the siblings' death, it is difficult to see how it could have lacked it previously. What is much more credible is that overall disvalue arises (as I have suggested) because of the adverse effects of the simultaneous existence of so many people in much the same place on the flourishing both of the parents and of the children themselves. If the tenth child's arrival is a tragedy, it is not intrinsically a tragedy, but at most a tragedy in the circumstances, all-things-considered.[14]

While Rolston, who is a believer in intrinsic value, could scarcely claim that this language is inapplicable to such matters, some of his readers might prefer to interpret his language about blessings and tragedies in a relational manner, and thus resist the above introduction of talk of intrinsic value. They could endorse his talk of the blessing comprised by the first two children because these children bless the union of the parents with fertility and fruitfulness; and they could claim that the arrival of the tenth child comprises a tragedy because the entire family is now overburdened, something the parents have reason to regret. But my point can be re-expressed in the language of relationships and blessings. For once again the deaths of siblings could deplete the number of children to below the same threshold, and the existence of the additional child would now count as a blessing on the basis just mentioned. Thus there is nothing intrinsically tragic about the arrival of the additional child; once again, the tragedy derives from the effects of the overall family situation. If all the children stay alive, but half the children are adopted by a childless aunt and uncle, there may be no tragedy for the family, although the environment might still be affected.

My suggestion is that we retain both the language of blessings and tragedy, which could serve to convey how in many cases the parents would perceive and understand their predicament, and also the language of intrinsic and instrumental value and disvalue, which avoids the need for everyone to endorse such perceptions, and which conveys interpersonal reasons for our welcoming or regretting, encouraging or discouraging the events to which it is applied. The language of value has the further advantage that, since it does not depend on intensional contexts, like cases must be judged alike, and that thus tenthness (and ordinality in general) will only correspond to a difference in value where it is shown to be relevant.

The next question to be considered concerns what is meant when Rolston says 'When the child comes, one has to be as humane as possible, but one will only be making the best of a tragic situation, and if the tenth child is reared, and has ten children in turn, that will only multiply the tragedy'. Who, precisely, must be as humane as possible, but might still consider not rearing the tenth child? The possibilities include poor parents in a Third World country, that country's government, and Western aid charities and their individual donors. Third World governments often lack the resources to supply the material needs of their citizens, and there would be something extremely patronising about the suggestion that it is Westerners, already on average taking a disproportionate share of the earth's resorces, who are to decide humanely whether the child is to be reared, even though Westerners are the people most obviously able to choose between saving nature and feeding the poor. Several features of the context suggest that the decision-makers are poor parents, who may do 'what humans have always done, making a resourceful use of nature to meet their own needs'.[15] But could it really be they who may instead 'try to save nature' and let the child go hungry?

In most cultures, parents are held to have a special responsibility to provide for their children, which takes precedence over other responsibilities. This may not be the last word on what the all-things-considered responsibility of the parents is; but in most countries the law requires parents or guardians to make this provision, on pain of considerable penalties. Thus, even if a reflective morality would not invariably support local expectations about parental duties, it would be unreasonable if the parents were to be expected to defy their country's law (and usually local custom too) in order to comply with reflective morality, even if reflective morality were somehow to urge infanticide. Thus the parents must be held to be justified in rearing the tenth child. And since they might themselves be tenth children of their parents, this judgement already supports the rearing of the tenth child of a tenth child.

This could still be a tragedy, all things considered. In my own view, it often would be. On the other hand, we have not yet heard enough about the situation of the poor parents to know this. For example, in some societies, large numbers of the population are childless monks; in such a context, if some adults have children at more than the replacement rate, that may be no problem. This would also be true of societies in which few people are celibate but fertility rates are low. Nevertheless, in many societies large families will often be a tragedy, all things considered, and should be discouraged, both by governments and aid agencies. But does this (or anything else) make population growth a cancer?

No. A cancer is not just 'an explosion of unregulated growth'. If it were, then species such as mushrooms, rabbits and locusts would often be cancerous. A cancer is also a growth bearing no positive intrinsic value itself which is also potentially fatal to a living creature capable of health, and who is thus, as has been argued more fully elsewhere[16] a potential bearer of intrinsic value.

But the suggestion that the current human population of the Earth is a cancer is deeply at variance with all this. On the one hand, unlike a cancer, this population consists of potential bearers of intrinsic value; and to represent such individuals (when numerous) as cancerous is to disregard this value, and to treat them as means only, and as nothing but dysfunctional ones too. On the other hand, what the collection of these intrinsically valuable individuals is supposed to be fatal to is the biosphere, which in the view of many including myself has no independent intrinsic value. The biosphere is still, of course, highly valuable, but this is because it is capable of generating bearers of intrinsic value such as individual humans and other creatures. Besides, if the suggestion is really that human beings might be a cancer because they could threaten each other, it is a fantastic hyperbole which serves to distract attention from ways in which these same human beings, in the same numbers, could avoid posing any such threats either to humanity or to other species.

I have no wish to deny that human numbers and activities are imperilling numerous other species, and that human numbers could easily grow to a level at which far more species would be threatened. But the possibility of extinctions has long been known, without usually inclining those aware of it to the vocabulary of pathology. Granted the strong grounds for preserving species, agents should certainly adopt concerted preservationist policies (and, where relevant, population policies to prevent unsustainable population growth too[17]), but need not simultaneously regard their own existence and agency as some kind of cosmic curse.

The discourse of human population as cancer is also dangerous. If, beyond certain numbers, humans comprise a cancer, then the motivations to save human life, to heal injury and to cure illness are likely to lapse. For if each individual existence beyond a certain numerical level is an evil, then (whatever humanitarianism may dictate) there must be virtue in letting such individuals die, if not in speeding the process. This discourse thus generates a reluctance to show solidarity with vulnerable humans, and can predispose those who endorse it to misanthropy. Morality is thus wrenched from its springs in sympathy, benevolence and mercy, and is even liable to be diverted from its concern for justice, in favour of some kind of global hygiene. The possibilities for racist or fascist outcomes are all too clear. Besides, if human

numbers beyond a certain level comprise a cancer, then the cancer is ourselves, the thinkers who think this thought, as much as other families or other peoples. At the very least, we should stop having children, even if we would be justified in remaining alive at all.

Thus the purportedly factual claim that population growth is cancerous turns out to carry unacceptable conceptual and normative implications. Rapid population growth is a real problem, but lacks these implications. Thus the depiction of population growth as cancer cannot be regarded as contributing to the case for withholding priority from feeding people.

6 The Delusion of the Neo-Malthusian Environmental Paradigm

Besides, the belief that population growth (sometimes supposedly combined with fecklessness) among rural people in the Third World is fatal to the environment and to sustainable development is often treated as an unchallengeable axiom among advisers of Western aid agencies in the grip of a preconceived neo-Malthusian environmentalist paradigm, and with total disregard for empirical evidence to the contrary. Allan Hoben has ably demonstrated this, and how the belief just mentioned has bedevilled the findings both of supposedly empirical research and of policy advisers.

Hoben's central case study concerns the Akamba of Kenya, whose land has become both greener and more productive through the same period as a continuation of human population growth which experts had claimed to be generating irreversible and hopeless desertification.[18] He also presents parallel case studies from Kordofan in the Sudan[19] and Kissidougou Prefecture in Guinea;[20] in both cases experts' claims about demographic pressures allegedly producing overgrazing, environmental degradation, deforestation and (in the Sudanese case) encroachment by the Sahara turn out to be constructions of outsiders who forced the phenomena to comply with an entrenched paradigm.

I am unable to claim that population growth *never* causes environmental degradation; thus the evidence which Rolston cites from Madagascar could well attest that it can,[21] unless possibly it is vitiated in parallel ways. Besides, Hoben's evidence of areas of Africa becoming greener relates (at least for his Kenyan and Guinean examples) to tree-planting on the part of local people, rather than to preservation of natural habitat. Yet this same evidence, combined with Hoben's account of how peoples such as the Akamba have been deprived of the best land during and since the colonial period,[22] raises doubts about claims of widespread poor land-use,[23] and about population growth driving people to colonise remaining areas of wilderness. Hence we should be cautious before supporting policies which might prohibit people introducing improved methods of agriculture, or before urging donor agencies to pressure African governments to require such often questionable policies as conditions of receiving aid packages.

In any case, the world population is going to increase before it stabilises; and it would be unfortunate if this larger population of the middle of this century is told by its philosophers and by their predecessors of today that many of its members ought not to have existed. Even if this is true, none of them will have been able to avoid existing; and suicide on the part of the conscientious ones is unlikely to improve matters.

Rather we have to plan for a planet with ten thousand million people (or more) living sustainably (even though a lower maximum would be desirable), and with sustainable wild habitats too. This requires both population policies (as in China), preservation policies (as in Kenya and Zimbabwe), and development policies which harness the energies of existing people and (in due course) of their descendants both for development and for preservation.[24]

In the long run, the ethical issue of whether we should ever give priority to saving nature over feeding people (to which the answer probably remains a heavily conditional 'yes') loses its significance. Agonising about this theoretical question should be replaced by devising policies of development and of preservation in which local people, including rural people, can participate, policies which encourage people both to save wildlife and to feed themselves.

Notes

I am grateful to the editor of *Environmental Values*, to several referees and to Holmes Rolston for comments on and criticisms of this essay, while taking full responsibility for its final form and content myself. I am also grateful to the participants in the Third International Jacobsen Philosophy Conference, held at Harare, Zimbabwe in March 1996, and to participants in a Seminar of the Department of Philosophy, University of Salzburg, held in May 1996, for their comments on a related paper. A German translation of that paper has appeared: Robin Attfield, 'Natur erhalten oder Menschen Ernähren?', *Conceptus: Zeitschrift für Philosophie*, XXIX.74, 1996, 27–45.

1 Rolston 1996, pp. 257–8.
2 Ibid., pp. 260–1.
3 Ibid., p. 259.
4 Ibid., p. 246.
5 Ibid., p. 245.
6 This is the sense widely used in, for example, development ethics circles. 'Development' in this sense could still fail on occasion to be change for the better, all things considered; but much so-called 'development' would (importantly) be denied the accolade of comprising development in this sense. At the same time, the criteria of development in this sense cohere well with those of social justice. Further, development in this sense typically involves sustainability, for the reasons given in the penultimate paragraph of this section.
7 Rolston, private communication of 11 April, 1996.
8 Rolston 1996, p. 256; he here cites Vitousek et al. 1986.
9 Sagoff 1995.
10 Rolston 1996, p. 256.
11 Ibid., p. 259.
12 Ibid., p. 254.
13 Ibid., p. 255.
14 Rolston considers that this was his sense of 'tragedy' too (private communication of April 11, 1996). The relation between population and flourishing is discussed in Attfield 1995a, chapter 10, 'Population and the Total View'.
15 Rolston 1996, p. 255 (previous paragraph).
16 Attfield 1995b.
17 I am indebted to Rolston (private communication of 11 April 1996) for pointing out the bearing of my earlier remarks about unsustainable development on population processes.
18 Hoben, 1995, pp. 19–21. Hoben here cites Tiffen and Mortimore 1992, and Tiffen, Mortimore and Gichuki 1994.
19 Hellden 1988. The current famine in Sudan is largely due to civil war.
20 Fairhead, Leach et al. 1992.
21 Rolston 1996, p. 256, where he cites Wilson 1992, p. 267, and Jolly 1980. Contrary evidence from Nigeria and elsewhere in West Africa is available in Lockwood 1995.

22 Hoben 1995, p. 17.
23 Hoben 1995, pp. 18–19.
24 I have revisited these issues in *The Ethics of the Global Environment*, 1999.

References

Aiken, William, and Hugh LaFollette (eds.), 1996. *World Hunger and Morality*, 2nd edn., Upper Saddle River, NJ: Prentice-Hall.

Attfield, Robin, 1995a. *Value, Obligation and Meta-Ethics*, Atlanta and Amsterdam: Rodopi.

Attfield, Robin, 1995b. 'Preferences, Health, Interests and Value', *Electronic Journal of Applied Philosophy*, 3:2.

Attfield, Robin, 1999. *The Ethics of the Global Environment*. Edinburgh: Edinburgh University Press.

Fairhead, James, Melissa Leach et al., 1992. *Forests of the Past? Archival, Oral and Demographic Evidence in Kissidougou Prefecture's Vegetation History*. COLA Working Paper, no. 1.

Hellden, Ulf, 1988. 'Desertification Monitoring: Is the Desert Encroaching?', *Desertification Control Bulletin*, 17: 8–12.

Hoben, Allan, 1995. *The Cultural and Political Construction of Environmental Policy in Africa*, Medford, MA: Global Development and Environment Institute

Jolly, Alison, 1980. *A World Like Our Own: Man and Nature in Madagascar*, New Haven: Yale University Press.

Lockwood, Matthew, 1995. 'Development Policy and the African Demographic Transition: Issues and Questions', *Journal of International Development*, 7(1): 1–23.

Rolston, Holmes, III, 1996. 'Feeding People versus Saving Nature?'. In William Aiken and Hugh LaFollette (eds.), *World Hunger and Morality*, 2nd edn., Upper Saddle River, NJ: Prentice-Hall, 244–63.

Sagoff, Mark, 1995. 'Carrying-Capacity and Ecological Economics', *BioScience*, 45(9): 610–20.

Tiffen, Mary, and Michael Mortimore, 1992. 'Environment, Population Growth and Productivity in Kenya: A Case Study of Machakos District', *Development Policy Review*, 10(4).

Tiffen, Mary, Michael Mortimore and Francis Gichuki, 1994. *More People, Less Erosion: Environmental Recovery in Kenya*, Chichester: John Wiley.

Vitousek, Peter M., Paul R. Ehrlich, Anne H. Ehrlich and Pamela A. Matson, 1986. 'Human Appropriation of the Products of Biosynthesis', *BioScience* 36: 368–73.

Wilson, E. O., 1992. *The Diversity of Life*, Cambridge, MA: Harvard University Press.

Editor's Note: Rolston replies to Attfield in "Saving Nature, Feeding People, and the Foundations of Ethics," *Environmental Values* 7 (1998): 349–57.

36

Integrating Environmentalism and Human Rights

James W. Nickel and Eduardo Viola

I The Greening of Human Rights

In this article, we argue that there are important contributions that the human rights and environmental movements can make to each other, and illustrate these by reference to Brazil. Because there are many significant similarities between the environmental and human rights movements,[1] cooperation between them has already occurred in many countries and there are important connections between their agendas. Both are predominantly post-World War II movements; both are international in scope; both are movements that find support among "conservatives" as well as "progressives"; both are committed to democratic political institutions; both support the survival of indigenous peoples; and both emphasize consciousness raising, individual engagement, and political activism as means of promoting their goals. There are, however, important areas of conflict between the human rights and environmental movements. These include conflicts over the right to have a large family, defended by some parts of the human rights movement, versus the need to avoid overpopulation, asserted by most environmental groups, and conflicts over the relative importance of improvements in the living standards of human populations versus environmental preservation and protection.

(1) *The right to a safe and healthy environment.* One important contribution that environmentalism can make to the human rights movement is

to persuade it to add a general right to a safe and healthy environment to the standard lists of rights – and to take it seriously as part of its agenda. Melissa Thorme has explored the case for a right to "a safe, healthy, and ecologically balanced environment."[2] James W. Nickel has defended a narrower right to a safe environment, focusing on threats to human life and health from technological and industrial processes and from the disposal of sewage and wastes. Nickel argues that this sort of right can pass the justificatory tests appropriate to all human rights.[3]

The recognition of a right to a safe environment is beginning to occur. A number of national constitutions now contain this right. For example, the Constitution of Honduras speaks of maintaining "a satisfactory environment for the protection of everyone's health"; the Constitution of South Korea declares a right "to a healthy and pleasant environment"; and the Constitution of Portugal speaks of a "healthy and ecologically balanced environment." The 1988 Constitution of Brazil has excellent – and extensive – environmental clauses, including one that asserts that "Everyone has the right to an ecologically balanced environment...."[4] The right to a safe environment has also been recognized in a few international human rights documents. For example, it is already found in the African Charter for Human and Peoples' Rights (1981), and will be part of the American Convention on Human Rights (1978) when the "Protocol of San Salvador" comes into force.[5] Finally, the right to a safe and healthy environment is one of the principles underlying several of the documents signed at the 1992 "Earth Summit" (UNCED) in Rio de Janeiro. These documents include the Rio Charter, Agenda 21, the Climate Convention, and the Biodiversity Treaty.[6] Although UNCED failed to achieve international consensus on strong measures for dealing with international environmental problems, it was successful in getting some key environmental ideas recognized as normative principles in international relations.

(2) *Seeing humans as part of nature.* Another contribution that environmentalism can make to the human rights movement is a broadened perspective that presents people as part of nature, as interacting extensively with biological and other natural systems, and as competitors with each other and with other animals for land and natural resources. In specific cases, this contribution will mean recognizing the environmental dimension of some human rights issues. For example, many killings in rural Brazil stem from conflicts over land and are driven by greed and economic desperation. Depriving indigenous groups of most of their territory through the encroachment of mainstream settlers may destroy these groups as effectively as mass murder. This perspective, if adopted, might also make human rights groups more supportive of attempts to control population size. Finally, seeing humans as part of nature might encourage submitting means of promoting and implementing human rights to evaluation from an ecological perspective. For example, such economic rights as a right to food, to a decent standard of living, or to employment need to be implemented in ways that are environmentally sound and sustainable.

(3) *Respecting nature.* A third contribution that environmentalism can make to the human rights movement is to get it to consider whether nature – including nonhuman animals – has moral claims of its own. A common theme in recent environmentalism is that nature deserves respect for its own sake – and perhaps even has rights of its own. If such respect for nature were accepted by the human rights movement, the rights of nature would then have to be balanced against the rights of humans. This possibility is a challenging prospect to many advocates of human rights since it calls into question not only the assumption that right holders have to be autonomous agents, but also the assumption that all moral duties are

directly or indirectly duties to humans. Whether these assumptions should be abandoned involves hard questions that won't be settled for a long time, either in philosophy or in popular beliefs. Although it will be difficult for the human rights movement to recognize powerful moral claims made on behalf of nature and balanced against human rights, theorists of human rights need to begin addressing these questions. Moreover, human rights activists – and particularly those who are opposed to population control measures – need to begin worrying about the costs to nature of respecting the rights of billions of humans.

II Human Rights and Environmentalism

In this section, we argue that the environmental movement, particularly in Brazil and countries like it,[7] has good reasons for adding concern for four areas of rights to its permanent agenda. Our overall approach is to try to show that some of the threats to human dignity, freedom, justice, and welfare, which the human rights movement takes seriously, are also threats to the goals or to the activities of the environmental movement. When these threats are shared, joint or similar responses are possible. In each case, we specify the threat and explain why it threatens a goal or method of environmentalism.

(1) *Rights against murder, violence, and arbitrary arrest that allow people to exercise their rights to express their views, protest, and engage in politics.* The murder of Chico Mendes in 1988 made it clear that opponents of environmental activists sometimes use violence to try to stop the activism they oppose.[8] In the Mendes case, the opponents were private parties, but governments also sometimes try to suppress environmental activists by threatening them with imprisonment or death.[9] Several traditional human rights are relevant to such threats. First, rights to life and liberty protect against extrajudicial execution, torture, and incarceration. Second, political rights such as freedom of speech, freedom of peaceful assembly, and freedom of political participation protect the rights of environmental activists to pursue their goals through political activism.

If environmental activists enjoyed effective protection of these rights, they would be able to defend their interests through legal and political means. For example, rubber tappers would not have to fear violence and death as the consequence of organizing and demonstrating to protect their traditional landholdings. The result of this change would be that attempts to appropriate these lands and turn them into cattle ranches would frequently be blocked. Extractive reserves and other forms of holdings for forest gatherers would have better chances of being created and protected.

The threat to human rights here is that landowners, or others who find their interests thwarted by people protesting and organizing on behalf of environmental preservation or the creation of extractive reserves, may hire gunmen to stop the protesting and organizing. Human rights against murder, violence, and torture, to free speech and press, and to engage in political activities protect against this kind of threat. Environmentalists need to be able to use the political arena to advance their ideas and programs. Hence, the environmental movement has good reason to incorporate permanently a commitment to people's human rights to protest, organize, and take political action on behalf of environmental causes. These rights need to be protected both against government agencies, who may attempt to jail the opponents of their policies, and against private parties who threaten with violence and death environmentalists who threaten their economic and political interests.

Brazilian environmentalists, who emerged under an authoritarian political regime, have been keenly aware of their vulnerability to violence and suppression, and hence emphasize the importance of promoting freedoms to speak, publish, protest, and engage in political activity.[10] The movements opposing the proposed Sao Paulo airport at Sete Quedas and opposing nuclear power in Brazil, for example, had a strong free speech aspect.

(2) *The rule of law.* The international human rights movement has put a lot of emphasis on the rule of law and on due process of law. It has been concerned that in the absence of a strong system of legal order and guarantees of fair trials, government officials and other powerful individuals are likely to be able to abuse governmental and legal powers to enrich themselves and to disadvantage or destroy their opponents. An effectively implemented system of legal order, including rights to

due process of law, allows disputes to be arbitrated in the courts by fair means rather than resolved by force and violence. The dangers that exist in the absence of the rule of law are threats not just to human rights but also to the values and methods of the environmental movement. Hence, the environmental movement has good reason for making concern for creating and maintaining the rule of law one of the standing concerns of its agenda.

An effective system of rule of law and due process in northern Brazil would block some of the means used by ranchers and developers to acquire large landholdings that are often burned and cleared. Like many parts of the American frontier in the nineteenth century, many parts of Amazonia are somewhat lawless. As a result, individuals are often vulnerable to crimes and other violations of their rights without legal redress; property titles are often unclear and are often "established" by force rather than by legal decision; and individuals who are taken into police custody are not assured of due process of law. Furthermore, the Amazon region is so large and travel is so arduous that law enforcement is extremely difficult. With regard to forest burning, this problem has been partially overcome by the use of satellite sensing and helicopter visits to burned areas by federal police. However, in general, getting the police to deal with serious violations of law is impeded by limited communications facilities and the lack of roads and other means of fast transport.

Absent rule of law, landowners and speculators are sometimes able to manipulate legal titles to their own advantage and are often able to ignore the legal claims to title of poor families who have resided and worked on the land for decades. The territories of Indian groups are vulnerable to invasion and are seldom defended effectively by local authorities. More broadly, environmentalists have pioneered systems for the legal regulation of pollution and land use that can only succeed when law is respected and generally enforced.

Brazilian environmentalists have not traditionally had much faith in law as a mechanism for environmental reform. Furthermore, they have tended to emphasize substantive rather than procedural rights. Nevertheless, over the long term, fuller realization of the rule of law and more emphasis on using suits initiated by environmental organizations to combat environmental problems will be essential to success in environmental protection. Some progress was made with the 1985 passage of a law for the "protection of diffuse interests." This law allows citizens and environmental organizations to sue polluters without risk of having to pay costs or penalties if their complaint is not successful. Most Brazilian environmental organizations, however, have not made much use of this law or the tactic of using lawsuits to initiate environmental change.

(3) *Indigenous peoples.* We remarked earlier that one point of agreement between the environmental and the human rights movements is that indigenous peoples should be allowed to survive and retain their cultures. Both of these movements are opposed to crowding out indigenous peoples and depriving them of their lands, even when doing so is thought to be a way of promoting economic development or better opportunities for the urban poor. Human rights advocates insist on the rights of indigenous peoples because they believe that these peoples have the same basic human rights to life and liberty as all other people, and that they are especially vulnerable to being killed, having their health destroyed, being put in a position where there traditional life styles are impossible, and being robbed of their lands. Environmentalists admire indigenous peoples because they live close to nature. They view the Indians of North and South America as having life styles that are models for sustainable use of natural resources and as being repositories of knowledge about nature that modern science may not have. Furthermore, reserves for Indians in Brazil are places where the forest is likely to be preserved rather than destroyed.

(4) *The right to education.* Ignorance that involves limited ability to read, count, understand natural processes such as the transmission of disease, and understand political issues and candidates is a barrier to the success of both the human rights movement and the environmental movement.

Ignorance is a barrier to the realization of human rights because uneducated people often lack knowledge of what rights they have and how to act to defend them. Ignorance is a barrier to environmental progress because uneducated people often lack knowledge of environmental problems and issues, how to avoid toxic substances, and how to live in ways that promote health.

The human rights movement has addressed these issues by declaring a universal human right to education. An effectively implemented right to education will require governments to make educational opportunities available to children and adults so that they can become literate, numerate, aware of their rights and duties, knowledgeable about health and nutrition, and aware of environmental concerns.

Free public education for the children of the lower classes in Brazil is often unavailable, and when it is available, it is often of very poor quality. The Brazilian environmental movement has emphasized the importance of environmental education, but hasn't addressed the issue of education more generally. Our contention is that those concerned with environmental protection in the Third World have good reason to include in their agenda a standing concern with the right to education.

(5) *Nutrition and social justice concerns.* Hunger and lack of the other necessities of life is an indignity, especially in such countries as Brazil, which have great wealth and natural resources. It is also harmful to many aspects of people's welfare, and makes it much less likely that its victims will succeed in becoming educated, knowledgeable about their rights, and prepared to take action to defend them. For these reasons and others, the international human rights movement has included the right to an adequate standard of living on nearly all of its list of rights.

There are at least two reasons why hunger and lack of the necessities of life are also threats to the values and methods of environmentalists.[11] One is that hungry children do not do well in school and are likely to drop out of school. Thus, the right to education is unlikely to be fully realized without taking steps to eliminate hunger. The second reason is that hunger and lack of the necessities of life makes people desperate and willing to degrade the environment.[12]

Immigration from the south and northeast of Brazil contributes substantially to devastation in the Amazon. The modernization of agriculture in the south has left many agricultural workers without jobs. People come to Amazon looking for a better deal, a chance to acquire some land. More effective programs to provide education, housing, and jobs to the poor would help reduce these problems. However, major expenditures in these areas are probably beyond the financial and institutional resources of the Brazilian government today, and there is real danger that large-scale programs of job creation or land distribution in Brazil will cause significant environmental problems of their own.

(6) *The international implementation model.* So far in this section, we have been concerned with particular substantive rights. Nevertheless, the environmental movement could also profitably adopt the implementation model used for international human rights. It is not a new idea,[13] but it is worth describing briefly in this context. First, environmentalists may find it useful to create a prominent international declaration of environmental norms analogous to the *Universal Declaration of Human Rights*. Second, after such an international declaration of a nonbinding nature is widely accepted, attempts can be made to embody the general environmental duties that it declares in multinational treaties, including implementation procedures such as standing committees within international organizations to encourage compliance and offer technical assistance, mandatory reports from states on their compliance with these duties and their implementation within domestic law, the investigation of complaints about the violation of these duties, and political pressure on states found to be in violation to make them change their practices and compensate victims. The development of such a system within the United Nations is currently underway.

III Conclusion

We have suggested that there is a lot of common ground between the environmental and human rights movements. Human rights need to be "greened," and trying to do so will mean looking closely at the links between development models, poverty and inequality, rights violations, and environmental degradation. On the other side, environmentalists have good reasons for endorsing a wide range of human rights. The success of their endeavors partially depends on the realization of certain human rights. This interconnection is not necessarily good news in such countries as Brazil, however, since it means that the success of environmental preservation requires more work, broader agendas, and greater costs. Creating effective rule of law all areas and improving nutrition and education will not be cheap or easy. Nevertheless, environmental and human rights issues cannot and should not be sharply separated.

Notes

1 When we speak of human rights, we have in mind the sorts of universal rights found in the *Universal Declaration of Human Rights* (1948) and other contemporary human rights documents. These rights are not the abstract rights of Locke and Jefferson (life, liberty, and something or other), but are rather more numerous and specific rights that address contemporary political and economic problems. They are responses to social and political abuses in particular areas. We take human rights to include: (1) rights of individual liberty, privacy, and autonomy such as the right to freedom of religion or the right to travel; (2) due process rights such as the right to a fair trial; (3) political rights such as the rights to assemble, protest and vote; (4) equality rights such as the rights to equality before the law and to freedom from discrimination; and (5) welfare rights such as the rights to adequate nutrition and to education. See James W. Nickel, *Making Sense of Human Rights* (Berkeley: University of California Press, 1987).

2 Melissa Thorme, "Establishing Environment as a Human Right," *Denver Journal of International Law and Policy* 19 (1991): 301.

3 James W. Nickel, "The Human Right to a Safe Environment," *Yale Journal of International Law* 18 (1993): 281–95.

4 The texts of such clauses can be found in Edith Brown Weiss, *In Fairness to Future Generations* (Dobbs Ferry, NY: Transnational Publishers 1989), p. 297. Although efforts to introduce a U.S. constitutional amendment creating a right to a safe environment have failed (for a proposed amendment see H. R. J. Res. 1205, 91st Cong., 2nd Sess. [1970]), the preamble of the U.S. National Environmental Policy Act (1970) sets the goal of assuring "for all Americans safe, healthful, productive, and esthetically and culturally pleasing surroundings."

5 The texts of these documents are available in Brownlie, *Basic Documents on Human Rights*, 2nd edn. (New York: Oxford University Press, 1981).

6 *Earth Summit Agenda 21: The United Nations Programme of Action from Rio* (New York: United Nations, 1992). See also Edward A. Parson, Peter M. Haas, and Marc A. Levy, "A Summary of the Major Documents Signed at the Earth Summit and the Global Forum," *Environment* 34 (October 1992): 12.

7 The twenty year history of the Brazilian environmental movement can be divided into two periods: a formative one (1971–86) oriented toward creating public awareness of environmental deterioration and a recent period (1987 on) oriented toward linking issues of environmental protection with sustainable economic development and emphasizing the creation of effective environmental organizations. Most of the

activities of Brazilian environmental groups in the formative period had a local focus, but there were some battles with a regional or national profile. In recent years the environmental movement has shown signs of increasing political maturity. The number of environmental groups grew from around four hundred in 1985 to around nine hundred in 1991. More importantly, environmental organizations came into being in areas other than the highly developed southern provinces, particularly the Northeast, Amazonia, and the Central-West region.

8 See Andrew Revkin, *The Burning Season: The Murder of Chico Mendes and the Fight for the Amazon Rain Forest* (Boston: Houghton Mifflin, 1990); Adrian Cowell, *The Decade of Destruction* (New York: Henry Holt, 1990).

9 See "Endangered Species: No, Not Owls or Elephants. Humans Who Fight to Save the Planet are Putting their Lives on the Line," *Time*, 27 April 1992, pp. 48–50. See also, "What Some Preach in Rio is Not What They Practice at Home," *New York Times*, 15 June 1992.

10 Brazil was under military rule from 1964 until 1986, and political oppression was severe between 1968 and 1976. This oppression involved suppression of political activity, censorship, arbitrary arrest, torture, murder, and disappearances. Constitutional democracy was restored in the mid-1980s, but severe human rights problems continue to exist. These include: (1) police torture and brutality, and murders committed by death squads ("urban violence"); (2) killings organized by landowners in conflicts over land in rural areas ("rural violence"); (3) killing and mistreatment of indigenous peoples; (4) violence against women; and (5) inadequate nu-

trition and education for more than half of the population. (The second most frequently occurs in the north of Brazil, particularly in areas where the presence of the state is weak or corrupt.) See Amnesty International, *Brazil: Torture and extrajudicial execution in urban Brazil* (New York: Amnesty International, 1990); *Brazil: Authorized Violence in Rural Areas.* (London: Amnesty International, 1988); *Brazil: Cases of Killings and Ill-Treatment of Indigenous People* (New York: Amnesty International, 1988).

11 Social equity and economic growth are matters that cannot be ignored by environmental movements in the Third World. In regard to social equity, the Brazilian environmental movement underwent a significant change between 1971 and 1986. In the early 1970s environmentalists did not have any impact on the popular sectors because they did not link their efforts with environmental and social crises. However, from the late 1970s on the environmental movement was strongly influenced by radical democratic ideas coming from the social movements that were struggling against the authoritarian regime. By 1986 many environmental activists had finally realized that building links with popular sectors was a crucial task.

12 Since the mid-1980s there has been a remarkable development in Brazil of what we might call "socio-environmentalism," in which social movements (that often have close ties to the Catholic Church) and labor unions have incorporated environmental concerns into their agendas and activities.

13 See *The World Charter for Nature* adopted by the United Nations General Assembly, 9 November 1982, UN Document A/37/51 (1982). See also Weiss, *In Fairness to Future Generations.*

37

Environmental Justice: An Environmental Civil Rights Value Acceptable to All World Views

Troy W. Hartley

History of the Environmental Justice Movement

Although the academic and civil rights communities first identified inequities in environmental protection in the 1970s,[1] it was an incident in 1982 that propelled environmental injustice, sometimes called environmental racism, into the public purview.[2] In 1982, in Warren County, North Carolina, a community mobilized in opposition to a proposed landfill for polychlorinated biphenyls (PCB) contaminated soils. Opposition forced the governor into weighing in on the decision. The governor selected the community of Afton for the landfill. Racial concerns were expressed by civil rights leaders. Afton was eighty-four percent black, while Warren County was sixty-four percent black and the state twenty-four percent black. In addition, technical and scientific communities in academia and government had previously expressed concerns about the Afton site. The water table was only five to ten feet below the surface and, like the majority of rural communities in America,[3] Afton residents relied on wells for their drinking water. Any significant release from the landfill could easily contaminate the groundwater aquifer, and as a result, expose the entire population of Afton to contaminants.[4] Grass-roots opposition followed the governor's decision and the movement took on the atmosphere of a civil rights campaign. During nonviolent civil disobedience over 400 people were arrested.[5]

Later in 1982, due in part to the Afton siting controversy, the District of Columbia's Congressional Delegate, Walter Fauntroy, called on the General Accounting Office (GAO) to investigate siting practices for hazardous waste landfills in EPA Region IV.[6] GAO found that while blacks represented twenty percent of Region IV's population, in communities surrounding three of the four commercial landfills in Region IV, blacks comprised more than fifty percent of the population.[7]

In 1986, the United Church of Christ sponsored a statistical assessment of the relationship between the location of hazardous waste sites and the racial and socioeconomic characteristics of the communities surrounding the sites. The analysis evaluated several racial and socioeconomic variables: race; mean household income; land values; historical land use; and proximity to waste generators. The report concluded that race was the most significant variable in determining the location of a commercial hazardous waste facility. Although mean household income was also statistically significant, there was a stronger correlation between race and commercial landfill location than exists between income and location.[8]

Throughout the 1980s a growing number of researchers in the academic community examined the problems of environmental injustices. Robert Bullard, a sociologist at the University of California at Riverside, is one of the leaders in this field. Bullard's book, *Dumping in Dixie*, examines how black residents in five southern communities addressed waste facilities in their neighborhoods.[9] Academic research in the 1980s helped placed environmental justice onto the political agenda. Nevertheless, Mohai and Bryant cited nine studies in the 1970s that identified inequities from air and hazardous waste pollution.[10] These earlier assessments generated little political momentum, despite the fact that eight of the nine demonstrated an inequitable distribution of pollution by race. Five of the eight that assess race relative to income for its correlation to pollution concluded that race was a more significant indicator than income.[11] Further research in the 1980s included other forms of inequities (for example, Hispanic farm workers and pesticide exposure; Native Americans and radiation or contaminated fish exposure) and the susceptibility of minority or low-income populations to risk.[12]

The academic and civil rights communities held a "Conference on Race and the Incidence of Environmental Hazards" at the University of Michigan in January 1990. Several academics and civil rights leaders presented papers, including one by Bullard on environmental blackmail.[13] A group of the presenters called the "Michigan Coalition" wrote to several government agencies, including the EPA, the Department of Health and Human Services, the White House's Council on Environmental Quality, and select members of the U.S. Congress, particularly the Congressional Black Caucus. The "Michigan Coalition" called for action on environmental injustices in minority and low-income communities.[14]

In July 1990, former EPA Administrator William K. Reilly established an Environmental Equity Workgroup to assess the problems of environmental injustice and make recommendations based on their findings. The workgroup concluded in July 1992 that there was a lack of data on equity and the environment because the EPA had not historically collected racial and socioeconomic data along with environment data. Nevertheless, the EPA concluded that the available data demonstrated disturbing trends. Concurrent with efforts to reverse the inequity trends, the workgroup called on the EPA to gather racial and socioeconomic data and incorporate it into risk assessments and risk management decisions. Other recommendations included an increased effort to identify high risk populations and target activities to reduce their environmental risks, promote the use of equity considerations in the rule-making process as well as all agency permit, grant, and compliance monitoring and enforcement procedures. The workgroup called for improved communication with minority and low-income communities and increased participation by these communities in the decision-making process. Lastly, the group concluded that the agency needed to address equity in its long-term strategic planning.[15]

By October 1991, at the first international conference on environmental justice, it was clear that environmental justice was squarely on the social and environmental agenda.[16] A union of social movements had occurred. Civil rights and environmental concerns were merged, despite the fact that the two had actually rejected each other for over twenty years.[17] The ethical considerations of such a union focuses on an area of environmental ethics that has lacked attention – that is, the distribution of environmental benefits among segments of society. Nevertheless, in the discussion below, I seek to demonstrate that environmental justice exists within the traditional ethical doctrines of Kant's rights and obligations.

Ethical Models and World Views

It is helpful to start with a brief discussion of hedonistic utilitarianism, Kantian rights and obligations, and Rawls' veil of ignorance to appreciate the world views that originate from these ethical models. World views guide and help persons understand the world, including environmental perspectives. Within this ethical structure, how does environmental justice fit in? In this discussion, my aim is to explain environmental justice as a fundamental value axiom that exists in all environmental world views, with the possible exception of hedonistic utilitarianism.

Utilitarian doctrine

Hedonistic, or narrow, utilitarianism bases moral utility on the principles of greatest happiness. Actions are morally right if they promote happiness (or pleasure) and wrong if they don't. All things desirable are desirable because there is inherent pleasure in them or they promote pleasure and avoid pain.[18] A conflict can arise between utility and justice when a discriminatory society produces a higher level of net happiness than a nondiscriminatory society.[19] It is this conflict that produced an environmental justice movement within the civil rights, minority, and low-income communities and challenges the traditional economic analysis of Mill's utilitarianism.

Within mainstream economic principles, the potential compensation criterion assesses the gains to a segment of society relative to the losses to another segment of society. If the gains outweigh the losses, then the action is beneficial to society. In theory, the winners could compensate the losers and society would still be ahead. In practice, compensation rarely occurs.[20]

Environmental justice rejects an assumption of the potential compensation criterion. The substitutability assumption states that individuals, knowing their preferences, can substitute one set of preferences for others.[21] That is, for low-income or minority communities, the preference for economic gains from the siting of polluting industry and jobs in their neighborhoods can be substituted for public health gained from a safer environment. The environmental justice movement and particularly Bullard's environmental blackmail concept challenges this traditionally held economic principle. Consistent with Taylor's view that utility and justice are incompatible,[22] the environmental blackmail concept questions whether it is just to subject minority or low-income communities to polluting industries at any level of compensation. One could still argue from a utilitarian viewpoint that jobs in highly polluting industries are often low paying. If the jobs paid more (that is, higher compensation), the community would be willing to put up with the pollution and reduced public health in exchange for greater economic wealth. To assess this presumption, it is helpful to review a siting example from upper New York state.

Residents of Yorkshire, a rural, low-income community of 3,850 people in upstate New York (not a predominantly minority community), rejected Browning Ferris Industries' plan to build a regional landfill for nontoxic wastes. BFI had offered the community an economic development package worth more than $1 million per year. The economic incentive package included the following promises: up to 100 jobs in a town that had been impacted by three recent plant closings; $1.6 million in annual fees to the city, which was enough to cut local taxes by three-quarters for the average family; $100 million in construc-

tion expenditures; and $1.15 million in annual grants to promote long-term economic development in Yorkshire (Yorkshire's annual town budget was only $810,000). During negotiations with the community, BFI offered local officials the authority to determine the source and type of wastes the landfill could accept. Nevertheless, seventy percent of Yorkshire's registered voters signed a petition opposing the landfill, and the town board voted unanimously to reject BFI's proposal.[23]

The potential compensation criterion assumes that a level of compensation (jobs and economic development assistance) can be found that is acceptable to the losers. The Yorkshire example challenges this assumption because an acceptable level of compensation could not be found. Bacow and Milkey came to a similar conclusion while assessing Massachusetts' efforts to overcome local opposition to hazardous waste facilities.[24] They asserted that past compensation experience reveals the social costs of hazardous waste facilities to be uncompensable.[25] The environmental justice movement would probably agree that the level of environmental degradation and reduced public health in minority and low-income communities is monetarily uncompensable.

Even if a utilitarian accepted an unequal distribution of environmental quality, doing so would not constitute an acceptance of unequal environmental protection under socially acceptable laws. The potential compensation criterion enables economists to justify an unequal distribution of environmental quality. The community with lower quality trades that quality for other preferred goods or is compensated in some other manner.[26] However, if socially acceptable rules constrained the economic system, the utilitarian would support the application and enforcement of those rules in an equitable manner.[27] For example, economists often site clearly defined and enforced property rights as a mechanism to address environmental problems.[28] Utilitarians would not support the inequitable enforcement of property rights, particularly because it could give one party an unfair economic advantage over another.

Kantian rights and obligations

Under a Kantian view, to have moral worth an action must be performed as a duty even to the detriment of one's inclinations.[29] Kantian ethics requires that actions not be aimed at any specific ends (for example, one's own inclination or utilitarian gains). Instead, moral action should be based on a principle or a moral rule.[30] To be a moral rule, the rule must be a categorical imperative. There are three formulations of the categorical imperative: (1) for a rule to be a moral law, it must be a universal law, legislatively valid for everyone; (2) the rule must treat all human beings as an ends and never merely as a means to an end; and (3) a person must recognize the rule as binding upon him or her, and thus, the person must act as if he or she is a member of an organized society of ends.[31] Kant held that through reason we know the categorical imperative to be true.[32] The environmental justice movement would, most likely, view a safe environment for all, low- or high-income and white or minority communities, as a moral law, satisfying the three formulations of a categorical imperative, and based on reason.

The Kantian aspects of the environmental justice movement are best demonstrated through the thoughts of some of its academic and political leaders. Bullard views environmental concerns as issues of equity and social justice as well as an issue of public health.[33] Bunyan Bryant and Paul Mohai of the University of Michigan consider environmental justice in terms of a "safe and clean environment as a basic right for all, regardless of race or color."[34] That is, a safe, clean environment is a fundamental human right, a moral law. Dorcetta Taylor, formerly of Yale University and now with the University of Michigan, has also noted that minorities participate in the environmental justice movement because it is based on principles of fairness and justice with a strong emphasis on civil rights and social justice.[35] The Environmental Justice Transition Group recommended to the Clinton administration's transition team that an environmental justice model be established that includes "a framework of equal justice and equal protection . . . to ensure every citizen's right to be free from pollution."[36] This approach need not go beyond an anthropocentric philosophy that views the environment as instrumentally valuable for human health reasons. The Kantian view of environmental justice has allowed the environmental justice movement to challenge the reductionist, utilitarian approach to environmental decision making without embracing more controversial, nonanthropocentric principles.

Rawls' veil of ignorance

John Rawls developed a process to establish just rules. Norton characterizes Rawls' philosophical model as a tool to reach a "reflective equilibrium" between a theory of justice and intuition.[37] Rawls' approach asks individuals familiar with social principles to reach consensus on a set of guiding principles for society to distribute gains and losses. Rawls places these individuals behind a veil of ignorance by omitting specific information, such as, the individual's own abilities, history, position in the imaginary society, and the time and place of that society. Because, Rawls holds, each individual may approach the problem from a viewpoint of self-interest and attempt to maximize his or her own gains, the participants behind the veil of ignorance are not told where they will end up in this society, thereby providing them with incentives to establish just principles that are fair to society's subordinate persons, just in case they turn out to be in that position themselves. In this way, the veil of ignorance serves the interests of all segments of society equally.[38]

Application of Rawls' hypothetical social contract to the burden of environmental risks helps identify environmental justice, for it is to the interest of all participants to apply equality at all levels of environmental risks and public health. The only exceptions are those individuals willing to gamble during Rawls' exercise. That is, if the disparity in wealth between one segment of society and another is great enough and creating that disparity causes lower environmental quality in minority or poorer areas, then some individuals may gamble in hopes that they are placed in the wealthier, nonminority areas. If such gambling occurs, Rawls' social contract fails to establish rules to provide an equitable burden of environmental risks.[39]

World views and environmental policy

Based on the principles of narrow utilitarianism, Kantian rights and obligations, or Rawls' veil of ignorance, world views characterize the application of ethical principles to the world, including environmental issues. Norton defines *world view* as a "constellation of beliefs, values, and concepts that give shape and meaning to the world a person experiences and acts within."[40] World views are not necessarily a complete philosophical belief in and of themselves; rather, they are an association of fundamental assumptions that are used to comprehend and act in the world. Central principles, or value axioms, are an underpinning of these assumptions and world views.

Although there is an emerging scientific consensus about environmental concerns, this consensus has not resulted in fewer environmental world views. Norton has identified and summarized seven: (1) Judeo-Christian stewardship; (2) deep ecology and related value systems; (3) transformationist/transcendentalism; (4) constrained economics; (5) scientific naturalism; (6) ecofeminism; and (7) pluralism/pragmatism.[41] None of these world views explicitly addresses the equitable distribution of environmental quality. Further, there are values or value axioms within these world views that conflict with justice, or a fair distribution of environmental quality. However, that fact alone does not defeat the argument that all world views can accept environmental justice. To the contrary, vastly different value axioms can coexist within a single world view or among several different environmental world views.[42]

While both Taylor and Raphael acknowledge a degree of incompatibility between utility and justice, they conclude that justice is a fundamental moral principle. An ethical system is inadequate if it cannot demonstrate a moral basis for justice.[43] From a purely Kantian perspective, justice is elemental to a moral community.[44] Justice is the most basic of social virtues and is needed as a basis for social ethics.[45] Many of the environmental world views are aligned with Kantian rights and obligations, and as a result have the social virtue of justice as a common denominator. Thus, there is no reason why each Kantian-derived environmental world view could not endorse environmental justice.

While the argument is a bit more difficult to make for environmental world views derived from hedonistic utilitarianism, the hypothesis still holds. For example, while not accepting an equal distribution of environmental quality, an advocate of a hedonistic utilitarian view or a constrained economic world view would accept equal application of the socially acceptable rules that protect

citizens from environmental risks.[46] The distinction made here between equal environmental quality and equal environmental protection under socially acceptable laws is crucial to the argument that all world views can accept environmental justice. If environmental justice is defined as equal environmental quality, then narrow utilitarianism cannot accept environmental justice. However, if environmental justice is equal environmental protection under the law, then utilitarianism more easily embraces it.[47] Nevertheless, independent of whether the argument presented here – that all world views can accept environmental justice – has been convincing or not, justice is conspicuously absent from the discussion of environmental ethics and world views.[48]

Incorporation of environmental justice into environmental policy appears more complicated than the acceptance of justice as part of environmental world views. What does it take to ensure that all citizens bear an equal environmental risk, or at least, that no single community shoulders more than a socially acceptable, minimum level of risk? Ensuring equal protection under current environmental laws and regulations will not necessarily result in an equal or an acceptable minimum level of environmental quality, particularly given that the laws themselves may contain inherent discrimination, whether intended or not. Throughout this discussion, equal protection has been defined as applying to and enforcing environmental laws equally regardless of the racial, ethnic, or socioeconomic characteristics of the surrounding community. The environmental justice movement argues that this definition is an inadequate view of equal protection, since disadvantaged communities start from a lower health standard than white communities.[49] Consequently, the environmental risks are compounded by the lower health standards and the impact of the same level of risk on the disadvantaged community is greater than on other communities. As a result, in order to ensure an equal or socially acceptable level of environmental quality, environmental protection, as defined above, must be applied unequally. Within the current statutory authority, it may not be possible to apply environmental protection in a sufficiently unequal manner to ensure an equal or socially acceptable level of environmental quality. These are the contentious policy issues of environmental justice that must be addressed by environmental policy makers.[50]

Conclusion

While environmental justice challenges narrow utilitarian views and promotes Kantian rights and obligations, the underpinnings of an environmental justice value axiom exists in all world views. Environmental justice does not present novel ideas to environmental ethics or world views, although it does present a distributional value axiom that is not prominent in the environmental ethics discussion. An effective environmental justice movement is forcing environmental inequities onto the policy agenda, and, as a result, environmental ethics too must discuss environmental justice.

Notes

1 In a report submitted to the Clinton administration's transition team, the Environmental Justice Transition Group described the environmental justice movement as "the confluence of three of America's greatest challenges: the struggle against racism and poverty; the effort to preserve and improve the environment; and the compelling need to shift social institutions from class division and environmental depletion to social unity and global sustainability." See Environmental Justice Transition Group, *Recommendations to the Presidential Transition Team for the U.S. Environmental Protection Agency on Environmental Justice Issues Submitted by the Environmental Justice Transition Group* (Washington, DC: The Lawyers' Committee for Civil Rights Under Law, 1992), p. 1. The Environmental Justice Transition Group was composed of several environmental justice organizations: Earth Island Institute; Gold Coast Tenants Organization; Indigenous Environmental Network; Lawyers' Committee for Civil Rights Under Law; Native Action; Southern Organizing Committee for Economic and Social Justice; Southwest Network for Environmental and Economic Justice; Southwest Organizing Project; and the United Church of Christ.

2 The United Church of Christ's Commission for Racial Justice accepts the following definition of racism: "Racism is racial prejudice plus power. Racism is the intentional or unintentional use of power to isolate, separate and exploit others. This use of power is based on a belief in superior racial origin, identity or supposed racial characteristics. Racism confers certain privileges on and defends the dominant group, which in turn sustains and perpetuates racism. Both consciously and unconsciously, racism is enforced and maintained by the legal, cul-

tural, religious, educational, economic, political, environmental and military institutions of societies. Racism is more than just a personal attitude; it is the institutionalized form of that attitude." See United Church of Christ, Commission for Racial Justice, *Toxic Wastes and Race in the United States: A National Report on the Racial and Socio-Economic Characteristics of Communities with Hazardous Waste Sites* (New York: United Church of Christ, 1987), p. ix. Feagin and Feagin define discrimination as "actions or practices carried out by dominant groups or their representatives, which have a differential and negative impact on members of subordinate groups." See J. R. Feagin and C. B. Feagin, *Discrimination American Style: Institutional Racism and Sexism*, 2nd augmented edn. (Malabar: R.E. Krieger Publishing, 1986), pp. 20–1. Freudian and cognitive psychology are often cited in discussions that distinguish unconscious racism from conscious, discriminatory actions. Racial prejudice within Freudian psychoanalytical theory is an attitude toward different groups that avoids a logical, reasoned reality test (Ego), not simply because it would take too much mental effort to conduct the reality check, but because the attitude itself fulfills a specific irrational function for the person. In psychoanalytical theory, racism is viewed as irrational because the secondary process (the Ego) – that is, reason – fails to control the primary process (the Id) – that is, desires, wishes, and instincts for pleasure. See M. Jahoda, *Race Relations and Mental Health* (New York: UNESCO, 1960), cited in Charles R. Lawrence III, "The Id, the Ego, and Equal Protection: Reckoning with Unconscious Racism," *Stanford Law Review* 39 (1987): 317–88.

3 Clean Sites, Inc., *Hazardous Waste Sites and the Rural Poor: A Preliminary Assessment* (Alexandria: Clean Sites, 1990), p. iv.

4 Populations are subject to greater risk (1) when exposure to the threat increases and (2) when there is higher biological susceptibility to the threat within the population. See Ken Sexton, "Cause for Immediate Concern: Minorities and the Poor Clearly Are More Exposed," *EPA Journal* 18 (1992): 38–9. For example, children have a higher biological susceptibility to detrimental health effects from lead exposure than adults. See Joel Schwartz and Ronnie Levin, "Lead: Example of the Job Ahead; Inner City Children Suffer Most," *EPA Journal* 18 (1992): 42–4.

5 HAZMED, *Final Report: Environmental Equity* (Silver Spring: Hazardous and Medical Waste Services, Inc., 1991), p. 2. This report was produced by a contractor for the EPA Environmental Equity Workgroup.

6 EPA Region IV is comprised of eight southern states: Alabama, Florida, Georgia, Kentucky, Mississippi;

North Carolina, South Carolina, and Tennessee. The EPA's regulations restrict the location of hazardous waste facilities and units, prohibiting sites on 100-year flood plans, areas of seismic activities, and locations with salt dome or bed formations, underground mines or caves. (See 40 Code of Federal Regulations, para. 264.18 and para. 265.18.) Further restrictions on acceptable locations for hazardous waste facilities are sometimes included in local land-use rules and decisions. The environmental justice movement has been critical of the EPA for not using its statutory authority more broadly to include socioeconomic variables in location standards, while the EPA has viewed the issue as predominantly a local land-use decision regulated by state and local government. (Personal communication, Karen Bergman, Office of Solid Waste and Emergency Response, U.S. Environmental Protection Agency, June 1993.)

7 HAZMED, *Final Report*, p. 23.
8 United Church of Christ, Commission for Racial Justice, *Toxic Wastes and Race in the United States: A National Report on the Racial and Socio-Economic Characteristics of Communities with Hazardous Waste Sites* (New York: United Church of Christ, 1987).
9 Robert Bullard, *Dumping in Dixie: Race, Class and Environmental Quality* (Boulder: Westview Press, 1990).
10 Paul Mohai and Bunyan Bryant, "Race, Poverty, and the Environment: The Disadvantaged Face Greater Risks," *EPA Journal* 18 (1992): 6–8. For examples cited by Mohai and Bryant, see Susan C. Cutter, "Community Concern: Social and Environmental Influences," *Environment and Behavior* 13 (1981): 105–24; Philip J. Landrigan and Richard L. Gross, "Chemical Wastes: Illegal Hazards and Legal Remedies," *American Journal of Public Health*, 71 (1981): 985–7; and Julian McCaull, "Discriminatory Air Pollution: If Poor, Don't Breathe," *Environment* 18 (1976): 26–31. For other examples, see J. E. Anderson, "U.S. Population Distribution and the Location of Hazardous Waste Sites," presented at the Population Association of America Annual Meeting (1986); P. Asch and J. J. Seneca, "Some Evidence on the Distribution of Air Quality," *Land Economics* 54 (1978): 278–97; B. J. Berry, *The Social Burdens of Environmental Pollution* (Cambridge: Ballinger Publishing, 1977); Robert Bullard, "Solid Waste Sites and the Black Houston Community," *Sociological Inquiry* 53 (1983): 273–88; Robert Bullard and Beverly H. Wright, "Endangered Environs: Dumping Grounds in a Sunbelt City," *Urban Resources* 2 (1985): 5–10; A. Myrick Freeman III, "The Distribution of Environmental Quality," ed. A. V. Kneese and R. M. Bower, *Environmental Quality Analysis* (Baltimore: Resources for the Future, 1972); L. P. Gianessi, H. P. Peskin, and

E. Wolf, "The Distributional Implications of National Air Pollution Damage Estimates," ed. F. T. Juster, *The Distribution of Economic Well-Being* (Cambridge: Ballinger Publishing, 1977); L. P. Gianessi, H. P. Peskin, and E. Wolf, "The Distributional Effects of Uniform Air Pollution Policy in the U.S.," *Quarterly Journal of Economics* May (1979): 281–301, F. Handy, "Income and Air Quality in Hamilton, Ontario," *Alternatives* 6 (1977): 18–24; and W. J. Kruvant, "People, Energy, and Pollution," ed. D. K. Newman and D. Days, *The American Energy Consumer* (Cambridge: Ballinger Publishing, 1976).

11 Ibid., p. 8.
12 For discussions of further research, see articles by Cynthia H. Harris and Robert C. Williams, "Research Directions: The Public Health Service Looks at Hazards to Minorities," *EPA Journal* 18 (1992): 40–1; Ivette Perfecto and Baldemar Velasqueo, "Farm Workers: Among the Least Protected; They Suffer the Most from Pesticides," ibid., pp. 13–14; Ken Sexton, "Cause for Immediate Concern: Minorities and the Poor Clearly Are More Exposed," ibid., pp. 38–9; D. R. Wernette and L. A. Nieves, "Breathing Polluted Air: Minorities are Disproportionately Exposed," ibid., pp. 16–17; and Patrick C. West, "Health Concerns for Fish-Eating Tribes? Government Assumptions Are Much Too Low," ibid., pp. 15–16.
13 The concept of environmental blackmail involves the public health price paid by communities that accept highly polluting industries in their neighborhoods in exchange for jobs and short-term economic gains. It challenges the belief that jobs are more important and of greater worth than public health. See Robert Bullard, "Environmental Blackmail in Minority Communities," in Bunyan Bryant and Paul Mohai, eds., *Race and the Incidence of Environmental Hazards: A Time for Discourse* (Boulder: Westview Press, 1992), p. 82.
14 Bunyan Bryant and Paul Mohai, "The Michigan Conference: A Turning Point," *EPA Journal* 18 (1992): 9.
15 EPA Environmental Equity Workgroup, *Environmental Equity: Reducing Risk for All Communities* (Washington: Office of Policy, Planning, and Evaluation, U.S. Environmental Protection Agency, 1992).
16 A logical extension of the domestic environmental justice movement is occurring at the international level. Economic and environmental policies of the First World have significant environmental impacts on the Third World, and racial and socioeconomic variables that impact international economic and environmental policies are worth consideration. The concept of environmental blackmail can easily be extended to the international arena.

17   Gale notes that social movements, such as the civil rights movement, viewed the environmental movement with distaste. See Richard P. Gale, "The Environmental Movement and the Left: Antagonists or Allies?" *Sociological Inquiry* 53 (1983): 179–99. The environmental movement was viewed as an establishment-sponsored concern designed to divert attention from fundamental civil rights. The civil rights community objected to the economic class, political ideology, and political strategies of the mainstream environmental movement. The civil rights movement preferred civil disobedience and economic boycotts to the willingness to negotiate with governments and the private sector embraced by the environmental movement. For a similar discussion, see Robert Bullard, *Dumping in Dixie: Race, Class and Environmental Quality* (Boulder: Westview Press, 1990) and Robert Collins, "Environmental Equity: A Law and Planning Approach to Environmental Racism," *Virginia Environmental Law Journal* 11 (1992): 495–546. While ultimately health risks from a poor environment may permanently unite elements of the civil rights interests with those of the environmental movement, fundamental strategic differences still exist today. For example, the environmental justice movement has criticized mainstream environmental organizations for ignoring their plight and failing to remove discriminatory practices in their own organizations. See John H. Adams, "The Mainstream Environmental Movement: Predominately White Memberships Are Not Defensible," *EPA Journal* 18 (1992): 25–7.

18   Paul Taylor, *Principles of Ethics: An Introduction* (Belmont: Wadsworth Publishing, 1975), p. 72.

19   Ibid., p. 109.

20   A. Myrick Freeman III, "The Ethical Basis of the Economic View of the Environment," in Donald Van De Veer and Christine Pierce, eds., *People, Penguins, and Plastic Trees* (Belmont: Wadsworth Publishing, 1986), p. 218.

21   Ibid., p. 221.

22   Taylor, *Principles of Ethics*, pp. 109–11.

23   Michael Weisskopf, "Even Cash for Trash Fails to Slow Landfill Backlash: Public Resistance Widens U.S. Garbage Gap," *Washington Post*, no. 115 (1992), pp. A1, A6–A7.

24   Lawrence S. Bacow and James R. Milkey, "Overcoming Local Opposition to Hazardous Waste Facilities: The Massachusetts Approach," *Harvard Environmental Law Review* 6 (1982): 265–305.

25   Ibid., p. 276.

26   Freeman, "The Ethical Basis," p. 218.

27   Taylor, *Principles of Ethics*, pp. 72–8.

28   See Terry L. Anderson and Donald R. Leal, *Free Market Environmentalism* (San Francisco: Pacific Research Institute for Public Policy, 1991).

29   D. W. Hamlyn, *A History of Western Philosophy* (New York: Viking Press, 1987), p. 236.

30   Taylor, *Principles of Ethics*, p. 85.

31   Taylor, *Principles of Ethics*, p. 85–6, and D. D. Raphael, *Moral Philosophy* (Oxford: Oxford University Press, 1981), pp. 55–7.

32   Raphael, *Moral Philosophy*, p. 59.

33   Bullard, *Dumping in Dixie*.

34   Bryant and Mohai, "The Michigan Conference," p. 9.

35   Dorcetta Taylor, "The Environmental Justice Movement: No Shortage of Minority Volunteers," *EPA Journal* 18 (1992): 23–5.

36   Environmental Justice Transition Group, *Recommendations to the Presidential Transition Team*, p. 2.

37   Bryan G. Norton, *Toward Unity Among Environmentalists* (New York: Oxford University Press, 1991), p. 90.

38   Raphael, *Moral Philosophy*, pp. 67–80.

39   Ibid., pp. 67–80, and Bryan Norton, personal communication, August 1992.

40   Norton, *Toward Unity Among Environmentalists*, p. 75.

41   Ibid., p. 197.

42   Norton, personal communication, August 1992. Also see Norton, *Toward Unity Among Environmentalists*, pp. 187–204.

43   Taylor, *Principles of Ethics*, p. 72.

44   Ibid., p. 78.

45   Raphael, *Moral Philosophy*, pp. 67, 76.

46   Taylor, *Principles of Ethics*, pp. 72–8.

47   One could argue that if a discriminatory society could produce a higher level of net happiness than a nondiscriminatory society, then the discriminatory society could be established through unequal protection under socially acceptable laws or simply different rules for different people. Under narrow utilitarianism, different rules for different people still demands equal application of the rules throughout each segment of society – that is, equal application of blatantly discriminatory rules. Unequal application of a socially acceptable, nondiscriminatory rule requires a consistent, unequal application of the socially acceptable rule to maximize utility. Consequently, narrow utilitarianism still adheres to a consistent application of a rule, whether that rule is blatantly or deceivingly discriminatory or whether the rule promotes environmental justice. I argue here that narrow utilitarianism can accept environmental justice because it supports the equal application of socially acceptable rules that constrain the economic system. See Taylor, *Principles of Ethics*, pp. 72–8.

48   Ironically, the environmental justice movement has levied criticism on the mainstream environmental movement for ignoring the plight of minority and low-income communities and for failing

Troy W. Hartley

to remove discriminatory practices in their own organizations. See Adams, "The Mainstream Environmental Movement"; Bullard, *Dumping in Dixie;* Collins, "Environmental Equity"; and Gale, "The Environmental Movement."

49 United Church of Christ, *Toxic Wastes and Race*, p. 7, and EPA Environmental Equity Workgroup, *Environmental Equity*, p. 11.

50 The policy ramifications of environmental justice deserve a far more thorough analysis. For a detailed discussion on what constitutes environmental justice in practice, see Vicki Been, "What's Fairness Got to Do With It? Environmental Justice and the Siting of Locally Undesirable Land Uses," *Cornell Law Review* 78 (1993): 1001–85.

38

Sustainability and Intergenerational Justice

Brian Barry

1 The Question

As temporary custodians of the planet, those who are alive at any given time can do a better or worse job of handing it on to their successors. I take that simple thought to animate concerns about what we ought to be doing to preserve conditions that will make life worth living (or indeed liveable at all) in the future, and especially in the time after those currently alive will have died ('future generations'). There are widespread suspicions that we are not doing enough for future generations, but how do we determine what is enough? Putting the question in that way leads us, I suggest, towards a formulation of it in terms of intergenerational justice.

A methodological principle to which I shall appeal more systematically in section 2 is that we shall make most headway in asking ethical questions about the future if we start by asking them about the present and then see how the results can be extended to apply to the future. The rationale for this procedure is that we are accustomed to thinking about relations among contemporaries and have developed a quite sophisticated apparatus to help us in doing so. We have no similar apparatus to aid our thoughts about relations between people living at different times. Rather than starting from scratch, then, my proposal is that we should move from the familiar to the unfamiliar, making whatever adaptations seem necessary along the way.

If we follow this precept, and start from relations among contemporaries, we shall immediately run into a contrast that virtually all moral systems draw, though they derive it differently and use different vocabularies, between what it would be desirable (virtuous, benevolent, supererogatory) to do for others and what it would be wrong not to do for them. We may be said to have a duty or an obligation to do things that it is wrong to do, though this entails taking the words outside their natural homes in, respectively, institutionally generated roles and constraints imposed within rule-governed activities (e.g. legal obligations or promissory obligations).

Another family of terms that fits in somewhere here is the one made up of 'just', 'unjust', 'justice', and 'injustice'. A broad conception would make 'unjust' roughly equivalent to 'wrong' or 'morally impermissible'. John Stuart Mill proposed a broad use in chapter 5 of *Utilitarianism*,[1] and I have myself employed a similarly broad conception of justice in a recent book.[2] However, we would not in normal usage describe murder or assault as unjust, even though they are paradigmatically wrong. Rather, we reserve terms from the 'justice' family for cases in which some distributive consideration comes into play. For the present purpose, it will make little difference whether we choose the broader or the narrower conception of justice. This is because the questions about intergenerational justice that are liable to create distinctive moral problems are very likely to be issues of justice in the narrow sense: cases where there is (or is believed to be) an intergenerational conflict of interest. Thus, suppose we could provide a benefit or avoid a loss to people in the future at some cost to ourselves, are we morally required to do it? This inter-temporal distributive question falls within the scope of justice in the narrow sense. It is quite true that we can also damage people in the future without benefiting ourselves. But such actions will normally be wrong in relation to contemporaries or at the very least recklessly imprudent. Thus, if the people living at a certain time devastate a large part of the world by fighting a nuclear war, that will obviously be bad for later generations (assuming that human life is not entirely wiped out). But its inflicting immense evils on subsequent people is of a piece, as it were, with its devastating effect on those alive at the time.

I qualified my equation of injustice and wrongness in the broad sense by saying only that they are roughly equivalent. I had in mind two ways in which we can behave wrongly but not unjustly. First, I take it to be uncontroversial that we can act wrongly in relation to non-human animals. It is, of course, controversial whether or not certain practices such as using them in medical experiments or raising them for food are wrong. But scarcely anybody would deny that some acts (e.g. torturing them for fun) are wrong. We can, I think, stretch 'duty' and 'obligation' further beyond their core applications to enable us to talk about duties or obligations to non-human animals. (Even here, though, the core applications exert a pull: we are especially liable to use the vocabulary of duty where a role-related responsibility is at issue.) In contrast, it does not seem to me that the concept of justice can be deployed intelligibly outside the context of relations between human beings. The reason for this is, I suggest, that justice and injustice can be predicated only of relations among creatures who are regarded as moral equals in the sense that they weigh equally in the moral scales.

The second way in which wrongness and injustice come apart is that it is possible to behave wrongly even where the interests of sentient beings are not involved. Here, it is controversial that there are really any cases in which we can treat 'nature' wrongly unless the interests of sentient beings are somehow affected. I shall defend the

claim below (section 5) though I shall there argue that the common move of appealing to the 'independent value of nature' is a mistaken one. For the present purpose, however, I can bracket the validity of the claim. Let me simply say that *if* it is in some circumstances wrong to behave in a certain way in relation to 'nature', there is no entity that can properly be described as a victim of injustice.[3] I also believe, incidentally, that talking about duties or obligations to 'nature' is misguided. My reason for holding this will, I hope, become apparent when I explain the sense in which I think we can behave wrongly in relation to 'nature'.

To sum up the discussion this far, behaving unjustly to future generations is wrong but (even in the broad conception of justice) it is not the only thing that those currently alive can do in relation to the distant future that is wrong. Injustice is, however, such a manifestly important aspect of wrongness that it is well worth the amount of attention it gets from political philosophers. Further, if we define 'distributive justice' to correspond to the narrow conception of justice, which focuses on conflicts of interest, we may say that questions about intergenerational justice are characteristically questions about intergenerational distributive justice.

With that by way of preamble, I can now set out very quickly what I see as the question to be asked about the ethical status of sustainability. This is as follows: Is sustainability (however we understand the term) either a necessary or a sufficient condition of intergenerational distributive justice?

2 Distributive Justice

In accordance with the methodological maxim that I laid down at the beginning, I shall approach the question of the demands of intergenerational justice via the question of the demands of distributive justice among contemporaries. The premiss from which I start is one of the fundamental equality of human beings. (It is precisely because this premiss does not make moral standing depend on the time at which people live that principles of justice valid for contemporaries are *prima facie* valid for intergenerational justice too.) Fundamental equality is, as John Stuart Mill said, 'the first principle of morals'. 'Bentham's dictum, "everybody to count for one, nobody for more than one"' is, as he noted, a specific application of it to the utilitarian calculus, telling us that pains and pleasures of equal intensity are to be given the same value in the calculus, regardless of the identity of the person to whom they belong.[4] An application that is not tied to utilitarianism is that different treatments of different people must be justified by adducing some morally relevant ground for different treatment. This is, of course, not saying a great deal until we know what are to count as morally relevant reasons. But even if we simply say that they are grounds which we ought reasonably to expect the person affected to accept freely, we shall rule out many historically prominent forms of domination and systematic inequality of rights, which have rested on nothing but the power of the beneficiaries to impose them.[5]

I do not know of any way of providing a justification for the premiss of fundamental equality: its status is that of an axiom. I will point out, however, that it is very widely accepted, at least in theory, and attempts to provide a rationale for unequal treatment at least pay lip service to the obligation to square it with the premiss of fundamental equality. Moreover, it seems to me that there is a good reason for this in that it is very hard to imagine any remotely plausible basis for rejecting the premiss. In any case, it is presupposed in what follows.

In brief compass, then, I shall propose four principles which are, I claim, theorems of the premiss of fundamental equality. These are as follows:

1 *Equal rights*. Prima facie, civil and political rights must be equal. Exceptions can be justified only if they would receive the well-informed assent of those who would be allocated diminished rights compared with others.
2 *Responsibility*. A legitimate origin of different outcomes for different people is that they have made different voluntary choices. (However, this principle comes into operation fully only against a background of a just system of rights, resources and opportunities.) The obverse of the principle is that bad outcomes for which somebody is not responsible provide a prima-facie case for compensation.
3 *Vital interests*. There are certain objective requirements for human beings to be able to live healthy lives, raise families, work at full capacity, and take a part in social and political life. Justice requires that a higher priority should be given to ensuring that all human beings have the

means to satisfy these vital interests than to satisfying other desires.
4 *Mutual advantage*. A secondary principle of justice is that, if everyone stands *ex ante* to gain from a departure from a state of affairs produced by the implementation of the above three principles, it is compatible with justice to make the change. (However, it is not unjust not to.)

What implications do these principles of justice have for justice between generations? Let me take them in turn.

1 *Equal rights*. I cannot see that this principle has any *direct* intergenerational application. For it would seem to me absurd to say, e.g. that it is unfair for a woman to have more rights in Britain now than a century ago, or unfair that a woman had fewer rights then. Surely, the principle of equal rights applies to contemporaries and only to contemporaries. However, the present generation may be able to affect the likelihood that there will be equal rights in the future. Thus, it seems to be a robust generalization that rights suffer at times when large challenges to a system demand rapid and co-ordinated responses. (To offer a relatively modest example, I would guess that all individual university teachers and departments have lost autonomy in the last twenty years.) The more environmental stress we leave our successors to cope with, therefore, the poorer prospects for equal rights.

2 *Responsibility*. This principle will clearly apply among people who are contemporaries in the future, as it does among people who are contemporaries today, to justify inequalities of outcome that arise from choice. But what place, if any, does it have in relations between different generations? People in the future can scarcely be held responsible for the physical conditions they inherit, so it would seem that it is unjust if people in future are worse off in this respect than we are. (This, of course, leaves open the question of what is the relevant criterion of being well off, and I shall take that up in the next section.) What future people may be held responsible for, however, is how many of them there are at any given time.

Clearly, if we take the view that the principle of responsibility applies to population size, it will have highly significant implications for the requirements of intergenerational justice. I shall pursue this further in section 4.

3 *Vital interests.* The fundamental idea that location in space and time do not in themselves affect legitimate claims has the immediate implication that the vital interests of people in the future have the same priority as the vital interests of people in the present. I shall take up the implications of this in section 4.

4 *Mutual advantage.* In theory, it would be possible for the principle of mutual advantage to have cross-generational implications. That is to say, it could be that there are intertemporally Paretian improvements to be made in comparison with a baseline constituted by the outcomes of the other principles working together. However, I think it quite implausible that there are. The scope of the principle in relation to the distant future is particularly limited because it is explicitly stated in terms of preferences, and the further into the future we look the less confidence we can have about the preferences that people will have.

An objection commonly made against a universalist theory of justice such as this one is that it does not provide an adequate account of motivation to conform to its demands. It is certainly true that it leaves a gap in a way that 'communitarian' accounts do not. Consider, for example, Avner de-Shalit's book *Why Posterity Matters.*[6] It seems to me that his account closes the gap only too successfully. For in essence what he is saying is that concern for people in the future is something we naturally have, to the extent that we see them as carrying on with projects that are dear to us, because that gives depth and meaning to our own lives. This is doubtless true to some degree, though it would seem more for some than for others, but (except to the extent that it can generate intragenerational obligations arising from the 'principle of fair play') it does not tell people that they have to do what they are not inclined to do anyway. Moreover, because it is a cross-generational form of communitarianism, it cannot offer any reason for people in rich countries to cut back so as to improve the prospects of future people in other communities. Yet that is, as it seems to me, the most important thing for a conception of intergenerational justice to deliver.

In almost all the world, there is discrimination against women: they have fewer legal rights than men, are poorly protected by the law, and even more by its administration, against domestic violence, they have restricted educational and occupational opportunities, and so on. In most countries there are (*de facto* or *de jure*) different grades of membership based on race, ethnicity, language, religion, or some other characteristic. Such practices have powerful beneficiaries and it might be said (and is by so-called communitarian political philosophers) that it is 'no use' applying universalistic criteria of justice and pointing out that according to these criteria practices such as these are unjust. The only 'useful' criticism is 'connected' criticism, which deploys already accepted ideas. But this means that criticism cannot get a foothold so long as those who discriminate on the basis of gender or ethnicity have an internally coherent rationale. Meanwhile, it remains none the less true that such practices are unjust. And even if that thought does not have any motivating effect on those within a country who are in a position to change things, it may motivate people outside to organize boycotts and lead international organizations to exclude such countries from the benefits of international trade and aid.

I believe that the core idea of universalism – that place and time do not provide a morally relevant basis on which to differentiate the weight to be given to the interests of different people – has an immense rational appeal. Its corollaries – the illegitimacy of slavery and the impermissibility of assigning women an inferior legal status, for example – have been acted on for the past two centuries in a significant part of the world, despite strongly entrenched interests and beliefs in opposition to them. In the past fifty years, concern for people who are distant in place and time has grown in a quite unprecedented way. The great question for the future is whether or not that concern will grow sufficiently to induce action of the kind called for by the demands of justice. But I can see no reason for supposing that those demands should be scaled back to match pessimistic predictions about the way in which that question will be answered, even if we believe pessimism to be a reasonable response to the evidence so far.

3 Sustainability

Many people who have thought seriously about the matter have reached the conclusion that the concept of sustainability is inherently incapable of carrying the burden it would have to bear if it were to constitute a basic building block in a theory of intergenerational justice. With due diffidence, as a non-expert, I should like to make two observations on the literature that I have read. I first note a tendency to elide an important distinction. I have in mind here on the one hand the problem of producing a definition of sustainability that is coherent and comprehensible, and on the other hand the problem of drawing out concrete policy implications from any such definition. It seems to me that the problem of application is undeniably enormous, but that this should not be allowed too readily to impugn the possibility of achieving a definition of the concept.

The other point that occurs to me about the pessimists is their propensity to cite disagreement about the concept of sustainability as a basis for dismissing it. But we need not despair so long as the disagreements reflect substantive differences of viewpoint. Thus, let us suppose that concern about sustainability takes its origins from the suspicion that I articulated at the beginning: the suspicion that we are shortchanging our successors. If we then take this to mean that we should not act in such a way as to leave them with less of what matters than we enjoy, and call that sustainability, it is clear that the content of sustainability will depend crucially on what we think matters. For example, one writer may assume that what matters is utility, understood as want-satisfaction. (Such a writer is unlikely to be anything other than an economist, but economists loom quite large in the literature of sustainability.) Others will disagree and propose some alternative. There is nothing either mysterious or discreditable about this. It is, in fact, exactly what we should expect.

The core concept of sustainability is, I suggest, that there is some X whose value should be maintained, in as far as it lies within our power to do so, into the indefinite future. This leaves it open for dispute what the content of X should be. I have already mentioned one candidate: utility, understood (as is orthodox in economics) as the satisfaction of wants or, as they are usually called, preferences. The obvious objection to this criterion is that wants are (quite reasonably) dependent on what is, or is expected to be, available. Perhaps people in the future might learn to find satisfaction in totally artificial landscapes, walking on the astroturf amid the plastic trees while the electronic

birds sing overhead. But we cannot but believe that something horrible would have happened to human beings if they did not miss real grass, trees, and birds.

The want-satisfaction criterion does not enable us to explain what would be wrong with such a world. This sheds light on the oft-noted tendency of economists to be disproportionately located at the 'brown' end of the spectrum on environmental issues. For economists are also, as I have already noted, the most significant adherents of the want-satisfaction criterion. Combine that criterion with a faith in the adaptability of human preferences and you have a formula that can easily generate optimism about the future. For it will seem plausible that almost any environmental degradation that does not actually undermine productive capacity will be compensable by advances in technology that we can safely assume will continue to occur.

If I am right that substantive disputes about the concept of sustainability reflect disagreements about what matters, we can begin to see why what appear superficially to be technical questions of definition are so intractable. Consider especially the arguments in the literature about the status of 'natural capital'. For someone who adopts want-satisfaction as a criterion, all resources are in principle fungible: if plastic trees are as satisfying as real ones, there is no reason for worrying about the destruction of the world's trees so long as the resources exist to enable plastic replacements to be manufactured in sufficient numbers. Those who insist that 'natural capital' must be preserved are in effect denying the complete fungibility of all capital. But what is this disagreement actually about? On the interpretation I wish to offer, this is not a disagreement that turns on some matter of fact. It would be quite possible to agree with everything that might be said in favour of fungibility and still deny that it amounts to a case against the special status of 'natural capital'. For the case in favour of giving the preservation of nature an independent value is that it is important in its own right. If future people are to have access to what matters, and unspoilt nature is an essential part of what matters, then it follows that loss of 'natural capital' cannot be traded off against any amount of additional productive capacity. (I leave until section 5 the idea that nature might have value independently of its contribution to human interests, broadly conceived.)

What helps to obscure the point at issue is the terminology of 'capital' itself. For this naturally suggests that what is going on is a technical dispute about the conditions of production. On this understanding of the matter, the proponents of 'natural capital' are insisting that production has a natural base that cannot be run down beyond a certain point without putting future production in jeopardy. But the 'fungibility' school are not committed to denying this. They insist on fungibility *in principle*; whether or not everything can be substituted for *in practice* is a matter of fact on which they do not have to be dogmatic. But if I am right the real dispute is at the level of principle, and is not perspicuously represented in terms of the properties of different kinds of capital.

'Capital' is a term that is inherently located within economic discourse. A mountain is, in the first instance, just a mountain. To bring it under the category of 'capital' – of any kind – is to look at it in a certain light, as an economic asset of some description. But if I want to insist that we should leave future generations mountains that have not been strip-mined, quarried, despoiled by ski-slopes, or otherwise tampered with to make somebody a profit, my point will be better made by eschewing talk about 'capital' altogether.

Let us dismiss the hypothesis that X is want-satisfaction. What, then, is it? On the strength of the objection urged against want-satisfaction, it might appear that what should be maintained for future generations is their chance to live a good life as we conceive it. But even if 'we' agreed on what that is (which is manifestly not the case), this would surely be an objectionable criterion for 'what matters'. For one of the defining characteristics of human beings is their ability to form their own conceptions of the good life. It would be presumptuous – and unfair – of us to pre-empt their choices in the future. (This is what is wrong with all utopias). We must respect the creativity of people in the future. What this suggests is that the requirement is to provide future generations with the opportunity to live good lives according to their conception of what constitutes a good life. This should surely include their being able to live good lives according to our conception but should leave other options open to them.

This thought leads me to the suggestion (for which I claim no originality) that X needs to be read as some notion of equal opportunity across generations. Unfortunately, however, the concept of equal opportunity is notoriously treacherous. Although, therefore, I do believe this to be the right answer, I have to confess that saying this is not doing a lot more than set out an agenda for further study.

To summarize an extensive and in places technical literature with desperate brevity, there are two natural approaches to the measurement of opportunity, both of which rapidly turn out to be dead ends. One is to count opportunities. This has the obvious drawback that three options that are very similar (three apples of the same variety) will have to be said to give more opportunity than two more dissimilar options (an apple and an orange). But why is a greater range more valuable? A natural response might be that a choice between a number of apples is fine if you are an apple-lover but leaves you out of luck otherwise, whereas a choice between an apple and an orange gives you two shots at getting something you like. We might be tempted to move from this to the conclusion that what makes a range of options valuable is the want-satisfying property of the most preferred item in it. From there it is a short step to identifying the value of a set of opportunities with the utility of the most preferred option in it.

Notice, however, that if we follow this path we shall have insensibly changed the subject. We began by asking for a measure of the *amount* of opportunity provided by a set of options. What we have now done is come up with a measure of the value of the opportunities provided by a set of options. Even if we concede that the value of the most preferred element is for certain purposes an appropriate measure of the value of a set of options, it is strikingly counterintuitive as a measure of the amount of opportunity offered by a set of options. Thus, for example, it entails that opportunity is not increased by adding any number of desirable options to a singleton choice set, so long as none of those added comes as far up the agent's preference scale as the one option with which we began.

Another way of seeing the inadequacy of this measure of opportunity is to note that it takes preferences as given. But the whole reason for our taking opportunities to be constitutive of X was that we could not accept utility based on given preferences as the criterion of X. If preferences in the future are such that plastic trees (the only kind, let us suppose, that are available) give as much satisfaction to people then as real trees do now to us, the amount of opportunity in the future is not diminished. Thus, if we embrace the measure of opportunity that equates it with the utility of the most preferred item in the choice set, we shall simply be back at utility as the criterion of X. All that will have happened is that it will have been relabelled 'opportunity'.

The notion of a range of opportunity cannot be reduced either to the sheer number of opportunities or to the utility of the most preferred option. We must define it in a way that tracks our reasons for wishing to make it our criterion of X in the first place. That means taking seriously the idea that conditions must be such as to sustain a range of possible conceptions of the good life. In the nature of the case, we cannot imagine in any detail what may be thought of as a good life in the future. But we can be quite confident that it will not include the violation of what I have called vital interests: adequate nutrition, clean drinking-water, clothing and housing, health care and education, for example. We can, in addition, at the very least leave open to people in the future the possibility of living in a world in which nature is not utterly subordinated to the pursuit of consumer satisfaction.

More work, as they say, needs to be done, but I cannot hope to undertake it within the bounds of this chapter. The most important contention that I have tried to establish in this section is that the concept of sustainability is irreducibly normative, so that disputes about its definition will inevitably reflect differing values. If, as I maintain, the root idea of sustainability is the conservation of what matters for future generations, its definition is inescapably bound up with one's conception of what matters.

4 Sustainability and Intergenerational Justice

Having said something about intergenerational justice and something about sustainability, it is time to bring them together. We can be encouraged about the prospect of a connection if I am correct in my contention that sustainability is as much a normative concept as is justice. And I believe that there is indeed a close connection. It may be recalled that the question that I formulated

at the end of section 1 asked if sustainability was either a necessary or a sufficient condition of intergenerational justice. It appears that sustainability is at least a necessary condition of justice. For the principle of responsibility says that, unless people in the future can be held responsible for the situation that they find themselves in, they should not be worse off than we are. And no generation can be held responsible for the state of the planet it inherits.

This suggests that we should at any rate leave people in the future with the possibility of not falling below our level. We cannot, of course, guarantee that our doing this will actually provide people in the further future with what we make possible. The next generation may, for all we can know, go on a gigantic spree and leave their successors relatively impoverished. The potential for sustaining the same level of X as we enjoy depends on each successive generation playing its part. All we can do is leave open the possibility, and that is what we are obliged by justice to do.

An objection sometimes raised to the notion that it would be unjust to let future generations fall below our standard (of whatever is to count as X) is that there is something arbitrary about taking the current position as the baseline. We are, it is argued, better off materially than our ancestors. Suppose we were to pursue policies that ran down resources to such an extent that people in future would be no better off than our ancestors were a hundred years (or two hundred years) ago. Why would that be unjust? What is so special about the present as the point of comparison? In reply, it must be conceded that the expression 'intergenerational justice' is potentially misleading – though perhaps it actually misleads only those who are determined to be misled. It is a sort of shorthand for 'justice between the present generation and future generations'. Because of time's arrow, we cannot do anything to make people in the past better off than they actually were, so it is absurd to say that our relations to them could be either just or unjust. 'Ought' implies 'can', and the only people whose fate we can affect are those living now and in the future. Taking the present as our reference point is arbitrary only in some cosmic sense in which it might be said to be arbitrary that now is now and not some other time. It is important, however, to understand that 'now' means 'now' in the timeless sense, not '1998'. Wilfred Beckerman suggested in a presentation to the seminar from which this chapter arose that there was something arbitrary in privileging 1998 from all dates in history as the benchmark of sustainability. So there would be. But in 1999 the benchmark will be 1999, and in 2099 it will be 2099. There are, as I have explained, excellent reasons for starting from now, whenever 'now' may be. But just as 'here' does not mean my flat (though that is where I am as I write this) so in the sentence 'We start from now' the meaning of 'now' is not rigidly designated.

We now have to face a question of interpretation so far left aside. This is: How are we to deal with population size? On one quite natural interpretation of the concept of sustainability, the X whose value is to be maintained is to be defined over individuals. The demands of justice will then be more stringent the larger we predict the future population to be. Suppose we were simply to extrapolate into the indefinite future growth rates of the order of those seen in past decades. On the hypothesis that numbers double every forty years or so, we shall have a world population after two centuries of around a hundred and fifty billion and in a further two centuries a population of five thousand billion. If the increase were spread evenly round the world, this would imply a population for the UK more than ten times the size of the whole current world population.

It is surely obvious that no degree of self-immiseration that those currently alive could engage in would be capable of providing the possibility of an equal level of X per head even that far inside the future. This would be so on any remotely plausible definition of X. (Indeed, we can be certain that some cataclysm would have occurred long before these numbers were reached.) But even far more modest increases in population would make it impossible to maintain X, if X is taken to include the preservation of so-called 'natural capital'.

This is worth emphasizing because the 'cornucopian' school of optimists about population, such as Julian Simon, cite in support of their ideas the alleged failures of early neo-Malthusians (from the mid-nineteenth century onward) to predict correctly the course of events. But I believe that the pessimists have already been proved right on a central point: the deleterious impact on the quality of life of sheer numbers. Thus, John Stuart Mill's forebodings a century and a half ago (in 1848 to be precise) have, it seems to me, proved quite uncannily prescient. All that he feared has already in large

measure come to pass, and every bit of future population increase will make things that much worse.

Mill was quite prepared to grant the 'cornucopian' premiss that material conditions might be able to keep up with a greatly expanded population (or even more than keep up with it). But he still insisted that the population increase should be regretted. 'A population may be crowded, though all be amply supplied with food and raiment...A world from which solitude is extirpated, is a very poor ideal...Nor is there much satisfaction in contemplating the world with nothing left to the spontaneous activity of nature; with every rood of land brought into cultivation, which is capable of growing food for human beings; every flowery waste or natural pasture ploughed up, all quadrupeds or birds which are not domesticated for man's use exterminated as his rivals for food, every hedgerow or superfluous tree rooted out, and scarcely a place left where a wild shrub or flower could grow without being eradicated as a weed in the name of improved agriculture.'[7]

Treating future population as parametric is in effect assuming it to be beyond human control. But any such assumption is obviously false. I suggest, therefore, that the size of future population should be brought within the scope of the principle of responsibility. We must define intergenerational justice on the assumption that 'the increase of mankind shall be under the guidance of judicious foresight', as Mill put it.[8] If future people choose to let population increase, or by default permit it to increase, that is to be at their own cost. There is no reason in justice for our having any obligation to accommodate their profligacy. Concretely, then, the conception of sustainability that makes it appropriate as a necessary condition of intergenerational justice may be formulated as follows: Sustainability requires at any point in time that the value of some X per head of population should be capable of being maintained into the indefinite future, on the assumption that the size of the future population is no greater than the size of the present population.

It is worth emphasizing again that we always start from now, and ask what sustainability requires. The question is: What amount of X could be maintained into the indefinite future, given things as they are now, on the assumption that future population will be the same then as now? The way in which 'now' is always moving would not matter if (a) the demands of sustainability were correctly assessed in 1998; (b) sustainability were achieved in 1998 and maintained thereafter; and (c) the assumption of stable population control were in fact accurate. If all these conditions were met, we could substitute '1998' for 'now', but not otherwise.

We know that stabilization of population is perfectly possible as a result of voluntary choices made by individuals because a number of Western countries have already arrived at the position at which the (non-immigrant) population is only barely replacing itself, if that. Although they stumbled into it without any particular foresight, the formula is now known and can be applied elsewhere. Women have to be educated and to have a possibility of pursuing rewarding occupations outside the home while at the same time compulsory full-time education and stringent child-labour laws make children an economic burden rather than a benefit.

Unfortunately, however, many countries have such a large proportion of their population below the age of fifteen that their numbers would double before stabilizing even if every female now alive had only two children. Stabilizing population at its current level in these countries can be achieved only if women have only one child. So long as a policy restricting women to one child is operated consistently across the board, it does not contravene any principle of intragenerational justice, and is a requirement of intragenerational justice. Combined, as it has been in China, with a focus on medical care and education for children, there can be no question that it offers the next generation the best chance of living satisfactory lives, and removes a huge burden on future generations.

At this point, however, we must expect the response, already anticipated in general terms, that whether or not this is just it simply conflicts too strongly with religious objections to contraception and abortion and to powerful pronatalist norms, especially in many parts of the world where great importance is attached to having a male heir. If we are impressed by this, we shall have to say that justice demands more of people than they can reasonably be expected to perform. But what follows from that? At this point, it seems to me unavoidable to enter into the question that I have so far left on one side: the concrete implications of any criterion of sustainability. Suppose we believed that it would be fairly easy to provide the conditions in which X (e.g. some conception of equal opportunity) could be maintained into the indefinite future for a population twice the existing one. We might then treat as parametric the predicted doubling of world population and redefine sustainability accordingly. But my own conjecture is that the criterion of sustainability already proposed is extremely stringent, and that there is little chance of its demands being met. If I am right about this, all we can do is get as close to that as we can, which means doing everything possible to reduce population growth as well as everything possible to conserve resources and reduce depletion.

What then about the future? Suppose that the demographers' (relatively optimistic) projection for world population is correct, so that it stabilizes some time in the next century at double its current size. If we stick to the proposition that intragenerational justice is always a problem for the current generation (because they are the only people in a position to do anything about it), the implication is that sustainability should be redefined by each generation as the indefinite continuation of the level of X over the existing population, whatever it is. Whether people in the past have behaved justly or not is irrelevant. But if I am right in thinking that we are going to fall short of maintaining sustainability even on the basis of the continuation of current population size, it seems highly unlikely that people in the future will achieve it on the basis of a population twice as large. The only ray of light is that getting from a stable population to a gently declining one would not be difficult (nothing like as difficult as stabilizing a rapidly expanding population), and that the power of compound interest means that even a gradual decline in numbers would suffice to bring world population back well below current levels over a matter of a few centuries.

My conclusion, after this vertiginous speculation, is that we would be doing very well to meet the criterion of sustainability that I originally proposed. The more we fail, and the more that world population is not checked in coming decades, the worse things will be in the future and the smaller the population at which it will be possible to maintain tolerable living conditions. Perhaps the right way to look at the matter is to think of population and resources (in the largest sense) as the two variables that enter into sustainability: we might then say that sustainability is a function of both. Realistically, any given generation can make only a limited impact on either. But what can at least then be said is that if some generation is failing to meet the condition of sustainability (defined in the standard way over a fixed population), it can at least be more just than otherwise towards its successors by ensuring that the dwindling resources will have to spread around over fewer people.

Interpreted on some such lines as these, sustainability is, I suggest, adequate as a necessary condition of intergenerational justice. Is it also a sufficient condition? I feel strongly inclined to say that it is: if we were to satisfy it, we would be doing very well, and it is hard to see that we could reasonably be expected to do more. My only hesitation arises from the application of the vital interests. (I noted in section 2 that this needed later discussion.) Obviously, if we give the principle of vital interests priority over the principle of responsibility, we are liable to be back at a version of the absurd idea that we are obliged to immiserate ourselves to a level capable of sustaining a hugely larger population if we predict there will be one. For if we predict an enormously greater number of people in the future, meeting their vital interests trumps any objective we might have. I have not specified priority relations among the principles, and I do not think this can be done across the board. The principles are guides to thinking, not a piece of machinery that can be cranked to grind out conclusions. However, in this case it seems to me that giving the principle of vital interests priority produces such absurd results that this cannot possibly be the right thing to do.

Even if we make the principle of vital interests subordinate to the principle of responsibility, there is still a feature of the principle of vital interests that is worth attention. So far 'generations' have been treated as collective entities: the question has been posed as one of justice between the present generation as a whole and future generations as wholes. But the principle of vital interests forces us to focus on the fates of individuals. Suppose we leave future generations as collectivities with 'enough' between them to satisfy the criterion of sustainability, but it is distributed in such a way that the vital interests of many will predictably fail to be met? Does this possibility suggest that the criterion of sustainability has to be supplemented in order to count as a sufficient condition of intergenerational justice?

What I think it shows is that the distinction between intergenerational and intragenerational justice cannot be made absolute. I pointed out in section 1 that some things that would be wrong in relation to people in the future (e.g. fighting a nuclear war) would in the first instance be wrong among those alive at the time. Similarly, the primary reason for our being able to predict that the vital interests of many people in the world will not be met in the future is that they are not being met in the present. Formally, I suggest we have to say that maldistribution in the future is intragenerational injustice in the future. But we must recognize that intragenerational injustice in the future is the almost inevitable consequence of intragenerational injustice in the present.

5 Beyond Justice

If the current generation meets the demands of justice, is that enough? In the broad sense of justice, we would not be doing wrong in relation to human beings if we met the demands of justice. But we can (as I said in section 1) behave wrongly in relation to non-human animals even though this does not fall within the scope of justice. If we factor this in, what difference does it make? As far as I can see, its main effect is to reinforce the importance of keeping the lid on population, since the pressure on the habitats of the remaining wild non-human animals are already being encroached on at an alarming rate as a consequence of the growth of population that has already occurred.

The remaining question is the one that divides environmentalists into those for whom the significance of the environment lies solely in its contribution to human (or if you like animal) welfare from those for whom the environment has some significance beyond that. (Perhaps talking about 'the environment' is itself prejudicial since it suggests something in the background to another thing that is more important. But I take it that the distinction is familiar enough in a variety of descriptions.) I have to confess that I cannot quite decide what I think about this question because I find it hard to focus on the question when it is put, as it often is, as one about the 'independent value of nature'. Let me explain.

In *Principia Ethica*, G. E. Moore sought to discredit Sidgwick's claim that nothing can be said to be good 'out of relation to human existence, or at least to some consciousness or feeling'.[9] To this end, he asked his reader to consider

the following case. Let us imagine one world exceedingly beautiful. Imagine it as beautiful as you can; put into it whatever on this earth you most admire – mountains, rivers, the sea, trees, and sunsets, stars and moon. Imagine these all combined in the most exquisite proportions so that no one thing jars against another but each contributes to increase the beauty of the whole. And then imagine the ugliest world you can possibly conceive. Imagine it simply one heap of filth, containing everything that is most disgusting to us, for whatever reason, and the whole, as far as maybe, without one redeeming feature. Such a pair of worlds we are entitled to compare: they fall within Prof. Sidgwick's meaning, and the comparison is highly relevant to it. The only thing we are not entitled to imagine is that any human being ever has or ever, by any possibility, *can*, live in either, can ever see and enjoy the beauty of the one or hate the foulness of the other. Well, even so, supposing them quite apart from any possible contemplation by human beings; still, is it irrational to hold that it is better that the beautiful world should exist, than the one that is ugly?[10]

It is surely obvious that the question is loaded, because the two worlds are already unavoidably being visited by us, at least in imagination. It requires a self-conscious effort to avoid being affected by that. But if I make that effort conscientiously, I have to say that the whole question strikes me as ridiculous. In what possible sense could the universe be a better or a worse place on one supposition rather than the other? It seems to me an abuse of our language to assume that the word 'good' still has application when applied to such a context.

If adherence to the 'deep ecological' or 'dark green' position entails giving Moore the answer he wanted about the two worlds, I have to be counted out. But I wonder if all (or even many) of those who wish to endorse such a position feel thereby committed to attaching an intrinsic value to nature in the sense suggested by Moore. And, quite apart from that biographical question, there is the philo-sophical question: is there any way of being 'dark green' that does not entail being committed to Moore's preferred answer about the two worlds?

I am inclined to think that there is an attitude (which I share) that is distinguishable from the first position but is perhaps misleadingly expressed in terms of the intrinsic value of nature. This is that it is inappropriate – cosmically unfitting, in some sense – to regard nature as nothing more than something to be exploited for the benefit of human beings – or other sentient creatures, if it comes to that. There is an obvious sense in which this is still somehow human-centred, because it is about the right way for human beings to think about nature. But the content of that thought could be expressed by talking about the intrinsic value of nature.

It is important to observe that what I am saying here is not to be equated with the kind of environmental utilitarianism put forward by Robert Goodin in his *Green Political Theory*.[11] According to this, we do as a matter of fact care about unspoilt nature – for example, even the most carefully restored site of open-cast mining is 'not the same' as the original, any more than a perfect copy of a statue is 'the same' as the original. A sophisticated utilitarianism will therefore take our concerns about nature into account and set more stringent limits on the exploitation of the environment than would be set by our merely regarding the environment as a factor of production. This enables us to press 'green' concerns but still within a framework that makes human interests the measure of all things.

What I am saying is quite different from this. For it is a purely contingent matter whether or not people have the attitude to nature attributed to them by Goodin or, if they do, how far it weighs in their utility function compared with, say, cheap hamburgers from the cattle raised on pasture created from the ravaged Brazilian rain forest. The view that I am proposing says bluntly that people behave wrongly if they act out of a wrong attitude to nature. Although this is in a sense a human-centred proposition, it cannot be captured in any utilitarian calculus, however extensive its conception of human well-being.

6 Conclusion

I want to conclude by saying that I can understand and indeed sympathize with the impatience that will undoubtedly be felt by any environmental activist into whose hands this might fall. (Jonathon Porritt eloquently expressed such sentiments – and not only in relation to my contribution – during the final session of the Keele seminars on social justice and sustainability.) What the activist wants is ammunition that can be used in the fight for greater ecological awareness and responsibility. Fine-drawn analyses of sustainability such as those offered here are hardly the stuff to give the troops. But is it reasonable to expect them to be?

Let me make what may at first sight seem an eccentric suggestion. This is that it is not terribly difficult to know what needs to be done, though it is of course immensely difficult to get the relevant actors (governmental and other) to do it. I do not deny that there are large areas of scientific uncertainty, and probably always will be (e.g. about global warming), since the interacting processes involved are so complex. But what I am claiming is that virtually everybody who has made a serious study of the situation and whose objectivity is not compromised by either religious beliefs or being in the pay of some multinational corporation has reached the conclusion that the most elementary concern for people in the future demands big changes in the way we do things. These could start with the implementation by all signatories of what was agreed on at the Rio Conference.

Moreover, whatever is actually going to get done in, say, the next decade, to move towards a sustainable balance of population and resources is going to be so pathetically inadequate that it really does not matter how far it falls short. We know the direction in which change is required, and we know that there is absolutely no risk that we shall find ourselves doing more than required. It really does not make any practical difference whether we think a certain given effort represents 10 percent of what needs to be done, or whether we think it is as much as 20 percent. Either way, we have good reason to push for more. If I am right about this, it explains the feeling among practitioners that philosophical analyses have little relevance to their concerns. For whether we make the demands of justice more or less stringent, it is going to demand more than is likely to get done in the foreseeable future. What then is the use of pursuing these questions?

One obvious answer is that as political philosophers we are concerned to discover the truth, and that is an adequate justification for our work. The agenda of a scholarly discipline has its own integrity, which is worthy of respect. Distributive justice among contemporaries and within the boundaries of a state has been at the centre of the dramatic revival of political philosophy in the last quarter century. Extending the inquiry into the nature of distributive justice beyond these limits is a natural and inevitable development. But I think that there is also something to offer to those who are not interested in pursuing these questions for their own sake. It is surely at least something to be able to assure those who spend their days trying to gain support for measures intended to improve the prospects of future generations that such measures do not represent optional benevolence on our part but are demanded by elementary considerations of justice. What I have aimed to do here is show that the application of ideas about justice that are quite familiar in other contexts have radical implications when applied to intergenerational justice, and that there is no reason why they should not be.

Notes

1 J. S. Mill, *Utilitarianism* (Indianapolis: Bobbs-Merrill, 1971), ch. 5. Mill defines justice as equivalent to the performance of 'duties of perfect obligation', which presupposes 'a wrong done, and some assignable person who is wronged' (p. 47). This is close to my wide conception of justice (see below) in that it rules out obligations to non-human animals and obligations to 'nature'. However, the requirement that there should be assignable persons who are wronged would rule out the possibility of behaving unjustly with respect to future generations, since they can scarcely be regarded as assignable.

2 B. Barry, *Justice as Impartiality* (Oxford: Clarendon Press, 1995), esp. ch. 4.

3 In a paper presented to the first of the three seminars from which this book emerged, Andrew Dobson wrote of 'the privileging of human welfare over justice to nature'. But perhaps this was not intended to carry a lot of theoretical freight ('Sustainabilities: An Analysis and a Typology', paper presented to the Social Justice and Sustainability Seminars, Keele University, UK, (1996), fo. 11). See also A. Dobson, *Justice and the Environment Conceptions of Environ-*

mental Sustainability and Dimensions of Social Justice (Oxford: Oxford University Press, 1998).

4 Mill (1971), 55–6.

5 In *Justice as Impartiality* I have set out the criterion of reasonable agreement more fully and worked out some of its implications.

6 A. de-Shalit, *Why Posterity Matters: Environmental Politics and Future Generations* (London: Routledge, 1995).

7 J. S. Mill, *Principles of Political Economy*, ed. Donald Winch (Harmondsworth, Penguin Books, 1970 [1848]), Book IV, ch. 5, 115–16.

8 Ibid. 117.

9 G. E. Moore, *Principia Ethica* (Cambridge: Cambridge University Press, 1903), 81.

10 Ibid. 83–4.

11 R. Goodin, *Green Political Theory* (Cambridge: Polity Press, 1992).

39

Democracy and Sense of Place Values in Environmental Policy

Bryan G. Norton and Bruce Hannon

An important problem of modern society is to understand how constraints on resource use can be democratically imposed. Recent authors have expressed deep concern about the possibility that resource shortages will lead to totalitarian governments. They hypothesize that such governments would be the only effective means to enforce constraints on resource use and protect the environment from the inevitable consequences of human population growth, overconsumption of natural resources and social chaos (Hannon 1985, Heilbroner 1974, Kennedy 1993, Ophuls 1977, 1992). Ludwig et al. (1993) have recently provided an elegant argument – based in fisheries management but apparently susceptible to startling generalization – which calls into question the ability of democratic governments with free market economies to protect renewable resources once there has been heavy capitalization and development of exploitative industries. Must societies of the next millennium be undemocratic if they are to protect their natural resources?

In this paper we address one important aspect of the search for a democratically supportable policy that will sustain resources for future generations – the comparative role of national/centralized, regional/state, and local communities in the development of environmental policy. We distinguish two approaches to the evaluation, development, and implementation of policies to protect resources and environments. The two approaches (we will call them "top-down" versus "bottom-

up") differ most essentially in that the top-down approach emphasizes centralized control and decision making, while the bottom-up approach attempts to protect, to the extent possible, local prerogatives in setting environmental policy. We will then show that the different approaches would require very different methodologies for gathering and aggregating data regarding environmental values, and that application of the two methodologies results in differing conceptions of the overall good of a society. We conclude with some general applications of our theory to the future of environmentally sensitive planning.

More and more authors and commentators on the environmental crisis endorse sense of place values as important components of our enjoyment and valuation of the environment (Ehrenfeld 1993; Norton and Hannon 1997; Sagoff 1993; Sale 1985; Seamon and Mugerauer 1985; Tuan 1977). The idea of sense of place is addressed in the literature of several disciplines – we will mention here key works in geography, anthropology, sociology, environmental ethics and social criticism, and especially ecological history, as well as in architectural and planning theory. We find the concept intriguing, in that the idea/concept is highly praised as important in several subdisciplines (such as phenomenological geography, historic preservation, and environmental ethics), but the concept itself has remained somewhat peripheral to the main subject matters of each of these disciplines. Perhaps the transdisciplinary nature of the concept, which has prevented its development within a single disciplinary paradigm, explains why the concept has not been given precise operational meaning or application. This lack of a shared operational meaning might at first recommend abandoning the term as too imprecise to serve as the basis for a scientific approach to policy formation and evaluation. We prefer, in contrast to this defeatist approach, to define the term within a transdisciplinary discourse rich enough to express aspects of the idea emphasized in several disciplines.

The concept of place has been most developed by *geographers*, especially by geographers in the phenomenological tradition (outstanding in this tradition is the work of Gould and White 1974, 1986; Relph 1976, Seamon 1979, Tuan 1971, 1974, 1977; also see the essays in Seamon and Mugerauer, 1985). While this work has created interesting conceptual ties with the tradition of philosophical phenomenology – especially the work of the German philosopher, Martin Heidegger (1958, 1962; and Vycinas 1961), it has not attracted much attention from more quantitative geographers. Consequently, while this literature has greatly expanded our qualitative understanding of the place-relatedness of humans, their institutions, and their cultures, it unfortunately has not been fully integrated into the broader theoretical and quantitative work of geographers. One promising direction in this area is geographical work that incorporates ecological theory – specifically hierarchy theory (an application of general systems theory to ecological systems) into large-scale, landscape-level geographical analysis. This work employs the ideas of hierarchy theory to develop more integrated conceptions of scale and interconnectedness in landscapes (Allen and Hoekstra 1992; Allen and Starr 1982; Collins and Glenn 1990; Holling 1992; Johnson 1993; Lavorel et al. 1993; McMahon et al. 1978; O'Neill et al., 1986). What remains puzzling, here, is how exactly the objectivist, hierarchical models, which seek scientific and culture-free "objective" truths of physical geography, relate to the subjectivist and culturally determined models of phenomenologists (Norton and Hannon, 1997).

Anthropology, sociology, and related social sciences have contributed to literature on the relationship of local and regional cultures to their environment and resource base; especially important have been several excellent accounts of successful systems of resource access and protection among indigenous cultures (see, for example, Gadgil and Berkes 1991; Gadgil and Guha 1992; Rappaport 1968). The relationship between societies and their resource base has been effectively studied in a new way by a group of environmental historians – the *ecological* historians – who have used a combination of ecological and social historical data to reconstruct the role of human institutions in the "development" of the new world by colonial and post-colonial societies. The breakthrough book in this area was William Cronon's *Changes in the Land* (1983), which surveyed the changes in the New England countryside as a result of the arrival of European colonists. Crosby (1986) offers a broadly similar account, but Crosby emphasizes introduced species as the agents of "ecological imperialism," while Cronon details the intricate interrelations of ecological processes with the dynamic of human institutions (Cronon 1983, 1991); we find Cronon's institutional/ecological account more illuminating in the context of issues emphasized in this paper. Cronon, Crosby, and also Worster (1979, 1985) have all added to our knowledge of the interrelations of social and natural history. This theoretical work has been followed by numerous studies which have applied similar methods to the social and ecophysical transformation that occurred in the landscapes of every region of the United States and a few foreign countries (see, for example, Gadgil and Guha 1992; Gutierrez 1991; Silver 1990). Many examples of this literature do not consider place relatedness explicitly, but it provides many local and regional examples of how changing social and economic institutions alter, contribute to, and in many cases destroy the distinctiveness and identity of a place.

The idea of place has also been discussed, although not extensively, in *environmental ethics and social criticism*. Murray Bookchin (1965, 1982) articulated the idea that ecology and social criticism both point toward smaller, decentralized communities with strong commitments to place, in opposition to centrally controlled societies and resource management regimes. Other popular authors and essayists, including Wendell Berry (see, especially, 1977) and a whole literary movement sometimes called Southern Agrarians, have been highly critical of top-down management of resources and have advocated a strong commitment to the distinctiveness of local places. Alan Gussow (no date, 1993) has explored sense of place in art and aesthetics. Sale (1985) provides a useful overview of the role of place in understanding human cultures, advocating

Bryan G. Norton and Bruce Hannon

a "bioregionalist" approach, while Sagoff (1992) explores the cultural and aesthetic aspects of sense of place values. Sagoff, incidentally, argues that Americans generally have a weak sense of place, and attributes this to both the mobility and commercialism of American society. Deep ecologists have advocated more attention to the concept of place, but in our view they have not successfully resolved the apparent conflict between the localism implied by emphasis on place, and the centralist, universalist, and Eurocentrist implications of their theory that all life has equal intrinsic value. In general, interest in these universal, extra-cultural values among environmental ethicists has reduced the importance of the concept of place in that discipline (Norton 1995a and b).

Among architects, planners, and designers there was considerable interest in place-relatedness in the late 1960s and 1970s, and there has been a revival of interest in the concept in the 1990s. Important early work ranges from concern for the cultural and physical distinctiveness of local communities (Briggs 1968; Lynch 1960, 1972; Moore et al. 1974) to phenomenological/aesthetic studies in architecture and planning theory (Norberg-Schulz 1979). Norberg-Schulz sharply separates objective from subjective aspects of place awareness, and then argues for a geographical determinism according to which cultural attitudes are determined by the physical structures of the environment (see, especially, chapter III.1). These issues have become intertwined with the question of the nature of the "spirit of place" or "genius loci," as it is sometimes called, as definitions of these ideas can vary according to the mix of physical and cultural factors assumed to determine the spirit of a place. More recent work ranges across the spectrum from approaches mainly descriptive of distinctive features of physical places (e.g., Hough 1990) to work with greater emphasis on cultural and perceptual aspects of place relatedness (e.g., Jackson 1994; Steele 1981). Daniel Kemmis (1990) provides both a provocative discussion of regionalism versus federalism in American politics and a useful application of the idea of place in local politics; also see J. K. Bullard (1991) for an account of professional specialization in a specific local place. Interestingly, Kemmis and Bullard have both been elected mayors of their cities (Missoula, Montana, and New Bedford, Massachusetts, respectively).

There has also been serious study of placelessness and loss of place. Important theoretical work

by Relph (1976) was preceded by empirical studies, funded by the National Institute of Mental Health in the 1960s and 1970s, which examined the lives of residents of Boston's West End before and after it was levelled for urban renewal. This work emphasized the psychological importance of attachment to place, and of a sense of grief at loss of one's place, even in an area considered by outsiders to be a "slum" (Brett 1980; Duhl 1963, including especially Fried 1963; Gans, 1962).

One area where consensus has not been reached is in the area of boundary-setting, and the related question of how rigid boundaries between places are assumed to be. This difference spans geography and planning, with physical geographers usually employing physically measured boundaries, while planners and phenomenological geographers follow anthropologists in emphasizing perception and cultural factors in the determination of boundaries between places.

Even if most individuals orient from a place, it is not clear whether this perceptual position translates into "neighborhoods" or whether neighborhoods have more shifting boundaries, depending on human issues and cultural similarities. See Galster (1986) for an incisive, empirical approach to these complex questions.

One important agreement among psychologists, geographers and planners is on the importance of distinguishing *place* from *location*. Despite their local mobility, migratory peoples can have a strong sense of place. This distinction was made sharply by the aesthetician Langer (1953), who argued that a gypsy camp is a *place* which is reestablished in many separate *locations* during migrations. In this case, the placement of wagons, etc. can create a sense of constant "place-orientation" at multiple locations. The ideas behind this distinction – that a sense of place emerges from an interaction of cultural and natural setting and that commitment to place is somewhat independent of location – may prove important to planners and environmental managers, because it raises the possibility of consciously building upon and strengthening a community's sense of place identity, even in the face of extraordinary mobility of populations. Of special interest here is the work of Proshansky (1978; Proshansky et al. 1983), who suggested the possibility that place-bonding may be to *types* of settlements as much as to particular locations, and thus may function transpatially. Feldman (1990), working in this tradition, reviews literature on "spatial identity" and presents data establishing loyalty to types of places, such as city, suburb, or small town. Hull (1992) explores Proshansky's hypothesis empirically, developing an operational notion of "place congruity."

If it is possible for individuals and communities to actively promote a positive sense of place, and if sense of place values in a community encourages protection of their local environments, it becomes an important question whether it is possible to adopt a policy of promoting a sense of local responsibility through strengthening the sense of place in a community. Unlike Sagoff, who, as we noted above, explains lack of sense of place by invoking population mobility, this approach treats the relationship between mobility and sense of place commitment as an empirical matter, and as an important area for active participation by local planners, who may function to develop a stronger sense of place commitment in highly mobile communities. We return to this point in the conclusion.

A survey of these varied literatures suggests that the concept of sense of place is much better understood, theoretically and empirically, than it once was, and that the concept may present opportunities for important applications in planning and in environmental management. Despite the increasing interest of environmentalists and planners in the idea of place, however, little has been done so far to operationalize this intriguing but elusive concept, and it has been given little emphasis in actual analyses of environmental values. As a result, important applications have not occurred because of the inability of practitioners of multiple disciplines to settle upon a concept that is operational and sufficiently transdisciplinary to unify insights from the disciplines, all of which address the subject of place from different perspectives and with differing emphases.

This lack of agreement regarding operationalization and application is well illustrated in a recent exchange published in *Resources*, the newsletter of the economic research institute, Resources for the Future. In response to a proposal by Mark Sagoff (1993), that protection of sense of place values be articulated as a criterion of good environmental management, the economist Raymond Kopp (1993) expresses disdain, rejecting the concept as "problematic as a basis for policy. If Congress and the regulatory agencies can figure out how to define environmental policy on [the basis of the concept of place], more power to them."

Kopp's summary dismissal of Sagoff's proposal as unworkable rests upon a key, implied premise. Kopp implies that sense of place values must prove themselves useful in guiding *national* environmental policy (through guidance to Congress and the regulatory agencies). Notice that this apparently unquestioned assumption functions in effect as a methodological stipulation, requiring that any measure of environmental values must be easily aggregable across space. Further, the remark might be taken to imply a preference for centralized control of resource use, a top-down system of environmental management that assumes federal sovereignty over state and local governments in conflicts regarding resource use. We hope we are not imputing too much to Kopp's remark; we worry, however, that a strong methodological preference for cross-scale aggregation of all values up to the national level may well bias environmental economists against sense of place values. Kopp, if we have understood him correctly, argues that sense of place values cannot be aggregated to guide a national environmental policy and, therefore, so much the worse for sense of place values as policy guides. This commitment to aggregating environmental values at the national level quite naturally discriminates against sense of place values, the accounts for which – almost by definition – must be kept local. Setting aside centralist and aggregationist biases, however, Kopp's argument can be reversed. If there is strong evidence for place-relativity of important environmental values, and local values and sovereignty are favored, it might be concluded: So much the worse for measures of value that aggregate at the national level but which cannot account for these locally placed values. Our purpose in this paper is to present a twofold argument. First, that there are local, place-relative values which are systematically missed if all environmental accounts must be kept in nationally aggregated accounts (such as market prices recorded as dollar values). And, second, that these values have an important role in charting a course toward a democratically acceptable approach to environmental policy and planning.

An Example

We introduce our argument for sense of place values by discussing a particular example – a farm family who has owned the same farm for several generations – and inquire how this family values its property, hypothesizing that some of these values cannot be captured within a market analysis of social values. We recognize that the example is a favorable one for our case, but we use it simply to establish the existence of nonmarketable sense of place values in one case. We discuss how widespread and how significant these values are below. For simplicity, we formulate the case as applying to land values, although we believe it applies to environmentally sensitive values more broadly, and perhaps to every "public good" in environmental valuation.

Consider the plight of a fourth-generation farm family who learns that an adjacent property is to be purchased under eminent domain provisions and provided as the site for a toxic waste treatment facility under a contract with the local municipality. Our family is offered a choice. If they wish to stay, they will be compensated for the decrease in their residential property value resulting from the siting or, if they prefer to move, they will be bought out at the estimated market value of their property before the siting. The amount offered in compensation, in case they stay, should in theory represent their property value lost by the change in the adjacent site. Determination of just compensation in the law is usually based on market values (Freeman 1993). It seems fair to ask whether in this case a "fair market value" approach does indeed represent complete compensation. Does fair market value capture all the values that are lost if the family decides that, while they do not want to move, they cannot accept the new risk and disruption, and decide to leave?

Apparently not. If the family accepts fair market compensation and then uses the money to purchase a farm elsewhere, they will be compensated for their economic loss, but they will not be compensated for the loss of their "home." Place-relative information such as how to avoid poison ivy on the way to the pond, what time of day to catch the largest fish, and a plethora of other practical and aesthetic details that will not be transmitted with the deed to the property cannot be carried to a new site.

These nontransferrable values are the countless pieces of information and experiences that are entwined with daily life, impossible to separate into fact and value. They represent generations of wisdom accumulated from specific experiences and encoded in the cultural information and atti-

tudes passed from generation to generation. We believe that these place-relative values appear in all cultures, though we expect that their specific form and content will be highly variable across cultures. To see the environmental connection, consider the extent to which loss of vernacular tradition in Florida architecture in favor of generic building techniques has both reduced the cultural distinctiveness of that semi-tropical state and also greatly increased demand for electrical energy.

At least some less technologically advanced cultures, especially those that have survived for many generations, have developed myths and cultural practices – often religious in nature – that have the effect of protecting the resource base (see, for example, Gadgil and Berkes 1991; Gadgil and Guha 1992; Rappaport 1968). These local myths and practices, which are part of the "cultural capital" of a region, are often eroded by "development," leaving local populations with neither traditional practices or trained scientists who might gauge the impacts of resource use. Because place-relative cultural values must be developed with intimate knowledge of local conditions, migration, especially toward modern cities, diminishes this cultural capital.

Return to the case of our family. If the loss of these values – the loss of a special relationship between people and a place – leaves the family diminished despite having received "fair compensation," what does society risk when these values are ignored in analyzing and shaping our environmental policies? There are specific experiences – a particular granddaughter learning to *like* to fish at her grandfather's side, or an apprentice learning the tricks of the trade for building a more comfortable Florida house, for example – which transmit values and information through experience, practice, and enjoyment that are too personal and place-specific to be exchanged with the sale of property. The sum of these values, practices and strategies constitute locally based cultural capital.

Now suppose our family sells and another, non-local, family, willing to accept the risks and disutilities of the site, subsequently purchases our family's property at a lower price (determined by its postsiting market value). Most of the place-relative values associated with the first family's long association with the land will not be transferred in the sale. The original family will leave the farm diminished, and the new family will acquire these positive place-oriented values only slowly, if at all. These effects represent a part of what economists have called "adjustment costs" (Hanemann 1993). This concept, which has been developed as a category of easily missed costs in computing the impacts of global warming, may be particularly applicable to locally originating values. Because long-term estimations of changes due to global warming compare two temporally distinct equilibria, Hanemann argues that it is important to consider the disequilibrium costs incurred in adjusting to accelerating environmental change. Values lost during a forced transition may represent a systematically undercounted category of costs, and locally disruptive changes such as sitings of noxious land uses can involve significant costs of this type. If we suppose, alternatively, that the siting goes forward and the land is no longer considered suitable for residential use at all, the land may be rezoned, making it a site for further difficult-to-site industries and facilities. These changes may make it an "attractive" site for further disputed industrial uses. The market value of the farm may then even increase as important place-related values are completely eradicated.

If this argument proves sound, it apparently entails that there exist significant, systematically overlooked externalities associated with large scale development activities, and with economies and regulations that encourage movement of industries, etc. These losses are losses in the cultural capital of a community, the bits of particular information and experiences that unite a people in a relationship with their resource base or, in ecological terms, their "habitat." At this level, a culture's integration with the larger biotic community – the plants, other animals, and physical forces that make up its habitat – represents both cultural capital and also an important part of the local identity of that culture. Having offered one (admittedly favorable) example to illustrate this local cultural capital, we proceed to examine some of the characteristics of this capital to determine how widespread this phenomenon is, and to inquire whether this cultural capital and the values it embodies could and should have a role in environmental policy analysis.

Characteristics of Sense of Place Values

It is worth noting several unusual characteristics of these sense of place values. We will describe five features of place-relative values: (1) conditionally transferrable, (2) local, (3) culturally constitutive, (4) pervasive, and (5) partially measurable.

Conditional transferrability

First we must note that nontransferrable sense of place values are not the only type of place-relative values. Indeed, many types of place-relative values are easily recognized and readily incorporated into a market-based analysis. A wonderful view across a valley or the sea, for example, is highly relative to a given site, but is readily included in a market analysis in societies in which such value is common; since the view is obvious to any buyer, the added value is reflected in the market price. Similarly, location near an already existing noxious industrial use lowers purchase prices. Our special concern here is with values that are similarly place relative but which cannot be observed by prospective buyers and which cannot therefore be reflected in the purchase price. Prices in free markets reflect values that are discoverable and exchangeable. The experience of a grandfather teaching his granddaughter to fish in the lake cannot be discovered by potential buyers, nor can it be exchanged. It can have value only to those who experience it and, therefore, if it has value, it is an extra-market value. Both transferrable and nontransferrable place-relative values affect the character of a place; our interest, here, is in the nontransferrable ones, however, because those will be most likely to be missed in a market analysis.

Locality

All sense of place values are place-relative in the sense that they emerge in a specific, local context. Philosophically, this means that actions constitutive of a culture gain their meaning in a specific place, and they are expressive of locally distinctive and highly variable culture, biogeographies, and physical features. Development by a person of a local sense of place is an important part of developing a sense of personal identity (Fried 1963; Relph 1976).

Place-orientation is complex and many-layered (Norberg-Schulz 1979). To paraphrase the geographer Yi-fu Tuan, "we need a sense of place and a sense of the space around our place" (Norton

Bryan G. Norton and Bruce Hannon

and Hannon 1997; Tuan 1971). Anthropologically, this means that one should expect as many senses of place as there are unique combinations of culture with varied types of natural communities that form the contexts of those cultures. Practically, it means that no environmental policy that ignores local variation and local experience can be expected to protect biological or cultural diversity. If the only values that get counted in our analyses of policy options are ones that can be aggregated without reference to perspective and scale, then the nontransferrable, place-relative values identified here will be "washed out" in the process of aggregation to higher levels.

Cultural constitutivity

The contextual knowledge that results from multigenerational interactions between a culture and its distinctive plants and animals ensures that sense of place will be highly variable across cultures and across natural physical systems. This variability expresses the creativity involved in a culture's adapting to varied challenges and opportunities as offered by their biogeographic context. These values can be thought of as representative of "options" – choices to enjoy particular experiences – as viewed from a local perspective. But they are also a series of possible connections to the land, connections that are mediated through patterns of choices. It will be the choices that our generation makes regarding these places, whether to lose or to continue them, that will determine the options of future generations. The fabric woven across generations by this process of interaction with local resources sets the broad outlines of the identity of a culture within its surroundings. It determines the physical context to which subsequent generations will adapt.

In this sense, the choices made by one generation create the context for the next generation's choices; but it is the combination of physical/ecological constraints and the reactions of a culture to them that constitute meaningful activity. Sense of place values, in this sense, capture the "options" open within a community (the patterns of learned behaviors and possibilities for innovation) *and*, at the same time, those behaviors give expression to locally based cultural meanings – they are individualized responses to a particular environment (see Norberg-Schulz 1979; Relph 1976).

Pervasiveness

While we have developed a quite specific example of private property values associated with experiences that are place-specific, the type of values identified here are by no means limited to this narrow case. We could re-tell the above story of the family, simply moving the experience of a grandparent teaching a grandchild to fish at the public access to the best local fishing lake. The difference in the cases is that, if an undesirable land use is sited near the public fishing site, the experience will be diminished, and the stock of sense of place values enjoyed by the family will decrease, but the family will almost certainly not be offered compensation of any kind. Indeed, it appears that there are similar losses in nonmarket values associated with many changes in the context of common access resources such as occur when the Forest Service clear-cuts land near a recreation area, because this action can negatively impact the quality of the experience of visitors to the area.

The type of values introduced in the favorable example can now be broadened. It is as if the fabric of future possibilities for a local culture is woven from choices in the present. Defense of place-relative values reflects the collective will of a people – the common embracing of a cultural identity – a collective decision to maintain an authentic relationship to its past, to its future, and to its natural context. The search for a cultural identity must respect and build upon the natural history of a place, which includes the practices that emerged historically, and it must also project values into the future.

Sense of place values emerge at the local level and are highly dependent on the context at that level; they represent the positive sense of community that, in best cases, arises between a people and the place in which their culture has been defined. These values are therefore "scaled" – they are associated with a particular level of a multiscalar system (see Norberg-Schulz, 1979; also, for some ecological theorizing relevant to this point, see Allen and Hoekstra 1992; Allen and Starr 1982; Collins and Glenn 1990; Holling 1992; Johnson 1993; Lavorel et al. 1993; McMahon et al. 1978; O'Neill et al. 1986). If one attempts to connect local values to a common scale (such as a monetary scale), and then to aggregate the community-level values of many communities to arrive at a "sum" for the nation, all of the richness and context-dependence of these locally originating values will be lost. These sense of place values cannot therefore be meaningfully monetized.

These values are also "scaled" in time – they emerge intergenerationally as the community accommodates itself to its habitat; new practices are adopted and passed from generation to generation in an ongoing process of culture-building. It may be useful to think of these values as "aspirations" or "community preferences" in contrast to economists' "individual preferences" as a second, and essential, aspect of human valuation (Norton 1994). Whereas preferences exist in the present and are taken as givens, aspirations exist on an intergenerational scale and they represent choices on the part of a society regarding the type of society it will be. The values that emerge on this level require intergenerational continuity, a continuity that should reflect itself across generations on the landscape. Choices each generation makes concerning the landscape govern the range of freedom of the future in the precise sense that the landscape will determine what options are open and what experiences are possible in the future (Norton 1995a). A commitment to sustainable use is a commitment to hold open certain options and the possibility of certain experiences. Because of this dynamic, intergenerational quality, sense of place values cannot be captured in a "snapshot" approach to ascertaining the aggregated preferences of a population at a moment in time.

Partial measurability

Sense of place values can be expressed as measurable differences in human behavior. We have argued that many sense of place values will not be captured in market transactions because they are so intimately intertwined with bits of knowledge and experience that are too place-specific to transmit at a real estate settlement. Again, our example is instructive. If the family had no positive attachment to the farm – if they were absentee owners or if they had just bought it and had not moved in yet, for example – they would probably be fully compensated for their loss if the price offered is indeed the fair market price. We can hypothesize that, if a family has a large stock of sense of place values, they will be more likely to refuse to accept a fair market price for their property, and their efforts (including, for example, legal fees and volunteer work) expended to protect the place itself provide a rough – or, lower-bound – measure of the strength of their commitment to their particular home place. Our emphasis on locally developed values as indicative of commitment to place leads us to take these costs very seriously in evaluating environmental impacts of large development projects and of national management of resources such as national parks and national forests. As an example of the power of local feeling, consider the State of Illinois' eighty million dollar attempt to site a radioactive waste storage facility in Martinsville, Illinois. A local citizen group of the small rural community with relatively high unemployment obtained contributions of nearly one-half million dollars in intervenor funding to organize expertise to defeat the project on several grounds. This remarkable effort was undertaken despite a state offer of over one million dollars per year in compensation to the community.

Willingness to accept the market value indicates an *economically* defensive stance – its motive is to protect the economic investment of the private landowner, but not the place itself, which is treated as having acceptable substitutes in alternative properties. Willingness to fight on against a siting *after fair market compensation has been offered* is indicative that something other than economic interests are being defended. In these cases, the economic model, which assumes there exists a rate of compensation that will make the person indifferent to loss of their home, seems inapplicable to an analysis of a positive commitment to *this* place, rather than to this and comparable places that could be purchased elsewhere. The values of home are in this sense separable from economic values embodied in the property; indeed, they are in an important sense nonfungible with economic values because they become obvious only when economic interests have been fully protected. When owners reject fair market value for their home, it is always possible to interpret their refusal to sell as economically motivated gaming. The difficulty of controlling for this confounding variable represents one of the major deterrents to the development of a more precise and measurable conception of sense of place values. But sense of place values, however difficult to measure directly because of the gaming effect, are necessary to explain behavior that is likely to be counter-productive economically.

Citizen actions to protect parks and preserves are often motivated by noneconomic goals. Another approach to quantifying values associated with particular places might be to pay attention to private landholders, gifts and below-value land sales by private landowners to environmental groups for preservation (Robert Mitchell, personal communication). Sense of place values therefore manifest themselves in connection with private goods (as in the case of our farm family) or they can be motivated by a public spirit. The point to be emphasized here is that these are significant and pervasive values and they are often systematically ignored in market valuations.

We feel justified in calling these place-relative values that cannot be measured in market transfers *positive sense of place values*. These are the values, the positive commitments – the aspirations – that are tied up with a particular place – which are not compensable in dollar terms. These values express commitment to a non-interchangeable connection to a particular place. A strong stock of positive sense of place values would represent intimate experience and relationships with the plants, animals, and ecosystems that are distinctive to their region. The idea of aspirations captures the sense of a cultural future, which must of course grow organically from a storied past, and it is these features that give distinctive value to a particular place (Rolston 1988). These aspirations, which correspond to intergenerationally created and protected cultural capital, cannot be understood independently of the resources – the opportunities and options expressed in the local biotic community. Nor can they be separated from the constraints that have been conquered by local technologies and local wisdom. These constraints give meaning to actions of individuals and communities who are integrated into a place (Norton 1995a). They emerge not so much in connection with particular acts and purchases, but rather as expressions of cultural identity and character (Page 1992). A good example of this type of value, from the political realm, would be the type of underlying political ideals (such as rule of law) that express themselves as a community writes a new constitution (Page 1977; Toman 1994). Whereas preferences expressed in markets may represent individual values as felt in the present, aspirations are group values that express themselves on a longer, intergenerational scale.

Notice also that aspirations can be more complex than preferences in the sense that, if one has an aspiration that one's children and grandchildren share and enjoy an experience (such as learning to fish in the family fishing hole) in the future, two conditions are implied: one hopes, first, that the fishing hole be unspoiled and accessible and, second, that the youngsters will enjoy that experience. So, in addition to the implied value of accessibility to means to fulfill a preference, aspirations represent also second-order preferences regarding what preferences future individuals will have and express. This feature of aspirations (Norton 1987; Sagoff 1986) introduces a level of complexity – they represent preferences over preferences – into the analysis that is impossible to capture in a uniscalar analysis such as that exemplified by microeconomics.

A Classification of Place-Relative Values

Drawing on our analysis of the example, we offer the following taxonomy of place-relative values:

1 Preferences associated with place
   a publicly observable benefits, risks, and disutilities associated with a place and adjacent land uses
   b recognizable and transferrable amenities (a nice view, fishing opportunities)
2 Place-oriented aspirations
   a enjoyments that depend for their value on the history and future of a place. These intimate values are expressed in a culture's relationship with their physical and ecological context – the geography, plants, and animals that constitute their environment/habitat – and they only emerge through participation in, and acquisition of knowledge about, the natural and cultural history of a place. They are values that are transmitted and experienced only by intimate contact among people who interact in a culture with a sense of natural as well as social history.
   b the value of the cultural and community continuity conserved when experiences of type (2a) are protected over generations.

While the values in category (1) are presumably captured in market transactions, values in category

(2) cannot be so captured, as argued above. They are, however, the very essence of any positive connection between a human culture and its place.

Measuring and Aggregating Sense of Place Values

Nontransferrable, place-relative values have measureable behavioral consequences. For example, we predict that communities with a large stock of these values are more likely to continue to contest land use decisions, incurring measurable costs, even after they have been offered compensation. Many of these costs are easily measurable – legal fees, for example – others are difficult to measure, but offer no problems in principle – such as donated time and efforts, etc. – while others, such as emotional pain experienced during a long legal battle, will never be measured accurately (Varlamoff 1993). The quantifiable expenses of opponents of a development plan (after having been offered market compensation) would nevertheless appear to provide a lower bound measure of place-relative values that are not transferred in fair-market sales.

The problem with these values is not so much that they are unmeasurable or unquantifiable in particular situations – any method of quantifying social values will include some easily measured and other difficult-to-measure values. But these values are so highly context-dependent that their character is lost when an attempt is made to aggregate them across many communities. We must therefore revisit Kopp's assumption in favor of nationally aggregatable data. Even if we were to develop quite precise measures of positive sense of place values for a given community, Kopp may well be correct in believing it is impossible to aggregate these "values" together to guide federal policy decisions because these values contain a nonfungible commitment to characteristics that are place-specific. These values are not additive with other values to achieve a grand, national total of welfare, because these values exist in so many different, and in some sense, incommensurable contexts. In particular, they embody values that emerge on multiple levels. These values do not aggregate because they are scale-specific (Norton 1995a).

The dispute here is not one about whether to *quantify* values; it is rather about whether to verti-

cally aggregate values across hierarchical levels, once a quantification has been achieved. And it is also about whether it is worthwhile to seek and use information that cannot be monetized and aggregated at the national level. Whereas a decision maker following the top-down approach would aggregate information to the highest decision level, treating decision making as a matter of computation of single-scaled values, a decision maker acting from the bottom-up would first sort decisions into various categories according to a scalar criterion. In the version we have developed, these categorizing decisions are based on an assessment of the scale of the problem and the social scale at which a response is appropriate (Norton 1995a; Norton and Ulanowicz 1992). Then, the decision maker asks, given the scale and level of dynamics at which we must address this particular environmental problem, what decision rule should apply in this context? Once a decision rule is chosen and goals have been formulated at the relevant governmental level, it should be possible to quantify data about the physical world and to quantify data regarding citizens' values affecting the decision. But on a multiscalar approach one would not expect that all of the data should be analyzable in terms of a single utility function of individuals and thereby aggregable upward in the decision hierarchy.

To illustrate the importance of the difference, consider two ways of making a decision regarding the placement of a long-term, low-level radioactive waste storage site. Suppose, first, it is noted that the risks and costs to society (considered as the set of all citizens in the nation) attendant upon having many decentralized storage sites are computed to be very large because, for example, security arrangements at many sites are either expensive or risky; or because there will be widespread stress on individuals because far more people will live near multiple sites than would live near a centralized site. A nationally aggregated decision made in the computational style, in other words, would apparently favor the choice of a single storage site in a remote area. But suppose that every local community refuses to accept the site. If we consider the siting to be a matter of the "right" of each local community to self-determination, respecting this right amounts to offering each local community a veto power. With such a multiscalar view of our governing system, in other words, it makes a lot of difference which questions are addressed first.

And in this sense the decision systems we offer are not computational, but emphasize careful categorization of risks and the values associated with them, seeking to characterize environmental problems in terms of their appropriate scale, and matching decisions to the appropriate governmental scale.

With a multiscalar view, every decision maker would accept the right to self-determination on the local level and would treat this universal veto as a given. The search for a national policy on radioactive waste storage would now be formulated with a whole different set of policy options. All options considered would be ones that respect the decisions of local governments not to accept the site. Admittedly, this approach may be idealistic in that we already possess – because of past decisions and activities – large stockpiles of waste requiring storage somewhere, which makes the apparent implication of the bottom-up approach inoperative as a complete solution. But this practical complication does not obscure the clear implication for future decisions of a commitment to local self-determination and enforceable local veto powers. Placing a high priority on local self-determination in effect constrains the options for a national policy, perhaps imposing the outcome that there must be a vast reduction in activities that create such waste. The point of such examples is to show that the choice of an aggregative approach to measuring environmental values tends to devalue local considerations that seem persuasive to members of local communities. If all communities reject a particular land use or even if a great number of them do, the message to the higher level would be to stop the imposition and seek another alternative. For example if no place can be found (due to local vetoes) for storage of low-level radioactive waste, then stop generating it and find substitutes. We could then dispense with cynical reports such as "Building Citizen Support for Responsible Low-Level Radioactive Waste Disposal Solutions: A Handbook for Grass Roots Organizers" (1995), published by the Nuclear Energy Institute, a trade organization consisting mainly of nuclear power utilities and manufacturers.

The special characteristic of hierarchically organized decision processes is that they recognize and meaningfully represent the apparently unavoidable asymmetries in space–time relationships. If actions of individuals are viewed as scale-specific within a multiscalar system, then the larger-scaled systems that provide the context for individual decisions appear as both constraints and opportunities available, locally, to individuals. The amount of forested land in an area offers an opportunity for a timber industry; but a limited quantity of high-quality forest also places a constraint on the development of such an industry. Opportunities provide an explanation of the behaviors of individual actors such as timber companies and their employees, but the constraints embodied in the limited extent of forest cover will determine, on a longer scale of time, the evolving character of the community in relationship to its natural context. Sustainable forestry, thus understood as including the sustenance of local culture and local ecological integrity, would in this sense be a *local* commitment and include local responsibility for forest protection (Norton and Hannon, 1997).

The problem is that in a nationally or internationally organized economy it is possible to "export" opportunities in the form of timber, but the associated constraints – the results of near-total deforestation such as erosion and siltation of streams – necessarily "stay at home". Thus it is "rational" for decisions made by multinational corporations in the context of international markets to change the character of a local community by deforesting it and then moving to a new forested area. Their profits will be exchangeable in the currency of larger-scale systems such as world markets (Clark 1974); the costs of their aggressive exploitation, the degradation of the natural resource, will be felt at the local level and will be lost from computations as the profits are summed at higher levels of geographic, social, and economic organization. Aggregated measures of rationality and single-scaled approaches to decision making therefore tend to over-estimate benefits and under-estimate costs because, in the arena of national economics, wealth will be created by the systematic transference of externalities to local communities as a byproduct of the exportation of their opportunities. Especially when international corporations can command federal subsidies through lobbying at the federal level, local communities will be hard put to resist such exploitation.

We have questioned Kopp's assumption that measures of environmental value must be expressed in terms that are aggregatable across space and time, exploring hierarchical systems of analysis which, unlike the single utility measures of mainstream economics, analyze values in a contextual and scale-sensitive manner. Multiscalar systems retain information of local importance in the process of developing a national policy, at the cost of giving up aggregability across scales. Sense of place values exist on many local levels and, within a hierarchical approach, these sense of place values would be satisfied locally before going on to address larger-scale questions of valuation. This creates a burden of proof on the powers of centralization to show why expressions of local goals should not trump centralized interests. If one favors local control and reestablishment of local responsibility, a multiscalar system of analysis which favors a bottom-up approach is more likely to achieve a democratic outcome than a policy process that emphasizes those values that can be aggregated to a national level. We should clarify that our preference for local control is not based on the assertion that all problems are local problems. Indeed, we expect that there will be many cases in which local governments must address large-scale environmental problems, including their contributions to global changes. Our point is that even to address international problems while ensuring democracy at the local level, decision structures must be organized in a bottom-up fashion.

Applications to Policy and Planning

We have sketched two approaches to environmental policy formation and valuation, and have noted that aggregation of values across all levels of environmental policy formation will promote policy goals – and the values that support them – favorable to a centralized decision process. Alternatively, a multiscalar organization of the process can be designed to be scale-sensitive and to encourage processes of valuation that emphasize locally developed environmental values. This approach eschews cross-level aggregation of values and instead recognizes the asymmetry of time-space relations, protecting local values at a local level. While we recognize that local cultures do sometimes destroy their resource base, local control has the advantage that information feedback loops are shorter and local populations may have to live with the consequences of reduced opportunities and economic options more directly than do

national and international corporations or national governments.

The evaluative, informational, and decision models we have proposed have been built from the bottom up, in that we have avoided the methodological requirement of cross-scale aggregability of value measures we propose. Our methodological choices have in this sense been guided by a persistent attempt to favor localism and values that are articulated locally, because we believe that centralized goal-setting for economic growth will inevitably favor large economic interests. These large interests will systematically export opportunities, leaving results of ignoring constraints behind as they move to fresher exploitable areas.

In closing we can return to the very large question with which we began this paper: is there any general approach to environmental policy formation that both protects resources *and* can be established democratically? If we think of democracies, broadly speaking, as governments that are responsive to the will of the people, it is possible to ask "which people?" and "How will their wills be aggregated?" In systems which are multiscalar (such as federal systems), it is possible to identify communities that exist at more than one level. It is comforting to think that, when such a system is working properly, "democracy" occurs at all levels, with the government at each level pursuing policies that are favored by the relevant community. A democratic national government would therefore pursue policies that are acceptable to people at all lower levels.

In the process of analysis, we have uncovered an important ambiguity in this conceptualization of the democratic process. We have shown that aggregating values from smaller to larger communities can bias policy analysis against local communities. We saw that Kopp and other neoclassical microeconomists set, as a methodological constraint/expectation, that all values expressed on all levels must be aggregable in common, fungible terms. On the view of democracy that emerges in this case, a democratic national government would pursue those policies that are indicated by the sum total of the aggregable preferences of all individuals, *quâ* individuals, at all lower levels of the society. It allows no statement by a local community of nonfungible, place-relative values. We have seen that, on the system assumed by Kopp, it will often be "rational" to impose a land use on a community despite opposition from that community because the strong local values of the opposition are swamped by the "common good" of millions of people from other communities who will reap the rewards of the government's imposition of a siting on this small community. The harshness of this approach can of course be mitigated by insisting, for example, that the few in the local community should be compensated from the gains of the many, perhaps with direct payments or with new schools, etc. These mitigative "bribes" take the form of subsidies flowing from the federal to the local level; they have the same impact as other federal subsidies for local resource extraction: they confuse the signals so that local governments will not perceive the consequences of nonsustainable use of their resources. This mitigation does not change the fact that the aggregative approach presupposes a "top-down" flow of control in the system. Policy is set on a national level and local communities are left with no choice but to negotiate the best "compensation package" they can get. The "good" of the society is determined at the national level through an aggregation of individual preferences; any local "goods" such as positive, nontransferrable sense of place values will have been lost because they are invisible among the market values that, on the view of mainstream economists, should guide national policies.

If, on the other hand, we relax the aggregability requirement on environmental values and think of environmental policy as hierarchically organized from the bottom up, locally developed values that are highly context-dependent may be instrumental in building many strong local communities in which individuals act upon a strong sense of local place. These local communities might, on this view, reject "fair compensation" for a siting simply because it is not consistent with their conception of their community. Values will be counted, voting will take place, etc., but the political outcomes at local community levels will stand on their own. They cannot be swamped and overridden by values that are aggregated at a larger scale. This difference in conception of the public good is the operational significance of the difference between a multiscalar and bottom–up approach to conception of environmental values and methods, and an aggregative and computational approach to policy with a national focus only.

Our theory suggests no less than an about-face in current trends toward centralized control in environmental policy formation. To some extent, we are calling for an end to federal and state sovereignty, and an end to "top-down" thinking in environmental policy. Our approach would, for example, shift the initiative for environmental policy development away from the federal to the local level. But it is important to realize that the approach can only work if devolution of federal control is accompanied by an end to federal subsidies and bail-outs. The point is to reestablish local *responsibility* for resource use and planning decisions, which requires both local control *and* a system in which local populations must accept the consequences of their actions.

One advantage of a compartmentalized, multiscalar, bottom-up system of many local controls is that it will reduce the impact of national economic lobbies. In the current system in which environmental policy goals are set on a national level, it is much easier for national industries to centralize their lobbying efforts. We hypothesize that it will be more difficult for national economic interests to control environmental decision making if it is decentralized.

Our argument also implies that we should provide local activists with resources by which to resist encroachment upon local prerogatives. In particular, new laws are needed to empower local activists to challenge proposed impositions of decisions that are motivated by the concerns of centralized, governmental power, often in collusion with large international businesses (Varlamoff 1993). More generally, our argument has several implications for planning and for the planning process.

First, once one draws the distinction between location and place, recognizing that it is possible to create a sense of place even among populations that change locations regularly, it is possible to advocate a strong role for planners as facilitators of a process of building and strengthening local sense of place. This process of community value articulation should be designed to build a stronger sense of place and a stronger inclination to defend the distinctiveness of local cultures. Planners, on this approach, could become key players in ecosystem management projects, encouraging local communities to articulate and develop their sense of place and local identity as a general guide to setting goals of environmental policy. This approach might also encourage closer cooperation of environmental and cultural/historical preservationists.

A second, related implication is that the process of devolution of responsibilities for environmental quality and regulation from the U.S. federal government to the states – a process that is certain to be accelerated by strong budget cuts at the U.S. Environmental Protection Agency – should be met with a process of social learning (Dewey 1984; Lee 1993). Local communities may, with the help of planner/facilitators, be able to seize as an opportunity the current trends away from federalism, using these events to strengthen local responsibility and control, and to build a healthy sense of the distinctiveness of particular places as broad guides to resource use and environmental protection (see Kemmis 1990). The processes of social learning described here must be iterative; they must encourage ongoing discussion of environmental goals and how those goals interact with socially and culturally expressed statements of the distinctiveness of particular places. This iterative process, well described by Lee (1993) and Gunderson, Holling, and Light (1995), emphasizes the interaction of professional scientists, environmental planners and managers, and the public in an experimental approach to proposing and testing environmental policy goals and policies.

These general implications all follow, directly or indirectly, from the main argument of this paper, that social values can only be protected if local communities can exert self-determination and a veto power in favor of locally originating and locally supportable norms to guide resource use. In general, then, a strengthened and more scientific conception of sense of place values, based on improved understanding of the role of place in developing a sense of community and a willingness to accept responsibility for local resources, may encourage a stronger role for planners in facilitating the articulation, public discussion, and revision of the goals of environmental management.

We recognize that return to local responsibility will be difficult and will require time to develop stronger, local senses of place and a commitment to protect the integrity of local places. But this may be the only route toward a democratically supportable approach to sustainable use of resources. We believe that it would also represent an important step toward introducing true democracy, which on the hierarchical bottom-up view of policy involves actions of government that are responsive to the needs of people and communities who live most intimately with their resources and within their habitat.

References

Allen, T. F. H., and Hoekstra, T. W. (1992). *Toward A Unified Ecology.* New York: Columbia University Press.

Allen, T. F. H., and Starr, T. B. (1982). *Hierarchy.* Chicago: University of Chicago Press.

Berry, W. (1977). *The Unsettling of America.* New York: Avon Books.

Bookchin, M. (1965). *Crisis in Our Cities.* Englewood Cliffs, NJ: Prentice-Hall.

——. (1982). *The Ecology of Freedom.* Palo Alto, Calif.: Cheshire Books.

Brett, J. M. (1980). "The Effect of Job Transfer on Employees and Their Families." In *Current Concerns in Occupational Stress,* ed. C. L. Cooper and R. Payne. New York: John Wiley and Sons.

Briggs, A. (1968). "The Sense of Place." In *The Fitness of Man's Environment,* Smithsonian Annual, II. Washington, D.C.: Smithsonian Institution Press.

Bullard, J. K. (1991). "The Specialty of Place." *Places 7,* no. 3: 72–9.

Clark, C. (1974). "The Economics of Over-Exploitation." *Science* 181: 630–4.

Collins, S. L., and Glenn, S. M. (1990). "A Hierarchical Analysis of Species Abundance Patterns in Grassland Vegetation." *American Naturalist* 135: 633–48.

Cronon, W. (1983). *Changes in the Land: Indians, Colonists, and the Ecology of New England.* New York: Hill and Wang.

——. (1991). *Nature's Metropolis: Chicago and the Great West.* New York: W.W. Norton.

Crosby, A. W. (1986). *Ecological Imperialism: The Biological Expansion of Europe, 900–1900.* Cambridge: Cambridge University Press.

Dewey, J. (1984). "The Public and Its Problems." In *The Later Works, 1925–1953, Volume 2.* Carbondale, Ill.: Southern Illinois University Press.

Duhl, L. J., ed. (1963). *The Urban Condition: People and Policy in the Metropolis.* New York: Basic Books.

Ehrenfeld, D. (1993). *Beginning Again: People and Nature in the New Millennium.* New York: Oxford University Press.

Feldman, R. (1990). "Settlement-Identity: Psychological Bonds with Home Places in a Mobile Society," *Environment and Behavior* 22: 183–229.

Freeman, A. M., III. (1993). *The Measurement of Environmental and Resource Values: Theory and Methods.* Washington, D.C.: Resources for the Future.

Fried, M. (1963). "Grieving for a Lost Home." In *The Urban Condition,* ed. L. J. Duhl, Basic Books: New York.

Bryan G. Norton and Bruce Hannon

Gadgil, M., and Berkes, F. (1991). "Traditional Resource Management Systems." *Resource Management and Optimization* 18: 127–41.

Gadgil, M. and Guha, R. (1992). *This Fissured Land: An Ecological History of India*. New Delhi and Berkeley: Oxford University Press and University of California Press.

Galster, G. C. (1986). "What is a Neighborhood? An Externality-Space Approach." *International Journal of Urban and Regional Research* 10: 243–63.

Gans, H. J. (1962). *The Urban Villagers: Group and Class in the Life of Italian Americans*. New York: The Free Press of Glencoe.

Gould, P., and White, R. (1974). *Mental Maps*. New York: Penguin Books.

——. (1986). *Mental Maps*. Second Edition. Boston: Allen & Unwin.

Gunderson, L., Holling, C. S., and Light, S. S. (1995). *Barriers and Bridges to the Renewal of Ecosystems and Institutions*. New York: Columbia University Press.

Gussow, A. (no date). *A Sense of Place: The Artist and the American Land*. San Francisco: Friends of the Earth/Seabury Press.

——. (1993). *The Artist as Native: Reinventing Regionalism*. San Francisco: Pomegranate Artbooks.

Gutierrez, R. (1991). *When Jesus Came, The Corn Mothers Went Away*. Stanford, Calif.: Stanford University Press.

Hanemann, M. (1993). "Assessing Climate Change Risks: Valuation of Effects." In *Assessing Surprises and Nonlinearities in Greenhouse Warming*, ed. J. Darmstadter and M. Toman. Washington, D.C.: Resources for the Future.

Hannon, B. (1985). "World Shogun." *Journal of Social and Biological Structures* 8: 329–41.

——. (1994). "Sense of Place: Geographic Discounting by People, Animals and Plants." *Ecological Economics* 10(2): 157–74.

Heidegger, M. (1958). "An Ontological Consideration of Place." In *The Question of Being*. New York: Twayne Publishers.

——. (1962). *Being and Time*. New York: Harper and Row.

Heilbroner, R. (1974). *An Inquiry into the Human Prospect*. New York: W.W. Norton.

Holling, C. S. (1992). "Cross-Scale Morphology, Geometry, and Dynamics of Ecosystems." *Ecological Monographs* 62(4): 447–502.

Hough, M. (1990). *Out of Place: Restoring Identity to the Regional Landscape*. New Haven: Yale University Press.

Hull, R. B. (1992). "Image Congruity: Place Attachment and Community Design." *Journal of Architecture and Planning Research* 9: 181–91.

Jackson, J. B. (1994). *A Sense of Place, a Sense of Time*. New Haven: Yale University Press.

Johnson, A. R. (1993). "Spatiotemporal Hierarchies in Ecological Theory and Modeling." From *2nd International Conference on Integrating Geographic Information Systems and Environmental Modeling*, Sept. 26–30, 1993, Breckenridge, Col.

Kemmis, D. (1990). *Community and the Politics of Place*. Norman, Okla.: University of Oklahoma Press.

Kennedy, P. (1993). *Preparing for the Twenty-First Century*. New York: Random House.

Kopp, R. J. (1993). "Environmental Economics: Not Dead but Thriving." *Resources for the Future*, Spring 1993, (111), 7–12.

Labao, L. (1994). "The Place of 'Place' in Current Sociological Research." *Environment and Planning A*, 26: 665–8.

Langer, S. (1953). *Feeling and Form*. New York: Charles Scribner's Sons.

Lavorel, S., Gardner, R. H., and O'Neill, R. V. (1993). "Analysis of Patterns in Hierarchically Structured Landscapes." *Oikos* 67: 521–8.

Lee, K. N. (1993). *Compass and Gyroscope: Integrating Science and Politics for the Environment*. Covelo, Calif.: Island Press.

Ludwig, D., Hilburn, R., and Walters, C. (1993). "Uncertainty, Resource Exploitation and Conservation: Lessons from History." *Science* 260 (April 2, 1993): 17–19.

Lynch, K. (1960). *The Image of the City*. Cambridge, Mass.: The MIT Press.

——. (1972). *What Time is This Place?* Cambridge, Mass.: The MIT Press.

McMahon, J. A., Phillips, D. A., Robinson, J. E., and Schimpf, D. J. (1978). "Levels of Organization: An Organism-Centered Approach." *Bioscience* 28: 700–4.

Moore, C., Allen, G., and Lyndon, D. (1974). *The Place of Houses*. New York: Holt, Rinehart and Winston.

Norberg-Schulz, C. (1979, U.S. Edition, 1980). *Genius Loci: Towards a Phenomenology of Architecture*. New York: Rizzoli.

Norton, B. G. (1987). *Why Preserve Natural Variety?* Princeton, NJ: Princeton University Press.

——. (1994). "Economists Preferences and the Preferences of Economists." *Environmental Values* 3: 311–32.

——. (1995a). "Ecological Integrity and Social Values: At What Scale?" *Ecosystem Health*: 228–41.

——. (1995b). "Applied Philosophy vs. Practical Philosophy: Toward an Environmental Policy Integrated According to Scale." In *Environmental Philosophy and Environmental Activism*, ed. D. Marietta and L. Embree. Lanham, Md., Rowman and Littlefield.

Norton, B. G., and Hannon, B. (1997). "Environmental Values: A Place-Based Theory." *Environmental Ethics* 19: 227–45.

Norton, B. G., and Ulanowicz, R. E. (1992). "Scale and Biodiversity Policy: A Hierarchical Approach." *Ambio* 21(3): 244–9.

Nuclear Energy Institute (1995). "Building Citizen Support for Responsible Low-Level Radioactive Waste Disposal Solutions: A Handbook for Grass Roots Organizers." Nuclear Energy Institute.

O'Neill, R. V., DeAngelis, D. L., Waide, J. B., and Allen, T. F. H. (1986). *A Hierarchical Concept of Ecosystems*. Princeton, NJ: Princeton University Press.

Ophuls, W. (1977). *The Politics of Scarcity: A Prologue to a Political Theory of the Steady State*. San Francisco: Freeman.

———. (1992). *The Politics of Scarcity Revisited: The Unraveling of the American Dream*. New York: Freeman.

Page, T. (1977). *Conservation and Economic Efficiency*. Baltimore: Johns Hopkins University Press.

———. (1992). "Environmental Existentialism." In *Ecosystem Health: New Goals for Environmental Management*, ed. R. Costanza, B. Norton, and B. Haskell. Covelo, Calif.: Island Press.

Proshansky, H. M. (1978). "The City and Self-Identity." *Environment and Behavior* 10: 147–70.

Proshansky, H. M., Favian, A. K., and Kaminoff, R. (1983). "Place Identity: Physical World Socialization of the Self." *Journal of Environmental Psychology*, 3: 57–83.

Rappaport, R. A. (1968). *Pigs for the Ancestors: Ritual in the Ecology of a New Guinea People*. New Haven: Yale University Press.

Relph, E. (1976). *Place and Placelessness*. London: Pion Limited.

Rolston, H. (1988). *Environmental Ethics: Duties to and Values in the Natural World*. Philadelphia: Temple University Press.

Sagoff, M. (1986). "Values and Preferences." *Ethics* 96(2): 301–16.

———. (1992). "Settling America: The Concept of Place in Environmental Ethics." *Journal of Energy, Natural Resources and Environmental Law* 12: 351–418.

———. (1993). "Environmental Economics: An Epitaph." *Resources (Newsletter of Resources for the Future)* Spring 1993 (111): 2–7.

Sale, K. (1985). *Dwellers in the Land*. San Francisco: Sierra Club Books.

Seamon, D. (1979). *A Geography of the Lifeworld*. London: Croom Helm.

Seamon, D., and Mugerauer, R., eds. (1985). *Dwelling, Place, and Environment*. New York: Columbia University Press.

Silver, T. (1990). *A New Face on the Countryside: Indians, Colonists, and Slaves in South Atlantic Forests, 1500–1900*. New York: Cambridge University Press

Steele, F. (1981). *The Sense of Place*. Boston: CBI Publishing Company.

Toman, M. (1994). "Economics and 'Sustainability': Balancing Tradeoffs and Imperatives." *Land Economics* 70: 399–413.

Tuan, Y.-F. (1971). *Man and Nature*. Resource Paper no. 10. Commission on College Geography, Washington, D.C.: Association of American Geographers.

———. (1974). *Topophilia: A Study of Environmental Perception, Attitudes, and Values*. Englewood Cliffs, NJ: Prentice-Hall.

———. (1977). *Space and Place: The Perspective of Experience*. Minneapolis: University of Minnesota Press.

Varlamoff, S. (1993). *The Polluters: A Community Fights Back*. Edna, Minn.: St. John's Publishing.

Vycinas, V. (1961). *Earth and Gods*. The Hague: Martinus Nijhoff.

Walters, C. (1986). *Adaptive Management of Renewable Resources*. New York: MacMillan.

Worster, D. (1979). *Dust Bowl: The Southern Plains in the 1930s*. New York: Oxford University Press.

———. (1985). *Rivers of Empire: Water, Aridity, and the Growth of the American West*. New York: Pantheon Books.

40

Environmental Awareness and Liberal Education

Andrew Brennan

Introduction

There is widespread agreement these days that among the biggest problems facing humankind are environmental ones. We may not face an environmental *crisis*, for ecological disasters and the accumulation of insults to planetary health are chronic, rather than critical, conditions. But we do face a crisis in our conception of ourselves and of our relations to our surroundings. Reflection on these matters is timely for the future both of humanity and of the many other species whose survival is in our hands.

Whenever society faces large problems, there is a tendency to think that either their roots or their solutions lie at least partly in the educational system. This is as true of environmental troubles as it is of football hooliganism, racism and child abuse. Predictably, then, many treatises on environmental issues, or green politics, call for improved environmental education.

The calls are often stated in a way that suggests not only concern with promoting what might be called *eco-literacy* within the community, but also a real concern with the nature of current educational provision. Indeed, some of the statements published in this connection are resonant, perhaps unconsciously, of the history of educational thinking in the liberal tradition. Compare, for example, the following statements. First this one:

Environmental education must look outward to the community. It should involve the individual in an active, problem-solving process within the context of specific realities, and it should encourage initiative, a sense of responsibility and commitment to build a better tomorrow. By its very nature, environmental education can make a powerful contribution to the renovation of the education process.

The second, somewhat earlier one, goes like this:

When we think that we all live on the earth, that we live in an atmosphere, that our lives are touched at every point by the influences of the soil, flora and fauna, by considerations of light and heat, and then think of what the school study of geography has been, we have a typical idea of the gap existing between the everyday experiences of the child and the isolated material supplied in such large measure by the school. This is but an instance, and one upon which most of us may reflect long, before we take the present artificiality of the school as other than a matter of course or necessity.

Both writers clearly think of there being potential in environmental studies for the renewal of the educational process. The first passage, however, comes from a UN declaration of 1977, while the second dates from a 1900 tract by John Dewey.[1]

The present paper explores, in a tentative way, some ideas about the connection between liberal education, in a sense to be defined, and environmental studies. If the argument in what follows is successful, it turns out that there is more to environmental education than simply the integration of a number of distinct studies and the merging of theory and practice. Both of these features were emphasized by Dewey, and are congenial to others who have followed in his footsteps. What the liberal tradition has not sufficiently emphasized, however, is a point about the organization of our thinking and our studies which can be made by introducing the notion of a *framework of ideas*.

Thinking in Frameworks, and its Effects

This is not the place to review the many different ways in which humans have made a potentially dangerous impact on planetary life-support systems. For the rest of the present paper, I assume that the reader is familiar, at least in outline, with the various challenges posed by pollution, species loss, the strain of increasing population and the global warming and other climatic changes which may be associated with changes in the proportions of atmospheric gases. However, consider not the existence of these dangers, nor the techniques for confronting them, but a series of more basic questions. These include 'Who is responsible for the environmental catastrophes we face?', 'What is their nature?', 'Why are they occurring?' A serious difficulty hinders giving answers to these questions.

For example, suppose a Marxist or an anarchist maintains that American and British environmental pollution is the result of capitalism's exploitative approach to nature. At first sight, we might think that there is some merit in this idea. Perhaps giving the market too much freedom, and failing to pass suitably tough environmental protection legislation does explain some of the problems. However, a glance at the situation in the planned economies of the Soviet Union and Eastern Europe shows that major environmental disasters are not the prerogative solely of free-market economies. There are no anarchist states we can study to see if a similar problem afflicts them.[2] Alternatively, some theorists might blame the Judaeo-Christian tradition for encouraging an attitude of

arrogance and dominance over the rest of the natural world. However, that same tradition can also fund a reverence for life and an approach of stewardship towards all created things.[3]

The difficulties just encountered are a symptom of a problem that runs deep. Failure in respect of these big questions is linked with the difficulty of saying anything helpful about environmental education. In the absence of a clear understanding of *why*, or *in what way*, our relations with nature have gone wrong we do not, in any ultimate sense, know what kind of problems we are facing.

A first requirement in making progress in discussions about environmental education is shared understanding of what such education should be about. If what has just been argued is plausible, then such education must provide materials for reflection on human beings and their behaviour. It follows that education for *eco-literacy* will be more than acquisition of certain kinds of technical competence. For if it is not clear just what problems we face, then it is certainly not clear that we are facing merely technical ones.

To gain a broad perspective on environmental education, we can put two questions:

(i) What kind of thinking has led into environmental predicaments?
(ii) Which educational strategies will help us improve our ways of thinking about natural systems and our relations to them?

To help tackle these, I now introduce the concept of a *framework of ideas*. A framework, in my sense, is a bit like what Hirst originally called a *form of knowledge*, and it is also like an *academic discipline*.[4] It also draws upon some of Rudolf Carnap's ideas on *linguistic frameworks*.[5] But, despite these affinities, it is more wide-ranging than any of the ones listed.[6]

Before venturing even a vague definition, here are some examples of frameworks. Since we are concerned with a complex subject-matter, namely human beings and their relations to their surroundings, I restrict attention to frameworks relevant to this alone. Moreover, I hope the examples make clear the difference between frameworks, in my sense, and the related conceptions of Carnap and Hirst.

Consider, for example, specific religions, like Judaism, Christianity, Buddhism or Islam. These provide frameworks of ideas, in my sense, because they provide a vocabulary and set of concepts for describing human beings and their relations to each other and to their surroundings. Note that the religions themselves are not academic disciplines, although there are academic disciplines devoted to studies within and related to the religions.

Further, each major religion also provides a point of view on its subject-matter which, for a time at least, can exclude other points of view. A Christian perspective, for example, may exclude a competing religious one, and it can also exclude various non-religious ones. Although Christianity and biology have lately become less hostile to each other, there seemed in the nineteenth century to be a clear choice between regarding human beings in terms of a religious, creationist perspective and regarding them in a biological, evolutionist one.[7]

Economics provides an example of a quite different framework. Although generated by what is nowadays an academic discipline, the framework of economics has its own vocabulary and concepts in terms of which to describe human beings and their relations; it provides the material for many different theories, including theories of the market, money and of economic behaviour. Moreover, once in the grip of economic thinking, whether Marxist or monetarist, we can start to think of humans solely in terms of that framework – as economic animals, expressing their desires and preferences through signals to each other mediated by the market or other economic mechanisms.

Switch attention now to the various physical sciences. Each of these also provides a rich enough account of human beings and their relationships to give us a distinctive point of view which, at least temporarily, seems to exclude others. Admittedly, the comprehensiveness and exclusiveness of various scientific viewpoints differ at different times. At the birth of modern physics, the issue of whether human beings were mere pieces of mechanistically-determined clockwork was a live issue in a way that it seems not to be so now. By contrast, sociobiological writers like Richard Dawkins have in recent years given the old bogey of determinism an evolutionary and genetic twist.

In the light of these examples, we can give a rough and ready account of frameworks along the following lines. A framework of ideas:

(i) provides a vocabulary and set of concepts for describing a certain subject matter,

(ii) provides the materials for *theorizing* about that subject-matter, and

(iii) gives a rich enough account of its subject-matter to provide a distinct *perspective* on it, a perspective which, once adopted, is capable of excluding (at least for a time) alternative perspectives.

Despite the vagueness of these conditions, two observations about frameworks seem plausible. First, we have a tendency to think in terms of frameworks; and, second, some frameworks have the capacity to seem comprehensive, exclude others, and provide ultimately satisfying answers to certain questions.

To appreciate the latter point, consider the following caricatures of economics and sociobiology. The former maintains, let us suppose, that humans are simply economic animals, while the latter insists that humans are no more than survival machines for their genes. These claims may become so elaborated through subsequent theorizing that they start to exert a strange force over us. It may start to seem plausible, as some economists have suggested, that even matters like the rights and wrongs of slavery or abortion are issues for the market to legislate on, not matters of individual or social conscience.[8] Or, to switch to the biological perspective, maybe keeping our promises or helping a stranger in difficulties are genetically programmed behaviours rather than the acts of decency we may normally think them to be.[9]

The very fact of juxtaposing the two frameworks may suggest a certain scepticism about the claims of either to comprehensiveness. It is certainly true that human beings are, among other things, economic animals. They are, also, among other things, the products of evolutionary processes. But they are religious, ethical, political, physical, aesthetic, beings as well. We do no justice to the richness of human life by trying to reduce everything to economic transactions or genetically-programmed behaviours. The core claims given in my previous caricatures are, it seems to me, obviously false. Yet it is striking that whole treatises have been written, and whole schools of thought founded, on just such false claims. There is a moral to be drawn from this, about which more will be said in the following section.

Finally, there need be no direct connection between a framework and either an academic discipline, a religion or a science. Ethics, for example, consists of sets of principles by which we order our personal lives, while politics deals with the modes of ordering the affairs of groups of people. Although these frameworks are the concern of some disciplines, including philosophy, sociology and political studies, they are not themselves academic disciplines. Yet they provide a rich vocabulary, together with conceptual and theoretical resources, that enable us to think about our relations to each other, our duties to our families and ourselves, the individual's relationship to the state, and even our relationship to the physical environment in which we live.

The framework of ethics can dominate our thinking in a distinctive way. It is possible to think of ourselves as ethical beings, and at the same as being to some extent at the mercy of conflicting social forces or biological drives. For some theorists it is not so much the case that ethical modes of thinking exclude other frameworks, but that the ethical has priority over everything else.[10] There are thus at least two different ways in which frameworks can claim authority. In the examples taken from economics and sociobiology, the framework claimed a certain reductive or simplifying role: all human transactions could supposedly be reduced to the economic, or the genetic. But we need not *reduce* all behaviour and relationships to the ethical in order to argue that ethical considerations have a compelling force compared with those derived from other sources. The authority of ethics is compatible with there being other things to say about any situation on which the ethical perspective has been brought to bear.

Limitations of Frameworks

If we grant that there are several rather large perspectives which bear on human life, our relations to each other and to the other living things with which we share the earth, we can try to establish certain principles about these frameworks and their operation.

The first is that not every mode of thinking in which we engage draws on just one framework.

When we approach some problems, we are quite clear that we have to draw on the methods, theories and techniques of several different frameworks. A clear example is the framework of *mathematics*, used by many different disciplines, from engineering to ecology. The field ecologist, however, is likely to draw not only on mathematics, but also on chemistry and several other frameworks to make sense of the flux of matter and energy in a community. Most of the sciences, then, with the exception of mathematics itself, call upon more than one framework.

A further principle is that some modes of thinking are reflections on the system of frameworks itself. That is, there are modes of thinking which have the system of points of view as their subject-matter, and so can be regarded as themselves being higher-level frameworks. Part of what is involved in the history of science, for example, is reflection on the scientific frameworks that have been adopted at one time or another. Portions of philosophy, sociology and certain forms of literary and artistic activity also involve reflection on various frameworks and this can be done quite explicitly (as in the present paper). Ironically enough, those parts of science which draw upon the perspectives of several frameworks are often regarded as less rigorous than those that involve just one or two frameworks. Hence mathematics and physics are sometimes thought to be considerably more demanding than ecology or psychology; but it is the latter which deal with the really complicated things. Persons and eco-systems, after all, are considerably more complex in respect of their properties and relations than are numbers or elementary particles.

A third principle is that certain frameworks have, at various times, a tendency to *hegemony*. This term is meant to refer to the *reductive* power of frameworks, identified in the previous section, rather than merely the tendency to dominate. Given the diversity of frameworks already mentioned, and the complexity of the subject-matter of human life and human relations to each other and to other things, it might seem odd that any tendency to hegemony exists. Yet, as already pointed out, there was a time not so long ago when the hegemony of physics was clear: and there is no shortage of examples in the history of humankind of the hegemony of certain religious frameworks. It is important to recognize the existence of the tendency to hegemony, and also to recognise that it carries dangers. For, as I will now briefly argue, there are at least two respects in which frameworks dealing with human beings and their relations to each other and their surroundings are bound to be inadequate.

The first inadequacy of any human-regarding framework is its limitation with respect to its *subject-matter*. Consider, for example, the claim that the framework of economics gives a complete account of the human situation. It is true that there is an economic dimension to many human transactions, at the level of the family, the local community, the workplace and so on. One aspect of our interactions with others can thus be captured by the concepts of economic theory, and different theories can give different explanations of our economic activities. But none of this goes to show that, for example, my relationship and commitment to my family can be expressed purely in terms of a cost–benefit analysis. On the contrary, family relationships involve emotions, duties, cares and responsibilities that lie beyond equations and monetary values. But if we were purely economic beings, the cost–benefit analysis would contain everything there is to know about family relationships.

The limitation just mentioned is perhaps fairly obvious to anyone who has not fallen entirely under the spell of economic thinking. But the point is a more general one. Any particular framework in terms of which we consider the human situation is bound to produce a description of its subject-matter relative to that framework. But the subject-matter is essentially multi-dimensional. And no single framework can capture what requires a multiplicity of frames of reference for its articulation.

The second inadequacy is a special case of the limitation just described, but for simplicity, we can regard it on its own. It concerns the limitation of the *scope of the central concepts* of a framework. This limitation is based on the fact that for each framework there are certain questions which cannot be put about its subject-matter, and therefore certain things that cannot be said.

Again, this feature can be illustrated by appeal to economics. Suppose, for example, that a problem arises in an economic analysis concerning the value to be given to historic buildings, natural woodlands, and a whole host of other things for which market values do not seem to match people's normal perceptions of value. Faced with the valuation of such things, some analysts might admit that their core concepts of (monetary) value simply had no application. Such an admission would reveal very clearly that the scope of the central concepts of economics is limited, that economics simply cannot discuss the value of a tree, a family or an archaeological site, for the simple reason that these values are not monetary ones. Instead of taking this course, however, many analysts embark on the ingenious programme of devising 'shadow prices' or 'contingent values' for such items.[11] The result has been confusion. For stretching economic value to cover these things fosters the dangerous illusion that everything has just one value which can be expressed in terms of a single, monetary measure.

Although the hegemony of economics is a matter for concern, economics is not the only case of a framework where problems arise from failure to admit the limits on the scope of central concepts. It can be argued that standard European ethical perspectives have also made it difficult to raise certain questions; but this has been seen not as a limitation on these perspectives but rather as showing the questions to be improper – again a dangerous illusion.

To illustrate this claim, consider questions about our obligations towards other living things. Some people still find it strange that environmentalists write, speak and act as if they regard plants, ecosystems and even land forms as having moral standing in our deliberations.[12] One source of such bewilderment is the fact that ethics has often been seen as a device for sorting out decisions and priorities among items with the particular properties of human beings. For example, because human beings are moral agents, or beings who group together into societies, it has been thought – naturally enough – that the scope of their moral obligations must be limited to other beings who are moral agents, or who group with them into societies.

However, the 'naturally enough' in the previous sentence simply calls attention to a problem with the scope of the central concepts in our ethical thinking. A framework that assumes that the only moral communities are groups of moral agents will find it hard to cope with the idea that other things (that are not themselves moral agents) can figure in our moral thinking. Other animals, for example, may have pains and pleasure and modes of flourishing, but they are not moral agents. Plants have no pleasures and pains as far as we know, still less have they any roles as moral agents. How is it then that people encounter feelings of restraint in their behaviour towards other animals and plants? Just as some economists try to assign monetary values to everything of value, so some moralists are highly ingenious in trying to explain away this everyday phenomenon. It may be argued, for example, that we do not owe respect *directly* to plants, but rather show restraint in our behaviour towards plants for the sake of others who want to enjoy the continued existence and flourishing of plants. What we thought, then, was concern for the oak tree or the rare marigold is *really* respect for others who value such things.[13]

Such contorted reasoning is forced on us by features of the ethical framework which make it difficult to raise certain options and put certain questions. To escape such latent forms of bias in our thinking is not easy. For we have to be aware of the framework of ideas in terms of which we are thinking, and then stand back to reflect on the fundamental assumptions of that framework. When we do so, the result can sometimes shock us out of our established modes of thinking. It is not comfortable. But only by doing so can we start to escape the inadequate perspectives of those frameworks that dominate our thinking on the problems that daily confront us.

New Aims for Liberal Education

These reflections on frameworks can now be related back to the initial puzzles about environmental education. Recall that we wanted to discover both what kind of thinking had led us into environmental difficulties and how best to improve our ways of thinking about nature. If what has been suggested so far is correct, then a major aim of education for environmental awareness must not only involve some acquaintance with the multiplicity of frameworks available to us, but also encourage reflection on the limitations associated with each. This, at least, is what I want to propose in the present section.

It may be that failure to reflect on such limitations is a factor in the environmental catastrophes we face: maybe they are, at least in part, a result of considering our actions under only one or two aspects. But reflection on such limitations is some-

thing that can be readily added to the characterization of a liberal education. More generally, our conception of what is involved in education, whether for environmental awareness or not, should be informed by an awareness that framework thinking can be a source of problems (as well as a means to solutions) and that *recognition* of the roles of frameworks of ideas, and their limitations, has a significant part to play in the development of the educated person.

A philosophy of education clearly has to relate the *aims* of education on the one hand to its *targets* on the other. One aim of education, according to a respectable tradition, is to expose the learner to a number of different areas of intellectual inquiry some of which will be what I have so far loosely characterized as frameworks of ideas. The aim of exposing learners to such 'forms of knowledge' is usually described in terms of the reigning disciplinary structure current in higher education at the time of writing.[14]

Even if a good liberal education involves exposure of the learner to a number of disciplines, the nature of this exposure will itself have to be adjusted to the group on which education is targeted. Although this is an obvious enough point, it is easily overlooked. If our target group is young children of primary age, for example, then the nature of their exposure to the forms of knowledge will be very different from the exposure of university undergraduates or mature students in continuing education. Indeed, how best to provide a liberal education for different target groups is a matter which involves extremely difficult questions.[15]

Sticking, for the moment, with the idea that a liberal education should, at least for some target groups, provide access to a range of disciplines, what other features of liberal education command widespread agreement? I think that, for theorists like Hirst and Peters, one point of exposure to a number of forms of knowledge is that each form will be found to have its own special validity. Thus, for example, historical modes of articulating experience will differ from religious or biological ones. But each form of knowledge brings, it is said, its own particular mode of justification, validation and explanation which marks it out as separate from the others.

Hirst made this point originally by reference to the peculiarity both of the logical structure of, and the criteria for truth within, each form of knowledge. If we recast Hirst's points, however, in terms of frameworks of ideas, we can still reach something like the same destination. History, sociology, psychology and biology all have fascinating theories to display and accounts to narrate of human beings and their relationships. Humans are in history, but also in society; they have minds and they are also biological beings. They are also, as we have already noted, economic, ethical and political animals. Given the complexity of the subjects we study, there is a clear case for the liberal ideal in education: if we do not expose learners to at least some of the many perspectives available on complex topics, then they will develop only simplistic attitudes to the wealth around them. Instead of helping them realise the richness of experience, education would equip them for only a superficial understanding of life.

These remarks gesture towards a line of argument rather than detailing it.[16] But let us suppose it is accepted in broad terms, and that we are in general well disposed to such an educational ideal. Although it may be implicit in the tradition of liberal educational theory, I would argue that there is another side to the ideal which is just as important as the considerations just given. A liberal education should not only involve the exposure to a number of frameworks and their associated perspectives, but *it should also generate reflection on the system of frameworks itself.*

Why is such reflection important? If we accept that each framework of ideas generates only a one-dimensional image of a multidimensional subject-matter, then it is clear that each framework is limited in scope. This has already been argued above. But then, for any complex subject-matter, no framework can give an intellectually satisfying or complete account of our knowledge or beliefs. If liberal education is to remove the blinkers from the learner's eyes, one way of doing this is by making sure that learners become aware of the tendency of some frameworks toward hegemony, and learn enough about the system of frameworks to resist this tendency.

To do this well in education will mean facing different challenges for different target groups. For example, the disciplinary structure of higher education can hardly be imposed in the primary school, as most theorists and teachers are well aware. Thanks to widespread adoption of Dewey's principles in British and American primary level

education, environmental studies (what Dewey called 'geography') are now widely recognized as important at that stage. Likewise, the integration of both academic and practical work, and of what happens inside the school with what happens outside, are well established features of much primary education.

Dewey would argue that his methods of education are designed to make the early learner start to become aware of the richness of experience. Our various modes of responding to puzzles and felt difficulties start to make it natural to think in terms of multiple perspectives, limited insights, partial glimpses of things that are themselves wonderfully complex and rich in new possibilities. A major challenge, however, is to translate the early work in the primary school into new forms of engagement with the world of experience without losing the benefits already achieved.[17]

At secondary level in the UK, we find a target group that has been treated rather differently from the earlier group. Greater integration of academic and practical work has recently come to seem a good idea. Before that there was considerable pressure to regard secondary education as exposing learners to a variety of academic disciplines, encouraging progressive specialization in a small number of these. These disciplines in which progressive specialization is supposed to occur reflect the history of sectional interests within the universities, and this structure is accepted with very little change within the polytechnics, and institutions of higher and further education.

The imposition of such structures from the top down has arguably been damaging for secondary education. Consider, for example, the problems posed by what Dewey identified as the isolation and artificiality of academic education. At its worst, an academic education imparts concepts to learners not in the context of experiences, puzzles and felt difficulties, but only in the context of other concepts. As a result, what is learned in the school, college or university can come to be regarded as different from what is encountered at first hand in the playground, the coffee bar, the sports field or the hillside. Our grasp of many issues, and even of what is happening in the world around us, can come to be increasingly *notional* rather than *real*.[18]

There is no easy answer to the problem posed by these particular reflections, although the problem itself is a serious one. Formal education is but one of many routes to personal growth and the development of individuality. We cannot expect tinkerings with the educational system and with the syllabus to have an overwhelming effect on the kind of citizens that exist tomorrow, but this is no reason for leaving things as they are. It may be that recent secondary syllabus revisions in Scotland and the rest of the UK signify a move towards Dewey's ideal. It has to be admitted, at the same time, that there is no widespread agreement that, even in the initial part of secondary education, there is a pivotal role to be played by environmental studies.

Eco-Literacy and Liberal Ideals

I conclude with some reflections on tertiary education, especially in universities. So far, I have argued that we bring frameworks of ideas to bear on experience. These frameworks may provide a fairly complete account of certain subjects, but are manifestly incomplete when brought to bear on complex items like human beings and their relationships with their surroundings. A liberal education should have the twin aims of exposing the learner to a number of such frameworks, while also making clear that each of them has its limitations.

Environmental studies – in the form of geography – were highly regarded by Dewey. What is special about them is that they are, in essence, multi-framework. There is no framework of ideas that is 'environmental', though there are ecological, physiological, geomorphological, and chemical perspectives to be mastered by the student of environmental science. As we extend our studies to the impact of human beings on the landscape and life forms, so we have to consider economic, political and sociological perspectives. Ironically, it is the very lack of a single framework of ideas that has led to the querying of the academic status of environmental studies. In other words, the more environmental scientists and geographers try to do justice to the complexity of their subject-matter, the more defensive they have to become about their status in institutions with rigid disciplinary structures.

Such a situation is indeed extraordinary. Let me emphasize that I am not here attacking the existence of specialization within the university, nor denying the cleverness and ingenuity associated with those disciplines which draw upon only one or two frameworks. But if the best minds are drawn only to such areas, and if high academic status is associated exclusively with them, then there is little hope for the future. We will not be able to get to grips with the problems that now confront humanity if we persist in seeing them as largely technical, largely economic, or whatever. A major priority in higher education, then, is to introduce awareness of the fact that single perspectives yield only limited views of complex problems.

We can thus think of the goal of education for eco-literacy as posing a challenge to be met in more or less grand ways. In a minimal way, we can think of exploiting the frameworks familiar to students in the various academic disciplines in order to provide them with some degree of environmental awareness. Although I have used the word 'exploit' here, we need to be cautious. For, as seen already, any framework will, by its nature, put limits on the questions to be raised, and indeed may prohibit the asking of certain questions at all.

None the less, we can think of ways in which the skills of students studying the physical sciences, engineering and architecture can be focused on environmental matters. They could, perhaps, be exposed to units on biological assessment and design, couched in vocabularies with which they are already familiar. Likewise students in business, accountancy and economics might usefully be exposed to units on the environmental impacts of industry. And, finally, humanities students could be offered units dealing with values and attitudes to conservation.

Not only would these schemes be worthy and easily grafted on to the existing disciplinary structures in higher education, but they could also be adapted in suitable ways for a different target group, namely students in secondary education. An additional point to commend them would be that, as public perceptions of environmental crisis intensify, as they almost certainly will, such units might prove increasingly popular. A problem does arise, I think, for the recommendations concerning humanities students. For they require something by way of content to provide a real, as opposed to a merely notional, grasp of the issues here. This content might best be provided at an earlier stage in the education system. Wherever it is provided it will involve first-hand exposure to

Andrew Brennan

environmental science and the concepts and methods of ecology.

A related reflection is that students in architecture, the sciences, economics and business may lack any real grasp of issues of value. Recall that within economics, for example, the term 'value' is often associated with techniques of cost–benefit analysis; but if anything is true about values it is that monetary value is not the whole story about what matters. Such reflections prompt the thought that there may be a grander, more radical, proposal to explore concerning environmental education.

What is striking about the proposal so far investigated is that it accepts current disciplinary structures and associated activities. But we might wonder whether it is appropriate to do this. Even if the structure of academic disciplines only changes relatively slowly, there need be no essential connection between this structure and the shape of academic provision. Indeed there is no general reason why teaching structures ought to reflect organizational ones. An important feature of university education as it is currently understood is that students have contact with those who are active in research in the various disciplines. But it by no means follows that the disciplines themselves should structure such contacts. On the contrary, a balanced educational provision, like a good meal, may involve a nourishing variety of courses, each embodying ingredients from several disciplines.

A grander proposal for making eco-literacy more widespread flows from these thoughts. We can perhaps best break away from modes of thought that draw on only one or two frameworks by providing *transdisciplinary* units and degree programmes which encourage multiframework thinking. Examples of these include degree programmes in human ecology, drawing upon the disciplines of various sciences as well as philosophy, politics and international law.[19] If we can produce enough graduates to whom such thinking is natural, then there is some chance that a wider range of responses to our environmental problems will be forthcoming.

Once there is general acceptance that good degree programmes need not be directly linked to disciplines, there would be scope for translating this recognition through the system to secondary education as well. Note that the current proposal is not meant as a threat to the disciplines themselves,

nor to the provision of the traditional specialist degree. I am not suggesting any general abandonment of framework thinking, or of academic disciplines; what I am suggesting is that the ideal of liberal education should include provision for modes of learning that encourage reflection on the system of frameworks and draw attention to the inherent limitations, as well as the strengths, of our various disciplines. Such provision, however, requires a greater range of multi-disciplinary involvement than is found in the traditional joint honours degree.

A final thought on real and notional approaches to problems is concerned with the question of what used to be called the *hidden curriculum*. Academic work can encourage a form of isolation from the very subject matter with which it deals. Dewey would have found it interesting that an institution may be keen to put on courses on ecology, energy conservation and the like while ignoring its own environmental impacts. For example, course handouts may not be printed on recycled paper, and classes may be held in poorly insulated, energy-wasting buildings. Although education for environmental awareness is a worthy goal, it is not purely a matter of syllabus, detaching educational provision from disciplinary frameworks and the rest. It is also a matter of becoming aware that there is an environmental dimension in all our dealings. If growing environmental awareness means that production and consumption within our society are seen as not purely economic phenomena, then it may also reinforce the perception that education is not just a matter of books, concepts and theories.

Liberal education, then, is not simply the introduction to a number of forms of knowledge, or frameworks, coupled with a recognition of their limitations. As writers like Peters, Hirst and Scheffler have also emphasized, it involves the teacher in displaying regard for certain norms and standards.[20] Traditionally, these have been the norms of rational inquiry, and the standards of civilized discourse. An extension of this to the institutional setting itself may not seem unduly controversial. But it would be no mean achievement for schools and universities to undertake an audit of their own environmental impacts. By so doing, and by setting institutional agendas that are environmentally sensitive, they would also contribute to the education both of their members and of the wider community.

Notes

This paper is an expanded version of an address given at a seminar entitled 'Education for Environmental Competence' at Airthrey Castle, Stirling, May, 1990. I am grateful for the contributions of participants at the ensuing discussion and to the Scottish Environmental Education Council and the University of Stirling Department of Educational Policy and Development for inviting me to take part in the seminar.

1 The Tiblisi declaration is quoted in Holdgate, M. W., Kassas, M. and White, G. F. *The World Environment 1972–82*, United Nations Environment Programme, Tycooly, Dublin, 1982, ch. 15. Dewey's comment is from the chapter 'Waste in Education' in *The School and Society*, revised 1915 and published in a combined volume with *The Child and the Curriculum*, University of Chicago Press, 1956, p. 76.
2 Whether 'green' political thought is distinct from traditional political positions, or is a variety of socialism, anarchism or liberalism, is very much a vexed question. For recent work, see Keekok Lee's *Social Philosophy and Ecological Scarcity*, Routledge, 1989.
3 The debate between different interpretations of Judaeo-Christian thought can be found in John Passmore's *Man's Responsibility for Nature*, second edition, Duckworth, 1980, and Robin Attfield's *The Ethics of Environmental Concern*, Basil Blackwell, 1983.
4 See the essays in Paul Hirst, *Knowledge and the Curriculum*, London, Routledge and Kegan Paul, 1974, especially 'Liberal Education and the Nature of Knowledge' and 'The Forms of Knowledge Revisited'.
5 See Rudolf Carnap, 'Empiricism, Semantics and Ontology', reprinted in *Meaning and Necessity*, enlarged edition, Chicago University Press, 1956.
6 There is a general difficulty in finding terminology to describe pervasive underlying themes in the thought of a culture. Francis Bacon, in his *Novum Organon* wrote about 'idols', but his terminology, like the terminology of 'ideology', suggests that the conceptions in question are false. Richard Routley and others have explored the notion of 'paradigms', a term borrowed from Thomas Kuhn – but they are large-scale complexes of ideas, attitudes and practices (see 'The Forms and Limits of Paradigms' in Elliot, R. and Gare, A., *Environmental Philosophy*, Milton Keynes, Open University Press, 1983).
7 For an account of a modern revival of this issue see Michael Ruse, 'A Philosopher at the monkey trial', *New Scientist* 93 (1982) 317–19. For further reading, see the same author's *Darwinism Defended: A Guide to the Evolution Controversies*, Reading, Mass., Addison-Wesley, 1982.
8 See G. Calabresi and A. D. Melamed, 'Property Rules, Liability Rules and Inalienability', *Harvard Law Review* 85, 1972, and H. Macauley, and B. Yandle *Environmental Use and the Market*, Lexington, Mass., Lexington Books, 1977. These views, along with the whole economic approach to environmental conservation, are critically discussed in Mark Sagoff's *The Economy of the Earth*, Cambridge University Press, 1988.
9 For a popular treatment, see Richard Dawkins, *The Selfish Gene*, Oxford University Press, 1976. More sophisticated is Michael Ruse's account of sociobiology in *Taking Darwin Seriously*, Basil Blackwell, 1986. For severe criticisms of the sociobiologists' programme, see Philip Kitcher, *Vaulting Ambition*, Cambridge, Mass., MIT Press, 1985.
10 Although there is a long tradition associated with the view that ethical considerations have a peculiarly compelling character, this has come under scrutiny from recent theorists. A helpful study is Bernard Williams, *Ethics and the Limits of Philosophy*, London, Fontana, 1985.
11 For a description and critique of such a process see Mark Sagoff, *The Economy of The Earth*. See also D. Pearce, A. Markandya and E. Barbier, *Blueprint for a Green Economy*, London, Earthscan, 1989.
12 There is a large literature on this issue. A flavour of what is at stake can be gleaned from E. Johnson, 'Treating the Dirt: Environmental Ethics and Moral Theory', in T. Regan (ed.) *Earthbound*, New York, Random House, 1984, and Andrew Brennan, 'The Moral Standing of Natural Objects', *Environmental Ethics* 6 (1984).
13 For a striking statement of this case see William F. Baxter, 'People or Penguins', in VanDeVeer, D. and Pierce, C. (eds.) *People, Penguins and Plastic Trees* (Wadsworth, 1986).
14 This is clear in the case of the essays by Paul Hirst already cited.
15 There is also a separate, but significant, problem posed for the liberal education tradition by the needs of those with mental deficits and learning difficulties. This issue is explored in a preliminary way in Andrew Brennan and Paul Dumbleton, 'Learning Difficulties and the Concept of a Person', *British Journal of Educational Studies*, 37, 1989.
16 They also overgeneralize. There are many routes to personal development, and it can be argued that the route favoured by theorists of liberal education is one among others, suitable perhaps for some learners for some of the time.
17 Dewey had a special reason for commending environmental studies as fundamental at all levels of schooling, for this fitted in with his ideal of unity in the sciences:

Andrew Brennan

The unity of all the sciences is found in geography. The significance of geography is that it presents the earth as the enduring home of the occupations of man ... The earth is the final source of all man's food. It is his continual shelter and protection, the raw material of all his activities, and the home to whose humanizing and idealizing all his achievement returns. *Child/School*, pp. 18–19.

18 Although the terminology of *real* and *notional* derives from John Henry Newman, it fits well with Dewey's emphasis on bridging the gap between the academic and the practical. Humanities students would not have real grasp of ecological science unless they did more than study some elementary texts and work with computer simulations (valuable though the latter undoubtedly are). The importance of field studies and first-hand acquaintance with natural systems cannot be overemphasized.

19 Some British universities are now moving towards offering such provision. Programmes in human ecology are well-established elsewhere in Europe, though still only in a handful of universities.

20 See, for one example, Israel Scheffler, 'Philosophical Models of Teaching', in *Reason and Teaching*, London, Routledge and Kegan Paul, 1973.

Index

Index

armour thyroid

Dr. Steven
Hotze, Health Happiness +
Hormones